Lecture Notes in Computer Science   13260

Founding Editors

Gerhard Goos, Germany
Juris Hartmanis, USA

Editorial Board Members

Elisa Bertino, USA
Wen Gao, China

Bernhard Steffen⬤, Germany
Moti Yung⬤, USA

Formal Methods

Subline of Lectures Notes in Computer Science

Subline Series Editors

Ana Cavalcanti, *University of York, UK*
Marie-Claude Gaudel, *Université de Paris-Sud, France*

Subline Advisory Board

Manfred Broy, *TU Munich, Germany*
Annabelle McIver, *Macquarie University, Sydney, NSW, Australia*
Peter Müller, *ETH Zurich, Switzerland*
Erik de Vink, *Eindhoven University of Technology, The Netherlands*
Pamela Zave, *AT&T Laboratories Research, Bedminster, NJ, USA*

More information about this series at https://link.springer.com/bookseries/558

Jyotirmoy V. Deshmukh ·
Klaus Havelund · Ivan Perez (Eds.)

NASA
Formal Methods

14th International Symposium, NFM 2022
Pasadena, CA, USA, May 24–27, 2022
Proceedings

 Springer

Editors
Jyotirmoy V. Deshmukh (iD)
University of Southern California
Los Angeles, CA, USA

Ivan Perez (iD)
National Institute of Aerospace
Hampton, VA, USA

Klaus Havelund (iD)
Jet Propulsion Laboratory
California Institute of Technology
Pasadena, CA, USA

ISSN 0302-9743 ISSN 1611-3349 (electronic)
Lecture Notes in Computer Science
ISBN 978-3-031-06772-3 ISBN 978-3-031-06773-0 (eBook)
https://doi.org/10.1007/978-3-031-06773-0

This Springer imprint is published by the registered company Springer Nature Switzerland AG
The registered company address is: Gewerbestrasse 11, 6330 Cham, Switzerland

Preface

The NASA Formal Methods (NFM) Symposium is a forum to foster collaboration between theoreticians and practitioners from NASA, academia, and industry, with the goal of identifying challenges and providing solutions to achieve assurance in mission-critical and safety-critical systems. The NASA Formal Methods Symposia welcome submissions on cross-cutting approaches that bring together formal methods and techniques from other domains. Topics covered by NFM 2022 included, but were not limited to, the following:

- Advances in formal methods

  - Interactive and automated theorem proving
  - SMT and SAT solving
  - Model checking
  - Static analysis
  - Runtime verification
  - Automated testing
  - Specification languages, textual and graphical
  - Refinement
  - Code synthesis
  - Design for verification and correct-by-design techniques
  - Requirements specification and analysis

- Integration of formal methods techniques

  - Use of machine learning and probabilistic reasoning in formal methods
  - Integration of formal methods into software engineering practices
  - Combination of formal methods with simulation and analysis techniques
  - Formal methods and fault tolerance, and self-healing systems
  - Formal methods and graphical modeling languages such as SysML, UML
  - Formal methods and autonomy

- Formal methods in practice

  - Experience reports of application of formal methods on real systems
  - Use of formal methods in systems engineering
  - Use of formal methods in education
  - Reports on negative results in the application of formal methods
  - Usability of formal method tools, and application in industry
  - Challenge problems for the formal methods community.

This volume contains the papers presented at NFM 2022, the 14th NASA Formal Methods Symposium, held at the California Institute of Technology (Pasadena, CA, USA) during May 24–27, 2022, and organized by JPL, the University of Southern California, the Formal Methods group at NASA Langley Research Center, and the

California Institute of Technology. NFM 2021 and NFM 2020 were held virtually and were organized by, respectively, the NASA Langley Research Center and the NASA Ames Research Center. Prior symposia were held in Houston, TX (2019), Newport News, VA (2018), Moffett Field, CA (2017), Minneapolis, MN (2016), Pasadena, CA (2015), Houston, TX (2014), Moffett Field, CA (2013), Norfolk, VA (2012), Pasadena, CA (2011), Washington, DC (2010), and Moffett Field, CA (2009). The series started as the Langley Formal Methods Workshop, and was held under that name in 1990, 1992, 1995, 1997, 2000, and 2008.

Papers were solicited for NFM 2022 under two categories: regular papers describing fully developed work and complete results, and short papers describing tools, experience reports, or work-in-progress with preliminary results. The symposium received 118 submissions for review, of which 93 were full papers and 25 were short papers. A total of 39 papers were accepted for publication: 33 full papers and six short papers. The submissions went through a rigorous review process where each paper was independently reviewed by at least three reviewers and then subsequently discussed by the Program Committee (PC).

In addition to the paper presentations, the symposium featured seven invited keynote speakers: Dines Bjørner (Technical University of Denmark, Denmark), Steve Chien (JPL, USA), Daniel Jackson (MIT, USA), Julia Lawall (Inria Paris, France), Sriram Sankaranarayanan (University of Colorado Boulder, USA), Alex Summers (University of British Columbia, Canada), and Emina Torlak (University of Washington, USA). The first day of the symposium included four tutorials presented by Edwin Brady (University of St. Andrews, UK), Ankush Desai (Amazon Web Services, USA), Anastasia Mavridou (KBR Inc./NASA Ames, USA), and Leonardo de Moura (Microsoft Research, USA) and Sebastian Ullrich (Karlsruhe Institute of Technology, Germany). Keynote speakers and tutorial presenters were invited to submit papers, which are also included in the proceedings.

The PC chairs are especially grateful to Richard Murray, our Local Chair, for making it possible to hold the symposium at the California Institute of Technology, as well as Monica Nolasco, for help with local arrangements. We would also like to thank our scientific advisor, Mani Chandy (California Institute of Technology), and the application advisors, Robert Bocchino (JPL), John Day (JPL), Maged Elasaar (JPL), Amalaye Oyake (Blue Origin), Nicolas Rouquette (JPL), and Vandi Verma (JPL).

The organizers are grateful to the authors for submitting their work to NFM 2022 and to all invited speakers for sharing their insights. NFM 2022 would not have been possible without the work of the outstanding Program Committee and additional reviewers, the support of the Steering Committee, the support of the California Institute of Technology, JPL, the University of Southern California, and the NASA Langley Research Center, and the general support of the NASA Formal Methods community.

The NFM 2022 website can be found at https://nfm2022.caltech.edu.

April 2022   Jyotirmoy V. Deshmukh
Klaus Havelund
Ivan Perez

Organization

Program Chairs

Jyotirmoy V. Deshmukh   University of Southern California, USA
Klaus Havelund   Jet Propulsion Laboratory, California Institute
                        of Technology, USA
Ivan Perez   National Institute of Aerospace, USA

Local Organizer

Richard M. Murray   California Institute of Technology, USA

Program Committee

Erika Ábrahám   RWTH Aachen University, Germany
Natalia Alexandrov   NASA, USA
Nikos Arechiga   Toyota Research Institute, USA
Julia Badger   NASA, USA
Stanley Bak   Stony Brook University, USA
Dirk Beyer   Ludwig-Maximilians-Universität München, Germany
Sylvie Boldo   Inria and Université Paris-Saclay, France
Borzoo Bonakdarpour   Michigan State University, USA
Betty H. C. Cheng   Michigan State University, USA
Alessandro Cimatti   Fondazione Bruno Kessler, Italy
Misty Davies   NASA, USA
John Day   Jet Propulsion Laboratory, California Institute of
                        Technology, USA
Ewen Denney   NASA, USA
Aaron Dutle   NASA, USA
Rüdiger Ehlers   Clausthal University of Technology, Germany
Yliès Falcone   Université Grenoble Alpes/Inria Grenoble, France
Chuchu Fan   MIT, USA
Marie Farrell   Maynooth University, Ireland
Martin Feather   Jet Propulsion Laboratory, California Institute of
                        Technology, USA
Lu Feng   University of Virginia, USA
Jean-Christophe Filliatre CNRS, France
Bernd Finkbeiner   CISPA Helmholtz Center for Information Security,
                        Germany
Alwyn Goodloe   NASA, USA
Kim Guldstrand Larsen   Aalborg University, Denmark
Arie Gurfinkel   University of Waterloo, Canada
Constance Heitmeyer   Naval Research Laboratory, USA

Kerianne Hobbs	Air Force Research Laboratory, USA
Gerard Holzmann	Nimble Research, USA
Bardh Hoxha	Toyota Research Institute North America, USA
Marieke Huisman	University of Twente, The Netherlands
Susmit Jha	SRI International, USA
Rajeev Joshi	Amazon Web Services, USA
Guy Katz	The Hebrew University of Jerusalem, Israel
Martin Leucker	University of Luebeck, Germany
Michael Lowry	NASA, USA
Leonardo Mariani	University of Milano Bicocca, Italy
Anastasia Mavridou	KBR/NASA Ames, USA
Natasha Neogi	NASA, USA
Dejan Nickovic	Austrian Institute of Technology, Austria
Corina Pasareanu	CMU/KBR/NASA Ames, USA
Doron Peled	Bar Ilan University, Israel
Pavithra Prabhakar	Kansas State University, USA
Giles Reger	Amazon Web Services, USA, and University of Manchester, UK
Nicolas Rouquette	Jet Propulsion Laboratory, California Institute of Technology, USA
Kristin Yvonne Rozier	Iowa State University, USA
Anne-Kathrin Schmuck	Max-Planck-Institute for Software Systems, Germany
Johann Schumann	KBR/NASA Ames, USA
Cristina Seceleanu	Mälardalen University, Sweden
Yasser Shoukry	University of California, Irvine, USA
Julien Signoles	CEA List/Université Paris-Saclay, France
Oleg Sokolsky	University of Pennsylvania, USA
Marielle Stoelinga	University of Twente, The Netherlands
Carolyn Talcott	SRI International, USA
Marcel Verhoef	European Space Agency, The Netherlands
Willem Visser	Amazon Web Services, USA
Huafeng Yu	Boeing Research and Technology, USA

Additional Reviewers

Anand, Ashwani
Andrès, Léo
Backeman, Peter
Barnat, Jiri
Bhayat, Ahmed
Borca-Tasciuc, Giorgian
Chawla, Abhinav
Chien, Po-Chun
Conrad, Esther
Das, Spandan

Dawson, Charles
Dobe, Oyendrila
Dolan, Sydney
Dross, Claire
Dureja, Rohit
Ferlez, James
Garcia-Contreras, Isabel
Girol, Guillaume
Goorden, Martijn
Grosen, Thomas M.

Gu, Rong
Guedri, Wissal
Hamilton, Nathaniel
Hansen, Jonas
Hsu, Tzu-Han
Jacquemin, Maxime
Johannsen, Chris
Kallwies, Hannes
Katis, Andreas
Kauffman, Sean
Kempa, Brian
Kochdumper, Niklas
Kolb, Christina
Lal, Ratan
Lammich, Peter
Lee, Nian-Ze
Lopuhaä-Zwakenberg, Milan
Mainhardt, Ana Maria
Marre, Bruno
Mata, Andrew
Meng, Yue
Neider, Daniel
Paskevich, Andrei
Prakash Nayak, Satya

Priya, Siddharth
Roussanaly, Victor
Rubbens, Robert
Sachenbacher, Martin
Schmitt, Frederik
Schmitz, Malte
Sheikhi, Sanaz
Slagel, Joseph
Slagel, Tanner
Soueidi, Chukri
Spiessl, Martin
Strub, Pierre-Yves
Su, Yusen
Thoma, Daniel
van den Bos, Petra
van Dijk, Tom
Vediramana Krishnan, Hari Govind
Wendler, Philipp
Winter, Stefan
Wu, Changshun
Xu, Kathleen
Yang, Xiaodong
Zhang, Songyuan
Zimmermann, Martin

Abstracts of Invited Tutorials

Total Functional Programming in Idris: A Tutorial

Edwin Brady ⓘ

School of Computer Science, University of St Andrews, Scotland, UK
ecb10@st-andrews.ac.uk
https://type-driven.org.uk/edwinb

Abstract. Idris is a pure functional programming language with dependent types. The type system allows precise specification and reasoning about program properties. Idris also supports *totality checking*. A total function is a function which returns a finite, non-empty prefix of a (possibly infinite) result in finite time. The analysis is necessarily incomplete, but Idris uses syntactic and semantic checks to check which functions are guaranteed to be total. In this tutorial, I will discuss total programming in Idris [2], both to show its practical benefits in writing robust and secure code, and to show how to write total programs in practice.

Overview

The tutorial is in two parts. In the first part, I show how to write total programs using recursion and corecursion. Recursive programs are checked for totality by checking how the size of inputs changes through recursive calls, using the size-change principle [3]. Corecursive functions are checked for totality by ensuring that all corecursive calls are *guarded* by a constructor. By combining recursive and corecursive functions and a notion of "fuel" [4], we have a Turing-complete language where individual components are guaranteed total. I also show how *views*, a concept enabled by dependent types [5], make total programming powerful and accessible. I illustrate these concepts with an example of a concurrent server program. In the second part, I show how to define and implement the views we have used to describe common patterns of recursion. This involves an *accessibility predicate* which we can use to prove that recursive functions reduce to a base case. In particular, I demonstrate domain predicates [1] in Idris, a method for proving termination of general recursive functions.

References

1. Bove, A., Capretta, V.: Modelling general recursion in type theory. Math. Struct. in Comp. Science **15**, 671–708 (2002). https://doi.org/10.1017/S0960129505004822
2. Brady, E.: Idris 2: quantitative type theory in practice. In: Møller, A., Sridharan, M. (eds.) 35th European Conference on Object-Oriented Programming (ECOOP 2021). Leibniz International Proceedings in Informatics (LIPIcs), vol. 194, pp. 9:1–9:26. Schloss Dagstuhl –

Leibniz-Zentrum für Informatik, Dagstuhl, Germany (2021). https://doi.org/10.4230/LIPIcs. ECOOP.2021.9, https://drops.dagstuhl.de/opus/volltexte/2021/14052
3. Lee, C.S., Jones, N.D., Ben-Amram, A.M.: The size-change principle for program termination. SIGPLAN Not. **36**(3), 81–92 (2001). https://doi.org/10.1145/373243.360210
4. McBride, C.: Turing-completeness totally free. In: Hinze, R., Voigtländer, J. (eds.) MPC 2015. LNCS, vol. 9129, pp 257–275. Springer, Cham (2015). https://doi.org/10.1007/978-3-319-19797-5_13
5. McBride, C., McKinna, J.: The view from the left. J. Funct. Program. **14**(1), 69–111 (2004). https://doi.org/10.1017/S0956796803004829,   http://www.journals.cambridge.org/abstract_ S0956796803004829

The Lean 4 Theorem Prover
and Programming Language: A Tutorial

Leonardo de Moura[1] and Sebastian Ullrich[2]

[1] Microsoft Research
leonardo@microsoft.com
[2] Karlsruhe Institute of Technology
sebastian.ullrich@kit.edu

Lean 4[1] is an implementation of the Lean interactive theorem prover (ITP) and programming language in Lean itself. It addresses many shortcomings of the previous versions and contains many new features. Lean 4 is fully extensible: users can modify and extend the parser, elaborator, tactics, decision procedures, pretty printer, and code generator. The new system has a hygienic macro system custom-built for ITPs. It contains a new typeclass resolution procedure based on tabled resolution, addressing significant performance problems reported by the growing user base. Lean 4 is also an efficient functional programming language based on a novel programming paradigm called functional but in-place. Efficient code generation is crucial for Lean users because many write custom-proof automation procedures in Lean itself.

The main goal of this tutorial is to introduce Lean 4 to potential users. Participants are assumed to have only a basic grounding in logic and (functional) programming. The tutorial is based on the book "Theorem Proving in Lean"[2] and examples from the "Lean 4 Language Manual"[3].

---

[1] http://leanprover.github.io/.

[2] https://leanprover.github.io/theorem_proving_in_lean4/title_page.html.

[3] https://leanprover.github.io/lean4/doc/.

Formally Reasoning about Distributed Systems using P

Ankush Desai

Amazon
ankushpd@amazon.com

Abstract. Distributed systems are notoriously hard to get right. Programmers need to reason about numerous control paths resulting from the myriad inter-leaving of messages and failures. Moreover, it is extremely difficult to sys-tematically test distributed systems, most control paths remain untested, and serious bugs can lie dormant for months or even years after deployment. These bugs can be in the design of the system itself or a gap between design and its implementation. Hence, there is need for tools and techniques that can enable developers to reason about correctness of their system in different phases of the development cycle, from design, to implementation and testing, and also after deployment in production.

To address these challenges, we have been developing P, a unified framework for reasoning about distributed systems. P is a state machine based programming language for modeling and specifying distributed systems. P supports several backend analysis engines (like model checking and symbolic execution) to check that the distributed system modeled in P satisfies the desired correctness specifications. Not only can a P program be systematically tested (e.g., model checking), but it can also be compiled into executable code. Essentially, P unifies modeling, specifying, implementing, and testing into one activity for the programmer. P is currently being used extensively inside Amazon (AWS) for analysis of complex distributed systems. P is also being used in academia for programming safe robotic systems. P was first used to implement and validate the USB device driver stack that ships with Microsoft Windows 8 and Windows Phone.

In this short informal article, we provide a quick overview of the challenges and key features in P that we believe helped in its adoption. Finally, we encourage the formal methods and distributed systems community to use and contribute to the open source P framework.

Keywords: Model checking · Formal methods · Distributed systems

1 Challenge: Programming Reliable Distributed Systems

Programming reliable distributed systems is challenging because of the need to reason about correctness in the presence of myriad possible interleaving of messages and failures. Unsurprisingly, it is common for developers to uncover correctness bugs after deployment. Formal methods (FM)[1] can play an important role in addressing this challenge. But the key requirement for *success*, especially, in an industrial setting, would be the ability to integrate FM in all the phases of development process, from system design, to implementation, to unit and integration testing, and even in production through runtime monitoring. Moreover, for most of the known applications of formal techniques for distributed systems in industrial setup, analysis performed during design phase (e.g., TLA+ [1]) has not been connected to popular techniques for validation/testing of the implementation (e.g., Jepsen [2], Chaos Monkey [3]). It is crucial for the adoption of formal methods that efforts invested in writing specifications during the design verification phase must not get wasted and should play an important role in the later phases of the software life cycle, e.g., during testing of implementation.

To summarize, there is a need to build an unified framework that can be used to perform analysis of distributed systems at design, implementation, and even in production with the capability to reuse developers efforts (e.g., artifacts like models and specifications) across different phases of the development cycle.

2   P Framework

P [4] is a state machine-based programming language for modeling and specifying complex distributed systems. The P framework has three important parts: (1) a **high-level state machine-based programming language**, allowing programmers to specify their system design as a collection of communicating state machines. P being a programming language (rather than a mathematical modeling language) has been one of the key reasons for its large-scale adoption; Developers find it easy to create formal models in a programming language with familiar syntax. The syntactic sugar of state machines, allows them capture the protocol as state machines which is how they normally think about complex system design. (2) it supports **scalable analysis engines** to check that the distributed system modeled in P satisfy the desired correctness specifications. P can also leverages distributed compute to scale exploration to large system design and has helped find critical bugs in complex systems. (3) we are actively developing automated to **check code conformance** and take steps towards bridging the gap between design models/specifications and the actual implementation. Each of these features have played an important role in the adoption of P.

In our limited experience of using P inside industry and academia, we have observed that P has helped developers in three critical ways: (1) **"P as a thinking tool"**: Writing formal specifications in P forced developers to think about their system design rigorously, and in turn helped in bridging gaps in their understanding of the system. A large fraction of the bugs were eliminated in the process of writing specifications

---

[1] Formal Methods is used leniently to refer to the wide area of techniques from model checking, to property-based testing, to runtime monitoring. Essentially, approaches that can be easily integrated into development process but does require engineers to create formal models and specifications of their system.

itself; (2) **"P as a bug finder"**: Model checking helped find corner case bugs in system design that were missed by stress and integration testing; (3) **"P helped boost developer velocity"**: After the initial overhead of creating the formal models, future updates and feature additions could be rolled out faster as these non-trivial changes are rigorously validated before implementing them. P is an open source project and we encourage the formal methods and distributed systems community to use and contribute to the framework.

Acknowledgements. P has always been a collaborative project between industry and academia. We sincerely thank all the contributors to P framework over the years.

References

1. TLA+. https://lamport.azurewebsites.net/tla/tla.html.
2. Jepsen. https://jepsen.io/.
3. Chaos Monkey. https://netflix.github.io/chaosmonkey/.
4. P. https://p-org.github.io/P/.

Contents

xx   Contents

Invited Keynotes

Formal Methods for Trusted Space Autonomy: Boon or Bane?

Steve A. Chien[✉][iD]

Jet Propulsion Laboratory, California Institute of Technology,
Pasadena, CA 91109-8099, USA
steve.a.chien@jpl.nasa.gov
https://ai.jpl.nasa.gov

Abstract. Trusted Space Autonomy is challenging in that space systems are complex artifacts deployed in a high stakes environment with complicated operational settings. Thus far these challenges have been met using the full arsenal of tools: formal methods, informal methods, testing, runtime techniques, and operations processes. Using examples from previous deployments of autonomy (e.g. the Remote Agent Experiment on Deep Space One, Autonomous Sciencecraft on Earth Observing One, WATCH on MER, IPEX, AEGIS on MER, MSL, and M2020, and the M2020 Onboard planner), we discuss how each of these approaches have been used to enable successful deployment of autonomy. We next focus on relatively limited use of formal methods (both prior to deployment and runtime methods). From the needs perspective, formal methods may represent the best chance for reliable autonomy. Testing, informal methods, and operations accommodations do not scale well with increasing complexity of the autonomous system as the number of text cases explodes and human effort for informal methods becomes infeasible. However from the practice perspective, formal methods have been limited in their application due to: difficulty in eliciting formal specifications, challenges in representing complex constraints such as metric time and resources, and requiring significant expertise in formal methods to apply properly to complex, critical applications. We discuss some of these challenges as well as the opportunity to extend formal and informal methods into runtime validation systems.

Keywords: Verification and validation · Flight software · Space autonomy · Artificial intelligence

1 Introduction

From the dawn of the space era, software has played a key role in the advancement of spaceflight. In the Apollo program, flight software in the Apollo Guidance Computer [16] enabled the astronauts to safely land on the Moon despite a radar configuration switch being set incorrectly.

© Springer Nature Switzerland AG 2022
J. V. Deshmukh et al. (Eds.): NFM 2022, LNCS 13260, pp. 3–13, 2022.
https://doi.org/10.1007/978-3-031-06773-0_1

Yet even with this success, the Apollo flight software development process encountered tremendous challenges [31], many of which would be quite familiar to flight software teams of today:

- inadequate memory available for software to meet stated requirements,
- evolving requirements,
- unit software being delivered to integration without any unit testing,
- late software deliveries jeopardizing project schedule (even the launch dates), and
- challenges in coordination between the teams distributed at NASA (Houston, TX and Huntsville, AL) and MIT (Cambridge, MA).

The Apollo program mitigated these challenges using methods that would be familiar to current flight software teams:

- revolutionary use of an interpreted "higher order language" rather than machine or assembly code
- requirements driven software development,
- reduction in scope of the software (reducing the fidelity of the Earth model used in lunar orbit, some attitude maneuver computations),
- development of significant infrastructure to support significant software testing (e.g. hardware and software simulations),
- institution of change control boards to restrict scope changes, and
- mitigating the distributed teams by having key personnel spend time co-location with other team elements.

In the end, the Apollo flight software delivered spectacularly, in no small part because of the tremendously talented team. The lessons learned from the Apollo flight software effort [31] would also come as no surprise to current flight software practitioners:

- documentation is crucial,
- verification must proceed through several levels,
- requirements must be clearly defined and carefully managed,
- good development plans should be created and executed, and
- more programmers do not mean faster development.

The Apollo flight software can be considered the "first" space autonomy flight software. The verification and validation process for this consisted primarily of extensive unit and system level testing. Although it is not described explicitly as such [31], informal methods must also have been heavily used in the form of code reviews and algorithm reviews.

But if we are to realize the incredible promise of autonomy in future space missions [10], which relies on reliable, trusted, autonomy flight software, what are the prospects for such software moving forward? We argue that all three major elements of validation and verification techniques will be critical as we move into an era of greater autonomy flight software: formal methods, informal methods, and testing. More precisely defined, verification typically refers to ensuring that the software meets a specification and validation ensuring that the software meets the customer/user needs. For the purposes of our discussion, the focus is on verification but some elements of user studies, acceptance testing and informal design reviews would also address validation. Also for the purposes of this paper we use the following informal definitions.

Testing - exercising software artifacts - units, combinations of units, and system level on inputs both within and beyond the design specifications.

Formal Methods - analytical and search based methods intended to prove specific positive or negative properties of software or algorithms. Examples formal methods include model checking and static code analyzers.

Informal Methods - includes design reviews, code reviews, safety analysis, and coding guidelines. Informal methods tend to be people and knowledge intensive which is both a strength and a weakness. Some application of Formal Methods that requires expert translation or re-implementation of an algorithm into a different modelling language might best be considered hybrid formal/informal methods with the manual translation being an informal method.

In the remainder of this paper, we first describe major autonomy software that has been flown in space (including development of Mars 2020 Autonomy Flight Software scheduled for deployment in 2023) and discuss the use of informal methods, formal methods, and testing to Verify and Validate said software.

We then discuss the promise and the challenges in growing the role of formal methods in developing increasingly robust, verified and validated autonomy flight software.

2 Past Verification and Validation of Autonomy Flight Software

While only a small fraction of space missions include significant autonomy flight software, because of the large number of space missions there have been numerous flights of autonomy software. In this section we survey prior flights of autonomy/artificial intelligence software and describe the use of testing, informal methods, and formal methods in their deployment.

2.1 Remote Agent Experiment

The Remote Agent Experiment (RAX) [30] flew a planner-scheduler, task executive, and mode identification and recovery software onboard NASA's Deep Space One mission for two periods totaling approximately 48 h in 1999. RAX represented the first spaceflight of significant AI software. RAX made extensive use of multiple software and hardware testbeds of varying fidelity [4] to Verify and Validate the RAX software.

The verification and validation of the onboard planner used novel methods for testing including definitions of test coverage, use of a logical domain specification to check plans for correctness (derived from the planner model) and also checks automatically derived from flight rules [13,33].

RAX was not only a significant advance in autonomy but also demonstrated significant use of formal methods for verification. Specifically, the executive was verified pre-flight using the SPIN model checker which identified several concurrency bugs [18]. Additionally, when an anomaly occurred during flight, an experiment was conducted to use formal methods to isolate the issue in a java surrogate for the flight code [17]. These successes are an excellent indicator of the utility of formal methods for AI/Autonomy software.

2.2 Autonomous Sciencecraft on Earth Observing One

The Autonomous Sciencecraft (ASE) flew onboard the Earth Observing One (EO-1) Mission and enables significant science-driven autonomy [9,27]. ASE flew the CASPER onboard planning system, the Spacecraft Command Language (SCL) task executive, and also Onboard Data Analysis software (including Support Vector Machine Learning). ASE later flew the Livingston 2 (L2) Mode Identification and Recovery software as a further flight experiment but L2 was not used operationally [19,20]. ASE enabled onboard analysis of acquired imagery and modification of the future mission plan to acquire more images based on image analysis. ASE originally was slated as a 6 month technology demonstration, but was so successful that it was approved for continued operational usage and was the primary missions operation software for EO-1 for the remainder of the mission 2004–2017 (over a dozen years). ASE represented flight of a considerable code base (over 100 K source lines of code (SLOC), primarily in C++ and C. Preparing this large code base for flight required overcoming significant software issues including memory allocation and code image size [34].

ASE was verified and validated using a combination of informal methods, formal methods, and testing [11]. Significant testing was performed on a range of software and hardware platforms of varying fidelity and included: requirements-based testing, unit testing, system-level testing, and scenario-based testing - including nominal, off nominal, and extrema scenarios.

ASE made heavy use of informal methods as well. A safety review was conducted studying over 80 potential ways in which incorrect operations could harm the spacecraft. ASE used a layered software and operations architecture with multiple redundant layers of: operations procedures, planner, executive, base flight software, and hardware. Therefore every layer could be used to redundantly enforce flight rules to protect the spacecraft. This layered architecture was very effective in enabling reliable operations.

ASE Verification and Validation had limited use of formal methods. Multiple static code checkers were used to check all ASE code. Automated code generation was used to generate of SCL checks from CASPER activity and resource specifications (this could be considered a form of runtime validation).

For a description of anomalies encountered during ASE operations and causes see [35]. It is worth noting that the majority of these anomalies could be considered systems engineering issues that were manifested in software, not core software errors (like pointer de-referencing or memory allocation issues).

2.3   WATCH/SPOTTER on Mars Exploration Rovers

WATCH/SPOTTER is image analysis software that was operationally qualified on the Mars Exploration Rovers (MER) mission [5] (WATCH is the MER software module name and SPOTTER is the name designated in publication(s)). WATCH was tested at the unit and subsystem level on testbeds ranging from workstation to the actual MER ground rover testbed. Informal methods were also used: coding guidelines, code walkthroughs, and software design document reviews. Standard code static analyzers were also applied as part of the project standard software process.

2.4   AEGIS on MER, MSL, and M2020

AEGIS is software used on the MER, MSL, and M2020 rover missions that allows the rover to acquire wide FOV imagery, find targets according to user specified science criteria, and target with narrow FOV sensors. AEGIS was originally developed for the MER mission Mini-TES and Pancam instruments[1] [12], updated for MSL with the Chemcam instrument [14], and is now in use on M2020 with the SuperCam instrument. AEGIS represents a significant code base at just under 30K lines of source code (SLOC).

Prior to deployment on all three rover missions, AEGIS was subjected to testing on testbeds ranging from workstations to actual ground rover testbeds. Informal methods were also applied such as code walkthroughs, software module reviews, and requirements analysis. Formal methods static code analyzers were also used as part of the normal software development process.

2.5   MSL FSW

While technically not all autonomy software, the Mars Science Laboratory (MSL) flight software development practices are worth considering as they represent the state of the practice for flight software development [21].

MSL heavily used a range of informal methods to ensure software quality including:

- risk-based coding rules (such as assertion density),
- design and code walkthroughs, and
- documentation requirements and reviews.

---

[1] Unfortunately the Mini-TES instrument failed before AEGIS-MER operational qualification so AEGIS was never able to be used with Mini-TES on MER on Mars.

Notably, the MSL project automated checking of the above software requirements.

MSL also conducted an extensive testing program on testbeds ranging from WSTS/linux workstation to flight testbeds.

Finally, MSL used formal methods in several ways. First, the SPIN model checker was used to search for concurrency issues in critical multithreaded code [21]. Second, significant amounts of code were automatically generated from higher-level specifications (such as controllers from statecharts). Third, MSL used the Coverity, Codesonar, Semmle, and Uno static code analyzers.

2.6   Intelligent Payload Experiment (IPEX)

IPEX [7] was a cubesat technology demonstration mission that demonstrated high throughput onboard processing for the HyspIRI Intelligent Payload Module (IPM) concept [8]. IPEX used the CASPER planner, a linux shell-based task executive, and numerous onboard instrument analysis software modules.

IPEX followed the same software processes as ASE. However, because IPEX was a much less complex spacecraft than EO-1 (specifically no active attitude control) the overall operations constraints were less complex. For IPEX the flight processor was running linux. This simplified the Verification and Validation process because there was very little difference between workstation and flight testbed environments - greatly facilitating testing. As with ASE, unit and system level testing, including nominal, off nominal, and extrema cases were performed. Informal methods included code, software module, and safety-based walkthroughs and reviews. Use of formal methods was limited to static code analyzers.

3   Current Validation of Autonomy Software: Onboard Planner for M2020

The Mars 2020 Mission is deploying an onboard scheduler to the Perseverance rover as this paper goes to press (Spring 2022) with a target operational date in 2023. This onboard scheduler would control most of the activities of the rover - including rover wake/sleep [28, 32]. This onboard scheduler must be fit within limited rover computing resources [15]. The onboard scheduler also utilizes flexible execution (which can be viewed as taking on the role of an executive) [1] and also supports a limited form of disjunction in plans [2]. The onboard planner represents a sizeable, complex code base at approximately 56K source lines of code (SLOC). The ground-based version of the automated scheduler [36] also has an explanation capability [3] to assist the ground operations team in understanding possible plans and outcomes.

The onboard planner is being verified using a combination of testing, informal methods, and formal methods. Testing includes unit test, systems test, and scenario tests. Specifically scenario testing includes approximately 1 year of operations data of the Perseverance rover since landing. Informal methods includes code walkthroughs, coding guidelines and rules (see MSL above), as well as design reviews and software documentation. Finally, formal methods include the use of static code analyzers as part of the M2020 software development process.

4 Discussion of Competing Verification and Validation Methods

In some sense, formal methods may be seen as more promising to achieve robust Verification and Validation to large scale, complex, autonomous systems. Consider the weaknesses of Testing and Informal Methods.

4.1 Limitations of Testing and Informal Methods

Testing can only reveal bugs, it cannot prove a software artifact bug-free. Residual defect rate refers to the defect rate in released software (e.g. post validation). Even the highly verified NASA space shuttle avionics software experienced 0.1 residual defects per KLOC [26] and leading-edge software companies experience a residual defect rate of 0.2 residual defects per KLOC [25]. A more broad reliability survey showed a residual defect rate of 1.4 per KLOC [29] and a Military system survey [6] showed a residual defect rate of 5–55 residual detects per KLOC. Additionally, testing can be extremely expensive both in terms of infrastructure (test drivers, simulators, oracles to evaluate tests) as well as time and computing power.

Informal methods can leverage significant human expert knowledge but are also incredibly time, labor, and expertise intensive and therefore add considerable expense to the software validation process.

4.2 Limitations of Formal Methods

Given the considerable weaknesses of testing and informal methods, one might consider why formal methods are not used. However consider the following challenges for application of formal methods to validation of autonomous space systems.

The Formal Specification Problem. Typically in order to apply formal methods, one needs three formal specifications: the target artifact, the algorithm/semantics, and the conditions to check. For example, when analyzing a computer program for race conditions, the target artifact is the program itself, the algorithm/semantics are the semantics of the programming language, and the conditions would be a formal specification of the "race conditions" one wishes to identify. If one is validating that a space system planner will generate valid plans, the target artifact might be the planner model, the algorithm/semantics might be the target planner algorithm for generating plans, and the conditions might be some specification of soundness or termination. The challenge of this approach is twofold. First, it is a tremendous amount of effort to derive the second and third specification, whose primary purpose is to enable the application of the formal methods analysis. Second, even if one is able to derive these specifications, they themselves are suspect and the process is only as good as these input specifications. E.g. recursively one might require a Verification and Validation process on these inputs as well.

The Representation Problem. Formal methods are challenged by expressive representations. Specifically, space applications are demanding in their requirements for: complex spatial representations of location, free space, pointing and geometry; mixed discrete and continuous quantities and resources; and use of multiple, variable resolution time systems. Any one of these presents considerable challenges for formal methods, space applications often include most if not all of these representational challenges simultaneously. On the other hand, practical problems are typically propositional (or at least bounded instances) so that the truly general representations (such as first order predicate logic) are not strictly required. Still, in order for formal methods to make further headway in Verification and Validation of space autonomous systems, further advances in domain modelling capability are needed.

The Tractability Problem. A formal methods proof that a property holds often is achieved by exhaustive search of some execution space (such as proving non concurrency of two elements may require searching the entire space of element orderings). For many space autonomy problems complete search of such a problem space is computationally intractable.

In some cases static source code analysis and logic model checking can been used to study the dual problem. Instead of exhaustively searching a problem space to prove a property, one searches in the problem space for violations of the property. In this way, even partial search can identify issues in the code [23]. This in some ways is more akin to testing but can achieve much greater coverage more rapidly (e.g. this approach can be considered a more efficient means of testing). Unfortunately, such approaches suffer similar drawbacks as testing - e.g. that they can only find issues and cannot (without complete search) indicate that no such issues exist.

Note also that increasing computing capabilities and swarm-based distributed methods of validation [22,24] spread computational difficulties of these approaches may be mitigated. However, because many of these search problems scale exponentially om problem specification (e.g. code size) progress can be elusive.

The Expertise Problem. Because of the above challenges, it often requires considerable expertise to apply formal methods to good effect. For example, the MSL concurrency analysis was performed by world class experts in formal methods. Because of the challenges described, one must not only be able to develop formal specifications, but one must understand how to build specifications that model the correct aspects of the application and are amenable to efficient analysis (e.g. this deeper application of formal methods is far from out of the box static code analyzers). In many respects, this is analogous to the situation with autonomy for space applications, in which considerable expertise in software, space, and operations is needed to develop and deploy critical autonomy software.

5 Conclusions

This paper has discussed prospects for an increasing role for formal methods in the verification and validation of autonomy flight software. We first surveyed a number of prior and ongoing developments of autonomy flight software and described their use of testing, informal methods, and formal methods. In all of these cases, the bulk of the effort consisted of testing and informal methods. With only a few notable exceptions (such as MSL code generation and Model checking of critical code), usage of formal methods was restricted to use of static code analyzers. We then discussed several challenges in application of formal methods that restrict its usage: The Formal Specification Problem, The Representation Problem, The Tractability Problem, and The Expertise Problem. Yet because of the inherent limitations of testing and informal methods, we are still optimistic and believe that formal methods are an essential tool in the development of space autonomy software in the future.

Acknowledgments. This work was performed at the Jet Propulsion Laboratory, California Institute of Technology, under a contract with the National Aeronautics and Space Administration.

References

1. Agrawal, J., Chi, W., Chien, S.A., Rabideau, G., Gaines, D., Kuhn, S.: Analyzing the effectiveness of rescheduling and flexible execution methods to address uncertainty in execution duration for a planetary rover. Robot. Auton. Syst. **140** (2021) 103758 (2021). https://doi.org/10.1016/j.robot.2021.103758
2. Agrawal, J., et al.: Enabling limited resource-bounded disjunction in scheduling. J. Aerosp. Inf. Syst. **18**(6), 322–332 (2021). https://doi.org/10.2514/1.I010908
3. Agrawal, J., Yelamanchili, A., Chien, S.: Using explainable scheduling for the mars 2020 rover mission. In: Workshop on Explainable AI Planning (XAIP), International Conference on Automated Planning and Scheduling (ICAPS XAIP), October 2020. https://arxiv.org/pdf/2011.08733.pdf
4. Bernard, D.E., et al.: The remote agent experiment. In: Deep Space One Technology Validation Symposium, Pasadena, CA, February 1999. https://ntrs.nasa.gov/api/citations/20000116204/downloads/20000116204.pdf
5. Castano, A., et al.: Automatic detection of dust devils and clouds at mars. Mach. Vis. Appl. **19**(5–6), 467–482 (2008)
6. Cavano, J., LaMonica, F.: Quality assurance in future development environments. IEEE Softw. **4**, 26–34 (1987)

7. Chien, S., et al.: Onboard autonomy on the intelligent payload experiment (IPEX) CubeSat mission. J. Aerosp. Inf. Syst. (JAIS) **14**(6), 307–315 (2016). https://doi.org/10.2514/1.I010386
8. Chien, S., Mclaren, D., Tran, D., Davies, A.G., Doubleday, J., Mandl, D.: Onboard product generation on earth observing one: a pathfinder for the proposed Hyspiri mission intelligent payload module. IEEE JSTARS Special Issue on the Earth Observing One (EO-1) Satellite Mission: Over a decade in space (2013)
9. Chien, S., et al.: Using autonomy flight software to improve science return on earth observing one. J. Aerosp. Comput. Inf. Commun. (JACIC) **2**, 196–216 (2005)
10. Chien, S., Wagstaff, K.L.: Robotic space exploration agents. Sci. Robot. (2017). https://www.science.org/doi/10.1126/scirobotics.aan4831
11. Cichy, B., Chien, S., Schaffer, S., Tran, D., Rabideau, G., Sherwood, R.: Validating the autonomous EO-1 science agent. In: International Workshop on Planning and Scheduling for Space (IWPSS 2004), Darmstadt, Germany, June 2004
12. Estlin, T., et al.: AEGIS automated targeting for the MER opportunity rover. ACM Trans. Intell. Syst. Technol. **3**(3), 1–19 (2012). Article No.: 50. https://doi.org/10.1145/2168752.2168764
13. Feather, M.S., Smith, B.: Automatic generation of test oracles–from pilot studies to application. Autom. Softw. Eng. **8**(1), 31–61 (2001)
14. Francis, R., et al.: AEGIS autonomous targeting for ChemCam on Mars Science Laboratory: deployment and results of initial science team use. Sci. Robot. **2** (2017). https://doi.org/10.1126/scirobotics.aan4582
15. Gaines, D., Rabideau, G., Wong, V., Kuhn, S., Fosse, E., Chien, S.: The Mars 2020 on-board planner: balancing performance and computational constraints. In: Flight Software Workshop, February 2022
16. George, A.: Margaret Hamilton led the NASA software team that landed astronauts on the moon (2019). https://www.smithsonianmag.com/smithsonian-institution/margaret-hamilton-led-nasa-software-team-landed-astronauts-moon-180971575/. Accessed 25 Mar 2022
17. Havelund, K., et al.: Formal analysis of the remote agent before and after flight. In: Lfm 2000: Fifth NASA Langley Formal Methods Workshop (2000)
18. Havelund, K., Lowry, M., Penix, J.: Formal analysis of a space-craft controller using spin. IEEE Trans. Softw. Eng. **27**(8), 749–765 (2001)
19. Hayden, S.C., Sweet, A.J., Christa, S.E.: Livingstone model-based diagnosis of earth observing one. In: AIAA Intelligent Systems Technical Conference. AIAA (2004). https://doi.org/10.2514/6.2004-6225
20. Hayden, S.C., Sweet, A.J., Shulman, S.: Lessons learned in the livingstone 2 on earth observing one flight experiment. In: AIAA Infotech@Aerospace. AIAA (2005). https://doi.org/10.2514/6.2005-7000
21. Holzmann, G.J.: Mars code. Commun. ACM **57**(2), 64–73 (2014)
22. Holzmann, G.J.: Cloud-based verification of concurrent software. In: Jobstmann, B., Leino, K.R.M. (eds.) VMCAI 2016. LNCS, vol. 9583, pp. 311–327. Springer, Heidelberg (2016). https://doi.org/10.1007/978-3-662-49122-5_15
23. Holzmann, G.J.: Test fatigue. IEEE Softw. **37**(4), 11–16 (2020)
24. Holzmann, G.J., Joshi, R., Groce, A.: Swarm verification techniques. IEEE Trans. Softw. Eng. **37**(6), 845–857 (2010)
25. Jones, C.: Applied Software Measurement. McGraw-Hill, New York (1991)
26. Joyce, E.: Is error free software possible? Datamation **35**(18), 749–765 (1989)
27. JPL-Artificial-Intelligence-Group: Autonomous sciencecraft web site (2017). https://ai.jpl.nasa.gov/public/projects/ase/. Accessed 25 Mar 2022

28. JPL-Artificial-Intelligence-Group: Mars 2020 onboard planner web site (2017). https://ai.jpl.nasa.gov/public/projects/m2020-scheduler/. Accessed 25 Mar 2022

29. Musa, J., et al.: Software Reliability: Measurement, Prediction, Application. McGraw-Hill, New York (1990)

30. Muscettola, N., Nayak, P.P., Pell, B., Williams, B.C.: Remote agent: to boldly go where no AI system has gone before. Artif. Intell. **103**(1–2), 5–47 (1998)

31. NASA: Chapter two: Computers on board the apollo spacecraft. In: Computers in Spaceflight: The NASA Experience. NASA. https://history.nasa.gov/computers/Ch2-6.html?mod=article_inline. Accessed 27 Mar 2022

32. Rabideau, G., et al.: Onboard automated scheduling for the Mars 2020 rover. In: Proceedings of the International Symposium on Artificial Intelligence, Robotics and Automation for Space, i-SAIRAS 2020, European Space Agency, Noordwijk, NL (2020)

33. Smith, B.D., Feather, M.S., Muscettola, N.: Challenges and methods in testing the remote agent planner. In: AIPS, pp. 254–263 (2000)

34. Tran, D., Chien, S., Rabideau, G., Cichy, B.: Flight software issues in onboard automated planning: Lessons learned on EO-1. In: International Workshop on Planning and Scheduling for Space (IWPSS 2004), Darmstadt, Germany, June 2004. https://ai.jpl.nasa.gov/public/papers/tran_iwpss2004.pdf

35. Tran, D., Chien, S., Rabideau, G., Cichy, B.: Safe agents in space: preventing and responding to anomalies in the autonomous sciencecraft experiment. In: Safety and Security in Multi Agent Systems Workshop (SASE-MAS), Autonomous Agents and Multi-Agent Systems Conference (AAMAS 2005), Utrecht, Netherlands, July 2005. https://ai.jpl.nasa.gov/public/papers/tran_sasemas2005_PreventingResponding.pdf

36. Yelamanchili, A., et al.: Ground-based automated scheduling for operations of the Mars 2020 rover mission. In: Proceedings Space Operations 2021, May 2021. https://spaceops.iafastro.directory/a/proceedings/SpaceOps-2021/SpaceOps-2021/6/manuscripts/SpaceOps-2021,6,x1385.pdf

An Essence of Domain Engineering
A Basis for Trustworthy Aeronautics and Space Software

Dines Bjørner[1,2]([⊠])

[1] DTU Compute, Technical University of Denmark, 2800 Kgs. Lyngby, Denmark
bjorner@gmail.com
[2] Technical University of Denmark, Fredsvej 11, 2840 Holte, Denmark
https://www.imm.dtu.dk/~dibj

Abstract. Before *software* can be *designed* one must have a reasonable grasp of its requirements. Before *requirements* can be *prescribed* one must have a reasonable grasp of the domain in which the software is to serve. So we must *study, analyse* and *describe* the application *domain*. We shall argue that *domain science & engineering* is a necessary prerequisite for requirements engineering, and hence software design. We survey elements of domain science & engineering – and exemplify some elements of domain descriptions. We finally speculate on the relevance of domain engineering in the context of and aeronautics and space.

Keywords: Formal methods · Philosophy · Software · Domain engineering · Requirements engineering

1 Introduction

A monograph has been published: [11, *Domain Science and Engineering*]. We immodestly claim that the contents of that monograph "heralds" a *new*, an *initial*, phase of software development—a *new area of study* within the exact sciences.

An aim of the present paper is to propagate awareness of the aim & objectives of that book and hence of this new field, also, of computer science – as labeled by the book title.

Another side-aim is to also introduce the possibility of a *Philosophy of Informatics*[1]. This, we think, is *a first* for computer & computing science, to be

---

[1] We take *informatics* to be an amalgam of mostly mathematical nature: computer & computing science and mathematics. Another such amalgam is *IT* which we consider as mostly of technological nature: electronics, plasma and quantum physics, etc. *Informatics*, to us, is a *universe of intellectual quality:* meeting customers expectations, correct wrt. specifications, etc. *IT* is then a *universe of material quantity:* smaller, bigger, faster, less costly, etc. The products of *informatics* [must] satisfy laws of mathematics, in particular of mathematical logic. The products of *IT* [must] satisfy the laws of physics.

Invited paper for the *The 14th NASA Formal Methods Symposium*, https://nfm2022.caltech.edu, May 24–27, 2022, Pasadena, California, USA.

© Springer Nature Switzerland AG 2022
J. V. Deshmukh et al. (Eds.): NFM 2022, LNCS 13260, pp. 14–51, 2022.
https://doi.org/10.1007/978-3-031-06773-0_2

"endowed" with a philosophy, as is mathematics [40], physics [13], life sciences [74], etc. Yes, we are aware of previous attempts[2] to include considerations of specific, detailed, technical issues of theoretical computer science as being of philosophical nature. But what we are suggesting, is, perhaps immodestly expressed, of a more foundational kind. In our treatment of a possible philosophy of informatics we shall *"dig deeper"*, as directed by [65–68].

The first four lines of the abstract expresses a dogma – the **Triptych**[3] dogma. In those lines we used the term 'reasonable'. By 'reasonable' we mean that we can rationally reason about the domain – as do physicists and mathematicians. To us that means that domain descriptions are expressed in some notation that allows logical reasoning. Here we shall use RSL, the Raise[4] Specification Language [27,28]. To express the analysis and description calculi of this paper we shall use an informal extension of RSL, one whose description functions yield RSL texts, RSL⁺Text.

This paper thus serves to propagate the dogma that software development proceeds from the study, analysis and informal and formal *domain descriptions*, via the "derivation" of *requirements prescriptions* from domain descriptions, to *software design*, "derived" from requirements prescriptions.

The paper presents a capsule view of the monograph. For the reasoning behind the various concepts and the technical details of the domain engineering method, its principles, techniques and tools, we refer to [11].

By a **method** we shall understand a set of principles and procedures for selecting and applying a number of techniques and tools for constructing an artifact. By a **formal method** we shall understand a method whose techniques and tools are given a mathematical understanding. By a **formal software development method** – in the context of the triptych dogma –we shall understand a formal method which is "built upon", i.e., utilizes, one or more formal specification languages, i.e., languages with formal syntax, formal semantics and proof systems, that are the used to describe, prescribe and design domain descriptions, requirements prescriptions and software – allowing formal tests [33], formal model checks [19] and formal proofs in order to verify these specifications and their transformations.

1.1   What Is a Domain?

By a *domain* we shall understand a *rationally describable*[5] area of a *discrete dynamics* segment of a *human assisted reality*, i.e., of the world, its *solid or fluid entities*: *natural* ["God-given"] and *artefactual* ["man-made"] parts, and its *living species entities*: *plants* and *animals* including, notably, *humans* [11, Sect. 4.2, Defn. 27]. In this paper we shall not cover the 'living species' aspects.

---

2   https://en.wikipedia.org/wiki/Philosophy_of_computer_science.
3   Triptych: a picture (such as an altarpiece) or carving in three panels side by side, or something composed or presented in three parts or sections especially, like a trilogy.
4   Raise: Rigorous approach to industrial software engineering.
5   By 'rationally describable' we mean that the specification, in this case the description, must allow for formal, i.e., logical reasoning.

1.2   Structure of Paper

There are four main sections of this paper. Section 2 discusses the problem of what must, unavoidably, be in any domain description. It does so on the background of the quest of philosophers – since antiquity – for understanding the world around us. Sections 3–4 summarise, respectively exemplify, a domain analysis & description method. The two sections go hand-in-hand. They have, sequentially, 'near-identical' subsections and paragraphs. Where some aspects of the method may be omitted in Sect. 3, Sect. 4 may exemplify also those aspects. Section 5 'speculates' on further perspectives of domain science & engineering. Its potential for application in aeronautics and space!

2   Philosophy: What Must be in any Domain Description?

Philosophy, since the ancient Greeks, have pondered over the question: *which are the absolutely necessary conditions for describing any world?*, that is: *what, if anything, is of such necessity, that it could under no circumstances be otherwise?*, or: *which are the necessary characteristics of any possible world?* We take these three as one-and-the-same question.

Philosophers, from *Aristotle* (384–322 BC) to *Immanuel Kant* (1724–1804), and onwards, have contributed to understanding this set of questions. We shall draw upon the works of the Danish Philosopher *Kai Sørlander* (1944) [65–68]. We shall therefore base our search for techniques and tools with which to analyse & describe domains in Sørlander's findings. This, in effect means, that we suggest a philosophy-basis for domain analysis & description! Next we shall therefore first summarise two thousand five hundred years of trying to answer the question with which we opened this section.

2.1   The Search

We shall focus only on one aspect of the philosophies of the very many philosophers that are mentioned below—namely their thinking wrt. *ontology*[6] and *epistemology*[7]; for many of these philosophers – from Plato onwards – this is, but a mere fraction of their great thinking.

This section borrows heavily from [68]. That book is only published in Danish. So the next three pages, till Sect. 3, is a terse summary of the first 130 pages of [68].

The Ancient Greeks. The quest for understanding the world around us appears to have started in ancient Greece. *Thales of Miletus* [51] (624/623–548/545 BC) claimed that everything originates from *water*. *Anaximander* [20] (610–546 BC) counter-claimed that 'apeiron' (the 'un-differentiated', 'the unlimited') was the origin. *Anaximenes* [50] (586–526 BC) counter-counter-claimed that *air* was the

---

[6] Ontology is the study of concepts such as *existence, being, becoming*, and *reality.*
[7] Epistemology is the study of properties, origin and limits for human knowledge.

basis for everything. *Heraklit of Efesos* [1] (540-480 BC) suggested that *fire* was the basis and that everything in nature *was in never-ending "battle"*. *Empedokles* [75] (490–430 BC) synthesized the above into the claim that there are four base elements: *fire, water, air* and *soil. Parminedes* [31] (515–470 BC) meant that everything that exists is *eternal and immutable. Demokrit* [1] (460–370 BC) argues that all is built from *atoms.* These were [some of] the *natural philosophers*, the *pre-Socrates* philosophers, the *ontologists*, of Ancient Greece.

The Sofists. Then came a period of so-called *sofists.* They maintained that we cannot reach understanding of the world through common sense. For a time they thus broke philosophical tradition. It was not their task to reach an understanding of that which exists. Such an understanding, they claimed, was an illusion; in that they seem to agree with today's modernism and post-modernism.

Socrates, Plato and Aristotle. Socrates (470–399 BC) [2] broke rank with this. For him it was a fundamental error to give up on the obligation of common, universal sense. Socrates, instead of reflecting on the general aspects of ontology, put the human in centrum. *Plato* [3] (427–347 BC) established a *Theory of Ideas* of "universal concepts" as of highest reality, that, however, seems to raise more questions than answering some. *Aristotle* [4] (384–322 BC) turned Plato's thinking upside-down: "concrete things" have primary existence and the universal concepts are abstractions. Aristotle made precise relations between the **modalities** of the *necessary*, the *real* and the *possible*, and suggested a list, [4, *Categories*], of ten **categories: substance, quantity, quality, relation, place, time, position, possession, acting** and **suffering**.

The "Middle Ages". Philosophical thinking – in the European sphere – from about 300 BC till about 1600 AC was dominated by religious thought – till shortly after the time of Martin Luther. From ontological arguments philosophy turned in the direction of epistemological arguments.

From Descartes to Hume. Then a number of philosophical schools succeeded one another. Sørlander shows that the philosophies of *Descartes* [23] (1596–1650), *Spinoza* [69] (1632–1677), *Leibniz* [45] (1646–1716), *Locke* [47] (1632–1704), *Berkeley* [7] (1685–1753) and *Hume* [38] (1711–1776) are individually inconsistent, and must thus be rejected.

Historicism. Sørlander also rejects the *'historicism'* philosophies, after *Immanuel Kant*, i.e., those of *Fichte* [42] (1762–1814), *Schelling* [6] (1775–1854) and *Hegel* [30] (1770–1831) as likewise individually inconsistent.

From Aristotle to Kant and Onwards …. Sørlander builds on the thinking of *Aristotle* [4] (384–322) and *Immanuel Kant* [43] (1724–1804). In doing so, Sørlander takes up a thread, lost for two hundred years of *"radical meaninglessness, loss of religion, the disappearance of [proper] philosophy – lost in the "historicism" of the 19th century and the "modernism" of the 20th century, in postmodernism's rejection of universal values, the possibility of objective knowledge, or solid foundation for human existence."* ... *"In this post-modern age nothing seems to be absolutely valid, there is no sharp boundary between fiction and science, everything is dissolved into uncertainty and individual interpretation"* No, says Sørlander, and builds a Philosophy based on rational reasoning. The current author, obviously, subscribes to the above!

Philosophies of Sciences. The science breakthroughs, in the late 1800s s and the early-to-mid 1900s,s, in mathematics, physics and biology, brought with it, independent of the 'historicism' of philosophy, philosophical investigations of these sciences.

Peano (1858–1932) [44] showed that some of **mathematics** could be understood axiomatically, i.e., logically. *Frege* (1848–1925) [25] contributed significantly to attempts to build an axiomatic basis for all of mathematics. On the basis of similar axiom systems *non-Euclidean Geometries* were then put forward[8]. *Principia Mathematica* [71, *Whitehead & Russell*] "grandiosely" attempted to axiomatise all of mathematics. *Gödel*'s (1906–1978) [29] *first incompleteness theorem* states that in any formal system $\mathbb{F}$ within which a certain amount of arithmetic can be carried out, there are statements of the language of $\mathbb{F}$ which can neither be proved nor disproved in $\mathbb{F}$. According to the second incompleteness theorem, such a formal system cannot prove that the system itself is consistent (assuming it is indeed consistent). These results have had a great impact on the philosophy of mathematics and logic.

Within **physics**, *Maxwell* (1831–1879) [48] *Planck* (1858–1947) [53] originated *quantum mechanics*. *Einstein*[9] (1879–1955), in 1905–1916 changed the study of physics with his *special* and *general theories of relativity*. *Bohr*[10] (1885–1962) [24] contributed with his understanding of the structure of atoms and with *quantum theory*. *Heisenberg* (1901–1976) [32] contributed further to quantum theory and is known for the uncertainty principle.

Darwin (1809–1882) [21, Origin of Species], *Wallace* (1823–1913) [70], and *Mendel* (1822–1884) [49] – as did Planck, Einstein, Bohr, Heisenberg, et al. for physics – founded modern **life sciences.**

These advances in mathematics and the natural sciences spurred some philosophers on to renewed studies – *"as from Kant!"*

The 20th Century. The *phenomenology of Husserl* (1859–1938) [39], *is the study of structures of consciousness as experienced from the first-person point of view*

---

[8] https://en.wikipedia.org/wiki/Non-Euclidean_geometry.

[9] https://en.wikipedia.org/wiki/Religious_and_philosophical_views_of_Albert_Einstein#Philosophical_beliefs.

[10] https://plato.stanford.edu/entries/qm-copenhagen/.

[Wikipedia]. Our consciousness, claims Husserl, is characterised by *intentionality:* an elementary directedness. Husserl's phenomenology appears to be inconsistent in the way it requires a study of our consciousness from "within", for example in the a-priory requirements that these concepts are introduced, not as a result of the study, but "beforehand".

It appeared then that philosophical studies along the lines *"what must inevitably be in any description of any domain"* additionally required consideration of our use of language. *Wittgenstein* (1889–1951) [72,73] and the *Logical Atomism* [52] of *Russell* (1872–1970) [59–62], made attempts in this direction, but failed. Wittgenstein realised that in his [73, *"Philosophisces Untersuchungen"*]. Logical atomism failed in not finding examples of propositions if they have to be logically independent of one another.

Logical Positivism, "coming out of" Vienna in the 1920s–1930s, rejected Russell's logical atomism and concentrated on the meaning of a sentence as being [the conditions for] its truth-value: one must be able to describe the circumstances under which the sentence can be verified. To them, in the early days, meaningful propositions, say, in any of the sciences, must have a common linguistic base. Eventually those theses also failed: Neither the verification-criteria, of, for example *Carnap* (1891–1970) [14–17], could be verified, nor could the falsification-criteria of *Popper* (1902–1994) [54–57] be falsified.

2.2 Sørlander's Findings

Three Cornerstones. We can claim that Sørlander bases his philosophical analyses on three "cornerstones": (A) an analysis and a conclusion of *"what it means to be rational"*; (B) an analysis and a conclusion of what it means to speak abut *"the meaning of a word"*; and (C) an analysis and a conclusion of the base point from which to start the philosophical inquiry into *"what must inevitably be in any domain description"*. We shall now review these three bases.

A: Rational Thinking. The following is adapted from [66, Chapter II, Sects. 4–5 *Common Sense and Motivation*]. Humans are physical entities. Thus we are characterisable by the causal conditions for moving around with purpose. To do so requires three conditions: We can *sense* our immediate situation. We have *feelings* that may result in incentives (encouragements). We have motoric apparatus that satisfy physical laws. These were the causal conditions for purposeful movements. Further: We possess languages by means of which to express propositions as to what we sense, our feelings and actions. We express propositions which reflect that *we know*, i.e., *have knowledge*, Finally we have *memory* from which we build *experience*. The above factors, after some further analysis, leads us to conclude that humans are *rational beings*.

B: The Implicit Meaning-Theory. The following is adapted from [67, Chapter III, especially Sect. 9 *The Meaning of a Word*, Pages 121–122]. On the basis of some simple considerations of what it means to express oneself by means of language, i.e., linguistically, Sørlander reaches the *interdependence* criterion. In saying, or writing, something, a choice is made. The chosen statement may be inconsistent with something else that one could have chosen to state. That means, that possible statements stand in consistence relations. What determines such relations? We can, firstly, say that these relations are determined by the meaning, of the designations used in the statements. Secondly we can say that meaning of the designations used in several statements which (thus must) stand in mutual consistence-relations. It is thus that we arrive at the necessary condition, *interdependence* criterion, also referred to as the *implicit meaning theory*, that *there is a mutual dependence between the meaning of designations and the consistence relations between statements.*

For computer scientists, this interdependence criterion is quite familiar. When defining an *abstract data type*—that is, its values and operations, as is, for example typical in algebraic semantics [63]—one states a number of propositions. They constrain values and operations, and, together, express their meaning.

C: The Possibility of Truth. The following is adapted from [68, Part III, Chapter 2 *"Basis & Method for the Philosophy"*]. Where Kant built on *human self-awareness*, Sørlander builds on the *possibility of truth*. One cannot deny that a proposition may be false. And one cannot accept that a proposition is both true and false. Hence the possibility of truth.

Building a Foundation

Logic, Relations, Transcendental Deduction, Space and Time. On the basis of *the principle of contradiction* and the *implicit meaning theory*. Kai Sørlander then motivates *the logical connectives* and, from these, *the associative, symmetry and transitive relations*, and, based on these, by *transcendental deduction*, reasons that *space* and *time* follows, not as, with Immanuel Kant, empirical facts, but as logical necessities.

Multiple, Uniquely Identifiable Entities and States. Again, in a rational manner, Sørlander, motivates that there must be an indefinite number of entities, that these are uniquely identifiable, and that they endure in possibly changing states.

Newton's Laws. Again, in a rational manner, Sørlander, motivates *movement* and *causality*, and, from these, again by *transcendental deductions*, *Newton's Laws*.

2.3   The Basis

The above, i.e., the rational deductions of what must be in any domain description, is then the foundation on which [11] and the present paper base their domain analysis & description approach.

3 Elements of Domain Science and Engineering

We embark on introducing a number of *domain analysis predicates*. These are not mathematical functions. They are informal in the sense of being applied by human *domain analysers cum describers*. They can not be formalised. That would require that we have a formal model of "the world"! Our domain analysis & description endeavour seeks such models! So the reader must bear with me: The delineations (cum definitions, characterisations) of the domain concepts that now follow must unavoidably be informal, yet sufficiently precise. Most are drawn from *The Shorter Oxford Dictionary of the English Language* [46, 2 vols., 1987].

3.1 Phenomena, Entities, Endurants and Perdurants

A *phenomenon*, ϕ, is an *entity*, is_entity(ϕ), if it can be *observed*, i.e., be seen or touched by humans, *or* that can be *conceived* as an *abstraction* of an entity; alternatively, a phenomenon is an entity *if it exists, it is "being", it is that which makes a "thing" what it is: essence, essential nature* [46, Vol. I, pg. 665]. If a phenomenon cannot be so described it is not an entity.

There are an indefinite number of entities in any domain. This follows from philosophic-analytic reasoning outlined by the philosopher Kai Sørlander [65–68]. We refer to [11, Sect. 2.2.3] for a summary.

By an *endurant*, is_endurant(e), we shall understand an entity, e, that can be observed, or conceived and described, as a "complete thing" at no matter which given snapshot of time; alternatively an entity is endurant if it is capable of *enduring*, that is *persist*, "hold out" [46, Vol. I, pg. 656]. Were we to "freeze" time we would still be able to observe the entire endurant.

By a *perdurant*, is_perdurant(e), we shall understand an entity, e, for which only a fragment exists if we look at or touch them at any given snapshot in time. Were we to freeze time we would only see or touch a fragment of the perdurant [46, Vol. II, pg. 1552].

External qualities of endurants of a manifest domain are, in a simplifying sense, those we, for example with our eyes blinded, can touch, hence manifestly "observe", and hence speak about abstractly.

Internal qualities of endurants of a manifest domain are those we, with our eyes open and with instruments, can measure.

3.2 Endurants

Figure 1 presents a graphic structure of the domain concepts such as we have and shall unveil them.

External Qualities. Our treatment of endurants "follow" the upper ontology of Fig. 1 in a left-to-right, depth-first traversal of the endurant "tree" (of Fig. 1).

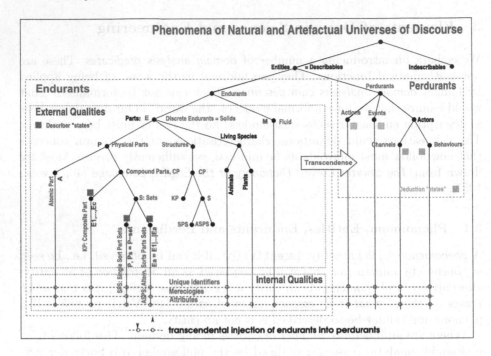

Fig. 1. A domain description ontology

Analysis Predicates. Endurants, e [is_endurant(e)], are either *solid* [is_-solid(e)]; or *fluid* [is_fluid(e)] (such as liquids, gases and plasmas). Solid endurants appears to be the "work-horse" of the domains we shall be concerned with. *Fluids* are presently further un-analysed. A *solid, e,* is either a *part* [is_-part(e)]; or a *structure* [is_structure(e)]; or a *living species* [is_living_-species(e)]. A *part, p,* is either an *atomic part* [is_atomic_part(p)]; or a *compound part* [is_compound_part(p)]. An *atomic part*, by definition, has no proper sub-parts. It is the domain analyser cum describer who decides which parts are atomic and which not. Atomic parts are further characterised by their internal qualities. A *compound part* is either a *composite part* [is_composite(p)]; or a *part set* [is_part_set(p)], A *part set* is either a *single sort part set* of parts of the same sort [is_single_sort_set(p)]; or an *alternative sort part set* of parts of two or more distinct sorts [is_alternative_sort_set(p)] – with two or more parts possibly being of the same sort.

A *composite* part consists of two or more parts (and could be modeled as a *Cartesian* of these). A *structure* is like a compound part but we omit recording its internal qualities[11]. A *living species* is either an *animal* [is_animal(e)]; or a *plant* [is_plant(e)]. An *animal* is either a *human* [is_human(e)]; or other.

---

[11] We could omit the concept of structure altogether and just allow compounds that do not have internal qualities.

Observers. Given a compound part we can observe its sub-parts and their sorts. We formulate these observers in RSL$^+$Text.

• • •

We remind the reader that the analysis and description processes are necessarily informal. That is, that it is the decision of the domain analyser cum describer as to whether an entity is an endurant or other, a part or other, etc. Next, in outlining, ever so briefly, the observer (cum describer) "functions", the describer must, repeatedly, decide that endurants are of definite sorts, and must, likewise repeatedly, choose names for endurant sorts. [11, Sect. 4.14] discusses that process in some detail. In reality, to determine, distinctness and names of sorts require a depth-first analysis, that is, one that analyses the internal qualities of the sort under investigation, then the external followed by internal qualities of possible sub-parts, et cetera, till atomic parts or fluids have been analysed, etc. In this section we first analyse external qualities. Analysis of internal qualities follow subsequently.

• • •

The next three observer functions reflect analyses pre-requisite to the subsequent description functions. In the formulas below we introduce two notions: The *name* of a type, say type E, as ηE, and the RSL text, of a type name, "E". ηE is an identifier whose value is "E".

Observe Single Sort Part Sets.

Observing a part, $p : P$, which is a set of endurants of the same sort, yields a pair of a set of endurants and the name of the endurant type.

value
  obs_single_sort_set: P $\rightarrow$ E-set $\times$ ηE

where E is to be further analysed and described.

Observe Alternative Sorts Part Sets.

Observing a part, $p : P$, which is a set of endurants of the possibly different sorts, yields a Cartesian of representative pairs[12] of endurants and names of their type.

value
  obs_alternative_sort_set: P $\rightarrow$ (E1 $\times\eta$E1)$\times$(E2 $\times\eta$E2)$\times$ ... $\times$(Em $\times\eta$Em)

where each Ei is to be further analysed and described.

Observe Composite Part.

Observing a part, $p : P$, which is a composite of endurants of [it is assumed] different sorts, yields a pair Cartesians of endurants, respectively their type.

value
  obs_composite: P $\rightarrow$ (E_1$\times$E_2$\times$...$\times$E_m) $\times$ (ηE_1$\times\eta$E_2$\times$...$\times\eta$E_m)

where each E_i is to be further analysed and described.

---

[12] By 'representative Cartesian of pairs' we mean that there is a pair of any part (of the set) and its type for every possible part type in the Cartesian.

Description Functions. There are three compound-part description functions. These are summarised in the RSL⁺Text form next.

We advocate first narrating all formal texts. The literal **type** prefix type and sort definitions. The literal **value** prefix predicate and function signatures and definitions. Proof obligations are required where sorts are expressed in terms of concrete types that may define something meaningless if not properly constrained.

Caveat: We remind the reader that the above *description functions*, really, are not mathematical functions: They are, in a sense, procedural guide-lines to be followed by *domain analysers cum describers:* they have to decide on which kind of parts they are dealing with, of which, already "discovered" or new sorts, hence sort names to ascribe these, etc.

The External Qualities Frames. The three frames next contain part descriptors for single sort sets, alternative sort sets, and composites.

```
─── describe_single_sort_set(p) as ───
let (_,ηE) = obs_single_sort_set(p) in
"Narration:
    ... on sorts ...
    ... on sort observers ...
    ... on axioms/proof obligations ...
Formalisation:
    type
        E
        Ps = P-set
    value
        obs_Ps: E → Ps  "
end
pre: is_single_sort_set(p)
```

```
─── describe_alternative_sorts_set(p) as ───
let ((_,ηE_1),...,(_,ηE_n))
    = obs_alternative_sorts_set(p) in
"Narration:
    ... on alternative sorts ...
    ... on sort observers ...
    ... on axioms/proof obligations ...
Formalisation:
    type
        Ea = E_1 | ... | E_n
        E_1 :: E1, ..., E_n :: En
        E1 == ..., ..., En == ...
    value
        obs_E_j: E → E_j [ j=1,...,n ]
    proof obligation
        [ disjointness of alt. sorts ]   "
end
pre: is_alternative_sorts_set(p)
```

```
─── describe_composite(p) as ───
let (_,({ηE1,...,ηEm})) =
    = obs_composite(p) in
"Narration:
    ... on sorts ...
    ... on sort observers ...
    ... on axiom/proof obligations ...
Formalisation:
    type
        E1, ..., Em
    value
        obs_Ei: E → Ei [ i:{1..m} ]
    proof obligation
        [ disjoint endurant sorts ]   "
end
pre: is_composite(p)
```

Initial Endurant State. An *endurant state* is any set of domain endurants.

Taxonomy. The taxonomy of a domain is given by the set of endurants sorts and their observers. A taxonomy can be given a graphic rendition such as shown in Fig. 2 on page 20.

Internal Qualities. *Internal qualities* of endurants of a manifest domain are, in a simplifying sense, those which we may not be able to see or "feel" when "touching" an endurant, but they can, as we now 'mandate' them, be reasoned about, as for *unique identifiers* and *mereologies*, or be measured by some *physical/chemical* means, or be "spoken of" by *intentional deduction*, and be reasoned about, as we do when we *attribute* properties to endurants. We refer to [11, *Sects. 2.2.3–4, 3.8, and 5.2–5.3*] for a fuller discussion of the concepts and unique identification and mereology.

Unique Identifiers. With each part sort P we associate a further undefined unique identifier sort Π and a similarly further undefined unique identifier observer **uid_P** such that for all distinct parts $p, p', ..., p''$ of sort P, $\text{uid\_P}(p)$, $\text{uid\_P}(p')$, ..., $\text{uid\_P}(p'')$, yield distinct unique identifiers $(\pi, \pi', ..., \pi'')$.

We refer to the leftmost of the three internal qualities frames on Page 13.

Mereology. "Mereology (from the Greek $\mu\epsilon\rho o\varsigma$ 'part') is a theory of part-hood *relations:* of the relations of part to whole and the relations of part to part within a whole"[13].

The mereology relations are here expressed in terms of the unique part identifiers. Let p:P (p of sort P) be a part with unique identifiers π. Let $\{p_1 : P_1, p_2 : P_2, ..., p_m : P_m\}$ be the set of parts (or respective sorts) to which p is [mereologically] related. We can express this by stating that mereo_P(p) = $\{\pi_1 : \Pi_1, \pi_2 : \Pi_2, ..., \pi_m : \Pi_m\}$, or **value** mereo_P: P→UI-set – i.e., as a set of unique identifiers. mereo_P is the mereology observer.

We shall deploy mereology practically. That is, we are not studying mereology. We are using the ideas of mereology for experimental research and engineering purposes.

For natural endurants, a typical relation is that of the topological *"next-to"*. For artefactual endurants typical relations, in addition to topological mereologies, make explicit how the designers of these artefacts *intended* their logical, not necessarily geographical relationship, to be: *"next-to"*, *"to-be-part-of"*, *"as-an-element-of-a-set"*, et cetera.

We refer to the middle of the three internal qualities frames on Page 13.

Attributes. Whereas unique identification and mereology are both of abstract, existential, logic nature, attributes are of concrete nature: physical, biological or historical nature. Attributes have values and attribute values are of types. *Two or more endurants that all have sets of attribute values of the same type, as well as the same unique identifier type and mereology types, are of the same sort. This is the endurant sort-determining mantra.*

From any part, $p:P$, we can thus identify a set of attribute type names, $\{A_{p_1}, A_{p_2}, ... A_{p_p}\}$, informally:

– *attrs_P*(a) **as** $\{\eta A_{p_1}, \eta A_{p_2}, ..., \eta A_{p_p}\}$.

Given a $p:P$, attr_A obtains the value of attribute A. The attr_A_{p_i}s are attribute observers of $p_i:P_i$.

We refer to the rightmost of the three internal qualities frames on Page 13.

Michael A. Jackson [41] has suggested a hierarchy of attribute categories.

---

[13] Achille Varzi: Mereology, http://plato.stanford.edu/entries/mereology/ 2009 and [18].

– *Static attributes:* values do not change.
– *Dynamic attributes:* values can change.
  Within the dynamic attribute category there are sub-categories.
  • *Inert attributes:* values are not determined by the endurant, but by "an outside" (e.g., other endurants).
  • Or *reactive attributes:* values which, if they change, change in response to external stimuli.
  • Or *active attributes:* values which change of the "own volition" of the part.
  We can define sub-categories of dynamic attributes.
    ∗ *Autonomous attributes:* values which change only on the "own volition" of the part.
    ∗ *Biddable attributes:* values, values that may be prescribed[14], but may fail to attain the prescribed value.
    ∗ And *programmable attributes:* values which are prescribed.

For our purposes we "reduce" these six categories to three, CAT = STA|MON|PRO:

– *static* [STA], (static values),
– *monitorable* [MON] (dynamic, except the programmable values), and the
– *programmable* (values) [PRO].

The Internal Qualities Frames. The three frames next contain part descriptors for unique identifiers, mereologies, and attributes.

```
——— unique_identifier_observer(p) as ———
"Narration:
    on unique identifier sort UI ...
    on unique identifier observer ...
    on uniqueness of identifiers ...
Formalisation:
type
    UI
value
    uid_P: P → UI
axiom
    [ disjoint UIs wrt. all sorts ]  "
```

```
——— mereology_observer(p) as ———
"Narration:
    on mereology type ...
    on mereology observer ...
    on mereology type constraints ...
Formalisation:
type
    MT = M(UI_i,...,UI_k)
value
    mereo_P: P → MT
axiom [ Well−formed Mereology ]
    A(MT): well−formed  "
```

```
——— describe_attributes(p) as ———
let { ηA_1,...,ηA_m } = attrs_P(p) in
"Narration:
    on attribute sorts ...
    on attribute sort observers ...
    attribute sort proof obligations ...
Formalisation:
type
    A_1, ..., A_m
value
    attr_A_1: P→A_1,
    attr_A_1: P→A_2,
    ...,
    attr_A_1: P→A_m
proof obligation [ Disjointness ]
    let P be any part sort in
    let a:(A_1|...|A_m) in
    is_A_i(a)≠is_A_j(a) [ i≠j, i,j:[ 1..m ] ]
    end end  "
end
```

---
[14] – by the transcendent part behaviour.

Intentional Pull. The concept of *intentional "pull"* is a concept which "parallels", we claim, the *gravitational pull* concept of physics.

For artefacts one can claim that certain parts $p:P$ are created in order to "serve" other parts $q:Q$, and vice versa: *roads serve to convey transport*, and *automobiles serve to transport goods.*

Historical events *time-stamp* record interactions between such parts p and q. So a historical attribute of p records its interaction with q, and a historical attribute of q records its interaction with p, and *"one cannot have one without the other"*, and this is what we mean by *intentional "pull"*!

Since we can talk about such events we can also model them as attributes. So introducing historical attributes for a sort P usually entails also introducing historical attributes for another sort Q, et cetera. And this consequentially implies that the domain analyser cum describer must express a necessary *intentional "pull" axiom* that expresses that *"one cannot have one without the other"*.

A classical example of intentional pull is found in *double bookkeeping* which states that every financial transaction has equal and opposite effects in at least two different accounts. It is used to satisfy the accounting equation: *Assets = Liabilities + Equity.*

3.3 Transcendental Deduction

"A *transcendental argument* is an argument which elucidates the conditions for the possibility of some fundamental phenomenon, whose existence is unchallenged or uncontroversial in the philosophical context in which the argument is propounded" [5, Anthony Brueckner, page 808]. "Such an argument proceeds deductively, from a premise of asserting the existence of some basic phenomenon (such as a meaningful discourse, conceptualisation of objective states of affairs, or the practice of making promises), to a conclusion asserting the existence of some interesting, substantive enabling conditions for that phenomenon" [5, Anthony Brueckner, page 808].

An **example** of a transcendental deduction is that of "morphing", for example, *automobile endurants* into *automobile perdurants.* That is: There is the automobile as, for example, shown at the dealer. It represents a *part*, an *endurant.* And there is the automobile "speeding" down the road. It represents a *behaviour*, a *perdurant.* The automobile as listed in the manufacturer's and car dealer's catalogues represents an *attribute* of manufacturers and dealers.

3.4 Perdurants

The emphasis is now on the **transcendental** deduction of **parts** into **behaviours**.

To explain what we mean by behaviours we first introduce *actions* and *events. Channels* will be introduced as a consequence of *interacting*, that is, *communicating* behaviours.

This section is necessarily a mere capsule view of Chapter 7 of [11]. Section 4.2, of the main example of this paper, should rectify some lacunae.

Actions, Events and Behaviours

Actions. By an *action* we shall understand something that occurs in time, lasting, however, no time, or, at least, we ignore time – considering actions as indivisible, taking place as the result of a "willed" [other] action, and usually changing the state $\xi{:}\varXi^{15}$.

The action may, or may not be based on some argument value.

value action: $[\,\mathsf{VAL}\,] \to \varXi \overset{\sim}{\to} \varXi$

Events. By an *event* we shall understand something that occurs in time, lasting, however, no time, taking place spontaneously, not as the result of a "willed" action, but possibly as the result of another event, and usually changing the state $\xi{:}\varXi$.

The event is usually not based on any argument value. The literal **Unit** can here be understood as a no argument value.

value event: $\mathbf{Unit} \to \varXi \overset{\sim}{\to} \varXi$

Behaviours. By a *behaviour* we shall then understand a set of sequences of actions, events and [other, sub-] behaviours, some of which relate to, i.e., *interact* with one another. Behaviours are uniquely identified, subject to the part mereology, and otherwise based on *static* (*constant*) attribute argument values, *dynamic monitorable* (*variable*) attribute argument values, *dynamic programmable* (*variable*) attribute argument values, and *channels* (for their interaction).

_____ *Behaviour Deduction, I: Signature* _____

value behaviour: Uid × Mereo × Static_VAL* × Mon_Attr_Name*
$\to$ Prgr_VAL* $\to$ in|out|in out ch... **Unit**

The literal **Unit** will here be understood as defining a never-ending behaviour. The signature, with **Unit**, expresses that if the process terminates no value is returned.

Channels. Interactions – between behaviours – are, as we model them, in RSL – as inspired by CSP [34–36,36,58,64], expressed in terms of CSP-like *channel* (ch) input/outputs: *ch[index]* ?, respectively *ch[index]* ! *value*, where *values* [based on internal qualities] are *communicated* over indexed channels.

A domain defines a number of *mereologies*, one for each part (of the *state*). These mereologies determine the *channels* to be *declared*. Given that any interesting, i.e., to us relevant, domain always consists of an indefinite, larger than 1,

---
[15] We shall forego explaining the state concept $\varXi$.

number of parts, the *common channel* for all behaviours is an index-able *channel array*[16]:

```
_____ Channel Deduction _____

channel {ch[ {i,j} ]|i,j:UI•{i,j}⊆ [ mereologies of the domain ]}:M
```

where M is the type of the values communicated.

Part Behaviours. Parts exist in a context of several parts. (The taxonomy, for example graphically represented, as in Fig. 2 on page 20, reflects these parts.) Part behaviours can therefore be expected to interact, i.e., to synchronise and communicate. A part behaviour can, consequently, be expected to alternate between either (a) doing an internal non-deterministic choice (⌈⌉) of 0, 1 or more "own work" behaviours, or (b) external non-deterministic choice (⌈⌉) offering [to accept] values from an alternative of 0, 1 or more other part behaviours. We can, schematically, summarise (a-b) as follows:

```
_____ Behaviour Deduction, II: Part Behaviour Definition Structure _____

value
    part_behav(...)(...) ≡
        (a) ⌈⌉ { own_behav_i(...)(...) | i ∈ {1..p} }
            ⌊⌋
        (b) ⌊⌋ { ext_behav_j(...)(...) | j ∈ {1..q} }
        where: p+q > 0
```

The ⌈⌉ and ⌊⌋ operators are the usual CSP operators on behaviours. The ⌊⌋ operator is like an "or" operator on behaviours. The ⌈⌉, ⌊⌋ and ⌊⌋ operators are commutative. We shall refer to either of the alternatives of the part_behav definition body as a part_alternative.

From Internal Qualities to Behaviour Arguments. By arguments of transcendental nature we shall assign unique part identifiers as static arguments of behaviours, part mereologies as determining channel communication, and part attributes as either static or dynamic arguments of behaviours.

```
_____ Behaviour Deduction, III: Signature, Part p:P _____

value
    behaviour_P: PI × mereo_P × Stat_Attr_Vals_P × Mon_Attr_Names
        → Prgr_Attr_Vals_P →
        → in|out|in out {ch[ {i,j} ] [ i,j ∈ mereology of P ]} Unit
```

---

[16] RSL does not have channel arrays. So this is a deviation from RSL.

Mon_Attr_Names makes use of *attrs_P*.

Part Alternative Behaviours. We shall express behaviours in terms of usually never-ending functions, behaviour![17] That is:

```
_____ Behaviour Deduction, IV: Alternative Part Definition, Part p:P _____

value
      alt_behav(uid_P(p),mereo_P(p),Stat_Attr_Vals_P(p),Mon_Attr_Names(p))
            (Prgr_Attr_Vals_P(p)) ≡
         let ui=uid_P(p), me=mereo_P(p), sta=Stat_Attr_Vals_P(p),
               mnl=Mon_Name_list(p), prgr=Prgr_Attr_Vals_P(p) in
         let prgr' = alt_behav_body(ui,me,sta,mnl)(prgr) in
         part_behav(ui,mereo,sta,mnl)(prgr') end end
```

Behaviour Clauses: Expressions and Statements. Further: alt_behav_body is a sequence of one or more action, event and sub-behaviour clauses – usually ending with an expression:

```
value
    behaviour_body(uid,mereo,sta_var)(prgr_var) ≡ clause_1 ; clause_2 ; ... ; clause_m
```

Clauses are either

- *s*, simple **statements**, or
- ch[...]! expression, **output statement**, or
- **let** pattern[18] = expression **in** ... **end**, value **decompositions**, or
- *e*, **expressions**[19], or
- clause_a ⌐ clause_b, internal non-deterministic clauses, or
- clause_a ▯ clause_b, external non-deterministic clauses, or
- clause_a ⌐⌐ clause_b, either/or non-deterministic clauses, or
- clause_a ‖ clause_b, parallel clauses, or
- **skip**, skip clause, or
- **stop**, abort function invocation.

Values of monitorable attributes, of name ηA[20], of parts p:P, are expressed as attr_val(uid)(σ) where attr_val is defined as:

```
value
      attr_val: PI → $\eta \mathbb{A}$ → $\Sigma$ → VAL
      attr_val(pi)($\eta A$)($\sigma$) ≡ attr_A(retr_P(pi)($\sigma$))
```

---

[17] *Parts* – being the bases for behaviours – persist, endure.

[18] where pattern – typically is a "grouping expression" over [free] identifiers.

[19] ch[{ui,uj}] ? is an expression.

[20] The type of attribute A names (a single element type) is ηA, and the value is "A". The type of all attribute names is $\eta \mathbb{A}$.

where σ is the endurants state:

type
  Σ = (P|Q|...|R)-**set**
value
  retr_P: PI $\rightarrow$ Σ
  retr_P(pi)(σ) $\equiv$ **let** p:P • p $\in$ σ • uid_P(pi) **in** p **end**

Initial System. Given a[n endurant] state, cf. Page 11, one can then define
[a corresponding perdurant] behaviour, namely the parallel ($\|$) composition of
an invocation of all the corresponding behaviours. This is exemplified as from
Item 69 on page 29.

3.5   The Domain Analysis and Description Process

1. There is the RSL[+]Text to be developed.
2. There is the $\mathcal{D}$omain.
3. The analyse_and_describe_domain process applies to a $\mathcal{D}$omain and yields, line
   12 an RSL[+]Text. That process proceeds "sequentially":

4. first external qualities, then
5. unique identifiers,
6. mereologies,
7. attributes,
8. channels

9. behaviour signatures,
10. behaviour definitions, and
11. initial system – yielding
12. a complete RSL[+]Text[21].

type
1. RSL[+]Text
2. $\mathcal{D}$
value
3. analyse_and_describe_domain: $\mathcal{D}$ $\rightarrow$ > RSL[+]Text
3. analyse_and_describe_domain(d) $\equiv$
4.   **let** es = analyse_and_describe_external_qualities(d) **in**
5.   **let** is = analyse_and_describe_unique_identifiers(es)(d) **in**
6.   **let** ms = analyse_and_describe_mereologies(es⊎is)(d) **in**
7.   **let** as = analyse_and_describe_attributes(es⊎is⊎ms)(d) **in**
8.   **let** cs = analyse_and_describe_channels(es⊎is⊎ms⊎as)(d) **in**
9.   **let** ss = analyse_and_describe_signatures(es⊎is⊎ms⊎as⊎cs)(d) **in**
10. **let** bs = analyse_and_describe_behaviours(es⊎is⊎ms⊎as⊎cs⊎ss)(d) **in**
11. **let** si = analyse_and_describe_initial_system(es⊎is⊎ms⊎as⊎cs⊎ss⊎bs)(d)(s)
12. **in** es ⊎ is ⊎ ms ⊎ as ⊎ cs ⊎ ss ⊎ bs ⊎ si **end end end end end end end end**

---

[21] The ⊎ operator merges RSL[+]Texts

4   An Example Domain Description

Initial Remark: *We shall illustrate core elements of a domain description of a road transport system. In doing so we really do not rely on the reader having already an idea as to what the terms of this road transport system mean – as we "slowly" unfold it. But at any stage, before the final, the informal meaning that You, the reader may ascribe to these terms, is not what the formulas express! At any stage, up to the point of the formal specification that we are unfolding, this specification denotes a space of meanings according to the RSL semantics [26]. Initially that space is very large. As we proceed the further formulas narrow down, restrict, the space. When, at the end, we think we have specified all that we need specify, the formulas define "exactly" what we mean by a road transport system. We shall continue this remark at the very end of this section, i.e., just before Sect. 5.*

● ● ●

The sectioning/paragraph structure of this section follows that of Sect. 3.

4.1   Endurants

External Qualities

13. We start by identifying and naming the universe of discourse, here a road transport system.
14. In a road transport system we can observe a structure of a composite in which we observe an aggregate of a road net and an aggregate of automobiles.
15. Road nets are here seen as structures of composites of aggregates of road links[22] and road hubs[23].
16. Link and Hub aggregates are set structures of Links, respectively Hubs.
17. Links and Hubs are considered atomic.
18. Automobile aggregates are set structures of automobiles.
19. Automobiles are considered atomic.

type
13. RTS
14. RN, AA
15. LS, HS
16. Ls = L-set, Hs = H-set
17. L, H
18. As = A-set
19. A

value
14. obs_RN: RTS → RN
14. obs_AA: RTS → AA
15. obs_LS: RN → LS
15. obs_HS: RN → HS
16. obs_Ls: LS → Ls
16. obs_Hs: HS → Hs
18. obs_As: AA → As

State

20. The state, σ,
21. of a road transport system *rts* consists of

---

[22] A link is a street segment delineated by street intersections.
[23] A hub is a street intersection of one or more links.

(a) the road net aggregate,   (d) the hubs,
(b) the automobile aggregate,
(c) the links,   (e) the automobiles.

22. For later use we also define the union of all links and hubs.

value   21c. $ls = \text{obs\_Ls}(\text{obs\_LS}(rn))$
21. rts:RTS   21d. $hs = \text{obs\_Hs}(\text{obs\_HS}(rn))$
20. $\sigma{:}\Sigma = \{rn\}\cup\{aa\}\cup ls\cup hs\cup as$ 21e. $as = \text{obs\_As}(aa)$
21a. $rn = \text{obs\_RN}(rts)$
21b. $aa = \text{obs\_AA}(rts)$ 22. $us{:}(\text{L}|\text{H})\text{-set} = ls \cup hs$

Taxonomy. Figure 2 presents a graphic rendition of the taxonomy of road transport systems.

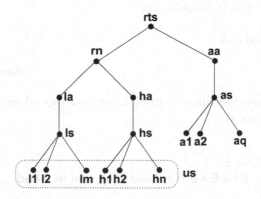

Fig. 2. Road transport system taxonomy

Internal Qualities

Unique Identifiers. Road traffic systems, aggregates of links and hubs, and sets of links, hubs and automobiles are endurant *structures*, hence have no internal qualities[24].

23. Road nets have unique identification,
24. automobile aggregates likewise,
25. links, hubs and automobiles also!

---

[24] – so we have decided!.

type
23. RNI
24. AAI
25. LI, HU, AI
value

23. uid_RN: RN → RNI
24. uid_AA: AA → AAI
25. uid_L: L→LI
25. uid_H:H→HI
25. uid_A:A→AI

Uniqueness of Parts.

26. All parts (of the state σ) have unique identification. This means that the number of state components equal the number of [their] unique identifiers.

value
26. $rni = $ uid_RN(rn), $aai=$uid_AA(aa),
26. $lis = \{$uid_L(l)|l:L•l$\in ls\}$,
26. $his = \{$uid_H(h)|h:H•h$\in hs\}$,
26. $ais = \{$uid_A(a)|a:A•a$\in as\}$,
26. σuis $= \{rni\}\cup\{aai\}\cup lis\cup his\cup ais$
axiom
26.   **card** $\sigma = $ **card** σuis

Retrieving Endurants.

27. Given any unique identifier, ui, in σuis, the "corresponding" endurant, e, can be retrieved from σ.

value
27.   retr_E: UI → Σ → E
27.   retr_E(ui)(σ) $\equiv$ **let** e:E • e $\in \sigma \wedge$ uid_E(e) $=$ ui **in** e **end**

Mereology.

28. The mereology of a road net aggregate is a pair of the unique identifier *of the automobile aggregate of the road transport system of which the road net is an aggregate,* and a pair of sets of the unique identifiers *of the links and hubs of the road transport system of which the road net is an aggregate.*
29. The mereology of an automobile aggregate is a pair of the unique identi-fiers *of the road net aggregate of the road transport system of which the automobile aggregate net is a part,* and a set of unique identifiers of auto-mobiles *of the automobile aggregate of the road transport system of which the automobile aggregate is a part.*
30. The mereology of a link is a pair of a two element set of hub identifiers and a set of identifiers of the automobiles that are allowed onto the link – *such that the hub and automobile identifiers are of the road transport system.*
31. The mereology of a hubs is a pair of a set of link identifiers and a set of identifiers of the automobiles that are allowed into the hub – *such that the link and automobile identifiers are of the road transport system.*

32. The mereology of an automobile is a pair of the identifier of *its* automobile aggregate and the set of identifiers of the links and hubs – *of the road net aggregate of the road transport system of which the automobile is a part it* is allowed to travel on.

33. The *slanted* texts above hint at axiomatic constraints.

type
28. RNM = AAI × (LI-set × HI-set)
29. AAI = RNI × AI-set
30. LM = HI-set × AI-set
31. HM = LI-set × AI-set
32. AM = AAI × (LI|RI)-set
value
28. mereo_RN: RN → RNM
29. mereo_AA: AA → AAM
30. mereo_L: L → LM
31. mereo_H: H → HM
32. mereo_A: A → AM
axiom

28. let (aai,(lis,his)) = mereo_RN(rn) in
28. aai = aai ∧ lis = lis ∧ his = his end
29. let (rni,ais) = mereo_AA(aa) in
29. rni = rni ∧ ais ⊆ ais end
30. ∀ l:L • l ∈ ls ⇒
30.   let (his,ais) = mereo_L(l) in
30.   his ⊆ his ∧ ais ⊆ ais end
31. ∀ h:H • h ∈ hs ⇒
31.   let (lis,ais) = mereo_H(h) in
31.   lis ⊆ lis ∧ ais ⊆ ais end
32. ∀ a:A • a ∈ as ⇒
32.   let (aai,ris) = mereo_H(a) in
32.   aai = aai ∧ ris ⊆ lis∪his end

Routes.

34. The observed road net defines a possibly infinite set of finite length routes:
    Basis Clauses:
35. The null sequence, ⟨⟩, of no links or hubs is a route.
36. Any one link or hub, u, of a road net forms a route, ⟨u⟩, of length one.
    Inductive Clauses:
37. Let r_i⌢⟨u_i⟩ and ⟨u_j⟩⌢r_j be two finite routes of a road net.
38. Let $u_{i_{ui}}$ and $u_{j_{ui}}$ be the unique identifiers for u_i, respectively u_j.
39. Let the road (hub or link) identifiers of mereology of u_i be uis and of u_j be ujs. If $u_{i_{ui}}$ is in uis and $u_{j_{ui}}$ is in ujs,
40. then r_i⌢⟨u_i, u_j⟩⌢r_j is a route of the road net.
    Extremal Clause:
41. Only such routes which can be formed by a finite number of applications of the clauses form a route.

type
34. R = (L|H)*
value
34 routes: RN $\overset{\sim}{\to}$ R-infset
34 routes(rn) ≡
35   let rs = {⟨⟩}
36   ∪ {⟨u⟩|u:(L|H)•u ∈ us} ∪
40   ∪ {ri⌢⟨ui⟩⌢⟨uj⟩⌢rj | ui,uj:(L|H) • {ui,uj} ⊆ us
37   ∧ ri⌢⟨ui⟩,⟨uj⟩⌢rj:R • {ri⌢⟨ui⟩,⟨uj⟩⌢rj} ⊆ rs
38,39   ∧ ui_ui = uid_U(ui) ∧ ui_ui ∈ xtr_UIs(ui)

38,41   ∧ uj_ui = uid_U(uj) ∧ uj_ui ∈ xtr_UIs(uj)} **in**
35   rs **end**

xtr_UIs: (L|H) → UI-set, xtr_UIs(u) ≡ **let** (uis,_)=mereo_(L|H)(u) **in** uis **end**

rs is the smallest [fixed point] set of finite routes that satisfy the equation 35.

42. We can also model routes, as identifier routes, IR, in terms of link and hub
    identifiers.
43. Given a road net we can examine whether it is strongly connected, i.e.,
    whether any link or hub can be reached from any other link or hub.
44. Et cetera!

type
42. IR = (LI|HI)*
value
42. i_routes: RN → IR-**infset**
42. i_routes(rn) ≡
42.   **let** rs = routes(rn) **in**
42.   { ⟨ uid_(L|H)(r[i]) | i:**Nat** • 1≤i≤**len** r ⟩ | r:R • r ∈ rs } **end**

43. is_connected_RN: RN → **Bool**
43. is_connected_RN(rn) ≡
43.   **let** rs = routes(rn) **in**
43.   ∀ u,u':(L|H) • {u,u'}⊆ *ls* ∪ *hs* ⇒ ∃ r:R • r ∈ rs and {u,u'} ⊆ **elems** r
43.   **end**

Attributes. We treat attributes only for atomic sorts. And we show only a very
few attribute examples.

Links.

45. Links have lengths.
46. Links have states – *sets of zero, one or two* pairs of hub identifiers – *of their
    hub mereology*[25].
47. Links have state spaces: a set of all relevant link states – *the link state must
    at any time be in its link state space.*

type
45. LEN
46. LΣ = (HI×HI)-**set**
47. LΩ = LΣ-**set**
value

---

[25] – zero expresses that the link is [currently] closed for traffic, one if it is [cur-
      rently] a one way link, in one or the other direction as indicated by the con-
      necting hub identifiers, or two if it is [currently] a two way link.

45. attr_LEN: L → LEN
46. attr_LΣ: L → LΣ
47. attr_LΩ: L → LΩ
axiom
46. $\forall$ l:L • l ∈ ls ⇒
46.   **let** (lσ,lω)=(attr_LΣ,attr_LΩ)(l) **in** lσ ∈ lω ∧
46. $\forall$ (hi′,hi″):(HI×HI) • (hi′,hi″)∈lσ ⇒ {hi′,hi″}⊆his **end**

Hubs.

48. Hubs have states: a set of pairs of link identifiers – *of its mereology.*[26]
49. Hubs have state spaces: the set of all relevant hub states – *the current hub state must at any time be in its hub state space.*

type
48. HΣ = (LI×LI)-**set**
49. HΩ = HΣ-**set**
value
48. attr_HΣ: H → HΣ
49. attr_HΩ: H → HΩ
axiom
48. $\forall$ h:H • h ∈ hs ⇒
49.   **let** (hσ,hω)=(attr_HΣ,attr_HΩ)(h) **in** hσ ∈ hω ∧
49. $\forall$ (li′,li″):(LI×LI) • (li′,li″)∈hσ ⇒ {li′,li″}⊆lis **end**

Automobiles.

50. Automobiles have positions on links or in hubs (programmable attributes).
   (a) An automobile on a link position is a triplet of (1) a link identifier *of the road net*, (2) and ordered pair of two hub identifiers *of the link mereology*, and (3) a real number properly between 0 and 1.[27]
   (b) An automobile at a hub position is a pair of (1) a hub identifier hi *of the road net*, and (2) an ordered pair of two link identifiers *li′ and li″ of the hub mereology*.[28]
51. Automobiles have a (programmable attribute) history of appearing, at times, at hubs or on links[29].
53c Automobiles have (monitorable attribute) speed and acceleration (plus or minus).

---

[26] – each pair, (li_j, li_k) expressing that automobiles may [currently] enter the hub from the links identified by li_j and leave the hub to the links identified by li_k.

[27] – expressing the fraction along the designated link between the two designated hubs. The type constructor :: is "borrowed" from VDM [22].

[28] – expressing that the automobile at hub hi is on its way between links designated by li′ and li″.

[29] We shall define that attribute in items 53c on the facing page.

52. Etc.

type
50.   APos = onL | atH
50a.   onL :: LI × (HI×HI) × F
50a.   F = **Real**, **invariant**: ∀ f:F • 0<f<1
50b.   atH :: HI × (LI×LI)
53c.   AHist
51.   Vel, Acc
52.   ...
value
50.   attr_APos: A → APos
51.   attr_Vel: A → Vel, attr_Acc: A → Acc
52.   ...
axiom
50.   ∀ a:A • a ∈ *as* ⇒
50.   **let** apos = attr_APos(a) **in**
50.   **case** apos:
50a.   onL(li,(fhi,thi),_) →
50a.   li ∈ *lis* ∧ **let** (his,_) = mereo_L(retr_L(li)(σ)) **in** {fhi,thi}⊆his **end**
50b.   atH(hi,(fli,tli)) →
50b.   hi ∈ *his* ∧ **let** (lis,_) = mereo_H(retr_H(hi)(σ)) **in** {fli,tli}⊆lis **end**
51.,52.   ...
50.   **end end**

Intentional Pull. We simplify the link, hub and automobile histories – aiming at just showing an essence of the intentional pull concept.

53. With links, hubs and automobiles we can associate history attributes.
   (a) Link history attributes time-stamp record, as an ordered list, the presence of automobiles.
   (b) Hub history attributes time-stamp record, as an ordered list, the presence of automobiles.
   (c) Automobile history attributes time-stamp record, as an ordered list, their visits to links and hubs.

type
53a.   LHist = AI $_{m}$→TIME*
53b.   HHist = AI $_{m}$→TIME*
53c.   AHist = (LI|HI) $_{m}$→TIME*

value
53a.   attr_LHist: L → LHist
53b.   attr_HHist: H → HHist
53c.   attr_AHist: A → AHist

Wellformedness of Event Histories.
Some observations must be made with respect to the above modelling of time-stamped event histories.

54. Each τ_ℓ : TIME* is an indefinite list. We have not expressed any criteria for the recording of events: *all the time, continuously* ! (?)
55. Each list of times, τ_ℓ : TIME*, is here to be in decreasing, *continuous* order of times.
56. Time intervals from when an automobile enters a link (a hub) till it first time leaves that link (hub) must not overlap with other such time intervals for that automobile.
57. If an automobile leaves a link (a hub), at time τ, then it may enter a hub (resp. a link) and then that must be at time τ' where τ' is some infinitesimal, sampling time interval, quantity larger that τ. Again we refrain here from speculating on the issue of sampling !
58. Altogether, ensembles of link and hub event histories for any given automobile define routes that automobiles travel across the road net. Such routes must be in the set of routes defined by the road net.

As You can see, there is enough of interesting modelling issues to tackle !

Formulation of an Intentional Pull.

59. An *intentional pull* of any road transport system, *rts*, is then if:
  (a) for any automobile, a, of *rts*, on a link, ℓ (hub, h), at time τ,
  (b) then that link, ℓ, (hub h) "records" automobile a at that time.
60. and:
  (c) for any link, ℓ (hub, h) being visited by an automobile, a, at time τ,
  (d) then that automobile, a, is visiting that link, ℓ (hub, h), at that time.

axiom
59a. $\forall$ a:A • a $\in$ *as* $\Rightarrow$
59a.   **let** ahist = attr_AHist(a) **in**
59a. $\forall$ ui:(LI|HI) • ui $\in$ **dom** ahist $\Rightarrow$
59b. $\forall$ τ:TIME • τ $\in$ **elems** ahist(ui) $\Rightarrow$
59b.   **let** hist $-$ is_LI(ui) $\rightarrow$ attr_LHist(retr_L(ui))(σ),
59b.   _ $\rightarrow$ attr_HHist(retr_H(ui))(σ) **in**
59b. τ $\in$ **elems** hist(uid_A(a)) **end end**
60. $\wedge$
60c. $\forall$ u:(L|H) • u $\in$ *ls*$\cup$*hs* $\Rightarrow$
60c.   **let** uhist = attr(L|H)Hist(u) **in**
60d. $\forall$ ai:AI • ai $\in$ **dom** uhist $\Rightarrow$
60d. $\forall$ τ:TIME • τ $\in$ **elems** uhist(ai) $\Rightarrow$
60d.   **let** ahist = attr_AHist(retr_A(ai))(σ) **in**
60d. τ $\in$ **elems** uhist(ai) **end end**

4.2   Perdurants

Behaviours. We show only the signature and definition of one aspect of one behaviour. That of an automobile at a hub. We refer to [11, Examples 82–83, pages 183–184] for the full set of signatures and definitions for link, hub and automobile behaviours.

Signatures.

61. automobile:
   (a) there is the usual "triplet" of arguments: unique identifier, mereology and static attributes;
   (b) then there are two programmable attributes: the automobile position (cf. Item 50 on page 24), and the automobile history (cf. Item 53c on page 25);
   (c) and finally there are the input/output channel references allowing communication between the automobile and the hub and link behaviours.
   We deviate from RSL in expression these signatures. The deviation amounts to a form of dependent types [37].
62. Similar signatures can be given for
   (a) link and
   (b) hub behaviours.

We omit the modelling of monitorable attributes.

value
61,61a automobile: ai:AI×(_,uis):AM×...
61b   → (apos:APos × ahist:AHist)
61c   → **in out** {ch[{ai,ui}]|ai:AI,ui:(HI|LI) • ai∈ais ∧ ui ∈ *uis*} **Unit**
62a   link: li:LI×(his,ais):LM×LΩ
62a   → LΣ
62a   → **in out** {ch[{li,ui}]|li:LI,ui:(AI|HI)-set • ai∈ais ∧ li ∈lis∪his} **Unit**
62b   hub: hi:HI×(_,ais):HM×HΩ
62b   → HΣ
62b   → **in out** {ch[{ai,ui}]|hi:HI,ai:AI • ai∈ais ∧ hi ∈ *uis*} **Unit**

We omit the pre-conditions.

Definitions: Automobile at a Hub.

63. We abstract automobile behaviour **at** a Hub (hi).
   (a) Either the automobile remains in the hub,
   (b) or, internally non-deterministically,
   (c) leaves the hub entering a link,
   (d) or, internally non-deterministically,
   (e) stops.
   (f) or, internally non-deterministically,
   (g) decides to communicate with the department of vehicles,
   (h) or, externally non-deterministically,
   (i) is contacted by department of vehicles,

We omit the definition of department_of_vehicle (i.e., automobile aggregate) behaviour.

63 automobile(ai,(aai,uis),...)(apos:atH(fli,hi,tli),ahist) ≡
63a   (automobile_remains_in_hub(ai,(aai,uis),...)(apos:atH(fli,hi,tli),ahist)
63b   ⌈⌉
63c   automobile_leaving_hub(ai,(aai,uis),...)(apos:atH(fli,hi,tli),ahist)
63d   ⌈⌉
63e   automobile_stop(ai,(aai,uis),...)(apos:atH(fli,hi,tli),ahist)
63f   ⌊⌋
63g   automobile_contacts_dv(ai,(aai,uis),...)(apos:atH(fli,hi,tli),ahist))
63h   [ ]
63i   dv_contacts_automobile(ai,(aai,uis),...)(apos:atH(fli,hi,tli),ahist)

64. [63a] The automobile remains in the hub:
   (a) the automobile remains at that hub, "idling",
   (b) informing ("first") the hub behaviour.

64 automobile_remains_in_hub(ai,(aai,uis),...)(apos:atH(fli,hi,tli),ahist) ≡
64   let τ = record_TIME() in
64b   ch[ai,hi] ! τ ;
64a   automobile(ai,(aai,uis),...)(apos,upd_hist(τ,hi)(ahist))
64   end

64a   upd_hist: (TIME×I) → (AHist|LHist|HHist) → (AHist|LHist|HHist)
64a   upd_hist(τ,i)(hist) ≡ hist † [i ↦ ⟨τ⟩⌢hist(i)]

65. [63c] The automobile leaves the hub entering a link:
   (a) tli, whose "next" hub, identified by thi, is obtained from the mereology
       of the link identified by tli;
   (b) informs the hub it is leaving and the link it is entering,
   (c) "whereupon" the vehicle resumes (i.e., "while at the same time" resum-
       ing) the vehicle behaviour positioned at the very beginning (0) of that
       link.

65 automobile_leaving_hub(ai,(aai,uis),...)(apos:atH(fli,hi,tli),ahist) ≡
65a   (let ({fhi,thi},ais) = mereo_L(retr_L(tli)(σ)) in assert: fhi=hi
65b   (ch[ai,hi] ! τ ‖ ch[ai,tli] ! τ) ;
65c   automobile(ai,(aai,uis),...)
65c   (onL(tli,(hi,thi),0),upd_hist(τ,tli)(upd_hist(τ,hi)(ahist))) end)

66. [63e] Or the automobile "disappears—off the radar" !

66 automobile_stop(ai,(aai,uis),...)(apos:atH(fli,hi,tli),ahist) ≡ stop

Similar behaviour definitions can be given for *automobiles on a link*, for *links* and
for *hubs*. Together they must reflect, amongst other things: the time continuity of
automobile flow, that automobiles follow routes, that automobiles, links and hubs
together adhere to the intentional pull expressed earlier, et cetera. A specification
of these aspects must be proved to adhere to these properties.

Initial System. The initial system is the parallel composition of

67. the road net aggregate behaviour,
68. the automobile aggregate behaviour,
69. all automobile behaviours,
70. all link behaviours, and
71. all hub behaviours.

value
67.   dept_of_roads(uid_RN(rn),mereo_RN(rn),...)(...)
68.   ‖ dept_of_vehicles(uid_AA(aa),mereo_AA(aa),...)(...)
69.   ‖ {automobile(uid_A(a),mereo_A(a),...)(attr_Apos(a),attr_AHist(a))|a:A•a∈as}
70.   ‖ {link(uid_L(l),mereo_L(l),(attr_LEN(l),attr_LΩ(l)))(attr_LΣ(l),attr_LHist(l))|l:L•l∈ls}
71.   ‖ {hub(uid_H(h),mereo_H(h),attr_HΩ(h))(attr_HΣ(h),attr_HHist(h))|h:H•h∈hs}

That's all folks! Neat!?

● ● ●

Initial Remark Reviewed: *Initially the narratives of the domain description were scant and their counterpart formalisations left many possible interpretations as to what these formal types and function signatures really meant. As the domain description proceeded – now with perdurants: channels and action, event and behaviour signatures and definitions – these meanings were narrowed down, considerably – focusing, finally, on yielding the properties that are deemed necessary and sufficient.*

5   Relevance to Aeronautics and Space

The specific relevance of domain engineering to aeronautics and space will be the subject of this section.

5.1   But First

As a preamble for briefly discussing the relevance of domain engineering to aeronautics and space, we 'complete' our treatment of domain engineering with three small notes.

Domain Modelling Experiments. It is appropriate to mention that the method, i.e., the principles, techniques and tools of domain analysis & description, has been "tuned & honed" by extensive "laboratory work". That is, there has been experimentally researched and developed a number of less-or-more "complete" domain models. In reverse chronological order we mention some:

– 2021: **Assembly Lines**, September, 2021. Techn. Univ. of Denmark
  www.imm.dtu.dk/~dibj/2021/assembly/assembly-line.pdf

- 2021: **Shipping**, April 2021. Techn. Univ. of Denmark
  www.imm.dtu.dk/~dibj/2021/ral/ral.pdf
- 2021: **Rivers and Canals**, March 2021. Techn. Univ. of Denmark
  www.imm.dtu.dk/~dibj/2021/Graphs/Rivers-and-Canals.pdf
- 2021: **A Retailer Market**, January 2021. Techn. Univ. of Denmark
  www.imm.dtu.dk/~dibj/2021/Retailer/BjornerHeraklit27January2021.pdf
- 2019: **Container Terminals**, ECNU, Shanghai, China
  www.imm.dtu.dk/~dibj/2018/yangshan/maersk-pa.pdf
- 2018: **Documents**, TongJi Univ., Shanghai, China
  www.imm.dtu.dk/~dibj/2017/docs/docs.pdf
- 2017: **Urban Planning**, TongJi Univ., Shanghai, China
  www.imm.dtu.dk/~dibj/2018/BjornerUrbanPlanning24Jan2018.pdf
- 2017: **Swarms of Drones**, Inst. of Softw., CAS, Peking, China
  www.imm.dtu.dk/~dibj/2017/swarms/swarm-paper.pdf
- 2013: **Road Transport**, Techn. Univ. of Denmark
  www.imm.dtu.dk/~dibj/road-p.pdf
- 2012: **Credit Cards**, Uppsala, Sweden
  www.imm.dtu.dk/~dibj/2016/credit/accs.pdf
- 2012: **Weather Information**, Bergen, Norway
  www.imm.dtu.dk/~dibj/2016/wis/wis-p.pdf
- 2010: **Web-based Transaction Processing**, Techn. Univ. of Vienna, Austria
  www.imm.dtu.dk/~dibj/wfdftp.pdf
- 2010: **The Tokyo Stock Exchange**, Tokyo Univ., Japan
  www.imm.dtu.dk/~db/todai/tse-1.pdf, www.imm.dtu.dk/~db/todai/tse-2.
  pdf
- 2009: **Pipelines**, Techn. Univ. of Graz, Austria
  www.imm.dtu.dk/~dibj/pipe-p.pdf
- 2007: **A Container Line Industry Domain**, Techn. Univ. of Denmark
  www.imm.dtu.dk/~dibj/container-paper.pdf
- 2002: **The Market**, Techn. Univ. of Denmark
  www.imm.dtu.dk/~dibj/themarket.pdf
- 1995–2004: **Railways**, Techn. Univ. of Denmark - a compendium
  www.imm.dtu.dk/~dibj/train-book.pdf

Requirements Engineering. If our objective for having a domain description
is that it serves as a basis for software development, then a [next] phase of
development is that of requirements engineering. Chapter 9 of [11] shows how to
systematically develop requirements from a domain description.

As we did for domain analysis & description, Sect. 3.5 on page 18, we can do
for requirements development: present an informal, but precise specification of
the *requirements analysis & description process*.

The "formalisation" below reveals an essence of [11, Chapter 9]. Namely that
the requirements development consists of three major stages: domain requirements, DR – which in turn consists of five steps, interface requirements, IR,
and machine requirements, MR. The stages of domain and interface requirements development can be further 'decomposed' into steps. The pseudo procedure names these steps. For details we refer to [11, Chapter 9]

value

       requirements_analysis_description: RSL$^+$Text$\to \mathcal{D} \to$

                                         ($\mathcal{D} \times \mathcal{D} \times ... \times \mathcal{D}) \to$ RSL$^+$Text

       requirements_analysis_description(rsl_txt)(d)(d1,...,dm) $\equiv$

DR: **let** dr=(**let** drp = domain_projection(rsl_txt)(d) **in**

                let dri = domain_requirements_instantiation(drp)(d) **in**

                let drd = domain_requirements_determination(dri)(d) **in**

                let dre = domain_requirements_extension(drd)(d) **in**

                let drf = domain_requirements_fitting(dre)((d1,...,dm),d)

                in drf **end end end end end**) **in**

IR: **let** irp = interface_requirements(drf)(d) **in**

MR: **let** mrp = machine_requirementsn(irp)(d)

           in mrp **end end end**

Here (d1,...,dm) are the "other" requirements with which ((dre),(...,d)) is to be fitted; mrp then represents the full set of requirements from which to develop, in a next phase, the software.

Software Design. The three monographs cum textbooks [8–10] show how to develop software from requirements prescriptions.

5.2   Air Traffic Control, ATC

On the background of the domain to requirements transformation, [11, Chapter 9], and a similar requirements to software design transformation [10], we now claim to have a rigorous path of development from domains to trustworthy software.

An domain, "close", informally speaking, to that of NASA's concerns, is *air traffic control, ATC*.

Future ATCs. Today's ATC is primarily radar-based and human-operated. Tomorrow's ATC appears headed for satellite-orientation and automation.[30]

We suggest, in this paper, that major US and European efforts for formulating the next generation ATCs be supported by *pre-domain* modeling experiments.

Models of proposed ATCs are neither domain models nor requirements models. They are models of virtual ATCs, as [12] formulates a family of models of automobile assembly lines. Such a family can be used to determine values of future ATC "parameters": which ATC components should undertake which

---

[30] We refer to:

- ICAO: https://www.icao.int/airnavigation/documents/ganp-2016-interactive.pdf
- US: https://www.faa.gov/nextgen/
- Europe: https://www.easa.europa.eu/domains/air-traffic-management

tasks, etc. Their modelling process can also, and this is something new, help experiment with alternative ATC-component or procedure proposals, as a form of "sounding boards".

A Model for Current ATC. In order to develop models for families of ATCs we suggest to first develop a model of the existing, worldwide ATC. A basis for such a model is illustrated in Fig. 3.

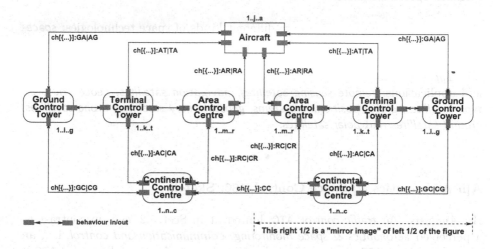

Fig. 3. Conventional air traffic control

Thus we challenge the reader to analyse & describe external qualities (as basically shown in Fig. 3), and states, then internal qualities, first unique identifiers, mereologies, and attributes; then external qualities, first channels, then behaviour signatures and definitions, and finally an initial state.

Now the modellers are well prepared for modelling future ATCs.

● ● ●

The above suggests that *domain modelling* problems related to aeronautics and space might also be a good idea!

5.3 An Aeronautics and Space Domain

To properly understand *the domain of aeronautics* &[31] *space* we must first analyse various facets of the domain as we see it today. Aeronautics & space, as an endeavour, is pursued in order to explore space, with space exploration missions "divided" into stages, deploying a variety of technologies, and satellites.[32]

---

[31] We shall use the ampersand, &, instead of 'and', to emphasize that we speak of one, consolidated topic, not two!.

[32] The following text is adapted from various NASA Web pages found under: https://www.nasa.gov.

[I] Types of Space Exploration. There are many kinds of space exploration: *earth observation satellites, spy satellites, communications satellites, military satellites, satellite navigation, space telescopes, space exploration* and *space tourism.*

[II] Stages of Space Exploration. There are common stages of missions: the *launch phase* (assembly, test, and launch operations), the *cruise phase*, the *encounter phase* and depending on the state of spacecraft health and mission funding, the *extended operations phase.*

[III] Space Technologies. There are different kinds of space technologies: *spacecraft, satellites, space stations* and *orbital launch.*

[IV] Types of Satellites and Applications. And there are many types of satellites and applications: *remote sensing satellites, navigation satellites, geocentric orbit type satellites, global positioning systems, geostationary satellites, drone satellites, ground satellites* and *polar satellites.*

• • •

A[n Aeronautics &] Space Control, ASC, Sketch.

An Analysis. Air traffic control, ATC, hinted at in Sect. 5.2, can, in contrast to a perceived *aeronautics & space monitoring, communication and control,* i.e., an *air space control,* ASC, it seems, be primarily characterised as follows: (a) ATC is concerned with only one kind of moveable entities: passenger and cargo aircraft whereas an ASC would have to deal with quite a variety of moveable entities; (b) ATC is independent of the multitude of national and international air carriers, whereas, it seems, today's national aeronautics & space efforts and their monitoring, communications and controls are fragmented into national agencies who are also the [main] stakeholders in the monitored, etc., space efforts; (c) ATC can, today, be partly identified in terms of *aircraft* (one, unifying concept), *ground control towers, terminal controls, area controls and continental controls*; and (d) ATC responsibility is shared by many (overflown) nations.

• • •

There is today an estimated 3.500 man-made space objects "up there", right now! Each such space "mission" lasting for up to many years. In contrast there is, today, an estimated 10.000 aircraft in flight at any moment. Each such flight lasting between 1/2 h and 14+ hours. *We proceed, therefore, on the assumption that a global, multi-nation co-ordinated ASC is required.*

• • •

The As Yet Unknowns. The above rather terse and simplified analysis left open a number of issues: (i) Can a perceived, "single", ASC be devised to handle all facets of space exploration, applications and technologies? (ii) Can a perceived ASC, of a next future, be "pinned down" to two or more separate physical, stationary parts (and behaviours) such as the *aircraft, ground control towers, terminal controls, area controls and continental controls*? (iii) Is it too early to consolidate matters? That is, do political concerns and technological advances stand in the way of consolidation?

A Suggestion. It is therefore suggested that the concepts of *domain science & engineering* be applied to the issues of whether (α) a national and/or an international, or a global, ASC; (β) one or several distinct ASCs, one per type of space exploration ([I]) or satellite ([IV]) or application ([IV]); and (γ) in case (β) recommends several, typed, ASCs, how to coordinate these.

In doing so *domain science & engineering* is being used not to model an existing, but a contemplated domain! Thus the modelling may involve modelling a variety of choices. In [12], the authors show how domain modelling can be formulated such that optimisation of assembly line production can be investigated. Similar possibilities could be investigated in connection with modelling proposed aeronautic & space control. Domain science & engineering may cast a new kind of light on these issues.

Thus it is suggested that the US Government FAA and NASA, and, in Europe, the EUROCONTROL and ESA, separately or jointly, and these in cooperation with many other space agencies[33], co-operate on researching and experimentally developing domain models for aeronautics & space.

6   Conclusion

The title of this paper had the prefix *'An Essence of'*. The *'An'*, rather than a *'The'*, shall indicate that there are many essential aspects of *domain engineering*. Some essences of *domain science & engineering* are (i) a basis in *philosophy*; (ii) an interpretation of *transcendental deduction*; (iii) *intentional pull*, an interpretation of *"gravitational pull"* being a core property of domains; and (iv) that domain analysis & description 'wavers' between *science* and *engineering*, being conducted in a context of more-or-less following *formal method principles, techniques* and *tools* – yet searching and deciding *informally* for the entities to analyse & describe.

---

[33] ICAO (UN), Roscosmos (Russia), CNSA (China), ISRO (India), JAXA (Japan), AEB (Brazil), CSA (Canada), ASA (Australia) and others.

There may be other 'essences'!³⁴ We refer to [11] for other aspects.

The proposed domain modelling method of this paper, and hence [11], raises a great many research issues:

- The issue of *intentional pull* is also only briefly sketched, paragraph *Intentional Pull* Sect., 3.2 on page 14.
- There is the issue of *the modelling of continuity*, illustrated in paragraph *Intentional Pull* of Sect. 4.1 on page 25. In modelling aeronautics & space there is a more general need for modelling continuity. 'Formal Methods', so far, has yet to "deliver" on this: the ability to freely alternate between discrete, logical models and continuous, say differential and integral calculus-based models.
- There is a carefully thought out and apparently complete analysis & description calculus for endurants, but there is no analysis & description calculus for perdurants!?

Acknowledgments. The front matter preface of [11] ends with an extensive list of acknowledgments. For this paper I repeat acknowledging three persons: *Kai Sørlander* from whose philosophical works and from our personal interaction I have benefited; my editor at Springer, *Ronan Nugent*, whose steadfast and tireless work also lies behind [11]; and *Klaus Havelund* for being a great discussion partner over now many years. I also thank the NASA Formal Methods Symposium for the invitation which has afforded me the possibility to correct, clarify and simplify a number of issues wrt. RSL, RSL⁺Text, and domain analysis and description methodology: its principles, techniques and tools.

References

1. Aaronson, S.: Quantum Computing since Democritus. Cambridge University Press, Cambridge (2013)
2. Ahbel-Rappe, S.: Socrates: A Guide for the Perplexed. A&C Black (Bloomsbury) (2011). ISBN 978-0-8264-3325-1
3. Ross, W.D., et al.: Plato's Theory of Ideas. Oxford University Press, Oxford (1963)
4. Aristotle: Categories. On Interpretation. Prior Analytics. Harvard University Press [Loebb Classical Library, translated by H.P. Cooke and Hugh Tredenick] (1938)
5. Audi, R.: The Cambridge Dictionary of Philosophy. Cambridge University Press, Cambridge (1995)

---

³⁴ It appears to have become fashionable to include the idea of 'essence' in the title of methods or books:

- https://essence.ivarjacobson.com/services/what-essence: *The Essence of Software Engineering. The SEMAT kernel.* Ivar Jacobson, Pan-Wei Ng, Paul E. McMahon, Ian Spence, and Svante Lidman. ACM Queue, October 24, 2012, Volume 10, issue 10.
- https://press.princeton.edu/books/hardcover/9780691225388/the-essence-of-software: *The Essence of Software: Why Concepts Matter for Great Design.* Daniel Jackson, Nov.16, 2021.

6. Berger, B., Whistler, D.: The Schelling Reader. Bloomsbury Publishing PLC, London (2020)
7. Berkeley, G.: Philosophical Works, Including the Works on Vision. Everyman edition, London (1975). (1713)
8. Bjørner, D.: Software Engineering, Vol. 1: Abstraction and Modelling. TTCS. Springer, Heidelberg (2006). https://doi.org/10.1007/3-540-31288-9
9. Bjørner, D.: Software Engineering, Vol. 2: Specification of Systems and Languages. TTCS. Springer, Heidelberg (2006). https://doi.org/10.1007/978-3-540-33193-3. Chapters 12–14 are primarily authored by Christian Krog Madsen
10. Bjørner, D.: Software Engineering, Vol. 3: Domains, Requirements and Software Design. TTCS. Springer, Heidelberg (2006). https://doi.org/10.1007/3-540-33653-2
11. Bjørner, D.: Domain Science & Engineering - A Foundation for Software Development. Monographs in Theoretical Computer Science. An EATCS Series. Springer, Cham (2021). https://doi.org/10.1007/978-3-030-73484-8
12. Bjørner, N., Levatich, M., Lopes, N.P., Rybalchenko, A., Vuppalapati, C.: Supercharging plant configurations using Z3. In: Stuckey, P.J. (ed.) CPAIOR 2021. LNCS, vol. 12735, pp. 1–25. Springer, Cham (2021). https://doi.org/10.1007/978-3-030-78230-6_1
13. Butterfield, J., Earmann, J. (eds.): Philosophy of Physics. Handbook of The Philosophy of Science. Elsevier (2006)
14. Carnap, R.: Der Logische Aufbau der Welt. Weltkreis, Berlin (1928)
15. Carnap, R.: The Logical Syntax of Language. Harcourt Brace and Co., New York (1937)
16. Carnap, R.: Introduction to Semantics. Harvard University Press, Cambridge (1942)
17. Carnap, R.: Meaning and Necessity, A Study in Semantics and Modal Logic. University of Chicago Press, Chicago (1947, 1956)
18. Casati, R., Varzi, A.C.: Parts and Places: The Structures of Spatial Representation. MIT Press, Cambridge (1999)
19. Clarke, E.M., Henzinger, T.A., Veith, H., Bloem, R.: Handbook of Model Checking. Springer, Cham (2018). https://doi.org/10.1007/978-3-319-10575-8
20. Couprie, D.L., Kocandrle, R.: Anaximander: Anaximander on Generation and Destruction. Briefs in Philosophy Series. Springer
21. Darwin, C.: Origin of Species. Penguin Putnam (2003). Introduction by Sir Julian Huxley
22. Dawes, J.: The VDM-SL reference guide, vol. 18. Pitman, London (1991)
23. Descartes, R.: Discours de la méthode. Texte et commentaire par Étienne Gilson. Vrin, Paris (1987)
24. Henry Folse, J.F. (ed.): Niels Bohr and the Philosophy of Physics: Twenty-First-Century Perspectives. Bloomsbury Academic (2019)
25. Frege, G. (ed.): Begriffsschrift - "a formula language, modelled on that of arithmetic, for pure thought". Verlag von Louis Nebert, Halle (1879)
26. George, C., Haxthausen, A.E.: The logic of the RAISE specification language. Comput. Artif. Intell. 22(3–4), 323–350 (2003). http://www.sav.sk/index.php?lang=en&charset=ascii&doc=journal&part=list_articles&journal_issue_no=882#abstract_2729
27. George, C.W., et al.: The RAISE Specification Language. The BCS Practitioner Series. Prentice-Hall, Hemel Hampstead (1992)

28. George, C.W., Haxthausen, A.E., Hughes, S., Milne, R., Prehn, S., Pedersen, J.S.: The RAISE Development Method. The BCS Practitioner Series. Prentice-Hall, Hemel Hampstead (1995)
29. Gödel, K.: Über formal unentscheidbare Sätze der Principia Mathematica und verwandter Systeme I. Monatshefte für Mathematik Physik **38**, 173–198 (1931). [English translation in van Heijenoort 1967, 596–616, and in Gödel, 1986, 144–195]
30. Hegel, G.W.F.: Wissenschaft der Logik. Hofenberg (2016). (1812–1816)
31. Heidegger, M.: Parminedes. Indiana University Press, Bloomington (1998)
32. Heisenberg, W.: Physics and Philosophy: The Revolution in Modern Science. Harper Perennial Modern Classics (2007)
33. Hierons, R.M., Bowen, J.P., Harman, M. (eds.): Formal Methods and Testing. LNCS, vol. 4949. Springer, Heidelberg (2008). https://doi.org/10.1007/978-3-540-78917-8
34. Hoare, C.A.R.: Communicating sequential processes. Commun. ACM **21**(8), 666–677 (1978)
35. Hoare, C.A.R.: Communicating Sequential Processes. C.A.R. Hoare Series in Computer Science, Prentice-Hall International (1985)
36. Hoare, C.A.R.: Communicating Sequential Processes. C.A.R. Hoare Series in Computer Science. Prentice-Hall International (1985). published electronically: usingcsp.com/cspbook.pdf (2004)
37. Hofmann, M.: Syntax and semantics of dependent types. In: Extensional Constructs in Intensional Type Theory. DISTDISS, pp. 13–54. Springer, London (1997). https://doi.org/10.1007/978-1-4471-0963-1_2
38. Hume, D.: Enquiry Concerning Human Understanding. Squashed Editions, Winster (2020). (1758)
39. Husserl, E.: Ideas. General Introduction to Pure Phenomenology. Routledge, Milton Park (2012)
40. Irvine, A.D. (ed.): Philosophy of Mathematics. Elsevier Science & Technology (2006)
41. Jackson, M.A.: Software Requirements & Specifications: A Lexicon of Practice, Principles and Prejudices. ACM Press, Addison-Wesley, Reading (1995)
42. James, D., Zoller, G.: Cambridge Companion to Fichte. Cambridge University Press, Cambridge (2016)
43. Kant, I.: Critique of Pure Reason. Penguin Books Ltd, London (2007). (1787)
44. Kennedy, H.C. (ed.): Selected works of Giuseppe Peano, with a biographical sketch and bibliography. Allen & Unwin, London (1973)
45. Leibniz, G.W.: The Philosophical Writings of Leibniz. Hassell Street Press, Stoke-on-Trent (2021)
46. Little, W., Fowler, H., Coulson, J., Onions, C.: The Shorter Oxford English Dictionary on Historical Principles. Clarendon Press, Oxford (1973, 1987). Two vols
47. Locke, J.: An Essay Concerning Human Understanding. Penguin Classics, London (1998). (1689)
48. Maxwell, J.C.: A Treatise on Electricity and Magnetism, 3rd edn., vol. 1–2. Dover reprint, Garden City (1954). (1892)
49. Mendel, G., Bateson, W. (eds.): Mendel's Principles of Heredity. Franklin Classics Trade Press, Minneapolis (2018)
50. Mercer, J.E.: The Mysticism of Anaximenes and the Air. Kessinger Publishing, LLC, Whitefish (2010)
51. O'Grady, P.: Thales of Miletus. Western Philosophy Series. Routledge, Milton Park (2002)

52. Pears, D.: Russell's Logical Atomism. Fontana Collins (1972)
53. Planck, M.: Eight Lectures on Theoretical Physics. Dover Publications, Garden City (2003). (1915)
54. Popper, K.R.: Logik der Forschung. Julius Springer Verlag, Vienna, Austria (1934). (1935). english version [56]
55. Popper, K.R.: The Logic of Scientific Discovery. Hutchinson of London, 3 Fitzroy Square, London W1, England (1959,... 1979), translated from [55]
56. Popper, K.R.: Conjectures and Refutations. The Growth of Scientific Knowledge. Routledge and Kegan Paul Ltd. (Basic Books, Inc.), 39 Store Street, WC1E 7DD, London, England (New York, NY, USA) (1963,...,1981)
57. Popper, K.R.: A Pocket Popper. Fontana Pocket Readers, Fontana Press, England (1983). An edited collection, Ed. David Miller
58. Roscoe, A.W.: Theory and Practice of Concurrency. C.A.R. Hoare Series in Computer Science. Prentice-Hall (1997). http://www.comlab.ox.ac.uk/people/bill. roscoe/publications/68b.pdf
59. Russell, B.: On denoting. Mind **14**, 479–493 (1905)
60. Russell, B.: The Problems of Philosophy. Home University Library, London (1912). oxford University Press paperback, 1959 Reprinted, 1971–2
61. Russell, B.: Introduction to Mathematical Philosophy. George Allen and Unwin, London (1919)
62. Russell, B.: "Preface". Our Knowledge of the External World. G. Allen & Unwin Ltd, London (1952)
63. Sannella, D., Tarlecki, A.: Foundations of Algebraic Semantics and Formal Software Development. Monographs in Theoretical Computer Science, Springer, Heidelberg (2012)
64. Schneider, S.: Concurrent and Real-Time Systems – The CSP Approach. World-wide Series in Computer Science. Wiley, Chichester (2000)
65. Sørlander, K.: Det Uomgængelige - Filosofiske Deduktioner [The Inevitable - Philosophical Deductions, with a foreword by Georg Henrik von Wright]. Munksgaard · Rosinante (1994). 168 pages
66. Sørlander, K.: Under Evighedens Synsvinkel [Under the viewpoint of eternity]. Munksgaard · Rosinante (1997). 200 pages
67. Sørlander, K.: Den Endegyldige Sandhed [The Final Truth]. Rosinante (2002). 187 pages
68. Sørlander, K.: Indføring i Filosofien [Introduction to The Philosophy]. Informations Forlag (2016). 233 pages
69. Spinoza, B.: Ethics, Demonstrated in Geometrical Order. The Netherlands (1677)
70. Wallace, A.R.: The Annotated Malaysian Archipelago. National University of Singapore Press, Singapore (2014). Edited by John Van Wyhe
71. Whitehead, A.N., Russell, B.: Principia Mathematica, 3 vols (1962). Cambridge University Press (1910, 1912, and 1913), second edition, 1925 (Vol. 1), 1927 (Vols 2, 3), also Cambridge University Press
72. Wittgenstein, L.J.J.: Tractatus Logico-Philosophicus. Oxford University Press, London (1961). (1921)
73. Wittgenstein, L.J.J.: Philosophical Investigations. Oxford University Press, Oxford (1958)
74. Wolfe, C.T., Huneman, P., Reydon, T.A. (eds.): History, Philosophy and Theory of the Life Sciences. Springer, Heidelberg (2013)
75. Wright, M.: Empedokles: The Extant Fragments. Hackett Publishing Company, Inc. (1995)

Concept Design Moves

Daniel Jackson[✉]

Massachusetts Institute of Technology, Cambridge, MA, USA
dnj@mit.edu

Abstract. Great designs are rarely inventions without precedent; more often they are skillful adaptations of earlier designs. Designers work by recognizing structures they have previously seen, and taking steps they have taken before. By making such *patterns* and *design moves* explicit, we can educate designers more effectively and promote good design. This paper explains *concepts*, a modular structure for describing software behavior that allows patterns to be recognized, and proposes three pairs of design moves for software design, illustrating their application in some widely used products.

Keywords: Software design · Design patterns · Design moves · Software concepts · Modularity

1 Introduction: Codifying Design Expertise

Accounts of design as a creative process often give the impression that design is mostly about coming up with entirely novel ideas. The fashionable term "ideation" reinforces this view, and suggests that insights emerge *ex nihilo* in the designer's mind. With the assumption that little can be done to make any individual designer more imaginative or creative, we tend to turn to a collaborative process to improve the outcome, for example by encouraging earlier prototyping, or by brainstorming with a diverse group of people. Such practices are helpful, but they are tangential to the substance of design.

1.1 Designers Bring Prior Knowledge

Instead, we might look to how experienced designers think, and try to make explicit (and learnable) the insights that they have gained over years of experience. From my own experience watching software designers in action, and from analyzing the occasions on which I have had design insights myself, I have concluded that design ideas do not appear in a vacuum, but are usually drawn from prior experience. This does not mean that the experienced designer is not creative. Precedents rarely match exactly, so identifying them demands insight (often in the form of an analogy or abstraction), and applying them requires adaptation and skill. Design is thus less about sudden inspiration and more about patient analogizing and adjustment. Innovation is no less important, but becomes less visible, being found not in a wholesale replacement of old ideas with new ones, but rather in subtle (and sometimes unexpected) details of reworking and refinement.

© Springer Nature Switzerland AG 2022
J. V. Deshmukh et al. (Eds.): NFM 2022, LNCS 13260, pp. 52–70, 2022.
https://doi.org/10.1007/978-3-031-06773-0_3

Design expertise, codified in an applicable form, can offer a shortcut to inexperienced designers, who can benefit from the accumulated wisdom of the community, and it can amplify the skills of experienced designers. In a sense, such codification is what thoughtful education in all practical areas seeks: to learn by doing, but where much of the doing has already been done (by others, in the past).

1.2 Standard Solutions and Moves

Different kinds of expertise might be codified, including: (a) standard solutions or *patterns*, which can be adopted in different contexts; (b) *design moves*, in which the solution is not provided, but instead a standard transformation from one solution to another; and (c) *methods* for applying these, e.g. for identifying relevant solutions or moves, and making whatever adjustments are needed to apply them in a new situation.

The first two categories of reusable expertise have been articulated in a variety of design fields. Notable examples include Alexander's design patterns [2, 3], which offer standard solutions in architecture and urban/landscape design, and Altshuller's TRIZ [26], which codified 40 design moves extracted from a study of thousands of patents for physical devices. The third category is addressed tangentially in some of the pattern literature, but has yet to be fully explored.

In software engineering, patterns have been formulated and widely adopted in many areas, including object-oriented programming [10], software architectures [23], enterprise applications [9], and user interfaces [27]. While many pattern collections are available, collections of design moves are harder to come by. Code refactoring [12] is a notable exception. Some of the most influential ideas about program structure might also be seen as design moves, most notably information hiding [21] and decoupling [22].

1.3 Design vs. Engineering

All of these examples in the software realm start from the point at which the observable behavior of the software has already been determined, and the problem is how to realize that behavior in code. The most far-reaching decisions—what the functions of the software will be, and how those functions will be organized—have already been made. The user's experience has been set; all that remains is the task of ensuring that the system will deliver its functions reliably and efficiently.

That task, of course, comprises all of programming and software architecture, and arguably user interface design also, so its importance should not be minimized. Nevertheless, our field has tended to focus on it at the expense of the more fundamental task of shaping the software's behavior. As Fred Brooks put it [5]: "The essence of a software entity is a construct of interlocking concepts... I believe the hard part of building software to be the specification, design, and testing of this conceptual construct, not the labor of representing it."

For this reason, I believe it's helpful to distinguish the terms *software design* and *software engineering*, reserving the first for the shaping of behavior and the second for structuring its implementation. This usage would accord with the way the term "design" is used in other fields. Adopting it is not a mere philological exercise, but a serious attempt to recognize the importance of design in its own right. As Mitchell Kapor wrote (paraphrasing slightly): "When you go to design a house you talk to an architect first, not an engineer. Why is this? Because the criteria for what makes a good building fall outside the domain of engineering. Similarly, in computer programs, the selection of the various components and elements of the application must be driven by the conditions of use. How is this to be done? By software designers." [20].

This paper proposes some design moves for software design. These moves depend on expressing the function of a software system using structures that I call *concepts*. I will explain first what concepts are, and then present the design moves, along with examples of their application. The idea of concepts is presented more fully in a recently published book [15], which also explains the design criteria on which the design moves are based, and includes many of the examples used in this paper—but does not articulate explicitly the idea of design moves.

Concepts are not the first attempt to identify patterns in software design prior to implementation. This work was inspired and influenced in particular by Michael Jackson's problem frames [18] and Martin Fowler's analysis patterns [8]. Patterns in data models have also been explored [13].

2   Concept Structuring

The behavior of a software system can be modeled as a set of interacting *concepts*. Each concept has its own state and a set of actions that update the state. Importantly, and in contrast to modules in the code, both the state and the actions are visible to the user.

The formulation of a concept's behavior is not novel. To a practitioner of formal methods, a concept is just a state machine, conventionally used to define entire systems in languages such as Alloy [16, 17], B [1], VDM [19] or Z [24]. To a software architect, a concept can be viewed as a service with a public API, like a microservice but smaller (perhaps a "nanoservice"), or as a domain (in the sense of domain-driven design [7]), with the state comprising a context that is even more "bounded" than usual. To a psychologist or social scientist, a concept is a little behavioral protocol that a user engages in, just like the protocols we use in everyday life (for example, in the way we add items to a shopping list and then check them off as we find the items in the store).

The Label concept (Fig. 1), for example, provides the functionality associated with labeling items and subsequently retrieving them through their labels. Some details of the description to note:

1. The term *Label* is overloaded to refer to the name of the concept (in the first line) and the set of labels (elsewhere). The concept is parameterized by *Item*, the type of items to be labeled.
2. The state and actions are defined using Alloy notation, augmented with a C-style update operator (and implicit frame conditions). Thus, for example, the formula

i.labels + = *l* in the *add_label* action says that the set of labels of the item *i* has *l* added to it.

3. The *clear_labels* action removes all the labels from an item, effectively removing the item from the concept's state.

4. The operational principle is one or more scenarios that demonstrate how the concept fulfills its purpose. In this case, the first says that if label *l* is added to item *i* and not removed, then performing a find on that label will return a set of items that includes *i*; the second says that if no addition of such a label occurs for an item, it will not be returned in a find on that label. The operational principle is intended to explain the basic operation of the concept and not all the details. Thus, it does not explain, for example, that a find on a set of labels returns the items that have all those labels, nor does it mention the *clear_labels* actions.

```
1   concept Label [Item]
2   purpose
3       classify items into overlapping categories
4   state
5       labels: Item -> set Label
6   actions
7       add_label (i: Item, l: Label)
8           i.labels += l
9       remove_label (i: Item, l: Label)
10          i.labels -= l
11      clear_labels (i: Item)
12          i.labels := none
13      find (ls: set Label): set Item
14          return {i: Item | ls in i.labels}
15  operational principle
16      if add_label (i, l) and no remove_label (i, l),
17          find (l) returns items including i
18      if no add_label (i, l), then find (l) returns items not including i
```

Fig. 1. An example concept: Label.

As another example, the Todo concept (Fig. 2) provides the basic functionality of a todo list, namely adding tasks to be displayed and marking them as done. Note that the *Task* type is not treated as a type parameter; the assumption is that task objects are generated by this concept, and that their details are not specified here. In the simplest case, a task would be just a text string.

```
1    concept Todo
2    purpose
3        track status of tasks
4    state
5        pending, done: set Task
6    actions
7        add_task (t: Task)
8            pending += t
9        remove_task (t: Task)
10           t in pending + done
11           pending -= t
12           done -= t
13       complete_task (t: Task)
14           t in pending
15           done += t
16           pending -= t
17       uncomplete_task (t: Task)
18           t in done
19           done -= t
20           pending += t
21   operational principle
22       following add_task (t), t is in pending until complete_task(t),
23           after which t is in done
```

Fig. 2. An example concept: Todo.

2.1 Concept Independence

Two important properties characterize concepts, distinguishing them from other behavioral structures (such as features [4] or object-oriented classes). First, each concept is *self-contained*: its behavior is defined without reference to other concepts, and concepts do not "use" each other in the way that one module or microservice in the code of a software system may use another, for example by making calls to it.

Second, concepts are *purposive*: each brings its own benefit that can be defined and evaluated without reference to another. These properties are different but nonetheless related; one can think of them both as forms of independence, the former in the realm of behavior and the latter in the realm of the needs or requirements that the behavior is intended to satisfy.

To achieve these properties, concept boundaries have to be drawn in certain ways, and not all increments of function can be described as concepts. In marked contrast, features can be used to organize the codebase of a system in almost arbitrary units. The rationale for the more restrictive notion of concept is that it ensures that concepts can be understood independently of one another, simplifying the user's mental model. Indeed, this independence of elements of a mental model is essential for its cognitive "robustness" [6]. It also allows the same concept to be instantiated in different systems, which brings benefits to both user (in terms of familiarity) and designer (in terms of reuse of design knowledge).

These properties are illustrated by the Label concept (Fig. 1). Self-containment means first that it includes the end-to-end functionality associated with labels: not only adding and removing labels, but actually using the labels to find items. It also means that, as reflected in the polymorphism of the concept, it relies on no properties of items except that they exist and can be distinguished, so it has no reliance on any other concept.

2.2 Concept Synchronization

Concepts are composed together to form an application. Since no concept uses the services of another, and every concept's behavior must be visible and intelligible to the user, traditional procedure call is not a suitable composition mechanism. Instead, we'll compose concepts by running them in parallel, synchronizing their actions where needed.

Synchronizations have the form "when action $A1$ happens in concept $C1$, action $A2$ happens in concept $C2$." An action in one concept can lead to any number of actions in other concepts. Synchronizations may also be conditioned on the states of the concepts. Synchronization is thus similar to the mechanism of an event-driven architecture, but there is an important distinction. A concept can refuse an action, and in that case a synchronization that would lead to that action must be blocked in its entirety. A synchronization is thus a kind of transaction, and its execution is all or nothing.

```
1    app todo-with-labels
2    include
3      Todo
4      Label [Todo.Task]
5    sync Todo.remove_task (t)
6      Label.clear_labels (t)
7    sync Todo.add_task (t)
8      Label.add_label (t, PENDING)
9    sync Todo.complete_task (t)
10     Label.remove_label (t, PENDING)
11   sync Label.remove_label (t, PENDING)
12     Todo.complete_task (t)
13   sync Label.add_label (t, PENDING)
14     Todo.uncomplete_task (t)
```

Fig. 3. An example synchronization.

This composition mechanism is borrowed from CSP [14]. In CSP, actions in two processes are synchronized when they have the same name, and in the resulting composition, a single shared action occurs for both processes. When process actions with different names are to be synchronized, a renaming operator is first applied. For concepts, it makes more sense to allow actions with different names to be synchronized, and for a single synchronization to result in multiple actions in the various participating concepts.

Despite this difference, a fundamental property of CSP is retained. Suppose a concept C has a specification $S(C)$, which you can think of as the set of permitted histories of actions (called traces in CSP). Let's say that an app conforms to the specification of C if every history of actions of the app, when restricted to those actions relevant to C, is a permitted history in $S(C)$. Then given two concepts $C1$ and $C2$, any composition $C1 \parallel C2$ will conform to both specifications $S(C1)$ and $S(C2)$. In other words, composition of concepts implements conjunction of specifications.

This is hardly surprising. Synchronization can never make a concept do an action it would not otherwise allow, and can therefore only restrict which actions happen. If this were not the case, a concept, once embedded in an app, might behave in an unfamiliar way, compromising the user's understanding of that concept as a distinct and separable unit of functionality.

In the absence of synchronization, a concept's actions are unconstrained, and may occur in any order consistent with the concept behavior. In practice, a user interface will limit which actions are available at any time, typically by offering certain groups of actions on certain pages, with traversal actions to navigate from page to page. Such limitations are rarely fundamental, however, and are unlikely to be imposed by the service layer that lies behind the user interface. They could in theory be described as synchronizations, but in most cases (especially for non-critical software) the effort of specifying them carefully will not be worthwhile, and they would be better addressed in the context of wireframing.

We can assemble a little application that combines the two concepts we defined earlier, allowing the user to add labels to tasks, using the label *PENDING* for tasks that are pending (Fig. 3). Some details to note:

1. The instantiation of the Label concept passes in the *Task* type of the Todo concept as a parameter, thus ensuring that the items manipulated by the Label concept are the tasks of the Todo concept.
2. The implicational structure of synchronizations is implicit. Thus, the first synchronization, for example, says that when a *remove_task* action happens in the Todo concept for task *t*, a corresponding *clear_labels* action happens in the Label concept for the same task.
3. The first synchronization is just a bit of book-keeping, ensuring that when a task is removed from the Todo concept, it doesn't remain as a labeled item in the Label concept. If it did, the removed task might appear when the user tries to find tasks by label.
4. The four remaining synchronizations bring a little magic: when a task is added, it automatically gets the *PENDING* label; and when the task is completed, the label is removed. Conversely, adding and removing the label changes the task status. This allows a user to filter tasks by their labels and by their task status at once, since the latter is now expressible with labels. (For simplicity, I've only included a *PENDING* label, but of course we could add a *COMPLETED* label too allowing the user to find completed tasks as well as *PENDING* tasks.)

The synchronizations of actions between the two concepts preserve an invariant: that the tasks classified as *pending* in the Todo concept are labeled as *PENDING* in the Label concept. You might think at first that this redundancy brings little benefit. But actually there's a valuable synergy at play. With the task classification now reflected in the labeling, the user can use the Label concept to perform filterings that might otherwise have needed additional functionality in the Todo concept. Imagine a user interface for this app: a button that filters tasks to those that are *pending* would, prior to this synchronization, have required a special implementation as a query over the state of the Todo concept, but now it can be implemented using the *find* action of Label. The benefit would be even greater if (as would occur in practice) the Label concept were extended to a rich query language, so that the *PENDING* status could be combined with other labels in conjunction and disjunction.

3 Design Moves: Mechanical Analogues

To introduce the concept design moves in an intuitive way, I'll use some familiar mechanical analogues. There are six design moves, organized into three pairs of duals. Each pair embodies some design tradeoffs; a move in one direction benefits some property P at the cost of some other property P', with its dual in the other direction benefitting P' at the cost of P.

3.1 Split/Merge

The split/merge pair (Fig. 4) trade off simplicity and directness of usage on the one hand with flexibility on the other. The first photocopier machines offered a single concept, Photocopy say. Today's all-in-one printers also provide photocopying, but no longer as its own concept. Instead, there are two distinct concepts, Print and Scan, each with its own collection of controls and customizations. By splitting the Photocopy concept into Print and Scan, the user now has more flexibility. Photocopying is still available as a synchronization of the two, but it is marginally less convenient.

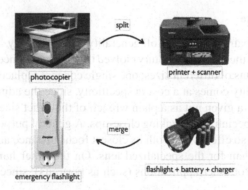

Fig. 4. Split-merge design moves.

For the dual, consider the emergency flashlight, whose single concept merges the distinct concepts of Flashlight, Battery and Charger. The merging brings a loss of flexibility: you can't use the batteries in another device, for example. But the gain in simplicity is significant, which is important especially for a device designed for use in emergencies. The merged concept also permits some special functionality, for example automatically turning the flashlight on when an outlet in which it has been charging loses power.

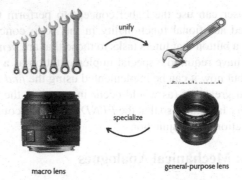

Fig. 5. Unify-specialize design moves.

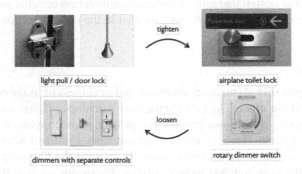

Fig. 6. Tighten-loosen design moves.

3.2 Unify/Specialize

The unify/specialize pair (Fig. 5) trade off generality and specificity. The invention of the adjustable wrench (in the mid-19th century) solved the problem of needing a collection of wrenches to handle nuts of different sizes; one single concept replaced multiple variants. Of course the generality comes at a cost in specificity, since the adjustable wrench isn't quite as good a fit for a given nut as a plain wrench of the exact size.

A macro lens is specialized for taking close-ups. A general purpose lens can be used for close-ups, but not so effectively: both its closest focus distance and smallest aperture are typically larger than for the specialized lens. On the other hand, a macro lens is usually less suitable for other applications (such as portraits), since its widest aperture is typically smaller.

3.3 Tighten/Loosen

The tighten/loosen pair (Fig. 6) trade off automation and control. In an aircraft toilet, the light and the door lock are synchronized tightly: you can't turn on the light without locking the door. The loss in flexibility (of a cleaner being able to keep the light on and door open) comes with the benefit of a passenger avoiding embarrassment of the door being opened while using the toilet.

The dual move, in which concept synchronization is loosened, can be seen in modern dimmer switches. The earliest switches coupled together the basic light switch concept and the dimmer concept: to turn the light off you had to first dim it all the way down. In modern designs, the two concepts can be operated independently, so that a light can be turned on and off while retaining the brightness setting.

4   Concept Design Moves: Software Examples

I'll now illustrate each of the design moves with an example from software, showing how the move was applied successfully in a familiar software product.

4.1   Split: Emergence of a Concept in Keynote

The Fullscreen concept (Fig. 7) has had a slow emergence. Initially, certain apps used full screen mode only for certain functions. Presentation apps such as Powerpoint and Keynote, in particular, would go full screen when the user switched from editing to presenting. Later, apps began to offer a full screen mode as an option during regular use. The final step came during the COVID-19 pandemic, when users began to make slide presentations in Zoom meetings, and needed a way to present *without* going full screen (so they could continue to see the other participants). Finally, Fullscreen became a concept in its own right that can be fully controlled independently of other concepts.

Fig. 7.   Keynote's fullscreen for edit (left) and non-fullscreen for play (right).

4.2   Merge: The Yellkey URL Shortener

The ShortURL and Expiry concepts have been known for a long time, although they weren't typically combined. Most URL shortening services generated a short URL that was permanent. The Expiry concept is used in a variety of contexts, and is often under user control (for example, to allow you to limit the access period for a shared document). The Yellkey URL shortener (Fig. 8) brought these two concepts together so tightly that they no longer appear to have any independent existence: when you request a short URL, you enter the long URL and an expiry time. No other action is provided, except of course the redirection in which short URLs are expanded. The benefit of this integration is that, by ensuring very short lifetimes for short URLs, a common word can be used in place of an unreadable sequence of random characters.

Fig. 8. Yellkey URL shortener.

4.3 Unify: MITs Moira Service

My own university offers a service for mailing lists called Moira (Fig. 9). The owner of a mailing list can be a single user, but it can also be a group of users. This is handy, because it permits the burden of maintaining the group to be spread amongst multiple administrators; it also supports the common case of a professor delegating control to an assistant.

In a deft design move, Moira's designers chose to reuse the mailing list concept for administrative groups too. Essentially, there is only a single concept, List say, which unifies two concepts, MailingList and AdminGroup, which might have been separated, but which share several key actions (notably adding and removing members). The unification simplifies the user interface and its implementation, and also offers the ability to treat an administrative group as a mailing list (so you can provide an email address for the administrators of a list to those who want to join or leave).

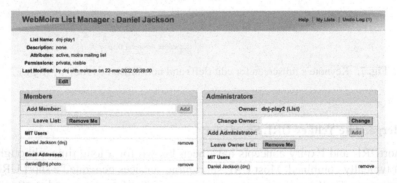

Fig. 9. MIT's Moira mailing list service.

But, as with all unifications, the move is not free of costs. A mailing list can include two types of members: internal users (who have MIT accounts, and are identified by their MIT user names) and external users (who do not have accounts, and are identified by their full email addresses). Because all administrative functions require login with an MIT user name, an external user cannot administer a mailing list. If you assign as the owner of a list a group comprising only external members, nobody can edit the list! It is also possible to create cyclic ownership—two mailing lists each of which serves as the administrative group for the other. Because the system is used by a relatively small community of mostly expert users, however, these problems do not appear to matter much in practice.

4.4 Specialize: Three Similar Concepts in Lightroom

Intentional specializations are harder to find in software, since software designers tend to favor unification over specialization, often to reduce implementation effort.

In Adobe Lightroom, there are three distinct concepts that all serve the purpose of classifying photos into a small number of fixed categories (Fig. 10). The Rating concept lets you rate a photo with some number of stars between zero and five; the Flag concept lets you mark a photo as picked or rejected (or neither); the ColorLabel concept lets you assign one of a few colors to a photo. These three distinct concepts are applied by Lightroom users mostly in one particular scenario: marking uploaded photos by quality prior to deleting some of them.

There are various differences between the concepts. The colors of the ColorLabel concept are not ordered; the Rating concept, in contrast, allows you to filter for photos with more than one star (for example). The Flag concept has a rather baroque built-in action called *refine* whose effect is to cause unflagged photos to be flagged as rejected, and picked photos to be unflagged. There is also a *delete-rejected* action which can then be applied to delete the photos that are now marked as rejected (and were previously the ones not picked).

Fig. 10. Lightroom ratings, flags and color labels.

In an early version of Lightroom, ratings and color labels were associated with files (so that if a photo belonged to multiple collections, any change in its rating or label would be seen in all of them), but flags were scoped by collection, so the same photo could have a flag in one collection but not another. This was a feature with legitimate uses, but it was removed, and flags were brought into line with ratings and color labels, presumably because users found it confusing that flag metadata was not saved to file.

Whether three distinct concepts are necessary here is not clear, but the cost of the additional complexity seems minor, and users seem to appreciate the choice.

4.5 Tighten: Page Scheduling in Hugo

Traditional blogging platforms such as WordPress and SquareSpace offer a Schedule concept that allows a blogger to author a post now but schedule it for publication at some date in the future. Blog posts also have metadata that includes a date which is often set by default to the date on which the post was created, and thus need not match the publication date.

In the Hugo static website generator, in contrast, scheduling is implicit. Files are written in markdown and contain a preamble giving the value of various metadata fields. The date field determines the date of publication, so all a user need do to schedule a post in the future is to enter the desired date in the file. Every file is treated uniformly, so any file on the website—not just a blog post—can be scheduled in this way.

This mechanism is a synchronization of Hugo's Metadata and Schedule concepts. The Metadata concept in its general form lets you associate properties with an object, retrieve them and sometimes also sort and filter collections of objects by their properties. In this design, the date field of a file is playing two roles: one (the basic Metadata role) is to show the date of a post on the website, and to sort posts by their dates in index pages; the other (the Schedule role) is to determine the date on which the post becomes visible. In fact, many of the other metadata fields in Hugo play additional roles of this sort via synchronization.

While elegant and flexible, the design is not without problems. Because the publication date of any file can be set in this way, it is possible if one is not careful to introduce inconsistencies in which a file and the files it references are published at different times, leading to broken links.

4.6 Loosen: Expert Control in ProCamera

Most digital cameras offer a rich Focus concept, often with many modes and settings, that sets the focal distance of the lens automatically, and an Exposure concept that sets the exposure (the aperture, shutter speed and sometimes also the ISO speed). In most cameras, the Focus concept offers an option in which the user can select a focal point somewhere in the image, and move it around (for example with a little joy stick on the back of the camera). In more advanced cameras, exposure can either be set by averaging over the scene, or by sampling a particular point (allowing the photographer to ensure that a face, for example, is correctly exposed). In almost all cameras, the Exposure point coincides with the Focus point.

Sometimes, however, the photographer wants to focus at one point and set exposure at another. In most cameras, this can be achieved by moving the focus point to the first point and setting "focus lock," and then moving it to the second point to set the exposure (or vice versa, using "exposure lock").

In ProCamera, a camera app for the iPhone, this complexity is eliminated by loosening the synchronization between the Focus and Exposure concepts. Unlike the conventional design, in which the target point of the Focus concept is used as the target point of the Exposure concept, each concept has its own point, so that focus and exposure can be sampled independently.

5   Solving Problems with Design Moves

To show how design moves might be used to fix design problems, let's consider some troubled designs.

5.1   Aspect Ratio in Fujifilm Cameras

Fujifilm makes a range of digital cameras that are widely admired for their physical design. Their cameras have been lauded especially for their manual controls, which allow almost all adjustments to be made directly by turning a dial or ring, and without having to navigate through menus. This is especially significant because, as in most cameras, the user interface design for the virtual controls is not as refined as the mechanical design.

One example can be found in the way one selects the aspect ratio (which can only be done by menu). Most mirrorless cameras (and some digital SLRs too) let you choose an aspect ratio that differs from the sensor's native ratio. This means wasting pixels, but allows a photographer to employ a different framing, and to visualize that framing in the viewfinder. The most common non-standard ratio is probably 1:1, since it matches Instagram's preferred ratio.

On Fujifilm cameras (Fig. 11), the ratio is set in the Image Size menu (whose name already suggests a problematic design). This menu is used also to set JPEG resolution. Thus, if you want a 1:1 ratio, for example, the menu offers three options for that ratio, combining it with L, M and S settings (for large, medium and small numbers of pixels in the recorded JPEG). A separate menu, called Image Quality, lets you choose to record just a raw file, or just a JPEG file, either in fine or normal quality, or to record both raw and JPEG, with either of the two JPEG quality options.

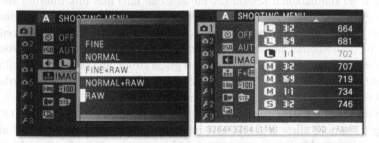

Fig. 11. Fujifilm image quality menu (left) and image size menu (right).

If you choose the option to store only raw files, and no JPEGs, the Image Size menu is greyed out, and the aspect ratio reverts to the default. You might imagine that this is because custom ratios are achieved by cropping the JPEG in-camera (which is true), and that they cannot therefore play a role for raw files (which is false). In fact, these cameras helpfully store a non-destructive crop in the raw file. But because of the strange design, if you want only raw files but with a custom ratio, you need to switch to the option to store JPEGs too, and then throw them away.

The remedy here seems straightforward. Ratio is not a proper concept in its own right; it has been merged into the Image Size concept as an additional feature. This is what I call "overloading by piggybacking": it seems as if the developer needed to find a place to insert the ratio feature and "piggybacked" it onto another concept. Applying a split and making Ratio a concept in its own right, so that the user could select the ratio independently of the JPEG size, would eliminate the problem of having to generate spurious JPEGs. It would also allow Fujifilm to support a larger number of ratios. Users are always asking for more (and there is even an online petition) but Fujifilm is presumably reluctant to do so, because of the combinatorial explosion it would produce in the Image Size menu (with its current design).

The Image Quality menu has a bad smell too in its mixing the choice of format (JPEG vs raw) and JPEG quality. There seems to be an opportunity to rework the entire menu system of digital cameras in a more systematic, concept-structured way.

5.2 Message Filters in Apple Mail

Apple Mail, the default mail client on macOS, includes several strongly related concepts: Rule, which lets you define a processing rule that when matched on a message performs some action (such as moving it to a given mailbox); Search, which lets you search for messages from particular senders or with certain subjects (amongst other things); and SmartMailbox, which lets you define a mailbox containing messages that meet certain criteria.

All three concepts involve filtering a set of messages using defined criteria. For Rule, the set comprises either incoming messages (by default), or the messages in a specified mailbox; for Search, the set comprises either all messages or the messages in selected mailboxes; and for SmartMailbox, it comprises all messages.

There is no fundamental reason (as far as I can tell) that this filtering should be specialized to the three concepts. And yet each concept has not only its own user interface, but also its own filtering options, and these options are incomparable. Thus, only Rule lets you filter on whether messages are encrypted or not; only Search lets you select messages in a mailbox whose name contains a given string; and only SmartMailbox lets you choose messages by the date when last viewed. Furthermore, Rule and SmartMailbox let you conjoin or disjoin multiple conditions; Search does not.

Applying the unify move to create a single, general filtering concept might improve this design. It would allow a single user interface for the filtering aspect of all three concepts, and it would allow more powerful filtering (especially for Search, which is very limited). It would also support converting a search into a rule or a smart mailbox. As with all unifications, there would be rough edges to handle: most notably, some warning would be desirable when a rule is applied only to incoming messages but contains a condition that does not apply to them (such as belonging to a given mailbox, or having been viewed already).

5.3 Event Deletion in Calendars

Calendar apps such as Apple Calendar and Google Calendar synchronize two concepts together: an Event concept (which lets you store and view upcoming events) and an

Invitation concept (which lets you send a request to a group of participants and receive replies). Obviously, the two concepts need to work in concert together, but in practice the synchronization has sometimes been too tight.

For years, Apple Calendar's predecessor iCal suffered from an amusing problem—although hardly amusing to users. If an event had an associated invitation, then deleting it would automatically send a reply that the invitation had been declined. This created a Catch-22 when you receive calendar spam: if you deleted the spam event, the reply would reveal to the spammer that your email address was legitimate, but if you left it, your calendar could fill up with spurious events. Various workarounds (such as moving the spam events to a new calendar and deleting the calendar in its entirety) were developed until Apple solved the problem by loosening the synchronization and offering users the option of deleting an event without declining the associated invitation.

This problem seems to have persisted longer in Google Calendar. A few years ago, seminars in our lab would routinely appear to be canceled, only for the organizer to assure people that the seminar was in fact going ahead. The problem, it turned out was that members of the lab mailing list received the seminar announcement in their email client, which in some cases automatically installed the event in their calendar. If someone then deleted their copy of the event, a message saying the event was canceled was sent to all (nearly 1,000!) members of the seminar mailing list, which was specified as a single participant in the seminar event.

It's unclear whether this problem remains in Google Calendar. In the official documentation for "Delete an event," there is no mention of deleting without canceling or sending a notification. Google Calendar does seem to present a "delete without notify" option in some cases, but according to one forum thread, only if the deletion is being requested by the owner of the event/invitation and not if by a recipient.

Fig. 12. Zoom reaction options.

5.4 Sticky Hands in Zoom

Finally, here is an example that seems to call for a tighten move. In Zoom, the RaisedHand concept operates entirely independently of other concepts, notably the Mute concept. And yet a common protocol for meetings has participants mute themselves until they want to talk; then raise their hand; then unmute when called upon. Unfortunately, people often forget to lower their hands, so the moderator is uncertain of whether or not to call on them again.

Introducing some synchronization here might help. One possibility would be to offer a special meeting mode in which only one participant who is not a host can be unmuted at a time; participants raise their hands to speak, and when a host selects someone, they are simultaneously unmuted, their hand is lowered, and the previous speaker muted.

The key point here is not that the design move is obvious or trivial. On the contrary, there are many pitfalls in designing this kind of behavior while trying to maintain a balance between simplicity and flexibility. What the design move offers is not a panacea but a way to frame the design space, by encouraging the designer to separate the design of the concepts and their actions from the way in which those actions are synchronized. A slightly different view of this problem is possible. In the current user interface of Zoom, the "raise hand" option appears when you click the "Reactions" button, along with other options such as displaying a clapping emoji (Fig. 12). This suggests that RaisedHand is not in fact a concept in its own right, but is a feature (comprising just the *raise-hand* action) that is subsumed by the Reaction concept. In this case, the appropriate design move might be first to apply a split so that RaisedHand is made a concept in its own right. That would allow a raised hand to have different behavior from a reaction. For example, a host might choose the next person to speak by clicking a button that changes their raised hand to a different icon (in contrast to reactions, which are controlled solely by the participant).

6 Discussion

The design moves described here should be viewed as an initial proposal. They are undoubtedly incomplete; they do not include, for example, some arguably even more fundamental moves (such as adjusting a novel concept to bring it into alignment with a familiar, existing concept). The distinctions between the moves are not always as clear as they might be. For example, while the general ideas of split and loosen are easy to distinguish, we saw in the context of the Zoom problem that whether one or the other applied depended on whether the raised-hand feature were viewed as a concept in its own right or just part of a Reaction concept.

I have also been a bit sloppy in identifying the exact boundaries of concepts. In the Apple Mail filtering case, for example, it seems likely that the unify design move would apply only to the filtering aspect of each of the three concepts Rule, Search and Smart-Mailbox, each of which would be composed with a unified Filter concept but would retain its own distinct identity. The same treatment might apply to the Moira case, so that instead of seeing the design as a unifying of MailingList and AdminGroup, it is seen as the factoring out of a unified (and shared) List concept.

Although much remains to be done, my hope is that this initial effort will inspire others to think about design in this way. Design will always remain a creative and uncertain activity, but a good design language and design structures can empower us to work with greater confidence and clarity.

Acknowledgments. Thank you to Geoffrey Litt, Joshua Pollock and Michael Jackson for helpful discussions about design moves, and to Akiva Jackson, Rachel Jackson and Rebecca Jackson for sharing their experiences and insights about troubled concepts. The author's research was supported in part by the National Science Foundation, under the Secure and Trustworthy Cyberspace (SATC) and Designing Accountable Software Systems (DASS) programs.

References

1. Abrial, J.-R.: The B-Book: Assigning Programs to Meanings. Cambridge University Press, Cambridge (2005)
2. Alexander, C.: A Pattern Language: Towns, Buildings, Construction. Oxford University Press, Oxford (1977)
3. Alexander, C.: Timeless Way of Building. Oxford University Press, Oxford (1979)
4. Batory, D., O'Malley, S.: The design and implementation of hierarchical software systems with reusable components. ACM Trans. Softw. Eng. Methodol. 1(4), 355–398 (1992)
5. Brooks, F.P.: No silver bullet—essence and accident in software engineering. In: Proceedings of the IFIP Tenth World Computing Conference, pp. 1069–1076 (1986)
6. de Kleer, J., Brown, J.S.: Mental models of physical mechanisms and their acquisition. In: Anderson, J.R. (ed.) Cognitive Skills and Their Acquisition, pp. 285–309. Lawrence Erlbaum (1981)
7. Evans, E.: Domain-Driven Design: Tackling Complexity in the Heart of Software. Addison-Wesley, Hoboken (2004)
8. Fowler, M.: Analysis Patterns: Reusable Object Models. Addison-Wesley Professional, Hoboken (1997)
9. Fowler, M.: Patterns of Enterprise Application Architecture. Addison-Wesley Professional, Hoboken (2002)
10. Gamma, E., Helm, R., Johnson, R., Vlissides, J.: Design Patterns: Elements of Reusable Object-Oriented Software. Addison-Wesley Professional, Hoboken (1994)
11. Greenberg, S., Buxton, B.: Usability evaluation considered harmful (some of the time). In: Proceedings of Computer Human Interaction (CHI 2008), April 2008
12. Griswold, W., Notkin, D.: Automated assistance for program restructuring. ACM Trans. Softw. Eng. Methodol. (TOSEM) 2(3), 228–269 (1993)
13. Hay, D.C.: Data Model Patterns. Dorset House (2011)
14. Hoare, C.A.R.: Communicating Sequential Processes. Prentice-Hall, Hoboken (1985)
15. Jackson, D.: The Essence of Software: Why Concepts Matter for Great Design. Princeton University Press, Princeton (2021)
16. Jackson, D.: Software Abstractions: Logic, Language, and Analysis. MIT Press, Cambridge (2012)
17. Jackson, D.: Alloy: a language and tool for exploring software designs. Commun. ACM 62(9), 66–76 (2019). https://cacm.acm.org/magazines/2019/9/238969-alloy
18. Jackson, M.: Problem Frames: Analysing & Structuring Software Development Problems. Addison-Wesley Professional, Boston (2000)
19. Jones, C.B.: Systematic Software Development Using VDM. Prentice Hall, Hoboken (1990)
20. Kapor, M.: A software design manifesto. Reprinted as Chapter 1 of [28]
21. Parnas, D.L.: On the criteria to be used in decomposing systems into modules. Commun. ACM 15(12), 1053–1058 (1972)
22. Parnas, D.L.: Designing software for ease of extension and contraction. IEEE Trans. Softw. Eng. 5, 2 (1979)
23. Shaw, M., Garlan, D.: Software Architecture: Perspectives on an Emerging Discipline. Pearson (1996)

24. Spivey, J.M.: The Z Notation: A Reference Manual. International Series in Computer Science, 2nd edn. Prentice Hall (1992). https://spivey.oriel.ox.ac.uk/wiki/files/zrm/zrm.pdf
25. Tognazzini, B.: First Principles of Interaction Design, revised & expanded (2014). https://ask tog.com/atc/principles-of-interaction-design
26. TRIZ (Wikipedia article). https://en.wikipedia.org/wiki/TRIZ
27. User Interface Design Patterns. https://ui-patterns.com
28. Winograd, T., Bennett, J., De Young, L., Hartfield, B. (eds.): Bringing Design to Software. Addison-Wesley, Boston (1996)

Automating Program Transformation with Coccinelle

Julia Lawall[(✉)] and Gilles Muller

Inria, Paris, France
{julia.lawall,gilles.muller}@inria.fr
https://coccinelle.gitlabpages.inria.fr/website/

Abstract. Coccinelle is a program matching and transformation engine for C code. This paper introduces the use of Coccinelle through a collection of examples targeting evolutions and bug fixes in the Linux kernel.

Keywords: Linux kernel · Coccinelle · Program transformation

1 Introduction

It is the dream of every programmer to have a tool that will automatically traverse their software and make any kind of changes that the programmer wants. Early efforts include sed and awk that permit developers to write simple search-and-replace patterns involving regular expressions [10,11]. Such tools are powerful, but regular expressions are hard to write, are error prone, have a limited view of the code, and are not aware of the programming language syntax. Tools designed according to the Visitor pattern [6], such as CIL [20], have been developed, but these require the user to become familiar with the visitor's chosen internal representation for the programming language. Must easier to use, common semantics-preserving changes, known as *refactorings*, were classified by Fowler [5], and are provided as a collection of black-box tools within integrated development environments such as Eclipse [3]. But in real software development, it is often necessary to perform changes that do not fit within a tidy collection of common refactorings. These include repetitive bug fixes, that intrinsically change the semantics of the code, and changes that respect the invariants that the developer knows, but that are difficult to automatically recover from the code base.

Coccinelle is a program matching and transformation engine for C code [15,22]. The goal of Coccinelle is to make it easy for software developers to express code transformations and apply these transformations across a large C code base. Coccinelle's transformation specification language SmPL (Semantic Patch Language) allows transformations to be expressed using code fragments, annotated with − and +, for lines to remove and add, respectively, mirroring the

Gilles Muller passed away before the writing of this paper. He initiated the Coccinelle project in 2004 and supported its development over the next 17 years.

J. V. Deshmukh et al. (Eds.): NFM 2022, LNCS 13260, pp. 71–87, 2022.
https://doi.org/10.1007/978-3-031-06773-0_4

familiar patch syntax [18]. Such pattern-matching rules can include scripts written in Python or OCaml, for greater expressiveness. Coccinelle was originally designed for updating Linux kernel device drivers to take into account evolutions in Linux kernel internal APIs [22], and accordingly supports a very large portion of the C language. It has been used in over 9000 Linux kernel commits, and is used in other C software projects, such as `wine` [25,27], `systemd` [26], and `git` [7].

Previous works on Coccinelle have presented the design of the tool [22], the semantics of its transformation language SmPL [1], the use of Coccinelle for finding bugs in Linux kernel code [16,23], and a retrospective after 10 years of use, including an enumeration and assessment of the design decisions [15]. Tutorials on Coccinelle have been presented at developer conferences, some of which are available as videos [12–14]. This paper takes advantage of the written format to make a deep dive into SmPL, to describe the reasoning that goes into constructing a semantic patch: how to identify a problem for which Coccinelle can be appropriate, how to sketch a solution for such a problem using SmPL, and how to iteratively make that solution more powerful and more automatic. Our examples focus on the Linux kernel, but should be applicable to other kinds of C software.

The rest of this paper is organized as follows. Section 2 provides some background on the Linux kernel, its development challenges, and the opportunities that it raises for automatic program transformation. Section 3 presents a simple and classic example, the transformation of a call to the kernel memory allocation function `kmalloc`, followed by a zeroing call to `memset`, into a single call to the zeroing kernel memory allocation function `kzalloc`. Section 4 scales this kind of transformation up to the detection of memory leaks involving kernel `device_node` structures. Section 5 considers detection of anomalies in the use of the Linux kernel memory allocation flags, GFP_KERNEL and GFP_ATOMIC. Each of these examples emphasizes the aspect of exploration facilitated by Coccinelle – the use of Coccinelle scales naturally from simple rules with a limited scope that may have false positives, but get the job done, to more complex rules that capture a wider variety of conditions in a more accurate way. It is hoped that this work can serve as a reference for a developer who wants to use Coccinelle for the first time or who wants to explore some of its more advanced features.

2   Background

The original and primary target of Coccinelle is the Linux kernel. The Linux kernel poses a huge maintenance challenge. It amounts to over 21 million lines of code in Linux v5.16 (January 2022), accepts contributions from over 4000 developers per year, and undergoes frequent and large-scale changes, motivated by security, performance, new hardware features, etc. As part of the Linux kernel's evolution, it often occurs that some API function is found to be unsuitable, the function is redefined in some way, and then the uses of the function have to be modified across the kernel. These modifications may involve changes in

Table 1. Usage of common functions in the files of Linux 5.16, `drivers/usb/atm`. ✓ indicates that the given API function is called at least once in the given file.

		cxacru.c	speedtch.c	ueagle-atm.c	usbatm.c	xusbatm.c
atm	`usbatm_usb_probe`	✓	✓	✓	–	✓
usb	`interface_to_usbdev`	✓	✓	✓	✓	✓
specific	`usb_submit_urb`	✓	✓	✓	✓	–
	`usb_set_intfdata`	–	✓	–	✓	✓
kernel	`request_firmware`	✓	✓	✓	–	–
generic	`wait_for_completion`	✓	–	–	✓	–
	`mutex_lock`	✓	–	✓	✓	–
	`init_timer`	✓	✓	–	✓	–
	`kzalloc`	✓	✓	✓	✓	–

the arguments and return values, triggering the need for further changes in the usage context.

Intuitively, sustaining the high rate of development on the huge code base of the Linux kernel may seem like an impossible task. Indeed one may think of one's own small software projects, where often one decides to just live with some unsuitable code structure to avoid the need to do all of the work required to change it. Scaling this work up to 21 million lines of code, and managing to make all the changes correctly is a real challenge.

A mitigating factor is that the Linux kernel code base contains a lot of repetition [2]. For example, consider the kernel API functions (Table 1) used in the various files of the Linux v5.16 directory `drivers/atm`, containing Asynchronous Transfer Mode (ATM) network device drivers. Many of the key kernel API functions are used in many of the drivers. This commonality occurs at all levels – we see functions that are specific to ATM drivers, functions that are generic to USB drivers, and functions that are generic to the entire kernel, including `kzalloc` for memory allocation, which we use as an initial case study in Sect. 3. This pattern raises hope that not only may these functions be reused across the various drivers, but they may also be used in similar ways. If this is the case, then it may be possible to automate any needed changes in their usage.

Repetitive API usages raise the opportunity for using a tool to script API usage changes. That is, rather than manually collecting the relevant files (*e.g.*, with `grep`) and then tracking down the relevant usage contexts (*e.g.*, with search in an editor), it could be faster and more reliable to write a transformation rule and then leave the job of finding the relevant code and making the changes to a transformation tool. This is the role of Coccinelle, that is the focus of this paper.

3 Coccinelle in a Nutshell, Illustrated by `kzalloc`

Coccinelle offers a pattern-based language for matching and transforming C code. It has been under development since 2005 and open source since 2008. An important goal of Coccinelle is to fit with the habits of Linux kernel developers. The Linux kernel follows an email-based development model, where developers exchange patches describing their proposed changes, and thus developers are used to creating, reading, and applying them. Accordingly, Coccinelle was designed to allow code changes to be expressed using patch-like code patterns. We refer to these as *semantic patches*, because they are like patches, but their application takes into account the program control flow, and thus part of its semantics.

A common use of Coccinelle is to reorganize a collection of one or more API functions. Accordingly, to present Coccinelle, we consider a simple example, the merging of uses of the kernel memory allocation function `kzalloc` followed by a zeroing of the allocated memory with `memset`, into a single call to the kernel zeroing memory allocation function `kzalloc`. An example of this change is shown, as a patch, in Fig. 1. The change itself is simple: replace `kmalloc` by `kzalloc` and drop the now redundant call to `memset`. Still, finding the opportunities for the change is complex: The calls to `kmalloc` and `memset` are typically not contiguous – as illustrated in Fig. 1, there is often at least some error-handling code in between them. Furthermore, some `kmalloc`s have no following `memset`s and some `memset`s have no preceding `kmalloc`s, so simply using `grep` to find calls to one or the other will return many irrelevant code locations. Finally, some `memset`s may serve to reinitialize a structure rather than initialize a just-allocated one. Even though calls to both `kmalloc` and `memset` are present, we do not want to create a call to `kzalloc` in these cases. Coccinelle is designed to help with these challenges.

```
1 @@ -1348,9 +1348,8 @@
2 - fh = kmalloc(sizeof(struct zoran_fh), GFP_KERNEL);
3 + fh = kzalloc(sizeof(struct zoran_fh), GFP_KERNEL);
4   if (!fh) {
5     dprintk(1,
6       KERN_ERR
7       "%s: zoran_open(): allocation of zoran_fh failed\n",
8       ZR_DEVNAME(zr));
9     return -ENOMEM;
10  }
11 - memset(fh, 0, sizeof(struct zoran_fh));
```

Fig. 1. An instance of the conversion of `kmalloc` and `memset` to `kzalloc`.

3.1 First Steps

To develop a `kmalloc-memset` semantic patch that is widely applicable across the Linux kernel code base, we take the patch of Fig. 1 as a starting point, and consider how it can be made more generic.

The first step is to consider what parts of the patch in Fig. 1 are generic to the change, and what parts are specific to a particular instance. For the `kmalloc-memset` transformation, it is necessary to have a call to `kmalloc` followed by a call to `memset`, where the second argument to `memset` should be 0.

These terms will thus appear in the semantic patch exactly as they appear in Fig. 1. On the other hand, some other terms in the patch of Fig. 1 are important, not for their specific content, but for their relationship to other terms appearing in the affected code. This is the case for 1) the return value of kmalloc (*i.e.*, fh) and the first argument of memset, which must be the same expression, 2) the first argument of kmalloc (the size of the allocated region), that becomes the first argument of the call to kzalloc and should be the third (size) argument of memset, and 3) the second argument of kmalloc that becomes the second argument of kzalloc. These terms appear in the semantic patch as *metavariables*, *i.e.*, variables that can match against any term in the source code, but that must be matched consistently. The metavariables are declared between the initial pair of @@, at the place of the affected line numbers in the standard patch. The metavariables are furthermore declared with their types; all of the metavariables that are relevant to this change have type expression. Finally, some terms are not important to the change, such as the if statement between the calls to kmalloc and memset. Such terms are removed, and replaced by "...".[1] "..." matches any control-flow path from a source code term matching the pattern before the "..." to a source code term matching the pattern after the "...". Furthermore, by default, all such execution paths that do not lead to an error return must satisfy these constraints.

The resulting semantic patch is shown in Fig. 2. It makes six changes in Linux v5.16, with no false positives. Figure 3 shows one change, in which the code separating the kmalloc and memset is more complex than a single if. All of the generated patches have been submitted to the Linux kernel. One received the feedback that a different zeroing function should be used (kcalloc). Four have been applied unchanged in linux-next as of March 25, 2022.

```
1 @@
2 expression res, size, flag;
3 @@
4 - res = kmalloc(size, flag);
5 + res = kzalloc(size, flag);
6   ...
7 - memset(res, 0, size);
```

Fig. 2. A first attempt at a kmalloc and memset to kzalloc semantic patch.

3.2 A Refinement

While our experiment with the semantic patch in Fig. 1 was completely successful on Linux v5.16, the semantic patch is not fully reliable. Figure 4 shows a false positive in net/sunrpc/auth_gss/gss_krb5_keys.c, in Linux v5.2. Here a kmalloc is indeed followed by a memset, according to our pattern, but the memset is used to reinitialize the data to 0 (just before freeing the data, for security reasons), rather than to initialize the data to 0 as done by kzalloc.

---

[1] To prevent misreading, in the text, we always enclose SmPL ... in quotes.

```
1 - port = kmalloc(sizeof(*port), GFP_KERNEL);
2 + port = kmalloc(sizeof(*port), GFP_KERNEL);
3   if (!port) {
4       rc = -ENOMEM;
5       goto __error;
6   }
7   rc = snd_seq_create_kernel_client(NULL, ...);
8   if (rc < 0)
9       goto __error;
10  system_client = rc;
11 - memset(port, 0, sizeof(*port));
```

Fig. 3. A successful change in sound/core/seq/oss/seq_oss_init.c.

```
1 - inblockdata = kmalloc(blocksize, gfp_mask);
2 + inblockdata = kzalloc(blocksize, gfp_mask);
3   if (inblockdata == NULL)
4           goto err_free_cipher;
5   ...
6   inblock.data = (char *) inblockdata;
7   inblock.len = blocksize;
8   ...
9   if (in_constant->len == inblock.len) {
10          memcpy(inblock.data, in_constant->data, inblock.len);
11  } else {
12          krb5_nfold(in_constant->len * 8, in_constant->data,
13                             inblock.len * 8, inblock.data);
14  }
15  ...
16 - memset(inblockdata, 0, blocksize);
17  kfree(inblockdata);
```

Fig. 4. An false positive for the kmalloc and memset semantic patch.

Indeed, by simply replacing the code between the kmalloc and the memset by "...", we have eliminated any constraints on the code found in the execution path between them. To limit the matches to the cases where the memset represents an initialization, we can add constraints on the matching of "..." using the keyword when. For inspiration, we consider how the allocated data is used in the false positive of Fig. 4. The data allocated by the call to kmalloc on line 1 is used in the right side of an assignment on line 6, creating an alias through which it is subsequently initialized on line 10 or 12. If such an assignment appears in the region matched by "...", then the memset is performing a reinitialization and should not be removed. This constraint is written as e = <+... res ...+> (Fig. 5, line 7), to indicate that the value returned by kmalloc, res, should not appear anywhere on the right-hand side of the assignment. Analogous to this example use, we also add constraints to ensure that the allocated data is not assigned to directly (line 8), or passed to another function (line 9), likely with the purpose of initializing it. Finally, we forbid loops, as the memset may be used to reinitialize the data on each iteration (lines 10–11). Figure 5 shows the resulting more robust semantic patch. On Linux v5.16, this semantic patch makes the same changes as the original one found in Fig. 2.

```
1  @@
2  expression res, size, flag, e, f;
3  statement S;
4  @@
5 -  res = kmalloc(size, flag);
6 +  res = kzalloc(size, flag);
7  ...  when != e = <+... res ...+>
8       when != (<+... res ...+>) = e
9       when != f(...,<+... res ...+>,...)
10      when != for(...;...;...) S
11      when != while(...) S
12 - memset(res, 0, size);
```

Fig. 5. A more robust `kmalloc` and `memset` to `kzalloc` semantic patch. Lines 3 and 7–11 are new.

3.3 A Second Refinement

Our semantic patch requires that the allocated data size be expressed in the same way in both the call to `kmalloc` (first argument) and the call to `memset` (third argument), to ensure that the sizes are the same. However, there are two common ways of indicating data sizes in the Linux kernel: `sizeof(T)`, where T is the type referenced by the data pointer, and `sizeof(*x)`, where x is the data pointer itself. Figure 6 shows a more flexible semantic patch allowing either style or a mixture.

```
1  @@
2  expression flag, e, f;
3  statement S;
4  type T;
5  T *res;
6  @@
7    res =
8 -        kmalloc
9 +        kzalloc
10            (\(sizeof(T)\|sizeof(*res)\), flag);
11 ...  when != e = <+... res ...+>
12       when != (<+... res ...+>) = e
13       when != f(...,<+... res ...+>,...)
14       when != for(...;...;...) S
15       when != while(...) S
16 -  memset(res, 0, \(sizeof(T)\|sizeof(*res)\));
```

Fig. 6. A more flexible `kmalloc` and `memset` to `kzalloc` semantic patch. Lines 4–5, 7–10, and 16 are new.

This semantic patch illustrates several new features:

- – and + need not be applied to complete lines of code (lines 7–10). The matching and transformation process is independent of any whitespace in the semantic patch.
- An expression metavariable can be declared to have a specific type (line 5). This can be a C-language type, or, as illustrated here, a type metavariable.

– A *disjunction*, here written as \(...\|...\), allows specifying a selection of patterns that can be allowed to match. The first match is chosen. A disjunction can also be written as (...|...), where the (, |, and) are in column 0.

This semantic patch finds two more opportunities for kzalloc, as compared to the one in Fig. 5, however it overlooks two opportunities as well, in which the size is not expressed as a single sizeof expression. For greater flexibility, we can create a single semantic patch consisting of Fig. 5 followed by Fig. 6, to find a larger set of transformation opportunities.

4   A Second Example: of_node_put

We next present a case study related to bug finding and fixing. Bug finding and fixing was not the original target of Coccinelle [22], but it can also involve searching for patterns of code and making repetitive changes accordingly, and thus Coccinelle can be useful in this case. While the previous example reorganizes a collection of API calls, this one finds the need for an API call that is missing, in a specific context. This example also illustrates how one instance of a change can be scaled up to many variants.

4.1   The Problem

We consider the case of iterators over collections of device_node structures. These structures are managed using reference counts. Forgetting to decrement a reference count when needed prevents the structure from ever being freed, causing a memory leak. As a concrete example, we consider the use of the for_-each_child_of_node iterator. Each iteration visits a device_node structure. To simplify the code, this iterator increases the reference count of the current node before executing the body of the loop, and then decreases the reference count of that node before moving on to the next iteration. Figure 7 shows a typical use of the iterator that benefits from these hidden reference count operations.

But, out of sight, out of mind. By hiding the management of the reference count in the normal case, the iterator hides the fact that explicit management of the reference count is needed in exceptional cases. Specifically, in the example of Fig. 8, if there is a jump out of the loop body via the return (line 7), the increment of the reference count is performed, but the decrement (of_node_put), that is performed by the iterator at the end of a loop iteration, is not executed. The solution is to add a call to of_node_put (line 6).

```
1 for_each_child_of_node(parent, child)
2     pnv_php_reverse_nodes(child);
```

Fig. 7. A simple use of for_each_child_of_node, from drivers/pci/hotplug/-pnv_php.c, Linux v5.16.

```
1  for_each_child_of_node(phandle->parent, node) {
2    alias_id = of_alias_get_id(node, clk_name);
3    if (alias_id >= 0 && alias_id < cmdq->gce_num) {
4      ...
5      if (IS_ERR(cmdq->clocks[alias_id].clk)) {
6 +      of_node_put(node);
7        return PTR_ERR(cmdq->clocks[alias_id].clk);
8      }
9    }
10 }
```

Fig. 8. A use of `for_each_child_of_node` that may case a memory leak, from `drivers/mailbox/mtk-cmdq-mailbox.c`, Linux v5.16, slightly simplified for conciseness.

The issue occurs not only for jumps via `return`, but also for `goto` and `break`. The jump out of the loop body can occur anywhere within the loop body and there may be multiple such jumps. There is also a large set of relevant iterators.

4.2 The Semantic Patch

Figure 9 shows the semantic patch for the case of `for_each_child_of_node` and `return`. This semantic patch uses "..." (line 9) to trace through each possible execution path in the loop body to find those where the reference count is decremented (line 11), where the `device_node` variable may be stored in some more global way that requires the reference count to remain raised (lines 13–17), and where there is a jump out of a loop (line 20). It is on the latter that an `of_node_put` should be inserted (line 19).

The semantic patch illustrates some more features of SmPL:

- Iterators: Iterators are not part of the C language, but are rather defined by the Linux kernel as macros. While many macros can be parsed as function calls, this is not possible for iterators, because an iterator amounts to a loop header. Accordingly, SmPL provides a special notation for declaring them. `iterator name` (line 2) allows declaring the name of a specific iterator, which is then parsed similarly to a `while` loop. `iterator` (line 5) allows declaring a metavariable that can match any iterator.
- Local variables: `local idexpression` (line 3) declares a metavariable that only matches a variable declared in the current function. This feature is important in this semantic patch, to ensure that the `device_node` does not escape the loop.
- Disjunction: (|) in the leftmost column indicates a choice between a selection of patterns. The `?` on the last pattern indicates that the `return` is optional; as in Fig. 7, some paths may not match any of the patterns.

```
 1 @@
 2 iterator name for_each_child_of_node;
 3 local idexpression n;
 4 expression e,e1;
 5 iterator i1;
 6 statement S;
 7 @@
 8  for_each_child_of_node(e,n) {
 9    ...
10 (
11    of_node_put(n);
12 |
13    e1 = n
14 |
15    return n;
16 |
17    i1(...,n,...) S
18 |
19 +  of_node_put(n);
20 ?  return ...;
21 )
22    ... when any
23 }
```

Fig. 9. for_each_child_of_node with no of_node_put before a return out of the loop.

– When any: By default, "..." matches a path that does not contain a match of any pattern appearing just before or after the "...". when any allows such matches. The effect of the when any on the second "..." is that the disjunction pattern matches the first instance of the pattern along each execution path through the loop body.

4.3 Scaling Up

In the previous semantic patch rule, the jump out of the loop is performed by a return. goto and break each introduce minor specific issues, and one can create a rule for each case. A second point of variation is the iterator name, and indeed new iterators can be introduced over time. The semantic patch in Fig. 10 addresses this issue, for a small selection of iterators, using a pair of rules.

The first rule (lines 1–20), named r (line 1), matches the complete loop in two ways, using a conjunction (&), analogous to the disjunction introduced previously. The first conjunct lists the names of specific iterators to match, while the second uses metavariables to capture the name of the iterator (i) and the number of arguments (len) before the device_node typed index variable. Note that the position of this index variable varies depending on the iterator.

The second rule (lines 22–44) then *inherits* from rule r the metavariables i (denoted r.i), representing the iterator name, and len, representing the offset of the index variable (denoted r.len). These inherited metavariables can then be used freely, like any other metavariable.

When applied to a given file, the semantic patch matches the first rule across the file, and collects possible bindings of the set of metavariables. The second rule is triggered once for each unique set of bindings of the metavariables that

```
 1 @r@
 2 local idexpression n;
 3 expression e;
 4 iterator name for_each_child_of_node, for_each_available_child_of_node,
 5   for_each_node_with_property;
 6 iterator i;
 7 statement S;
 8 expression list [len] es;
 9 @@
10 (
11 (
12 for_each_child_of_node(e,n) S
13 |
14 for_each_available_child_of_node(e,n) S
15 |
16 for_each_node_with_property(n,e) S
17 )
18 &
19 i(es,n,...) S
20 )
21
22 @@
23 local idexpression n;
24 expression e1;
25 iterator r.i,i1;
26 expression list [r.len] es;
27 statement S;
28 @@
29 i(es,n) {
30   ...
31 (
32   of_node_put(n);
33 |
34   e1 = n
35 |
36   return n;
37 |
38   i1(...,n,...) S
39 |
40 + of_node_put(n);
41 ? return ...;
42 )
43   ... when any
44 }
```

Fig. 10. for_each_child_of_node with no of_node_put before a jump out of the loop.

it inherits. Thus, the second rule will be applied to the entire file up to three times, depending on how many of the iterators mentioned in r are used in the file, and thus the number of bindings of rule r's i and len metavariables.

4.4 Impact

Figure 11 shows the number of files in each release of the Linux kernel between v4.0 (April 2015) and v5.16 (January 2022) that are missing an of_node_put() within a use of one of the iterators for_each_node_-by_name, for_each_node_by_type, for_each_compatible_node, for_each_-matching_node, for_each_matching_node_and_match, for_each_child_of_-node, for_each_available_child_of_node, or for_each_node_with_property.

We collected this information using the `for_each_child.cocci` semantic patch that has been part of the Linux kernel distribution since v5.10 (December 2020).

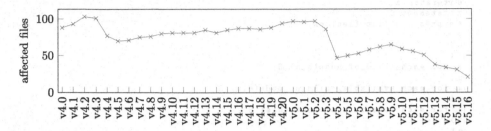

Fig. 11. Number of files missing uses of `of_node_put` as detected by the `for_each_child.cocci` semantic patch found in the Linux kernel.

Over most of the time shown (April 2015–January 2022), the number of affected files has slowly increased, as, for example, new files have been added that do not contain the required code. The large dips from version v4.3 to version v4.4 and then from version v5.2 to version v5.4 were due in part to the use of Coccinelle to add the needed calls at a large scale. In recent years, there has been a steady decline, starting with Linux v5.10, in which a semantic patch addressing the need for `of_node_put` was added into the Linux kernel. Developers and continuous integration tools can use this semantic patch to add the missing calls even before the code is integrated into a mainline Linux kernel release, breaking the steady upward trend seen in previous releases.

5   A Third Example: Inconsistent Atomicity Flags

Our final example shows how Coccinelle can be used to collect information across a complete code base, and to report anomalies in the collected information as potential bugs. Similar reasoning has been used effectively in various prior approaches for mining API usage rules [4,8,17]. We how this idea can be used in a lightweight way with Coccinelle. A challenge is that Coccinelle works on one file at a time, and within each file on one function (or other top-level declaration) at a time. We show how Coccinelle's scripting language interface, allowing the use of scripts written in OCaml or Python, makes collecting and processing information across an entire code base possible.

5.1   The Problem

Our example relates to the use of the Linux kernel flags `GFP_KERNEL` and `GFP_ATOMIC` that are commonly passed to memory allocation functions to indicate whether the function may sleep or not to wait for memory to be available, respectively. Essentially, `GFP_KERNEL` should be used when no lock is held, and

GFP_ATOMIC should be used when a lock is held. The challenge is that holding a lock is an interprocedural property; taking a lock in one function means that the lock is held in the execution of all called functions, until the lock is released.

Detecting whether a caller may hold a lock is particularly difficult for function pointers, which the Linux kernel uses extensively. Figure 12 shows an example, representing an interface to a network device driver. The choice of GFP_KERNEL or GFP_ATOMIC depends on whether locks are held at the call sites of these function pointers. Such call sites are typically located in other files, and thus are not accessible to Coccinelle when processing the file that contains this interface definition and the definitions of the referenced functions. The call sites may be subject to further interprocedural locking effects that are difficult to analyze.

```
1 static struct platform_driver moxart_mac_driver = {
2         .probe  = moxart_mac_probe,
3         .remove = moxart_remove,
4         .driver = {
5                 .name           = "moxart-ethernet",
6                 .of_match_table = moxart_mac_match,
7         },
8 };
```

Fig. 12. Collection of function pointers representing an interface to the MOXA ART Ethernet (RTL8201CP) driver (`drivers/net/ethernet/moxa/moxart_ether.c`).

5.2   The Solution

Rather than search for the function-pointer call sites and the contexts in which they occur, we instead explore what information we can infer by assuming that the function stored in a particular structure member is always called in the same way. This assumption implies that if no locking code is present in the function itself, then either GFP_KERNEL will always be used by all functions stored in a given structure member, or GFP_ATOMIC will always be used. A mixture would imply that either our hypothesis is false, and the function pointer is called in different contexts, or that the function is using an incorrect flag.

The structure of the semantic patch is roughly as follows. First, it will pass over the code base to collect the names of all functions containing a reference to GFP_KERNEL and the names of all functions containing a reference to GFP_-ATOMIC. In each case, it identifies the structure member storing the function, if any. Finally, after collecting this information across the entire code base, for each structure member, it compares the number of functions in each category. If there is a large number of functions in one category and a small number of functions in the other, it is possible that inappropriate flags are being used, and the relevant code should be further investigated.

The semantic patch starts as shown below, by defining some hash tables to collect information from across the code base. This rule is indicated as initial-ize:ocaml (line 1), meaning that it is run before the treatment of any files, and

that it contains OCaml script code. Such script code is passed directly to the
OCaml interpreter, and is not processed by Coccinelle in any way.

```
1 @initialize:ocaml@
2 @@
3 let atbl = Hashtbl.create 101 (* collect functions using GFP_ATOMIC *)
4 let ktbl = Hashtbl.create 101 (* collect functions using GFP_KERNEL *)
```

Next, the semantic patch matches uses of GFP_KERNEL and GFP_ATOMIC, first
identifying a use, then detecting whether the containing function is stored in a
structure member, and finally, if so, storing the location of the reference in the
appropriate hash table. The rules for each flag are independent, and are thus
shown in parallel in Fig. 13, although in the actual semantic patch, one sequence
of rules comes after the other. The first rule in the GFP_ATOMIC case (lines 1–14
on the right of Fig. 13) is more complex than the first rule in the GFP_KERNEL
(lines 1–5 on the left of Fig. 13); in the former case we have to ensure that the
code is not executed when a lock is locally held, which is verified by ensuring that
there is no subsequent lock release before the taking of another lock is optionally
reached (lines 8–14), considering some common lock functions.

```
1 @r1@                                    1 identifier f;
2 identifier f;                           2 position p;
3 position p;                             3 @@
4 @@                                      4 f@p(...,GFP_ATOMIC,...)
5 f@p(...,GFP_KERNEL,...)                 5 ... when != spin_unlock(...)
6                                         6     when != spin_unlock_irqrestore(...)
7 @s1@                                    7     when != spin_unlock_bh(...)
8 identifier i,j,fn;                      8 (
9 identifier f1 :                         9 spin_lock(...);
10   script:ocaml(r1.p)                   10 |
11   {f1=(List.hd p).current_element};    11 spin_lock_irqsave(...);
12 @@                                      12 |
13 struct i j = { .fn = f1, };            13 ?spin_lock_bh(...);
14                                         14 )
15 @script:ocaml@                          15
16 p << r1.p;                             16 @s2@
17 i << s1.i;                             17 identifier i,j,fn;
18 fn << s1.fn;                           18 identifier f1 :
19 @@                                      19   script:ocaml(r2.p)
20 Common.hashadd ktbl (i,fn) p           20   {f1=(List.hd p).current_element};
                                          21 @@
                                          22 struct i j = { .fn = f1, };
                                          23
                                          24 @script:ocaml@
                                          25 p << r2.p;
                                          26 i << s2.i;
                                          27 fn << s2.fn;
                                          28 @@
                                          29 Common.hashadd atbl (i,fn) p
```

Fig. 13. Collection of information about occurrences of GFP_KERNEL and GFP_ATOMIC.

The semantic patch concludes with a straightforward finalize:ocaml rule
that iterates over one of the hash tables, and for each structure member compares
the number of pointed functions using GFP_KERNEL or GFP_ATOMIC. The output
can be freely tailored to be more complete, possibly including false positives, or to
only include the most likely anomalies, possibly creating false negatives. Among

the results, we observe that, in Linux 5.16, 7 functions in the `probe` member of a `platform_driver` structure, as illustrated in Fig. 12, use `GFP_ATOMIC`, while 2627 use `GFP_KERNEL`. Checking the 7 cases reveals that they should be converted to use `GFP_KERNEL`. Patches making these changes have been submitted to the Linux kernel, and appear in the `linux-next` version of March 10, 2022.

6   Related Work

Automated program transformation has a long history. We focus on work specifically related to Coccinelle. Lawall and Muller give an overview of the design decisions of Coccinelle, its impact, and closely related work [15]. Martone and Lawall provides a tutorial in using Coccinelle, similar to that presented here, but targeting high-performance computing [19]. Kang *et al.* [9] explore the use of Coccinelle for Java. Outside of the Coccinelle team, Nielsen *et al.* [21] propose a transformation system something like Coccinelle to meet the needs of JavaScript programs. Some Coccinelle-like features have recently been added to the Java source-code analysis and transformation tool Spoon [24].

7   Conclusion

Coccinelle has facilitated thousands of lines of changes in the Linux kernel and other software projects. By making it possible to easily write complex patterns, describing code fragments and their context, Coccinelle enables an alternate, cross cutting view of a large code base. Coccinelle has been a source of fun and pride for its developers. We hope that the reader will have a chance to try Coccinelle, and will enjoy using it too.

Availability: Coccinelle is available from many Linux distributions, and from the Coccinelle website: https://coccinelle.gitlabpages.inria.fr/website/

Acknowledgments. Yoann Padioleau and René Rydhof Hansen were postdocs working on Coccinelle in its earliest days, and contributed greatly to the design and implementation. Nicolas Palix has also maintained parts of Coccinelle over the years. Recent interns who contributed greatly to the code base include Jaskaran Singh and Keisuke Nishimura. The initial work on Coccinelle was funded in part by the French ANR and the Danish FTP. Recently, Inria has supported the continued maintenance of Coccinelle, with the help of Sébastien Hinderer and then Thierry Martinez. We are also deeply grateful for the feedback and support from the Linux kernel developer community. Keisuke Nishimura and Michele Martone also gave helpful feedback on drafts of this paper. We thank the organizers of NFM22 for the invitation to present this work.

References

1. Brunel, J., Doligez, D., Hansen, R.R., Lawall, J., Muller, G.: A foundation for flow-based program matching using temporal logic and model checking. In: POPL, pp. 114–126, January 2009

2. Casazza, G., Villano, U., Merlo, E., Antoniol, G., DiPenta, M.: Identifying clones in the Linux kernel. In: Proceedings First IEEE International Workshop on Source Code Analysis and Manipulation (2001)
3. Eclipse (2022). https://www.eclipse.org/ide/
4. Engler, D.R., Chen, D.Y., Chou, A.: Bugs as deviant behavior: a general approach to inferring errors in systems code. In: Marzullo, K., Satyanarayanan, M. (eds.) SOSP, pp. 57–72. ACM (2001)
5. Fowler, M.: Refactoring: Improving the Design of Existing Code. Addison-Wesley, Boston (2002)
6. Gamma, E., Helm, R., Johnson, R., Vlissides, J.: Design Patterns: Elements of Reusable Object-Oriented Software. Addison-Wesley, Boston (1995)
7. Git, September 2021. https://github.com/git/git/tree/master/contrib/coccinelle
8. Le Goues, C., Weimer, W.: Specification mining with few false positives. In: Kowalewski, S., Philippou, A. (eds.) TACAS 2009. LNCS, vol. 5505, pp. 292–306. Springer, Heidelberg (2009). https://doi.org/10.1007/978-3-642-00768-2_26
9. Kang, H.J., Thung, F., Lawall, J., Muller, G., Jiang, L., Lo, D.: Semantic patches for Java program transformation (experience report). In: ECOOP. LIPIcs, vol. 134, pp. 22:1–22:27 (2019)
10. Kernighan, B.: UNIX: A History and a Memoir. Kindle Direct Publishing (2019)
11. Kernighan, B.W., Pike, R.: The UNIX Programming Environment. Prentice Hall, Hoboken (1984)
12. Lawall, J.: An introduction to Coccinelle bug finding and code evolution for the Linux kernel. Suse Labs (2014). https://www.youtube.com/watch?v=buZrNd6XkEw
13. Lawall, J.: Keynote: Inside the mind of a coccinelle programmer. Linux Security Summit (2016). https://www.youtube.com/watch?v=xA5FBvuCvMs
14. Lawall, J.: Coccinelle: 10 years of automated evolution in the Linux kernel. Linaro Connect (2019). https://www.youtube.com/watch?v=LOsluYTzdMg
15. Lawall, J., Muller, G.: Coccinelle: 10 years of automated evolution in the Linux kernel. In: USENIX ATC, pp. 601–614 (2018)
16. Lawall, J.L., Brunel, J., Palix, N., Hansen, R.R., Stuart, H., Muller, G.: WYSIWIB: exploiting fine-grained program structure in a scriptable API-usage protocol-finding process. Softw. Pract. Exp. **43**(1), 67–92 (2013)
17. Li, Z., Zhou, Y.: PR-Miner: Automatically extracting implicit programming rules and detecting violations in large software code. In: ESEC-FSE (2005)
18. MacKenzie, D., Eggert, P., Stallman, R.: Comparing and Merging Files With Gnu Diff and Patch. Network Theory Ltd, January 2003. Unified Format section. http://www.gnu.org/software/diffutils/manual/html_node/Unified-Format.html
19. Martone, M., Lawall, J.: Refactoring for performance with semantic patching: case study with recipes. In: Jagode, H., Anzt, H., Ltaief, H., Luszczek, P. (eds.) ISC High Performance 2021. LNCS, vol. 12761, pp. 226–232. Springer, Cham (2021). https://doi.org/10.1007/978-3-030-90539-2_15
20. Necula, G.C., McPeak, S., Rahul, S.P., Weimer, W.: CIL: intermediate language and tools for analysis and transformation of C programs. In: Horspool, R.N. (ed.) CC 2002. LNCS, vol. 2304, pp. 213–228. Springer, Heidelberg (2002). https://doi.org/10.1007/3-540-45937-5_16
21. Nielsen, B.B., Torp, M.T., Møller, A.: Semantic patches for adaptation of JavaScript programs to evolving libraries. In: ICSE, pp. 74–85. IEEE (2021)
22. Padioleau, Y., Lawall, J., Hansen, R.R., Muller, G.: Documenting and automating collateral evolutions in Linux device drivers. In: EuroSys 2008, Glasgow, Scotland, pp. 247–260. ACM, March 2008

23. Palix, N., Thomas, G., Saha, S., Calvès, C., Lawall, J., Muller, G.: Faults in Linux 2.6. ACM Trans. Comput. Syst. **32**(2), 4:1–4:40 (2014)
24. Spoon, March 2022. https://github.com/INRIA/spoon
25. Stefaniuc, M.: Coccinelle scripts for Wine, September 2021. https://github.com/mstefani/coccinelle-wine
26. Systemd, February 2022. https://github.com/systemd/systemd/tree/main/coccinelle
27. WineHQ: Static analysis, February 2016. https://wiki.winehq.org/Static_Analysis

The Prusti Project: Formal Verification for Rust

Vytautas Astrauskas[1], Aurel Bílý[1], Jonáš Fiala[1], Zachary Grannan[2],
Christoph Matheja[3], Peter Müller[1], Federico Poli[1],
and Alexander J. Summers[2(⊠)]

[1] Department of Computer Science, ETH Zurich, Zurich, Switzerland
[2] University of British Columbia, Vancouver, Canada
alex.summers@ubc.ca
[3] Technical University of Denmark, Kongens Lyngby, Denmark

Abstract. Rust is a modern systems programming language designed
to offer both performance and static safety. A key distinguishing feature
is a strong type system, which enforces by default that memory is either
shared or mutable, but never both. This guarantee is used to prevent
common pitfalls such as memory errors and data races. It can also be used
to greatly simplify formal verification, as we demonstrated by developing
the Prusti verifier, which can verify rich correctness properties of Rust
programs with a very modest annotation overhead. In this paper, we
provide an overview of the Prusti project. We outline its main design
goals, illustrate examples of its use, and discuss important outcomes from
the perspectives of a user, a verification expert, and a tool developer.

Keywords: Rust · Deductive verification · Separation logic

1 Introduction

Systems programming languages have traditionally had one dominating design
goal: performance. To achieve this goal they give programmers maximum freedom in organising their code and data. They allow unrestricted aliasing and
freely bypassing the safety checks of the language, for instance through unchecked
type casts. This freedom enables the development of highly efficient programs,
but also makes it all too easy to introduce errors and vulnerabilities, such as
buffer overflows, memory errors, data races, and subtle functionality bugs.

Rust is a modern systems programming language that is built on a different
premise: it is designed to maximise *both* performance and static safety. Rust
employs a strong type system that prevents many common errors at compile
time. In particular, it eradicates memory errors (e.g. accessing uninitialised or
freed memory), various sources of program crashes (e.g. null-dereferencing), and
data races. In cases where the type system is too restrictive, programmers can
escape into unsafe Rust, which permits direct pointer manipulation like in traditional systems programming languages. However, according to Rust's design philosophy [25,32], unsafe operations are typically confined to libraries and encap-
sulated behind safe abstractions, while client code is written in safe Rust [5,30].

© Springer Nature Switzerland AG 2022
J. V. Deshmukh et al. (Eds.): NFM 2022, LNCS 13260, pp. 88–108, 2022.
https://doi.org/10.1007/978-3-031-06773-0_5

This design makes Rust a promising target for program verification. Not only does Rust's type system prevent certain errors, such that verification need not deal with them, but it also provides strong compiler-enforced restrictions on aliasing and mutable state, which can be leveraged to simplify verification. There is also an important social motivation: Rust is often chosen for projects with high safety and security requirements, whose members are likely open to program verification as an additional means of achieving these requirements.

To explore this opportunity, we started the Prusti project in 2017. Prusti [6] is a general-purpose deductive verifier for Rust. We had three key design goals:

1. *Enable the verification of expressive program properties.* These go beyond the absence of exceptions (called *panics* in Rust, e.g. due to overflows or out-of-bounds accesses) to include invariants of data types, and more-general functional correctness properties. We initially focused on safe Rust code, but a designated goal of the Prusti project has been to generate self-contained proofs that are valid independently of the guarantees of safe Rust. For the properties guaranteed by safe Rust, this so-called *core proof* is redundant (assuming Rust's type system is sound), but it forms a reusable basis for layering correctness arguments for more complex properties on top, and (eventually) extending verification to common usages of unsafe code.

2. *Reduce the annotation burden for programmers by leveraging Rust's design.* Prusti addresses this goal along two dimensions. First, it reduces the *complexity* of annotations. Safe Rust's restrictions on aliasing and mutations allow Prusti to use annotations based on Rust expressions, without the need to expose programmers to non-trivial logics such as separation logic [39,43]. The resulting annotations are similar to classical contracts [35], but enable sound, modular verification of heap-manipulating programs.

   Second, Prusti reduces the *amount* of necessary annotations. Mainstream verification techniques such as separation logic or dynamic frames [29] require a large upfront investment to declare and manipulate predicates and ghost state that describe the shape of data structures, and to prove memory safety as the basis for more advanced properties. In contrast, Prusti extracts this information automatically from Rust's type system, allowing programmers to focus immediately on the functional properties they care about.

3. *Integrate smoothly into the workflow of Rust programmers.* Integrating verification tools into development workflows is widely regarded as a major obstacle for their adoption [18]. Prusti simplifies integration in two ways:

   First, since Prusti requires no upfront investment, it enables a workflow where programmers can incrementally write more annotations to obtain stronger guarantees. It offers a mode that does not check panic freedom, such that it can be run on unannotated Rust programs. Panic freedom can generally be proved by adding a small (often zero) number of simple annotations (e.g. function preconditions); richer properties can be expressed and proved by adding postconditions and invariants.

   Second, Prusti integrates smoothly into the compiler infrastructure. It operates on the same representations of programs that the Rust compiler uses. This avoids discrepancies with the compiler (which, in the absence of a formal language specification serves as a working definition) and makes sure the verifier does not drift out of sync as the Rust language and compiler evolve. It also gives a unified view on potential errors: verification issues are reported in the same way as compilation errors.

In this paper, we give an overview of the Prusti verifier and discuss the central design decisions and relevant outcomes so far from the perspective of a user (Sect. 2), a verification expert (Sect. 3), and a tool developer (Sect. 4). We discuss related work (Sect. 5) and conclude with some directions for future work (Sect. 6).

2   Prusti from a User's Perspective

We first consider the Prusti verifier from a Rust progammer's perspective. Prusti builds upon the standard Rust compiler `rustc`. The command `prusti-rustc` can be used as a drop-in replacement for `rustc` to verify individual files; the command `cargo prusti` uses Rust's package manager `cargo` to run Prusti on Rust projects. Alternatively, Prusti can be used through an extension for Visual Studio Code (VSCode), which is a popular editor for Rust programming [49].

A key feature of Prusti is that it supports incremental verification with an initial annotation effort of (almost) *zero*: developers get guarantees beyond those of safe Rust and useful feedback by just running Prusti on their code; they can then choose to invest more effort to obtain more powerful guarantees. We will illustrate Prusti's capabilities by proving increasingly complex properties for safe Rust programs. Further details and examples are available online [47].

2.1   (Almost) Zero-Cost Verification

By default, Prusti checks that a Rust program will not *panic* (terminate with an unrecoverable error) at runtime, whether due to an explicit `panic!(...)` call[1] or e.g. due to bounds-checks and integer overflows. Prusti can perform these checks directly on the input program, with *no* modification and *no* user-supplied annotations; in particular, it does not require the specifications of data structures and side-effects required as upfront investment by verification techniques for other imperative languages. For many examples, the checks for panic freedom succeed immediately; others require a small amount of simple annotations. In the following, we present examples for both cases.

As a first example, consider the Rust function in Fig. 1, which performs a binary search for a value `key` on a slice of integers `a`, i.e. a contiguous subsequence of the elements in a collection. Compiling this function with `rustc` produces no errors. However, running `prusti-rustc` reveals a potential bug: the statement `let mid = (low+high)/2` on line 7 might overflow for a very large slice `a`. This automatically detected bug is non-trivial: it remained undetected for years in a similar implementation provided by the Java standard library [9].

---

[1] or its siblings `unreachable!()`, `unimplemented!()`, `assert!(false)`, etc.

```
1  fn search(a: &[i32], key: i32)
2          -> Option<usize> {
3    let mut low = 0;
4    let mut high = a.len();
5    while low < high {
6      // Addition may overflow
7      let mid = (low+high) / 2;
8      // Bound check at runtime
9      let mid_val = a[mid];
10     if mid_val < key {
11       low = mid + 1;
12     } else if mid_val > key {
13       high = mid;
14     } else {
15       return Some(mid);
16     }
17   }
18   return None;
19 }
```

Fig. 1. Buggy binary search.

```
> prusti-rustc search.rs
error: [Prusti: verification error]
assertion might fail with attempt to
add with overflow
 --> search.rs:7:5
  |
7 |      let mid = (low+high) / 2;
  |      ^^^^^^^^^^^^^^^^^^^^^^^^^


5  while low < high {
6    body_invariant!(high <= a.len());
7    let mid = low + ((high-low) / 2);
8    assert!(mid < high);
9    let mid_val = a[mid];
     // ...
17 }
```

Fig. 2. Reported error and fixed loop.

Whenever Prusti fails to verify the absence of panics, it reports potential issues like compiler errors, as in Fig. 2 (upper half); these naturally benefit from any IDE highlighting of errors. Programmers can understand and handle such warnings as if Prusti were a stricter compiler for Rust.

We can fix the bug by rewriting line 7 to let mid = low + ((high-low)/2). Now Prusti is able to infer both that high-low cannot underflow (from the loop guard: low < high) and that low + ((high-low)/2) cannot overflow.

While this property can be proved without any help from the programmer, others require annotations. Prusti verifies loops according to the guarantees of the Rust type system and any user-provided loop invariants. After fixing the overflow error in our example, Prusti cannot show that, in every loop iteration, the slice access a[mid] (line 9) is within bounds. To establish this it suffices to add a simple loop invariant[2] stating that, during every iteration, high <= a.len() holds just inside the loop body. The annotated code accepted by Prusti is shown in Fig. 2 (lower half). Prusti proves that the loop invariant holds (inductively); the invariant, along with the loop guard mid < high and the (implicit) unsigned types of these index variables, allows Prusti to prove that a[mid] is safe).

This simplest way of using Prusti requires almost no user annotation: Prusti's underlying reasoning accounts for path conditions, value ranges and (not shown here) non-aliasing guarantees implied by rustc's type-checking. Additional local properties of interest can be added with standard Rust assert macros (e.g. line 8 in Fig. 2), and checked statically with Prusti rather than (only) at runtime; the initial friction in using Prusti this way is as low as for using a code linter.

---

[2] In slight contrast to classical loop invariants, a body_invariant!(...) need only hold for every loop iteration *reaching* this location inside the loop body.

2.2   Modular Verification of User-Specified Contracts

After using Prusti for proving panic freedom, developers may decide to invest
annotation effort step-by-step to obtain stronger correctness guarantees about
their Rust code. To this end, every function can be annotated with a *contract*: a
specification consisting of pre- and postconditions. Functions are verified modularly against these contracts: when verifying calls to the function, only its
contract and type signature are used, not its concrete implementation. Besides
facilitating scalability and supporting recursion, a modular approach enables
decoupling verification of client code from e.g. specific library implementations.

Continuing our example from Fig. 1, consider the following contract:

```
1  #[requires(a.len() < usize::MAX / 2)]
2  #[ensures(if let Some(idx) = result { idx < a.len() && a[idx] == key }
3          else { true })]
4  fn search(a: &[i32], key: i32) -> Option<usize> { /* ... */ }
```

Specifications in Prusti consist of (a large subset of) side-effect free Rust expressions with a few carefully chosen extensions, as we discuss below. The above
postcondition ensures(...) uses the special Prusti variable result to refer to the
function's return value[3]. It specifies that whenever search returns some position
idx, then the value a[idx] equals the search key. Prusti checks this property and
also that the slice access a[idx] in the postcondition is in bounds.

The precondition requires(...) states that search can be called only on slices
whose length is at most half of the largest number of type usize—Prusti will
report an error if a caller attempts to pass a longer slice. Under this precondition,
the original overflow bug could never be triggered, and Prusti can also verify the
unmodified code from Fig. 1 (for calls allowed by the precondition).

2.3   The Prusti Specification Language

We will now explain and illustrate numerous features of Prusti's specification
language via its usage on a binary search tree (BST), given by:

```
1  // A binary search tree data structure (elements should be sorted)
2  pub enum Tree<T: Ord> {
3      Node(T, Box<Tree<T>>, Box<Tree<T>>),
4      Empty,
5  }
```

Every element of a Tree is either an Empty leaf or a Node storing pointers to its
left and right subtree, and a value of (generic) type T; the bound on T requires
that this type must implement the Ord trait so that values can be compared. We
assume that this BST represents a set, i.e. duplicate entries will never be stored.

Prusti's specification syntax (e.g. for pre- and postconditions) reuses Rust
expressions as far as possible. Not *all* Rust expressions are accepted: the evaluation of expressions used in specifications must not have side-effects (specifications

---

[3] The if let construct is standard Rust, branching on whether the value can be
pattern-matched against Some(idx) (taking the second branch if not, i.e. for None).

should not affect program execution), and must be deterministic and terminate, to ensure that specifications have an intuitive meaning for programmers (a clear mathematical interpretation for the verifier). Prusti identifies a *pure subset* of Rust with the above properties allowed in specifications, including dereferencing, branching, pattern-matching etc.., as used in our `search` postconditions above.

Importantly, Prusti allows calls to *functions* within specifications, *if* they have the Prusti-specific attribute `#[pure]`. The body of a function labelled as pure must fall into Prusti's pure Rust fragment described above. As of now, Prusti checks that pure functions have no side-effects and are deterministic (termination checking is not yet performed, but will be added in the near future).

A common case of pure functions are queries (or *getters*) of a data structure, such as the `contains` function below, which often appear in specifications.

```
1  impl<T: Ord> Tree<T> {
2    #[pure]
3    pub fn contains(&self, find_value: &T) -> bool {
4      // ... with the natural (recursive) definition in Rust ...
```

This function is implemented as a straightforward recursive traversal over the BST [48], naturally satisfying the requirements for a pure function[4]. As `contains` is declared pure, Prusti will treat it analogously to a mathematical function and unroll its definition (in a bounded way, to avoid non-termination) instead of relying solely on the function's contract (as for ordinary methods). Annotating the function as pure suffices for proving simple code such as the following:

```
1  let v = 0;
2  let t = Tree::Node(v, Box::new(Tree::Empty), Box::new(Tree::Empty));
3  assert!(t.contains(&v));
```

While it is reassuring that such unit-test-like programs can be statically verified automatically, the real power of pure functions is that they provide API-specific building blocks for defining richer functional specifications, as we show next.

Type Invariants. Our next goal is to specify that `Tree` objects maintain a fundamental invariant, namely that they model binary search trees. Assume, for the moment, that we already have a specification of the search tree property given by a pure method `bst_invariant(&self) -> bool`. Prusti's `#[invariant(...)]` annotation then allows us to directly attach the invariant to the `Tree` type:

```
1  #[invariant(self.bst_invariant())]
2  pub enum Tree<T: Ord> {
```

Now, Prusti will ensure that whenever a `Tree` instance is passed as function argument or return value, the invariant is guaranteed; it is correspondingly assumed for function parameters (by the callee) and return values (by the caller).

---

[4] Values of generic type `T` are compared with the library function `cmp` from trait `Ord`, which is specified to satisfy the standard properties of total orders using an *external specification*; this Prusti feature is explained in Sect. 2.4.

```
1  predicate! {
2    pub fn bst_invariant(&self) -> bool {
3      if let Tree::Node(value, left, right) = self {
4          forall(|i: &T| left.contains(i)   ==
5              (matches!(i.cmp(value), Less   ) && self.contains(i)))
6          && forall(|i: &T| right.contains(i) ==
7              (matches!(i.cmp(value), Greater) && self.contains(i)))
8      } else { true }
9    }
10 }
```

Fig. 3. Predicate expressing the invariant of a binary search tree.

Quantifiers and Predicates. Our invariant `bst_invariant` needs to capture the following informal search tree property: any value v of type T in the left (resp. right) subtree of a BST instance t with root value v' is smaller (resp. greater) than v' according to T's ordering. Rather than implementing this property as a pure function in Rust, the above description suggests *quantifying* over all values. Prusti specifications may contain both universal (syntax: `forall(|vars| expr)`) and existential (syntax: `exists(|vars| expr)`) quantifiers, where the declaration of quantified variables `vars` is analogous to declaring Rust closure parameters.

We can now precisely define our intended invariant with this powerful mix of logical quantifiers and pure functions denoting data-structure-specific abstractions. However, since quantifiers are not Rust expressions, the invariant itself cannot be defined in a Rust function. Instead, Prusti provides the feature of *predicates*, which are similar to (pure) Rust functions whose bodies can be any expression allowed in Prusti's specification language. Our formal Prusti specification of the invariant is shown in Fig. 3. Prusti checks that predicates are only ever invoked in specifications; they cannot be called from executable code (general quantifiers need not have an executable semantics).

Old Expressions. Now that we have established the search tree property as an invariant of `Tree`, we may decide to add further contracts to functions working with trees. For instance, Fig. 4 shows a method `insert` that inserts a new value into a binary search tree; it is equipped with a simple postcondition (line 1) stating that, once the function terminates, the tree contains the new value. Since `insert` mutates the given tree, we may also want to make sure that, apart from adding the new value, no other values have been added or removed. Prusti specifications can include `old(...)` expressions in postconditions to refer to the memory before execution of the function's body. As shown in lines 2–3, we can then specify that, for all values except the new one, the function `contains` returns the same result when executed on the tree before and after running `insert`.

Pledges. One of the most advanced specification features Prusti adds to its base language of Rust expressions tackles specification of *reborrowing*: func-

```
1  #[ensures(self.contains(&new_value))]
2  #[ensures(forall(|i: &T| !matches!(new_value.cmp(i), Equal)
3                      ==> self.contains(i) == old(self).contains(i)))]
4  pub fn insert(&mut self, new_value: T) {
5      if let Tree::Node(value, left, right) = self {
6          match new_value.cmp(value) {
7              Equal => (),
8              Less => left.insert(new_value),
9              Greater => right.insert(new_value),
10         }
11     } else {
12         *self = Tree::Node(new_value,
13                         Box::new(Tree::Empty), Box::new(Tree::Empty))
14     }
15 }
```

Fig. 4. Insertion into a binary search tree.

tions that both take and return mutable references. An example is the function `get_root_value` below, which hands out a reference to the root value of the tree.

```
1  pub fn get_root_value(&mut self) -> &mut T {
2      if let Tree::Node(value, _, _) = self { value } else { panic!() }
3  }
```

Rust's type system (generally forbidding the combination of usable aliases and mutability) makes the reference `self` *blocked* after calling this function, until the returned reference's lifetime expires (it is no longer used). This creates an interesting challenge if (as we did for Prusti) one wants a specification language which is in-keeping with both Rust expression syntax and its typing rules, to aid programmer understanding. The key challenges [6] are: (1) one wants to specify guarantees that will be true for `self` *once it becomes accessible again*, but in the post-state of the call one cannot (according to the type system) talk about the blocked reference to `self`, and (2) *some* facts that one cares about cannot even be determined in the post-state of this call, since the value that the root will have when the reborrow expires is *not yet known*: it depends on what the caller does with the returned reference to this root value.

Prusti solves both problems with *pledges* [6], a novel specification feature which allows one to express specifications about points in the *future* of this call, when the returned reborrow expires. Pledges use two specification constructs: `after_expiry(e)` (which describes what e's value *will be* once the returned reference expires), and `before_expiry(e)` (which describes e's value *just before* the returned reference expires). Using these constructs, one can write e.g. a postcondition `after_expiry(self.contains(before_expiry(result)))`, to express that once the returned reference `result` expires, the BST `self` is guaranteed to contain whatever value `result` stores by the time it expires. More examples are discussed in our earlier paper [6].

```
1  #[requires(matches!(self, Tree::Node(..)))]
2  #[assert_on_expiry(
3    // Must hold before result can expire
4    if let Tree::Node(_, left, right) = old(self) {
5      forall(|i: &T| left.contains(i)
6                    ==> matches!(i.cmp(result), Less)) &&
7      forall(|i: &T| right.contains(i)
8                    ==> matches!(i.cmp(result), Greater))
9    } else { false },
10   // A postcondition of 'get_root_value' after result expires
11   if let Tree::Node(ref value, _, _) = self {
12     matches!(value.cmp(before_expiry(result)), Equal)
13   } else { false }
14 )]
15 pub fn get_root_value(&mut self) -> &mut T {
16   if let Tree::Node(value, _, _) = self { value } else { panic!() }
17 }
```

Fig. 5. A rich specification combining many Prusti and Rust features.

Given our desired BST invariant, client code should modify the root's value only in a way that guarantees to preserve the BST invariant. This can be enforced with the more-advanced pledge construct `assert_on_expiry(e',e)`. This construct expresses `after_expiry(e)` and, in addition, asserts e' at the point where the reborrowed reference expires. To demonstrate the expressiveness of these features combined, we show a very general specification for `get_root_value` in Fig. 5, which exploits the power of Prusti's specifications to combine pledges, old expressions, pure functions, quantifiers along with standard Rust features. Notably, the constraint on the reborrowed reference `result` relates only its (single) value to the old version of the tree: the rest of the tree structure is guaranteed immutable while the reborrow is live, and Prusti's underlying separation logic proof (discussed in the next section) captures this directly.

2.4   Incremental Verification in Practice

As illustrated above, Prusti's design enables developers to verify a codebase by incrementally trading annotation effort for stronger guarantees. In this subsection, we report on preliminary experiences from an ongoing project in which Prusti is used this way to analyse the ibc [21] crate, an implementation of the Interblockchain Communication Protocol [19] containing >20,000 lines of code.

At the time of our first experiments, Prusti could run on roughly 70% of the functions in the two crates (495/716 and 545/738) analysed; the remainder used features unsupported by the verifier. Without specifications the vast majority of these functions were proved panic-free automatically. Prusti identified a small number of potential panics, due to manual `assert!` calls (conceptually expressing preconditions) or potential overflows due to expressions such as `self.revision_height + delta` where `delta` was a `u64` function parameter. Making manual `assert!`s into preconditions (which are then checked at call sites!) is easy since Prusti's specifications can be Rust expressions; adding preconditions to rule out overflows was also simple, e.g. this precondition for the case above:

```
1  #[requires(u64::MAX - self.revision_height >= delta)]
2  pub fn add(&self, delta: u64) -> Height { /* ... */ }
```

This ruled out language-level panics for all supported functions, but (as is common) the code also uses standard library functions such as `Option.unwrap()`, which panic at runtime if called incorrectly. To extend Prusti's reach to uncovering such panics, we need to add a precondition for `Option.unwrap()`, but since this is standard library code, we also can't (and don't want to) edit it.

For this purpose, Prusti offers the *external specifications* (`extern_spec`) feature, which allows attaching contracts to functions (including library functions) separately from their implementation[5]. Such specifications look like a regular implementation block for a Rust type except that functions have no bodies (mimicking Rust's trait declaration syntax).

For instance, the following external specification makes sure that calls to `Option.unwrap()` won't cause panics, which is naturally expressed as a Prusti specification by identifying `is_some` as a pure method:

```
1  #[extern_spec]
2  impl<T> std::option::Option<T> {
3    #[pure]
4    fn is_some(&self) -> bool;
5
6    #[requires(self.is_some())]
7    fn unwrap(self) -> T;
8  }
```

As a user, one can take an incremental approach to adding such specifications to called functions, adding those which are most worthwhile for the user's goals. For our panic-freedom pass, we pragmatically focused on the most widely used functions known to panic (from `Option<T>` and `Result<T>`), which already gave us stronger guarantees than our initial run with no such specifications.

After ruling out (most) panics in this way, we added specifications to check important domain-specific requirements, for example, that the height and time of each block in the blockchain increases monotonically. We used Prusti to verify that various functions in the `ibc` crate maintain these monotonicity invariants.

Inevitably for such a large codebase, we found functions that use currently unsupported language features. We *can* still attach contracts to such functions, which will subsequently be used by Prusti to deal with calls. We can tell Prusti not to check these specifications with a `#[trusted]` annotation. For example, in `ibc`, some time-related functions, such as `from_nanos` below, relied on unsupported types exposed by the `chrono` [28] crate and were marked as `#[trusted]`. The specification below expresses that `from_nanos` returns a valid result (rather than the error case of `Result`) if the `u64` parameter `nanos` fits within an `i64`, but Prusti does not check the function's body to verify that the specification holds.

---

[5] External specifications can also be used for functions inside the same crate, allowing developers to apply Prusti without modifying source files, if desired.

```
1 #[trusted]
2 #[ensures(nanos <= i64::MAX as u64 ==> result.is_ok())]
3 pub fn from_nanos(nanos: u64) -> Result<Timestamp, TryFromIntError> {
4   let nanos = nanos.try_into()?;
5   Ok(Timestamp {time: Some(Utc.timestamp_nanos(nanos))})
6 }
```

While trusted specifications must be written carefully, they enable developers to pragmatically focus on specifying and proving those properties they consider most relevant without imposing an excessive verification burden.

These features provide a further degree of freedom in the verification workflow: developers may initially use many #[trusted] annotations in a first iteration, and later attempt to reduce the number of trusted functions in subsequent iterations. As such, both trusted functions and external specifications further facilitate the incremental verification of realistic Rust code using Prusti.

3   Prusti from a Verification Expert's Perspective

At the heart of Prusti lies the *core proof*, i.e. a memory safety proof written in separation logic [23,39,43], the de-facto standard for verifying resource-manipulating programs. Conceptually, the Prusti project explores three main questions, upon which we will reflect in this section:

1. To what extent can intuitive reasoning about most Rust programs be captured by an off-the-shelf separation logic?
2. To what extent can the generation of core proofs be automated?
3. To what extent can core proofs be leveraged for verifying interesting functional correctness properties?

3.1   Core Proofs in an Off-the-Shelf Separation Logic

Separation logic nowadays comes in numerous flavours, ranging from simple logics for verifying sequential heap-manipulating code to highly specialised variants targeting intricate concurrency or weak-memory models (cf. [39]). It is thus not surprising (but still very challenging!) that one can construct *some* separation logic which allows precise reasoning about all aspects of Rust's memory model; RustBelt [27] is the most impressive attempt in that direction so far.

By contrast, the Prusti project aims to enable *intuitive* formal reasoning about *most* Rust code. We believe that this approach matches Rust's design philosophy of enabling "fearless programming": *safe Rust* code, i.e. code without any *direct* usages of unsafe language features should be understandable, without low-level concerns. Recent studies [5,16] confirm that Rust code in the wild largely adheres to this philosophy: the vast majority of function implementations are written in safe Rust; they *may* call functions that are implemented using unsafe features, but shield clients from these details through encapsulation.

More concretely, Prusti embeds an annotated Rust program (cf. Sect. 2) in the Viper intermediate verification language [38], which is based on Implicit

Dynamic Frames (IDF)—a variant of traditional separation logics with a clear formal connection to standard separation logic [40]. Building upon an off-the-shelf logic has the advantage that the overall soundness of the embedding is analogous to soundness arguments that are well-understood for separation logic reasoning; it also allows us to draw on substantial prior work and expertise, particularly when it comes to proof automation.

The original Prusti paper [6] describes the embedding in detail. Overall, we found that the read and write capabilities governed by Rust's flow sensitive type system have almost identical properties to the assertions governing heap accesses in IDF. In particular, Rust structs can be modelled as (possibly nested and recursive) *predicates* representing unique access to a type instance. Moreover, moves and simple usages of Rust's shared and mutable borrows resemble ownership transfers in the permission reading of separation logic assertions [10]; *reborrowing* is modelled directly by *magic wands*: when a reborrowed reference is passed back to a caller, it comes with a magic wand representing the ownership of all borrowed-from locations *not* currently in the proof.

Prusti's underlying logic champions simplicity and fits well into Rust's overall design philosophy: at every point in Prusti's core proof, there is direct representation of ownership in separation logic terms. This is different from RustBelt [27], where ownership and the connection between reborrowed and borrowed-from locations is handled via an indirection through a custom *lifetime logic* designed to express general semantic requirements on how lifetimes are manipulated, including via ad hoc manual policies implemented by unsafe code.

However, the simplicity of Prusti's underlying logic has also made some (safe) Rust features harder to incorporate. One key example is struct types with explicit *lifetime parameters* (used to accommodate reference-typed fields), for which it is sometimes convenient to treat the struct as a single resource, and sometimes convenient to consider it as multiple individual resources borrowed for a certain lifetime. RustBelt achieves this via the more fine-grained resources of its lifetime logic; it is unclear whether this complexity is inevitable.

3.2   Full Automation of Core Proofs for Type-Checked Rust

As explained above, Prusti's underlying model introduces nested and potentially recursive predicates to model instances of Rust types. However, general reasoning about such separation logic predicates is known to be undecidable [3,22]. Verifiers such as Viper require additional annotations to guide reasoning about predicates, e.g. by inserting explicit statements to *unfold* and *fold* predicate definitions into a Viper program. For example, when a field of a struct is accessed in the Rust program, this requires unfolding the predicate modelling the capabilities for accessing the struct; the obtained capabilities cannot always be re-folded into a predicate since the field might be borrowed or moved-out.

While fold and unfold statements cannot be inferred automatically for *arbitrary* code with recursive predicates, Prusti infers them automatically for type-correct Rust code. The essential point is that the Rust compiler, when enforcing the flow-sensitive typing rules for the language, requires book-keeping similar to that of unfolding and folding our predicates. For example, enforcing the check that fields moved out from a struct are (all) moved back in before the struct can be returned is conceptually analogous to refolding its corresponding predicate definition in Prusti's model.

Prusti performs a pass over the encoded Rust program to add the necessary fold and unfold operations: essentially it performs a symbolic execution, tracking the accessible places at each program point and their current depth of unfolding (differentiating, say, between a struct being accessible and its fields being accessible). In addition to fold/unfold annotations, Prusti also infers all of the necessary Viper annotations for reasoning about magic wands [45] modelling reborrows. In all, the annotations required make up a large chunk of the generated Viper code, but they are generated *fully automatically* for all Rust programs supported by Prusti. This degree of automation is challenging to achieve but (we believe) an important objective for a tool that tries to raise the conceptual level at which a user interacts with a verifier. It ensures that Prusti users do not have to understand the sometimes intricate logical encoding of their programs. To our knowledge, Prusti was the first tool to be able to automatically produce formal proofs about a substantial fragment of Rust that could be automatically checked by a program verifier.

3.3   Incorporating Rich Functional Specifications

Prusti's underlying logic is Viper's dialect of Implicit Dynamic Frames. Although closely related to separation logic, a key feature of this logic is that one can conjoin functional specifications concerning heap *values* directly onto the resources such as permissions and predicate instances. In this sense, once the core proof is in place, layering functional specifications on top comes essentially for free.

Our first versions of Prusti exploited this technical feature to embed *all* aspects of user-written specifications (i.e. Rust annotations) into corresponding expressions in the generated Viper code, i.e. the core proof. A more-recent extension of Prusti's core model equips each predicate instance with a *snapshot*: a value used as a mathematical identity for the current state of the (possibly composite) portion of the program memory accessible via this predicate. This technique originates (we believe) from the implementation of the VeriFast program verifier [24], and is also used extensively in Viper's symbolic execution engine [46]. RustHornBelt [33] uses a similar technique to layer functional specification on top of RustBelt [27] predicates. Snapshots simplify encoding properties guaranteed by reasoning methodologies *other than* the basic separation logic framing built into Prusti's core proofs. For example, (in work with Fabian Wolff) we use the flexibility provided by snapshots to layer guarantees about the heap on top of the core proof to extend Prusti's support for a rich class of specifications about Rust closures [52].

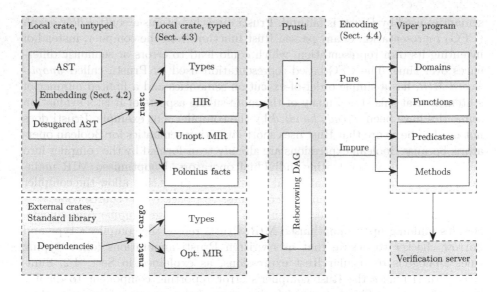

Fig. 6. Overview of Prusti's encoding process.

4   Prusti from a Tool Engineer's Perspective

Prusti targets real-world code in Rust, itself a mature and complex language. Accordingly, Prusti is designed to reuse existing functionality from the Rust compiler whenever possible, in order to reduce the implementation burden and faithfully maintain compatibility with the constantly-evolving Rust ecosystem.

4.1   Architecture and Design Overview

Prusti is implemented as a *compiler driver*, reusing the standard `rustc` compiler extensively; its overall workflow is presented in Fig. 6. Prusti launches and interacts with a full instance of `rustc`, used both for its program representations and analysis results (second column; cf. Sect. 4.3). To have Prusti-specific specification features (Sect. 2.3) type-checked analogously to regular Rust expressions (including error-reporting), Prusti performs a *specification embedding*, reusing existing Rust features whose type-checking rules are analogous (top-left; cf. Sect. 4.2). Prusti has `rustc` map the sources for both the program and (embedded) specifications down to `rustc`'s mid-level representations as for standard compilation. Prusti performs its own analyses (third column), and assimilates all necessary information to generate a Viper program (last column) that it sends to a further Prusti component which performs verification through a Viper wrapper. If verification fails, Prusti maps the Viper errors to user-readable Rust errors reported via the compiler API.

The compiler driver architecture is used by popular tools such as Clippy [11] and Miri [36]; it has two main advantages. First, it raises confidence that the semantics used by Prusti is faithful. Prusti directly obtains a control-flow graph (CFG) representation of any parsed Rust function from the compiler, instead of inventing its own representation, which could lead to errors or semantic differences over time. The CFG-based representation used by Prusti, called *unoptimised MIR*, has a simple order-of-execution semantics and a limited number of statements; at this stage, many of the more-subtle aspects of Rust's evaluation semantics have been *already handled* by the compiler. For example, Prusti does not need to be aware that Rust uses short-circuiting semantics for Boolean operators, because Boolean expressions are already transformed by the compiler into multiple statements evaluating individual operators. Unoptimised MIR maintains all type-checker information, along with back-links that allow the compiler (and thus also Prusti) to translate error messages back to the source code.

Second, the above architecture enables Prusti to reuse compiler components. Besides building upon unoptimised MIR, Prusti reuses the compiler's type and borrow checker to ensure that user-written Prusti annotations follow typing rules analogous to regular Rust expressions, as explained in Sect. 4.2. Similarly, Prusti reuses the Rust compiler's error reporting component to display verification errors. This way, the default syntax of the reports is familiar to Rust programmers and the compiler can be configured to report machine-readable errors. The latter simplifies integrating Prusti with other tools. For example, IDE extensions like the official Prusti Assistant extension for Visual Studio Code, but even Prusti-unaware tools such as Rust-analyzer [44], can be configured to report Prusti verification errors generated by running `cargo-prusti` instead of `cargo check`.

4.2 Specification Embedding

Prusti-specific annotations (e.g. method contracts) are implemented with *procedural macros* [1]. These macros are defined to generate nothing when compiled using the regular Rust compiler. However, when compiled with Prusti, a *specification embedding* is performed: to make the compiler both type-check and translate (to MIR) these specifications, corresponding methods are added to the program. For Prusti-specific constructs the specification embedding is more involved, replacing them with usages of Rust features which have the right type-checking requirements. For example, quantifiers (Sect. 2.3) are embedded as *closures*.

Prusti uses a Pratt parser [41] to perform the embedding of Prusti-specific constructs, before invoking the `syn` [13] Rust parser on the result, yielding an AST representation. The resulting specification expressions are embedded into the bodies of methods with unique names. Prusti constructs a mapping between these generated methods (called *specification items*) and the relevant construct in the original source code (e.g. for a precondition, the method it is a precondition of). By feeding the program augmented with specification items through the compiler, we both check that the specifications type-check and can obtain corresponding MIR representations of the specifications. The type-checking and evaluation semantics reflected by this translation to MIR are those of standard `rustc`; this approach reuses the standard semantics of the Rust language for specification checking and compilation.

4.3 Compiler Interface

Prusti obtains various information from `rustc`'s data structures, as illustrated in the second column of Fig. 6. Given how Rust compilation works, different information is available (and used by Prusti) for the *local* crate (i.e. the crate being compiled/verified) and *external* crates (the dependencies of the local crate).

Local Crate. For the local crate, Prusti obtains a high-level AST representation (HIR), the type definitions, the unoptimised CFGs of the functions (MIR), and borrow-checker information (Polonius facts), defining the compiler-determined lifetimes of references. Prusti uses HIR, in which function names have already been associated to their definition, to retrieve specifications embedded in specification items, as described in Sect. 4.2. Prusti uses type definitions to generate Viper predicate definitions for the core proof (cf. Sect. 3), while unoptimised MIR is used to generate the corresponding Viper code itself (cf. Sect. 4.4).

The compiler offers various versions of MIR at different stages during the compilation process. Prusti uses the *unoptimised* version because it is the only one on which the borrow-checker runs. This also has a semantic advantage, since we do not need to worry whether compiler optimisations preserve the strong type properties that Prusti exploits[6]. Prusti uses the results from the Polonius borrow-checker, also called *facts*, to automate the generation of annotations such as folding and unfolding of Viper predicates (cf. Sect. 3.2).

Previously, the compiler API did not expose Polonius facts, but the compiler developers were very supportive in accepting our proposed additions to the API [4]. Our changes have since been used by at least one other static analysis tool, Flowistry [12], to access precise aliasing information.

External Crates. For external crates, the compiler offers strictly less information than for the local one, primarily for performance reasons. Type definitions and *optimised* MIR are available (Prusti uses the former to encode calls), but the HIR, the unoptimised MIR, and the Polonius facts are not present. Since Prusti's overall methodology is modular, the only real limitation this imposes is that any Prusti specifications written *in* an external crate will not be seen. As explained in Sect. 2.4, Prusti supports external specifications to be applied to these functions from the local crate. Nonetheless, following the example of the MIRAI static analyser [17], we believe that, in the future, previously-compiled Prusti specifications could be recovered for external crates from a combination of the optimised MIR and persisting some information to disk between compilations.

---

[6] See for example https://github.com/rust-lang/rust/issues/46420 for an optimisation that used to copy non-duplicable mutable references.

4.4   Encoding to Viper

Finally, Prusti uses the information assembled from the Rust compiler to encode an annotated Rust program to a Viper program for verification. As shown in the right half of Fig. 6, there are *two* different encodings: a *pure encoding* to Viper expressions and an *impure encoding* to Viper statements.

Pure Encoding. Prusti's pure encoding is used for specifications and pure functions (which may be invoked from within specifications), and is necessary as Viper specifications must be Viper expressions (which are side-effect-free, unlike statements, which are a distinct notion in Viper).

Pure Rust expressions (cf. Sect. 2.3) are encoded to Viper expressions using a backwards symbolic execution through their CFG, starting from the variable which stores the final result (easily determined in MIR); the steps are reminiscent of a standard weakest-precondition calculation.

To represent Rust values in pure code, Prusti uses the snapshot technique presented in Sect. 3.3. Snapshots are encoded to Viper domains; that is, abstract type definitions with uninterpreted functions and axioms that describe the relation between the snapshot of a type and the snapshot of its inner instances (e.g. variants of an enumeration or fields of a structure). These are computed from the compiler's type definitions.

Impure Encoding. Like the pure encoding, the impure encoding processes the unoptimised MIR and analyses the CFG of a method. However, in the impure case, the output is a Viper *method* containing heap-mutating statements. Viper methods can also contain goto statements, which allows us to encode the MIR CFG without having to reconstruct loops or standard control flow structures.

To encode mutable references, Prusti needs to know the program point at which references expire and which places receive the no-longer-borrowed ownership, such that magic wands that encode the ownership flow can be applied in the right order to form the core proof. To do so, Prusti elaborates the borrow-checker facts to automatically compute a directed acyclic graph (DAG) of the borrowing relations for each program point: each node with exit edges represents a reference and each edge points to the places that it blocks. When a set of references expire, a topological sort of the DAG determines the order in which the magic wands associated to the edges should be applied. This *Reborrowing DAG* is generalised to appropriately account for conditional paths through the CFG.

5   Related Work

RustBelt [27] is a long-standing verification project for Rust. RustBelt focuses on proving that abstractions provided by internally unsafe libraries are safe; verification is performed in Coq [8] over a simplified language based on Rust. By contrast, Prusti is designed for general-purpose verification (with an emphasis on safe Rust), and directly uses the representations in the Rust compiler.

Several verification approaches have been developed which avoid explicitly modelling Rust's memory (and aliasing) for safe Rust (only). Electrolysis [50] applied *purification* of such programs to convert them to functional programs to be verified in Lean [37]. More recently, RustHorn [34] and Creusot [14] leverage Rust's ownership semantics to model mutable references using a technique similar to prophecy variables [2] rather than explicitly modelling the heap. The soundness of the approach was shown in RustHornBelt [33], a unification of RustBelt and RustHorn. To our knowledge, automatic generation of core proofs in these underlying models remains an open problem. Although not for Rust, the Move Prover [15] employs a reborrowing DAG similar to Prusti's, although it then employs techniques similar to purification to eliminate heap reasoning.

Several automated static analysers have been developed for Rust, including the abstract interpreter MIRAI [17]. The Kani Rust Verifier [51] applies bounded model-checking. Other tools analyse the generated LLVM: e.g. Klee Rust performs symbolic testing [31], Smack applies bounded verification [7], Project Oak [42] provides an evolving portfolio of complementary tools. None of these tools use the ownership guarantees of the type system, to our knowledge.

Stacked Borrows [26] is another formal model for Rust aiming to precisely define notions of *undefined behaviour* for the Rust language; it is accompanied by the interpreter Miri [36], which can be used to dynamically check for rule violations. We are not aware of corresponding static tools based on this model.

6   Conclusions and Future Work

We have presented the Prusti project, and reflected on its key features and most-notable design decisions from three different perspectives: for users, verification experts, and authors of other Rust analysis tools. From a user's perspective, notable features include the close relationship between specifications and Rust expressions, and the flexible trade-offs between annotation effort and richness of guarantees, which supports incremental usage of the tool on large-scale projects. For verification experts, a notable goal is the reuse of long-standing program reasoning techniques for reasoning about (primarily) safe Rust code. For tool builders, the extensive reuse of compiler data structures, analyses and error reporting mechanisms has proven powerful; these techniques are largely reusable.

A key goal for future work to benefit users is to enable richer specifications (when desired), via built-in types (such as mathematical sets) and add dedicated features for *ghost code*, as well as improving verification performance. Of more interest to verification experts, we are exploring the adaptation of Prusti's core model and proofs to both structs with lifetime parameters and some usages of unsafe code. On the tooling front, we aim to support persistence of compiled Prusti specifications, and offering built-in specifications for common Rust libraries.

Acknowledgements. We warmly thank Nicholas D. Matsakis, Nick Cameron, Derek Dreyer and Ralf Jung for extensive discussions and feedback in the early stages of this project, and are very grateful to Florian Hahn for his work on a precursor to Prusti [20], as well as numerous Master's and undergraduate students who have since contributed via projects.

This work was partially funded by the Swiss National Science Foundation (SNSF) (Grant No. 200021_169503), the Natural Sciences and Engineering Research Council of Canada (NSERC) (ref. RGPIN-2020-06072), Amazon Research Awards, Meta (then Facebook) Research and the Interchain Foundation.

References

1. Procedural macros documentation (2022). https://doc.rust-lang.org/reference/procedural-macros.html
2. Abadi, M., Lamport, L.: The existence of refinement mappings. In: Proceedings of the 3rd Annual Symposium on Logic in Computer Science, pp. 165–175, July 1988. https://www.microsoft.com/en-us/research/publication/the-existence-of-refinement-mappings/, lICS 1988 Test of Time Award
3. Antonopoulos, T., Gorogiannis, N., Haase, C., Kanovich, M., Ouaknine, J.: Foundations for decision problems in separation logic with general inductive predicates. In: Muscholl, A. (ed.) FoSSaCS 2014. LNCS, vol. 8412, pp. 411–425. Springer, Heidelberg (2014). https://doi.org/10.1007/978-3-642-54830-7_27
4. Astrauskas, V.: Enable compiler consumers to obtain MIR: Body with Polonius facts. https://github.com/rust-lang/rust/pull/86977
5. Astrauskas, V., Matheja, C., Poli, F., Müller, P., Summers, A.J.: How do programmers use unsafe Rust? Proc. ACM Program. Lang. 4(OOPSLA), 1–27 (2020)
6. Astrauskas, V., Müller, P., Poli, F., Summers, A.J.: Leveraging rust types for modular specification and verification. Proc. ACM Program. Lang. 3(OOPSLA), 147:1–147:30 (2019). https://doi.org/10.1145/3360573
7. Baranowski, M., He, S., Rakamarić, Z.: Verifying rust programs with SMACK. In: Lahiri, S.K., Wang, C. (eds.) ATVA 2018. LNCS, vol. 11138, pp. 528–535. Springer, Cham (2018). https://doi.org/10.1007/978-3-030-01090-4_32
8. Bertot, Y., Castéran, P.: Interactive Theorem Proving and Program Development: Coq'Art: The Calculus of Inductive Constructions. In: Texts in Theoretical Computer Science. An EATCS Series, pp. XXV–472. Springer, Heidelberg (2013). https://doi.org/10.1007/978-3-662-07964-5
9. Bloch, J.: Extra, extra - read all about it: Nearly all binary searches and merge-sorts are broken, June 2006. https://ai.googleblog.com/2006/06/extra-extra-read-all-about-it-nearly.html
10. Bornat, R., Calcagno, C., O'Hearn, P., Parkinson, M.: Permission accounting in separation logic. In: Proceedings of the 32nd ACM SIGPLAN-SIGACT Symposium on Principles of Programming Languages, pp. 259–270 (2005)
11. Clippy developers: Clippy: A collection of lints to catch common mistakes and improve your Rust code. https://github.com/rust-lang/rust-clippy
12. Crichton, W.: Flowistry: Information flow for Rust. https://github.com/willcrichton/flowistry
13. Tolnay, D.: Parser for Rust source code (2021). https://crates.io/crates/syn
14. Denis, X., Jourdan, J.H., Marché, C.: The Creusot environment for the deductive verification of Rust programs (2021)
15. Dill, D., Grieskamp, W., Park, J., Qadeer, S., Xu, M., Zhong, E.: Fast and reliable formal verification of smart contracts with the Move prover. arXiv preprint arXiv:2110.08362 (2021)
16. Evans, A.N., Campbell, B., Soffa, M.L.: Is rust used safely by software developers? In: 2020 IEEE/ACM 42nd International Conference on Software Engineering (ICSE), pp. 246–257. IEEE (2020)

17. Facebook: MIRAI: an abstract interpreter for the Rust compiler's mid-level inter-mediate representation. https://github.com/facebookexperimental/MIRAI
18. Garavel, H., Beek, M.H., Pol, J.: The 2020 expert survey on formal methods. In: ter Beek, M.H., Ničković, D. (eds.) FMICS 2020. LNCS, vol. 12327, pp. 3–69. Springer, Cham (2020). https://doi.org/10.1007/978-3-030-58298-2_1
19. Goes, C.: The interblockchain communication protocol: an overview. arXiv preprint arXiv:2006.15918 (2020)
20. Hahn, F.: Rust2Viper: building a static verifier for Rust. Master's thesis, ETH Zurich (2015)
21. Informal Systems Inc. and ibc-rs authors: Rust implementation of the Inter-Blockchain Communication (IBC) protocol (2021). https://docs.rs/ibc
22. Iosif, R., Rogalewicz, A., Vojnar, T.: Deciding entailments in inductive separation logic with tree automata. In: Cassez, F., Raskin, J.-F. (eds.) ATVA 2014. LNCS, vol. 8837, pp. 201–218. Springer, Cham (2014). https://doi.org/10.1007/978-3-319-11936-6_15
23. Ishtiaq, S.S., O'Hearn, P.W.: BI as an assertion language for mutable data structures. In: POPL, pp. 14–26. ACM (2001)
24. Jacobs, B., Smans, J., Philippaerts, P., Vogels, F., Penninckx, W., Piessens, F.: VeriFast: a powerful, sound, predictable, fast verifier for C and Java. In: Bobaru, M., Havelund, K., Holzmann, G.J., Joshi, R. (eds.) NFM 2011. LNCS, vol. 6617, pp. 41–55. Springer, Heidelberg (2011). https://doi.org/10.1007/978-3-642-20398-5_4
25. Jung, R.: The scope of unsafe, January 2016. https://www.ralfj.de/blog/2016/01/09/the-scope-of-unsafe.html
26. Jung, R., Dang, H.H., Kang, J., Dreyer, D.: Stacked borrows: an aliasing model for Rust. Proc. ACM Program. Lang. 4(POPL), 1–32 (2019)
27. Jung, R., Jourdan, J.H., Krebbers, R., Dreyer, D.: RustBelt: securing the foundations of the Rust programming language. Proc. ACM Program. Lang. 2(POPL), 1–34 (2017)
28. Seonghoon, K., et al.: Chrono: Date and Time for Rust (2021). https://docs.rs/chrono
29. Kassios, I.T.: The dynamic frames theory. Formal Aspects Comput. 23(3), 267–289 (2011)
30. Klabnik, S., Nichols, C.: Unsafe Rust (2022). https://doc.rust-lang.org/book/ch19-01-unsafe-rust.html
31. Lindner, M., Aparicius, J., Lindgren, P.: No panic! Verification of Rust programs by symbolic execution. In: 2018 IEEE 16th International Conference on Industrial Informatics (INDIN), pp. 108–114. IEEE (2018)
32. Matsakis, N.D.: Unsafe abstractions (2016). http://smallcultfollowing.com/babysteps/blog/2016/05/23/unsafe-abstractions
33. Matsushita, Y.: Extensible functional-correctness verification of rust programs by the technique of prophecy. Master's thesis, University of Tokyo (2021)
34. Matsushita, Y., Tsukada, T., Kobayashi, N.: RustHorn: CHC-based verification for Rust programs. In: ESOP, pp. 484–514 (2020)
35. Meyer, B.: Design by contract. In: Mandrioli, D., Meyer, B. (eds.) Advances in Object-Oriented Software Engineering, pp. 1–50. Prentice Hall (1991)
36. Miri developers: Miri: An interpreter for Rust's mid-level intermediate representation. https://github.com/rust-lang/miri

37. de Moura, L., Kong, S., Avigad, J., van Doorn, F., von Raumer, J.: The lean theorem prover (system description). In: Felty, A.P., Middeldorp, A. (eds.) CADE 2015. LNCS (LNAI), vol. 9195, pp. 378–388. Springer, Cham (2015). https://doi.org/10.1007/978-3-319-21401-6_26

38. Müller, P., Schwerhoff, M., Summers, A.J.: Viper: a verification infrastructure for permission-based reasoning. In: Jobstmann, B., Leino, K.R.M. (eds.) VMCAI 2016. LNCS, vol. 9583, pp. 41–62. Springer, Heidelberg (2016). https://doi.org/10.1007/978-3-662-49122-5_2

39. O'Hearn, P.: Separation logic. Commun. ACM **62**(2), 86–95 (2019)

40. Parkinson, M.J., Summers, A.J.: The relationship between separation logic and implicit dynamic frames. Log. Methods Comput. Sci. **8**(3:01), 1–54 (2012)

41. Pratt, V.R.: Top down operator precedence. In: Proceedings of the 1st Annual ACM SIGACT-SIGPLAN Symposium on Principles of Programming Languages, pp. 41–51 (1973)

42. Reid, A., Church, L., Flur, S., de Haas, S., Johnson, M., Laurie, B.: Towards making formal methods normal: meeting developers where they are. arXiv preprint arXiv:2010.16345 (2020)

43. Reynolds, J.C.: Separation logic: a logic for shared mutable data structures. In: Proceedings 17th Annual IEEE Symposium on Logic in Computer Science, pp. 55–74. IEEE (2002)

44. Rust-analyzer developers: Rust-analyzer: A Rust compiler front-end for ides. https://github.com/rust-analyzer/rust-analyzer

45. Schwerhoff, M., Summers, A.J.: Lightweight support for magic wands in an automatic verifier. In: 29th European Conference on Object-Oriented Programming (ECOOP 2015), vol. 37, pp. 614–638. Schloss Dagstuhl-Leibniz-Zentrum für Informatik (2015)

46. Schwerhoff, M.H.: Advancing automated, permission-based program verification using symbolic execution. Ph.D. thesis, ETH Zurich (2016)

47. The Prusti Team: Prusti User Guide (2020). https://viperproject.github.io/prusti-dev/user-guide/

48. The Prusti Team: Prusti NFM 2022 Online Appendix (2022). https://github.com/viperproject/prusti-dev/tree/master/prusti-tests/tests/verify_overflow/pass/nfm22

49. The Rust Survey Team: Rust survey 2019 results: Rust blog, April 2020. https://blog.rust-lang.org/2020/04/17/Rust-survey-2019.html

50. Ullrich, S.: Simple verification of Rust programs via functional purification. Master's thesis, Karlsruher Institut für Technologie (KIT) (2016)

51. VanHattum, A., Schwartz-Narbonne, D., Chong, N., Sampson, A.: Verifying dynamic trait objects in Rust (2022)

52. Wolff, F., Bílý, A., Matheja, C., Müller, P., Summers, A.J.: Modular specification and verification of closures in Rust. Proc. ACM Program. Lang. **5**(OOPSLA), 1–29 (2021)

Reachability Analysis for Cyber-Physical Systems: Are We There Yet?

Xin Chen[1] and Sriram Sankaranarayanan[2]([⊠])

[1] University of Dayton, Dayton, USA
[2] University of Colorado Boulder, Boulder, USA
srirams@colorado.EDU

Abstract. Reachability analysis is a fundamental problem in verification that checks for a given model and set of initial states if the system will reach a given set of unsafe states. Its importance lies in the ability to exhaustively explore the behaviors of a model over a finite or infinite time horizon. The problem of reachability analysis for Cyber-Physical Systems (CPS) is especially challenging because it involves reasoning about the continuous states of the system as well as its switching behavior. Each of these two aspects can by itself cause the reachability analysis problem to be undecidable. In this paper, we survey recent progress in this field beginning with the success of hybrid systems with affine dynamics. We then examine the current state-of-the-art for CPS with nonlinear dynamics and those driven by "learning-enabled" components such as neural networks. We conclude with an examination of some promising directions and open challenges.

1 Introduction

Formal verification techniques attempt to exhaustively explore the behaviors of computational models that include *finite state machines* that model sequential circuits and network protocols; *push-down machines* that model function calls/returns in software; *Petri-net models* of concurrent systems or *timed automata* that model the execution of real-time systems. In each of the instances above, the reachability problem asks given a model, an initial set of configurations and a target unsafe set, whether the system starting at some initial state can reach an "unsafe" state in some finite number of steps. A reachability analyzer will either provide a proof that the unsafe set is not reachable or a *witness* execution that shows how to reach an unsafe state starting from an initial state.

Reachability analysis has been a powerful tool for checking properties of hardware circuits and software programs with success stories arising from their ability to discover bugs in these systems or prove their absence through exhaustive verification [20,26,27,40,42,48,68,69,75,117]. Since the early 90s, the formal methods and control theory communities have investigated so-called "hybrid" or "Cyber-Physical Systems" (CPS), that model computation interacting closely with a physical environment. Such systems have been mathematically captured by formalisms such as hybrid automata, that combine the evolution of continuous states through ordinary differential equations (ODEs) with discrete mode switches modeled using finite state automata. CPS include systems from a variety of safety-critical areas such as medical devices,

© Springer Nature Switzerland AG 2022
J. V. Deshmukh et al. (Eds.): NFM 2022, LNCS 13260, pp. 109–130, 2022.
https://doi.org/10.1007/978-3-031-06773-0_6

control systems that help fly airplanes, power systems and autonomous vehicles. Modeling these systems and reasoning about the set of all reachable states can go a long way towards guaranteeing safe operation during deployment.

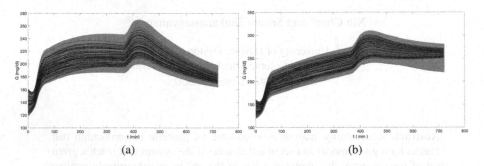

(a)   (b)

Fig. 1. Reachable sets (in gray) showing the possible blood glucose levels of a patient controlled by two different instantiations of an automated insulin infusion algorithm taken from Chen et al. [34]. Simulation trajectories are shown in black. The analysis proves for instance (a) that the blood glucose levels remain below 260 mg/dl over a 24 h period, whereas for instance (b) it is unable to establish that bound.

Consider the block diagram of an insulin infusion control system for patients with type-1 diabetes taken from our previous work [34]. Here, $b(t)$ represents external user commanded insulin, $u(t)$: the insulin infused to patient, $G(t)$, blood glucose level of the patient, $n(t)$: sensor measurement error (noise), $G_s(t)$: glucose level estimated/ reported by sensor, and $u_c(t)$:

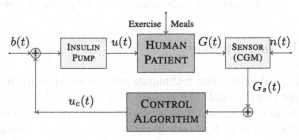

Fig. 2. Block diagram of an insulin infusion control system.

insulin infusion commanded by the algorithm. The patient's blood glucose level is modeled using nonlinear human insulin-glucose model coupled with a controller that switches between various levels of insulin, based on the sensed blood glucose level of the patient. The reachable set estimates computed using the tool Flow* [33] establishes bounds the possible blood glucose levels over a 24 h time period. Such a flowpipe can be used to establish upper and lower bounds on the value of the blood glucose levels as shown in Fig. 1. Further details are available from our ARCH 2017 paper [34] (Fig. 2).

In this paper, we present a brief overview of reachability analysis for Cyber-Physical Systems. We begin by formulating the problem in a formal manner and discuss cases when the problem is known to be decidable along with a brief mention of the broad class of approaches taken to solve the reachability problem. We focus on set-based techniques for systems with linear dynamics wherein powerful tools such as SpaceEx [56] and Hylaa [18] have pushed the state of the art to large hybrid systems with thousands of state variables. We then present some of the approaches for nonlinear systems, while illustrating why the problem is much more challenging when the dynamics are nonlinear. We discuss emerging areas of interest, including reachability analysis for neural networks. This paper is not meant to be an exhaustive survey of results in this area. A recent survey by Althoff et al. is recommended for the reader who wishes to learn more about set-based techniques [4]. The main purposes of this article are to (a) illustrate why the problem is important but challenging; (b) highlight some important approaches to the problem; and (c) highlight a few emerging areas where efficient and precise reachability analysis techniques will play an important role.

2   Hybrid Systems and Reachability Analysis

In this section, we will briefly review some of the fundamental concepts that include (a) models of hybrid (Cyber-Physical) systems; (b) the reachability analysis problem; (c) decidable cases for the problem and (d) a brief overview of existing approaches.

A Brief History: The formal study of hybrid (Cyber-Physical) systems was initiated in the early 1990s from the computer science and the control communities. In the controls community, the consideration of hybrid control systems began in the late 1980s as an attempt to formalize supervisory control wherein discrete-event systems are used to represent "higher level" decision making which may switch between multiple "lower level" control strategies to interact with a continuous plant [13]. Early modeling efforts for such systems include the work of Peleties and DeCarlo [97], Gollu and Varaiya [64] and Benveniste and Le Guernic [22]. In the computer science community, the problem of modeling and reasoning about reactive systems naturally led to the consideration of timed systems followed by hybrid systems [88]. The timed-automaton model of Alur and Dill augments automata with finitely many clocks that can trigger transitions between states which may in turn reset these clocks [10,11]. Hybrid systems can then be modeled augmenting these further with physical quantities that evolve according to simple differential equations [8,89,96].

The hybrid automaton model was proposed in order to unify the continuous evolution of state variables with switching due to mode changes within a single formalism. Detailed descriptions are available elsewhere [7,84,114].

Example 1. Figure 3 illustrates a hybrid automaton with four modes $\{m_1, \ldots, m_4\}$, continuous state variables $\{x_1, x_2, x_3\}$ and an external time-varying disturbance input w lying in the range $[-0.25, 0.25]$. The dynamics inside each mode and the transitions between modes are also shown. The transitions are defined by guards and reset maps, as shown in the figure. The figure also shows 5000 trajectories with randomly sampled initial conditions starting from mode m_1 and $x_1 \in [0.3, 0.5], x_2 \in [0.2, 0.4], x_3 \in [0, 0.4]$ with the disturbance in the range $[-0.25, 0.25]$. Each mode is shown in a different color. We note that only 6 out of the 5000 trajectories reach mode m_2 (green).

The example above shows the need for exhaustive simulations, since "corner case behaviors" that violate safety properties are often a concern. We have encountered more

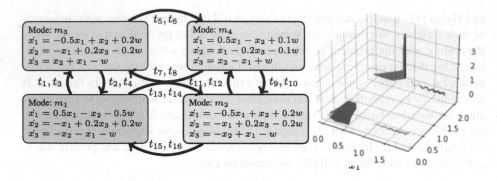

IDs	Guard	Reset	IDs	Guard	Reset
t_1, t_{11}	$x_2 \geq 1$	none	t_2, t_9	$x_2 \leq 1$	none
t_3, t_{12}	$x_2 \leq 0$	$x_2 := 1.9, x_3 := 0$	t_4, t_{10}	$x_2 \geq 2$	$x_2 := 0.1, x_3 := 0$
t_5, t_{13}	$x_1 \geq 1$	none	t_7, t_{15}	$x_1 \leq 1$	none
t_6, t_{14}	$x_1 \leq 0$	$x_1 := 1.9, x_3 := 0$	t_8, t_{16}	$x_1 \geq 2$	$x_1 := 0.1, x_3 := 0$

Fig. 3. Description of hybrid automaton and randomly simulated trajectories.

realistic systems wherein nearly 100 million random simulations do not expose a safety violation that can be discovered quite easily by a more exhaustive approach [121].

2.1 Reachability Analysis

Rather than rely on finitely many simulations, we wish to exhaustively explore the set of reachable states of a hybrid system, in order to decide if a given set of unsafe states is reachable starting from a set of initial conditions. This is known as the *reachability analysis* problem.

Definition 1 (Reachability Problem). *Given a hybrid system $\mathcal{H}$, initial set of states X_0, unsafe set X_u and time horizon T, is there any trajectory that starts from some state in X_0 and reaches some state in X_u, within the given time horizon T?*

The reachability analysis problems can be *finite time horizon* problems where T is finite, or *infinite time horizon* problems if $T = \infty$. Naturally, the latter class of problems are harder than the former. Although a finite time horizon seems restrictive, there are many reasons why it is important: (a) often, it is known that failures would manifest within a finite time horizon if at all; (b) in many cases the reachability analysis problem has uncertain time varying parameters that makes the model invalid for infinite time horizons; or (c) the infinite time horizon problem is often harder to solve than the finite time horizon problem.

Reachability analysis is a fundamental verification problem for hybrid systems. Important correctness properties of hybrid systems are naturally posed as safety properties. Reachability analysis can also be used as a primitive step for reasoning about more complex liveness properties. Therefore, the question of decidability of reachability problem is of great interest. Unfortunately, it is known that the reachability analysis problem is undecidable for all but the simplest classes of hybrid systems.

Asarin, Maler and Pnueli showed that hybrid systems with piece-wise constant dynamics (the simplest dynamics possible) already have an undecidable reachability problems for systems with 3 or more state variables [15]. Specifically, their model considers a partitioning of the state-space by convex polyhedra where each partition has its dynamics of the form $\dot{\vec{x}} = \vec{c}$ for a fixed $\vec{c}$. At the same time, the reachability analysis problem is undecidable for non-linear dynamical systems without any switching [94]. The finite time horizon reachability problem for linear dynamical systems (also known as the "continuous Skolem-Pisot problem" [21]) has been shown to be decidable provided an open number-theoretic conjecture called the Schaunel conjecture is true [36]. Broadly, we note that undecidability arises separately from the presence of switching between modes even if the dynamics are simple, or just from the continuous dynamics themselves without switching. The reachability problem for systems combining both switching and linear/non-linear dynamics is thus a computationally hard problem.

In the past three decades since these results, a number of sub-classes of hybrid automata have been identified for which the reachability problem is decidable, starting with Henzinger et al. [71] who defined the class of *initialized rectangular hybrid automata*. Subsequently, O-minimal hybrid systems that allow for a more general class of dynamics in each mode were introduced by Laffarriere et al. [82]. These have been generalized by Vladimerou et al. [118]. In general, decidability results place restrictions on the form of transitions between modes as well as the dynamics in each mode. These restrictions ensure that the resulting system has a finite bisimulation quotient which can be used to check any temporal logic property. However, such restrictions are often not met by the systems which we are interested in reasoning about. As a result, numerous approaches attempt to solve the reachability problem by *over-approximating* the reachable set of states, or proposing a semi-algorithm that may not terminate in the worst case. The former class of approaches can help us conclude that the unsafe states are not reachable but fail to provide concrete counterexamples, whereas the latter class of approaches can fail by exhausting computational resources. We will now summarize a few approaches for solving the reachability analysis problem.

Abstraction-Based Techniques: The goal is to construct a finite-state abstraction that can be refined, possibly using counterexamples. Once the abstraction is constructed, we solve the reachability problem on this abstraction. If the unsafe set in the abstract state-space cannot be reached, we conclude the same for the original system. However, abstract counterexamples can be *spurious*: i.e., they need not correspond to a real execution of the concrete system. This can be addressed by refining the abstraction to rule away such counterexamples [9,12,41,61]. Interestingly, the abstractions need not necessarily be finite state. For instance, Prabhakar et al. present an approach that considers rectangular hybrid automata as abstractions [102]. Hybridization is yet another approach that relies on locally abstracting nonlinear dynamics by linear dynamics while accounting for the error [46]. Abstraction-based approaches are quite versatile since they can be applied to a large class of hybrid systems with nonlinear dynamics. However, these approaches typically resort to tiling the state-space into discrete cells in order to handle complex nonlinear dynamics. This often limits the number of state variables that can be treated by these techniques.

Dynamic Programming (Hamilton-Jacobi) Approaches: In this approach, the more general problem of controlling a hybrid system (with control and disturbance inputs) is considered as a game between two players. The goal is to characterize a controllable region (termed as the viability kernel), a subset of the state-space which excludes the undesired set of states, such that the controller can keep the system within this region no matter what disturbance signal is applied. This approach was proposed by Lygeros, Tomlin and Sastry [85], and leads to a partial differential equation (PDE) that needs to be solved in order to compute the controllable region. Subsequent work by Mitchell and Tomlin uses level-set methods to solve this PDE [92,93]. The dynamic programming approach is quite powerful: it applies to nonlinear systems and can compute a set of control strategies for guaranteeing safety. We note, however, that the reachability problems we have considered thus far do not involve control inputs. However, solving PDEs requires expensive numerical methods whose complexity can be exponential in the number of state variables.

Deductive Approaches: Deductive approaches are based on proving that the unsafe states are unreachable from the initial set by obtaining *(positive) invariant sets* of the hybrid system, and proving that these sets contain the initial set but exclude the unsafe set. Such invariants can be synthesized automatically using techniques from optimization and algebraic geometry [60,103,110,115]. However, invariant construction techniques are quite limited in the kind of systems that can be proven correct. In general, they play a supporting role inside a theorem prover that is built on top of a logic that supports reasoning about hybrid systems. The work of Platzer et al. has constructed the rich framework of differential dynamic logic [99,101] and integrated this inside a theorem prover Keymaera [98,100]. In general, deductive approaches can prove that unsafe sets are not reachable. It is incumbent upon the user to deduce how the failure of a proof can lead to the construction of a counterexample.

Set-Propagation: Set propagation approaches rely on a chosen family of sets to represent sets of states (examples include ellipsoids, polyhedra, Taylor models) [4]. At each step, the reachable set is represented as a union of sets in this family. These algorithms propagate these sets for a small time step Δ so that an approximation that is valid for time up to t is now valid for time up to $t + \Delta$. By repeatedly iterating this process, an over-approximation of the reachable sets up to a finite time horizon T is produced. Set propagation techniques have been investigated extensively for linear systems beginning with the pioneering work on the tool HyTech for rectangular hybrid automata [70] and followed by a quick succession of approaches for richer classes of hybrid systems permitting nonlinear dynamics [14,112]. Currently, set propagation techniques are capable of analyzing linear dynamical systems with more than a billion state variables [19], linear hybrid systems with hundreds of state-variables [56] and nonlinear systems with tens of state variables [33]. Due to the over-approximate nature of these techniques, they are unable to produce concrete counter-example. Furthermore, these approaches are mostly restricted to finite time horizon problems.

However, there are successful reachability analysis techniques that fail to fit neatly into any of the categories above, or deserve to be described on their own.

Constraint Solving Approaches: An important class of approaches uses constraint solvers to show that no counterexample trace with a given length/time bound exists for a reachability problem. Ratschan and She achieve this by constructing an abstraction that is refined using ideas borrowed from constraint programming [105]. Franzle et al. use a bounded-model checking approach that encodes the reachability problem as a set of constraints [55,72]. More recently, Kong et al. build on top of their previous work on the dReal solver for nonlinear constraints [57] to build a reachability analyzer called dReach [80]. An important advantage of constraint solvers lies in their ability to search in a *non chronological* manner. I.e, they can search for counterexamples or prove their absence without necessarily having to start from time $t = 0$. However, the same factors that make the problem challenging hamper their performance. For one, the ability to reason about dynamical systems inside a constraint solver is a challenge. dReach uses other reachability analysis tools for nonlinear dynamical systems to approximate the solution to ODEs. Another challenge lies in choosing how to iteratively subdivide a large state-space during constraint solving in order to zero in on a counterexample or rule out counterexamples altogether.

Falsification: Whereas most approaches cited so far focus on *verification*, which is typically defined as "the process of establishing the truth, accuracy, or validity of something", approaches for *falsification* focus on disproving correctness by searching for a counterexample that establishes that an unsafe state is reachable starting from some initial state. Recently, there have been many approaches towards falsification based on using robustness of trajectory (its minimum distance to the unsafe set) as a fitness function that is minimized repeatedly using optimization [1]. Although they do not have guarantees of exhaustiveness, falsification techniques have been more successful in the industry wherein they provide a form of "smart fuzz-testing" for CPS [49,78].

3 Set-Propagation Approaches

In this section, we present the so-called set propagation approach for solving the reachability analysis problem. These approaches construct an over-approximation of the reachable set by (a) choosing a family of set representations such as ellipsoids to over-approximate sets of states; and (b) iteratively propagating the reachable state over-approximation forward in time according to the semantics of the hybrid automaton. Rather than attempt an exhaustive survey, we will briefly describe these approaches and highlight some of the successes. As mentioned earlier, a comprehensive survey of many of these techniques is available elsewhere [4]. Set-propagation approaches are analogous to techniques such as symbolic model checking and abstract interpretation that are commonly used for verifying digital circuits and computer software [16,45].

3.1 Linear Hybrid Systems

Linear Hybrid Systems (LHS) are characterized by multiple modes (also known as locations) and continuous states $\vec{x}$. A configuration, also called a state, of an LHS is denoted by a pair $(\vec{x}, \ell)$ such that $\vec{x}$ is the current valuation of the state variables and ℓ is the current location. Starting from an initial state, an LHS evolves in the following way.

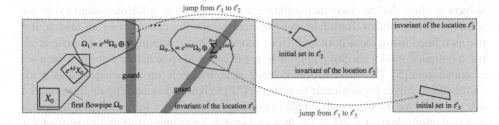

Fig. 4. Flowpipe construction for LHS.

Continuous Evolution. The state variable values change continuously within the location invariant under the continuous dynamics which is a linear ODE in the form of $\dot{x} = A\vec{x} + B\vec{w}$ associated with the current location. The parameters $\vec{w}$ are used to represent range-bounded uncertainties if there is any, and the invariant is defined by a conjunction of linear constraints over $\vec{x}$. In a continuous evolution, the location of the system does not change, and the values of $\vec{x}$ should satisfy the invariant.

Discrete Jump. The discrete dynamics of an LHS is defined by a set of transitions. The system instantly updates its current location according to the specification of a transition. More precisely, a transition can be made by satisfying the following requirements: (a) The current and new locations should be the start and end locations respectively of the transition; (b) The current state variable values should satisfy the transition *guard* which is defined by a conjunction of linear constraints over $\vec{x}$. A transition may also update the state variables $\vec{x}$ according to its linear reset rule.

Set-propagation approaches for LHS compute reachable sets for a bounded time horizon $[0, T]$[1]. We illustrate the main algorithm in Fig. 4. Starting from a given initial state set X_0, the algorithm first over-approximates the reachable set by a convex set Ω_0 in the time interval of $[0, \delta]$ which is called the first time step according to a given step size $\delta > 0$. Next, we iteratively compute the sets $\Omega_1, \ldots, \Omega_{N-1}$, that are over-approximations of the reachable sets over the time intervals $[\delta, 2\delta], \ldots, [(N-1)\delta, N\delta]$, respectively, until $N\delta \geq T$. This step is usually done by repeatedly computing the flowpipes using the recurrent relation $\Omega_i = e^{A\delta}\Omega_{i-1} \oplus V$ wherein V is a convex set containing the impact from all uncertainties in a one-step evolution. When there is an invariant associated to the location, the flowpipes should also be intersected with it in order to exclude the unreachable states outside of the invariant. Finally, we compute over-approximations for the reachable sets under all possible discrete jumps, which

---

[1] Such reachable sets are often called flowpipes following the early work of Feng Zhao [120].

themselves form initial sets in new locations. The algorithm repeatedly performs the three steps mentioned above, until all of executions in the time horizon are explored.

In order to represent sets, existing approaches use geometric objects such as polytopes [39,66,70,109], zonotopes [62] and ellipsoids [81], or symbolic representations for convex sets such as support functions [83]. These representations are closed under key operations that are performed by the reachability algorithms, including linear transformation and Minkowski sum in computing the recurrence relation. However, it is still challenging to handle discrete jumps, the main difficulty comes from the computation of the intersection with transition guards. Although a few of the representations such as polytopes are closed under intersections with sets defined by linear constraints, no representation can efficiently perform all the required set operations. Hence, much effort has been devoted to developing effective and efficient over-approximation algorithms for various intersection types, including ellipsoid/ellipsoid intersections [106], zonotope/hyperplane intersections [63], zonotope/polyhedron [3,5], and support function/support function [65]. The approaches are integrated into verification tools such as SpaceEx [56] and CORA [2].

Besides the above set-based approaches, a novel approach by Duggirala et al. focuses on producing approximations at discrete time points using numerical simulations and the super-position principle for linear dynamics [51]. Such a technique is used in the tool Hylaa [18].

3.2   Nonlinear Hybrid Systems

NonLinear Hybrid Systems (NLHS) have an analogous structure to LHS except that the continuous dynamics may be defined by nonlinear ODEs, the guards and invariants may be defined by nonlinear constraints, and the reset rules of the jumps may also be nonlinear. Due to these nonlinearities, the reachability analysis on NLHS calls for a different class of approaches. The challenges are from answering the following two questions: *(i) How to compute the flowpipes for nonlinear ODEs?* and *(ii) How to compute nonlinear flowpipe/guard intersections?* We may categorize existing approaches as follows:

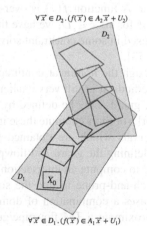

$\forall \vec{x} \in D_2 . (f(\vec{x}) \in A_2\vec{x} + U_2)$

$\forall \vec{x} \in D_1 . (f(\vec{x}) \in A_1\vec{x} + U_1)$

Fig. 5. Illustration of conservative linearization for nonlinear ODEs

Conservative Linearization of ODEs: It has already been shown that flowpipes for nonlinear ODEs can be effectively computed by repeatedly calling the following steps: (1) Conservatively linearizing the ODE to a range-bounded linear differential inclusion in the form of $\dot{\vec{x}} \in A\vec{x} + U$ in a local neighborhood in the state space; (2) Computing the flowpipes for the linear differential inclusion in the neighborhood. The algorithm goes to the step (1) with the last flowpipe which almost exceeds the neighborhood.

Althoff et al. [6] presented a framework that computing the reachable sets for a nonlinear system by conservatively linearizing the ODE on the fly. The linearization error is controlled by splitting the reachable sets. A more complex framework for over-approximating a nonlinear ODE by an LHS, which is also called *hybridization*, is presented by Dang et al. [46,47]. The approach computes bounded state subspaces which are called *hybridization domain* along the system executions, and linearizes the dynamics in those subspaces. Then the flowpipes can be obtained using an existing method for linear dynamics. Figure 5 illustrates hybridization approach. The flowpipes for the nonlinear ODE $\dot{\vec{x}} = f(\vec{x})$ are computed based on two linear differential inclusions, each of which is an over-approximation of the nonlinear dynamics in its hybridization domain.

Verified Set-Valued Integration: Verified integration are set-based techniques which were introduced to provide guaranteed solutions for *initial value problems*: i.e., find $\vec{x}(t)$ for some time $t > 0$ for an ODE defined by $\dot{\vec{x}} = f(\vec{x}, t)$ with an initial condition $\vec{x}(0) \in X_0$. The main idea of the techniques is to iteratively compute a reachable set over-approximation over a time step. In each integration step, starting from the over-approximation set obtained at the end of the previous step, a new set which is guaranteed to contain the reachable set in the current step is computed by a set-based arithmetic such as interval arithmetic, and then verified by ensuring the contractiveness of the Picard operator over the set [91]. Several well-developed interval-based integration methods have already been implemented and released as tools such as VNODE-LP [95] and CAPD [77]. In order to better control the overestimation, Berz and Makino [25,87] developed the Taylor model-based integration approach. A *Taylor Model (TM)* is denoted by a pair (p, I) such that p is a polynomial and I is an interval remainder. A function $f(\vec{x})$ is over-approximated by a TM $(p(\vec{x}), I)$ over an interval domain, if for all $\vec{x} \in D$, we have that $f(\vec{x}) \in p(\vec{x}) + I$. Verified integration methods are also used in some constraint solving-based verification tools such as iSAT [54] and dReach [58].

Although the nonlinear continuous dynamics of an NLHS can be handled by the above methods, it is still very challenging to deal with the flowpipe/guard intersections since the guards may be defined by nonlinear constraints. Many reachability analysis frameworks or tools compute these intersections by constraint solving. Ariadne [23,24] uses intervals which are obtained from merging the interval solutions of the constraints defining the guard and flowpipes. In [104], Ramdani and Nedialkov described a method to compute an intersection by solving a constraint satisfiability problem, and use branch-and-prune to find the solution boxes. The method developed by Chen et al. [32] uses a combination of domain contraction and range over-approximation to over-approximate a TM flowpipe/guard intersection by a TM, and it is later implemented in the tool Flow* [33].

Besides, some other approaches such as the technique implemented in the tool C2E2 [50] which uses set propagation method under the hood but simulates trajectories to construct discrepancy functions.

We have briefly described reachability analysis techniques based on set-propagation in this section. Whereas the approaches for linear hybrid systems can now be considered *mature* by most reasonable standards, the same cannot be said for general nonlinear hybrid systems. For instance, our own tool Flow* supports many different heuristic strategies for computing reachable sets efficiently. The choice of such a strategy requires setting time steps, polynomial orders, aggregation heuristics and many other details that are internal to the algorithm. However, different choices of these parameters yield vastly different results in terms of computation speed and the overestimation error in the results. Understanding the interplay between these parameters will help improve the usability of nonlinear reachability analysis techniques.

4   Scaling up Reachability Analysis

In this section, we briefly describe some novel approaches that have been applied to scale up reachability analysis, especially for nonlinear systems. As discussed previously, the work of Bak et al. cleverly exploits the sparsity in the system's dynamics as well as the properties of the initial and unsafe sets to compute the projections of the reachable sets over linear systems with billions of state variables [19]. In this section, we will discuss some recent work on scaling up reachability analysis.

Exploiting Monotonicity: Monotone systems are those where there is a partial order between states in the state-space such that if $\vec{x}(0) \preceq \vec{y}(0)$ for two initial states, then $\vec{x}(t) \preceq \vec{y}(t)$ for the respective trajectories encountered starting from these initial states. Monotonicity is natural in many types of systems such as traffic networks. Coogan and Arcak show how monotone systems lend themselves to efficient computation of abstractions that can be used to solve reachability analysis problems [43,44]. In fact, their work also extends the classic notion of monotonicity to apply to a wider class of systems. Under these monotonicity assumptions, it can be shown that the reachable set for a hyper-rectangular set is obtained precisely by simulating two diagonally opposite corner points. As a result, it is possible to solve verification problems for monotone systems with large state spaces.

Exploiting Symmetries: Another approach that exploits special structure in the system concerns symmetries in the system description. These symmetries can be discrete symmetries wherein permutations of the state variables can lead to the original system back. The permutations define an equivalence class amongst the state variables, and therefore, a smaller system can be obtained by "lumping" system variables together in a natural manner. This approach has been shown to work for nonlinear systems derived from gene regulatory networks [28]. However, its application requires that the initial conditions of the lumped variables agree with each other. Another approach considers continuous (Lie) symmetries, including invariance of the system's dynamics to translations and rotations of the coordinate frames. This is a powerful approach that can be exploited to speed up reachability analysis. Maidens and Arcak exploit symmetries for backward reachability in order to synthesize controllers using the dynamic programming framework [86]. A different approach to ensuring efficiency by exploiting symmetry is considered by Sibai et al. [111], particularly for the case when a system involves multiple agents. Their approach uses previously caches reachable set computations: for instance, some set $X_{t+\Delta}$ is reachable from some other set X_t in time Δ.

Symmetry allows us to reuse this information for a different set Y that may not be the same as X_t but related to it through a transformation. An almost identical approach was also adopted (independently) by the second author jointly with Chou and Yoon, wherein they show how reachable sets can be pre-computed offline in order to support rapid table lookups to perform predictive runtime monitoring [38]. This approach was designed specifically to exploit invariance to rotation and translations for vehicle models.

Decompositions Based on System Structure: Decompositions are a very promising approach to reducing reachability problems for systems over higher dimensional state-spaces into problems that involve multiple systems over a subset of the state variables. The key idea is to consider how the state-variables in the dynamics depend on each other through a dependency graph.

Figure 6 shows an example of a Dubin's vehicle with a "sampled-data" control strategy where the control inputs u_1, u_2 are computed using the state at a previous time step. Therefore, for the duration of a time step Δ, they may be thought of as a constant. Thus, instead of considering 4 state variables together, the reachability algorithm can separately integrate the subsystems for ψ, v and use these in turn to separately compute reachable set estimates for x, y. These are effectively systems with a sin-

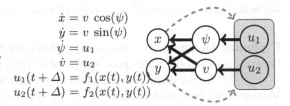

$$\dot{x} = v \, \cos(\psi)$$
$$\dot{y} = v \, \sin(\psi)$$
$$\dot{\psi} = u_1$$
$$\dot{v} = u_2$$
$$u_1(t + \Delta) = f_1(x(t), y(t))$$
$$u_2(t + \Delta) = f_2(x(t), y(t))$$

Fig. 6. A 2 dimensional Dubin's vehicle model and its dependency graph. The dashed line shows feedback from the vehicle position at a previous time step to the control inputs at the subsequent time step.

gle state variable. This idea was considered independently by Mo Chen et al. [29,30] in the context of the Hamilton-Jacobi approach and by the authors of this paper in the context of nonlinear set-based reachability [35]. In both cases, a dependency graph is constructed and decomposed into strongly connected components. Furthermore, our work also focused on approximate methods by "cutting" continuous feedback loops. Decomposition methods are very powerful in that they allow us to treat "loosely coupled" systems with hundreds of state variables. Recently, Sankaranarayanan used a tree-width decomposition approach to consider overlapping partitions of the system variables. The system is then projected into multiple abstract subsystems each involving one of the partitions. The key idea is that the partitions can exchange information using an algorithm inspired by belief propagation [108].

Although, we have presented a few promising approaches to scaling up reachability analysis, there are currently numerous challenges that require new approaches. We mention a few promising areas for future work.

Model Order Reductions: The reachability problem for large CPS often involve safety properties that are expressed over very few system variables. It is thus interesting to consider techniques akin to model-order reductions that can speed up reachability analysis. Model-order reductions have been explored in the past by using standard approaches in that area to reduce the dimensionality of the state-space [37,67]. However, these approaches do not preserve soundness. Recent approaches that have exploited the fact that initial conditions and unsafe sets involve a few of the system variables with great success and without sacrificing soundness for linear dynamical systems [19]. A new general approach to such reductions that allows us to avoid computing reachability information for "unnecessary" state variables in a sound manner is needed.

Koopman Operator-Based Linearization: Another promising approach is to convert linear systems into nonlinear systems in a higher dimensional space through the theory of Koopman operators [90]. The key idea here is to consider a new state-space in terms of functions $\{f_1(\vec{x}), \ldots, f_N(\vec{x})\}$ wherein the derivative of each f_i can be written as an affine function of the other functions. This helps us abstract the trajectories of the system by a linear system. Reachability analysis over this system gives us reachable set over-approximations of the original nonlinear systems. The key here is to discover appropriate basis functions f_i (so-called Koopman invariant subspace), and there is no guarantee that these functions will be polynomials. Earlier work by Sankaranarayanan explored an iterative approach to discovering a basis where f_i are all polynomials [107]. However, there is no guarantee that such a basis would exist. More recently, Bak et al. present an algorithm that assumes that a Koopman-invariant subspace is known or approximated through techniques such as dynamic mode decomposition. It then shows how the resulting reachability analysis problem can be solved [17]. In general, ideas such as Koopman operator-based linearization provide alternatives to existing ways of abstracting nonlinear dynamics which could be an interesting way forward to make reachability analysis more scalable.

5   Neural Network Controlled Systems

With the rapid development of machine learning techniques, more and more CPS are using learning-enabled components such as neural networks for making decisions in strategic situations. Since most of such learning-enabled CPS are safety-critical, it is important to develop new methods for ensuring their safety. However, most of the verification methods developed for pure discrete or even hybrid systems can hardly be applied due to the complex system behavior produced by the interaction between the learning-enabled components and the others.

Recently, a great amount of work has been devoted to developing new formal methods for verifying *neural network controlled systems (NNCS)* which are a basic class of learning-enabled CPS but very challenging to verify. Figure 7 shows the formal model of NNCS. It is a class of sampled-data systems in which the plant, i.e., the continuous dynamics, is defined by an ODE over the state variable(s) x and the control input(s) u, while the controller is a *Feed-forward Neural Network (FNN)*. Given a control step size $\delta_c > 0$, at the time $t = k\delta_c$ for every $k = 0, 1, \ldots$, the controller reads the current state of the plant and computes the control input which will be used immediately for δ_c-time, i.e., in the current control step, by the plant. Since a control input is obtained from the

FNN, the computation time is ignored in the system execution due to the fast response
of neural networks.

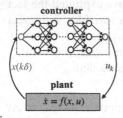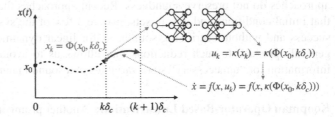

Fig. 7. Model of NNCS   **Fig. 8.** Dependency on the initial state

NNCS are continuous systems but not necessarily differentiable due to the non-differentiable activation functions such as ReLU in the neural networks. Given an NNCS, the system execution from an initial state x_0 is deterministic and can be defined by a flow map function Φ such that $\Phi(x_0, t)$ denotes the system state at a future time $t \geq 0$. According to the behavior of NNCS, for $k = 0, 1, \ldots, x_k = \Phi(x_0, k\delta_c)$ is the initial state of the $(k+1)$-st control step, and the control input used in that step is derived as $u_k = \kappa(x_k)$ wherein $\kappa(\cdot)$ denotes the input-output mapping of the FNN controller. Hence, not only the reachable states but also the control inputs in a system execution are determined by the initial state x_0. Figure 8 illustrates the dependency between a reachable state and the initial state. In the case of a set X_0 of initial states, the exact reachable set at a time $t \geq 0$ is denoted by $\Phi(X_0, t) = \{\Phi(x_0, t) \mid x_0 \in X_0\}$, and the set of the control inputs used in the $(k + 1)$-st step is given by $U_k = \kappa(X_k)$ wherein $X_k = \Phi(X_0, k\delta_c)$. The core technique in a reachability analysis approach for NNCS is an algorithm to over-approximate the range of the flow map Φ over a time interval w.r.t. a given set of initial states.

Most of the existing reachability analysis methods use a set-propagation scheme to compute over-approximate reachable set segments, i.e., flowpipes, over a finite number K of control steps. Starting with a given initial set $\hat{X}_0 = X_0$, the main algorithm repeatedly performs the following two steps to compute the flowpipes in the $(k + 1)$-st control step for $k = 0, 1, \ldots, K - 1$:

(i) *Computing the output range of the controller.* In this step, a set $\hat{U}_k$ which is guaranteed to contain all of the control inputs in U_k is computed.

(ii) *Flowpipe computation for the plant.* The step computes the flowpipes for the plant ODE $\dot{x} = f(x, u)$ with the local initial set $\hat{X}_k$ and the control input range $u \in \hat{U}_k$. Then the local initial set of the next iteration is computed as $\hat{X}_{k+1}$ which is an over-approximation of $\Phi(X_0, (k + 1)\delta_c)$.

They can be classified as follows, based on the over-approximation schemes.

Directly Over-Approximating Reachable Sets. A reachability analysis algorithm on NNCS can be developed as a combination use of a method for computing FNN output ranges and an existing flowpipe construction technique for ODEs. To do so, one may need to use a uniform set representation for FNN output ranges and ODE flowpipes. Many FNN output ranges analysis techniques [53,59,74,79,116,119] can be extended and work cooperatively with the existing reachability tools for ODEs [2,33,95]. The main advantage of this scheme is twofold. Firstly, there is no need to develop a new technique from scratch, and the correctness of the composed approach can be proved easily based on the correctness of the existing methods. Secondly, the performance of the approach is often good since it can use well engineered tools as primitives. However, on the other hand, the relationship between the control inputs and the plant states (see Fig. 8) are not explicitly represented in this approach. This may lead to a overestimation when the plant dynamics is nonlinear or the initial set is large, making the resulting bounds less useful in proving properties of interest.

Over-Approximating Flow Map Functions. More accurate over-approximations can be obtained if a reachability method tries to over-approximate the flow map function Φ instead of its image. It is well-known that functional over-approximations such as TMs have an apparent advantage in accuracy over the pure range over-approximation methods for nonlinear dynamical systems [31]. Recent work has applied interval, polynomial and TM arithmetic to obtain over-approximations for NNCS flow maps [52,73,76]. Those techniques are often able to compute more accurate flowpipes than the methods in Category (A). On the other hand, the functional over-approximation methods are often computationally expensive due to the computation of nonlinear multivariate polynomials for tracking the dependencies.

Neural Network Control Systems are an emerging area that has seen an explosion of interest in the recent years. Persistent challenges include the need to handle ever larger networks and also the need to integrate rich sensor inputs from sensors such as camera and LiDAR. This poses a hard modeling challenge that requires us to link the state of the system with the possible inputs that these sensors may provide. The work of Shoukry et al. presents an interesting case for solving this challenge when the system's operating environment is known [113]. This paper represents a very promising line of work that can benefit from further investigation.

6 Conclusions

We have thus far introduced a wide variety of techniques that have been explored for solving the reachability analysis of CPS, integrating ideas from diverse disciplines, ranging from Logic to control theory. We have also briefly surveyed exciting new frontiers, including the emerging topic of verifying safety of systems controlled by neural networks. While it is clear that the research on reachability analysis techniques have come a long way, numerous challenges remain. For one, many of the techniques remain inaccessible to control engineers due to many reasons. There is a gap between the rich expressive modeling formalisms that are used by engineers such as Simulink/Stateflow, and the capabilities of existing reachability analysis tools that work on hybrid automata models. The translation from one to another is not simple. Tools like C2E2 are seeking to bridge this gap by allowing model specifications inside Stateflow [50], but more needs to happen along this front before such tools can be said to be developer friendly. Besides these practical concerns, there are numerous open challenges and new frontiers. One such area that has not been mentioned in this survey concerns the reachability analysis of stochastic hybrid systems. Another open area concerns reachability analysis for systems whose feedback control inputs are specified in an *implicit manner*: i.e., they are specified as minimizers of some cost functions. Such systems arise from many domains such as model-predictive control algorithms or physics-based models that are described using potential fields.

To conclude, we revisit the question in the title *"Are we there yet?"*. Briefly, we would conclude at this time that reachability analysis of CPS has *gone places* without yet arriving at a destination!

Acknowledgments. We thank Klaus Havelund for helpful comments and suggestions. Sankaranarayanan gratefully acknowledges support from the NSF through award numbers 1815983, 1836900 and 1932189. Chen gratefully acknowledges the support from the US Air Force Research Laboratory (AFRL) under contract FA8650-16-C-2642. All opinions are those of the authors and not necessarily of NSF or AFRL.

References

1. Abbas, H., Fainekos, G., Sankaranarayanan, S., Ivancic, F., Gupta, A.: Probabilistic temporal logic falsification of cyber-physical systems. ACM Trans. Embedded Comput. Syst. (TECS) **12**(12s), 95 (2013)
2. Althoff, M.: An introduction to CORA 2015. In: Proceedings of ARCH 2015, EPiC Series in Computer Science, vol. 34, pp. 120–151. EasyChair (2015)
3. Althoff, M., Stursberg, O., Buss, M.: Computing reachable sets of hybrid systems using a combination of zonotopes and polytopes. Nonlinear Anal. Hybrid Syst **4**(2), 233–249 (2010)
4. Althoff, M., Frehse, G., Girard, A.: Set propagation techniques for reachability analysis. Annu. Rev. Control Robot. Auton. Syst. **4**, 369–395 (2021)
5. Althoff, M., Krogh, B.H.: Avoiding geometric intersection operations in reachability analysis of hybrid systems. In: Proceedings of HSCC 2012, pp. 45–54. ACM (2012)
6. Althoff, M., Stursberg, O., Buss, M.: Reachability analysis of nonlinear systems with uncertain parameters using conservative linearization. In: Proceedings of CDC 2008, pp. 4042–4048. IEEE (2008)
7. Alur, R.: Principles of Cyber-Physical Systems. MIT Press, Cambridge (2015)
8. Alur, R., Courcoubetis, C., Henzinger, T.A., Ho, P.-H.: Hybrid automata: an algorithmic approach to the specification and verification of hybrid systems. In: Grossman, R.L., Nerode, A., Ravn, A.P., Rischel, H. (eds.) HS 1991-1992. LNCS, vol. 736, pp. 209–229. Springer, Heidelberg (1993). https://doi.org/10.1007/3-540-57318-6_30
9. Alur, R., Dang, T., Ivančićl, F.: Counter-example guided predicate abstraction of hybrid systems. In: Garavel, H., Hatcliff, J. (eds.) TACAS 2003. LNCS, vol. 2619, pp. 208–223. Springer, Heidelberg (2003). https://doi.org/10.1007/3-540-36577-X_15
10. Alur, R., Dill, D.: Automata for modeling real-time systems. In: Paterson, M.S. (ed.) ICALP 1990. LNCS, vol. 443, pp. 322–335. Springer, Heidelberg (1990). https://doi.org/10.1007/BFb0032042
11. Alur, R., Dill, D.L.: A theory of timed automata. Theoret. Comput. Sci. **126**, 183–235 (1994)

12. Alur, R., Henzinger, T.A., Lafferriere, G., Pappas, G.: Discrete abstractions of hybrid systems. Proc. IEEE **88**(7), 971–984 (2000)
13. Antsaklis, P.J., Passino, K.M., Wang, S.J.: An introduction to autonomous control systems. IEEE Control Syst. Mag. **11**(4), 5–13 (1991)
14. Asarin, E., Dang, T., Maler, O.: The d/dt tool for verification of hybrid systems. In: Brinksma, E., Larsen, K.G. (eds.) CAV 2002. LNCS, vol. 2404, pp. 365–370. Springer, Heidelberg (2002). https://doi.org/10.1007/3-540-45657-0_30
15. Asarin, E., Maler, O., Pnueli, A.: Reachability analysis of dynamical systems having piecewise-constant derivatives. Theoret. Comput. Sci. **138**, 35–66 (1995)
16. Baier, C., Katoen, J.-P.: Principles of Model Checking. MIT Press, Cambridge (2008)
17. Bak, S., Bogomolov, S., Duggirala, P.S., Gerlach, A.R., Potomkin, K.: Reachability of black-box nonlinear systems after Koopman operator linearization. In: Analysis and Design of Hybrid Systems (ADHS), IFAC-PapersOnLine, vol. 54, pp. 253–258. Elsevier (2021)
18. Bak, S., Duggirala, P.S.: HyLAA: a tool for computing simulation-equivalent reachability for linear systems. In: Proceedings of HSCC 2017, pp. 173–178. ACM (2017)
19. Bak, S., Tran, H.-D., Johnson, T.T.: Numerical verification of affine systems with up to a billion dimensions. In: HSCC 2019, pp. 23–32. Association for Computing Machinery, New York (2019)
20. Ball, T., Rajamani, S.K.: The SLAM project: debugging system software via static analysis. In: POPL 2002: Proceedings of the 29th ACM SIGPLAN-SIGACT Symposium on Principles of Programming Languages, pp. 1–3. ACM, New York (2002)
21. Bell, P.C., Delvenne, J.-C., Jungers, R.M., Blondel, V.D.: The continuous Skolem-Pisot problem. Theoret. Comput. Sci. **411**(40), 3625–3634 (2010)
22. Benveniste, A., Le Guernic, P.: Hybrid dynamical systems theory and the signal language. IEEE Trans. Autom. Control **35**(5), 535–546 (1990)
23. Benvenuti, L., et al.: Reachability computation for hybrid systems with Ariadne. In: Proceedings of the 17th IFAC World Congress. IFAC Papers-OnLine (2008)
24. Benvenuti, L., Bresolin, D., Collins, P., Ferrari, A., Geretti, L., Villa, T.: Ariadne: dominance checking of nonlinear hybrid automata using reachability analysis. In: Finkel, A., Leroux, J., Potapov, I. (eds.) RP 2012. LNCS, vol. 7550, pp. 79–91. Springer, Heidelberg (2012). https://doi.org/10.1007/978-3-642-33512-9_8
25. Berz, M., Makino, K.: Verified integration of ODEs and flows using differential algebraic methods on high-order Taylor models. Reliable Comput. **4**, 361–369 (1998)
26. Beyer, D., Henzinger, T.A., Jhala, R., Majumdar, R.: The software model checker BLAST. STTT **9**(5–6), 505–525 (2007)
27. Blanchet, B., et al.: A static analyzer for large safety-critical software. In: Programming Language Design & Implementation, pp. 196–207. ACM Press (2003)
28. Cardelli, L., Tribastone, M., Tschaikowski, M., Vandin, A.: Symbolic computation of differential equivalences. ACM SIGPLAN Not. **51**, 137–150 (2016)
29. Chen, M., Herbert, S.L., Vashishtha, M.S., Bansal, S., Tomlin, C.J.: Decomposition of reachable sets and tubes for a class of nonlinear systems. arXiv e-prints (2017)
30. Chen, M., Herbert, S., Tomlin, C.: Exact and efficient Hamilton-Jacobi-based guaranteed safety analysis via system decomposition. In: IEEE International Conference on Robotics and Automation (ICRA) (2017). arXiv:1609.05248
31. Chen, X.: Reachability analysis of non-linear hybrid systems using Taylor models. Ph.D. thesis, RWTH Aachen University (2015)
32. Chen, X., Ábrahám, E., Sankaranarayanan, S.: Taylor model flowpipe construction for non-linear hybrid systems. In: Proceedings of the 33rd IEEE Real-Time Systems Symposium (RTSS 2012), pp. 183–192. IEEE Computer Society (2012)

33. Chen, X., Ábrahám, E., Sankaranarayanan, S.: Flow*: an analyzer for non-linear hybrid systems. In: Sharygina, N., Veith, H. (eds.) CAV 2013. LNCS, vol. 8044, pp. 258–263. Springer, Heidelberg (2013). https://doi.org/10.1007/978-3-642-39799-8_18

34. Chen, X., Dutta, S., Sankaranarayanan, S.: Formal verification of a multi-basal insulin infusion control model. In: Workshop on Applied Verification of Hybrid Systems (ARCH), p. 16. Easychair (2017)

35. Chen, X., Sankaranarayanan, S.: Decomposed reachability analysis for nonlinear systems. In: IEEE Real Time Systems Symposium (RTSS), pp. 13–24. IEEE Press (2016)

36. Chonev, V., Ouaknine, J., Worrell, J.: On the skolem problem for continuous linear dynamical systems. In: ICALP 2016, LIPIcs, vol. 55, pp. 100:1–100:13. Schloss Dagstuhl - Leibniz-Zentrum für Informatik (2016)

37. Chou, Y., Chen, X., Sankaranarayanan, S.: A study of model-order reduction techniques for verification. In: Abate, A., Boldo, S. (eds.) NSV 2017. LNCS, vol. 10381, pp. 98–113. Springer, Cham (2017). https://doi.org/10.1007/978-3-319-63501-9_8

38. Chou, Y., Yoon, H., Sankaranarayanan, S.: Predictive runtime monitoring of vehicle models using Bayesian estimation and reachability analysis. In: International Conference on Intelligent Robots and Systems (IROS), pp. 2111–2118. IEEE Press (2020)

39. Chutinan, A., Krogh, B.: Computing polyhedral approximations to flow pipes for dynamic systems. In: Proceedings of IEEE CDC. IEEE Press (1998)

40. Clarke, E., Kroening, D., Lerda, F.: A tool for checking ANSI-C programs. In: Jensen, K., Podelski, A. (eds.) TACAS 2004. LNCS, vol. 2988, pp. 168–176. Springer, Heidelberg (2004). https://doi.org/10.1007/978-3-540-24730-2_15

41. Clarke, E., Fehnker, A., Han, Z., Krogh, B., Stursberg, O., Theobald, M.: Verification of hybrid systems based on counterexample-guided abstraction refinement. In: Garavel, H., Hatcliff, J. (eds.) TACAS 2003. LNCS, vol. 2619, pp. 192–207. Springer, Heidelberg (2003). https://doi.org/10.1007/3-540-36577-X_14

42. Edmund, M., Clarke, O.G., Peled, D.A: Model Checking. MIT Press, Cambridge (1999)

43. Coogan, S.: Mixed monotonicity for reachability and safety in dynamical systems. In: 2020 59th IEEE Conference on Decision and Control (CDC), pp. 5074–5085. IEEE Press (2020)

44. Coogan, S., Arcak, M.: Efficient finite abstraction of mixed monotone systems. In: Girard, A., Sankaranarayanan, S. (eds.) HSCC 2015, pp. 58–67. ACM (2015)

45. Cousot, P.: Principles of Abstract Interpretation. MIT Press, Cambridge (2021)

46. Dang, T., Maler, O., Testylier, R.: Accurate hybridization of nonlinear systems. In: Proceedings of HSCC 2010, pp. 11–20. ACM (2010)

47. Dang, T., Testylier, R.: Hybridization domain construction using curvature estimation. In: Proceedings of HSCC 2011, pp. 123–132. ACM (2011)

48. Delmas, D., Souyris, J.: Astrée: from research to industry. In: Nielson, H.R., Filé, G. (eds.) SAS 2007. LNCS, vol. 4634, pp. 437–451. Springer, Heidelberg (2007). https://doi.org/10.1007/978-3-540-74061-2_27

49. Donzé, A.: BreachFlows: simulation-based design with formal requirements for industrial CPS (extended abstract). In: Workshop on Autonomous Systems Design (ASD 2020). OpenAccess Series in Informatics (OASIcs), vol. 79, pp. 5:1–5:5 (2020)

50. Duggirala, P.S., Mitra, S., Viswanathan, M., Potok, M.: C2E2: a verification tool for stateflow models. In: Baier, C., Tinelli, C. (eds.) TACAS 2015. LNCS, vol. 9035, pp. 68–82. Springer, Heidelberg (2015). https://doi.org/10.1007/978-3-662-46681-0_5

51. Duggirala, P.S., Viswanathan, M.: Parsimonious, simulation based verification of linear systems. In: Chaudhuri, S., Farzan, A. (eds.) CAV 2016. LNCS, vol. 9779, pp. 477–494. Springer, Cham (2016). https://doi.org/10.1007/978-3-319-41528-4_26

52. Dutta, S., Chen, X., Sankaranarayanan, S.: Reachability analysis for neural feedback systems using regressive polynomial rule inference. In: Ozay, N., Prabhakar, P. (eds.) Proceedings of HSCC 2019, pp. 157–168. ACM (2019)

53. Dutta, S., Jha, S., Sankaranarayanan, S., Tiwari, A.: Output range analysis for deep feed-forward neural networks. In: Dutle, A., Muñoz, C., Narkawicz, A. (eds.) NFM 2018. LNCS, vol. 10811, pp. 121–138. Springer, Cham (2018). https://doi.org/10.1007/978-3-319-77935-5_9

54. Eggers, A., Ramdani, N., Nedialkov, N., Fränzle, M.: Improving SAT modulo ODE for hybrid systems analysis by combining different enclosure methods. In: Barthe, G., Pardo, A., Schneider, G. (eds.) SEFM 2011. LNCS, vol. 7041, pp. 172–187. Springer, Heidelberg (2011). https://doi.org/10.1007/978-3-642-24690-6_13

55. M. Fränzle, C. Herde, S. Ratschan, T. Schubert, Teige, T.: Efficient solving of large non-linear arithmetic constraint systems with complex Boolean structure. JSAT–J. Satisfiability Boolean Model. Comput. 1, 209–236 (2007). Special Issue on SAT/CP Integration

56. Frehse, G., Le Guernic, C., Donzé, A., Cotton, S., Ray, R., Lebeltel, O., Ripado, R., Girard, A., Dang, T., Maler, O.: SpaceEx: scalable verification of hybrid systems. In: Gopalakrish-nan, G., Qadeer, S. (eds.) CAV 2011. LNCS, vol. 6806, pp. 379–395. Springer, Heidelberg (2011). https://doi.org/10.1007/978-3-642-22110-1_30

57. Gao, S., Kong, S., Clarke, E.M.: dReal: an SMT solver for nonlinear theories over the reals. In: Bonacina, M.P. (ed.) CADE 2013. LNCS (LNAI), vol. 7898, pp. 208–214. Springer, Heidelberg (2013). https://doi.org/10.1007/978-3-642-38574-2_14

58. Gao, S., Kong, S., Clarke, E.M.: Satisfiability modulo odes. In: Proceedings of FMCAD 2013, pp. 105–112. IEEE (2013)

59. Gehr, T., Mirman, M., Drachsler-Cohen, D., Tsankov, P., Chaudhuri, S., Vechev, M.T.: AI2: safety and robustness certification of neural networks with abstract interpretation. In: Pro-ceedings of S& P 2018, pp. 3–18. IEEE Computer Society (2018)

60. Ghorbal, K., Sogokon, A., Platzer, A.: A hierarchy of proof rules for checking positive invariance of algebraic and semi-algebraic sets. Comput. Lang. Syst. Struct. 47, 19–43 (2017)

61. Ghosh, R., Tomlin, C.J.: Symbolic reachable set computation of piecewise affine hybrid automata and its application to biological modeling: Delta-Notch protein signaling. IEE Trans. Syst. Biol. 1(1), 170–183 (2004)

62. Girard, A.: Reachability of uncertain linear systems using zonotopes. In: Morari, M., Thiele, L. (eds.) HSCC 2005. LNCS, vol. 3414, pp. 291–305. Springer, Heidelberg (2005). https://doi.org/10.1007/978-3-540-31954-2_19

63. Girard, A., Le Guernic, C.: Zonotope/hyperplane intersection for hybrid systems reach-ability analysis. In: Egerstedt, M., Mishra, B. (eds.) HSCC 2008. LNCS, vol. 4981, pp. 215–228. Springer, Heidelberg (2008). https://doi.org/10.1007/978-3-540-78929-1_16

64. Gollu, A., Varaiya, P.: Hybrid dynamical systems. In: Proceedings of the 28th IEEE Con-ference on Decision and Control, vol. 3, pp. 2708–2712 (1989)

65. Le Guernic, C., Girard, A.: Reachability analysis of hybrid systems using support functions. In: Bouajjani, A., Maler, O. (eds.) CAV 2009. LNCS, vol. 5643, pp. 540–554. Springer, Heidelberg (2009). https://doi.org/10.1007/978-3-642-02658-4_40

66. Halbwachs, N., Proy, Y.-E., Roumanoff, P.: Verification of real-time systems using linear relation analysis. Formal Methods Syst. Des. 11(2), 157–185 (1997)

67. Han, Z., Krogh, B.: Reachability analysis of hybrid control systems using reduced-order models. In: Proceedings of the American Control Conference, vol. 2, pp. 1183–1189, Jan-uary 2004

68. Harrison, J.: Formal methods at Intel - an overview. In: Proceedings of the Second NASA Formal Methods Symposium (NFM) (2010)

69. Havelund, K., Pressburger, T.: Model checking JAVA programs using JAVA PathFinder. Int. J. Softw. Tools Technol. Trans. 2(4), 366–381 (2000)

70. Henzinger, T.A., Ho, P.-H.: HyTech: the Cornell hybrid technology tool. In: Antsaklis, P., Kohn, W., Nerode, A., Sastry, S. (eds.) HS 1994. LNCS, vol. 999, pp. 265–293. Springer, Heidelberg (1995). https://doi.org/10.1007/3-540-60472-3_14

71. Henzinger, T.A., Kopke, P.W., Puri, A., Varaiya, P.: What's decidable about hybrid automata? J. Comput. Syst. Sci. **57**(1), 94–124 (1998)

72. Herde, C., Eggers, A., Franzle, T., Teige, M.: Analysis of hybrid systems using HySAT. In: Third International Conference on Systems 2008. ICONS 2008, pp. 13–18. IEEE (2008)

73. Huang, C., Fan, J., Li, W., Chen, X., Zhu, Q.: ReachNN: reachability analysis of neural-network controlled systems. ACM Trans. Embed. Comput. Syst. **18**(5s), 106:1–106:22 (2019)

74. Huang, X., Kwiatkowska, M., Wang, S., Wu, M.: Safety verification of deep neural networks. In: Majumdar, R., Kunčak, V. (eds.) CAV 2017. LNCS, vol. 10426, pp. 3–29. Springer, Cham (2017). https://doi.org/10.1007/978-3-319-63387-9_1

75. Ivančić, F., Shlyakhter, I., Gupta, A., Ganai, M.K.: Model checking C programs using f-soft. In: ICCD, pp. 297–308. IEEE Computer Society (2005)

76. Ivanov, R., Carpenter, T.J., Weimer, J., Alur, R., Pappas, G.J., Lee, I.: Verifying the safety of autonomous systems with neural network controllers. ACM Trans. Embed. Comput. Syst. **20**(1), 7:1–7:26 (2021)

77. Kapela, T., Mrozek, M., Pilarczyk, P., Wilczak, D., Zgliczyński, P.: CAPD - a rigorous toolbox for computer assisted proofs in dynamics. Technical report, Jagiellonian University (2010)

78. Kapinski, J., Deshmukh, J.V., Jin, X., Ito, H., Butts, K.R.: Simulation-guided approaches for verification of automotive powertrain control systems. In: American Control Conference, ACC 2015, Chicago, IL, USA, 1–3 July 2015, pp. 4086–4095. IEEE (2015)

79. Katz, G., Barrett, C., Dill, D.L., Julian, K., Kochenderfer, M.J.: Reluplex: an efficient SMT solver for verifying deep neural networks. In: Majumdar, R., Kunčak, V. (eds.) CAV 2017. LNCS, vol. 10426, pp. 97–117. Springer, Cham (2017). https://doi.org/10.1007/978-3-319-63387-9_5

80. Kong, S., Gao, S., Chen, W., Clarke, E.: dReach: δ-reachability analysis for hybrid systems. In: Baier, C., Tinelli, C. (eds.) TACAS 2015. LNCS, vol. 9035, pp. 200–205. Springer, Heidelberg (2015). https://doi.org/10.1007/978-3-662-46681-0_15

81. Kurzhanski, A.B., Varaiya, P.: Ellipsoidal techniques for reachability analysis. In: Lynch, N., Krogh, B.H. (eds.) HSCC 2000. LNCS, vol. 1790, pp. 202–214. Springer, Heidelberg (2000). https://doi.org/10.1007/3-540-46430-1_19

82. Lafferriere, G., Pappas, G., Sastry, S.: O-minimal hybrid systems. Math. Control Sig. Syst. **13**, 1–21 (2000)

83. Guernic, C.L., Girard, A.: Reachability analysis of linear systems using support functions. Nonlinear Anal. Hybrid Syst. **4**(2), 250–262 (2010). IFAC World Congress 2008

84. Lygeros, J.: Lecture notes on hybrid systems (2004). Notes for ENSIETA short course

85. Lygeros, J., Tomlin, C., Sastry, S.: Controllers for reachability specifications for hybrid systems. Automatica **35**(3), 349–370 (1999)

86. Maidens, J., Arcak, M.: Exploiting symmetry for discrete-time reachability computations. IEEE Control Syst. Lett. **2**(2), 213–217 (2018)

87. Makino, K., Berz, M.: Remainder differential algebras and their applications. In: Berz, M., et al. (eds.) Computational Differentiation: Techniques, Applications, and Tools, pp. 63–75. SIAM (1996)

88. Maler, O.: Amir Pnueli and the dawn of hybrid systems. In: Proceedings of the Hybrid Systems: Computation and Control, pp. 293–295. Association for Computing Machinery (2010)

89. Maler, O., Manna, Z., Pnueli, A.: Prom timed to hybrid systems. In: de Bakker, J.W., Huizing, C., de Roever, W.P., Rozenberg, G. (eds.) REX 1991. LNCS, vol. 600, pp. 447–484. Springer, Heidelberg (1992). https://doi.org/10.1007/BFb0032003
90. Mauroy, A., Mezić, I., Susuki, Y. (eds.): The Koopman Operator in Systems and Control. LNCIS, vol. 484. Springer, Cham (2020). https://doi.org/10.1007/978-3-030-35713-9
91. Meiss, J.D.: Differential Dynamical Systems. SIAM Publishers (2007)
92. Mitchell, I.: Toolbox of level-set methods. Technical report, UBC Department of Computer Science Technical Report TR-2007-11 (2007)
93. Mitchell, I., Tomlin, C.J.: Level set methods for computation in hybrid systems. In: Lynch, N., Krogh, B.H. (eds.) HSCC 2000. LNCS, vol. 1790, pp. 310–323. Springer, Heidelberg (2000). https://doi.org/10.1007/3-540-46430-1_27
94. Moore, C.: Unpredictability and undecidability in dynamical systems. Phys. Rev. Lett. **64**, 2354–2357 (1990)
95. Nedialkov, N.S.: Implementing a rigorous ode solver through literate programming. In: Rauh, A., Auer, E. (eds.) Modeling. Design, and Simulation of Systems with Uncertainties, volume 3 of Mathematical Engineering, chapter Mathematical Engineering, pp. 3–19. Springer, Berlin Heidelberg (2011)
96. Nicollin, X., Olivero, A., Sifakis, J., Yovine, S.: An approach to the description and analysis of hybrid systems. In: Grossman, R.L., Nerode, A., Ravn, A.P., Rischel, H. (eds.) HS 1991-1992. LNCS, vol. 736, pp. 149–178. Springer, Heidelberg (1993). https://doi.org/10.1007/3-540-57318-6_28
97. Peleties, P., DeCarlo, R.: A modeling strategy with event structures for hybrid systems. In: Proceedings of the 28th IEEE Conference on Decision and Control, vol. 2, pp. 1308–1313 (1989)
98. Platzer, A.: Logical Foundations of Cyber-Physical Systems, 1st edn. Springer, Cham (2018). https://doi.org/10.1007/978-3-319-63588-0
99. Platzer, A., Clarke, E.: Computing differential invariants of hybrid systems as fixedpoints. Formal Methods Syst. Des. **35**(1), 98–120 (2009)
100. Platzer, A., Quesel, J.-D.: KeYmaera: a hybrid theorem prover for hybrid systems (system description). In: Armando, A., Baumgartner, P., Dowek, G. (eds.) IJCAR 2008. LNCS (LNAI), vol. 5195, pp. 171–178. Springer, Heidelberg (2008). https://doi.org/10.1007/978-3-540-71070-7_15
101. Platzer, A., Quesel, J.-D.: Logical verification and systematic parametric analysis in train control. In: Egerstedt, M., Mishra, B. (eds.) HSCC 2008. LNCS, vol. 4981, pp. 646–649. Springer, Heidelberg (2008). https://doi.org/10.1007/978-3-540-78929-1_55
102. Prabhakar, P., Duggirala, P.S., Mitra, S., Viswanathan, M.: Hybrid automata-based CEGAR for rectangular hybrid systems. Formal Methods Syst. Des. **46**(2), 105–134 (2015). https://doi.org/10.1007/s10703-015-0225-4
103. Prajna, S., Jadbabaie, A.: Safety verification of hybrid systems using barrier certificates. In: Alur, R., Pappas, G.J. (eds.) HSCC 2004. LNCS, vol. 2993, pp. 477–492. Springer, Heidelberg (2004). https://doi.org/10.1007/978-3-540-24743-2_32
104. Ramdani, N., Nedialkov, N.S.: Computing reachable sets for uncertain nonlinear hybrid systems using interval constraint-propagation techniques. Nonlinear Anal. Hybrid Syst. **5**(2), 149–162 (2011)
105. Ratschan, S., She, Z.: Safety verification of hybrid systems by constraint propagation based abstraction refinement. In: Morari, M., Thiele, L. (eds.) HSCC 2005. LNCS, vol. 3414, pp. 573–589. Springer, Heidelberg (2005). https://doi.org/10.1007/978-3-540-31954-2_37
106. Ros, L., Sabater, A., Thomas, F.: An ellipsoidal calculus based on propagation and fusion. IEEE Trans. Syst. Man Cybern. Part B **32**(4), 430–442 (2002)
107. Sankaranarayanan, S.: Change of basis abstractions for non-linear hybrid systems. Nonlinear Anal. Hybrid Syst **19**, 107–133 (2016)

108. Sankaranarayanan, S.: Reachability analysis using message passing over tree decompositions. In: Lahiri, S.K., Wang, C. (eds.) CAV 2020. LNCS, vol. 12224, pp. 604–628. Springer, Cham (2020). https://doi.org/10.1007/978-3-030-53288-8_30

109. Sankaranarayanan, S., Dang, T., Ivančić, F.: Symbolic model checking of hybrid systems using template Polyhedra. In: Ramakrishnan, C.R., Rehof, J. (eds.) TACAS 2008. LNCS, vol. 4963, pp. 188–202. Springer, Heidelberg (2008). https://doi.org/10.1007/978-3-540-78800-3_14

110. Sankaranarayanan, S., Sipma, H., Manna, Z.: Constructing invariants for hybrid systems. Formal Methods Syst. Des. **32**(1), 25–55 (2008)

111. Sibai, H., Mokhlesi, N., Fan, C., Mitra, S.: Multi-agent safety verification using symmetry transformations. In: TACAS 2020. LNCS, vol. 12078, pp. 173–190. Springer, Cham (2020). https://doi.org/10.1007/978-3-030-45190-5_10

112. Silva, B.I., Richeson, K., Krogh, B.H., Chutinan, A.: Modeling and verification of hybrid dynamical system using checkmate. In: ADPM 2000 (2000). http://www.ece.cmu.edu/~webk/checkmate

113. Sun, X., Khedr, H., Shoukry, Y.: Formal verification of neural network controlled autonomous systems. In: HSCC, pp. 147–156. ACM (2019)

114. Tabuada, P.: Verification and Control of Hybrid Systems: A Symbolic Approach. Springer, New York (2009). https://doi.org/10.1007/978-1-4419-0224-5

115. Tiwari, A., Khanna, G.: Nonlinear systems: approximating reach sets. In: Alur, R., Pappas, G.J. (eds.) HSCC 2004. LNCS, vol. 2993, pp. 600–614. Springer, Heidelberg (2004). https://doi.org/10.1007/978-3-540-24743-2_40

116. Tran, H.-D., et al.: NNV: the neural network verification tool for deep neural networks and learning-enabled cyber-physical systems. In: Lahiri, S.K., Wang, C. (eds.) CAV 2020. LNCS, vol. 12224, pp. 3–17. Springer, Cham (2020). https://doi.org/10.1007/978-3-030-53288-8_1

117. Visser, W., Havelund, K., Brat, G., Park, S.J., Lerda, F.: Model checking programs. Autom. Softw. Eng. **10**(2), 203–232 (2003)

118. Vladimerou, V., Prabhakar, P., Viswanathan, M., Dullerud, G.: STORMED hybrid systems. In: Aceto, L., Damgård, I., Goldberg, L.A., Halldórsson, M.M., Ingólfsdóttir, A., Walukiewicz, I. (eds.) ICALP 2008. LNCS, vol. 5126, pp. 136–147. Springer, Heidelberg (2008). https://doi.org/10.1007/978-3-540-70583-3_12

119. Wang, S., Pei, K., Whitehouse, J., Yang, J., Jana, S.: Formal security analysis of neural networks using symbolic intervals. In: Proceedings of USENIX Security 2018, pp. 1599–1614. USENIX Association (2018)

120. Zhao, F.: Automatic analysis and synthesis of controllers for dynamical systems based on phase-space knowledge. Ph.D. thesis (1998)

121. Zutshi, A., Sankaranarayanan, S., Deshmukh, J., Jin, X.: Symbolic-numeric reachability analysis of closed-loop control software. In: Hybrid Systems: Computation and Control (HSCC), pp. 135–144. ACM Press (2016)

Regular Submissions

Towards Better Test Coverage: Merging Unit Tests for Autonomous Systems[†]

Josefine B. Graebener[(✉)], Apurva Badithela, and Richard M. Murray

California Institute of Technology, Pasadena, CA 91125, USA
{jgraeben,apurva,murray}@caltech.edu

Abstract. We present a framework for merging unit tests for autonomous systems. Typically, it is intractable to test an autonomous system for every scenario in its operating environment. The question of whether it is possible to design a single test for multiple requirements of the system motivates this work. First, we formally define three attributes of a test: a test specification that characterizes behaviors observed in a test execution, a test environment, and a test policy. Using the merge operator from contract-based design theory, we provide a formalism to construct a merged test specification from two unit test specifications. Temporal constraints on the merged test specification guarantee that non-trivial satisfaction of both unit test specifications is necessary for a successful merged test execution. We assume that the test environment remains the same across the unit tests and the merged test. Given a test specification and a test environment, we synthesize a test policy filter using a receding horizon approach, and use the test policy filter to guide a search procedure (e.g. Monte-Carlo Tree Search) to find a test policy that is guaranteed to satisfy the test specification. This search procedure finds a test policy that maximizes a pre-defined robustness metric for the test while the filter guarantees a test policy for satisfying the test specification. We prove that our algorithm is sound. Furthermore, the receding horizon approach to synthesizing the filter ensures that our algorithm is scalable. Finally, we show that merging unit tests is impactful for designing efficient test campaigns to achieve similar levels of coverage in fewer test executions. We illustrate our framework on two self-driving examples in a discrete-state setting.

Keywords: Testing of autonomous systems · Assume-guarantee contracts · Receding horizon synthesis

1 Introduction

Rigorous test and evaluation of autonomous systems is imperative for deploying autonomy in safety-critical settings [25]. In the case of testing self-driving

---

J. B. Graebener and A. Badithela—Contributed equally to this work.
The code for examples given in this paper can be found at: https://github.com/jgraeb/MergeUnitTests.

© Springer Nature Switzerland AG 2022
J. V. Deshmukh et al. (Eds.): NFM 2022, LNCS 13260, pp. 133–155, 2022.
https://doi.org/10.1007/978-3-031-06773-0_7

cars, operational tests are constructed manually by experienced test engineers and can be combined with test cases generated in simulators using falsification techniques [11]. In addition, operational testing of self-driving cars on the road is expensive, and would need to be repeated after every design iteration [13]. In this paper, we pose the question of whether it is possible to check multiple requirements in a single test execution. Addressing this question is the first step towards optimizing for the largest number of test requirements checked in as few operational tests as possible.

The study of principled approaches to testing, verification and validation is a relatively young but growing research area. In the formal methods community, *falsification* is the technical term referring to the study of optimization algorithms, typically black-box, and sampling techniques to search for inputs that result in the system-under-test violating its formal requirements on input-output behavior [1,2,8,9,12,24]. Falsification algorithms require a metric defined over temporal logic requirements to quantitatively reason about the degree to which a formal requirement has been satisfied. Assuming that the design of the autonomous system is black-box, falsification algorithms seek to find inputs that minimize the metric associated with satisfying formal requirements. The reasoning here is that minimizing this metric brings the system closer to violating its *requirements*, thus being a critical test scenario [14]. Formal methods literature uses *falsification* and *testing* interchangeably. In addition to manually constructing operational tests, falsification is used to find critical scenarios in simulation and the test environment parameters characterizing these critical scenarios are used for operational testing [11]. Falsification aims to find parameters of the test environment that lead the system to violate its *requirements*. However, our approach is different in that we construct a test with respect to a test specification,

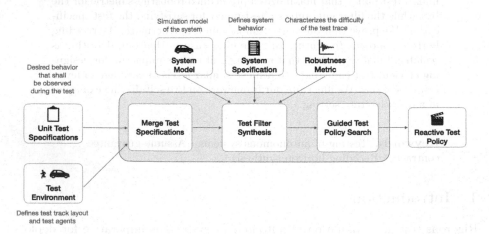

Fig. 1. Overview of the proposed framework. The blocks the left represent the inputs to the algorithm that define the unit tests, the blocks on the top represent inputs describing the system under test, the building blocks of our approach are shown in the blue shaded box, and the test policy is the result of the algorithm. (Color figure online)

which characterizes a set of desired test executions. For example, consider an autonomous car on a test track. The requirement for the autonomous car is to drive around the track and follow traffic rules while the human drivers of the test vehicles are instructed to drive in a specific fashion (ex: maintaining some distance between each other). These guidelines given to the test drivers constitute the test specification, which is not known to the system-under-test. Instead of considering all possible test environment policies, the test specification restricts the space of scenarios that our test policy search algorithm searches over. It also leverages reactivity: test scenarios are not planned in advance, but the test environment agents will react depending on the actions taken by the system under test.

Our contributions are the following. First, we formally characterize a test by three attributes, a test specification, a test environment and a test policy. Second, we leverage the merge operator from assume-guarantee contract theory to merge two unit test specifications into a merged specification, resulting in a single test that checks the test specifications of both unit tests. Furthermore, if necessary, we characterize temporal constraints on the merged test specification. Finally, we use Monte Carlo Tree Search (MCTS) to search for a test environment policy corresponding to the test specification, and use receding horizon synthesis techniques to prevent the search procedure from exploring policies that violate the test specification. This framework is illustrated in Fig. 1.

2   Background

In this work, we choose Linear Temporal Logic (LTL) to represent the system and test specifications. LTL is a temporal logic language for describing linear-time properties over traces of computer programs and formally verifying their properties [23]. Although first introduced to formally describe properties of computer programs, LTL has been used for formal methods applications in control such as temporal logic synthesis of planners and controllers [15,17,26].

Definition 1 (Linear Temporal Logic (LTL) [3]). Given a set of atomic propositions AP, the *syntax* of LTL is given by the following grammar:

$$\varphi ::= \text{true} \mid a \mid \varphi_1 \wedge \varphi_2 \mid \neg\varphi \mid \bigcirc \varphi \mid \varphi_1 \mathcal{U} \varphi_2 \tag{1}$$

where $a \in AP$ is an atomic proposition, $\wedge$ (and) and $\neg$ (not) are logic operators, and $\bigcirc$ (next) and $\mathcal{U}$ (until) are temporal operators. Other temporal operators such as $\square$ (always), $\lozenge$ (eventually), $\square\lozenge$ (always eventually), and $\lozenge\square$ (eventually always) can be derived. Let φ be an LTL formula over the set of atomic propositions AP. The *semantics* of LTL are inductively defined over an infinite sequence of states $\sigma = s_0 s_1 s_2 \ldots$ as follows: i) If $p \in AP$, $s_i \models p$ iff p evaluates to true at s_i, ii) $s_i \models \neg\varphi$ iff $s_i \not\models \varphi$, iii) $s_i \models \varphi_1 \wedge \varphi_2$ iff $s_i \models \varphi_1 \wedge s_i \models \varphi_2$, iv) $s_i \models \bigcirc\varphi$ iff $s_{i+1} \models \varphi$, v) $s_i \models \varphi_1 \mathcal{U} \varphi_2$ iff $\exists j > i$ such that for all $k \in [i,j)$, $s_k \models \varphi_1$ and $s_j \models \varphi_2$. An infinite sequence $\sigma = s_0 s_1 \ldots$ satisfies an LTL formula φ, denoted by $\sigma \models \varphi$, iff $s_0 \models \varphi$.

In our framework, we consider a fragment of LTL specifications in the class of generalized reactivity of rank 1 $(GR(1))$ [22]. $GR(1)$ specifications are expressive for capturing safety ($\Box$), liveness ($\Diamond$), and recurrence ($\Box\Diamond$) requirements that are relevant to several autonomous systems [17, 26]. A $GR(1)$ formula φ is as follows,

$$\varphi = (\varphi_e^{\text{init}} \wedge \Box\varphi_e^s \wedge \Box\Diamond\varphi_e^f) \rightarrow (\varphi_s^{\text{init}} \wedge \Box\varphi_s^s \wedge \Box\Diamond\varphi_s^f), \tag{2}$$

where the subscript s refers to the robotic system for which a reactive controller is being synthesized, and φ_s^{init}, $\Box\varphi_s^s$, and $\Box\Diamond\varphi_s^f$, define respectively, the initial requirements, safety requirements and recurrence requirements on the system denoted by s. Similarly, φ_e^{init}, $\Box\varphi_e^s$, and $\Box\Diamond\varphi_e^f$, define requirements on the environment e of the system s. Furthermore, synthesis for $GR(1)$ formulas has time complexity $O(|V|^3)$, where $|V|$ is the size of the state space [22].

Assume-Guarantee Contracts. Contract-based design was first developed as a formal modular design methodology for analysis of component-based software systems [7, 18, 19], and later applied for the design and analysis of complex autonomous systems [10, 20]. In this work, we adopt the mathematical framework of assume-guarantee contracts presented in [5, 21].

Definition 2 (Assume-Guarantee Contract). Let Λ be an alphabet and $\mathcal{B}(\Lambda)$ be the set of all behaviors over Λ. A component M over the alphabet Λ is defined as $M \subseteq B(\Lambda)$. Then an *assume-guarantee contract* $\mathcal{C}$ is defined as a pair $\mathcal{C} = (A, G)$, where A is a set of behaviors for assumptions on the environment in which the component operates, and G is a set of behaviors for the guarantees that the component provides, assuming its assumptions on the environment are met. M is an implementation of a contract, $M \models \mathcal{C}$, if and only if $M \subseteq G \wedge \neg A \Leftrightarrow M \wedge (A \wedge \neg G) = \emptyset$ [4].

In this work, the assumptions and guarantees constituting assume-guarantee contracts are LTL formulas. To facilitate the contract algebra, we will consider contracts in their *saturated* form, where a contract is defined as $\mathcal{C} = (A, A \rightarrow G)$. In Sect. 3 we define system and test specifications with LTL and borrow operators from assume-guarantee contract theory in Sect. 4.1 to formally define the merge of two unit tests.

3   Problem Setup

First we define the system under test, which we will refer to as *system* for brevity, and its corresponding system specification. We assume that the system, the system specification, and the controller are provided by the designer of the system and cannot be modified when designing the test.

Definition 3 (Transition System). A *transition system* is a tuple $\mathcal{T} := (Q, \rightarrow)$, where Q is a set of states and $\rightarrow \subseteq Q \times Q$ is a transition relation. If $\exists$ a transition from $q_1 \in Q$ to $q_2 \in Q$, we write $q_1 \rightarrow q_2$.

Definition 4 (System). Let $\mathbb{V}_S$ be the set of system variables, and let Q_{sys} be the set of all possible valuations of $\mathbb{V}_{sys}$. A *system* S is a transition system $\mathcal{T}_{sys} = (Q_{sys}, \rightarrow_{sys})$, where the transition relation $\rightarrow_{sys}$ is defined by the dynamics of the system.

Definition 5 (System Specification). A *system specification* φ_{sys} is the $GR(1)$ formula,

$$\varphi_{sys} = (\varphi_{test}^{init} \wedge \Box \varphi_{test}^{s} \wedge \Box \Diamond \varphi_{test}^{f}) \rightarrow (\varphi_{sys}^{init} \wedge \Box \varphi_{sys}^{s} \wedge \Box \Diamond \varphi_{sys}^{f}), \tag{3}$$

where φ_{sys}^{init} is the initial condition that the system needs to satisfy, φ_{sys}^{s} encode system dynamics and safety requirements on the system, and φ_{sys}^{f} specifies recurrence goals for the system. Likewise, φ_{test}^{init}, φ_{test}^{s}, and φ_{test}^{f} represent assumptions the system has on the test environment.

The system is evaluated in a test environment, which comprises of both the test track and test agents. A *test* is characterized by the *test environment*, a *test specification*, and a *test policy*. Our approach differs from falsification in that we are not generating a test strategy to stress test the system for $\varphi_{sys}^{init} \wedge \Box \varphi_{sys}^{s} \wedge \Box \Diamond \varphi_{sys}^{f}$. Instead, we synthesize a test for a new concept—a test specification—which describes the set of behaviors we would like to see in a test. For example, an informal version of a test specification is requiring test agents to "drive around the test track at a fixed speed while maintaining a certain distance from each other".

Definition 6 (Test Environment). Let $\mathbb{V}_{test}$ be the set of test environment variables, and let Q_{test} be the set of all possible valuations of $\mathbb{V}_{test}$. A *test environment* T is a transition system $\mathcal{T}_{test} = (Q_{test}, \rightarrow_{test})$, where the transition relation $\rightarrow_{test}$ is defined by the dynamics of the test agents.

Definition 7 (Test Specification). A *test specification* φ_{test} is the $GR(1)$ formula,

$$\varphi_{test} := (\varphi_{sys}^{init} \wedge \Box \varphi_{sys}^{s} \wedge \Box \Diamond \varphi_{sys}^{f}) \rightarrow (\varphi_{test}^{init} \wedge \Box \varphi_{test}^{s} \wedge \Box \Diamond \varphi_{test}^{f} \wedge \Box \psi_{test}^{s} \wedge \Box \Diamond \psi_{test}^{f}), \tag{4}$$

where φ_{sys}^{init}, φ_{sys}^{s} and φ_{sys}^{f}, φ_{test}^{init}, φ_{test}^{s} and φ_{test}^{f} are propositional formulas from Eq. (3). Additionally, $\Box \psi_{test}^{s}$ and $\Box \Diamond \psi_{test}^{f}$ describe the safety and recurrence formulas for the test environment in addition to the dynamics of the test environment known to the system. Note that the system is unaware of these additional specifications on the test environment, and the test specification is such that the system is allowed to satisfy its requirements. Defining the test specification in this manner allows for i) synthesizing a test in which the system, if properly designed, can meet φ_{sys}, and ii) specifying additional requirements on the test environment, unknown to the system at design time. We assume that test specifications are defined *a priori*; we leave finding relevant test specifications to future work.

Let $\mathcal{T}_{\mathrm{prod}} = (Q_{\mathrm{prod}}, \rightarrow_{\mathrm{prod}})$ be a turn-based product transition system constructed from $\mathcal{T}_{\mathrm{sys}}$ and $\mathcal{T}_{\mathrm{test}}$, where $Q_{\mathrm{prod}} := Q_{\mathrm{sys}} \times Q_{\mathrm{test}}$, and $\rightarrow_{\mathrm{prod}} \subseteq Q_{\mathrm{prod}} \times Q_{\mathrm{prod}}$. In particular, for every transition $(s, s') \in \rightarrow_{\mathrm{sys}}$, we have $((s, t), (s', t)) \in \rightarrow_{\mathrm{prod}}$ where $t \in Q_{\mathrm{test}}$. Similarly, for every transition $(t, t') \in \rightarrow_{\mathrm{test}}$, we have $((s, t), (s, t')) \in \rightarrow_{\mathrm{prod}}$ where $s \in Q_{\mathrm{sys}}$.

Definition 8 (Game Graph). Let V_{sys} and V_{test} be copies of the states Q_{prod}. Let E_{sys} denote the set of transitions $((s, t), (s', t)) \in \rightarrow_{\mathrm{prod}}$, and let E_{test} denote the set of transitions $((s, t), (s, t')) \in \rightarrow_{\mathrm{prod}}$ for some $s, s' \in Q_{\mathrm{sys}}$ and $t, t' \in Q_{\mathrm{test}}$. Then the *game graph* $G = (V, E)$ is a directed graph with vertices $V := V_{\mathrm{sys}} \cup V_{\mathrm{test}}$ and edges $E := E_{\mathrm{sys}} \cup E_{\mathrm{test}}$.

Definition 9 (Policy). On the game graph G, a policy for the system is a function $\pi_{\mathrm{sys}} : V^* V_{\mathrm{sys}} \rightarrow V_{\mathrm{test}}$ such that $(s, \pi_{\mathrm{sys}}(w \cdot s)) \in E_{\mathrm{sys}}$, where $s \in V_{\mathrm{sys}}$ and $w \in V^*$. Similarly defined, π_{test} denotes the test environment policy, where $*$ is the Kleene star operator.

Definition 10 (Test Execution). A *test execution* $\sigma = v_0 v_1 v_2 \ldots$ starting from vertex $v_0 \in V$ is an infinite sequence of states on the game graph G. Since G is a turn-based game graph, the states in the test execution alternate between V_{sys} and V_{test}, so if $V_1 \in V_{\mathrm{sys}}$, then $v_{i+1} = \pi_{\mathrm{sys}}(v_0 \ldots V_1)$. Let $\sigma_{\pi_{\mathrm{sys}} \times \pi_{\mathrm{test}}}(s_0)$ be the test execution starting from state $s_0 \in V_{\mathrm{sys}}$ for policies π_{sys} and π_{test}. Let Σ denote the set of all possible test executions on G. A robustness metric $\rho : \Sigma \rightarrow \mathbb{R}$ is a function evaluated assigning a scalar value to a test execution.

Problem 1. Given system and environment transition systems, $\mathcal{T}_{\mathrm{sys}}$ and $\mathcal{T}_{\mathrm{test}}$, two unit test specifications $\varphi_{\mathrm{test},1}$ and $\varphi_{\mathrm{test},2}$, and a robustness metric ρ, find a test policy π^*_{test}, such that

$$\pi^*_{\mathrm{test}} = \underset{\pi_{\mathrm{test}}}{\arg\max} \ \rho(\sigma_{\pi_{\mathrm{sys}} \times \pi_{\mathrm{test}}})$$

$$\text{s.t.} \quad \sigma_{\pi_{\mathrm{sys}} \times \pi_{\mathrm{test}}} \models (\varphi_{\mathrm{test},1} \wedge \varphi_{\mathrm{test},2}), \quad \forall \pi_{\mathrm{sys}} \models \varphi_{\mathrm{sys}}, \tag{5}$$

Running Example—Lane Change. Consider the example of lane change illustrated in Fig. 2. The system (red car) must merge into the lower lane before the track ends, and must not collide with the test environment agents (blue cars). Thus, the liveness requirement of changing lanes, $\varphi^f_{\mathrm{sys}} := (y_{\mathrm{sys}} = 2)$, and the safety requirement of not colliding with test agent i, $\neg(y_{\mathrm{sys}} = y_{\mathrm{test},i} \wedge x_{\mathrm{sys}} = x_{\mathrm{test},i}) \in \varphi^s_{\mathrm{sys}}$, constitute part of the system specification φ_{sys}. In the two unit tests, we have the system changing into the other lane in front of and behind a tester car, respectively, and in the merged test, it finished its lane change maneuver in between the tester cars.

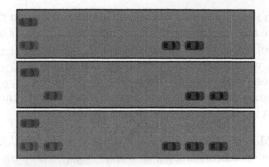

Fig. 2. Lane change example with initial (left) and final (right) configurations. The x-coordinates are numbered from left to right, and y-coordinates are numbered top to bottom, starting from 1. The system (red) is required to merge into the lower lane without colliding. Merging in front of (top), behind (center), or in between (bottom) tester agents (blue). (Color figure online)

4   Merging Unit Tests

In this section, we will outline our main approach for merging unit tests. First, we define the notion of a merged test and use the merge operator for merging test specifications and add temporal constraints to the test specification, if necessary. Then, we construct an auxiliary graph corresponding to the merged test specification and describe the synthesis of the test policy filter on this auxiliary graph using a receding horizon approach.

4.1   Merging Test Specifications

The merge, also known as strong merge, operator of two contracts $\mathcal{C}_1$ and $\mathcal{C}_2$ is defined as follows,

$$\mathcal{C}_1 \cdot \mathcal{C}_2 = (a_1 \wedge a_2, (a_1 \wedge a_2) \rightarrow [(a_1 \rightarrow g_1) \wedge (a_2 \rightarrow g_2)]) \tag{6}$$

In addition to *strong merge*, contract theory defines other operators over a pair of contracts such as *composition* and *conjunction* [5,21]. Among all these operators, strong merge is the only operator that requires assumptions from both unit contracts (and as a result, unit test specifications) to hold true. Thus, we choose the strong merge operator to derive the merged test specification. Given two unit test specifications, $\varphi_{\text{test},1}$ and $\varphi_{\text{test},2}$, we can construct the corresponding contracts $\mathcal{C}_1 = (a_1, a_1 \rightarrow g_1)$ and $\mathcal{C}_2 = (a_2, a_2 \rightarrow g_2)$, where $a_i = (\varphi_{\text{sys}}^{init} \wedge \Box\varphi_{\text{sys}}^s \wedge \Box\Diamond\varphi_{\text{sys}}^f)$ being the assumptions on the system (under test), and $g_i = (\varphi_{\text{test},i}^{init} \wedge \Box\varphi_{\text{test},i}^s \wedge \Box\Diamond\varphi_{\text{test},i}^f \wedge \Box\psi_{\text{test},i}^s \wedge \Box\Diamond\psi_{\text{test},i}^f)$ being the guarantees for unit test i.

Remark 1. We make the following modifications to guarantees g_i for brevity. First, we assume that the only recurrence requirements in the test specification is $\Box\Diamond\psi_{test,i}^f$, which is not a part of the system's assumptions on the environment. Second, we assume that the merged test environment $\mathcal{T}_{test,m}$ is a simple product transition system of the unit test environments, $\mathcal{T}_{test,1}$ and $\mathcal{T}_{test,2}$. On the merged test environment, we assume that the initial conditions $\varphi_{test,1}^{init}$ and $\varphi_{test,2}^{init}$ are equivalent, and test environment dynamics $\varphi_{test,1}^s$ and $\varphi_{test,2}^s$ are equivalent. Therefore, in merging the two unit specifications, we refer to the test guarantees as $g_{t,i} = \Box\psi_{test,i}^s \wedge \Box\Diamond\psi_{test,i}^f$.

Definition 11 (Merged Test). From the merged contract $\mathcal{C}_m := (a_m, a_m \rightarrow g_m) = \mathcal{C}_1 \cdot \mathcal{C}_2$, the specification $\varphi_{test,m} = a_m \rightarrow g_m$, where $a_m = a_1 \wedge a_2$, and $g_m = [(a_1 \rightarrow g_1) \wedge (a_2 \rightarrow g_2)]$ is the *merged test specification*. A test environment policy $\pi_{test,m}$ for merged test specification $\varphi_{test,m}$ results in a test execution $\sigma \models \varphi_{test,m}$.

Lemma 1. *Given unit test specifications $\varphi_{test,1}$ and $\varphi_{test,2}$ such that $\varphi_{test,m} = a_m \rightarrow g_m$ is the corresponding merged test specification. Then, for every test execution $\sigma \models \varphi_{test,m}$ such that $\sigma \models a_m$, we also have that $\sigma \models \varphi_{test,1}$ and $\sigma \models \varphi_{test,2}$.*

Proof. Suppose $\mathcal{C}_1$ and $\mathcal{C}_2$ are the assume-guarantee contracts corresponding to unit test specifications $\varphi_{test,1}$ and $\varphi_{test,2}$. Applying strong merge operator on contracts $\mathcal{C}_1$ and $\mathcal{C}_2$, we get:

$$
\begin{aligned}
\mathcal{C}_1 \cdot \mathcal{C}_2 &= (a_1 \wedge a_2, (a_1 \wedge a_2) \rightarrow [(a_1 \rightarrow g_1) \wedge (a_2 \rightarrow g_2)]) \\
&= (a_1 \wedge a_2, \neg a_1 \vee \neg a_2 \vee (g_1 \wedge g_2)).
\end{aligned}
\tag{7}
$$

Thus, the merged test specification $\varphi_{test,m} = \neg a_1 \vee \neg a_2 \vee (g_1 \wedge g_2)$ requires either one of the assumptions to not be satisfied, or for both the guarantees hold. Since $\sigma \models a_m = a_1 \wedge a_2$, and $\sigma \models \varphi_{test,m}$, we get that $\sigma \models \varphi_{test,1}$ and $\sigma \models \varphi_{test,2}$. □

A key point in our framework is that we select g_1 and g_2 to guide the test search, that is, we do not allow merged test policies that vacuously satisfy the merged test specification. This allows the test environment to always give the system an opportunity to satisfy its specification. If assumptions ever get violated, that is because of the system, and not the design of the test.

Returning to our lane change example, we define the unit test specifications as merging *behind* a car and merging *in front* of a car. The respective saturated assume guarantee contracts are defined as $\mathcal{C}_1 = (a_1, a_1 \rightarrow g_1)$ and $\mathcal{C}_2 = (a_2, a_2 \rightarrow g_2)$ with $a_1 = \varphi_{sys}^{init} \wedge \Box\varphi_{sys}^s \wedge \Box\Diamond(y = 2)$ and $g_1 = \Box\Diamond(y = y_1 = 2 \wedge x = x_1 + 1)$, and $a_2 = \varphi_{sys}^{init} \wedge \Box\varphi_{sys}^s \wedge \Box\Diamond(y = 2)$ and $g_2 = \Box\Diamond(y = y_2 = 2 \wedge x = x_2 - 1)$ being the assumptions and guarantees of the two individual tests. Thus, after applying the strong merge operation to the two contracts, the guarantee of the merged test specification for the lane change example is,

$$
g_m = \Box\Diamond(y = y_1 = 2 \wedge x = x_1 + 1) \wedge \Box\Diamond(y = y_2 = 2 \wedge x = x_2 - 1). \tag{8}
$$

4.2   Temporal Constraints on the Merged Test Specification

Definition 12 (Temporally constrained tests). For a test trace σ, let σ_t be the suffix of the trace, starting at time t. Let t_{S1}, t_{S2} be times such that $\sigma_{t_{S1}} \models \varphi_{\text{test},1}$ and $\sigma_{t_{S2}} \models \varphi_{\text{test},2}$, and assume there exists a time t_{F1} such that $t_{F1} = min(t)$ for all t, $t > t_{S1}$ such that $\sigma_{t_F 1} \not\models \varphi_{\text{test},1}$ and assume that there exists a time t_{F2} such that $t_{F2} = min(t)$ for all t, $t > t_{S2}$ such that $\sigma_{t_{F2}} \not\models \varphi_{\text{test},2}$. Then if $t_{S1} = t_{S2} = t_1$ and $t_{F1} = t_{F2} = t_2$ the tests are *parallel-merged* in the interval $t \in [t_1, t_2]$. If $t_{S1} < t_{S2}$ and $t_{F1} < t_{F2}$, or $t_{S1} > t_{S2}$ and $t_{F1} > t_{F2}$, the tests are *temporally constrained*.

In this section, we will outline when the merged test specification requires a more constrained temporal structure. To ensure that the test execution will provide the desired information, we need to make certain that each test specification is sufficiently checked. For example, consider the lane change example. There exist many executions in which one of the unit tests is satisfied (i.e. the car merges in front of a vehicle), but it is not guaranteed that the other specification is satisfied as well. Therefore these two tests can be parallel-merged. In contrast to this there exist test specifications where satisfying one will trivially satisfy the other. Then we are not able to distinguish which specification was checked, thus these unit tests should not be parallel-merged to ensure that during the test there is a point in time where each test specification is satisfied individually.

Proposition 1. *If for two test specifications $\varphi_{\text{test},1}$ and $\varphi_{\text{test},2}$, and the set of all test executions Σ, we have $\sigma \models \varphi_{\text{test},1} \iff \sigma \models \varphi_{\text{test},2} \; \forall \sigma \in \Sigma$, then these tests cannot be parallel-merged. Instead, the temporal constraint must be enforced on $g_{t,1}$ and $g_{t,2}$.*

Proof. We refine the general specification in Eq. (7), which allows any temporal structure, to include the temporal constraints in the guarantees. The temporally constrained merged test specification is thus defined as $\varphi'_{\text{test},m} = a_m \to g'_m$, with

$$g'_m = (\neg a_1 \lor \neg a_2 \lor (\Diamond(g_{t,1} \land \neg g_{t,2}) \land \Diamond(\neg g_{t,1} \land g_{t,2}) \land (g_1 \land g_2))). \tag{9}$$

Because any trace σ satisfying $\varphi'_{\text{test},m}$ will also satisfy $\varphi_{\text{test},m}$, $\sigma \models \varphi'_{\text{test},m} \Rightarrow \sigma \models \varphi_{\text{test},m}$. Any test trace satisfying this specification will consist of at least one occurrence of visiting a state satisfying $g_{t,1}$ and not $g_{t,2}$ and vice versa. Thus the guarantees of the specifications for each unit test, $g_{t,1}$ and $g_{t,2}$ are checked individually during the merged test which satisfies the temporal constraints. $\square$

4.3   Receding Horizon Synthesis of Test Policy Filter

Since the test specification characterizes the set of possible test executions, we need a policy for the test environment that is consistent with the test specification. In this section, we detail the construction of an auxiliary game graph and algorithms for receding horizon synthesis of the test specification on the auxiliary game graph. This filter will then be used to find the test policy (detailed in Sect. 4.4).

Auxiliary Game Graph G_{aux}. Assume we are given a game graph $G = (V, E)$ constructed according to Definition (8), and a (merged) test specification $\varphi_{\mathrm{test},m}$ in $GR(1)$ form as in Eq. (4). Then, for each recurrence requirement in the test specification, $\Box\Diamond\psi_{\mathrm{test}}^{f}$, we can find a set of states $\mathcal{I} = \{i_1, \dots, i_n\} \subseteq V$ that satisfy the propositional formula ψ_{test}^{f}. For each $i \in \mathcal{I}$, there exists a non-empty subset of vertices $V^s \subseteq V$ that can be partitioned into $\{\mathcal{V}_0^i, \dots, \mathcal{V}_n^i\}$. We follow [26] in partitioning the states; $\mathcal{V}_k^i$ is the set of states in V that is exactly k steps away from the goal state i. From this partition of states, we can construct a partial order, $\mathcal{P}^i = (\{\mathcal{V}_0^i, \dots, \mathcal{V}_n^i\}, \leq)$, such that $\mathcal{V}_l^i \leq \mathcal{V}_{l-1}^i$ for all $l \in \{0, \dots, n\}$. This partial order will be useful in the receding horizon synthesis of the test policy outlined below [26]. We construct an auxiliary game graph $G_{\mathrm{aux}} = (V_{\mathrm{aux}}, E_{\mathrm{aux}})$ (illustrated in Fig. 3) to accommodate any temporal constraints on the merged test specification before proceeding to synthesize a filter for the test policy. Without loss of generality, we elaborate on the auxiliary graph construction in the case of one recurrence requirement in each unit specification, but this approach can be easily extended to multiple progress requirements. An illustration of the auxiliary graph is given in Fig. 3. Let $\varphi_{\mathrm{test},1}$ and $\varphi_{\mathrm{test},2}$ be the two unit test specifications, with $\psi_{\mathrm{test},1}^{f}$ and $\varphi_{\mathrm{test},2}^{f}$, respectively. First, we make three copies of the game graph $G = (V, E)$—$G_{\varphi_{\mathrm{test},1} \vee \varphi_{\mathrm{test},2}} = (V_{1\vee2}, E_{1\vee2})$, $G_{\varphi_{\mathrm{test},1}} = (V_1, E_1)$, and $G_{\varphi_{\mathrm{test},2}} = (V_2, E_2)$. Note that, $V_{1\vee2}$, V_1 and V_2 are all copies of V, but are denoted differently for differentiating between the vertices that constitute G_{aux}, and a similar argument applies to edges of these subgraphs. Let $\mathcal{V}_0^i = \bigcup \mathcal{V}_0^{i_j} \subseteq V_{1\vee2}$ be the set of states in $G_{\varphi_{\mathrm{test},1} \vee \varphi_{\mathrm{test},2}}$ that satisfy propositional formula $\psi_{\mathrm{test},1}^{f}$. Likewise, the set of states $\mathcal{V}_0^k \subseteq V_{1\vee2}$ satisfy the propositional formula $\psi_{\mathrm{test},2}^{f}$.

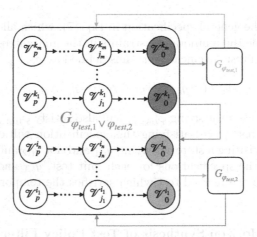

Fig. 3. Auxiliary game graph construction for the merged test specification of unit test specifications $\varphi_{\mathrm{test},1}$ and $\varphi_{\mathrm{test},2}$. Subgraphs $G_{\varphi_{\mathrm{test},1} \vee \varphi_{\mathrm{test},2}}$, $G_{\varphi_{\mathrm{test},1}}$ and $G_{\varphi_{\mathrm{test},2}}$ are copies of the game graph G constructed per Definition 8. In $G_{\varphi_{\mathrm{test},1} \vee \varphi_{\mathrm{test},2}}$, the sets of states at which the progress propositional formulas of test specifications, $\varphi_{\mathrm{test},1}$ and $\varphi_{\mathrm{test},2}$, are satisfied are shaded yellow and blue, respectively. (Color figure online)

Now, we connect the various subgraphs through the vertices in $\mathcal{V}_0^i$ and $\mathcal{V}_0^k$. Let (v_0^k, u) be an outgoing edge from a node $v_0^k \in \mathcal{V}_0^k$, and let u_1 be the vertex in subgraph $G_{\text{test},1}$ that corresponds to vertex u in $G_{\varphi_{\text{test},1} \vee \varphi_{\text{test},2}}$. Remove edge (v_0^k, u) and add the edge (v_0^k, u_1). Likewise, every outgoing edge from $\mathcal{V}_0^i \cup \mathcal{V}_0^k$ in $G_{\varphi_{\text{test},1} \vee \varphi_{\text{test},2}}$ is replaced by adding edges to $G_{\varphi_{\text{test},1}}$ and $G_{\varphi_{\text{test},2}}$. On subgraphs $G_{\varphi_{\text{test},1}}$ and $G_{\varphi_{\text{test},2}}$, vertices are partitioned and partial orders are constructed once again for $\psi_{\text{test},1}^f$ and $\psi_{\text{test},2}^f$, respectively. From $\mathcal{V}_0^i$ defined on the nodes of the graph $G_{\varphi_{\text{test},1}}$, every outgoing edge is replaced by a corresponding edge to $G_{\varphi_{\text{test},1} \vee \varphi_{\text{test},2}}$. Subgraph $G_{\varphi_{\text{test},2}}$ is connected back to $G_{\varphi_{\text{test},1} \vee \varphi_{\text{test},2}}$ in a similar manner. The construction of the auxiliary graph G_{aux} and partial order $\mathcal{P}^i$ is summarized in Algorithm 2. Our choice of constructing the auxiliary graph in this manner is amenable to constructing a simple partial order as outlined below.

Assumption 1. For unit test specifications $\varphi_{\text{test},1}$ and $\varphi_{\text{test},2}$ with recurrence specifications φ_1^p and φ_2^p, respectively, such that $\varphi_1^p = \Box\Diamond\psi_{\text{test},1}^f$ and $\varphi_2^p = \Box\Diamond\psi_{\text{test},2}^f$. Suppose there exist partial orders $\mathcal{P}^i = (\{\mathcal{V}_n^i, \ldots, \mathcal{V}_0^i\}, \leq)$ and $\mathcal{P}^k = (\{\mathcal{V}_m^k, \ldots, \mathcal{V}_0^k\}, \leq)$ on G corresponding to $\psi_{\text{test},1}^f$ and $\psi_{\text{test},2}^f$, respectively. Assume that at least one of the following is true: (a) there exists an edge (u_1, v_2) where $u_1 \in \mathcal{V}_0^i$ and $v_2 \in \mathcal{V}_j^k$ for some $j \in 1, \ldots, m$, (b) there exists an edge (u_2, v_1) where $u_2 \in \mathcal{V}_0^k$ and $v_1 \in \mathcal{V}_j^i$ for some $j \in 1, \ldots, n$.

Lemma 2. *If Assumption 1 holds, there exists a partial order on G_{aux} for the merged recurrence propositional formula, $\psi_{test,m}^f$, where $\psi_{test,m}^f$ is the propositional formula that evaluates to true at: (i) all $v \in V_{1\vee2}$ such that $v \models \psi_{test,1}^f \wedge \psi_{test,2}^f$, (ii) all $v \in V_1$ such that $v \models \psi_{test,1}^f$, and (iii) all $v \in V_2$ such that $v \models \psi_{test,2}^f$.*

Proof. Let $\mathcal{V}_0^m \subseteq V_{\text{aux}}$ denote the non-empty set of states at which $\psi_{\text{test},m}^f$ evaluates to true. Then, let $\mathcal{V}_j^m \subseteq V_{\text{aux}}$ be the subset of states that is at least j steps away from a vertex in $\mathcal{V}_0^m$. Then, we can construct the partial order $\mathcal{P}^m = (\{\mathcal{V}_l^m, \ldots, \mathcal{V}_0^m\}, \leq)$, where l is the distance of the farthest vertex connected to $\mathcal{V}_0^m$. The subset of vertices $\bigcup_j \mathcal{V}_j^m \subseteq V_{\text{aux}}$ is non-empty because $\mathcal{V}_0^m$ is non-empty. Furthermore, from Assumption 1, if (a) holds, there exists a $j \in \{1, \ldots, l\}$ such that $\mathcal{V}_j^m \cap \mathcal{V}_0^i$ is non-empty. Likewise, if (b) holds, there exists a $j \in \{1, \ldots, l\}$ such that $\mathcal{V}_j^m \cap \mathcal{V}_0^k$ is non-empty. Therefore, for some $j \in \{1, \ldots, l\}$ there exists a test execution σ over the game graph G_{aux} such that $\sigma \models \Box\Diamond\psi_{\text{test},m}^f$. □

Remark 2. If Assumption 1 is not true, the unit tests corresponding to test specifications $\varphi_{\text{test},1}$ and $\varphi_{\text{test},2}$ cannot be merged.

Receding Horizon Synthesis on G_{aux}. We leverage receding horizon synthesis to scalably compute the set of states $\mathcal{W}$ from which the test environment can realize the test specification on the system in a test execution. Note that we are not synthesizing a test strategy using the receding horizon approach, instead using $\mathcal{W}$ as a filter on a search algorithm (MCTS) that finds an optimal test policy. Further details on applying receding horizon strategies for temporal logic planning can be found in [26]. A distinction in our work is that there can be multiple states in graph G_{aux} that satisfy a progress requirement on the test specification.

For a test specification $\varphi_{\text{test},1}$ with progress propositional formula $\square\lozenge\psi^f_{\text{test},1}$, let $\mathcal{I}$ be the set of states on G_{aux} at which $\psi^f_{\text{test},1}$ evaluates to true. Specifically, for some goal $i \in \mathcal{I}$, if the product state starts at j steps from i (i.e. $v \in \mathcal{V}^i_{j+1}$), the test environment is required to guide the product state to $\mathcal{V}^i_{j-1}$. The corresponding formal specification for the test environment is,

$$\psi^i_j = (v \in \mathcal{V}^i_{j+1} \wedge \Phi \wedge \square\varphi^s_{\text{sys}} \wedge \square\lozenge\varphi^f_{\text{sys}}) \rightarrow (\square\lozenge(v \in \mathcal{V}^i_{j-1}) \wedge \square\varphi^s_{\text{test}} \wedge \square\psi^s_{\text{test}} \wedge \square\Phi), \tag{10}$$

where Φ is the invariant condition that ensures that ψ^i_j is realizable. See [26] for further details on how this invariant can be constructed. Since there are $|\mathcal{I}|$ different ways to satisfy the goal requirement $\psi^f_{\text{test},1}$, and the test specification requires that we satisfy $\psi^f_{\text{test},1}$ for at least one $i \in \mathcal{I}$. To capture this in the receding horizon framework the test execution must progress to at least one $i \in \mathcal{I}$, formally stated as,

$$\Psi^{\mathcal{I}}_j = \vee_{i \in \mathcal{I}} \psi^i_j. \tag{11}$$

Thus, the set of states from which the test environment has a strategy that satisfies the specification in Eq. (11) is the short horizon filter, denoted by $\mathcal{W}^{\mathcal{I}}_j$. Let $j_{\max}$ denote the supremum of all shortest paths from a vertex $v \in V$ to some $i \in \mathcal{I}$. Then, overall test policy filter is the union of short-horizon test policy filters,

$$\mathcal{W}^{\mathcal{I}} = \bigcup_{j=1}^{j_{\max}} \mathcal{W}^{\mathcal{I}}_j. \tag{12}$$

The synthesis of $\mathcal{W}^{\mathcal{I}}$ and its use as a test policy filter in the MCTS procedure used to find the test environment policy is outlined in Algorithm 1. Note, that this receding horizon approach to generating a filter $\mathcal{W}$ can be applied on any $GR(1)$ specification and its corresponding game graph. For the merged test specification, $\mathcal{W}^{\mathcal{I}}$ is generated on G_{aux} where $\mathcal{I}$ is the set of states corresponding to $\psi^f_{\text{test},m}$, and for simplicity, we apply the following arguments on G_{aux}. Let $G_{\mathcal{W}^{\mathcal{I}}} = (V_{\mathcal{W}}, E_{\mathcal{W}})$ be the subgraph of G_{aux} induced by $\mathcal{W}^{\mathcal{I}}$ such that $V_{\mathcal{W}} = \mathcal{W}^{\mathcal{I}} \subseteq V_{\text{aux}}$ and $E_{\mathcal{W}} = \{(u,v) \in E_{\text{aux}} | u \in \mathcal{W}^{\mathcal{I}} \wedge v \in \mathcal{W}^{\mathcal{I}}\}$.

On $\mathcal{W}^{\mathcal{I}}$ as a Test Policy Filter. Inspired by work on shield synthesis [6], we use the winning set $\mathcal{W}^{\mathcal{I}}$ as a filter to guide rollouts in the Monte Carlo Tree Search sub-routine for finding the test policy. Since $\Psi^{\mathcal{I}}_j$ is a disjunction of short-horizon $GR(1)$ specifications, it is possible that an execution always satisfies $\Psi^{\mathcal{I}}_j$ without ever satisfying the progress requirement $\square\lozenge\psi^f_{\text{test}}$. This happens when the test execution makes progress towards some $i \in \mathcal{I}$ but never actually reaches a goal in $\mathcal{I}$, resulting in a live lock. Further details addressing this are given in the Appendix. We *assume* that the graph is constructed such that there are no such cycles. In addition to using $W^{\mathcal{I}}$ to ensure that $\Psi_j^{\mathcal{I}}$ will always be satisfied, we enforce progress by only allowing the search procedure to take actions that will lead to a state which is closer to one of the goals $i \in \mathcal{I}$. Thus, the search procedure will ensure that for every state $v_l \in \mathcal{V}_l^i$, the control strategy for the next horizon will end in $v_{l'} \in \mathcal{V}_k^i$, such that $k \leq l$ for at least one goal $i \in \mathcal{I}$.

Fig. 4. Illustration of the intersection of the winning sets for the unit specification. V_{test} are depicted as circles and V_{sys} as rhombi. The black states lie in the intersection and the filter will ensure that only these states are being searched. The orange intersection represents the set of traces of the merged test specification.

Theorem 1. *Receding horizon synthesis of test filter $W^{\mathcal{I}}$ is such that any test execution σ on $G_{W^{\mathcal{I}}}$ starting from an initial state in $V_{\mathcal{W}} \cap V$ satisfies the test specification in Eq. (4).*

Proof. For the recurrence formula of the merged test specification, $\Box\Diamond\psi_{\text{test},m}^f$, suppose there exists a single vertex on G_{aux} that satisfies $\psi_{\text{test},m}^f$. Then, it is shown in [26] that if there exists a partial order $(\{\mathcal{V}_p^i, \ldots, \mathcal{V}_0^i\}, \leq)$ on G_{aux}, we can find a set of vertices $\mathcal{W}^i \subseteq V_{\text{aux}}$, such that every test execution σ that remains in $\mathcal{W}^i$, will satisfy the safety requirements $\Box\varphi_{\text{test}}^s$ and $\Box\psi_{\text{test}}^s$, and the invariant Φ. Furthermore, given the partial order $(\{\mathcal{V}_p^i, \ldots, \mathcal{V}_0^i\}, \leq)$, one can find a test policy to ensure that the σ makes progress along the partial order such that for some $t > 0$, $\sigma_t \in \mathcal{V}_0^i$. However, in case of multiple vertices in G_{aux} that satisfy $\psi_{\text{test},m}^f$, we need to extend the receding horizon synthesis to specification $\Psi_j^{\mathcal{I}}$. We construct the filter $W^{\mathcal{I}}$ and also check that for every test execution σ, there exists $i \in \mathcal{I}$ such that for every $k \geq 0$, $\sigma_k \in \mathcal{V}_j^i$ and $\sigma_{k+1} \in \mathcal{V}_{j'}^i$. Therefore, because the auxiliary game graph is assumed to not have cycles, the test execution makes progress on the partial order of at least one $i \in \mathcal{I}$ at each timestep, thus eventually satisfying $\psi_{\text{test},m}^f$. Thus every execution of our algorithm will satisfy Eq. (4). $\qquad\square$

Algorithm 1. Merge Unit Tests $(\varphi_{\text{test},1}, \varphi_{\text{test},2}, \varphi_{\text{sys}}, \mathcal{T}_{\text{sys}}, \mathcal{T}_{\text{test},1}, \mathcal{T}_{\text{test},2}, \rho)$

Input: Unit test specifications $\varphi_{\text{test},1}$ and $\varphi_{\text{test},2}$, system specification φ_{sys}, System $\mathcal{T}_{\text{sys}}$, unit test environments, $\mathcal{T}_{\text{test},1}$ and $\mathcal{T}_{\text{test},2}$, and quantitative metric of robustness ρ,

Output: Merged test specification $\varphi_{\text{test},m}$, Merged test environment $\mathcal{T}_{\text{test},m}$, Merged test policy $\pi_{\text{test},m}$

1: $\mathcal{C}_1, \mathcal{C}_2 \leftarrow$ Construct contracts for $\varphi_{\text{test},1}$ and $\varphi_{\text{test},2}$
2: $\mathcal{T}_{\text{test}} \leftarrow \mathcal{T}_{\text{test},1} \times \mathcal{T}_{\text{test},2}$ Merged test environment
3: $\mathcal{T}_{\text{prod}} \leftarrow \mathcal{T}_{\text{sys}} \times \mathcal{T}_{\text{test}}$ Product transition system
4: $G \leftarrow$ Game graph from product transition system $\mathcal{T}_{prod}$
5: $\mathcal{C}_m := (a_m, a_m \rightarrow g_m) \leftarrow$ strong merge$(\mathcal{C}_1, \mathcal{C}_2)$ Constructing the merged specification
6: $\varphi_{\text{test},m} \leftarrow a_m \rightarrow g_m$ Merged test specification
7: $G_{\text{aux}} \leftarrow$ Auxiliary game graph.
8: $\mathcal{I} = \{s \in \mathcal{V}_{\text{aux}} | s \models \psi_{\text{test},m}^f\}$ Defining goal states and partial orders
9: **for** $i \in \mathcal{I}$ **do**
10:     $\mathcal{P}^i := \{(\mathcal{V}_p^i, \ldots, \mathcal{V}_0^i)\} \leftarrow$ Partial order for goal i
11:     $\psi_j^i \leftarrow$ Receding horizon specification for goal i at distance j
12: **end for**
13: $\mathcal{W}^{\mathcal{I}} := \{\mathcal{W}_j^i\} \leftarrow$ Test policy filter for goal i at a distance of j
14: $\pi_{\text{test},m} \leftarrow$ Searching for test policy guided by $\mathcal{W}^{\mathcal{I}}$
15: **return** $\varphi_{\text{test},m}, \mathcal{T}_{\text{test},m}, \pi_{\text{test},m}$

4.4 Searching for a Test Policy

To find the merged test policy $\pi_{text,m}$, we use Monte-Carlo Tree Search (MCTS), which is a search method that and combines random sampling with the precision of a tree search. Using MCTS with an upper confidence bound (UCB) was introduced in [16] as upper confidence bound for trees (UCT) which guarantees that given enough time and memory, the result converges to the optimal solution. We use MCTS to find $\pi_{\text{test,m}}^*$, the approximate solution to Problem 1 for the merged test. We apply the filter that was generated according to the approach detailed in Sect. 4.3 to constrain the search space as shown graphically in Fig. 4.

Proposition 2. *Algorithm 1 is sound.*

Proof. This follows by construction of the algorithm and the use of MCTS with UCB. Given a test policy π_{test} and a system policy π_{sys}, for every resulting execution $\sigma_{\pi_{\text{sys}} \times \pi_{\text{test}}}$ starting from an initial state in $\mathcal{W}^{\mathcal{I}}$, it is guaranteed that $\sigma \models \varphi_{\text{test},m}$ by Theorem 1. This is because for any action chosen by the test environment according to the policy π_{test} found by MCTS, we are guaranteed to remain in $\mathcal{W}^{\mathcal{I}}$ for any valid system policy π_{sys}. If $\mathcal{W}^{\mathcal{I}} = \emptyset$ or the initial state is not in $\mathcal{W}^{\mathcal{I}}$, the algorithm will terminate before any rollout is attempted and no policy is returned. It can be shown that the probability of selecting the optimal action converges to 1 as the limit of the number of rollouts is taken to infinity. For convergence analysis of MCTS, please refer to [16]. □

Complexity Analysis. The time complexity of $GR(1)$ synthesis is in the order of $O(|N|^3)$, where $|N|$ is the size of the state space. To improve the scalability, our algorithm uses a receding horizon approach to synthesize the winning sets, which reduces the time complexity significantly, please prefer to [26]. The complexity for MCTS is given as $O(ijkl)$ with j the number of rollouts, k the branching factor of the tree, l the depth of the tree, and i the number of iterations. In our approach the filter reduces the size of the search space, for a visualization refer to Fig. 4. The number of rollouts and iterations are design variables, that can be chosen to ensure convergence. More details on the complexity of MCTS for the lane change example can be found in the Appendix.

Definition 13 (Coverage). A test execution σ *covers* a test specification φ_{test} if the test execution non-trivially satisfies the test specification, that is, $\sigma \models \varphi_{\text{test}}$ and $\sigma \models \varphi_{\text{sys}}^{init} \wedge \Box \varphi_{\text{sys}}^{s} \wedge \Box \Diamond \varphi_{\text{sys}}^{f}$. A set of test executions $T = \{\sigma_1, \ldots, \sigma_n\}$ *covers* the set of test specifications $\Phi := \{\varphi_{\text{test},1}, \ldots, \varphi_{\text{test},m}\}$ iff for each test specification $\varphi_{\text{test}} \in \Phi$, there exists a test execution $\sigma_j \in T$ such that σ_j *covers* $\varphi_{\text{test},1}$.

Optimizing for the smallest set of test executions that cover a set of test specifications is combinatorial in the number of test specifications. In this work, we outlined an algorithm for merging two unit tests. In future work, given N unit tests, we will consider the problem of constructing a smaller set of N' merged test specifications with upper bounds on N'/N.

Lemma 3. *Given a set of unit test specifications,* $\Phi_T := \{\varphi_{test,1}, \ldots, \varphi_{test,N}\}$ *such that N test executions are are required to cover Φ, i.e. one test execution for each test specification, merging unit tests results in N' test executions that cover Φ where $N' \leq N$. The equality holds iff no two unit tests in Φ can be merged.*

Proof. If at least a pair of test specifications in Φ can be merged, it is possible to characterize a set of test specifications Φ' such that the cardinality of Φ', N', is always smaller than N. If each test specification in Φ' has a test execution, then we have $N' < N$ test executions. □

5   Examples

We implemented the examples as a discrete gridworld simulation in Python, where the system controller is non-deterministic and the test agents follow the test policy generated by our framework. We use the Temporal Logic and Planning Toolbox (TuLiP) to synthesize the winning sets [27] and online MCTS to find the test policy. Videos of the results can be found in the linked GitHub repository.

5.1   Lane Change

For our discrete lane change example, we define $\rho(\sigma)$ as the x-value of the cell in which the system finished its lane change maneuver. We search for the test policy that satisfies the test specification in Eq. (8) as explained in Sect. 4. Snapshots of the resulting test execution are depicted in Fig. 5.

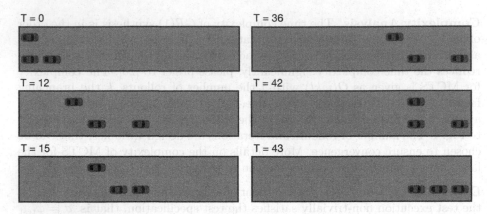

Fig. 5. Snapshots during the execution of the test generated by our framework. The system under test (red car) needs to merge onto the lower lane between the two test agents (blue cars). (Color figure online)

Unprotected Left-Turn at Intersection. Consider the example of an autonomous vehicle (AV) crossing an intersection with the intention of taking a left-turn. The test agents are a car approaching the intersection from the opposite direction and a pedestrian crossing the crosswalk to the left of the AV under test. The intersection layout can be seen in Fig. 6. The individual tests are defined to be waiting for a car, and waiting for a pedestrian while taking a left turn. The unit specification for waiting for the pedestrian are defined according to Eq. (4), with

$$\varphi_{sys}^{init} = (\mathbf{x}_S \in I_S), \quad \Box\Diamond\varphi_{sys}^f = \Diamond(\mathbf{x}_S \in \mathcal{S}_G), \quad \Box\Diamond\psi_{test}^f = \Diamond(\mathbf{x}_S \in \mathcal{S}_P \wedge \mathbf{x}_P \in T_P),$$
(13)

with $\mathbf{x}_S$ the system coordinates, I_S the initial state of the system, $\mathcal{S}_G$ the set of desired goal states after the left turn, $\mathbf{x}_P$ the pedestrian coordinates, and $\mathcal{S}_P$ the states in which the car must wait for the pedestrian if the pedestrian is in a state in T_P. Similarly we define the specification for waiting for the tester car (detailed in the Appendix).

The robustness metric is assumed to be the time until the traffic light changes to red starting the moment the system executes a successful left turn, and minimizing this metric results in a difficult test execution. Next, we merge unit test contracts, and derive the resulting merged test specification. According to Proposition 1, this merged specification needs to include the temporal constraints as defined in Eq. (9). In this example, waiting for the tester car and waiting for the pedestrian trivially imply each other in this example. Any execution of the system waiting at the intersection will satisfy both unit specifications. Thus we need to find a test where the system waits for just the tester car at some time during the test execution and waits for the tester pedestrian at another time during the test execution. We follow the approach detailed in Sect. 4.3 to generate the auxiliary graph for this example, with the terminal states corresponding

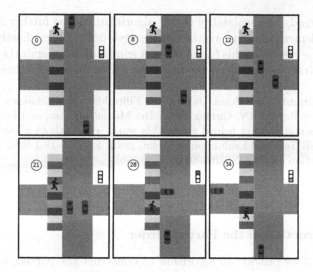

Fig. 6. Snapshots during the execution of the unprotected left turn test generated by our framework. The autonomous vehicle (AV) under test (red) should take an unprotected left turn and wait for the pedestrian and the car (blue) individually, which are agents of the test environment. In the snapshots at time steps 8 and 12, the AV waits just for the car, and in time step 21 it waits just for the pedestrian. (Color figure online)

to a successful left turn through the intersection after satisfying the temporally constrained merged test specification. The graph for this example is illustrated in Fig. 3, with test, 1 and test, 2 being the subscripts for the first and second unit test specification. We then generate the test policy filter by constructing a partial order for the goal states and synthesizing the winning sets with the receding horizon strategy detailed in Sect. 4.3. Finally, applying this test filter on MCTS to find the test policy. Figure 6 shows snapshots from a test execution resulting from a test policy generated by Algorithm 1. As expected, we see the system first waiting for the tester car to pass the intersection. Even after the tester car passes, the pedestrian is still traversing the crosswalk, causing the system to wait for the pedestrian, satisfying the temporally constrained merged test specification.

6 Conclusion and Future Work

In this work, we presented a framework for merging unit test specifications. While we applied this framework to two discrete-state examples in the self-driving domain, this framework can be applied to test other autonomous systems as well. This paper details the mathematical and algorithmic foundation for merging two unit tests. This technique could be used as a subroutine to optimize for a small set of tests that cover several unit specifications. The winning set structure of the unit specifications could be leveraged to decide which unit specifications should be merged. The scalability of our algorithm can be further improved by symbolic implementations to synthesize the test policy filter. Lastly, we would like to show the results of this framework on continuous dynamical systems with a discrete abstraction for which the test policy filter can be synthesized.

Acknowledgements. We thank Dr. Ioannis Filippidis, Dr. Tichakorn Wongpirom-sarn, Íñigo Íncer Romeo, Dr. Qiming Zhao, Dr. Michel Ingham, and Dr. Karena Cai for valuable discussions that helped shape this work. The authors acknowledge funding from AFOSR Test and Evaluation program, grant FA9550-19-1-0302 and National Science Foundation award CNS-1932091.

7   Appendix

7.1   Construction of the Partial Order

In Algorithm 2 we provide an algorithm to construct the partial order and the auxiliary game graph.

7.2   Live Lock

Depending on the construction of the partial order, the test could end up in a live lock. This is a result of planning over a short horizon for a disjunction of specifications, ψ_j^i, each of which specifies progress on different partial orders. An example of naively applying $\mathcal{W}^{\mathcal{I}}$ as a filter is given in Fig. 7b, where an execution can get stuck in the loop $(\mathcal{V}_2^1 \rightarrow \mathcal{V}_3^2 \rightarrow \mathcal{V}_2^2 \rightarrow \mathcal{V}_3^1 \rightarrow \ldots)$, where progress towards goals 1 and 2 happens infinitely often but neither of the goals are reached. Consider the example of a roundabout, where the system always makes progress towards one of the exits while driving around the roundabout, even if it never chooses to take an exit. To address this, we propose removing a goal from $\mathcal{I}$ that the test execution has stopped making progress towards, and store it in $\mathcal{I}'$. If $\mathcal{I}$ becomes empty before one of the goals are reached, we reset $\mathcal{I}$ to have all goals stored in $\mathcal{I}'$.

Remark 3. This approach to ensuring that the test execution reaches one of the goals $i \in \mathcal{I}$ requires that eventually, there exists a path.

Algorithm 2. Construction of Partial Order and Auxiliary Graph

Input: Game graph $G = (V, E)$, propositional formulas $\psi_{\text{test},1}^f$ and $\psi_{\text{test},2}^f$ constituting the progress requirements of unit test specifications

Output: Auxiliary game graph G_{aux}

1: $G_{\varphi\text{test},1\vee\varphi\text{test},2} := (V, E) \leftarrow G$ Initialize subgraph
2: $G_{\varphi\text{test},1} := (V_1, E_1) \leftarrow G$ Initialize subgraph
3: $G_{\varphi\text{test},2} := (V_2, E_2) \leftarrow G$ Initialize subgraph
4: $[\mathcal{P}_{\varphi\text{test},1\vee\varphi\text{test},2}^i, \mathcal{P}_{\varphi\text{test},1\vee\varphi\text{test},2}^k] \leftarrow$ Partial order$(G_{\varphi\text{test},1\vee\varphi\text{test},2}, [\psi_{\text{test},1}^f, \psi_{\text{test},2}^f])$
5: $\mathcal{P}_{\varphi\text{test},1}^i \leftarrow$ Partial order$(G_{\varphi\text{test},1}, \psi_{\text{test},1}^f)$
6: $\mathcal{P}_{\varphi\text{test},2}^k \leftarrow$ Partial order$(G_{\varphi\text{test},2}, \psi_{\text{test},2}^f)$
7: $E_{\varphi\text{test},1\vee\varphi\text{test},2}^r \subseteq E$ Deleting outgoing edges from $\mathcal{V}_0^i \cup \mathcal{V}_0^k \subseteq V$ within $G_{\varphi\text{test},1\vee\varphi\text{test},2}$

8: $E_{\varphi\text{test},1\vee\varphi\text{test},2}^a$ Adding edges from $\mathcal{V}_0^i \cup \mathcal{V}_0^k \subseteq V$ to subgraphs $G_{\varphi\text{test},1}$ and $G_{\varphi\text{test},2}$
9: $E_{\varphi\text{test},1}^r \subseteq E_1$ Deleting outgoing edges from $\mathcal{V}_0^i \subseteq V_1$ within $G_{\varphi\text{test},1}$
10: $E_{\varphi\text{test},1}^a$ Adding edges from $\mathcal{V}_0^i \subseteq V_1$ to subgraph $G_{\varphi\text{test},1\vee\varphi\text{test},2}$
11: $E_{\varphi\text{test},2}^r \subseteq E_2$ Deleting outgoing edges from $\mathcal{V}_0^k \subseteq V_2$ within $G_{\varphi\text{test},2}$
12: $E_{\varphi\text{test},2}^a$ Adding edges from $\mathcal{V}_0^k \subseteq V_2$ to subgraph $G_{\varphi\text{test},1\vee\varphi\text{test},2}$
13: $V_{\text{aux}} = V \cup V_1 \cup V_2$
14: $E_{\text{aux}} = (E \setminus E_{\varphi\text{test},1\vee\varphi\text{test},2}^r) \cup (E_1 \setminus E_{\varphi\text{test},2}^r) \cup (E_2 \setminus E_{\varphi\text{test},2}^r) \cup E_{\varphi\text{test},2}^a \cup E_{\varphi\text{test},1}^a \cup E_{\varphi\text{test},1\vee\varphi\text{test},2}^a$
15: $G_{\text{aux}} = (V_{\text{aux}}, E_{\text{aux}})$
16: **return** $G_{\text{aux}}, \mathcal{P}_{\varphi\text{test},1\vee\varphi\text{test},2}^i, \mathcal{P}_{\varphi\text{test},1\vee\varphi\text{test},2}^k, \mathcal{P}_{\varphi\text{test},1}^i, \mathcal{P}_{\varphi\text{test},2}^k$

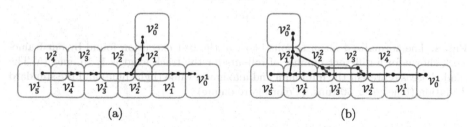

(a)   (b)

Fig. 7. Sketch of receding horizon winning set with and without cycle.

7.3   Example: Lane Change

On the lane change example, we analyzed the convergence of MCTS as the search procedure. Figure 8 shows that the terminal cost (robustness metric) reaches the maximum value with a relatively low number of rollouts. This is due to the fact that we are applying our framework to a problem with a relatively small action space for the test environment, using the test policy filter, and MCTS as an online policy. Even though the state space of the lane change example grows significantly with an increase of the track length, the actions that the testers can take are at maximum four (both move, both stay, one moves/one stays). With the use of the winning set and depending on the positions of the system and testers, the number of possible actions can be smaller. Because only

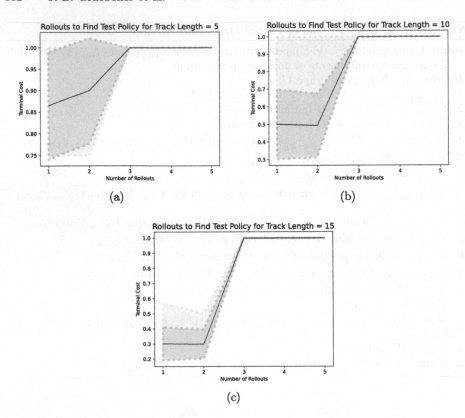

Fig. 8. The normalized mean terminal cost of the test execution found by our framework shown for a different number of rollouts for the track lengths 5, 10, and 15. The shaded areas represent the minimum and maximum value (light blue) and the standard deviation (blue) over 50 runs. (Color figure online)

actions that remain in the winning set for the specification can be chosen, the search procedure quickly finds a policy that maximizes the cost. The number of iterations used by the online MCTS depends on the actions of the system and is upper bounded by the maximum duration of the test. As we find a search procedure online, every time that the test environment has to take its turn, MCTS executes the specified number of rollouts to choose the next action, and this continues until the test is finished.

In Fig. 9 the runtime for the winning set synthesis is shown. We compare the runtime of the receding horizon approach to the synthesis of the full horizon winning set for each goal location at once. While the runtimes for both approaches increase significantly, the full horizon approach is already unable to generate a winning set for a track length of 11 for the same specifications.

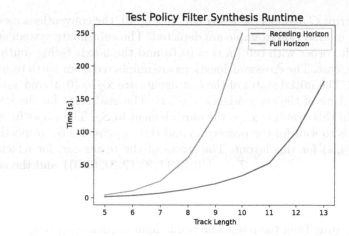

Fig. 9. The computation time required to generate the winning set filter with the receding horizon approach and by computing the entire winning set for each possible goal at once. The experiments were run on a MacBook Pro with a 2.3 GHz Quad-Core Intel Core i7 processor with 32 GB RAM.

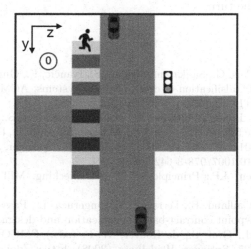

Fig. 10. Layout of the unprotected left turn at intersection example. The system starts in cell (7,4) and wants to reach the goal cell (0,3), while the initial positions of the test agents are at the beginning of the road and crosswalk. (Color figure online)

7.4   Example: Unprotected Left Turn

The test specification for waiting for the test car is specified according to Eq. (4), with

$$\varphi_{sys}^{init} = (\mathbf{x}_S \in I_S), \quad \Box\Diamond\varphi_{sys}^{f} = \Diamond(\mathbf{x}_S \in \mathcal{S}_G), \quad \Box\Diamond\psi_{test}^{f} = \Diamond(\mathbf{x}_S \in \mathcal{S}_C \wedge \mathbf{x}_C \in T_C),$$
$$(14)$$

where the subscript C denotes the tester car. In Fig. 10, the conventions used for the left turn at intersection example are depicted. The coordinate system starts in the upper left corner with cell $(y, z) = (0, 0)$ and the y-axis facing south and the z-axis facing east. The crosswalk locations are numbered from north to south, starting with 0. The initial states of the test agents are $\mathbf{x}_C = (0, 3)$ and $\mathbf{x}_P = 0$, and the initial state of the system is $\mathbf{x}_S = (7, 4)$. The goal state for the system is $\mathbf{x}_G = (0, 3)$. In this example $\mathbf{x}_G$ is the only element in $\mathcal{S}_g$. The states in which the system needs to wait for the pedestrian and the car, $\mathcal{S}_P$ and $\mathcal{S}_P$ respectively, are both $\mathbf{x} = (4, 4)$ for this layout. The states of the tester car, for which the system has to wait are given as $\mathcal{T}_C = \{(0, 3), (1, 3), (2, 3), (3, 3)\}$ and the states of the pedestrian, for which the system has to wait are $\mathcal{S}_P = \{1, 2, 3, 4, 5\}$, which represent the cells on the crosswalk, that map to grid coordinates. Note that if the pedestrian is in cell 0, the system is not required to wait for the pedestrian, as she is too far away from the road. The traffic light sequence is predetermined, the light will be green for a fixed number of time steps t_g, followed by t_y time steps of yellow and red for t_r time steps. We are assuming that the system designer supplied the robustness metric as the time until the traffic light turns red, resulting in a harder test the closer the light is to red once the system successfully takes the turn.

References

1. Abbas, H., Fainekos, G., Sankaranarayanan, S., Ivančić, F., Gupta, A.: Probabilistic temporal logic falsification of cyber-physical systems. ACM Trans. Embedded Comput. Syst. (TECS) **12**(2s), 1–30 (2013)
2. Annpureddy, Y., Liu, C., Fainekos, G., Sankaranarayanan, S.: S-TALiRo: a tool for temporal logic falsification for hybrid systems. In: Abdulla, P.A., Leino, K.R.M. (eds.) TACAS 2011. LNCS, vol. 6605, pp. 254–257. Springer, Heidelberg (2011). https://doi.org/10.1007/978-3-642-19835-9_21
3. Baier, C., Katoen, J.P.: Principles of Model Checking. MIT press, Cambridge (2008)
4. Benveniste, A., Caillaud, B., Ferrari, A., Mangeruca, L., Passerone, R., Sofronis, C.: Multiple viewpoint contract-based specification and design. In: de Boer, F.S., Bonsangue, M.M., Graf, S., de Roever, W.-P. (eds.) FMCO 2007. LNCS, vol. 5382, pp. 200–225. Springer, Heidelberg (2008). https://doi.org/10.1007/978-3-540-92188-2_9
5. Benveniste, A., et al.: Contracts for system design. Found. Trends Electron. Des. Autom. **12**(2–3), 124–400 (2018)
6. Bloem, R., Könighofer, B., Könighofer, R., Wang, C.: Shield synthesis: In: Baier, C., Tinelli, C. (eds.) TACAS 2015. LNCS, vol. 9035, pp. 533–548. Springer, Heidelberg (2015). https://doi.org/10.1007/978-3-662-46681-0_51
7. Dijkstra, E.W.: Guarded commands, non-determinacy and formal derivation of programs. Commun. ACM **18**(8), 453–457 (1975)
8. Dreossi, T., Donzé, A., Seshia, S.A.: Compositional falsification of cyber-physical systems with machine learning components. J. Autom. Reason. **63**(4), 1031–1053 (2019)
9. Dreossi, T., et al.: VERIFAI: a toolkit for the design and analysis of artificial intelligence-based systems. arXiv preprint arXiv:1902.04245 (2019)

10. Filippidis, I., Murray, R.M.: Layering assume-guarantee contracts for hierarchical system design. Proc. IEEE **106**(9), 1616–1654 (2018)
11. Fremont, D.J., et al.: Formal scenario-based testing of autonomous vehicles: From simulation to the real world. In: 2020 IEEE 23rd International Conference on Intelligent Transportation Systems (ITSC), pp. 1–8. IEEE (2020)
12. Ghosh, S., Berkenkamp, F., Ranade, G., Qadeer, S., Kapoor, A.: Verifying controllers against adversarial examples with Bayesian optimization. In: 2018 IEEE International Conference on Robotics and Automation (ICRA), pp. 7306–7313. IEEE (2018)
13. Kalra, N., Paddock, S.M.: Driving to safety: how many miles of driving would it take to demonstrate autonomous vehicle reliability? Transp. Res. Part A: Policy Pract. **94**, 182–193 (2016)
14. Klischat, M., Liu, E.I., Holtke, F., Althoff, M.: Scenario factory: creating safety-critical traffic scenarios for automated vehicles. In: 2020 IEEE 23rd International Conference on Intelligent Transportation Systems (ITSC), pp. 1–7. IEEE (2020)
15. Kloetzer, M., Belta, C.: A fully automated framework for control of linear systems from temporal logic specifications. IEEE Trans. Autom. Control **53**(1), 287–297 (2008)
16. Kocsis, L., Szepesvári, C.: Bandit based Monte-Carlo planning. In: Fürnkranz, J., Scheffer, T., Spiliopoulou, M. (eds.) ECML 2006. LNCS (LNAI), vol. 4212, pp. 282–293. Springer, Heidelberg (2006). https://doi.org/10.1007/11871842_29
17. Kress-Gazit, H., Fainekos, G.E., Pappas, G.J.: Temporal-logic-based reactive mission and motion planning. IEEE Trans. Robot. **25**(6), 1370–1381 (2009)
18. Lamport, L.: Win and sin: predicate transformers for concurrency. ACM Trans. Programm. Lang. Syst. (TOPLAS) **12**(3), 396–428 (1990)
19. Meyer, B.: Applying' design by contract'. Computer **25**(10), 40–51 (1992)
20. Nuzzo, P., et al.: A contract-based methodology for aircraft electric power system design. IEEE Access **2**, 1–25 (2013)
21. Passerone, R., Íncer Romeo, Í., Sangiovanni-Vincentelli, A.L.: Coherent extension, composition, and merging operators in contract models for system design. ACM Trans. Embedded Comput. Syst. (TECS) **18**(5s), 1–23 (2019)
22. Piterman, N., Pnueli, A., Sa'ar, Y.: Synthesis of reactive(1) designs. In: Emerson, E.A., Namjoshi, K.S. (eds.) VMCAI 2006. LNCS, vol. 3855, pp. 364–380. Springer, Heidelberg (2005). https://doi.org/10.1007/11609773_24
23. Pnueli, A.: The temporal logic of programs. In: 18th Annual Symposium on Foundations of Computer Science (SFCS 1977), pp. 46–57. IEEE (1977)
24. Sankaranarayanan, S., Fainekos, G.: Falsification of temporal properties of hybrid systems using the cross-entropy method. In: Proceedings of the 15th ACM International Conference on Hybrid Systems: Computation and Control, pp. 125–134 (2012)
25. Seshia, S.A., Sadigh, D., Sastry, S.S.: Towards verified artificial intelligence. arXiv preprint arXiv:1606.08514 (2016)
26. Wongpiromsarn, T., Topcu, U., Murray, R.M.: Receding horizon temporal logic planning. IEEE Trans. Autom. Control **57**(11), 2817–2830 (2012)
27. Wongpiromsarn, T., Topcu, U., Ozay, N., Xu, H., Murray, R.M.: Tulip: a software toolbox for receding horizon temporal logic planning. In: Proceedings of the 14th International Conference on Hybrid Systems: Computation and Control, pp. 313–314 (2011)

Quantification of Battery Depletion Risk Made Efficient

Holger Hermanns and Gilles Nies[✉]

Universität des Saarlandes, Saarland Informatics Campus, Saarbrücken, Germany
{hermanns,nies}@cs.uni-saarland.de

Abstract. Rechargeable batteries are the backbone of our mobile and wireless way of life. In the context of model-based battery depletion estimation, the kinetic battery model (KiBaM) pairs modelling convenience with prediction accuracy. This paper proposes algorithms to analyze energy budgets with respect to a rechargeable stochastic KiBaM with capacity bounds. Concretely, we present two different approaches to narrowly bound the cumulative depletion risk induced by a sequence of possibly noisy tasks. One of them enables adaptive discretization of the (provably) relevant portion of the charge space. The other avoids this discretization by instead propagating charge percentiles iteratively, resulting in safe bounds on the depletion risk. Both approaches have their particular strengths with respect to applicability, precision, space and runtime complexity. We provide empirical evidence of their characteristics on the basis of a representative example.

Keywords: Battery Power · Kinetic Battery Model · Depletion Risk Estimation · Adaptive Discretization · Percentile Propagation

1 Introduction

Rechargeable battery technology is nowadays built into almost every portable device, and is the acclaimed enabler of electric mobility. For battery electric vehicles, *range anxiety* is the fear of the vehicle occupants to get stranded on the way to a destination due to battery depletion. Efficient and precise methods for model-based estimation of battery depletion risks are needed in order to outstrip range anxiety as a major barrier to large scale adoption of all-electric cars. Due to the omnipresence of rechargeable batteries, estimation methods for battery depletion risks actually have a much broader application range, from earth-orbiting satellites, to autonomous vacuum robots, to wearable smartwatches, to energy buffers in power grids. In the context of model-based battery depletion estimation, the kinetic battery model (KiBaM) [9] pairs modelling convenience with prediction accuracy and constitutes the premier consensus model relative to the simplistic linear battery model and much more complex electro-chemical models [8]. As such, the KiBaM, or one of its many extensions [4,11,14] is often used when investigating the lifetime of a system [3,11], inferring suitable capacity limits [1], planning

© Springer Nature Switzerland AG 2022
J. V. Deshmukh et al. (Eds.): NFM 2022, LNCS 13260, pp. 156–174, 2022.
https://doi.org/10.1007/978-3-031-06773-0_8

and scheduling of tasks [13] and by now has found its way into widely used tools such as UPPAAL as first-class citizen [7].

Recently proposed extensions to the KiBaM are [6]: *(i)* the incorporation of capacity bounds when charging, *(ii)* uncertainty in the initial battery state, useful to reflect manufacturing tolerances and self-discharging while inactive, and *(iii)* imprecision or noise in battery loads. These extensions have been motivated especially by low-Earth orbit applications [5,10,12]. In this setting, it has become apparent that precise and efficient estimates of battery depletion risks are much harder to calculate than in a purely deterministic setting. This paper addresses this challenge.

We start off from the existing, universally applicable discretization algorithm, which safely approximates the entire battery state distribution [6]. This is enhanced to an *adaptive discretization* approach that keeps only a relevant neighborhood of the state of charge space (Section 3.2). This enables the use of smaller and more focussed representations without altering precision, which in turn implies better runtime and space efficiency at the cost of a negligible computational overhead. This improved method inherits all the merits from the previous version.

Additionally, we propose an approach that avoids discretization of the charge space entirely. It instead directly estimates the quantity of interest, the depletion risk (Section 3.3). The computation harvests analytical insights for the computation of charge percentiles, thereby providing bounds on the depletion risk of the entire initial charge distribution. The approach however comes with mild restrictions on the class of initial charge distributions it supports. Iterative applications of this so-called *percentile propagation* scheme, result in arbitrarily tight and preconfigurable bounding of the true depletion risk.

We discuss both these approaches in great detail, and empirically evaluate (Section 4) their effectiveness with respect to runtime and memory requirements. Percentile propagation comes with a precision level configurable a priori and can play out its strengths especially on scenarios with low noise. On the other hand, adaptive discretization is conceptually bound to higher space requirements which pays off for higher noise scenarios, with the precision being revealed a posteriori only. All experimental results and the code are made available as an artefact.

2   Battery Kinetics

The *Kinetic Battery Model* (KiBaM) is an energy storage model that models the state of charge (SoC) of a battery by splitting it into two disjoint portions, namely *(i)* the available charge $A(t)$, the portion of stored charge that is directly available to be consumed or replenished, *(ii)* the bound charge $B(t)$, the portion of stored charge that is considered chemically bound inside the battery, and is not immediately available. These quantities can be considered unitless and abstract for mathematical and analytical purposes, and we will denote battery states as rowvectors $[a; b]$, throughout this paper. The battery is strained by a *load* $\ell(t)$ that represents charging and discharging if $\ell(t) < 0$ and $\ell(t) > 0$, respectively. If there is no load (i.e. $\ell = 0$) we speak of a *resting* period.

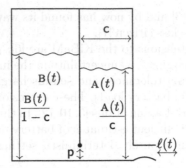

Fig. 1. The two-wells illustration of the KiBaM.

The principle behind the KiBaM is that one type of charge is converted into the other over time via diffusion, depending on the amount of each type of charge currently in the battery. For this reason the KiBaM is often depicted as two interconnected wells holding fluid as depicted on the right above, as seen in Figure 1. The model is characterized by two parameters, the first of which being the *width* parameter $c \in]0, 1[$. It corresponds to the width of the available charge well, while $1 - c$ is the width of the bound charge well. The second parameter, the *diffusion rate* parameter $p > 0$, is the factor of proportionality of the difference in fluid levels of both wells, namely $A(t)/c$ and $B(t)/1 - c$, and thus governs the speed with which bound charge is converted to available charge and vice-versa. Among other characteristics, these parameters are usually estimated for a specific battery type, and are likely subject to change as the battery ages.

KiBaM ODE System. Mathematically, the KiBaM state of charge evolves as indicated by two coupled differential equations given in Equation 1.

$$\dot{A}(t) = -\ell(t) + p \left(\frac{B(t)}{1 - c} - \frac{A(t)}{c} \right)$$
$$\dot{B}(t) = \qquad p \left(\frac{A(t)}{c} - \frac{B(t)}{1 - c} \right) \qquad (1)$$

The dynamics of the KiBaM account for a couple of non-linear effects that can be observed in real-world batteries, which makes the model at hand highly relevant, as is made clear by related literature [8].

We denote SoCs by row vectors $[a; b]$, and denote the set of all SoCs by $\mathbb{S}$. We say that a SoC is *in equilibrium* iff no diffusion is taking place, i.e $\frac{a}{c} = \frac{b}{1-c}$. We interpret operations on SoCs to be componentwise, hence for an arithmetic operator $\star$, and for any comparison operator $\triangleright$ we have

$$[a_0; b_0] \star x := \begin{cases} [a_0 \star a_1; b_0 \star b_1] & \text{if } x = [a_1; b_1] \\ [a_0 \star k; b_0 \star k] & \text{if } x = k \in \mathbb{R} \end{cases}$$

and

$$[a_0; b_0] \triangleright x := \begin{cases} a_0 \triangleright a_1 \wedge b_0 \triangleright b_1 & \text{if } x = [a_1; b_1] \\ a_0 \triangleright k \wedge b_0 \triangleright k & \text{if } x = k \in \mathbb{R} \end{cases}.$$

Load model. The load model we want to investigate is described by *tasks* and sequences thereof. A *task* (Δ, ℓ) is a pair of a positive time duration $\Delta > 0$ and a load ℓ with which the battery is strained throughout that time duration, i.e. for $0 \leq t < \Delta$, we have $\ell(t) = \ell$. We denote the set of tasks by $\mathbb{T} :=$ $\mathbb{R}_{>0} \times \mathbb{R}$. A sequence of tasks thus induces a piecewise constant load sequence. It is possible to derive a solution of the ODEs at time Δ, for instance by using Laplace transforms. We can capture all of the above formally, by introducing an operator on tasks and SoCs, as a vector valued linear map, taking the initial available and bound charge a_0 and b_0 as argument. Thus we denote the successor SoC of $[a_0; b_0]$ as application of an operator $\mathbb{K}$, i.e. $\mathbb{K}_{(\Delta,\ell)}[a_0; b_0]$. The choice of piecewise constant load sequences is necessary to enable efficient handling of depletion and saturation scenarios outlined in the next section. In most practical cases, like a processor executing an arithmetic operation, the generated load sequences can be considered piecewise constant, or loads can easily be collapsed into a single constant load by averaging. However, there are instances in which the load is inherently non-linear. Charging via solar panels is such an example, as the panel's efficiency is highly dependent on temperature, which decreases as it is hit by sun light. In such cases the load is abstracted into a constant load, for instance by considering mean efficiencies.

Depletion and Capacity Limits. So far, the operator $\mathbb{K}$ is defined on any given SoC and its evolution potentially spans the entire range of SoCs, including the negatives. We instead define the region of critically low SoCs in terms of a given battery depletion level depl, which in turn induces depletion thresholds on available and bound charge quantities by $[\underline{a}; \underline{b}] := [c; 1 - c] \cdot \text{depl}$. We refer to a SoC S as *safe* iff $S > [\underline{a}; \underline{b}]$. Safe SoCs can sustain a discharging task for a non-zero duration without depleting. We let $\perp := [\underline{a}; \underline{b}]$, denote the *canonical* depletion SoC. SoC S is *depleted* if its *available charge* is lower than the depletion threshold, i.e. if $a \leq \underline{a}$. For depletion, only the available charge dimension is decisive, because this is when a battery-powered system stops operating. We do not differentiate between depleted SoCs, as none of them can support any further discharging.

Real-world batteries are evidently not infinite energy storage devices. The KiBaM does not reflect this, since the $\mathbb{K}$-operator can attain arbitrarily large values. We enforce a capacity limit of cap $\in \mathbb{R}_{>\text{depl}}$, which induces limits $[\overline{a}; \overline{b}] := [c; (1 - c)] \cdot \text{cap}$ on available and bound charge. We call a SoC *saturated* and *over-saturated*, iff $a = \overline{a}$ and $a > \overline{a}$, respectively. Just as for depletion, the *available charge* is the decisive quantity for saturation.

Charging and discharging are not fully symmetric: A depleted SoC can no longer power its task, contrary to a saturated SoC that *continues to operate*, but changes its further charging behavior. In this case a *sufficiently* high charging load ℓ induces that only the bound charge increases due to diffusion while the available charge stays at the capacity limit: This is the case if $\ell \leq \text{p}(b_0/(1 - c) - \text{cap})$. Stated differently, the *least* bound charge to compensate the diffusion given ℓ is $b_\ell^{\text{sat}} := \frac{\ell}{\text{p}}(1-c)+\overline{b}$. For a sufficient load, the subsequent evolution of the bound charge is given by $\text{B}_\Delta^{\text{sat}}(b_0) = e^{-ck\Delta} \cdot b_0 + \left(1 - e^{-ck\Delta}\right) \cdot \overline{b}$, with $k = \text{p}/\text{c}(1 - \text{c})$. We lift this evolution to an operator on SoCs $\mathbb{K}_\Delta^{\text{sat}}$ by $\mathbb{K}_\Delta^{\text{sat}}[a; b] := [a; \text{B}_\Delta^{\text{sat}}(b)]$.

Evolution across Saturation. Each non-saturated SoC will eventually become saturated via indefinite charging. We are interested in the time point of saturation, since this is when the dynamics of the battery change. So, with $\overline{\Delta}$ identifying the time point at which the first component of $\mathbb{K}_{(\overline{\Delta},\ell)}S$ is exactly $\overline{a}$, and with $\delta := \Delta - \overline{\Delta}$ being the remainder of the task, we can express the SoC of a KiBaM after powering a given task (Δ, ℓ) by splitting, if needed, the evolution at $\overline{\Delta}$. This results in an operator $\mathbb{K}$,

$$\mathbb{K}_T S := \begin{cases} \bot, & \text{if } S = \bot \text{ or } \mathbb{K}_T S \text{ is depleted} \\ \mathbb{K}_\delta^{\text{sat}} \circ \mathbb{K}_{(\overline{\Delta},\ell)}S & \text{if } \mathbb{K}_T S \text{ is over-saturated} \\ \mathbb{K}_T S, & \text{otherwise} \end{cases}.$$

Note that $\mathbb{K}$ is invariant with respect to the canonical depletion SoC $\bot$ (first case), even if T is a charging task, reflecting that the battery-powered device can no longer sustain operation. The correctness of the development in the next sections hinges on the following two very intuitive properties, both of which can be proven via case distinctions and investigation of the sign of partial derivatives of $\mathbb{K}$.

Lemma 1. *Let Δ be a positive duration, S, S_0, S_1 be SoCs, ℓ_0, ℓ_1 be loads, and T be a task. We have*

$$\ell_0 \geq \ell_1 \implies \overline{\mathbb{K}}_{(\Delta,\ell_0)}S \leq \overline{\mathbb{K}}_{(\Delta,\ell_1)}S \quad \text{and} \quad S_0 \leq S_1 \implies \overline{\mathbb{K}}_T S_0 \leq \overline{\mathbb{K}}_T S_1.$$

The computational nature of $\overline{\mathbb{K}}$ is problematic, because $\overline{\Delta}$ is transcendental [6], thus we resort to under- and over-approximations. A simplistic approximation is the interval $[0, \Delta]$, but saturation time points can easily be approximated up to a chosen width ε by an iterative interval halving scheme: Starting from the interval $[0, \Delta]$, we test the exact midpoint of the interval for saturation. The midpoint becomes the new right endpoint $\overline{\Delta}_\downarrow$ if the battery is already over-saturated midway, otherwise it becomes the new left endpoint $\overline{\Delta}_\uparrow$. We repeat this step until the width of the interval $[\overline{\Delta}_\uparrow, \overline{\Delta}_\downarrow]$ falls below ε, and return the interval.

To enclose the true evolution of the SoC across saturation, we will adjust the load ℓ we work with so that instead saturation is reached at precisely $\overline{\Delta}_\uparrow$, respectively $\overline{\Delta}_\downarrow$. In order to derive the load reaching saturation from a SoC S precisely at, say Δ, we solve $\mathbb{K}_{(\Delta,\ell)}S = [\overline{a}; \bullet]$ for ℓ (which is straightforward) and denote by $\overline{\ell}_\Delta S$ its solution. With this, we define operators $\overline{\mathbb{K}}^\uparrow$ and $\overline{\mathbb{K}}^\downarrow$ that approximate $\overline{\mathbb{K}}$. They both agree with $\overline{\mathbb{K}}$ unless $\mathbb{K}_{(\Delta,\ell)}S$ is over-saturated for task (Δ, ℓ) and SoC S, while in that case we define

$$\overline{\mathbb{K}}^\downarrow_{(\Delta,\ell)}S := \mathbb{K}_{\delta_\uparrow}^{\text{sat}} \circ \overline{\mathbb{K}}_{(\overline{\Delta}_\uparrow, \overline{\ell}_{\overline{\Delta}_\uparrow})}S \quad \text{and} \quad \overline{\mathbb{K}}^\uparrow_{(\Delta,\ell)}S := \mathbb{K}_{\delta_\downarrow}^{\text{sat}} \circ \mathbb{K}_{(\overline{\Delta}_\downarrow, \overline{\ell}_{\overline{\Delta}_\downarrow})}S$$

where $\delta_\downarrow := \Delta - \overline{\Delta}_\downarrow$ and $\delta_\uparrow := \Delta - \overline{\Delta}_\uparrow$. Figure 2 illustrates how we handle the saturation time point scenario of the $\overline{\mathbb{K}}^\downarrow$- and $\overline{\mathbb{K}}^\uparrow$-operators. Indeed, $\overline{\mathbb{K}}^\downarrow$ and $\overline{\mathbb{K}}^\uparrow$ bound the actual KiBaM SoC evolution: For any SoC S and any task $T \in \mathbb{T}$ we have $\overline{\mathbb{K}}^\uparrow_T S \leq \overline{\mathbb{K}}_T S \leq \overline{\mathbb{K}}^\downarrow_T S$.

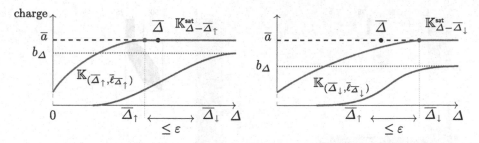

Fig. 2. An illustration of the $\overline{\mathbb{K}}^{\downarrow}$-operator (left) and the $\overline{\mathbb{K}}^{\uparrow}$-operator (right). $\overline{\mathbb{K}}^{\downarrow}$ makes the available charge (red) hit the saturation limit $\bar{a}$ at $\overline{\Delta}_{\uparrow}$ prior to actual saturation at $\overline{\Delta}$, which leads to an *over-approximation* of the SoC, while with $\overline{\mathbb{K}}^{\uparrow}$ this happens afterwards at $\overline{\Delta}_{\downarrow}$, inducing a SoC *under-approximation*, and this order transfers to the bound charges (blue).

Stochastic Battery Kinetics. In order to treat the KiBaM as a stochastic object, we consider the initial SoC $[a_0; b_0]$ as being random, reflecting the real phenomenon of uncertain initial charge levels, rooted in wear and manufacturing variances [2] as well as self discharging rates during a battery's shelf life. The distribution of a random SoC is described by a triple $\langle \bar{f}, f, z \rangle$, where $\bar{f}$ is a one-dimensional density function, describing how the bound charge is distributed under the condition that the battery is saturated, f is a joint density over the non-saturated SoC space, and finally $z \in [0, 1]$ that is the cumulative probability of depletion, i.e. the likelihood of the battery depleting withing a given time horizon. A random $[A; B]$ is said to be distributed according to a SoC distribution $\langle \bar{f}, f, z \rangle$, and write $[A; B] \sim \langle \bar{f}, f, z \rangle$ if for any measurable set $X \subseteq \mathbb{S}$, we have

$$\mathbf{Pr}[S \in X] = \iint_{[a;b] \in X} f(a, b) \, \mathrm{d}a \, \mathrm{d}b \; + \int_{[\bar{a};b] \in X} \bar{f}(b) \, \mathrm{d}b \; + \; z \mathbb{I}_{\perp \in X}$$

where $\mathbb{I}_{\varphi}$ denotes the indicator function of a condition φ. In Figure 3a, we visualize a SoC distribution as three stacked heatmaps: On the very top resides a one-dimensional heatmap depicting $\bar{f}$, in the middle sits the two-dimensional density of the non-saturated safe portion f and on the bottom the accumulated depletion risk z as a color-coded probability value. The red checkered area represents unsafe SoCs. In addition, we consider the load ℓ that is imposed on a battery as being a random quantity as well, reflecting, for example, measurement noise. Thus, the load on the battery is considered a random variable L, independent of the SoC, distributed as given by an associated probability density function g. We write $L \sim g$ with $g : \mathbb{R} \to \mathbb{R}$, and refer to tasks with random load as *noisy tasks*.

3   Algorithms

Up to this point, most of what has been covered has been presented (possibly using different notation) in earlier work [6]. We now turn to the question how to efficiently compute the SoC distribution resulting from a certain sequence of possibly noisy tasks. This is a problem of major concern in applications.

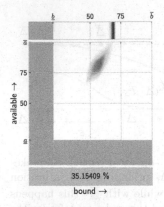 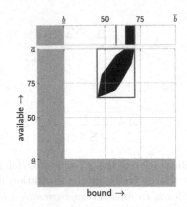

(a) A SoC distribution.   (b) A SoC distribution's support and its bounding box.

Fig. 3. A SoC distribution, its support and bounding box.

Along the way, we need to refer to the charge portion for which a certain task is saturating or depleting. For a task T and available charge level $\tilde{a}$ we call the set $\{S \mid \mathbb{K}_T S = [\tilde{a}; \bullet]\}$ the $\tilde{a}$-*target boundary* of T. Specifically, fixing $\tilde{a} := \underline{a}$ gives the *depletion boundary* of T, and $\tilde{a} := \overline{a}$ the *saturation boundary*. We visualize these concepts in the SoC space in Figure 4.

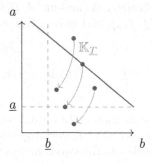 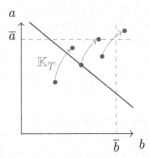

Fig. 4. A discharging task's depletion boundary (left) and charging task's saturation boundary (right), with illustrative $\overline{\mathbb{K}}$-mappings of SoCs.

Assuming a discharging task $\underline{T}$, the red line indicates the depletion boundary of $\underline{T}$. Any SoC (represented in the figure as blue dots) above and to the right of the depletion boundary remains safe after $\underline{T}$, while SoCs below and to the left of the boundary are rendered unsafe. SoCs that are part of the boundary reach a SoC of the form $[\underline{a}; b]$, for some b.

Analogously, for a charging task $\overline{T}$, the SoCs above and to the right of the saturation boundary are over-saturated after $\overline{T}$, while SoCs below and to the left of the boundary remain unsaturated. SoCs that are situated exactly on the boundary end up saturated. As the above example already indicates, the target boundaries are linear in the SoC space and are strictly monotonically decreasing (can be shown by investigating the sign of the derivative). We write $a_{\overline{T}}^{\tilde{a}}(b)$ or $b_{\overline{T}}^{\tilde{a}}(a)$ to denote the target boundary ($\tilde{a}$ omitted if clear from context). $a_{\overline{T}}^{\tilde{a}}(b)$ describes the available charge on the boundary as function of the bound charge, and vice-versa for $b_{\overline{T}}^{\tilde{a}}(a)$. As a consequence, the SoC S on T's target boundary that minimizes (maximizes) $\mathbb{K}_T S = [\tilde{a}; b_\Delta]$ is at the left (right) domain boundary.

3.1 Static Discretization

To track SoC distributions along noisy task sequences, past work has discretized noisy tasks with finite support into discretized noisy tasks and SoC distributions into discretized SoC distributions [6]. For the former, the task support is divided into a number of equi-sized chunks. For each chunk, the entirety of the probability mass contained is concentrated into its left-hand endpoint to get an over-approximation, and in the right-hand endpoint to get an under-approximation. The discretization of SoC distributions is similar: One constructs a two-dimensional $N \times N$ grid with equi-sized grid cells on the SoC space between depletion and saturation limits, and condenses the probability mass of each grid-cell into the bottom-left (the smallest SoC in the cell) and top-right corners (the largest SoC in the cell) to under- and over-approximate the original distribution, respectively. Powering a task then means $\overline{\mathbb{K}}^{\uparrow}$- and $\overline{\mathbb{K}}^{\downarrow}$-mapping each cell's appropriate corner-point, and rounding the result to the appropriate corner-point of the cell it landed in, thereby amassing approximation errors proportional to the size of grid-cells. Given that the grid stays invariant, we call this scheme *static discretization* (SD).

3.2 Adaptive Discretization

In most scenarios, the initial SoC of a battery is located in only a small portion of the SoC space: This is because the operation of battery-powered systems usually starts with an (almost) fully charged and equilibrated battery. This leads to just a localized neighborhood of grid-cells actually carrying non-zero probability mass, while much of the rest of the grid is empty. In the following we generalize this discretization scheme by bounding boxes: Instead of putting a grid on the entire SoC space, we put a grid only on a rectangular, localized neighborhood of the actual support of the initial SoC distribution, and propagate this neighborhood along a task sequence, exploiting properties of the $\mathbb{K}$-operators to keep these neighborhoods as tight as possible. This way, grid-cells remain as small as possible, which entails minimal approximation errors with every tasks. We refer to this scheme as *adaptive discretization* (AD). In Figure 3b we visualize a bounding box of a SoC distribution.

Definition 1. A bounding box $\mathfrak{B}$ of a SoC distribution $\langle \bar{f}, f, z \rangle$ is a triple of intervals $\langle A, B, \overline{B} \rangle$ such that

$$\text{supp}(f) \subseteq A \times B \subseteq [\underline{a}, \overline{a}] \times [\underline{b}, \overline{b}] \quad and \quad \text{supp}(\bar{f}) \subseteq \{\overline{a}\} \times \overline{B} \subseteq \{\overline{a}\} \times [\underline{b}, \overline{b}].$$

In Figure 3b above we display the support (black) and its bounding box (blue) for the SoC distribution shown before. Before we transform the SoC distribution according to $\mathbb{K}$, we compute the successor bounding box, denoted by $\overline{\mathbb{K}}_T \mathfrak{B}$, from task T and the initial bounding box $\mathfrak{B} := \langle A, B, \overline{B} \rangle$. The successor box can be computed in a modular fashion, meaning that we can combine the successors of each of the two components $\overline{\mathbb{K}}_T[A; B] := \overline{\mathbb{K}}_T \langle A, B, \emptyset \rangle$ and $\overline{\mathbb{K}}_T \overline{B} := \overline{\mathbb{K}}_T \langle \emptyset, \emptyset, \overline{B} \rangle$ into a bounding box of the successor SoC distribution. To this end, we start by introducing the notion of subsumption and closure of bounding boxes, by essentially lifting the subset relation and the union operation on intervals.

Definition 2 (Subsumption). Let $\mathfrak{B}_0 := \langle A_0, B_0, \overline{B}_0 \rangle$ and $\mathfrak{B}_1 := \langle A_1, B_1, \overline{B}_1 \rangle$ be boxes. We denote by $\mathfrak{B}_0 \sqsubseteq \mathfrak{B}_1$ that $\mathfrak{B}_0$ is subsumed by $\mathfrak{B}_1$. Subsumption is defined as $\mathfrak{B}_0 \sqsubseteq \mathfrak{B}_1 := A_0 \subseteq A_1 \wedge B_0 \subseteq B_1 \wedge \overline{B}_0 \subseteq \overline{B}_1$.

Definition 3 (Closure of boxes). Let $\mathfrak{B}_0 := \langle A_0, B_0, \overline{B}_0 \rangle$ and $\mathfrak{B}_1 := \langle A_1, B_1, \overline{B}_1 \rangle$ be two boxes. The closure of $\mathfrak{B}_0$ and $\mathfrak{B}_1$, denoted by $\mathfrak{B}_0 \sqcup \mathfrak{B}_1$ is defined componentwise by $\mathfrak{B}_0 \sqcup \mathfrak{B}_1 := \langle A_0 \sqcup A_1, B_0 \sqcup B_1, \overline{B}_0 \sqcup \overline{B}_1 \rangle$, where $M \sqcup N$ is defined as $[min(M \cup N), max(M \cup N)]$ provided both M and N are non-empty. Otherwise, $M \sqcup N$ returns M if $N = \emptyset$, or otherwise N. The closure of countably many boxes $\bigsqcup_{i=0}^{N} \mathfrak{B}_i$ is defined inductively.

The following properties will in the sequel be used throughout without explicit reference. For two boxes $\mathfrak{B}_0$ and $\mathfrak{B}_1$, we have $\mathfrak{B}_0 \sqcup \mathfrak{B}_1 \sqsupseteq \mathfrak{B}_0$ and $\mathfrak{B}_0 \sqcup \mathfrak{B}_1 \sqsupseteq \mathfrak{B}_1$. Furthermore, if $\langle \bar{f}, f, z \rangle$ is a SoC distribution with bounding box $\mathfrak{B}_0$ then each $\mathfrak{B}_1$ with $\mathfrak{B}_0 \sqsubseteq \mathfrak{B}_1$ is also a bounding box of $\langle \bar{f}, f, z \rangle$.

Successor bounding box if charging. We now focus on how to compute the successor box $\overline{\mathbb{K}}_T \mathfrak{B}$, where T is a charging task, since charging is the most involved scenario. The basic principle is to track the smallest and the largest SoCs, given by the left and right endpoints of the box intervals, respectively. By Lemma 1 these SoCs remain the extreme SoCs after T, and therefore the successor box still accounts for the entire support of the successor SoC distribution. Certain intermediate SoCs are of specific interest: If the bounding box $\mathfrak{B}$ is cut by T's saturation boundary, then a part of the box contributes to the *saturated* part of the successor box $\overline{\mathbb{K}}_T \mathfrak{B}$, while the other part remains *unsaturated*, and thus contributes to the unsaturated part of the successor box $\overline{\mathbb{K}}_T \mathfrak{B}$. Since the saturation boundary is monotonically decreasing, the left-most intersection point with the box decides where the unsaturated part of the successor box ends, and where the saturated part of the successor box starts. The resulting bounding box can then easily be composed from both parts by $\overline{\mathbb{K}}_T[A; B] \sqcup \overline{\mathbb{K}}_T \overline{B}$.

Definition 4. *Let* $A = [a^\uparrow, a^\downarrow]$ *and* $B = [b^\uparrow, b^\downarrow]$, *then*

$$
\mathbb{K}_T[A; B] := \begin{cases}
\langle \emptyset, \emptyset, [b_{\mathsf{sat}}^{\min}, b_{\mathsf{sat}}^{\max}] \rangle, & \text{if } a_T(b^\uparrow) < a^\uparrow \\
\langle [a_{\mathsf{mid}}^{\min}, a_{\mathsf{mid}}^{\max}], [b_{\mathsf{mid}}^{\min}, b_{\mathsf{mid}}^{\max}], \emptyset \rangle, & \text{if } a_T(b^\downarrow) > a^\downarrow \\
\langle [a_{\mathsf{mid}}^{\min}, \overline{a}], [b_{\mathsf{mid}}^{\min}, b_{\mathsf{hit}}^{\mathsf{top}}], [b_{\mathsf{hit}}^{\mathsf{top}}, b_{\mathsf{sat}}^{\max}] \rangle, & \text{if } b_T(a^\downarrow) \in B \\
\langle [a_{\mathsf{mid}}^{\min}, \overline{a}], [b_{\mathsf{mid}}^{\min}, b_{\mathsf{hit}}^{\mathsf{left}}], [b_{\mathsf{hit}}^{\mathsf{left}}, b_{\mathsf{sat}}^{\max}] \rangle, & \text{if } a_T(b^\uparrow) \in A
\end{cases}
$$

where $\quad [\bullet; b_{\mathsf{sat}}^{\min}] := \overline{\mathbb{K}}_T^\uparrow[\overline{a}; \overline{b}^\uparrow], \quad [a_{\mathsf{mid}}^{\min}; b_{\mathsf{mid}}^{\min}] := \mathbb{K}_T[a^\uparrow; b^\uparrow], \quad [\bullet; b_{\mathsf{hit}}^{\mathsf{top}}] := \mathbb{K}_T[a^\downarrow; b_T(a^\downarrow)]$

$\qquad\quad [\bullet; b_{\mathsf{sat}}^{\max}] := \overline{\mathbb{K}}_T^\downarrow[\overline{a}; \overline{b}^\downarrow], \quad [a_{\mathsf{mid}}^{\max}; b_{\mathsf{mid}}^{\max}] := \mathbb{K}_T[a^\downarrow; b^\downarrow], \quad [\bullet; b_{\mathsf{hit}}^{\mathsf{left}}] := \mathbb{K}_T[a_T(b^\uparrow); b^\uparrow].$

To compute the successor of the saturated part, we need to incorporate the additional scenario of saturated SoCs temporarily becoming unsaturated due to diffusion. The decisive value is the least diffusion-compensating bound charge b_ℓ^{sat}, which separates the box into a perpetually saturated portion (use $\mathbb{K}^{\mathsf{sat}}$), and a transiently unsaturated portion (use $\overline{\mathbb{K}}^\uparrow/\overline{\mathbb{K}}^\downarrow$).

Definition 5. *For* $\overline{B} = [\overline{b}^\uparrow, \overline{b}^\downarrow]$ *and* $T := (\Delta, \ell)$ *we define*

$$
\mathbb{K}_T \overline{B} := \begin{cases}
\langle \emptyset, \emptyset, [\mathrm{B}_\Delta^{\mathsf{sat}}(\overline{b}^\uparrow), \mathrm{B}_\Delta^{\mathsf{sat}}(\overline{b}^\downarrow)] \rangle, & \text{if } b_\ell^{\mathsf{sat}} < \overline{b}^\uparrow \\
\langle [a_{\mathsf{mid}}^{\min}, a_{\mathsf{mid}}^{\max}], [b_{\mathsf{mid}}^{\min}, b_{\mathsf{mid}}^{\max}], \emptyset \rangle, & \text{if } b_T(\overline{a}) > \overline{b}^\downarrow \\
\langle \emptyset, \emptyset, [b_{\mathsf{sat}}^{\min}, b_{\mathsf{sat}}^{\max}] \rangle, & \text{if } b_T(\overline{a}) < \overline{b}^\uparrow \wedge b_\ell^{\mathsf{sat}} > \overline{b}^\downarrow \\
\langle [a_{\mathsf{mid}}^{\min}, \overline{a}], [b_{\mathsf{mid}}^{\min}, b_{\mathsf{ret}}], [b_{\mathsf{ret}}, \mathrm{B}_\Delta^{\mathsf{sat}}(\overline{b}^\downarrow)] \rangle, & \text{if } b_T(\overline{a}) \in \overline{B} \wedge b_\ell^{\mathsf{sat}} \in \overline{B} \\
\langle \emptyset, \emptyset, [b_{\mathsf{sat}}^{\min}, \mathrm{B}_\Delta^{\mathsf{sat}}(\overline{b}^\downarrow)] \rangle, & \text{if } b_T(\overline{a}) < \overline{b}^\uparrow \wedge b_\ell^{\mathsf{sat}} \in \overline{B} \\
\langle [a_{\mathsf{mid}}^{\min}, \overline{a}], [b_{\mathsf{mid}}^{\min}, b_{\mathsf{ret}}], [b_{\mathsf{ret}}, b_{\mathsf{sat}}^{\max}] \rangle, & \text{if } b_T(\overline{a}) \in \overline{B} \wedge b_\ell^{\mathsf{sat}} > \overline{b}^\downarrow
\end{cases}
$$

where $\quad [\bullet; b_{\mathsf{sat}}^{\min}] := \overline{\mathbb{K}}_T^\uparrow[\overline{a}; \overline{b}^\uparrow], \quad [a_{\mathsf{mid}}^{\min}; b_{\mathsf{mid}}^{\min}] := \mathbb{K}_T[\overline{a}; \overline{b}^\uparrow], \quad [\bullet; b_{\mathsf{ret}}] := \mathbb{K}_T[\overline{a}; b_T(\overline{a})],$

$\qquad\quad [\bullet; b_{\mathsf{sat}}^{\max}] := \overline{\mathbb{K}}_T^\downarrow[\overline{a}; \overline{b}^\downarrow], \quad [a_{\mathsf{mid}}^{\max}; b_{\mathsf{mid}}^{\max}] := \mathbb{K}_T[\overline{a}; \overline{b}^\downarrow].$

Note that we use $\overline{\mathbb{K}}^\uparrow$ and $\overline{\mathbb{K}}^\downarrow$ whenever there is saturation, thus the computed box is slightly larger than the exact one. It however subsumes the latter, and hence constitutes a valid bounding box.

Successor bounding box if discharging or resting. Essentially the dual idea applies to discharging: *(i)* Instead of saturation there might be depletion. Therefore, if the depletion boundary cuts the box into a depleting part and a non-depleting part, the left-most intersection point provides the smallest non-depleting SoC and hence the lower-left corner of the unsaturated part of $\overline{\mathbb{K}}_T \mathfrak{B}$. *(ii)* The saturated part of $\overline{\mathbb{K}}_T \mathfrak{B}$ is empty, and the top-right cornerpoint of the unsaturated part is determined as the largest among the right endpoint of $\overline{B}$, and the top-right cornerpoint of $[A; B]$. For resting, we can simply propagate the box as is, using $\mathbb{K}$.

Successor bounding box of noisy tasks. Lastly, in order to lift the above from tasks (Δ, ℓ) to discretized noisy tasks (Δ, γ), we need to compute the successor bounding box, for each load instance in the support of γ and build their closure, i.e. $\overline{\mathbb{K}}_{(\Delta,\gamma)}\mathfrak{B} := \bigsqcup_{\ell\in\mathrm{supp}(\gamma)}\overline{\mathbb{K}}_{(\Delta,\ell)}\mathfrak{B}$. The fact that this indeed provides a valid bounding box is witnessed by Lemma 1 and the properties of subsumption.

Algorithm. With all of the above in place, we are ready to formalize an algorithm that tracks an initial SoC distribution $\langle \bar{f}, f, z\rangle$ along a sequence of discretized noisy tasks $(T_i)_{i=0}^M$. A pseudo-code formulation is given in Algorithm 1. It first discretizes the initial SoC at hand, and then iteratively propagates discretized SoC distributions along discretized noisy tasks, by determining the successor box via the closure of boxes induced by the support of the noisy task loads, placing a grid into the successor box, and finally mapping the cells of the current grid onto the cells of the successor grid in an under- and over-approximating fashion.

In : A SoC distribution $\langle \bar{f}, f, z\rangle$ with bounding box $\mathfrak{B}$, a sequence of
    discretized noisy tasks $(T_i)_{i=0}^M$ and a grid size N.
Out: Two discrete SoC distributions bounding $\overline{\mathbb{K}}_{(T_i)_{i=0}^M}\langle \bar{f}, f, z\rangle$

1 $\mathfrak{B}^\uparrow := \mathfrak{B}$; $\mathfrak{B}^\downarrow := \mathfrak{B}$

2 $D^\downarrow, D^\uparrow :=$ discretizations of $\langle \bar{f}, f, z\rangle$ with box $\mathfrak{B}$

3 **foreach** $(\Delta, \gamma) \in (T_i)_{i=0}^M$ **do**

4 | $\mathfrak{B}^\uparrow := \overline{\mathbb{K}}_{(\Delta,\gamma)}\mathfrak{B}^\uparrow$; $\mathfrak{B}^\downarrow := \overline{\mathbb{K}}_{(\Delta,\gamma)}\mathfrak{B}^\downarrow$

5 | Place $N \times N$ grid in both $\mathfrak{B}^\uparrow$ and $\mathfrak{B}^\downarrow$

6 | $D^\uparrow := \overline{\mathbb{K}}^\uparrow_{(\Delta,\gamma)}D^\uparrow$ with box $\mathfrak{B}^\uparrow$; $D^\downarrow := \overline{\mathbb{K}}^\downarrow_{(\Delta,\gamma)}D^\downarrow$ with box $\mathfrak{B}^\downarrow$

7 **return** $D^\downarrow$, $D^\uparrow$

Algorithm 1: The AD algorithm in pseudo-code.

3.3   Percentile Propagation

The algorithm developed above supports (almost) any initial SoC distribution as well as load distributions, by appropriate discretization of both. The price of this generality is that of precision. Due to the permanent rounding of SoCs onto the grid-cell cornerpoints, estimates diverge the longer the task sequence we apply.

We now discuss a different approach that does not attempt to track the entire distribution, but aims at a precise estimate of the cumulative depletion risks induced by a possibly very long task sequence. Often the depletion risk constitutes the most crucial information of an energy budget analysis of a battery powered system. By restricting to a certain, relevant, class of initial SoC distributions we are indeed able to estimate that risk precisely. The idea is to exploit monotonicity of the operator $\overline{\mathbb{K}}$ (Lemma 1), in the sense that if a SoC S depletes when strained by a task sequence $(T_i)_{i=0}^n$, then every SoC *smaller than* S must also deplete. Additionally, if S is *greater than* q percent of all the initially supported SoCs, we can deduce that the depletion risk is *at least* q. Dually, if S does not deplete, then depletion risk is *at most* q. Since the depletion risk is bounded by 0 and 1, the idea is to iteratively tighten the bounds around the depletion risk by probing and propagating certain *percentiles* of the initial distribution until the bounds exhibit a difference less than a given $\varepsilon_\perp$. We refer to this paradigm as *percentile propagation* PP.

However, clearly not all SoCs are pairwise either *smaller than* or *greater than*, because $\leq$ is not a total order. Therefore we need to restrict this idea to initial SoC distributions that do not contain two pairwise incomparable SoCs with respect to $\leq$. Luckily, this is not an unrealistic assumption, since batteries that have had enough time to equilibrate exhibit exactly such initial SoC distributions. These distributions basically degenerate to one-dimensional distributions, since each SoC $[a; b]$ is uniquely defined by the sum of its components $a + b$.

For a cumulative density function (CDF) F the q–percentile is given by the generalized inverse of F, $F^{-1}(q) := \inf_{x \in \mathbb{R}} \{F(x) \geq q\}$. The infimum is needed because F is not necessarily invertible in the functional sense.

To lift the notion of percentiles to SoCs, we consider distributions over the total charge stored in a battery, since it uniquely defines SoCs supported by the SoC distribution with the above restrictions in place.

Definition 6. *Let* $\langle \bar{f}, f, z \rangle$ *be a SoC distribution such that* $(\{\bar{a}\} \times \operatorname{supp}(\bar{f})) \cup \operatorname{supp}(f)$ *is a totally ordered set with respect to* $\leq$. *We define* h *as follows:*

$$h(c) := \begin{cases} \bar{f}(b), & \text{if } c = \bar{a} + b \wedge [\bar{a}; b] \in \{\bar{a}\} \times \operatorname{supp}(\bar{f}) \\ f(a, b), & \text{if } c = a + b \wedge [a; b] \in \operatorname{supp}(f) \\ 0, & \text{otherwise} \end{cases}$$

Then, the $(z + q)$*–percentile of* $\langle \bar{f}, f, z \rangle$ *is the unique SoC* $[a; b]$ *such that* $c = a + b$ *is the (conventional)* q*–percentile of* h, *for* $0 \leq q \leq 1 - z$.

The function h essentially constitutes a diagonal sweep of the SoC space, cumulatively "picking up" SoCs in the appropriate order. The function is well-defined if, for every position of the sweep diagonal (red line), it intersects the support of $\langle \bar{f}, f, z \rangle$ (blue) in at most one single SoC, like in the following visual example:

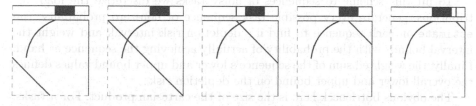

SoC distributions are inherently non-continuous because they are by definition separated into three distinct parts. In conclusion, SoC percentiles are not unique without the infimum operation. With a few restrictions, however, we are able to fulfill all the necessary assumptions to drop the infimum operator. In order to avoid technical problems, let's therefore assume that the *initial* SoC distribution exhibits no initial depletion risk, and that the entire probability mass is exclusively supported by either $\bar{f}$ or f. Again these assumptions are not very restrictive. For instance, a saturated battery (i.e. the entire probability mass is in $\bar{f}$), or a battery in full equilibrium (i.e. the entire probability mass is situated on the diagonal of f) are valid scenarios.

Depletion risk approximation. We now give a pseudo-code algorithm to bound the depletion risk within an interval of arbitrary width, given a sequence of tasks and an initial SoC distribution meeting the criteria from above.

The algorithm initially bounds the depletion risk z with the interval $[0, 1]$. We then keep halving the interval $[z_\uparrow, z_\downarrow]$ iteratively in the following sense. We look at q, the midpoint of $z_\downarrow$ and $z_\uparrow$, and check whether the q–percentile depletes when strained with $(T_i)_{i=0}^N$ using both approximation operators $\overline{\mathbb{K}}^\uparrow$ and $\overline{\mathbb{K}}^\downarrow$. If the $\overline{\mathbb{K}}^\downarrow$ trace exhibits depletion, we deduce that the depletion risk is at least q, and thus assign $z_\uparrow := q$. If the $\overline{\mathbb{K}}^\uparrow$ trace does not exhibit depletion, we conclude that the depletion risk is at most q, and assign $z_\downarrow := q$. If the approximations disagree, we narrow the approximation corridor, by gradually increasing the saturation time point precision $\varepsilon_{\overline{\Delta}}$, until they eventually agree. We keep increasing the precision by a factor of 0.1 and recompute the approximations until a consensus is reached, upon which we reset the precision $\varepsilon_{\overline{\Delta}}$ to its initial value. If said consensus is depletion, we update the lower bound $z_\uparrow := q$, otherwise the upper bound $z_\downarrow := q$, for the same reason as above. Finally, after having narrowed down the interval surrounding the true depletion risk enough, we return the current interval.

Algorithm. The function `estimate` in Algorithm 2 formalizes the above in pseudo-code. Notably, the `estimate` function describes a semi-decision procedure. Divergence may happen if the q–percentile currently under investigation corresponds to the true depletion risk z_N, and the task sequence causes battery saturation at least once. In this case, the $\overline{\mathbb{K}}^\uparrow$-, $\overline{\mathbb{K}}^\downarrow$-approximations never reach a consensus, no matter how precisely we estimate the saturation time points. In all other cases, the approximations eventually agree, and the algorithm terminates, because we halve the interval in each iteration, eventually undershooting $\varepsilon_\perp$ in width.

To lift this scheme to sequences of noisy tasks we discretize the load distributions, generate every possible task sequence of non-zero probability, run `estimate` on each sequence to find it's depletion risk interval, and weight the interval bounds with the probability of actually achieving the sequence at hand. Finally, the weighted sum of the sequence's lower and upper bound values defines the overall lower and upper bound on the depletion risk.

The obvious bottleneck here is the size of the cartesian product. For n tasks, each supporting k loads, the cartesian product has k^n members, for which we run `estimate`. For $k = 1$, the cartesian product degenerates to one single task sequence. With a generative implementation of the cartesian product, we don't need to store every trace in memory, but rather the state of the generator, which takes $O(n)$ space. Thus, this paradigm excels in space efficiency.

In : SoC distribution $\langle \bar{f}, f, z \rangle$, discretized noisy tasks $(\Delta_i, \gamma_i)_{i=0}^N$, $\varepsilon > 0$
Out: Interval bounding the depletion risk of $\overline{\mathbb{K}}_{(\Delta_i, \gamma_i)_{i=0}^N} \langle \bar{f}, f, z \rangle$

1 **Function** estimate($\langle \bar{f}, f, z \rangle$, $(T_i)_{i=0}^N$, ε):
  In : A SoC distribution $\langle \bar{f}, f, z \rangle$, a task sequence $(T_i)_{i=0}^N$ and $\varepsilon > 0$
  Out: Interval $[z_\uparrow, z_\downarrow]$ of width at most ε with $z_N \in [z_\uparrow, z_\downarrow]$

2 | $[z_\uparrow, z_\downarrow] := [0, 1]$

3 | **while** $z_\downarrow - z_\uparrow \geq \varepsilon$ **do**

4 | | $q := (z_\downarrow + z_\uparrow)/2$

5 | | $[a_q; b_q] := q$–percentile SoC of $\langle \bar{f}, f, z \rangle$

6 | | $S_\uparrow, \ S_\downarrow := \overline{\mathbb{K}}^\uparrow_{(T_i)_{i=0}^N}[a_q; b_q], \ \overline{\mathbb{K}}^\downarrow_{(T_i)_{i=0}^N}[a_q; b_q]$ with precision $\varepsilon_{\overline{\Delta}}$

7 | | **if** $S_\uparrow = \bot$ **then** $z_\uparrow := q$

8 | | **else if** $S_\downarrow \neq \bot$ **then**

9 | | | **do**

10 | | | | $\varepsilon_{\overline{\Delta}} := 0.1 \cdot \varepsilon_{\overline{\Delta}}$

11 | | | | $S_\uparrow, S_\downarrow := \overline{\mathbb{K}}^\uparrow_{(T_i)_{i=0}^N}[a_q; b_q], \overline{\mathbb{K}}^\downarrow_{(T_i)_{i=0}^N}[a_q; b_q]$ with precision $\varepsilon_{\overline{\Delta}}$

12 | | | **while** $S_\uparrow \neq S_\downarrow$

13 | | | reset $\varepsilon_{\overline{\Delta}}$

14 | | | **if** $S_\downarrow = \bot = S_\uparrow$ **then** $z_\uparrow := q$ **else** $z_\downarrow := q$

15 | | **else** $z_\downarrow := q$

16 | **return** $[z_\uparrow, z_\downarrow]$

17 $[z_\uparrow, z_\downarrow] := [0, 0]$

18 **foreach** $(\ell_j)_{j=0}^N \in \mathrm{supp}(\gamma_0) \times \cdots \times \mathrm{supp}(\gamma_N)$ **do**

19 | $p := \prod_{k=0}^N \gamma_k(\ell_k)$

20 | $[z'_\uparrow, z'_\downarrow] := \text{estimate}(\langle \bar{f}, f, z \rangle, (\Delta_j, \ell_j)_{j=0}^N, \varepsilon)$

21 | $z_\uparrow := z_\uparrow + p \cdot z'_\uparrow; \ z_\downarrow := z_\downarrow + p \cdot z'_\downarrow$

22 **return** $[z_\uparrow, z_\downarrow]$

Algorithm 2: The PP algorithm in pseudo-code.

4 Evaluation

We now cross-compare the performance of the algorithms presented. All experiments were run on an Intel(R) Core(TM) i7-10510U CPU @ 1.80 GHz-2.30 GHz and 16 GB RAM.

Comparison of SD and AD. In order to achieve a satisfying sample size of task sequences we synthesize tasks from a Markovian probabilistic load process, to ensure that the sequences exhibit a minimal degree of structure. The generated tasks are of duration $\Delta \sim \mathcal{U}[50, 500]$, and exhibit loads $\ell \sim \mathcal{U}[-30, -5]$ for charging, loads $\ell \sim \mathcal{U}[5, 30]$ for discharging and $\ell = 0$ for resting. The synthesis excludes consecutive resting tasks, but allows consecutive charging as well as discharging

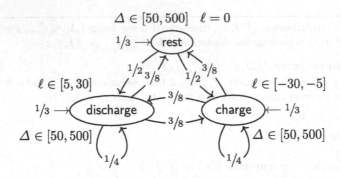

Fig. 5. A graph representation of the Markovian load process we used to synthesize (noisy) task sequences. The edge labels describe jump probabilities, while the state annotations describe the intervals loads ℓ and durations Δ are sampled from. Ingoing arrows into states represent the initial state distribution. The sampled durations and loads are taken uniformly at random from the annotated intervals. The loads then serve as the location parameter of a normal distribution.

tasks, albeit with a slight bias against this. Figure 5 provides a graph representation of the load process, a slightly altered version of the Process introduced in [6]

The battery is instantiated with a capacity of 300 000 J, c = 0.5 (thus, $\bar{a} = \bar{b} = 150000$) with a depletion threshold depl = 0.5, and various values for the diffusion parameter p. Its initial SoC is uniformly distributed on the set $\bar{a}[0.65, 0.75] \times [0.65, 0.75]\bar{b}$ discretized to different grid sizes N. The sampled load ℓ serves either as a single load, i.e. task, or as the location parameter of a normal distribution $\mathcal{N}(\ell, 1.5)$ for noisy tasks. In this case, the load distributions are truncated and discretized into 10 samples.

SD was run on 50 generated task sequences of length 150 with grid sizes $N = 500, 750, 1000, 1250$ and 1500. For each run, we determine a grid size for AD that induces a result of the same precision via binary search with the lowest and the largest grid size being 0 and the grid size used for SD, and report the relative runtime of AD with the found grid size. The runs producing a singleton interval (either 0 or 1, i.e. both approximations agree on sure survival or depletion) were discarded, because AD can find these essentially with a 1×1 grid. The aggregated results of the evaluation are depicted in Figure 6.

A comparison of the left and the middle plot shows that the faster the diffusion (larger diffusion parameter p), the more efficient AD becomes relative to SD, both in terms of runtime and grid size. The reason is, that the support of the SoC distribution is less spread out, and thus occupies a smaller portion of the bounding box, meaning we have less cells carrying a non-zero probability mass. The right and middle plot showcase a similar difference, but here the spread is caused by noise in the task loads.

The results paint a relatively clear picture of overall superiority of AD over SD, in terms of space as well as runtime efficiency.

Comparison of AD and PP. We first evaluate AD and PP on simple task sequences. We assume a battery (cap = 300 000 J, c = 0.5, p = 0.0005, depl

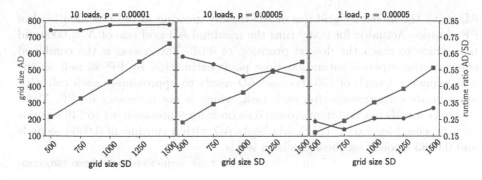

Fig. 6. Evaluation of SD vs. AD. Grid size for SD (x-axes) is plotted against mean grid size needed by AD to produce a similar solution (red squares) and against mean ratio of runtimes AD/SD for the determined grid (blue bullets).

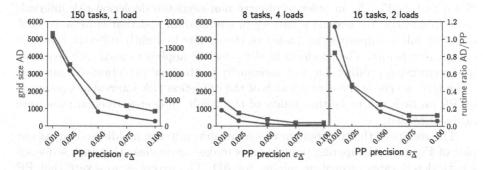

Fig. 7. Evaluation of PP vs AD. Precision for PP (x-axes) is plotted against mean grid size that AD needed to produce a similar solution (red squares) and against mean ratio of runtimes AD/PP for the determined grid (blue bullets).

$= 0.5$) that is in equilibrium and that is between 60% and 80% full, i.e. on the set $S := \{x \cdot [c; 1 - c] \mid x \in [0.6, 0.8] \cdot \mathsf{cap}\}$, and construct the initial SoC distribution $\langle \bar{f}, f, z \rangle$ such that f is a uniform distribution on S. Note that $\leq$ is indeed a total order on S.

Similar to the previous comparison, we run PP on 50 task sequences of length 150 from the load process with precision levels $\varepsilon_{\perp} = 0.1, 0.075, 0.05, 0.025$ and 0.01. For each run, we determine a grid size for AD that induces a depletion risk interval that is as narrow or narrower than $\varepsilon_{\perp}$. This can be achieved via binary search with the lowest and the largest grid size being 0 and 6000, and report the relative runtime of AD with the found grid size. The boundary of 6000 was chosen for time reasons. It is worth mentioning that AD uses the simplistic version of the saturation time point algorithm (which allows an efficient vectorized implementation), while PP uses the iterative version with $\varepsilon_{\overline{\Delta}} = 0.1$. The runs producing a singleton interval (either 0 or 1) were again discarded. The aggregated results of the evaluation are depicted in the leftmost plot of Figure 7. We observe that here PP is up to 4 orders of magnitude faster than

AD, with the necessary grid size of AD rapidly growing as the precision level of PP shrinks. Actually, for many runs the maximal AD grid size of $N = 6000$ did not suffice to reach the desired precision of 0.01. The reason is the combined effect of the superior saturation time point estimation by PP as well as the task sequence length of 150, because AD needs to approximate each cell with appropriate cornerpoints after each task, which is not necessary for PP. Mean runtimes for AD reached from around 6 seconds for a precision 0.1 to 140 seconds with precision level 0.01. PP clearly beats AD with a runtime of 0.0064 seconds and 0.0083 seconds on these precision levels.

In order to compare PP and AD on noisy task sequences, we chose two configurations, namely sequences of 8 tasks, each supporting 4 loads, as well as sequences of 16 tasks, each supporting only 2 loads. Both scenarios result in the same workload of 65 536 possible load sequences for PP. For the former configuration we needed to alter the load process to allow loads from the interval $[5, 45]$ and $[-45, -5]$, in order to observe non-singleton depletion risk intervals more frequently. We assume a battery in equilibrium and that is between 60% and 65% full. Comparing the quality of the results is slightly different from the comparison before. The precision level $\varepsilon_\perp$ for PP applies to each task sequence in the cartesian product, but not necessarily to the final depletion risk interval. Therefore, we chose the actual width of the depletion risk interval as computed by PP on each run to be the quality of the result. Singleton interval runs were again discarded.

The results of the two configurations are shown in the middle and rightmost plot of Figure 7. Comparing the two plots makes again clear that task sequence length deteriorates estimation quality for AD. The extent is so severe that PP actually beats AD for precision level $\varepsilon_\perp = 0.01$ in terms of runtime for 16 tasks, while AD was way faster for only 8 tasks.

5 Conclusion

This paper has introduced two KiBaM-based algorithms, AD and PP, to estimate the cumulative depletion risk of rechargable battery-powered systems subject to stochastic fluctuations in both the initial battery state and the loads imposed on the battery. AD generalizes the previously introduced discretization algorithm by making its focus follow the relevant neighborhood of the actual battery state, thereby improving both runtime and memory efficiency. On the other hand, PP harvests the KiBaM's order-preserving properties to iteratively narrow down the depletion risk of relevant classes of initial charge distributions.

After examining the evaluation of AD and PP a few points are worth being highlighted. First, we point out that AD is the universally applicable algorithm that can be run on any initial SoC distribution, while PP requires mild conditions on the initial charge to be fulfilled. The consequence of this is, that AD can be used to analyze systems which are already in operation, while PP is only suitable for inactive (and fully equilibriated systems) or fully charged systems. On noisy task instances with large supports, chances are that PP does not perform well, but it still provides an alternative with low space requirements, and comes with an a priori configurable precision level. On the other hand, if high precision is required, and the task sequences are long, AD requires large grids that do not directly translate into a precision level. AD has high space requirements, with the precision being revealed a posteriori only. Additionally, PP only estimates the depletion risk, which most of the time is the quantity of interest. If instead the entire final distribution is required, for example to examine where the surviving probability mass ends up at the very end of the task sequence, AD is the algorithm that should be used.

Acknowledgement. This work was partially supported by ERC Proof of Concept Grant 966770 (LEOpowver), by EU Horizon 2020 Grant 101008233 (MISSION), and by DFG grant 389792660 as part of TRR 248 – CPEC.

References

1. Boker, U., Henzinger, T.A., Radhakrishna, A.: Battery transition systems. In: Jagannathan, S., Sewell, P. (eds.) The 41st Annual ACM SIGPLAN-SIGACT Symposium on Principles of Programming Languages, POPL '14, San Diego, CA, USA, January 20–21, 2014. pp. 595–606. ACM (2014). https://doi.org/10.1145/2535838.2535875
2. Buchmann, I. Inc, C.E.: Batteries in a Portable World: A Handbook on Rechargeable Batteries for Non-engineers. Cadex Electronics (2001). https://books.google.de/books?id=YIBhAAAACAAJ
3. Cloth, L., Jongerden, M.R., Haverkort, B.R.: Computing battery lifetime distributions. In: 37th Annual IEEE/IFIP International Conference on Dependable Systems and Networks (DSN'07). pp. 780–789 (2007). https://doi.org/10.1109/DSN.2007.26
4. Fenner, G., Stringini, L., Rangel, C., Canha, L.: Comprehensive model for real battery simulation responsive to variable load. Energies **14**, 3209 (05 2021). https://doi.org/10.3390/en14113209
5. Fraire, J.A., Nies, G., Hermanns, H., Bay, K., Bisgaard, M.: Battery-aware contact plan design for LEO satellite constellations: The ulloriaq case study. In: IEEE Global Communications Conference, GLOBECOM 2018, Abu Dhabi, United Arab Emirates, December 9–13, 2018. pp. 1–7. IEEE (2018). https://doi.org/10.1109/GLOCOM.2018.8647822
6. Hermanns, H., Krcál, J., Nies, G.: How is your satellite doing? battery kinetics with recharging and uncertainty. Leibniz Trans. Embed. Syst. **4**(1), 04:1–04:28 (2017). https://doi.org/10.4230/LITES-v004-i001-a004
7. Ivanov, D., Larsen, K.G., Schupp, S., Srba, J.: Analytical solution for long battery lifetime prediction in nonadaptive systems. In: McIver, A., Horváth, A. (eds.) Quantitative Evaluation of Systems - 15th International Conference, QEST 2018, Beijing, China, September 4–7, 2018, Proceedings. Lecture Notes in Computer Science, vol. 11024, pp. 173–189. Springer (2018). https://doi.org/10.1007/978-3-319-99154-2_11
8. Jongerden, M.R., Haverkort, B.R.: Which battery model to use? IET Softw. **3**(6), 445–457 (2009). https://doi.org/10.1049/iet-sen.2009.0001
9. Manwell, J.F., McGowan, J.G.: Lead acid battery storage model for hybrid energy systems. Solar energy **50**(5), 399–405 (1993)

10. Nies, G., Stenger, M., Krčál, J., Hermanns, H., Bisgaard, M., Gerhardt, D., Haverkort, B., Jongerden, M., Larsen, K.G., Wognsen, E.R.: Mastering operational limitations of leo satellites - the gomx-3 approach. Acta Astronautica **151**, 726–735 (2018). https://doi.org/10.1016/j.actaastro.2018.04.040, https://www.sciencedirect.com/science/article/pii/S009457651730321

11. Rao, V., Singhal, G., Kumar, A., Navet, N.: Battery model for embedded systems. In: 18th International Conference on VLSI Design held jointly with 4th International Conference on Embedded Systems Design. pp. 105–110 (2005). https://doi.org/10.1109/ICVD.2005.61

12. Stock, G., Fraire, J.A., Mömke, T., Hermanns, H., Babayev, F., Cruz, E.: Managing fleets of LEO satellites: Nonlinear, optimal, efficient, scalable, usable, and robust. IEEE Trans. Comput. Aided Des. Integr. Circuits Syst. **39**(11), 3762–3773 (2020). https://doi.org/10.1109/TCAD.2020.3012751

13. Wognsen, E.R., Hansen, R.R., Larsen, K.G.: Battery-aware scheduling of mixed criticality systems. In: Margaria, T., Steffen, B. (eds.) Leveraging Applications of Formal Methods, Verification and Validation. Specialized Techniques and Applications - 6th International Symposium, ISoLA 2014, Imperial, Corfu, Greece, October 8–11, 2014, Proceedings, Part II. Lecture Notes in Computer Science, vol. 8803, pp. 208–222. Springer (2014). https://doi.org/10.1007/978-3-662-45231-8_15

14. Zhang, Q., Li, Y., Shang, Y., Duan, B., Cui, N., Zhang, C.: A fractional-order kinetic battery model of lithium-ion batteries considering a nonlinear capacity. Electronics **8**, 394 (04 2019). https://doi.org/10.3390/electronics8040394

Hierarchical Contract-Based Synthesis
for Assurance Cases

Timothy E. Wang[1](✉), Zamira Daw[1], Pierluigi Nuzzo[2], and Alessandro Pinto[1]

[1] Raytheon Technologies Research Center, Berkeley, CA 94705, USA
{timothy.wang,zamira.daw,alessandro.pinto}@rtx.com
[2] University of Southern California, Los Angeles, CA 90089, USA
nuzzo@usc.edu

Abstract. An automatic synthesis problem is often characterized by
an overall goal or specification to be satisfied, the set of all possible
outcomes, called the design space, and an algorithm for the automatic
selection of one or more members from the design space that are provably guaranteed to satisfy the overall specification. A key challenge in
automatic synthesis is the complexity of the design space. In this paper,
we introduce a formal model, termed *hierarchical contract nets*, and a
framework for the efficient automatic synthesis of hierarchical contract
nets, based on a library of refinement relations between contracts and
contract nets. We show, via the application of automatic synthesis of
assurances cases, that hierarchical contract-based synthesis can mitigate
the design space complexity problem. We also show that the approach
can bring both the benefits of automating the creation of assurance cases
and ensuring that the knowledge from the argumentation experts is captured and reflected in the synthesized assurance cases.

Keywords: Contracts · Automated synthesis · Assurance case ·
Certification

1 Introduction

Program synthesis consists of automatically finding a program in an underlying
programming language that satisfies a user intent captured by a specification.
This problem, which has long been considered a holy grail [1] of computer science, can be traced back to Alonzo Church's synthesis problem [2], albeit posed
in the context of circuits rather than programs. From the perspective of formal
verification, program synthesis is closely tied to deductive theorem proving, on
which the earliest known work traces back to the beginning of theoretical computer science [3]. Subsequent developments in deductive theorem proving have
resulted in proof assistants that can be used for program extractions [4], where
the extracted program is a solution to the program synthesis problem.

The idea behind program synthesis holds several attractions, including (i)
automating the task of low-level programming away from error-prone manual

J. V. Deshmukh et al. (Eds.): NFM 2022, LNCS 13260, pp. 175–192, 2022.
https://doi.org/10.1007/978-3-031-06773-0_9

implementations, and (ii) providing a provable guarantee of the correctness of the program by virtue of the correct-by-construction method. Moreover, the concept has analogues in many fields, from logic synthesis to robust control and architecture design exploration [5]. In its logical underpinnings, the core synthesis problem is the problem of deciding an existential formula in second-order logic [6]. However, a general, systematic strategy for solving synthesis problems remains "notoriously challenging" [1].

The inherent challenges stem from the very large search space of possible solutions, the complexity of the specification, and the ambiguities of the user intent. Moreover, any attempt at a generic approach is often outperformed by special purpose synthesis methods with narrowly tailored search strategies adapted for the application at hand. For example, synthesis problems in robust control are solved by restricting the design space or the specification to have a certain structural property, e.g., convexity. Similarly, in program synthesis, possible programs are restricted to certain syntactical templates [7].

In this paper, we address these challenges via a hierarchical synthesis approach based on contracts and a library of pre-crafted parts that captures the knowledge of the domain experts. The goal of the automated synthesis procedure is to construct a solution using all or some parts from the library. While the synthesis process is fully automatic, the library may be manually constructed. The design space is then purposefully constrained, which allows harnessing complexity. However, we do not restrict to any language or syntax *a priori*, except that the possible outcomes be expressed as finite collections of collections of contracts.

Contracts have shown to offer effective mechanisms to analyze system requirements and behaviors in a modular way for the design of complex hardware and software systems [8–12]. A contract consists of a pair of specifications called assumptions and guarantees. Intuitively, the assumptions express the set of environments that the system or software operate in, and the guarantees express the set of possible implementations of the system or software. A system component can then be captured by a contract. Contracts can be "combined" in the same way as components are combined to form the overall system. In this paper, we denote a collection of contracts, their interconnections, and the associated algebra for composition as a *contract net*. Depending on the specific contract operations (e.g., composition or conjunction), a contract net can represent either a collection of components or a collection of different views of a system.

A preorder can be established over contracts via a binary refinement relation $\preceq$ such that C_2 refines C_1, written $C_2 \preceq C_1$, implies, intuitively, that contract C_1 can be replaced by contract C_2. In system design, if component M_2 satisfies C_2, then it can be swapped in for any component M_1 satisfying C_1 while still guaranteeing that the overall specification C_1 is satisfied. In this paper, we establish a similar notion of ordering between a contract and a contract net. The relation $\preceq$, the contract, and the contract net form an atomic *hierarchical contract net (HCN)*, and our reference library is a collection of atomic HCNs. By restricting the design space to the power-set of a finite collection of HCNs, its complexity is reduced. Intuitively, each atomic HCN refers to a component (contract) of the system, a collection of sub-components that can be manually created by the domain experts (contract net), and the preorder relation linking them, i.e., an indication that the collection of sub-components, when combined together based on some algebra, refines the component.

By the hierarchical structure of the HCN, each of the sub-components of an atomic HCN can be linked with another collection of sub-components to form other atomic HCNs, and so on. The synthesis procedure itself starts with a top-level contract net (root) and, for each of the contracts within the top-level contract net, it searches the library for any contract nets that can refine the contract based on the established pre-order relation. If one such contract net is found, then the contract net is connected with the contract, thus forming an HCN. The synthesis procedure performs this recursively until all the "leaf" contracts of the resulting HCN cannot be refined by any other contract net in the library.

Program synthesis from component libraries is undecidable, in general [13, 14]. Imposing a bound on the number of selected components to achieve decidability, by relying on a library of predefined components (and contracts), possibly including refinement relations, has also been proposed for automated verification [15] and synthesis [16,17] in the context of linear temporal logic (LTL) contracts. This paper rethinks the synthesis problem within the general, hierarchical framework offered by HCNs. Moreover, while the main idea of hierarchical contract-based synthesis seems straightforward, its practical implementation in the context of various industry-scale synthesis problems hinges on addressing some critical challenges:

1. The size of the library can be very large and the library construction is prohibitively expensive.
2. The complexity of formally verifying the preorder relations can lead to tractability issues depending on the complexity of the specifications captured by the contracts.

This paper focuses on these challenges. We introduce a technical approach to address them in Sects. 2 and 3 based on hierarchical contract networks and a library-based synthesis algorithm. Section 4 presents the application of hierarchical contract-based synthesis to the automatic generation of assurance cases. Finally, Sect. 5 draws some conclusions.

2   Hierarchical Contract Networks

We first provide a brief overview of the theory of specifications and contracts [9] used in this paper. A specification theory is a triple $(\mathcal{S}, \|, \leq)$, where $\mathcal{S}$ is a set of specifications, $\| : \mathcal{S} \times \mathcal{S} \rightarrow \mathcal{S}$ is a parallel composition operator over specifications, and $\leq \subseteq \mathcal{S} \times \mathcal{S}$ is a reflexive and transitive refinement relation. A specification is a pair $S = (V_S, \phi_S)$, where V_S is a set of variables and ϕ_S is a formula over V_S. The parallel composition of two specifications $S = (V_S, \phi_S)$ and

$T = (V_T, \phi_T)$ is a new specification $S||T = (V_S \cup V_T, \phi_S \wedge \phi_T)$. Finally, a specification (V_S, ϕ_S) refines a specification (V_T, ϕ_T), written $(V_S, \phi_S) \leq (V_T, \phi_T)$, if
and only if $V_T \subseteq V_S$ and $\phi_S \implies \phi_T$ is valid. The contract theory that we are
going to use is based on this specification theory.

Definition 1. *A contract is a pair of specifications* $((V, A), (V, G))$*, shortened
as* (A, G)*, where* V *is a set of variables and* A *and* G *are referred to as assumptions and guarantees, respectively. Given a contract* (A, G)*, its normal form is*
$(A, A \implies G)$*.*

The environment semantics of a contract is the set of specifications that
refines the assumptions: $[\![C]\!]_{env} = \{E \in \mathcal{S} | E \leq A\}$, $\mathcal{S}$ denoting the set of all
the specifications in the theory. The implementation semantics of a contract
is the set of specifications that refines the guarantees G under assumptions A:
$[\![C]\!]_{impl} = \{I \in \mathcal{S} | I \leq (A \implies G)\}$. Two contracts are semantically *equivalent*
if their environment and implementation semantics are the same, respectively.
A contract $C = (A, G)$ is semantically equivalent to its normal form. A contract
C is *compatible* if there exists a valid environment semantics for it, i.e., A is
satisfiable, and *consistent* if there exists a valid implementation semantics, i.e.,
$A \implies G$ is satisfiable. We also say that C is *feasible* when $A \wedge G$ is satisfiable.

Contracts can also be related by a refinement relation $\preceq$. A contract $C' =
(A', G')$ refines $C = (A, G)$ if and only if $[\![C']\!]_{env} \supseteq [\![C]\!]_{env}$ and $[\![C']\!]_{impl} \subseteq
[\![C]\!]_{impl}$. It can be shown that this condition corresponds to $A \leq A'$ and $G' \leq
(A \implies G)$.

A contract C is a common dominator of two contracts C_1 and C_2 if and only
if the following conditions hold: (i) $\forall I_1 \in [\![C_1]\!]_{impl}$ and $\forall I_2 \in [\![C_2]\!]_{impl}, I_1 || I_2 \in
[\![C]\!]_{impl}$; (ii) for all environments $E \in [\![C]\!]_{env}$: $\forall I_1 \in [\![C_1]\!]_{impl}, E||I_1 \in [\![C_2]\!]_{env}$,
and $\forall I_2 \in [\![C_2]\!]_{impl}, E||I_2 \in [\![C_1]\!]_{env}$. Given two contracts C_1 and C_2, their
composition $C = C_1 || C_2$, if it exists, is their most specific common dominator,
i.e., C is a common dominator of both, and for any common dominator C',
$C \preceq C'$ holds. Composition is associative and commutative.

2.1   Contract Networks and Library

We first give the definition of contract network and then introduce the concept
of library for automatic synthesis.

Definition 2. *A contract network (net) is a tuple* $N := (\mathbb{C}, ||, \kappa)$*, consisting of
a collection of contracts* $\mathbb{C} = \{C_1, \ldots, C_n\}$*, the composition operation* $||$ *over the
contracts, and a set of formulas* κ *encoding relations over the variables* V *of the
contracts in* $\mathbb{C}$*.*

The semantics of a contract net N are given by the composite contract $C_N =
C_1 || \cdots || C_n || (\top, \kappa_1) || \cdots || (\top, \kappa_{|\kappa|})$ where $|\kappa|$ is the cardinality of κ and
$\top$ denotes the Boolean value *true*. We can then extend the standard refinement
relation between contracts to also formalize a substitutability relation between a
net N and a contract C, so that the contract net N can replace C in all contexts
where C works.

Certain synthesis problems deal with specific classes of contracts and a restricted set of possible refinements into contract networks for each class. Let $\mathcal{C}$ denote a class of contracts, $\mathcal{P}(\mathcal{C})$ the powerset of contracts, i.e., contract networks in the class, and $\preceq \subseteq \mathcal{C} \times \mathcal{P}(\mathcal{C})$ the refinement relation between contracts and contract networks in the class. We could then define a *library* as the tuple $\mathcal{L} = (\mathcal{C}, \preceq)$. We use the library to capture a set of high-level components (contracts) as well as atomic components, i.e., components whose contracts are not related to any network in the library. A library can then encapsulate the different ways in which contracts can be refined by contract networks, perhaps following a set of architectural patterns that are used in system or software design. Notice, however, that there are no limitations on the size of the library. In principle, a contract can be associated with any large number of networks in the library.

A synthesis framework based on such a library would present two challenges: the library could be too large to specify and the algorithm would need to search over a large number of contracts. In the following, we detail how we address the first issue via (1) the re-definition of the library over equivalence classes of contracts, and (2) a weaker notion of refinement called *conditional refinement*.

Consider an equivalence relation $\sim$ over the set of specification $\mathcal{S}$, such that if $S \leq T$, and $S' \sim S$, then there exists $T' \sim T$ such that $S' \leq T'$. The equivalence relation extends to a contract theory built over such a specification theory. If the contract set of a library is endowed with such an equivalence relation, then the library is amenable to a more compact representation, including only a set of representative refinement relations, since a single relation of the form $N \preceq C$ can represent a potentially large class of relations of the form $N' \preceq C'$, where $C' \sim C$ and $N' \sim N$ hold. To make the representation even more compact, we also leverage the notion of conditional refinement, which we introduce with a concrete example below.

Consider the case of two refinements $N_1 \preceq C_1 = (A_1, G)$ and $N_2 \preceq C_2 = (A_2, G)$ and assume that there exists A such that $A_1 = A \wedge A_1'$ and $A_2 = A \wedge A_2'$. Then, we can factor out a common contract (A, G) and represent the two refinement relations as refinements of the same contract (A, G) subject to additional conditions, such that $N_1 \preceq_{A_1'} (A, G)$ and $N_2 \preceq_{A_2'} (A, G)$ hold. This method enables halving the number of contracts in this simple example. In the following section, we discuss how a weaker notion of refinement, namely, conditional refinement, enables such compact representations.

2.2   Conditional Refinement and Hierarchical Contract Networks

Definition 3. C_2 *conditionally refines* C_1 *under specification* φ, *written* $C_2 \preceq_\varphi C_1$, *if and only if* $A_1 \wedge \varphi$ *is satisfiable and* $\varphi \implies (C_2 \preceq C_1)$.

The following theorem shows that a conditional refinement amounts to strengthening the environment assumptions of the contract being refined.

Theorem 1. *The conditional refinement* $C_2 \preceq_\varphi C_1$ *is equivalent to*

$$(A_2, G_2) \preceq (A_1 \wedge \varphi, G_1). \tag{1}$$

Proof. Note that $\varphi \implies (C_2 \preceq C_1)$ is true if and only if the following implications are true:

$$\varphi \implies (A_1 \implies A_2), \tag{2}$$

$$\varphi \implies ((A_2 \implies G_2) \implies (A_1 \implies G_1)). \tag{3}$$

Note that (2) is equivalent to

$$A_1 \wedge \varphi \implies A_2, \tag{4}$$

and (3) is equivalent to

$$(A_2 \implies G_2) \implies ((A_1 \wedge \varphi) \implies G_1). \tag{5}$$

Consider the normal forms of (A_2, G_2) and $(A_1 \wedge \varphi, G_1)$, which are $(A_2, A_2 \implies G_2)$ and $(A_1 \wedge \varphi, A_1 \wedge \varphi \implies G_1)$. We observe that $(A_2, G_2) \preceq (A_1 \wedge \varphi, G_1)$ is equivalent to $A_1 \wedge \phi \implies A_2$ and $(A_2 \implies G_2) \implies (A_1 \wedge \varphi \implies G_1)$, which are precisely (4) and (5). □

The conditional refinement relation extends to a contract network N and a contract C. For the rest of this paper, with an abuse of notation, we refer to both relations as conditional refinements. Moreover, we use conditional refinement as an element of the library $\mathcal{L}$.

Definition 4. *A conditional refinement of the library $\mathcal{L}$ is a tuple (N, φ, C) such that N conditionally refines C under φ, i.e., $N \preceq_\varphi C$.*

In the following, we use a function with the same name as an element of a tuple to return the tuple member itself, e.g., $A(C)$ returns the assumption of the contract C, $\mathbb{C}(N)$ returns the set of contracts in the contract network N, and $\varphi(R)$ returns the conditional formula of refinement R. Figure 1 illustrates how conditional refinement can be used for synthesis. Let the top-level requirement of a design be modeled by C_0 and let φ_0 be its assumption, capturing all the valid environments for the design, shown as the solid gray box in the figure. φ_0 can be very large, e.g., it may represent the set of all the possible operating conditions of an autonomous aircraft, including all the possible airport settings, all the hours of the day, and the possible weather and traffic conditions. It is, however, possible that certain components of the design only operate under a subset of the environments satisfying ϕ_0, e.g., an autoland component C_1 may work during the daylight hours, in good weather and in medium air traffic conditions. Conditional refinement enables a mechanism for the selection of library components based on further restrictions of the environment in which the system is expected to work. In this example, we have that $C_1 \preceq_{\phi_1} C_0$, i.e., the autoland component C_1 satisfies C_0 under the conditions posed by ϕ_1.

We now introduce a notion of transitivity for conditional refinements.

Definition 5. *Given $C_2 \preceq_{\phi_2} C_1$ and $C_1 \preceq_{\phi_1} C_0$, we say that conditional refinements $\preceq_{\phi_i}$ are conditionally transitive, i.e., $C_2 \preceq_{\phi'} C_0$ holds with $\phi' \equiv \phi_2 \wedge \phi_1$.*

Given: $C_0 = (\phi_0, true), C_1 = (A_1, true), C_2 = (A_2, true), C_3 = (A_3, true), C_1 \preccurlyeq_{\phi_1} C_0, C_2 \preccurlyeq_{\phi_2} C_1,$ and $C_3 \preccurlyeq_{\phi_3} C_1$

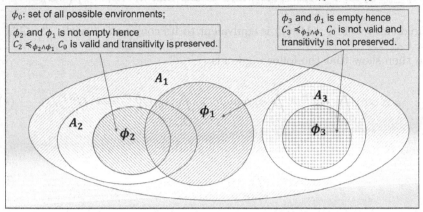

Fig. 1. A library of conditional refinements.

Conditional transitivity between C_2, C_1, and C_0 subject to ϕ' is well defined only if $A_0 \wedge \phi_1 \wedge \phi_2$ is satisfiable, A_0 being the assumptions of C_0, since, by Theorem 1, $C_2 \preceq_{\phi'} C_0$ is equivalent to $(A_2, G_2) \preceq (A_0 \wedge \phi_1 \wedge \phi_2, G_0)$. If $A_0 \wedge \phi_1 \wedge \phi_2$ is unsatisfiable, then the contract $C_0' = (A_0 \wedge \phi_1 \wedge \phi_2, G_0)$ admits no environment. This is illustrated in Fig. 1, where $\phi_3 \wedge \phi_1$ is unsatisfiable, hence the conditional refinement $C_3 \preceq_{\phi_3 \wedge \phi_1} C_0$ is undefined. The following result shows that conditional transitivity holds for conditional refinements between contract networks.

Theorem 2. *Given a contract $C = (A, G)$, a contract network $N = (\mathbb{C} = \{C_1, \ldots, C_M\}, \|, \kappa)$, and contract networks $N_i = (\mathbb{C}_i, \|, \kappa_i)$ for $i = 1, \ldots, M$. Assume that $N \preceq_\phi C$, $N_i = (\mathbb{C}_i, \|, \kappa_i) \preceq_{\phi_i} C_i$ for $i = 1, \ldots, M$, and $A \wedge \phi \wedge \bigwedge_{i=1}^M \phi_i$ is satisfiable. Then, the following holds:*

$$N' = \left(\bigcup_{i=1}^M \mathbb{C}_i, \|, \kappa \wedge \bigwedge_{i=1}^M \kappa_i \right) \preceq_{\phi \wedge \bigwedge_{i=1}^M \phi_i} C. \tag{6}$$

Proof. The satisfiability condition on $A \wedge \phi \wedge \bigwedge_{i=1}^M \phi_i$ ensures that the conditional refinement $N' \preceq_{\phi \wedge \bigwedge_{i=1}^M \phi_i} C$ is defined (see Definition 3). First, we show that the guarantees of C are strengthened by N'. Let G^{NF} be the guarantees of the normal form of a contract, i.e., $G^{NF} := A \implies G$; we show that

$$\kappa \wedge \phi \wedge \bigwedge_{i=1}^M \kappa_i \wedge \phi_i \wedge \bigwedge_{C_k \in \bigcup_{i=1}^M \mathbb{C}_i} G_k^{NF} \implies G^{NF}. \tag{7}$$

Since $N_i \preceq_{\phi_i} C_i$ for $i = 1, \ldots, M$, which means that $\kappa_i \wedge \phi_i \wedge \bigwedge_{C_k \in \mathbb{C}_i} G_k^{NF} \implies$ G_i^{NF} holds for $i = 1, \ldots, M$, (7) is equivalent to its conjunction with $\bigwedge_{C_i \in \mathbb{C}} G_i^{NF}$. We can then show that the following holds:

$$\kappa \wedge \phi \wedge \bigwedge_{C_i \in \mathbb{C}} G_i^{NF} \wedge \bigwedge_{i=1}^M \kappa_i \wedge \phi_i \wedge \bigwedge_{C_k \in \bigcup_{i=1}^M \mathbb{C}_i} G_k^{NF} \implies G^{NF}. \tag{8}$$

Moreover, $N \preceq_\phi C$ implies that the following holds:

$$\kappa \wedge \phi \wedge \bigwedge_{C_i \in \mathbb{C}} G_i^{NF} \implies G^{NF}. \tag{9}$$

From (9), we conclude that (8) is true. We then show that the assumptions of C are weakened via refinement, that is,

$$\kappa \wedge \phi \wedge A \wedge \bigwedge_{i=1}^M \kappa_i \wedge \phi_i \wedge \bigwedge_{C_k \in \bigcup_{i=1}^M \mathbb{C}_i \setminus \{C_j\}} G_k^{NF} \implies A_j. \tag{10}$$

For $C_j \in \mathbb{C}_J$, $J \in [1, M]$, (10) is equivalent to

$$\kappa \wedge \phi \wedge A \wedge \alpha \wedge \kappa_J \wedge \phi_J \wedge \bigwedge_{C_l \in \mathbb{C}_J \setminus \{C_j\}} G_l^{NF} \implies A_j, \tag{11}$$

in which

$$\alpha := \bigwedge_{i \neq J} \kappa_i \wedge \phi_i \wedge \bigwedge_{C_k \in \bigcup_{i \neq J} \mathbb{C}_i} G_k^{NF}. \tag{12}$$

Because $N_i \preceq_{\phi_i} C_i$, (11) is equivalent to its conjunction with $\bigwedge_{C_i \in \mathbb{C} \setminus \{C_J\}} G_i^{NF}$, i.e.,

$$\kappa \wedge \phi \wedge A \wedge \bigwedge_{C_i \in \mathbb{C} \setminus \{C_J\}} G_i^{NF} \wedge \alpha \wedge \kappa_J \wedge \phi_J \wedge \bigwedge_{C_l \in \mathbb{C}_J \setminus \{C_j\}} G_l^{NF} \implies A_j. \tag{13}$$

By $N \preceq_\phi C$, (13) is equivalent to its conjunction with A_J, i.e.,

$$\kappa \wedge \phi \wedge A \wedge \bigwedge_{C_i \in \mathbb{C} \setminus \{C_J\}} G_i^{NF} \wedge \alpha \wedge \kappa_J \wedge \phi_J \wedge A_J \wedge \bigwedge_{C_l \in \mathbb{C}_J \setminus \{C_j\}} G_l^{NF} \implies A_j. \tag{14}$$

Since $N_J \preceq_{\phi_J} C_J$, (14) is valid and holds for any $C_J \in \bigcup_{i=1}^M \mathbb{C}_i$ since $J \in [1, M]$ was arbitrary. $\square$

We now define what is a *hierarchical contract network* (HCN).

Definition 6. *A hierarchical contract network is a graph with the nodes being contract networks, and each edge links a contract of a node with another node, indicating a conditional refinement relation between the two. There exists only one node in an HCN, denoted as the top-level node, which is not linked by a refinement relation to a contract of any other node in the graph.*

Intuitively, the simplest, or *atomic*, HCN is a conditional refinement from the library (see Definition 4), in which a network N_1 conditionally refines $C(N)$, where N contains one contract C. In an HCN, zero or more contracts of a node could be conditionally refined by another node, i.e., $N_i \preceq_{\phi_i} C_i(N)$ for zero or more $C_i \in \mathbb{C}(N)$. Moreover, a contract could be linked to more than one node, i.e., $N_1 \preceq_{\phi_1} C(N), N_2 \preceq_{\phi_2} C(N), \ldots, N_M \preceq_{\phi_M} C(N)$. This results in an HCN containing multiple *hierarchies*, in which each hierarchy represents a different outcome of a refinement process. In this case, there are M different hierarchies. An HCN is hierarchical in the sense that $N_1 \preceq_{\phi_1} C_1(N), N_2 \preceq_{\phi_2} C_1(N_1), \ldots, N_M \preceq_{\phi_M} C_1(N_{M-1})$.

In summary, let $\preceq_\phi \subseteq C \times \mathcal{P}(C)$ denote a set of conditional refinements. A library can be compactly represented as the pair $\mathcal{L} = (C/\sim, \preceq_\phi)$. Given a library $\mathcal{L}$ and a contract network N with one contract C, the synthesis problem turns into a search over the library to replace contracts with contract networks via possible refinements until no more replacements can be found.

3   Automatic Synthesis

The synthesis algorithm leverages a *well-formed* component library to ensure soundness and termination. The definitions of a library and a well-formed library are given in Sect. 3.1 while the synthesis algorithm is described in Sect. 3.2.

3.1   Well-Formed Library

Definition 7. *A library $\mathcal{L}$ is a tuple $(C, \mathcal{R}, \mathcal{N})$, where C is a collection of contracts, $\mathcal{N}$ is a collection of contract networks such that $\forall N \in \mathcal{N}, \mathbb{C}(N) \in 2^C$, and $\mathcal{R} \subseteq \mathcal{N} \times C$ is a collection of conditional refinements.*

A *well-formed* library, defined as follows, ensures that the synthesis algorithm terminates.

Definition 8. *A library $\mathcal{L}$ is well-formed if and only if all of the following conditions are satisfied:*

1. *All conditional refinements hold, i.e., $\forall R \in \mathcal{R}(\mathcal{L})$, where $R = (C, \varphi, N)$, $N \preceq_\varphi C$.*
2. *There is no circularity in the library, i.e., there does not exist a sequence of conditional refinements $R_i = (N_i, \varphi_i, C_i), i = 1, \ldots, M$, such that $N_1 \preceq_{\varphi_1} C_1$, $C_2 \in \mathbb{C}(N_1)$ and $N_2 \preceq_{\varphi_2} C_2, \ldots, C_M \in \mathbb{C}(N_{M-1})$ and $N_M \preceq_{\varphi_M} C_M$, $\bigwedge_{i=1}^M \varphi_i$ is satisfiable, and there exists a contract $C_{M+1} \in \mathbb{C}(N_M)$ such that $C_1 \preceq C_{M+1}$.*

The first item in Definition 8 ensures that all the conditional refinements in the library hold, which, as described in Theorem 2, is one of the conditions for the algorithm to be sound. The second condition ensures that the algorithm will always terminate. In fact, conditional refinement enables the possibility of having a sequence of refinements which leads back to the initial contract C_1 of the sequence. Consider, for example, the following contracts: $C_0 = (x \geq 0, true)$, $C_1 = (x \geq 1, true)$, and ϕ defined as $x \geq 1$. Clearly, $C_1 \preceq_\phi C_0$ holds, and since $C_0 \preceq C_1$, the synthesis algorithm will not terminate. In this paper, we do not directly address how to ensure that there are no circularities in the library, leaving it as future work. However, we include a runtime check for circularity in a tool implementation of the algorithm described in the next section.

3.2   Synthesis Algorithm

As summarized in Algorithm 1, the main function of the synthesis algorithm returns a hierarchical contract network H containing the set of all satisfying hierarchies if all the pre-conditions are satisfied. The inputs to the algorithm include the library $\mathcal{L}$, a contract network $\tilde{N}$ consisting of only one contract $\tilde{C}$ representing the top-level specification to be satisfied by the output H, a set of formulas $\mathcal{X}$ that are assumed to hold, a set of system contexts I, and the formula Φ which is a conjunction of all the conditions of the conditional refinements used in the construction of the hierarchy (for example, see $A \wedge \phi \wedge \bigwedge_{i=1} \phi_i$ used in Theorem 2). The system contexts I is a set of constants which provides information about the system under design or assurance depending on the application of the synthesis procedure. The formula Φ is initialized to A, which is the assumption of the contract in $\tilde{N}$. The pre-conditions require that the library of components $\mathcal{L}$ be well-formed and that the contract network $\tilde{N}$ admit at least one environment and at least one implementation when $\mathcal{X}$ holds.

The function $findRefinements$ enables a full search of the library for any contract that might refine the leaf contract of the synthesized H at some iteration of the algorithm. This enables the algorithm to find potential refinements in the library which are not explicitly added by a human user, thus reducing the manual effort in creating the library. The instantiation function $inst_{ren,I}$ is parameterized by the system contexts I and a bijective mapping $ren : V(C) \to I$ from the variables of the contract $V(C)$ to the system contexts I. It takes in a contract C and returns an *instantiated* contract $\tilde{C}$ such that

$$\tilde{C} = (A[v_i \leftarrow ren(v_i)], G[v_i \leftarrow ren(v_i)]) . \tag{15}$$

The inverse of $inst_{ren,I}$, $inst_{ren,I}^{-1}$, returns C given $\tilde{C}$. The instantiation function induces an equivalence relation over the contracts, i.e., $C \sim \tilde{C}$. Furthermore, the $inst_{ren,I}$ function is overloaded for contract networks and refinements. For a contract network N, $inst_{ren,I}$ returns

$$\tilde{N} = ((inst_{ren,I}(C_1), \ldots, inst_{ren,I}(C_M)), ||, \kappa[v_i \leftarrow ren(v_i)]) . \tag{16}$$

Algorithm 1. Synthesize a satisfying hierarchical contract net H from a library $\mathcal{L}$, a top-level specification represented by the contract net $\tilde{N}$, a set of facts about the system and other axioms $\mathcal{X}$, and a set of system contexts I.

Require: $\mathcal{L}$ is well-formed, Φ is satisfiable, $\tilde{N}$ is consistent, compatible, and feasible.
Ensure: Termination and an output satisfying HCN H.

```
 1: function main_{L,I,X}(Ñ, Φ)
 2:     for C̃_j ∈ Ñ do
 3:         R ← findRefinements(C̃_j, L)
 4:         for R_k ∈ R, R_k = (C_j, φ_+, N_k) do
 5:             R̃_k ← inst_{ren,I}(R_k, C̃_j)
 6:             Φ' ← φ_+ ∧ X ∧ Φ
 7:             if sat?(Φ') then
 8:                 getEdges(C̃_j) ← getEdges(C̃_j) ∪ Ñ_k
 9:                 Φ ← φ_+ ∧ Φ
10:     for C̃_j ∈ Ñ_i do
11:         for Ñ_m ∈ getEdges(C̃_j) do
12:             main_{L,I,X}(Ñ_m, Φ)

13: function findRefinements(C̃_j, L)
14:     C_j ← inst_{ren,I}^{-1}(C̃_j)
15:     for C_i ∈ L do
16:         if C_i ⪯ C_j then
17:             for R_i ∈ L do
18:                 if C_i = C(R_i) then
19:                     R ← insert(R, R_i)
```

For refinements, $inst_{r,I}$ takes in a refinement $R = (C, \varphi, N)$ and contract $\tilde{C}$ and returns

$$\tilde{R} = (\tilde{C}, \varphi[v_i \leftarrow ren(v_i)], \tilde{N}). \tag{17}$$

In this paper, we consider contracts expressed in a first order logic language. Satisfaction and refinement checks are then translated into satisfiability modulo theory [18] (SMT) problems and solved using a state-of-art SMT solver [19]. While SMT solving can be computationally expensive, for the application in this paper, we have primarily used quantifier-free formulas. In the few instances in which we use quantifiers, those formulas are restricted to one universal quantifier over uninterpreted functions.

4   Application: Assurance Cases

In this section, we give a brief introduction to assurance cases, describe the application of hierarchical contract-based synthesis for the automatic generation of assurance cases, and provide a case study of synthesis of assurance cases for aerospace software certification.

An assurance case (AC) is a collection of structured arguments that are supported by evidence, intended to argue that a claim about the system or software is true to some acceptable level of confidence. Since the Goal Structuring Notation [20] (GSN) is a popular notation for writing ACs, for the purpose of illustration, in this section, we describe the typical structure of an AC by using elements from this notation, e.g., claims (goals), strategy, assumptions, justifications, contexts, and solutions. We discuss how ACs can be formalized in terms of HCNs in Sect. 4.1.

The top claim is the overall objective of the assurance case, e.g., stating that the system is safe. A strategy describes the approach used to make the argument. An example of such strategy for the top-level claim that "the system is safe" is to argue that the claim can be supported if each of the identified hazards of the system has been mitigated. This sort of strategy typically results in the decomposition of a higher-level claim into a set of lower-level claims, or sub-claims. A solution is one or more pieces of evidence that directly support a claim without additional intermediate arguments. Solutions are the leaf nodes of an AC. Assumptions are additional propositions that need to be true for a strategy to be valid, but do not need to be backed up by any other arguments. For example, the strategy "each of the identified hazards of the system has been mitigated" used to infer that the system is safe is obviously not sound if one does not assume that all the hazards have been identified. Finally, the justification provides the reasons why a strategy is adopted.

4.1   Assurance Case as a Hierarchical Contract Network

Instead of viewing an assurance case as a set of structured arguments, one can also view it as representing an evolving assurance process. This system-theoretic viewpoint of assurance cases naturally leads to modeling them as HCNs. In an HCN, each contract provides an abstraction for a step in the assurance process. The top-level element of the HCN, a contract network N_0 containing one or more contracts, is an abstraction of the entire assurance process, of which the outcome is that the system satisfies some safety or security goal up to some level of acceptance. Each contract C_i in N_0 has guarantees G_i, which form the top-level claims of the assurance case (and relate to the top-level claim in the GSN notation). The refinements of N_0 amount to the decomposition of the assurance process into a collection of smaller processes, each with its own sub-claims. This decomposition relates intuitively to the decomposition of claims into sub-claims in a GSN-based notation.

While contract guarantees map directly to claims, the role of contract assumptions is less intuitive. As an example, consider the following contract, where the set $Haz_{sys} := \{h \in Hazards | present(h, system)\}$ is by definition the set of all the hazards of the system:

$$A := \bigwedge_{i=1}^{M} belongs(h_i, Haz_{sys}) \wedge (\forall h \in Haz_{sys} : \bigvee_{i=1}^{M}(h = h_i))$$
$$G := \bigwedge_{i=1}^{M} mitigated(h_i). \tag{18}$$

The guarantees directly map to a claim stating that the hazards h_i, $i = 1, \ldots, M$, have been mitigated. The assumptions require, instead, that the hazards h_i belong to the system, and that these are the only hazards for the system. On the other hand, the assumption in GSN is a proposition (unsupported by other arguments or evidence within the AC) that is used to support the argument for another claim. A GSN assumption (e.g., "all hazards of the system have been identified") can then be mapped to a predicate of the contract assumption as well as to part or to the whole of a condition φ in a conditional refinement. Likewise, a GSN strategy can also be mapped to part or to the whole of the condition in a conditional refinement. For example, the condition below captures both the assumption (by definition of Haz_{sys}) that all hazards of the system have been identified and the argumentation strategy arguing that the system is safe because all hazards of the system have been mitigated.

$$\varphi_1 = \bigwedge_{i=1}^{M} belongs(h_i, Haz_{sys}) \wedge (\forall h \in Haz_{sys} : \bigvee_{i=1}^{M}(h = h_i))$$
$$\wedge \bigwedge_{i=1}^{M} mitigated(h_i) \implies safe(system). \tag{19}$$

4.2   Case Study: Assurance Cases for Certification

A certification process evaluates whether the risk of a software system is acceptable for its intent. The evaluation criteria are usually defined in certification standards, which encapsulate domain knowledge and best practices for a specific industry. To streamline the certification process, the Overarching Properties (OPs) [21] concept has been developed with support of NASA and certifying agencies including the Federal Aviation Administration (FAA) and the European Aviation Safety Agency (EASA). OPs provide the flexibility to propose different means of compliance by showing that the product possesses the three OPs: *Intent* (the system has been specified correctly), *Correctness* (the system has been correctly implemented), and *Innocuity* (the system is safe).

This case study aims to demonstrate how the synthesis of assurance cases can be used to generate OP certification arguments for an autopilot based on an assurance case library inspired by best practices presented in RTCA DO-178C, DO-331, and DO-333. The autopilot has a flight stack, to perform estimation and control of a drone, and a middleware that supports communication and hardware integration. System-level requirements (SLR) are formally defined in computation tree logic (CTL) while high-level requirements (HLR) are modeled using automata. Low-level requirements (LLR) for the flight stack are then modeled in Simulink (LLR6-10), from which code is automatically generated. For the middleware, LLR are written, instead, in natural language (LLR1-5) and manually implemented in C.

A set of "partial" assurance cases in our library (atomic HCNs) related to the intent property is shown in Fig. 2. Every assurance case has only one reasoning step, so that the synthesis algorithm can explore multiple combinations from the library. AC1 specifies that the system needs to possess the *Intent*, *Correctness*, and *Innocuity* OPs. AC2 specifies that, to possess *Intent*, the specification must

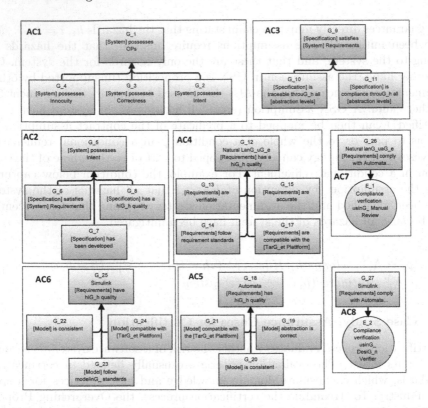

Fig. 2. Pictorial representation (following a GSN-based notation) of a library of "partial" AC patterns used in the synthesis process for the case study.

be developed, have high quality, and satisfy the SLR. AC3 shows that traceability and compliance between SLR and HLR is required to satisfy SLR. AC1, AC2, and AC3 are general assurance cases that can be applied to any system. On the other hand, showing that the specification has high quality is specific to the type of specification being considered. As AC4 shows, natural-language requirements require properties such as verifiability, accuracy, conformance to standards, and compatibility with the target. In the absence of a formal representation of these requirements, as it may be the case for legacy software, these properties may still need to be checked using manual reviews. To ensure the quality of a formal representation, e.g., based on automata or a Simulink model, for example, we need to check that the abstraction accurately represents the intended specification. In these cases, certain verifiability properties can be intrinsically enforced by the adoption of a formal language. In a similar way, AC7 and AC8 show patterns that describe how to check if LLR, specified using Simulink models or natural language, comply with HLR, specified using automata. Compliance can be checked by either using a verification tool, in the case of Simulink models, or manual review, in the case of natural-language requirements.

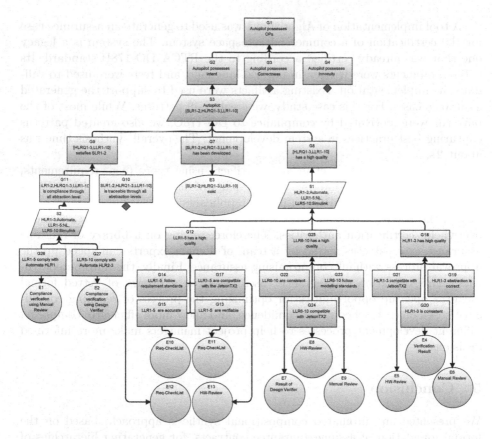

Fig. 3. Pictorial representation (following a GSN-based notation) of the result from the synthesis algorithm.

Based on this library, the synthesis tool explores 8 candidates, including all the possible combinations of the library patterns (atomic HCNs). The number of candidates is reduced when considering the top-level claim for the system and the available development process, as shown in Fig. 3. The claims of the library nets are instantiated and connected to their premises and sub-claims based on the evaluation of the conditional refinement relations. The claims represented with a green diamond have not been developed because the algorithm did not find any contract network that satisfies the refinement relationship. The pattern AC2 is instantiated based on the requirement set of the autopilot associated with the claim in G2. The algorithm also instantiates different patterns to refine G8 based on the type or requirement: AC4 for natural-language requirements, AC6 for requirements specified using Simulink models, and AC5 for formal requirements. Being able to instantiate patterns for groups of artifacts of the same type, in this case requirements, reduces the number of refinement evaluations and facilitates the interpretation of the argument.

A tool implementation of Algorithm 1 was used to generate an assurance case for the certification of a commercial aerospace system. The system is a legacy one that was already certified according to the RTCA DO-178B standard. Its 676 requirements were written in natural language, and tests were used to validate the implementation. Existing artifacts were used to support the generated assurance cases. For this case study, we created 40 patterns. While most of the patterns were motivated by compliance to DO-178C, we also created patterns capturing best practices in system development. The overall synthesis time was about 2 s.

Overall, grouping the certification artifacts using types (e.g., requirements, test cases, reviews) helps improve the scalability of the synthesis algorithm. Especially in the context of OPs, as different applicants can develop different arguments, the heterogeneity and size of the space of possible assurance cases can overwhelm certification authorities. Therefore, relying on a library of reusable assurance case patterns vetted by a team of domain experts can speed up the approval process without compromising assurance. Finally, the automated synthesis and validation of assurance cases based on a library of vetted formal patterns open up opportunities for optimizing the process of reaching compliance based on cost, schedule, or confidence, and allow more efficiently comparing different development processes to help project managers make more informed decisions.

5 Conclusion

We presented an automated compositional synthesis approach, based on the formal foundation of assume-guarantee contracts, for generating hierarchies of interconnected contracts, i.e., hierarchical contract networks, to satisfy a system-level specification. The approach employs a library of components, encoded using atomic hierarchical contract nets, that captures the domain knowledge and a satisfiability modulo theory (SMT)-based synthesis procedure that is fully automated. We presented the synthesis algorithm and its application to the automatic generation of assurance cases. We illustrated how assurance cases can be formally represented using hierarchical contract networks and provided a case study on creating assurance cases for software certification in the aerospace domain. The proposed approach provides the correct balance between automation and knowledge representation capabilities that is demanded for the construction of certification arguments in safety-critical applications. In future work, we want to also explore this synthesis approach for system design with potentially other specification languages, such as Simulink. In this context, refinement checking of contracts over streams is more of a challenge for SMT solving than the quantifier-free fragment that we have mostly utilized for assurance cases.

Acknowledgments. Distribution Statement A (Approved for Public Release, Distribution Unlimited). This research was developed with funding from the Defense Advanced Research Projects Agency (DARPA) contract FA875020C0508. The views, opinions, or findings expressed are those of the authors and should not be interpreted as representing the official views or policies of the Department of Defense or the U.S. Government.

References

1. Gulwani, S., Polozov, O., Singh, R., et al.: Program synthesis. Found. Trends Programm. Lang. **4**(1–2), 1–119 (2017)
2. Church, A.: Application of recursive arithmetic to the problem of circuit synthesis. J. Symbol. Logic **28**(4) (1963)
3. Turing, A.M.: Checking a large routine. In: Report of a Conference on High Speed Automatic Calculating Machines, pp. 67–69 (1949)
4. Bertot, Y., Castéran, P.: Interactive theorem proving and program development: Coq'Art: the calculus of inductive constructions. Springer Science & Business Media (2013)
5. Nuzzo, P., Bajaj, N., Masin, M., Kirov, D., Passerone, R., Sangiovanni-Vincentelli, A.L.: Optimized selection of reliable and cost-effective safety-critical system architectures. IEEE Trans. Comput.-Aided Des. Integr. Circ. Syst. **39**(10), 2109–2123 (2020)
6. David, C., Kroening, D.: Program synthesis: challenges and opportunities. Philos. Trans. Royal Soc. A: Math. Phys. Eng. Sci. **375**(2104), 20150403 (2017)
7. Alur, R., et al.: Syntax-guided synthesis. IEEE (2013)
8. Benveniste, A., et al.: Contracts for system design. PhD thesis, Inria (2012)
9. Sebastian, S., et al.: Moving from specifications to contracts in component-based design. In: Fundamental Approaches to Software Engineering (2012)
10. Sangiovanni-Vincentelli, A., Damm, W., Passerone, R.: Taming dr. Frankenstein: Contract-based design for cyber-physical systems. Eur. J. Control **18**, 217–238 (2012)
11. Nuzzo, P., Sangiovanni-Vincentelli, A.L., Bresolin, D., Geretti, L., Villa, T.: A platform-based design methodology with contracts and related tools for the design of cyber-physical systems. In: Proceedings of the IEEE (2015)
12. Benveniste, A., et al.: Contracts for System Design. Werner Damm (2018)
13. Pneuli, A., Rosner, R.: Distributed reactive systems are hard to synthesize. In: Proceedings Annual Symposium on Foundations of Computer Science, pp. 746–757 (1990)
14. Lustig, Y., Vardi, M.Y.: Synthesis from component libraries. In: de Alfaro, L. (ed.) FoSSaCS 2009. LNCS, vol. 5504, pp. 395–409. Springer, Heidelberg (2009). https://doi.org/10.1007/978-3-642-00596-1_28
15. Iannopollo, A., Nuzzo, P., Tripakis, S., Sangiovanni-Vincentelli, A.: Library-based scalable refinement checking for contract-based design. In: 2014 Design, Automation Test in Europe Conference Exhibition (DATE) (2014)
16. Iannopollo, A., Tripakis, S., Sangiovanni-Vincentelli, A.: Constrained synthesis from component libraries. Sci. Comput. Programm. **171**, 21–41 (2019)
17. Iannopollo, A., Tripakis, S., Sangiovanni-Vincentelli, A.: Specification decomposition for synthesis from libraries of LTL assume/guarantee contracts. In: Design, Automation Test in Europe Conference Exhibition (DATE), pp. 1574–1579 (2018)
18. Barrett, C., Tinelli, C.: Satisfiability modulo theories. In: Handbook of Model Checking, pp. 305–343. Springer, Cham (2018). https://doi.org/10.1007/978-3-319-10575-8_11

19. de Moura, L., Bjørner, N.: Z3: an efficient SMT solver. In: Ramakrishnan, C.R., Rehof, J. (eds.) TACAS 2008. LNCS, vol. 4963, pp. 337–340. Springer, Heidelberg (2008). https://doi.org/10.1007/978-3-540-78800-3_24
20. Kelly, T., Weaver, R.: The goal structuring notation-a safety argument notation. In: Proceedings of the Dependable Systems and Networks 2004 Workshop on Assurance Cases, p. 6. Citeseer (2004)
21. Holloway, C.M.: Understanding the Overarching Properties. NASA Langley Research Center (2019)

Verified Probabilistic Policies for Deep Reinforcement Learning

Edoardo Bacci◉ and David Parker(✉)◉

University of Birmingham, Birmingham, UK
{exb461,d.a.parker}@bham.ac.uk

Abstract. Deep reinforcement learning is an increasingly popular technique for synthesising policies to control an agent's interaction with its environment. There is also growing interest in formally verifying that such policies are correct and execute safely. Progress has been made in this area by building on existing work for verification of deep neural networks and of continuous-state dynamical systems. In this paper, we tackle the problem of verifying *probabilistic* policies for deep reinforcement learning, which are used to, for example, tackle adversarial environments, break symmetries and manage trade-offs. We propose an abstraction approach, based on interval Markov decision processes, that yields probabilistic guarantees on a policy's execution, and present techniques to build and solve these models using abstract interpretation, mixed-integer linear programming, entropy-based refinement and probabilistic model checking. We implement our approach and illustrate its effectiveness on a selection of reinforcement learning benchmarks.

1 Introduction

Reinforcement learning (RL) is a technique for training a policy used to govern the interaction between an agent and an environment. It is based on repeated explorations of the environment, which yield rewards that the agent should aim to maximise. *Deep reinforcement learning* combines RL and deep learning, by using neural networks to store a representation of a learnt reward function or optimal policy. These methods have been increasingly successful across a wide range of challenging application domains, including for example, autonomous driving [30], robotics [19] and healthcare [49].

In safety critical domains, it is particularly important to assure that policies learnt via RL will be executed safely, which makes the application of *formal verification* to this problem appealing. This is challenging, especially for deep RL, since it requires reasoning about multi-dimensional, continuous state spaces and complex policies encoded as deep neural networks.

There are several approaches to assuring safety in reinforcement learning, often leveraging ideas from formal verification, such as the use of temporal logic to specify safety conditions, or the use of abstract interpretation to build discretised models. One approach is *shielding* (e.g., [1]), which synthesises override

© Springer Nature Switzerland AG 2022
J. V. Deshmukh et al. (Eds.): NFM 2022, LNCS 13260, pp. 193–212, 2022.
https://doi.org/10.1007/978-3-031-06773-0_10

mechanisms to prevent the RL agent from acting upon bad decisions; another is *constrained* or *safe* RL (e.g. [17]), which generates provably safe policies, typically by restricting the training process to safe explorations.

An alternative approach, which we take in this paper, is to verify an RL policy's correctness after it has been learnt, rather than placing restrictions on the learning process or on its deployment. Progress has been made in the formal verification of policies for RL [6] and also for the specific case of deep RL [3,4,28], in the latter case by building on advances in abstraction and verification techniques for neural networks; [3] also exploits the development of efficient abstract domains such as *template polyhedra* [42], previously applied to the verification of continuous-space and hybrid systems [7,16].

A useful tool in reinforcement learning is the notion of a *probabilistic policy* (or *stochastic policy*), which chooses randomly between available actions in each state, according to a probability distribution specified by the policy. This brings a number of advantages (similarly to mixed strategies [39] in game theory and contextual bandits [34]), such as balancing the exploration-exploitation tradeoff [18], dealing with partial observability of the environment [40], handling multiple objectives [47] or learning continuous actions [38].

In this paper, we tackle the problem of verifying the safety of probabilistic policies for deep reinforcement learning. We define a formal model of their execution using (continuous-state, finite-branching) *discrete-time Markov processes*. We then build and solve sound abstractions of these models. This approach was also taken in earlier work [4], which used Markov decision process abstractions to verify deep RL policies in which actions may exhibit failures.

However, a particular challenge for probabilistic policies, as generated by deep RL, is that policies tend to specify very different action distributions across states. We thus propose a novel abstraction based on *interval Markov decision processes* (IMDPs), in which transitions are labelled with intervals of probabilities, representing the range of possible events that can occur. We solve these IMDPs, over a finite time horizon, which we show yields *probabilistic guarantees*, in the form of upper bounds on the actual probability of the RL policy leading the agent to a state designated to be unsafe.

We present methods to construct IMDP abstractions using template polyhedra as an abstract domain, and mixed-integer linear programming (MILP) to reason symbolically about the neural network policy encoding and a model of the RL agent's environment. We extend existing MILP-based methods for neural networks to cope with the softmax encoding used for probabilistic policies. Naive approaches to constructing these IMDPs yield abstractions that are too coarse, i.e., where the probability intervals are too wide and the resulting safety probability bounds are too high be useful. So, we present an iterative refinement approach based on sampling which splits abstract states via cross-entropy minimisation based on the uncertainty of the over-approximation.

We implement our techniques, building on an extension of the probabilistic model checker PRISM [32] to solve IMDPs. We show that our approach successfully verifies probabilistic policies trained for several reinforcement learning benchmarks and explore trade-offs in precision and computational efficiency.

Related Work. As discussed above, other approaches to assuring safety in reinforcement learning include shielding [1,5,25,31,52] and constrained or safe RL [13,17,21–23,26,37,45]. By contrast, we verify policies independently, without limiting the training process or imposing constraints on execution.

Formal verification of RL, but in a *non-probabilistic* setting includes: [6], which extracts and analyses decision trees; [28], which checks safety and liveness properties for deep RL; and [3], which also uses template polyhedra and MILP to build abstractions, but to check (non-probabilistic) safety invariants.

In the *probabilistic* setting, perhaps closest is our earlier work [4], which uses abstraction for finite-horizon probabilistic verification of deep RL, but for non-probabilistic policies, thus using a simpler (MDP) abstraction, as well as a coarser (interval) abstract domain and a different, more basic approach to refinement. Another approach to generating formal probabilistic guarantees is [14], which, unlike us, does not need a model of the environment and instead learns an approximation and produces probably approximately correct (PAC) guarantees. Probabilistic verification of neural network policies on partially observable models, but for *discrete* state spaces, was considered in [10].

There is also a body of work on verifying continuous space probabilistic models and stochastic hybrid systems, by building finite-state abstractions as, e.g., interval Markov chains [33] or interval MDPs [11,36], but these do not consider control policies encoded as neural networks. Similarly, abstractions of discrete-state probabilistic models use similar ideas to our approach, notably via the use of interval Markov chains [15] and stochastic games [27].

2   Background

We first provide background on the two key probabilistic models used in this paper: *discrete-time Markov processes* (DTMPs), used to model RL policy executions, and *interval Markov decision processes* (IMDPs), used for abstractions.
Notation. We write $Dist(X)$ for the set of discrete probability distributions over a set X, i.e., functions $\mu : X \rightarrow [0,1]$ where $\sum_{x \in X} \mu(x) = 1$. The support of μ, denoted supp(μ), is defined as supp$(\mu) = \{x \in X \mid \mu(x) > 0\}$. We use the same notation where X is uncountable but where μ has finite support. We write $\mathcal{P}(X)$ to denote the powerset of X and v^i for the ith element of a vector v.

Definition 1 (Discrete-time Markov process). *A (finite-branching) discrete-time Markov process is a tuple $(S, S_0, \mathbf{P}, AP, L)$, where: S is a (possibly uncountably infinite) set of states; $S_0 \subseteq S$ is a set of initial states; $\mathbf{P} : S \times S \rightarrow [0,1]$ is a transition probability matrix, where $\sum_{s' \in \text{supp}(\mathbf{P}(s,\cdot))} \mathbf{P}(s,s') = 1$ for all $s \in S$; AP is a set of atomic propositions; and $L : S \rightarrow \mathcal{P}(AP)$ is a labelling function.*

A DTMP begins in some initial state $s_0 \in S_0$ and then moves between states at discrete time steps. From state s, the probability of making a transition to state s' is $\mathbf{P}(s,s')$. Note that, although the state space of DTMPs used here is continuous, each state only has a finite number of possible successors. This is always true for our models (where transitions represent policies choosing between a finite number of actions) and simplifies the model.

A *path* through a DTMP is an infinite sequence of states $s_0 s_1 s_2 \ldots$ such that $\mathbf{P}(s_i, s_{i+1}) > 0$ for all i. The set of all paths starting in state s is denoted $Path(s)$ and we define a probability space Pr_s over $Path(s)$ in the usual way [29]. We use atomic propositions (from the set AP) to label states of interest for verification, e.g., to denote them as safe or unsafe. For $b \in AP$, we write $s \models b$ if $b \in L(s)$.

The probability of reaching a b-labelled state from s within k steps is:

$$Pr_s(\Diamond^{\leqslant k} b) = Pr_s(\{s_0 s_1 s_2 \cdots \in Path(s) \mid s_i \models b \text{ for some } 0 \leqslant i \leqslant k\})$$

which, since DTMPs are finite-branching models, can be computed recursively:

$$Pr_s(\Diamond^{\leqslant k} b) = \begin{cases} 1 & \text{if } s \models b \\ 0 & \text{if } s \not\models b \wedge k=0 \\ \sum_{s' \in \text{supp}(\mathbf{P}(s,\cdot))} \mathbf{P}(s, s') \cdot Pr_{s'}(\Diamond^{\leqslant k-1} b) & \text{otherwise.} \end{cases}$$

To build abstractions, we use interval Markov decision processes (IMDPs).

Definition 2 (Interval Markov decision process). *An* interval Markov decision process *is a tuple* $(S, S_0, \mathbf{P}, AP, L)$, *where: S is a finite set of states; $S_0 \subseteq S$ are initial states; $\mathbf{P} : S \times \mathbb{N} \times S \to (\mathbb{I} \cup 0)$ is the interval transition probability function, where $\mathbb{I}$ is the set of probability intervals $\mathbb{I} = \{[a, b] \mid 0 < a \leqslant b \leqslant 1\}$, assigning either a probability interval or the probability exactly 0 to any transition; AP is a set of atomic propositions; and $L:S \to \mathcal{P}(AP)$ is a labelling function.*

Like a DTMP, an IMDP evolves through states in a state space S, starting from an initial state $s_0 \in S_0$. In each state $s \in S$, an action j must be chosen. Because of the way we use IMDPs, and to avoid confusion with the actions taken by RL policies, we simply use integer indices $j \in \mathbb{N}$ for actions. The probability of moving to each successor state s' then falls within the interval $\mathbf{P}(s, j, s')$.

To reason about IMDPs, we use *policies*, which resolve the nondeterminism in terms of actions and probabilities. A policy σ of the IMDP selects the choice to take in each state, based on the history of its execution so far. In addition, we have a so-called *environment policy* τ which selects probabilities for each transition that fall within the specified intervals. For a policy σ and environment policy τ, we have a probability space $Pr_s^{\sigma,\tau}$ over the set of infinite paths starting in state s. As above, we can define, for example, the probability $Pr_s^{\sigma,\tau}(\Diamond^{\leqslant k} b)$ of reaching a b-labelled state from s within k steps, under σ and τ.

If ψ is an event of interest defined by a measurable set of paths (e.g., $\Diamond^{\leqslant k} b$), we can compute (through *robust value iteration* [48]) lower and upper bounds on, e.g., maximum probabilities, over the set of all allowable probability values:

$$Pr_s^{\max \min}(\psi) = \sup_\sigma \inf_\tau Pr_s^{\sigma,\tau}(\psi) \quad \text{and} \quad Pr_s^{\max,\max}(\psi) = \sup_\sigma \sup_\tau Pr_s^{\sigma,\tau}(\psi)$$

3   Modelling and Abstraction of Reinforcement Learning

We begin by giving a formal definition of our model for the execution of a reinforcement learning system, under the control of a probabilistic policy. We also define the problem of verifying that this policy is executed safely, namely that the probability of visiting an unsafe system state, within a specified time horizon, is below an acceptable threshold.

Then we define abstractions of these models, given an abstract domain over the states of the model, and show how an analysis of the resulting abstraction yields probabilistic guarantees in the form of sound upper bounds on the probability of a failure occurring. In this section, we make no particular assumption about the representation of the policy, nor about the abstract domain.

3.1 Modelling and Verification of Reinforcement Learning

Our model takes the form of a controlled dynamical system over a continuous n-dimensional state space $S \subseteq \mathbb{R}^n$, assuming a finite set of *actions* A performed at discrete time steps. A (time invariant) *environment* $E : S \times A \to S$ describes the effect of executing an action in a state, i.e., if s_t is the state at time t and a_t is the action taken in that state, we have $s_{t+1} = E(s_t, a_t)$.

We assume a reinforcement learning system is controlled by a *probabilistic policy*, i.e., a function of the form $\pi : S \to Dist(A)$, where $\pi(s)(a)$ specifies the probability with which action a should be taken in state s. Since we are interested in verifying the behaviour of a particular policy, not in the problem of learning such a policy, we ignore issues of partial observability. We also do not need to include any definition of rewards.

Furthermore, since our primary interest here is in the treatment of probabilistic policies, we do not consider other sources of stochasticity, such as the agent's perception of its state or the environment's response to an action. Our model could easily be extended with other discrete probabilistic aspects, such as the policy execution failure models considered in [4].

Combining all of the above, we define an *RL execution model* as a (continuous-space, finite-branching) *discrete-time Markov process* (DTMP). In addition to a particular environment E and policy π, we also specify a set $S_0 \subseteq S$ of possible *initial states* and a set $S_{fail} \subseteq S$ of *failure states*, representing *unsafe* states.

Definition 3 (RL execution model). *Assuming a state space $S \subseteq \mathbb{R}^n$ and action set A, and given an environment $E : S \times A \to S$, policy $\pi : S \to Dist(A)$, initial states $S_0 \subseteq S$ and failure states $S_{fail} \subseteq S$, the corresponding RL execution model is the DTMP $(S, S_0, \mathbf{P}, AP, L)$ where $AP = \{fail\}$, for any $s \in S$, fail $\in L(s)$ iff $s \in S_{fail}$ and, for states $s, s' \in S$:*

$$\mathbf{P}(s, s') = \sum \{\pi(s)(a) \mid a \in A \text{ s.t. } E(s, a) = s'\}.$$

The summation in Definition 3 is required since distinct actions a and a' applied in state s could result in the same successor state s'.

Then, assuming the model above, we define the problem of verifying that an RL policy executes safely. We consider a fixed time horizon $k \in \mathbb{N}$ and an error probability threshold p_{safe}, and the check that the probability of reaching an unsafe state within k time steps is always (from any start state) below p_{safe}.

Definition 4 (RL verification problem). *Given a DTMP model of an RL execution, as in Definition 3, a time horizon $k \in \mathbb{N}$ and a threshold $p_{safe} \in [0,1]$, the RL verification problem is to check that $Pr_s(\lozenge^{\leqslant k} fail) \leqslant p_{safe}$ for all $s \in S_0$.*

In practice, we often tackle a *numerical* version of the verification problem, and instead compute the worst-case probability of error for any start state $p^+ = \inf\{Pr_s(\lozenge^{\leqslant k} fail) \mid s \in S_0\}$ or (as we do later) an upper bound on this value.

3.2   Abstractions for Verification of Reinforcement Learning

Because our models of RL systems are over continuous state spaces, in order to verify them in practice, we construct finite *abstractions*. These represent an over-approximation of the original model, by grouping states with similar behaviour into *abstract states*, belonging to some abstract domain $\hat{S} \subseteq \mathcal{P}(S)$.

Such abstractions are usually necessarily nondeterministic since an abstract state groups states with similar, but distinct, behaviour. For example, abstraction of a probabilistic model such as a discrete-time Markov process could be captured as a Markov decision process [4]. However, a further source of complexity for abstracting *probabilistic policies*, especially those represented as deep neural networks, is that states can also vary widely with regards to the probabilities with which policies select actions in those states.

So, in this work we represent abstractions as *interval MDPs* (IMDPs), in which transitions are labelled with intervals, representing a range of different possible probabilities. We will show that solving the IMDP (i.e., computing the maximum finite-horizon probability of reaching a failure state) yields an upper bound on the corresponding probability for the model being abstracted.

Below, we define this abstraction and state its correctness, first focusing separately on abstractions of an RL system's environment and policy, and then combining these into a single IMDP abstraction.

Assuming an abstract domain $\hat{S} \subseteq \mathcal{P}(S)$, we first require an *environment abstraction* $\hat{E} : \hat{S} \times A \rightarrow \hat{S}$, which soundly over-approximates the RL environment $E : S \times A \rightarrow S$, as follows.

Definition 5 (Environment abstraction). *For environment $E : S \times A \rightarrow S$ and set of abstract states $\hat{S} \subseteq \mathcal{P}(S)$, an environment abstraction is a function $\hat{E} : \hat{S} \times A \rightarrow \hat{S}$ such that: for any abstract state $\hat{s} \in \hat{S}$, concrete state $s \in \hat{s}$ and action $a \in A$, we have $E(s,a) \in \hat{E}(\hat{s},a)$.*

Additionally, we need, for any RL policy π, a *policy abstraction* $\hat{\pi}$, which gives a lower and upper bound on the probability with which each action is selected within the states grouped by each abstract state.

Definition 6 (Policy abstraction). *For a policy $\pi : S \rightarrow Dist(A)$ and a set of abstract states $\hat{S} \subseteq \mathcal{P}(S)$, a policy abstraction is a pair $(\hat{\pi}_L, \hat{\pi}_U)$ of functions of the form $\hat{\pi}_L : \hat{S} \times A \rightarrow [0,1]$ and $\hat{\pi}_U : \hat{S} \times A \rightarrow [0,1]$, satisfying the following: for any abstract state $\hat{s} \in \hat{S}$, concrete state $s \in \hat{s}$ and action $a \in A$, we have $\hat{\pi}_L(\hat{s},a) \leqslant \pi(s,a) \leqslant \hat{\pi}_U(\hat{s},a)$.*

Finally, combining these notions, we can define an *RL execution abstraction*, which is an IMDP abstraction of the execution of an policy in an environment.

Definition 7 (RL execution abstraction). *Let E and π be an RL environment and policy, DTMP $(S, S_0, \mathbf{P}, AP, L)$ be the corresponding RL execution model and $\hat{S} \subseteq \mathcal{P}(S)$ be a set of abstract states. Given also a policy abstraction $\hat{\pi}$ of π and an environment abstraction $\hat{E}$ of E, an RL execution abstraction is an IMDP $(\hat{S}, \hat{S}_0, \hat{\mathbf{P}}, AP, \hat{L})$ satisfying the following:*

- *for all $s \in S_0$, $s \in \hat{s}$ for some $\hat{s} \in \hat{S}_0$;*
- *for each $\hat{s} \in \hat{S}$, there is a partition $\{\hat{s}_1, \ldots, \hat{s}_m\}$ of $\hat{s}$ such that, for each $j \in \{1, \ldots, m\}$ we have $\hat{\mathbf{P}}(\hat{s}, j, \hat{s}') = [\hat{\mathbf{P}}_L(\hat{s}, j, \hat{s}'), \hat{\mathbf{P}}_U(\hat{s}, j, \hat{s}')]$ where:*

$$\hat{\mathbf{P}}_L(\hat{s}, j, \hat{s}') = \sum \left\{ \hat{\pi}_L(\hat{s}_j, a) \mid a \in A \text{ s.t. } \hat{E}(\hat{s}_j, a) = \hat{s}' \right\}$$
$$\hat{\mathbf{P}}_U(\hat{s}, j, \hat{s}') = \sum \left\{ \hat{\pi}_U(\hat{s}_j, a) \mid a \in A \text{ s.t. } \hat{E}(\hat{s}_j, a) = \hat{s}' \right\}$$

- *$AP = \{fail\}$ and $fail \in \hat{L}(\hat{s})$ iff $fail \in L(s)$ for some $s \in \hat{s}$.*

Intuitively, each abstract state $\hat{s}$ is partitioned into groups of states $\hat{s}_j$ that behave the same under the specified environment and policy abstractions. The nondeterministic choice between actions $j \in \{1, \ldots, m\}$ in abstract state $\hat{s}$, each of which corresponds to the state subset $\hat{s}_j$, allows the abstraction to overapproximate the behaviour of the original DTMP model.

Finally, we state the correctness of the abstraction, i.e., that solving the IMDP provides upper bounds on the probability of policy execution resulting in a failure. This is formalised as follows (see the appendix for a proof).

Theorem 1. *Given a state $s \in S$ of an RL execution model DTMP, and an abstract state $\hat{s} \in \hat{S}$ of the corresponding abstraction IMDP for which $s \in \hat{s}$:*

$$Pr_s(\lozenge^{\leqslant k} fail) \leqslant Pr_{\hat{s}}^{\max \max}(\lozenge^{\leqslant k} fail).$$

In particular, this means that we can tackle the RL verification problem of checking that the error probability is below a threshold p_{safe} for all possible start states (see Definition 4). We can do this by finding an abstraction for which $Pr_{\hat{s}}^{\max \max}(\lozenge^{\leqslant k} fail) \leqslant p_{safe}$ for all initial abstract states $\hat{s} \in \hat{S}_0$.

Although $Pr_{\hat{s}}^{\max \min}(\lozenge^{\leqslant k} fail)$ is not necessarily a *lower* bound on the failure probability, the value may still be useful to guide abstraction refinement.

4   Template-Based Abstraction of Neural Network Policies

We now describe in more detail the process for constructing an IMDP abstraction, as given in Definition 7, to verify the execution of an agent with its environment, under the control of a probabilistic policy. We assume that the policy is encoded in neural network form and has already been learnt, prior to verification, and we use template polyhedra to represent abstract states.

The overall process works by building a k-step unfolding of the IMDP, starting from a set of initial states $\hat{S}_0 \subseteq S$. For each abstract state $\hat{s}$ explored during this process, we need to split $\hat{s}$ into an appropriate partition $\{\hat{s}_1, \ldots, \hat{s}_m\}$. Then, for each $\hat{s}_j \in \hat{s}$ and each action $a \in A$, we determine lower and upper bounds on the probabilities with which a is selected in states in $\hat{s}_j$, i.e., we construct a *policy abstraction* $(\hat{\pi}_L, \hat{\pi}_U)$. We also find the successor abstract state that results from executing a in $\hat{s}_j$, i.e., we build an *environment abstraction* $\hat{E}$. Construction of the IMDP then follows directly from Definition 7.

In the following sections, we describe our techniques in more detail. First, we give brief details of the abstract domain used: bounded polyhedra. Next, we describe how to construct policy abstractions via MILP. Lastly, we describe how to partition abstract states via *refinement*. We omit details of the environment abstraction since we reuse the symbolic post operator over template polyhedra given in [3], also performed with MILP. This supports environments specified as linear, piecewise linear or non-linear systems defined with polynomial and transcendental functions. The latter is dealt with using linearisation, subdividing into small intervals and over-approximating using interval arithmetic.

Further details of the algorithms in this section can be found in [2].

4.1 Bounded Template Polyhedra

Recall that the state space of our model $S \subseteq \mathbb{R}^n$ is over n real-valued variables. We represent abstract states using *template polyhedra* [42], which are convex subsets of $\mathbb{R}^n$, defined by constraints in a finite set of *directions* $\Delta \subset \mathbb{R}^n$ (in other words, the facets of the polyhedra are normal to the directions in Δ). We call a fixed set of directions $\Delta \subset \mathbb{R}^n$ a *template*.

Given a (convex) abstract state $\hat{s} \subseteq \mathbb{R}^n$, a Δ-polyhedron of $\hat{s}$ is defined as the tightest Δ-polyhedron enclosing $\hat{s}$:

$$\cap\{\{s : \langle \delta, s \rangle \leqslant \sup\{\langle \delta, s \rangle : s \in \hat{s}\}\} : \delta \in \Delta\},$$

where $\langle \cdot, \cdot \rangle$ denotes scalar product. In this paper, we restrict our attention to *bounded* template polyhedra (also called *polytopes*), in which every variable in the state space is bounded by a direction of the template, since this is needed for our refinement scheme.

Important special cases of template polyhedra are *rectangles* (i.e., intervals) and *octagons*. Later, in Sect. 5, we will present an empirical comparison of these different abstract domains applied to our setting, and show the benefits of the more general case of template polyhedra.

4.2 Constructing Policy Abstractions

We focus first on the abstraction of the RL policy $\pi : S \to Dist(A)$, assuming there are k actions: $A = \{a_1, \ldots, a_k\}$. Let π be encoded by a neural network comprising n input neurons, l hidden layers, each containing h_i neurons ($1 \leqslant i \leqslant l$), and k output neurons, and using ReLU activation functions.

The policy is encoded as follows. We use variable vectors $z_0 \dots, z_{l+1}$ to denote the values of the neurons at each layer. The current state of the environment is fed to the input layer z_0, each hidden layer's values are as follows:

$$z_i = \text{ReLU}(W_i z_{i-1} + b_i) \text{ for } i = 1, \dots, l$$

and the output layer is $z_{l+1} = W_{l+1} z_l$, where each W_i is a matrix of weights connecting layers $i-1$ and i and each b_i is a vector of biases. In the usual fashion, $\text{ReLU}(z) = \max(z, 0)$. Finally, the k output neurons yield the probability assigned by the policy to each action. More precisely, the probability that the encoded policy selects action a_j is given by p_j based on a softmax normalisation of the output layer:

$$p_j = \text{softmax}(z_{l+1})^j = \frac{e^{z_{l+1}^j}}{\sum_{i=1}^{k} e^{z_{l+1}^i}}$$

For an abstract state $\hat{s}$, we compute the policy abstraction, i.e., lower and upper bounds $\hat{\pi}_L(\hat{s}, a_j)$ and $\hat{\pi}_U(\hat{s}, a_j)$ for all actions a_j (see Definition 6), via mixed-integer linear programming (MILP), building on existing MILP encodings of neural networks [9,12,46]. The probability bounds cannot be directly computed via MILP due to the nonlinearity of the softmax function so, as a proxy, we maximise the corresponding entry (the jth logit) of the output layer ($l+1$). For the upper bound (the lower bound is computed analogously), we optimise:

$$
\begin{aligned}
\text{maximize} \quad & z_{l+1}^j \\
\text{subject to} \quad & z_0 \in \hat{s}, \\
& 0 \leqslant z_i - W_i z_{i-1} - b_i \leqslant M z_i' \text{ for } i = 1, \dots, l, \\
& 0 \leqslant z_i \leqslant M - M z_i' \qquad\qquad \text{for } i = 1, \dots, l, \\
& 0 \leqslant z_i' \leqslant 1 \qquad\qquad\qquad\quad \text{for } i = 1, \dots, l, \\
& z_{l+1} = W_{l+1} z_l,
\end{aligned}
\tag{1}
$$

over the variables $z_0 \in \mathbb{R}^n$, $z_{l+1} \in \mathbb{R}^k$ and $z_i \in \mathbb{R}^{h_i}$, $z_i' \in \mathbb{Z}^{h_i}$ for $1 \leqslant i \leqslant l$.

Since abstract state $\hat{s}$ is a convex polyhedron, the initial constraint $z_0 \in \hat{s}$ on the vector of values z_0 fed to the input layer is represented by $|\Delta|$ linear inequalities. ReLU functions are modelled using a big-M encoding [46], where we add integer variable vectors z_i' and $M \in \mathbb{R}$ is a constant representing an upper bound for the possible values of neurons.

We solve $2k$ MILPs to obtain lower and upper bounds on the logits for all k actions. We then calculate bounds on the probabilities of each action by combining these values as described below. Since the exponential function in softmax is monotonic, it preserves the order of the intervals, allowing us to compute the bounds on the probabilities achievable in $\hat{s}$.

Let $x_{lb,i}$ and $x_{ub,i}$ denote the lower and upper bounds, respectively, obtained for each action a_i via MILP (i.e., the optimised values z_{l+1}^i in (1) above). Then, the upper bound for the probability of choosing action a_j is $y_{ub,j}$:

$$y_{ub,j} = \text{softmax}(z_{ub,j}) \quad \text{where} \quad z^i_{ub,j} = \begin{cases} x_{ub,i} & \text{if } i = j \\ 1 - x_{lb,i} & \text{otherwise} \end{cases}$$

and where $z_{ub,j}$ is an intermediate vector of size k. Again, the computation for the lower bound is performed analogously.

4.3   Refinement of Abstract States

As discussed above, each abstract state $\hat{s}$ in the IMDP is split into a partition $\{\hat{s}_1, \ldots, \hat{s}_m\}$ and, for each $\hat{s}_i$, the probability bounds $\hat{\pi}_L(\hat{s}_i, a)$ and $\hat{\pi}_U(\hat{s}_i, a)$ are determined for each action a. If these intervals are two wide, the abstraction is too coarse and the results uninformative. To determine a good partition (i.e., one that groups states with similar behaviour in terms of the probabilities chosen by the policy), we use *refinement*, repeatedly splitting $\hat{s}_i$ into finer partitions.

We define the *maximum probability spread* of $\hat{s}_i$, denoted $\Delta_{\hat{\pi}}^{\max}(\hat{s}_i)$, as:

$$\Delta_{\hat{\pi}}^{\max}(\hat{s}_i) = \max_{a \in A}(\hat{\pi}_U(\hat{s}_i, a) - \hat{\pi}_L(\hat{s}_i, a))$$

and we refine $\hat{s}_i$ until $\Delta_{\hat{\pi}}^{\max}(\hat{s}_i)$ falls below a specified threshold ϕ. Varying ϕ allows us to tune the desired degree of precision.

When refining, our aim is minimise $\Delta_{\hat{\pi}}^{\max}(\hat{s}_i)$, i.e., to group areas of the state space that have similar probability ranges, but also to minimise the number of splits performed. We try to find a good compromise between improving the accuracy of the abstraction and reducing partition growth, which generates additional abstract states and increases the size of the IMDP abstraction.

Calculating the range $\Delta_{\hat{\pi}}^{\max}(\hat{s}_i)$ can be done by using MILP to compute each of the lower and upper bounds $\hat{\pi}_L(\hat{s}_i, a)$ and $\hat{\pi}_U(\hat{s}_i, a)$. However, this may be time consuming. So, during the first part of refinement for each abstract state, we sample probabilities for some states to compute an underestimate of the true range. If the sampled range is already wide enough to trigger further refinement, we do so; otherwise we calculate the exact range of probabilities using MILP to check whether there is a need for further refinement.

Each refinement step comprises three phases, described in more detail below: (i) sampling policy probabilities; (ii) selecting a direction to split; (iii) splitting. Figure 1 gives an illustrative example of a full refinement.

Sampling the Neural Network Policy. We first generate a sample of the probabilities chosen by the policy within the abstract state. Since this is a convex region, we sample state points within it randomly using the Hit & Run method [44]. We then obtain, from the neural network, the probabilities of picking actions at each sampled state. We consider each action a separately, and then later split according to the most promising one (i.e., with the widest probability spread across all actions). The probabilities for each a are computed in a *one-vs-all* fashion: we generate a point cloud representing the probability of taking that action as opposed to any other action.

Fig. 1. Sampled policy probabilities for one action in an abstract state (left) and the template polyhedra partition generated through refinement (right).

The number of samples used (and hence the time needed) is kept fixed, rather than fixing the density of the sampled points. We sample 1000 points per abstract state split but this parameter can be tuned depending on the machine and the desired time/accuracy tradeoff. This ensures that ever more accurate approximations are generated as the size of the polyhedra decreases.

Choosing Candidate Directions. We refine abstract states (represented as template polyhedra) by bisecting them along a chosen direction from the set Δ used to define them. Since the polyhedra are bounded, we are free to pick any one. To find the direction that contributes most to reducing the probability spread, we use cross-entropy minimisation to find the optimal boundary at which to split each direction, and then pick the direction that yields the lowest value.

Let $\tilde{S}$ be the set of sampled points and $\tilde{Y}_s$ denote the true probability of choosing action a in each point $s \in \tilde{S}$, as extracted from the probabilistic policy. For a direction δ, we project all points in $\tilde{S}$ onto δ and sort them accordingly, i.e., we let $\tilde{S} = \{s_1, \ldots, s_m\}$, where $m = |\tilde{S}|$ and index i is sorted by $\langle \delta, s_i \rangle$. We determine the optimal boundary for splitting in direction δ by finding the optimal index k that splits $\tilde{S}$ into $\{s_1, \ldots, s_k\}$ and $\{s_{k+1}, \ldots, s_m\}$. To do so, we first define the function $Y_i^{k,\delta}$ classifying the ith point according to this split:

$$Y_i^{k,\delta} = \begin{cases} 1 \text{ if } i \leqslant k \\ 0 \text{ if } i > k \end{cases}$$

and then minimise, over k, the binary cross entropy loss function:

$$H(Y^{k,\delta}, \tilde{Y}) = -\frac{1}{m} \sum_{i=1}^{m} \left(Y_i^{k,\delta} \log(\tilde{Y}_{s_i}) + (1 - Y_i^{k,\delta}) \log(1 - \tilde{Y}_{s_i}) \right)$$

which reflects how well the true probability for each point $\tilde{Y}_s$ matches the separation into the two groups.

One problem with this approach is that, if the distribution of probabilities is skewed to strongly favour some probabilities, a good decision boundary may not be picked. To counter this, we perform sample weighting by grouping the sampled probabilities into small bins, and counting the number of samples in each bin to calculate how much weight to give to each sample.

Abstract State Splitting. Once a direction δ and bisection point s_k are chosen, the abstract state is split into two with a corresponding pair of constraints that splits the polyhedron. Because we are constrained to the directions of the template, and the decision boundary is highly non-linear, sometimes the bisection point falls close to the interval boundary and the resulting slices are extremely thin. This would cause the creation of an unnecessarily high number of polyhedra, which we prevent by imposing a minimum size of the split relative to the dimension chosen. By doing so we are guaranteed a minimum degree of progress and the complex shapes in the non-linear policy space which are not easily classified (such as non-convex shapes) are broken down into more manageable regions.

5   Experimental Evaluation

We evaluate our approach by implementing the techniques described in Sect. 4 and applying them to 3 reinforcement learning benchmarks, analysing performance and the impact of various configurations and optimisations.

5.1   Experimental Setup

Implementation. The code is developed in a mixture of Python and Java. Neural network manipulation is done through Pytorch [51], MILP solution through Gurobi [20], graph analysis with `networkX` [50] and cross-entropy minimisation with Scikit-learn [41]. IMDPs are constructed and solved using an extension of PRISM [32] which implements robust value iteration [48]. The code is available from https://github.com/phate09/SafeDRL.

Benchmarks. We use the following three RL benchmark environments:

(i) Bouncing ball [24]: The agent controls a ball with height p and vertical velocity v, choosing to either hit the ball downward with a paddle, adding speed, or do nothing. The ball accelerates while falling and bounces on the ground losing 10% of its energy; it eventually stops bouncing if its height is too low and it is out of reach of the paddle. The initial heights and speed vary. In our experiments, we consider two possible starting regions: "large" ($S_0 = L$), where $p \in [5, 9]$ and $v \in [-1, 1]$, and "small" ($S_0 = S$), where $p \in [5, 9]$ and $v \in [-0.1, 0]$. The safety constraint is that the ball never stops bouncing.

(ii) Adaptive cruise control [3]: The problem has two vehicles $i \in \{lead, ego\}$, whose state is determined by variables x_i and v_i for the position and speed of each car, respectively. The lead car proceeds at constant speed ($28\,\mathrm{m\,s^{-1}}$), and the agent controls the acceleration ($\pm 1\,\mathrm{m\,s^{-2}}$) of *ego* using two actions. The

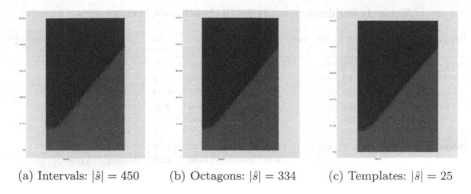

(a) Intervals: $|\hat{s}| = 450$ (b) Octagons: $|\hat{s}| = 334$ (c) Templates: $|\hat{s}| = 25$

Fig. 2. Policy abstractions for an abstract state from the adaptive cruise control benchmark, using different abstract domains (see Fig. 1 for legend).

range of possible start states allows a relative distance of $[3, 10]$ metres and the speed of the ego vehicle is in $[26, 32]$ m/s. Safety means preserving $x_{lead} \geqslant x_{ego}$.

(iii) Inverted pendulum: This benchmark is a modified (discrete action) version of the "Pendulum-v0" environment from the OpenAI Gym [8] where an agent applies left or right rotational force to a pole pivoting around one of its ends, with the aim of balancing the pole in an upright position. The state is modelled by 2 variables: the angular position and velocity of the pole. We consider initial conditions of an angle $[-0.05, 0.05]$ and speed $[-0.05, 0.05]$. Safety constitutes remaining within a range of positions and velocities such that an upright position can be recovered. This benchmark is more challenging than the previous two: it allows 3 actions (noop, push left, push right) and the dynamics of the system are highly non-linear, making the problem more complex.

Policy Training. All agents have been trained using proximal policy optimisation (PPO) [43] in actor-critic configuration with Adam optimiser. The training is distributed over 8 actors with 10 instances of each environment, managing the collection of results and the update of the network with `RLlib` [35]. Hyperparameters have been mostly kept unchanged from their default values except the learning rate and batch size which have been set to 5×10^{-4} and 4096, respectively. We used a standard feed forward architecture with 2 hidden layers (size 32 for the bouncing ball and size 64 for the adaptive cruise control and inverted pendulum problems) and ReLU activation functions.

Abstract Domains. The abstraction techniques we present in Sect. 4 are based on the use of template polyhedra as an abstract domain. As special cases, this includes rectangles (intervals) and octagons. We use both of these in our experiments, but also the more general case of arbitrary bounded template polyhedra. In the latter case, we choose a set of directions by sampling a representative portion of the state space where the agent is expected to operate, and choosing appropriate slopes for the directions to better represents the decision boundaries. The effect of the choice of different template can be seen in Fig. 2 where

Table 1. Verification results for the benchmark environments

Benchmark environment	k	Abs. dom.	φ	Contain. check	Num. poly.	Num. visited	IMDP size	Prob. bound	Runtime (min.)
Bouncing ball	20	Rect	0.1	✓	337	28	411	0.0	1
($S_0 = S$)	20	Oct	0.1	✓	352	66	484	0.0	2
Bouncing ball	20	Rect	0.1	✓	1727	5534	7796	0.63	30
($S_0 = L$)	20	Oct	0.1	✓	2489	3045	6273	0.0	33
	20	Rect	0.1	✗	18890	0	23337	0.006	91
	20	Oct	0.1	✗	13437	0	16837	0.0	111
Adaptive cruise	7	Rect	0.33	✓	1522	4770	10702	0.084	85
control	7	Oct	0.33	✓	1415	2299	6394	0.078	60
	7	Temp	0.33	✓	2440	2475	9234	0.47	70
	7	Rect	0.5	✓	593	1589	3776	0.62	29
	7	Oct	0.5	✓	801	881	3063	0.12	30
	7	Temp	0.5	✓	1102	1079	4045	0.53	34
	7	Rect	0.33	✗	11334	0	24184	0.040	176
	7	Oct	0.33	✗	7609	0	16899	0.031	152
	7	Temp	0.33	✗	6710	0	14626	0.038	113
	7	Rect	0.5	✗	3981	0	8395	0.17	64
	7	Oct	0.5	✗	2662	0	5895	0.12	52
	7	Temp	0.5	✗	2809	0	6178	0.16	48
Inverted	6	Rect	0.5	✓	1494	3788	14726	0.057	71
pendulum	6	Rect	0.5	✗	5436	0	16695	0.057	69

we show a representative abstract state and how the refinement algorithm is affected by the choice of template: as expected, increasing the generality of the abstract domain results in a smaller number of abstract states.

Containment Checks. Lastly, we describe an optimisation implemented for construction of IMDP abstractions, whose effectiveness we will evaluate in the next section. When calculating the successors of abstract states to construct an IMDP, we sometimes find that successors that are partially or fully contained within previously visited abstract states. Against the possible trade-off of decreasing the accuracy of the abstraction, we can attempt to reduce the total size of the IMDP that is constructed by aggregating together states which are fully contained within previously visited abstract states.

5.2   Experimental Results

Table 1 summarises the experimental results across the different benchmark environments; k denotes the time horizon considered. We use a range of configurations, varying: the abstract domain used (rectangles, octagons or general template polyhedra); the maximum probability spread threshold ϕ and whether the containment check optimisation is used.

The table lists, for each case: the number of independent polyhedra generated, the number of instances in which polyhedra are contained in previously visited abstract states and aggregated together; the final size of the IMDP abstraction (number of abstract states); the generated upper bound on the probability of encountering an unsafe state from an initial state; and the runtime of the whole process. Experiments were run on a 4-core 4.2 GHz PC with 64 GB RAM.

Verification successfully produced probability bounds for all environments considered. Typically, the values of k shown are the largest time horizons we could check, assuming a 3 h timeout for verification. The majority of the runtime is for constructing the abstraction, not solving the IMDP.

As can be seen, the various configurations result in different safety probability bounds and runtimes for the same environments, so we are primarily interested in the impact that these choices have on the trade-off between abstraction precision and performance. We summarise findings for each benchmark separately.

Bouncing Ball. These are the quickest abstractions to construct and verify due to the low number of variables and the simplicity of the dynamics. For both initial regions considered, we can actually verify that it is fully safe (maximum probability 0). However, for the larger one, rectangles (particular with containment checks) are not accurate enough to show this.

Two main areas of the policy are identified for refinement: one where it can reach the ball and should hit it and one where the ball is out of reach and the paddle should not be activated to preserve energy. But even for threshold $\phi = 0.1$ (lower than used for other benchmarks), rectangular abstractions resulted in large abstract states containing most of the other states visited by the agent, and which ultimately overlapped with the unsafe region.

Adaptive Cruise Control. On this benchmark, we use a wider range of configurations. Firstly, as expected, for smaller values of the maximum probability spread threshold ϕ, the probability bound obtained is lower (the overestimation error from the abstraction decreases, making it closer to the true maximum probability) but the abstraction size and runtime increase. Applying the containment check for previously visited states has a similar effect: it helps reduce the computation time, but at the expense of overapproximation (higher bounds)

The choice of abstract domain also has a significant impact. Octagons yield more precise results than rectangles, for the same values of ϕ, and also produce smaller abstractions (and therefore lower runtime). On the other hand, general template polyhedra (chosen to better approximate the decision boundary) do not appear to provide an improvement in time or precision on this example, instead causing higher probability bounds, especially when combined with the containment check. Our hypothesis is that this abstract domains groups large areas of the state space (as shown in Fig. 2) and this eventually leads to overlaps with the unsafe region.

Inverted Pendulum. This benchmark is more challenging and, while we successfully generate bounds on the probability of unsafe behaviour, for smaller values of ϕ and other abstract domains, experiments timed out due to the high number of abstract states generated and the time needed for MILP solution. The abstract states generated were sufficiently small that the containment check could be used to reduce runtime without increasing the probability bound.

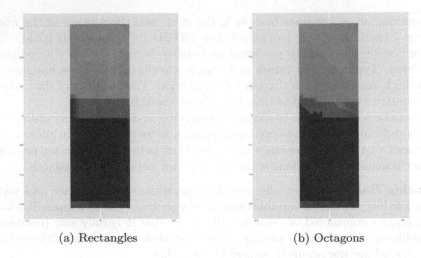

(a) Rectangles   (b) Octagons

Fig. 3. Refined policy abstractions from the inverted pendulum benchmark (Color figure online)

Figure 3 illustrates abstraction applied to a state space fragment from this benchmark using both rectangles and octagons. It shows the probability of choosing one of three actions, coded by RGB colour: *noop* (red), *right* (green) and *left* (blue), The X axis represents angular speed and the Y axis represents the angle of the pendulum in radians. Notice the grey area towards the centre where all 3 actions have the same probability, the centre right area with yellow tints (red and green), and the centre left area with purple tints (red and blue). Towards the bottom of the heatmap, the colour fades to green as the agent tries to push the pendulum so that it spins and balances once it reaches the opposite side.

6   Conclusion

We presented an approach for verifying probabilistic policies for deep reinforcement learning agents. This is based on a formal model of their execution as continuous-space discrete time Markov process, and a novel abstraction represented as an interval MDP. We propose techniques to implement this framework with MILP and a sampling-based refinement method using cross-entropy minimisation. Experiments on several RL benchmarks illustrate its effectiveness and show how we can tune the approach to trade off accuracy and performance.

Future work includes automating the selection of an appropriate template for abstraction and using lower bounds from the abstraction to improve refinement.

Acknowledgements. This project has received funding from the European Research Council (ERC) under the European Union's Horizon 2020 research and innovation programme (grant agreement No. 834115, FUN2MODEL).

Appendix: Proof of Theorem 1

We provide here a proof of Theorem 1, from Sect. 3, which states that:

Given a state $s \in S$ of an RL execution model DTMP, and abstract state $\hat{s} \in \hat{S}$ of the corresponding controller abstraction IMDP for which $s \in \hat{s}$, we have:

$$Pr_s(\Diamond^{\leqslant k} fail) \leqslant Pr_{\hat{s}}^{\max \max}(\Diamond^{\leqslant k} fail)$$

By the definition of $Pr_{\hat{s}}^{\max \max}(\cdot)$, it suffices to show that there is *some* policy σ and *some* environment policy τ in the IMDP such that:

$$Pr_s(\Diamond^{\leqslant k} fail) \leqslant Pr_{\hat{s}}^{\sigma, \tau}(\Diamond^{\leqslant k} fail) \tag{2}$$

Recall that, in the construction of the IMDP (see Definition 7), an abstract state $\hat{s}$ is associated with a partition of subsets $\hat{s}_j$ of $\hat{s}$, each of which is used to define the j-labelled choice in state $\hat{s}$. Let σ be the policy that picks in each state s (regardless of history) the unique index j_s such that $s \in \hat{s}_{j_s}$. Then, let τ be the environment policy that selects the upper bound of the interval for every transition probability. We use function $\hat{\mathbf{P}}_\tau$ to denote the chosen probabilities, i.e., we have $\hat{\mathbf{P}}_\tau(\hat{s}, j_s, \hat{s}') = \hat{\mathbf{P}}_U(\hat{s}, j_s, \hat{s}')$ for any $\hat{s}, j_s, \hat{s}'$.

The probabilities $Pr_{\hat{s}}^{\sigma, \tau}(\Diamond^{\leqslant k} fail)$ for these policies, starting in $\hat{s}$, are defined similarly to those for discrete-time Markov processes (see Sect. 2):

$$Pr_{\hat{s}}^{\sigma, \tau}(\Diamond^{\leqslant k} fail) = \begin{cases} 1 & \text{if } \hat{s} \models fail \\ 0 & \text{if } \hat{s} \not\models fail \wedge k = 0 \\ \sum_{\hat{s}' \in \mathrm{supp}(\hat{\mathbf{P}}(\hat{s}, j_s, \cdot))} \hat{\mathbf{P}}(\hat{s}, j_s, \hat{s}') \cdot Pr_{\hat{s}'}^{\sigma, \tau}(\Diamond^{\leqslant k-1} fail) & \text{otherwise.} \end{cases}$$

Since this is defined recursively, we prove (2) by induction over k. For the case $k = 0$, the definitions of $Pr_s(\Diamond^{\leqslant 0} fail)$ and $Pr_{\hat{s}}(\Diamond^{\leqslant 0} fail)$ are equivalent: they equal 1 if $s \models fail$ (or $\hat{s} \models fail$) and 0 otherwise. From Definition 7, $s \models fail$ implies $\hat{s} \models fail$. Therefore, $Pr_s(\Diamond^{\leqslant 0} fail) \leqslant Pr_{\hat{s}}^{\sigma, \tau}(\Diamond^{\leqslant 0} fail)$.

Next, for the inductive step, we will assume, as the inductive hypothesis, that $Pr_{s'}(\Diamond^{\leqslant k-1} fail) \leqslant Pr_{\hat{s}'}^{\sigma, \tau}(\Diamond^{\leqslant k-1} fail)$ for $s' \in S$ and $\hat{s}' \in \hat{S}$ with $s' \in \hat{s}'$. If $\hat{s} \models fail$ then $Pr_{\hat{s}}^{\sigma, \tau}(\Diamond^{\leqslant k} fail) = 1 \geqslant Pr_s(\Diamond^{\leqslant k} fail)$. Otherwise we have:

$$
\begin{aligned}
& Pr_{\hat{s}}^{\sigma, \tau}(\Diamond^{\leqslant k} fail) \\
= & \textstyle\sum_{\hat{s}' \in \mathrm{supp}(\hat{\mathbf{P}}_\tau(\hat{s}, j_s, \cdot))} \hat{\mathbf{P}}_\tau(\hat{s}, j_s, \hat{s}') \cdot Pr_{\hat{s}'}(\Diamond^{\leqslant k-1} fail) && \text{by defn. of } \sigma \text{ and } Pr_{\hat{s}}^{\sigma, \tau}(\Diamond^{\leqslant k} fail) \\
= & \textstyle\sum_{\hat{s}' \in \mathrm{supp}(\hat{\mathbf{P}}_U(\hat{s}, j_s, \cdot))} \hat{\mathbf{P}}_U(\hat{s}, j_s, \hat{s}') \cdot Pr_{\hat{s}'}(\Diamond^{\leqslant k-1} fail) && \text{by defn. of } \tau \\
= & \textstyle\sum_{a \in A} \pi_U(\hat{s}, a) \cdot Pr_{\hat{E}(\hat{s}_j, a)}(\Diamond^{\leqslant k-1} fail) && \text{by defn. of } \hat{\mathbf{P}}_U(\hat{s}, j, \hat{s}') \\
\geqslant & \textstyle\sum_{a \in A} \pi(s, a) \cdot Pr_{\hat{E}(\hat{s}_j, a)}(\Diamond^{\leqslant k-1} fail) && \text{since } s \in \hat{s} \text{ and by Defn.6} \\
\geqslant & \textstyle\sum_{a \in A} \pi(s, a) \cdot Pr_{E(s, a)}(\Diamond^{\leqslant k-1} fail) && \text{by induction and since, by} \\
& && \text{Defn. 5, } E(s, w) \in \hat{E}(\hat{s}_j, w) \\
= & \textstyle\sum_{s' \in \mathrm{supp}(\mathbf{P}(s, \cdot))} \mathbf{P}(s, s') \cdot Pr_{s'}(\Diamond^{\leqslant k-1} fail) && \text{by defn. of } \mathbf{P}(s, s') \\
= & Pr_s(\Diamond^{\leqslant k} fail) && \text{by defn. of } Pr_s(\Diamond^{\leqslant k} fail)
\end{aligned}
$$

which completes the proof.

References

1. Alshiekh, M., Bloem, R., Ehlers, R., Könighofer, B., Niekum, S., Topcu, U.: Safe reinforcement learning via shielding. In: Proceedings of 32nd AAAI Conference on Artificial Intelligence (AAAI 2018), pp. 2669–2678 (2018)
2. Bacci, E.: Formal Verification of Deep Reinforcement Learning Agents. Ph.D. thesis, School of Computer Science, University of Birmingham (2022)
3. Bacci, E., Giacobbe, M., Parker, D.: Verifying reinforcement learning up to infinity. In: Proceedings 30th International Joint Conference on Artificial Intelligence (IJCAI 2021), pp. 2154–2160 (2021)
4. Bacci, E., Parker, D.: Probabilistic guarantees for safe deep reinforcement learning. In: Bertrand, N., Jansen, N. (eds.) FORMATS 2020. LNCS, vol. 12288, pp. 231–248. Springer, Cham (2020). https://doi.org/10.1007/978-3-030-57628-8_14
5. Bastani, O.: Safe reinforcement learning with nonlinear dynamics via model predictive shielding. In: Proceedings of the American Control Conference, pp. 3488–3494 (2021)
6. Bastani, O., Pu, Y., Solar-Lezama, A.: Verifiable reinforcement learning via policy extraction. In: Proceedings of 2018 Annual Conference on Neural Information Processing Systems (NeurIPS 2018), pp. 2499–2509 (2018)
7. Bogomolov, S., Frehse, G., Giacobbe, M., Henzinger, T.A.: Counterexample-guided refinement of template polyhedra. In: TACAS (1), pp. 589–606 (2017)
8. Brockman, G., Cheung, V., Pettersson, L., Schneider, J., Schulman, J., Tang, J., Zaremba, W.: OpenAI Gym, June 2016
9. Bunel, R., Turkaslan, I., Torr, P., Kohli, P., Kumar, P.: A unified view of piecewise linear neural network verification. In: Proceedings of 32nd International Conference on Neural Information Processing Systems (NIPS 2018), pp. 4795–4804 (2018)
10. Carr, S., Jansen, N., Topcu, U.: Task-aware verifiable RNN-based policies for partially observable Markov decision processes. J. Artif. Intell. Res. **72**, 819–847 (2021)
11. Cauchi, N., Laurenti, L., Lahijanian, M., Abate, A., Kwiatkowska, M., Cardelli, L.: Efficiency through uncertainty: scalable formal synthesis for stochastic hybrid systems. In: 22nd ACM International Conference on Hybrid Systems: Computation and Control (2019)
12. Cheng, C.-H., Nührenberg, G., Ruess, H.: Maximum resilience of artificial neural networks. In: D'Souza, D., Narayan Kumar, K. (eds.) ATVA 2017. LNCS, vol. 10482, pp. 251–268. Springer, Cham (2017). https://doi.org/10.1007/978-3-319-68167-2_18
13. Cheng, R., Orosz, G., Murray, R.M., Burdick, J.W.: End-to-end safe reinforcement learning through barrier functions for safety-critical continuous control tasks. In: AAAI, pp. 3387–3395. AAAI Press (2019)
14. Delgrange, F., Ann Now e, G.A.P.: Distillation of RL policies with formal guarantees via variational abstraction of Markov decision processes. In: Proceedings of 36th AAAI Conference on Artificial Intelligence (AAAI 2022) (2022)
15. Fecher, H., Leucker, M., Wolf, V.: *Don't Know* in probabilistic systems. In: Valmari, A. (ed.) SPIN 2006. LNCS, vol. 3925, pp. 71–88. Springer, Heidelberg (2006). https://doi.org/10.1007/11691617_5
16. Frehse, G., Giacobbe, M., Henzinger, T.A.: Space-time interpolants. In: Chockler, H., Weissenbacher, G. (eds.) CAV 2018. LNCS, vol. 10981, pp. 468–486. Springer, Cham (2018). https://doi.org/10.1007/978-3-319-96145-3_25
17. Fulton, N., Platzer, A.: Safe reinforcement learning via formal methods: toward safe control through proof and learning. In: AAAI, pp. 6485–6492. AAAI Press (2018)

18. García, J., Fernández, F.: Probabilistic policy reuse for safe reinforcement learning. ACM Trans. Autonomous Adaptive Syst. **13**(3), 1–24 (2018)
19. Gu, S., Holly, E., Lillicrap, T.P., Levine, S.: Deep reinforcement learning for robotic manipulation with asynchronous off-policy updates. In: Proceedings of 2017 IEEE International Conference on Robotics and Automation (ICRA 2017), pp. 3389–3396 (2017)
20. Gurobi Optimization, LLC: Gurobi Optimizer Reference Manual (2021)
21. Hasanbeig, M., Abate, A., Kroening, D.: Logically-constrained neural fitted q-iteration. In: AAMAS, pp. 2012–2014. IFAAMAS (2019)
22. Hasanbeig, M., Abate, A., Kroening, D.: Cautious reinforcement learning with logical constraints. In: AAMAS, pp. 483–491. International Foundation for Autonomous Agents and Multiagent Systems (2020)
23. Hunt, N., Fulton, N., Magliacane, S., Hoang, T.N., Das, S., Solar-Lezama, A.: Verifiably safe exploration for end-to-end reinforcement learning. In: Proceedings of 24th International Conference on Hybrid Systems: Computation and Control (HSCC 2021) (2021)
24. Jaeger, M., Jensen, P.G., Guldstrand Larsen, K., Legay, A., Sedwards, S., Taankvist, J.H.: Teaching stratego to play ball: optimal synthesis for continuous space MDPs. In: Chen, Y.-F., Cheng, C.-H., Esparza, J. (eds.) ATVA 2019. LNCS, vol. 11781, pp. 81–97. Springer, Cham (2019). https://doi.org/10.1007/978-3-030-31784-3_5
25. Jansen, N., Könighofer, B., Junges, S., Serban, A., Bloem, R.: Safe reinforcement learning using probabilistic shields. In: Proceedings of 31st International Conference on Concurrency Theory (CONCUR 2020), vol. 171, pp. 31–316 (2020)
26. Jin, P., Zhang, M., Li, J., Han, L., Wen, X.: Learning on Abstract Domains: A New Approach for Verifiable Guarantee in Reinforcement Learning, June 2021
27. Kattenbelt, M., Kwiatkowska, M., Norman, G., Parker, D.: A game-based abstraction-refinement framework for Markov decision processes. Formal Methods Syst. Des. **36**(3), 246–280 (2010)
28. Kazak, Y., Barrett, C.W., Katz, G., Schapira, M.: Verifying deep-RL-driven systems. In: Proceedings of the 2019 Workshop on Network Meets AI & ML, NetAI@SIGCOMM 2019, pp. 83–89. ACM (2019)
29. Kemeny, J., Snell, J., Knapp, A.: Denumerable Markov Chains, 2nd edn. Springer (1976)
30. Kendall, A., et al.: Learning to drive in a day. In: ICRA, pp. 8248–8254. IEEE (2019)
31. Könighofer, B., Lorber, F., Jansen, N., Bloem, R.: Shield synthesis for reinforcement learning. In: Margaria, T., Steffen, B. (eds.) ISoLA 2020. LNCS, vol. 12476, pp. 290–306. Springer, Cham (2020). https://doi.org/10.1007/978-3-030-61362-4_16
32. Kwiatkowska, M., Norman, G., Parker, D.: PRISM 4.0: verification of probabilistic real-time systems. In: Gopalakrishnan, G., Qadeer, S. (eds.) CAV 2011. LNCS, vol. 6806, pp. 585–591. Springer, Heidelberg (2011). https://doi.org/10.1007/978-3-642-22110-1_47
33. Lahijania, M., Andersson, S.B., Belta, C.: Formal verification and synthesis for discrete-time stochastic systems. IEEE Trans. Autom. Control **60**(8), 2031–2045 (2015)
34. Langford, J., Zhang, T.: The epoch-greedy algorithm for contextual multi-armed bandits. Adv. Neural. Inf. Process. Syst. **20**(1), 96–1 (2007)

35. Liang, E., et al.: RLlib: abstractions for distributed reinforcement learning. In: Dy, J., Krause, A. (eds.) Proceedings of the 35th International Conference on Machine Learning. Proceedings of Machine Learning Research, vol. 80, pp. 3053–3062. PMLR, 10–15 July 2018

36. Lun, Y.Z., Wheatley, J., D'Innocenzo, A., Abate, A.: Approximate abstractions of Markov chains with interval decision processes. In: Proceedings of 6th IFAC Conference on Analysis and Design of Hybrid Systems (2018)

37. Ma, H., Guan, Y., Li, S.E., Zhang, X., Zheng, S., Chen, J.: Feasible Actor-Critic: Constrained Reinforcement Learning for Ensuring Statewise Safety (2021)

38. Mnih, V., et al.: Asynchronous methods for deep reinforcement learning. In: Balcan, M.F., Weinberger, K.Q. (eds.) Proceedings of 33rd International Conference on Machine Learning, vol. 48, pp. 1928–1937. PMLR (2016)

39. Osborne, M.J., et al.: An Introduction to Game Theory, vol. 3. Oxford University Press, New York (2004)

40. Papoudakis, G., Christianos, F., Albrecht, S.V.: Agent modelling under partial observability for deep reinforcement learning. In: Proceedings of the Neural Information Processing Systems (NeurIPS) (2021)

41. Pedregosa, F., et al.: Scikit-learn: machine learning in Python. J. Mach. Learn. Res. **12**, 2825–2830 (2011)

42. Sankaranarayanan, S., Sipma, H.B., Manna, Z.: Scalable analysis of linear systems using mathematical programming. In: Cousot, R. (ed.) VMCAI 2005. LNCS, vol. 3385, pp. 25–41. Springer, Heidelberg (2005). https://doi.org/10.1007/978-3-540-30579-8_2

43. Schulman, J., Wolski, F., Dhariwal, P., Radford, A., Klimov, O.: Proximal policy optimization algorithms. arXiv:1707.06347 (2017)

44. Smith, R.L.: Efficient Monte Carlo procedures for generating points uniformly distributed over bounded regions. Oper. Res. **32**(6), 1296–1308 (1984)

45. Srinivasan, K., Eysenbach, B., Ha, S., Tan, J., Finn, C.: Learning to be Safe: Deep RL with a Safety Critic (2020)

46. Tjeng, V., Xiao, K., Tedrake, R.: Evaluating Robustness of Neural Networks with Mixed Integer Programming (2017)

47. Vamplew, P., Dazeley, R., Barker, E., Kelarev, A.: Constructing stochastic mixture policies for episodic multiobjective reinforcement learning tasks. In: Nicholson, A., Li, X. (eds.) AI 2009. LNCS (LNAI), vol. 5866, pp. 340–349. Springer, Heidelberg (2009). https://doi.org/10.1007/978-3-642-10439-8_35

48. Wolff, E., Topcu, U., Murray, R.: Robust control of uncertain Markov decision processes with temporal logic specifications. In: Proceedings of 51th IEEE Conference on Decision and Control (CDC 2012), pp. 3372–3379 (2012)

49. Yu, C., Liu, J., Nemati, S., Yin, G.: Reinforcement learning in healthcare: a survey. ACM Comput. Surv. **55**(1), 1–36 (2021)

50. Networkx - network analysis in python. https://networkx.github.io/. Accessed 07 May 2020

51. Pytorch. https://pytorch.org/. Accessed 07 May 2020

52. Zhu, H., Magill, S., Xiong, Z., Jagannathan, S.: An inductive synthesis framework for verifiable reinforcement learning. In: Proceedings of the ACM SIGPLAN Conference on Programming Language Design and Implementation (PLDI), pp. 686–701. Association for Computing Machinery, June 2019

NNLander-VeriF: A Neural Network Formal Verification Framework for Vision-Based Autonomous Aircraft Landing

Ulices Santa Cruz[✉] and Yasser Shoukry

University of California Irvine, Irvine, CA, USA
{usantacr,yshoukry}@uci.edu

Abstract. In this paper, we consider the problem of formally verifying a Neural Network (NN) based autonomous landing system. In such a system, a NN controller processes images from a camera to guide the aircraft while approaching the runway. A central challenge for the safety and liveness verification of vision-based closed-loop systems is the lack of mathematical models that captures the relation between the system states (e.g., position of the aircraft) and the images processed by the vision-based NN controller. Another challenge is the limited abilities of state-of-the-art NN model checkers. Such model checkers can reason only about simple input-output robustness properties of neural networks. This limitation creates a gap between the NN model checker abilities and the need to verify a closed-loop system while considering the aircraft dynamics, the perception components, and the NN controller. To this end, this paper presents NNLander-VeriF, a framework to verify vision-based NN controllers used for autonomous landing. NNLander-VeriF addresses the challenges above by exploiting geometric models of perspective cameras to obtain a mathematical model that captures the relation between the aircraft states and the inputs to the NN controller. By converting this model into a NN (with manually assigned weights) and composing it with the NN controller, one can capture the relation between aircraft states and control actions using one augmented NN. Such an augmented NN model leads to a natural encoding of the closed-loop verification into several NN robustness queries, which state-of-the-art NN model checkers can handle. Finally, we evaluate our framework to formally verify the properties of a trained NN and we show its efficiency.

Keywords: Neural network · Formal verification · Perception

1 Introduction

Machine learning models, like deep neural networks, are used heavily to process high-dimensional imaging data like LiDAR scanners and cameras. These data

This work was supported by the National Science Foundation under grant numbers #2002405 and #2013824.

driven models are then used to provide estimates for the surrounding environment which is then used to close the loop and control the rest of the system. Nevertheless, the use of such data-driven models in safety-critical systems raises several safety and reliability concerns. It is unsurprising the increasing attention given to the problem of formally verifying Neural Network (NN)-based systems.

The work in the literature of verifying NNs and NN-based systems can be classified into *component-level* and *system-level* verification. Representatives of the first class, namely *component-level* verification are the work on creating specialized decision procedures that can reason about input-output properties of NNs [2,8,10,11,17,18,20,25,26]. In all these works, the focus is to ensure that inputs of the NN that belong to a particular convex set will result in NN outputs that belong to a defined set of outputs. Such input-output specification allows designers to verify interesting properties of NN like robustness to adversarial inputs and verify the safety of collision avoidance protocols. For a comparison between the details and performance of these NN model checkers, the reader is referred to the annual competition on verification of neural networks [1]. Regardless of the improvements observed every year in the literature of NN model checkers, verifying properties of perception and vision-based systems as a simple input-output property of NNs is still an open challenge.

On the other hand, *system-level* verification refers to the ability of reasoning about the temporal evolution of the whole system (including the NNs) while providing safety and liveness assurance [7,12,23,24]. A central challenge to verify systems that rely on vision-based systems and other high-bandwidth signals (e.g., LiDARs) is the need to explicitly model the imaging process, i.e., the relation between the system state and the images created by cameras and LiDARs [23]. While first steps were taken to provide formal models for LiDAR based systems [23], very little attention is given to perception and vision-based systems. In particular, current state-of-the-art aims to avoid modeling the perception system formally, and instead focus on the use of abstractions of the perception system [14,19]. Unfortunately, these abstractions are only tested on a set of samples and lack any formal guarantees in their ability to model the perception system formally. Other techniques use the formal specifications to guide the generation of test scenarios to increase the chances of finding a counterexample but without the ability to formally prove the correctness of the vision-based system [12].

Motivated by the lack of formal guarantees of the abstractions of perception components [14,19], we argue in this paper for the need to formally model such perception components. Fortunately, such models were historically investigated in the literature of machine vision before the explosion of using data-driven approaches in machine learning [9,21]. While these physical/geometrical models of perception were shown to be complex to design vision-based systems with high performance, we argue that these models can be used for verification. In other words, we employ the philosophy of data-driven design of vision-based systems and model-based verification of such systems.

In this paper, we employ our philosophy above to the problem of designing a vision-based NN that controls aircraft while approaching runways to perform autonomous landing. Such a problem enjoys geometric nature that can be exploited to develop a geometrical/physical model of the perception system, yet represent an important real-world problem of interest to the autonomous systems designers. In particular, we present NNLander-VeriF, a framework for formal verification of vision-based autonomous aircraft landing. This framework provides several contributions to the state of the art:

- The proposed framework exploits the geometry of the autonomous landing problem to construct a formal model for the image formation process (a map between the aircraft states and the image produced by the camera). This formal model is designed such that it can be encoded as a neural network (with manually chosen weights) that we refer to as the perception NN. By augmenting the perception NN along with the NN controller (which maps camera images into control actions), we obtain a formal relation between the aircraft states and the control action that is amenable to verification.
- The proposed framework uses symbolic abstraction of the physical dynamics of the aircraft to divide the problem of model checking the system-level safety and liveness properties into a set of NN robustness queries (applied to the augmented NN obtained above). Such robustness queries can be carried out efficiently using state-of-the-art component-level NN model checkers.
- We evaluated the proposed framework on a NN controller trained using imitation learning.

2   Problem Formulation

Notation. We will denote by $\mathbb{N}$, $\mathbb{B}$, $\mathbb{R}$ and $\mathbb{R}^+$ the set of natural, Boolean, real, and non-negative real numbers, respectively. We use $||x||_\infty$ to denote the infinity norm of a vector $x \in \mathbb{R}^n$. Finally, we denote by $\mathcal{B}_r(c)$ the infinity norm ball centered at c with radius r, i.e., $\mathcal{B}_r(c) = \{x \in \mathbb{R}^n \mid ||c - x||_\infty \leq r\}$.

Aircraft Dynamical Model. In this paper, we will consider an aircraft landing on a runway. We assume the states of the aircraft to be measured with respect to the origin of the Runway Coordinate Frame (shown in Fig. 1(left)), where positions are: ξ_x is the axis across runway; ξ_y is the altitude, and ξ_z is the axis along runway. We consider only one angle ξ_θ which represents the pitch rotation around x axis of the aircraft. The state vector of the aircraft at time $t \in \mathbb{N}$ is denoted by $\xi^{(t)} \in \mathbb{R}^4 = [\xi_\theta^{(t)}, \xi_x^{(t)}, \xi_y^{(t)}, \xi_z^{(t)}]^T$ and is assumed to evolve over time while being governed by a general nonlinear dynamical system of the form $\xi^{(t+1)} = f(\xi^{(t)}, u^{(t)})$ where $u^{(t)} \in \mathbb{R}^m$ is the control vector at time t. Such nonlinear dynamical system is assumed to be time-sampled from an underlying continuous-time system with a sample time equal to τ.

Runway Parameters. We consider runway that consists of two line segments L and R. Each line segment can be characterized by its start and end point (measured also in the Runway Coordinate Frame) i.e. $L = [(L_x, 0, L_z), (L_x, 0, L_z + r_l)]$ and $R = [(R_x, 0, R_z), (R_x, 0, R_z + r_l)]$, with $R_x = L_x + r_w$ and $R_z = L_z$ where r_w

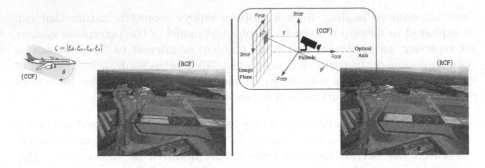

Fig. 1. Main coordinate frames: Runway (RCF), Camera (CCF) and Pixel (PCF).

and r_l refers to the runway width and length (standard international runways are designed with $r_w = 40$ m wide and $r_l = 3000$ m).

Camera Model. We assume the aircraft is equipped with a monochrome camera $\mathcal{C}$ that produces an image I of $q \times q$ pixels. Since the camera is assumed to be monochromatic, each pixel in the image I takes a value of 0 or 1. The image produced by the camera depends on the relative location of the aircraft with respect to the runway. In other words, we can model the camera $\mathcal{C}$ as a function that maps aircraft states into images, i.e., $\mathcal{C} : \mathbb{R}^4 \to \mathbb{B}^{q \times q}$. Although the images created by the camera depend on the runway parameters, for ease of notation, we drop this dependence from our notation in $\mathcal{C}$.

We utilize an ideal pinhole camera model [21] to capture the image formation process of this camera. In general, a point $p = (p_x, p_y, p_z)$ in the Runway Coordinate Frame (RCF) is mapped into a point $p' = (p'_{x_{CCF}}, p'_{y_{CCF}}, p'_{z_{CCF}})$ on the Camera Coordinate Frame (CCF) using a translation and rotation transformations defined by [13]:

$$
\begin{bmatrix} p'_{x_{CCF}} \\ p'_{y_{CCF}} \\ p'_{z_{CCF}} \\ 1 \end{bmatrix} = \begin{bmatrix} 1 & 0 & 0 & x \\ 0 & \cos\theta & \sin\theta & y \\ 0 & -\sin\theta & \cos\theta & z \\ 0 & 0 & 0 & 1 \end{bmatrix} \begin{bmatrix} p_x \\ p_y \\ p_z \\ 1 \end{bmatrix}
\tag{1}
$$

The camera then converts the 3-dimensional point p' on the camera coordinate frame into two-dimensional point p'' on the Pixel Coordinate Frame (PCF) as:

$$
p'' = \left(p''_{x_{PCF}}, p''_{y_{PCF}} \right) = \left(\left\lfloor \frac{q_{x_{PCF}}}{q_{z_{PCF}}} \right\rfloor, \left\lfloor \frac{q_{y_{PCF}}}{q_{z_{PCF}}} \right\rfloor \right)
\tag{2}
$$

where:

$$
\begin{bmatrix} q_{x_{PCF}} \\ q_{y_{PCF}} \\ q_{z_{PCF}} \end{bmatrix} = \begin{bmatrix} \rho_w & 0 & u_0 \\ 0 & -\rho_h & v_0 \\ 0 & 0 & 1 \end{bmatrix} \begin{bmatrix} f & 0 & 0 & 0 \\ 0 & f & 0 & 0 \\ 0 & 0 & 1 & 0 \end{bmatrix} \begin{bmatrix} p'_{x_{CCF}} \\ p'_{y_{CCF}} \\ p'_{z_{CCF}} \\ 1 \end{bmatrix}
\tag{3}
$$

and f is the focal length of the camera lens, W is the image width (in meters), H is the image width (in meters), WP is the image width (in pixels), HP is the image height (in pixels), and $u_0 = 0.5 \times \text{WP}$, $v_0 = 0.5 \times \text{HP}$, $\rho_w = \frac{\text{WP}}{\text{W}}$, $\rho_h = \frac{\text{HP}}{\text{H}}$.

What is remaining is to map the coordinates of $p'' = (p''_{x_{\text{PCF}}}, p''_{y_{\text{PCF}}})$ into a binary assignment for the different $q \times q$ pixels. But first, we need to check if p'' is actually inside the physical limits of the Pixel Coordinate Frame (PCF) by checking:

$$\text{visible} = \begin{cases} \text{yes} & |p''_{x_{\text{PCF}}}| \leq \frac{W}{2} \ \vee \ |p''_{y_{\text{PCF}}}| \leq \frac{H}{2} \\ \text{no} & \text{otherwise} \end{cases} \tag{4}$$

Whenever the point p'' is within the limits of PCF, then the pixel $I[i,j]$ should be assigned to 1 whenever the index of the pixel matches the coordinates $(p''_{x_{\text{PCF}}}, p''_{y_{\text{PCF}}})$, i.e.:

$$I[i,j] = \begin{cases} 1 & (p''_{x_{\text{PCF}}} == i - 1) \wedge (p''_{y_{\text{PCF}}} == j - 1) \wedge \text{visible} \\ 0 & \text{otherwise} \end{cases} \tag{5}$$

for $i, j \in (1, 2, 3...\text{WP})$. Where for simplicity, we set $\text{HP} = \text{WP}$ for square images. This process of mapping a point p in the Runway Coordinate Frame (RCF) to a pixel in the image I is summarized in Fig. 1 (right).

Neural Network Controller. The aircraft is controlled by a vision based neural network $\mathcal{NN}$ controller that maps the images I created by the camera C into a control action, i.e., $\mathcal{NN} : \mathbb{B}^{q \times q} \to \mathbb{R}^m$. We confine our attention to neural networks that consist of multiple layers and where Rectified Linear Unit (ReLU) are used as the non-linear activation units.

Problem Formulation. Consider the closed-loop vision based system Σ defined as:

$$\Sigma : \left\{ \ \xi^{(t+1)} = f(\xi^{(t)}, \mathcal{NN}(C(\xi^{(t)}))). \right.$$

A trajectory of the closed loop system Σ that starts from the initial condition ξ_0 is the sequence $\{\xi^{(t)}\}_{t=0, \xi^{(0)}=\xi_0}^{\infty}$. Consider also a set of initial conditions $\mathcal{X}_0 \subset \mathbb{R}^4$. We denote by $\Sigma^{\mathcal{X}_0}$ the trajectories of the system Σ that starts from $\mathcal{X}_0$, i.e.,

$$\Sigma^{\mathcal{X}_0} = \bigcup_{\xi_0 \in \mathcal{X}_0} \{\xi^{(t)}\}_{t=0, \xi^{(0)}=\xi_0}^{\infty}.$$

We are interested in checking if the closed-loop system meets some specifications that are captured using Linear Temporal Logic (LTL) (or a Bounded-Time LTL) formula φ. Examples of such formulas may include, but are not limited to:

- $\varphi_1 := \Diamond\{\xi_\theta = 0 \wedge \xi_y = 0\}$ which means that the aircraft should *eventually* reach an altitude of zero while the pitch angle is also zero. Satisfying φ_1 ensures that the aircraft landed on the ground.
- $\varphi_2 := \Box\{\xi_z \leq 3000\}$ which ensures the aircraft will *always* land before the end of the runway (assuming a runway length that is equal to 3000 m).

For the formal definition of the syntax and semantics of LTL and Bounded-Time LTL formulas, we refer the reader to [5]. Given a formula φ that specifies correct landing, our objective is to design a bounded model checking framework that verifies if all the trajectories $\Sigma^{\mathcal{X}_0}$ satisfy φ (denoted by $\Sigma^{\mathcal{X}_0} \models \varphi$).

3   Framework

The verification problem described in Sect. 2 is challenging because it needs to take into account the nonlinear dynamics of the aircraft f, the image formation process captured by the camera model $\mathcal{C}$, and the neural network controller $\mathcal{NN}$.

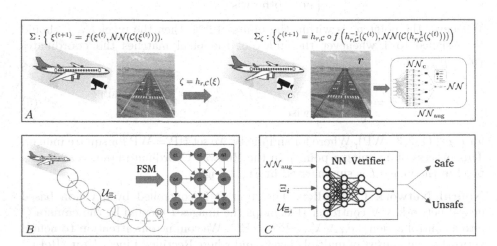

Fig. 2. Main elements of the proposed NNLander-VeriF framework: (A): construction of the augmented neural network that captures both perception and control, (B:) symbolic analysis of aircraft trajectories, (C:) neural network verification.

Our framework starts by re-modeling the pinhole camera model as a ReLU based neural network (with manually designed weights) that we refer to as the perception neural network $\mathcal{NN}_\mathcal{C}$. To facilitate this re-modeling, we need first to apply a change of coordinates to the states of the dynamical systems. We refer to the states in the new coordinates as ζ, i.e., $\zeta = h(\xi)$. By augmenting $\mathcal{NN}_\mathcal{C}$ along with the neural network controller $\mathcal{NN}$, one can obtain an augmented neural network $\mathcal{NN}_{\mathrm{aug}} : \mathbb{R}^n \to \mathbb{R}^m$ defined as $\mathcal{NN}_{\mathrm{aug}} = \mathcal{NN} \circ \mathcal{NN}_\mathcal{C}$ and a simplified closed-loop dynamics, in the new coordinates, written as:

$$\Sigma : \left\{ \zeta^{(t+1)} = g(\zeta^{(t)}, \mathcal{NN}_{\mathrm{aug}}(\zeta^{(t)})). \right.$$

Now, assume that we are given (i) a region Ξ in the new coordinate system and (ii) the maximal set of control actions (denoted by $\mathcal{U}_\Xi$) that can be applied at Ξ while ensuring the system adhere to the specification φ. Given this pair $(\Xi, \mathcal{U}_\Xi)$ one can always ensure that the augmented neural network $\mathcal{NN}_{\mathrm{aug}}$ will produce actions in the set $\mathcal{U}_\Xi$ whenever its inputs are restricted to Ξ by checking the following property:

$$\forall \zeta \in \Xi.(\mathcal{NN}_{\mathrm{aug}}(\zeta) \in \mathcal{U}_\Xi) \tag{6}$$

which can be easily verified using existing neural network model checkers [10,18, 20]. In other words, checking the augmented neural network against the property above ensures that all the images produced within the region Ξ will force the neural network controller $\mathcal{NN}$ to produce control actions that are within the set of allowable actions $\mathcal{U}_\Xi$.

To complete our framework, we need to partition the state-space into regions $(\Xi_1, \Xi_2, \ldots)$. Each region is a ball parametrized by a center ζ_i and a radius ϵ. For each region, our framework will compute the set of allowable control actions at each of these regions $(\mathcal{U}_{\Xi_1}, \mathcal{U}_{\Xi_2}, \ldots)$. Our framework will also parametrize each set $\mathcal{U}_{\Xi_i}$ as a ball with center c_i and radius μ_i, i.e., $\mathcal{U}_{\Xi_i} = \{u \in \mathbb{R}^4 \mid \|u - c_i\| \le \mu_i\}$. The computations of the pairs $(\Xi_i, \mathcal{U}_{\Xi_i})$ can be carried out using the knowledge of the aircraft dynamics f. In summary, and as shown in Fig. 2, our framework will consist of the following steps:

- **(A) Compute the augmented neural network**: Using the physical model of the pinhole camera, our framework will re-model the pinhole camera $\mathcal{C}$ as a neural network that can be augmented with the neural network controller to produce a simpler model that is amenable for verification.
- **(B) Compute the set of allowable control actions**: We use the properties of the dynamical system f to compute the set of safe control actions $\mathcal{U}_{\Xi_i}$ for each partition Ξ_i of the state space.
- **(C) Apply the neural network model checker**: We use the neural network model checkers to verify that $\mathcal{NN}_{\text{aug}}$ satisfies (6) for each identified pair $(\Xi, \mathcal{U}_{\Xi_i})$.

The remainder of this paper is devoted to providing details for the steps required for each of the three phases above.

4 Neural Network Augmentation

In this section, we focus on the problem of using the geometry of the runway to develop a different mathematical model for the camera $\mathcal{C}$. As argued in the previous section and shown in Fig. 3, our goal is to obtain a model with the same structure of a neural network (i.e., consists of several layers and neurons) and contains only ReLU activation units. We refer to this new model as $\mathcal{NN}_\mathcal{C}$.

The main challenge to construct $\mathcal{NN}_\mathcal{C}$ is the fact that ReLU based neural networks can only represent piece-wise affine (or linear) functions [22]. Nevertheless, the camera model $\mathcal{C}$ is inherently nonlinear due to the optical projection present in any camera. Such non-linearity can not be expressed (without any error) via a piece-wise affine function. To solve this problem, we propose a change of coordinates to the aircraft states h. Such change of coordinates is designed to eliminate part of the camera's non-linearity while allowing the remainder of the model to be expressed as a piece-wise affine transformation.

Change of Coordinates: Recall the runway consists of line segments L and R (defined in Sect. 2). Instead of measuring the state of the aircraft by the

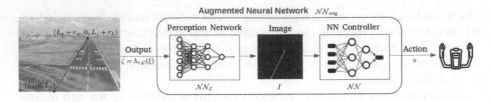

Fig. 3. Augmented network $\mathcal{NN}_{\text{aug}}$ maps the output ζ to control action u.

vector $\zeta = [\xi_\theta, \xi_x, \xi_y, \xi_z]$, we propose measuring the state of the aircraft by the projections of the end points of the lines L and R on the Pixel Coordinate Frame PCF. Formally, we define the change of coordinates as:

$$\zeta = h_{r,\mathcal{C}}(\xi) = \begin{bmatrix} \zeta_1 \\ \zeta_2 \\ \zeta_3 \\ \zeta_4 \\ \zeta_5 \end{bmatrix} = \begin{bmatrix} \rho_w f \frac{L_x+\xi_x}{L_z\cos(\xi_\theta)+\xi_z} + u_0 \\ -\rho_h f \frac{L_z\sin(\theta)+\xi_y}{L_z\cos(\xi_\theta)+\xi_z} + v_0 \\ \rho_w f \frac{L_x+\xi_x}{(L_z+r_L)\cos(\xi_\theta)+\xi_z} + u_0 \\ -\rho_h f \frac{(L_z+r_L)\sin(\xi_\theta)+\xi_y}{(L_z+r_L)\cos(\xi_\theta)+\xi_z} + v_0 \\ \zeta_1\zeta_4 - \zeta_2\zeta_3 \end{bmatrix} \tag{7}$$

where $f, \rho_h, \rho_w, v_0, u_0$ are the camera physical parameters as defined in Sect. 2. In other words, the pair (ζ_1, ζ_2) is the projection of the start point of the runway $(L_x, 0, L_z)$ onto the Pixel Coordinate Frame PCF (while ignoring the flooring operator for now). Similarly, the pair (ζ_3, ζ_4) is the projection of the endpoint of the runway $(L_x, 0, L_z + r_L)$ onto the PCF frame. Indeed, we can define a similar set of variables for the other line segment of the runway, R. The dependence of this change of coordinates on the camera parameters (e.g., the focal length f) and the runway parameters justifies the subscripts in our notation $h_{r,\mathcal{C}}$. We refer to the new state-space as Ξ.

Before we proceed, it is crucial to establish the following result.

Proposition 1. *The change of coordinates function $h_{r,\mathcal{C}}$ is bijective.*

The proof of such proposition is based on ensuring that the inverse function $h_{r,\mathcal{C}}^{-1}$ exists. For brevity, we will omit the details of this proof. Since $h_{r,\mathcal{C}}$ is bijective, we can re-write the closed-loop dynamics of the system as:

$$\Sigma_\zeta : \left\{ \zeta^{(t+1)} = h_{r,\mathcal{C}} \circ f\left(h_{r,\mathcal{C}}^{-1}(\zeta^{(t)}), \mathcal{NN}(\mathcal{C}(h_{r,\mathcal{C}}^{-1}(\zeta^{(t)})))\right) \right. \tag{8}$$

Indeed, if Σ_ζ satisfies the property φ then do the original system Σ and vice versa, thanks for the fact that $h_{r,\mathcal{C}}$ is bijective. This is captured by the following proposition:

Proposition 2. *Consider the dynamical systems Σ and Σ_ζ. Consider a set of initial states $\mathcal{X}_0$ and an LTL formula φ, the following holds:*

$$\Sigma^{\mathcal{X}_0} \models \varphi \Longleftrightarrow \Sigma_\zeta^{\Xi_0} \models \varphi$$

where $\Xi_0 = \{h_{r,c}(\xi) \mid \xi \in \mathcal{X}_0\}$.

Neural Network-Based Model for Perception: While the model of the pinhole camera (defined in Eq. (1)–(5)) focuses on mapping individual points into pixels, we aim here to obtain a model that maps the entire runway lines R and L into the corresponding binary assignment for each pixel in the image. Therefore, it is insufficient to analyze the values of $\zeta_1, \ldots, \zeta_4$ which encodes the start point (ζ_1, ζ_2) and the endpoint (ζ_3, ζ_4) of the runway line segments on the PCF. To correctly generate the final image $I \in \mathbb{B}^{q \times q}$, we need to map *every* point between (ζ_1, ζ_2) and (ζ_3, ζ_4) into the corresponding pixels.

While the pinhole camera (defined in Eq. (1)–(4)) uses the information in the Pixel Coordinate Frame (PCF) to compute the values of each pixel, we instead rely on the information in the Camera Coordinate Frame (CCF) to avoid the nonlinearities added by the flooring operator in (2) and the logical checks in (4)–(5). For each pixel, imagine a set of four line segments AB, BC, CD, DA in the Pixel Coordinate Frame (PCF) that defines the edges of each pixel (see Fig. 4 for an illustration). To check if a pixel should be set to zero or one, it is enough to check the intersection between the line segment $(\zeta_1, \zeta_2) - (\zeta_3, \zeta_4)$ and each of the lines A–B, B–C, C–D, D–A. Whenever an intersection occurs, the pixel should be assigned to one.

To intersect one of the pixel edges, e.g., the edge $A - B = (A_x, A_y) - (B_x, B_y)$, with the line segment $(\zeta_1, \zeta_2) - (\zeta_3, \zeta_4)$, we proceed with the standard line segment intersection algorithm [6] which compute four values named O_1, O_2, O_3, O_4 as:

$$O_1 = \zeta_1(A_y - B_y) + \zeta_2(B_x - A_x) + A_x B_y - A_y B_x \tag{9}$$

$$O_2 = \zeta_3(A_y - B_y) + \zeta_4(B_x - A_x) + A_x B_y - A_y B_x \tag{10}$$

$$O_3 = -\zeta_1(A_y) + \zeta_2(A_x) + \zeta_3(A_y) - \zeta_4(A_x) + \zeta_5 \tag{11}$$

$$O_4 = -\zeta_1(B_y) + \zeta_2(B_x) + \zeta_3(B_y) - \zeta_4(B_x) + \zeta_5 \tag{12}$$

The line segment algorithm [6] detects an intersection whenever the following condition holds:

$$(\text{sign}(O_1) \neq \text{sign}(O_2)) \wedge (\text{sign}(O_3) \neq sign(O_4)) \tag{13}$$

Luckily, we can organize the equations (9)–(13) in the form of a neural network with a Rectifier Linear Activation Unit (ReLU). ReLU nonlinearity takes the form of $\text{ReLU}(x) = \max\{x, 0\}$. To show this conversion, we first note that the values of A_x, A_y, B_x, B_y are constant and well defined for each pixel. So assuming the input to such a neural network is the vector ζ, one can use equations (9)–(12) to assign the weights to the input layer of the neural network (as shown in Fig. 4). To check the signs of $O_1, \ldots, O_4$, we recall the well-known identity for numbers of the same sign:

$$\text{sign}(a) = \text{sign}(b) \iff |a + b| - |a| - |b| = 0 \tag{14}$$

The absolute function can be implemented directly with a ReLU using the identity:

$$|x| = \max\{x, 0\} + \max\{-x, 0\}. \tag{15}$$

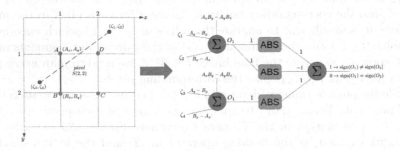

Fig. 4. Line-segment intersection algorithm: The runway line (in red) as seen by the camera intersects the pixel edge A–B (in blue), this single edge intersection is detected by using a layer of six ReLU's. (Color figure online)

The process above has to be repeated four times (to account for all edges A–B, B–C, C–D, D–A of a pixel). Finally, to check that at least one intersection occurred, we compute the minimum across the results from all the intersections. Calculating the minimum itself can be implemented directly with a ReLU using the identity:

$$min\{a, b\} = \frac{a + b}{2} - \frac{|a - b|}{2}. \tag{16}$$

The overall neural network requires $68 \times q \times q$ ReLU neurons for each projected line segment. The final architecture is shown in Fig. 5. We refer to the resulting neural network as $\mathcal{NN}_\mathcal{C}(\zeta^{(t)})$.

It is direct to show that the constructed neural network $\mathcal{NN}_\mathcal{C}(\zeta^{(t)})$ will produce the same images obtained by the pinhole camera model $\mathcal{C}$, i.e.,

$$\mathcal{C}(h_{r,\mathcal{C}}^{-1}(\zeta^{(t)})) = \mathcal{NN}_\mathcal{C}(\zeta^{(t)})$$

Finally, by substituting in (8), we can now re-write the closed-loop dynamics as:

$$\Sigma_\zeta : \left\{ \zeta^{(t+1)} = g\left(h_{r,\mathcal{C}}^{-1}(\zeta^{(t)}), \mathcal{NN}_{\text{aug}}(\zeta^{(t)})\right) \right. \tag{17}$$

where $\mathcal{NN}_{\text{aug}} = \mathcal{NN} \circ \mathcal{NN}_\mathcal{C}$ and $g = h_{r,\mathcal{C}} \circ f$.

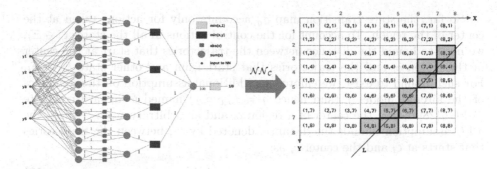

Fig. 5. $\mathcal{NN}_C$ checks the intersection between line segment $(\zeta_1, \zeta_2) - (\zeta_3, \zeta_4)$ and all edges of each cell pixel of the final image.

5 Identifying the Allowable Control Actions Using Symbolic Abstractions

As shown in Sect. 3, our framework aims to split the verification of the dynamical system (17) into several NN model checking queries. Each query will verify the correctness of the closed-loop system within a region (or a symbol) Ξ_i of the state space. To prepare for such queries, we need to compute a set of input/output pairs $(\Xi_i, \mathcal{U}_{\Xi_i})$ with the guarantee that all the control inputs inside each $\mathcal{U}_{\Xi_i}$ will produce trajectories that satisfy the specifications φ. In this section, we provide details of how to compute the pairs $(\Xi_i, \mathcal{U}_{\Xi_i})$.

State Space Partitioning: Given a partitioning parameter ϵ, we partition the new coordinate space of ζ into L regions $\Xi_1, \Xi_2, \ldots, \Xi_L$ such that each Ξ_i is an infinity-norm ball with radius ϵ and center c_i. For simplicity of notation, we keep the radius ϵ constant within all the regions Ξ_i. However, the framework is generic enough to account for multi-scale partitioning schemes similar to those reported in the literature of symbolic analysis of hybrid systems [15].

Obtain Symbolic Models: Given the regions $\Xi_1, \Xi_2, \ldots$, the next step is to construct a *finite-state abstraction* for the closed loop system (17). Such finite state abstraction takes the form of a finite state machine $\Sigma_q = (S_q, \sigma_q)$ where S_q is the set of finite states and $\sigma_q : S_q \to 2^{S_q}$ is the state transition map of the finite state machine, defined as:

$$S_q = \{1, 2, \ldots L\} \quad \text{and} \quad j \in \sigma_q(i) \iff g\left(h_{r,C}^{-1}(c_i), \mathcal{NN}_{\text{aug}}(c_i)\right) \in \Xi_j. \quad (18)$$

In other words, the finite state machine (FSM) has a number of states L that is equal to the number of regions Ξ_i, i.e., each finite state symbolically represents a region. A transition between the state i and j is added to the state transition map σ_q whenever applying the NN controller to the center of the region i (i.e., c_i) will force the next state of the system to be within the region Ξ_j. The value of $g\left(h_{r,C}^{-1}(c_i), \mathcal{NN}_{\text{aug}}(c_i)\right)$ can be directly computed by evaluating the neural network $\mathcal{NN}_{\text{aug}}$ at the center c_i followed by evaluating the function g.

So far, the state transition map σ_q accounts only for actions taken at the center of the region. To account for the control actions in all the states $\zeta_i \in \Xi_i$, we need to bound the distance between the trajectories that start at the center of the region c_i and the trajectories that start from any other state $\zeta_i \in \Xi_i$. For such bound to exist, we enforce an additional assumption on the dynamics of the aircraft model f (and hence $g = h_{r,c} \circ f$) named δ forward complete (δ-FC) [28]. Given the center of a region c_i and an arbitrary state $\zeta_i \in \Xi_i$, the δ-FC assumption bounds the distance, denoted by δ_ζ, between the trajectories that starts at ζ_i and the center c_i as:

$$\delta_\zeta \leq \beta(\epsilon, \tau) + \gamma(\|\mathcal{NN}_{\mathrm{aug}}(c_i) - \mathcal{NN}_{\mathrm{aug}}(\zeta_i)\|_\infty, \tau) \tag{19}$$

where τ is the sample time used to obtain the dynamics f (as explained in Sect. 2) and β and γ are class K_∞ functions that can be computed from the knowledge of the dynamics f. Such δ-FC assumption is shown to be mild and does not require the aircraft dynamics to be stable. For technical details about the δ-FC assumption and the computation of the functions β and γ, we refer the reader to [27]. Given the inequality (19), we can revisit the definition of the state transition map σ_q to account for all possible trajectories as:

$$j \in \sigma_q(i) \iff g\left(h_{r,c}^{-1}(c_i), \mathcal{NN}_{\mathrm{aug}}(c_i)\right) + \delta_\zeta \in \Xi_j. \tag{20}$$

With such a modification, it is direct to show the following result:

Proposition 3. *Consider the dynamical systems Σ_ζ and Σ_q. Consider also a set of initial conditions Ξ_0 and a specification φ. The following holds:*

$$\Sigma_q^{\mathcal{S}_0} \models \varphi \Rightarrow \Sigma_\zeta^{\Xi_o} \models \varphi$$

where $\mathcal{S}_0 = \{i \in \{1, \ldots, L\} \mid \exists \zeta_0 \in \Xi_0 : \zeta_0 \in \Xi_i\}$.

This proposition follows directly from Theorem 4.1 in [28].

Compute the Set of Allowable Control Actions: Unfortunately, computing the norm $\|\mathcal{NN}_{\mathrm{aug}}(c_i) - \mathcal{NN}_{\mathrm{aug}}(\zeta_i)\|_\infty$ (and hence δ_ζ) is challenging. As shown in [16], computing such norm is NP-hard and existing tools in the literature focus on computing an upper bound for such norm. Nevertheless, the bounds given by the existing literature constitute large error margins that will render our approach severely conservative.

To alleviate the problem above, we use the inequality (19) in a "backward design approach". We first search for the maximum value of δ_ζ that renders Σ_q compatible with the specification. To that end, we substitute the norm $\|\mathcal{NN}_{\mathrm{aug}}(c_i) - \mathcal{NN}_{\mathrm{aug}}(\zeta_i)\|_\infty$ with a dummy variable μ. By iteratively increasing the value of μ, we will obtain different Σ_q, one for each value of μ. We use a bounded model checker for each value of μ to verify if the resulting Σ_q satisfies the specification. We keep increasing the value of μ until the resulting Σ_q no longer satisfies φ. We refer to this value as $\mu_{\max}$. What is remaining is to ensure that the neural network indeed respects the bound:

$$\|\mathcal{NN}_{\mathrm{aug}}(c_i) - \mathcal{NN}_{\mathrm{aug}}(\zeta_i)\|_\infty \leq \mu_{\max}$$

Algorithm 1. LanderNN-VeriF

Input: $\Xi, \Xi_0, \varphi, \epsilon, \tau, \beta, \gamma, \mathcal{NN}_{\mathrm{aug}}, T, \overline{\mu}, \underline{\mu}, f, h, h^{-1}$
Output: STATUS

1: $\{\Xi_1, \Xi_2, \ldots, \Xi_L\} = $ Partition_into_regions(Ξ, ϵ)
2: $\mu = \underline{\mu}$
3: **while** statusFSM == UNSAT **do**
4:    $\Sigma_q = $ Create_FSM$(f, h, h^{-1}, \tau, \beta, \gamma, \mathcal{NN}_{aug}, \Xi_{1..L}, \mu)$
5:    statusFSM = Check_FSM(φ, Σ_q, T)
6:    **if** $\mu \leq \overline{\mu}$ **then**
7:        $\mu = $ Increase_MU(μ)
8:    **end if**
9: **end while**
10: **for** i $= 1$ to L **do**
11:    STATUS_NN[i] = NN_Verifier$(\mathcal{NN}_{aug}, \Xi_i, \mu)$
12:    **if** STATUS_NN[i] == SAT **then**
13:        STATUS = UNSAFE
14:    **else**
15:        STATUS = SAFE
16:    **end if**
17: **end for**
18: **return** STATUS

To that end, we define the set of allowable control actions $\mathcal{U}_{\Xi_i}$ as:

$$\mathcal{U}_{\Xi_i} = \mathcal{B}_{\mu_{\max}}(\mathcal{NN}_{\mathrm{aug}}(c_i))$$

It is then direct to show the following equivalence:

$$\|\mathcal{NN}_{\mathrm{aug}}(c_i) - \mathcal{NN}_{\mathrm{aug}}(\zeta_i)\|_\infty \leq \mu_{\max} \iff \forall \zeta \in \Xi_i.(\mathcal{NN}_{\mathrm{aug}}(\zeta) \in \mathcal{U}_{\Xi_i})$$

where $\mathcal{U}_{\Xi_i} = \mathcal{B}_{\mu_{\max}}(\mathcal{NN}_{\mathrm{aug}}(c_i))$. Luckily, the right-hand side of this equivalence is precisely what neural network model checkers are capable of verifying. Algorithm 1 summarizes this discussion. The following result captures the guarantees provided by the proposed framework:

Proposition 4. *The LanderNN-VeriF algorithm (Algorithm 1) is sound but not complete.*

6   Numerical Example

We illustrate the results in this paper using a vision-based aircraft landing system. We use a fixed-wing aircraft model defined using the guidance kinematic model [3], where orientations (in Rads) are defined by the course angle χ (rotation around y_{CCF} axis), pitch angle θ (rotation around x_{CCF} axis) and V_g denotes the total Aircraft velocity relative to the ground. We further simplify the system by keeping the course angle pointing towards the runway ($\chi = 0$), similarly velocity is kept as constant. Moreover, $\dot{\theta}$ (Rad/s) is regarded as the control input u. According to this model, the state vector of the aircraft evolves over time while being governed by the following dynamical system [3]:

$$\xi_z^{(t+1)} = \xi_z^{(t)} + V_g\tau \cos{(\xi_\theta^{(t)})} \tag{21}$$

$$\xi_y^{(t+1)} = \xi_y^{(t)} + V_g\tau \sin{(\xi_\theta^{(t)})} \tag{22}$$

$$\xi_\theta^{(t+1)} = \xi_\theta^{(t)} + u^{(t)}\tau \tag{23}$$

where τ is the sampling time. For our simulations we consider $V_g = 25\frac{m}{s}$ and $\tau = 0.1$. Moreover based on airport standards we consider the runway segments (in meters) defined by $L = [(L_x, 0, L_z), (L_x, 0, L_z + r_l)]$ and $R = [(R_x, 0, R_z), (R_x, 0, R_z + r_l)]$ where $R_x = 20$, $L_x = -20$, $R_z = 0$, $L_z = 0$, $r_l = 3000$. For the camera parameters we consider images of 16×16 pixels and focal length of $400\,\text{mm}$.

We note that the system dynamics (21)–(23) is a δ-FC system. In particular, by using the method [27] and the δ-FC Lyapunov function $\mathcal{V}(\xi, \xi') = \|\xi - \xi'\|_2^2$ one can show that:

$$\beta(\zeta_1, \zeta_2, \zeta_3, \tau) = \sqrt{8}\sqrt{\zeta_1^2 + \zeta_2^2 + \zeta_3^2}\;e^\tau \tag{24}$$

$$\gamma(\mu, \tau) = \sqrt{V_g(e^{2\tau} - 1)\mu} \tag{25}$$

We work on the output space set $D = [\zeta_1 \times \zeta_2 \times \zeta_3] = [0, 16] \times [0, 16] \times [0, 16]$ of Σ_ζ with a precision $\epsilon = 1$, thus our discretized grid consists of 16^3 cubes.

We used Imitation Learning to train a fully connected ReLU Neural Network controller ($\mathcal{NN}$) of 2 layers with 128 Neurons each. Trajectories from different initial conditions were collected and used to train the network. Our objective is to verify that the aircraft landing using the trained $\mathcal{NN}_{aug}$ satisfies the safety specification $\phi = \Box \neg q_{unsafe}$ where $q_{unsafe} = [\xi_z = 800, \xi_y = 200, \xi_\theta = 1]$ which corresponds to an unsafe region while landing.

In what next, we report the execution time to verify the trained network. All experiments were executed on an Intel Core i7 processor with 50 GB of RAM. First, we implemented our Vision Network ($\mathcal{NN}_C$) for images of 16×16 pixels using Keras. Similarly, we used Keras composition libraries to merge the controller and perception networks into the augmented network ($\mathcal{NN}_{aug}$), a landing trajectory using $\mathcal{NN}_{aug}$ is shown in Fig. 6 and its corresponding camera view is shown in Fig. 7.

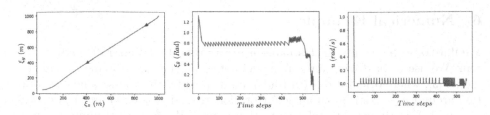

Fig. 6. Aircraft landing using augmented controller $\mathcal{NN}_{aug}$. Left: aircraft position (ξ_y, ξ_z); Middle: aircraft angle (ξ_θ); Right: aircraft control ($u = \mathcal{NN}_{aug}$).

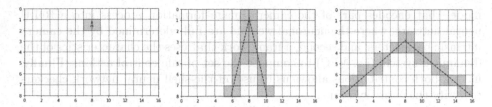

Fig. 7. Landing camera view using 16×16 pixels resolution. Left: $\xi^1 = [1000, 1000, \frac{\pi}{4}]$, Middle: $\xi^{300} = [400, 300, \frac{\pi}{8}]$, Right: $\xi^{1000} = [5, 5, 0]$.

We used a Boolean SAT solver named SAT4J [4] to implement the Check_FSM function in Algorithm 1. The finite state machine Σ_q was encoded using a set of Boolean variables and our implementation performed a bounded model checking for the generated FSMs (the bounded model checking horizon was set to 20). We constructed FSMs with the following values $\mu = [0.1, 0.2, 0.3, 0.6, 0.8, 0.9, 1.1]$ until a value of $\mu_{max} = 1.1$ was found. The execution time for creating Σ_q and verifying its properties with the bounded model checker increased monotonically from 2000 seconds for $\mu = 0.1$ to 7000 seconds for $\mu = 1.1$. As expected, the higher the value of μ, the higher the number of transitions in Σ_q, and the higher the time needed to create and verify.

Finally, we used PeregriNN [20] as the NN model checker. Figure 8 reports the execution time for verifying the neural network property in 100 random regions, and Fig. 9 in regions 1 to 500. The average execution time was 76 s per region and the NN was found to be safe and satisfying the specification φ.

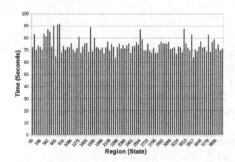

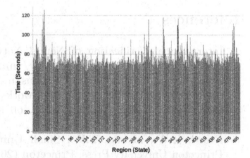

Fig. 8. Execution time for verifying φ in 100 different random regions.

Fig. 9. Execution time for verifying φ in regions 1 to 500.

7 Conclusion and Future Work

Due to the recent surge in vision-based autonomous systems, it is becoming increasingly important to provide frameworks to facilitate its formal verification. In this work we have proposed two key contributions: first, a generative model that encodes part of the camera image formation process into a ReLU neural network, where the neuronal weights are fully determined by the camera intrinsic parameters, and second, a framework that uses the characteristics of the dynamical system (i.e. δ-FC) to compute the set of safe control actions; Finally, having both contributions allows us to use off-the-shelf neural network checkers to verify the entire system.

At the same time, there are some limitations. First, the generative model we developed insists on modeling the image formation process with a piecewise affine (PWA) function which facilitates encoding it as a ReLU network. However, this restriction may in odds with realistic scenarios which may not be captured exactly by CPWA functions. Nevertheless, it is widely known that CPWA functions can approximate general nonlinear functions with some error. This also leads to the second limitation, namely, the inability to consider noise in the image formation process. Finally, the number of pixels has a direct effect on the scalability of the framework, as a consequence further improvements are required to build more concise finite-state machine abstractions of the physical system.

Moving forward, we plan to extend our approach in different directions to account for the aforementioned limitations. First, we seek to generalize the framework to account for uncertainties in the camera model, the image formation model, and the environment. Second, we intend to process more complex image features (e.g. combinations of multiple lines and curvatures) by developing better generative models with provable error bounds. Finally, we aim to verify the robustness of neural network controllers to external disturbances (e.g., wind) while developing better scalable algorithms.

References

1. International Verification of Neural Networks Competition 2020 (VNN-COMP 2020). https://sites.google.com/view/vnn20
2. Bak, S., Tran, H.-D., Hobbs, K., Johnson, T.T.: Improved Geometric path enumeration for verifying ReLU neural networks. In: Lahiri, S.K., Wang, C. (eds.) CAV 2020, Part I. LNCS, vol. 12224, pp. 66–96. Springer, Cham (2020). https://doi.org/10.1007/978-3-030-53288-8_4
3. Beard, R.W., Mclain, T.W.: Small Unmanned Aircraft: Theory and Practice. Princeton University Press, Princeton (2012)
4. Berre, D.L., Parrain, A.: The Sat4j library. Boolean Model. Comput. **7**, 59–64 (2010)
5. Clarke, E.M., Henzinger, T.A., Veith, H., Bloem, R., et al.: Handbook of Model Checking, vol. 10. Springer, Heidelberg (2018). https://doi.org/10.1007/978-3-319-10575-8
6. Cormen, T., Leiserson, C., Rivest, R., Stein, C.: Introduction to Algorithms. The MIT Press, Cambridge (2003)
7. Cruz, U.S., Ferlez, J., Shoukry, Y.: Safe-by-repair: a convex optimization approach for repairing unsafe two-level lattice neural network controllers. arXiv preprint arXiv:2104.02788 (2021)

8. Ehlers, R.: Formal verification of piece-wise linear feed-forward neural networks. In: D'Souza, D., Narayan Kumar, K. (eds.) ATVA 2017. LNCS, vol. 10482, pp. 269–286. Springer, Cham (2017). https://doi.org/10.1007/978-3-319-68167-2_19
9. Faugeras, O., Faugeras, O.A.: Three-Dimensional Computer Vision: A Geometric Viewpoint. MIT Press, Cambridge (1993)
10. Ferlez, J., Khedr, H., Shoukry, Y.: Fast BATLLNN: fast box analysis of two-level lattice neural networks. In: Proceedings of the 25th ACM International Conference on Hybrid Systems: Computation and Control (2022)
11. Ferlez, J., Shoukry, Y.: Bounding the complexity of formally verifying neural networks: a geometric approach. In: 2021 60th IEEE Conference on Decision and Control (CDC), pp. 5104–5109. IEEE (2021)
12. Fremont, D.J., Chiu, J., Margineantu, D.D., Osipychev, D., Seshia, S.A.: Formal analysis and redesign of a neural network-based aircraft taxiing system with VERIFAI. In: Lahiri, S.K., Wang, C. (eds.) CAV 2020, Part I. LNCS, vol. 12224, pp. 122–134. Springer, Cham (2020). https://doi.org/10.1007/978-3-030-53288-8_6
13. Hartley, R., Zisserman, A.: Multiple View Geometry in Computer Vision. Cambridge University Press, Cambridge (2003)
14. Hsieh, C., Joshi, K., Misailovic, S., Mitra, S.: Verifying controllers with convolutional neural network-based perception: a case for intelligible, safe, and precise abstractions. arXiv preprint arXiv:2111.05534 (2021)
15. Hsu, K., Majumdar, R., Mallik, K., Schmuck, A.K.: Multi-layered abstraction-based controller synthesis for continuous-time systems. In: Proceedings of the 21st International Conference on Hybrid Systems: Computation and Control (part of CPS Week), pp. 120–129 (2018)
16. Kallus, N., Zhou, A.: Assessing disparate impact of personalized interventions: identifiability and bounds. Adv. Neural Inf. Process. Syst. **32** (2019)
17. Katz, G., Barrett, C., Dill, D.L., Julian, K., Kochenderfer, M.J.: Reluplex: an efficient SMT solver for verifying deep neural networks. In: Majumdar, R., Kunčak, V. (eds.) CAV 2017, Part I. LNCS, vol. 10426, pp. 97–117. Springer, Cham (2017). https://doi.org/10.1007/978-3-319-63387-9_5
18. Katz, G., et al.: The marabou framework for verification and analysis of deep neural networks. In: Dillig, I., Tasiran, S. (eds.) CAV 2019, Part I. LNCS, vol. 11561, pp. 443–452. Springer, Cham (2019). https://doi.org/10.1007/978-3-030-25540-4_26
19. Katz, S.M., Corso, A.L., Strong, C.A., Kochenderfer, M.J.: Verification of image-based neural network controllers using generative models. arXiv preprint arXiv:2105.07091 (2021)
20. Khedr, H., Ferlez, J., Shoukry, Y.: PEREGRiNN: penalized-relaxation greedy neural network verifier. In: Silva, A., Leino, K.R.M. (eds.) CAV 2021, Part I. LNCS, vol. 12759, pp. 287–300. Springer, Cham (2021). https://doi.org/10.1007/978-3-030-81685-8_13
21. Ma, Y., Soatto, S., Kosecka, J., Sastry, S.S.: An Invitation to 3-D Vision: From Images to Geometric Models, vol. 26. Springer, Heidelberg (2012). https://doi.org/10.1007/978-0-387-21779-6
22. Nagamine, T., Mesgarani, N.: Understanding the representation and computation of multilayer perceptrons: a case study in speech recognition. In: International Conference on Machine Learning, pp. 2564–2573. PMLR (2017)
23. Sun, X., Khedr, H., Shoukry, Y.: Formal verification of neural network controlled autonomous systems. In: Proceedings of the 22nd ACM International Conference on Hybrid Systems: Computation and Control, pp. 147–156 (2019)
24. Sun, X., Shoukry, Y.: Provably correct training of neural network controllers using reachability analysis. arXiv preprint arXiv:2102.10806 (2021)

25. Tran, H.-D., et al.: NNV: the neural network verification tool for deep neural networks and learning-enabled cyber-physical systems. In: Lahiri, S.K., Wang, C. (eds.) CAV 2020, Part I. LNCS, vol. 12224, pp. 3–17. Springer, Cham (2020). https://doi.org/10.1007/978-3-030-53288-8_1
26. Wang, Y.S., Weng, L., Daniel, L.: Neural network control policy verification with persistent adversarial perturbation. In: International Conference on Machine Learning, pp. 10050–10059. PMLR (2020). https://proceedings.mlr.press/v119/wang20v.html
27. Zamani, M.: Control of cyber-physical systems using incremental properties of physical systems. Ph.D. thesis (2012)
28. Zamani, M., Pola, G., Mazo, M., Jr., Tabuada, P.: Symbolic models for nonlinear control systems without stability assumptions. IEEE Trans. Autom. Control 57(7), 1804–1809 (2012)

The Black-Box Simplex Architecture
for Runtime Assurance
of Autonomous CPS

Usama Mehmood, Sanaz Sheikhi[(✉)], Stanley Bak, Scott A. Smolka,
and Scott D. Stoller

Department of Computer Science, Stony Brook University, Stony Brook, NY, USA
{umehmood,ssheikhi,sbak,sas,stoller}@cs.stonybrook.edu

Abstract. The Simplex Architecture is a runtime assurance framework
where control authority may switch from an unverified and potentially
unsafe *advanced controller* to a backup *baseline controller* in order to
maintain the safety of an autonomous cyber-physical system. In this
work, we show that runtime checks can replace the requirement to statically verify safety of the baseline controller. This is important as there
are many powerful control techniques, such as model-predictive control
and neural network controllers, that work well in practice but are difficult to statically verify. Since the method does not use internal information about the advanced or baseline controller, we call the approach
the *Black-Box Simplex Architecture*. We prove the architecture is safe
and present two case studies where (i) model-predictive control provides
safe multi-robot coordination, and (ii) neural networks provably prevent
collisions in groups of F-16 aircraft, despite the controllers occasionally
outputting unsafe commands.

Keywords: Black-Box Simplex · Runtime assurance · Autonomous
CPS

1 Introduction

Autonomous cyber-physical systems (CPS) have the potential to transform vital
domains such as transportation, health-care, and energy management. As these
systems perform complex functions, they often require complex designs. Moreover, since autonomous CPS interact with the physical world, they are typically
safety-critical. Formal analysis, however, can be difficult for complex systems.

In the development of such CPS, powerful control techniques such as model-
predictive control and deep reinforcement learning are increasingly being used
instead of traditional controller design techniques. Such trends exacerbate the
safety verification problem. Additionally, there is increasing interest in systems
that can *learn in the field*, changing their behaviors based on observations. Classical verification strategies are poorly suited for such designs.

© Springer Nature Switzerland AG 2022
J. V. Deshmukh et al. (Eds.): NFM 2022, LNCS 13260, pp. 231–250, 2022.
https://doi.org/10.1007/978-3-031-06773-0_12

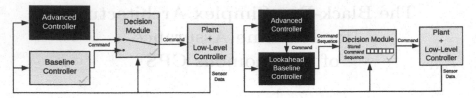

(a) Traditional Simplex Architecture   (b) Black-Box Simplex Architecture

Fig. 1. The Black-Box Simplex Architecture guarantees safety despite a black-box advanced controller and a black-box baseline controller.

One approach for dynamically providing safety for systems with complex and unverified components is *runtime assurance* [9], where the state of the plant is monitored at runtime to mitigate possible imminent violations of formal properties. A well-known runtime assurance technique is the Simplex Control Architecture [36,37], which has been applied to a wide range of systems [10,30,32]. In the original Simplex Architecture, shown in Fig. 1(a), the *baseline controller* (BC) and the *decision module* (DM) are part of the trusted computing base. The DM monitors the state of the system and switches control from the *advanced controller* (AC) to the BC if using the former could result in a safety violation in the near future. The original Simplex Architecture requires creating a provably safe BC, which can be difficult. In this work, we eliminate this requirement through a greater reliance on runtime verification.

In the proposed *Black-Box Simplex Architecture* (BSA), shown in Fig. 1(b), the BC (now referred to as the *Lookahead Baseline Controller* (LBC)), no longer needs to be statically verified, and can even be incorrect. The tradeoff is that the DM performs more extensive runtime checking and stores backup command sequences from previous computation steps. The DM performs simulation or reachability analysis based on a known system model. If the DM's computation time is too large, BSA keeps the system safe by switching control to a stored command sequence generated at an earlier step by the LBC and checked for safety by the DM. The specifics of the approach will be discussed in Sect. 2.

We prove two theorems about this architecture: (i) safety is always guaranteed, and (ii) when the baseline and advanced controllers perform well (to be formally defined in Sect. 2), the architecture is transparent: the advanced controller appears to have full control of the system. The practicality of these assumptions and the utility of the BSA architecture itself is demonstrated through two significant case studies. In the first, a multi-robot coordination system uses a BC based on a model-predicative control algorithm with a potential-field approach for collision avoidance. Such a setup is difficult to statically verify as it depends on the online solution of a nonlinear optimization problem. In the second, a mid-air collision avoidance system for groups of F-16 aircraft is created from imperfect logic encoded in neural networks. A preview of the second case study is shown in Fig. 2, where directly using the neural networks causes a collision (left), but the Black-Box Simplex approach safely navigates the scenario, resulting in an emergent maneuver similar to a roundabout (right).

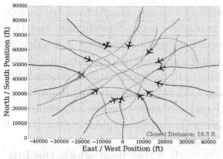
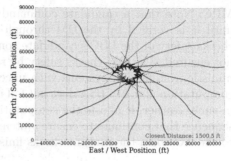

(a) Original System (unsafe, the two red aircraft collide)

(b) Black-Box Simplex (safe, snapshot shown at closest distance)

Fig. 2. Black-Box Simplex safely navigates complex scenarios. In the 15-aircraft case, all aircraft cross the circle while maintaining a 1500 ft separation distance.

The rest of the paper is organized as follows. Section 2 presents a formal definition of the Black-Box Simplex Architecture, including proofs of safety and transparency. Section 3 features two case studies implementing the architecture. Section 4 discusses related work and Sect. 5 offers our concluding remarks.

2   Black-Box Simplex

The traditional Simplex Architecture, shown in Fig. 1(a), preserves the safety of the system while permitting the use of an unverified AC. It does this by using the AC in conjunction with a verified BC and a verified DM. The DM cannot simply check if the next state is safe, as cyber-physical systems have inertia and it may be too late to take corrective action. Rather, the verified design of a Simplex system usually requires offline reasoning with respect to a trusted BC and the system dynamics.

If the system dynamics are linear and the admissible states are defined with linear constraints, a state-feedback BC and a DM can be synthesized by solving a linear matrix inequality [36]. If the system dynamics or constraints are nonlinear, however, there is no direct approach to create a trusted BC and DM. This prevents more widespread use of the traditional Simplex Architecture.

The proposed Black-Box Simplex Architecture removes the requirement that the BC is statically verified, allowing provable safety with both an unverified AC and an unverified BC. Its architecture is shown in Fig. 1(b). Apart from eliminating the need to establish safety of the BC, BSA differs from the traditional Simplex Architecture in other important ways. First, the AC shares its command with the LBC instead of passing it directly to the DM. Second, the LBC uses this command as the starting point of a *candidate safe command sequence*. (Sanaz: inconsistant with Sect. 3.2).

Candidate command sequences may be generated using state-of-the-art controller designs, including neural networks trained with reinforcement learning or

MPC. Note that a candidate command sequence is not guaranteed to be safe until it is verified by the DM through a runtime check. Specifically, the DM checks safety of the LBC's candidate command sequence, rejecting it if safety is not ensured. The DM checks safety by running simulations (rollouts) for deterministic systems; for systems with uncertainty, it performs online reachability computation [2,4,21]. BSA does not fail if the DM cannot finish the computation in time. Rather, it aborts the computation and switches to a backup command sequence that continues to ensure system safety. It can subsequently switch back to the AC when the runtime checks finish in time.

As long as the AC drives the system through states from which the LBC can recover, it continues to actuate the system. However, if the LBC fails to compute a candidate command sequence that maintains safety—due to a fault of the unverified AC or the unverified BC, or due to excessive computation time for any of the components—the DM can still recover the system using the safe command sequence from the previous step. Note that the DM does not generate any command sequences. It only performs runtime checks and stores command sequences to maintain a safe backup plan at all times.

The applicability of BSA depends on the feasibility of two system-specific steps: (i) constructing candidate command sequences and (ii) proving their safety at runtime. For some systems, a safe command sequence can simply bring the system to a stop. An autonomous car, for example, could have a safe command sequence that steers the car to the side of the road and then stops. A safe sequence for a drone might direct it to the closest emergency landing location. For an rapidly-moving autonomous fixed-wing aircraft swarm, a safe sequence could fly all aircraft in non-intersecting circles to allow time for human intervention. Proving safety of a given command sequence can also be challenging and depends on the system dynamics. For nondeterministic systems, this could involve performing reachability computations at runtime [2,4,21]. Such techniques assume an accurate system model is available in order to compute reachable sets. Notice that traditional offline control theory also requires this assumption, so we do not view it as overly burdensome.

In BSA, although both controllers are unverified, we do not combine them into a single unverified controller. This allows for a logical separation of concerns, where the AC focuses on making progress on the mission, and the BC focuses on generating safe backup plans.

2.1 Formal Definition of Black-Box Simplex

We formalize the behavior and requirements for the components of the Black-Box Simplex Architecture in order to prove properties about the system's behavior.

Plant Model. We consider discrete-time plant dynamics, modeled as a function

$$f(\underbrace{x_i}_{\text{state}}, \underbrace{u_i}_{\text{input}}, \underbrace{w_i}_{\text{disturbance}}) = \underbrace{x_{i+1}}_{\text{next state}} \tag{1}$$

where $i \in \mathbb{Z}^+$ is the time step, $x_i \in \mathcal{X}$ is the system state, $u_i \in \mathcal{U}$ is a control input command, and $w_i \in \mathcal{W}$ is an environmental disturbance. We sometimes also consider a *deterministic* version of the system, where the disturbance w_i can be taken to be zero at every step.

Admissible States. The system is characterized by a set of operational constraints which include physical limits and safety properties. States that satisfy all the operational constraints are called *admissible states*.

Candidate Command Sequences. A single-input command is some $u \in \mathcal{U}$, and a k-length sequence of commands is written as $\overline{u} \in \mathcal{U}^k$. The length of a sequence can be written as $\overline{u}_{\text{len}} = k$, where we also can take the length of a single command, $u_{\text{len}} = 1$. We use Python-like notation for subsequences, where the first element in a sequence is $\overline{u}[0]$, and the rest of the sequence is $\overline{u}[1:]$.

Decision Module. The decision module in Black-Box Simplex stores a command sequence $\overline{s}$, which we sometimes call the decision module's state. The behavior of the DM is defined through two functions, dm_{update} and dm_{step}. The dm_{update} function attempts to modify the DM's stored command sequence:

$$dm_{\text{update}}(\underbrace{x}_{\text{state}}, \underbrace{\overline{s}}_{\text{cur seq}}, \underbrace{\overline{t}}_{\text{proposed seq}}) = \underbrace{\overline{s'}}_{\text{new seq}} \tag{2}$$

where if $\overline{s'} = \overline{t}$ then we say that the proposed command sequence is *accepted*; otherwise $\overline{s'} = \overline{s}$ and we say that it is *rejected*. Correctness conditions on dm_{update} are given in Sect. 2.2. Note that the DM will accept a safe command sequence from the AC even if the previous command sequence from the AC was rejected because it was unsafe. As in [28], we refer to this as *reverse switching*, since it switches control back to the AC.

The dm_{step} function produces the next command u to apply to the plant, as well as the next step's command sequence $\overline{s'}$ for the DM:

$$dm_{\text{step}}(\underbrace{\overline{s}}_{\text{cur seq}}) = (\underbrace{u}_{\text{next input}}, \underbrace{\overline{s'}}_{\text{next seq}}) \tag{3}$$

where $u = \overline{s}[0]$ and $\overline{s'}$ is constructed from $\overline{s}$ by removing the first command (if the current sequence $\overline{s}$ has only one command then it is repeated):

$$\overline{s'} = \begin{cases} \overline{s} & \text{if } \overline{s}_{\text{len}} = 1 \\ \overline{s}[1:] & \text{otherwise} \end{cases}$$

Controllers. The AC and LBC are defined using functions of the system state. In particular, the AC is defined by a function $ac(x) = u$, where $u \in \mathcal{U}$ is a single command. BSA's *look-ahead baseline controller* is defined by $lbc(x) = \overline{u}$, where

$\overline{u} \in \mathcal{U}^k$ is a k-length command sequence. The LBC outputs candidate command sequences that start with a given command, specifically, the command proposed by the AC. These can be defined with a function $lbc_{ac}(x) = \overline{u}$, with $\overline{u}[0] = ac(x)$. We generally drop the subscript on lbc, as it is clear from context.

Execution Semantics. At step i, given system state x_i and DM state $\overline{s_i}$, the next system state x_{i+1} and next DM state $\overline{s_{i+1}}$ are computed with the following sequence of steps: (1) $z_i = ac(x_i)$; (2) $\overline{t_i} = lbc(x_i)$, with $\overline{t_i}[0] = z_i$; (3) $\overline{s_i'} = dm_{\mathsf{update}}(x_i, \overline{s_i}, \overline{t_i})$; (4) $(u_i, \overline{s_{i+1}}) = dm_{\mathsf{step}}(\overline{s_i'})$; (5) $x_{i+1} = f(x_i, u_i, w_i)$, for some disturbance $w_i \in \mathcal{W}$.

2.2   Safety and Transparency Theorems

We define several relevant concepts and then state and prove safety and transparency theorems for Black-Box Simplex.

Definition 1 (Safe System Execution). *A system execution is called* safe *if and only if the system state is admissible at every step.*

Safety can be ensured by following a permanently safe command sequence from a given system state.

Definition 2 (Permanently Safe Command Sequence). *Given state x_i, a k-length* permanently safe command sequence *$\overline{s_i} \in \mathcal{U}^k$ is one where the state x_j is admissible at every step $j \geq i$, where $(u_i, \overline{s_{i+1}}) = dm_{\mathsf{step}}(\overline{s_i})$, and $x_{i+1} = f(x_i, u_i, w_i)$, for every choice of disturbance $w_i \in \mathcal{W}$.*

That is, the system state will remain admissible when applying each command in the sequence $\overline{s_i}$, and then repeatedly using the last command forever, according to the semantics of dm_{step}. More general definitions of permanently safe command sequences could be considered, such as repeating a suffix rather than just the last command. For simplicity we do not explore this here.

We define recoverable commands to be commands that result in states that have permanently safe command sequences.

Definition 3 (Recoverable Command). *Given state x_i, a* recoverable command *u is one where there exists a permanently safe command sequence from x_{i+1}, where $x_{i+1} = f(x_i, u, w_i)$, for every choice of disturbance $w_i \in \mathcal{W}$.*

Optimal decision modules are defined by requiring the dm_{update} function accept all sequences that can guarantee future safety.

Definition 4 (Optimal Decision Module). *An* optimal decision module *has a dm_{update} function that accepts $\overline{t}$ at state x if and only if $\overline{t}$ is a permanently safe command sequence starting from x.*

A correct DM is one which only accepts sequences that can guarantee future safety. A correct DM, by this definition, could reject every command sequence.

Definition 5 (Correct Decision Module). *A correct decision module has a dm_{update} function that accepts $\bar{t}$ at state x only if $\bar{t}$ is a permanently safe command sequence starting from x.*

The role of the BC is to try to keep the system safe. An optimal look-ahead BC can be defined as one that always produces a permanently safe command sequence when it exists. This is optimal in the sense that during system execution, it allows the DM to override the AC as infrequently as possible while still guaranteeing safety. This notion of optimality can be defined with respect to a specific advanced controller ac.

Definition 6 (Optimal Look-Ahead Baseline Controller). *Given state x with $u = ac(x)$, if there exists a permanently safe command sequence $\bar{s}$ from x with $\bar{s}[0] = u$, then an* optimal look-ahead baseline controller *will always produce a permanently safe command sequence $\bar{t}$, with $\bar{t}[0] = u$.*

Note that $\bar{t}$ may differ from $\bar{s}$, as there can be multiple permanently safe command sequences from the same state.

Theorem 1 (Safety). *Given initial state x_0 along with an initial permanently safe command sequence $\bar{s_0}$, if the decision module is correct, then the system's execution is safe regardless of the outputs of the advanced controller ac and look-ahead baseline controller lbc.*

Proof. The command executed at each step comes from the state of the decision module $\bar{s_i}$, which maintains the invariant that $\bar{s_i}$ is always a permanently safe command sequence from the current system state $\bar{x_i}$. The dm_{update} function can only replace a permanently safe command sequence with another permanently safe command sequence. Since initially, $\bar{s_0}$ is permanently safe, then by induction on the step number, the decision module's command sequence at every step is permanently safe, and so the system's execution is safe.

Although safety is important, achieving only safety is trivial, as a decision module can simply reject all new command sequences. A runtime assurance system must also have a transparency property, where the advanced controller retains control in sufficiently well-designed systems.

Theorem 2 (Transparency). *If (i) from every state x_i encountered, the output of the advanced controller $ac(x_i) = z_i$ is a recoverable command, (ii) the look-ahead baseline controller is optimal, and (iii) the decision module is optimal, then the input command used to actuate the system at every step is the advanced controller's command, z_i.*

Proof. The proof proceeds by stepping through an arbitrary step i of the execution semantics defined in Sect. 2.1. Since the output of the advanced controller $ac(x_i) = z_i$ is assumed to be recoverable, there exists a permanently safe command sequence from x_i that starts with z_i. By the definition of an optimal look-ahead baseline controller, since there exists a permanently safe command sequence, the output $lbc(x_i) = \bar{t}$ must also be a permanently safe command sequence, with $\bar{t}[0] = z_i$ as required by the definition of a look-ahead baseline controller. In step (3) of the execution semantics, $dm_{\mathsf{update}}(x_i, \overline{s_i}, \overline{t_i}) = \overline{s_i'}$. Since $\bar{t}$ is a permanently safe command sequence and the decision module is optimal, the command sequence will be accepted by the decision module, and so $\overline{s_i'} = \bar{t}$. Step (4) of the execution semantics produces u_i, which is the first command in the sequence $\bar{t}$. As shown before, this command is equal to z_i, which is used in step (5) of the execution semantics to actuate the system. This reasoning applies at every step, and so the advanced controller's command is always used.

Discussion. There are several practical considerations with the described approach. For example, the black-box controllers may not only generate unsafe commands, but a controller implementation may fail to generate a command at all, for example, entering an infinite loop. To account for such behaviors, a runtime cap can be used with a default command sequence assumed if the DM receives no input. For increased protection, the black-box controllers can be isolated on dedicated hardware [3] so that they do not, for example, crash a shared operating system. Also, the DM's analysis of the command sequence is nontrivial and could involve a runtime reachability computation. If this may take too long, we again could use a runtime cap. This means that the practicality of the architecture depends on the efficiency of runtime reachability methods, an active area of research orthogonal to this work.

Another consideration is the feasibility of coming up with permanently safe command sequences. For systems where landing or coming to a stop is considered safe, remaining there forever will be permanently safe. Other approaches, which we use the case studies in the next section, rely on geometric arguments to show permanent safety. Methods from control theory could also be used for this, such as computing forward invariant sets [16] or using a locally stable controller. For example, using the indirect method of Lyapnuov, a closed-loop system's equilibrium point x^* can be proven to be stable using linearization, along with conservative bounds on its basin of attraction [27]. The BC would then strive to get the system into the basin of attraction of x^*, and then use the locally stable controller to ensure indefinite future safety. Directly using the locally stable controller as the BC, however, would be overly conservative, as it would not allow the system to leave the (potentially small) basin of attraction.

3   Case Studies

In this section, we apply the approach to two case studies: a multi-robot coordination system, and a mid-air collision avoidance system for groups of F-16 aircraft.

3.1   Multi-robot Coordination

We consider a multi-agent system (MAS), indexed by $\mathcal{M} = \{1, ..., n\}$, of planar robots modeled with discrete-time dynamics of the form:

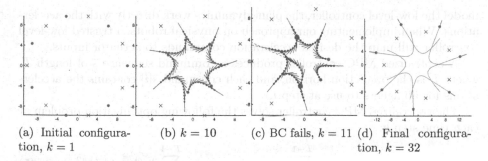

(a) Initial configuration, $k = 1$ (b) $k = 10$ (c) BC fails, $k = 11$ (d) Final configuration, $k = 32$

Fig. 3. Simulation of the MAS with 7 robots. The DM performs system recovery after the BC produces an unsafe command sequence. The BC's proposed path is shown in part (c) at $k = 11$, where the two dotted red lines intersect, indicating the future paths of the agents cross. We represent current positions as red dots, future positions corresponding to the safe/unsafe command sequences as green/blue dots, velocities as blue lines, and agent trajectories as grey curves. (Color figure online)

$$p_i(k + 1) = p_i(k) + dt \cdot v_i(k), \quad |v_i(k)| < v_{max}$$
$$v_i(k + 1) = v_i(k) + dt \cdot a_i(k), \quad |a_i(k)| < a_{max} \qquad (4)$$

where p_i, v_i, $a_i \in \mathbb{R}^2$ are the position, velocity and acceleration of agent i, respectively, at time step k, and $dt \in \mathbb{R}^+$ is the time step. The magnitudes of velocities and accelerations are bounded by v_{max} and a_{max}, respectively. The acceleration a_i is the control input for agent i. The combined state of all agents is denoted as $x = [p_1^T, v_1^T, ..., p_n^T, v_n^T]^T$, and their accelerations are $a = [a_1^T, ..., a_n^T]^T$.

In the initial configuration, the agents are equally spaced on the boundary of a circle and are at rest. Agent i's goal is to reach a target location r_i, located on the opposite side of the circle. The initial configuration of the MAS is shown in Fig. 3(a), where the agents and their target locations are represented as red dots and blue crosses, respectively. The safety property is absence of inter-agent collisions. A pair of agents is considered to collide if the Euclidean distance between them is less than a non-negative threshold d_{min}. Thus, the safety property is that $\|p_i - p_j\| > d_{min}$ for all pairs of agents $i, j \in \mathcal{M}$ with $i \neq j$.

Both the AC and the BC are designed using centralized Model Predictive Control (MPC), which produces command sequences as part of the solution of a nonlinear optimization problem. For collision avoidance, we use a potential field formulation [19] in both the AC and BC. While the AC tries to reach the target positions on the opposite side of the circle, the BC has a simpler goal of having each agent leave the circle. Note that numerical methods for global nonlinear optimization, such as MATLAB's `fmincon` used in our implementation, do not provide a guaranteed optimal solution. To create unsafe variants of the controllers, we simply limit the number of iterations used for optimization.

The AC only outputs the first command of the command sequence, whereas the BC produces the full command sequence. Both the AC and the BC are high-level controllers that produce accelerations. In our simulations, we do not

model the low-level controller; the plant dynamics work directly with the accelerations. When implementing our approach on physical robots, a trusted low-level
controller will map the desired acceleration commands to actuator inputs.

A centralized MPC controller produces a command sequence $\bar{s}$ of length T,
where T is the prediction horizon, and each command $\bar{s}[i]$ contains the accelerations for all agents to use at step i.

The centralized MPC controller solves the following optimization problem at
each time step k:

$$\underset{a(k|k),\dots,a(k+T-1|k)}{\arg\min} \sum_{t=0}^{T-1} J(k+t \mid k) + \lambda \cdot \sum_{t=0}^{T-1} \|a(k+t \mid k)\|^2 \tag{5}$$

where $a(k + t \mid k)$ and $J(k + t \mid k)$ are the predictions made at time step k for
the values at time step $k + t$ of the accelerations and the centralized (global)
cost function J, respectively. The first term is the sum of the centralized cost
function, evaluated for T time steps, starting at time step k. It encodes the
control objective. The second term, scaled by a weight $\lambda > 0$, penalizes large
control inputs.

Advanced Controller. The centralized cost function J_{ac} for the AC contains
two terms: (1) a *separation* term based on the inverse of the squared distance
between each pair of agents (potential field term for collision avoidance); and
(2) a *target seeking* term based on the distance between the agent and its target
location.

$$J_{ac} = \omega_s \sum_{i>j} \frac{1}{\|p_i - p_j\|^2} + \omega_t \sum_i \|p_i - r_i\|^2 \tag{6}$$

where $\omega_s, \omega_t \in \mathbb{R}$ are the weights of the separation term and target seeking
terms. The separation term promotes inter-agent spacing but does not guaran-
tee collision avoidance. The AC generates a command sequence by solving the
optimization problem in Eq. 5, with J replaced by J_{ac}. The first command in
that sequence is the AC's command; it is passed to the LBC.

Baseline Controller. The centralized cost function J_{bc} for the BC contains
two terms. As in Eq. 6, the first term is the separation term (collision avoidance
based on potential fields). The second term is a *divergence* term which forces
the agents to move out of the circle by aligning their velocities with rays radially
pointing out of the center of the circle.

$$J_{bc} = \omega_s \sum_{i>j} \frac{1}{\|p_i - p_j\|^2} + \omega_d \sum_i \left(1 - \frac{(p_i - c) \cdot v_i}{|p_i - c||v_i|}\right) \tag{7}$$

where $\omega_s, \omega_d \in \mathbb{R}$ are the weights of the separation term and the divergence
term, and c is the center of the circle containing the initial configuration of the
robots and their target locations. The control law for the BC is Eq. 5, with J
replaced by J_{bc}. A zero acceleration is appended to the end of the BC's command
sequence to help establish collision freedom for all future time steps.

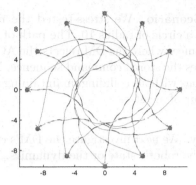

Fig. 4. Stress test of robotic MAS with 12 robots reaching their targets. Trajectory segments where stored command sequences are used are shown in blue. (Color figure online)

Decision Module. The LBC combines accelerations from the AC and the BC, producing the command sequence $\bar{t} = [ac(x), bc(x'), \mathbf{0}]$, where x' is the next state after executing $ac(x)$ in state x. The function $dm_{\mathsf{update}}(x, \bar{s}, \bar{t})$ accepts the proposed command sequence $\bar{t}$ if and only if $\bar{t}$ is a permanently safe command sequence. For this system, a command sequence $\bar{t}$ is considered permanently safe in a state x if it satisfies the following two conditions. First, for all states in the state trajectory obtained by executing $\bar{t}$ from x, the Euclidean distance between every pair of distinct agents is at least d_{min}. Second, in the final state, for all pairs of distinct agents, the rays extending from their positions and in the directions of their velocities do not intersect. Any pair of agents that satisfies the second condition will not collide in the future, since the last command in the sequence $\bar{t}$ has zero acceleration. The initial permanently safe command sequence is a zero acceleration for all agents, as the agents start at rest.

MPC Parameters. In our case study, we use the following MPC parameters: $dt = 0.3 \ sec$, $d_{min} = 1.7$, $a_{max} = 1.5$, and $v_{max} = 2$. The length of the prediction horizon for MPC is $T_{ac} = T_{bc} = 10$.

Successful Recovery After Failure. We first consider seven robotic agents initialized on a circle centered at the origin, with a radius of 10. The initial state of the system is shown in Fig. 3(a). At $k = 11$, the BC produces an unsafe command sequence. The state trajectory corresponding to the unsafe sequence is shown in blue. As shown in Fig. 3(c), the final paths of the two agents corresponding to the larger red dots cross after simulating the current state forward with the unsafe sequence. Hence, at $k = 11$, the DM rejects the proposed command sequence and shifts control to the previous safe command sequence, which safely recovers the system. Here, we purposefully did not return control to the AC to demonstrate how the stored command sequence keeps the agents safe[1].

---

[1] A video of the simulation is available at https://youtu.be/bcVJBkGgnxA.

Reverse Switching Scenario. We stress-tested the multi-robot system by initializing 12 agents on a circle of radius 10. The path of the agents is shown in Fig. 4. There are 10 instances where the DM rejects the AC's proposed command sequence and instead uses the stored command sequence. Nonetheless, all agents reach their target locations without colliding, maintaining a minimum separation of 1.724 between any pair of agents[2].

Handling Uncertainty. We next investigate the DM's runtime overhead when there is uncertainty in the robot's state or the dynamics. The former case arises when the sensors used to determine the positions and velocities are subject to sensor noise. The latter case could be used to account for modeling errors, through disturbances on the positions and velocities at each step.

We continue to use the same MPC strategy as before; thus, the controllers ignore the uncertainty when generating proposed command sequences. Only the logic used by the DM to accept or reject command sequences is modified to account for uncertainty. We examine the scenario shown before in Fig. 3(b). To account for the uncertainty, we perform an online reachability computation. To do this, we use efficient methods for reachability for linear systems based on zonotopes [11], which we implement in Python. Briefly, a zonotope is a set of states represented as an affine transformation of a unit box. The unit box is associated with a number of *generator vectors*, where each generator vector corresponds to one dimension of the box. The computational efficiency of propagating sets over time using zonotopes relates to the number of generators. Each agent has four state variables, two for position and two for velocity. The composed system with seven agents has 28 state variables.

In the situation shown in Fig. 5(a), the current state is assumed to have uncertainty independently in both position and velocity with an L^2 norm of 0.1. We use a 16-sided polygon to bound this uncertainty. In the plot, the deterministic simulation is given, along with black polygons for each agent that show the states that might be reachable at each step due to the sensor uncertainty. The uncertainty in the velocity causes the set to expand over time, since the open-loop command sequence does not attempt to compensate for the uncertainty. The zonotope representation of the composed system needs 112 generator vectors to represent the initial states, which remains constant at every time step.

In the situation shown in Fig. 5(b), the initial state has very little error, but the dynamics is modified to have disturbances at each step. For each component of each agent's position and velocity, we allow an external disturbance value to be added in the range $[-0.02, 0.02]$. Since each agent has four independent disturbances, the zonotope representation of the composition will have 28 new generators added at each step. After 12 steps, the final zonotope will have a total of 364 generators.

---

[2] A video of the simulation is available at https://youtu.be/qmk31jS6B2Y.

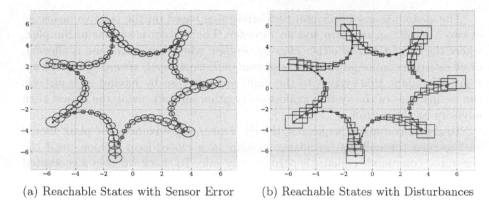

(a) Reachable States with Sensor Error   (b) Reachable States with Disturbances

Fig. 5. Zonotope reachability computes future states with uncertainty.

Runtime. To measure runtime, we used a standard laptop with a 2.70 GHz Intel Xeon E-2176M CPU and 32 GB RAM. The method is fast. For the case of sensor uncertainty, computing the box bounds of the reachable set at all the steps takes about 1.5 ms. With uncertainty, even though the number of generators grows over time, it is not large enough to significantly affect the runtime. The computation with disturbances requires about 2 ms to complete. We believe such execution times are sufficiently fast for use in the decision module.

3.2 Multi-aircraft Collision Avoidance

Our second evaluation system guarantees collision avoidance for groups of aircraft. We use a full six-degrees-of-freedom F-16 simulation model [14], based on dynamics taken from an Aerospace Engineering textbook [38]. Each aircraft is modeled with 16 state variables, including positional states, positional velocities, rotational states, rotational velocities, an engine thrust lag term, and integrator states for the low-level controllers. These controllers actuate the system using the typical aircraft control surfaces—the ailerons, elevators, and rudder—as well as by setting the engine thrust. The system evolves continuously with piece-wise nonlinear differential equations, where the function that computes the derivative given the state is provided as Python code. In order to match the discrete-time plant model in Definition 1, we periodically select a control strategy with a frequency of once every two seconds. The model further includes high-level autopilot logic for waypoint following, which we reuse in the advanced controller.

For the collision-avoidance baseline controller, our controller is based on the ACAS Xu system designed for collision avoidance in unmanned aircraft [20]. While the original system was designed using a partially observable Markov decision process (POMDP), the resultant controller was encoded in a large look-up table that used hundreds of gigabytes of storage [15]. To make the system more practical, one early approach considered a downsampling process followed by a lossy compression using neural networks [15,17]. We use these downsampled neural networks as the BC and refer to this as the original system.

The system issues horizontal turn advisories based on the relative positions of two aircraft, an *ownship* and an *intruder*. The system is similar to Simplex, where the output can be either *clear-of-conflict*, where any command is allowed, or an override command that is one of *weak-left, weak-right, strong-left* or *strong-right*. We adapt this system to the multi-aircraft case by having each aircraft run an instance of the system against every other aircraft, using the closest turn advisory as the output.

To create command sequences, the BC repeatedly advances the plant model and re-runs the collision avoidance system in a closed-loop fashion until the generated command sequence is permanently safe. To check whether a generated command sequence is permanently safe, the DM checks that (i) each aircraft's state stays within the model limits (e.g., no aircraft enters a stall), (ii) all aircraft obey the safety distance constraint at all times, and (iii) the execution ends in a state where the roll angle of each aircraft has been small (less than $15°$) and the distances between all pairs of aircraft has been increasing consecutively for several seconds. If all aircraft continue to fly straight and level from such a configuration, their distance would increase and no collisions would occur in the future.

As with the multi-robot scenario, we examine cases where the initial aircraft state x_0 has all aircraft starting evenly-spaced, facing towards the center of a circle with a given initial diameter. Each aircraft has an initial velocity of 807 ft/s and an initial altitude of 1000 ft, both of which are maintained throughout the maneuver by the lower-level controllers. The AC commands each aircraft to fly towards a waypoint past the opposite side of the circle, which would cause a collision at the center. The safety property requires maintaining horizontal separation. The *near mid-air collision cylinder* (NMAC) uses a safe horizontal separation of 500 ft [24], although we will vary this in our evaluation. For the initial permanently safe command sequence s_0, we have each aircraft fly in clockwise circles forever, which avoids collisions.

In addition to the AC being unsafe, the baseline controller should not be fully trusted for many reasons. The original POMDP formulation was not proven formally correct, not to mention the downsampling and lossy neural network compression. While some research has examined proving open-loop properties for the neural network compression [5,6,17], these do not imply *closed-loop* collision avoidance. Further, we use a multi-aircraft adaptation of the system, which could also lead to problems. Although aspirationally, the system should handle up to 30 intruders [15], in practice most analysis has been performed on two aircraft scenarios. Finally, the intended physical system response to the collision-avoidance commands is that *weak-left* and *weak-right* should cause turning at $1.5°$ per second, whereas *strong-left* and *strong-right* turn at $3.0°$ per second [15]. However, turning an aircraft in the F-16 model (as well as in the real world) is not an instantaneous process, and requires first performing a roll maneuver before the heading angle begins to change. For these reasons, the BC in this scenario is also an unverified component, and we will show scenarios where it misbehaves. Nonetheless, we will compose the incorrect AC with the incorrect BC to create a safe collision-avoidance system by using BSA.

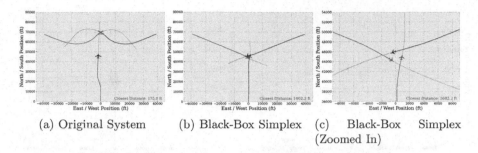

(a) Original System   (b) Black-Box Simplex   (c) Black-Box Simplex (Zoomed In)

Fig. 6. Black-Box Simplex is safe. In the three-aircraft case, the original system fails, whereas BSA maintains the 1500 ft separation.

We now elaborate on three scenarios: (i) a three aircraft case, which shows the safety of the system despite unsafe outputs, (ii) a four aircraft case, which shows the increased transparency of BSA, and (iii) a 15 aircraft case, which shows safe navigation of a complex scenario. Also, a seven aircraft case is presented in the appendix of extended report[3], which shows the safety condition can be easily customized.

In all the plots in this section, we show snapshots at the time when the distance between the two closest aircraft is smallest. The two red aircraft are the closest pair, and their distance is printed in the bottom right of each figure. The solid line shows the historic path of each aircraft, and the dotted line is the future trajectory.

Three Aircraft Scenario. The original collision avoidance system was designed with two aircraft in mind, an ownship and an intruder. We adapted it to the multi-aircraft case, but this mismatch between the system design assumptions and usage scenario can lead to problems. In Fig. 6, we show such a scenario, where the initial circle diameter is 90,000 ft. In Fig. 6(a), the minimum distance between the top two aircraft is 175 ft, violating the near mid-air collision safety distance. The other two subplots show the system using BSA with a safety distance of 1500 ft; the minimum separation is 1602 ft, which satisfies the constraint.

Four Aircraft Scenario. Figure 7 shows a four-aircraft scenario using an initial circle diameter of 70,000 ft. In this case, both designs have safe executions. Using the original system leads to a minimum separation of 5342 ft, whereas the minimum separation with Black-Box Simplex is 1600 ft, much closer to the 1500 ft safety-distance constraint used in the DM. Although both systems are safe, from the plots it is clear that the Black-Box Simplex version is more transparent, in the sense that it produces smaller modifications to the direct-line trajectories commanded by the AC.

---

[3] https://arxiv.org/abs/2102.12981.

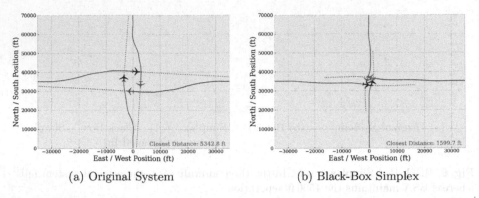

(a) Original System   (b) Black-Box Simplex

Fig. 7. Black-Box Simplex is more transparent. For the four aircraft case, the original system is significantly more intrusive than Black-Box Simplex, which overrides commands just enough to guarantee the 1500 ft separation requirement.

Fifteen Aircraft Scenario. Finally, we demonstrate the system's ability to safely navigate complex scenarios. For this, we use a 15 aircraft scenario, with an initial circle diameter of 90,000 ft. With 15 aircraft, the composed system has 240 real-valued state variables, each of which evolves according to piecewise nonlinear differential equations. The plot for this system was shown in the introduction in Fig. 2. While the original system is unsafe, Black-Box Simplex has a minimum separation of 1500.5 ft, just above the 1500 ft safety constraint used in the DM. Another surprising observation is that in some of the cases, such as this 15-aircraft case and the seven-aircraft case shown in the appendix of the extended report(see Footnote 3), the aircraft perform something similar to a roundabout maneuver. This is an emergent behavior, not something explicitly hardcoded or anticipated. A video of this case is also available online[4].

Runtime. The existing implementation uses numerical integration for the dynamics with an adaptive-step explicit Runge-Kutta scheme of order 5(4) from Python's `scipy` package. On our laptop platform with default accuracy parameters, this runs at about 55 times faster than real-time per aircraft.

4   Related Work

Reachability-based verification methods for black-box systems for waypoint following with uncertainty have been recently investigated in the ReachFlow framework [21]. ReachFlow builds upon the Flow* reachability tool [8], which is unlikely to scale to systems like the 240-variable 15-aircraft scenario.

A framework for safe trajectory planning using MILP for piecewise-linear vehicle models is presented in [33,34]. The method relies on the ability of an MPC controller to produce command sequences where the terminal state in the

---

[4] https://youtu.be/Bhn0uqKCj7Q.

prediction horizon is constrained to lie within a safe invariant set. This provides a safe back-up command sequence for the next step in case the system fails to find a safe sequence. The scope of this work is limited to MPC, and it is not clear how to extend it to other types of controllers. Moreover, the conditions for switching back from the stored return trajectory are not formalized.

In the Contingency Model Predictive Control framework [1], an MPC controller maintains a contingency plan in addition to the nominal or desired plan to ensure safety during an identified potential emergency. Like BSA, the initial command is common to both plans. In this framework, both plans must be generated using their custom version of MPC, whereas Black-Box Simplex works with independent baseline and advanced controllers of any design.

Similar frameworks have been considered for autonomous vehicles, using failsafe backup plans and reachability analysis [22]. In this case, the target was planning for autonomous vehicles where most likely trajectories are used for other vehicles but safety can still be provided if emergency maneuvers are performed instead. Other ideas such as Safety Net Control [35] extend the approach to use backreachability and underapproximations of nonlinear reachable sets while taking computation time into account.

Designing safe switching logic for a given baseline controller is related to the concept of computing viability kernels [31] (closed controlled-invariant subsets) in control theory. This often requires set operations which can be inefficient in high-dimensional spaces with nonlinear dynamics, although there has been some progress on this [18,23].

Simplex designs have also been considered that use a combination of offline analysis with online reachability [4]. Again, though, reachability computation is currently intractable for large nonlinear systems, and requires symbolic differential equations. Other work has used Simplex to provide safety guarantees for neural network controllers with online retraining [29]. In these approaches, the baseline controller must be verified ahead of time.

Online simulation-based methods have also been investigated to secure power grids from insider attacks [25]. As with this work, fast online simulation is critical, although the goal there is system security not safe high-level control design.

The design of the MPC controllers for our multi-robot case study is similar to Control Barrier Function methods [7,12] and Implicit Active Set Invariance Filtering [13]. There, a runtime assurance system was used to provide minimally perturbed advanced controller commands, computed using a constrained-optimization problem. However, the optimization problem might become infeasible or global nonlinear optimization could perform poorly at one of the steps at runtime, causing this method to be unsafe. With Black-Box Simplex, failure of the baseline controller does not compromise safety.

5   Conclusions

We have presented the Black-Box Simplex Architecture, a methodology for constructing safe CPS from unverified black-box high-level controllers. Unlike the classical Simplex design, the baseline controller does not need to be statically verified and can even be incorrect. The tradeoff is that the decision module performs more extensive runtime checking and stores backup command sequences produced by the black-box baseline controller at previous time steps. The complexity of runtime checking depends on the nature of the system model. For deterministic models, simulation suffices. However, if the model has uncertainty then we need to perform online reachability analysis.

BSA reduces the difficult problem of proving high-level safety to a simpler problem of *performance optimization*: ensuring that the runtime checking completes before a decision is needed. The practicality of the approach was demonstrated through two significant case studies, including a mid-air collision avoidance system for groups of F-16 aircraft created from imperfect logic encoded in neural networks. This case study involves a highly complex nonlinear system with over a hundred dimensional variables and a neural-network-based controller. Black-Box Simplex provides a feasible path for runtime verification of systems that are otherwise unverifiable in practice.

Acknowledgement. This material is based upon work supported by National Science Foundation (NSF) under grant numbers OIA-2134840, OIA-2040599, CCF-1918225, CCF-1954837 and CPS-1446832, the Office of Naval Research (ONR) under grants N000142112719 and N000142212156, and the Air Force Office of Scientific Research (AFOSR) under award numbers FA9550-19-1-0288, FA9550-21-1-0121, FA9550-22-1-0450. Any opinions, findings, and conclusions or recommendations expressed in this material are those of the author(s) and do not necessarily reflect the views of the NSF, United States Air Force or the United States Navy. An early version of this work was presented in the CAADCPS 2021 workshop under the title "Safe CPS from Unsafe Controllers" [26].

References

1. Alsterda, J.P., Brown, M., Gerdes, J.C.: Contingency model predictive control for automated vehicles. In: 2019 American Control Conference (ACC), pp. 717–722 (2019). https://doi.org/10.23919/ACC.2019.8815260
2. Althoff, M., Dolan, J.M.: Online verification of automated road vehicles using reachability analysis. IEEE Trans. Robot. **30**(4) (2014)
3. Bak, S., Chivukula, D.K., Adekunle, O., Sun, M., Caccamo, M., Sha, L.: The system-level simplex architecture for improved real-time embedded system safety. In: 2009 15th IEEE Real-Time and Embedded Technology and Applications Symposium, pp. 99–107. IEEE (2009)
4. Bak, S., Johnson, T.T., Caccamo, M., Sha, L.: Real-time reachability for verified simplex design. In: 35th IEEE Real-Time Systems Symposium (RTSS 2014). IEEE Computer Society, Rome, December 2014
5. Bak, S., Liu, C., Johnson, T.: The second international verification of neural networks competition (VNN-COMP 2021): summary and results. arXiv preprint arXiv:2109.00498 (2021)
6. Bak, S., Tran, H.D., Hobbs, K., Johnson, T.T.: Improved geometric path enumeration for verifying Relu neural networks. In: Proceedings of the 32nd International Conference on Computer Aided Verification (2020)

7. Borrmann, U., Wang, L., Ames, A.D., Egerstedt, M.: Control barrier certificates for safe swarm behavior. In: Egerstedt, M., Wardi, Y. (eds.) ADHS. IFAC-PapersOnLine, vol. 48, pp. 68–73. Elsevier, Amsterdam (2015)
8. Chen, X., Ábrahám, E., Sankaranarayanan, S.: Flow*: an analyzer for non-linear hybrid systems. In: Sharygina, N., Veith, H. (eds.) CAV 2013. LNCS, vol. 8044, pp. 258–263. Springer, Heidelberg (2013). https://doi.org/10.1007/978-3-642-39799-8_18
9. Clark, M., et al.: A study on run time assurance for complex cyber physical systems. Technical report, Air Force Research Laboratory, Aerospace Systems Directorate (2013)
10. Desai, A., Ghosh, S., Seshia, S.A., Shankar, N., Tiwari, A.: SOTER: a runtime assurance framework for programming safe robotics systems. In: 49th Annual IEEE/IFIP International Conference on Dependable Systems and Networks, DSN 2019, Portland, OR, USA, 24–27 June 2019. IEEE (2019)
11. Girard, A.: Reachability of uncertain linear systems using zonotopes. In: Morari, M., Thiele, L. (eds.) HSCC 2005. LNCS, vol. 3414, pp. 291–305. Springer, Heidelberg (2005). https://doi.org/10.1007/978-3-540-31954-2_19
12. Gurriet, T., Mote, M., Ames, A.D., Feron, E.: An online approach to active set invariance. In: Conference on Decision and Control. IEEE (2018)
13. Gurriet, T., Mote, M., Singletary, A., Feron, E., Ames, A.D.: A scalable controlled set invariance framework with practical safety guarantees. In: 2019 IEEE 58th Conference on Decision and Control (CDC), pp. 2046–2053. IEEE (2019)
14. Heidlauf, P., Collins, A., Bolender, M., Bak, S.: Verification challenges in f-16 ground collision avoidance and other automated maneuvers. In: 5th International Workshop on Applied Verification of Continuous and Hybrid Systems. EPiC Series in Computing, EasyChair (2018)
15. Julian, K.D., Kochenderfer, M.J., Owen, M.P.: Deep neural network compression for aircraft collision avoidance systems. J. Guid. Control. Dyn. 42(3), 598–608 (2019)
16. Kapinski, J., Deshmukh, J.: Discovering forward invariant sets for nonlinear dynamical systems. In: Cojocaru, M.G., Kotsireas, I.S., Makarov, R.N., Melnik, R.V.N., Shodiev, H. (eds.) Interdisciplinary Topics in Applied Mathematics, Modeling and Computational Science. SPMS, vol. 117, pp. 259–264. Springer, Cham (2015). https://doi.org/10.1007/978-3-319-12307-3_37
17. Katz, G., Barrett, C., Dill, D.L., Julian, K., Kochenderfer, M.J.: Reluplex: an efficient SMT solver for verifying deep neural networks. In: Majumdar, R., Kunčak, V. (eds.) CAV 2017. LNCS, vol. 10426, pp. 97–117. Springer, Cham (2017). https://doi.org/10.1007/978-3-319-63387-9_5
18. Kaynama, S., Maidens, J., Oishi, M., Mitchell, I.M., Dumont, G.A.: Computing the viability kernel using maximal reachable sets. In: Proceedings of the 15th ACM International Conference on Hybrid Systems: Computation and Control, pp. 55–64 (2012)
19. Khatib, O.: Real-time obstacle avoidance for manipulators and mobile robots. In: Cox, I.J., Wilfong, G.T. (eds.) Autonomous Robot Vehicles, pp. 396–404. Springer, New York (1986). https://doi.org/10.1007/978-1-4613-8997-2_29
20. Kochenderfer, M.J., Chryssanthacopoulos, J.: Robust airborne collision avoidance through dynamic programming. Project Report ATC-371 130, Lincoln Laboratory, Massachusetts Institute of Technology (2011)
21. Lin, Q., Chen, X., Khurana, A., Dolan, J.: ReachFlow: an online safety assurance framework for waypoint-following of self-driving cars. In: 2020 IEEE/RSJ International Conference on Intelligent Robots and Systems (IROS) (2020)

22. Magdici, S., Althoff, M.: Fail-safe motion planning of autonomous vehicles. In: 2016 IEEE 19th International Conference on Intelligent Transportation Systems (ITSC), pp. 452–458. IEEE (2016)
23. Maidens, J.N., Kaynama, S., Mitchell, I.M., Oishi, M.M., Dumont, G.A.: Lagrangian methods for approximating the viability kernel in high-dimensional systems. Automatica **49**(7), 2017–2029 (2013)
24. Marston, M., Baca, G.: ACAS-Xu initial self-separation flight tests. Technical report, NASA (2015)
25. Mashima, D., Chen, B., Zhou, T., Rajendran, R., Sikdar, B.: Securing substations through command authentication using on-the-fly simulation of power system dynamics. In: IEEE International Conference on Communications, Control, and Computing Technologies for Smart Grids (2018)
26. Mehmood, U., Bak, S., Smolka, S.A., Stoller, S.D.: Safe cps from unsafe controllers. In: Proceedings of the Workshop on Computation-Aware Algorithmic Design for Cyber-Physical Systems, pp. 26–28 (2021)
27. Murray, R.M., Li, Z., Sastry, S.S., Sastry, S.S.: A Mathematical Introduction to Robotic Manipulation. CRC Press, Boca Raton (1994)
28. Lee, R., Jha, S., Mavridou, A., Giannakopoulou, D. (eds.): NFM 2020. LNCS, vol. 12229. Springer, Cham (2020). https://doi.org/10.1007/978-3-030-55754-6
29. Phan, D.T., Grosu, R., Jansen, N., Paoletti, N., Smolka, S.A., Stoller, S.D.: Neural simplex architecture. In: Lee, R., Jha, S., Mavridou, A., Giannakopoulou, D. (eds.) NFM 2020. LNCS, vol. 12229, pp. 97–114. Springer, Cham (2020). https://doi.org/10.1007/978-3-030-55754-6_6
30. Phan, D., Yang, J., Grosu, R., Smolka, S.A., Stoller, S.D.: Collision avoidance for mobile robots with limited sensing and limited information about moving obstacles. Formal Methods Syst. Des. **51**(1), 62–86 (2017). https://doi.org/10.1007/s10703-016-0265-4
31. Saint-Pierre, P.: Approximation of the viability kernel. Appl. Math. Optim. **29**(2), 187–209 (1994)
32. Schierman, J., et al.: Runtime assurance framework development for highly adaptive flight control systems. Report AD1010277, Defense Technical Information Center (2015)
33. Schouwenaars, T., Valenti, M., Feron, E., How, J.: Implementation and flight test results of MILP-based UAV guidance. In: 2005 IEEE Aerospace Conference, pp. 1–13 (2005)
34. Schouwenaars, T.: Safe trajectory planning of autonomous vehicles. Ph.D. thesis, Massachusetts Institute of Technology (2006)
35. Schurmann, B., Klischat, M., Kochdumper, N., Althoff, M.: Formal safety net control using backward reachability analysis. IEEE Trans. Autom. Control (2021)
36. Seto, D., Krogh, B., Sha, L., Chutinan, A.: The simplex architecture for safe online control system upgrades. In: Proceedings of the 1998 American Control Conference. ACC (IEEE Cat. No. 98CH36207), vol. 6. IEEE (1998)
37. Sha, L.: Using simplicity to control complexity. IEEE Softw. **18**(4), 20–28 (2001). https://doi.org/10.1109/MS.2001.936213
38. Stevens, B.L., Lewis, F.L., Johnson, E.N.: Aircraft Control and Simulation. Wiley, New York (2015)

Case Studies for Computing Density of Reachable States for Safe Autonomous Motion Planning

Yue Meng[1](✉), Zeng Qiu[2], Md Tawhid Bin Waez[2], and Chuchu Fan[1]

[1] Massachusetts Institute of Technology, Cambridge, USA
mengyue@mit.edu
[2] Ford Motor Company, Dearborn, USA

Abstract. Density of the reachable states can help understand the risk of safety-critical systems, especially in situations when worst-case reachability is too conservative. Recent work provides a data-driven approach to compute the density distribution of autonomous systems' forward reachable states online. In this paper, we study the use of such approach in combination with model predictive control for verifiable safe path planning under uncertainties. We first use the learned density distribution to compute the risk of collision online. If such risk exceeds the acceptable threshold, our method will plan for a new path around the previous trajectory, with the risk of collision below the threshold. Our method is well-suited to handle systems with uncertainties and complicated dynamics as our data-driven approach does not need an analytical form of the systems' dynamics and can estimate forward state density with an arbitrary initial distribution of uncertainties. We design two challenging scenarios (autonomous driving and hovercraft control) for safe motion planning in environments with obstacles under system uncertainties. We first show that our density estimation approach can reach a similar accuracy as the Monte-Carlo-based method while using only 0.01X training samples. By leveraging the estimated risk, our algorithm achieves the highest success rate in goal reaching when enforcing the safety rate above 0.99.

Keywords: Reachability analysis · State density estimation · Online planning · Liouville Theorem · Neural network

1 Introduction

Verifying and enforcing the safety of the controlled systems is crucial for applications such as air collision avoidance systems [28], space exploration [32], and autonomous vehicles. It is still a challenging problem to perform online verification and controller synthesis for high-dimensional autonomous systems involving complicated dynamics and uncertainties because of the scalability issue in verification and the absence of the analytical form to describe system trajectories.

Reachability analysis is one of the main techniques used for rigorously validating the system's safeness [17,19,26,27,53] and controller synthesis [21,33,40,50].

© Springer Nature Switzerland AG 2022
J. V. Deshmukh et al. (Eds.): NFM 2022, LNCS 13260, pp. 251–271, 2022.
https://doi.org/10.1007/978-3-031-06773-0_13

In reachability analysis, one computes the reachable set, defined as the set of states where the system (with the control inputs) can be driven to from the initial conditions, under the system dynamics and physical constraints. Take the aircraft collision avoidance system as an example: the system safety can be guaranteed if all the future space that the airplane can reach (under physical constraints) will not overlap with obstacles. However, computing the reachable states is proved to be undecidable in general (e.g., polynomial dynamical systems with degrees larger than 2) [24] and is also empirically time-consuming, limiting applications to simple dynamics (e.g., linear systems) or low-dimension systems.

Besides, using worst-case reachability for safety analysis will usually return a binary result ("yes" or "no"), regardless of the initial state distribution and the uncertainty in the systems. The focus on the "worst-case" makes the corresponding reachability-based planning methods "conservative" or "infeasible" when the initial state has a large uncertainty. Consider a robot navigating in an environment with obstacles and state uncertainty - when a collision is inevitable in the worst case (though the worst case is a rare event), the planning algorithm will fail to return any safety-guaranteed control policies but to let the robot stop. Hence in those cases, we need a way to quantify the risk/probability of the undesired event (e.g., collision) happening and guide controller designs.

In this paper, we present a probabilistic and reachability-based planning framework for safety-critical applications. Inspired by [42], we first learn the system flow maps and the density evolution by solving the Liouville partial differential equation (PDE) using Neural Networks from collected trajectory data. Instead of using the exact reachability analysis tool [54] for reachable states probability estimation, we use Barycentric interpolation [25], which can handle more complicated systems (dimension > 4) and sharply reduces the processing time compared to [42]. In addition, by picking different numbers of sampled points, our algorithm can flexibly control the trade-off between estimation efficiency and accuracy. Leveraging this density estimation technique, our planning framework (illustrated in Fig. 1) verifies the safety of the system trajectory via a segment-by-segment checking. If one segment becomes unsafe, we perturb around the reference trajectory to find a safe alternative, and plan for the rest of the trajectory. The process repeats until all segments are enforced to be safe.

We conduct experiments on two challenging scenarios (autonomous car and hovercraft control with uncertainties). Our estimated reachable states density distribution is informative as it reflects the contraction behavior of the controllers and highlights the places that the system is more likely to reach. Quantitatively, compared to Monte Carlo density estimation, our approach can achieve a similar accuracy while only using 0.01X training samples. We test our density-based planning algorithm in 20 randomly generated testing environments (for each system), where we achieve the highest success rate in goal reaching with high safety rate (measured by one minus the collision rate) compared to other baselines.

Our contributions are: (1) we are the first group to study the use of learned reachability density in safe motion planning to ensure probabilistic safety for complicated autonomous systems, (2) our approach can estimate state density and conduct safe planning for systems with nonlinear dynamics, state uncertainty, and disturbances, and (3) we design both qualitative and quantitative experiments for two challenging systems to validate our algorithm being accurate, data-efficient and achieving the best overall performance for the goal reaching success rate and safety.[1]

2   Related Work

Reachability analysis has been a powerful tool for system verification. The related literature has been extensively studied in [2,10,12,37]. However, few of those have been tackling the problem of calculating reachable set density distribution. Hamilton Jacobian PDE has been used to derive the exact reachable sets in [6,10,43], but this approach does not compute the density. Many data-driven methods can compute reachable sets with probabilistic guarantees using scenario optimization [14,56], convex shapes [7,35,36], support vector machines [3,48], and nonparametric methods [13,51]. However, they cannot estimate state density distribution. [20] estimates human policy distribution using a probabilistic model but requires state discretization. [39] uses the Liouville equation to maximize the backward reachable set for only polynomial system dynamics. In [1], the authors discretize the system to Markov Chains (MC) and perform probabilistic analysis on MC. This approach is computation-heavy for online safety checks.

Recently, with Neural Networks (NN) development, there has been a growing interest in studying worst-case reachability for NN [30,31,42,54,55,57] or NN-controlled systems [17,19,26,27,53]. Among those, [42] leverages the exact reachability method [54] and the Liouville Theorem to perform reachability analysis and reachable set density distribution. This approach finds the probability density function transport equation by solving the Liouville PDE using NN. It shows high accuracy in density estimation compared with histogram, kernel density estimation [11], and Sigmoidal Gaussian Cox Processes methods [15]. Hence, we choose this approach to verify the autonomous systems' safety and to conduct safe motion planning.

There have been various motion planning techniques for autonomous systems, and we refer the interested readers to these surveys [22,23,44]. Most approaches use sampling-based algorithms [29], state lattice planners [41,46], continuous optimization [8,47], and deep neural networks [9,58]. Reachable sets have also been used for safe motion planning for autonomous systems [21,33,40,50]. However, worst-case reachability-based methods only treat reachability as a binary "yes" or "no" problem without considering the density distribution of the reachable states. This boolean reachability setting makes the reachability-based motion planner conservative when the collision is inevitable in the worst case (but only happens at a very low probability) thus the system cannot reach the goal state. In this paper, we integrate the density-based reachability estimation method in [42] with model predictive control to improve the goal reaching success rate while enforcing the systems' safety in high probability.

---

[1] The code is available at https://github.com/mengyuest/density_planner.

3 Problem Formulation

Consider a controlled system $\dot{q} = f(q, u)$ where $q \in \mathcal{Q} \subseteq \mathbb{R}^d$ denotes the system state (e.g., position and heading) and $u \in \mathcal{U} \subseteq \mathbb{R}^z$ denotes the control inputs (e.g., thrust and angular velocity). For a given control policy $\pi : \mathcal{Q} \to \mathcal{U}$, the system becomes an autonomous system $\dot{q} = f(q, \pi(q)) = f_\pi(q)$ that the future state q_t at time t will only depends on the initial state q_0. We assume the initial state $q_0 \in \mathcal{Q}_0 \subseteq \mathcal{Q}$. Then, the forward reachable set at time t is defined as:

$$\mathcal{Q}_t = \{q_t \mid q_0 \in \mathcal{Q}_0, \dot{q} = f_\pi(q)\} \tag{1}$$

Assume the initial state q_0 follows a distribution $\mathcal{D}$ with the support $\mathcal{Q}_0$. Given obstacles $\{\mathcal{O}_i \subseteq \mathbb{R}^p\}_{i=1}^M$ in the environment, we aim to compute the probability for colliding with obstacles and the forward probabilistic reachability defined below:

Definition 1 (Collision probability estimation). *Given a system $\dot{q} = f_\pi(q)$ with initial state distribution $\mathcal{D}$, compute the probability for states colliding with an obstacle $\mathcal{O}$ at time t: $P_t(\mathcal{O}) = \text{Prob}\{q_0 \sim \mathcal{D}, \dot{q} = f_\pi(q), \Pi(q_t) \in \mathcal{O}\}$ where $\Pi : \mathcal{Q} \to \mathbb{R}^p$ projects the system state to the space that the obstacle $\mathcal{O}$ resides.*

Definition 2 (Forward probabilistic reachability estimation). *Given a system $\dot{q} = f_\pi(q)$ with initial state distribution $\mathcal{D}$, for each time step t, estimate the forward reachable set $\mathcal{Q}_t$ and the probability distribution $\{(\mathcal{A}_i, P_t(\mathcal{A}_i))\}_{i=1}^{N_t}$. Here $\mathcal{A}_1, ..., \mathcal{A}_{N_t}$ is a non-overlapping partition for $\mathcal{Q}_t$, i.e., $\mathcal{A}_i \cap \mathcal{A}_j = \varnothing, \forall i \neq j$, $\bigcup_{i=1}^{N_t} \mathcal{A}_i = \mathcal{Q}_t$.*

Assume π is a tracking controller: $\pi(q) = u(q, q^{ref})$ with a reference trajectory $\{q_t^{ref}\}_{t=1}^T$ of length T first generated from a high-level planner with commands $U^{ref} = \{u_t^{ref}\}_{t=1}^T$. Define the *total collision risk*:

$$\text{Prob(colliding)} = P_c(U^{ref}) = \sum_{t=1}^T \sum_{i=1}^M P_t(\mathcal{O}_i) \tag{2}$$

We are interested in the following problem:

Definition 3 (Safety verification and planning problem). *Given a system $\dot{q} = f_\pi(q)$ with initial state distribution $\mathcal{D}$ and reference control commands U^{ref}, verify the total collision risk $P_c(U^{ref}) \leq \gamma$, where γ is a tolerant collision risk threshold. If not, plan a new command $\tilde{U}^{ref}$ to ensure $P_c(\tilde{U}^{ref}) \leq \gamma$*

In this paper, the details about the dynamic systems $\dot{q} = f_\pi(q)$ and controllers $\pi(q) = u(q, q^{ref})$ are listed in the A and B.

4 Technical Approaches

Inspired by [42], we design a sample-based approach to compute the reachability and the density distribution for the system described in the previous section and further leverage these results for trajectory planning for autonomous systems.

4.1   Data-driven Reachability and Density Estimation

Our framework is built on top of a recently published density-based reachability analysis method [42]. From the collected trajectory data, [42] learns the system flow map and the state density concentration function jointly, guided by the fact that the state density evolution follows the Liouville partial differential equation (PDE). With the set-based reachability analysis tools RPM [54], they can estimate the bound for the reachable set probability distribution.[2]

For the autonomous system defined in Sect. 3, we denote the density function $\rho : \mathcal{Q} \times \mathbb{R} \to \mathbb{R}^{\geq 0}$ which measures how states distribute in the state space at a specific time step. The density function is completely determined by the underlying dynamics f_π and the initial density map $\rho_0 : \mathcal{Q} \to \mathbb{R}^{\geq 0}$ according to the Liouville PDE [16].

$$\frac{\partial \rho}{\partial t} + \nabla \cdot (\rho \cdot f_\pi) = 0, \quad \rho(q, 0) = \rho_0(q) \tag{3}$$

We define the flow map $\Phi : \mathcal{Q} \times \mathbb{R} \to \mathcal{Q}$ such that $\Phi(q_0, t)$ is the state at time t starting from q_0 at time 0. The density along the trajectory $\Phi(q_0, t)$ is an univariate function of t, i.e., $\rho(t) = \rho(\Phi(q_0, t), t)$. If we consider the augmented system with states $[q, \rho]$, from Eq. 3 we can get the dynamics of the augmented system:

$$\begin{bmatrix} \dot{q} \\ \dot{\rho} \end{bmatrix} = \begin{bmatrix} f_\pi(q) \\ -\nabla \cdot f_\pi(q)\rho \end{bmatrix} \tag{4}$$

To compute the state and the density at time T from the initial condition $[q_0, \rho_0(q_0)]$, one can solve the Eq. 4 and the solution at time T will give the desired density value. To accelerate the computation process for a large number of initial points, we use neural networks to estimate the density $\rho(q, t)$ and the flow map $\Phi(q, t)$. Details for the network training are introduced in Sect. 3 of [42].

4.2   Reach Set Probability Estimation

As mentioned in [42], when the system state is high (≥ 4), it is either infeasible (due to the numerical issue in computing for polyhedra) or too time-consuming to generate RPM results for probability estimation. The state dimension will become 7–10 for a 2D car control or a 3D hovercraft control problem after including the reference control inputs. If we use other worst-case reachability analysis tools such as [17] to compute the probability, the reachable set will be too conservative and the planner will not return a feasible solution (other than stop) because the reachable states will occupy the whole state space regardless of the choice of the reference controls. Therefore, we use a sample-based approach to estimate the probability of the reachable sets, as introduced in the following.

To estimate the probability in Prob. 1, we first uniformly sample initial states $\{q_0^i\}_{i=1}^{N_s}$ from the support of the distribution ρ_0 and use the method in Sect. 4.1

---

[2] For details about computing the probability of the reachable state, we refer the interested readers to [42](Appendix B).

to estimate the future states and the corresponding densities at time t denoted as $\{(q_t^i, \rho_t(q_t^i))\}_{i=1}^{N_s}$. We approximate the forward reachable set $\mathcal{Q}_t$ defined in Eq. 1 as the convex hull of $\{q_t^i\}_{i=1}^{N_s}$, and denote it as $\mathcal{CH}_t$. Then, based on $\{(q_t^i, \rho_t(q_t^i))\}_{i=1}^{N_s}$, we use the linear interpolation to estimate the density distribution $\hat{\rho}_t(\cdot)$ at time t. Finally, we uniformly sample points q_s within the convex hull $\mathcal{CH}_t$, and the probability for the system reaching $\mathcal{A}$ can be computed as:

$$\mathrm{Prob}(q_t \in \mathcal{A}) \approx \frac{\sum_{q_s \sim \mathcal{CH}_t} \mathbb{1}\{q_s \in \mathcal{A}\}\hat{\rho}_t(q_s)}{\sum_{q_s \sim \mathcal{CH}_t} \hat{\rho}_t(q_s)} \tag{5}$$

Here are some remarks for our approach. The probabilistic guarantee about estimation accuracy is provided in [42][Appendix A]. Besides, our approach will return probability zero if the ground truth probability of reaching $\mathcal{A}$ is zero. Moreover, compared to the set-based approach RPM, which has poor scalability because of the number of polyhedral cells growing exponentially to the system state dimension, our sample-based approach is fast, and the runtime can be controlled by selecting different numbers of sampled points as a trade-off between efficiency and accuracy.

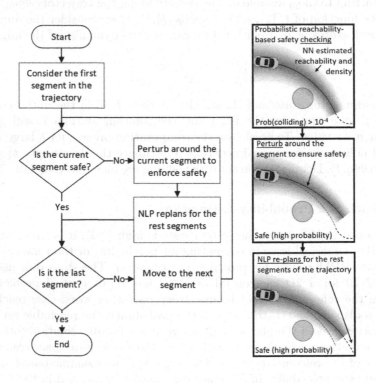

(a) Flow chart of the algorithm   (b) Planning process

Fig. 1. The safe planning algorithm.

4.3   Motion Planning Based on Reachability Analysis

After estimating the reachable states and density for the autonomous system under a reference trajectory, we utilize the results to plan feasible trajectories to ensure the collision probability is under a tolerable threshold.

In this paper, the reference trajectory is generated using nonlinear programming (NLP). Given the origin state q_{origin}, the destination state q_{dest}, the physical constraints $u_{min} \leq u \leq u_{max}$ and M obstacles $\{(x_i^o, y_i^o)\}_{i=0}^{M-1}$ (with radius $\{r_i\}_{i=0}^{M-1}$) in the environment, discrete time duration Δ_t and total number of timesteps T, we solve an NLP using CasADI [5] to generate a reference trajectory, which consists of N trajectory segments $\xi_0, ..., \xi_{N-1}$ (each segment ξ_j has length L and is generated by $q_{j \cdot L}$ and u_j). The details about this nonlinear optimization formulation can be found in Appendix C

Then for each segment ξ_j, with the uncertainty and disturbances considered, we use the approach in Sect. 4.2 to estimate the system's reachable states as well as their density. If the total collision risk defined in Eq. 2 is below a predefined threshold (10^{-4} in our case), we call the current trajectory "safe". Otherwise, we call the trajectory "unsafe" and adjust for the current trajectory segment. Notice that the traditional reachability-based planning is just a special case when we set this threshold to 0.

To ensure fast computation for the planning, we use the perturbation method to sample candidate trajectory segments around this "unsafe" trajectory segment ξ_j (by adding Δu to the reference control commands) and again use the method in Sect. 4.2 to verify whether the candidate is "unsafe", until we find one segment $\tilde{\xi}_j$ that is "safe", and then we conduct the NLP starting from the endpoint of the segment $\tilde{\xi}_j$. We repeat this process until all the trajectory segments are validated to be "safe". The whole process is summarized in Algorithm 1.

Given enough sampled points with guaranteed correctness in approximating state density and forward reachable set, the algorithm is sound because the produced control inputs will always ensure the system is "safe". However, our algorithm is not complete because: (1) in general, the nonlinear programming is not always feasible, and (2) the perturbation method might not be able to find a feasible solution around the "unsafe" trajectory. The first point can be addressed by introducing slack variables to relax for the safety and goal-reaching constraints. The second point can be tackled by increasing the tolerance probability threshold of collision.

5   Experiments

We investigate our approach in autonomous driving and hovercraft navigation applications under the following setup: given an environment with an origin point, a destination region, and obstacles, the goal for the agent at the origin point is to reach the destination while avoiding all the obstacles. Notice that this is a very general setup to encode the real-world driving scenarios because: (1) the road boundaries and other irregular-shaped obstacles can be represented

---

Algorithm 1. Reachability-based Planning Algorithm

Input: Origin S_0, destination S_N, NLP constraints
Output: Reference trajectories $\xi_0, \xi_1, \cdots, \xi_{N-1}$

1: $i \leftarrow 0$
2: **while** $i < N$ **do**
3:     Generate segments $\xi_i, ..., \xi_{N-1}$ from S_i to S_N using NLP
4:     **for** $j = i : N$ **do**
5:         Use the method in Sect. 4.2 to check whether the trajectory segment ξ_j is "safe".
6:         **if** The trajectory is "safe" **then**
7:             Continue
8:         **else**
9:             Perturb the segment ξ_j to search for a possible "safe" segment $\tilde{\xi}_j$ (goes from S_j to close to S_{j+1}).
10:            $\xi_j \leftarrow \tilde{\xi}_j$
11:            $S_{j+1} \leftarrow \tilde{S}_{j+1}$
12:        **end if**
13:     **end for**   ▷ By far, $S_0 \rightarrow S_{j+1}$ is "safe"
14:     $i \leftarrow j + 1$ ▷ Next step will inspect $S_{j+1} \rightarrow \cdots S_N$
15: **end while**

---

by using a set of obstacles, and (2) other road participants (pedestrians, other driving cars) can be modeled as moving obstacles. Here we consider only the center of mass of the car/hovercraft in rendering reachable sets and planning (we can bloat the radius of the obstacle to take the car/hovercraft length and width into account). In Sect. 5.1, we evaluate the reachability and density for the system under a fixed reference trajectory. In Sect. 5.2, we leverage the reachability and density result to do trajectory re-planning when the system is "unsafe".

We collect 50,000 trajectories from the simulator, with randomly sampled initial states, reference trajectories, and disturbances. Each trajectory has 50 timesteps with a duration of 0.02s at each time step. Then, we select 40,000 for the training set and 10,000 for the evaluation set and train a neural network for estimating the future states and the density evolution mentioned in [42]. We use a fully connected ReLU-based neural network with 3 hidden layers and 128 hidden units in each layer. We train the neural network for 500k epochs, using stochastic gradient descent with a batch size of 256 and a learning rate of 0.1. The code is implemented in PyTorch [45], and the training takes less than an hour on an NVidia RTX 2080Ti GPU.

5.1   Reachable States and Density Estimation

In this section, we first conceptually show how our approach of estimating reachable states and density can benefit safety-critical applications. As depicted in

Fig. 4, a car plans to move to the destination (the red arrow) while avoiding all the obstacles on the road. The initial state of the car (X,Y position, and heading angle) and the disturbance follow a Gaussian distribution. The high-level motion planner has already generated a reference trajectory (the blue line in Fig. 4), with the uncertainty owing to the initial state estimation error and the disturbance. We will show that our approach can estimate the state density distribution and reachable state accurately and can help to certify that the planned reference trajectory is not colliding with obstacles in high probability.

Visualizations of the Estimated Reachability and Density Heatmap.
Using the method introduced in Sect. 4.2, we can first estimate the tracking error density distribution and marginalize it to the 2D XY-plane to get the probability heatmaps (as shown in Fig. 2(a)–(d)). Then we can transform it to the reference trajectory and check whether it has an intersection with the obstacles in the environment (as shown in Fig 2(e)).

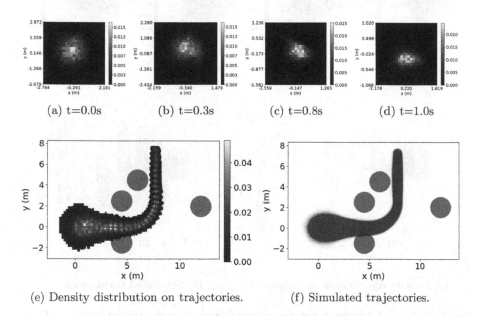

(a) t=0.0s   (b) t=0.3s   (c) t=0.8s   (d) t=1.0s

(e) Density distribution on trajectories.   (f) Simulated trajectories.

Fig. 2. Estimated density (for states in (a)–(d) and along the trajectory in (e)) for the car model. The states are shown to concentrate on reference trajectory (blue line in (e)), and the collision risk is very low. (Color figure online)

To verify the correctness of our estimated reachable states and density, we also sample a large number of states from the initial state distribution and use the ODE to simulate actual car trajectories, as shown in Fig. 2(b). Comparing Fig. 2(a) with Fig. 2(b), we find out in both cases that the vehicle will have a collision with the bottom obstacle. In addition, our density result also shows that the risk of the collision is very low ($\mathrm{Prob(colliding)} \leq 10^{-4}$ as shown in Sect. 5.1), which is reasonable because the majority of the states will be converging to the reference trajectory (as indicated from Fig. 2(a)–(d)). Only a few outlier trajectories will intersect with the obstacle. We also conduct this experiment with the Hovercraft system (3D scenarios), where the results in Fig. 3 reflect similar contraction behaviors, and the probability of colliding with the obstacles is very low (thus, we do not need to do planning in this stage).

Visually, our results are more informative than the pure reachability analysis because ours reflects the tracking controller's contraction behavior and illustrates that the colliding event is in very low probability. The following subsection will further quantify this probability and compare it with a traditional probability estimation method.

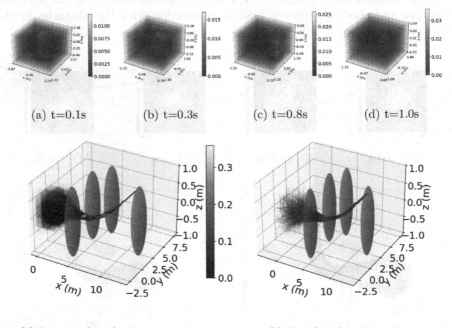

(a) t=0.1s   (b) t=0.3s   (c) t=0.8s   (d) t=1.0s

(e) Density distribution on trajectories.   (f) Simulated trajectories.

Fig. 3. Estimated density (for states in (a)–(d) and along the trajectory in (e)) for the hovercraft model. The states are shown to concentrate on reference trajectory (blue line in (e)), and the collision probability is very low. (Color figure online)

Comparison with Monte-Carlo Based Probability Estimation. Our visualization result in Sect. 5.1 reflects that under some initial conditions, the vehicle might hit the obstacle. Although Fig. 2 shows that the likelihood of the clash is very low, we want to quantify the risk of the collision to benefit future

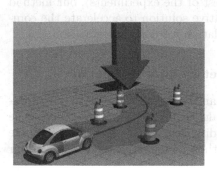

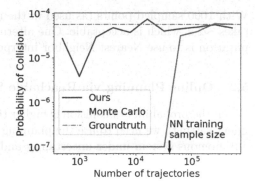

Fig. 4. A vehicle plans to reach the red arrow while avoiding all the obstacles. Blue region shows the reference trajectory and uncertainty. (Color figure online)

Fig. 5. Estimation of collision probability with respect to sample size.

decisions (e.g., choosing the policy with the lowest collision probability or with the lowest value at risk (VaR) [38]). However, it is intractable to derive the ground-truth probability of collision for general non-linear systems. Therefore, we compare our estimation result with the Monte Carlo approximation (this is done by generating a considerable amount of simulations and counts for the frequency of the collision.

We try different numbers of samples (from 500 to 512000) and compare our approach to the Monte Carlo estimation. As shown in Fig. 5, the groundtruth probability of collision (where we approximated by sampling 5×10^7 trajectories and compute the collision rate) is approximately 5×10^{-5}. The Monte Carlo approach fails to predict meaningful probability results until increasing the sample size to 64000. In contrast, our approach can give a non-trivial probability estimation using only 500 examples, less than 0.01X the samples needed for the Monte Carlo approach.

The black vertical arrow in Fig. 5 corresponds to the 40000 sample size (the number of samples we have used offline for our neural network training). The corresponding result is already as stable as the Monte Carlo approach which requires more than 64000 samples. Furthermore, our approach can be adapted to any initial condition for the same car dynamic system without retraining or fine-tuning, making it possible for downstream tasks like online planning, as introduced in the following section.

In terms of the computation time (for 512000 points), our approach requires 2.3X amount of time (31.8 s) as needed for the Monte Carlo method (14.1 s), mainly because that the Delaunay Triangulation method [34] used for state-space partition in the linear interpolation has the complexity of $O(N^{\lfloor d/2 \rfloor})$ [52] for N data points in the d-dimension system. Thus the run time will grow about quadratically to the number of sample points in our case (state dimension=4).

With 1000 sampled points (as used in the rest of the experiments), our method takes ~2 s, which is acceptable. One alternative solution to accelerate the computation is to use Nearest Neighbor interpolation for density estimation.

5.2 Online Planning via Reachable Set Density Estimation

When the probability of collision is higher than the threshold (10^{-4} in our experiment setting), we need to use the planning algorithm to ensure the safety of the autonomous system under uncertainty and disturbance. We first show how the planning algorithm works in Sect. 5.2, and then quantitative assessment of our algorithm is conducted in Sect. 5.2.

Demonstration for an Example. We conduct experiments to demonstrate how our proposed reachability-based planning framework works for autonomous driving cars and hovercraft applications. In Fig. 6, a car is moving from left to right of the map while avoiding collisions with obstacles. After checking for the first segment's safety (Fig. 6(a)), the algorithm finds out the probability of the collision is higher than 10^{-4}. Thus it starts to plan for the first segment (the red line in Fig. 6(b)) around the reference trajectory (the blue line in Fig. 6(b)). Moreover, after it updates the reference trajectory using the NLP solver (the blue line in Fig. 6(c)) based on the perturbed segment, the algorithm detects the next segment as "unsafe." Hence it plans again to enforce the collision probability is below 10^{-4} (Fig. 6(c)). Another example in a 3D scenario is shown in Fig. 7, where the hovercraft perturbs for the first segment and then later verifies that the next two segments are all "safe", hence the whole trajectory in Fig. 7(c) is "safe."

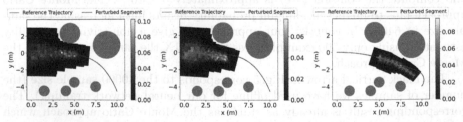

(a) t=0, "unsafe" detected. (b) t=0, perturb to "safe". (c) t=1, perturb to "safe".
Prob(colliding) $\geq 10^{-4}$ Prob(colliding) $\leq 10^{-4}$ Prob(colliding) $\leq 10^{-4}$

Fig. 6. Demonstration for the re-planning algorithm for the 2D car experiment. For each trajectory segment, if the probability of collision is higher than a predefined threshold, we denote the trajectory segment as "unsafe", otherwise, we denote the trajectory segment as "safe". (Color figure online)

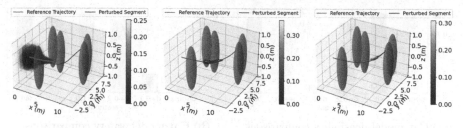

(a) t=0, perturb to "safe". (b) t=1, "safe" is verified. (c) t=2, "safe" is verified.
Prob(colliding) $\leq 10^{-4}$ Prob(colliding) $\leq 10^{-4}$ Prob(colliding) $\leq 10^{-4}$

Fig. 7. Demonstration for the re-planning algorithm for the 3D hovercraft experiment. For each trajectory segment, if the probability of collision is higher than a predefined threshold, we denote the trajectory segment as "unsafe", otherwise, we denote the trajectory segment as "safe".

Evaluation of Trajectory Planning Performance. To illustrate the advantage of our approach in enforcing the system safety, we design 20 testing environments with randomly placed obstacles (while ensuring the initial reference trajectory is feasible from the NLP solver) for the autonomous car system and the hovercraft control system. We compare our framework with several baseline methods: the "original" approach just uses the initial reference trajectory (without any planning process), the "$d =$?" approach denotes the distance-based planning methods with the safety distance threshold set as d (the larger d is, the more conservative and safer the algorithm will be, at the cost of infeasible solutions), the "reach" approach uses estimated reachable tube computed from the sampled convex hull $\mathcal{CH}$ introduced in Sect. 4.2 to do safe planning.

We measure the performances of different methods using two metrics: feasibility and safety. *Feasibility* is defined as the frequency that the algorithm can return a plausible solution (but might be unsafe) to reach the designed destination. Over all feasible solutions, *safety* is defined as the expected collision probability. Intuitively, the feasibility measures the successful rate of the goal reaching, and the "safety" measures how "reliable" the planner is.

As shown in Fig. 8(a)(b) for the car experiments, compared to the "reach" method (which just uses reachable tubes to do planning) and a distance-based planning method ("$d = 1.0$"), our approach can achieve a similar safety rate, while having 0.29–0.76 higher feasibility (due to less conservative planning). Though we are 0.059 less in feasibility than the "original" and the "$d = 0.1$" baselines, they lead to 3772X–4574X collision rates than ours (due to our approach being less aggressive in planning). Compared to the "$d = 0.2$" method, we are 0.06 better in feasibility (0.94 vs 0.88) while being only 0.2X in collision rate (0.000025 vs 0.000125), we also get a lower collision rate . A similar trend can also be observed from the hovercraft experiment (Fig. 8(c)(d)). Hence, our approach achieves the best overall performance by considering feasibility and safety.

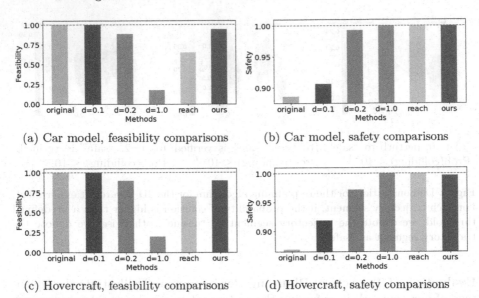

(a) Car model, feasibility comparisons   (b) Car model, safety comparisons

(c) Hovercraft, feasibility comparisons   (d) Hovercraft, safety comparisons

Fig. 8. Feasibility and safety comparisons. Our method achieves the best trade-off between the feasibility and the safety, with close to 100% safety and 0.2X–4X improvement in feasibility comparing to high-safety methods. Here "original" uses nonlinear programming for planning ,"d =?" denotes the distance-based re-planning with the safety distance d, "reach" uses estimated reachable tube to do re-planning, and "ours" leverages both the reachable tube and the corresponding density to do re-planning. More details can be found in Sect. 5.2

5.3   Discussions

While our approach can accurately estimate the collision probability and the motion planner using our estimated density can achieve the highest goal reaching rate compared to other baselines when enforcing the safety rate above 0.99, we admit there are assumptions and limitations in our method.

First we assume the neural network can learn a perfect state dynamic and state density evolution, which is not always satisfied due to the model capacity and the complexity of the system. The proof in [42][Appendix A] shows the generalization error bound for this learning framework, which indicates one possible remedy is to collect more training trajectories.

Besides, we assume the sampled trajectories from the simulator are following the same distribution as for the real world trajectories. This assumption might create biases in the density concentration function and the flow map estimation. One way to resolve this issue is to further fine-tuning the neural network using the real world data at the inference stage.

The first limitation of our approach is lacking guarantee for the convergence of the planning algorithm. The success planning rate of our method depends on the perturbation range (how far the control policy can deviate from the reference policy) and the perturbation resolution (the minimum difference between two candidate policies). There are also optimization-based methods, such as stochastic gradient descent [4], that can converge with probabilistic guarantee derived from the Robbins-Siegmund theorem [49]. Using optimization-based method for density-based planning is left to our future work.

The second limitation of our planning framework is the computation time. This is mainly due to our risk computation step in Eq. 2, as mentioned in Sect. 5.1. Although our proposed probability computation method can handle higher dimension systems than [42], the complexity of the Delaunay Triangulation process in our framework grows in the power of $\lfloor d/2 \rfloor$ for a d-dimensional system. In practice, one can use less number of sample points to reduce the computation time. Another alternative is to use other interpolation methods (e.g., Nearest Neighbor interpolation) for d-dimensional space.

6   Conclusion

We propose a data-driven framework for probabilistic verification and safe motion planning for autonomous systems. Our approach can accurately estimate collision risk, using only 0.01X training samples compared to the Monte Carlo method. We conduct experiments for autonomous driving and hovercraft control, where the car (hovercraft) with state uncertainty and control input disturbances plans to move to the destination while avoiding all the obstacles. We show that our approach can achieve the highest goal reaching rate among all approaches that can enforce the safety rate above 0.99. For future works, we manage to develop verification approaches for cases that consider (1) other road participants' presence and intention and (2) more complicated sensory inputs, such as LiDAR measurements or even raw camera inputs.

Acknowledgement. The Ford Motor Company provided funds to assist the authors with their research, but this article solely reflects the opinions and conclusions of its authors and not any Ford entity. The authors would also want to thank Kyle Post for providing constructive suggestions regarding experiment designs, figures, and paper writings.

Appendix

A   Car Model Dynamic and Controller Designs

The dynamics for the rearwheel kinematic car model [18] is:

$$\dot{q} = \begin{bmatrix} \dot{x} \\ \dot{y} \\ \dot{\theta} \end{bmatrix} = \begin{bmatrix} \cos\theta & 0 \\ \sin\theta & 0 \\ 0 & 1 \end{bmatrix} \begin{bmatrix} v \\ \omega \end{bmatrix} \tag{6}$$

where (x, y) denotes the position of the vehicle's center of mass, θ denotes vehicle's heading angle, and v, ω are the velocity and angular velocity control inputs. Given a reference trajectory generated from the motion planner $(x^{ref}, y^{ref}, \theta^{ref})^T$, the error for the car model is:

$$
\begin{bmatrix} e_x \\ e_y \\ e_\theta \end{bmatrix} = \begin{bmatrix} \cos(\theta) & \sin(\theta) & 0 \\ -\sin(\theta) & \cos(\theta) & 0 \\ 0 & 0 & 1 \end{bmatrix} \begin{bmatrix} x - x^{ref} \\ y - y^{ref} \\ \theta - \theta^{ref} \end{bmatrix} \tag{7}
$$

The Lyapunov-based controller is designed as:

$$
\begin{cases} v = v^{ref} \cos(e_\theta) + k_1 e_x + d_v \\ \omega = \omega^{ref} + v^{ref}(k_2 e_y + k_3 \sin(e_\theta)) + d_\omega \end{cases} \tag{8}
$$

where k_1, k_2, k_3 are the coefficients for the controller and d_v and d_ω are the controller disturbances.

B   Hovercraft Model Dynamic and Controller Designs

The hovercraft is the model tested in 3D scenarios. The dynamics for the hovercraft [18] is:

$$
\dot{q} = \begin{bmatrix} \dot{x} \\ \dot{y} \\ \dot{z} \\ \dot{\theta} \end{bmatrix} = \begin{bmatrix} \cos\theta & 0 & 0 \\ \sin\theta & 0 & 0 \\ 0 & 1 & 0 \\ 0 & 0 & 1 \end{bmatrix} \begin{bmatrix} v \\ v_z \\ \omega \end{bmatrix} \tag{9}
$$

where (x, y, z) denotes the 3D position of the hovercraft's center of mass, θ denotes the heading angle of the hovercraft in the xy-plane, v (and ω) denotes the velocity (and angular velocity) in the xy-plane, v_z denotes the velocity along the z-axis. When a reference trajectory $(x^{ref}, y^{ref}, z^{ref}, \theta^{ref})^T$ is introduced, the error for the car model is:

$$
\begin{bmatrix} e_x \\ e_y \\ e_z \\ e_\theta \end{bmatrix} = \begin{bmatrix} \cos(\theta) & \sin(\theta) & 0 & 0 \\ -\sin(\theta) & \cos(\theta) & 0 & 0 \\ 0 & 0 & 1 & 0 \\ 0 & 0 & 0 & 1 \end{bmatrix} \begin{bmatrix} x - x^{ref} \\ y - y^{ref} \\ z - z^{ref} \\ \theta - \theta^{ref} \end{bmatrix} \tag{10}
$$

The Lyapunov-based controller is designed as:

$$
\begin{cases} v = v^{ref} \cos(e_\theta) + k_1 e_x + d_v \\ v_z = v_z^{ref} + k_4 e_z + d_{v_z} \\ \omega = \omega^{ref} + v^{ref}(k_2 e_y + k_3 \sin(e_\theta)) + d_\omega \end{cases} \tag{11}
$$

where k_1, k_2, k_3, k_4 are the coefficients for the controller and d_v, d_{v_z} and d_ω are the corresponding disturbances.

C Nonlinear Programming for Controller Synthesize

The goal of this section is to find a control sequence $\{u_j\}_{j=0}^{N-1}$ for the car (or the hovercraft, we use "robot" to represent them in the following context) starting from $q_{origin} \in \mathbb{R}^d$ to reach the goal state $q_{dest} \in \mathbb{R}^d$ in T time steps, while satisfying the physical constraints and avoiding colliding with the surrounding obstacles (M obstacles in total) in the environment. We use the forward Euler method to compute the ODE $\dot{q} = f(q, u)$, with each time step duration as Δt. Each control input u_j will last for $L = \lceil \frac{T}{N} \rceil$ steps. For the physical constraints, we set up the maximum and minimum allowed value for the control inputs as $u_{max}, u_{min} \in \mathbb{R}^z$. We represent the obstacles as circles (and spheres in 3D scenarios). The i-th obstacle has a center position $\bar{q}_i^o \in \mathbb{R}^2$ ($\bar{q}_i^o \in \mathbb{R}^3$ in 3D scenarios) and a radius $r_i \in \mathbb{R}^+$ (we use $\bar{q}_j$ to represent the robot position at time j, to distinguish with the full robot state q_j). We formulate the optimization process as followed:

$$
\begin{aligned}
\min_{u_{0:N-1}} \quad & \sum_{i=0}^{M-1} \sum_{j=0}^{T} \gamma_{i,j}^2 \\
\text{s.t.} \quad & q_0 = q_{origin} \\
& q_T = q_{dest} \\
& u_{min} \le u_j \le u_{max}, \forall j = 0...N-1 \\
& q_{j \cdot L+k+1} = q_{j \cdot L+k} + f(q_{j \cdot L+k}, u_j)\Delta t, \forall j = 0...N-1, \forall k = 0...L-1 \\
& |\bar{q}_j - \bar{q}_i^o|^2 + \gamma_{i,j}^2 \ge r_i^2, \forall i = 0..., M-1, \forall j = 0, ..., T
\end{aligned}
$$
(12)

where the first two constraints make sure the robot starts from the initial point and will reach the goal point, the third and forth constraints enforce the physical constraints and the robot dynamic, and the last constraint ensure the robot will not hit obstacles at any time. For feasibility issues, slack variables $\gamma_{i,j}$ are introduced to relax the collision avoidance constraint (the robot safety will be checked and ensured during the online planning process after this optimization process).

References

1. Abate, A.: Probabilistic Reachability for Stochastic Hybrid Systems: Theory, Computations, and Applications. University of California, Berkeley (2007)
2. Agha, G., Palmskog, K.: A survey of statistical model checking. ACM Trans. Model. Comput. Simul. (TOMACS) **28**(1), 1–39 (2018)
3. Allen, R.E., Clark, A.A., Starek, J.A., Pavone, M.: A machine learning approach for real-time reachability analysis. In: 2014 IEEE/RSJ International Conference on Intelligent Robots and Systems, pp. 2202–2208. IEEE (2014)
4. Amari, S.: Backpropagation and stochastic gradient descent method. Neurocomputing **5**(4–5), 185–196 (1993)

5. Andersson, J.A.E., Gillis, J., Horn, G., Rawlings, J.B., Diehl, M.: Casadi: a software framework for nonlinear optimization and optimal control. Math. Program. Comput. **11**(1), 1–36, 2019

6. Bansal, S., Tomlin, C.: Deepreach: A deep learning approach to high-dimensional reachability. arXiv preprint arXiv:2011.02082 (2020)

7. Berndt, A., Alanwar, A., Johansson, K.H., Sandberg, H.: Data-driven set-based estimation using matrix zonotopes with set containment guarantees. arXiv preprint arXiv:2101.10784 (2021)

8. Chen, J., Liu, C., Tomizuka, M.: Foad: fast optimization-based autonomous driving motion planner. In: 2018 Annual American Control Conference (ACC), pp. 4725–4732. IEEE (2018)

9. Chen, L., Xuemin, H., Tian, W., Wang, H., Cao, D., Wang, F.-Y.: Parallel planning: a new motion planning framework for autonomous driving. IEEE/CAA J. Autom. Sin. **6**(1), 236–246 (2018)

10. Chen, M., Tomlin, C.J.: Hamilton-jacobi reachability: some recent theoretical advances and applications in unmanned airspace management. Ann. Rev. Control Robot. Autonom. Syst. **1**, 333–358 (2018)

11. Chen, Y., Ahmadi, M., Ames, A.D.: Optimal safe controller synthesis: a density function approach. In: 2020 American Control Conference (ACC), pp. 5407–5412. IEEE (2020)

12. International competition on verifying continuous and hybrid systems. https://cps-vo.org/group/ARCH/FriendlyCompetition. Accessed 18 June 2021

13. Devonport, A., Arcak, M.: Data-driven reachable set computation using adaptive gaussian process classification and Monte Carlo methods. In: 2020 American Control Conference (ACC), pp. 2629–2634. IEEE (2020)

14. Devonport, A., Arcak, M.: Estimating reachable sets with scenario optimization. In: Learning for Dynamics and Control, pp. 75–84. PMLR (2020)

15. Donner, C., Opper, M.: Efficient bayesian inference of sigmoidal gaussian cox processes. https://doi.org/10.14279/depositonce-8398 (2018)

16. Ehrendorfer, M.: The liouville equation and prediction of forecast skill. In: Predictability and Nonlinear Modelling in Natural Sciences and Economics, pp. 29–44. Springer (1994)

17. Everett, M., Habibi, G., Jonathan, P.: How Efficient reachability analysis of closed-loop systems with neural network controllers. arXiv preprint arXiv:2101.01815 (2021)

18. Fan, C., Miller, K., Mitra, S.: Fast and guaranteed safe controller synthesis for nonlinear vehicle models. In: Lahiri, S.K., Wang, C. (eds.) CAV 2020. LNCS, vol. 12224, pp. 629–652. Springer, Cham (2020). https://doi.org/10.1007/978-3-030-53288-8_31

19. Fan, J., Huang, C., Chen, X., Li, W., Zhu, Q.: ReachNN*: a tool for reachability analysis of neural-network controlled systems. In: Hung, D.V., Sokolsky, O. (eds.) ATVA 2020. LNCS, vol. 12302, pp. 537–542. Springer, Cham (2020). https://doi.org/10.1007/978-3-030-59152-6_30

20. Fridovich-Keil, D., et al.: Confidence-aware motion prediction for real-time collision avoidance1. Int. J. Robot. Res. **39**(2–3), 250–265 (2020)

21. Gerdts, M., Xausa, I.: Avoidance trajectories using reachable sets and parametric sensitivity analysis. In: Hömberg, D., Tröltzsch, F. (eds.) CSMO 2011. IAICT, vol. 391, pp. 491–500. Springer, Heidelberg (2013). https://doi.org/10.1007/978-3-642-36062-6_49

22. Goerzen, C., Kong, Z., Mettler, B.: A survey of motion planning algorithms from the perspective of autonomous uav guidance. J. Intell. Robot. Syst. **57**(1), 65–100 (2010)
23. González, D., Pérez, J., Milanés, V., Nashashibi, F.: A review of motion planning techniques for automated vehicles. IEEE Trans. Intell. Transp. Syst. **17**(4), 1135–1145 (2015)
24. Hainry, E.: Decidability and undecidability in dynamical systems. In: Research Report (2009)
25. Hormann, K.: Barycentric interpolation. In: Approximation Theory XIV: San Antonio 2013, pp. 197–218. Springer (2014)
26. Hu, H., Fazlyab, M., Morari, M., Pappas, G.J.: Reach-sdp: Reachability analysis of closed-loop systems with neural network controllers via semidefinite programming. In: 2020 59th IEEE Conference on Decision and Control (CDC), pp. 5929–5934. IEEE (2020)
27. Ivanov, R., Weimer, J., Alur, R., Pappas, G.J., Lee, I.: Verisig: verifying safety properties of hybrid systems with neural network controllers. In: Proceedings of the 22nd ACM International Conference on Hybrid Systems: Computation and Control, pp. 169–178 (2019)
28. Julian, K.D., Kochenderfer, M.D.: Reachability analysis for neural network aircraft collision avoidance systems. J. Guidance Control Dyn. **44**(6), 1132–1142 (2021)
29. Karaman, S., Frazzoli, E.: Sampling-based algorithms for optimal motion planning. Int. J. Robot. Res. **30**(7), 846–894 (2011)
30. Katz, G., Barrett, C., Dill, D.L., Julian, K., Kochenderfer, M.J.: Reluplex: an efficient SMT solver for verifying deep neural networks. In: Majumdar, R., Kunčak, V. (eds.) CAV 2017. LNCS, vol. 10426, pp. 97–117. Springer, Cham (2017). https://doi.org/10.1007/978-3-319-63387-9_5
31. Katz, G., et al.: The marabou framework for verification and analysis of deep neural networks. In: Dillig, I., Tasiran, S. (eds.) CAV 2019. LNCS, vol. 11561, pp. 443–452. Springer, Cham (2019). https://doi.org/10.1007/978-3-030-25540-4_26
32. Kornfeld, R.P., Prakash, R., Devereaux, A.S., Greco, M.E., Harmon, C.C., Kipp, D.M.: Verification and validation of the mars science laboratory/curiosity rover entry, descent, and landing system. J. Spacecraft Rockets **51**(4), 1251–1269 (2014)
33. Kousik, S., Vaskov, S., Fan, B., Johnson-Roberson, M., Vasudevan, R.: Bridging the gap between safety and real-time performance in receding-horizon trajectory design for mobile robots. Int. J. Robot. Res. **39**(12), 1419–1469 (2020)
34. Lee, D.T., Schachter, B.J.: Two algorithms for constructing a delaunay triangulation. Int. J. Comput. Inf. Sci. **9**(3), 219–242 (1980)
35. Lew, T., Pavone, M.: Sampling-based reachability analysis: A random set theory approach with adversarial sampling. arXiv preprint arXiv:2008.10180 (2020)
36. Liebenwein, L., Baykal, C., Gilitschenski, I., Karaman, S., Rus, D.: Sampling-based approximation algorithms for reachability analysis with provable guarantees. RSS (2018)
37. Liu, C., Arnon, T., Lazarus, C., Strong, C., Barrett, C., Kochenderfer, M.J.: Algorithms for verifying deep neural networks. arXiv preprint arXiv:1903.06758 (2019)
38. Majumdar, A., Pavone, M.: How should a robot assess risk? towards an axiomatic theory of risk in robotics. In: Amato, N.M., Hager, G., Thomas, S., Torres-Torriti, M. (eds.) Robotics Research. SPAR, vol. 10, pp. 75–84. Springer, Cham (2020). https://doi.org/10.1007/978-3-030-28619-4_10
39. Majumdar, A., Vasudevan, R., Tobenkin, M.M., Tedrake, R.: Convex optimization of nonlinear feedback controllers via occupation measures. Int. J. Robot. Res. **33**(9), 1209–1230 (2014)

40. Manzinger, S., Pek, C., Althoff, M.: Using reachable sets for trajectory planning of automated vehicles. IEEE Trans. Intell. Veh. 6(2), 232–248 (2020)
41. McNaughton, M., Urmson, C., Dolan, J.M., Lee, J.W.: Motion planning for autonomous driving with a conformal spatiotemporal lattice. In: 2011 IEEE International Conference on Robotics and Automation, pp. 4889–4895. IEEE (2011)
42. Meng, Y., Sun, D., Qiu, Z., Waez, M.T.B., Fan, C.: Learning density distribution of reachable states for autonomous systems. arXiv preprint arXiv:2109.06728 (2021)
43. Mitchell, I.M., Bayen, A.M., Tomlin, C.J.: A time-dependent hamilton-jacobi formulation of reachable sets for continuous dynamic games. IEEE Trans. Autom. Control 50(7), 947–957 (2005)
44. Paden, B Čáp, M., Yong, S.Z., Yershov, D., Frazzoli, E.: A survey of motion planning and control techniques for self-driving urban vehicles. IEEE Trans. Intell. Veh. 1(1), 33–55 (2016)
45. Paszke, A., et al.: Pytorch: an imperative style, high-performance deep learning library. Adv. Neural Inf. Process. Syst. 32, 8026–8037 (2019)
46. Pivtoraiko, M., Knepper, R.A., Kelly, A.: Differentially constrained mobile robot motion planning in state lattices. J. Field Robot. 26(3), 308–333 (2009)
47. Qian, X., Altché, F., Bender, P., Stiller, C., de La Fortelle, A.: Optimal trajectory planning for autonomous driving integrating logical constraints: an miqp perspective. In: 2016 IEEE 19th International Conference on Intelligent Transportation Systems (ITSC), pp. 205–210. IEEE (2016)
48. Rasmussen, M., Rieger, J., Webster, K.N.: Approximation of reachable sets using optimal control and support vector machines. J. Comput. Appl. Math. 311, 68–83 (2017)
49. Robbins, H., Siegmund, D.: A convergence theorem for non negative almost supermartingales and some applications. In: Optimizing Methods in Statistics, pp. 233–257. Elsevier (1971)
50. Shkolnik, A., Walter, M., Tedrake, R.: Reachability-guided sampling for planning under differential constraints. In 2009 IEEE International Conference on Robotics and Automation, pp. 2859–2865. IEEE (2009)
51. Thorpe, A.J., Ortiz, K.R., Oishi, M.M.K.: Data-driven stochastic reachability using hilbert space embeddings. arXiv preprint arXiv:2010.08036 (2020)
52. Toth, C.D., O'Rourke, J., Goodman, J.E.: Handbook of Discrete and Computational Geometry. CRC Press (2017)
53. Tran, H.D., et al.: NNV: the neural network verification tool for deep neural networks and learning-enabled cyber-physical systems. In: Lahiri, S.K., Wang, C. (eds.) CAV 2020. LNCS, vol. 12224, pp. 3–17. Springer, Cham (2020). https://doi.org/10.1007/978-3-030-53288-8_1
54. Vincent, J.A., Schwager, M.: Reachable polyhedral marching (rpm): A safety verification algorithm for robotic systems with deep neural network components. arXiv preprint arXiv:2011.11609 (2020)
55. Xiang, W., Tran, H.D., Johnson, T.T.: Output reachable set estimation and verification for multilayer neural networks. IEEE Trans. Neural Netw. Learn. Syst. 29(11), 5777–5783 (2018)
56. Xue, B., Zhang, M., Easwaran, A., Li, Q.: PAC model checking of black-box continuous-time dynamical systems. IEEE Trans. Comput.-Aid. Des. Integr. Circ. Syst. 39(11), 3944–3955 (2020)

57. Yang, X., Tran, H.-D., Xiang, W., Johnson, T.: Reachability analysis for feedforward neural networks using face lattices. arXiv preprint arXiv:2003.01226 (2020)
58. Zeng, W.: End-to-end interpretable neural motion planner. In: Proceedings of the IEEE/CVF Conference on Computer Vision and Pattern Recognition, pp. 8660–8669 (2019)

Towards Refactoring FRETish Requirements

Marie Farrell[✉], Matt Luckcuck, Oisín Sheridan, and Rosemary Monahan

Department of Computer Science and Hamilton Institute, Maynooth University, Co.,
Kildare, Ireland
{marie.farrell,matt.luckcuck,rosemary.monahan}@mu.ie,
oisin.sheridan.2019@mumail.ie

Abstract. Like software, requirements evolve and change frequently
during the development process. Refactoring is the process of reorganis-
ing software without changing its behaviour, to make it easier to understand and modify. We propose refactoring for formalised requirements
to reduce repetition in the requirement set so that they are easier to
maintain as the system and requirements evolve. This work-in-progress
paper describes our motivation for and initial approach to refactoring
requirements in NASA's Formal Requirements Elicitation Tool (FRET).
This work was directly triggered by our experience with an industrial
aircraft engine software controller use case. In this paper, we reflect on
the requirements that were obtained and, with a view to their maintainability, propose and outline functionality for refactoring FRETISH requirements.

Keywords: Refactoring · Formal requirements · FRET

1 Introduction and Background

Detailed requirements elicitation is an important step in the software development process. This often begins with a set of natural-language requirements,
which then evolve as the project progresses, as additional functionality is added,
and as bugs reveal unintended or unsafe system behaviour. For safety-critical
systems, requirements can often be drawn from standards or regulator guidance, and verifying that the system's design and implementation preserve these
requirements can be an integral part of securing approval to use the system.

The authors thank Georgios Giantamidis, Stylianos Basagiannis, and Vassilios A. Tsa-
chouridis (United Technologies Research Center, Ireland) for their collaboration in the
requirements elicitation process; and Anastasia Mavridou (KBR/NASA Ames Research
Center, USA) for her help with FRET.

This research was financially supported by the European Union's Horizon 2020 research
and innovation programme under the VALU3S project (grant No 876852). This project
is also funded by Enterprise Ireland (grant No IR20200054). The funders had no role
in study design, data collection and analysis, decision to publish, or preparation of the
manuscript.

J. V. Deshmukh et al. (Eds.): NFM 2022, LNCS 13260, pp. 272–279, 2022.
https://doi.org/10.1007/978-3-031-06773-0_14

Formal methods can provide robust verification that gives developers and regulators the confidence that the system functions correctly and safely. However, natural-language requirements can be difficult to express in the logical formalisms that formal methods use. Tools such as NASA's Formal Requirements Elicitation Tool (FRET) plug this gap by providing a structured natural requirements language (called FRETISH) that has an underlying temporal logic semantics, which can be used directly as input to formal methods tools [3, 8].

Through examining recent work [4], we see that sets of natural-language requirements can contain many similar requirements, as well as dependencies between requirements. This makes the necessary task of maintaining the requirements tedious and error-prone, as the system and its requirements evolve.

In software engineering, refactoring is the process of improving the structure of the software without altering its functionality [7]. An example is using the EXTRACT METHOD refactoring, which extracts a large piece of code into a method, to simplify and modularise the program. This is often used when the same functionality is repeated throughout the program. Here we investigate how to use refactoring to simplify and modularise requirements.

The cleaner code produced by refactoring is easier to maintain, examine, understand and update. Like software, requirements often go through several iterations before they are complete. Even then, they may need updating, if an error is found or a new feature is added. This means that their structure is almost as important as the software that they specify.

We view the maintenance of a requirements set to have similar benefits to the maintenance of software, namely that the requirements can be modified more easily with a reduced potential for human error. The notion of refactoring requirements is not new and has been previously explored in [13]. Here, we introduce the idea for FRET through examining how refactoring can be applied to the FRETISH requirements for an aircraft engine controller system.

Within the VALU3S project[1], we elicited and formalised requirements for an aircraft engine software controller use case with our industrial partner [5, 9]. We are now constructing formal models of the system to verify the requirements against, and generating verification conditions from the requirements. At this stage, it is important that our FRETISH requirements are easy to maintain and update, should new or modified functionality be developed. As a result, we are devising an approach to refactoring these requirements to reduce repetition and aid the maintainabilty of the requirements set. We take inspiration from prior work on refactoring natural-language requirements [13] and apply it to formal requirements with an additional step to check that the refactored requirement preserves the meaning of its unrefactored counterpart.

This work-in-progress paper explores how formalised FRET requirements can be refactored, and illustrates our refactoring process via our industrial, aerospace use case. We begin by providing a brief analysis of the requirements in our use case and introduce refactoring for FRETISH requirements. We then discuss the ways in which refactoring might be suppoorted in FRET.

---

[1] https://valu3s.eu/.

Table 1. UC5_R_1–UC5_R_4 of the natural-language requirements for the aircraft engine controller. These 4 requirements are mainly concerned with continued operation of the controller in the presence of sensor faults [5].

ID	Description
UC5_R_1	Under sensor faults, while tracking pilot commands, control objectives shall be satisfied (e.g., settling time, overshoot, and steady state error will be within predefined, acceptable limits)
UC5_R_2	Under sensor faults, during regulation of nominal system operation (no change in pilot input), control objectives shall be satisfied (e.g., settling time, overshoot, and steady state error will be within predefined, acceptable limits)
UC5_R_3	Under sensor faults, while tracking pilot commands, operating limit objectives shall be satisfied (e.g., respecting upper limit in shaft speed)
UC5_R_4	Under sensor faults, during regulation of nominal system operation (no change in pilot input), operating limit objectives shall be satisfied (e.g., respecting upper limit in shaft speed)

2   Refactoring Requirements

This section provides an overview and brief analysis of the requirements that we elicited for the aircraft engine software controller use case (originally presented in [5]) and describes our approach to refactoring them.

2.1   Analysis: Aircraft Engine Controller Requirements

Previously, we presented 14 natural-language requirements for an industrial aircraft engine controller which we formalised using FRET [5]. Table 1 contains the first 4 of these requirements, which were constructed independently by our industrial partner. It was clear to us from the outset that these requirements were repetitive, for example the phrase '*Under sensor faults*' appears in several requirements (4/14 in total).

To preserve traceability between the natural language requirements and their corresponding FRETISH encodings we opted for a one-to-one mapping, where each natural-language requirement corresponds to one (parent) requirement in FRETISH. FRETISH requirements have the following structure and fields:

  scope condition **component shall** timing **response**

Here, the **scope** and timing fields are optional. Users specify a condition under which a **component** shall satisfy a **response**. For example the FRETISH encoding of UC5_R_1 is: if((sensorFaults)&(trackingPilotCommands)) **Controller shall satisfy (controlObjectives)**. '*Under sensor faults*' maps to the boolean sensorFaults, and the other requirements (Table 1) follow a similar structure.

Since we adopted a one-to-one mapping, the repetition of '*Under sensor faults*' is mirrored by the repetition of sensorFaults in the FRETISH requirements. We refer to these repeated pieces as requirement *fragments*. We identified 7 fragments in our 14 abstract requirements, and each fragment was repeated in between 4 and 7 of the 14 requirements. Figure 1 shows the dependencies between the requirements and specific fragments and includes the natural-language description of the fragments themselves.

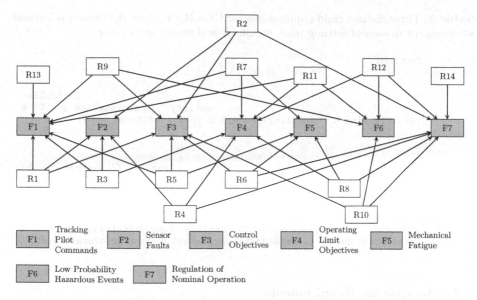

Fig. 1. Dependency graph: arrows indicate a 'depends on' relationship between requirements (white boxes) and fragments (grey boxes).

Once the high-level requirements were encoded in FRETISH, we elicited 28 detailed child requirements that expanded the definitions of the abstract terms in the 14 parent requirements [5]. UC5_R_1 has 3 child requirements (Table 2). Each of these contains the expanded, more detailed definition of `sensorFaults`:

`(sensorValue(S) > nominalValue + R) | (sensorValue(S) < nominalValue - R) | (sensorValue(S) = null)`

As expected, this repetition of definitions in the child requirements makes the requirements set more difficult to maintain, because changes to the definition of one fragment cause updates in multiple places. For example, if the definition of `sensorFaults` were to change, as it did during the elicitation process, then 8 of the 28 child requirements would require updating. This process is time-consuming, tedious, and error prone. A better approach would be to update the definition of `sensorFaults` in one place and avoid this duplication of effort.

`sensorFaults` corresponds to one detailed clause in each child requirement, but this was not the case for all fragments. For example, `trackingPilotCommands` corresponds to a condition (`when (diff(r(i),y(i))>E)`) and a timing constraint (`until (diff(r(i),y(i))<e)`). An automatic approach to refactoring FRETISH requirements would be even more helpful in similar situations where an abstract requirement corresponds to multiple detailed clauses.

Next, we outline our approach to refactoring FRETISH requirements, taking inspiration from prior work on refactoring natural-language requirements.

Table 2. Three distinct child requirements for UC5_R_1 capture the correct behaviour with respect to each of settling time, overshoot and steady state error.

ID	FRETISH
UC5_R_1.1	when (diff(r(i),y(i)) > E) if((sensorValue(S) > nominalValue + R) | (sensorValue(S) < nominalValue - R) | (sensorValue(S) = null) & (pilotInput => setThrust = V2) & (observedThrust = V1)) **Controller** shall until (diff(r(i),y(i)) < e) **satisfy (settlingTime >= 0) & (settlingTime <= settlingTimeMax) & (observedThrust = V2)**
UC5_R_1.2	when (diff(r(i),y(i)) > E) if((sensorValue(S) > nominalValue + R) | (sensorValue(S) < nominalValue - R) | (sensorValue(S) = null)& (pilotInput => setThrust = V2) & (observedThrust = V1)) **Controller** shall until (diff(r(i),y(i)) < e) **satisfy (overshoot >= 0) & (overshoot <= overshootMax) & (observedThrust = V2)**
UC5_R_1.3	when (diff(r(i),y(i)) > E) if((sensorValue(S) > nominalValue + R) | (sensorValue(S) < nominalValue - R) | (sensorValue(S) = null)& (pilotInput => setThrust = V2)& (observedThrust = V1)) **Controller** shall until (diff(r(i),y(i)) < e) **satisfy (steadyStateError >= 0) & (steadyStateError <= steadyStateErrorMax) & (observedThrust = V2)**

2.2   Refactoring Requirements

We briefly show how we specialise the classical refactoring, EXTRACT METHOD [7], to requirements. EXTRACT METHOD extracts code into a method, so that it can be called rather than copying code snippets. Our specialisation is based on the EXTRACT REQUIREMENT refactoring in [13]; but with an extra step, facilitated by FRET's automatic translation of requirements to temporal logic.

We begin by creating a new requirement to contain the behaviour that we wish to extract. We then replace the extracted behaviour in the original requirement with a reference to the new one. Finally, we check that the restructuring has not altered the behaviour of the original requirement, and we propagate this change throughout the requirements set.

EXTRACT REQUIREMENT allows us to define the sensorFaults fragment in one place. Then, individual requirements essentially 'call' the fragment in a similar way to method calls in object oriented programming languages. Supporting this 'calling' capability in FRET is part of our current work.

We chose FRET because it facilitates the formal verification that an implementation obeys its requirements. We intend to translate FRETISH requirements into other formalisms for verification [9]; so it is important that they are easy to maintain, if and when formal methods tools find problems in the system.

When refactoring the FRETISH encodings of requirements we can formally verify that the refactoring preserves the semantics of the original requirements. The Linear-time Temporal Logic (LTL) representation FRET generates enables us to perform the 'compile and test' step that is included in software refactoring [7] but not previously addressed for refactoring natural-language requirements [13]. Specifically, this involves checking that the temporal logic version of the requirements before refactoring has taken place is the same as that after (i.e. that the behaviour has not changed). This can be achieved by checking that the two temporal logic formulae are equivalent; or that the refactored requirement implies the original.

There are many other refactorings that might be applied such as the PULL UP METHOD refactoring that also helps to remove code duplication. This is particularly relevant for the child requirements and is used to eliminate duplication in sibling subclasses [7]. We are currently investigating how this might be applied in our requirements set.

3   Towards FRET-Supported Refactoring

FRET does not currently support refactoring. This section outlines our initial investigations into how automatic refactoring functionality could be included.

FRET requirements are not aware of one another. For example, although one requirement might depend on another requirement, it cannot *call the* other requirement in the way that a program can call a method. Requirements can be linked by a parent-child relationship but this is superficial at present, although it is useful from a user-perspective for maintaining traceability as requirements evolve.

We propose an additional requirement type, called FRAGMENT, that can be called from other requirements. This will involve updating the FRET interface and will lead to minor modifications to the generation of LTL specifications. FRET uses an in-built bank of templates to generate the LTL semantics for each requirement [8]. Templates take the form: [<*scope-option*>, <*condition-option*>, <*timing-option*>]. Since each FRAGMENT will be a specialised requirement, each will produce a template. When generating the LTL semantics for a requirement that references a FRAGMENT, it will be necessary to combine the templates of the FRAGMENT and the requirement to produce a complete template.

In general we think that combining templates can be achieved by taking the union of the *scope, condition*, and *timing* fields (respectively). However, we can also see specific situations where this simple approach might fail; e.g., if we combine two distinct timing options, should they be summed or should one take precedence (if so, which one)? We leave this investigation as future work.

Users should be able to refactor existing requirements *and* create fragments from scratch. Refactoring existing requirements could be realised, similarly to refactoring code in Eclipse[2], by selecting the part of a requirement to become a FRAGMENT and selecting (from a context-menu) that it should be extracted. The FRET interface should also provide the option to 'create FRAGMENT'.

When refactoring existing requirements, FRET should check that the original and refactored requirements (including the extracted FRAGMENT(s)) are equivalent. FRET already checks the equivalence of the past- and future-time LTL for each requirement, this step performs a similar check between requirements.

FRET links to the CoCoSim [2] and Copilot [12] verification tools. The translations to these tools would now require an extra step to address refactored

---

[2] Eclipse: https://www.eclipse.org/ide/.

requirements. A naive approach would involve recombining the fragments, effectively 'unrefactoring' the requirement. This would be hidden from the user, with the fully expanded requirement only appearing in the generated verification conditions. However, if the user wanted to edit the generated conditions, the original problems with repetition in the requirements would reappear.

A more sophisticated approach would carry the refactoring relationship through to the generated conditions. For example, in CoCoSim, guarantees would be generated corresponding to the fragments, but investigating how these guarantees are combined whilst preserving the semantics of the requirement is future work.

Recent work has formally verified the FRET design using the PVS theorem prover [3]. The changes that we propose in this paper by including a designated FRAGMENT requirement type and related refactoring functionality would need to be similarly verified to preserve the trustworthiness and integrity of FRET. This would likely involve extending the PVS specification and associated denotational semantics in [3] to support and verify the refactoring features that we propose.

4   Conclusion

This paper presents our work-in-progress on refactoring FRET requirements, which is directly motivated by our specification of an industrial aircraft engine controller use case. We demonstrated that repetition in natural-language requirements can cause difficulty when maintaining a set of corresponding formalised requirements, and presented an approach to refactoring requirements that extends an existing approach in the literature. We have also outlined how we intend to implement this in FRET as future work.

Other FRET studies have not encountered such a strong need for refactoring [1,6,10]. However, these do not directly involve an industry partner throughout the requirements elicitation and formalisation process. Our study is unique, since it is the first published use of FRET in an industrial case study where development of the system is ongoing [5]. That said, recent FRETISH requirements for a liquid mixer [11] exhibit some repetition, so may benefit from our refactoring approach. Investigating refactoring for FRET in other use cases is an important avenue of future work.

References

1. Bourbouh, H., et al.: Integrating formal verification and assurance: an inspection rover case study. In: Dutle, A., Moscato, M.M., Titolo, L., Muñoz, C.A., Perez, I. (eds.) NFM 2021. LNCS, vol. 12673, pp. 53–71. Springer, Cham (2021). https://doi.org/10.1007/978-3-030-76384-8_4
2. Bourbouh, H., Garoche, P.L., Loquen, T., Noulard, É., Pagetti, C.: CoCoSim, a code generation framework for control/command applications an overview of CoCoSim for multi-periodic discrete Simulink models. In: European Congress on Embedded Real Time Software and Systems (2020)

3. Conrad, E., Titolo, L., Giannakopoulou, D., Pressburger, T., Dutle, A.: A compositional proof framework for FRETish requirements. In: Proceedings of the 11th ACM SIGPLAN International Conference on Certified Programs and Proofs, pp. 68–81 (2022)
4. Deshpande, G., Arora, C., Ruhe, G.: Data-driven elicitation and optimization of dependencies between requirements. In: International Requirements Engineering Conference, pp. 416–421. IEEE (2019)
5. Farrell, M., Luckcuck, M., Sheridan, O., Monahan, R.: FRETting about requirements: formalised requirements for an aircraft engine controller. In: Gervasi, V., Vogelsang, A. (eds.) Requirements Engineering: Foundation for Software Quality. REFSQ 2022. LNCS, vol. 13216, pp. 96–111. Springer, Cham (2022). https://doi.org/10.1007/978-3-030-98464-9_9
6. Farrell, M., Mavrakis, N., Ferrando, A., Dixon, C., Gao, Y.: Formal modelling and runtime verification of autonomous grasping for active debris removal. Front. Robot. AI **8**, 639282 (2022)
7. Fowler, M., Beck, K.: Refactoring: improving the design of existing code. The Addison-Wesley object technology series. Addison-Wesley (1999)
8. Giannakopoulou, D., Pressburger, T., Mavridou, A., Schumann, J.: Automated formalization of structured natural language requirements. Inf. Software Technol. **137**, 106590 (2021)
9. Luckcuck, M., Farrell, M., Sheridan, O., Monahan, R.: A methodology for developing a verifiable aircraft engine controller from formal requirements. In: IEEE Aerospace Conference (2022)
10. Mavridou, A., et al.: The ten Lockheed martin cyber-physical challenges: formalized, analyzed, and explained. In: International Requirements Engineering Conference, pp. 300–310. IEEE (2020)
11. Mavridou, A., Katis, A., Giannakopoulou, D., Kooi, D., Pressburger, T., Whalen, M.W.: From Partial to global assume-guarantee contracts: compositional realizability analysis in FRET. In: Huisman, M., Păsăreanu, C., Zhan, N. (eds.) FM 2021. LNCS, vol. 13047, pp. 503–523. Springer, Cham (2021). https://doi.org/10.1007/978-3-030-90870-6_27
12. Perez, I., Dedden, F., Goodloe, A.: Copilot 3. Technical report, NASA/TM-2020-220587, National Aeronautics and Space Administration (2020)
13. Ramos, R., et al.: Improving the Quality of Requirements with Refactoring. In: Simpósio Brasileiro de Qualidade de Software, pp. 141–155. Sociedade Brasileira de Computação (2007)

Neural Network Compression of ACAS Xu Early Prototype Is Unsafe: Closed-Loop Verification Through Quantized State Backreachability

Stanley Bak[1(✉)] and Hoang-Dung Tran[2]

[1] Stony Brook University, Stony Brook, NY, USA
stanley.bak@stonybrook.edu
[2] University of Nebraska-Lincoln, Lincoln, NE, USA
dtran30@unl.edu

Abstract. ACAS Xu is an air-to-air collision avoidance system designed for unmanned aircraft that issues horizontal turn advisories to avoid an intruder aircraft. Due the use of a large lookup table in the design, a neural network compression of the policy was proposed. Analysis of this system has spurred a significant body of research in the formal methods community on neural network verification. While many powerful methods have been developed, most work focuses on open-loop properties of the networks, rather than the main point of the system—collision avoidance—which requires closed-loop analysis.

In this work, we develop a technique to verify a closed-loop approximation of the system using *state quantization* and *backreachability*. We use favorable assumptions for the analysis—perfect sensor information, instant following of advisories, ideal aircraft maneuvers and an intruder that only flies straight. When the method fails to prove the system is safe, we refine the quantization parameters until generating counterexamples where the original (non-quantized) system also has collisions.

Keywords: Neural network verification · ACAS Xu · Reachability

1 Introduction

The Airborne Collision Avoidance System X (ACAS X) is a mid-air collision avoidance system under development [26], with the ACAS Xu variant focused on collision avoidance for unmanned aircraft [20]. Originally designed offline using dynamic programming and Markov decision processes (MDPs) [21], the large rule table was compressed by a factor of 1000 using a set of neural networks [19]. The proposed system is an example of a neural network control system (NNCS), where the system's execution alternates between the aircraft dynamics and a neural network controller. As collision avoidance is safety-critical, analysis of the neural networks has spurred a significant body of research on neural network

© Springer Nature Switzerland AG 2022
J. V. Deshmukh et al. (Eds.): NFM 2022, LNCS 13260, pp. 280–298, 2022.
https://doi.org/10.1007/978-3-031-06773-0_15

verification. Most existing work, however, focuses on *open-loop* verification, such as property ϕ_3 from the original work [20], which states, "if the intruder is directly ahead and is moving towards the ownship, [a turn will be commanded]." Open-loop properties can be expressed in terms of constraints over the inputs and outputs of a single execution of the neural network. However, satisfying open-loop properties does not prove the system is safe, as this requires reasoning with the physical system dynamics—how the aircraft responds to turn commands. Also, the system is running continuously and may change advisories at a future time, complicating safety analysis. Verification of closed-loop safety of provided collision avoidance system under all designed operating conditions is thus a sort of grand challenge.

While verification of neural networks is continuously improving, an intriguing alternate approach has recently been proposed based on input quantization [15]. Rather than verifying the neural network directly, which requires reasoning about the semantics at each layer, the system's execution semantics are changed to round the inputs to a discrete set of possible values before running the network. To be clear, this type of quantization is a preprocessing layer before the network runs; it does not change the representation of the floating-point values inside the network itself. Through input quantization, proving open-loop properties of a neural network is reduced to the problem of *network execution* for each of a finite set of possible inputs. Due to the possibility of combinatorial explosion, this strategy can only work if the number of inputs is small, which is often the case for neural networks used in control systems. When the strategy is applicable, however, it enjoys several advantages: (i) batch execution of neural networks is often used in training and so optimized hardware like GPUs can be leveraged to enumerate the possible inputs for verification, (ii) the performance of the final quantized system approximates the performance of the original neural network and the approximation can be tuned through the quantization parameters, and (iii) the verification method only requires execution, and works regardless of the network size, the network architecture, or the layer types, unlike most neural network verification methods. In the context of verification, however, quantization has only been considered for open-loop properties.

In this work, we propose an approach to formally verify quantized closed-loop NNCS. Although the technique is general, we focus primarily on proving safety for quantized version of the well-studied aircraft collision avoidance neural network benchmark. Two key ideas are needed to make this work: (1) we perform *state quantization* rather than input quantization and (2) we use *back-reachability* from the unsafe states to reduce the number of partitions. We prove the approach is sound and complete, in the sense that by continuing to refine quantization parameters, either the quantized system will eventually be proven safe or an unsafe counterexample will be found in the original system. When the method fails to prove safety of quantized closed-loop system, we refine the quantization values until discovering cases where the original (unquantized) version of the system fails. We also show that with stricter assumptions on the ownship aircraft's velocity, the quantized system can guarantee safety.

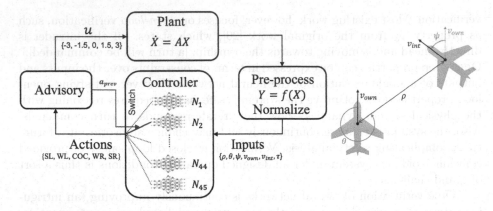

Fig. 1. The closed-loop air-to-air collision avoidance system design.

2   Background and Problem Formulation

We next review key aspects of the system design, proof assumptions, and provide background on $\mathcal{AH}$-Polytopes before formulating the safety verification problem.

2.1   Collision Avoidance System Design

We are interested in safety verification and falsification of the *closed-loop* air-to-air collision avoidance system [20,21] depicted in Fig. 1. The system computes advisory commands to control an ownship aircraft with physical dynamics described by a set of ordinary differential equations (ODEs), trying to avoid collisions with a nearby intruder.

A detailed description of the inputs and actions in the system is shown in Table 1. The system receives 7 inputs about the state of an ownship and a nearby intruder aircraft, $\mathcal{I} = \{\rho, \theta, \psi, v_{own}, v_{int}, \tau, a_{prev}\}$, and produces one of five possible advisories for the ownship, $\mathcal{A} = \{\text{COC, WL, WR, SL, SR}\}$.

The turn advisories in the system are generated by 45 deep ReLU neural networks with 6 layers and 50 neurons per layer for each network. Control switches between different neural networks $N_{a_{prev},\tau}$ based on the previous advisory a_{prev} (total of 5 choices) and the time until loss of vertical separation $\tau = \{0, 1, 5, 10, 20, 50, 60, 80, 100\}$ (total of 9 choices). For example, the network $N_{5,3}$ will be invoked if the previous advisory is $a_{prev} = \text{SR}$ and $\tau = 5$. If the ownship and the intruder are at the same altitude, then $\tau = 0$ and only five neural network controllers need to be used, $N_{1,1}, N_{2,1}, N_{3,1}, N_{4,1}$, and $N_{5,1}$.

2.2   Assumptions and Plant Model

Before we describe the plant model used in analysis, we first state our system assumptions: (i) the intruder flies in straight-line trajectories with constant speed, (ii) the ownship flies with constant speed and its heading is adjusted every second (the NNCS control period), (iii) the actions correspond to heading changes in the intruder of 1.5 deg/sec for weak turn commands, 3.0 deg/sec for strong turns and 0.0 deg/sec for clear-of-conflict commands [19], (iv) there is no sensor noise and (v) advisories are followed exactly and immediately. Many of these are fairly strong and the real system would need to be robust to maneuvering intruders, pilot delay and sensor noise. From a safety proof perspective, however, we would want the system to *at least* be safe under these ideal assumptions.

To model the state of the system with these assumptions, we use Cartesian coordinates. The values $x_{own}, y_{own}, x_{int}, y_{int}$ refer to the x and y positions of the ownship and the intruder; $v_{own} = \sqrt{(v_{own}^x)^2 + (v_{own}^y)^2}$ and $v_{int} = \sqrt{(v_{int}^x)^2 + (v_{int}^y)^2}$ are the speed of the ownship and the intruder; θ_{own} and θ_{int} are the heading of the ownship and the intruder w.r.t the x axis. The system performs idealized turn maneuvers modeled with Dubins aircraft dynamics:

$$
\begin{aligned}
\dot{x}_{own} &= v_{own}^x = v_{own}cos(\theta_{own}) \\
\dot{y}_{own} &= v_{own}^y = v_{own}sin(\theta_{own}) \\
\dot{x}_{int} &= v_{int}^x = v_{int}cos(\theta_{int}) \\
\dot{y}_{int} &= v_{int}^y = v_{int}sin(\theta_{int})
\end{aligned}
\tag{1}
$$

Equation 1 does not show clearly how the aircraft can be controlled by changing their heading. Taking derivatives of the Eq. 1 one more time and noticing that $\dot{\theta}_{own}$ is a constant between advisories, $\dot{\theta}_{own} = (\pi/180)u = c(rad/s)$, and then taking $\dot{\theta}_{int} = 0$, we obtain the following 8-d linear system dynamics:

$$
\begin{bmatrix}
\dot{x}_{own} \\
\dot{y}_{own} \\
\dot{v}_{own}^x \\
\dot{v}_{own}^y \\
\dot{x}_{int} \\
\dot{y}_{int} \\
\dot{v}_{int}^x \\
\dot{v}_{int}^y
\end{bmatrix}
=
\begin{bmatrix}
0 & 0 & 1 & 0 & 0 & 0 & 0 & 0 \\
0 & 0 & 0 & 1 & 0 & 0 & 0 & 0 \\
0 & 0 & 0 & -c & 0 & 0 & 0 & 0 \\
0 & 0 & c & 0 & 0 & 0 & 0 & 0 \\
0 & 0 & 0 & 0 & 0 & 0 & 1 & 0 \\
0 & 0 & 0 & 0 & 0 & 0 & 0 & 1 \\
0 & 0 & 0 & 0 & 0 & 0 & 0 & 0 \\
0 & 0 & 0 & 0 & 0 & 0 & 0 & 0
\end{bmatrix}
\begin{bmatrix}
x_{own} \\
y_{own} \\
v_{own}^x \\
v_{own}^y \\
x_{int} \\
y_{int} \\
v_{int}^x \\
v_{int}^y
\end{bmatrix}
\tag{2}
$$

Table 1. Input variables used to produce a turn advisory.

Input	Units	Description	Action	Description
ρ	ft	Distance between ownship and intruder	SL	Strong left turn at 3.0 deg/s
θ	rad	Angle to intruder w.r.t ownship heading	WL	Weak left at turn 1.5 deg/s
ψ	rad	Heading of intruder w.r.t ownship	COC	Clear of conflict (do nothing)
v_{own}	ft/s	Velocity of ownship	WR	Weak right turn at 1.5 deg/s
v_{int}	ft/s	Velocity of intruder	SR	Strong right turn at 3.0 deg/s
τ	s	Time until loss of vertical separation		
a_{prev}		previous advisory		

The linear model described in Eq. 2 is valid for only one control step, with a fixed control signal u, which may be either $-3, -1.5, 0, 1.5$ or 3 deg/s depending on the specific command. Therefore, this model can be considered as a piece-wise linear model of the system. From the plant state variables, we can obtain the inputs for the neural network controller which are expected to in radial coordinates as follows.

$$\theta_{own} = arctan(\frac{v_{own}^y}{v_{own}^x}), \quad \theta_{int} = arctan(\frac{v_{int}^y}{v_{int}^x}),$$

$$\rho = \sqrt{(x_{int} - x_{own})^2 + (y_{int} - y_{own})^2}, \tag{3}$$

$$\theta = arctan(\frac{y_{int} - y_{own}}{x_{int} - x_{own}}) - \theta_{own}, \quad \psi = \theta_{int} - \theta_{own}.$$

2.3 Reachability with $\mathcal{AH}$-Polytopes

An $\mathcal{AH}$-polytope is a set representation that informally is an affine transformation of a half-space polytope, where the affine transformation and polytope terms are explicitly kept separate. Although the name is fairly recent [27], this set representation has often been used in reachability analysis for linear systems [2,5] and neural networks [4,30], where it is also called a linear star set [8], constrained zonotope [28], affine form [12], or symbolic orthogonal projection [11].

Importantly for this work, discrete-time reachability of systems with linear dynamics, $\dot{x} = Ax$, can be expressed exactly using this set representation, as it amounts to a linear transformation of the entire set by the matrix exponential e^{At}, where t is the time step. Further, operations like intersections can be performed exactly on $\mathcal{AH}$-polytopes, as well as linear optimization over the sets.

Definition 1 ($\mathcal{AH}$-Polytope). *An $\mathcal{AH}$-Polytope is a tuple $\Theta = \langle V, c, C, d \rangle$ that represents a set of states as follows:*

$$[\![\Theta]\!] = \{x \in \mathbb{R}^n \mid \exists \alpha \in \mathbb{R}^m, \ x = V\alpha + c \wedge C\alpha \leq d\}.$$

Proposition 1 (Affine Mapping). *An affine mapping of an $\mathcal{AH}$-Polytope $\Theta = \langle V, c, C, d \rangle$ with a mapping matrix W and an offset vector b is a new $\mathcal{AH}$-Polytope $\Theta' = \langle V', c', C', d' \rangle$ in which $V' = WV$, $c' = Wc + b$, $C' = C$, $d' = d$.*

Proposition 2 (Linear Transformation). *A linear transformation of an $\mathcal{AH}$-Polytope with a matrix W is an affine mapping using mapping matrix W and an offset vector of $b = 0$.*

Proposition 3 (Intersection). *The intersection of $\Theta = \langle V, c, C, d \rangle$ and a half-space $\mathcal{H} = \{x \mid Gx \leq g\}$ is a new $\mathcal{AH}$-Polytope $\Theta' = \langle V', c', C', d' \rangle$ with $c' = c$, $V' = V$, $C' = [C; GV]$, $d' = [d; g - Gc]$.*

Proposition 4 (Linear Optimization). *Linear optimization in given a direction $w \in \mathbb{R}^n$ over a star set $\Theta = \langle V, c, C, d \rangle$ can be solved with linear programming as follows: $\min(w^T x)$, s.t. $x \in \Theta = w^T c + \min(w^T V\alpha)$, s.t. $C\alpha \leq d$.*

2.4   Safety Problem Formulation

Verifying the safety of the closed-loop system means proving the absence of *unsafe paths* under all operating conditions. For simplified presentation, we consider a discrete-time version of the problem, where we only check for collisions once a second when the system is activated. Our analysis could be extended to continuous time through *conservative time-discretization* approaches from hybrid systems reachability analysis [10], which essentially bloat the initial set and then perform discrete-time analysis.

Definition 2 (Path). *A path is written as $s_1 \xrightarrow{\alpha_1} s_2 \xrightarrow{\alpha_2} \ldots \xrightarrow{\alpha_{n-1}} s_n$, where successive values of s_i and s_{i+1} correspond to the state of the system one second apart according to the plant dynamics in Eq. 2. The command α_i is the system output from state s_i using $\alpha_{prev} = \alpha_{i-1}$, with s_1 using the COC network. Paths can either be in-plane, where $\dot{\tau} = 0$ and $\tau = 0$ in all states and so the $N_{1,*}$ networks get used to generate all commands, or out-of-plane, where $\dot{\tau} = -1$. In the out-of-plane case, each state in the path should decrease τ by one second.*

An unsafe path has s_1 as an initial state and s_n as an unsafe state.

Definition 3 (Initial State). *An initial state of the state of the system is one where the aircraft are outside of the system's operating range ($\rho > 60760$ ft).*

Definition 4 (Unsafe State). *Unsafe states are defined to be any states in the near mid-air collision (NMAC) cylinder [25], where the horizontal separation ρ is less than 500 ft and the time to loss of vertical separation τ is zero seconds.*

The operating conditions where the system should ensure safety are extracted based on the training ranges used for the original neural networks [20,21]. The system should be active when the distance between aircraft $\rho \in [0, 60760]$ ft, otherwise clear-of-conflict is commanded. The valid values for the ownship velocity are $v_{own} \in [100, 1200]$ ft/sec, valid values for intruder velocity are $v_{int} \in [0, 1200]$ ft/sec, and the angular inputs θ and ψ are both between $-\pi$ and π.

3   Quantized State Backreachability

Our verification strategy is to compute the backwards reachable set of states from all possible unsafe states, trying to a find a path that begins with an initial state. We first partition the unsafe states along state quantization boundaries.

3.1   Partitioning the Unsafe States

Since the system advisories are only based on relative positions and headings, we eliminate symmetry by assuming that at the time of the collision the intruder is flying due east and at the origin. We then consider all possible positions of the ownship to account for all possible unsafe states. Three quantization parameters are used in the analysis: q_{pos} to quantize positions, q_{vel} to quantize velocities,

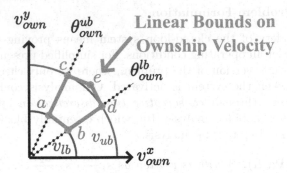

Fig. 2. The ownship velocity range and heading angle range are used to create linear bounds on v_{own}^x and v_{own}^y by connecting the points a, b, c, d and e.

and q_θ to quantize the heading angle. Based on these parameters, we partition the unsafe states into 8-d $\mathcal{AH}$-polytopes covering the entire set of possible unsafe states. The eight dimensions correspond to the system states in the linear dynamics in Eq. 2, including positions x, y, and velocities v^x, v^y for both the ownship and intruder. Associated with each partition, we also enumerate the five possible previous commands α_{prev} and two possibilities for whether there is a relative vertical velocity—whether the time to loss of vertical separation is fixed at 0 or decreasing, $\dot{\tau} \in \{0, -1\}$.

To create partitions, the x_{own} and y_{own} values are divided into a grid based on q_{pos}. The intruder position (x_{int}, y_{int}) is set to $(0,0)$. The intruder and ownship velocities are partitioned based on q_{vel}, which gets reflected in the x and y velocity state variables for the two aircraft. The intruder is moving due east, so $v_{int}^y = 0$ and v_{int}^x is set to the range of intruder velocities corresponding to the current partition. The heading of the angle of the ownship is partitioned based on q_θ, where each partition has a lower and upper bound on the heading $[\theta_{own}^{lb}, \theta_{own}^{ub}]$. From the current range of values for the ownship heading and the range of values for the ownship velocity, we can construct linear bounds on v_{own}^x and v_{own}^y. This is done by connecting five points, a, b, c, d and e, where a and b are the points at two extreme angles and minimum velocity, c and d are the two extreme angles and max velocity, and e is the point at the intersection of the tangent lines of the maximum velocity circle at c and d. A visualization is shown in Fig. 2. We generally use $q_\theta = 1.5$ deg (as it makes for a cleaner backreachability step), which guarantee all possible v_{own}^x, v_{own}^y values are covered.

3.2 Backreachability from Each Partition

Once a covering of the entire set of unsafe states is performed, for each partition we compute the *exact* set of predecessor states that can lead to the states in the partition at a previous step. This process is repeated until either no predecessors

```
Function: check_state, Recursively checks safety of predecessors
Input     : State set: S, Prev cmd: α_prev, Time to loss of vertical separation: τ
Output   : Verification Result (safe or unsafe)
1  P = backreach_step(S, α_prev) // state set of one-step predecessors
2  τ_prev = τ − τ̇ // τ̇ is fixed at either 0 or -1
3  for α_prevprev in [COC, WL, WR, SL, SR] do
4  │    predecessor_quanta ← List()
5  │    all_correct ← TRUE
6  │    for q in possible_quantized_states(P) do
7  │    │    if run_network(α_prevprev, τ_prev, q) = α_prev then
8  │    │    │    predecessor_quanta.append(q)
9  │    │    │    if ρ_min(q) > 60760 then
10 │    │    │    │    return unsafe // predecessor is valid initial state
11 │    │    else
12 │    │    │    all_correct ← FALSE
13 │    end
14 │    if all_correct then
15 │    │    // recursive case without splitting
16 │    │    if check_state(P, α_prevprev, τ_prev) = unsafe then
17 │    │    │    return unsafe
18 │    │    end
19 │    else
20 │    │    // recursive case with splitting along quantum boundaries
21 │    │    for q in predecessor_quanta do
22 │    │    │    T ← quantized_to_state_set(q)
23 │    │    │    Q ← T ∩ P
24 │    │    │    if check_state(Q, α_prevprev, τ_prev) = unsafe then
25 │    │    │    │    return unsafe
26 │    │    │    end
27 │    │    end
28 end
29 return safe
```

Algorithm 1: High-level algorithm for single partition backreachability.

exist or an initial state predecessor is found[1], as described in Definition 3. In the latter case, a path exists from an initial state to a partition of the unsafe states in the quantized closed-loop system. Otherwise, if no partitions contain unsafe paths, then the quantized closed-loop system is safe.

The check_state function in Algorithm 1 recursively computes and checks predecessors. The input is a state set S, which is initially an 8-d partition of the unsafe states represented as an $\mathcal{AH}$-Polytope, as well as the associated value of α_{prev} and the time to loss of vertical separation, $\tau = 0$ in all unsafe states.

In line 1, backreach_step is called, which returns the predecessor set of states as an $\mathcal{AH}$-polytope P. This is done by taking the linear derivative matrix

---

[1] Degenerate paths could theoretically exist of infinite length that never include a valid initial state, but we did not observe this occurring in practice.

A_c from Eq. 2 with the value of c corresponding to α_{prev}, and then computing the matrix exponential $W = e^{-A_c}$. The resulting matrix is the solution matrix for the system one second prior. A linear transformation of the $\mathcal{AH}$-polytope S is then performed by W in order to obtain $\mathcal{P}$. In line 2, the value of the time to loss of vertical separation at the previous step τ_{prev} is computed. This either always equals 0 if $\dot{\tau} = 0$ for the current partition corresponding to in-plane flight, or increases by 1 at each call to check_state if $\dot{\tau} = -1$ for out-of-plane flight.

Next, the algorithm computes states in $\mathcal{P}$ where the command produced by the networks was α_{prev} and the time to loss of vertical separation was the value at the previous step, τ_{prev}. This requires iterating over the five possible networks that could have been used at the prior state (the loop on line 3). For each network (corresponding to α_{prevprev}), we check each quantized state in $\mathcal{P}$ (line 6).

The possible_quantized_states returns a list of *quantized states*, which are 5-tuples of integers, $q = (dx, dy, \theta_{own}, v_{own}, v_{int})$. The dx and dy terms correspond to the difference in positions between the intruder and ownship, divided by the position quantum q_{pos}. The θ_{own} term is the heading angle divided by q_θ, and the velocities v_{own} and v_{int} are the fixed aircraft velocities, integer divided by q_{vel}. The function computes the possible quantized states by using linear programming to find $\mathcal{P}$'s bounding box, and then looping over possible quantized states to check for feasibility when intersected with $\mathcal{AH}$-polytope $\mathcal{P}$.

Line 7 runs the neural network corresponding to α_{prevprev} on quantized state q to check if the correct command (α_{prev}) is obtained. This process requires converting from the quantized state (a 5-tuple of integers) to continuous inputs for the neural network. To do this, we use Eq. 3, noting that the θ_{own} is quantized using q_θ, θ_{int} is always 0, and the computation of ρ and θ uses the dequantized value of dx and dy ($x_{int} - x_{own}$ is taken to be $\frac{q_{\text{pos}}}{2} + dx * q_{\text{pos}}$).

When the network output matches the required α_{prev} command, line 8 adds the quantized state to the valid list of predecessors predecessor_quanta. Otherwise, line 12 sets the all_correct flag to false, since some of the quantized states are not valid predecessors. Line 10 checks if the predecessor state satisfies the initial state condition, in which case an unsafe path has been found. On this line, $\rho_{\text{min}}(q)$ is the minimum aircraft separation distance in the quantized state q, which must be greater than 60760 ft in an initial state.

After classifying each quantized predecessor state, either all quantized states had the correct output or some did not. Based on this, we either recursively call check_state on the entire set $\mathcal{P}$ (line 16), or we split the set $\mathcal{P}$ into parts, and only recursively call check_state on parts that had the correct output. On line 22, quantized_to_state_set returns the 8-d continuous states corresponding to the quantized state q, which is then intersected with $\mathcal{P}$ before being recursively passed to check_state. When splitting is performed, it is possible that no states had the correct output (predecessor_quanta may be empty).

An illustration of the algorithm is provided in Fig. 3. In the figure, the set $\mathcal{P}$ is covered by nine quantized states returned by possible_quantized_states (the dots on the right side). Of these nine, eight have a correct output (blue

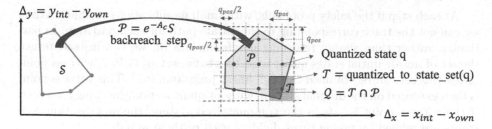

Fig. 3. Illustration of Algorithm 1 given state set $\mathcal{S}$.

dots), and one has an incorrect output (red dot). In this case, the algorithm would split the set $\mathcal{P}$ into eight parts and call check_state on each recursively[2].

We next prove the described algorithm is sound with respect to the safety of the quantized closed-loop system.

Theorem 1 (Soundness). *If* check_state *returns* safe *for every partition, the quantized closed-loop system is safe.*

Proof. We proceed by contraction. Assume the quantized closed-loop system is unsafe and so these exists a finite path from an initial state to an unsafe state, $s_1 \xrightarrow{\alpha_1} s_2 \xrightarrow{\alpha_2} \ldots \xrightarrow{\alpha_{n-1}} s_n$. Since the unsafe state partitioning covers the full set of unsafe states, the unsafe state s_n is in some partition. We can follow the progress of $s_n \in \mathcal{S}$, through check_state at each recursive call.

At each call, $s_i \in \mathcal{S}$ has a predecessor $s_{i-1} \in \mathcal{P}$ that gets to s_i using command α_{i-1}. In the call to check_state, α_{prev} will be α_{i-1}. The value of τ_{prev} is incremented at each call on line 2 and so always correctly corresponds to s_{i-1}. Since $s_{i-1} \in \mathcal{P}$, s_{i-1} will also be in one of the quantized states q_{i-1} checked on line 6. The existence of the counterexample path segment $\xrightarrow{\alpha_{i-2}} s_{i-1} \xrightarrow{\alpha_{i-1}} s_i$ means that the condition on line 7 will be true when $\alpha_{\text{prevprev}} = \alpha_{i-2}$, and so q_{i-1} will be added to predecessor_quanta. Since s_{i-1} is both in $\mathcal{P}$ and in the state set corresponding to a quantized state in predecessor_quanta, it will be used in a recursive call to check_state. This argument can be repeated for all states in the unsafe path back to the initial state s_1, which would have been returned as unsafe on line 10 rather than used in a recursive call. This contradicts the assumption that check_state returned safe for every partition. $\square$

3.3 Falsification of Original (Unquantized) System

The algorithm in the previous section can be used to efficiently find unsafe paths of the original, unquantized, closed-loop neural network control system. This is done by repeatedly calling the algorithm with smaller and smaller quantization constants q_{pos}, q_{vel} and q_θ and checking the quantized system for safety.

---

[2] An implementation optimization could be to reduce this splitting into only three parts. Three is the minimum in this case, since $\mathcal{AH}$-polytopes must be convex.

At each step if the safety proof fails, with small modifications to check_state we can get the trace corresponding to the unsafe path for each partition. In particular, rather than simply returning unsafe on line 10, we can instead return the set of unsafe initial states quantized_to_state_set(q) $\cap$ $\mathcal{P}$. A witness point inside this set can be obtained through linear programming[3]. This witness point is then executed on the original system, without quantization, checking for safety. If the witness point is safe in the non-quantized system, the quantization constants are refined by taking turns dividing each of them in half.

Theorem 2 (Completeness). *By following the falsification approach above and repeatedly refining q_{pos}, q_{vel} and q_θ, either we will prove the quantized system is safe or find an unsafe trace in the original, unquantized system.*

Proof. First, consider the case that the system is *robustly unsafe*, which we define as there existing a ball $\mathcal{B}_{init}$ of initial states of radius $\delta > 0$ that all follow the same command sequence $\alpha_1, \alpha_2, \ldots, \alpha_n$ and end in the unsafe set. Since all the initial states follow the same command sequence, the linear transformations corresponding to the commands $\alpha_1, \alpha_2, \ldots, \alpha_n$, which we call $A_{c_1}, A_{c_2}, \ldots, A_{c_n}$ can be multiplied together into a single matrix that transforms initial states to unsafe states, $A_C = A_{c_n} \ldots A_{c_2} A_{c_1}$. The matrix A_C is invertible since all the transformations corresponding to each command $A_{c_1}, A_{c_2}, \ldots, A_{c_n}$ are invertible. The matrix A_C being invertible means that since the volume of the ball in the initial states $\mathcal{B}_{init}$ is nonzero, the corresponding set of states in the unsafe set is an ellipsoid with nonzero volume, which we call $\mathcal{E}_{unsafe}$. Through refinement of the quantization parameters q_{pos}, q_{vel} and q_θ, eventually a partition will be entirely contained in $\mathcal{E}_{unsafe}$. When this happens, every witness point of the quantized counterexample from that partition will be in $\mathcal{B}_{init}$, and so will be an initial state of an unsafe oath of the original, unquantized system.

Perhaps less practically, even if the original system is not robustly unsafe, the process still will theoretically terminate when finite-precision numbers are used in the non-quantized system, such as with air-to-air collision avoidance neural networks that use 32-bit floats. As the quantization values are halved, the difference between the unsafe state in the quantized and nonquantized system is also reduced, until it reaches numeric precision.   □

The second case may seem like one needs to split the entire state space up to machine precision, which would make it very impractical. However, if the goal is to search for counterexamples, then the process can first refine the regions that were found as unsafe using the previous quantization values, in a depth-first search manner. In this way, when the system is unsafe the process would not need to immediately refine the entire state space in order to find these counterexamples. Also keep in mind that the quantized system being safe is a valid outcome of this refinement process, and this does not mean that the original, unquantized system, is safe.

---

[3] For witness points, we use the Chebyshev center of the six-dimensional state polytope (removing y_{int} and v_{int}^y since they are fixed at zero), as it helps avoid numerical issues that can occur at the boundaries of the set.

4   Evaluation

We implemented the approach and set out to prove the safety of quantized closed-loop air-to-air collision avoidance system[4]. We ran the measurements on an Amazon Web Services (AWS) Elastic Computing Cloud (EC2) server with a `c6i.metal` instance type, which has a 3.5 GHz Intel Xeon processor with 128 virtual CPUs, and 256 GB memory. The algorithm is easily parallelized as proofs for each partition of the unsafe states can be checked independently.

4.1   Complete Proof of Safety Attempt

We first attempted a proof of safety for the entire range of unsafe states for ACAS Xu. For this, we started with large quantization values, $q_{pos} = 500$ ft, q_{vel} = 100 ft/sec, and $q_\theta = 1.5$ deg. In this case, the unsafe near-mid-air collision circle of radius 500 ft can be covered with 4 partitions, the complete velocity range of the ownship [100, 1200] needs 11 partitions, the velocity of the intruder [0, 1200] needs 12 partitions, the heading angle of the ownship is divided into $\frac{360 \text{ deg}}{1.5 \text{ deg}} = 240$ partitions, and there are 5 choices for the α_{prev} and two possibilities to check for $\dot{\tau}$. Multiplying these together, we get a total of 1267200 partitions of the unsafe states, each of which we pass to `check_state` (Algorithm 1).

This quickly, within a minute, finds counterexamples in the quantized system. When the witness initial states of the quantized counterexample are replayed on the original non-quantized system, according to the falsification algorithm from Sect. 3.3, these were also found to be unsafe! The exact runtime before an unsafe case is found depends on the order in which the partitions are searched, but we found that although changing this did affect the counterexample produced, the runtime was usually less than a minute. Two of the unsafe cases are shown in Fig. 4 in parts (a) and (b).

In the situation shown in Fig. 4(a), the intruder starts beyond the range of the network ($\rho > 60780$ ft). As soon as the intruder gets in range, a turn is commanded, but the velocity of the ownship is slow and a collision still occurs. This situation looks like it could be fixed by increasing the range of the system beyond 60780 ft—likely requiring retraining the networks—to allow a turn to be commanded earlier. Alternatively, perhaps adding a "do not turn" option as a possible output would be another way to address this scenario (clear-of-conflict could allow the ownship to maneuver as desired which may be unsafe here).

Figure 4(b) shows another unsafe case found that is particularly concerning. This is a tail-chase scenario, although the ownship is already moving away from the straight-line trajectory of the intruder. The system nonetheless commands a turn and actively maneuvers the ownship aircraft back into the path of the intruder. This situation demonstrates one of the dangers of the collision risk metric used to evaluate the effectiveness of many air-to-air collision avoidance systems, which compares the number of near mid-air collisions (NMAC) with

---

[4] The code and instructions to reproduce all the results are online: https://github.com/stanleybak/quantized_nn_backreach/releases/tag/NFM2022_submitted.

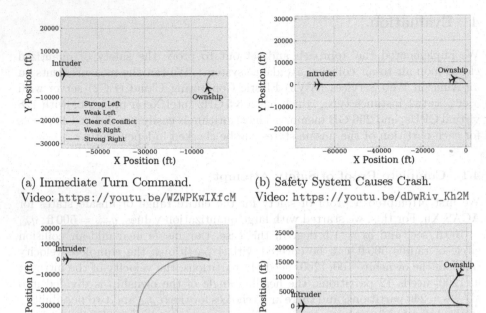

(a) Immediate Turn Command.
Video: https://youtu.be/WZWPKwIXfcM

(b) Safety System Causes Crash.
Video: https://youtu.be/dDwRiv_Kh2M

(c) Fast Ownship and $\tau > 0$.
Video: https://youtu.be/F_bykLR9lJw

(d) Slow Intruder.
Video: https://youtu.be/7B_-k0qpZTo

Fig. 4. Unsafe counterexamples found in the original non-quantized NNCS. Step-by-step traces of the counterexamples are provided in the appendix of the extended report: https://arxiv.org/abs/2201.06626.

and without the system using a large number of simulations. Although a system can be effective by this metric, in specific cases it may still create collisions that would not otherwise have occurred, as demonstrated in this scenario.

4.2 Proving Safety in More Limited Operating Conditions

As the proof of safety for the entire operating range failed, we next tried to prove safety in restricted operating conditions. Many of the unsafe situations found, including the two above, had a slow ownship velocity and a fast intruder. By making the ownship fast enough, we hypothesized collisions could be avoided.

When we restricted the range of v_{own} to be in $[1000, 1200]$ ft/sec, using q_{pos} = 250 ft, q_{vel} = 50 ft/sec, and q_θ = 1.5 deg, we were able to guarantee safety of the quantized closed-loop neural network control system. The proof required checking 3.7 million cases and took about 32 min. The longest runtime for any single call to check_state (checking a single partition) was 63 s.

Reducing v_{own} further to [950, 1000] ft/sec made the quantized system unsafe. Following the falsification approach from Sect. 3.3, we refined the quantization parameters until we were able to find a counterexample in the original unquantized closed loop system. In this case, the ownship was moving with $v_{own} = 964.1$ ft/sec, and the time to loss of vertical separation τ was initially 75 secs (the quantized system was safe for in-plane flight, with $\dot{\tau} = 0$). This case is shown in Fig. 4(c).

From the other side, we can alternatively attempt to prove safety under the assumption that the intruder is slow without restricting the ownship's velocity. In this case, the method also finds unsafe counterexamples in the unquantized system, such as the 159 s trace shown in Fig. 4(d) with $v_{int} = 390.1$ ft/sec. The full trace for this situation is provided in the appendix of the extended report[5] and has a peculiar characteristic. The command switch from weak-left to strong-right a few seconds before the collision corresponds to the relative position angle θ wrapping from $-\pi$ to π. This discontinuity in the network input between successive steps is a strong candidate root cause of the eventual near mid-air collision.

4.3   Comparison with Other Approaches

As far as we are aware, the proposed method is the first to provide safety guarantees while varying all of the operating conditions of the neural network compression of the collision avoidance system.

One related technique, based on computing discrete abstractions and forward reachability was able to provide safety guarantees for the similar Horizontal CAS [17]. This system is simpler to analyze: the inputs were modified to take in Cartesian state variables, the operating range was smaller ($\rho < 50000$), there were fewer neural networks in the system, each of which had half as many neurons per layer, and critically, fixed velocities of $v_{own} = 200$ and $v_{int} = 185$ were considered, rather than using velocity ranges. Despite these simplifications, analysis took 227 CPU hours, mostly on the neural network analysis step to analyze 74 million partitions. For a comparison, we analyzed the larger neural networks in this work with the proposed state quantization and backreachability method, using the same fixed v_{own} and v_{int} values. Using a quantized system with $q_{pos} = 250$ ft and $q_\theta = 1.5$ deg, the method proved safety of all 38400 partitions of the unsafe states in 60.6 s. Also note that while the Horizontal CAS discrete abstraction approach can sometimes prove safety, it would be poor at generating counterexamples, as abstract reachability overapproximates the true reachable set; abstract counterexamples do not correspond to real counterexamples. In contrast, the backwards reachability performed in Algorithm 1 is exact with respect to the quantized system, and the gap between the quantized and original system can be reduced by refining the quantization parameters, making it highly effective for counterexample generation.

---

[5] https://arxiv.org/abs/2201.06626.

We also compared our method with simulation-based analysis, which cannot provide guarantees about system safety but should be able to find unsafe counterexamples if enough simulations are attempted, as the system was shown to be unsafe. In earlier work [18], 1.5 million encounters were simulated for the original neural network compression to evaluate the risk of collisions, sampling from probability distributions of actual maneuvers and taking into account sensor noise. We evaluated the same number of simulations without sensor noise and sampling over the entire set of operating conditions, in order to match the assumptions used in the safety proof. We generated uniform random initial states by considering an initial $\rho \in [60760, 63160]$ and θ, ψ, v_{own} and v_{int} in their entire operating range. When considering $\dot{\tau} = -1$, we assigned the initial value of τ between 25 and 160 s, as the unsafe case in Fig. 4(d) was a 159 s trace. We repeated the process of running 1.5 million simulations one hundred times each for both $\dot{\tau} = -1$ and $\dot{\tau} = 0$, in order to account for statistical noise.

In the $\dot{\tau} = 0$ case, each batch of 1.5 million simulations found on average 17.07 unsafe paths. The unsafe cases were dominated by situations where the intruder velocity was low and the ownship velocity was high. The mean value of v_{int} was 997.8, with a standard deviation of 147.5. The lowest values of v_{int} over the unsafe cases in all 150 million simulations was 927.6, whereas Fig. 4(d) showed a case with $v_{int} = 390.1$ found with our approach. The mean value of v_{own} in the unsafe cases was 133.4 with a standard deviation of 43.0. The greatest value of v_{own} over all the unsafe cases found with 150 million simulations was 452.3, whereas our approach found an in-plane case with $v_{own} = 881.6$.

The performance of simulation analysis for the out-of-plane case is even worse, as the initial state must also correctly choose the value of the time to loss of vertical separation τ in order to find a collision. Each batch of 1.5 million simulations with $\dot{\tau} = -1$ had on average 0.07 unsafe simulations. The maximum ownship velocity v_{own} in the unsafe cases had a mean of 175.4 with a standard deviation of 77.9. The greatest value of v_{own} over the unsafe cases found in all 150 million simulations was 343.0, whereas our approach found a case with $v_{own} = 964.1$, as shown before in Fig. 4(c).

Overall, while simulation analysis may find some unsafe cases, it would be difficult to find the extreme velocity cases discovered with the proposed approach. Further, simulation analysis is incomplete and cannot prove safety for the system under subsets of operating conditions as was done in Sect. 4.2.

5   Related Work

Simulation-Based Safety Analysis. The air-to-air collision avoidance system was originally evaluated using 1.5 million simulations [22] based on Bayesian statistical encounter models. This uses relaxed assumptions compared with our work, such as allowing for changes in acceleration. The output of such analysis is not a yes/no assessment of safety, as the system can clearly be unsafe if the intruder is faster than the ownship and maneuvers adversarially, but rather a risk score assessment of the change in safety compared to without using the system. Via simulation, given a bounded uncertainty in sensing and control, the probability of near-mid-air-collision was about 10^{-4} [18]. Although simulations show that the system may be unsafe, we do not know if the collision occurs due to the uncertainty or the system itself. In this work, we could show that the system itself was unsafe, even if we have perfect sensing and control.

Verification of NNCS. The Verisig approach [14] verifies a NNCS by transforming a network with a sigmoidal neural network controller to an equivalent hybrid system that can be analyzed with Flow* [6], a well-known tool for verifying nonlinear hybrid systems. Another method [9,13] combines polynomial approximation of the neural network controller with the plant's physical dynamics to construct a tight overapproximation of the system's reachable set. The star set approach [29] shows that the exact reachable set of an NNCS with a linear plant model and a ReLU neural network controller can be computed, although this is expensive when initial states are large. These methods build upon open-loop neural network verification algorithms [23,31], which can be difficult to scale to large complex networks [3] and can sometimes lose soundness due to floating-point numeric issues [34]. The proposed quantization analysis only needs to execute neural networks, and so does not suffer from these problems.

Verification of the Closed-loop Air-to-Air Collision Avoidance System. Existing works have verified NNCS with a single neural network controller on a small set of initial states [16]. The closed-loop system involves switching between multiple neural networks and has a large set of initial states, creating a unique challenge for verification. The simplified Horizontal CAS system was analyzed using fast symbolic interval analysis for neural network controllers [33] to construct a discrete abstraction [17]. This method can consider sensor uncertainty, inexact turn commands, and pilot delay, although simplified assumptions are made, as discussed in Sect. 4.3. Recently, the same system as this work has been verified with extensions of the symbolic interval method [7] and with star-based reachability [24] in nnv [32] and nnenum [1]. These approaches use forward reachability analysis and provide sound but not complete verification results. However, verification has only been demonstrated for specific scenarios with small sets of initial states, not the full operating conditions considered here.

6 Conclusion

In this work, we set out to prove the *closed-loop* safety of one of the most popular benchmarks for neural network verification methods, using a new algorithm based on state quantization and backreachability. In principle, the approach scaled sufficiently well to be able to verify the system under all valid initial states and aircraft velocities. However, the proof process instead found many unsafe scenarios where the original, unquantized system had near mid-air collisions, despite ideal assumptions on sensors and maneuvering. Compared with random simulation-based analysis, we could find counterexamples at more extreme velocities, as well as provide proofs of safety of the quantized closed-loop system in more limited scenarios.

The approach is could be attractive for certification. A system with a quantization layer behaves like a large lookup table, and the method is therefore effective on any size network with any layer type, and may even be applicable to other machine learning approaches. The trade-off of quantization is usually a small degradation in performance of the controller, with a significant benefit of reducing analysis complexity and allowing for the possibility of verification.

Acknowledgement. This material is based upon work supported by the NSF EPSCoR First Award, the Air Force Office of Scientific Research and the Office of Naval Research under award numbers FA9550-19-1-0288, FA9550-21-1-0121, FA9550-22-1-0450 and N00014-22-1-2156. Any opinions, findings, and conclusions or recommendations expressed in this material are those of the author(s) and do not necessarily reflect the views of the NSF, US Air Force or US Navy.

References

1. Bak, S.: nnenum: verification of ReLU neural networks with optimized abstraction refinement. In: Dutle, A., Moscato, M.M., Titolo, L., Muñoz, C.A., Perez, I. (eds.) NFM 2021. LNCS, vol. 12673, pp. 19–36. Springer, Cham (2021). https://doi.org/10.1007/978-3-030-76384-8_2
2. Bak, S., Duggirala, P.S.: HyLAA: a tool for computing simulation-equivalent reachability for linear systems. In: Proceedings of the 20th International Conference on Hybrid Systems: Computation and Control. HSCC 2017 (2017)
3. Bak, S., Liu, C., Johnson, T.: The second international verification of neural networks competition (VNN-COMP 2021): Summary and results. arXiv preprint arXiv:2109.00498 (2021)
4. Bak, S., Tran, H.-D., Hobbs, K., Johnson, T.T.: Improved geometric path enumeration for verifying ReLU neural networks. In: Lahiri, S.K., Wang, C. (eds.) CAV 2020. LNCS, vol. 12224, pp. 66–96. Springer, Cham (2020). https://doi.org/10.1007/978-3-030-53288-8_4
5. Bak, S., Tran, H.D., Johnson, T.T.: Numerical verification of affine systems with up to a billion dimensions. In: Proceedings of the 22Nd ACM International Conference on Hybrid Systems: Computation and Control, pp. 23–32. HSCC 2019. ACM, New York, NY, USA (2019)
6. Chen, X., Ábrahám, E., Sankaranarayanan, S.: Flow*: an analyzer for non-linear hybrid systems. In: Sharygina, N., Veith, H. (eds.) CAV 2013. LNCS, vol. 8044, pp. 258–263. Springer, Heidelberg (2013). https://doi.org/10.1007/978-3-642-39799-8_18
7. Clavière, A., Asselin, E., Garion, C., Pagetti, C.: Safety verification of neural network controlled systems. In: 2021 51st Annual IEEE/IFIP International Conference on Dependable Systems and Networks Workshops (DSN-W), pp. 47–54. IEEE (2021)
8. Duggirala, P.S., Viswanathan, M.: Parsimonious, simulation based verification of linear systems. In: Chaudhuri, S., Farzan, A. (eds.) CAV 2016. LNCS, vol. 9779, pp. 477–494. Springer, Cham (2016). https://doi.org/10.1007/978-3-319-41528-4_26
9. Dutta, S., Chen, X., Sankaranarayanan, S.: Reachability analysis for neural feedback systems using regressive polynomial rule inference. In: Proceedings of the 22nd ACM International Conference on Hybrid Systems: Computation and Control, pp. 157–168 (2019)

10. Forets, M., Schilling, C.: Conservative time discretization: a comparative study. arXiv preprint arXiv:2111.01454 (2021)
11. Hagemann, W.: Reachability analysis of hybrid systems using symbolic orthogonal projections. In: Biere, A., Bloem, R. (eds.) CAV 2014. LNCS, vol. 8559, pp. 407–423. Springer, Cham (2014). https://doi.org/10.1007/978-3-319-08867-9_27
12. Han, Z., Krogh, B.H.: Reachability analysis of large-scale affine systems using low-dimensional polytopes. In: Hespanha, J.P., Tiwari, A. (eds.) HSCC 2006. LNCS, vol. 3927, pp. 287–301. Springer, Heidelberg (2006). https://doi.org/10.1007/11730637_23
13. Huang, C., Fan, J., Li, W., Chen, X., Zhu, Q.: ReachNN: reachability analysis of neural-network controlled systems. ACM Trans. Embedded Comput. Syst. (TECS) 18(5s), 1–22 (2019)
14. Ivanov, R., Weimer, J., Alur, R., Pappas, G.J., Lee, I.: Verisig: verifying safety properties of hybrid systems with neural network controllers. In: Proceedings of the 22nd ACM International Conference on Hybrid Systems: Computation and Control, pp. 169–178 (2019)
15. Jia, K., Rinard, M.: Verifying low-dimensional input neural networks via input quantization. In: Drăgoi, C., Mukherjee, S., Namjoshi, K. (eds.) SAS 2021. LNCS, vol. 12913, pp. 206–214. Springer, Cham (2021). https://doi.org/10.1007/978-3-030-88806-0_10
16. Johnson, T.T., et al.: ARCH-COMP21 category report: Artificial intelligence and neural network control systems (AINNCS) for continuous and hybrid systems plants. EPiC Ser. Comput. 80, 90–119 (2021)
17. Julian, K.D., Kochenderfer, M.J.: Guaranteeing safety for neural network-based aircraft collision avoidance systems. In: 2019 IEEE/AIAA 38th Digital Avionics Systems Conference (DASC), pp. 1–10. IEEE (2019)
18. Julian, K.D., Kochenderfer, M.J., Owen, M.P.: Deep neural network compression for aircraft collision avoidance systems. J. Guid. Control. Dyn. 42(3), 598–608 (2019)
19. Julian, K.D., Lopez, J., Brush, J.S., Owen, M.P., Kochenderfer, M.J.: Policy compression for aircraft collision avoidance systems. In: 2016 IEEE/AIAA 35th Digital Avionics Systems Conference (DASC), pp. 1–10. IEEE (2016)
20. Katz, G., Barrett, C., Dill, D.L., Julian, K., Kochenderfer, M.J.: Reluplex: an efficient SMT solver for verifying deep neural networks. In: Majumdar, R., Kunčak, V. (eds.) CAV 2017. LNCS, vol. 10426, pp. 97–117. Springer, Cham (2017). https://doi.org/10.1007/978-3-319-63387-9_5
21. Kochenderfer, M.J., Chryssanthacopoulos, J.: Robust airborne collision avoidance through dynamic programming. Massachusetts Institute of Technology, Lincoln Laboratory, Project Report ATC-371 130 (2011)
22. Kochenderfer, M.J., Edwards, M.W., Espindle, L.P., Kuchar, J.K., Griffith, J.D.: Airspace encounter models for estimating collision risk. J. Guid. Control. Dyn. 33(2), 487–499 (2010)
23. Liu, C., Arnon, T., Lazarus, C., Barrett, C., Kochenderfer, M.J.: Algorithms for verifying deep neural networks. arXiv preprint arXiv:1903.06758 (2019)
24. Lopez, D.M., Johnson, T.T., Tran, H.D., Bak, S., Chen, X., Hobbs, K.: Verification of neural network compression of ACAS Xu lookup tables with star set reachability. In: AIAA Scitech 2021 Forum. AIAA, January 2021
25. Marston, M., Baca, G.: ACAS-Xu initial self-separation flight tests. http://hdl.handle.net/2060/20150008347 (2015)
26. Olson, W.A.: Airborne collision avoidance system x. Tech. rep, MASSACHUSETTS INST OF TECH LEXINGTON LINCOLN LAB (2015)

27. Sadraddini, S., Tedrake, R.: Linear encodings for polytope containment problems. In: 2019 IEEE 58th Conference on Decision and Control (CDC), pp. 4367–4372. IEEE (2019)
28. Scott, J.K., Raimondo, D.M., Marseglia, G.R., Braatz, R.D.: Constrained zonotopes: a new tool for set-based estimation and fault detection. Automatica **69**, 126–136 (2016)
29. Tran, H.D., Cai, F., Diego, M.L., Musau, P., Johnson, T.T., Koutsoukos, X.: Safety verification of cyber-physical systems with reinforcement learning control. ACM Trans. Embedded Comput. Syst. (TECS) **18**(5s), 1–22 (2019)
30. Tran, H.D., et al.: Star-based reachability analysis of deep neural networks. In: International Symposium on Formal Methods, pp. 670–686. Springer (2019)
31. Tran, H.D., Xiang, W., Johnson, T.T.: Verification approaches for learning-enabled autonomous cyber-physical systems. IEEE Design & Test (2020)
32. Tran, H.-D., et al.: NNV: the neural network verification tool for deep neural networks and learning-enabled cyber-physical systems. In: Lahiri, S.K., Wang, C. (eds.) CAV 2020. LNCS, vol. 12224, pp. 3–17. Springer, Cham (2020). https://doi.org/10.1007/978-3-030-53288-8_1
33. Wang, S., Pei, K., Whitehouse, J., Yang, J., Jana, S.: Formal security analysis of neural networks using symbolic intervals. In: 27th USENIX Security Symposium, pp. 1599–1614 (2018)
34. Zombori, D., Bánhelyi, B., Csendes, T., Megyeri, I., Jelasity, M.: Fooling a complete neural network verifier. In: International Conference on Learning Representations (2020)

ZoPE: A Fast Optimizer for ReLU Networks with Low-Dimensional Inputs

Christopher A. Strong[1]($\boxtimes$), Sydney M. Katz[2], Anthony L. Corso[2], and Mykel J. Kochenderfer[2]

[1] Department of Electrical Engineering, Stanford University, Stanford, USA
christopher_strong@berkeley.edu
[2] Department of Aeronautics and Astronautics, Stanford University, Stanford, USA
{smkatz,acorso,mykel}@stanford.edu

Abstract. Deep neural networks often lack the safety and robustness guarantees needed to be deployed in safety critical systems. Formal verification techniques can be used to prove input-output safety properties of networks, but when properties are difficult to specify, we rely on the solution to various optimization problems. In this work, we present an algorithm called ZoPE that solves optimization problems over the output of feedforward ReLU networks with low-dimensional inputs. The algorithm eagerly splits the input space, bounding the objective using zonotope propagation at each step, and improves computational efficiency compared to existing mixed-integer programming approaches. We demonstrate how to formulate and solve three types of optimization problems: (i) minimization of any convex function over the output space, (ii) minimization of a convex function over the output of two networks in series with an adversarial perturbation in the layer between them, and (iii) maximization of the difference in output between two networks. Using ZoPE, we observe a 25× speedup on property 1 of the ACAS Xu neural network verification benchmark compared to several state-of-the-art verifiers, and an 85× speedup on a set of linear optimization problems compared to a mixed-integer programming baseline. We demonstrate the versatility of the optimizer in analyzing networks by projecting onto the range of a generative adversarial network and visualizing the differences between a compressed and uncompressed network.

Keywords: Neural network verification · Global optimization · Convex optimization · Safety critical systems

1 Introduction

The incorporation of deep neural networks (DNNs) into safety critical systems is limited by our ability to provide guarantees on their behavior [1,2]. Neural network verification tools aim to provide these guarantees by proving whether a network satisfies a given input-output property [3]. When input-output relationships are difficult to specify, analyzing a system may require the solution to an optimization problem [4].

© Springer Nature Switzerland AG 2022
J. V. Deshmukh et al. (Eds.): NFM 2022, LNCS 13260, pp. 299–317, 2022.
https://doi.org/10.1007/978-3-031-06773-0_16

In this paper, we focus on solving optimization problems involving feedforward ReLU networks with low-dimensional inputs. Neural networks that control dynamical systems from state estimates often have low input dimension. For example, the ACAS Xu networks for aircraft collision avoidance have a five-dimensional input [2]. Additionally, semantic perturbations to high dimensional spaces can be analyzed through low dimensional networks [4]. When the input space is low-dimensional, it can more easily be decomposed into smaller regions, each defining a simpler optimization problem. We leverage this insight by rapidly dividing the input space into smaller regions that can be more tightly approximated, realizing a significant performance gain and finding the optimal value to a desired tolerance.

We consider the following three optimization problems, each of which is motivated by an application related to verifying the behavior of safety critical systems:

- Minimizing a convex function of the output of a network. This problem can be used to reason about the actions of a control network [5,6]. It can also be used to evaluate a generative adversarial network (GAN), which is a network architecture often used to model high-dimensional data distributions, by calculating the recall metric [4,7].
- Minimizing a convex function of the output of two networks in series subject to an adversarial attack at the output of the first network. This problem can be used to consider adversarial attacks on the input of a network when the input space is itself modeled by another network [8].
- Maximizing the difference between the outputs of two networks given the same input. This problem can be used to compare a compressed and uncompressed network.

Minimizing a convex function of the output can be used to solve many neural network verification problems [3,9]. The other two problems have received less attention in the literature.

In this work, we propose the **Zo**notope **P**ropagation with **E**agerness (ZoPE) optimizer, which solves these optimization problems to a desired tolerance by (i) eagerly breaking down the problem by splitting the input region, and (ii) relying on zonotope propagation to reason about the output reachable set from each input region. We consider a more "eager" solver to be one which spends less time on its bounding functions before splitting. We evaluate the optimizer through runtime comparisons and qualitative demonstrations. We solve four of the standard ACAS Xu neural network verification benchmarks, and compare to state-of-the-art neural network verification tools ERAN [10], NNENUM [11], and MARABOU [12]. On property 1, which can be solved as a linear optimization problem over the output of the network, we observe a speedup of over 25× compared to the next best tool. We also evaluate the runtime of ZoPE on a batch of linear optimization problems from Katz, Corso, Strong, and Kochenderfer [4] and compare against a baseline that mirrors REFINEZONO's approach to verifying the ACAS Xu benchmark [10]. We observe a speedup of 85×. Lastly, we demonstrate how ZoPE can be used as a tool to evaluate a generative adversarial network (GAN) and how it can be used to compare compressed to non-compressed networks.

There have been numerous recent works in the field of neural network verification. These approaches often focus on networks with piecewise linear activation functions, such as the rectified linear unit (ReLU), and frequently take the form of a branch and bound search [13]. Our optimizer does the same. Many break the verification problem into subproblems by case-splitting on the activation function or dividing the input domain [11,12,14–17]. A survey by Liu, Arnon, Lazarus, Strong, Barrett, and Kochenderfer [3] compares these verification algorithms.

Many neural network verification tools can be extended to solve optimization problems [9,18]. Inspired by this idea, the proposed optimizer uses components from several verifiers—it eagerly splits the input domain like RELUVAL [16], propagates zonotopes like DEEPZ [19], combines zonotope propagation with input splitting like REFINEZONO [20], and can optimize functions on the output like MIPVERIFY [18]. The pieces we drew from these different approaches were chosen in order to eagerly break down the input space while still limiting the overapproximation at each step. We expected rapidly splitting would have an advantage on networks with low-dimensional inputs that hadn't been fully explored by existing optimizers.

This paper contains the following contributions:

- A unified optimizer for three global optimization problems over low input dimension ReLU networks. These problems are of interest for verifying safety critical systems.
- A comparison of this new optimizer to existing verifiers and optimizers demonstrating a significant improvement against the state of the art when optimizing affine functions.
- Demonstrations of optimization problems which project onto the range of a network and find the maximum difference between two networks.

2   Background

In this section we introduce notation, discuss the standard neural network verification problem, and compare it to the optimization problems that we focus on. We view a network f as representing a function

$$f : \mathbb{R}^{n_{in}} \to \mathbb{R}^{n_{out}}$$

We will only consider feedforward ReLU networks.

Geometric Objects and Operations. We will make use of several geometric objects. The first is a hyperrectangle, the generalization of a rectangle to n-dimensional space, which is defined by a center $\mathbf{c} \in \mathbb{R}^n$ and a radius $\mathbf{r} \in \mathbb{R}^n$ such that

$$H = \{\mathbf{x} \in \mathbb{R}^n \mid \mathbf{c} - \mathbf{r} \preceq \mathbf{x} \preceq \mathbf{c} + \mathbf{r}\}$$

where $\preceq$ is the elementwise $\leq$ between two vectors.

Hyperrectangles are a special case of a more general class of geometric objects called zonotopes, which can be defined as an affine transform of the unit hypercube. A zonotope Z can be represented using matrix $\mathbf{G} \in \mathbb{R}^{n \times m}$ whose columns are referred to as generators, and a vector $\mathbf{c} \in \mathbb{R}^n$ which is the center of the zonotope as

$$Z = \{\mathbf{y} \in \mathbb{R}^n \mid \mathbf{y} = \mathbf{G}\mathbf{x} + \mathbf{c}, -1 \leq x_i \leq 1 \; \forall i = 1, \dots, m\}$$

Zonotopes are a subset of polytopes, and have symmetry about their center. Optimizing a linear function over a hyperrectangle or a zonotope can be done analytically instead of by solving a linear program [21,22].

We will also use the Minkowski sum between two sets X and Y defined as

$$X \oplus Y = \{\mathbf{x} + \mathbf{y} \mid \mathbf{x} \in X, \mathbf{y} \in Y\}$$

This can be visualized as padding one set with the other.

Zonotope Propagation. A vital component of our approach will be finding an overapproximation of the output reachable set for a given input region. There are a variety of techniques to find symbolic or concrete descriptions of such a set [3,16,19]. One approach, used in the neural network verification tool DEEPZ [19], propagates zonotopes through a network layer by layer. After each layer the respective zonotope is an overapproximation of the reachable set for that layer. The new zonotope is formed elementwise, with overapproximation introduced for any dimension in the input zonotope that can be both negative and positive. For dimensions where this is true, an additional generator is introduced into the zonotope. The cost of computing this overapproximation is linear in the number of existing generators. We refer readers to the original paper, in particular Theorem 3.1, for details on this procedure [19]. We will make use of this algorithm in our optimizer, although in principal other overapproximate output reachable sets could be used. Exploring these alternatives is a promising direction for future work.

3   Optimization Problems

The field of neural network verification has focused on checking input-output properties with yes or no answers. Formally, for input sets $\mathcal{X}$ and $\mathcal{Y}$ a neural network verification tool tells us whether the property

$$\mathbf{x} \in \mathcal{X} \implies \mathbf{y} \in \mathcal{Y} \tag{1}$$

holds [3]. Recent work has explored extending these tools to solve optimization problems [9]. In this work, we would like to address several optimization problems involving neural networks. In each problem we will only consider optimizing over hyperrectangular or zonotopic input sets.

Minimizing a Convex Function on the Range of a Network. Our first problem of interest is to minimize a convex function on the output of a network. We can write this problem as

$$\underset{\mathbf{x}}{\text{minimize}} \quad g(f(\mathbf{x})) \tag{2}$$
$$\text{subject to} \quad \mathbf{x} \in \mathcal{X}$$

where g is a convex function. This can be used to solve a variety of neural network verification problems as defined in Eq. (1). We can view the problem of projecting onto the range of a network as a special case with

$$g(f(\mathbf{x})) = \|f(\mathbf{x}) - \mathbf{y}_0\| \tag{3}$$

An example use case is when f is a generative adversarial network (GAN). By solving this optimization problem we can find the closest possible generated image to a ground truth image.

Noise Buffer. We would like to optimize over the output of two networks in series with an adversarial perturbation applied between the two networks. This can be formulated as

$$\underset{\mathbf{x},\mathbf{z}}{\text{minimize}} \quad g(f_2(f_1(\mathbf{x}) + \mathbf{z}))) \tag{4}$$
$$\text{subject to} \quad \mathbf{x} \in \mathcal{X}$$
$$\mathbf{z} \in Z$$

where Z is a zonotope of allowed perturbations and f_1 and f_2 are our two networks in series. The addition of $\mathbf{z}$ from the set Z can be viewed as padding the output manifold of the first network. We will limit g to be convex in this work. For an example of its use, consider if f_1 is a generative model and f_2 is a control network. By solving this optimization problem, we can evaluate the behavior of the controller with inputs defined by the generative model and subject to adversarial perturbations. Of note, this noise buffer optimization problem could also be put into the form of the first optimization problem in Eq. (2) by considering an augmented input space that parameterizes the noise, then connecting those extra inputs to the intermediate layer with skip connections or a larger network. However, this could substantially increase the input dimension, so we focus on the framing of the problem given in Eq. (4) and leave a comparison with the alternative framing for future work.

Network Difference. A third optimization problem of interest is to determine how different the output of two networks can be if they take in the same input. We can write this as

$$\underset{\mathbf{x}}{\text{maximize}} \quad \|f_1(\mathbf{x}) - f_2(\mathbf{x})\|_p \tag{5}$$
$$\text{subject to} \quad \mathbf{x} \in \mathcal{X}$$

for ℓ_p norm with $p \geq 1$. For an example of its use, consider if f_1 is a large network and f_2 is a smaller "compressed" network that attempts to mimic the behavior of f_1. By solving this optimization problem, we can evaluate how closely f_1 and f_2 will match. The non-convexity of this problem comes both from the network's non-convexity and from the fact that we would like to maximize rather than minimize a convex function.

4   Approach

Our proposed approach takes the form of a branch and bound search for the optimum value. The components within this branch and bound search will vary between optimization problems but share some common elements, including input splitting and zonotope propagation. Below we first sketch the general branch and bound algorithm and then discuss how it can be applied to each of the optimization problems of interest.

4.1   Optimization with Branch and Bound

Branch and bound is an approach to optimization which repeatedly breaks down a problem into smaller sub-problems, bounding the optimal value of each sub-problem as it goes, and using those bounds to prune regions of the search space [23,24]. Suppose we would like to minimize an objective over some region. The branch and bound algorithm requires three functions: (i) SPLIT, (ii) UPPER-BOUND, and (iii) LOWERBOUND. The function SPLIT splits a problem into multiple subproblems, LOWERBOUND finds a lower bound on the optimal value for a sub-problem, and UPPERBOUND(f)inds an upper bound on the optimal value for a sub-problem. The algorithm maintains a priority queue of subproblems ordered by their associated lower bound on the objective from LOWERBOUND, with highest priority given to the subproblem with the lowest lower bound. Some or all subproblems will also have associated upper bounds on their optimal value from UPPERBOUND. At each step, the subproblem with lowest lower bound is removed from the queue and split. Each new subproblem then has its lower bound evaluated and is added back onto the queue. The new subproblems may have an upper bound on their minimum objective evaluated as well, and those that don't inherit the upper bound of their parent subproblem.

The *optimality gap* at any point is given by the difference between the lowest lower bound and the lowest upper bound across the open subproblems (those in the priority queue). If the optimality gap ever falls below a tolerance $\epsilon \geq 0$, the algorithm can return with a value within ϵ of the global optimum. The subproblems with lower bound greater than the lowest upper bound are effectively pruned, as they will never be revisited in the search for the optimum. If we would like to maximize instead of minimize an objective, we can reframe the problem as minimizing the negative of the original objective. Many neural network verification tools can be viewed as performing a branch and bound search for violations of a property [13].

In our case, the problem will correspond to an input set $\mathcal{X}$ that we would like to optimize over, and the subproblems will be regions from this original set. In this work we will only consider zonotope input sets, which includes hyperrectangles. In order to solve the optimization problems described in Sect. 3 with the generic branch and bound algorithm, we will describe how to implement the three functions required: (i) SPLIT, (ii) UPPERBOUND, and (iii) LOWERBOUND.

4.2 Split, UpperBound, LowerBound

We will start by addressing SPLIT, which will be common to each of the problems we would like to solve. For a zonotope input set $Z_{in} \subseteq \mathbb{R}^{n_{in}}$ defined by n_{gen} generators $G \in \mathbb{R}^{n_{in} \times n_{gen}}$ and center $c \in \mathbb{R}^{n_{in}}$, we choose to split along the generator with largest ℓ_2 norm using Proposition 3 from the work of Althoff, Stursberg, and Buss [25]. This approach splits a zonotope into two zonotopes, but these zonotopes may have a non-empty intersection. Their union will be guaranteed to contain the original zonotope.

For a hyperrectangular input set, we choose the dimension with largest radius and split the hyperrectangle halfway along that dimension into two hyperrectangles. The interiors of the hyperrectangles will have an empty intersection. We experimented with a simple gradient based splitting heuristic but did not see an improvement to the performance. This may have been the result of the particular geometry of these networks. The computation required for the zonotope propagation at each step depends on the number of network activation regions, which are sets where the activation pattern of the network is constant, that overlap with the current input region. As a result, we conjecture that a splitting strategy which aims to mold the subregions to match the geometric structure of the activation regions may be beneficial. Other gradient or duality based input splitting heuristics from neural network verification tools may lead to better splits and should be explored in the future [16,26]. Since we rely on splitting the input space, we expect our approach to scale poorly to high dimensions.

The approach to UPPERBOUND will also be similar across our problems. For the upper bound on the optimization problem over a region, we will evaluate the objective for a single point in the region. As an achievable objective, this will always upperbound the minimum achievable objective. We choose to evaluate the center of our input region. We experimented with a first order method to choose the point to evaluate but found limited benefit, and as a result chose to keep the heuristic of using the center point for simplicity. The optimality gap depends on two factors: the value of the achievable objective and the size of the input region. The overapproximation from propagating the input region is often more substantial, so choosing a better achievable objective does little to improve runtime. As a result, even with a better heuristic there is a limit to the performance gains from the LOWERBOUND function. Many adversarial attacks could be repurposed to perform some local exploration for this step [27], and the tradeoff between the runtime of the UPPERBOUND function and the ability to reduce the optimality gap sooner could be explored. For the noise buffer problem, to find an upperbound we hold the input to the first network constant at the cell's center, leading to an output $\mathbf{y}_1$ from the first network. To account for points in the buffered region, we then optimize our objective over the second network with input given by the padded region $\{\mathbf{y}_1\} \oplus Z$.

Next, we will focus on LOWERBOUND for each of the optimization problems, which differs depending on the problem type. This function must map from a zonotopic or hyperrectangular input region $\mathcal{X}$ to a lower bound on the objective value.

Minimizing a Convex Function on the Range of a Network. To lower bound a convex function over the output, we first propagate the input set $\mathcal{X}$ to a zonotopic output set Z_{out} with generator $\mathbf{G}_{\text{out}} \in \mathbb{R}^{n_{\text{out}} \times n_{\text{gen}}}$ and center $\mathbf{c}_{\text{out}} \in \mathbb{R}^{n_{\text{out}}}$ which overapproximates the true output reachable set for this region. We then solve the convex program

$$\begin{array}{ll} \underset{\mathbf{z}}{\text{minimize}} & g(\mathbf{z}) \\ \text{subject to} & \mathbf{z} \in Z_{\text{out}} \end{array} \tag{6}$$

The constraint $\mathbf{z} \in Z_{\text{out}}$ is a set of linear constraints which can be written by introducing variables $\mathbf{x} \in \mathbb{R}^{n_{\text{gen}}}$ to get

$$\begin{array}{ll} \underset{\mathbf{z},\mathbf{x}}{\text{minimize}} & g(\mathbf{z}) \\ \text{subject to} & -1 \leq x_i \leq 1 \quad i = 1, \ldots, n_{\text{gen}} \\ & \mathbf{z} = \mathbf{G}_{\text{out}}\mathbf{x} + \mathbf{c}_{\text{out}} \end{array} \tag{7}$$

We will return the optimal value p^* of this convex program as the lower bound.

If g is an affine function $g(\mathbf{y}) = \mathbf{a}^\top \mathbf{y} + b$, then the solution is analytic and is given by

$$p^* = \mathbf{c}_{\text{out}}^\top \mathbf{a} + \left\| \mathbf{G}_{\text{out}}^\top \mathbf{a} \right\|_1 + b \tag{8}$$

where $\mathbf{G}$ is the generator matrix for the zonotope and $\mathbf{c}$ is the center of the zonotope [28]. Computing this expression will typically be much faster than solving a convex program, giving a large speedup when optimizing an affine function.

Additionally, checking whether the output of a network is always contained within a polytope $\mathcal{P} = \{\mathbf{x} \mid \mathbf{A}\mathbf{x} \leq \mathbf{b}, \mathbf{A} \in \mathbb{R}^{n \times m}, \mathbf{b} \in \mathbb{R}^n\}$ can be accomplished by maximizing the maximum violation of the polytope's constraints. We will denote the ith row of $\mathbf{A}$ as $\mathbf{a}_i^\top$. This problem could either be solved with the above framework through n separate queries with the negative violation of the ith constraint as the objective $g(\mathbf{y}) = -\mathbf{a}_i^\top \mathbf{y} - b_i$, or through a single query with $g(\mathbf{y}) = -\max_i(\mathbf{a}_i^\top \mathbf{y} - b_i)$ This objective is the negative of a pointwise maximum of affine functions, so is concave. Fortunately, although g is concave, minimizing g over a zonotope can be accomplished with one linear optimization per row of $\mathbf{A}$, each of which is analytical. As a result, checking whether the output of a network is always contained within a polytope $\mathcal{P}$ can be performed through n separate queries which solve a single linear optimization at each step, or through a single query which solves n linear optimizations at each step.

Lastly, if we are projecting onto the range of a network with $g(\mathbf{y}) = \|\mathbf{y} - \mathbf{y}_0\|$, the choice of norm will affect the complexity of the optimization problem over a zonotope. For example, with ℓ_1 or ℓ_∞ norms this can be formulated as a linear program, while for the ℓ_2 norm it will be a quadratic program. Future work could explore using faster projection algorithms instead of solving a convex program at each step which may yield significant speedups.

Noise Buffer. We would like to optimize a function over two networks in series with a buffer of allowed perturbations Z after the first layer. This is equivalent to taking the Minkowski sum of the output manifold of the first network and the buffer. We would like to find a lower bound on the objective that will approach the true objective as the input cell grows smaller. We first propagate the cell through the first network to get a zonotope $Z_{1_{out}}$ which overapproximates the reachable set. We then take the Minkowski sum of this zonotope with our buffer to get

$$Z_{\text{buffered}} = Z_{1_{out}} \oplus Z = \{\mathbf{z}_{1_{out}} + \mathbf{z} \mid \mathbf{z}_{1_{out}} \in Z_{1_{out}}, \mathbf{z} \in Z\}$$

Since zonotopes are closed under Minkowski sums, the resulting object will still be a zonotope [29].

Our problem now becomes trying to lower bound our function g on this buffered set. As our input cell becomes small, $Z_{1_{out}}$ does as well, and Z_{buffered} approaches the size of the buffer. Since the buffered zonotope will not become arbitrarily small, if we were to just propagate Z_{buffered} through the second network, we would incur some steady state error in our lower bound. To avoid this overapproximation, we can solve the optimization problem from the buffered zonotope to the output exactly. If the dimension of the intermediate space is low, we could apply the algorithm we have already given for optimizing convex functions over a single network. If the dimension is high, we can use another optimization strategy such as encoding the second network using mixed-integer constraints as done by NSVERIFY, MIPVERIFY, and ERAN [10,18,30], then adding the objective and solving the resulting optimization problem with an off-the-shelf MIP solver such as Gurobi or GLPK. Since this approach nests another full optimization problem over the second half of the network within each step of the original branch and bound, we expect the runtime to scale poorly as the size of the perturbation set Z and the complexity of the second network grow, which may limit the use of the proposed approach for this type of analysis.

In summary, to get a lower bound we (i) overapproximate the set passing through the first network, then (ii) solve the resulting optimization problem over the second network with input set given by a buffered zonotope.

Network Difference. Our goal is to find the maximum difference in the output of two networks over an input region. Since we are maximizing a function, we are interested in finding an upper bound on the objective over our input cell. We start by propagating the input cell through the first network to get $Z_{1_{out}}$ and the second network to get $Z_{2_{out}}$. We can then tightly overapproximate each of these zonotopes as hyperrectangles H_1 and H_2 by finding their maximum and minimum value in each elementary direction. Each of these operations can be performed analytically. Once we have these two hyperrectangular overapproximations, we are interested in solving

$$\underset{\mathbf{h}_1, \mathbf{h}_2}{\text{maximize}} \quad \|\mathbf{h}_1 - \mathbf{h}_2\|_p$$
$$\text{subject to} \quad \mathbf{h}_1 \in H_1 \tag{9}$$
$$\mathbf{h}_2 \in H_2$$

whose optimal value will upper bound the true maximum distance in this region. Let $\mathbf{c}_1$ and $\mathbf{c}_2$ be the centers of H_1 and H_2 and $\mathbf{r}_1$ and $\mathbf{r}_2$ be the radius of H_1 and H_2 in each elementary direction. An analytical solution to this optimization problem is given by

$$\mathbf{h}_1^* = \mathbf{c}_1 + \text{sign}(\mathbf{c}_1 - \mathbf{c}_2) \odot \mathbf{r}_1$$
$$\mathbf{h}_2^* = \mathbf{c}_2 + \text{sign}(\mathbf{c}_2 - \mathbf{c}_1) \odot \mathbf{r}_2$$
$$d^* = \|\mathbf{h}_1^* - \mathbf{h}_2^*\|_p$$

where $\odot$ represents elementwise multiplication and d^* is the optimal value. See Appendix A.1 for a derivation of this analytical solution. Returning d^* as defined above will upper bound the objective function.

4.3 Implementation

Each of the approaches described in Sect. 4.2 were implemented in a Julia package.[1] This repository also has code to reproduce the benchmarks on our optimizer in Sect. 5. The zonotope propagation and zonotope splitting is performed with the LazySets library.[2] For solving linear and mixed-integer linear programs we use Gurobi and for solving other convex programs we use Mosek, both of which have a free academic license.[3] The implementation is modular and is intended to be easily extended to solve other optimization problems.

5   Experimental Results

We apply ZoPE to a variety of problems, first comparing its runtime to existing solvers on the ACAS Xu benchmark and linear optimization problems. We then showcase how it can be used to solve problems with more complex objectives. In several of these experiments we use a conditional GAN trained to represent images from a wing-mounted camera on a taxiing aircraft. The conditional GAN has four inputs, two of which are the crosstrack position and heading while the other two are latent inputs. We also use a state estimation network which

---

[1] Source is at https://github.com/sisl/NeuralPriorityOptimizer.jl.
[2] Source is at https://github.com/JuliaReach/LazySets.jl.
[3] Available at https://www.gurobi.com and https://www.mosek.com.

takes as input a 128-dimensional image of the taxiway and outputs the state of the aircraft. The GAN and state estimation network can be combined in series. All timing is done on a single core of an Intel Xeon 2.20 GHz CPU and with an optimality gap of 1×10^{-4} unless otherwise specified. All queries use hyperrectangular input sets; in future work it would be valuable to explore the runtime consequences when splitting non-hyperrectangular input zonotopes as well.

5.1 ACAS Xu Benchmark

The ACAS Xu neural network verification benchmark contains a set of properties on networks trained to compress the ACAS Xu collision avoidance system and is often used to benchmark verification tools [2,15]. We will consider properties 1, 2, 3, and 4 introduced by Katz, Barrett, Dill, Julian, and Kochenderfer [15]. We compare to the neural network verification tools MARABOU [12], NNENUM [11], and ERAN [10,19,20,31]. See Appendix A.2 for details on how each solver was configured. Property 1 can be evaluated by maximizing a linear function, while properties 2, 3, and 4 can be evaluated by minimizing the convex indicator function to the output polytope associated with the property or by minimizing the distance to the output polytope associated with the property. Viewed in another way, property 1 can be solved by asking the question "Is the network always contained in a polytope?" while property 2 can be solved by asking the question "Does the network ever reach a polytope?" For property 1 each step is analytical, while for properties 2, 3, and 4 at each step we apply a quick approximate check for intersection, and if it is indeterminate we solve a linear program. Each verification tool was run on a single core.

Figure 1 shows the performance of the optimizer on four ACAS properties. ZoPE achieves a speedup of about 25× on property 1. We remain competitive with the other tools on properties 2, 3, and 4, where we may need to solve a linear program at each step.

5.2 Optimizing Convex Functions

We first evaluate ZoPE maximizing a linear objective. We run queries on a network composed of the conditional GAN concatenated with the image-based control network. This combined network was introduced by Katz, Corso, Strong, and Kochenderfer [4] and has an input of two states and two latent dimensions. The objective function corresponds to the control effort. The baseline we compare against divides the state dimensions into hyperrectangular cells, propagates a zonotope through each cell with DEEPZ's approach, then uses the resulting bounds to formulate a mixed-integer program and find the optimum for that cell. Since we run these queries sequentially, each mixed-integer program also has a constraint that the objective should be larger than the best seen so far. The strategy of interleaving splitting and MIP calls mirrors REFINEZONO's approach to verifying the ACAS Xu networks [10]. Table 1 shows more than an 85× speedup of our approach over the baseline. The efficiency of ZoPE relies heavily

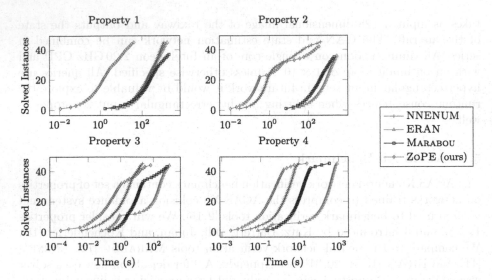

Fig. 1. Comparison of Solvers on ACASXu Properties 1, 2, 3, and 4 with a 300s timeout.

Table 1. Performance on linear optimization problems. 25 queries in different regions of the input space are run on a single network. The network was introduced in Katz, Corso, Strong, and Kochenderfer [4] and consists of a conditional GAN concatenated with an image-based controller. The performance of the MIP approach with a variety of discretizations of the state space is shown. For example, MIP 3×3 corresponds to an optimizer which for each query (i) discretizes the input space into a 3×3 grid, then (ii) for each cell in the grid finds bounds on each node using the approach of DEEPZ, and (iii) solves the resulting MIP using Gurobi.

Approach	Total time (s)
MIP 3×3	3728
MIP 5×5	1171
MIP 10×10	1610
MIP 15×15	2473
ZoPE (ours)	**13.5**

on the computational cost of finding bounds for the objective over a zonotope. As a result, like with ACAS property 1 we see substantially better performance than existing tools when optimizing an objective with only analytical operations at each step.

Next, we demonstrate using the proposed optimizer to project an image onto the output manifold of a conditional GAN. The GAN has a finite, convex support for its latent variables. This allows us to project onto the range of the network, under some ℓ_p norm, by minimizing the convex objective function in Eq. (3). Figure 2 shows several images and their corresponding closest generated images

True Images

Generated Images

Fig. 2. Closest generated images (bottom row) to a set of true images (top row) with distance measured by the ℓ_2 norm.

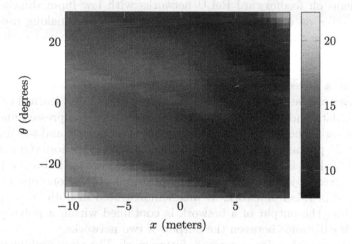

Fig. 3. The maximum output distance in L1 norm of two networks over the state space.

from the GAN. The visual similarity between the two rows gives some evidence that the GAN is capturing the desired images in its output manifold. However, we still see some slight differences between the images. The degree of these differences can be used to measure how closely the GAN captures each training datapoint, giving a recall metric to evaluate a GAN and inform hyperparameter choice, as was done in Katz, Corso, Strong, and Kochenderfer [4]. Note that this analysis, and the sense of "closeness" in this context, depends on the norm used for the projection.

5.3 Maximum Distance Between Compressed and Original Networks

By finding the maximum distance between the outputs of two networks as described in Sect. 4.2, we can evaluate how well a compressed network mimics the behavior of an original uncompressed network. We validate this technique on a large conditional GAN, with two input states to be conditioned on, two latent dimensions, four layers with 256 ReLUs each, and a 128 dimensional output layer. The second "compressed" network has the same input and output spaces, but only two layers with 128 ReLUs each. We use a required optimality gap of 0.1. The heatmap in Fig. 3 shows the maximum difference in the output of these networks across a slice of the state space. These maximum differences, or an approximation thereof, could be used to retrain the network in regions where the difference is large.

6   Conclusion

In this work, we introduced an algorithm for solving a wide variety of optimization problems on feedforward ReLU networks with low input dimension. The algorithm relies on eagerly splitting the input space and making use of zonotope propagation through the network to bound the optimum at each step. We observe a speedup of 25× on property 1 of the ACAS Xu benchmark compared to several existing verification tools, and 85× on a linear optimization benchmark compared to a mixed-integer programming baseline. We also demonstrate how the optimizer can be used to analyze how closely a GAN has learned to replicate its training data and how it can be used to compare a compressed and uncompressed network. The optimizer was implemented modularly and was made available as a Julia package at https://github.com/sisl/NeuralPriorityOptimizer.jl so as to flexibly allow for a reader to explore solving other optimization problems. Any non-convex objective which can be optimized over a zonotope can readily be optimized in this framework, as was demonstrated in both our approach to check whether the output of a network is contained within a polytope and to maximize the distance between the output of two networks.

There are several major avenues for future work. The often prohibitive growth of the runtime with the input dimension, depth, and width of the network remains as a significant challenge for this and other exact optimizers. One direction of interest would be to develop more specialized lower bound functions for particular problems. For example, faster intersection or projection algorithms may be applied to some problems where our implementation solves a convex program at each step. We could also incorporate and compare some of the optimizations that ERAN makes use of; for example, mixing mixed-integer program solves in with the splitting, tightening the propagated zonotopes, or propagating polytopes instead of zonotopes. Another would be to consider how to scale up to high-dimensional input spaces, and consider what a more eager splitting strategy looks like in those contexts. Lastly, we could find other optimization problems of interest over neural networks that could be solved with the same or a similar framework.

Acknowledgments. We would like to acknowledge support from Eric Luxenberg, Haoze Wu, Gagandeep Singh, Chelsea Sidrane, Joe Vincent, Changliu Liu, Tomer Arnon, and Katherine Strong.

Funding in support of this work is from DARPA under contract FA8750-18-C-009, the NASA University Leadership Initiative (grant #80NSSC20M0163), and the National Science Foundation Graduate Research Fellowship under Grant No. DGE-1656518. Any opinions, findings, and conclusions or recommendations expressed in this material are those of the authors and do not necessarily reflect the views of DARPA, any NASA entity, or the National Science Foundation.

A   Appendix

A.1   Maximum Distance Between Points in Two Hyperrectangles

We would like to derive an analytical solution for the maximum distance given by a p-norm with $p \geq 1$ between two hyperrectangles H_1 and H_2. We will let $\mathbf{c}_1$ and $\mathbf{c}_2$ be the centers of H_1 and H_2, and $\mathbf{r}_1$ and $\mathbf{r}_2$ be the radii of H_1 and H_2. The maximum distance can be found by solving the following optimization problem

$$\underset{\mathbf{h}_1, \mathbf{h}_2}{\text{maximize}} \quad \|\mathbf{h}_1 - \mathbf{h}_2\|_p$$
$$\text{subject to} \quad \mathbf{h}_1 \in H_1$$
$$\mathbf{h}_2 \in H_2$$

The p-norm for finite p is defined as

$$\|\mathbf{x}\|_p = (\sum_{i=1}^n |(\mathbf{x})_i|^p)^{\frac{1}{p}}$$

We expand the objective of our maximization problem to be

$$(\sum_{i=1}^n (|(\mathbf{h}_1)_i - (\mathbf{h}_2)_i|^p))^{\frac{1}{p}}$$

and since $x^{\frac{1}{p}}$ is monotonically increasing on the non-negative reals for $p \geq 1$, we can remove the power of $\frac{1}{p}$ giving us the equivalent problem

$$\underset{\mathbf{h}_1, \mathbf{h}_2}{\text{maximize}} \quad \sum_{i=1}^n (|(\mathbf{h}_1)_i - (\mathbf{h}_2)_i|^p)$$
$$\text{subject to} \quad \mathbf{h}_1 \in H_1 \tag{10}$$
$$\mathbf{h}_2 \in H_2$$

Now we see that the constraints $\mathbf{h}_1 \in H_1$ and $\mathbf{h}_2 \in H_2$ apply independent constraints to each dimension of $\mathbf{h}_1$ and $\mathbf{h}_2$. We also note that the objective can be decomposed coordinate-wise. As a result, in order to solve this optimization problem, we will need to solve n optimization problems of the form

$$\underset{(\mathbf{h}_1)_i, (\mathbf{h}_2)_i}{\text{maximize}} \quad |(\mathbf{h}_1)_i - (\mathbf{h}_2)_i|^p$$
$$\text{subject to} \quad (\mathbf{c}_1)_i - (\mathbf{r}_1)_i \leq (\mathbf{h}_1)_i \leq (\mathbf{c}_1)_i + (\mathbf{r}_1)_i \tag{11}$$
$$(\mathbf{c}_2)_i - (\mathbf{r}_2)_i \leq (\mathbf{h}_2)_i \leq (\mathbf{c}_2)_i + (\mathbf{r}_2)_i$$

Since x^p is monotonically increasing for $p \geq 1$ we can equivalently maximize $|(\mathbf{h}_1)_i - (\mathbf{h}_2)_i|$. We show an analytic form for the maximum by checking cases. If $(\mathbf{c}_2)_i$ is larger than $(\mathbf{c}_1)_i$, the maximum will be found by pushing $(\mathbf{h}_2)_i$ to its upper bound and $(\mathbf{h}_1)_i$ to its lower bound. Conversely, if $(\mathbf{h}_1)_i$ is larger than

$(\mathbf{h}_2)_i$, the maximum will be found by pushing $(\mathbf{h}_1)_i$ to its upper bound and $(\mathbf{h}_2)_i$ to its lower bound. If $(\mathbf{c}_1)_i$ is equal to $(\mathbf{c}_2)_i$, then we can arbitrarily choose one to push to its lower bound and the other to push to its upper bound—we select $(\mathbf{h}_1)_i$ to go to its upper bound and $(\mathbf{h}_2)_i$ to go to its lower bound. As a result we have the optimal inputs

$$(\mathbf{h}_1)_i^* = (\mathbf{c}_1)_i + \mathrm{sign}((\mathbf{c}_1)_i - (\mathbf{c}_1)_i)(\mathbf{r}_1)_i$$
$$(\mathbf{h}_2)_i^* = (\mathbf{c}_2)_i + \mathrm{sign}((\mathbf{c}_2)_i - (\mathbf{c}_2)_i)(\mathbf{r}_2)_i$$

where the sign function is given by

$$\mathrm{sign}(x) = \begin{cases} 1.0 & x \geq 0 \\ -1.0 & x < 0 \end{cases}$$

Then, backtracking to our original problem and vectorizing gives us the analytical solution to this optimization problem with optimal value d^*

$$\mathbf{h}_1^* = \mathbf{c}_1 + \mathrm{sign}(\mathbf{c}_1 - \mathbf{c}_2) \odot \mathbf{r}_1$$
$$\mathbf{h}_2^* = \mathbf{c}_2 + \mathrm{sign}(\mathbf{c}_2 - \mathbf{c}_1) \odot \mathbf{r}_2$$
$$d^* = \|\mathbf{h}_1^* - \mathbf{h}_2^*\|_p$$

where the sign function is applied elementwise. This completes our derivation of the analytical solution for the maximum distance between two points contained in two hyperrectangles.

A.2   Verifier Configuration for the Collision Avoidance Benchmark

This section describes how each verifier was configured for the collision avoidance benchmark discussed in Sect. 5.1. Table 2 summarizes the non-default parameters for each solver and the location where the parameter was set. Both NNENUM and ERAN by default make use of parallelization, and MARABOU has a parallel mode of operation, but for this experiment we restrict all tools to a single core. We ran the experiments on a single core to try to separate the aspects of how each solver was parallelized from what we viewed as the core of its algorithmic approach. We expect ZOPE would parallelize well, especially on more challenging problems. The hyperparameters we ran for ERAN may be better suited for multiple cores than a single core, so further comparison could explore these in more depth. Additionally, the timing results from the Verification of Neural Networks 2020 competition[4] for several properties for ERAN were slower than we expected from the change in hardware and the restriction to a single core. Exploring the tool further, we observed that on several problem instances it would return back a failed status before reaching a timeout. On these same instances we saw that ERAN would find several inputs that were almost counterexamples, for example with a margin of 1×10^{-6} from violating the property,

---

[4] https://sites.google.com/view/vnn20/vnncomp.

Table 2. Non-default verifier parameters

Solver	Parameter	Value	Location
MARABOU			
	Split-threshold	1	Command line argument
	INTERVAL_SPLITTING_FREQUENCY	1	GlobalConfiguration.cpp file
NNENUM			
	Settings.NUM_PROCESSES	1	acasxu_all.py file
ERAN			
	use_parallel_solve	True	__main__.py file
	Processes	1	__main__.py file
	Domain	Deeppoly	Command line argument
	Complete	True	Command line argument
	timeout_milp	10	Command line argument
	Numproc	1	Command line argument
ZoPE			
	stop_gap	1×10^{-4}	acas_example.jl
	stop_frequency	1	acas_example.jl

flag these as potential counter-examples, then move on. It is possible that the root cause of the abnormalities we observed affected timing results. On problems where ERAN did return a status the results were consistent with the ground truth.

The parameters were chosen based off of a mix of recommendations from developers on their best configuration for the collision avoidance benchmark or existing documented settings for this benchmark. For example, ERAN's parameters were based off of the VNN20 competition as found at https://github.com/GgnDpSngh/ERAN-VNN-COMP/blob/master/tf_verify/run_acasxu.sh. The code for for MARABOU,[5] NNENUM,[6] ERAN,[7] and our optimizer ZoPE[8] is available for free online.

References

1. Bojarski, M., et al.: End to end learning for self-driving cars, Technical Report (2016). http://arxiv.org/abs/1604.07316
2. Julian, K.D., Kochenderfer, M.J., Owen, M.P.: Deep neural network compression for aircraft collision avoidance systems. AIAA J. Guid. Control Dyn. **42**(3), 598–608 (2019)
3. Liu, C., Arnon, T., Lazarus, C., Strong, C., Barrett, C., Kochenderfer, M.J.: Algorithms for verifying deep neural networks. Found. Trends® Optim. **4**(3–4), 244–404 (2021)

---

[5] https://github.com/NeuralNetworkVerification/Marabou.
[6] https://github.com/stanleybak/nnenum.
[7] https://github.com/eth-sri/eran.
[8] https://github.com/sisl/NeuralPriorityOptimizer.jl.

4. Katz, S.M., Corso, A.L., Strong, C.A., Kochenderfer, M.J.: Verification of image-based neural network controllers using generative models. In: Digital Avionics Systems Conference (DASC) (2021)
5. Julian, K.D., Lee, R., Kochenderfer, M.J.: Validation of image-based neural network controllers through adaptive stress testing (2020)
6. Katz, S.M., Julian, K.D., Strong, C.A., Kochenderfer, M.J.: Generating probabilistic safety guarantees for neural network controllers. Mach. Learn. , 1–29 (2021). https://doi.org/10.1007/s10994-021-06065-9
7. Kynkäänniemi, T., Karras, T., Laine, S., Lehtinen, J., Aila, T.: Improved precision and recall metric for assessing generative models. In: Advances in Neural Information Processing Systems (NeurIPS) (2019)
8. Mirman, M., Gehr, T., Vechev, M.: Robustness certification with generative models. In: ACM SIGPLAN International Conference on Programming Language Design and Implementation (2021)
9. Strong, C.A., et al.: Global optimization of objective functions represented by ReLU networks. Mach. Learn. 2010.03258 (2021). https://doi.org/10.1007/s10994-021-06050-2
10. Singh, G., Gehr, T., Püschel, M., Vechev, M.T.: Boosting robustness certification of neural networks. In: International Conference on Learning Representations (2019)
11. Bak, S., Tran, H.-D., Hobbs, K., Johnson, T.T.: Improved geometric path enumeration for verifying ReLU neural networks. In: Lahiri, S.K., Wang, C. (eds.) CAV 2020. LNCS, vol. 12224, pp. 66–96. Springer, Cham (2020). https://doi.org/10.1007/978-3-030-53288-8_4
12. Katz, G., et al.: The Marabou framework for verification and analysis of deep neural networks. In: Dillig, I., Tasiran, S. (eds.) CAV 2019. LNCS, vol. 11561, pp. 443–452. Springer, Cham (2019). https://doi.org/10.1007/978-3-030-25540-4_26
13. Bunel, R., Mudigonda, P., Turkaslan, I., Torr, P., Lu, J., Kohli, P.: Branch and bound for piecewise linear neural network verification. J. Mach. Learn. Res. **21**(2020), 1–39 (2020)
14. Ehlers, R.: Formal verification of piece-wise linear feed-forward neural networks. In: D'Souza, D., Narayan Kumar, K. (eds.) ATVA 2017. LNCS, vol. 10482, pp. 269–286. Springer, Cham (2017). https://doi.org/10.1007/978-3-319-68167-2_19
15. Katz, G., Barrett, C., Dill, D.L., Julian, K., Kochenderfer, M.J.: Reluplex: an efficient SMT solver for verifying deep neural networks. In: Majumdar, R., Kunčak, V. (eds.) CAV 2017. LNCS, vol. 10426, pp. 97–117. Springer, Cham (2017). https://doi.org/10.1007/978-3-319-63387-9_5
16. Wang, S., Pei, K., Whitehouse, J., Yang, J., Jana, S.: Formal security analysis of neural networks using symbolic intervals. In: USENIX Security Symposium 2018, pp. 1599–1614 (2018)
17. Wu, H., et al.: Parallelization techniques for verifying neural networks. CoRR, vol. abs/2004.08440 (2020). arXiv: 2004.08440
18. Tjeng, V., Xiao, K., Tedrake, R.: Evaluating robustness of neural networks with mixed integer programming. In: International Conference on Learning Representations (2017)
19. Singh, G., Gehr, T., Mirman, M., Püschel, M., Vechev, M.T.: Fast and effective robustness certification. In: Advances in Neural Information Processing Systems (NeurIPS) (2018)
20. Singh, G., Gehr, T., Püschel, M., Vechev, M.: An abstract domain for certifying neural networks. In: Proceedings of the ACM on Programming Languages, vol. 3, no. POPL, pp. 1–30 (2019)

21. Fujishige, S.: Submodular Functions and Optimization. Elsevier (2005)
22. Kitahara, T., Sukegawa, N.: A simple projection algorithm for linear programming problems. Algorithmica **81**(1), 167–178 (2019)
23. Lawler, E.L., Wood, D.E.: Branch-and-bound methods: a survey. Oper. Res. **14**(4), 699–719 (1966)
24. Kochenderfer, M.J., Wheeler, T.A.: Algorithms for Optimization. MIT Press, Cambridge (2019)
25. Althoff, M., Stursberg, O., Buss, M.: Reachability analysis of nonlinear systems with uncertain parameters using conservative linearization. In: IEEE Conference on Decision and Control (CDC), pp. 4042–4048 (2008)
26. Rubies-Royo, V., Calandra, R., Stipanovic, D.M., Tomlin, C.: Fast neural network verification via shadow prices. arXiv preprint arXiv:1902.07247 (2019)
27. Yuan, X., He, P., Zhu, Q., Li, X.: Adversarial examples: attacks and defenses for deep learning. IEEE Trans. Neural Netw. Learn. Syst. **30**(9), 2805–2824 (2019)
28. Althoff, M., Frehse, G.: Combining zonotopes and support functions for efficient reachability analysis of linear systems. In: IEEE Conference on Decision and Control (CDC), pp. 7439–7446 (2016)
29. Althoff, M.: On computing the Minkowski difference of zonotopes. arXiv preprint arXiv:1512.02794 (2015)
30. Lomuscio, A., Maganti, L.: An approach to reachability analysis for feedforward ReLU neural networks. arXiv preprint arXiv:1706.07351 (2017)
31. Singh, G., Ganvir, R., Püschel, M., Vechev, M.: Beyond the single neuron convex barrier for neural network certification. In: Advances in Neural Information Processing Systems (NeurIPS), vol. 32, pp. 15 098–15 109 (2019)

Permutation Invariance of Deep Neural Networks with ReLUs

Diganta Mukhopadhyay[1]([✉]), Kumar Madhukar[2], and Mandayam Srivas[1]

[1] Chennai Mathematical Institute, Chennai, India
digantam@cmi.ac.in
[2] Indian Institute of Technology Delhi, Delhi, India
madhukar@cse.iitd.ac.in

Abstract. We look at the problem of verifying *permutation invariance* in Deep Neural Networks (DNNs) – if certain permutations are applied on the inputs, its effect on the outputs will also be a permutation (possibly identity). These properties surface in many interesting practical applications of DNNs, e.g. consider the aircraft collision avoidance system that guides an aircraft to turn right if the sensory inputs suggest an intruder aircraft coming from the left, and *vice-versa*. The naive way of verifying such properties – using two copies of the network and a standard DNN verification technique, e.g. Reluplex – is impracticable as the complexity of this task is exponential in the network size. This paper proposes a sound, abstraction-based technique to establish permutation invariance in DNNs with ReLU as the activation function. The technique computes an over-approximation of the reachable states, and an under-approximation of the safe states, and propagates this information across the layers, both forward and backward. The novelty of our approach lies in a useful *tie-class* analysis, that we introduce for forward propagation, and a scalable 2-polytope under-approximation method that escapes the exponential blow-up in the number of regions during backward propagation. Experiments demonstrate that our method compares favorably with the existing state-of-the-art in DNN verification.

1 Introduction

Artificial neural networks are now ubiquitous. They are increasingly being allowed and used to handle increasingly more complex tasks, that used to be unimaginable for a machine to perform. This includes driving cars, playing games, maneuvering air traffic, recognizing speech, interpreting images and videos, creating art, and numerous other things. While this is exciting, it is crucial to understand that neural networks are responsible for a lot of decision making, some of which can have disastrous consequences if gone wrong. Consider a DNN that is being used to suggest the direction in which an aircraft

The authors are thankful to TCS Research, Pune, India. A substantial part of this work was done when the first two authors were associated with TCS Research, as an intern and as an employee, respectively.

© Springer Nature Switzerland AG 2022
J. V. Deshmukh et al. (Eds.): NFM 2022, LNCS 13260, pp. 318–337, 2022.
https://doi.org/10.1007/978-3-031-06773-0_17

must turn to avoid a possible collision with an intruder aircraft. Informally, such a network is well-behaved if it asks the own ship to turn right (left) when an intruder approaches from the left (right). Consider another network that takes four inputs – the cards dealt to the players in a game of contract bridge – and decides which team can bid *game*. Loosely speaking, if you exchange the hands of partners (*north* and *south*, or *east* and *west*), the decision would not change. However, it will change if, say, you exchange north's hand with east. Such *permutation invariance* properties, for certain permutations at input and output layers, are important to the correctness and robustness of these networks.

Formally, given a DNN $\mathcal{N}$, permutations σ_{in} and σ_{out}, two vectors B_1 and B_2 of dimension as large as the input size of the neural network and a positive real M, the permutation invariance is defined as: *if the inputs of the network lie between B_1 and B_2 component-wise, then permuting the input of the network by σ_{in} leads to the output being permuted by σ_{out} up to a tolerance of M. That is,*

$$B_1 \leq x \leq B_2 \Rightarrow |\sigma_{out}(\mathcal{N}(x)) - \mathcal{N}(\sigma_{in}(x))| \leq M$$

Permutation invariance of DNNs is really a two-safety property, i.e. it can be verified using existing techniques for safety verification of feed-forward neural networks (FFNNs), by composing two copies of the network. A straightforward way to do this would be to encode the network and the property as SMT constraints, and solve it using Z3 [4]. It is invariably more efficient, however, to use specially designed solvers and frameworks such as Reluplex [12] and Marabou [13,14]. Still, these methods do not scale well, and are particularly inapplicable in this case (which requires doubling the network size), as the worst-case complexity of FFNN verification is exponential in the size of the input network.

This paper proposes a technique to verify permutation invariance properties in DNNs with ReLU (Rectified Linear Unit) activation function. Our technique computes, at each layer, an over-approximation of the reachable states (moving forward from the input layer), and also an under-approximation of the safe states (moving backward from the final layer at which the property is specified). If the reachable states fall entirely within the safe region in any of the layers, the property is established. Otherwise, we obtain a witness to exclusion at each layer and do a spuriousness check to see if there is an actual counterexample.

The novelty of our approach lies in the way we propagate information across layers. For the forward propagation of reachable states, as affine regions, we have introduced the notion of *tie classes*. The purpose of tie classes is to group together the *Relu* nodes that will always get inputs of the same sign. This grouping cuts down on the branching required to account for active and inactive states of all the *Relu* nodes during forward propagation. Intuitively, tie classes let us exploit the behavioral symmetry of the network, with respect to the inputs and the permutation. The backward propagation relies on convex polytope propagation. During the propagation one may have to account for multiple cases, based on the possible signs of the inputs to the *Relu* nodes (corresponding to each quadrant of the space in which the polytope resides), leading to an exponential blow-up in the worst case. We address this by proposing a 2-polytope under-approximation method that is efficient (does not depend on LP/SMT solving), scalable, as well as effective. Note that the forward propagation may also be done using convex polytope propagation (which is how it is usually done, e.g. [19]), but it requires computing the convex hull each time, which is an expensive operation. In contrast, tie-class analysis helps us propagate the affine regions efficiently.

The core contributions of this paper are: *i*) an approach for verifying permutation invariance, based on novel forward- and backward-propagation techniques (Sect. 4), *ii*) a proof of soundness of the proposed approach (in the Appendix), and *iii*) a tool and an experimental evaluation of our approach (Sect. 5).

2   Preliminaries

We represent vectors in n-dimensional space as row matrices, i.e., with one row and n columns. A linear transform T from and n dimensional space to an m dimensional space can then be represented by a matrix M with n rows and m columns, and we have: $T(\boldsymbol{x}) = \boldsymbol{x}M$.

Convex Polytopes. A convex polytope is defined as a conjunction of a set of linear constraints indexed by i of the form $\boldsymbol{x}.\boldsymbol{v}_i \leq c_i$, for fixed (column) vectors $\boldsymbol{v}_i$ and constants c_i. Geometrically, it is a convex region in space enclosed within a set of planar boundaries. Symbolically, we can represent a convex polytope by arranging all the $\boldsymbol{v}_i$s into the columns of a matrix M, and letting the components of a row vector $\boldsymbol{b}$ to be constants b_i: $\boldsymbol{x}M \leq \boldsymbol{b}$.

Pullback. The *pullback* of a convex polytope P (given by $\boldsymbol{x}M_P^{n \times k} \leq \boldsymbol{b}_p$), over an affine transform T (given by $\boldsymbol{x} \to \boldsymbol{x}M_T^{m \times n} + \boldsymbol{t}_T$), is defined as the set of all points $\boldsymbol{x}$ such that $T(\boldsymbol{x})$ lies inside P, i.e., $T(\boldsymbol{x}) \in P \Leftrightarrow \boldsymbol{x}M_T M_P \leq \boldsymbol{b}_P - \boldsymbol{t}_T M_P$.[1]

Affine Region. An n-dimensional affine subspace is the set of all points generated by linear combinations of a set of *basis* vectors $\boldsymbol{v}_i, 0 \leq i < k$, added to a *center* $\boldsymbol{c}$: $\{\boldsymbol{x} \mid \boldsymbol{x} = (\Sigma_{i=0}^{k-1}\alpha_i \boldsymbol{v}_i) + \boldsymbol{c}$, for some real $\alpha_i\}$.
We define an *affine region* as a constrained affine subspace by bounding the values of α to be between -1 and 1. Formally, an affine region $A[B_A, \boldsymbol{c}]$ generated by a set of basis vectors $\boldsymbol{v}_i, 0 \leq i < k$, represented by a matrix $B_A^{k \times n}$, is defined as the following set of points: $\boldsymbol{x} \in A \Leftrightarrow (\exists \boldsymbol{\alpha}. \ \boldsymbol{x} = \boldsymbol{\alpha}B_A + \boldsymbol{c} \wedge |\boldsymbol{\alpha}| \leq 1)$.

Pushforward. The *pushforward* (A_T) of an affine region A (defined by B_A and $\boldsymbol{c}_A$), across an affine transform T, (given by $\boldsymbol{x} \to \boldsymbol{x}M_T + \boldsymbol{t}_T$), is the set of points: $\boldsymbol{x} \in A_T \Leftrightarrow (\exists \boldsymbol{\alpha}. \ \boldsymbol{x} = \boldsymbol{\alpha}B_A M_T + \boldsymbol{c}_A M_T + \boldsymbol{t}_T \ , \ |\boldsymbol{\alpha}| \leq 1)$. This is the image of A under T. (In a DNN context, a separate M_T and $\boldsymbol{t}_T$ is associated with each layer that is constructed from the weights and bias used at that layer.)

DNN Notation and Conventions. We number the layers of the neural network as 0, 1, 2, and so on, upto $n - 1$. A layer is said to consist of an affine transform followed by a *Relu* layer. The affine transform of layer i is given by $\boldsymbol{x} \to \boldsymbol{x}W_i + \boldsymbol{b}_i$, where W_i are the weights and $\boldsymbol{b}_i$ are biases. We denote the input

---

[1] We use bold face to denote vectors, and $A^{p \times q}$ means P is a $p \times q$ matrix.

vectors by x_0 feeding into the affine transform of layer 0, and in general for $i > 0$, the input of layer i's affine transform (the output of the $i - 1^{th}$ layer's $Relu$) as x_i. The output of layer i's affine transform (the input to layer i's $Relu$) is labeled as y_i. Finally, the output is x_n. Also, we maintain copies of each variable's original and permuted value (using a primed notation). So, we have:

$$x_0, x_0' \to xW_0 + b_0 \to y_0, y_0' \to Relu \to x_1, x_1' \to xW_1 + b_1 \to y_1, y_1' \to Relu \to$$
$$\cdots y_{n-1}, y_{n-1}' \to Relu \to x_n, x_n'$$

Here, W_i and b_i represent the action of the layer on the joint space of x_i and x_i'. Then, the invariance property we wish to verify has the following form:

$$B_1 \le x_0, x_0' \le B_2 \wedge x_0' = \sigma_{in}(x_0) \Rightarrow |x_n' - \sigma_{out}(x_n)| \le M$$

Note that the precondition here is an affine region and the postcondition is a conjunction of linear inequalities, involving permutations.

3   Informal Overview

Algorithm 1. Overview of our approach

1: **inputs:** $\mathcal{N}, n, pre, post$
2: **globals:** reach$[n]$, safe$[n]$

3:    reach$[0] \leftarrow initPre(pre, \mathcal{N})$
4:    safe$[n-1] \leftarrow initPost(post, \mathcal{N})$
5:    **for** $i \in [1 \ldots n)$ **do**
6:       reach$[i] \leftarrow forwardPropagate($reach$[i-1], \mathcal{N})$
7:    **for** $i \in [n-2 \ldots 0)$ **do**
8:       safe$[i] \leftarrow backwardPropagate($safe$[i+1], \mathcal{N})$
9:    **for** $i \in [1 \ldots n)$ **do**
10:      **if** (reach$[i] \wedge \neg$safe$[i]$) is unsatisfiable **then**
11:         **return** *property holds*
12:      **else**   ▷ there must be a satisfying witness
13:         *spuriousnessCheck(witness, i)*

Algorithm 1 presents an overview of our approach. The input to it is the network $\mathcal{N}$ with n layers, and the invariance property given as a (*pre, post*) pair of formulas. The algorithm begins by converting the pre-condition to an affine region by calling *initPre* (line 3) and expressing the postcondition as a convex polytope by calling *initPost* (line 4), without any loss of precision (see Sect. 3.1). Then it propagates the affine region forward, to obtain an over-approximation of the set of reachable values as an affine region at each subsequent layers (line 6). Similarly, an under-approximation of the safe region – as a union of two convex polytopes – is calculated at each layer, propagating the information backward from the output layer (line 8). The property holds if the reachable region at any layer is contained within the safe region (lines 9–13).

If the inclusion check does not succeed, the algorithm attempts to construct an actual counterexample from the witness to the inclusion check failure (see Algorithm 2). In general, pulling back the witness to the first layer is as hard as pulling back the postcondition. So, we try to find several individual input points that lead to something close to the witness at the layer where the inclusion fails,

---

Algorithm 2. Spariouness checking algorithm

1: **procedure** *spuriousnessCheck* (*counterexample, layer*)
2:     *cexes* ← [*counterexample*]   ▷ list of potential counterexamples
3:     **while** *cexes* ≠ ∅ ∧ *layer* > 0 **do**
4:         *prevCexes* ← ∅   ▷ collect (approximate) pullbacks in the prev. reach
5:         **for** *cex* ∈ *cexes* **do**
6:             *prevCexes* << *pullBackCex*(*cex, layer, N*) ∩ *reach*[*layer* − 1]
7:         *cexes* ← *prevCexes*; *layer* ← *layer* − 1
8:     **if** *cexes* = ∅ **then**
9:         **return** *inconclusive*   ▷ pullback failed, no potential counterexamples
10:     **for** *cex* ∈ *cexes* **do**
11:         **for** *j* ∈ [0 . . . *n*) **do**   ▷ forward simulation of the counterexample
12:             *cex* ← *simulateLayer*(*cex, j, N*)
13:             **if** cex ∈ safe[*j*] **then**   ▷ spurious c'example, move on to the next one
14:                 **break**
15:         **return** (*property failed, cex*)   ▷ actual counterexample found
16:     **return** *inconclusive*   ▷ all potential counterexamples are safe

---

allowing us to check a number of potential counterexamples. In lines 5–6 (Algorithm 2) we repeatedly apply *pullBackCex* and collect these approximate pull back points layer by layer backwards until the input layer. We now simulate these points forward to check if the output of the DNN lies within the safe region in lines 11–17. If for any point it does not, we have successfully constructed a counterexample. Otherwise, if we cannot find any potential counterexamples (line 10), or if all the potential counterexamples are safe (line 17), the witness represents a spurious counterexample and the algorithm returns *inconclusive*. Before getting into the details of *forwardPropagate*, *backwardPropagate*, and *pullBackCex*, we present an example and describe the pre-processing part of our algorithm.

3.1   Running Example

Consider the neural network shown in Fig. 1. Here, we have separated the result of computing the weighted sum from that of the application of the *Relu* into separate nodes, represented by dashed and solid circles respectively. Also, we show the weights as labels on the arrows coming into a combination point (dark circles), and biases as labels of arrows emerging from the point. The arrows for weights that are 0 been omitted. The values at (output of) each node in the network for the input in the range [0.5 0] are shown in the diagram at that node. This network has the following symmetry property: $0 \leq x_{00}, x_{01}, x'_{00}, x'_{01} \leq 1 \wedge x_{00} = x'_{01} \wedge x_{01} = x'_{00} \Rightarrow |[x_{20}\ x_{21}] - [x'_{21}\ x'_{20}]| \leq 0.1$. This expresses the fact that flipping the inputs leads to the outputs being flipped, σ_{in} and σ_{out} both flip the components.

Preprocessing: The W_i and b_i are calculated as follows: If the weights and bias of layer i are W^i and b^i, then $W_i = \begin{bmatrix} W^i & 0 \\ 0 & W^i \end{bmatrix}$ and $b_i = [b^i\ b^i]$ as we need to track both the original and permuted values at each layer. For this example:

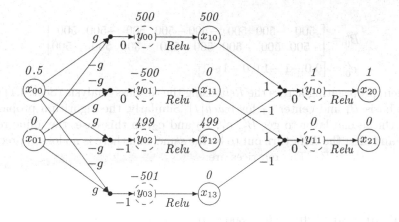

Fig. 1. $\sigma = (0\rightarrow1, 1\rightarrow0)$, $g = 1000$

$W_0 =$

$$\begin{bmatrix} 1000 & -1000 & 1000 & -1000 & 0 & 0 & 0 & 0 \\ -1000 & 1000 & -1000 & 1000 & 0 & 0 & 0 & 0 \\ 0 & 0 & 0 & 0 & 1000 & -1000 & 1000 & -1000 \\ 0 & 0 & 0 & 0 & -1000 & 1000 & -1000 & 1000 \end{bmatrix}$$

$W_1 = \begin{bmatrix} 1 & 0 & 0 & 0 \\ 0 & 1 & 0 & 0 \\ -1 & 0 & 0 & 0 \\ 0 & -1 & 0 & 0 \\ 0 & 0 & 1 & 0 \\ 0 & 0 & 0 & 1 \\ 0 & 0 & -1 & 0 \\ 0 & 0 & 0 & -1 \end{bmatrix}$

$b_0 = \begin{bmatrix} 0 & 0 & -1 & -1 & 0 & 0 & -1 & -1 \end{bmatrix}$

$b_1 = \begin{bmatrix} 0 & 0 & 0 & 0 \end{bmatrix}$

Action of *initPre* **and** *initPost*: Now, *initPre* calculates *reach*[0] as the following affine region given by basis B_0 and center c_0, and *initPost* expresses *safe*[2] as a convex polytope:

reach[0] :   **safe[2]** :

$$\exists \alpha : [x_0 \ x_0'] = \alpha B_0 + c_0, \ |\alpha| \le 1$$

$$B_0 = \begin{bmatrix} 0.5 & 0 & 0 & 0.5 \\ 0 & 0.5 & 0.5 & 0 \end{bmatrix}$$

$$c_0 = \begin{bmatrix} 0.5 & 0.5 & 0.5 & 0.5 \end{bmatrix}$$

$$[x_2 \ x_2'] \begin{bmatrix} 1 & 0 & -1 & 0 \\ 0 & 1 & 0 & -1 \\ 0 & -1 & 0 & 1 \\ -1 & 0 & 1 & 0 \end{bmatrix} \le [0.1 \ 0.1 \ 0.1 \ 0.1]$$

$$(1)$$

Forward Propagation: *ForwardPropagate* then propagates (1) across the layers to get affine regions that are over-approximations for the reachable region for that layer. While propagation across the linear layer can be done easily via matrix multiplication, propagating across the *Relu* layer is in general hard, since we need to take into account all possible branching behaviors. We do this via a tie class analysis (Sect. 4.1) that exploits the inherent symmetry of the network and precondition. For this network, propagating across the first linear layer gives us an affine region given by the basis and center:

$$B_0' = \begin{bmatrix} 500 & -500 & 500 & -500 & -500 & 500 & -500 & 500 \\ -500 & 500 & -500 & 500 & 500 & -500 & 500 & -500 \end{bmatrix}$$

$$c_0' = \begin{bmatrix} 0 & 0 & -1 & -1 & 0 & 0 & -1 & -1 \end{bmatrix}$$

Then, propagating across the *Relu* using the tie class analysis (Sect. 4.1) gives us the basis B_1 and center c_1 for *reach*[1]. Similarly, the algorithm propagates across the second layer to get B_1', c_1', B_2 and c_2. In this case, the affine region before and after the *Relu* turn out to be the same, and there is no loss in precision going from B_1' to B_2. The matrices are:

$B_1 =$

$$\begin{bmatrix} 500 & 0 & 0 & 0 & 0 & 500 & 0 & 0 \\ -500 & 0 & 0 & 0 & 0 & -500 & 0 & 0 \\ 0 & -500 & 0 & 0 & -500 & 0 & 0 & 0 \\ 0 & 500 & 0 & 0 & 500 & 0 & 0 & 0 \\ 0 & 0 & 500 & 0 & 0 & 0 & 0 & 500 \\ 0 & 0 & -500 & 0 & 0 & 0 & 0 & -500 \\ 0 & 0 & 0 & -500 & 0 & 0 & -500 & 0 \\ 0 & 0 & 0 & 500 & 0 & 0 & 500 & 0 \end{bmatrix}$$

$c_1 = \begin{bmatrix} 0 & 0 & 0 & 0 & 0 & 0 & 0 & 0 \end{bmatrix}$

$B_1', B_2 =$

$$\begin{bmatrix} 500 & 0 & 0 & -500 \\ -500 & 0 & 0 & 500 \\ 0 & -500 & -500 & 0 \\ 0 & 500 & 500 & 0 \\ -500 & 0 & 0 & -500 \\ 500 & 0 & 0 & 500 \\ 0 & 500 & 500 & 0 \\ 0 & -500 & -500 & 0 \end{bmatrix}$$

$c_1', c_2 = \begin{bmatrix} 0 & 0 & 0 & 0 \end{bmatrix}$

$$(2)$$

Inclusion Check: Now, we see that if we substitute x with the form given in *reach*[2] given by B_2 and c_2 above into *safe*[2] from Eq. 1, the right side of the inequality in *safe*[2] is a matrix multiplication that evaluates to 0. So, *reach*[2] is included in *safe*[2]. This is done by an algorithm (Sect. 4.3) that checks this using an LP solver, and since it succeeds in this case, it returns *property holds*.

Note that for this example, it was unnecessary to perform any back propagation of the *safe*[i] to previous layers, as the inclusion check succeeded at the output layer. In general, back propagation (Sect. 4.2) would be performed to compute under-approximations. Spuriousness check (Sect. 4.3) will be needed if the inclusion check fails.

4   Forward and Backward Propagation

An input precondition of the form $B_1 \le [x_0, x_0'] \le B_2$ with $x_0' = \sigma(x_0)$ can always be converted into an equivalent affine region characterized by the formula $\exists \alpha : [x_0 \ x_0'] = \alpha V + c$, $|\alpha| \le 1$ by making corresponding components of V the same according to σ, shifting the origin of V and scaling. This gives us *reach*[0]. Similarly, a postcondition of the form $|x_n' - \sigma_{out}(x_n)| \le M$ can be written as the convex polytope $|[x_n \ x_n']L| \le M$ where each column of L calculates one of the differences of corresponding components, giving us *safe*$_n$. Having *reach*[0] and *safe*$_n$, we move on to forward and backward propagation.

4.1 Forward Propagation Using Tie Classes

Let $reach[j] = \{[x_j \ x_j'] \mid \exists \alpha : [x_j \ x_j'] = \alpha B_j + c_j, \ |\alpha| \leq 1\}$, be the affine region representing an over-approximation of reachable points at the input to layer j; $forwardPropagate$ constructs $reach[j + 1]$ as an affine region that is an over-approximation for the set of all points produced when $reach[j]$ is propagated to the input of layer $j + 1$. $reach[j + 1]$, is constructed by forward propagating $reach[j]$ first across the affine transform at j to produce an affine region A_j, which is then further forward propagated across the $Relu$ layer.

Forward propagation across the linear transform given by $x \rightarrow xW_j + b_j$ is straightforward and precise as it can be computed as a simple linear pushforward across W_j, i.e., $A_j([y_j \ y_j']) \Leftrightarrow (\exists \alpha : [y_j \ y_j'] = \alpha B_j' + c_j', \ |\alpha| \leq 1)$, where $B_j' = B_j W_j$ is the new basis and $c_j' = c_j W_j + b_j$ is the new center.

Propagating A_j across $Relu$ is more complex and challenging as it requires, in general, a detailed case analysis of the polarity and strength of the components of the basis vectors and the scaling α; rather than performing it precisely, $reach[j + 1]$ is constructed as an affine region that over-approximates the $Relu$ image. Several methods can be used to construct an over-approximation that make different tradeoffs between precision and efficiency. One can construct the smallest affine region (or polytope) that includes all the reachable values possible across the $Relu$ [19]. Computing the smallest region can be inefficient as it is an optimization problem requiring several expensive LP or convex-hull calls. Our method efficiently constructs an over-approximate affine region that, while sub-optimal, does not need any LP calls and is effective for checking permutation invariance properties.

Our method to construct the over-approximate affine region relies on looking for similarities in the polarity of the components of the vectors belonging to $reach[j]$ that are preserved when a $Relu$ is applied to the region. For this, we introduce the notion of tie $classes$ associated with an affine region.

Propagating over Relu with Tie Classes. Given an affine region A defined by a basis v_i and center c we define a binary relation, $tied$, over the set of indices[2] denoting the components of any vector x in A as follows.

Definition 1 (Tied). *Given an affine region A characterized by the condition $\exists \alpha_i : x = \sum_i \alpha_i v_i + c, \ |\alpha_i| \leq 1$, and two indices i_1 and i_2 in the index set, we say i_1 and i_2 are tied iff for every vector x in A the components at i_1 and i_2 have the same sign.*

The binary relation being $tied$ is an equivalence relation on the index set of vectors x that generates an equivalence class defined as follows.

Definition 2 (Tie Class). *A tie class for an affine region A is the equivalence class (partitioning) of the index set for the vectors in A induced by the equivalence relation tied for A.*

---

[2] We assume the indices range from 0 to $n - 1$ for vectors of size n.

Consider the affine region generated by the basis v_i and c: $v_0 = [1\ 0\ 0\ 2]$, $v_1 = [0\ 1\ 0.5\ 0]$, $c = [0.5\ 2\ 1\ 1]$. For this region, the indices 0 and 3 are tied because for every vector in the region the component 3 is always 2 times the component 0 , since the component 3 of the v_i and the c are 2 times the component 0. Similarly, indices 1 and 2 are tied as well. For this region, the tie equivalence class is $\{0 : \{0, 3\}, 1 : \{1, 2\}\}$

Tie Class Based Transformation of Basis Vectors. To help construct the basis vectors for the over-approximation of the output of *Relu*, we define a transformation of the set of basis vectors at the input to *Relu*. For each tie class j in the equivalence class induced, and each vector v_i in the input basis set, we construct a vector $v_i''^j$ by setting all the components of v_i that are not in the tie class j to 0. Similarly, we get a c^j from c for each tie class j. For the example above, we have:

$$v_0'^0 = [1\quad 0\quad 0\quad 2]\quad v_1'^0 = [0\quad 0\quad 0\quad\quad 0]\quad c^0 = [0.5\quad 0\quad 0\quad 1]$$
$$v_0'^1 = [0\quad 0\quad 0\quad 0]\quad v_1'^1 = [0\quad 1\quad 0.5\quad 0]\quad c^1 = [0\quad\quad 2\quad 1\quad 0]$$

Lemma 1. *Given* $x = \sum_i \alpha_i v_i + c$, *we can write* $Relu(x) = \sum_{i,j} \alpha_i''^j v_i''^j + \sum_j \beta_j c_j$ *where each* $\alpha_i''^j$ *is either* α_i *or is* 0, *and each* β_j *is either* 0 *or* 1. *Moreover, the components of* $Relu(x)$ *with indices in a tie class* j *are* 0 *iff* $\alpha_i''^j$ *and* β_j *are* 0.

This lemma[3] states that there exists an oracle that, given an x in *reach*$[j]$, can determine whether to set each $\alpha_i''^j$ to α_i or 0 and each β_j to 0 or 1 so that we can express $Relu(x)$ in the above form. Regardless of what the oracle chooses we can always replace the condition $\alpha_i''^j = \alpha_i \lor \alpha_i''^j = 0$ with $|\alpha_i''^j| \le 1$ as an over-approximation. Now, if we can somehow replace $\sum_j \beta_j c_j$ with a single vector, we will have found our output affine region. The following theorem proves that we can replace this sum with $Relu(c)$.

Theorem 1. *Given* $x = \sum_i \alpha_i v_i + c, |\alpha_i| \le 1$, *in an affine region* A, *there are scalars* $\alpha_i''^j$ *such that:*

1. $Relu(x) = \sum_{i,j} \alpha_i''^j v_i''^j + Relu(c)$
2. $|\alpha_i''^j| \le 1$ *for all* i *and* j.

The above theorem ensures that if we relax the condition on $\alpha_i''^j$ to $|\alpha_i''^j| \le 1$, the affine region obtained an over-approximation for the Relu image of A. Given v_i and c, it is easy to compute $v_i''^j$ and $Relu(c)$ if we know what the tie classes are, since this only involves setting certain components to 0. All we need to do now is compute the tie classes for the given v_i and c.

---

[3] A more detailed version of the paper including an appendix with all the proofs and other details is available at https://arxiv.org/abs/2110.09578.

Algorithm 3. Checking tiedness

1: **inputs:** $A, \vec{v_i}, \vec{c}, i_1, i_2$
2: **if** $\forall j : \frac{v_j^{i_1}}{v_j^{i_2}} = \frac{c^{i_1}}{c^{i_2}}$ **then return** *tied*
3: **else if** $\vec{c_{i_1}} \geq 0$ and $\vec{c_{i_2}} \geq 0$ **then**
4:     **if** i_1 or i_2 component of some $\vec{x} \in A < 0$
    then return *not tied*
5:     **else return** *tied*
6: **else if** $\vec{c_{i_1}} < 0$ and $\vec{c_{i_2}} < 0$ **then**
7:     **if** i_1 or i_2 component of some $\vec{x} \in A > 0$
    then return *not tied*
8:     **else return** *tied*
9: **else return** *not tied*

Computing Tie Classes. To compute tie classes, for every pair of indices i_1 and i_2, we check whether i_1 and i_2 are tied, and then group them together. One way to check if two i_1 and i_2 are in the same tie class using two LP queries involving the α_i: one which constrains the value of component i_1 of x to positive and component i_2 to negative, and vice versa. If any of these are feasible, i_1 and i_2 cannot be in the same tie class. Else, they are in the same tie class. This needs to be repeated for each pair of i_1 and i_2, which amounts to $n * (n-1)$ LP calls for n *Relu* nodes, which is inefficient. Instead, we state another property of tie classes that will allow us to compute the tie classes more efficiently:

Theorem 2. *Two indices i_1 and i_2 are in the same tie class if and only if one of the following is true:*

1. *The i_1 and i_2 components of $\boldsymbol{x}$ are always both positive.*
2. *The i_1 and i_2 components of $\boldsymbol{x}$ are always both negative.*
3. *The vector formed by the i_1 and i_2 components of the $\boldsymbol{v_k}$ and c are parallel. In other words, if v_k^l is the l-component of $\boldsymbol{v_k}$, and c^l is the l component of $\boldsymbol{c}$, then $[v_1^{i_1}, v_2^{i_1}, \cdots c^{i_1}] = k[v_1^{i_2}, v_2^{i_2}, \cdots c^{i_2}]$ for some real $k > 0$.*

Algorithm 3 uses Theorem 2 to check if i_1 and i_2 are in the same tie class. The queries in lines 5, 7, 12 and 14 can be reduced to looking for α_j such that $\sum_j \alpha_j v_j^{i_1} + c^{i_1} < 0$. Such queries can be solved via an LP call, but we use Lemma 2 to avoid LP calls and check these queries efficiently.

Lemma 2. *The maximum and minimum values of $\sum_i \alpha_i v_i$, for real α_i, fixed real v_i, constrained by $|\alpha_i| \leq 1$, are $\sum_i |v_i|$ and $-\sum_i |v_i|$ respectively.*

If the network has a lot of inherent symmetry with respect to the input permutation, it is more likely for different neurons in the same layer to be tied together, leading to larger tie classes. This, in turn, reduces the number of basis vectors required to construct our over-approximation of the *Relu* image, and improves the quality of the over-approximation. Thus, we can expect our over-approximation to perform well for checking permutation invariance.

4.2 Backward (Polytope) Propagation

Given a convex polytope $P : \boldsymbol{x}L \leq \boldsymbol{u}$, we aim to symbolically construct a region that reasonably under-approximates *WeakestPrecond(Layer, P)*. Back propagating P across the linear part of a layer is easy as it can be done precisely by simply pulling back P across the affine transform of the layer.

Back propagating it across *Relu* is challenging as *WeakestPrecond*(*Relu*, *P*) may potentially touch all of the exponentially many "non-positive" quadrants. For each non-positive quadrant Q, relu acts on the points in the quadrant by projecting them linearly to the positive quadrant. If this projection is given by $Relu(\boldsymbol{x}) = \boldsymbol{x}\Pi_Q$, we have $Relu(\boldsymbol{x})L \leq \boldsymbol{u} \Leftrightarrow \boldsymbol{x}\Pi_Q L \leq \boldsymbol{u}$. Thus, the inverse image of P over *Relu* restricted to each quadrant is itself a polytope, giving us exponentially many polytopes in *WeakestPrecond*(*Relu*, *P*). Therefore, exact backpropagation is infeasible, and we look for under-approximations to *WeakestPrecond*(*Relu*, *P*).

A sound single polytope solution is to use $P \wedge \boldsymbol{x} \geq 0$ ignoring the entire "non-positive" region at the input, but this is too imprecise. Our compromise solution is to use a union of two polytopes: one that includes the positive region $P \wedge \boldsymbol{x} \geq 0$ and another that includes as much of the non-positive region as possible. To construct a polytope under-approximating the non-positive regions using inexpensive linear algebraic techniques, we use two separate methods, depending on whether P includes the 0 vector or not.

Case 1, P Does not include 0: Of all the non-positive quadrants, we choose the quadrant Q_c that has the center point of *reach*[i]. Then, we take the polytope corresponding to the inverse image of P over *Relu* restricted to Q_c as the under-approximation for the non-positive region. This center point based heuristic for choosing a quadrant is motivated by the fact that if the center point of *reach*[i] is in Q_c, we know that at-least a part of *reach*[i] must be in Q_c.

$$\boldsymbol{x}\begin{bmatrix} 1 & -1 \\ 1 & -1 \\ 1 & -1 \end{bmatrix} \leq \begin{bmatrix} 2 & -1 \end{bmatrix} \quad (3) \qquad \boldsymbol{x}\begin{bmatrix} 0 & 0 & 0 \\ 0 & 1 & 0 \\ 0 & 0 & 1 \end{bmatrix}\begin{bmatrix} 1 & -1 \\ 1 & -1 \\ 1 & -1 \end{bmatrix} = \boldsymbol{x}\begin{bmatrix} 0 & 0 \\ 1 & -1 \\ 1 & -1 \end{bmatrix} \leq \begin{bmatrix} 2 & -1 \end{bmatrix} \quad (4)$$

For example, consider the polytope given in Eq. 3. This touches all of the 7 non-positive quadrants, and so there will be one polytope for each of these in *WeakestPrecond*(*Relu*, *P*). Let us say the center point *reach*[i] is in the quadrant where the first component of $\boldsymbol{x}$ is negative, and all other components are non-negative. In this component, *Relu* acts by setting the first component to 0, and Π_Q is given by the identity matrix with the uppermost leftmost element set to 0. Then, following the calculations before, Eq. 4 gives us the polytope for the negative side region.

Case 2, P includes the 0 vector: If 0 is inside P, there is a high chance for the center of *reach*[i] to lie inside the all-negative quadrant, and for the above method to produce $\boldsymbol{x} \leq 0$ as the non-positive polytope. While this polytope may potentially cover a large number of the points in *reach*[i], the polytope touches P only at the origin. Thus, points in *reach*[i] that are close to the origin may not be covered. We therefore try to do better by extending $\boldsymbol{x} \leq 0$ a region of the form $\boldsymbol{x} \leq \boldsymbol{\eta}$, where all components of $\boldsymbol{\eta}$ are non-negative.

We notice that $\boldsymbol{x} \leq \boldsymbol{\eta} \Rightarrow 0 \leq Relu(\boldsymbol{x}) \leq \boldsymbol{\eta}$. Thus, $\boldsymbol{\eta}$ should satisfy the soundness condition $\forall \boldsymbol{y} \; 0 \leq \boldsymbol{y} \leq \boldsymbol{\eta} \Rightarrow \boldsymbol{y}L \leq \boldsymbol{u}$. To cover as many points as possible in the region, we try to maximize the "volume" $\prod_i \eta_i$, where η_i are the components of $\boldsymbol{\eta}$. If P has a single linear inequality, we can do this by constraining η to the boundary, and solving for the gradient of $\prod_i \eta_i$ to be 0. This reduces to solving a set of linear inequalities. We repeat this procedure for each inequality j in P to get an η_j and take the component-wise minimum to get the final η. For example, the columns 1 and 2 of polytope 5 below give us the η_1 and η_2 in Eq. 6.

$$x \begin{bmatrix} 1 & 2 \\ 2 & 1 \end{bmatrix} \leq [2 \; 2] \quad (5) \qquad\qquad \begin{aligned} \eta_1 &= [1 \; 0.5], \eta_2 = [0.5 \; 1] \\ \eta &= min(\eta_1, \eta_2) = [0.5 \; 0.5] \end{aligned} \quad (6)$$

Thus, we backpropagate a polytope across *Relu* to get a union of two polytopes. If we repeat this process at each layer, the number of polytopes will double at each layer, leading to an exponential blowup. To avoid this, we keep this 2-polytope under-approximation only to perform inclusion check (line 10 in Algorithm 1). The polytope corresponding to the negative region is dropped before it is subsequently back propagated further into earlier layers.

4.3   Inclusion Checking and Counterexample Propagation

Our goal is to check whether *reach*[i], given by basis B and center c, is included in *safe*[i], given as union of $P_1 : xL_1 \leq u_1$ and $P_2 : xL_2 \leq u_2$.

The first challenge in inclusion checking comes from the fact that *safe* is a disjunction of two polytopes. In the case when P comes from **Case 2** above, we notice that the two polytopes P_1 and P_2 lie entirely in the opposite sides of the plane separating the selected quadrant from the positive quadrant. This allows us to reduce the inclusion check to seeing if all points in *reach*[i] on each side of the plane lie entirely inside the corresponding polytope. For **Case 1** we do not have any such separating plane, but here inclusion holds iff for all i, all points in *reach*[i] above the $x_i \geq \eta_i$ plane lies in the positive side polytope. Thus, in both cases, we have reduced inclusion checking to a query of the form $(\exists \alpha : x = \alpha B + c \wedge |\alpha| \leq 1 \wedge x.v \geq k) \Rightarrow xL \leq u$.

To solve the above query, we pull $xL \leq u$ and $x.v \leq k$ back to the space of α using the linear transform given by B and c to get P_α and K_α respectively. This gives us a bounded polytope inclusion query, which can be solved by optimizing the objective given by each inequality of P_α with K_α as constraint. This we solve via an LP call, thus reducing inclusion checking to multiple simple LP calls.

If the inclusion fails, we obtain a point w that witnesses the violation of the inclusion at layer i. Since back-propagating this witness to the input layer to generate a counterexample is in general as hard as backpropagating the *safe* regions, in *pullBackCex* we generate multiple approximate back-propagations of w across a layer, which map to points close to w when taken across the layer. We do this by first generating several candidate back-propagated points x in the *reach* randomly. Then, we project each x towards the pullback of w with respect to the action of the layer restricted to x's quadrant. Finally, we discard all x that under the action of the layer lead to points that have euclidean distance more than D from w, where D is a parameter that we tune. Doing this backwards layer by layer gives us many points in the input layer which approximately map to w, and we check if these violate the property.

4.4   Example (continued from Sect. 3.1)

Details of *initPre*: For the input points $[x_{00}\ x_{01}\ x'_{00}\ x'_{01}\ ]$, $x_{00} = x'_{01}$, and $x_{01} = x'_{00}$. This can be expressed as saying that $[x_{00}\ x_{01}\ x'_{00}\ x'_{01}\ ]$ is a linear combination of the rows of: $\begin{bmatrix} 1\ 0\ 0\ 1 \\ 0\ 1\ 1\ 0 \end{bmatrix}$.

Now, as the points also have components in the range $[0, 1]$, we can shift the origin to 0.5 and scale by 0.5 to get the affine region $\alpha B_0 + c_0$, $|\alpha| \le 1$ with

$$B_0 = \begin{bmatrix} 0.5 & 0 & 0 & 0.5 \\ 0 & 0.5 & 0.5 & 0 \end{bmatrix} \quad c_0 = [0.5\ 0.5\ 0.5\ 0.5]$$

Forward Propagation Across Layer 1: Now, we follow the algorithm as it pushes 1 forward across the layers of the network to get the postconditions at various points. Firstly, 1 is pushed forward across linear layer 0 by taking the pushforward with respect to W_0 and b_0 to get:

$$B'_0 = \begin{bmatrix} 500 & -500 & 500 & -500 & -500 & 500 & -500 & 500 \\ -500 & 500 & -500 & 500 & 500 & -500 & 500 & -500 \end{bmatrix}$$
$$c'_0 = [0\ 0\ -1\ -1\ 0\ 0\ -1\ -1]$$

Now, the algorithm performs the tie class analysis to push B'_0 and c'_0 across the *Relu* to get B_1 and c_1. Here, using 3 of Theorem 2 the algorithm determines that the tie classes of the columns are $\{0, 5\}$, $\{1, 4\}$, $\{2, 7\}$, $\{3, 6\}$. We note that if x_0 and x'_0 are related by the permutation that swaps the components, the pairs of variables in each of the above tie class will actually have the same value. Thus, the tie class is capturing a weaker over-approximation of this strict symmetry property. Now, for each tie class, all the columns of all the basis vectors in B'_0 not in the tie class is set to 0, and collecting the resulting vectors gives us B_1; c_1 is simply given by $Relu(c'_0)$. As before, B_1 is pushed across linear layer 1 to get B'_1. Both these matrices are given in Eq. 2 in Sect. 3.1. Again, the algorithm performs a tie class analysis, getting $\{0, 3\}$ and $\{1, 2\}$. This again is a weakening of the fact that these pairs of variables are actually equal. Note that the basis B_2 gotten on the other side of the *Relu* in this case is actually the same as B'_1.

5   Experiments

We have implemented this in Python, using the *numpy* and *scipy* libraries for linear algebra and LP solving, respectively. Our experiments were run on an Intel i7 9750H processor with 6 cores and 12 threads with 32 GB RAM. The artifacts are available for evaluation at https://github.com/digumx/permcheck/tree/nfm22.

We have compared our algorithm with the Marabou [13,14] implementation of the Reluplex [12] on a few DNNs of various sizes with the following target behavior: for n inputs, there should be n outputs so that if input i is the largest among all the inputs, output i should be 1. These networks have three layers excluding the input layer, with sizes $2n(n-1)$, $n(n-1)$ and n respectively. Formally, we check that $0 \leq \boldsymbol{x} \leq 1 \Rightarrow |\sigma(\mathcal{N}(\boldsymbol{x})) - \mathcal{N}(\sigma(\boldsymbol{x}))| \leq \epsilon$, where σ represents the permutation sending $1 \rightarrow 2, 2 \rightarrow 3 \cdots n \rightarrow 1$ cyclically, and ϵ varies across the experiments. Note that if the network follows the target behavior, then this property should hold.

We first demonstrate our algorithm on a set of hand-crafted networks solving the above problem for which we have manually fixed the weights. The network has been manually engineered so that the first and second layers perform pairwise comparisions of the input, and the third layer combines the results of these comparisions logically to produce the output.

In general, as the input to the above DNN varies within the precondition region, the input to the *Relu* nodes can regularly switch between positive and negative. This can potentially lead to an exponential blowup in the number of case-splits. However, since permuting the inputs of this DNN leads to a more complicated permutation of the intermediate layers, intuitively we should be able to easily verify the property using an effective abstraction. The columns labelled *Safe* of Table 1 compares the time taken by our algorithm and by Marabou on these networks and demonstrates that the over-approximation and under-approximation used in our algorithm form an effective abstraction for this example, and is likely to be so for similar, symmetric networks.

We also test our algorithm on an unsafe problem using the same hand-crafted network from the previous example. To do so, we change the permutation on the output side to be the identity permutation, leading to a property that clearly should never hold. The results are given in the columns labelled *Unsafe* of Table 1 and show that our counterexample search is able to find counterexamples in a way that is competitive with Marabou, especially for networks with 8 or more inputs.

Table 1. Comparison of Marabou and our algorithm on safe and unsafe synthetic networks

Inputs	Size	Safe			Unsafe		
		Our algorithm	Marabou		Our algorithm	Marabou	
			Time	Splits		Time	Splits
3	21	0.074	4.833	2046	0.048	0.187	68
4	40	0.112	>100.8	>11234	0.074	0.202	38
5	65	0.163	>101.9	>5186	0.132	0.267	47
6	96	0.269	>100.1	>2243	0.233	0.603	60
7	133	0.493	>106.8	>1533	0.422	1.085	64
8	176	0.911	>126.5	>475	0.809	71.89	299
9	225	1.477	>183.9	>467	1.508	5.011	91
10	280	2.276	>158.7	>394	2.157	29.09	202

Finally, we compare the performance of our algorithm with Marabou on two sets of trained DNNs. The first is a set of DNNs for the same problem that have been trained using SGD to have the target behavior described above, using a large number of randomly generated input and corresponding correct output for training. We compare the algorithms on trained networks of various sizes, and with various values of ϵ.

The results (Table 2) show that for these examples, most networks are unsafe, and as the size of the network increases, both our algorithm and Marabou is able to find counterexamples. However, the time taken by Marabou increases significantly for the larger networks, eventually timing out for the largest examples, while our algorithm scales much better. The table also shows that for smaller networks Marabou performs better than our algorithm. We believe this is due to the inefficiencies in our prototype implementation compared to Marabou. For some small networks, our algorithm is unable to find a proof or counterexample, however we believe this issue can be handled with a counterexample guided refinement procedure in the future (Fig. 2).

Table 2. Comparison of Marabou and our algorithm on trained networks. the time is given in *seconds*.

Network				Our algorithm		Marabou		
n	Size	ϵ	Accuracy	Time	Result	Time	Splits	Result
3	21	0.1	94.0%	0.023	CEX	0.023	10	CEX
3	21	0.5	100%	0.249	INCONS	0.034	16	CEX
3	21	0.9	100%	0.204	INCONS	1.330	274	SAFE
5	65	0.1	97.1%	0.197	CEX	0.684	35	CEX
5	65	0.5	99.5%	0.188	CEX	0.682	35	CEX
6	96	0.1	98.0%	0.012	CEX	3.070	85	CEX
6	96	0.3	98.6%	0.018	CEX	3.138	85	CEX
7	133	0.1	87.5%	0.011	CEX	5.651	84	CEX
7	133	0.3	96.1%	0.012	CEX	5.810	86	CEX
8	176	0.1	65.7%	0.012	CEX	44.42	258	CEX
8	176	0.3	68.5%	1.584	CEX	42.80	258	CEX
9	255	0.1	58.4%	1.193	CEX	>120.3	>228	TO
9	255	0.3	70.2%	1.310	CEX	>127.9	>179	TO
10	280	0.1	20.8%	4.040	CEX	>130.4	>58	TO
10	280	0.3	31.0%	3.966	CEX	>125.0	>58	TO

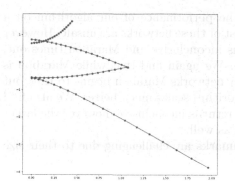

Fig. 2. Example craft paths (Color figure online)

The second set of examples involve DNNs that we have trained to solve a smaller-scale simpler version of the collision avoidance problem. Here, we consider a craft moving through 2D space with a given initial position and velocity under a given constant acceleration. The DNN must take as input the initial position, velocity and constant acceleration for a pair of crafts and determine weather they will collide. In the attached figure, the green plots show the trajectory of a non-colliding pair of crafts, and the red plots show the trajectory of a colliding pair in the dataset. There is an inherent symmetry to this problem: if we swap the two crafts, the output of the DNN should remain the same. We generated a dataset of 100000 pairs of craft position, velocity and acceleration, labeled as colliding and non-colliding. On this dataset we trained (using SGD) DNNs with various sizes, and used them to compare Marabou and our method on the problem of verifying invariance under swapping for different values of ϵ. The data is given in the Table 3.

Table 3. Comparison of Marabou and our algorithm on collision avoidance networks.

Network			Our algorithm		Marabou		
Size	ϵ	Accuracy	Time	Result	Time	Splits	Result
33	0.1	76.4%	0.059	CEX	0.123	27	CEX
33	0.5	97.2%	0.337	CEX	0.312	40	CEX
33	0.7	99.5%	1.440	INCONS	0.325	47	CEX
33	0.9	100%	1.679	INCONS	>121.0	>12466	TO
52	0.1	81.6%	0.093	CEX	0.808	26	CEX
52	0.7	98.9%	10.13	INCONS	5.692	140	CEX
52	0.9	100%	10.94	INCONS	>121.0	>4084	TO
90	0.1	90.0%	0.433	CEX	10.13	100	CEX
90	0.5	98.6%	1.906	CEX	10.07	101	CEX
90	0.9	100%	36.25	INCONS	>121.0	>745	TO
138	0.1	92.3%	0.564	CEX	27.52	108	CEX
138	0.9	99.9%	31.34	INCONS	>121.0	> 274	TO
318	0.1	91.7%	2.328	CEX	>121.0	>118	TO
318	0.3	94.9%	2.373	CEX	>121.0	>118	TO
318	0.5	96.8%	2.445	CEX	>121.0	>118	TO
488	0.1	92.5%	10.15	CEX	>121.0	>6	TO
488	0.3	94.5%	9.932	CEX	>121.0	>6	TO

The results (Table 3) demonstrate the performance of our algorithm on a realistic example. Again we find that most of these networks are unsafe. However for some networks our algorithm returns inconclusive and Marabou times out, and these networks may indeed be safe. We again find that while Marabou is faster on smaller networks, for the larger networks Marabou begins to time out more and more frequently, while our algorithm scales much better. We also find that for certain networks, our algorithm returns inconclusive, however the larger of these networks are hard for Marabou as well.

Though small in number, our benchmarks are challenging due to their size and complexity of verification. We attribute the efficiency of our approach to a number of design elements that are crucial in our approach – a layer by layer analysis, abstractions (that help reduce case-splits), under-approximations (that lead to good counterexamples), algebraic manipulations instead of LP/SMT calls, etc. A downside of our algorithm is that it may sometimes return *inconclusive*. A counterexample-guided refinement procedure can help tackle this issue.

6 Related Work

The field of DNN verification has gained significant attention in recent years. DNNs are increasingly being used in safety- and business-critical systems, making it crucial to formally argue that the presence of ML components do not compromise on the essential and desirable system-properties. Efforts in formal verification of neural networks have relied on abstraction-refinement [7,15,16], constraint-solving [1,5,6,20], abstract interpretation [9,17,18], layer-by-layer search [10,21], two-player games [22], dependency analysis [3] and several other approaches [11,23].

The most closely related work to ours is using a DNN verification engine such as Reluplex [12] and Marabou [13,14] to verify permutation invariance properties by reasoning over two copies of the network. Reasoning over multiple copies also comes up in the context of verifying Deep Reinforcement Learning Systems [8]. However, verification of DNNs is worst-case exponential in the size of the network and therefore our proposal to handle permutation invariance directly (instead of multiplying the network-size) holds a lot of promise.

Polytope propagation has been quite useful in the context of DNN verification (e.g. [19,24]). In the case of forward propagation, however, it requires computing the convex hull each time, which is an expensive. In contrast, our tie-class analysis helps us propagate the affine regions efficiently. In the backward direction, even though we rely on convex polytope propagation, we mitigate the worst-case exponential blow-up by using a 2-polytope under-approximation method that does not depend on LP or SMT solving, and is both scalable and effective.

In general, the complexity of a verification exercise can be mitigated by abstraction techniques, e.g. [2,7] for DNNs. The essential idea is to let go of an exact computation, which is achieved by merging of neurons in [7]. In [15], the authors propose construction of a simpler neural network with fewer neurons, using interval weights, to over-approximate the output range of the original neural network. Our work is similar in spirit, in that it avoids exact computation unless really necessary for establishing the property. In practice, these techniques can even be used complementary to one another.

7 Conclusion

We presented a technique to verify permutation invariance in DNNs, based on novel forward- and backward-propagation methods. Our approach is sound (not just for permutation invariance properties, but for general safety properties too), efficient, and scalable. It is natural to wonder whether the approximately computed reach and safe regions may be refined to eliminate spurious counterexamples, and continue propagation till the property is proved or refuted. Our approach is definitely amenable to a counterexample-guided refinement. In particular, the spurious counterexamples can guide us to split *Relu* nodes (to refine over-approximations), and add additional safe regions (to refine under-approximations). This would require us to maintain sets of affine regions and convex polytopes at each layer, which is challenging but an interesting direction to pursue.

References

1. Akintunde, M., Lomuscio, A., Maganti, L., Pirovano, E.: Reachability analysis for neural agent-environment systems. In: Thielscher, M., Toni, F., Wolter, F., (eds.), Principles of Knowledge Representation and Reasoning: Proceedings of the Sixteenth International Conference, KR 2018, Tempe, Arizona, 30 October - 2 November 2018, pp. 184–193. AAAI Press (2018)
2. Ashok, P., Hashemi, V., Křetínský, J., Mohr, S.: DeepAbstract: neural network abstraction for accelerating verification. In: Hung, D.V., Sokolsky, O. (eds.) ATVA 2020. LNCS, vol. 12302, pp. 92–107. Springer, Cham (2020). https://doi.org/10.1007/978-3-030-59152-6_5
3. Botoeva, E., Kouvaros, P., Kronqvist, J., Lomuscio, A., Misener, R.: Efficient verification of relu-based neural networks via dependency analysis. In: Proceedings of the AAAI Conference on Artificial Intelligence, vol. 34, no. 04, 3291–3299 (2020)
4. de Moura, L., Bjørner, N.: Z3: an efficient SMT solver. In: Ramakrishnan, C.R., Rehof, J. (eds.) TACAS 2008. LNCS, vol. 4963, pp. 337–340. Springer, Heidelberg (2008). https://doi.org/10.1007/978-3-540-78800-3_24
5. Dutta, S., Jha, S., Sankaranarayanan, S., Tiwari, A.: Output range analysis for deep feedforward neural networks. In: Dutle, A., Muñoz, C., Narkawicz, A. (eds.) NFM 2018. LNCS, vol. 10811, pp. 121–138. Springer, Cham (2018). https://doi.org/10.1007/978-3-319-77935-5_9
6. Ehlers, R.: Formal verification of piece-wise linear feed-forward neural networks. In: D'Souza, D., Narayan Kumar, K. (eds.) ATVA 2017. LNCS, vol. 10482, pp. 269–286. Springer, Cham (2017). https://doi.org/10.1007/978-3-319-68167-2_19
7. Elboher, Y.Y., Gottschlich, J., Katz, G.: An abstraction-based framework for neural network verification. In: Lahiri, S.K., Wang, C. (eds.) Computer Aided Verification. pp. pp. 43–65. Springer International Publishing, Cham (2020)

8. Eliyahu, T., Kazak, Y., Katz, G., Schapira, M.: Verifying learning-augmented systems. In: Kuipers, F.A., Caesar, M.C. (eds.), ACM SIGCOMM 2021 Conference, Virtual Event, USA, 23–27 August 2021, pp. 305–318. ACM (2021)

9. Gehr, T., Mirman, M., Drachsler-Cohen, D., Tsankov, P., Chaudhuri, S., Vechev, M.: Ai2: safety and robustness certification of neural networks with abstract interpretation. In: 2018 IEEE Symposium on Security and Privacy (SP), Los Alamitos, CA, USA, IEEE Computer Society, May 2018

10. Huang, X., Kwiatkowska, M., Wang, S., Wu, M.: Safety verification of deep neural networks. In: Majumdar, R., Kunčak, V. (eds.) CAV 2017. LNCS, vol. 10426, pp. 3–29. Springer, Cham (2017). https://doi.org/10.1007/978-3-319-63387-9_1

11. Jacoby, Y., Barrett, C., Katz, G.: Verifying recurrent neural networks using invariant inference. In: Hung, D.V., Sokolsky, O. (eds.) ATVA 2020. LNCS, vol. 12302, pp. 57–74. Springer, Cham (2020). https://doi.org/10.1007/978-3-030-59152-6_3

12. Katz, G., Barrett, C., Dill, D.L., Julian, K., Kochenderfer, M.J.: Reluplex: an efficient SMT solver for verifying deep neural networks. In: Majumdar, R., Kunčak, V. (eds.) CAV 2017. LNCS, vol. 10426, pp. 97–117. Springer, Cham (2017). https://doi.org/10.1007/978-3-319-63387-9_5

13. Katz, G., et al.: The marabou framework for verification and analysis of deep neural networks. In: Dillig, I., Tasiran, S. (eds.) CAV 2019. LNCS, vol. 11561, pp. 443–452. Springer, Cham (2019). https://doi.org/10.1007/978-3-030-25540-4_26

14. Kazak, Y., Barrett, C.W., Katz, G., Schapira, M.: Verifying deep-rl-driven systems. In: Proceedings of the 2019 Workshop on Network Meets AI & ML, NetAI@SIGCOMM 2019, Beijing, China, 23 August 2019, pp. 83–89. ACM (2019)

15. Prabhakar, P., Afzal, Z.R.: Abstraction based output range analysis for neural networks. In: Wallach, H.M., Larochelle, H., Beygelzimer, A., d'Alché-Buc, F., Fox, E.B., Garnett, R. (eds.), Advances in Neural Information Processing Systems 32: Annual Conference on Neural Information Processing Systems 2019, NeurIPS 2019, 8–14 December 2019, Vancouver, BC, Canada, pp. 15762–15772 (2019)

16. Pulina, L., Tacchella, A.: An abstraction-refinement approach to verification of artificial neural networks. In: Touili, T., Cook, B., Jackson, P. (eds.) CAV 2010. LNCS, vol. 6174, pp. 243–257. Springer, Heidelberg (2010). https://doi.org/10.1007/978-3-642-14295-6_24

17. Singh, G., Gehr, T., Mirman, M., Püschel, M., Vechev, M.T.: Fast and effective robustness certification. In: Bengio, S., Wallach, H.M., Larochelle, H., Grauman, K., Cesa-Bianchi, N., Garnett, R. (eds.), Advances in Neural Information Processing Systems 31: Annual Conference on Neural Information Processing Systems 2018, NeurIPS 2018, December 3–8, 2018, Montréal, Canada, pp. 10825–10836 (2018)

18. Singh, G., Gehr, T., Püschel, M., Vechev, M.T.: An abstract domain for certifying neural networks. Proc. ACM Program. Lang. 3(POPL), 41:1–41:30 (2019)

19. Sotoudeh, M., Thakur, A.V.: SyReNN: a tool for analyzing deep neural networks. In: TACAS 2021. LNCS, vol. 12652, pp. 281–302. Springer, Cham (2021). https://doi.org/10.1007/978-3-030-72013-1_15

20. Tjeng, V., Xiao, K.Y., Tedrake, R.: Evaluating robustness of neural networks with mixed integer programming. In: ICLR (2019)

21. Wicker, M., Huang, X., Kwiatkowska, M.: Feature-guided black-box safety testing of deep neural networks. In: Beyer, D., Huisman, M. (eds.), Tools and Algorithms for the Construction and Analysis of Systems - 24th International Conference, TACAS 2018, Held as Part of the European Joint Conferences on Theory and Practice of Software, ETAPS 2018, Thessaloniki, Greece, 14–20 April 2018, Proceedings, Part I, volume 10805 of LNCS, pp. 408–426. Springer (2018)

22. Wu, M., Wicker, M., Ruan, W., Huang, X., Kwiatkowska, M.: A game-based approximate verification of deep neural networks with provable guarantees. Theor. Comput. Sci. **807**, 298–329 (2020)

23. Xiang, W., Tran, H., Johnson, T.T.: Output reachable set estimation and verification for multilayer neural networks. IEEE Trans. Neural Netw. Learn. Syst. **29**(11), 5777–5783 (2018)

24. Zhang, H., Shinn, M., Gupta, A., Gurfinkel, A., Le, N., Narodytska, N.: Verification of recurrent neural networks for cognitive tasks via reachability analysis. In: Giacomo, G.D. (eds.) et al., ECAI 2020–24th European Conference on Artificial Intelligence, 29 August-8 September 2020, Santiago de Compostela, Spain, August 29 - September 8, 2020 - Including 10th Conference on Prestigious Applications of Artificial Intelligence (PAIS 2020), volume 325 of Frontiers in Artificial Intelligence and Applications, pp. 1690–1697. IOS Press (2020)

Configurable Benchmarks for C Model Checkers

Xaver Fink, Philipp Berger[(✉)][iD], and Joost-Pieter Katoen[iD]

RWTH Aachen University, Aachen, Germany
{berger,katoen}@cs.rwth-aachen.de

Abstract. Software model checkers employ many different techniques. During various competitions, the capabilities of these verification tools are compared on a wide variety of benchmarks. Our aim is to get insight into which code characteristics are "hard" for software model checkers. To that end, we present a software tool that automatically generates C benchmark programs that are intended as stress tests for software model checkers. The parameters of the generated C programs, e.g., program size, types of operation, are controllable, and programs can be tweaked, e.g., floats can be replaced by integers and pointer dereferencing can be used for variable accesses. Our tool enables a systematic comparison of software verifiers. We illustrate its usage by evaluating the top verifiers from the SV-COMP 2022 reachability category and analyze what makes benchmarks hard for these tools and how well these tools scale, both in terms of code related to the property at hand as well as in terms of code that is unrelated to it.

1 Introduction

Software model checkers verify essential properties of program code such as reachability and safety. Model checking tools for various programming languages exist; this paper focuses on verifying ANSI C programs. Software model checking is notoriously hard. It attempts to tackle a problem that is inherently undecidable. Software model checkers are in fact no pure model checkers, but use techniques from various domains [14]: model checking (such as abstraction-refinement), deductive verification (e.g. loop invariant synthesis), abstract interpretation (using abstract domains) and satisfiability (modulo theory) checking.

The capability and precision of software model checkers are annually compared in verification competitions such as the annual Competition on Software Verification (SV-COMP) [2]. As an important by-product of these competitions, a set of benchmarks is provided to the research community which grows with each issue of the competition. Many benchmarks are provided by the tool builders of the competing software model checkers and often focus on specific new algorithmic developments. As a result, the benchmark code is usually not consistent in size and properties used, which, in general, is great but makes it impossible to study the impact of specific code features and -size. Some papers show that

© Springer Nature Switzerland AG 2022
J. V. Deshmukh et al. (Eds.): NFM 2022, LNCS 13260, pp. 338–354, 2022.
https://doi.org/10.1007/978-3-031-06773-0_18

exposing software model checkers to industrial code indeed shows significant weaknesses [10,21].

The aim of this work is to get insight into which code characteristics are "hard" for software model checkers. To that end, we present a software tool that automatically generates C benchmark programs that are intended as stress tests for software model checkers. The parameters of the generated C programs, e.g., program size, types of operation and data, are controllable, and programs can be tweaked, e.g., floats can be replaced by integers and pointer dereferencing can be used for variable accesses. The generated programs are reactive in nature, i.e., infinite loops in which in each iteration signal variables are set non-deterministically, statements are executed in a lock-step manner and a property check is carried out. These closed-loop programs are popular in the automotive domain and can be obtained automatically from block-based Simulink models, see [1]. Figure 1 provides an overview of our benchmark-generation tool.

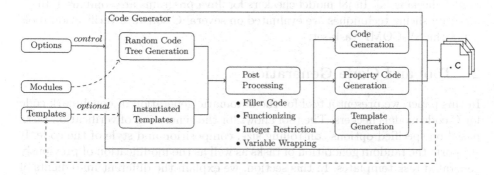

Fig. 1. An overview over the inner working of the benchmark generation tool.

Our tool enables a systematic comparison of software verifiers and is publicly available. We show its usage by performing a number of extensive experiments using the top verifiers from the SV-COMP 2022 "ReachSafety" category investigating their *robustness*—both in terms of verification outcome as well as model-checking performance—against code changes that do not affect the validity of the property at hand. Our experiments address questions such as:

- What is the effect of adding arbitrary, innocent code?
- What is the impact of variable wrapping (as array, struct, etc.)?
- What is the effect of wrapping expressions by function calls?
- What is the effect of using pointer for variable accesses?
- What is effect of floating-point variables and arithmetic?, and
- How scalable are software model checkers?

Our experiments give some interesting and unexpected insights, and are statistically analyzed in the paper.

Related Work. Bug detection in model checkers using fuzzing is presented in [22]. Soundness and precision is analyzed using benchmarks generated from seed programs in [15]. Automatic code generation is discussed in several works. A translation tool for the generation of programming language code from existing, hand-crafted Event-B models is presented in [17]. [13] presents a framework for synthesizing benchmark tasks from formal specifications and translation into C, Java or Petri nets, used in the RERS competition [12]. While task size and -hardness are configurable, it is not possible to apply transformations for differential analysis or control code connectivity. In [1] industrial-grade C-code, generated from Simulink, is benchmarked with an industrial verification software. This study was repeated in [21] with academic verification tools such as 2LS, CPACHECKER and others.

There exist several reports and evaluations comparing specific verification approaches. A comparison of static program analysis with model checking is performed in [20]. In another work traditional testing methods are compared to model checking [4]. In [8] model checkers for Java programs are compared. In [7] program slicing techniques are evaluated on several C software verification tools using the SV-COMP task-set.

2   Tool and Code Generation

In this paper, we present a tool for the automatic generation of benchmark code for C code model checkers. The tool allows for the generation of verification tasks based on specified options controlling size, composition and style of the code. It supports the random generation of tasks as well as the modification of previously generated task templates. In this section, we explain the different ingredients of our tool as indicated in Fig. 1.

Code Structure. The generated verification tasks follow the structure presented in Fig. 2. The tasks consist of an infinite loop as typical for reactive systems. The system being modeled can be standalone or downstream of other, similar components, modeled by signal variables that change their value within a specified range non-deterministically at the start of every iteration. Execution in such systems happens in (forced) lockstep in a predefined, known and fixed order. Such systems are popular in automotive engineering and can be auto-coded to C for embedded systems using Simulink from block-based Simulink models. The structure of generated verification tasks into requirements in this work is inspired by the tasks encountered in [1].

Requirements. A requirement defines the behavior of one or more *output variables*, whose values are defined using expressions over variables and constants as input. An output can also be an input, but we require it to be distinctly marked using the `last_i(var, steps)` function (internally), realized by distinct copies in the code for allowing the verification access to earlier values. Figure 3 shows an example requirement which defines `var2` based on other inputs. From every such definition of an output variable we derive properties, essentially describing the same behavior as the conditional assignment expression. One or more

```
1   extern void reach_error();
2   int main() {
3     initialize();
4     while(1) {
5       nondet_var_update();
6       step();
7       if(!property())
8         reach_error();
9       shift_last_variables();
10    }}
11
```

Fig. 2. The basic structure of the generated code.

requirements form the loop body of the code, where they are executed in an infinite loop with non-deterministic updates to all external input variables before each step. Non-deterministic initialization and updates to the variables based on defined variable ranges allow for model checking of all possible system behaviors. On generating the code, we try not to impose any unnecessary restrictions on the order and the type of operations. Necessary restrictions include prohibition of undefined behavior and arithmetic problems like division by zero, which we achieve by over-approximation of value ranges, see Sect. 2.1. This diversity can be helpful in "fuzzing" edge cases (see e.g.[1]).

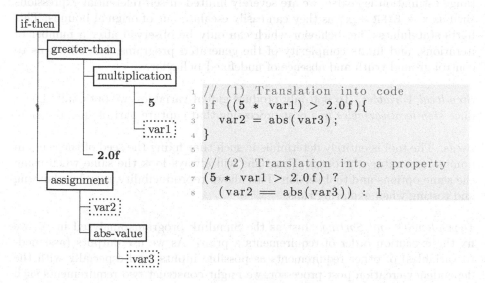

Fig. 3. Code representation in the tool: internal, property and functional.

---

[1] https://github.com/ultimate-pa/ultimate/issues/578.

Templates. A template is a piece of C code including all internal supplemental information in a non-human-readable format. Its purpose is being used by further code-gen and/or post-processing, e.g. in differential analysis of `float` vs. `int`, where multiple programs are generated from the same base template. It is not meant to be hand-crafted, only exported as the result of a call to the tool.

2.1   Code Generation

Type Widening and Expression Conditioning. When generating code, restrictions regarding allowed types and values need to be passed along the generated tree of operations. Similarly, we need to gauge possible value ranges of generated expressions when considering variables for expression generation. Instead of full-blown model checking or applying SMT solving, we rely on a simplified over-approximation consisting of a range and list of excluded values. When considering an integer division for example, we disallow 0. Similarly, as we do not allow over- or underflows on signed integers or floating-point variables as to not risk undefined behavior or `Inf`-values, we enforce limits smaller than the maximum of the datatype.

Limitations of the Tool. While we can generate functions by way of extracting parts of the code tree and placing them into functions, no recursive functions may be generated this way. The current version does not generate any dynamic pointer arithmetic or otherwise non-trivial access via pointers. As our expression range estimation is coarse, we are severely limited in self-referential expressions such as `x = EXPR + x;` as they can easily escalate out of original bounds. This hurts statefulness, i.e. behavior which can only be observed after a number of iterations, and limits complexity of the generated programs, but allows us to control ground truth and absence of undefined behavior.

Step-local Variables. To not only produce global variables, we optionally introduce *step-local variables* in a post-processing that capture part of an expression.

Seeds. The tool is entirely deterministic such that fixing the seed of the random number generator, the output programs will always look the same when using the same options and tool version. This allows reproducibility, easy bug hunting and testing when exploring runs.

Dependencies and Sorting. Just as the Simulink programs analyzed in [1], we fix the execution order of requirements a priori. As we use outputs (assigned-to variables) of other requirements as possible inputs, and especially with the dependency-creation post-processor, we might construct two requirements such as `x = y + c;` and `y = 0.5 * x;`. Since there is a mutual dependence on the output of the other being available, we break this cycle by introducing an explicit `last`, e.g. `y = 0.5 * last(x);`, accessing the value of the previous iteration. Now a clear ordering can be established.

Tool and Availability. The tool is publicly available at https://github.com/moves-rwth/c-code-generator. It is written in Java 11 and consists of about 23k LOC. Development of its core has taken about 30 person-months.

3   Benchmarking the Open-Source Verifiers

The experiments were performed on a machine with four AMD Opteron 6172 processors, 192 GB DDR3 memory at 1333 MHz MHz on Debian 11 running kernel 5.14.0-0.bpo.2-amd64. Each benchmark verification run was restricted to 15 min of CPU time, 15 GB of memory and at most eight CPU cores, unless otherwise noted. These restrictions were chosen based on the SV-COMP specifications to account for verification tool optimizations.

3.1   Verification Tool Setup

We evaluate the experiments by benchmarking verification runs of six academic verification tools with historically good performance on reachability properties. Based on the performance in the category "ReachSafety" of the SV-COMP 2022[2] we chose 2LS [16], CPACHECKER [3], ESBMC [9], PESCO [18], SYMBIOTIC [6] and ULTIMATE AUTOMIZER [11].

For all verification tools we used the version and verification parameters supplied for the ReachSafety Category of SV-COMP 2022. One exception is SYMBIOTIC, for which we had to replace its shipped version of libz3 with a build compatible with our host CPUs. We note that this might influence the tool-performance. While we would have liked to include VERIABS, the winner of the ReachSafety category in SV-COMP 2022, its license allows use only within SV-COMP 2022 and the competition benchmarks.

3.2   Verification Task Creation

The individual verification tasks were created using our tool. The verification task sets for each configuration were generated by a PowerShell wrapper script. The wrapper script produces the following output for each configuration:

- .c-File and corresponding .yml-File for each verification task,
- .json-File containing file-statistics for each verification task,
- .xml-Files for each verification tool containing Benchexec task definitions,
- multiple helper scripts.

In general, we create 100 tasks (files) per configuration and test. However, the tool is capable of producing a higher number of tasks without difficulties. All created files, the tool and generated data can be found in the artifact.

3.3   Benchmarking Setup

For reliable and reproducible results, we rely on the Benchexec framework with the SV-COMP 2022 configuration. Benchexec is a benchmarking framework developed at the LMU Munich, designed to reliably measure and limit resource

---
[2] https://sv-comp.sosy-lab.org/2022/systems.php.

usage using the cgroups feature of the Linux kernel [5]. Its successful usage in the annual Competitions on Software Verification of recent years make it a great tool for our purposes. We set up our environment based on the instructions for Execution and Reproduction of the SV-COMP 2022 benchmarks[3].

3.4   Experiment I: Effect of Filler Code

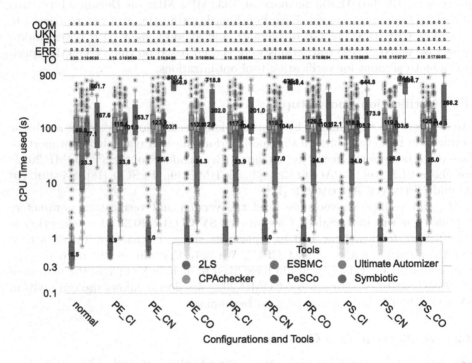

Fig. 4. Influence of filler code on CPU time used. P is the position of inserted code (End, Random, Start), C the connection type (inputs, outputs, nothing).

Table 1. Wilcoxon rank sum results on runtimes in Fig. 4 between unchanged and modified code. We use $p < 0.05$ as threshold.

Tool	PE_CI	PE_CN	PE_CO	PR_CI	PR_CN	PR_CO	PS_CI	PS_CN	PS_CO
2LS	2.2E−06	4.1E−09	4.0E−08	7.9E−07	4.2E−10	1.1E−08	9.9E−07	1.4E−08	3.8E−08
CPA	1.9E−02	3.8E−04	5.7E−03	9.5E−03	5.5E−04	1.3E−04	1.1E−02	1.4E−03	8.7E−04
ESBMC	6.2E−01	5.8E−01	6.0E−01	7.8E−01	6.1E−01	6.6E−01	7.3E−01	5.2E−01	5.9E−01
PESCO	4.3E−03	1.3E−03	1.8E−03	7.2E−03	3.7E−03	1.0E−04	4.2E−03	8.6E−03	9.9E−04
SYMB	6.6E−01	NA	5.3E−01	4.3E−01	NA	7.3E−01	5.9E−01	NA	3.2E−01
UA	NA	NA	NA	NA	NA	NA	NA	NA	NA

---

[3] https://gitlab.com/sosy-lab/benchmarking/competition-scripts/#instructions-for-execution-and-reproduction.

Here, we investigate the influence of additional code on the model checking time of the requirement. The programs studied in [1] often contained large disjunct parts together with unused functions and variables. The size of the property ($\approx$50 operations) under test stays constant over all configurations and benchmarks. The filler code is made up of $\approx$50 operations and is subject to the same generation conditions as the property of interest. An expression such as y = 0.5 * x; would count as two operations (one assignment and one multiplication).

Our tool supports three possible options for the location of filler code: in front of the real code (**S**), behind it (**E**) or randomly placed (even within, **R**). We fully control the flow of information between both code parts: we can either have no connection (neither input- nor output variables are shared, **N**), shared input meaning the external input signals are used read-only by both code parts (**I**) and consecutive, where the filler code uses outputs generated by the real code as read-only inputs (**O**). Correctness of the property in question is not influenced by the filler code in any way.

Figure 4 shows box-plots of the processing times including the median. The top lines show the number of instances that resulted in state "out of memory" (OOM), "unknown" (UKN), "false negative" (FN), "error" (ERR) and "time-out" (TO). The configuration "normal" provides a baseline, containing only the property under test and no additional code. For example, the leftmost blue entry, marked in the color of the corresponding tool 2LS, shows the median runtime (0.5s), upper and lower quartils, outliers towards the top and eight timeouts.

For determining whether the changes in runtime are significant, we employ the *Wilcoxon rank sum test with continuity correction* as provided by R^4 on all runtimes $\leq$ TO (900s) that resulted in "true". The values given in Table 1 are the p-values, meaning a lower value equals a higher probability for the two sample sets being from different populations, implying a significance in observed difference. We say the shift in runtime is significant iff $p < 0.05$. If less than five data points are available, we instead put "NA". As all results other than "true" are not considered in this test, we manually evaluate them.

When reviewing Table 1, we can see that for all tools but ESBMC, all configurations show a significant, positive shift. Thus, we—considering available space and time—focus on "PS_CN" for further analysis, as this configuration, with no connection between parts, gives the tools the best possible chance of ignoring the disjunct code.

We now fix the placement and connection type of the filler code and instead test different amounts (scaling). The results are given in Fig. 5. The number of operators added as filler is given in the configuration name. The configuration "normal" with $\approx$50 operations again provides a baseline with no filler coded added. SYMBIOTIC can solve almost no instances, regardless of filler presence, with 92% timeouts even in the best case. ULTIMATE AUTOMIZER similarly has many timeouts. They are therefore not considered any further. The box-plot of CPACHECKER in the 500-configuration and those of 2LS and PESCO in 250 and 500 are skewed by the large amount of instances running into timeout. As the results of the model checker in cases of timeout or error are not known, they are

---

[4] https://stat.ethz.ch/R-manual/R-devel/library/stats/html/wilcox.test.html.

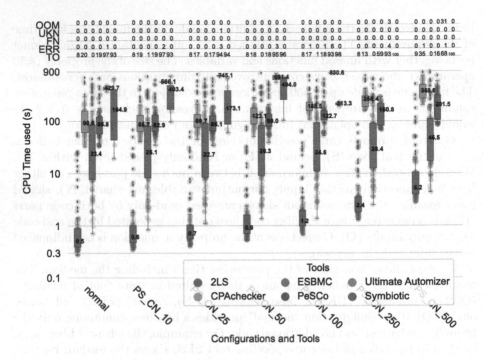

Fig. 5. Influence of filler code on CPU time used. Position and connection are fixed to "start" and "nothing", but the amount of filler is varied.

ignored. All relevant tools show significant impact of additional code on runtime, and, keeping the loglog-scale (the amount of code also grows exponentially) in mind, at least a linear influence of its size. This is an important insight, as, due to the connection type, the filler code should potentially be easily handled by slicing and static analysis. Even SYMBIOTIC, which implements program slicing, is heavily influenced by unconnected filler code.

Conclusion: Code size, even when mostly unrelated to the property in question, hugely influences model checking times.

3.5 Experiment II: Effect of Variable Wrapping

Many real-world programs use arrays or structs. To simulate this and its effect on model checking, we use post-processors that "wrap" all global variables in a program. We use code with ≈30 operations as base. The *array wrapper* (**A**) creates one array per type, often with more than one dimension for added complexity. The *struct wrapper* (**S**) creates one struct around all variables. The *pointer wrapper* (**P**) creates a type-correct pointer for every variable and replaces every access, read and write, by a pointer operation. With the combination AP (arrays accessed through pointer) we found an issue in 2LS which does not support pointer access inside arrays[5].

---

[5] https://github.com/diffblue/2ls/issues/159.

Table 2. Wilcoxon rank sum results on runtimes in Fig. 5 between unchanged and modified code. We use $p < 0.05$ as threshold.

Tool	PS_CN_10	PS_CN_25	PS_CN_50	PS_CN_100	PS_CN_250	PS_CN_500
2LS	7.3E–02	2.8E–04	7.3E–09	1.8E–13	1.3E–18	3.2E–21
CPA	9.0E–01	1.3E–01	2.7E–03	1.8E–13	1.5E–19	1.2E–20
ESBMC	9.7E–01	7.7E–01	5.5E–01	4.1E–01	1.4E–01	1.4E–03
PESCO	2.8E–01	2.3E–01	6.3E–03	1.2E–06	4.2E–06	3.2E–11
SYMB	3.2E–01	6.3E–01	NA	NA	NA	NA
UA	NA	NA	NA	NA	NA	NA

Table 3. Wilcoxon rank sum results on runtimes in Fig. 6 between code with and without variable wrapping. We use $p < 0.05$ as threshold.

Tool	Array	Pointer	Struct	Array + Pointer	Struct + Pointer
2LS	7.8E–09	1.5E–10	6.1E–01	NA	4.2E–10
CPA	7.5E–02	4.8E–07	1.8E–02	NA	3.8E–07
ESBMC	2.2E–01	NA	9.3E–01	NA	NA
PESCO	5.4E–07	1.1E–15	5.7E–01	NA	3.4E–17
SYMB	8.6E–01	NA	8.6E–01	NA	NA
UA	NA	NA	NA	NA	NA

The box-plots in Fig. 6 show the runtime on the unmodified code (column "normal") and the wrapped variants. As SYMBIOTIC and ULTIMATE AUTOMIZER in the base case only solve less than 10% and 18%, respectively, we ignore them in the comparison. With almost all wrapping types, we see a significant impact on results - large numbers of timeouts, unknown and errors. For some tools and configurations, we observe a *decrease* in median runtime. We believe this stems from the large number of timeouts combined with not all tasks containing "hard" properties due to the relatively low code size. With a small code size, the probability of containing every type of operation is small. This experiment shows that only structs are handled without a significant increase in runtime, and even that with slightly elevated error rates. Combining arrays and pointers or structs and pointers brings even the most mature and well-known tools to their knees Table 3.

Conclusion: While many tools are capable of handling features such as pointers or arrays, their combined complexity seems to offer a large opportunity for improvement.

3.6 Experiment III: Loop vs. Straight-line Code

While the program structure generated by our tool in general contains an outer infinite loop, we introduced the option to replace it by a bounded `for`-loop, for which we can fix the bound k to a constant. This allows us to easily generate

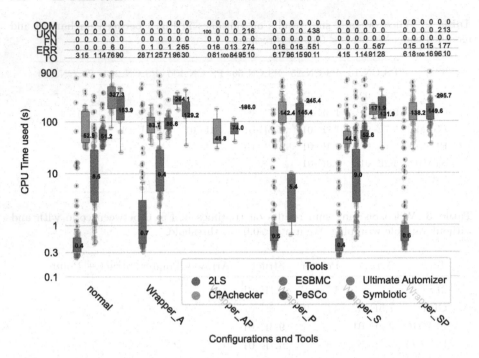

Fig. 6. Influence of wrappers on CPU time used. Wrapping types are Array, Pointer, Struct and the combinations Array + Pointers and Struct + Pointers.

"straight-line code". We performed statistical analysis on the difference between "_1loop" (straight-line code) and "_while" (infinite-loop code) to analyze the significance of differences, shown in Table 4. The prefix of the indicated configuration is the amount of operations in the generated code (25, 50 and 100). With rising code size, the rate of timeouts increases. SYMBIOTIC and ULTIMATE AUTOMIZER run into timeout in almost all instances, barring any relevant analysis. CPACHECKER, in the 25 and 50 operations configuration, where the number of timeouts is still low, shows a significant impact of the outer loop type. And while most tools show an increase in median processing time, only ESBMC shows a *significant* difference across all sizes. Of course, the reason can also be that ESBMC is the only tool capable of exploiting the missing loop.

Conclusion: For the checked code sizes, only ESBMC is significantly influenced by the presence/absence of an infinite outer loop, while we can not make any such claims about 2LS , CPACHECKER and PESCO , as the timeouts and errors blur the picture.

3.7   Experiment IV: Effect of Code Structure

Aside from loops, many structural properties of code can potentially impact model checking performance. Regarding our selection, the problem of analyzing functions concerning inter-procedural data-flow is long known [19]. Our "functionizing" post-processor randomly replaces arbitrary sub-expressions by

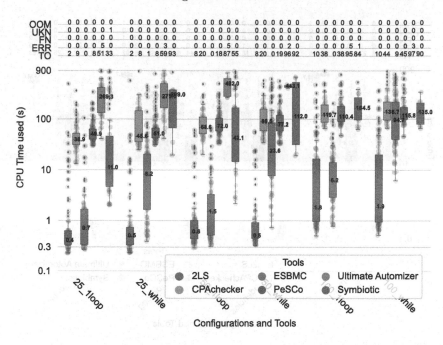

Fig. 7. Influence of loop presence on CPU time used.

Table 4. Wilcoxon rank sum results on runtimes in Fig. 7 between loop- and straight-line code. We use $p < 0.05$ as threshold.

Tool	25 Ops	50 Ops	100 Ops
2LS	4.8E–01	8.8E–01	8.1E–01
CPA	1.9E–03	3.2E–02	1.9E–01
ESBMC	1.3E–15	6.2E–22	2.0E–25
PESCO	3.6E–01	4.4E–01	4.5E–01
SYMB	5.7E–03	1.8E–01	6.8E–01
UA	7.4E–01	NA	NA

function calls to newly created functions encapsulating the cut sub-expression, where constants and variables within are randomly either used as function parameters or kept as is. For a second experiment, we interconnect the code further by aggressively replacing (external non-deterministic) input variables with outputs from other requirements in the program, reducing the number of variables but increasing dependencies. Lastly, we use the "step locals" post-processing to transform part of expressions into local variable assignments, as this can have side effects on expression optimization. The resulting runtimes are shown in Fig. 8. A statistical evaluation comparing the column "normal" with the three modified code variants is presented in Table 5. We can see no significant change in runtimes for "Dependencies" and "StepLocals", but both

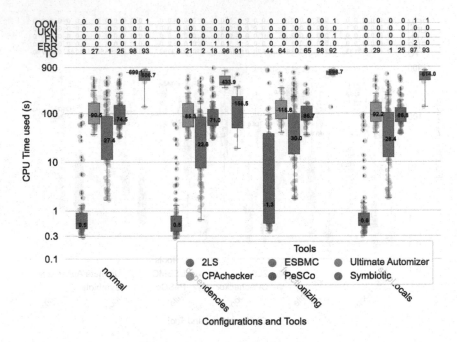

Fig. 8. Influence of code structure on CPU time used.

"Functionizing" shows such change for 2LS. In the case of "Functionizing", a significant increase in timeouts for 2LS, CPACHECKER and PESCO is visible (Table 5).

Conclusion: From the analyzed structural modifications and code sizes, functionizing has the strongest impact on model checking runtimes with large amounts of timeouts.

3.8   Experiment V: Influence of Floating-point Arithmetic

Table 5. Wilcoxon rank sum results on runtimes in Fig. 8 between unmodified and restructured code.

Tool	Dependencies	Functionizing	StepLocals
2LS	1.2E-01	4.6E-06	3.2E-01
CPA	2.4E-01	1.9E-01	5.5E-01
ESBMC	1.8E-01	6.2E-01	9.2E-01
PESCO	4.6E-01	2.4E-01	3.1E-01
SYMB	4.3E-02	7.0E-01	7.0E-01
UA	NA	NA	NA

We use $p < 0.05$ as threshold.

Table 6. Wilcoxon rank sum results on runtimes in Fig. 9 between unchanged and modified code.

Tool	NO_FLOATS
2LS	1.0E-03
CPA	3.6E-12
ESBMC	4.1E-05
PESCO	1.5E-06
SYMB	NA
UA	3.2E-02

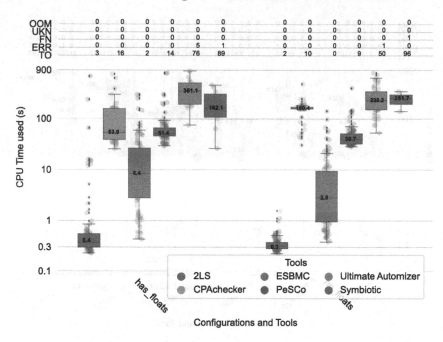

Fig. 9. Influence of floats on CPU time used.

Floating-point arithmetic is often regarded as *hard* for model checking. For a direct comparison on its influence, we generate a set of benchmark tasks including floating-point variables and operations on them. We then derive a second set of benchmark tasks from this set, where all floating-point variables and constants are replaced by integer equivalents. Since overall form, type of operations, number of assignments, etc. are the same, we believe this gives good insight into impact of floating-points on verification performance. Figure 9 presents the resulting runtimes (left half with floats, right half without). SYMBIOTIC, even though it fails on more "no_floats"-instances than those with floats, solves not enough tasks for further analysis. For the remaining tools, we observe a significant change in verification time needed when operating only on integers and reduced timeout-rates. 2LS, ESBMC, PESCO and ULTIMATE AUTOMIZER all solve more instances and faster when no floats are present. The most significant change, however, we see with CPACHECKER, and unexpectedly so, in the other direction. This behavior warrants further analysis in the future. From logs, the presence of floats seems to change the initial verification strategy to one apparently more suited to the tasks at hand. Additionally, the variance is greater for the floating-point case for all tools.

Conclusion: Aside from CPACHECKER *, floating-point presence significantly increases model checking complexity.* For multi-technique tools, the automated initial algorithm selection might also have significant influence.

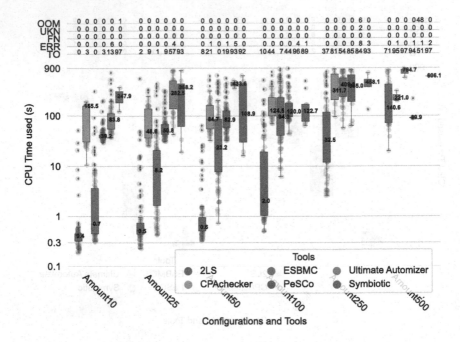

Fig. 10. Influence of code size on CPU time used.

3.9 Experiment VI: Effect of Code Size

As we are interested in how well model checkers scale, experimenting with different code sizes is an obvious choice. We can easily configure how many operations should be generated. For these benchmarks, we impose no type restrictions (floating-point, etc.) but also do not apply any post processing such as functionizing or step-local variables.

Figure 10 presents the results for six different code sizes (ranging from 10 to 500 operations). SYMBIOTIC and ULTIMATE AUTOMIZER are unable to solve a significant amount of tasks even with small programs. The number of timeouts rises quickly for all tools, which skews their results and median. Considering the loglog-scale, we observe potential exponential growth in 2LS, CPACHECKER and PESCO.

Conclusion: Of course the low number of data points in general and high number of timeouts towards the greater code sizes prevent us from drawing any strong conclusions, but, as perhaps expected, code size could have an exponential impact on model checking runtime.

4 Epilogue

This paper presents a tool for generating targeted C-code benchmarks and reported on six experiments using such generated code. While the tool and code certainly have limitations regarding structure, parallelism and depth of state, we were able to target specific properties of interest such as unrelated code, structured variables, functions, presence of loops and floating-points and overall code size. With the presented results, we gained reproducible insight into the strengths and weaknesses of the software model checkers and possible areas of improvement: a high impact of functions always called at only one point, unrelated code which could potentially be sliced, the occurrence of floating-point variables and how they influence algorithm selection and problems with combinations of pointers, arrays and structs. Since these are features often observed in industrial systems, we believe these to be relevant areas of improvement for making model checking more viable in practice.

Future Work. We plan to support automatic loop generation, deeper stateful systems and generating programs with violated properties. These programs require at least one execution to reach that part of the program, which requires extensive knowledge about reachability and satisfiability of generated conditions. Additionally, we want to harvest the extensive knowledge about the generated programs for a cluster-analysis of what floating-point operations impact the runtime the most. Including existing, specialized commercial model checkers in our experiments could help highlight relevant directions for future research.

5   Artifact

The replication artifact can be found at https://doi.org/10.5281/zenodo. 6392205. All scripts, generated code, data and plots are included. See `README.md` in the artifact for instructions and usage examples.

Acknowledgments. We thank Fabian Hippler and Felix Faber for their continuing support and work.

References

1. Berger, P., Katoen, J.-P., Ábrahám, E., Waez, M.T.B., Rambow, T.: Verifying auto-generated C code from simulink. In: Havelund, K., Peleska, J., Roscoe, B., de Vink, E. (eds.) FM 2018. LNCS, vol. 10951, pp. 312–328. Springer, Cham (2018). https://doi.org/10.1007/978-3-319-95582-7_18
2. Beyer, D.: Software verification: 10th comparative evaluation (SV-COMP 2021). In: TACAS 2021. LNCS, vol. 12652, pp. 401–422. Springer, Cham (2021). https://doi.org/10.1007/978-3-030-72013-1_24
3. Beyer, D., Keremoglu, M.E.: CPACHECKER: a tool for configurable software verification. In: Gopalakrishnan, G., Qadeer, S. (eds.) CAV 2011. LNCS, vol. 6806, pp. 184–190. Springer, Heidelberg (2011). https://doi.org/10.1007/978-3-642-22110-1_16
4. Beyer, D., Lemberger, T.: Software verification: testing vs. model checking. In: HVC 2017. LNCS, vol. 10629, pp. 99–114. Springer, Cham (2017). https://doi.org/10.1007/978-3-319-70389-3_7

5. Beyer, D., Löwe, S., Wendler, P.: Reliable benchmarking: requirements and solutions. Int. J. Softw. Tools Technol. Transf. **21**(1), 1–29 (2019)
6. Chalupa, M., Novák, J., Strejcek, J.: Symbiotic 8: parallel and targeted test generation - (competition contribution). In: FASE. LNCS, vol. 12649, pp. 368–372. Springer (2021)
7. Chalupa, M., Strejček, J.: Evaluation of program slicing in software verification. In: Ahrendt, W., Tapia Tarifa, S.L. (eds.) IFM 2019. LNCS, vol. 11918, pp. 101–119. Springer, Cham (2019). https://doi.org/10.1007/978-3-030-34968-4_6
8. Cordeiro, L.C., Kroening, D., Schrammel, P.: Benchmarking of java verification tools at the software verification competition (SV-COMP). ACM SIGSOFT Softw. Eng. Notes **43**(4), 56 (2018)
9. Gadelha, M.Y.R., Menezes, R., Monteiro, F.R., Cordeiro, L.C., Nicole, D.A.: ESBMC: scalable and precise test generation based on the floating-point theory - (competition contribution). In: FASE. LNCS, vol. 12076, pp. 525–529. Springer (2020)
10. Groce, A., Havelund, K., Holzmann, G., Joshi, R., Xu, R.-G.: Establishing flight software reliability: testing, model checking, constraint-solving, monitoring and learning. Ann. Math. Artif. Intell. **70**(4), 315–349 (2014). https://doi.org/10.1007/s10472-014-9408-8
11. Heizmann, M., et al.: Ultimate automizer and the search for perfect interpolants. In: Beyer, D., Huisman, M. (eds.) TACAS 2018. LNCS, vol. 10806, pp. 447–451. Springer, Cham (2018). https://doi.org/10.1007/978-3-319-89963-3_30
12. Howar, F., Jasper, M., Mues, M., Schmidt, D., Steffen, B.: The RERS challenge: towards controllable and scalable benchmark synthesis. Int. J. Softw. Tools Technol. Transf. **23**(6), 917–930 (2021). https://doi.org/10.1007/s10009-021-00617-z
13. Jasper, M.: Synthesizing realistic verification tasks. Ph.D. thesis, Technical University of Dortmund, Germany (2021)
14. Jhala, R., Majumdar, R.: Software model checking. ACM Comput. Surv. **41**(4), 21:1–21:54 (2009)
15. Klinger, C., Christakis, M., Wüstholz, V.: Differentially testing soundness and precision of program analyzers. In: ISSTA, pp. 239–250. ACM (2019)
16. Malík, V., Schrammel, P., Vojnar, T.: 2LS: heap analysis and memory safety. In: TACAS 2020. LNCS, vol. 12079, pp. 368–372. Springer, Cham (2020). https://doi.org/10.1007/978-3-030-45237-7_22
17. Méry, D., Singh, N.K.: Automatic code generation from event-b models. In: SoICT, pp. 179–188. ACM (2011)
18. Richter, C., Wehrheim, H.: PeSCo: predicting sequential combinations of verifiers. In: Beyer, D., Huisman, M., Kordon, F., Steffen, B. (eds.) TACAS 2019. LNCS, vol. 11429, pp. 229–233. Springer, Cham (2019). https://doi.org/10.1007/978-3-030-17502-3_19
19. Sharir, M., Pnueli, A., et al.: Two Approaches to Interprocedural Data Flow Analysis. New York University, Courant Institute of Mathematical Sciences (1978)
20. Vorobyov, K., Krishnan, P.: Comparing model checking and static program analysis: a case study in error detection approaches. In: Proceedings of SSV (2010)
21. Westhofen, L., Berger, P., Katoen, J.-P.: Benchmarking software model checkers on automotive code. In: Lee, R., Jha, S., Mavridou, A., Giannakopoulou, D. (eds.) NFM 2020. LNCS, vol. 12229, pp. 133–150. Springer, Cham (2020). https://doi.org/10.1007/978-3-030-55754-6_8
22. Zhang, C., Su, T., Yan, Y., Zhang, F., Pu, G., Su, Z.: Finding and understanding bugs in software model checkers. In: ESEC/SIGSOFT FSE, pp. 763–773. ACM (2019)

Assume-Guarantee Reasoning
with Scheduled Components

Cong Liu[1]([⊠]), Junaid Babar[1], Isaac Amundson[1], Karl Hoech[1], Darren Cofer[1],
and Eric Mercer[2][ID]

[1] Applied Research and Technology, Collins Aerospace, Charlotte, USA
{cong.liu,junaid.babar,isaac.amundson,karl.hoech,
darren.cofer}@collins.com
[2] Brigham Young University, Provo, USA
egm@cs.byu.edu

Abstract. Contract-based assume-guarantee reasoning can be used to improve the scalability of model checking by decomposing complex verification problems. In previous work, we demonstrated this approach for systems modeled using the Architecture Analysis and Design Language (AADL) assuming a synchronous model of computation. This allows non-deterministic ordering of parallel components and generally results in an over-approximation of real behavior. This paper describes an approach to incorporating an execution schedule in the assume-guarantee reasoning. We define our semantic interpretation of contracts when components are executed according to this schedule, more accurately reflecting the behavior of the system implementation. We introduce virtual scheduling events which tie AADL timing and execution semantics to contracts. A case study based on a simple unmanned air vehicle surveillance system is provided to illustrate our approach.

Keywords: Assume-guarantee · Compositional verification · Model checking · Model based system engineering · AADL · Scheduling semantics

1 Introduction

Formal verification of cyber-physical systems can be a daunting task due to the *state explosion problem* [5]. We tackle this challenge from two angles. First, we use a compositional verification technique [6,23] to decompose the reasoning on the global state space into a number of localized problems for each component separately. The system proof is constructed from the individual component proofs. Second, we assume that the components execute in a static sequential order. We do not consider all possible execution orders; in other words, non-determinism due to scheduling decisions is excluded. In fact, in many safety-critical applications the actual implementation executes according to a pre-defined schedule [2] to achieve real-time performance requirements.

© Springer Nature Switzerland AG 2022
J. V. Deshmukh et al. (Eds.): NFM 2022, LNCS 13260, pp. 355–372, 2022.
https://doi.org/10.1007/978-3-031-06773-0_19

Previous work has not incorporated component execution times or ordering imposed by a component execution schedule. As a result, an analysis performed at the model level may produce results that deviate from the actual behavior of the system implemented from the model. Our objective is to refine our compositional verification approach to capture this aspect of the design and ensure that analysis results faithfully represent the system implementation.

The Architecture Analysis and Design Language (AADL) was developed to capture the important design concepts in distributed real-time embedded systems [10]. AADL captures both the hardware and software architecture in a hierarchical format, offering a high degree of flexibility and supporting incremental development in which an architecture is refined to add increasing levels of detail.

In AADL, an architecture model includes component interfaces, connections, and execution characteristics, but not component implementations. It describes the interactions between components and their arrangement in the system, but the lowest level components themselves are "black boxes." Their implementations must be described separately using model-based behavioral specification languages or traditional programming languages, which may be included by reference in the architecture model.

In previous work, we developed the Assume Guarantee Reasoning Environment (AGREE) [8], a language and tool for compositional verification of AADL models. The behavior of a model is described by *contracts* [4] specified for each component. A contract contains a set of *assumptions* about the component's inputs and a set of *guarantees* about the outputs. The guarantees of a component must be true provided that the component's assumptions are true. The goal of an AGREE analysis is to prove that each component's contract is entailed by the contracts of its subcomponents. Guarantees on a leaf-level component must be verified to hold by its implementation.

AGREE was originally developed to reason about systems that execute synchronously. These systems have straightforward translations to *Lustre* [13], a synchronous dataflow language interpreted by the model checkers used by AGREE. However, many systems that are modeled in AADL do not behave synchronously. Ideally one can implement a communication protocol between components, such as Physically Asynchronous Logically Synchronous (PALS) [20], that allows the abstraction of synchronous communication to be sound. However, for many systems this is not the case.

In this paper, we extend the AGREE framework to enable the verification of *scheduled* AADL models. We introduce virtual scheduling events, which tie AADL timing and scheduling semantics to AGREE contracts. This enhancement enables AGREE to take the software execution schedule into account in the analysis. Furthermore, it enables formal verification of a new class of embedded system architectures.

This paper is organized as follows. First we illustrate the motivation of our work using simple examples in Sect. 2. We then provide an informal description of our interpretation of the scheduling semantics in Sect. 3, followed by formal definitions of the model in Sect. 4. We present the modeling of the semantics in

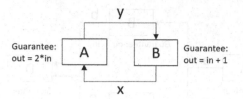

Fig. 1. A simple feedback system

the AGREE AADL annex and Lustre backend in Sect. 6 and Sect. 7, respectively. We demonstrate usage of the model in a case study in Sect. 8. Related work is presented in Sect. 9. We discuss our conclusion and future work in Sect. 10.

2 Motivating Examples

First, we will illustrate the key semantic difference between the synchronous model used in the original AGREE framework and the proposed model. Consider an AADL model that consists of two threads A and B, as shown in Fig. 1. All ports are data ports. The behavior of each thread is indicated by its AGREE contract. The output of thread A is double its input and the output of thread B increments its input by one. By the synchronous semantics, the value of signal x and y at computation step n is defined by the solution to the two equations $y_n = 2x_n$ and $x_n = y_n + 1$, for all $n \in N$. This results in $x = (-1, -1, \ldots)$, $y = (-2, -2, \ldots)$ for all time. However, if the two threads execute in a sequential order $(ABAB...)$, letting x_0, y_0 denote the initial value of x and y, respectively, an intuitive interpretation of the execution semantics is $y_1 = 2x_0, x_1 = y_1 + 1, y_2 = 2x_1....$ If $x_0 = 0$ and $y_0 = 0$, this results in $x = (0, 1, 3, 7, \ldots)$ and $y = (0, 0, 2, 6, \ldots)$. The example shows that the behavior of a synchronous model is defined by the solution(s) to systems of mathematical equations (or inequalities) at each instant, while the behavior of the scheduled components is defined through iterations over time.

We are aware that the Lustre compiler rejects all syntactic loops. A one-step delay (the **pre** operator) could be added between A and B, resulting in an implied schedule and legal Lustre code. Since an AGREE analysis does not compile the generated Lustre code but instead interprets it via one of the underlying model checkers, we do not face the same limitation and can compute a solution for synchronous execution whenever one exists.

Now consider an AADL model that consists of four threads A, B, C, D, as shown in Fig. 2. Again, all ports are data ports. Thread A outputs the sequence of all natural numbers. Threads B and C simply copy their inputs to their outputs. Thread D subtracts the second (bottom) input value from the first (top) input value. Given a schedule $(ACABD)^*$, suppose we want to prove that the primary output d is a sequence of ones (ignoring the initial prefix). This can be achieved with the proposed model, since thread B only copies even numbers, and thread C only copies odd numbers. However, it cannot be proved directly with the

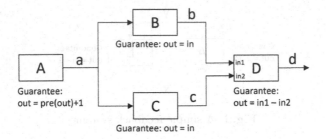

Fig. 2. A simple downsampling system

```
thread A
    features
        Input: in data port Base_Types::Integer;
        Output: out data port Base_Types::Integer;
    properties
        Dispatch_Protocol => Periodic;
        Period => 500ms;
        Compute_Execution_Time => 6ms .. 8ms;
    annex agree {**
        assume "A input": Input > prev(Input, 0);
        guarantee "A output": Output = Input + prev(Output, 0);
    **};
end A ;
```

Fig. 3. A simple integrator AADL model in AGREE

synchronous model, where d is a sequence of zeroes. Note that in the example, threads B and C essentially downsample the data stream from thread A. To model this kind of behavior, we require a mechanism significantly more complex than *delays*.

Note that if the schedule is $(ABCD)^*$, the output d is a sequence of zeroes (ignoring the initial prefix), matching the behavior of the synchronous model. This indicates that the execution order could have an impact on the system behavior. As we will show later, our model is not a variant of Kahn Process Network [15], like Lee's Synchronous Dataflow [18], where any execution order results in the same system behavior. Therefore, it makes sense to tie a system-level property to a specific schedule of the components.

3   Overview of the Model

We now discuss in detail our semantic interpretation of AGREE contracts on scheduled components. Consider the AADL model of an integrator, shown in Fig. 3. We assume that an execution time slot is assigned to the thread. The first question that we face is when the contracts shall hold. In a synchronous model, contracts hold at every instant. However, with scheduled execution, it is reasonable to assume that the contract may not hold when the component is not activated. But once it is activated, shall a contract hold throughout the entire execution or just at certain instants? Second, how shall *Input* (referred to in the contract) be interpreted? One interpretation is that it refers to the input value at the time when the contract is evaluated, which may vary during the execution. Another interpretation is that it refers to the input value when the component starts its execution. In other words, there is a notion of *sample and hold*. This interpretation is consistent with the *frozen* inputs described in the AADL V2 standard. Third, how shall the *prev* operator be interpreted? In a synchronous model, it refers to the previous instant. However, with scheduled execution, it seems reasonable to interpret *prev* as the previous activation (i.e. the value when the component was last activated). If the contracts hold throughout the activation, a more sensible interpretation is that at the first instant during activation, it refers to the previous activation. Then at each following instant, it refers to the last updated value in the current activation. This interpretation is adopted in the *activation condition* in SCADE [9] and the *clock* mechanism in SIGNAL [3].

We believe that AGREE contracts are intended to model requirements [26], not implementations. Guarantees model the component requirements, and assumptions model the environmental constraints that are used to verify the component requirements. Following the AADL *input-compute-output* model, assumptions are said to hold at the start of the execution (i.e. *dispatch*) when the inputs are read. The guarantees shall be satisfied at the end of the execution (i.e. *complete*) when the outputs are written. This interpretation has a few implications. First, since we adopt the AADL *frozen inputs* concept, any reference to *Input* refers to the input value that was read in at dispatch. Second, a component's assigned time slot does not necessarily exactly match its execution time window. If the time slot is greater than its execution time, we interpret the start and end of the time slot as *dispatch* and *complete*, respectively. Otherwise, we claim that a *preemption* has occurred. Third, each contract is examined exactly once in each activation. Thus, we interpret the *prev* operator as the previous activation. Fourth, the guarantees are not models of the *transient* behavior during an execution. Instead, we interpret them as constraints on the *steady-state* outputs at the end of activation.

We assume that the requirements do not contain real-time constraints. Modeling such constraints in AGREE is discussed in [1]. However, this does not mean that AGREE contracts cannot model timer based requirements. In practice, a timer is usually implemented as a counter, whose limit (constant) is calculated based on the frequency of its execution. The counter is activated periodically and increments by only one during each activation, independent of the execution time. This is consistent with our interpretation.

Thus, for each component we introduce two distinctive events, *dispatch* and *complete*, to model the start and end of its activation, respectively. Similarly, for a system (consisting of components), the two events model the start and end of a scheduling cycle. The two events shall appear in pairs and alternate, with *dispatch* appearing before *complete*. We introduce the notion of *well-ordered* in Sect. 4 to capture this pattern.

In SCADE and SIGNAL, when a component is not activated, its outputs retain their previous values. We extend this output freeze time window to *complete* events, including activation. We understand that in practice the actual output values may change during activation. We choose this because we interpret the *guarantees* as steady-state requirements of outputs at *complete*. Output values between *dispatch* and *complete* are undefined. Thus, we model them using the last output values, so that the outputs are well-defined at every instant.

We inherit the same notion of composition used in the current AGREE framework. A connection between two components means their contracts refer to the same signal. This, combined with a schedule and the output freeze rule, essentially simulates communication based on *shared variables*. When the producer is not activated, its outputs hold the last values. When the consumer is activated, it reads the last values from the producer. The communication may also be viewed as a FIFO queue, where the queue size is one. This means the proposed model only supports limited AADL *event* data port communication.

We only consider single-machine schedules. The scheduler ensures that at most one component is activated at a time. For a preemptive schedule, we require that a component can only be preempted by another component if they do not have connections. Thus, there is no ambiguity on the order of read and write or the variable value referenced in the contracts.

We assume that the system-level inputs do not change values throughout a scheduling cycle. In practice, this means that there may exist a queue that holds the system-level input messages, which are periodically sampled by the components, or the inputs may come from another system, which is inactive while the system under consideration is active.

The input freeze rule may imply that the assumptions could be examined at *complete*, instead of *dispatch*. Thus, we may not really need the *dispatch* event. We keep it mainly for two reasons. First, the assumptions in general could depend on previous outputs. In our model, the outputs are updated at *complete*. So the output values at *dispatch* may be different from the values at the corresponding *complete*. Therefore, it is important to distinguish between the two events to avoid ambiguity of the output values. Second, keeping the pair (*dispatch*, *complete*) may help users to better understand the AGREE counterexample trace, particularly with a preemptive schedule.

The original schedule is often specified in the form of a sequence of time slots assigned to the components. The schedule could come from an AADL real-time scheduling tool such as Cheddar [25], or from a scheduler provided by an RTOS/Microkernel vendor, such as seL4 [17]. To properly model the schedule in AGREE, the component execution time has to be considered. Consider the example shown in Fig. 4 with two scheduled components A and B. We refer to the original schedule and its model in AGREE as the real-time schedule and AGREE schedule, respectively. Given the same real-time schedule, due to the different execution time C_A of A, two different AGREE schedules are created. In Fig. 4(a), since C_A is equal to the time slots assigned to A, the end of the each time slot is modeled as *complete*. In Fig. 4(b), since the first time slot assigned

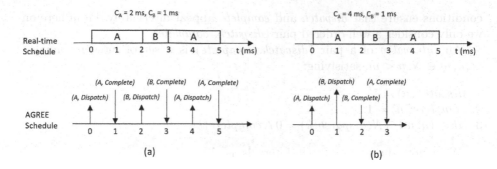

Fig. 4. Models of real-time schedule in AGREE

to A is less than its execution time, the end of the first time slot is interpreted as *preemption*, instead of *complete*.

4 Formal Definitions

In this section we formally define the proposed model.

Signal. A *signal* x is a function $x : N \to V$, where N is the set of natural numbers including zero, and V is a value set. A signal is *Boolean* if the value set is the Boolean domain. We use $x(n)$ to denote the value of signal x at instant n.

Port. Let Q be a set of ports. For each port $q \in Q$, a set V_q denotes the values that may be assigned to port q. A signal x_q at port q is a function $x_q : N \to V_q$. A *trace* σ_Q of Q is an assignment of a signal x_q to each port q in Q. We use Σ_Q to denote the set of all traces of Q. Given a set $Q' \subseteq Q$, the *projection* of a trace σ_Q onto Q' is the assignment of signal x_q to each port q in Q', as defined in σ_Q. We denote the projection as $\sigma_Q|_{Q'}$.

Dispatch and Complete. Two Boolean signals *dispatch* and *complete* are *well-ordered* if

1. $\forall n \in N, dispatch(n) \neq 1 \lor complete(n) \neq 1$,
2. $\forall n \in N, dispatch(n) = 1 \implies \exists m \in N, m > n, complete(m) = 1$,
3. $\forall m \in N, complete(m) = 1 \implies \exists n \in N, n < m, dispatch(n) = 1$,
4. $\forall n, m \in N, n < m, dispatch(n) = 1 \land dispatch(m) = 1 \implies \exists k \in N, n < k < m, complete(k) = 1$.
5. $\forall n, m \in N, n < m, complete(n) = 1 \land complete(m) = 1 \implies \exists k \in N, n < k < m, dispatch(k) = 1$.

The first condition requires that *dispatch* and *complete* are mutually exclusive. The second and third conditions state that *dispatch* and *complete* appear in pairs, and in each pair *dispatch* appears before *complete*. The fourth and fifth conditions ensure that *dispatch* and *complete* appear alternately. From here on we only consider a well-ordered pair (*dispatch*, *complete*).

An *interval* δ of a pair (*dispatch*, *complete*) is a set of integers $[n, m] \cap N, n, m \in N, n < m$, satisfying:

1. $dispatch(n) = 1$,
2. $complete(m) = 1$,
3. $\forall k \in (n, m) \cap N, dispatch(k) = 0 \wedge complete(k) = 0$.

We denote the set of all such intervals as Δ.

Component. A (scheduled) *component* c is a tuple $(I_c, O_c, A_c, P_c, dispatch_c, complete_c)$, where:

- I_c is a finite set of ports, called *inputs*,
- O_c is a finite set of ports disjoint from I_c, called *outputs*,
- A_c and P_c are two past-time LTL formulas on a trace $\sigma_c \in \Sigma_{I_c \cup O_c}$, called *assumptions* and *guarantees*, respectively,
- (*dispatch_c*, *complete_c*) is a pair of *well-ordered* Boolean signals.

The *behaviors* of a component c are a set $\Sigma_c \subseteq \Sigma_{I_c \cup O_c}$, such that $\forall \sigma_c \in \Sigma_{I_c \cup O_c}, \sigma_c \in \Sigma_c$ if and only if the following propositions hold:
The *assumptions* hold at *dispatch*. That is,

$$dispatch_c(n) \implies (\sigma_c, n) \models A_c, \forall n \in N. \qquad (1)$$

Inputs freeze between *dispatch* and *complete*. That is,

$$x(i) = x(j), \forall i, j \in \delta \cap N, \forall \delta \in \Delta, \forall x \in \sigma_c|_{I_c}. \qquad (2)$$

The *guarantees* hold at *complete*. That is,

$$complete_c(n) \implies (\sigma_c, n) \models P_c, \forall n \in N. \qquad (3)$$

Outputs freeze between *completes*. That is,

$$\neg complete_c(n) \implies y(n) = y(n-1), \forall n \in N, n > 0, \forall y \in \sigma_c|_{O_c}. \qquad (4)$$

Equations 1, 2, 3, and 4 represent the specification of a scheduled component.

Connection. Two components $c, c', c \neq c'$ are said to be *connected* if

$$O_c \cap I_{c'} \neq \varnothing \vee O_{c'} \cap I_c \neq \varnothing. \qquad (5)$$

Note that by definition the intersection of a component's inputs and outputs is empty. Thus, we forbid a component from connecting to itself.

Schedule. Let C be a finite set of components, a *schedule* ϕ of C with *length* $T \in N$ is a partial function $[1, T] \cap N \rightarrow C \times \{\mathsf{Dispatch}, \mathsf{Complete}\}$, where $\mathsf{Dispatch}$ and $\mathsf{Complete}$ are two strings, satisfying:

1. $\forall i \in \text{dom } \phi, c \in C, \phi(i) = (c, \text{Dispatch}) \implies \exists j \in \text{dom } \phi, j > i, \phi(j) = (c, \text{Complete})$,
2. $\forall j \in \text{dom } \phi, c \in C, \phi(j) = (c, \text{Complete}) \implies \exists i \in \text{dom } \phi, i < j, \phi(i) = (c, \text{Dispatch})$,
3. $\forall i, j \in \text{dom } \phi, i < j, c \in C, \phi(i) = (c, \text{Dispatch}) \wedge \phi(j) = (c, \text{Dispatch}) \implies \exists k \in \text{dom } \phi, i < k < j, \phi(k) = (c, \text{Complete})$,
4. $\forall i, j \in \text{dom } \phi, i < j, c \in C, \phi(i) = (c, \text{Complete}) \wedge \phi(j) = (c, \text{Complete}) \implies \exists k \in \text{dom } \phi, i < k < j, \phi(k) = (c, \text{Dispatch})$,
5. $\forall i, j \in \text{dom } \phi, i < j, c, c' \in C, c \neq c', \phi(i) = (c, \text{Dispatch}) \wedge \phi(j) = (c', \text{Dispatch}) \wedge \forall k \in \text{dom } \phi, i < k < j, \phi(k) \neq (c, \text{Complete}) \implies c, c'$ are not connected,
6. $\forall i, j, k \in \text{dom } \phi, i < j < k, c, c' \in C, c \neq c', \phi(i) = (c, \text{Dispatch}) \wedge \phi(j) = (c', \text{Dispatch}) \wedge \phi(k) = (c, \text{Complete}) \implies \exists n \in \text{dom } \phi, j < n < k, \phi(n) = (c', \text{Complete})$.

The first four conditions ensure the pair (Dispatch, Complete) associated with a component is *well-ordered* in a schedule. The fifth condition allows a component to be *preempted* by another component if the two have no connection. The sixth condition ensures that the scheduling events of two components are interleaved in a proper order. A schedule is *minimal* if ϕ is a *total* function. This means that at each instant there is either a *dispatch* or a *complete*. A schedule is *fair* if ϕ is *surjective*. This means that every component is scheduled to execute at least once. If a schedule is minimal and non-preemptive, we could simplify the notation and denote the schedule as a function that maps $[1, |C|] \cap N$ to C, as shown in the previous examples.

Given a schedule ϕ of components C, the *dispatch* and *complete* signals of each component $c \in C$ are defined as follows: $\forall i \in N$,

$$
dispatch_c^\phi(i) = \begin{cases} 1, & \text{if } \phi(i \mod T) = (c, \text{Dispatch}) \\ 0, & \text{otherwise} \end{cases}, \tag{6}
$$

$$
complete_c^\phi(i) = \begin{cases} 1, & \text{if } \phi(i \mod T) = (c, \text{Complete}) \\ 0, & \text{otherwise} \end{cases}. \tag{7}
$$

System. A set C of components are said to be *compatible* if no two components share the same output. That is,

$$
\forall c_i, c_j \in C, c_i \neq c_j, O_{c_i} \cap O_{c_j} = \varnothing. \tag{8}
$$

A *system* S is a tuple $(C, \phi, I_s, O_s, A_s, P_s, dispatch_s, complete_s)$, where:

- C is a set of compatible, scheduled components,
- ϕ is a schedule of C,
- $I_s = \cup_{\forall c \in C} I_c - \cup_{\forall c \in C} O_c$,
- $O_s = \cup_{\forall c \in C} O_c$,

- A_s and P_s are two past-time LTL formulas on a trace $\sigma_s \in \Sigma_{I_s \cup O_s}$, called system-level *assumptions* and *guarantees*, respectively,

- $dispatch_s(i) = \begin{cases} 1, & \text{if } i \mod T = 1 \\ 0, & \text{otherwise} \end{cases}, \forall i \in N,$

- $complete_s(i) = \begin{cases} 1, & \text{if } i \mod T = 0 \\ 0, & \text{otherwise} \end{cases}, \forall i \in N, i > 0.$

We have $I_s \cup O_s = \cup_{\forall c \in C}(I_c \cup O_c)$. The *behaviors* of a system S are a set $\Sigma_s \subseteq \Sigma_{I_s \cup O_s}$, such that $\forall \sigma_s \in \Sigma_{I_s \cup O_s}$,

$$\sigma_s \in \Sigma_s \iff \forall c \in C, \exists \sigma_c \in \Sigma_c, \sigma_s|_{I_c \cup O_c} = \sigma_c. \tag{9}$$

Informally, a trace of a system's ports is a behavior of the system if and only if its projection onto any component's ports is a behavior of the component. This implies that a system behavior maps the connected ports to the same signal. We use δ_s to denote an *interval* of the pair $(dispatch_s, complete_s)$. And we use Δ_s to denote the set of all such intervals. Given a system S and a trace $\sigma_s \in \Sigma_{I_s \cup O_s}$, we define the following propositions:

The system-level *assumptions* hold at *dispatch*. That is,

$$dispatch_s(n) \implies (\sigma_s, n) \models A_s, \forall n \in N. \tag{10}$$

Inputs freeze between dispatch and complete. That is,

$$x(i) = x(j), \forall i, j \in \delta_s \cap N, \forall \delta_s \in \Delta_s, \forall x \in \sigma_s|_{I_s}. \tag{11}$$

The system-level *guarantees* hold at *complete*. That is,

$$complete_s(n) \implies (\sigma_s, n) \models P_s, \forall n \in N. \tag{12}$$

Equations 10–12 represent the system specification of a set of scheduled components. Our verification goal is to prove that the system behaviors satisfy the system specification. Note that we do not define the system output freeze rule. This is because (in our context) the system under consideration is always active. The rule would make sense in the assume-guarantee reasoning at a higher level in the hierarchy, where the system is viewed as a periodically activated component.

5   Assume-Guarantee Reasoning

Scheduled components lend themselves to hierarchical assume-guarantee reasoning in a manner similar to that in [26]. The verification conditions to prove a system of unscheduled components correct are formalized in *past-time linear temporal logic* (PLTL) [16]. The two PLTL operators necessary for the verification conditions are $\mathbf{G}$ (globally) and $\mathbf{H}$ (historically). These are defined over a trace of the system, π, and a moment of evaluation in the trace, i, as follows:

$$(\pi, i) \models \mathbf{G}(f) \iff \forall j \geq i, (\pi, j) \models f$$
$$(\pi, i) \models \mathbf{H}(f) \iff \forall 0 \leq j \leq i, (\pi, j) \models f$$

Globally is invariant from the current moment into the future and historically is invariant from the beginning to the current moment.

We define $\mathbb{I}_c$ to be the set of components providing input to some component c in the system, and we define $\mathbb{O}$ to be the set of components that provide the output for the system. An unscheduled system, $S = (I, O, A, P)$, is correct if and only if for all π and for all $i \geq 0$ the following holds:

$$\forall c \in C \; \mathbf{G}(\mathbf{H}(A \wedge \bigwedge_{c' \in \mathbb{I}_c} P_{c'}) \implies A_c) \wedge$$
$$\mathbf{G}(\mathbf{H}(A \wedge \bigwedge_{c' \in \mathbb{O}} P_{c'}) \implies P)$$

The first condition checks the input assumptions on each component under the system assumptions and upstream component guarantees. The second checks the output guarantees of the system under the system assumptions and component guarantees providing the output. If both conditions hold, then the system is said to be *correct*, meaning that $\mathbf{G}(\mathbf{H}(A) \implies P)$ holds.

The verification conditions are extended to scheduled components by adding a notion of *dispatch* and *complete* to the verification conditions. We define a predicate $same(X)$ that is true in the first moment, and after that, true at any moment if and only if the signals in the set X are unchanged from the previous moment. We also define the predicate δ_c^ϕ to be true if the current moment is in a dispatch interval for the component c according the schedule.

The assumptions in a scheduled component must hold at dispatch, and the guarantees of the same component must hold at complete. A component also assumes that its inputs are invariant through the dispatch interval and it guarantees that the outputs are invariant between complete cycles. These requirements are captured in the following predicates where x is a component:

$$\mathbb{D}_x^\phi(A_x) = \left[\left(dispatch_x^\phi \wedge A_x\right) \vee \left(\delta_x^\phi \wedge same(I_x)\right)\right]$$
$$\mathbb{C}_x^\phi(P_x) = \left[\left(complete_x^\phi \wedge P_x\right) \vee \left(\neg complete_x^\phi \wedge same(O_x)\right)\right]$$

$\mathbb{D}_x^\phi(A_x)$ relies on the scheduling interval, δ_x^ϕ, for the input assumption to hold. The guarantee on the output hold is more direct relying only on the current value of $complete_x^\phi$.

A scheduled system, $S = (C, \phi, I, O, A, P)$, is correct if and only if for all π and for all $i \geq 0$ the following holds:

$$\forall c \in C \; \mathbf{G}\left[\mathbf{H}\left(\mathbb{D}_S^\phi(A) \wedge \bigwedge_{c' \in \mathbb{I}_c} \mathbb{C}_{c'}^\phi(P_{c'})\right) \implies \mathbb{D}_c^\phi(A_c)\right] \wedge$$

$$\mathbf{G}\left[\mathbf{H}\left(\mathbb{D}_S^\phi(A) \wedge \bigwedge_{c' \in \mathbb{O}} \mathbb{C}_{c'}^\phi(P_{c'})\right) \implies \left(complete_s^\phi \wedge P_s\right)\right]$$

Here the system itself has a dispatch cycle in the schedule as discussed in the prior section. The first set of verification conditions, one condition in the set for each component, checks compatibility between connected components. Component outputs that are consumed by downstream components as inputs must have

```
thread WaypointPlanManagerService_thr
    features
        AutomationResponse: in event data port CMASI::AutomationResponse.i;
        MissionCommand: out event data port CMASI::MissionCommand.i;
    annex agree {**
        eq Dispatch: bool;
        eq Complete: bool;

        guarantee Sem_WPM_Output_Event_Hold_MissionCommand "Output event freeze" :
            not Complete => (event(MissionCommand) = prev(event(MissionCommand), false));
        guarantee Sem_WPM_Output_Data_Hold_MissionCommand "Output data freeze" :
            not Complete => (true -> (MissionCommand = pre(MissionCommand)));

        assume Req_WPM_Good_Automation_Response "Input valid automation response":
            Dispatch => (event(AutomationResponse) => WELL_FORMED_AUTOMATION_RESPONSE(AutomationResponse));

        guarantee Req_WPM_Good_Mission_Command "Output valid mission commands" :
            Complete => (event(MissionCommand) => WELL_FORMED_MISSION_COMMAND(MissionCommand));
    **};
end WaypointPlanManagerService_thr;
```

Fig. 5. Modeling of scheduling semantics in AGREE

guarantees strong enough to satisfy input assumptions at dispatch. These must also respect the input freeze required by the consuming component.

The second condition is for the system outputs. Components producing system outputs must have guarantees strong enough to imply that the system guarantees hold at complete. Unlike components though, there is no output hold requirement for the system because outputs appear depending on when components producing those outputs complete. As before, if all of the verification conditions hold, then a scheduled system is said to be correct. Correct means that for the schedule $\phi\prime$, $\mathbf{G}\left[\mathbf{H}\left(\mathbb{D}_S^{\phi\prime}(A)\right) \implies \mathbb{C}_S^{\phi\prime}(P)\right]$ holds. Here the internal components of the system are completely abstracted away, and the system itself is just some scheduled component in $\phi\prime$ belonging to a larger system.

6   AGREE Model

The scheduling semantics can often be directly modeled in the AADL AGREE annex. At the component level, this requires introducing two Boolean variables *dispatch* and *complete*, augmenting the original *assumptions* and *guarantees* with *dispatch* and *complete*, respectively, and adding additional *guarantees* to enforce the output freeze rule. We often omit the assumptions of frozen inputs, as they are trivially satisfied by the schedule definition, the output freeze rule, and the system-level assumptions.

Figure 5 shows a simplified AADL model originally developed on the DARPA CASE program [19]. The first two *guarantees* are added to freeze the outputs between completions. Also the original contract (the assumption and the third *guarantee*) are augmented with *dispatch* and *complete*. In practice, we find that direct modeling is helpful to clarify the semantics with users. However, in general it could be a complex task, particularly if the contracts depend on past history. In the next section, we will discuss how the Lustre backend model is used to handle the general case.

```
node CircularCounter (init: int, incr: int, reset: bool)
returns (count: int);
let
    count = if reset then init
              else init-> (pre(count) + incr);
tel;

const PERIOD :    int = 10;

eq tick : int = CircularCounter(1, 1, prev(tick = PERIOD, false));

assume "Schedule ABACD" :
    A_Dispatch = (tick = 1 or tick = 5) and
    A_Complete = (tick = 2 or tick = 6) and
    B_Dispatch = (tick = 3) and
    B_Complete = (tick = 4) and
    C_Dispatch = (tick = 7) and
    C_Complete = (tick = 8) and
    D_Dispatch = (tick = 9) and
    D_Complete = (tick = 10);
```

Fig. 6. Modeling schedule with circular counter in AGREE

At the system level, we use a circular counter to model a cyclic schedule in AGREE. The counter updates at every instant. Once it reaches the limit, it resets to one at the next instant. We set the limit to the period of the schedule.

Based on the current count, the counter triggers a corresponding scheduling event. Figure 6 shows an AGREE model of the schedule ($ABACD$).

7 LUSTRE Backend Model

AGREE translates an AADL model and its annotated contracts into a dialect [12] of the Lustre language, and then queries a user-selected model checker to perform the verification. The dialect includes an expression called *condact*, which is similar to the activation condition in SCADE. It clocks a node call expression as follows: *condact(cond, node(node_inputs, node_outputs), init_outputs)*. If the Boolean signal *cond* is true, the clocked node *node* is activated and updates its local and output signals. Otherwise, the node keeps the previous value of the local and output signals. Before the first activation, the node outputs values are set to *init_outputs*. We are aware that the standard Lustre language introduced similar temporal operators like *when* and *current*. We use *condact* simply because it is supported by our default model checker JKind [12].

AGREE translates an AADL thread to a Lustre node in a *constraint* style, in which the thread input and output ports are both mapped to the node input signals. Thus, the *condact* expression does not automatically freeze the thread outputs. We add assertions to enforce the output freeze rule, and we use the thread *complete* signal to clock the node. The *complete* signal is triggered by the circular counter shown in Fig. 6. Figure 7 shows an example of using *condact* to model a scheduled AADL thread.

```
assert condact(WPM_Complete, WPM(WPM_ASSUME_HIST, WPM_ASSUME0, WPM_AutomationResponse_EVENT,
               WPM_AutomationResponse, WPM_MissionCommand_EVENT, WPM_MissionCommand), true);

assert (not WPM_Complete) => (true -> (WPM_MissionCommand = pre(WPM_MissionCommand)));
assert (not WPM_Complete) => (WPM_MissionCommand_EVENT = (false -> pre(WPM_MissionCommand_EVENT)));
assert (not WPM_Complete) => (WPM_ASSUME0 = (true -> pre(WPM_ASSUME0)));
```

Fig. 7. Modeling scheduling semantics with *condact* in lustre

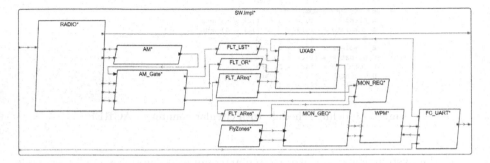

Fig. 8. UAV software architecture model in AADL

8   Case Study

The approach presented in this paper was applied to the BriefCASE toolchain [7], which was developed on the DARPA CASE program to assist engineers in the design of inherently cyber-resilient embedded systems. As part of the demonstration effort, a UAV surveillance system architecture was modeled in AADL. Figure 8 shows the architecture of the UAV mission computer software, which receives commands from a ground station to conduct surveillance along a geographical feature, such as a river. The software generates a flight plan adhering to a set of keep-in and keep-out zones, which is then sent to the UAV flight controller.

The baseline design included the UxAS [24] flight planning component, waypoint plan manager, UART driver, radio driver, and fly-zone database. These components were associated with varying levels of trustworthiness. In particular, UxAS was treated as blackbox software and deemed potentially security-compromised since it was an open-source component developed by a third party. BriefCASE includes tools that analyze architecture models and generate requirements corresponding to vulnerabilities in the design. The BriefCASE cyber-resiliency tool was then used to address the requirements by transforming the model, thereby mitigating the corresponding vulnerabilities. The transformations inserted eight high-assurance components into the model including an attestation manager, attestation gate, two monitors, and four filters. AGREE behavioral specifications for these components were provided, describing their intended functionality.

The hardened model (baseline plus high-assurance components) contained 13 threads, all of which were mapped to a single mission computer processor running

```
fun WellformedCASE_RF_Msg(msg : CASE_RF_Msg.Impl, src : int64.i, dst : int64.i ) : bool =
    WellformedCASE_MsgHeader(msg.header, src, dst);
fun WellformedCASE_MsgHeader(hdr : CASE_MsgHeader.Impl, src : int64.i, dst : int64.i ) : bool =
    (hdr.src = src) and (hdr.dst = dst) and (hdr.trusted = true) and (hdr.HMAC = true);
fun WellformedCASE_UART_Msg(msg : CASE_UART_Msg.Impl) : bool =
    msg.crc = true;
assume "Radio receives well-formed messages" :
    event(radio_recv) => WellformedCASE_RF_Msg(radio_recv, GS_ID, UAV_ID);
assume "UART receives well-formed messages" :
    event(uart_recv) => WellformedCASE_UART_Msg(uart_recv);
guarantee "Radio sends well-formed messsages" :
    event(radio_send) => WellformedCASE_RF_Msg(radio_send, UAV_ID, GS_ID);
guarantee "UART sends well-formed messages" :
    event(uart_send) => WellformedCASE_UART_Msg(uart_send);
```

Fig. 9. Model of assumptions and well-formedness properties in AGREE

the seL4 microkernel (chosen for its formally verified separation guarantees). An seL4 domain schedule was added to the model with all threads designated to run once per scheduling cycle with a period of 500 ms. The processor time allocated to each thread ranged from 2 ms (filters and monitors) to 100 ms (UxAS). The verification goal was to prove that the key system security properties were satisfied by the hardened model with the components executing according to the seL4 domain schedule.

We note that although *event* and *event data* ports were used in the UAV AADL model, they were intended to model the event-triggered execution of periodic threads. In addition, since each thread executed once every scheduling cycle, the number of queued events or data was always equal to or less than one, making this model suitable for the application of our modeling framework.

The following system-level security properties were to be verified in the presence of the seL4 domain schedule: (a) the output UART and RF messages are *well-formed*, (b) the system only responds to trusted sources, and (c) the waypoints generated are *geo-fenced*. The encoding of the well-formedness property and its assumptions is shown in Fig. 9.

Our framework was able to prove these properties in less than 2 min on a PC with 2.6 GHz CPU and 32 GB RAM. The verification results are shown in Fig. 10.

The case study is reflective of a development workflow in which we first verify that the component contracts hold under a synchronous dataflow model. As the design is refined and an execution schedule for each component is specified, we want to show that the system properties continue to hold. Our new framework enables such verification, providing assurance of intended behavior at runtime.

9 Related Work

The AADL standard by itself does not have a well-defined execution semantics. In order to formally verify an AADL model, it is often translated to a formal model, like timed automata [11], Lustre [14], and Real-Time Maude [22]. Then a formal method is applied to analyze the translated model.

Property	Result
✓ ✓ Verification for SW.Impl	26 Valid
✓ ✓ Contract Guarantees	11 Valid
✓ FC_UART assume: [Req001_UARTDriver] Assumes recv_data only gets well formed CASE_UART_Msg.Impl types	Valid (31s)
✓ FC_UART assume: [Req002_UARTDriver] The UART shall receive valid mission commands	Valid (36s)
✓ RADIO assume: The radio receives well-formed messages	Valid (32s)
✓ WPM assume: [Req_WPM_Good_Automation_Response] The Waypoint Manager shall receive valid automation response	Valid (36s)
✓ WPM assume: [Req_WPM_Good_AirVehicle_State] The Waypoint Manager shall receive well-formed air vehicle state messages	Valid (32s)
✓ WPM assume: [Req002_WPM] The set of waypoints received will not have duplicates in them	Valid (36s)
✓ Subcomponent Assumptions	Valid (36s)
✓ The radio_send outputs only well formed CASE_RF_Msg.impl types	Valid (36s)
✓ The uart_send outputs only well formed CASE_UART_Msg.impl types	Valid (36s)
✓ The system only responds to trusted sources	Valid (1m 19s)
✓ The uart_send waypoints are geo-fenced	Valid (1m 56s)
> ✓ This component consistent	1 Valid
> ✓ FC_UART consistent	1 Valid
> ✓ RADIO consistent	1 Valid
> ✓ FlyZones consistent	1 Valid
> ✓ UXAS consistent	1 Valid
> ✓ WPM consistent	1 Valid
> ✓ AM consistent	1 Valid
> ✓ AM_Gate consistent	1 Valid
> ✓ FLT_AReq consistent	1 Valid
> ✓ FLT_OR consistent	1 Valid
> ✓ FLT_LST consistent	1 Valid
> ✓ MON_REQ consistent	1 Valid
> ✓ FLT_ARes consistent	1 Valid
> ✓ MON_GEO consistent	1 Valid
> ✓ Component composition consistent	1 Valid

Fig. 10. Use case verification results in AGREE

In *aadl2sync* [14], the AADL behavior models are translated to synchronous programs mainly for simulation. *aadl2sync* uses activation condition to model sporadic execution of software components. By contrast, our proposed framework focuses on simulating detailed timed behavior in the presence of clock drift. Moreover, we focus on the formal verification of system properties based on component requirements, which in general do not completely define component behavior.

Metzler et al. [21] use an iterative and incremental approach to prove safety properties of concurrent programs. Their technique starts with a proof under a specific schedule, and then in each following iteration gradually relaxes the scheduling constraints. The iteration stops when all possible executions are explored or a counterexample is generated. Unlike our component model, their programs are "white boxes", allowing their schedule to interleave instructions between programs. In comparison, our basic scheduling unit is a software thread. In each iteration, the model checking problem is still challenging. In this context, our compositional verification approach makes sense.

10   Conclusion and Future Work

Based on the AGREE framework, we presented an approach to assume-guarantee reasoning with scheduled components. The proposed model of computation differs from the synchronous model used in the current framework. We introduced virtual scheduling events to tie the AADL execution semantics to AGREE contracts. Our approach was applied to the compositional verification of a UAV model developed on the DARPA CASE program.

In the proposed model, the queue associated with an AADL event or event data port is limited to size of one. This limitation is due to our domain of interest. One interesting future task is to extend the modeling framework to allow a larger queue size. Given a *balanced* schedule, the maximum size of each queue is a constant that can be calculated from the schedule.

Acknowledgment. This work was funded by DARPA contract HR00111890001. The views, opinions and/or findings expressed are those of the author and should not be interpreted as representing the official views or policies of the Department of Defense or the U.S. Government.

We would like to thank John Hatcliff and Robby for many helpful discussions to clarify our understanding of the AADL semantics. We also want to thank David Hardin and anonymous reviewers for their comments that greatly improved the paper.

References

1. Backes, J.D., Whalen, M.W., Gacek, A., Komp, J.: On implementing real-time specification patterns using observers. In: International Symposium on NASA Formal Methods. pp. 19–33. Springer (2016)
2. Baker, T., Shaw, A.: The cyclic executive model and Ada. In: Real-Time Systems Symposium, pp. 120–129. IEEE (1988)
3. Benveniste, A., Le Guernic, P., Jacquemot, C.: Synchronous programming with events and relations: the SIGNAL language and its semantics. Science of Computer Programming 16(2), 103–149 (1991)
4. Champion, A., Gurfinkel, A., Kahsai, T., Tinelli, C.: CoCoSpec: A mode-aware contract language for reactive systems. In: International Conference on Software Engineering and Formal Methods. pp. 347–366. Springer (2016)
5. Clarke, E.M., Klieber, W., Nováček, M., Zuliani, P.: Model checking and the state explosion problem. In: Meyer, B., Nordio, M. (eds.) Tools for Practical Software Verification: LASER 2011, pp. 1–30. Springer (2012).
6. Clarke, E., Long, D., McMillan, K.: Compositional model checking. In: Fourth Annual Symposium on Logic in Computer Science, pp. 353–362. IEEE (1989)
7. Cofer, D., Amundson, I., Babar, J., Hardin, D., Slind, K., Alexander, P., Hatcliff, J., Robby, R., Klein, G., Lewis, C., Mercer, E., Shackleton, J.: Cyberassured systems engineering at scale. IEEE Secur. Priv. **01**, 2–14 (2022)
8. Cofer, D., Gacek, A., Backes, J., Whalen, M.W., Pike, L., Foltzer, A., Podhradsky, M., Klein, G., Kuz, I., Andronick, J., Heiser, G., Stuart, D.: A formal approach to constructing secure air vehicle software. Computer 51(11), 14–23 (2018)
9. Colaço, J.L., Pagano, B., Pouzet, M.: SCADE 6: a formal language for embedded critical software development. In: International Symposium on Theoretical Aspects of Software Engineering, pp. 1–11. IEEE (2017)
10. Feiler, P., Gluch, D.: Model-Based Engineering with AADL: An Introduction to the SAE Architecture Analysis & Design Language. Addison-Wesley Professional (2012)
11. Frana, R., Bodeveix, J.P., Filali, M., Rolland, J.F.: The AADL behaviour annex - experiments and roadmap. In: International Conference on Engineering of Complex Computer Systems, pp. 377–382. IEEE (2007)
12. Gacek, A., Backes, J., Whalen, M., Wagner, L.G., Ghassabani, E.: The JKind model checker. In: International Conference on Computer Aided Verification. pp. 20–27. Springer (2018)

13. Halbwachs, N., Caspi, P., Raymond, P., Pilaud, D.: The synchronous data flow programming language LUSTRE. Proceedings of the IEEE 79(9), 1305–1320 (1991)
14. Jahier, E., Halbwachs, N., Raymond, P., Nicollin, X., Lesens, D.: Virtual execution of AADL models via a translation into synchronous programs. In: International Conference on Embedded Software, pp. 134–143. ACM (2007)
15. Kahn, G.: The semantics of a simple language for parallel programming. In: Rosenfeld, J.L. (ed.) Information Processing, Proceedings of the 6th IFIP Congress 1974, pp. 471–475. North-Holland (1974)
16. Kamp, J.A.W.: Tense Logic and the Theory of Linear Order. Ph.D. thesis, UCLA (1968)
17. Klein, G., et al.: seL4: formal verification of an OS kernel. In: ACM Symposium on Operating Systems Principles, pp. 207–220. ACM (2009)
18. Lee, E.A., Messerschmitt, D.G.: Static scheduling of synchronous data flow programs for digital signal processing. IEEE Trans. Comput. 36(1), 24–35 (1987)
19. Mercer, E., Slind, K., Amundson, I., Cofer, D., Babar, J., Hardin, D.: Synthesizing verified components for cyber assured systems engineering. In: 24th International Conference on Model Driven Engineering Languages and Systems, pp. 205–215. IEEE (2021)
20. Meseguer, J., Ölveczky, P.C.: Formalization and correctness of the PALS architectural pattern for distributed real-time systems. Theor. Comput. Sci. 451, 1–37 (2012)
21. Metzler, P., Suri, N., Weissenbacher, G.: Extracting safe thread schedules from incomplete model checking results. International Journal on Software Tools for Technology Transfer 22(5), 565–581 (2020)
22. Ölveczky, P.C., Boronat, A., Meseguer, J.: Formal semantics and analysis of behavioral AADL models in real-time Maude. In: Hatcliff, J., Zucca, E. (eds.) Formal Techniques for Distributed Systems. pp. 47–62. Springer (2010)
23. Pnueli, A.: In transition from global to modular temporal reasoning about programs. In: Logics and Models of Concurrent Systems, sub-series F: Computer and System Science, pp. 123–144. Springer-Verlag (1985)
24. Rasmussen, S., Kingston, D., Humphrey, L.: A brief introduction to unmanned systems autonomy services (UxAS). In: International Conference on Unmanned Aircraft Systems, pp. 257–268. IEEE (2018)
25. Singhoff, F., Legrand, J., Nana, L., Marcé, L.: Scheduling and memory requirements analysis with AADL. In: Annual ACM SIGAda International Conference on Ada, pp. 1–10. ACM (2005)
26. Whalen, M.W., Gacek, A., Cofer, D., Murugesan, A., Heimdahl, M.P., Rayadurgam, S.: Your what is my how: iteration and hierarchy in system design. IEEE Softw. 30(2), 54–60 (2013)

Stateful Black-Box Fuzzing of Bluetooth Devices Using Automata Learning

Andrea Pferscher[✉] and Bernhard K. Aichernig[iD]

Institute of Software Technology, Graz University of Technology, Graz, Austria
{apfersch,aichernig}@ist.tugraz.at

Abstract. Fuzzing (aka fuzz testing) shows promising results in security testing. The advantage of fuzzing is the relatively simple applicability compared to comprehensive manual security analysis. However, the effectiveness of black-box fuzzing is hard to judge since the internal structure of the system under test is unknown. Hence, in-depth behavior might not be covered by fuzzing. This paper aims at overcoming the limitations of black-box fuzzing. We present a stateful black-box fuzzing technique that uses a behavioral model of the system under test. Instead of manually creating the model, we apply active automata learning to automatically infer the model. Our framework generates a test suite for fuzzing that includes valid and invalid inputs. The goal is to explore unexpected behavior. For this, we test for conformance between the learned model and the system under test. Additionally, we analyze behavioral differences using the learned state information. In a case study, we evaluate implementations of the Bluetooth Low Energy (BLE) protocol on physical devices. The results reveal security and dependability issues in the tested devices leading to crashes of four out of six devices.

Keywords: Automata learning · Fuzz testing · Model-based fuzzing · Bluetooth Low Energy

1 Introduction

The Internet of Things (IoT) connects billions of devices, and the number of connected devices will increase with the pervasion of new communication protocols. One popular protocol for short-range communication is Bluetooth. The introduction of Bluetooth Low Energy (BLE) made Bluetooth also available for low-energy devices in the IoT. Nowadays, manufacturers advertise BLE as a key communication technology that could make wired communication obsolete in some applications. For example, Texas Instruments [21] motivates the use of BLE chips for the automotive industry. They suggest that BLE can replace wires that connect sensors in a vehicle. Further automotive applications include, e.g., the use of the smartphone as a "virtual" key. These proposals stress the need for thorough testing techniques to ensure the safety and security of the user.

© Springer Nature Switzerland AG 2022
J. V. Deshmukh et al. (Eds.): NFM 2022, LNCS 13260, pp. 373–392, 2022.
https://doi.org/10.1007/978-3-031-06773-0_20

Fuzzing (aka fuzz testing) is a security and robustness testing technique. Fuzzing aims to reveal unexpected behavior, e.g. crashes. For this, fuzzing executes a large number of randomly generated test cases that include invalid or unusual inputs. One problem in fuzzing is the definition of a termination criterion for testing. In a white- or gray-box setting, coverage measurements, e.g. code coverage, create the possibility to define termination criteria. However, assuming a black-box environment hampers coverage measurements. One solution to obtain behavioral coverage for black-box fuzzing is the extension of fuzzing by model-based testing. Garbelini et al. [17] used model-based fuzzing to reveal security issues in BLE devices. They manually created a generic model based on the BLE specification. However, the manual creation of a model can be an error-prone process and additionally requires the ongoing effort of keeping the model up-to-date.

Instead of manual modeling, automata learning automatically creates behavioral models of black-box components from observed system behavior. In practice, automata learning has successfully been applied to show flaws in communication protocols like (D)TLS [14,30], TCP [13], SSH [15], or MQTT [37]. These learning applications deduce behavioral inconsistencies by comparing learned models against the specification.

In this paper, we present a stateful black-box fuzzer that tests BLE devices. For this, we combine automata learning and fuzzing. In preliminary work, Aichernig et al. [2] proposed learning-based fuzzing for MQTT servers. In contrast to their work, we do not learn one generic model for all devices, but rather base our proposed fuzzing technique on individual learned models for every BLE device. This is motivated by the observation in our previous work [26], where BLE devices behaved differently. The learned models show that functionalities might not be available or only after a specific message sequence. Hence, learning a generic model from one device is not feasible. Unlike Aichernig et al. [2], we do not only test one specific input. Instead we fuzz several packets from different layers of the BLE stack. Additionally, we extended the learning-based fuzzing framework with a counterexample analysis technique that automatically investigates unexpected behavior. Our results show that all BLE devices contain behavioral inconsistencies, security, or robustness issues. As a result, we were able to crash four out of the six investigated devices.

The contribution of this paper is threefold. First, we propose a stateful black-box fuzzing framework for fuzzing BLE devices. Second, we present the conducted case study that is based on six BLE devices. Last, we provide the code of the learning-based fuzzing framework **online**[1] [25].

The paper is structured as follows. Section 2 discusses the needed background. In Sect. 3, we introduce the developed learning-based fuzzing framework. Section 4 presents the case study on learning-based fuzzing of the BLE devices. We discuss related work in Sect. 5, and conclude our work with a discussion and an outlook on future work in Sect. 6.

---

[1] https://git.ist.tugraz.at/apferscher/ble-fuzzing.

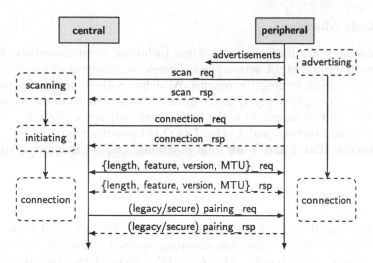

Fig. 1. Bluetooth sequence diagram including the connection procedure and the start of the pairing procedure. The figure is taken from our previous work [26].

2   Preliminaries

2.1   Bluetooth Low Energy

Bluetooth Low Energy (BLE) is part of the Bluetooth specification [6] since version 4.2 and enables communication via Bluetooth also for low energy devices. Compared to the Bluetooth classic, BLE builds upon a different protocol stack.

Figure 1 shows the sequence chart of the connection procedure between two BLE devices. We distinguish between two roles of the devices: the central and the peripheral device. In the remaining of the paper, we refer to the central and peripheral devices as *central* and *peripheral*. The central initiates the connection, whereas the peripheral is available for the establishment of a connection. For example, a central would be a smartphone that connects to a peripheral like a smartwatch. The peripheral is initially in an *advertising* state sending advertisements. The central starts in the *scanning* state by scanning for advertisements via performing a scan_req. The peripheral's response either contains an advertisement or a scan response, both are referred to in Fig. 1 as scan_rsp. Then the central enters the *initiating* state by sending a connection_req that is answered by a connection_rsp. Next, a negotiation phase starts, where parameters like maximum transmission unit (MTU) or Bluetooth version are agreed upon. Note that also the peripheral may request parameters from the central, which should be answered. The BLE specification does not specify which parameters must be negotiated. Hence, the establishment of a connection might be different for every BLE device. Afterward, the devices are connected and the pairing procedure can start. We distinguish between *legacy* and *secure* pairing, which differ in the encryption key-exchange procedure. A connection can be terminated by sending an additional scan_req or by a termination indication (termination_ind).

2.2   Mealy Machine

Mealy machines are finite state machines including state transitions that are labeled with input/output action pairs. Therefore, Mealy machines represent a modeling formalism for reactive systems. We define a Mealy machine as a 6-tuple $\mathcal{M} = \langle Q, q_0, I, O, \delta, \lambda \rangle$ where Q is the finite set of states, q_0 is the initial state, I is the finite set of inputs, O is the finite set of outputs, $\delta : Q \times I \rightarrow Q$ is the state-transition function, and $\lambda : Q \times I \rightarrow O$ is the output function.

We assume that δ and λ are total functions, i.e., $\mathcal{M}$ is input enabled and deterministic. Let $s \in (I \times O)^*$ be a sequence of alternating inputs and outputs, where $s_I \in I^*$ is the corresponding input sequence and $s_O \in O^*$ the output sequence. We denote the empty sequence as ϵ and upgrade a single element to a sequence of size one. We write $s \cdot s'$ for the concatenation of two sequences s and s'. We extend δ and λ for sequences. Let $\delta^* : Q \times I^* \rightarrow Q$ be a function that returns the target state after executing an input sequence from a source state. Similarly, we define $\lambda^* : Q \times I^* \rightarrow O^*$ which returns the corresponding output sequence that is observable on executing an input sequence starting at a given state. Let S_I be the set of all possible input sequences in $\mathcal{M}$. We denote that two Mealy machines $\mathcal{M} = \langle Q, q_0, I, O, \delta, \lambda \rangle$ and $\mathcal{M}' = \langle Q', q_0', I, O, \delta', \lambda' \rangle$ are behavioral equivalent if $\forall s_I \in S_I : \lambda^*(q_0, s_I) = \lambda'^*(q_0', s_I)$. Consequently, a counterexample to conformance between $\mathcal{M}$ and $\mathcal{M}'$ is an input sequence $s_I \in S_I$ where $\lambda^*(q_0, s_I) \neq \lambda'^*(q_0', s_I)$.

2.3   Automata Learning

Automata learning creates behavioral models of black-box systems using system observations. In automata learning, we distinguish between two main directions: passive and active learning. Passive learning infers a behavioral model from a given data set, e.g., log files. Therefore, the quality of the learned behavioral model depends on the provided data. Active learning creates a behavioral model by actively querying the System Under Learning (SUL). For this, we require an interface to the SUL that enables query execution and observation of outputs.

Many state-of-the-art learning algorithms build upon the L^* algorithm proposed by Dana Angluin [3]. Her seminal work introduces the minimally adequate teacher framework that comprises two members: the learner and the teacher. The learner's objective is to create a minimal Deterministic Finite Automaton (DFA) that represents a hidden regular language. The teacher knows this regular language. To learn the DFA, the learner asks the teacher two different types of queries. First, the learner asks if a word is part of the language. We denote such queries as membership queries. Based on the answers to the membership queries, the learner creates an initial hypothesis. This hypothesis is then provided to the teacher. Since the learner asks for equivalence between the hypothesis and the SUL, the second query type is named equivalence queries. The teacher answers equivalence queries either by confirming that the provided hypothesis conforms to the regular language or by returning a counterexample that shows the non-conformance between the hypothesis and the SUL. In the case of non-conformance, the learner creates new membership queries based on the counterexample and then proposes a new hypothesis. This procedure repeats until a conforming hypothesis is provided. The L^* algorithm has been extended for various behavioral system types. Shahbaz and Groz [34] propose Angluin-style learning for reactive systems, where the behavior is formalized by Mealy machines. For this, the learner asks output queries instead of membership queries. Output queries include an input sequence, and the teacher responds with the corresponding output sequence. Since the efficiency of L^*-based algorithms depends on the considered alphabet, active learning does not scale well for systems with large input and output space. To overcome this issue, Aarts et al. [1] introduce a mapper component that enables learning with an abstracted alphabet.

The assumption of a teacher with a perfect equivalence oracle is not practical. Therefore, conformance testing implements the equivalence oracle. For this, a conformance relation must be defined. Assuming that an implementation represents a hidden Mealy machine $\mathcal{I}$, Tretmans [38] defines the implementation relation $\mathcal{I}$ **imp** $\mathcal{S}$ between an implementation $\mathcal{I}$ and a Mealy machine specification $\mathcal{S}$. We denote conformance between $\mathcal{I}$ and $\mathcal{S}$ based on the behavioral equivalence of Mealy machines. In automata learning, conformance testing aims to test that a proposed hypothesis $\mathcal{H}$ conforms to a black-box implementation $\mathcal{I}$, i.e., testing that $\mathcal{H}$ **imp** $\mathcal{I}$ is satisfied. Since the behavioral conformance between two Mealy machines is based on equivalence, $\mathcal{I}$ **imp** $\mathcal{H} \Leftrightarrow \mathcal{H}$ **imp** $\mathcal{I}$ holds. Assuming that a finite set of input sequences $S'_I \subseteq S_I$ adequately represents the behavior of $\mathcal{I}$, we can define the following conformance relation for learning:

$$\mathcal{H} \text{ imp } \mathcal{I} \Leftrightarrow \forall s'_I \in S'_I : \lambda^*_{\mathcal{H}}(q_0^{\mathcal{H}}, s'_I) = \lambda^*_{\mathcal{I}}(q_0^{\mathcal{I}}, s'_I). \tag{1}$$

2.4 Fuzzing

Fuzzing aims at finding unexpected behavior of the System Under Test (SUT) by executing a large number of tests. To trigger unexpected behavior, executed tests not only contain valid inputs, but also invalid or unusual inputs. The first fuzzing framework was introduced by Miller et al. [22] to test UNIX utilities.

We categorize fuzzing based on three access levels to the SUT: white, gray, and black box. In white-box fuzzing access to the code is given. White-box techniques, e.g. SAGE [19], apply symbolic execution to generate inputs that also execute in-depth behavior. Gray-box fuzzer, e.g. american fuzzing loop (AFL) [40], are based on instrumented binary code, which enables reasoning about covered behavior. In black-box fuzzing, no access to the system's code is assumed. Böhme et al. [7] distinguish between mutational and generational black-box techniques. Mutational fuzzers generate random inputs by modifying an initial input, e.g. via bit-flipping. Generational fuzzers require a priori knowledge about the input structure of the SUT, e.g., the packet structure of the tested protocol.

The main problem in black-box fuzzing is the assurance of sufficient test coverage. To overcome this problem, Aichernig et al. [2] presented a generational black-box fuzzer that is based on active automata learning. Figure 2 illustrates

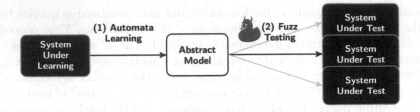

Fig. 2. Concept of learning-based fuzzing technique proposed by Aichernig et al. [2].

the proposed two-step procedure of learning-based fuzzing. First, Aichernig et al. learn a behavioral model of the SUL. Since learning would not be feasible using all possible inputs, an abstracted alphabet is considered. The learned abstract model is then used for model-based fuzzing of other SUTs which represent different implementations of the SUL. The learned model is on a more abstract level than the SUTs. Therefore, Aichernig et al. extend the model-based testing technique with a so-called fuzzing mapper. The fuzzing mapper generates fuzzing inputs by concretizing the abstract inputs to invalid and valid inputs. The stateful fuzzer then identifies behavioral differences between the model and the SUTs.

3   Methodology

In the following, we present a fuzzing framework that combines automata learning and fuzzing to create a stateful black-box fuzzing technique. Figure 3 illustrates our proposed learning-based fuzzing framework. The framework consists of three components: the system interface, the active automata learning component, and the stateful fuzzer. The presented technique is a two-step procedure. First, we use active automata learning to generate a behavioral model of the SUT. Second, we fuzz the SUT based on the learned model. In the following sections, we describe the details of each component.

3.1   System Interface

The system interface comprises the SUT and an adapter that enables communication to the SUT. We assume that the SUT is a reactive black-box system, where we can execute inputs and observe outputs. Furthermore, we require the SUT to be resettable via inputs sent by the adapter.

Our testing targets are BLE devices. To communicate with a black-box BLE device, we require another BLE device as part of our adapter component. The device used in the adapter is controlled by us and enables the transmission of manually crafted BLE packets to the SUT. In the context of Fig. 1, the adapter device represents the central, whereas the SUT acts as peripheral. Hence, the SUT initially distributes BLE advertisements. The used learning algorithm and conformance testing technique require that the SUT can be reset to the initial

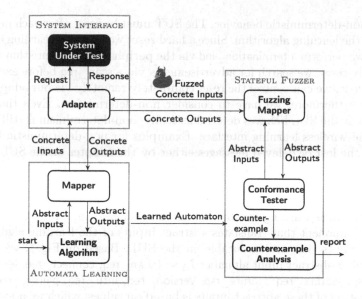

Fig. 3. The proposed framework for learning-based fuzzing of BLE devices comprises three components: the system interface, the learning component, and the fuzzer.

advertising state. We assume that the BLE connection can be terminated by performing termination_ind or scan_req. After the connection is terminated, we expect that the peripheral again enters the advertising state. A reset via BLE messages is assumed to be equal to a hard reset, e.g., via pressing the reset button on the device.

Garbelini et al. [17] provide a firmware for the central that enables the transmission of manually crafted BLE packets. Using Python and the library SCAPY [31], we can draft BLE packets and send them via the central to the peripheral, i.e. the SUT. Vice versa, we parse received packets from the peripheral by the central again using SCAPY.

3.2 Automata Learning

The automata learning component implements a framework that deduces a behavioral model from the observations returned by the system interface. Since we require for fuzzing that the behavior in every state for all inputs is defined, we apply an L^*-based automata learning algorithm. We applied an improved variant of the L^* algorithm proposed by Shahbaz and Groz [34] that learns a Mealy machine of a reactive system.

The L^*-based learning algorithm requires the SUL to be deterministic and resettable. Due to the wireless setup, we have to take care of non-deterministic behavior and a sufficient reset procedure. For this, we use an updated version of the learning framework for BLE devices presented in our previous work [26]. The updates include a different reset implementation and a more fault-tolerant handling of non-deterministic behavior. The SUT must be reset after each performed query by the learning algorithm. Since a hard reset would make learning a tedious process, we perform a termination_ind via the peripheral. To ensure that the SUT is properly reset, we search for advertisements via a scan_req before executing a query. Hence, we can control the reset completely remotely via our adapter component. Furthermore, we have to consider non-determinism. Even though, we assume that the SUL behaves deterministically, non-determinism is still possible due to the wireless learning interface. Examples for non-deterministic behavior could be the lost or delayed messages either by the adapter or the SUL. In case of non-determinism, we repeat the query and apply a majority selection to select the most commonly observed value.

Similar to our previous technique [26], we consider an abstracted input alphabet which makes learning feasible within an adequate time. Figure 3 shows the mapper component that translates abstract inputs of the learning algorithm to concrete inputs that are executable on the SUL. Based on Fig. 1, we consider the following abstract input alphabet $I_A = \{$scan_req, connect_req, length_req, length_rsp, feature_req, feature_rsp, version_req, mtu_req, pairing_req$\}$. The concretization of these abstract inputs is based on values, which we assume to be valid BLE packets that lead to similar responses each time they are sent. The concrete values are mainly based on preset values provided by SCAPY. For example, the mapper translates the abstract input version_req to BTLE($access\_addr$)/ BTLE_DATA()/BTLE_CTRL()/LL_VERSION_IND($version$), where the fields $access\_addr$ and $version$ are defined by the mapper. The mapper then forwards the concrete packet to the system interface and waits for a response. The received concrete packets from the system interface are then translated by the mapper to an abstract output. The output abstraction removes field values from the packets and considers only the packet type name provided by SCAPY.

3.3   Stateful Fuzzer

The stateful fuzzer is the third component in our learning-based fuzzing framework and executes the last step in our fuzzing technique. Our proposed stateful fuzzer aims to find and analyze counterexamples to the conformance between the provided hypothesis and the SUT. The stateful fuzzer takes the learned automaton as input and has access to the interface of the SUT.

In contrast to other model-based fuzzers [2,17], our technique does not require a generic behavioral model of the SUT. According to Garbelini et al. [17], the manual creation of a generic BLE model is tedious due to the underspecified connection procedure in the BLE specification [6]. Furthermore, we cannot follow the learning-based fuzzing technique proposed by Aichernig et al. [2], since there does not exist any SUL that implements a generic model of the BLE protocol. The results of previous work [26] show that the learned model differs for every BLE device. Differences arise due to limitations of functionality, e.g. no support for BLE pairing, or functionality that is only available after a certain input sequence.

Our fuzzing technique is based on model-based testing and the conformance relation used in the fuzzing component follows the one during active automata learning. However, we need to adapt this conformance relation, since our fuzzing technique aims at testing if the provided SUT $\mathcal{I}$ implements the behavior defined by the provided automaton $\mathcal{H}$. Therefore, we test if $\mathcal{I}$ **imp** $\mathcal{H}$ holds. The provided automaton $\mathcal{H}$ specifies the behavior on an abstract level. Due to the abstraction, we define conformance based on the abstract input and output alphabet. Let T_A, where $T_A \subseteq I_A^*$, be a finite set of abstract input sequences. For this, we denote conformance between the provided automaton $\mathcal{H}$ and the SUT $\mathcal{I}$ for fuzzing as follows:

$$\mathcal{I} \text{ imp } \mathcal{H} \Leftrightarrow \forall t_A \in T_A : \lambda_\mathcal{I}^*(q_0^\mathcal{I}, t_A) = \lambda_\mathcal{H}^*(q_0^\mathcal{H}, t_A). \tag{2}$$

Note that λ^* returns a sequence of abstract outputs for the provided abstract input sequence. Let I^* be the set of possible concrete input sequences. The stateful fuzzer aims at finding a concrete input sequence $t \in I^*$ that shows for the corresponding abstract input sequence $t_A \in I_A^*$ that $\lambda_\mathcal{I}^*(q_0^\mathcal{I}, t_A) \neq \lambda_\mathcal{H}^*(q_0^\mathcal{H}, t_A)$ is fulfilled. In the remainder of this work, we denote $t \in I^*$ as test sequence and the corresponding $t_A \in I_A^*$ as abstract test sequence.

We generate abstract test sequences that consist of three parts $p \cdot f \cdot s$, where $p \in I_A^*$ is the prefix of the sequence, $f \in I_A$ is a fuzzing input, and $s \in I_A^*$ is the suffix of the test sequence. The prefix p represents an *access sequence* to a state in the behavioral model. The *access sequence* is an abstract test sequence that defines the shortest sequence to reach a state in the behavioral model starting from the initial state, where the access sequence for the initial state is the empty sequence ϵ. We can guarantee state coverage for fuzzing by generating for every access sequence corresponding test sequences. The fuzzing input f is a randomly selected abstract input that is later concretized by fuzzing techniques. The suffix s is a sequence of randomly selected inputs.

The fuzzing mapper translates the abstract test sequence to a concrete test sequence. The generation of concrete inputs differs for the three parts of the test sequence. The prefix p and the suffix s correspond to valid BLE packets similar to the translation during learning. The fuzzing input f is differently generated. The fuzzing mapper selects concrete fuzzed values for fields in the BLE packet based on given value ranges. For every packet, we fuzz exactly one field and if the packet has several fields randomly one field is chosen. The selection of the concrete value is based on randomness. For some fields, a set of possible values is given, whereas others are limited by minimum and maximum values. Additionally, for fields that are limited by an upper and lower bound, the selection of boundary values is preferred. For example, if the abstract input is a connect_req, then the concrete BLE packet in SCAPY syntax is BTLE() / BTLE_ADV(...) / BTLE_CONNECT_REQ(*interval, timeout,* ...). The fuzzing mapper concretizes the fields and chooses exactly one field to be fuzzed. For example, the mapper selects to fuzz the field *timeout*. Next, the fuzzer randomly picks a value between 0 and $2^{16} - 1$, since the BLE specification considers two bytes for the *timeout* field. The fuzzing mapper similarly translates all other fields as in the learning phase. Note that the fuzzed fields might be invalid according to the BLE specification. Considering the given example, the BLE specification defines the supervision timeout to be within 100 ms and 32 s, which corresponds to *timeout* values between 10 and 3 200.

We check after each executed input on the SUT $\mathcal{I}$ if the received output deviates from the defined output in the hypothesis $\mathcal{H}$. If this is the case, we stop the execution of the test sequence and truncate the test sequence after the first non-corresponding output. The counterexample to the conformance between $\mathcal{I}$ and $\mathcal{H}$ is then provided to the counterexample analysis component. Before we start the analysis, we try to reproduce the found counterexample. To avoid the reporting of counterexamples due to connection errors and non-deterministic behavior, we require to observe the found counterexample again within n_{cex} attempts.

If we found a reproducible counterexample, we perform the counterexample analysis. The counterexample analysis examines unexpected state transitions revealed by the fuzzing input. Based on the W-Method [9], we use the *characterization set* to calculate possible different state transitions between $\mathcal{I}$ and $\mathcal{H}$. The characterization set contains input sequences that generate a unique set of output sequences for every state. By the execution of input sequences of the characterization set, we aim to identify if an unexpected output leads to a different state. Since the characterization set might change for the extended fuzzing input alphabet, we extend the characterization set always by the input alphabet. The advantage of performing an L^*-based learning algorithm in advance is that the characterization set can be automatically derived from the data structures used during learning. Note that this counterexample analysis only hints at a possible target state. For example, a BLE connection might terminate on an invalid request. In this case, we would observe a transition to the initial state. To check the actual state equivalence, a more comprehensive conformance test would be required. The counterexample analysis is also limited by n_{cex} repetitions in the case of connection errors or non-deterministic behavior.

To make conformance testing feasible, we limit the size of T_A by $n_{\mathrm{fuzz}} \in \mathbb{N}$ and the size of the suffix s for each trace by $n_{\mathrm{suffix}} \in \mathbb{N}$. All executed test sequences, including the counterexample analysis, are stated in a final report that is generated after the conformance test. In the case that the SUT crashes, the report includes all executed traces up to the crash.

4   Evaluation

We evaluated our learning-based fuzzing technique on six different BLE devices. In the following, we present the practical setup for learning and fuzzing the BLE devices. Furthermore, we discuss the issues found by learning-based fuzzing. Our learning-based fuzzing framework, implemented in Python 3.9, and the learned automata are available **online**[2] [25]. We ran all experiments on an Apple Mac-Book Pro 2019 with an Intel Quad-Core i5 (2.4 GHz) and 8 GB RAM.

---

[2] https://git.ist.tugraz.at/apferscher/ble-fuzzing.

Table 1. Investigated BLE devices

Manufacturer (Board)	SoC	Application
Texas Instruments (LAUNCHXL-CC2640R2)	CC2640R2F	Project Zero
Texas Instruments (LAUNCHXL-CC2650)	CC2650	Project Zero
Texas Instruments (LAUNCHXL-CC26X2R1)	CC2652R1	Project Zero
Cypress (CY8CPROTO-063-BLE)	CYBLE-416045-02	Find Me Target
Cypress (Raspberry Pi 4 Model B)	CYW43455	bluetoothctl
Nordic (decaWave DWM1001-DEV)	nRF52832	Nordic GATTS

4.1 General Setup

Table 1 lists the six evaluated BLE devices. Our evaluation includes five devices that were already considered in previous work [26] and an additional device from Texas Instruments (CC2652R1). All of the selected devices implement the BLE 5 standard. The selection involves devices from different manufacturers that were also part of the case study by Garbelini et al. [17]. We extended our selection to popular boards, e.g., the Raspberry Pi 4. Furthermore, we aimed to identify behavioral differences between boards of the same manufacturer. All devices run an example application that sends BLE advertisements and allows a connection with the central. We refer to the BLE devices by their System on Chip (SoC) name. As central for learning and fuzzing, we used the Nordic nRF52840 Dongle and the Nordic nRF52840 Development Kit. We flashed both devices with custom firmware provided by Garbelini et al. [17].

To learn behavioral models of the BLE devices, we followed the learning setup presented in our previous work [26]. We used an adapted version of the learning library AALPY [23] (v1.1.5) which implements Rivest and Shapire's [28] improved L^* for Mealy machines. The learning library was extended by a method to calculate the characterization set, which is now included in v1.1.7. For the creation of BLE packets, we used an adapted version of the library SCAPY [31] (v2.4.4), where the used updates are available in v2.4.5.

Similar to our previous work [26], we adapted the considered input alphabet for the CC2640R2F to learn deterministic behavioral models, since the SoC behaves non-deterministically on some input sequences. We learned three different deterministic models of the CC2640R2 using a decreased input alphabet. The first variation considers the abstracted input alphabet I_A, introduced in Sect. 3.2, without pairing_req, the second without feature_req, and the third without length_req. For fuzzing, we separately tested each behavioral model against the SoC CC2640R2 with the corresponding reduced input alphabet.

For CC2651R1 and CYW43455, we required a different learning setup since the consecutive performing of connection_req led disproportionately often to connection errors. For these SoCs, we established a connection before executing a test sequence. Considering Fig. 1, we started learning in the initiating phase of the central after the connection_req. After executing the test sequence, a termination indication was performed to cancel the connection. Furthermore,

Table 2. Overview on fuzzing results. The *-symbol denotes that learning and fuzzing starts after the connection_req. Two SoCs crash before executing 1 000 queries.

SoC	States	Fuzzing rounds	Crashes	Queries	CEX
CC2640R2F (no pairing_req)	6	4	3	1 280	27
CC2640R2F (no feature_req)	11	5	5	928	50
CC2640R2F (no length_req)	11	5	5	767	39
CC2650	5	4	3	1 375	28
CC2652R1*	4	5	5 (6)	919	39
CYBLE-416045-02	3	2	1	1 413	38
CYW43455*	16	1	0	2 652	197
nRF52832	5	1	0	2 258	113

we decrease the learning alphabet to $I'_A = \{\text{length\_req}, \text{length\_rsp}, \text{feature\_req},$ feature_rsp, version_req, mtu_req, pairing_req$\}$. Hence, we solely learned for these devices the behavior during the parameter negotiation phase until the initiation of the pairing procedure.

For the conformance check during fuzzing, we define the minimum number of generated test sequences to $n_{\text{fuzz}} = 1\,000$. Since we want to create a stateful fuzzer, we defined the actual number of performed tests depending on the number of states. Let $n \in \mathbb{N}$ be the number of states of the provided learned model, then the number of generated test sequences per state is defined as follows $\lceil \frac{n_{\text{fuzz}}}{n} \rceil$. In previous work [26], we observed that the SUT might behave non-deterministically due to lost or delayed packets. Additionally, we check if a valid connection can be established before executing a test sequence. If not, we note down a connection error. We also require an error-handling behavior for the conformance testing. For each performed query, we set the maximum number of non-deterministic errors $n_{\text{nondet}} = 20$ and connection errors $n_{\text{errors}} = 20$. In case the BLE device crashed due to the execution of a fuzzed input, the conformance check stops after observing n_{errors} connection errors. For the counterexample analysis, the maximum attempts to reproduce the counterexample is $n_{\text{cex}} = 5$.

4.2   Fuzzing Results

Table 2 shows the learning-based fuzzing results for the investigated BLE SoCs. For every SoC, we list the number of states of the learned Mealy machine. The learned behavioral models of the SoCs that we already considered in the previous case study [26] did not change except for CYW43455. For CYW43455, we updated the BLUEZ version and used a different example application. Due to the update, the behavior on the connection_req changes, since consecutive connection_req lead more frequently to connection errors.

The *Fuzzing Rounds* indicate the number of performed conformance testing attempts performed by our stateful fuzzer. The stateful fuzzer aims to execute $\lceil \frac{1\,000}{n} \rceil \cdot n$ test sequences, where n is the number of states. However, four out of the six investigated SoCs crashed during the execution of our fuzzing technique.

In the case of a crash, we identify the cause of the crash. For example, whether a BLE packet with a fuzzed field causes the crash. In Sect. 4.3, we provide examples for fuzzed fields that led to a crash. If there exists such a field, we exclude the fuzzing of it in the next fuzzing execution. If the cause for crashing is not obvious, we repeat the stateful fuzzing without any changes a second time.

Looking at the number of crashes reported in Table 2, we not only see that four out of six SoCs crash, but, more seriously, two SoCs (CC2640R2F and CC2652R1) crash on every execution. Hence, we could not execute at least 1 000 fuzzed test sequences without crashing the devices. For the CC2652R1, we recognized an additional crash during the learning setup.

The column *Queries* reports the number of performed test sequences on the SoC during fuzzing. This number also includes the executions for the repetition of counterexamples and the following state analysis. The column *CEX* shows the number of found counterexamples to the conformance between the learned model and the SoC. Note that the number of counterexamples does not conclude that the SoC behaves erroneously. Instead, a high number of counterexamples more likely indicates that we observe more countermeasures against invalid inputs. In case of crashes, we take the number of performed tests and counterexamples from the fuzzing execution that executed the most test sequences.

The execution of conformance testing including the counterexample analysis took on average 5.6 h for non-crashing runs. However, this average runtime does not include the runtime of the nRF52832, since it has an extraordinary high runtime of 42.2 h. This observation conforms to the learning results we obtained in previous work [26] where the interaction with nRF52832 was more time-consuming than with other devices. We detect crashes within 12.6 min and 22.2 h. We assume that there is a high potential for optimization of the time to detect crashes due to the immediately performed counterexample analysis and the high number of accepted connection errors n_{errors}.

4.3 Bug Hunt

Table 3 presents the found vulnerabilities, and anomalies to the BLE specification [6] or compared to other devices. We found four different crash scenarios denoted by an identifier (ID) starting with a "C". Furthermore, we present two anomalies, A1 and A2, to the BLE specification and another two, A3 and A4, that shows a unique behavior compared to all other devices. The last finding of our paper reveals a security vulnerability (identified by V1) which allows a reduction of the key's entropy during the pairing procedure.

Connection crashes (C1-C4). All three investigated SoCs from Texas Instruments crashed due to performing connection requests (C1-C4). The crash C1 requires no input modification. Instead, a sequence of valid inputs crashes the CC2651R1. During learning, we observed that the CC2651R1 crashes on a sequence of non-fuzzed connection_req. For example, the execution of the following sequence of valid inputs leads to a crash on the CC2651R1:

scan_req · connection_req · connection_req.

Table 3. List of found crashes and anomalies. The identifiers (IDs) of crashes start with a "C", behavioral anomalies with an "A", and other vulnerabilities with a "V".

ID	Issue	SoCs
C1	Crash on consecutive connection_req	CC2652R1
C2	Crash on connection_req($interval$)	CC2640R2F, CC2650, CYBLE-416045-02
C3	Crash on connection_req($timeout$)	CC2640R2F, CC2650
C4	Crash on connection_req($latency$)	CC2640R2F, CC2650
A1	Multiple responses to version_req	CC2652R1
A2	Accepting pairing_req($max\_kex\_size :> 16$)	CYW43455
A3	Connection termination on length_rsp	nRF52832
A4	Unknown behavior on length_{req, rsp}($max\_\{tx, rx\}\_bytes$)	CC2652R1
V1	Key size reduction on pairing_req($max\_kex\_size : [7, 16]$)	All devices (except CYBLE-416045-02)

With the support of Texas Instruments, we identified the origin of this issue in the installed application software. The running application stops sending advertisements after two consecutive connections. Additionally, the connection cannot be reset, since no further scan_req are accepted. Hence, the device is inaccessible.

The crashes C2-C4 were caused by fuzzed fields of the connection_req. The fields that crashed the devices CC2640R2F and CC2650 were *latency, timeout,* and *interval.* Invalid values of the field interval (C1) also crashed one BLE device of Cypress (CYBLE-416045-02). We assume that issues relate to CVE-2019-19193 which has been reported by Garbelini et al. [17]. According to Garbelini et al., this issue has been fixed by the manufacturers.

Multiple Answers to Version Requests (A1). Figure 4 illustrates a simplified learned model of the CC2651R1. This model shows that every version_req is always answered by a version indication. The BLE specification [6] defines that an already answered version_ind should not be answered again.

Anomalies in Length Requests and Responses. A comparison of the learned models shows that the nRF52832 is the only SoC that terminates the BLE connection and returns to the initial state if an unexpected length_rsp is performed. We observed that behavior even though the length_rsp did not contain any fuzzed fields. Furthermore, our counterexample analysis revealed an anomalous behavior for the CC2651R1 (A4). We trigger the anomaly by performing a length_rsp or length_req, where we fuzzed the fields max_tx_bytes or max_rx_bytes. After this, we execute a non-fuzzed mtu_req or pairing_req. Executing this sequence, the CC2651R1 enters a state, where only empty BLE data packets are received for all inputs except those that reset the connection. A4 also violates the BLE specification, since none of the further requests is appropriately answered. Furthermore, this unknown state cannot be exited by performing another valid length_req.

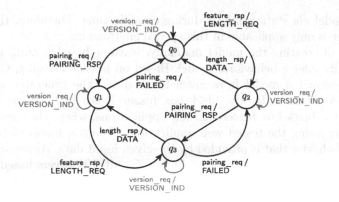

Fig. 4. Model learned of CC2652R1. For clarity, some transitions are not displayed. The complete model is available online [25].

Key Size Acceptance in Pairing Request (V1, A2). We see for all tested SoCs, except for the CYLBE-416045-02, that a reduction of the maximum key size during the pairing request is possible (V1). The test fails on the CYLBE-416045-02 since the SoC does not accept any pairing_req. By performing a pairing_req, the requesting party proposes some parameters for the pairing, e.g., the maximum key size of the long-termkey (LTK) that is later used to distribute session keys for a secure connection. The BLE specification defines that the key size field needs to be within 7 and 16 bytes. Downgrade attacks, e.g. the KNOB attack [4], show that accepting low key sizes decreases the entropy of the LTK and, therefore, enables brute-forcing of the used key. All devices, except CYLBE-416045-02, accept a key with an entropy of 7 bytes. Additionally, fuzzing the accepted key sizes shows that CYW43455 accepts pairing_req that contains maximum key sizes greater than 16 bytes.

5 Related Work

In practice, protocol state fuzzing proved itself a useful tool to reveal security issues and behavioral anomalies of communication protocols, e.g. TCP [13], SSH [15], TLS [30], DTLS [14], 802.11 4-way handshake [36], MQTT [37], OpenVPN [11], and QUIC [27]. In the literature, this technique is also known as learning-based testing where the SUT is tested via active automata learning. Hence, our learning-based fuzzer also performs protocol state fuzzing during learning the behavioral models of the BLE devices.

Several black-box fuzzers for network protocols exist, e.g. *boofuzz* (former Sulley) [24] or *GitLab Protocol Fuzzer Community Edition* (former Peach) [18]. They require user-defined input generators and guidance to in-depth paths. To enable stateful black-box fuzzing model-based techniques have been proposed. *SNOOZE* [5] is a model-based fuzzer for network protocols. However, input generators, as well as the model, must be manually crafted. Another model-based fuzzer for telecommunication protocols is *T-Fuzz* [20]. T-Fuzz extracts the required model via static analysis during compile time. Therefore, this model-based fuzzer is only applicable in this special environment.

Instead of creating the model manually, learning-based fuzzing techniques automatically infer a behavioral model. Based on passive learning, Comparetti et al. [10] extract a model from given input data. The generated model can then be used as input for the black-box fuzzer Peach [18]. Doupé et al. [12] also present a black-box fuzzer for web applications, where they generate the model via crawling the tested web application. However, passive learning can cover only behavior that is provided by the given input data. Aichernig et al. [2] presented a learning-based fuzzing technique for MQTT servers based on active automata learning. Different from our technique, they learned the model of one SUL, which they assume contained the most conforming behavior. This model is then used to fuzz other implementations of the tested system. The assumption of a generic model might hamper the applicability of learning-based fuzzing. Our results show that such an approach would not be feasible for BLE devices. In contrast to our technique, they fuzzed only one specific input field type and based their conformance tests on random traces which does not provide any guarantees about in-depth state coverage.

Bluetooth attacks and vulnerability collections like *BlueBorne* [32], *BLEED-INGBIT* [33], *KNOB* [4], *BLESA* [39], *Frankenstein* [29], *SweynTooth* [17] and *BrakTooth* [16] reveal severe issues in the Bluetooth protocol. Ruge et al. [29] detected issues concerning Bluetooth classic and BLE. They propose a frame-work that fuzzes an emulated chip firmware. Since no over-the-air communi-cation is required the time efficiency of fuzzing can be significantly improved. However, preparing the firmware for emulation is tedious. The motivation for our work originates from the fuzzing framework proposed by Garbelini et al. [17]. Instead of providing a handcrafted general model, we extend the model-based fuzzing framework by automata learning. This allows us to create more BLE device-specific input sequences. Furthermore, behavioral differences become vis-ible through the learned individual models. Additionally, we extend our fuzzer by a counterexample analysis tool that reports unknown state transitions or states.

6   Conclusion

6.1   Summary

We presented a learning-based fuzzing technique for BLE devices. Our proposed method is based on a black-box assumption. To achieve in-depth testing, we require a behavioral model of the SUT. Instead of manually crafting the model, we used automata learning to automatically generate the model. Using the learned model, we created a stateful black-box fuzzer. Furthermore, we extended our fuzzer with a counterexample analysis tool that examines unknown behavior. Our evaluation revealed anomalies and security issues in the tested BLE devices. Additionally, our fuzzer crashed four out of six devices.

6.2   Discussion

The missing ability to measure coverage limits the applicability of black-box fuzzing. To overcome this limitation, black-box fuzzing extended by model-based testing techniques shows promising results [17,20]. However, manually crafting models might be an error-prone process. In learning-based fuzzing, we extend fuzzing by automata learning to automatically create behavioral models. Still, our previous work [26] showed that the creation of a fault-tolerant interface for learning a remote physical device might not be straightforward. Nevertheless, this work has to be only done once. Our work indicates that the learning interface can then be easily extended to a stateful black-box fuzzer. The availability of distinct behavioral models enables checking for behavioral differences. Furthermore, we can automatically analyze found counterexamples.

6.3   Future Work

In future work, we propose advancements for learning as well as for fuzzing. For learning, we want to consider other modeling formalisms. Evaluating communication protocols shows that non-deterministic behavior hampers deterministic learning. Modeling this non-deterministic behavior might also hint at faulty behavior. Additionally, the work of Garbelini et al. [17] revealed several vulnerabilities during the pairing procedure of the BLE protocol. For this, we will extend our learning framework to deduce behavioral models of the pairing procedure. For fuzzing, we plan to adapt our generation of fuzzed inputs with a search-based technique. By defining a reward function for test sequences, we might cover more error-handling behavior of the SUT. Regarding our proposed counterexample analysis, we saw that fuzzed inputs revealed not yet observed behavior. Smeters et al. [35] used fuzzing as an equivalence oracle during learning. Following an akin idea, we can extend our learned models by the information that we already gained during the counterexample analysis. With this, we can generate models that also formalize error-handling behavior.

Acknowledgement. This work is funded by the TU Graz LEAD project *Dependable Internet of Things in Adverse Environments*, by the *LearnTwins* project (No 880852) from the Austrian Research Promotion Agency (FFG), and by *AIDOaRt* project (grant agreement No 101007350) from the ECSEL Joint Undertaking (JU). The JU receives support from the European Union's Horizon 2020 research and innovation programme and Sweden, Austria, Czech Republic, Finland, France, Italy, and Spain. We would like to thank Maximilian Schuh for providing support for the BLE devices and the authors of the SweynTooth paper for creating an open-source BLE interface. Furthermore, we thank the anonymous reviewers for their useful remarks.

References

1. Aarts, F., Jonsson, B., Uijen, J., Vaandrager, F.W.: Generating models of infinite-state communication protocols using regular inference with abstraction. Formal Methods Syst. Des. **46**(1), 1–41 (2015). https://doi.org/10.1007/s10703-014-0216-x

2. Aichernig, B.K., Muškardin, E., Pferscher, A.: Learning-based fuzzing of IoT message brokers. In: 14th IEEE Conference on Software Testing, Verification and Validation, ICST 2021, Porto de Galinhas, Brazil, 12–16 April 2021, pp. 47–58. IEEE (2021). https://doi.org/10.1109/ICST49551.2021.00017

3. Angluin, D.: Learning regular sets from queries and counterexamples. Inf. Comput. 75(2), 87–106 (1987). https://doi.org/10.1016/0890-5401(87)90052-6

4. Antonioli, D., Tippenhauer, N.O., Rasmussen, K.: Key negotiation downgrade attacks on Bluetooth and Bluetooth Low Energy. ACM Trans. Priv. Secur. 23(3), 14:1–14:28 (2020). https://doi.org/10.1145/3394497

5. Banks, G., Cova, M., Felmetsger, V., Almeroth, K.C., Kemmerer, R.A., Vigna, G.: SNOOZE: Toward a stateful network protocol fuzzer. In: Katsikas, S.K., López, J., Backes, M., Gritzalis, S., Preneel, B. (eds.) Information Security, 9th International Conference, ISC 2006, Samos Island, Greece, 30 August–2 September 2006, Proceedings. Lecture Notes in Computer Science, vol. 4176, pp. 343–358. Springer (2006). https://doi.org/10.1007/11836810_25

6. Bluetooth SIG: Bluetooth core specification v5.3. Standard (2021). https://www.bluetooth.com/specifications/specs/core-specification/

7. Böhme, M., Cadar, C., Roychoudhury, A.: Fuzzing: Challenges and reflections. IEEE Softw. 38(3), 79–86 (2021). https://doi.org/10.1109/MS.2020.3016773

8. Capkun, S., Roesner, F. (eds.): 29th USENIX Security Symposium, USENIX Security 2020, 12–14 August 2020. USENIX Association (2020). https://www.usenix.org/conference/usenixsecurity20

9. Chow, T.S.: Testing software design modeled by finite-state machines. IEEE Trans. Software Eng. 4(3), 178–187 (1978). https://doi.org/10.1109/TSE.1978.231496

10. Comparetti, P.M., Wondracek, G., Krügel, C., Kirda, E.: Prospex: Protocol specification extraction. In: 30th IEEE Symposium on Security and Privacy (S&P 2009), 17–20 May 2009, Oakland, California, USA, pp. 110–125. IEEE Computer Society (2009). https://doi.org/10.1109/SP.2009.14

11. Daniel, L., Poll, E., de Ruiter, J.: Inferring OpenVPN state machines using protocol state fuzzing. In: 2018 IEEE European Symposium on Security and Privacy Workshops, EuroS&P Workshops 2018, London, United Kingdom, 23–27 April 2018, pp. 11–19. IEEE (2018). https://doi.org/10.1109/EuroSPW.2018.00009

12. Doupé, A., Cavedon, L., Kruegel, C., Vigna, G.: Enemy of the state: A state-aware black-box web vulnerability scanner. In: Kohno, T. (ed.) Proceedings of the 21th USENIX Security Symposium, Bellevue, WA, USA, 8–10 August 2012, pp. 523–538. USENIX Association (2012). https://www.usenix.org/conference/usenixsecurity12/technical-sessions/presentation/doupe

13. Fiterau-Brostean, P., Janssen, R., Vaandrager, F.W.: Combining model learning and model checking to analyze TCP implementations. In: Chaudhuri, S., Farzan, A. (eds.) Computer Aided Verification - 28th International Conference, CAV 2016, Toronto, ON, Canada, July 17–23, 2016, Proceedings, Part II. Lecture Notes in Computer Science, vol. 9780, pp. 454–471. Springer (2016). https://doi.org/10.1007/978-3-319-41540-6_25

14. Fiterau-Brostean, P., Jonsson, B., Merget, R., de Ruiter, J., Sagonas, K., Somorovsky, J.: Analysis of DTLS implementations using protocol state fuzzing. In: Capkun and Roesner [8], pp. 2523–2540. https://www.usenix.org/conference/usenixsecurity20/presentation/fiterau-brostean

15. Fiterau-Brostean, P., Lenaerts, T., Poll, E., de Ruiter, J., Vaandrager, F.W., Verleg, P.: Model learning and model checking of SSH implementations. In: Erdogmus, H., Havelund, K. (eds.) Proceedings of the 24th ACM SIGSOFT International SPIN Symposium on Model Checking of Software, Santa Barbara, CA, USA, 10–14 July 2017, pp. 142–151. ACM (2017). https://doi.org/10.1145/3092282.3092289

16. Garbelini, M.E., Chattopadhyay, S., Bedi, V., Sun, S., Kurniawan, E.: BRAKTOOTH: Causing havoc on Bluetooth link manager. https://asset-group.github.io/disclosures/braktooth/braktooth.pdf (2021). Accessed 8 Jan 2022

17. Garbelini, M.E., Wang, C., Chattopadhyay, S., Sun, S., Kurniawan, E.: SweynTooth: Unleashing mayhem over Bluetooth Low Energy. In: Gavrilovska, A., Zadok, E. (eds.) 2020 USENIX Annual Technical Conference, USENIX ATC 2020, 15–17 July 2020, pp. 911–925. USENIX Association (2020). https://www.usenix.org/conference/atc20/presentation/garbelini

18. Gitlab.org: Gitlab protocol fuzzer community edition. https://gitlab.com/gitlab-org/security-products/protocol-fuzzer-ce. Accessed 8 Jan 2022

19. Godefroid, P., Levin, M.Y., Molnar, D.A.: SAGE: Whitebox fuzzing for security testing. ACM Queue 10(1), 20 (2012). https://doi.org/10.1145/2090147.2094081

20. Johansson, W., Svensson, M., Larson, U.E., Almgren, M., Gulisano, V.: T-Fuzz: Model-based fuzzing for robustness testing of telecommunication protocols. In: Seventh IEEE International Conference on Software Testing, Verification and Validation, ICST 2014, 31 March 2014–4 April 2014, Cleveland, Ohio, USA, pp. 323–332. IEEE Computer Society (2014). https://doi.org/10.1109/ICST.2014.45

21. Le, K.T.: Bluetooth Low Energy and the automotive transformation. https://www.ti.com/lit/wp/sway008/sway008.pdf. Accessed 29 Dec 2021

22. Miller, B.P., Fredriksen, L., So, B.: An empirical study of the reliability of UNIX utilities. Commun. ACM 33(12), 32–44 (1990). https://doi.org/10.1145/96267.96279

23. Muškardin, E., Aichernig, B.K., Pill, I., Pferscher, A., Tappler, M.: AALpy: An active automata learning library. Innovations Syst. Softw. Eng. (2022). https://doi.org/10.1007/s11334-022-00449-3

24. Pereyda, J.: boofuzz: Network protocol fuzzing for humans. https://github.com/jtpereyda/boofuzz. Accessed 8 Jan 2022

25. Pferscher, A.: Stateful black-box fuzzing of BLE devices using automata learning. https://git.ist.tugraz.at/apferscher/ble-fuzzing. Accessed 9 Jan 2022

26. Pferscher, A., Aichernig, B.K.: Fingerprinting Bluetooth Low Energy devices via active automata learning. In: Huisman, M., Pasareanu, C.S., Zhan, N. (eds.) Formal Methods - 24th International Symposium, FM 2021, Virtual Event, 20–26 November 2021, Proceedings. Lecture Notes in Computer Science, vol. 13047, pp. 524–542. Springer (2021). https://doi.org/10.1007/978-3-030-90870-6_28

27. Rasool, A., Alpár, G., de Ruiter, J.: State machine inference of QUIC. CoRR abs/1903.04384 (2019). http://arxiv.org/abs/1903.04384

28. Rivest, R.L., Schapire, R.E.: Inference of finite automata using homing sequences. Inf. Comput. 103(2), 299–347 (1993). https://doi.org/10.1006/inco.1993.1021

29. Ruge, J., Classen, J., Gringoli, F., Hollick, M.: Frankenstein: Advanced wireless fuzzing to exploit new Bluetooth escalation targets. In: Capkun and Roesner [8], pp. 19–36. https://www.usenix.org/conference/usenixsecurity20/presentation/ruge

30. de Ruiter, J., Poll, E.: Protocol state fuzzing of TLS implementations. In: Jung, J., Holz, T. (eds.) 24th USENIX Security Symposium, USENIX Security 15, 12–14 August 2015, Washington, D.C., USA, pp. 193–206. USENIX Association (2015). https://www.usenix.org/conference/usenixsecurity15/technical-sessions/presentation/de-ruiter

31. Rohith Raj, S., Rohith, R., Moharir, M., Shobha, G.: SCAPY - A powerful interactive packet manipulation program. In: 2018 International Conference on Networking, Embedded and Wireless Systems (ICNEWS), pp. 1–5 (2018). https://doi.org/10.1109/ICNEWS.2018.8903954

32. Seri, B., Livne, A.: Exploiting BlueBorne in Linux-based IoT devices. Armis, Inc (2019). https://www.armis.com/research/blueborne/. Accessed 8 Jan 2022

33. Seri, B., Vishnepolsky, G., Zusman, D.: BLEEDINGBIT: The hidden attack surface within BLE chips. Armis, Inc (2019). https://www.armis.com/research/bleedingbit/. Accessed 8 Jan 2022

34. Shahbaz, M., Groz, R.: Inferring Mealy machines. In: Cavalcanti, A., Dams, D. (eds.) FM 2009, Eindhoven, The Netherlands, 2–6 November 2009. Proceedings. Lecture Notes in Computer Science, vol. 5850, pp. 207–222. Springer (2009). https://doi.org/10.1007/978-3-642-05089-3_14, https://doi.org/10.1007/978-3-642-05089-3

35. Smetsers, R., Moerman, J., Janssen, M., Verwer, S.: Complementing model learning with mutation-based fuzzing. CoRR abs/1611.02429 (2016). http://arxiv.org/abs/1611.02429

36. Stone, C.M., Chothia, T., de Ruiter, J.: Extending automated protocol state learning for the 802.11 4-way handshake. In: López, J., Zhou, J., Soriano, M. (eds.) Computer Security - 23rd European Symposium on Research in Computer Security, ESORICS 2018, 3–7 September 2018, Barcelona, Spain, Proceedings, Part I. Lecture Notes in Computer Science, vol. 11098, pp. 325–345. Springer (2018). https://doi.org/10.1007/978-3-319-99073-6_16

37. Tappler, M., Aichernig, B.K., Bloem, R.: Model-based testing IoT communication via active automata learning. In: 2017 IEEE International Conference on Software Testing, Verification and Validation, ICST 2017, 13–17 March 2017, Tokyo, Japan, pp. 276–287. IEEE Computer Society (2017). https://doi.org/10.1109/ICST.2017.32

38. Tretmans, J.: Model based testing with labelled transition systems. In: Hierons, R.M., Bowen, J.P., Harman, M. (eds.) Formal Methods and Testing, An Outcome of the FORTEST Network, Revised Selected Papers. Lecture Notes in Computer Science, vol. 4949, pp. 1–38. Springer (2008). https://doi.org/10.1007/978-3-540-78917-8_1

39. Wu, J., et al.: BLESA: Spoofing attacks against reconnections in Bluetooth Low Energy. In: Yarom, Y., Zennou, S. (eds.) 14th USENIX Workshop on Offensive Technologies, WOOT 2020, 11 August 2020. USENIX Association (2020). https://www.usenix.org/conference/woot20/presentation/wu

40. Zalewski, M.: American fuzzy lop. https://lcamtuf.coredump.cx/afl/ (2013). Accessed 2 Jan 2022

From Verified Scala to STIX File System Embedded Code Using Stainless

Jad Hamza[1], Simon Felix[2], Viktor Kunčak[1]([✉]), Ivo Nussbaumer[2], and Filip Schramka[2]

[1] EPFL IC LARA, Lausanne, Switzerland
{jad.hamza,viktor.kuncak}@epfl.ch
[2] Ateleris GmbH, Brugg, Switzerland
{simon.felix,ivo.nussbaumer,filip.schramka}@ateleris.ch

Abstract. We present an approach for using formal methods in embedded systems and its evaluation on a case study. In our approach, the developers describe the system in a restricted subset of the high-level programming language Scala. We then use 1) a verification system to formally prove properties of such Scala program, and 2) a source-to-source translator to map Scala to C code. We have adapted the Stainless verification system to support constructs for describing embedded software (more machine integer types and early returns) and to support verification patterns needed for embedded systems code (array swap operation, pre-allocated and initialized memory, constant-length arrays). The implemented C code translator generates code that can be compiled with compilers such as GCC and integrated into larger C applications.

We evaluate our approach on a case study of a file system of an instrument on the Solar Orbiter satellite. We have ported around a thousand lines of C code to Scala. We wrote specification and proof hints to make the code verify. Stainless verified the absence of run-time errors, as well as function preconditions, postconditions, and data structure invariants. The generated C code was integrated into the existing code base and exhibits very similar code size, memory use, and performance. In this process we identified multiple bugs in the well-tested code base, which were fixed in-orbit.

Keywords: Formal verification · Embedded system · File system · Flight software · Scala · Stainless

1 Introduction

This paper includes our experience in using and adapting Stainless, a verifier for the Scala programming language [18], for a software component of a mission-critical system. Mission- and safety-critical systems such as trains, cars, aircraft,

In the original version of this chapter, Fig. 3 is missing. The correction can be found at https://doi.org/10.1007/978-3-031-06773-0_46

Work financially supported by the Swiss Space Center project Embedded Flight Software Verification (ESOVER).

© Springer Nature Switzerland AG 2022, corrected publication 2022
J. V. Deshmukh et al. (Eds.): NFM 2022, LNCS 13260, pp. 393–410, 2022.
https://doi.org/10.1007/978-3-031-06773-0_21

satellites and space probes contain embedded software that must be at all cost free of bugs. While extensive testing prevents many bugs, we aim to raise the correctness standard by additionally leveraging *formal verification* in the development process. With formal verification, we model the behavior of a program and prove that, under well-defined assumptions, the program behaves as expected in all executions.

Our use of Stainless is motivated by the knowledge of the tool by some of us, as well by our desire to make the experience appealing from both software development and verification experience point of view. Whereas our target application is a component of a custom file system, we choose to use a general-purpose tool, instead of a specialized one that may achieve higher automation [1,8,11,12,23], in part because we aim to arrive at conclusions and methodologies that generalize to other pieces of embedded software and because we wish to make assumptions of formal proof more explicit. Furthermore, formal verification tools may take several decades to become mature and develop a user community [21,30,32], an effort that is amortized over more use cases with general-purpose techniques. On the extreme end of this spectrum, interactive theorem provers have had long continued history of use and have high degree of trustworthiness. At the same time, they may appear unusual to developers accustomed to widely used programming languages. It is therefore natural to try and use a general-purpose and relatively mature verification tool while still remaining close to project source code. We found that Stainless enabled us to pursue this approach. While the original target of Stainless is (sequential) functional code, it has gained several features along the years, including support for imperative code. We show in this case study how Stainless can be used to verify real-world embedded code.

The experience that was driving our approach was formally verifying a portion of the file system of Spectrometer Telescope for Imaging X-rays, used onboard the Solar Orbiter satellite. We ported parts of the C code in this software to Scala and verified it using Stainless. Thanks to the use of Stainless, the resulting code was shown free from buffer and arithmetic overflows, two common problems in C. Furthermore, we also verified and proved additional properties, specified as invariants, preconditions, and postconditions.[1]

Using a Scala source to C source translator we incorporated into Stainless, we mapped the verified Scala code automatically to C, and used it as a drop-in replacement for the original C code in the existing system. Using this approach we were able to incrementally verify increasingly large components of the existing system, gradually replacing them with C code generated from verified Scala source.

Making this case study possible required us to add a new execution path to Stainless, which does not use Java Virtual Machine but C source code as target, without using memory allocation. Using C source code allowed us to use the gcc compiler available for a wide range of platforms, including LEON3 [15] soft

---

[1] A repository containing an illustrative fragment of the code we ported to Scala code and verified is https://github.com/epfl-lara/STIX-showcase.

core on which the software is deployed. Our translator generates readable code similar in structure to the Scala input.

To accommodate the use of unsigned machine integer types of various lengths, we extended the Scala front end of Stainless with libraries and incorporated support into our C code generator to handle these C data types, generating code that efficiently interacts with the surrounding embedded C code.

A design choice of Stainless is to not use global variables but instead use the pattern of passing (possibly implicitly declared) parameters to functions, thus documenting program side effects. This approach is a simple version of *object capability discipline*, advocated as part of a type discipline for actor-based Scala concurrency [17]. In our work, we identify a combination of source code patterns (use of implicit parameters and initial values of default parameters) and code generation to respect this design choice. Consequently, we were able to support writing arguably reasonable Scala code that can be mapped to the embedded code with statically allocated and initialized memory.

1.1 Contributions

This paper makes the following contributions:

- We present an extension of the Stainless verifier for handling embedded-style imperative code with statically allocated memory, fixed-sized arrays, early returns, and additional bitvector data types (Sect. 4).
- We show how to generate suitable embedded C code using source-to-source translation from Scala input to C code, extending a previous code generation approach of the Leon system [2] to recognize statically allocated memory use as well as to systematically eliminate specification-only (ghost) code (Sect. 5).
- As a case study, we present our experience in rewriting parts of the Spectrometer Telescope for Imaging X-rays (STIX) file system to Scala code, proving the absence of run-time errors, memory errors, as well as invariants, preconditions and postconditions. We have integrated the generated C code into the original project without loss of performance (Sect. 6).

1.2 Related Work

Cogent [1] is a high-level language specifically designed for formal verification of file systems. It features a compiler whose correctness is formally proven in the Isabelle proof assistant [31]. The authors of [1] wrote a file system and proved high-level properties. Other works strive for more automation using general techniques but tuned to file system models [8], or focus on finding bugs [23] instead of proving their absence. Interactive theorem provers have great expressive power for checking arbitrarily complex proofs, and they contain frameworks that help automate verification in various domains, including file systems [11,12]. In contrast, in our approach, we write the specification in Scala, the same language (and in the same place) as the actual code. Dafny [27] has many similarities to Stainless; it was used in [9] to implement and verify operational crash-consistency file system models at a higher level of abstraction but was also used for low-level code in other projects [20].

SPARK Ada and other tools by AdaCore are alternative single-language options for high assurance software. Whereas Ada has the advantage of being designed for verification, it is not a functional language and does not support higher-order functions. We believe that functional programming is a strong basis for formal reasoning. That said, the approach of Stainless with preconditions and postconditions results in similar code in many cases, so it may even be possible to perform source-to-source translation between these two languages.

A parallel approach to our C code generator in Stainless (which started in its predecessor, Leon [2]) has been the development of SLang [33], a subset of Scala from which, among others, C code can be generated. In comparison to SLang, Stainless uses Scala itself for contracts, supports higher-order functions, and permits certain forms of subtyping. Stainless uses Scala 2 and Scala 3 compilers as front ends, benefiting from type checks and type-informed transformations performed early in the Scala compiler pipeline. Stainless itself does not use macros, but its Scala 3 version is compatible with inline functions in the input Scala code.

The Verified C Compiler VCC [4,13] could be likely used to directly verify C code and has the advantage of supporting concurrency, though it also uses a different specification language than the implementation language. Before using Stainless to verify STIX code, a subset of authors tested CBMC [24] and Frama-C [14] on other parts of the code base. Both tools did not scale to the size of the code and struggled to work with the idioms in the application code and operating system. We suspect that both tools could have produced better results, had we invested more time. We suspect no tool will work out of the box entirely, even if it is designed to not require annotations as modular verification does. Because our Stainless-based verification approach results in C code, we could use tools like CBMC and Frama-C on the generated code to detect errors in the code generation step. In this project we rely on a code generation facility mapping a subset of Scala to C. Building such code generation implementation within a foundational framework such as CompCert [28] or CakeML [26] would further improve the confidence in the resulting generated code.

2   STIX Instrument Onboard Solar Orbiter—Background

The Spectrometer Telescope for Imaging X-rays (STIX [25]) onboard ESA's Solar Orbiter satellite is a hard X-ray imaging spectrometer. STIX observes hard X-ray bremsstrahlung emissions from solar flares and provides information about the hottest flare plasmas. The instrument and the satellite are shown in Fig. 1. The satellite was launched in early 2020; the STIX instrument was turned on a few days later.

The STIX hardware consists of several custom application-specific integrated circuits (ASIC) and sensors, a radiation-hardened field-programmable gate array (FPGA), 128 MB DRAM, 2 MB SRAM, 1 MB EEPROM and 16 GB

Fig. 1. *Left:* STIX images X-ray sources using moiré patterns produced by two tungsten grids placed in front of a sensor. *Center:* Solar Orbiter being prepared for launch. *Right:* Solar Orbiter completed its second Venus flyby maneuver November 2021.

flash memory. The FPGA implements logic for real-time data processing, and a LEON3 [15] soft microprocessor. This SPARC V8-compatible soft microprocessor executes the flight software, which is the focus of this work. Owed to the limited energy budget and number of logic gates, the soft microprocessor runs at 20 MHz and is equipped with only 1 kB data and instruction caches. The system is under soft realtime constraints – missing interrupts means losing scientific data. The complete system processes up to 800'000 events per second and outputs a telemetry data stream of at most 700 bits per second.

The flight software is a self-contained C program, which is statically linked to the real-time operating system RTEMS [7]. To work around known bugs in the CPU a special, patched, GCC version is used to compile the software. The 36'418 non-comment code lines compile to 370 KB binary code. The flight software does not perform any dynamic memory allocation to prevent memory fragmentation. All data structures sizes are statically allocated at compile time. During development, several techniques were used to increase the robustness of the flight software: compiler warnings were enabled, static code analysis tools were run regularly, manual testing, automated end-to-end test scripts and unit-tests for certain subsystems were used.

Our verification efforts focused on the file system which manages the data stored on the 16 GB flash memory.

3 Background on Stainless Verifier

In this section, we highlight key features of Stainless verifier that we used to perform verification and, subsequently, code generation. Stainless was derived from Leon verification and synthesis system, which was originally designed to verify first-order recursive purely functional programs [36]. It was subsequently extended to support higher-order functions [37] and simple non-shared mutable data verified via a translation to functional code [5,6]. Foundations and soundness of a substantial fragment of Stainless, including function termination, was presented using an expressive dependent type system, whose soundness is shown using a set-of-terms model [18]. When given Scala code, Stainless can process it in the *verification pipeline*. The typical deployment of Stainless programs (until the work in this paper) has been to compile them using Scala compiler and run on the Java Virtual Machine.

The verification pipeline of Stainless transforms high-level abstractions in the input program to simpler functional programming constructs which can be handled by our internal type-checker [18]. Our type-checker is not a typical type-checker in the sense that it not only ensures that "standard" types (such as int) are respected, but it also supports user-annotated assertions, and function pre- and postconditions in the form of boolean-typed expressions, which are encoded using *refinement types*.

The type-checker generates *verification conditions* for all annotations, which are formulas with recursive functions. All verification conditions must be checked to be true to ensure that assertions are indeed true for all possible function inputs respecting preconditions, and that function preconditions are respected at call-sites in all cases. In Stainless, verification conditions are checked using Inox[2], a solver for formulas written as functional programs with recursive functions, and which uses function unfolding [36] and SMT solvers (Z3 [16], CVC4 [3], Princess [34]) as backends.

4   Adapting the Verifier for Embedded Software

Despite the fact that Stainless was used to verify tens of thousands of lines of Scala code before, it was not suitable initially for verification of imperative embedded code.

4.1   Circumventing Stainless Aliasing Restrictions

When transforming away imperative features in the verification pipeline, Stainless checks that there is no *aliasing*, i.e. no two pointers to the same object. This greatly simplifies the transformation into a functional program, and therefore makes verification tractable for the solver.

The original file system code was written in a way that there could be several pointers to the same *control blocks* in the file system. Stainless would detect the aliasing and not transform the code. We made some adjustments to the STIX code ported to Scala in order to circumvent this restriction. Namely, all control blocks are stored in a global array, and wherever we needed to store a control block, we stored the index in the array instead. All control blocks accesses therefore go through the global array and there is no more aliasing.

4.2   Early Return Statements

The STIX code that we ported has early **return** statements in several places. We added a phase (`ReturnElimination`) in the verification pipeline to transform return statements into functional code. An often-used idea to translate

---

[2] https://github.com/epfl-lara/inox

imperative code into functional code is to use a form of continuation monad in order to know, at each point of the code (e.g. after a loop iteration), whether the code has already returned or not. To prove correctness in while loops containing return statements, we added the ability to specify a `noReturnInvariant`, which is an invariant that holds after each loop iteration except after a return.

5   Scala to C Translation for Embedded Software

To enable the deployment of embedded code, we incorporated the C code generator from the Leon system [2] into Stainless and used it as the starting point for our source-to-source generator. The code generation pipeline need not transform away imperative features into functional ones. For example, assignments and while loops remain mostly untranslated, as they can be directly mapped to their equivalents in C. The code generation pipeline shares some of the early phases with the verification pipeline, for example resolving method overrides and Scala class inheritance (`MethodLifting`). After that, we transform the program to an internal representation, where we perform some more transformations to produce a C program:

- `GhostElimination` removes all the ghost code specific verification,
- `Normalisation` flattens the block structure of a program, to avoid blocks within expressions (supported by Scala but not by C),
- `Referencing` adds references and dereferences where appropriate, as objects are passed by references in Scala, without explicit references,
- `IR2C` transforms classes to structs and enums.

In this section, we describe improvements we made in the C code generation pipeline [2] after porting it from the Leon system. These changes are what made it possible to write realistic components of the file system and generate C code with expected memory use and runtime behavior.

5.1   Unsigned Integers of Various Bit Lengths

The existing C code makes extensive use of several unsigned integer types (`uint8`, `uint16`, `uint32`), which were not supported by Stainless at the beginning of the project. The reason is that the Java Virtual Machine does not have support for native unsigned integers, and therefore, neither does Scala.

On the other hand, the used SMT backends support arbitrary-length bitvectors with signed and unsigned operations. We thus decided to add a Stainless library for signed and unsigned integers of arbitrary length (1 to 256), which is mapped in the verification pipeline to SMT bitvectors, and in the compilation pipeline to C signed/unsigned types, for bit lengths natively supported by C.

The library supports converting between signed and unsigned types, as well as narrowing and widening the bit length. These operations include appropriate checks (which can be locally or globally disabled) to detect overflows.

5.2 Mutable Global State

The verification pipeline of Stainless does not support verifying code with mutable global variables. We used a common Scala idiom to simulate global state: implicitly passing extra mutable objects to functions that need to read or write the global state. We split the global state into several groups of mutable variables, and each object has its own **case class** definition and corresponds to one such group. This has the benefit of explicitly showing in the function signature which parts, if any, of the global state are accessed by this function, and could be viewed as an effect system [22].

In the code generation pipeline, we remove these extra parameters from functions, and we leave three options to the user:

a. *(default)* Add a global declaration in the generated C code with a default value for each field of the case class. Additional annotations in Scala code, e.g. **static** or **volatile**, are carried over.
b. Add a global declaration in the generated C code without an initial value (implicitly zero-initialized), or
c. Do not add a global declaration. This is useful to refer to an existing variable declared in the existing C code, unknown to Stainless.

To ensure that this transformation is correct, we perform the following checks in the Scala code, for each case class S representing a global state portion. 1) Functions can take as argument at most one parameter of type S. 2) One function which does take such an argument is allowed to create instances of S, with default values, and pass it to other functions. 3) Instances of S can only be read, written to, or passed to other functions; instances cannot be copied or let-bound. These checks ensure that it is safe to remove parameters typed S and compile their read and write accesses to global C variables accesses.

5.3 Specifications and Ghost Elimination

We write the properties that we want to verify as preconditions (**require**), postconditions (**ensuring**), and code assertions (**assert**). Stainless is able to prove simple properties automatically, but more complex properties (e.g. sortedness of an array) require additional annotations in the form of:

a. functions to describe the property,
b. functions (lemmas) to prove that the property is maintained after an operation (e.g. insertion of an element in the array),
c. calls to these lemmas in the places where we need to prove the property.

During compilation, the preconditions (except in exported functions), postconditions, assertions, and additional annotations are eliminated in a *ghost elimination* phase. As such, they do not incur any performance overhead in the final executable.

In general, preconditions of exported functions are transformed into runtime assertions in C. For specific preconditions, the user can use the **require** keyword from `stainless.lang.StaticChecks` to denote that this precondition should not be compiled, even in an exported function. In general, this is unsafe as we do not know whether external function calls will respect these preconditions, but still useful for preconditions that may be too expensive to check at runtime (see one example Sect. 6.1), or preconditions that use Stainless features which are supported by the verification pipeline but not supported by the code generation pipeline.

5.4   Declarations Followed by `memset`

The following is a common idiom in C to initialize structures:

```
myStruct s;
memset(&s, 0, sizeof(s));
```

In Scala, this corresponds to declaring a variable `s` of (case) class `myStruct`, with all fields set to 0. When some fields have arrays, which themselves contains structs with other arrays inside, a single statement declaration in Stainless of such a struct would be complex and would contain expressions such as `Array.fill` that are in general not supported by our translation to C. In the particular case where we encounter a complex declaration in Stainless that contains only zeroes (or `Array.fill`'s with zeroes), we generate the idiom above instead.

In Scala, we can access array lengths, which we translate to structs containing a pointer, and an integer length (*bounded pointers*) in C. However, when an array is part of a struct, this makes the `memset` idiom above unusable, because `memset` would just set the pointer to 0 instead of setting the pointer to a preallocated memory region. In our case study, the length of arrays contained in structs are known at compile-time, and we compile them to fixed-length arrays, without storing the length as an extra variable, as shown in Fig. 2, so the memset idiom is applicable.

5.5   Pure Functions

Because of the aliasing restrictions that we discussed in Sect. 4.1, Stainless contains an effect analysis that is able to determine which parts of the code mutate global state, and which parts are *pure*. We use this analysis during code generation to output purity annotations in the C code. Such annotations trigger additional optimizations in GCC, for example replacing deterministic function calls with constant values.

6   Experience with Case Study

We next present our experience in porting parts of the file system code from C to the subset of Scala supported by Stainless, and annotating it to prove the absence of run-time errors that Stainless always checks for, as well as proving additional invariants, preconditions, and postconditions.

```
case class MyStruct(ar: Array[Int]) {
    require(ar.length == 100)
}
```

```
typedef struct {
    int *underlying;
    int length;
} array_int;

typedef struct {
    array_int ar;
} MyStruct;
```

```
typedef struct {
    int ar[100];
} MyStruct;
```

Fig. 2. *Top:* a case class in Scala containing an array whose length is specified using a class invariant to be constant. *Left:* The generated C struct contains both a pointer and an array length when the class invariant is missing. *Right:* When a constant array length is specified as class invariant, the generated C struct contains a fixed-length array member instead.

6.1 Verified Properties and Statistics

The ported parts of the file system consist of around 6'000 lines of Scala code. This code contains 5'220 explicit and implicit verification conditions, all of which are proven (see Table 1). Initial verification takes 2'562 s[3], but verification completes in 86 s when using cached results from previous runs.

All of our data structures are array-based. Consequently, Stainless generates verification conditions for all array accesses and has to prove that all indices are within array bounds. To make verification of these bound checks feasible, we had to add invariants about the array lengths in function preconditions and in structures containing arrays, and we added invariants on integer indices in while loops. We show below a few examples of other higher-level properties we verified.

Insertion into a Sorted Array. The file system manages some data in a (fixed-length) sorted array. Insertion in this array uses an insertion sort that (1) looks for the index i where to insert an element by dichotomy, (2) shift all elements with lower priority to make place in the array, (3) assign the element to insert at index i.

As explained in Sect. 4.1, the verification pipeline that we use for imperative code only supports limited forms of aliasing. Therefore, shifting mutable elements in an array is not possible, because an assignment of the form ar(i+1) = ar(i) creates two aliases to the object initially stored in ar(i). This problem led to the introduction of a new swap(ar, i, i+1) operation that swaps two mutable elements in an array without creating aliases. We were able to prove strong

---

[3] Measured on a MacBook Pro, Intel Core i9 2.3 GHz 8-Core, 32 GB RAM.

Table 1. Summary of the verification conditions.

Verification Condition	#	Verification Condition	#
Precondition	1546	Non-negative measure	57
Postcondition	1051	Strict arithmetic on shift	52
Array index within bounds	556	Measure decreases	19
Unsigned to signed overflow	518	Multiplication overflow	18
Class invariant	501	Division by zero	15
Subtraction overflow	284	Narrowing too large unsigned int	14
Addition overflow	246	Division overflow	6
Match exhaustiveness	128	Local invariant	5
Body assertion	124	Negation overflow	3
Signed to unsigned requires ≥ 0	74	Remainder by zero	3

enough invariants in the while loops implementing the steps (1) and (2) above to show that the array remains sorted after insertion of new elements.

Counting Blocks with a Specific Status. The flash memory managed by the file system is organized in blocks, each containing 256 kB data. During system initialization, each Flash block transitions from the initial state to one of the following states: *free, used, error,* or *bad*. Blocks in state *error* contain bit flips which are not correctable with the employed error correction codes. Those blocks can be reused for new data in the future. In extreme cases, the Flash hardware itself can fail due to aging or radiation. This leads to *bad* blocks, which should never be used anymore.

Instrument operators want to know how many blocks are in which state to assess the state of the flash memory. We store the number of blocks in each state in global counters. It is therefore natural to define an invariant that states that these global counters actually correspond to the number of control blocks with a specific status.

We defined the invariant using the recursive function countStatus that counts the blocks with a given status. Proving the invariant further required proving lemmas that explain how countStatus changes after updating the status of a block, which is not trivial given the recursive nature of *countStatus*. Specifically, it requires proving additional lemmas, which state the desired properties as postconditions, and which are themselves defined recursively following the countStatus pattern to simulate proofs by induction on the executions of countStatus.

6.2 General Improvements to Stainless

During the project, we continuously improved Stainless, either by fixing bugs, or implementing new features. In total, we merged around 150 pull requests related to this project in the public Stainless code base, and around 25 in the public code base of Inox, our backend solver.

To deal with a project this size we had to make performance improvements, for instance by supporting more recent backend SMT solvers (Z3 4.8.12 with its experimental "new core" option, CVC4 1.8), or by reducing the amount of duplication in the generated verification conditions.

To make solving of some verification conditions possible, we had to extend the `opaque` keyword to control at each call-site whether function bodies are visible to the solver[4]. Before, Stainless only supported the `opaque` keyword with per-function granularity.

6.3 Identified Bugs in the STIX File System Code

During this project we identified a number of implementation bugs in the existing file system code, of which we highlight two examples. First, we uncovered a potential buffer overflow due to an off-by-1 error in a data structure. The way the buffer was used prevented this problem from ever surfacing, but otherwise innocent changes might trigger the bug in the future, if left unfixed. Second, the type system of Scala helped identify a case where an incompatible `enum` type was returned by a function. Even though these bugs have no real-world ramifications, we patched the in-orbit instrument in December 2021.

6.4 Using Stainless Without Prior Formal Verification Experience

Our team consists of experts that worked on the original file system implementation, and verification experts that were concerned with improvements to Stainless verification and code generation, as well as help in specification and verification.

Our experience with Stainless confirmed the expectation that formal verification of code is challenging without prior experience in the field.

First, it takes time to get accustomed to the language, in this case Scala subset supported by Stainless. For example, programmers cannot use the standard Scala class libraries or certain high-level abstractions, because they are unverified or rely on dynamic memory allocation. Instead, to write embedded code in Scala, basic data structures must be implemented first. The resulting code is similar to the C implementation, but benefits from a richer type system. With these building blocks in place, we quickly adjusted to the way some constructs have to be expressed (e.g. enumerations, pass by reference, global variables).

A bigger challenge is specifying correct and verifiable properties. Some properties are straightforward to express or have proof obligations even generated automatically, like absence of arithmetic overflows or out of bound accesses. Other properties require recursive lemmas to encode inductive proofs in Stainless. The examples in Sect. 6.1 were only verifiable with assistance by the formal verification experts in the group.

---

[4] Thanks to Georg Stefan Schmid for an implementation idea of this feature.

The file `callgraph.pdf` hasn't been created from `callgraph.dot` yet.
Run 'dot -Tpdf -o callgraph.pdf callgraph.dot' to create it.
Or invoke LATEX with the -shell-escape option to have this done automatically.

Fig. 3. Flight Software using the file system (top), and the hardware drivers (bottom) were not modified. Only the file system was ported to Scala. Bridge functions, written in C, connect the two implementations when function signatures differ.

```
static array_uint8 toGenCArray(const void* x, int len) {
    return (array_uint8) { (uint8_t*)x, len };
}
void stream_write(MemStream_s* _s, void* _buf, uint32_t _bytes) {
    stream_write_scala(_s, toGenCArray(_buf, _bytes));
}
```

Fig. 4. Converting raw pointers to bounded arrays is trivial, due to the low level of C code. GCC optimizes these conversions, making it a zero-cost abstraction.

6.5 Integration into the Existing C Code Base

In most cases, the generated C code can be integrated trivially in the existing C code base, because it has identical signatures. However, some concepts can be expressed in multiple ways in C. For example, the existing C code freely mixes arrays, raw pointers and bounded pointers, whereas the generated C code represents arrays as structs. Similarly, the existing code exploits the liberal C type system and preprocessor macros, which the generated code does not do. In such cases, it becomes necessary to convert between different representations at the interfaces. The required conversions are implemented as small, inlined functions with negligible overhead (Fig. 4). The call graph in Fig. 3 of the FSWrite function shows the STIX flight software and hardware drivers written in C, the file system in Scala, and how the bridge functions act as interfaces in-between.

6.6 Generated Code Performance, Memory, and Code Size Impact

In this case study we generate approximately 1 kLOC of C code from around 6 kLOC of Scala code (for implementation, specification and proof hints), which replaces a similar number of original C code. We compared the original flight software C code to the generated C code quantitatively and qualitatively. We focus our attention on file system metadata operations and microbenchmarks. The measurements were performed on an engineering model of the flight hardware. The engineering model contains 62'022 files in 7 partitions. During boot, the file system initialization code reads and processes all flash blocks. The next three tests operate on a particular file in the file system. A file is read, deleted, and finally written again. These operations perform a name-based lookup internally. Finally, we perform in-memory data microbenchmarks: endianness conversion

Table 2. Quantitative comparison between the original, hand-written C code and automatically generated C code. The reported sizes include the benchmark code. We report averaged results from 250 runs.

	Original C	Generated C	
Code size	513 072 bytes	514 368 bytes	(+0.3%)
Data size	21 824 bytes	21 744 bytes	(−0.4%)
Boot time	539 288 ms	560 305 ms	(+3.9%)
Read file (32 kb)	183 ms	176 ms	(−3.8%)
Write file (32 kb)	238 ms	242 ms	(+1.7%)
Delete file	5 ms	9 ms	(+55.6%)
Little-Endian decoding (224 kb)	404 ms	199 ms	(−50.7%)
Little-Endian encoding (224 kb)	797 ms	1006 ms	(+26.2%)
Compression (10^6 samples)	20 506 ms	20 566 ms	(+0.3%)

and sample compression. It is important to note that we compare the generated C code to a hand-tuned C implementation. The performance is comparable to the original C code for high-level operations (Table 2).

Significant increases in code size would not be acceptable: The CPU instruction cache has a limited capacity of only 256 instructions and significant performance drops occur when inner loops exceed this limit. Measurements confirm that the code and data sizes stayed almost identical. This is expected, as we carefully declared the data structures to correspond exactly to their existing C counterparts to ensure interoperability. The small data size reduction is caused by the replacement of a look-up table in the C version with an equivalent look-up function in Scala. The manual inspection of the resulting assembly code shows that GCC produces virtually identical outputs for inner loops in both cases.

We found that minor, innocent differences between the original and generated C code can have significant performance effects. For example, the extreme performance gaps observed in the Endian conversion microbenchmarks are not a result of major differences in the original and generated C code, but instead the result of different inlining decisions of the GCC compiler.

For quick operations, like file deletion, the performance overhead of bridge functions (see previous chapter) can become significant. However, the overhead is acceptable in the context of the overall system for our use case.

7   Discussion and Conclusions

We have presented an approach for verifying embedded software implementations. The approach can be used to incrementally verify software by rewriting parts of it in a memory safe language and using source-to-source translation to produce C code that integrates into a large software ecosystem written in C.

To make this approach work, we needed to make substantial improvements to the original verifier, which was initially aimed at functional programs with memory allocated on the heap. We improved support for bitvector data types, including unsigned data types not present on the JVM. Furthermore, we added supported non-local **return** from functions, translating such code to compute a value of Either type (disjoint sum) encoding normal or early return outcome. We introduced new specification constructs for loops with such early returns.

A substantial change was to accommodate the use of global, statically allocated memory. We preserved the design of Stainless where developers must use parameters to pass mutable parts of the heap and thus document function side effects. The design is convenient in Scala because function parameters can be declared implicit and omitted at the function call sites. To ensure that generated code uses only statically allocated memory that is appropriately initialized, we proposed a model that specifies initial values of fields of cases classes. Our code generator also recognizes data structure invariants that constrain Scala array sizes to be compile-time reducible to a constant; it maps such arrays to C arrays of constant size.

The executable Scala code we wrote in our case study has imperative flavor, so one may ask whether the use of Scala and Stainless was justified. We argue that it is justified, for several reasons. The first reason is the ability to use Scala as a unified memory-safe Scala notation for both code and specifications. Indeed, even in imperative code of our case study, all control structures we used remain valid Scala; the language remains memory safe by design. Moreover, majority of lines of code in the case study is non-executable Scala code used to express preconditions, post-conditions, invariants, and proof hints (such as intermediate assertions and recursive functions expressive inductive proofs). These specification (ghost) constructs widely use functional programming idioms with recursive functions and recursive data types. Ghost code never executes in the resulting system: Stainless proves it correct and eliminates it during code generation. The net result is that executable code is efficient, yet the developer has used constructs that belong to the same language for both code and specifications. In particular, for aspects of code that are purely functional, Scala functions serve as their own specification. This in contrast to verification systems where implementation and specification live in separate domains, which often results in unnecessary specification effort and a steeper learning curve for users.

Using our approach we verified components of the file system on the STIX instrument of the Solar Orbiter satellite. In this process we have identified and corrected several errors in the original system. We then established that the ported component of the code is free of run-time errors and that it satisfies basic invariants. The code size and performance of the generated code were on par with the original C code. We thus hope we presented a piece of evidence for feasibility of formal verification in embedded system domain.

One possibly misleading aspect of our case study is that we started with an existing C code base, so one may be tempted to attribute a necessary cost to porting C to Scala. Of course, having an existing C code is not necessary for developing new systems: they can be written in Scala and Stainless to start with, taking verification goal into consideration from the beginning. Developing libraries of verified Stainless code in the future would thus make formally verified approach more cost effective and avoid the danger of errors in existing or interface code. Our work thus may help realize the vision [19] of using Scala broadly as a modern language for for mission critical systems, creating synergies with the other uses of Scala in runtime monitoring [35], simulation [29], and probabilistic safety assessment [10].

References

1. Amani, S., et al.: Cogent: verifying high-assurance file system implementations. In: Conte, T., Zhou, Y. (eds.) Proceedings of the Twenty-First International Conference on Architectural Support for Programming Languages and Operating Systems, ASPLOS 2016, Atlanta, GA, USA, 2–6 April 2016, pp. 175–188. ACM (2016). https://doi.org/10.1145/2872362.2872404
2. Antognini, M.: Extending Safe C Support In Leon. Master's thesis, EPFL (2017). http://infoscience.epfl.ch/record/227942
3. Barrett, C., et al.: CVC4. In: Gopalakrishnan, G., Qadeer, S. (eds.) CAV 2011. LNCS, vol. 6806, pp. 171–177. Springer, Heidelberg (2011). https://doi.org/10.1007/978-3-642-22110-1_14
4. Beckert, B., Moskal, M.: Deductive verification of system software in the verisoft XT project. Künstliche Intell. **24**(1), 57–61 (2010). https://doi.org/10.1007/s13218-010-0005-7
5. Blanc, R.W., Kneuss, E., Kuncak, V., Suter, P.: An overview of the Leon verification system: verification by translation to recursive functions. In: Scala Workshop (2013)
6. Blanc, R.W.: Verification by Reduction to Functional Programs. Ph.D. thesis, EPFL, Lausanne (2017). https://doi.org/10.5075/epfl-thesis-7636, http://infoscience.epfl.ch/record/230242
7. Bloom, G., Sherrill, J.: Scheduling and thread management with RTEMS. ACM Sigbed Rev. **11**(1), 20–25 (2014)
8. Bornholt, J., Kaufmann, A., Li, J., Krishnamurthy, A., Torlak, E., Wang, X.: Specifying and checking file system crash-consistency models. In: Conte, T., Zhou, Y. (eds.) Proceedings of the Twenty-First International Conference on Architectural Support for Programming Languages and Operating Systems, ASPLOS 2016, Atlanta, GA, USA, 2–6 April 2016, pp. 83–98. ACM (2016). https://doi.org/10.1145/2872362.2872406
9. Bornholt, J., Kaufmann, A., Li, J., Krishnamurthy, A., Torlak, E., Wang, X.: Specifying and checking file system crash-consistency models. In: Proceedings of the Twenty-First International Conference on Architectural Support for Programming Languages and Operating Systems, pp. 83–98 (2016)
10. Buyse, M., Delmas, R., Hamadi, Y.: ALPACAS: a language for parametric assessment of critical architecture safety. In: Møller, A., Sridharan, M. (eds.) 35th European Conference on Object-Oriented Programming (ECOOP 2021). Leibniz International Proceedings in Informatics (LIPIcs), vol. 194, pp. 5:1–5:29. Schloss Dagstuhl - Leibniz-Zentrum für Informatik, Dagstuhl, Germany (2021). https://doi.org/10.4230/LIPIcs.ECOOP.2021.5
11. Chajed, T., Chen, H., Chlipala, A., Kaashoek, M.F., Zeldovich, N., Ziegler, D.: Certifying a file system using crash Hoare logic: correctness in the presence of crashes. Commun. ACM **60**(4), 75–84 (2017). https://doi.org/10.1145/3051092

12. Chajed, T., Tassarotti, J., Theng, M., Jung, R., Kaashoek, M.F., Zeldovich, N.: GoJournal: a verified, concurrent, crash-safe journaling system. In: Brown, A.D., Lorch, J.R. (eds.) 15th USENIX Symposium on Operating Systems Design and Implementation, OSDI 2021, 14–16 July 2021, pp. 423–439. USENIX Association (2021). https://www.usenix.org/conference/osdi21/presentation/chajed

13. Cohen, E., et al.: VCC: a practical system for verifying concurrent C. In: Berghofer, S., Nipkow, T., Urban, C., Wenzel, M. (eds.) Theorem Proving in Higher Order Logics, 22nd International Conference, TPHOLs 2009, Munich, Germany, 17–20 August 2009. Proceedings. Lecture Notes in Computer Science, vol. 5674, pp. 23–42. Springer (2009). https://doi.org/10.1007/978-3-642-03359-9_2

14. Cuoq, P., Kirchner, F., Kosmatov, N., Prevosto, V., Signoles, J., Yakobowski, B.: Frama-C. In: Eleftherakis, G., Hinchey, M., Holcombe, M. (eds.) SEFM 2012. LNCS, vol. 7504, pp. 233–247. Springer, Heidelberg (2012). https://doi.org/10.1007/978-3-642-33826-7_16

15. Daněk, M., Kafka, L., Kohout, L., Sýkora, J., Bartosiński, R.: The LEON3 processor. In: UTLEON3: Exploring Fine-Grain Multi-Threading in FPGAs, pp. 9–14. Springer (2013). https://doi.org/10.1007/978-1-4614-2410-9

16. de Moura, L., Bjørner, N.: Z3: an efficient SMT solver. In: Ramakrishnan, C.R., Rehof, J. (eds.) TACAS 2008. LNCS, vol. 4963, pp. 337–340. Springer, Heidelberg (2008). https://doi.org/10.1007/978-3-540-78800-3_24

17. Haller, P., Loiko, A.: LaCasa: lightweight affinity and object capabilities in Scala. In: Proceedings of the 2016 ACM SIGPLAN International Conference on Object-Oriented Programming, Systems, Languages, and Applications, pp. 272–291. Association for Computing Machinery, New York, NY, USA (2016). https://doi.org/10.1145/2983990.2984042

18. Hamza, J., Voirol, N., Kunčak, V.: System FR: formalized foundations for the Stainless verifier. Proc. ACM Program. Lang. 3(OOPSLA) (2019). https://doi.org/10.1145/3360592

19. Havelund, K., Bocchino, R.: Integrated modeling and development of component-based embedded software in Scala. In: Margaria, T., Steffen, B. (eds.) Leveraging Applications of Formal Methods, Verification and Validation - 10th International Symposium on Leveraging Applications of Formal Methods, ISoLA 2021, 17–29 October 2021, Rhodes, Greece, Proceedings. Lecture Notes in Computer Science, vol. 13036, pp. 233–252. Springer (2021). https://doi.org/10.1007/978-3-030-89159-6_16

20. Hawblitzel, C., et al.: Ironclad apps: end-to-end security via automated Full-System verification. In: 11th USENIX Symposium on Operating Systems Design and Implementation (OSDI 14), pp. 165–181. USENIX Association, Broomfield, CO, October 2014. https://www.usenix.org/conference/osdi14/technical-sessions/presentation/hawblitzel

21. Inria, C., contributors: Early history of coq. https://coq.inria.fr/refman/history.html (2021)

22. Jouvelot, P., Gifford, D.K.: Algebraic reconstruction of types and effects. In: Wise, D.S. (ed.) Conference Record of the Eighteenth Annual ACM Symposium on Principles of Programming Languages, Orlando, Florida, USA, 21–23 January 1991, pp. 303–310. ACM Press (1991). https://doi.org/10.1145/99583.99623

23. Kim, S., Xu, M., Kashyap, S., Yoon, J., Xu, W., Kim, T.: Finding bugs in file systems with an extensible fuzzing framework. ACM Trans. Storage 16(2), 10:1–10:35 (2020). https://doi.org/10.1145/3391202

24. Kroening, D., Tautschnig, M.: CBMC – C bounded model checker. In: Ábrahám, E., Havelund, K. (eds.) TACAS 2014. LNCS, vol. 8413, pp. 389–391. Springer, Heidelberg (2014). https://doi.org/10.1007/978-3-642-54862-8_26

25. Krucker, S., et al.: The spectrometer/telescope for imaging X-rays (STIX). Astronom. Astrophys. **642**, A15 (2020)

26. Kumar, R., Myreen, M.O., Norrish, M., Owens, S.: CakeML: a verified implementation of ML. In: Jagannathan, S., Sewell, P. (eds.) The 41st Annual ACM SIGPLAN-SIGACT Symposium on Principles of Programming Languages, POPL 2014, 20–21 January 2014, San Diego, CA, USA, pp. 179–192. ACM (2014). https://doi.org/10.1145/2535838.2535841

27. Leino, K.R.M.: Dafny: an automatic program verifier for functional correctness. In: Clarke, E.M., Voronkov, A. (eds.) LPAR 2010. LNCS (LNAI), vol. 6355, pp. 348–370. Springer, Heidelberg (2010). https://doi.org/10.1007/978-3-642-17511-4_20

28. Leroy, X.: Formal verification of a realistic compiler. Commun. ACM **52**(7), 107–115 (2009). https://doi.org/10.1145/1538788.1538814

29. Mehlitz, P., Shafiei, N., Tkachuk, O., Davies, M.: RACE: building airspace simulations faster and better with actors. In: 2016 IEEE/AIAA 35th Digital Avionics Systems Conference (DASC), pp. 1–9 (2016). https://doi.org/10.1109/DASC.2016.7777991

30. Moore, J.S.: Milestones from the Pure Lisp theorem prover to ACL2. Formal Aspects Comput. **31**(6), 699–732 (2019). https://doi.org/10.1007/s00165-019-00490-3

31. Nipkow, T., Paulson, L.C., Wenzel, M.: Isabelle/HOL: a proof assistant for higher-order logic, vol. 2283. Springer Science & Business Media (2002). https://doi.org/10.1007/3-540-45949-9_5

32. Paulson, L.C., Nipkow, T., Wenzel, M.: From LCF to Isabelle/HOL. Formal Aspects Comput. **31**(6), 675–698 (2019). https://doi.org/10.1007/s00165-019-00492-1

33. Robby, Hatcliff, J.: Slang: the Sireum programming language. In: Margaria, T., Steffen, B. (eds.) Leveraging Applications of Formal Methods, Verification and Validation (ISoLA), pp. 253–273. Springer International Publishing, Cham (2021). https://doi.org/10.1007/978-3-030-89159-6_17

34. Rümmer, P.: A constraint sequent calculus for first-order logic with linear integer arithmetic. In: Cervesato, I., Veith, H., Voronkov, A. (eds.) LPAR 2008. LNCS (LNAI), vol. 5330, pp. 274–289. Springer, Heidelberg (2008). https://doi.org/10.1007/978-3-540-89439-1_20

35. Shafiei, N., Havelund, K., Mehlitz, P.C.: Actor-based runtime verification with MESA. In: Deshmukh, J., Nickovic, D. (eds.) Runtime Verification - 20th International Conference, RV 2020, 6–9 October 2020, Los Angeles, CA, USA, Proceedings. Lecture Notes in Computer Science, vol. 12399, pp. 221–240. Springer (2020). https://doi.org/10.1007/978-3-030-60508-7_12

36. Suter, P., Köksal, A.S., Kuncak, V.: Satisfiability modulo recursive programs. In: Yahav, E. (ed.) SAS 2011. LNCS, vol. 6887, pp. 298–315. Springer, Heidelberg (2011). https://doi.org/10.1007/978-3-642-23702-7_23

37. Voirol, N., Kneuss, E., Kuncak, V.: Counter-example complete verification for higher-order functions. In: Scala Symposium (2015)

On the Termination of Borrow Checking in Featherweight Rust

Étienne Payet[1] (ID), David J. Pearce[2](✉)(ID), and Fausto Spoto[3](ID)

[1] LIM, Université de La Réunion, Saint Denis, France
etienne.payet@univ-reunion.fr
[2] Victoria University of Wellington, Wellington, New Zealand
david.pearce@ecs.vuw.ac.nz
[3] Dipartimento di Informatica, Università di Verona, Verona, Italy
fausto.spoto@univr.it

Abstract. A distinguished feature of the Rust programming language is its ability to deallocate dynamically-allocated data structures as soon as they go out of scope, without relying on a garbage collector. At the same time, Rust lets programmers create references, called *borrows*, to data structures. A static borrow checker enforces that borrows can only be used in a controlled way, so that automatic deallocation does not introduce dangling references. Featherweight Rust provides a formalisation for a subset of Rust where borrow checking is encoded using flow typing [40]. However, we have identified a source of non-termination within the calculus which arises when typing environments contain cycles between variables. In fact, it turns out that well-typed programs cannot lead to such environments—but this was not immediately obvious from the presentation. This paper defines a simplification of Featherweight Rust, more amenable to formal proofs. Then it develops a sufficient condition that forbids cycles and, hence, guarantees termination. Furthermore, it proves that this condition is, in fact, maintained by Featherweight Rust for well-typed programs.

Keywords: Borrowing · Type checking · Rust · Termination

1 Introduction

The Rust programming language is seeing widespread use in areas such as system programming [1,6,9,27], blockchain systems [15,36], smart contracts [2,57] and more [3,7]. A key feature of Rust is its ability to automatically deallocate dynamically allocated data when it goes out of scope. This differs from most other programming languages, that either: require programmers to free data structures explicitly (*e.g.*, C/C++); or, rely on garbage collection to free

Work supported by the SafePKT subproject of the LEDGER MVP Building Programme of the European Commission. Goal of the project is the analysis of Rust code used in the PKT blockchain (https://pkt.cash).

J. V. Deshmukh et al. (Eds.): NFM 2022, LNCS 13260, pp. 411–430, 2022.
https://doi.org/10.1007/978-3-031-06773-0_22

unreachable data (*e.g.*, Java, C#, etc.). The former approach is error prone (*e.g.*, use-after-free or free-after-free errors), whilst the latter is safe but costly (garbage collection consumes resources and data may not be released in a timely fashion).

In Rust, each data structure is *owned* by a variable [46]. Once that variable goes out of scope, the data is freed as well. Rust also allows data to be lent temporarily (*e.g.*, as a function parameter) using *borrows*, which can be seen as pointers in traditional programming languages (but without ownership). Since borrows are access paths into data structures, the type checker of Rust must enforce strict rules on their creation and lifetime. For example, a location cannot be mutated as long as a borrow to it exists. To support this, data is divided into two categories: that which can be *copied* (*e.g.*, primitives); and that which must be *moved* (*e.g.*, mutable borrows). For the latter, assignments result in a transfer of ownership from rightvalue to leftvalue. The Rust compiler performs *borrow checking* to statically check that borrows are used safely (*i.e.* that automatic deallocation does not create dangling pointers, that multithreaded code does not generate race conditions, etc.).

Featherweight Rust (FR) formalises a subset of Rust and includes a proof of correctness for borrow checking [40]. In particular, borrow checking is formalised as a flow-sensitive type system, whose types include primitives (such as int), dynamically allocated data structures (collectively represented by a boxing operator) and borrows of leftvalues, both for *reading* (immutable borrows) and *writing* (mutable borrows). The type system rules are given by structural induction on the syntax of the Rust source code, and are hence well-founded. However, they use, internally, a procedure to type leftvalues. Since borrows include other leftvalues, we have discovered this procedure may enter an infinite loop and, in such case, the borrow checker would not terminate.

Contribution. This paper provides a sufficient condition which ensures that the borrow checker for Featherweight Rust terminates [40]. Our insight is that, for well-typed programs, this condition already holds for typing environments created during borrow checking. Hence, this is not a bug in Featherweight Rust *per se*, but rather an important condition which was left implicit. Our approach shows that data structures are *linearizable* at run time and, hence, that our condition holds for the specific kind of type environments the borrow checker builds during execution. This result is important in order to increase confidence in the borrow checker of Rust. Moreover, it provides a notion of well-foundness for the recursion used in the borrow checker, that future work can exploit in order to prove other properties by induction. For example, this is a necessary step towards a mechanical proof of Featherweight Rust.

2   Overview

This section illustrates various aspects of Rust related to memory allocation and borrowing, and provides an initial connection with Featherweight Rust (FR). A more detailed introduction to Rust can be found elsewhere [46,47].

Rust deallocates the data owned by a variable as soon as that variable goes out of scope. Consider the following, where the `Box::new(13)` allocates a new box (*i.e.* location) on the heap which contains the integer 13:

```
1  fn deallocate1() -> i32 {      // accepted by the borrow checker
2      let x = Box::new(13);
3      return 17;
4  }
```

Local variable x goes out of scope at the end of the function, hence Rust deallocates the box there, automatically. Assignments move the ownership of a value to their leftvalue. Consider the following:

```
1  fn deallocate2() {             // rejected by the borrow checker
2      let x = Box::new(13);
3      {
4          let y = x;
5      }
6      println!("{}", x);
7  }
```

The assignment moves ownership of the box from x to y. Since y goes out of scope when the inner block ends, the box is deallocated there. Consequently, the print statement is trying to use deallocated data, *i.e.* it is trying to access a dangling pointer. Correctly, the borrow checker of Rust rejects this. Consider the following function now:

```
1  fn ok1() -> Box<i32> {         // accepted by the borrow checker
2      let x = Box::new(13);
3      return x;
4  }
```

Here, ownership of the box is transferred from x to the return value, and subsequently to the caller of the function. When variable x reaches the end of its scope it no longer owns a value and, hence, Rust does not deallocate anything inside ok1.

Things become more complicated if borrows of data structures exist. For instance, the following function tries to return a borrow of a data structure that has been already deallocated:

```
1  fn dangling() -> &Box<i32> { // rejected by the borrow checker
2      let i = Box::new(13);
3      let result = &i;
4      return result;
5  }
```

Local variable i owns the box and, when it goes out of scope at the end of the function, the box is deallocated. Variable **result** takes an *immutable borrow* of i (roughly a pointer to i without ownership). Thus, when the box is deallocated, **result** becomes a dangling pointer which cannot safely be returned. Again,

Rust rejects this function. Roughly, the borrow checker for FR [40] computes the following *typing* (or *type environment*) at the end of the function:

$$\{i \rightarrow \Box\,\mathsf{int}, \mathsf{result} \rightarrow \&i\}$$

For simplicity, FR uses `int` to collectively represent integer types in Rust (*e.g.*, `i32`, `i64`, etc.). Likewise, $\Box T$ corresponds with `Box<T>` and provides the only form of dynamically allocated data in FR. Finally, $\&w$ (resp. $\&\mathsf{mut}\ w$), where w is a leftvalue, is the type of an immutable (resp. mutable) borrow. Furthermore, since the borrow checker allows arbitrary leftvalues here (*i.e.* not just variables), we can have types such as $\&**y$.

Mutable borrows are a sort of temporary ownership of a value. As a consequence, that value can be modified only through the borrow, for the whole duration of the borrow. Any other attempt to modify the value is rejected. Consider for instance the following function:

```
1  fn writes_to_borrowed() { // rejected by the borrow checker
2      let v = 13;
3      let w = 17;
4      let mut y = &v;
5      let x = &y;
6      y = &w;
7      println!("{}{}{}{}", x, y, v, w);
8  }
```

Here, the `y=&w` statement is trying to modify the leftvalue `y` that, however, has been borrowed at the previous line. Correctly, the borrow checker rejects this function. It computes the following typing just before the `y=&w` statement:

$$\{v \rightarrow \mathsf{int}, w \rightarrow \mathsf{int}, y \rightarrow \&v, x \rightarrow \&y\}$$

from where it is apparent that y is borrowed and, therefore, the subsequent assignment `y=&w` is rejected.

Borrows in previous examples are immutable: the borrowed value can be read from them, but cannot be modified from them. Borrows can also be mutable, meaning that they allow one to modify the borrowed value, with the dereference operator `*`. In this sense, a mutable borrow takes full responsibility about the borrowed value, for its whole lifetime. When a mutable borrow to a value exists, that value cannot be written *nor read* from any other path. Consider for instance the following function:

```
1  fn reads_mutably_borrowed() { // rejected by the borrow checker
2      let mut z = 13;
3      let y = &mut z;
4      let x = z;
5      println!("{}{}{}", x, y, z);
6  }
```

The statement x=z tries to read z, that has been mutably borrowed at the previous line. Hence, the borrow checker rejects this function. It computes the typing

$$\{z \rightarrow \text{int}, y \rightarrow \&\text{mut } z\}$$

just before x=z, from where it is apparent that z is mutably borrowed there. Furthermore, if line 4 above was replaced with let x=&z, the program would still be rejected.

3 Preliminaries

This section provides a formal, simplified presentation of Featherweight Rust (FR) [40]. This retains the key features of FR relevant to our discussion but, for brevity, omits other aspects. Roughly speaking, the main simplifications are:

- **Compatibility.** The original formulation of FR supports a notion of *partial type*. This allows the "shadow" of a variable's type to be retained in the environment after it has been moved, such that subsequent re-assignments can be checked for compatibility. Since this is not important here, we reduce these shadow types to a single "dangling" type.
- **Borrows.** The original formulation of FR models borrows using *sets* of leftvalues. This allows FR to be easily extended with control-flow constructs, but is not strictly necessary for the core calculus. Since this makes our presentation more complex without adding anything significant, we restrict borrows to a single leftvalue.
- **Misc.** We have transformed some definitions, originally given as typing rules, into functions (such as **type** and **move** later). This makes them more compact and simplifies proofs involving them.

Definition 1 (LVals). *We assume a set of variables* Vars. *A context* $\kappa \subseteq$ Vars *is a finite set of variables in scope. The set* LV_κ *of leftvalues over* κ *is:*

$$w ::= x \mid *w, \text{where } x \in \kappa.$$

The root *of a leftvalue is then defined as:*

$$\text{root}(x) = x \quad \text{if } x \in \text{Vars}$$
$$\text{root}(*w) = \text{root}(w).$$

Definition 2 (Expressions). *The set of* expressions e *is defined as follows where i ranges over integer literals:*

$$e ::= i \mid w \mid \&w \mid \&\text{mut } w \mid \text{box } e$$

Definition 3 (Terms). *We assume a set* Lifetimes *of lifetimes l which decorate blocks of code. The set of terms t is defined as (where $x \in$ Vars and $l \in$ Lifetimes):*

$$t ::= w = e \mid \text{let mut } x = e \mid \{ t_1 ; \ldots ; t_n \}^l$$

Intuitively, variables declared in a block with lifetime l have lifetime l and are deallocated at the end of the block. Lifetimes are important for the borrow checker to ensure borrows do not outlive their referents and become dangling. The following illustrates a simple (invalid) program:

$$\{ \texttt{let mut x} = 0; \texttt{ let mut p} = \&\texttt{x}; \{ \texttt{let mut y} = 1; \texttt{ p} = \&\texttt{y}; \}^\texttt{m} \}^1$$

This program creates a dangling reference when the inner block completes and, hence, is rejected by the borrow checker.

The types used in FR are a simplification of those found in Rust, and include only primitive types (such as int) or structures dynamically allocated in memory (collectively represented by a box), but can also refer to a borrow or mutable borrow of a leftvalue.

Definition 4 (Types). *The set of* types *over a context κ is defined as follows (where $\texttt{w} \in \mathsf{LV}_\kappa$):*

$$\mathsf{T}_\kappa ::= \texttt{ int} \mid \&\texttt{w} \mid \&\texttt{mut w} \mid \square\, \mathsf{T}_\kappa \mid \texttt{dangling}$$

Here, type dangling is given to a variable whose value has been *moved*, that is, assigned to another owner.[1] Consequently, the value exists but cannot be accessed from that variable anymore.

Definition 5 (Declared Types). *The set of* declared types, *T^l, over κ associates types with lifetimes. We define $|T^l| = T$ and $\mathsf{lifetime}(T^l) = l$.*

Rust distinguishes types with *copy semantics* and types with *move semantics*. Values whose type has copy semantics are copied upon reading, while values whose type has move semantics are *moved* instead, in the sense that their original container loses the ownership to the value. Only mutable borrows and dynamically allocated data (*i.e.* boxes) have move semantics.

Definition 6 (Copy and Move). *Let $T \in \mathsf{T}_\kappa$. Then T has move semantics, and we write $\mathsf{move}(T)$, if and only if $T = \&\texttt{mut w}$ or $T = \square\, T'$ for some T'. In all other cases, T has copy semantics, and we write $\mathsf{copy}(T)$.*

Another useful notion is that of *full* types. They are types that do not contain dangling. This notion is important because, as we will see in Sect. 4, only values with full type can be borrowed in Rust.

Definition 7 (Full type). *A type $T \in \mathsf{T}_\kappa$ is full if and only if dangling does not occur inside T. We write it as $\mathsf{full}(T)$.*

We define now the typings, or type environments, that is, information about the types of the variables in scope at a given program point, with their lifetime.

---

[1] This is a simplification of the dangling(T) type in [40], that embeds the *shadow* type T of a value that has been moved away.

Definition 8 (Typing). *Given a context κ, a typing τ over κ is a map from each variable $v \in \kappa$ to a type T and a lifetime l. We write this as $\tau(v) = T^l$.*

The types used in a typing can include borrows and mutable borrows. The basic idea of the borrow checker is that the root of the borrowed leftvalues (mutable or not) can only be used in a restricted way [40].

Definition 9 (Read/Write Prohibited). *Let κ be a context and τ a typing over κ. Then $w \in LV_\kappa$ is read prohibited in τ, written as readProhibited(w, τ), if root(w) occurs in a mutable borrow inside τ. Moreover, w is write prohibited in τ, written as writeProhibited(w, τ), if root(w) occurs in a borrow or in a mutable borrow inside τ.*

A typing provides type and lifetime information for variables in scope, and this naturally extends to leftvalues. The following is a translation[2] of Def. 3.11 in [40]. It can be seen as a recursive algorithm for typing leftvalues and, as such, it is heavily used in the borrow checker. The algorithm queries the typing when the leftvalue is actually a variable, and dereferences borrows and boxes when the leftvalue contains one or more $*$ operations, further recurring in the case of borrows. Types int and dangling cannot be dereferenced, hence the algorithm fails on them.

Definition 10 (LVal Typing). *Given a context κ, a typing τ over κ and $w \in LV_\kappa$, the partial function* type(w, τ) *yields the type and lifetime of w in τ:*

$$\text{type}(x, \tau) = \tau(x)$$

$$\text{type}(*w, \tau) = \begin{cases} undefined & if\ \text{type}(w, \tau)\ is\ undefined \\ undefined & if\ |\text{type}(w, \tau)| = \text{dangling} \\ undefined & if\ |\text{type}(w, \tau)| = \text{int} \\ \text{type}(w', \tau) & if\ |\text{type}(w, \tau)| = \&w' \\ \text{type}(w', \tau) & if\ |\text{type}(w, \tau)| = \&\text{mut}\ w' \\ T^l & if\ \text{type}(w, \tau) = (\Box\, T)^l. \end{cases}$$

Definition 10 is clearly recursive, both on the structure of w and on the leftvalues contained in the borrows or mutable borrows that occur in the typing. In general, that recursion is not well-founded. In algorithmic terms, this means that this algorithm for typing leftvalues might not terminate. Consider for instance the typing $\{x \rightarrow \&*x\}$: the definition of type$(*x, \tau)$ ends in an infinite loop. This example can be arbitrarily complicated, through the use of more involved cycles that pass through more variables. As a consequence, the natural question is to understand when the recursion in Definition 10 is well-founded and if that is always the case when it is used by the borrow checker of Featherweight Rust.

---

[2] This definition is given as a type system in [40] and as a recursive function here.

4   Borrow Checking

The borrow checker is formalized as a *flow-sensitive* type system [39] whose rules bind the typing τ *before* the evaluation of a term t to the typing τ' *after* that evaluation. We write this as $\tau, l \vdash t \dashv \tau'$, where l is the *enclosing* lifetime of t (*i.e.* that of the enclosing block). On expressions, the typing rules provide the inferred type T of the expression as well: $\tau, l \vdash e : T \dashv \tau'$.

4.1   Typing Expressions

T-Const. This rule applies to integer constants. Their evaluation yields a value of type int and does not modify the typing:

$$\overline{\tau, l \vdash i : \text{int} \dashv \tau}$$

T-Copy. This rule applies to leftvalues whose type has copy semantics. Their evaluation yields their value, while the typing remains unchanged. The rule requires that the leftvalue can be accessed for reading:

$$\frac{T^m = \text{type}(w, \tau) \quad \text{copy}(T) \quad \neg\text{readProhibited}(w, \tau)}{\tau, l \vdash w : T \dashv \tau}$$

T-Move. This rule applies to leftvalues whose type has move semantics. Their evaluation yields their value, but the ownership of the value is moved away from the leftvalue. Because of this, the typing gets modified, by letting the old container of the value get the dangling type (*i.e.* so it cannot be used anymore). As a consequence, reading, from a leftvalue, a value with move semantics amounts to writing into its old container and requires write permission:

$$\frac{T^m = \text{type}(w, \tau) \quad \text{move}(T) \quad \neg\text{writeProhibited}(w, \tau)}{\tau, l \vdash w : T \dashv \text{move}(w, \tau)}$$

where the move function modifies the binding for the root of w:

$$\text{move}(w, \tau) = \tau[\text{root}(w) \mapsto \text{strike}(w, \tau(\text{root}(w)))]$$

with

$$\text{strike}(x, T^l) = \text{dangling}^l$$
$$\text{strike}(*w, (\Box\, T)^l) = (\Box\, |\text{strike}(w, T^l)|)^l.$$

The function strike is undefined otherwise. We note also there are no cases for borrows since one cannot move out of a borrow in Rust.

T-ImmBorrow. The evaluation of a borrow expression requires the borrowed leftvalue to be readable and have full type (only values with full type can be borrowed in Rust):

$$\frac{\text{full}(|\text{type}(w, \tau)|) \quad \neg\text{readProhibited}(w, \tau)}{\tau, l \vdash \&w : \&w \dashv \tau}$$

<u>T-MutBorrow</u>. The evaluation of a mutable borrow expression requires the borrowed leftvalue to be writable and have full type (only values with full type can be borrowed in Rust). Moreover, Rust requires that the borrowed leftvalue never traverses an immutable borrow:

$$\frac{\mathsf{full}(|\mathsf{type}(\mathsf{w}, \tau)|) \quad \neg\mathsf{writeProhibited}(\mathsf{w}, \tau) \quad \mathsf{mutable}(\mathsf{w}, |\tau(\mathsf{root}(\mathsf{w}))|, \tau)}{\tau, l \vdash \&\mathrm{mut}\ \mathsf{w} : \&\mathrm{mut}\ \mathsf{w} \dashv \tau}$$

where

$$\mathsf{mutable}(x, T, \tau) = true$$

$$\mathsf{mutable}(*\mathsf{w}, \square\,T, \tau) = \mathsf{mutable}(\mathsf{w}, T, \tau)$$

$$\mathsf{mutable}(*\underbrace{*\cdots*}_{n}x, \&\mathrm{mut}\ \mathsf{w}, \tau) = \mathsf{mutable}(\underbrace{*\cdots*}_{n}\mathsf{w}, |\tau(\mathsf{root}(\mathsf{w}))|, \tau).$$

<u>T-Box</u>. The evaluation of a box expression simply recurs on the boxed expression:

$$\frac{\tau, l \vdash \mathsf{e} : T \dashv \tau'}{\tau, l \vdash \mathsf{box}\ \mathsf{e} : \square\,T \dashv \tau'}$$

4.2 Typing Terms

<u>T-Block</u>. The execution of a block of statements simply recurs on each statement. At the end, the variables declared inside the block get dropped away. We assume that variables cannot be redefined inside a block, hence there is no risk of a name clash.

$$\frac{\tau, l \vdash \mathsf{t}_1 \dashv \tau_1 \quad \cdots \quad \tau_{n-1}, l \vdash \mathsf{t}_n \dashv \tau'}{\tau, l \vdash \{\mathsf{t}_1; \ldots; \mathsf{t}_n\}^m \dashv \mathsf{drop}(m, \tau')}$$

where

$$\mathsf{drop}(m, \tau) = \{x \to T^l \mid x \in \mathsf{dom}(\tau),\ \tau(x) = T^l \text{ and } l \neq m\}.$$

<u>T-Declare</u>. The declaration of a fresh variable x evaluates its initialization expression e and binds x to the type of e, decorated with the lifetime of the block of code where the declaration is evaluated:

$$\frac{x \notin \mathsf{dom}(\tau) \quad \tau, l \vdash \mathsf{e} : T \dashv \tau'}{\tau, l \vdash \mathrm{let}\ \mathrm{mut}\ x = \mathsf{e} \dashv \tau'[x \to T^l]}$$

<u>T-Assign</u>. The assignment of a value to a leftvalue w requires w to be writable. In that case, the assigned expression is evaluated and assigned to w. This is modelled through the write function below. Since w can be more complex than a single variable, the assignment might actually update a variable in a mutable borrow reachable from the root of w. This is reflected in the (quite complex) definition of write, that we take from [40] where more details can be found:

$$\frac{\tau, l \vdash \mathsf{e} : T \dashv \tau' \quad \tau'' = \mathsf{write}(\tau', \mathsf{w}, T) \quad \neg\mathsf{writeProhibited}(\mathsf{w}, \tau'')}{\mathsf{survives}(T, \mathsf{lifetime}(\mathsf{type}(\mathsf{w}, \tau)), \tau')}{\tau, l \vdash \mathsf{w} = \mathsf{e} \dashv \tau''}$$

where

$$\mathsf{write}(\tau, \underbrace{* \cdots *}_{n} x, T) = \mathsf{apply}(x, \mathsf{update}(\tau, n, |\tau(x)|, T))$$

where

$$\mathsf{update}(\tau, 0, T', T) = \langle \tau, T \rangle$$
$$\mathsf{update}(\tau, n + 1, \square\, T', T) = \mathsf{expand}(\mathsf{update}(\tau, n, T', T))$$
$$\mathsf{update}(\tau, n + 1, \&\mathtt{mut}\ w, T) = \langle \mathsf{write}(\tau, \underbrace{* \cdots *}_{n} w, T), \&\mathtt{mut}\ w \rangle$$

and

$$\mathsf{apply}(y, \langle \tau, T \rangle) = \tau[y \rightarrow T^l] \quad \text{where}\ \mathsf{lifetime}(\tau(y)) = l$$
$$\mathsf{expand}(\langle \tau, T \rangle) = \langle \tau, \square\, T \rangle.$$

It is important to observe that if write modifies a type, it is that of x or that of variables inside the mutable borrows in τ.

Function $\mathsf{survives}(T, m, \tau)$ determines if all leftvalues contained in the borrows or mutable borrows inside the type T have a type whose lifetime is m or is larger than m. Hence they *survive* to the end of the lifetime m. The motivation of this constraint in rule T-Assign is to guarantee that, when a variable v can reach another variable v', the lifetime of v' is equal or larger than the lifetime of v. Otherwise, the deallocation of v' (at the end of its lifetime) would leave a dangling reference reachable from v.

Consider for instance the following illegal program.

$$\{\mathtt{let\ mut}\ x = \mathtt{box}\ 0;\ \mathtt{let\ mut}\ y = \&\mathtt{mut}\ *x;\ *x = 1\}^l$$

Let us apply the typing rules above starting from $\tau_1 = \{\}$.

- (T-Const) $\tau_1, l \vdash 0 : \mathtt{int} \dashv \tau_1$.
- (T-Box) $\tau_1, l \vdash \mathtt{box}\ 0 : \square\,\mathtt{int} \dashv \tau_1$.
- (T-Declare) As $x \notin \mathsf{dom}(\tau_1)$, for $\tau_2 = \tau_1[x \rightarrow (\square\,\mathtt{int})^l] = \{x \rightarrow (\square\,\mathtt{int})^l\}$ we have $\tau_1, l \vdash \mathtt{let\ mut}\ x = \mathtt{box}\ 0 \dashv \tau_2$.
- (T-MutBorrow) By Definition 10, we have $\mathsf{type}(x, \tau_2) = \tau_2(x) = (\square\,\mathtt{int})^l$, hence $\mathsf{type}(*x, \tau_2) = \mathtt{int}^l$, so $|\mathsf{type}(*x, \tau_2)| = \mathtt{int}$. Therefore, $|\mathsf{type}(*x, \tau)|$ is full because dangling does not occur in it. Moreover, $\neg\mathsf{writeProhibited}(*x, \tau_2)$ holds because $\mathsf{root}(*x) = x$ does not occur in a borrow nor in a mutable borrow inside τ_2. Finally, $\mathsf{mutable}(*x, |\tau_2(\mathsf{root}(*x))|, \tau_2) = \mathsf{mutable}(*x, |\tau_2(x)|, \tau_2) = \mathsf{mutable}(*x, \square\,\mathtt{int}, \tau_2) = \mathsf{mutable}(x, \mathtt{int}, \tau_2) = true$. Consequently, we have $\tau_2, l \vdash \&\mathtt{mut}\ *x : \&\mathtt{mut}\ *x \dashv \tau_2$.
- (T-Declare) As $y \notin \mathsf{dom}(\tau_2)$, for $\tau_3 = \tau_2[y \rightarrow (\&\mathtt{mut}\ *x)^l]$, we have $\tau_2, l \vdash \mathtt{let\ mut}\ y = \&\mathtt{mut}\ *x \dashv \tau_3$.
- (T-Const) $\tau_3, l \vdash 1 : \mathtt{int} \dashv \tau_3$.
- (T-Assign) We have $\mathsf{write}(\tau_3, *x, \mathtt{int}) = \mathsf{apply}(x, \mathsf{update}(\tau_3, 1, |\tau_3(x)|, \mathtt{int})) = \mathsf{apply}(x, \mathsf{update}(\tau_3, 1, \square\,\mathtt{int}, \mathtt{int}))$. Moreover, we have $\mathsf{update}(\tau_3, 1, \square\,\mathtt{int}, \mathtt{int}) =$

expand(update($\tau_3, 0$, int, int)) = expand($\langle \tau_3$, int$\rangle$) = $\langle \tau_3, \square$ int$\rangle$. Consequently, write($\tau_3, *x$, int) = apply($x, \langle \tau_3, \square$ int$\rangle$) = $\tau_3[x \rightarrow (\square$ int$)^l$] = τ_3. However, $\neg$writeProhibited($*x, \tau_3$) does not hold because root($*x$) = x occurs in the mutable borrow &mut $*x$ inside τ_3. Therefore, (T-Assign) cannot be applied.

5   Termination

This section provides a sufficient condition for the termination of the typing algorithm for leftvalues in Definition 10. It is based on the idea that the Rust type system forces programmers to build *linear* data structures. This translates into a notion of *linearization* for typings, meaning that they map variables in a way that does not allow cycles: each variable is mapped into a type that only contains variables of strictly lower ranks.

The same condition, with a similar proof, can be used to prove that the other recursive functions used in the typing rules in Sect. 4 terminate, namely, mutable and write. The proof is identical and we have chosen type as a representative.

Definition 11. *A typing τ over a context κ is* linearizable *if there exists an injective function $\phi : \kappa \rightarrow \mathbb{N}$ such that, for every $x \in \kappa$, if v occurs in $\tau(x)$ then $\phi(x) > \phi(v)$. We say that $\phi(y)$ is the ϕ-rank of y, or just the rank of y when ϕ is clear from the context.*

As an example, suppose $\kappa = \{x, y\}$ where $\tau = \{x \rightarrow \&y^l, y \rightarrow int^l\}$, then $\phi = \{x \rightarrow 1, y \rightarrow 0\}$ is a suitable linearisation. A linearizable typing induces an ordering between leftvalues: either the number of dereferences decreases, or the rank of their roots decreases.

Definition 12. *Given a context κ and a linearizable typing τ over κ, the relation $>$ between leftvalues is the minimal relation such that*

1. *$*w > w$ for every $w \in LV_\kappa$, and*
2. *$w_1 > w_2$ if $\phi(root(w_1)) > \phi(root(w_2))$, for every $w_1, w_2 \in LV_\kappa$.*

Proposition 1. *The relation $>$ from Definition 12 is well-founded.*

Proof. Assume by contradiction that $>$ is not well-founded. Then there is an infinite sequence of leftvalues $s = w_0 > w_1 > \cdots > w_n > \cdots$. Since, in the first rule of Definition 12, it is root($*w$) = root(w) and consequently $\phi(root(*w)) = \phi(root(w))$, we conclude that the rank of the root of the leftvalues decreases at most $|\kappa|$ times in s or remains constant. Hence, there is a finite k such that $\phi(root(w_k)) = \phi(root(w_{k+i}))$ for all $i \geq 0$. This means that, from k onwards, only rule 1 of Definition 12 applies. But that rule strictly decreases the size of the leftvalues and consequently cannot be applied indefinitely. This is incompatible with the hypothesis that s is infinite.   □

Since $>$ is well-founded, it can be used in proofs by induction, as below.

Proposition 2. *If a typing τ over κ is linearizable, then the algorithm for computing* type *in Definition 10 terminates.*

Proof. We actually prove a stronger statement, namely that, given $w \in LV_\kappa$:

1. type(w, τ) terminates;
2. if a variable v occurs in type(w, τ) then $\phi(\text{root}(w)) > \phi(v)$.

We proceed by induction on w.

- The base case is when w is actually the variable x of lowest rank. By Definition 10, it is type$(x, \tau) = \tau(x)$ hence it terminates and no variable occurs in it, since (Definition 11) the rank of those variables should be even lower, which is impossible.
- Assume now that both 1 and 2 hold for all leftvalues w'' such that $w > w''$. If w is a variable x, then type$(x, \tau) = \tau(x)$ hence type(w, τ) terminates and every variable v that occurs in $\tau(x)$ is such that $\phi(x) > \phi(v)$ (Definition 11). Hence both 1 and 2 hold for w as well. If, instead, $w = *w''$ for a suitable w'', then $w > w''$ (Definition 12) and by inductive hypothesis we know that 1 and 2 hold for w''. The computation of type$(*w'', \tau)$ first recurs on type(w'', τ) (Definition 10).
  - In the first, second and third case of Definition 10, also the computation of type$(*w'', \tau)$ terminates and property 2 is vacuously true.
  - In the sixth case of Definition 10, the computation of type$(*w'', \tau)$ terminates and $|\text{type}(w'', \tau)| = \Box |\text{type}(*w'', \tau)|$. Since w'' and $*w''$ have the same root, condition 2 lifts from w'' to $*w''$.
  - In the fourth and fifth case of Definition 10, by inductive hypothesis we know that 2 holds for w'' and consequently the root of w' in Definition 10 has lower rank than the root of w''. That is, $w'' > w'$. By inductive hypothesis, both 1 and 2 hold for w'. Hence type(w', τ) terminates and type$(*w'', \tau)$ terminates and yields type(w', τ). Every variable that occurs in type(w', τ) has lower rank than root$(w'') = \text{root}(w)$. Therefore, both 1 and 2 hold for w also in this case. $\Box$

6   Preservation of Linearizability

This section proves that the rules from Sect. 4 preserve linearizability: when applied from a linearizable typing τ, they can only lead to a linearizable typing τ'. By Proposition 2, this means that the recursion used for typing leftvalues in those rules is well-founded, hence a borrow checker that implements those typing rules terminates (assuming that it starts from the empty, linearizable typing). The proof proceeds by rule induction.

Some rules from Sect. 4 obviously preserve linearizability, since they do not modify the typing (for them, $\tau = \tau'$). This is the case of rules T-Const, T-Copy, T-ImmBorrow and T-MutBorrow. Rule T-Box preserves linearizability by a simple application of rule induction.

For rule T-Move, it is $\tau' = \mathsf{move}(w, \tau)$. The intuition is that strike can only make the set of variables in the right-hand side of the typing smaller. Therefore, it can never make τ' non-linearizable. This is proved below.

Lemma 1. *If T-Move is applied from a linearizable typing τ and leads to a typing τ', then also τ' is linearizable.*

Proof. By definition of move, the only difference between τ and τ' is at $r = \mathsf{root}(w)$. The variables that occur in $\tau'(r)$ are included in those that occur in $\tau(r)$ (strike can only strike away part of the type $\tau(r)$). Hence the same function ϕ that exists for τ (Definition 11) shows that τ' is linearizable. □

Rule T-Block is used at the end of a block of code, where the set S of local variables declared in the block goes out of scope. It removes the type bindings for the variables in S from the initial typing τ, through function drop. Therefore, T-Block preserves linearizability, by rule induction and by the following result, whose intuition is that the removal of bindings from a typing can never make it non-linearizable.

Lemma 2. *If drop is applied from a linearizable typing τ and leads to a typing τ', then also τ' is linearizable.*

Proof. The difference between τ and τ' is that τ' is missing some bindings for some variables that have been projected away. Therefore, the same function ϕ that exists for τ (Definition 11) can be used to show that τ' is linearizable. □

Rule T-Declare models the declaration of a new variable x, bound to an expression e. The evaluation of e leads to a typing τ' that, by rule induction, is linearizable. As a final step, this rule enlarges τ' with a binding for x. Since x is fresh ($x \notin \mathsf{dom}(\tau)$), variable x does not occur in the right-hand side of that binding. Namely, the rule leads to a new typing $\tau'' = \tau'[x \rightarrow T^l]$ where T^l is the type of e, such that x does not occur in T. Therefore, the next result entails that T-Declare preserves linearizability.

Lemma 3. *Let τ be a linearizable typing for the context κ; let $x \notin \kappa$, $T \in \mathsf{T}_\kappa$ (hence x does not occur in T) and l be a lifetime. Then $\tau' = \tau[x \rightarrow T^l]$ is linearizable as well.*

Proof. Consider the function ϕ that shows that τ is linearizable (Definition 11). Let us extend ϕ into an injective function ϕ' that gives x the highest rank:

$$\phi' = \phi\left[x \rightarrow 1 + \max_{y \in \kappa} \phi(y)\right].$$

Given $y \in \kappa$, it is $\phi'(y) = \phi(y) > \phi(v)$ if there is v that occurs in $\tau(y) = \tau'(y)$. Since x is fresh, v is distinct from x and we conclude that $\phi'(y) > \phi'(v)$ if v occurs in $\tau'(y)$. Since x does not occur in T, it is $\phi'(x) = 1 + \max_{y \in \kappa} \phi(y) > \phi(v) = \phi'(v)$ if v occurs in $T^l = \tau'(x)$. □

Rule T-Assign computes the type T of the value of the assigned expression e, which leads to a typing τ'. By rule induction, τ' is linearizable. Then the rule writes that value into a leftvalue w. It performs this by computing $\tau'' = \mathsf{write}(\tau', \mathsf{w}, T)$. The following result shows that τ'' is linearizable as well.

Lemma 4. *Let τ be a linearizable typing for the context κ; let $\mathsf{w} \in \mathsf{LV}_\kappa$ and $T \in \mathsf{T}_\kappa$. Let $\tau' = \mathsf{write}(\tau, \mathsf{w}, T)$ be the application of function write in rule T-Assign, used there to assign the type T to w. Then τ' is linearizable as well.*

Proof. The function write modifies a set of variables $v_1, \ldots, v_n$ in τ to compute τ'. The type of the other variables remains unchanged from τ to τ'. Since the type system guarantees that borrowed variables are not modified [40], this means that $v_1, \ldots, v_n$ do not occur in the borrows in τ. Moreover, the variables in the borrows in T do not contain $v_1, \ldots, v_n$, because such variables are either $x = \mathsf{root}(\mathsf{w})$, and the rule T-Assign forbids the presence of x in the borrows in T ($\neg$writeProhibited in rule T-Assign); or they are inside mutable borrows in τ (last case of update), in which case they would be mutably borrowed and the type system would have forbidden to read mutably borrowed variables in order to compute the type T (see rule T-MutBorrow). This means that such $v_1, \ldots, v_n$ only occur in the left-hand side of the bindings of τ'. Consider now the function ϕ that shows that τ is linearizable (Definition 11). Let us extend ϕ into an injective function ϕ' that gives $v_1, \ldots, v_n$ the highest ranks:

$$\phi' = \phi \left[v_i \to i + \max_{y \in \kappa \setminus \{v_1, \ldots, v_n\}} \phi(y) \,\middle|\, 1 \leq i \leq n \right].$$

For every $y \in \kappa \setminus \{v_1, \ldots, v_n\}$, it is $\phi'(y) = \phi(x) > \phi(v) = \phi'(v)$ if v occurs in $\tau(y) = \tau'(y)$. Moreover, by construction, $\phi'(v_i) > \phi(v) = \phi'(v)$ if v occurs in $\tau'(v_i)$. That is, ϕ' is linearizable as well. $\square$

7   Related Work

Reed provided an early formalisation of Rust called "Patina" which shares some similarities with FR [43]. For example, it employs a flow-sensitive type system for characterising borrow checking which operates over a "shadow" heap. However, the scope was significantly larger and, as such, soundness was not established. Likewise, Wang *et al.* presented a formal, executable operational semantics for Rust called KRust [51]. This was defined in $\mathbb{K}$—a rewrite-based executable semantic framework particularly suited at developing operational semantics [45]. A large subset of Rust was defined in this way and partially validated against the official Rust test suite. Another example is that of Weiss *et al.*, who presented an unpublished system called *Oxide* which bears striking similarity with FR [54]. Oxide was also inspired by Featherweight Java to produce a relatively lean formalisation of Rust. Again, it includes a far larger subset of Rust than FR (perhaps making it more *middleweight* than *featherweight*). There are also differences, as Oxide doesn't model boxes explicitly and has no clear means to model heap-allocated memory. The comprehensive work of Jung *et al.* provides a machine-checked formalisation for a realistic subset of Rust [18]. This includes various notions of concurrency and extends to libraries using `unsafe` features by identifying *library-specific verification conditions* which must be satisfied to ensure overall safety. However, concessions were understandably necessary given the enormity of this formalisation task (which, in fact, amounts to roughly 17.5KLOC of Coq). For example, the system presented does not resemble the surface syntax of Rust but, rather, is more akin to the *Mid-level Intermediate Representation (MIR)* used within the Rust compiler. Underpinning this development is *Iris*—a framework for high-order concurrent separation logic [20–22]. This enables, for example, a notion of *borrow propositions* which correspond with borrowing in Rust. Later work also adapted RustBelt to account for relaxed memory operations and, in the process, uncovered a previously unknown data race in `Arc` [10]. Separately, Jung *et al.* explored compiler optimisations in the context of unsafe code [19]. This is challenging because, within unsafe code, the usual guarantees provided by Rust may not hold (*e.g.*, multiple mutable borrows of the same location can exist). The proposed system, *Stacked Borrows*, provides an operational semantics for memory accesses in Rust. This introduces a strong notion of *undefined behaviour* such that a compiler is permitted to ignore the possibility of such programs when applying optimisations (roughly in line with how C compilers handle undefined behaviour [35]).

The potential hazards of `unsafe` code have been a considerable focus of academic work and, indeed, numerous bugs and security advisories have already been uncovered in real-world programs [5,56]. Large-scale studies indicate the potential effects of unsafe code can propagate widely [14] and that, whilst unsafe code is typically small and self-contained, it is most often used for interoperability with external systems [4]. As such, interest has been growing in using state-of-the-art verification tools here. For example, Rudra employs a straightforward static analysis to scan for bug patterns related to error handling [5]. Nevertheless, the tool identified 74 new CVE's (including two in the standard library). In a similar vein, MIRCHECKER employs a mixed-domain static analysis to track both numeric and symbolic values and operates directly on Rust's Mid-level Intermediate Representation (MIR) [30]. Amongst other things, for this example, this tool can detect integer overflows and use-after free errors in unsafe code. Another good example is SMACK [8,11] which translates LLVM IR to Boogie/Z3 and was recently extended to Rust [7]. CRUST [48] is similar, but uses CBMC [24] as the backend. CRUST specifically focuses on memory safety violations (such as multiple mutable references to the same data). An interesting feature is support for automatically deriving "proof drivers" using a technique reminiscent of that for test case generation [38]. KLEE employs symbolic execution and was also extended to support Rust [31,32]. Unlike CRUST this tool considers a larger number of errors, including arithmetic overflow and buffer overruns (*i.e.*, not just those related to memory unsafety). Prusti exploits automated theorem proving as the core technique, building on Viper [3]. This makes Prusti more comparable with tools such as Dafny [25,26] and Whiley [41,42,49] which require additional programmer annotations to verify memory-safety properties (*e.g.* adding specifications to clarify method side-effects, etc.). However, Prusti exploits aliasing information inherent in Rust programs to avoid much of this. Instead, programmers can focus on specifying properties of interest, such as the absence of arithmetic overflow or buffer overruns. Unfortunately, Prusti does not consider unsafe code (though it presumably could be managed with further specification). Other relevant tools here include Miri [19,37] (a partially symbolic interpreter for MIR), RustHorn [34] (a specialised verifier based on Constrained Horn Clauses) and RUPAIR (a tool for detecting buffer overflows) [16]. We also note verification techniques developed to tackle specific features of Rust, such as *closures* [55] and *trait objects* [50]. Several works have also focused on dynamic approaches which typically limit the effect unsafe code can have. For example, XRust partitions the heap such that memory accessed in unsafe code is isolated from that of safe code [33]. Similarly, Galeed preserves the memory safety guarantees of Rust in using (unsafe) C++ code [44]. Again, this works by isolating the heap accessible in Rust from that accessible within C++. Wang *et al.* also employ segregated heaps for Rust/C++ applications within the secure enclave capability offered by Intel SGX [52,53].

Finally, researchers have been exploring the use of Rust's type system for statically enforcing strong guarantees. For example, Levy *et al.* report on experiences developing an Embedded OS in Rust [29]. They argued that *"At first examination, Rust seems perfectly suited for this task"*. Unfortunately, they were hindered by ownership in Rust preventing otherwise safe resource sharing. For example, an interrupt handler could not retain a mutable borrow of a shared resource (*e.g.*, a network stack). Such situations are not safe in general. However, in their particular setting this was safe due to guarantees provided by the OS and, to workaround, they instead relied on unsafe code. In subsequent work, they further reduced this unsafe code to a single trusted primitive, TakeCell [27,28]. This is similar to Cell but instead of copying values out as Cell does (which can introduce overhead), it provides a mechanism for code to execute "within" the cell with, effectively, zero overhead. As such, it provides a form of mutual exclusion. Similarly, Jespersen *et al.* describe a library for implementing session types in Rust which was an adaptation of communication patterns in Servo [17]. Session types require a linear usage of channels which naturally fits with the ownership in Rust and, as such, afforded some safety guarantees [23]. It is also interesting to note that Rust is the primary language used to develop Mozilla's experimental rendering engine, Servo, and accounts for some 800KLOC. Anderson *et al.* examined how the use of Rust here addresses many common security issues [1]. For example, the use of uninitialised memory has led to problems in Firefox. They argue many aspects of Rust (*e.g.*, good interoperation with C) make it well suited here, but found situations where its ownership model was problematic, such as for data structures which do not assume a single owner *"in order to provide multiple traversal APIs without favoring the performance of one over the other"*. In a similar vein, Emre *et al.* consider the problem of automatically translating C programs into safer Rust programs [13]. Whilst noting many challenges, their aim, amongst other things, was to minimise the use of `unsafe` code and `mut` annotations. Finally, Dewey *et al.* focus on the integrity of the Rust type checker itself as this underlies many of the safety guarantees provided by Rust [12]. By leveraging techniques from constraint logic programming, they managed to fuzz test the Rust compiler using over 900M automatically generated programs and, in the process, uncovered numerous bugs.

8 Conclusion

This paper has provided a proof of termination for the borrow checker of Featherweight Rust. As a consequence, it supports the use of that framework for the specification and analysis of the behaviour of Rust programs. The proof is based on the particular property of Rust, that imposes a strict discipline to programmers, so that only linearizable data structures can be constructed at run time. In this sense, the proof sheds more light on the reason of such design choice of the language.

References

1. Anderson, B., et al.: Engineering the servo web browser engine using Rust. In: Proceedings of the ICSE, pp. 81–89 (2016)
2. Ashouri, M.: Etherolic: a practical security analyzer for smart contracts. In: Proceedings of the SAC, pp. 353–356. ACM Press (2020)
3. Astrauskas, V., Müller, P., Poli, F., Summers, A.J.: Leveraging Rust types for modular specification and verification. In: Proceedings of the OOPSLA, page Article 147 (2019)
4. Astrauskas, V., Matheja, C., Poli, F., Müller, P., Summers, A.J.: How do programmers use unsafe Rust? In: Proceedings of the OOPSLA, pp. 136:1–136:27 (2020)
5. Bae, Y., Kim, Y., Askar, A., Lim, J., Kim, T.: RUDRA: finding memory safety bugs in Rust at the ecosystem scale. In: Proceedings of the SOSP (2021, to appear)
6. Balasubramanian, A., Baranowski, M.S., Burtsev, A., Panda, A., Rakamari, Z., Ryzhyk, L.: System programming in Rust: beyond safety. OS Rev. **51**(1), 94–99 (2017)
7. Baranowski, M., He, S., Rakamarić, Z.: Verifying Rust programs with SMACK. In: Proceedings of the ATVA, pp. 528–535 (2018)
8. Barnett, M., Chang, B.-Y.E., DeLine, R., Jacobs, B., Leino, K.R.M.: Boogie: a modular reusable verifier for object-oriented programs. In: de Boer, F.S., Bonsangue, M.M., Graf, S., de Roever, W.-P. (eds.) FMCO 2005. LNCS, vol. 4111, pp. 364–387. Springer, Heidelberg (2006). https://doi.org/10.1007/11804192_17
9. Bornholt, J., et al.: Using lightweight formal methods to validate a key-value storage node in Amazon S3. In: Proceedings of the SOSP, pp. 836–850. ACM Press (2021)
10. Dang, H.-H., Jourdan, J.-H., Kaiser, J.-O., Dreyer, D.: RustBelt meets relaxed memory. In: Proceedings of the POPL, page Article 34 (2020)
11. de Moura, L., Bjørner, N.: Z3: an efficient SMT solver. In: Ramakrishnan, C.R., Rehof, J. (eds.) TACAS 2008. LNCS, vol. 4963, pp. 337–340. Springer, Heidelberg (2008). https://doi.org/10.1007/978-3-540-78800-3_24

12. Dewey, K., Roesch, J., Hardekopf, B.: Fuzzing the Rust typechecker using CLP (t). In: Proceedings of the ASE, pp. 482–493. IEEE (2015)

13. Emre, M., Schroeder, R., Dewey, K., Hardekopf, B.: Translating C to safer Rust, pp. 1–29 (2021)

14. Evans, A.N., Campbell, B., Soffa, M.L.: Is Rust used safely by software developers? In: Proceedings of the ICSE, pp. 246–257. ACM Press (2020)

15. Hjálmarsson, F.Þ., Hreiðarsson, G.K., Hamdaqa, M., Hjálmtýsson, G.: Blockchain-based e-voting system. In: Proceedings of the CLOUD, pp. 983–986 (2018)

16. Hua, B., Ouyang, W., Jiang, C., Fan, Q., Pan, Z.: Rupair: towards automatic buffer overflow detection and rectification for Rust. In: Proceedings of the ACSAC, pp. 812–823. ACM Press (2021)

17. Jespersen, T.B.L., Munksgaard, P., Larsen, K.F.: Session types for Rust. In: Proceedings of the Workshop on Generic Programming (WGP), pp. 13–22 (2015)

18. Jung, R., Jourdan, J., Krebbers, R., Dreyer, D.: RustBelt: securing the foundations of the Rust programming language. In: Proceedings of the POPL, pp. 1–34 (2018)

19. Jung, R., Dang, H.-H., Kang, J., Dreyer, D.: Stacked borrows: an aliasing model for Rust. In: Proceedings of the POPL, page Article 41 (2020)

20. Jung, R., Krebbers, R., Birkedal, L., Dreyer, D.: Higher-order ghost state. In: Proceedings of the ICFP, pp. 256–269. ACM Press (2016)

21. Jung, R., Krebbers, R., Jourdan, J.-H., Bizjak, A., Birkedal, L., Dreyer, D.: Iris from the ground up: a modular foundation for higher-order concurrent separation logic. JFP **28**, e20 (2018)

22. Kaiser, J.-O., Dang, H.-H., Dreyer, D., Lahav, O., Vafeiadis, V.: Strong logic for weak memory: reasoning about release-acquire consistency in iris. In: Proceedings of the ECOOP, vol. 74, pp. 17:1–17:29. Schloss Dagstuhl - Leibniz-Zentrum für Informatik (2017)

23. Kokke, W.: Rusty variation: deadlock-free sessions with failure in Rust. In: Proceedings of the ICE, pp. 48–60 (2019)

24. Kroening, D., Tautschnig, M.: CBMC – C bounded model checker. In: Ábrahám, E., Havelund, K. (eds.) TACAS 2014. LNCS, vol. 8413, pp. 389–391. Springer, Heidelberg (2014). https://doi.org/10.1007/978-3-642-54862-8_26

25. Rustan, K., Leino, M.: Developing verified programs with Dafny. In: Joshi, R., Müller, P., Podelski, A. (eds.) VSTTE 2012. LNCS, vol. 7152, p. 82. Springer, Heidelberg (2012). https://doi.org/10.1007/978-3-642-27705-4_7

26. Leino, K.R.M.: Dafny: an automatic program verifier for functional correctness. In: Clarke, E.M., Voronkov, A. (eds.) LPAR 2010. LNCS (LNAI), vol. 6355, pp. 348–370. Springer, Heidelberg (2010). https://doi.org/10.1007/978-3-642-17511-4_20

27. Levy, A., Campbell, B., Ghena, B., Pannuto, P., Dutta, P., Levis, P.: The case for writing a kernel in Rust. In: Proceedings of the APSYS, pp. 1:1–1:7 (2017)

28. Levy, A., et al.: Multiprogramming a 64kb computer safely and efficiently. In: Proceedings of the SOSP, pp. 234–251. ACM Press (2017)

29. Levy, A.A., et al.: Ownership is theft: experiences building an embedded OS in Rust. In: Proceedings of the Workshop on Programming Languages and Operating Systems, pp. 21–26 (2015)

30. Li, Z., Wang, J., Sun, M., Lui, J.C.S.: MirChecker: detecting bugs in Rust programs via static analysis. In: Proceedings of the CCS, pp. 2183–2196. ACM Press (2021)

31. Lindner, M., Aparicius, J., Lindgren, P.: No panic! Verification of Rust programs by symbolic execution. In: Proceedings of the INDIN, pp. 108–114 (2018)

32. Lindner, M., Fitinghoff, N., Eriksson, J., Lindgren, P.: Verification of safety functions implemented in Rust - a symbolic execution based approach. In: Proceedings of the INDIN, pp. 432–439 (2019)

33. Liu, P., Zhao, G., Huang, J.: Securing unsafe Rust programs with XRust. In: Proceedings of the ICSE, pp. 234–245. ACM Press (2020)

34. Matsushita, Y., Tsukada, T., Kobayashi, N.: RustHorn: CHC-based verification for rust programs. In: ESOP 2020. LNCS, vol. 12075, pp. 484–514. Springer, Cham (2020). https://doi.org/10.1007/978-3-030-44914-8_18

35. Memarian, K., et al.: Exploring C semantics and pointer provenance. In: Proceedings of the POPL, pp. 67:1–67:32 (2019)

36. Ning, P., Qin, B.: Stuck-me-not: a deadlock detector on blockchain software in Rust. Procedia Comput. Sci. **177**, 599–604 (2020)

37. Olson, S.: Miri: an interpreter for Rust's mid-level intermediate representation. Technical report (2016)

38. Pacheco, C., Ernst, M.D.: Randoop: feedback-directed random testing for Java. In: Proceedings of the OOPSLA (Companion), pp. 815–816 (2007)

39. Pearce, D.J.: Sound and complete flow typing with unions, intersections and negations. In: Proceedings of the VMCAI, pp. 335–354 (2013)

40. Pearce, D.J.: A lightweight formalism for reference lifetimes and borrowing in Rust. ACM TOPLAS **43**(1), Article 3 (2021)

41. Pearce, D.J., Groves, L.: Designing a verifying compiler: lessons learned from developing Whiley. In: SCP, pp. 191–220 (2015)

42. Pearce, D.J., Utting, M., Groves, L.: An introduction to software verification with Whiley. In: Bowen, J.P., Liu, Z., Zhang, Z. (eds.) SETSS 2018. LNCS, vol. 11430, pp. 1–37. Springer, Cham (2019). https://doi.org/10.1007/978-3-030-17601-3_1

43. Reed, E.: Patina: a formalization of the Rust programming language. Technical report (2015)

44. Rivera, E., Mergendahl, S., Shrobe, H.E., Okhravi, H., Burow, N.: Keeping safe Rust safe with Galeed. In: Proceedings of the ACSAC, pp. 824–836. ACM Press (2021)

45. Rosu, G., Serbanuta, T.: An overview of the K semantic framework. JLAP **79**(6), 397–434 (2010)

46. Rust Team: The Rust programming language. doc.rust-lang.org/book/. Accessed 05 Jan 2016

47. Rust Team: The rustonomicon - the dark arts of advanced and unsafe Rust programming. doc.rust-lang.org/nomicon/. Accessed 31 Mar 2020

48. Toman, J., Pernsteiner, S., Torlak, E.: Crust: a bounded verifier for Rust. In: Proceedings of the ASE, pp. 75–80 (2015)

49. Utting, M., Pearce, D.J., Groves, L.: Making Whiley Boogie! In: Proceedings of the IFM, pp. 69–84 (2017)

50. VanHattum, A., Schwartz-Narbonne, D., Chong, N., Sampson, A.: Verifying dynamic trait objects in Rust. In: Proceedings of the ICSE-SEIP (2022, to appear)

51. Wang, F., Song, F., Zhang, M., Zhu, X., Zhang, J.: KRust: a formal executable semantics of Rust. In: Proceedings of the TASE, pp. 44–51 (2018)

52. Wang, H., et al.: Towards memory safe enclave programming with Rust-SGX. In: Proceedings of the CCS, pp. 2333–2350. ACM Press (2019)

53. Wang, P., et al.: Building and maintaining a third-party library supply chain for productive and secure SGX enclave development. In: Proceedings of the ICSE-SEIP, pp. 100–109. ACM Press (2020)

54. Weiss, A., Patterson, D., Matsakis, N.D., Ahmed, A.: Oxide: The essence of Rust (2019)

55. Wolff, F., Bílý, A., Matheja, C., Müller, P., Summers, A.J.: Modular specification and verification of closures in Rust. In: Proceedings of the OOPSLA, pp. 1–29 (2021)
56. Xu, H., Chen, Z., Sun, M., Zhou, Y.: Memory-safety challenge considered solved? An empirical study with all Rust CVEs. CoRR, abs/2003.03296 (2020)
57. Zhang, F., et al.: The Ekiden platform for confidentiality-preserving, trustworthy, and performant smart contracts. IEEE S&P 18(3), 17–27 (2020)

More Programming Than Programming: Teaching Formal Methods in a Software Engineering Programme

James Noble(✉)(iD), David Streader, Isaac Oscar Gariano(iD),
and Miniruwani Samarakoon

School of Engineering and Computer Science, Victoria University of Wellington,
Wellington, New Zealand
kjx@comp.vuw.ac.nz
http://ecs.vuw.ac.nz/~kjx

Abstract. Formal methods for software correctness are critical to the future of software engineering—and so must be an essential part of software engineering education. Unfortunately, formal methods are often resisted by students due to perceived difficulty, mathematicity, and practical irrelevance. We redeveloped our software correctness course by taking a programming intensive approach, using the solver-aided language Dafny to provide instant formative feedback via automated assessment. Our redeveloped course increased student retention and resulted in the best evaluation for the course for at least ten years.

Keywords: Formal methods · Software engineering · Education · Dafny

1 Introduction

In the last 20 years, formal methods for software verification have moved from an esoteric research topic [38] to a set of increasingly practical tools, and from doctoral study to undergraduate degrees. Victoria University of Wellington's Computer Science and Software Engineering programmes include a course, SWEN324 "Software Correctness" that teaches software verification. We often call this course "Programming Made Hard" because 100 students repeat the assignments they completed years ago in introductory programming courses, but now must specify those programs' behaviour and verify that their implementations meet those specifications. In 2020 we redesigned SWEN324 using the solver-aided Dafny language, supported by Leino's Dafny textbook [36]; we are just finishing teaching the 2021 version of the course at time of writing. Students and teaching staff found the use of Dafny very positive: the 2020 course offering received the highest overall evaluation for at least ten years.

Although very positive overall, students found Dafny difficult to learn and to use, and our informal observations as teachers are that many of these difficulties stem from "accidental" complexity introduced by the Dafny tool. This accidental complexity obscures the "essential" complexity of learning the fundamentals of software verification, and then applying those techniques to verifying simple programs [9]. In this paper we reflect on our experience teaching SWEN324, focusing particularly on our course design and issues with formal tooling.

© Springer Nature Switzerland AG 2022
J. V. Deshmukh et al. (Eds.): NFM 2022, LNCS 13260, pp. 431–450, 2022.
https://doi.org/10.1007/978-3-031-06773-0_23

2 Background

Formal verification of software systems has been a significant research topic for in computer science for 50 years or more [28]. Tools such as Dafny, SAW, SPIN are increasingly mature enough to support industrial application [23,47] but the main barrier to adoption remains a lack of software engineers trained in their use [20]. To address this problem, there have been a number of studies on the usability of formal methods, and tools that support formal verification. Beckert and Grebing [6] for example used the Cognitive Dimensions framework [22] to evaluate the usability of the KeY proof tool; Grebing and Ulbrich [21] followed this up with a user study.

Tools have also been (re)designed to better support programmers in the task of verifying their programs. Whereas the Dafny tool, although interactive, requires programmers to verify their whole program statically, Gradual Dafny [18] allows programmers to choose between static ("assert") and dynamic (run time "assume") verification for each invariant. Other gradual verification approaches have shown similar promise at partial verification, but with choices embodied in the tools themselves [3,5,45,48]. Coming at the problem from the other side, Müller & Ruskiewicz [41] demonstrated how standard program debuggers could be used to debug verification failures, by generating a modified program that reproduced the failure when run, and Christakis [12] integrated concolic testing tools and lower level solver debuggers into Dafny's IDE.

More recently, some of the most interesting recent program verification work has been using the Rust language [8]. Eschewing garbage collection, Rust has an ownership types system that is used to manage memory allocation, object lifetimes, and permissible inter-object references. Program verification tools such as Prusti [4] and RustBelt [29] leverage ownership information to support verification without needing memory structures to be described separately.

Finally, as formal methods' industrial use has increased, so has their relevance to education [10,15,17,30]; Zhumagambetov [50] offers a relatively recent systematic literature review. Aceto and Ingolfsdottir [1], for example, have described a recent course at the University of Reykjavik, where students can participate in a three week intensive formal methods course at first year. Yatapanage [49] describes a recent second year course taught at De Montfort University that applied formal methods to concurrent programming—although the paper's title highlights most students' concerns when approaching this topic "*Students Who Hate Maths and Struggle with Programming*". Kamburjan and Gratz [30] showed how a custom interactive proof tool can generate a positive effect on student engagement; Körner and Krings [32] describe how pedagogical changes to inquiry-based learning can support the user of formal tools. In some ways closest to the approach we present here, Ettinger describes how Dafny has been used for six years at Ben-Gurion University to support teaching refinement-style "correct-by-construction" programming [16], and Blazy describes a similar course based on Why3 [7]. Güdemann describes how verification tools can even support similar learning strategies even in applied computer science courses taught using C [24].

3 SWEN324 Software Correctness

Formal methods have been taught as part of Computer Science and Software Engineering programmers at VUW since 1984. Unfortunately, formal methods are often resisted by students due to perceived difficulty, mathematicity, and practical irrelevance—and SWEN324 had similar problems. In 2021 we had the opportunity to redevelop the course, as a companion to a relatively new course SWEN326 "Safety Critical Systems", that focused on correct software engineering in a wider context, including software processes, testing, and abstract modelling (based on Alloy). This meant that we were able to refocus SWEN324 specifically on formal methods for software correctness based on program proof.

Traditional Formal Course: We initially considered staying with a relatively straightforward, "traditional" formal methods course, introducing students to propositional and predicate logic, then working up through weakest preconditions to Hoare logics and their application in describing and reasoning about software systems, culminating in pencil-and-paper proofs. After some debate, it was decided that this was not appropriate for several reasons. In particular, our students have already taken compulsory courses including Boolean algebra and logic (as mathematics) and discrete logic (as physics) during first year: we do not want students to regard this as "another maths or physics course"—our earlier experience with such courses suggested that such a course would not be popular [42]. On the other hand, our programme is heavily based around programming, with all engineering majors requiring a full first year computer science programme, and software engineering majors keen to take practical elective courses to develop programming skill and experience [42, 43].

Abstract Formal Modelling: We also considered taking an approach based on abstract formal modelling. High-level tools, such as TLA+ [33], Alloy [27] or SPIN [26], support reasoning and mechanised checking of systems' properties, based on abstract models of those systems, rather than actual programming and source code. It is clear that these kinds of abstract formal models can play an important role in software engineering projects, at least in project's the early stages, supporting design validation before a single line of code has been written. Indeed, we had earlier taught a first-year course (SWEN102) that attempted to give a gentle introduction to formal methods within a more general context of software modelling, beginning with UML and moving through to Alloy [42]. The idea was to present formal and informal approaches as different points in a spectrum of approaches to describing software systems, rather than being totally different subjects. We also wanted to ensure that students see software modelling as a useful way of understanding systems, rather than just an exercise in learning new notations, so we felt it was important that any formal notation we used be supported by tools which allowed students to explore the consequences of the models they created. This course was mostly successful on its own terms: even first year students were generally capable of domain modelling using Alloy, of translating functional requirements into Alloy properties, and then able to analyse the Alloy models to demonstrate that the requisite properties held (or explain why they did not).

Unfortunately, our SWEN102 course was never widely popular: for better or for worse, our cohort, privilege programming, over pretty much every other software engineering activity or practice. For the SWEN102 approach to work, we first had to successfully "sell" modelling, and then second to "sell" the advantage of formal models over informal ones—where students simply did not see the relevance of the models to the programming/software engineering tasks the expected to undertake. On the other hand: SWEN102 demonstrated that even our early undergraduate students were capable of learning formal tools, constructing formal models, and handling propositional and predicate logic.

Formalism as Programming: For this reason, we decided to base our SWEN324 course redesign on the reverse of the traditional approach. Rather than progressing bottom up from propositional logic to predicate logic, Hoare logic, and eventually perhaps experimenting with a practical tool, we aimed to progress top down: starting with programming language based tool, and then using that high-level tool as a context in which we can present and teach the key concepts of software correctness—while offering the majority of students an experience that feels like programming, rather than like doing mathematics.

The latest version of this course—SWEN324 "Software Correctness" – adopted the Dafny programming language and associated toolset, based on the Z3 solver and the Visual Studio Code. Dafny provides what Leino has called "auto-active" verification [37] in which verification is seamlessly incorporated into development practices and the toolchain. It may be clearer to think of this approach as *implicit* verification where programmers annotate their programs with preconditions, postconditions, variants, invariants, as in Eiffel [40], and do not interact directly with formal models or e.g. proof trees. This is in contrast to *explicit* verification technologies such as Coq [11,44] where programmers must interact with solvers by directly building proofs and proof trees, potentially even extracting programs from those proofs. Dafny's implicit approach still offers many guarantees: Dafny attempts to prove programs totally correct by default, so recursive methods and loops often require programmers to give variants to prove termination, and loops in particular generally require invariants to prove correctness. Array and pointer accesses typically require invariants, assertions, or preconditions to ensure all accesses are within bounds and variables are initialised and non-null. This means that Dafny programmers (and thus students) interact with Dafny's underlying prover indirectly, at arm's length, in terms of definitions in their programs and constructs in the Dafny language, rather than having to learn explicit representations of proof.

Choice of Dafny: Dafny was selected for a number of pragmatic reasons: it is well supported by a team in Amazon's Automated Reasoning Group led by Rustan Leino, has substantial publicly available on-boarding and tutorial material, including a full book by Leino [36], an online playground at Rise4Fun, documentation available online, and a developing academic community—and, frankly, because what little experience the course staff had with suitable tools seemed most transferable to Dafny. Based on our earlier experience, we hoped Dafny would offer a number of advantages over Alloy, or more sophisticated tools like Coq [44] or Why3 [7]. First, Dafny offers a concrete, ASCII-compliant syntax—being restricted to ASCII means students should feel some familiarity with the notation: students would not need to learn how to type, let alone pronounce, relatively esoteric characters such as α, δ, or o (little were we to know how familiar alpha, delta, and omicron would become). Dafny's syntax and semantics being based on C♯ and Java should also be familiar. Students can use the development toolsets they already know, such as VS Code, Eclipse, Git—particularly important for students who need tools such as screen readers, magnifiers, or voice control to complete their work.

Second, because Dafny is well supported by a toolset, we are able to rely on Dafny itself to provide students rapid formative feedback—simply by requiring students to submit their solutions via the Dafny verifier. In a very real sense, we are able to leverage the "essential difficulty" of formal verification of correctness—that no only must students implement a correct program, but they must also convince the Dafny prover that their implementation is correct—to aid the students in that task. In simple cases, where students' focus on implementing programs, we can directly supply students with the Dafny specifications and the tool itself will provide feedback: either their program verifies against the specification, or it does not. Where students' focus is on writing specifications, we can allow students to verify their solutions against hidden "oracle" specifications, and again Dafny can check that the students' specifications capture important properties described by the oracles, or more straightforwardly, that the students' specifications and the oracles are mutually consistent [19].

Finally, because Dafny is relatively mature, there is a fair amount of material available online, which students are able to access as necessary. We were also able to use a draft version of Leino's *Program Proofs* textbook [36].

Continuous Automated Feedback: The ability for Dafny to provide feedback, and that this course was targeted at third-year students—experienced both in programming and in tertiary study—lead us to make this automated feedback a central feature of the course. Again based on our department's practice in teaching programming—with which our students are very familiar!—we provide that feedback in two ways.

First, our "lectures" are centred around a weekly series of small "mastery" questions about Dafny and verification, served from a simple website. This is similar to the existing Dafny Rise4Fun website, but simpler: we discuss this further in the next section. The weekly questions are released at the start of each week, and students may discuss the questions, may work in groups, ask for answers, and make any number of attempts at answering them—but are expected to answer the vast bulk of these questions correctly. The time in "lectures" allows students to discuss any of the questions with the class, lead by the course staff—in practice, the website lets us know which questions students are currently finding difficult, and so we use that to guide choices. Because of the very liberal rules around answering the mastery questions, we can work out the solution to any weekly question in class, and even demonstrate the correct answer and show it verifying: if students choose to pay little attention and just copy the provided answer, so be it.

Second, we also incorporate automated feedback into larger summative individual assignments (again, we provide examples in the next section). Students can submit answers to the assignments as many times as necessary: by running each submission through the Dafny verifier, students then get immediate feedback about their submission. This feedback is quite terse (just the number of assertions verified, or not verified) because it is not intended to replace students' use of IDEs or to substitute for their own attempts at verification—rather it is so students can judge their progress through the course, and in particular, to know when they have completed each part of each assignment. We are careful to ensure that every important concept required by the summative assignments are covered by weekly questions before the assignment is due. Thus, while we can discuss the summative assignments only in broad outline, we can (and do) refer students to the relevant weekly questions which we can discuss in as much detail and at as much length as necessary.

Course Design: As with all VUW engineering courses, SWEN324 is offered in one twelve week semester, generally split into two six-week half-semesters. Figure 1 shows the ideal course plan (for COVID reasons, an extra week's break was substituted at week 9 in 2020 and week 3 in 2021). There are four main topics in the course: learning Dafny as a programming language; writing Dafny (method) specifications; verifying those specifications against Dafny programs; and handling objects with mutable state.

Week	Topic	Assignment
1.	**Introduction** — overview, industrial use [25, 13]	
2.	**Programming** — pre- and post-conditions	
3.	**Data** — inductive data types, pattern matching	A1 Programming (10%)
4.	**Recursion** — totality, termination	
5.	**Structural Recursion** — over inductive types	
6.	**Iteration** — loops, variants	
	Midterm break	
	Midterm break	A2 Specifying Programs (15%)
7.	**Loops** – loop invariants and variants	
8.	**Recursion vs Iteration** — tail recursion	
9.	**Recursion vs Iteration** — specs. vs. programs	
10.	**Objects** — mutable structures and validity	A3 Verifying Programs (15%)
11.	**Ownership** — ownership of representation	
12.	**Proofs** — Dafny "assert" vs "calc"	
15.		A4 Reasoning about Systems (40%)

Fig. 1. SWEN324 course plan.

Course Content: The resulting course covers most of the content Leino's *Programs Proofs* [36], although it does not explicitly address the foundational material. In more detail: we address essentially all the "core" features of Dafny circa 2020, i.e. Dafny version 2.3.0. This included Dafny methods and classes (imperative, and mutable); functions and inductive datatypes (immutable, finitary); pre and postconditions; predicates (Boolean functions); assumptions and assertions; compiled vs ghost code, well-founded recursion and explicit termination measures, pattern matching, destructors; built-in collections (arrays, sets, maps); loops, invariants, and variants; recursive specifications of iterative programs (including transformations between general recursion, tail recursion, and iteration); and representation invariants for dynamic data structures.

There are only two chapters of material from *Program Proofs* that we intentionally overlook. Chapter 2 presents the mathematical foundations of Dafny's program logic, based on Hoare Logic and Weakest Preconditions. Where necessary, we discuss Dafny's semantics informally: we have not needed to refer the formal definitions. Chapter 5 presents the notion of proof and Dafny's constructs (function lemmas, `calc` blocks) that can support programmers in making explicit proofs. Perhaps more surprisingly we have not needed this material either. Because Dafny is an *implicit* verification system, students do not need to build proof objects, and they are not even able to see what proofs Dafny's solver many have constructed!

Course Assessment: The overall assessment of the course is shown in Fig. 2. A significant fraction of the assessment supports the formative mastery questions, with the balance taken up by four summative assignments, one for each part, and a reflective essay. Each part of the course is addressed by around 25 weekly formative mastery questions. Students who complete all the mastery questions and the first assignment are well on the way to obtaining a bare pass; students who are hoping for an "excellent" grade must complete most of the assignments correctly.

Weekly Overview Questions (Dafny, open)	20%
Assignment A1: Programming (Dafny, individual)	10%
Assignment A2: Specifying (Dafny, individual)	15%
Assignment A3: Verifying (Dafny, individual)	15%
Assignment A4: Reasoning (20% Dafny, 20% essay, individual)	40%

Fig. 2. SWEN304 assessment items.

These assessment weights also guide students time. VUW courses of this size (15 points) are rated at 150 h over the whole trimester—nominally 10 h per week over 15 weeks—12 lecture weeks and a three-week assessment period at the end. Allowing approx. 25 h (2 h per week) to attend lectures, and another 25 h for background reading, installing software, navigating Git, etc., that leaves 100 h of assessed work. The assessment percentages offer a rough guide to the amount of time students should aim to spend on each piece of work.

Course Objectives: The resulting course objectives are that, by the end of the course, students should be able to:

1. Explain what it means for a system to be correct, what engineering techniques we can use to increase confidence in correctness, and why this is important.
2. Use formal structures such as sets, functions, relations and sequences to model software systems.
3. Use formal notations to specify desired properties of software systems, such as assertions, pre- and postconditions, variants, and invariants.
4. Use formal tools to check that systems correctly implement their desired properties.
5. Use formal reasoning to explain why a particular system is correct with respect to a specification.

The first objective is primarily tested by the essay: the other objectives by the assignments and mastery questions.

4   Assessment

To quote Tom Angelo [2], *"most students are going to try to 'study to the test.'"*. What is assessed is what we can expect students to (try to) learn. This is why we have restructured SWEN324 around questions and assignments with automated feedback, rather e.g. than traditional lecture content. In this section we present examples of the assessment items we designed for SWEN324, to demonstrate the kind of problems students are able to solve during the course.

4.1   Weekly Overview Questions

As discussed above, 20% of the assessment in SWEN324 is in the form of formative weekly questions. Students can choose to answer any question at any time, and make repeated attempts to answer each question. The point is formative, to support learning, rather than summative evaluation—although the system records when each student successfully answers each question. Students can repeat completed questions (e.g. to experiment with alternative solutions)—the question stays listed as completed.

Figure 3 shows the rudimentary web system that presents these questions to students. The left-hand pane shows some Dafny code including a place-holder "[???]"; this placeholder is replaced by whatever students type in to the right-hand pane. This system was originally built by our colleague Marco Servetto to help students revise their Java knowledge, and is well integrated with the other systems which we use in the school: we have re-purposed this tool for Dafny.

The question in Fig. 3 (titled "First Past the Post") is addressing a basic definition of Boolean algebra: what is Dafny's Boolean "exclusive-or" operator. This question shows the advantage of the placeholder mechanism: potential solutions are necessarily restricted to fit within the syntactic context of the placeholder. The solution to this question is Dafny's "! =" operator.

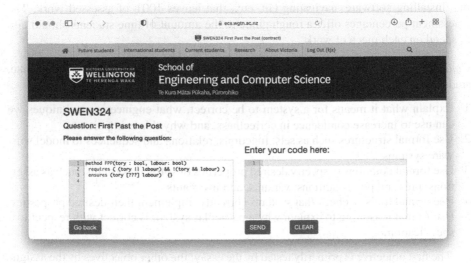

Fig. 3. Web interface for weekly questions.

Figure 4 shows the course-wide overview of the summary questions, showing how many students have completed each question. This proved very used in tracking students' progress through the course overall, and in choosing lecture topics (i.e. which questions we will discuss and then answer in lectures). Generally we aim to pick questions where that top 10–20% of students have answered successfully (we can lure them into the discussion of their solutions) but the bulk of the class has not (so that they are interested in learning how to solve those questions). This also allows us to choose not to revisit questions that the vast majority of the class has already answered, even if some stragglers have not—rather than taking up everyone's class time with well understood topics. Rather, we can direct stragglers e.g. to the recordings of the lectures where we have answered those questions, or arrange to provide individual support.

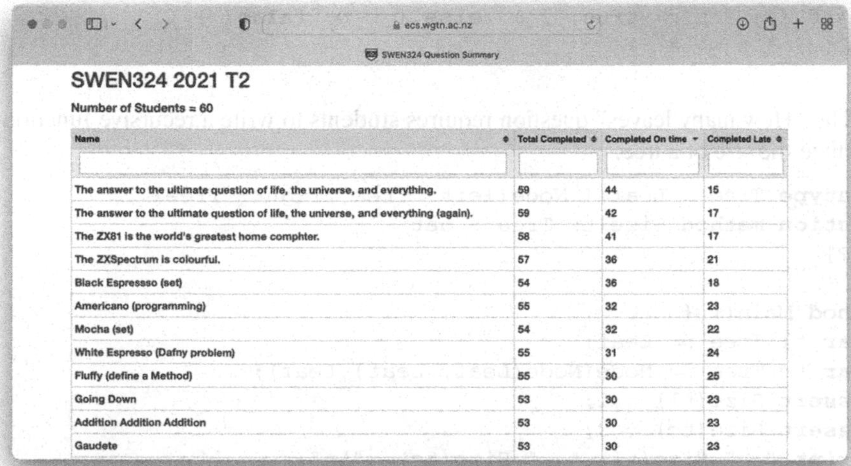

SWEN324 2021 T2

Number of Students = 60

Name	Total Completed	Completed On time	Completed Late
The answer to the ultimate question of life, the universe, and everything.	59	44	15
The answer to the ultimate question of life, the universe, and everything (again).	59	42	17
The ZX81 is the world's greatest home comphter.	58	41	17
The ZXSpectrum is colourful.	57	36	21
Black Espressso (set)	54	36	18
Americano (programming)	55	32	23
Mocha (set)	54	32	22
White Espresso (Dafny problem)	55	31	24
Fluffy (define a Method)	55	30	25
Going Down	53	30	23
Addition Addition Addition	53	30	23
Gaudete	53	30	23

Fig. 4. Overview of student progress.

It is worth reiterating that these questions are at least as important as resources or content or prompts for lecture sessions, as questions that students must answer by themselves. Fairly early on, for example, there is a relatively simple question that most students get wrong:

```
//complete the following method which returns the "real"
//sum and product of its two real arguments
method SumAndDifference(a : real, b : real) [???]
```

```
//Hint: https://www.youtube.com/watch?v=kqFPDrDWAHs
```

The point of this question is that the question title ("We'll look at them together then we'll take them apart") and method name ("SumAndDifference") are inconsistent with the comment on the method ("//.."real" sum and product"). This inconsistency was originally introduced in error, however we kept it because of the valuable in-class discussion it engendered, about how comments can be misleading, as can method names, or alternatively tests or specifications can be incorrect. As it happens, here the comment is wrong: the automated test indeed requires sum and difference not sum and product.

The "First Past the Post" question illustrates how we use Dafny to revise Boolean algebra. The questions get rather more sophisticated as the course progresses. For example, the "Very Logical, Mr Spock" question also tests Boolean algebra, but requires students to understand how a method's control flow and assignments are summarised by postconditions ("**ensures**"):

```
method logical(a : bool, b : bool, c : bool) returns (t : bool)
  ensures [???]
{
 t := false;
 if (b) {
    if (a) { t := true; } }  else { t := false; }
 if (c) { t := a; }
}
```

The "How many leaves" question requires students to write a recursive function to calculate the size of a tree:

```
datatype Tree = Leaf | Node(left: Tree, right: Tree)
function method Size(t: Tree): nat
[???]

method Main() {
   var tl: Tree := Leaf;
   var tc: Tree := Node(Node(Leaf, Leaf),Leaf);
   assert Size(tl) = 1;
   assert Size(tc) = 3;
   print "⌴⌴",Size(tl),"⌴⌴",Size(tc), "\n";


}
```

The "Hopalong" question requires students to define a termination measure, as Dafny programs are total by default:

```
//insert a decreases clause so Dafny can prove termination
function hopalong(q: int, x : int, y : int, z : int) : int
  [???]
{
 var modulo := (x + y + z) % 3;

q + if (y ≤ 0) ∨ (z ≤ 0) ∨ (x ≤ 0) then 0 else
if (modulo = 0) then (hopalong(q+1, x + 3, y - 1, z + 2))
    else if (modulo = 1) then (hopalong(q+3, x - 3, y , z - 1))
    else (hopalong(q+5, x + 2, y, z - 10))
}
```

Our final example is an excerpt of the last of the weekly questions—the full example presents 90 lines of code to students; another 30 lines of code for method implementations are omitted. This question is rather more complex, requiring students to implement both the "Valid()" predicate to describe the class invariant of a complex mutable object, and to manipulate the "Repr" ghost field that must track the auxiliary implementation objects owned by the stack:

```
datatype StackModel = Empty | Push(val : int, prev : StackModel)

class Stack {
    var values : array<int>
    var capacity : nat
    var size : nat

    ghost const Repr : set<object>

//Define these two methods so that the hidden code below works
//   constructor(capacity_ : nat)
//   predicate Valid()
[???]

    method push(i : int)
        requires Valid()
        ensures Valid()
        modifies Repr
        ensures capacity = old(capacity)
/*omitted*/
```

4.2 Assignments

The four Dafny assignments are very similar to the overview questions in spirit—but with two main differences: they are undertaken using whichever Dafny IDE students choose (usually Visual Studio Code); and students must upload complete Dafny files into the school's standard submission system, rather than using a specialised web interface. Assignment questions are significantly larger than weekly questions. Whereas the overview questions typically aim to teach one single verification concept or Dafny construct, the assignments typically require students to combine techniques and link concepts together. To guide students' work, we again ensure rapid feedback by reporting the results of Dafny attempting to verify each submission, and we allow students to submit work any number of times. Space does not permit us to include full details of assignment questions here—however some of the more interesting questions included:

1. Add annotations to the code of a vector sum (A1) or small sorting network (A1).
2. Print out the text of the song "Ten Green Bottles" (exactly as supplied, 1743 characters) but with a program shorter than 750 characters (A1).
3. Calculate the income tax payable by an individual New Zealander (A1).
4. Calculate with Carolingian duodecimal currency or interval arithmetic (A2).
5. Verify functional implementations of sets, lists, and maps (A2, A3).
6. Test if a string is a Palindrome (A4).
7. Implement search trees (A3), tries (A3), or balanced trees (A4).
8. Implement an object-oriented mutable map (A4).

These questions obviously get harder as they go along. The first questions either ask students to annotate existing code, or write code without specifications to introduce students to the language. Even here, however, apparently simply programs such as "Ten Green Bottles" (which we do not verify against any external specifications) still require significant verification effort to be accepted by Dafny—at least four or five lines of annotation out of a 25-line solution. Dafny needs to prove termination, and that all array accesses are in bounds, and this necessitates preconditions constraining arguments on all subsidiary methods and functions. The final assignment questions are as complex as the final data structure examples from *Program Proofs*.

4.3   Essay

A reflective essay provides the last 20% of the course. This is the final assessment component that students complete—although due to VUW's regulations, it is due together with the fourth Dafny assignment, as late as possible in the term. The core rubric for the essay is straightforward: to write no more than 750 words reflecting on students' "experience with verified programming in Dafny to ensure software correctness', in the style of a blog post aimed to communicate to other students, developers, or software engineers. Students are invited to select a problem (typically from the final assignment, but "in case of emergency" they may choose any programming problem) and then explain how they used Dafny to specify, implement, and verify their chosen problem; to discuss which features of Dafny made this easier (or harder); and if they had to do it again, what they would do differently and why.

This essay fulfills two important purposes in the course design. Towards higher marks, a VUW "A−" grade is 80%: a student who completes all the assignments perfectly but chose not to attempt the essay would get that grade. The essay thus enables us to distinguish the truly outstanding "A+" students from the merely excellent "A" or "A−": students. At the other end of the grade distribution, reasonable attempts at the weekly questions and the first two assignments should yield 40%: an essay that demonstrates merely "adequate evidence of learning" is then sufficient to pass the course.

5   Experience with Dafny

Mathematics may still be taught via pencil and paper (or LaTeX) but these days teaching programming is impossible without a toolchain: a language implementation, a development environment, and the other accoutrements students expect. Our course design teaches verification as a specially intense kind of programming ("More programming than programming is our motto" [46])—this requires a toolchain that is reliable, scalable, and supported enough to cope with daily use by hundreds of students. Luckily, we found the current versions Dafny were certainly good enough for our purposes: we were able to spend the vast majority of our efforts in teaching the practices and principles of verification, rather than working around problems and bugs in the tools. While we encountered roughly one serious bug during each course offering so far, the Dafny project team resolved them assiduously. Our overall experience with Dafny was very positive.

Probably the biggest issue we encountered was just finding the resources – notably staff time and effort—to support rapid feedback via automated marking of the weekly questions and the assignments. The problem was not so much the necessary infrastructure, which is essentially a one-off cost, but the advance preparation needed for automated marking of every assignment. Basically, marking must be complete before an assignment can be released, rendering it no longer possible to write underspecified assignments which point students in a general direction, wait until the assignment deadline, and then take as much time as necessary *after the students have submitted their work* to work out the marks, the desired solutions, or even *whether solutions are possible*. All this work must now be completed beforehand.

That said, we did strike three more technical issues that could be addressed via changes to Dafny's design:

Program Testing: We encourage students to start by testing their implementations, because it is easier to verify code that is correct than it is to verify incorrect code:-). Dafny's tight integration of proving and programming unfortunately means that programs cannot easily be tested until they are fully verified. We observed students continually "commenting out" assertions and preconditions to be able to test their programs, and then undoing those comments to undertake verification. There are four related problems here.

First, Dafny's requirements to prove all memory accesses safe, and that all programs terminate, often mean even simple programs have to be heavily annotated just to compile. A method to swap two array elements will require array reads and writes to be in bounds; the obvious (and best practice) solution is to define method preconditions which ensure method arguments are in bounds: but now all callers of the method must themselves do enough to meet those preconditions.

Second, while annotations, assumptions, and non-totality declarations etc. can be used to remove the need for some of these checks, they still require students to annotate their programs explicitly, i.e. so students always have to deal with the checks even if just to tell Dafny to ignore them!

Third, while Dafny does support command line options to e.g. ignore verification and compile and run programs directly, verification is an all-or-nothing, static affair: either verification is attempted for the whole program, or all specification and verification constructs are ignored.

Fourth (and finally) the options to control verification are buried in the command line, and are not surfaced in the Visual Studio Code IDE.

Following the example of Gradual Dafny [18] and Gradual Verification [3,5,48] more generally should make testing easier. Ideally students would be able to run programs in a "test mode" where Dafny checks as many assertions, assumptions, and pre- and postconditions as possible dynamically. Students could then express a series of unit tests as Dafny assertions: if the program verifies, well and good; but if not, they would still have the option of running the program and using print statements or host debuggers to interrogate program state. Recent Dafny releases [34] now support an `expect` statement that does Gradual Dafny style dynamic checking: implementing this option may be as simple as translating Dafny's verification condition as `expects` rather than `asserts`.

Verification Debugging: Much of the work of verifying Dafny programs involves students annotating their code—adding require and ensure clauses and assertions until the verifier has enough information to discharge its proof obligations. Students find this hard because it is not obvious what Dafny "knows" at any given program point: which assertions Dafny is able to prove, which assertions Dafny is able to refute, and which assertions Dafny is unable to answer (i.e. where the prover times out). We also observed cases where Dafny is unable to verify an assertion because it does not have enough information about variable values—this is particularly prevalent in code where e.g. students have forgotten to write method postconditions, or have not realised a particular postcondition is necessary. This manifests as Dafny being unable to verify an assertion about a method's return value, and simultaneously unable to verify the negation of that same assertion. Even good students find this situation intensely frustrating. Ideally Dafny would be able to give programmers more information about what it knows, e.g. by querying its underlying solver [12].

Mutable Object Structure: Dafny is one of the few tools that can verify programs built from composite structures of mutable objects using class invariants and representation sets. In practice, this requires either explicit definitions of "Valid" and "Repr" attributes [36] which are verbose and complex, or implicit definitions generated via the "autocontracts" attribute [35] which are concise but opaque. Few students were able to use either mechanism effectively. Perhaps by building on work verifying Rust programs, such as Prusti [4] and RustBelt [29], it should be possible to add ownership annotations to fields and parameters, to check those annotations as with Rust's borrow checker [14,31,39] and thus extend the implicit definitions already generated by autocontracts.

We also encountered a number of pragmatic issues that arose with Dafny, but which appear to be consequences of Dafny's design choices, and as such are less amenable to technical fixes.

Idiosyncrasies: Dafny's syntax is sometimes idiosyncratic, which students found hard to follow. To give just one example, here are a method and function to add two numbers:

```
method addM (a : int, b : int) returns (c : int) { c := a + b; }
function method addF (a : int, b : int) : int { a + b }
```

The syntax for declaring the return values are different (**returns** vs :); the syntax for actually returning the results are different; a final semicolon is mandatory in the method and forbidden in the function. Adding insult to injury, methods and functions then perform very differently in the verifier:

```
0    var m := addM(x,y);
1    var f := addF(x,y);
2    assert m = x + y;    //Fails to verify
3    assert f = x + y;    //Verifies
```

Dafny verifies the assertion on line 4, because functions are incorporated into the verification context. Dafny fails to verify the assertion on line 3, however, because methods are always abstracted by their postconditions, and the declaration of addM omits postconditions. There are reasons for these choices, but they do make the language more difficult to learn.

Implicit vs. Explicit Verification: We have described as taking an implicit (aka "auto-active" [37]) approach to verification. Our students, or Dafny programmers in general, do not construct proofs explicitly, in some verification domain that reflects on the base domain of the program: rather they work in an extended programming language domain. That is, students focus on programs, and program verification, but not on the foundations of logic, programming languages, and critically, not on proof. Our teaching practice builds on this implicit approach: students definitely need an implicit understanding of the underlying formal concepts—because they will be incapable of completing any work without that understanding—but we present those concepts completely within the programming approach: we don't discuss the semantics of programming languages, weakest preconditions, the kind of inferences Dafny's underlying solver is making, let alone how it works. We approach software verification in the same way that most software engineering courses approach statically-typed languages: students can understand the benefits, and use the type systems, but could not give a type-theoretic explanation for why their programs don't compile.

Arguably the biggest weakness of this implicit approach is that it sidesteps the question of proof. Dafny does not illustrate proofs of programs (other than symbolic dumps designed for debugging Dafny). As a result, we do not expose students to formal proofs, and in fact students never need to understand what a proof is.

We do teach that Dafny assertions can be used as "hints" to the verifier checker; we also show how Dafny (ghost) functions can be used within specifications or assertions to embody lemmas that Dafny cannot find itself. In the latter part of the course, questions require (ghost) data and methods to model the state of imperative objects. We mention Dafny's calc statement that supports line-by-line reasoning only in passing.

We consider this a trade-off worth making: the course stays focused on program verification, through a programming lens, and we use the time to allow students to complete more significant examples with more complex verification constructs, rather than teaching proof and necessarily working on smaller examples.

6   Evaluation

As part of VUW's quality assurance process, we conducted a standard evaluation of SWEN324. Under the terms of that process, we can only report the quantitative results here. The quantitative questions employed a 5-point Likert scale ("Strongly Agree/Agree/Neither Agree nor Disagree/Strongly Disagree" unless otherwise noted) and employ both objective and affective questions. We received 19 questionnaires from 88 students nominally enrolled in the course when the evaluations where conducted.

Based on the quantitative feedback, over 70% of students either agreed or strongly agreed that the course was well organised, and that its objectives were communicated well. 70% of students considered the workload "about right", although of the balance, 20% considered the workload "too much" or "far too much" while only 5% considered that it was "too little".

Considering quality measures, most students considered the course overall as "very good" (58%) or "excellent" (21%)—although one outlier did rank the course as "poor". Apart from that outlier, all evaluated students agreed or strongly agreed that what they had learned in the course had been valuable, and over half that the course had stimulated interest in the subject "a great deal". This results in a median overall score or 2.0 "very good". Compared with other courses in the faculty, that is a slightly worse median (1.9), but perhaps more relevant are comparisons with earlier offerings of more traditional versions of the course. Over the last ten years, across many iterations of the course, these have ranged from 3.8 "Poor" to 2.3 (approaching "Good") with most offerings around 2.6–2.7—i.e. this version seems substantially better.

Finally, given the focus of our course design on online tools and automatic marking to provide rapid feedback, it is gratifying that 80% of students agreed or strongly agreed that the "online components of the course contributed to my learning". Over 90% agreed or strongly agreed that "Assessment tasks have helped me to learn" and that "I received helpful feedback on my progress." This is about as strong evidence for the benefits of the "programming style" approach we adopted in SWEN324, and the use of automated marking and feedback, that one is ever likely to receive.

Overall we consider the experiment of our redesign of SWEN324 a success. Following this programming-centric approach, almost all students were able to demonstrate enough engagement with practical software verification to pass the course, and those students who chose to put in the necessary time and effort were able to complete quite significant verification tasks. In spite of the "mastery" approach taken in much of the course, the final assignments and essays, were sufficient to ensure a good spread of grades across the course.

We are aware that the practical, pragmatic, programming focus of this approach has some trade-offs and costs. While students are able to program with Dafny, their knowledge of logic and indeed of formal methods and software verification is latent, i.e. implicit. For example, students would be able to propose preconditions for a given Dafny function (e.g. to avoid array bounds errors or invalid computation), and given interaction with a Dafny IDE, to write preconditions that Dafny could verify: many students could argue informally about why such preconditions were necessary. Because the knowledge is not explicit, they would not be able to present the formal rationale for those preconditions, to derive them from e.g. weakest preconditions, or to produce a formal proof that those preconditions would definitely rule out crashes at run time. We had hoped that these topics could be addressed in a follow-on fourth-year course, however it seems we will not have that opportunity.

The other costs were essentially resources: all students needed access to the Dafny tool at all times; technical support from tutors thus needed to be provided whenever possible. Automated marking (both weekly questions and assignments) was essential to maintaining that programming focus, and directly supported learning. Preparing the automated questions, and then validating them by verifying several different solutions also required significant time and effort, by both tutors and academic staff. Some of this effort (e.g. weekly questions) could be amortised over multiple offerings of the course, but most institutions would need to refresh the main assignments for each course offering—at least in institutions without very strong honour code traditions that prevent sharing solutions across cohorts.

7 Conclusion

Getting code to work is one thing.
Proving it does what it's supposed to is something else.
Convincing Dafny you've proved it does what it's supposed to
is something else entirely.

"Motto for a Software Correctness Course"
Thomas J. "Tad" Peckish (attrib.), twitter, Oct 4 2020

Formal methods are becoming more popular in software engineering practice, and accordingly more common in software engineering education course work. This shift has implications for how we teach: a course that aims to ensure every computer science or software engineering student has understanding of formal methods, and some basic exposure to formal tools, must necessarily be different to a course that (explicitly or implicitly) aims to prepare students for graduate work. We have described our experience in redeveloping our formal methods course to be for the many, not the few; by employing tool and strategies typically used to teach programming, rather than those of mathematics. So far, this approach has been fruitful: most students who enroll in the course are able to pass it; are able to actually complete some small problems using Dafny; and overall consider the course worthwhile. The key factors supporting this outcome were the Dafny tool, which is now sufficiently mature to be used at this scale, and the necessary time and effort to prepare weekly questions and assignments in advance to support feedback via automatic marking. We hope to continue with work, both to integrate formal methods ever more tightly into teaching programming, and to investigate how tools such as Dafny can best support this approach.

Acknowledgements. Thanks to Rustan Leino and James Wilcox for all their help with Dafny; to our colleagues Marco Servetto for the "marcotron" weekly question system, to Royce Brown, Christo Muller, and the ECS technical staff for their support with the course automation; to Lindsay Groves, longtime custodian of Formal Methods at VUW through various iterations (COMP202, SWEN202, SWEN224, SWEN324); to the reviewers for their helpful comments; and above all to the students who choose to stay with SWEN324 in spite of everything.

This work was supported in part by the Royal Society of New Zealand Marsden Fund Grant VUW1815, and by a gift from Agoric.

References

1. Aceto, L., Ingólfsdóttir, A.: Introducing formal methods to first-year students in three intensive weeks. In: Ferreira, J.F., Mendes, A., Menghi, C. (eds.) FMTea 2021. LNCS, vol. 13122, pp. 1–17. Springer, Cham (2021). https://doi.org/10.1007/978-3-030-91550-6_1
2. Angelo, T.: A teacher's dozen-fourteen general research-based principles for improving higher learning. AAHE Bulletin (1993)
3. Arlt, S., Rubio-González, C., Rümmer, P., Schäf, M., Shankar, N.: The gradual verifier. In: Badger, J.M., Rozier, K.Y. (eds.) NFM 2014. LNCS, vol. 8430, pp. 313–327. Springer, Cham (2014). https://doi.org/10.1007/978-3-319-06200-6_27
4. Astrauskas, V., Müller, P., Poli, F., Summers, A.J.: Leveraging rust types for modular specification and verification. Proc. ACM Program. Lang. 3(OOPSLA), 1–30 (2019)
5. Bader, J., Aldrich, J., Tanter, É.: Gradual program verification. In: VMCAI 2018. LNCS, vol. 10747, pp. 25–46. Springer, Cham (2018). https://doi.org/10.1007/978-3-319-73721-8_2
6. Beckert, B., Grebing, S.: Evaluating the usability of interactive verification systems. In: COMPARE, pp. 3–17. Citeseer (2012)
7. Blazy, S.: Teaching deductive verification in Why3 to undergraduate students. In: Dongol, B., Petre, L., Smith, G. (eds.) FMTea 2019. LNCS, vol. 11758, pp. 52–66. Springer, Cham (2019). https://doi.org/10.1007/978-3-030-32441-4_4
8. Bornholt, J., et al.: Using lightweight formal methods to validate a key-value storage node in amazon S3. In: Proceedings of the ACM SIGOPS 28th Symposium on Operating Systems Principles, pp. 836–850 (2021)
9. Brooks, F., Kugler, H.: No silver bullet, April 1987
10. Cerone, A., Roggenbach, M. (eds.): FMFun 2019. CCIS, vol. 1301. Springer, Cham (2021). https://doi.org/10.1007/978-3-030-71374-4
11. Chlipala, A.: Certified Programming with Dependent Types: A Pragmatic Introduction to the CoQ Proof Assistant. MIT Press, Cambridge (2013)
12. Christakis, M., Leino, K.R.M., Müller, P., Wüstholz, V.: Integrated environment for diagnosing verification errors. In: Chechik, M., Raskin, J.-F. (eds.) TACAS 2016. LNCS, vol. 9636, pp. 424–441. Springer, Heidelberg (2016). https://doi.org/10.1007/978-3-662-49674-9_25
13. Cook, B.: Formal reasoning about the security of amazon web services. In: Chockler, H., Weissenbacher, G. (eds.) CAV 2018. LNCS, vol. 10981, pp. 38–47. Springer, Cham (2018). https://doi.org/10.1007/978-3-319-96145-3_3
14. Dietl, W., Dietzel, S., Ernst, M.D., Muşlu, K., Schiller, T.W.: Building and using pluggable type-checkers. In: Proceedings of the 33rd International Conference on Software Engineering, pp. 681–690 (2011)
15. Dongol, B., Petre, L., Smith, G. (eds.): FMTea 2019. LNCS, vol. 11758. Springer, Cham (2019). https://doi.org/10.1007/978-3-030-32441-4
16. Ettinger, R.: Lessons of formal program design in Dafny. In: Ferreira, J.F., Mendes, A., Menghi, C. (eds.) FMTea 2021. LNCS, vol. 13122, pp. 84–100. Springer, Cham (2021). https://doi.org/10.1007/978-3-030-91550-6_7
17. Ferreira, J.F., Mendes, A., Menghi, C. (eds.): FMTea 2021. LNCS, vol. 13122. Springer, Cham (2021). https://doi.org/10.1007/978-3-030-91550-6
18. Figueroa, I., García, B., Leger, P.: Towards progressive program verification in Dafny. In: Proceedings of the XXII Brazilian Symposium on Programming Languages, pp. 90–97 (2018)
19. Flannery-Dailey, F., Wagner, R.L.: Wake up! Gnosticism and Buddhism in the Matrix. J. Religion Film 5(2), 4 (2001)
20. Garavel, H., Beek, M.H., Pol, J.: The 2020 expert survey on formal methods. In: ter Beek, M.H., Ničković, D. (eds.) FMICS 2020. LNCS, vol. 12327, pp. 3–69. Springer, Cham (2020). https://doi.org/10.1007/978-3-030-58298-2_1

21. Grebing, S., Ulbrich, M.: Usability recommendations for user guidance in deductive program verification. In: Ahrendt, W., Beckert, B., Bubel, R., Hähnle, R., Ulbrich, M. (eds.) Deductive Software Verification: Future Perspectives. LNCS, vol. 12345, pp. 261–284. Springer, Cham (2020). https://doi.org/10.1007/978-3-030-64354-6_11
22. Green, T.R.G., Petre, M.: Usability analysis of visual programming environments: a 'cognitive dimensions' framework. J. Vis. Lang. Comput. 7(2), 131–174 (1996)
23. Greengard, S.: The Internet of Things. MIT Press, Cambridge (2021)
24. Güdemann, M.: Online teaching of verification of C programs in applied computer science. In: Ferreira, J.F., Mendes, A., Menghi, C. (eds.) FMTea 2021. LNCS, vol. 13122, pp. 18–34. Springer, Cham (2021). https://doi.org/10.1007/978-3-030-91550-6_2
25. Hawblitzel, C., et al.: IronFleet: proving safety and liveness of practical distributed systems. Commun. ACM 60(7), 83–92 (2017)
26. Holzmann, G.J.: The SPIN Model Checker: Primer and Reference Manual. Addison-Wesley, Boston (2003)
27. Jackson, D.: Software Abstractions: Logic, Language, and Analysis. MIT Press, Cambridge (2006)
28. Jones, C.B., Misra, J.: Theories of Programming: The Life and Works of Tony Hoare. Morgan & Claypool, Williston (2021)
29. Jung, R., Jourdan, J.H., Krebbers, R., Dreyer, D.: RustBelt: securing the foundations of the rust programming language. Proc. ACM Program. Lang. 2(POPL), 1–34 (2017)
30. Kamburjan, E., Grätz, L.: Increasing engagement with interactive visualization: formal methods as serious games. In: Ferreira, J.F., Mendes, A., Menghi, C. (eds.) FMTea 2021. LNCS, vol. 13122, pp. 43–59. Springer, Cham (2021). https://doi.org/10.1007/978-3-030-91550-6_4
31. Klabnik, S., Nichols, C.: The Rust Programming Language (Covers Rust 2018). No Starch Press, San Francisco (2019)
32. Körner, P., Krings, S.: Increasing student self-reliance and engagement in model-checking courses. In: Ferreira, J.F., Mendes, A., Menghi, C. (eds.) FMTea 2021. LNCS, vol. 13122, pp. 60–74. Springer, Cham (2021). https://doi.org/10.1007/978-3-030-91550-6_5
33. Lamport, L.: Specifying Systems: The TLA+ Language and Tools for Hardware and Software Engineers. Pearson, London (2002)
34. Leino, K.R.M.: Dafny 3.0.0 release. https://github.com/dafny-lang/dafny/-rcleases/tag/v3.0.0
35. Leino, K.R.M.: Developing verified programs with Dafny. In: 2013 35th International Conference on Software Engineering (ICSE), pp. 1488–1490. IEEE (2013)
36. Leino, K.R.M.: Program Proofs. Available from Lulu.com (2020)
37. Leino, K.R.M., Moskal, M.: Usable auto-active verification. In: Usable Verification Workshop (UV10) (2010)
38. Rustan, K., Leino, M., Nelson, G.: An extended static checker for modula-3. In: Koskimies, K. (ed.) CC 1998. LNCS, vol. 1383, pp. 302–305. Springer, Heidelberg (1998). https://doi.org/10.1007/BFb0026441
39. Markstrum, S., Marino, D., Esquivel, M., Millstein, T., Andreae, C., Noble, J.: JavaCOP: declarative pluggable types for java. ACM Trans. Program. Lang. Syst. (TOPLAS) 32(2), 1–37 (2010)
40. Meyer, B.: Touch of Class. Springer, Heidelberg (2009). https://doi.org/10.1007/978-3-540-92145-5
41. Müller, P., Ruskiewicz, J.N.: Using debuggers to understand failed verification attempts. In: Butler, M., Schulte, W. (eds.) FM 2011. LNCS, vol. 6664, pp. 73–87. Springer, Heidelberg (2011). https://doi.org/10.1007/978-3-642-21437-0_8
42. Noble, J., Pearce, D.J., Groves, L.: Introducing Alloy in a software modelling course. In: 1st Workshop on Formal Methods in Computer Science Education (FORMED) (2008)

43. Pang, A., Anslow, C., Noble, J.: What programming languages do developers use? A theory of static vs dynamic language choice. In: 2018 IEEE Symposium on Visual Languages and Human-Centric Computing (VL/HCC), pp. 239–247. IEEE (2018)
44. Paulin-Mohring, C.: Introduction to the Coq proof-assistant for practical software verification. In: Meyer, B., Nordio, M. (eds.) LASER 2011. LNCS, vol. 7682, pp. 45–95. Springer, Heidelberg (2012). https://doi.org/10.1007/978-3-642-35746-6_3
45. Pearce, D.J., Groves, L.: Designing a verifying compiler: lessons learned from developing Whiley. Sci. Comput. Program. 113, 191–220 (2015)
46. Scott, R.: Blade runner. Motion Picture (1982)
47. Wayne, H.: Temporal logic. In: Practical TLA+, pp. 97–110. Apress, Berkeley (2018). https://doi.org/10.1007/978-1-4842-3829-5_6
48. Wise, J., Bader, J., Wong, C., Aldrich, J., Tanter, É., Sunshine, J.: Gradual verification of recursive heap data structures. Proc. ACM Program. Lang. 4(OOPSLA), 1–28 (2020)
49. Yatapanage, N.: Introducing formal methods to students who hate maths and struggle with programming. In: Ferreira, J.F., Mendes, A., Menghi, C. (eds.) FMTea 2021. LNCS, vol. 13122, pp. 133–145. Springer, Cham (2021). https://doi.org/10.1007/978-3-030-91550-6_10
50. Zhumagambetov, R.: Teaching formal methods in academia: a systematic literature review. In: Cerone, A., Roggenbach, M. (eds.) FMFun 2019. CCIS, vol. 1301, pp. 218–226. Springer, Cham (2021). https://doi.org/10.1007/978-3-030-71374-4_12

Zone Extrapolations in Parametric Timed Automata

Johan Arcile[✉] and Étienne André[iD]

Université de Lorraine, CNRS, Inria, LORIA, 54000 Nancy, France
johan.arcile@univ-lorraine.fr

Abstract. Timed automata (TAs) are an efficient formalism to model and verify systems with hard timing constraints, and concurrency. While TAs assume exact timing constants with infinite precision, parametric TAs (PTAs) leverage this limitation and increase their expressiveness, at the cost of undecidability. A practical explanation for the efficiency of TAs is zone extrapolation, where clock valuations beyond a given constant are considered equivalent. This concept cannot be easily extended to PTAs, due to the fact that parameters can be unbounded or can take arbitrary rational values. In this work, we propose several definitions of extrapolation for PTAs based on the M-extrapolation, and we study their correctness. Our experiments show an overall decrease of the computation time and, most importantly, allow termination of some previously unsolvable benchmarks.

Keywords: Parametric timed automata · Abstraction · Parameter synthesis · Reachability · Liveness · IMITATOR

1 Introduction

Timed automata (TAs) [1] represent an efficient and expressive formalism to model and verify systems, able to specify both hard timing constraints and concurrency; TAs are one of the most expressive decidable formalisms with timing constraints. However, TAs assume exact timing constants with infinite precision, which may not be realistic in practice; in addition, they assume full knowledge of the model, preventing verification at an early development phase. Parametric timed automata (PTAs) leverage these limitations, by allowing unknown timing constants in the model—at the cost of undecidability: the mere emptiness of the parameter valuations set for which a given (discrete) location is reachable (called *reachability emptiness*) is undecidable [2].

A practical explanation for the efficiency of TAs for reachability properties is *(zone) extrapolation*, where clock valuations beyond a given constant are considered to be equivalent. Since the seminal work [1], several works improved the

This work is partially supported by the ANR-NRF French-Singaporean research program ProMiS (ANR-19-CE25-0015).

quality and efficiency of zone extrapolation, by considering different constants per clock [12,13] or extending extrapolation to liveness properties [23,25]. This concept cannot be easily extended to PTAs, due to the fact that parameters can be unbounded, or converge toward infinitely small values.

Extrapolation in TAs. Daw and Tripakis first introduced the *extrapolation* abstraction in [18] as a mean to obtain a finite simulation of the state space of TAs. The extrapolation abstraction preserves reachability properties and is based on the largest constant appearing in any state of the model, which can be computed syntactically from the constants present in its guards and invariants. In [12] Behrmann *et al.* redefine this abstraction with individual clock bounds (i.e., the largest constant is computed for each clock) and will later refer to it in [13] as the M-extrapolation. Experiments are performed using UPPAAL [22]. Tripakis [25] showed that the M-extrapolation is correct for checking emptiness of timed Büchi automata, i.e., checking for accepting cycles in TAs.

Parameter Synthesis for PTAs. Most non-trivial decision problems are undecidable for PTAs (see [3] for a survey). As a consequence exact synthesis is usually out of reach, except for small numbers of clocks or of parameters (see, e.g., [2,14,17]). For general subclasses (without bound on the number of variables), exact synthesis results are very scarce. Some fit in the L/U-PTAs subclass[1] [20], and notably in the subclasses called U-PTAs (resp. L-PTAs) [16], where each timing parameter is constrained to be always compared to a clock as an upper (resp. lower) bound, i.e., of the form $x \leq p$ (resp. $p \leq x$). The only known situations when exact reachability-synthesis (i.e., synthesis of all parameter valuations for which a given location is reachable) can be achieved for subclasses of PTAs are *i)* for U-PTAs (resp. L-PTAs) over *integer-valued* timing parameters [16]; *ii)* for the whole PTA class, over *bounded and integer-valued* parameters (which reduces to TAs) [21]; and *iii)* for reset-update-to-parameters-PTAs ("R-U2P-PTAs"), in which all clocks must be updated (possibly to a parameter) whenever a clock is compared to a parameter in a guard [7]. On the negative side, even L/U-PTAs show negative results for synthesis: while reachability-emptiness is decidable for L/U-PTAs [20], reachability-synthesis is intractable (its result cannot be represented using a finite union of polyhedra) [21]; and even in the very restricted subclass of U-PTAs without invariant, TCTL-emptiness (i.e., emptiness of the parameter valuations set for which a TCTL formula is valid) is undecidable [6].

We performed a first attempt to define an extrapolation for PTAs in [8]: we adapted the M-extrapolation to the context of PTAs, although restricted to *bounded* parameter domains only. No implementation was provided. In [15], the authors also define an extrapolation very similar to [8]. Compared to [8], we reuse here some of the definitions of [8], and we significantly extend the definition of extrapolations; we also consider several subclasses of models, as well as liveness properties; we also conduct an experimental evaluation.

---

[1] While "L/U" means in both cases "lower-upper (bound)", L/U-PTAs are a completely different concept from LU-extrapolation for (P)TAs.

Contributions. We propose several definitions of extrapolation for PTAs, and study their correctness. In the context of bounded parameter domains, we extend the parametric M-extrapolation from [8] to individual clock bounds. Those extrapolations are combined with results from [16] to cope with the issue raised by unbounded parameters. We notably consider variants of the U-PTAs and L-PTAs. We show that, on the subclass of (unbounded) PTAs on which they apply, those abstractions preserve not only reachability-synthesis but also cycle-synthesis ("liveness"). We conduct experiments using the parametric timed model checker IMITATOR [4], including on the most general class (rational-valued, possibly unbounded parameters). With the aforementioned negative theoretical results in mind, our evaluation focuses on evaluating the speed enhancement, and the increase of termination chances for our case studies. We show that, overall, extrapolation decreases the verification time and, most importantly, can effectively help solving previously unsolvable benchmarks.

Outline. We introduce the necessary preliminaries in Sect. 2. The M-extrapolation in the bounded context (partially reusing results from [8]) is studied in Sect. 3. Section 4 adapts the M-extrapolation to the unbouded context for reachability properties. Liveness properties are discussed in Sect. 5. Finally, Sect. 6 benchmarks the abstractions, and Sect. 7 concludes the paper.

2   Preliminaries

Throughout this paper, we assume a set $\mathbb{X} = \{x_1, \ldots, x_H\}$ of *clocks*, i.e., real-valued variables that evolve at the same rate. A clock valuation is a function $w : \mathbb{X} \to \mathbb{R}_+$. We write $\vec{0}$ for the clock valuation assigning 0 to all clocks. Given $d \in \mathbb{R}_+$, $w + d$ denotes the valuation s.t. $(w + d)(x) = w(x) + d$, for all $x \in \mathbb{X}$. Given $R \subseteq \mathbb{X}$, we define the *reset* of a valuation w, denoted by $[w]_R$, as follows: $[w]_R(x) = 0$ if $x \in R$, and $[w]_R(x) = w(x)$ otherwise.

We assume a set $\mathbb{P} = \{p_1, \ldots, p_K\}$ of *parameters*, i.e., unknown constants. A parameter *valuation* v is a function $v : \mathbb{P} \to \mathbb{Q}$. Given two valuations v_1, v_2, we write $v_1 \geq v_2$ whenever $\forall p \in \mathbb{P}$, $v_1(p) \geq v_2(p)$.

In the following, we assume $\bowtie \in \{<, \leq, =, \geq, >\}$. A *constraint* C over $\mathbb{X} \cup \mathbb{P}$ is a conjunction of inequalities of the form $lt \bowtie 0$, where lt is a linear term over $\mathbb{X} \cup \mathbb{P}$ of the form $\sum_{1 \leq i \leq H} \alpha_i x_i + \sum_{1 \leq j \leq K} \beta_j p_j + d$, with $x_i \in \mathbb{X}$, $p_j \in \mathbb{P}$, and $\alpha_i, \beta_j, d \in \mathbb{Z}$. We also refer to constraints as their geometrical representation, i.e., of *convex polyhedron*. We denote by $\bot$ the constraint over $\mathbb{P}$ corresponding to the empty set of parameter valuations.

Given a parameter valuation v, $v(C)$ denotes the constraint over $\mathbb{X}$ obtained by replacing each parameter p in C with $v(p)$. Likewise, given a clock valuation w, $w(v(C))$ denotes the expression obtained by replacing each clock x in $v(C)$ with $w(x)$. We say that v *satisfies* C, denoted by $v \models C$, if the set of clock valuations satisfying $v(C)$ is nonempty. Given a parameter valuation v and a clock valuation w, we denote by $w|v$ the valuation over $\mathbb{X} \cup \mathbb{P}$ such that for all clocks x, $w|v(x) = w(x)$ and for all parameters p, $w|v(p) = v(p)$. We use the notation $w|v \models C$ to indicate that $w(v(C))$ evaluates to true. We say that C is *satisfiable* if $\exists w, v$ s.t. $w|v \models C$.

We define the *time elapsing* of C, denoted by $C^{\nearrow}$, as the constraint over $\mathbb{X}$ and $\mathbb{P}$ obtained from C by delaying all clocks by an arbitrary amount of time. That is, $w'|v \models C^{\nearrow}$ iff $\exists w : \mathbb{X} \to \mathbb{R}_+, \exists d \in \mathbb{R}_+$ s.t. $w|v \models C \wedge w' = w + d$.

Given $R \subseteq \mathbb{X}$, we define the *reset* of C, denoted by $[C]_R$, as the constraint obtained from C by resetting the clocks in R, and keeping the other clocks unchanged. We denote by $C{\downarrow}_{\mathbb{P}}$ the projection of C onto $\mathbb{P}$, i.e., obtained by eliminating the variables not in $\mathbb{P}$ (e.g., using Fourier-Motzkin [24]).

A *simple clock guard* is an inequality of the form $x \bowtie \sum_{1 \leq i \leq K} \alpha_i p_i + z$, with $p_i \in \mathbb{P}$, and $\alpha_i, z \in \mathbb{Z}$. A *clock guard* is a constraint over $\mathbb{X} \cup \mathbb{P}$ defined by a conjunction of simple clock guards. Given a clock guard g, we write $w \models v(g)$ if the expression obtained by replacing each x with $w(x)$ and each p with $v(p)$ in g evaluates to true.

PTAs. Parametric timed automata (PTAs) extend timed automata with parameters within guards and invariants in place of integer constants [2].

Definition 1 (PTA). *A PTA $\mathcal{A}$ is a tuple $\mathcal{A} = (\Sigma, L, \ell_0, L_F, \mathbb{X}, \mathbb{P}, \mathbb{D}, I, E)$, where: i) Σ is a finite set of actions, i) L is a finite set of locations, iii) $\ell_0 \in L$ is the initial location, iv) $L_F \subseteq L$ is a set of accepting locations, v) $\mathbb{X}$ is a finite set of clocks, vi) $\mathbb{P}$ is a finite set of parameters, vii) $\mathbb{D} : \mathbb{P} \to (\mathbb{Q} \cup \{-\infty\}) \times (\mathbb{Q} \cup \{+\infty\})$ is the parameter domain, viii) I is the invariant, assigning to every $\ell \in L$ a clock guard $I(\ell)$, ix) E is a finite set of edges $e = (\ell, g, a, R, \ell')$ where $\ell, \ell' \in L$ are the source and target locations, $a \in \Sigma$, $R \subseteq \mathbb{X}$ is a set of clocks to be reset, and g is a clock guard.*

Let $\mathbb{G}(\mathcal{A})$ denote the set of all simple clock guards of the PTA $\mathcal{A}$, i.e., all simple clock guards being a conjunct within a guard or an invariant of $\mathcal{A}$. Given a clock $x \in \mathbb{X}$, we denote by $\mathbb{G}^x(\mathcal{A}) \subseteq \mathbb{G}(\mathcal{A})$ the set of simple clock guards where x appears, i.e., is bound by a non-0 coefficient. A clock x of $\mathcal{A}$ is said to be a *parametric clock* if it is compared to at least one parameter (with a non-0 coefficient) in at least one guard of $\mathbb{G}^x(\mathcal{A})$.

The parameter domain of a PTA is the admissible range of the parameters. Given p, given $\mathbb{D}(p) = (b^-, b^+)$, $\mathbb{D}^-(p)$ denotes b^- while $\mathbb{D}^+(p)$ denotes b^+. The admissible valuations for p are therefore $[\mathbb{D}^-(p), \mathbb{D}^+(p)]$ (the domain is *closed* unless on the side of an infinite bound). A *bounded* parameter domain assigns to each parameter a minimum and a maximum rational bound. In that case, $\mathbb{D}^-(p_i) > -\infty$ and $\mathbb{D}^+(p_i) < +\infty$. A bounded parameter domain can be seen as a hyperrectangle in K dimensions. Any parameter that is not bounded is *unbounded*. Note that an unbounded parameter can still have a lower bound or an upper bound $\in \mathbb{Q}$. A PTA is *bounded* if its parameter domain is bounded; otherwise, it is *unbounded*.

Given a parameter valuation v, we denote by $v(\mathcal{A})$ the non-parametric structure where all occurrences of a parameter p_i have been replaced by $v(p_i)$. We denote as a *timed automaton* any structure $v(\mathcal{A})$, by assuming a rescaling of the constants: by multiplying all constants in $v(\mathcal{A})$ by the least common multiple of their denominators, we obtain an equivalent (integer-valued) TA [1].

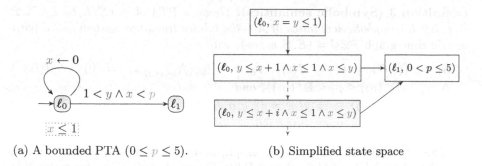

(a) A bounded PTA $(0 \leq p \leq 5)$.   (b) Simplified state space

Fig. 1. A bounded PTA and its infinite state space.

Example 1. Figure 1a displays a bounded PTA. We have $\mathbb{G}(\mathcal{A}) = \{x \leq 1, 1 < y, x < p\}$, $\mathbb{G}^x(\mathcal{A}) = \{x \leq 1, x < p\}$, and $\mathbb{G}^y(\mathcal{A}) = \{1 < y\}$. The valuation of p can be any rational value in $[0, 5]$. Therefore, this PTA can be seen as the abstract representation for an infinite number of TAs.

Definition 2 (Semantics of a TA). *Given a PTA* $\mathcal{A} = (\Sigma, L, \ell_0, L_F, \mathbb{X}, \mathbb{P}, \mathbb{D}, I, E)$ *and a parameter valuation* v, *the concrete semantics of* $v(\mathcal{A})$ *is given by the timed transition system* $(S, s_0, \rightarrow)$, *with*

- $S = \{(\ell, w) \in L \times \mathbb{R}_{\geq 0}^H \mid w \models v(I(\ell))\}$, $s_0 = (\ell_0, \vec{0})$,
- $\rightarrow$ *consists of the (continuous) delay and discrete transition relations:*
  - *delay transitions:* $(\ell, w) \xmapsto{d} (\ell, w + d)$, *with* $d \in \mathbb{R}_{\geq 0}$, *if* $\forall d' \in [0, d], (\ell, w + d') \in S$;
  - *discrete transitions:* $(\ell, w) \xmapsto{e} (\ell', w')$, *if* $(\ell, w), (\ell', w') \in S$, *and there exists* $e = (\ell, g, a, R, \ell') \in E$, *such that* $w' = [w]_R$, *and* $w \models v(g)$.

Moreover, we write $(\ell, w) \xrightarrow{(d,e)} (\ell', w')$ for a combination of a delay and discrete transition if $\exists w'' : (\ell, w) \xmapsto{d} (\ell, w'') \xmapsto{e} (\ell', w')$.

Given a TA $v(\mathcal{A})$ with concrete semantics $(S, s_0, \rightarrow)$, we refer to the states of S as the *concrete states* of $v(\mathcal{A})$. A *run* of $v(\mathcal{A})$ is an alternating sequence of concrete states of $v(\mathcal{A})$ and pairs of edges and delays starting from the initial state s_0 and is of the form $s_0, (d_0, e_0), s_1, \cdots s_i, (d_i, e_i), \cdots$ with $i = 0, 1, \ldots$, $e_i \in E$, $d_i \in \mathbb{R}_{\geq 0}$ and $s_i \xrightarrow{(d_i, e_i)} s_{i+1}$. The set of all (finite or infinite) runs of a TA $v(\mathcal{A})$ is $\mathrm{Runs}(v(\mathcal{A}))$. Given a concrete state $s = (\ell, w)$, we say that s is *reachable* in $v(\mathcal{A})$ (and by extension that ℓ is reachable, or that $v(\mathcal{A})$ visits ℓ) if s appears in a run of $v(\mathcal{A})$. An infinite run is *accepting* if it visits infinitely often (at least) one location $\ell \in L_F$.

Symbolic Semantics of PTAs. Let us now recall the symbolic semantics of PTAs (see e.g., [5,20]). A symbolic state is a pair (ℓ, C) where $\ell \in L$ is a location, and C is a constraint over $\mathbb{X} \cup \mathbb{P}$ called its associated *parametric zone*.

Definition 3 (Symbolic semantics). *Given a PTA* $\mathcal{A} = (\Sigma, L, \ell_0, L_F, \mathbb{X}, \mathbb{P}, \mathbb{D}, I, E)$, *the symbolic semantics of* $\mathcal{A}$ *is the labeled transition system called* parametric zone graph $\mathcal{PZG} = (E, \mathbf{S}, \mathbf{s}_0, \Rightarrow)$, *with*

- $\mathbf{S} = \{(\ell, C) \mid C \subseteq I(\ell)\}$, $\mathbf{s}_0 = (\ell_0, (\bigwedge_{1 \le i \le H} x_i = 0)^{\nearrow} \wedge I(\ell_0) \wedge \bigwedge_{1 \le j \le K} \mathbb{D}^-(p_j) \le p_j \le \mathbb{D}^+(p_j))$, *and*
- $((\ell, C), e, (\ell', C')) \in \Rightarrow$ *if* $e = (\ell, g, a, R, \ell') \in E$ *and* $C' = ([[(C \wedge g)]_R \wedge I(\ell'))^{\nearrow} \wedge I(\ell')$, *with* C' *satisfiable.*

That is, in the parametric zone graph, nodes are symbolic states, and arcs are labeled by *edges* of the original PTA. Given $(\mathbf{s}, e, \mathbf{s}') \in \Rightarrow$, we write $\mathbf{s}' = \mathsf{Succ}(\mathbf{s}, e)$. Given a concrete state $s = (\ell, w)$ and a symbolic state $\mathbf{s} = (\ell', C)$, we write $s \in \mathbf{s}$ whenever $\ell = \ell'$ and $w \models C$.

Example 2. Figure 1b displays the parametric zone graph of the PTA in Fig. 1a. Blue states represent an infinite sequence (i being the number of times the looping transition was taken).

Computation Problems. Given a class of decision problems $\mathcal{P}$ (reachability, etc.), we consider the problem of synthesizing the set (or part of it) of parameter valuations v such that $v(\mathcal{A})$ satisfies φ. Here, we mainly focus on reachability (i.e., "does there exist a run that reaches some given location?") and liveness (i.e., "does there exist a run that visits a given location infinitely often?").

3 M- and $\vec{M}$-extrapolation for Bounded PTAs

3.1   Recalling M-extrapolation

In this subsection, we recall some results from [8,13], where the classical "k-extrapolation" used for the zone-abstraction of TAs is adapted to PTAs. While this part is not clearly a contribution of the current manuscript, we redefine some concepts from [8], and provide several original examples.

The maximal constant M is the maximum value that can appear in the guards and invariants of the PTA. When those constraints are parametric expressions, we compute the maximum value that the expression can take over any parameter valuation within the (bounded) parameter domain $\mathbb{D}$ (this maximal value is unique since expressions are linear).

Given a simple clock guard g of the form $x \bowtie \sum_{1 \le i \le K} \alpha_i p_i + z$ we define $C_{maxg}(g) = \sum_{1 \le i \le K} \alpha_i \gamma_i + z$ where *i)* $\gamma_i = \mathbb{D}^-(p_i)$ if $\alpha_i < 0$, *ii)* $\gamma_i = \mathbb{D}^+(p_i)$ if $\alpha_i > 0$, and *iii)* $\gamma_i = 0$ otherwise.

Example 3. Consider the simple clock guard $g : x \le 2p_1 - p_2 + 1$ and $p_1 \in [2,5]$, and $p_2 \in [-3, 4]$; then $C_{maxg}(g) = 2 \times 5 - (-3) + 1 = 14$.

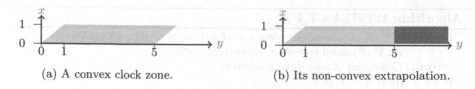

(a) A convex clock zone.   (b) Its non-convex extrapolation.

Fig. 2. Example illustrating the non-convex parametric extrapolation.

Definition 4 (Maximal constant). *Given a bounded PTA $\mathcal{A}$, for any clock $x \in \mathbb{X}$, the maximal constant for clock x is $C^x_{max}(\mathcal{A}) = \max_{g \in \mathbb{G}^x(\mathcal{A})} C_{maxg}(g)$ furthermore, the maximal constant of the PTA is $C_{max}(\mathcal{A}) = \max_{g \in \mathbb{G}(\mathcal{A})} C_{maxg}(g)$.*

Example 4. Consider again Fig. 1a. Then, $C^x_{max}(\mathcal{A}) = 5$ and $C^y_{max}(\mathcal{A}) = 1$.

Let us recall from [13] the notion of bisimulation based on M:

Lemma 1 ([13, Lemma 1]). *Let $\mathcal{A}$ be a TA. Given clock x, let $M(x)$ be an integer constant greater than or equal to $C^x_{max}(\mathcal{A})$. Let w, w' be two clock valuations. Let $\equiv_M$ be the relation defined as $w \equiv_M w'$ iff $\forall x \in \mathbb{X}$: either $w(x) = w'(x)$ or $(w(x) > M(x)$ and $w'(x) > M(x))$. The relation $\mathcal{R} = \{((\ell, w), (\ell, w')) \mid w \equiv_M w'\}$ is a bisimulation relation.*

Example 5. Let us recall the motivation for the use of an extrapolation, through the PTA $\mathcal{A}$ in Fig. 1a. After i times through the loop, we get constraints in ℓ_0 of the form $y - x \leq i$. The maximal constant is $C_{max}(\mathcal{A}) = 5$. After five loops, y can be greater than 5. Therefore, we can apply on y the classical k-extrapolation used for TAs (from [13]) of the corresponding zone. More specifically, we consider that when $y > k$, the bounds on y can be ignored. The obtained polyhedron is non-convex, but can be split into two convex ones, one where $y \leq k$ (the part without extrapolation) and one with $y > k$ (the part with extrapolation). This is depicted in Fig. 2 where Fig. 2a is the original clock zone ($y \leq x + 5 \wedge x \leq 1 \wedge x \leq y$) and Fig. 2b is its non-convex extrapolation (($x \leq y \leq 5 \wedge x \leq 1) \vee (y \geq 5 \wedge 0 < x \leq 1)$).

Let us now formally recall from [8] the concept of M-extrapolation for PTAs. First, we recall the *cylindrification* operation, which consists in *unconstraining x*.

Definition 5 (Cylindrification [8]). *For a polyhedron C and variable x, we denote by $\mathsf{Cyl}_x(C)$ the cylindrification of C along variable x, i.e., $\mathsf{Cyl}_x(C) = \{w \mid \exists w' \in C, \forall x' \neq x, w'(x') = w(x') \text{ and } w(x) \geq 0\}$.*

The (M, x)-extrapolation is an operation that splits a polyhedron into two polyhedra such that clock x is either less than or equal to M, or is strictly greater than M while being independent from the other variables.

Definition 6 ((M, x)-extrapolation [8]). *Let C a polyhedron. Let $M \in \mathbb{N}$ and x be a clock. The (M, x)-extrapolation of C, denoted by $\mathsf{Ext}^M_x(C)$, is defined as:*

$$\mathsf{Ext}^M_x(C) = \big(C \cap (x \leq M)\big) \cup \big(\mathsf{Cyl}_x(C \cap (x > M))\big) \cap (x > M)\big).$$

Algorithm 1: EEF($\mathcal{A}$, s, T, **P**)

---

input : A PTA $\mathcal{A}$, a symbolic state s = (ℓ, C), a set of target locations T, a
set **P** of passed states on the current path
output: Constraint K over the parameters

1   **if** $\ell \in T$ **then** $K \leftarrow C\!\downarrow_{\mathbb{P}}$;
2   **else**
3      $K \leftarrow \perp$;
4   **if** s $\notin$ **P** **then**
5   **for** *each outgoing e from ℓ in $\mathcal{A}$* **do**
6            $K \leftarrow K \cup \mathsf{EEF}(\mathcal{A}, \mathsf{Ext}_{\mathbb{X}}^{M}(\mathsf{Succ}(\mathsf{s}, e)), T, \mathbf{P} \cup \{\mathsf{s}\})$;

7   **return** K

Given s = (ℓ, C), we write $\mathsf{Ext}_x^M(\mathsf{s})$ for $\mathsf{Ext}_x^M(C)$.

We can now consistently define the M-extrapolation operator.

Definition 7 (M-extrapolation [8]). *Let $M \in \mathbb{N}$ and $\mathbb{X}$ be a set of clocks. The $(M, \mathbb{X})$-extrapolation operator $\mathsf{Ext}_{\mathbb{X}}^{M}$ is defined as the composition (in any order) of all Ext_x^M, for all $x \in \mathbb{X}$. When clear from the context we omit $\mathbb{X}$ and only write M-extrapolation.*

[8, Lemma 1] shows that the order of composition of (M, x)-extrapolation does not impact its results, i.e., $\mathsf{Ext}_x^M\!\left(\mathsf{Ext}_y^M(C)\right) = \mathsf{Ext}_y^M\!\left(\mathsf{Ext}_x^M(C)\right)$, and [8, Lemma 5] shows that given a symbolic state s of a PTA and a non-negative integer M greater than $C_{max}(\mathcal{A})$, for any clock x and parameter valuation v such that $(\ell, w) \in v(\mathsf{Ext}_x^M(\mathsf{s}))$ is a concrete state, there exists a state $(\ell, w') \in v(\mathsf{s})$ such that (ℓ, w) and (ℓ, w') are bisimilar.

3.2 Synthesis with Extrapolation

We now recall the reachability-synthesis algorithm, formalized in [21], and then enhanced with extrapolation (and "integer hull"—unused here) in [8]. We adapt here to our notations a version of reachability-synthesis with the extrapolation.

The goal of EEF given in Algorithm 1 ("E" stands for "extrapolation", "EF" denotes reachability) is to synthesize valuation solutions to the reachability-synthesis problem. EEF proceeds as a post-order traversal of the symbolic reachability tree, and collects all parametric constraints associated with the target locations T. In contrast to the classical reachability-synthesis algorithm EF formalized in [21], it recursively calls itself (line 6) with the *extrapolation* of the successor of the current symbolic state (this difference is highlighted in yellow in Algorithm 1).

Algorithm 1 is correct (i.e., sound and complete):[2]

Theorem 1. *Let $\mathcal{A}$ be a PTA with initial symbolic state s_0, and $T \subseteq L$ a set of target locations. Assume EEF($\mathcal{A}, \mathsf{s}_0, T, \emptyset$) terminates. We have:*

---

[2] The proofs of all our results are in a technical report [10].

1. *Soundness: If $v \in \mathsf{EEF}(\mathcal{A}, \mathbf{s}_0, T, \emptyset)$ then T is reachable in $v(\mathcal{A})$;*
2. *Completeness: For all v, if T is reachable in $v(\mathcal{A})$ then $v \in \mathsf{EEF}(\mathcal{A}, \mathbf{s}_0, T, \emptyset)$.*

3.3 Extending the M-extrapolation to Individual Bounds

Our first technical contribution is to extend the extrapolation from [8] to *individual* clock bounds, instead of a global one, in the line of what has been proposed for non-parametric TAs [13].

Definition 8 ($\vec{M}$-extrapolation). *Let $\vec{M} = \{M(x_1), \dots, M(x_H)\}$ be a set of non-negative integer constants. The $\vec{M}$-extrapolation, denoted by $\mathsf{Ext}_{\mathbb{X}}^{\vec{M}}$, is the composition (in any order) of all $\mathsf{Ext}_x^{M(x)}$ for all $x \in \mathbb{X}$.*

All we need to do for the results from [8] to hold on the $\vec{M}$-extrapolation is to adapt [8, Lemmas 1 and 5].

Lemma 2. *For all polyhedra C, integers $M(x), M(x') \geq 0$ and clock variables x and x', we have $\mathsf{Ext}_x^{M(x)}\big(\mathsf{Ext}_{x'}^{M(x')}(C)\big) = \mathsf{Ext}_{x'}^{M(x')}\big(\mathsf{Ext}_x^{M(x)}(C)\big)$.*

We now extend [8, Lemma 5] to $\mathsf{Ext}^{\vec{M}}$:

Lemma 3 ($\vec{M}$ and bisimilarity). *Let $\mathcal{A}$ be a PTA and $\mathbf{s}$ be a symbolic state of $\mathcal{A}$. Let x be a clock, $M(x) \in \mathbb{N}$ greater than or equal to $C_{max}^x(\mathcal{A})$, v be a parameter valuation and $(\ell, w) \in v(\mathsf{Ext}_x^{M(x)}(\mathbf{s}))$ be a concrete state. There exists a state $(\ell, w') \in v(\mathbf{s})$ such that (ℓ, w) and (ℓ, w') are bisimilar.*

Given $M \in \mathbb{N}$, given a vector $\vec{M}$, note that, whenever $\vec{M}(x) \leq M$ for all $x \in \mathbb{X}$, then the $\vec{M}$-extrapolation is necessarily coarser than the M-extrapolation.

Let $\vec{M}$ be such that, for all x, $\vec{M}(x) = C_{max}^x(\mathcal{A})$. Let $\vec{\mathsf{EEF}}$ denote the modification of EEF where $\mathsf{Ext}_{\mathbb{X}}^{M}$ is replaced with $\mathsf{Ext}_{\mathbb{X}}^{\vec{M}}$ (line 6 in Algorithm 1). That is, instead of computing the M-extrapolation of each symbolic state, we compute its $\vec{M}$-extrapolation. Figure 3 illustrates its effect on the state space of Fig. 1a.

Proposition 1. *Let $\mathcal{A}$ be a PTA with initial symbolic state $\mathbf{s}_0$, and $T \subseteq L$ a set of target locations. Assume $\vec{\mathsf{EEF}}(\mathcal{A}, \mathbf{s}_0, T, \emptyset)$ terminates. We have:*

1. *Soundness: If $v \in \vec{\mathsf{EEF}}(\mathcal{A}, \mathbf{s}_0, T, \emptyset)$ then T is reachable in $v(\mathcal{A})$;*
2. *Completeness: For all v, if T is reachable in $v(\mathcal{A})$ then $v \in \vec{\mathsf{EEF}}(\mathcal{A}, \mathbf{s}_0, T, \emptyset)$.*

4 $\vec{M}$-extrapolation on Unbounded PTAs

In this section, we extend the $\vec{M}$-extrapolation to subclasses of (unbounded) PTAs. This requires to be able to identify for each clock $x \in \mathbb{X}$ a constant $M(x)$ such that given a symbolic state $\mathbf{s}$ and a parameter valuation v, for any concrete state in $v(\mathsf{Ext}_x^{M(x)}(\mathbf{s}))$ there exists a bisimilar state in $v(\mathbf{s})$, i.e., Lemma 3 holds. We will consider *(i)* L-PTAs and U-PTAs (Sect. 4.1), *(ii)* bounded PTAs with additional *unbounded* lower-bound or upper-bound parameters (Sect. 4.2), and *(iii)* the full class of PTAs to which we apply extrapolation only on bounded parameters (Sect. 4.3).

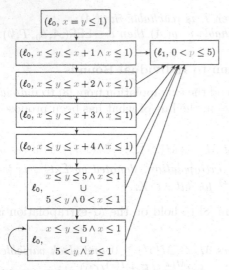

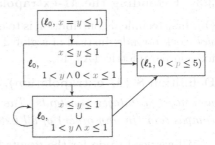

(b) Simplified state space of Fig. 1a with $\vec{M}$-extrapolation where $M(x) = 5$ and $M(y) = 1$. As $\vec{M}$-extrapolation differentiates the maximal constant of each clock, the extrapolation is applied on y after only one loop.

(a) Simplified state space of Fig. 1a with M-extrapolation.

Fig. 3. Comparison between M-extrapolation and $\vec{M}$-extrapolation.

4.1 $\vec{M}$-extrapolation on Unbounded L-PTAs and U-PTAs

Definition 9 (L-PTA and U-PTA [16]). *A PTA $\mathcal{A}$ is an L-PTA (resp. U-PTA) if, for each guard $x \bowtie \sum_{1 \leq i \leq K} \alpha_i p_i + z$ of $\mathbb{G}(\mathcal{A})$, for all i with $\alpha_i \neq 0$:*

- *$\alpha_i > 0$ and $\bowtie \in \{\geq, >\}$ (respectively $\bowtie \in \{<, \leq\}$), or*
- *$\alpha_i < 0$ and $\bowtie \in \{<, \leq\}$ (respectively $\bowtie \in \{\geq, >\}$).*

L-PTAs and U-PTAs feature a well-known monotonicity property: enlarging a parameter valuation in a U-PTA (resp. decreasing in an L-PTA) can only *add* behaviors, as recalled in the following lemma:

Lemma 4 ([16]). *Given a U-PTA (resp. L-PTA) $\mathcal{A}$, given two valuations v_1, v_2 with $v_1 \leq v_2$ (resp. $v_1 \geq v_2$), then $\mathsf{Runs}(v_1(\mathcal{A})) \subseteq \mathsf{Runs}(v_2(\mathcal{A}))$.*

For any L-PTA $\mathcal{A}$, as per [16, Theorem 3], there exists a constant bound N, such that for all valuations v_1, v_2 with $v_1 \geq v_2 \geq v_N$ (where v_N denotes the parameter valuation assigning N to each parameter), if $v_2(\mathcal{A})$ provides an infinite accepting run then so does $v_1(\mathcal{A})$. A dual result is shown for U-PTAs. Formally:

Lemma 5 ([16, Theorems 3 and 6]). *Given a U-PTA (resp. L-PTA) $\mathcal{A}$ with N the constant bound defined in [16], given two valuations $v_1 \geq v_N$ and $v_2 \geq v_N$, there exists an infinite accepting run in $v_1(\mathcal{A})$ iff there exists an infinite accepting run in $v_2(\mathcal{A})$.*

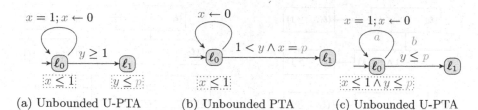

Fig. 4. Three toy PTAs

Computation of $\widehat{N}$. Given an L-PTA (respectively U-PTA) $\mathcal{A}$, the value given in [16] is $N = k(R+1) + c + 1$ (respectively $N = 8k(R+1) + c + 1$), where k is the number of parametric clocks of $\mathcal{A}$, R is the number of clock regions obtained when the parameter valuation is 0 for all parameters, and c is the greatest non-parametric constant in absolute value among all linear expressions. More precisely, all linear expression being of the form $\sum_{1 \le i \le H} \alpha_i x_i + \sum_{1 \le j \le K} \beta_j p_j + d \bowtie 0$, c is the maximum over all $|d|$. Although k and c are obtained syntactically, R needs to be computed. As N acts as a lower bound, using an over-approximation of R would still guarantee the correctness of Lemma 5. From [1, Lemma 4.5], the number of clock regions is bounded by $\widehat{R} = 2^{|\mathbb{X}|}|\mathbb{X}|! \prod_{x \in \mathbb{X}}(2c_x + 2)$ with $\mathbb{X}$ the set of clocks and c_x the greatest constant over x (either as a upper or lower bound)—which can both be obtained syntactically. We define $\widehat{N}$ as the constant defined in [16] for an L-PTA (resp. U-PTA) $\mathcal{A}$, where we use $\widehat{R}$ instead of R.

Formal Results. We first adapt Lemma 5 to our new constant $\widehat{N}$:

Lemma 6. *Given a U-PTA (resp. L-PTA) $\mathcal{A}$, given two valuations $v_1 \ge v_{\widehat{N}}$ and $v_2 \ge v_{\widehat{N}}$, there exists an infinite accepting run in $v_1(\mathcal{A})$ iff there exists an infinite accepting run in $v_2(\mathcal{A})$.*

Proof. From the fact that we use in the computation of $\widehat{N}$ an over-approximation on the number of clock regions (with $R \le \widehat{R}$), giving $N \le \widehat{N}$.

We can now prove the correctness of extrapolation for unbounded L-PTAs and U-PTAs. Let $\widehat{M} = \{M(x_1), \ldots, M(x_H)\}$ such that $M(x_i)$ is the maximal constant of clock x_i when bounding all unbounded parameters with $\widehat{N}$. Let $\widehat{\mathsf{EEF}}$ denote the modification of EEF where $\mathsf{Ext}_{\mathbb{X}}^M$ is replaced with $\mathsf{Ext}_{\mathbb{X}}^{\widehat{M}}$.

Example 6. Figure 5 illustrates the effects of the $\widehat{M}$-extrapolation on the unbounded U-PTA of Fig. 4a. Figure 5a displays its (simplified) infinite state space. The valuation of p can be any value in $\mathbb{Q}_+$. Figure 5b shows the state space obtained with the $\widehat{M}$-extrapolation. Note that the state space is now finite.

Proposition 2. *Let $\mathcal{A}$ be an L-PTA or U-PTA with initial state s_0, and $T \subseteq L$ a set of target locations. Assume $\widehat{\mathsf{EEF}}(\mathcal{A}, \mathsf{s}_0, T, \emptyset)$ terminates. We have:*

1. *Soundness: If $v \in \widehat{\mathsf{EEF}}(\mathcal{A}, \mathsf{s}_0, T, \emptyset)$ then T is reachable in $v(\mathcal{A})$;*
2. *Completeness: For all v, if T is reachable in $v(\mathcal{A})$ then $v \in \widehat{\mathsf{EEF}}(\mathcal{A}, \mathsf{s}_0, T, \emptyset)$.*

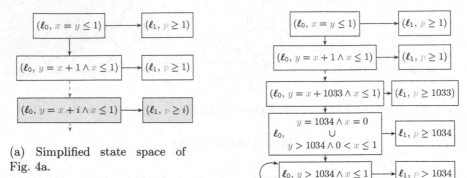

(a) Simplified state space of Fig. 4a.

(b) Simplified state space of Fig. 4a with the $\widehat{M}$-extrapolation where $M(x) = 1$ and $M(y) = 1034$, computed using $\widehat{N}$. The dashed link represents a succession of 1031 intermediate states where the value of y grows from $x + 1$ to $x + 1033$.

Fig. 5. Example of an unbounded PTA generating an infinite state space.

4.2 $\vec{M}$-extrapolation on PTAs with Unbounded Lower or Upper Bound Parameters

The method described previously can be adapted to a subclass of PTAs that can be turned into L-PTAs or U-PTAs (only) for the sake of computing the constant bound $\widehat{N}$. Let us first define this subclass:

Definition 10 (bPTA+L and bPTA+U). *Let $\mathcal{A}$ be a PTA. $\mathcal{A}$ is a bounded PTA with unbounded lower-(resp. upper-)bound parameters, or bPTA+L (resp. bPTA+U), if for each guard $x \bowtie \sum_{1 \leq i \leq K} \alpha_i p_i + z$ of $\mathbb{G}(\mathcal{A})$, for all i:*

- *$\mathbb{D}(p_i) \in \mathbb{Q} \times \mathbb{Q}$ (i.e., p_i is bounded), or $\alpha_i = 0$, or*
- *$\alpha_i > 0$ and $\bowtie \in \{\geq, >\}$ (respectively $\bowtie \in \{<, \leq\}$), or*
- *$\alpha_i < 0$ and $\bowtie \in \{<, \leq\}$ (respectively $\bowtie \in \{\geq, >\}$).*

Let $\mathcal{A}$ be a bPTA+L (resp. bPTA+U). We denote by $\overline{\mathcal{A}}$ the L-PTA (resp. U-PTA) obtained from $\mathcal{A}$ by valuating the bounded parameters as follows: we replace each bounded parameter p_i within a guard or invariant with its lower bound $\mathbb{D}^-(p_i)$ if it appears negatively ($\alpha_i < 0$) or with its upper bound $\mathbb{D}^+(p_i)$ otherwise. Formally:

Definition 11 (Bounded valuation of a bPTA+L or bPTA+U). *Let $\mathcal{A}$ be a bPTA+L (resp. bPTA+U). Let $\overline{\mathcal{A}}$ be the modification of $\mathcal{A}$ where for each guard $x \bowtie \sum_{1 \leq i \leq K} \alpha_i p_i + z \in \mathbb{G}(\mathcal{A})$, for each bounded $p_i \in \mathbb{P}$, i) if $\alpha_i < 0$, p_i is replaced by $\mathbb{D}^-(p_i)$, ii) if $\alpha_i > 0$, p_i is replaced by $\mathbb{D}^+(p_i)$, and iii) p_i is replaced with 0 otherwise.*

Example 7. To illustrate Definition 10 we modify Fig. 4a by adding a bounded parameter. Figure 6a is a bPTA+U $\mathcal{A}$ with q bounded between 1 and 2, and p

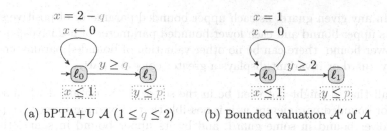

(a) bPTA+U $\mathcal{A}$ ($1 \leq q \leq 2$)   (b) Bounded valuation $\mathcal{A}'$ of $\mathcal{A}$

Fig. 6. A bPTA+U and its bounded valuation.

unbounded. Figure 6b is the bounded valuation $\mathcal{A}'$ of $\mathcal{A}$, as defined in Definition 11. Note that in this example $\mathcal{A}'$ does not describe a behavior that belongs to $\mathcal{A}$, as parameter q is valuated to 1 in the guard where it occurs with a negative sign, while it is valuated to 2 in the guard where it occurs with a positive sign. It will nevertheless be useful to exhibit a constant bound for $\mathcal{A}$.

Correctness of the Transformation. Clearly, if $\mathcal{A}$ is a bPTA+L (resp. bPTA+U) then $\overline{\mathcal{A}}$ is an L-PTA (resp. U-PTA).

Lemma 7. *Let $\mathcal{A}$ be a bPTA+L (resp. bPTA+U). Then $\overline{\mathcal{A}}$ is an L-PTA (resp. U-PTA).*

Proof. Assume $\mathcal{A}$ is a bPTA+L (resp. bPTA+U). When building $\overline{\mathcal{A}}$, any occurrence of a bounded parameter is replaced by its constant bounds. In addition, all unbounded parameters from $\mathcal{A}$ are, by Definition 10, lower-bound (resp. upper-bound) parameters. Therefore, the only remaining parameters in $\overline{\mathcal{A}}$ are lower-bound (resp. upper-bound) parameters. Therefore, $\overline{\mathcal{A}}$ is an L-PTA (resp. U-PTA).

Method. Our method is then as follows: given a bPTA+L (resp. bPTA+U) $\mathcal{A}$, *i)* we construct the L-PTA (resp. U-PTA) $\overline{\mathcal{A}}$, and *ii)* we then compute the bound $\widehat{N}$ on the obtained L-PTA (resp. U-PTA) $\overline{\mathcal{A}}$ (using the technique given in Sect. 4.1). Let $\overline{N}$ denote the computed bound.

Let $\overline{M} = \{M(x_1), \ldots, M(x_H)\}$ such that $M(x_i)$ is the maximal constant of clock x_i when bounding in $\mathcal{A}$ all unbounded parameters with $\overline{N}$. Let $\overline{\mathsf{EEF}}$ denote the modification of EEF where $\mathsf{Ext}_{\mathsf{X}}^{M}$ is replaced with $\mathsf{Ext}_{\mathsf{X}}^{\overline{M}}$.

Proposition 3. *Let $\mathcal{A}$ be a bPTA+L or bPTA+U with initial state $\mathbf{s}_0$, and $T \subseteq L$ a set of target locations. Assume $\overline{\mathsf{EEF}}(\mathcal{A}, \mathbf{s}_0, T, \emptyset)$ terminates. We have:*

1. *Soundness: If $v \in \overline{\mathsf{EEF}}(\mathcal{A}, \mathbf{s}_0, T, \emptyset)$ then T is reachable in $v(\mathcal{A})$;*
2. *Completeness: For all v, if T is reachable in $v(\mathcal{A})$ then $v \in \overline{\mathsf{EEF}}(\mathcal{A}, \mathbf{s}_0, T, \emptyset)$.*

Lemma 8. *The bounded valuation $\overline{\mathcal{A}}$ of a PTA $\mathcal{A}$ guarantees for each constraint in the model to give the greatest possible constant bound for all valuations in the set of bounded parameters of $\mathcal{A}$.*

Proof. In any given guard, as each upper bounded parameter of positive sign is set to its upper bound and each lower bounded parameter of negative sign is set to its lower bound, there can be no other valuation of bounded parameters such that any guard or invariant displays a greater constant part.

Recall that $\overline{\mathcal{A}}$ might not even be in the set of PTAs obtained when setting values for bounded parameters, as it is possible that a given parameter is replaced by its lower bound in some guard, and by its upper bound in some other. It guarantees, however, that the value of the constant bound for any of the PTA obtained by valuating bounded parameters is no greater than $\overline{N}$.

We can proceed with the proof of Proposition 3:

Proof. Let $\mathcal{A}'$ be any bounded valuation of $\mathcal{A}$. By definition, $\mathcal{A}'$ is either an L-PTA or a U-PTA. From Lemma 8, we know that $\overline{N}$ is greater than the constant bound of $\mathcal{A}'$. By Proposition 2, we know that the extrapolation of $\mathcal{A}'$ is sound and complete when defining $M(x)$ as the maximal constant of clock x when bounding all unbounded parameters with $\widehat{N}$. As $\overline{N} > \widehat{N}$, the extrapolation is still sound and complete for any valuation in the set of bounded parameters of $\mathcal{A}$.

4.3   Partial $\vec{M}$-extrapolation on General PTAs

Finally, it is possible to perform a *partial* extrapolation on any PTA $\mathcal{A}$, by extrapolating only the clocks that are only compared to the set of bounded parameters $\mathbb{P}_{bound}$ of $\mathcal{A}$. That is, for a given guard or invariant g of the form $x \bowtie \sum_{1 \le i \le K} \alpha_i p_i + z$, the maximum value $C_{maxg}(g) = \sum_{1 \le i \le K} \alpha_i \gamma_i + z$ where *i)* $\gamma_i = \mathbb{D}^-(p_i)$ if $\alpha_i < 0$, *ii)* $\gamma_i = \mathbb{D}^+(p_i)$ if $\alpha_i > 0$, and *iii)* $\gamma_i = 0$ otherwise. Note that γ_i may be ∞ or $-\infty$ if p_i is not an unbounded parameter. As a result, the maximal constant of any clock $x_i \in \mathbb{X}$ compared to unbounded parameter is equal to ∞. Therefore, $M(x_i) \in \vec{M} = \infty$—which amounts to never applying extrapolation on x_i. A (simple) formal result is given in [10].

Example 8. In Fig. 4b, x is compared to p which is neither a lower bound nor an upper bound parameter. Therefore, this PTA is not in any of the previous classes on which it is possible to compute a constant bound. However, we can apply a partial extrapolation, i.e., the extrapolation is only applied on y, for which there exists a maximal constant $C_{max}^y(\mathcal{A}) < \infty$. The analysis using IMITATOR returns quickly (in $< 0.1\,s$) the expected result $0 \le p \le 1$, while it cannot be solved without extrapolation (i.e., the algorithm would not terminate).

5   Beyond Reachability in bPTA+L and bPTA+U

We saw in Sect. 4 that it was possible to apply extrapolation on unbounded L-PTAs and U-PTAs with additional bounded parameters. However, we only proved correctness for reachability properties. In this section, we study liveness.

In the context of unbounded parameters, the $\widehat{M}$-extrapolation cannot be used directly to check liveness properties, as it might produce false positives. The U-PTA in Fig. 4c exemplifies why the parametric extrapolation is not correct for cycle synthesis on unbounded PTAs. With this automaton, the state space is infinite with y growing without bound: after i loops, we have $y = x + i \leq p$. The expected result of a cycle synthesis is $\bot$ (no valuation yields a cycle), but an exploration of the state space would not terminate. If we try applying the $\widehat{M}$-extrapolation, we obtain $M(x) = 1$ and $M(y) = 522$ as greatest constants, computed using $\widehat{N}$ (Sect. 4.1). After 522 loops, the valuation of y can be greater than $M(y)$, and we obtain a self-looping state where $y > 522$ and $p > 523$. As a result, the $\widehat{M}$-extrapolation will synthesize a cycle for $p > 523$, while there should be none. This behavior is due to the invariant $y \leq p$ being removed by the cylindrification of clock y. Note that this is not possible with bounded parameters (or general TAs) because any invariant $y \leq t$, with t a given constant, would necessarily contradict the constraint $y > M$. Indeed, M being by definition the greatest constant of clock y, $M \geq t$ and thus $y > M \cap y \leq t = \emptyset$.

A solution to fix that issue is to ensure the invariant is not ignored, by bounding p by the constant $\widehat{N}$ (522 in this case). In general, bounding all parameters by $\widehat{N}$ ensures no false positive are present, but might include false negative in the form of upper bounds (those we introduced to bound the parameters). However, we know from [16, Theorems 3 and 6] that in an L-PTA or a U-PTA, if there is an infinite accepting run for a parameter valuation v with $v(p) \geq \widehat{N}$, then this run exists for all valuations v' with $v(p) \geq \widehat{N}$. Therefore, in a U-PTA, the upper bound on p can be removed on any results that contains "$p = \widehat{N}$". This method can be applied on the classes of models on which we have defined a extrapolation using the constant bound $\widehat{N}$ (i.e., bPTA+L and bPTA+U).

In the case of our example from Fig. 4c, this means constraining the model with $p \leq 522$. As a result, the $\widehat{M}$-extrapolation will synthesize no cycles, which is correct. Now, imagine a model with the same constant bound over parameter $\widehat{N} = 522$, but such that the expected result is $400 < p$. The $\widehat{M}$-extrapolation on the constrained model will synthesize $400 < p \leq 522$—which contains $p = 522$. We can then remove the upper bound on p and obtain the correct result, i.e., $400 < p$.

6   Experiments

We implemented the aforementioned extrapolation in IMITATOR [4]; all operations on parametric zones are computed by polyhedral operations, using PPL [11]. We consider the full class of PTAs, over (potentially unbounded) rational-valued parameters. We applied the extrapolation on the bPTA+L/bPTA+U subclass from Sect. 4.2 when it was possible, and the partial $\widehat{M}$-extrapolation from Sect. 4.3 otherwise (i.e., extrapolation is applied to each clock whenever possible). We conducted experiments on a library of standard PTA benchmarks [9]. We used an Intel Core i5-4690K with 4 GHz.[3]

We tabulate our results in Table 1. The first and main outcome is the two lines for "all models" (in bold): on the entire benchmark set (119 models and 177 properties), the average execution time is 954 s without extrapolation, and 824 s with; in addition, the normalized average (always taking 1 for the slowest of both algorithms and rescaling the second one accordingly) is 0.89 without and 0.91 with. Both metrics are complementary, as the average favors models with large verification times, while normalized average gives the same weight to all models, including those of very small verification times. The outcome is that the extrapolation decreases the average time by 14 %, and increases the normalized average time by 1.5 %, which remains near-to-negligible.

We only tabulate in Table 1 results with the most significant difference, i.e., with a gap of more than 1 s with a ratio $\frac{min}{max} > 2$ (and only one property per model). Put it differently, other models show little difference between both versions. "reach" denotes reachability synthesis; "liveness" denotes the synthesis of valuations leading to at least one infinite run.

Recall that, even on the most restrictive syntactic subclass of PTAs we considered (L-PTAs and U-PTAs), no exact algorithm for reachability-synthesis over rational-valued parameters is known, and therefore our algorithms (including with extrapolation) come with no guarantee of termination. On the entire benchmarks set, 39 properties (over 33 models) do not terminate without extrapolation; this figure reduces to 33 properties (over 29 models) when applying extrapolation. (No analysis terminating without extrapolation would lead to non-termination when adding extrapolation.)

On the models where there is a significant difference between with and without extrapolation, tabulated in Table 1, the extrapolation is sometimes significantly faster, sometimes significantly slower. Most importantly, extrapolation allows termination of some so far unsolvable models. The slower cases are due to the fact that our implementation in IMITATOR needs to keep each symbolic state *convex*—this is required by the internal polyhedral structure. Therefore, when a clock is extrapolated, this increases the number of states in the state space (a given extrapolated symbolic state can be potentially split into up to $2^{|X|}$ new symbolic states via a single outgoing transition).

All in all, our experiments suggest that, despite a few models (tabulated in Table 1) where the presence or absence of extrapolation has a significant difference of execution time, adding extrapolation remains overall harmless, with even an average decrease of 14 % in the execution time. Most importantly, it allows to solve so far unsolvable benchmarks—which we consider as the main outcome. This suggests to use extrapolation by default for synthesis in PTAs.

---

[3] Source, benchmarks, raw results and full table are available at doi.org/10.5281/zenodo.5824264. We used a fork of IMITATOR 3.1 "Cheese Artichoke" extended with extrapolation functions (exact version: v3.1.0+extrapolation).

Table 1. Execution times for our experiments. T.O. denotes an execution unfinished after 3,600 s. (We use this value for means computation.) Normalized mean is the ratio to the worst execution times. Cells color represents the difference in performance for a given row: the lighter the better.

Model	Property	No extrapolation (s)	$\overline{M}$-extrapolation (s)
FischerPS08-4	reach	10.6	4.8
FMTV_2	reach	0.7	2.3
fischerPAT3	reach	1.9	0.8
SLAF14_5	reach	12.6	74.4
spsmall	reach	0.4	19.3
SSLAF13_test2	reach	2869.8	1399.1
synthRplus	reach	T.O.	0.2
Cycle1	liveness	T.O.	0.001
infinite-5	liveness	T.O.	0.006
infinite-5_6	liveness	T.O.	0.004
exU_noloop	liveness	1.1	7.7
Mean (models from Table 1 only)		1572.5	137.1
Normalized mean (models from Table 1 only)		0.697	0.490
Mean (all models)		954.4	823.8
Normalized mean (all models)		0.891	0.905

7 Conclusion and Perspectives

We proposed several definitions of zone extrapolation for parametric TAs. We proposed a first implementation (in IMITATOR), and showed that, while extrapolation is harmless for most models, it can also decrease the computation time of larger models and, most importantly, can lead to termination (exact synthesis) of previously unsolvable benchmarks. Considering the difficulty of parameter synthesis for timed models, we consider it a non-trivial and promising step.

A limitation of our implementation (discussed in Sect. 6) is that it only handles *convex* zones. Using the non-convex polyhedral structures offered by PPL [11] may dramatically reduce the number of symbolic states. However, they are much more costly than their convex counterparts—this should be experimentally compared.

Another perspective concerns the computation of the constant bounds $\widehat{N}$, for which one needs to compute the number R of clock regions. Our current implementation uses its over-approximation $\widehat{R}$. Computing the actual number of clock regions before applying the extrapolation may considerably reduce the analysis time for larger models.

Finally, we plan to go beyond this work by adapting the LU-extrapolation from [13] to PTAs, a theoretically coarser abstraction for which implementation is not trivial. Algorithms from [19] may prove useful to this purpose.

Acknowledgements. The authors would like to thank the reviewers for their comments, and Dylan Marinho for his help in providing the models and automation tools that were used for the benchmarking presented in this paper.

References

1. Alur, R., Dill, D.L.: A theory of timed automata. TCS **126**(2), 183–235 (1994). https://doi.org/10.1016/0304-3975(94)90010-8
2. Alur, R., Henzinger, T.A., Vardi, M.Y.: Parametric real-time reasoning. In: Kosaraju, S.R., Johnson, D.S., Aggarwal, A. (eds.) STOC, pp. 592–601. ACM, New York (1993). https://doi.org/10.1145/167088.167242
3. André, É.: What's decidable about parametric timed automata? Int. J. Softw. Tools Technol. Transfer **21**(2), 203–219 (2017). https://doi.org/10.1007/s10009-017-0467-0
4. André, É.: IMITATOR 3: synthesis of timing parameters beyond decidability. In: Silva, A., Leino, K.R.M. (eds.) CAV 2021. LNCS, vol. 12759, pp. 552–565. Springer, Cham (2021). https://doi.org/10.1007/978-3-030-81685-8_26
5. André, É., Chatain, T., Encrenaz, E., Fribourg, L.: An inverse method for parametric timed automata. Int. J. Found. Comput. Sci. **20**(5), 819–836 (2009). https://doi.org/10.1142/S0129054109006905
6. André, É., Lime, D., Ramparison, M.: TCTL model checking lower/upper-bound parametric timed automata without invariants. In: Jansen, D.N., Prabhakar, P. (eds.) FORMATS 2018. LNCS, vol. 11022, pp. 37–52. Springer, Cham (2018). https://doi.org/10.1007/978-3-030-00151-3_3
7. André, É., Lime, D., Ramparison, M.: Parametric updates in parametric timed automata. LMCS **17**(2), 13:1–13:67 (2021). https://doi.org/10.23638/LMCS-17(2:13)2021
8. André, É., Lime, D., Roux, O.H.: Integer-complete synthesis for bounded parametric timed automata. In: Bojańczyk, M., Lasota, S., Potapov, I. (eds.) RP. LNCS, vol. 9328, pp. 7–19. Springer (2015). https://doi.org/10.1007/978-3-319-24537-9
9. André, É., Marinho, D., van de Pol, J.: A benchmarks library for extended parametric timed automata. In: Loulergue, F., Wotawa, F. (eds.) TAP 2021. LNCS, vol. 12740, pp. 39–50. Springer, Cham (2021). https://doi.org/10.1007/978-3-030-79379-1_3
10. Arcile, J., André, É.: Zone extrapolations in parametric timed automata. Technical Report abs/2203.13173, arXiv (2022). https://arxiv.org/abs/2203.13173
11. Bagnara, R., M., H.P., Zaffanella, E.: The Parma Polyhedra Library: Toward a complete set of numerical abstractions for the analysis and verification of hardware and software systems. Sci. Comput. Programm. **72**(1–2), 3–21 (2008). https://doi.org/10.1016/j.scico.2007.08.001
12. Behrmann, G., Bouyer, P., Fleury, E., Larsen, K.G.: Static guard analysis in timed automata verification. In: Garavel, H., Hatcliff, J. (eds.) TACAS 2003. LNCS, vol. 2619, pp. 254–270. Springer, Heidelberg (2003). https://doi.org/10.1007/3-540-36577-X_18
13. Behrmann, G., Bouyer, P., Larsen, K.G., Pelánek, R.: Lower and upper bounds in zone-based abstractions of timed automata. STTT **8**(3), 204–215 (2006). https://doi.org/10.1007/s10009-005-0190-0
14. Beneš, N., Bezděk, P., Larsen, K.G., Srba, J.: Language emptiness of continuous-time parametric timed automata. In: Halldórsson, M.M., Iwama, K., Kobayashi, N., Speckmann, B. (eds.) ICALP 2015. LNCS, vol. 9135, pp. 69–81. Springer, Heidelberg (2015). https://doi.org/10.1007/978-3-662-47666-6_6
15. Bezděk, P., Beneš, N., Barnat, J., Černá, I.: LTL parameter synthesis of parametric timed automata. In: De Nicola, R., Kühn, E. (eds.) SEFM 2016. LNCS, vol. 9763, pp. 172–187. Springer, Cham (2016). https://doi.org/10.1007/978-3-319-41591-8_12

16. Bozzelli, L., La Torre, S.: Decision problems for lower/upper bound parametric timed automata. FMSD **35**(2), 121–151 (2009). https://doi.org/10.1007/s10703-009-0074-0

17. Bundala, D., Ouaknine, J.: On parametric timed automata and one-counter machines. Inf. Comput. **253**, 272–303 (2017). https://doi.org/10.1016/j.ic.2016.07.011

18. Daws, C., Tripakis, S.: Model checking of real-time reachability properties using abstractions. In: Steffen, B. (ed.) TACAS 1998. LNCS, vol. 1384, pp. 313–329. Springer, Heidelberg (1998). https://doi.org/10.1007/BFb0054180

19. Herbreteau, F., Srivathsan, B., Walukiewicz, I.: Better abstractions for timed automata. Inf. Comput. **251**, 67–90 (2016). https://doi.org/10.1016/j.ic.2016.07.004

20. Hune, T., Romijn, J., Stoelinga, M., Vaandrager, F.W.: Linear parametric model checking of timed automata. JLAP **52-53**, 183–220 (2002). https://doi.org/10.1016/S1567-8326(02)00037-1

21. Jovanović, A., Lime, D., Roux, O.H.: Integer parameter synthesis for real-time systems. TSE **41**(5), 445–461 (2015). https://doi.org/10.1109/TSE.2014.2357445

22. Larsen, K.G., Pettersson, P., Yi, W.: UPPAAL in a nutshell. STTT **1**(1-2), 134–152 (1997). https://doi.org/10.1007/s100090050010

23. Li, G.: Checking timed büchi automata emptiness using LU-abstractions. In: Ouaknine, J., Vaandrager, F.W. (eds.) FORMATS 2009. LNCS, vol. 5813, pp. 228–242. Springer, Heidelberg (2009). https://doi.org/10.1007/978-3-642-04368-0_18

24. Schrijver, A.: Theory of Linear and Integer Programming. Wiley, New York (1986)

25. Tripakis, S.: Checking timed Büchi automata emptiness on simulation graphs. ACM Trans. Comput. Logic **10**(3), 15:1–15:19 (2009). https://doi.org/10.1145/1507244.1507245

Exemplifying Parametric Timed Specifications over Signals with Bounded Behavior

Étienne André[1]([✉])(iD), Masaki Waga[2](iD), Natuski Urabe[3](iD),
and Ichiro Hasuo[3,4](iD)

[1] Université de Lorraine, CNRS, Inria, LORIA, 54000 Nancy, France
`eandre93430@lipn13.fr`
[2] Kyoto University, Kyoto, Japan
[3] National Institute of Informatics, Tokyo, Japan
[4] The Graduate University for Advanced Studies, SOKENDAI, Tokyo, Japan

Abstract. Specifying properties can be challenging work. In this paper, we propose an automated approach to exemplify properties given in the form of automata extended with timing constraints and timing parameters, and that can also encode constraints over real-valued signals. That is, given such a specification and given an admissible automaton for each signal, we output concrete runs exemplifying real (or impossible) runs for this specification. Specifically, our method takes as input a specification, and a set of admissible behaviors, all given as a subclass of rectangular hybrid automata, namely timed automata extended with arbitrary clock rates, signal constraints, and timing parameters. Our method then generates concrete runs exemplifying the specification.

Keywords: Specification · Timed automata · Hybrid automata · Signals

1 Introduction

Model checking has had a lot of successes in the last decades (see, e.g., [27]). Still, its use in the industry can be seen as slightly disappointing, considering its high advantages in providing system designers with formal guarantees in the correctness of their system. This is especially true for *quantitative* model checking, that considers systems extended with quantities such as probabilities, time, costs... Among the explanations, one reason is the high expertise required by model checking users to master the model, the specification and their semantics. Even domain experts may do manual errors, leading to specifications with a completely different behaviors from the expectations. These issues may then only be solved using a tedious debugging phase.

This work is partially supported by ERATO HASUO Metamathematics for Systems Design Project (No. JPMJER1603), JST and by the ANR-NRF French-Singaporean research program ProMiS (ANR-19-CE25-0015).

© Springer Nature Switzerland AG 2022
J. V. Deshmukh et al. (Eds.): NFM 2022, LNCS 13260, pp. 470–488, 2022.
https://doi.org/10.1007/978-3-031-06773-0_25

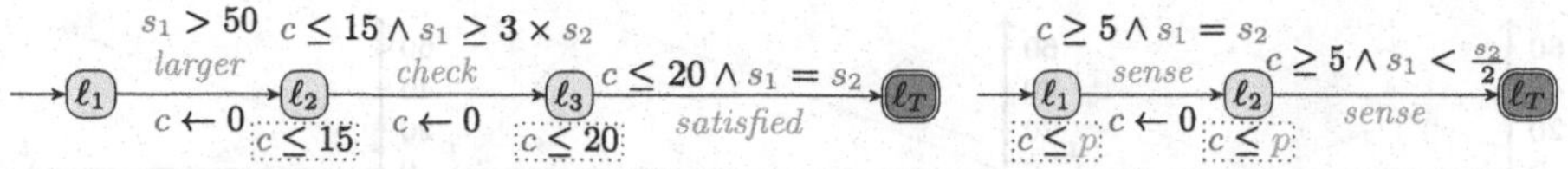

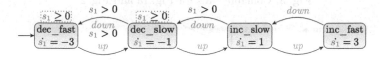

(a) Non-parametric specification   (b) Parametric specification

Fig. 1. Examples of PTAS

$$s_1 > 0 \qquad s_1 > 0 \qquad down$$

$$\boxed{\begin{matrix}\text{dec\_fast}\\ \dot{s}_1 = -3\end{matrix}} \xrightarrow[up]{\begin{matrix}down\\ s_1 > 0\end{matrix}} \boxed{\begin{matrix}\text{dec\_slow}\\ \dot{s}_1 = -1\end{matrix}} \xrightarrow[up]{down} \boxed{\begin{matrix}\text{inc\_slow}\\ \dot{s}_1 = 1\end{matrix}} \xrightarrow[up]{down} \boxed{\begin{matrix}\text{inc\_fast}\\ \dot{s}_1 = 3\end{matrix}}$$

Fig. 2. An example of SBA

Contribution. In this work, we propose an approach to exemplify concrete continuous evolutions of signals over time, according to a specification. We introduce as a specification formalism *parametric timed automata with signals (PTASs)* as an extension of (parametric) timed automata [2,3]: our PTASs use the full power of timed automata, with clocks compared to constants, and add the possibility to specify *signal (linear) constraints*, such as "$s_1 \geq 3 \times s_2$". This allows us to easily express specifications of the form "whenever signal s_1 is larger than 50, then within at most 15 time units, it holds that $s_1 \geq 3 \times s_2$ and then, within at most 20 more time units, both signals are equal ($s_1 = s_2$)". Figure 1a depicts the PTAS encoding this specification (where c is a clock, while s_1 and s_2 are signals), i.e., ℓ_T is reachable whenever the specification is met for some execution. In addition, we allow for *timing parameters* (unknown constants), thus enabling parametric specifications mixing discrete actions, signal constraints and timing parameters all together, such as "after a first sensing (action *sense*) occurring within $[5, p]$, it holds that $s_1 = s_2$, and after a second sensing occurring within $[5, p]$, it holds that $s_1 < \frac{s_2}{2}$", where p is a timing parameter. The PTAS encoding this specification is given in Fig. 1b. In this latter case, the exemplification comes in the form of a concrete valuation for p *and* an evolution of the signals satisfying the specification.

In order to bound the possible signal behaviors, we introduce as additional input *signal bounding automata* (SBA), i.e., automata bounding the admissible behaviors of the signals. These SBAs can be gathered from a (rough) knowledge from the system under consideration; they can also be used to search among the widely variety signals satisfying the specification e.g., driving with/without acceleration/deceleration. In addition, thanks to the SBAs, we avoid generating irrelevant signals, e.g., signals with unrealistically large value change even in the negative example generation. Our SBAs assign signals an arbitrary (but piecewise constant) derivative, according to some guards. For example, an SBA could allow signal s to alternate between slowly ($\dot{s} = 1$) and rapidly ($\dot{s} = 3$) growing—or decreasing; this latter SBA is depicted in Fig. 2.

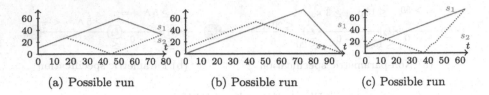

Fig. 3. Concrete runs for Fig. 1a and Fig. 2

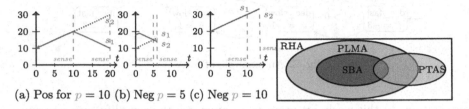

(a) Pos for $p = 10$ (b) Neg $p = 5$ (c) Neg $p = 10$

Fig. 4. Positive and negative runs for
Fig. 1b

Fig. 5. Formalisms

We generate not only *positive* ("correct") exemplifications, but also *negative* ("incorrect", i.e., that do *not* match the specification). The crux behind this is that, in order to illustrate a specification, we may need both positive and negative examples that are close to the boundary. See Fig. 4 for an example.

Example 1. Let $\mathcal{A}$ be the PTAS in Fig. 1a; let $\mathcal{A}_1$ be the SBA in Fig. 2, and let $\mathcal{A}_2$ be the SBA in Fig. 2 where s_1 is replaced with s_2. We assume initially $s_1, s_2 \in [0, 10]$. Given the PTAS $\mathcal{A}$ and the 2 SBAs $\mathcal{A}_1$ and $\mathcal{A}_2$ bounding the behavior of s_1 and s_2, our framework automatically generates several signal evolutions satisfying the specification; we give 3 of them in Fig. 3. Observe that they present 3 very different evolutions of the signals, with different initial valuations, evolution rates, and final valuations.

Our approach is given in Fig. 6. More specifically, our contributions are:

1. We introduce three formalisms, all being subclasses of rectangular hybrid automata [22], namely *parametric timed automata with signals* (PTASs) to express specifications, *signal bounding automata* (SBAs) to bound the behavior of each signal, and *parametric linear multi-rate automata* (PLMAs) that will be used for the parallel composition of the aforementioned formalisms; the relationship between these classes is given in Fig. 5;
2. We equip PLMAs with both a concrete and a symbolic semantics;
3. We propose an exemplification algorithm for PLMAs, yielding concrete parameter valuations together with positive and negative runs;
4. We implement our framework into the IMITATOR model checker [5];
5. We show the applicability of our approach on a set of specifications.

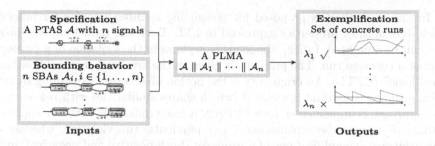

Fig. 6. Our general approach

Outline. Section 2 reviews related works. Section 3 recalls the necessary preliminaries. Then, Sect. 4 introduces the general class of parametric linear multirate automata (PLMAs), as well as two subclasses used in the subsequent approach. Section 5 formally defines our specification exemplification problem. Section 6 is the core of our contribution, proposing to exemplify specifications using techniques to exhibit parameter valuations and concrete runs for reachability properties in PLMAs. Section 7 exemplifies our approach on a set of specifications. Section 8 concludes and proposes future works.

2   Related Works

There are several works [14,23,33,35] to visualize counterexamples of a formal specification. One of the closest works to ours is STLInspector [35]. Given a signal temporal logic (STL) [28] formula φ, STLInspector generates a signal s differentiating φ and a mutated formula φ'. Similarly, in [33], concrete traces are automatically generated, that satisfy or violate an STL formula. Such signals are generated by SMT. A difference between [33] and [35] is that [33] considers linear (as opposed to rectangular) predicates. Another related work is ShapEx [14]. Given a shape expression [31] φ, ShapEx generates signals represented by φ based on a sampling-based algorithm. Compared with most of these related works, the main difference with our approach is the use of *signal bounding automata*: since most of the existing techniques generate a signal without bounding the admissible behaviors, an unrealistic signal may be generated. Another difference, especially from SMT-based approaches, is that it is easy for our automata-based approach to generate various signals by covering various paths of the automaton. In contrast, for example, [33] requires an additional constraint, called a *blocking constraint*, to generate various signals. Nevertheless, the use of SMT in the analysis of an automaton (much like nuXmv [17]) is future work. In addition, most of these works utilize MITL [29], STL [28], or an extension of regular expressions. Our approach takes as input a more general, automata-based formalism (using notably timing parameters and multi-rate variables), not restricted to a given logic. We note that one can translate a formula in most of these logics to a timed automaton, which our formalism captures. See e.g., [11,15] for translation of such logical expressions to timed automata.

In [32], a method is proposed for *visualizing* counterexamples for function block diagrams, of properties expressed in LTL. Both the model and the property can be animated. In [18], the focus is *explaining* the violation of a property against a concrete run. The property is given in the low-level "control flow temporal logic" (CFTL). An originality is the notion of *severity*, explaining by how much a timing constraint is violated (which shares similarities with *robustness*). The approach is implemented into VYPR2. A main difference with our approach is that [18] targets the explanation of *one* particular run violation, whereas we seek arbitrary exemplifications of a property (both positive and negative), independently of a run. Visualization of specifications was also considered, e.g., for Z specification [26] and for a DSL based on Event-B [36].

Another direction to tackle the difficulty of specification writing is translation of a natural language description to a temporal logic formula, e.g., [21].

Finally, our new notion of *signal bounding automaton*, used to bound the possible behavior of the signals, can be reminiscent of the recent model-bounded monitoring framework, which we introduced in [37]. In that paper, we used a rough over-approximation to bound the possible behaviors while performing monitoring of a black-box system. Similar idea is also used in [13] to bound the signal space in the falsification problem by a timed automaton [2].

The main originality of our work is *i)* the use of quantitative specifications (involving notably continuous time, timing parameters and signals), and *ii)* the use of signal bounding automata to bound the admissible behaviors.

3   Preliminaries: Constraints and Rect. Hybrid Automata

We assume a set $\mathbb{V} = \{v_1, \ldots, v_H\}$ of real-valued continuous variables. Different from timed automata "clocks" [2], our variables (closer to hybrid systems' "continuous variables") can have different rates, and turn negative. A variable valuation is $\mu : \mathbb{V} \to \mathbb{R}$. We write $\mathbf{0}$ for the variable valuation assigning 0 to all variables. Given $d \in \mathbb{R}$, and a flow (or rate) function $f : \mathbb{V} \to \mathbb{Q}$ assigning each variable with a flow (i.e., the value of its derivative), we define the time elapsing function te as follows: $te(\mu, f, d)$ is the valuation such that $\forall v \in \mathbb{V} : te(\mu, f, d)(v) = \mu(v) + f(v) \times d$. Given $R \subseteq \mathbb{V}$, we define the *reset* of a valuation μ, denoted by $[\mu]_R$, as follows: $[\mu]_R(v) = 0$ if $v \in R$, and $[\mu]_R(v) = \mu(v)$ otherwise.

We assume a set $\mathbb{P} = \{p_1, \ldots, p_M\}$ of *(timing) parameters*. A parameter *valuation* λ is $\lambda : \mathbb{P} \to \mathbb{Q}_+$. We assume $\bowtie \in \{<, \leq, =, \geq, >\}$. A *parametric linear term* over $\mathbb{V} \cup \mathbb{P}$ is of the form $\sum_{1 \leq i \leq H} \alpha_i v_i + \sum_{1 \leq j \leq M} \beta_j p_j + d$, with $v_i \in \mathbb{V}$, $p_j \in \mathbb{P}$, and $\alpha_i, \beta_j, d \in \mathbb{Q}$. A *parametric linear inequality* is $plt \bowtie 0$, where plt is a parametric linear term. A *parametric linear constraint* $\mathbf{C}$ (i.e., a convex polyhedron) over $\mathbb{V} \cup \mathbb{P}$ is a conjunction of parametric linear inequalities. Given $\mathbf{C}$, we write $\mu \models \lambda(\mathbf{C})$ if the expression obtained by replacing each v with $\mu(v)$ and each p with $\lambda(p)$ in $\mathbf{C}$ evaluates to true.

Let $\mathcal{I}(\mathbb{R})$ denote the set of all intervals over $\mathbb{R}$. We first recall rectangular hybrid automata (RHAs), a subclass of hybrid automata. Our definition involves (timing) parameters; parameters could be seen as syntactic sugar for a subset of variables (i.e., variables of arbitrary initial value and of zero rate throughout the automaton), but we still add them explicitly as they will explicitly appear in subsequent subclasses of RHAs.

Definition 1 (RHA). *A rectangular hybrid automaton (RHA) $\mathcal{A}$ is a tuple $\mathcal{A} = (\Sigma, L, \ell_0, F, \mathbb{V}, V_0, \mathbb{P}, I, f, E)$, where: 1) Σ is a finite set of actions, 2) L is a finite set of locations, 3) $\ell_0 \in L$ is the initial location, 4) $F \subseteq L$ is the set of accepting locations, 5) $\mathbb{V}$ is a finite set of variables, 6) $V_0 : \mathbb{V} \to \mathcal{I}(\mathbb{R})$ is the initial set of variable valuations, 7) $\mathbb{P}$ is a finite set of parameters, 8) I is the invariant, assigning to every $\ell \in L$ a parametric linear constraint $I(\ell)$ over $\mathbb{V} \cup \mathbb{P}$, 9) f is the flow (or rate), assigning to every $\ell \in L$ and $v \in \mathbb{V}$ a flow $f(\ell, v) \in \mathcal{I}(\mathbb{R})$, 10) E is a finite set of edges $e = (\ell, g, a, R, \ell')$ where $\ell, \ell' \in L$ are the source and target locations, $a \in \Sigma$, $R \subseteq \mathbb{V}$ is a set of variables to be reset, and g is a parametric linear constraint over $\mathbb{V} \cup \mathbb{P}$.*

Parallel Composition. RHAs can be *composed* using synchronized product (see e.g., [34, Definition 4]) in a way similar to finite-state automata. The synchronized product of n RHAs $\mathcal{A}_i, i \in \{1, \ldots, n\}$, denoted by $\mathcal{A}_1 \parallel \mathcal{A}_2 \parallel \cdots \parallel \mathcal{A}_n$, is an RHA [20]. Of importance is that, in a composed location, the global flow constraint is the *intersection* of the local component flow constraints.

We do not give the concrete semantics of this formalism, as we will manipulate a subclass called parametric linear multi-rate automaton (PLMA).

4 Parametric Linear Multi-rate Automata

Timed automata extend finite-state automata with clocks (i.e., real-valued variables evolving at the same constant rate 1), that can be compared with integer constants along transitions ("guards") or within locations ("invariants"). Parametric timed automata (PTAs) extend TAs with parameters within guards and invariants in place of integer constants [3], i.e., allowing inequalities of the form $v \bowtie p$ (simple guards) or sometimes $v - v' \bowtie p$ (diagonal constraints), where $v, v' \in \mathbb{V}$ and $p \in \mathbb{P}$. Here, we extend PTAs notably with: *i)* multi-rate clocks (called *variables*), i.e., each clock can have an arbitrary (but constant) rational rate in each location; and *ii)* linear constraints over variables and parameters, instead of the usual definition $v \bowtie p$. We first define parametric linear multi-rate automata (PLMA) with their syntax (Sect. 4.1) and semantics (Sect. 4.2); we then propose two other subformalisms of RHAs (Sect. 4.3) used subsequently in this paper.

4.1 Syntax

We extend (P)TAs with (constant) *flows*; in the absence of timing parameters, this formalism is usually called *multi-rate timed automata* [1,19]. Also note that, different from TA clocks, our variables can possibly turn *negative*. In addition, we extend the usual syntax of clock guards to our aforementioned definition of *parametric linear constraints*.

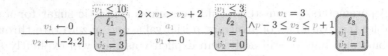

Fig. 7. A PLMA example

Definition 2 (PLMA). *An RHA* $\mathcal{A} = (\Sigma, L, \ell_0, F, \mathbb{V}, V_0, \mathbb{P}, I, f, E)$ *is a para-metric linear multi-rate automaton (PLMA) if:* $\forall \ell \in L, \forall v \in \mathbb{V} : f(\ell, v) \in \mathbb{Q}$.

That is, a PLMA is an RHA where all flows are constant. Observe that the flow is taken in $\mathbb{Q}$, which includes negative rates and zero-rates (also called *stopwatches* [16]). A PLMA is *strongly deterministic* if $\forall \ell \in L, \forall a \in \Sigma, |\{(\ell_1', g', a', R', \ell_2') \in E \mid \ell_1' = \ell \wedge a' = a\}| \leq 1$.

Example 2. Consider the PLMA in Fig. 7. In the PLMA figures, we use notation $\dot{v}_i = d$ in location ℓ_j to denote $f(\ell_j, s_i) = d$. This PLMA contains two variables v_1 and v_2, and one parameter p. ℓ_1 is the initial location, while ℓ_3 is the (only) accepting location. We have $V_0(v_1) = [0, 0]$ and $V_0(v_2) = [-2, 2]$.

Given λ, we denote by $\lambda(\mathcal{A})$ the non-parametric structure where all occurrences of a parameter p_i have been replaced by $\lambda(p_i)$. We call such a structure a *linear multi-rate automaton* (LMA). Note that, whenever all rates are 1 ($\forall \ell \in L, \forall v \in \mathbb{V}, f(\ell, v) = 1$), all guards and invariants are of the form $v \bowtie d$, $d \in \mathbb{Q}_+$, and all variables are initially 0 (i.e., $\forall v \in \mathbb{V} : V_0(v) = \{0\}$), then the resulting structure is a *timed automaton* [2].

4.2 Semantics

Concrete Semantics of LMAs. The semantics of LMAs is close to that of multi-rate automata, extended with linear constraints over variables.

Definition 3 (Semantics of an LMA). *Given a PLMA* $\mathcal{A} = (\Sigma, L, \ell_0, F, \mathbb{V}, V_0, \mathbb{P}, I, f, E)$, *and a parameter valuation* λ, *the semantics of* $\lambda(\mathcal{A})$ *is given by the timed transition system (TTS)* $(S, S_0, \rightarrow)$, *with*

- $S = \{(\ell, \mu) \in L \times \mathbb{R}^H \mid \mu \models \lambda(I(\ell))\}$,
- $S_0 = \{(\ell_0, \mu) \mid \mu \models \lambda(I(\ell_0)) \wedge \forall v : \mu(v) \in V_0(v)\}$,
- $\rightarrow$ *consists of the discrete and (continuous) delay transition relations:*
  1. *discrete transitions:* $(\ell, \mu) \overset{e}{\mapsto} (\ell', \mu')$, *if* $(\ell, \mu), (\ell', \mu') \in S$, *and there exists* $e = (\ell, g, a, R, \ell') \in E$, *such that* $\mu' = [\mu]_R$, *and* $\mu \models \lambda(g)$.
  2. *delay transitions:* $(\ell, \mu) \overset{d}{\mapsto} (\ell, te(\mu, f(\ell), d))$, *with* $d \in \mathbb{R}_+$, *if* $\forall d' \in [0, d], (\ell, te(\mu, f(\ell), d')) \in S$.

Moreover we write $(\ell, \mu) \overset{(d,e)}{\longrightarrow} (\ell', \mu')$ for a delay transition followed by a discrete transition if $\exists \mu'' : (\ell, \mu) \overset{d}{\mapsto} (\ell, \mu'') \overset{e}{\mapsto} (\ell', \mu')$.

Given an LMA $\lambda(\mathcal{A})$ with concrete semantics $(S, S_0, \rightarrow)$, we refer to the states of S as the *concrete states* of $\lambda(\mathcal{A})$. A *concrete run* of $\lambda(\mathcal{A})$ is an alternating sequence of concrete states of $\lambda(\mathcal{A})$ and pairs of edges and delays starting from an initial state $s_0 \in S_0$ of the form $s_0, (d_0, e_0), s_1, \cdots$ with $i = 0, 1, \ldots, e_i \in E$, $d_i \in \mathbb{R}_+$ and $s_i \xrightarrow{(d_i, e_i)} s_{i+1}$. Given $s = (\ell, \mu)$, we say that s is *reachable* in $\lambda(\mathcal{A})$ if s appears in a run of $\lambda(\mathcal{A})$. By extension, we say that ℓ is reachable. A run ρ is said to be *accepting* if there exists $\ell \in F$ such that ℓ is reachable along ρ.

A *negative run* of $\lambda(\mathcal{A})$ is an alternating sequence of states (ℓ_i, μ_i) and pairs of edges and delays of the form $(\ell_0, \mu_0), (d_0, e_0), (\ell_1, \mu_1), \cdots$ with $i = 0, 1, \ldots, e_i \in E$ and $d_i \in \mathbb{R}_+$, which is not a concrete run of $\lambda(\mathcal{A})$. That is, there exists some i such that (ℓ_i, μ_i) is not a concrete state of $\lambda(\mathcal{A})$, or $(\ell_i, \mu_i) \xrightarrow{(d_i, e_i)} (\ell_{i+1}, \mu_{i+1})$ does not belong to the semantics of $\lambda(\mathcal{A})$. To distinguish from negative runs, we will sometimes refer to concrete runs as *positive* runs.

Example 3. Consider again the PLMA $\mathcal{A}$ in Fig. 7, and let λ be such that $\lambda(p) = 12$. Consider the following run ρ of $\lambda(\mathcal{A})$: $(\ell_1, (0, -2)), (e_1, 3.8)$, $(\ell_2, (0, 9.4)), (e_2, 3), (\ell_3, (3, 9.4))$, where e_1 is the edge from ℓ_1 to ℓ_2 in Fig. 7, and e_2 is the edge from ℓ_2 to ℓ_3. (As an abuse of notation, we write $(\ell_0, (0, -2))$ for (ℓ_0, μ_0) where $\mu_0(v_1) = 0$ and $\mu_0(v_2) = -2$.) Observe that, after 3.8 time units in ℓ_1, we have $v_1 = 2 \times 3.8 = 7.6$ (which satisfies invariant $v_1 \leq 10$) while $v_2 = 9.4$; therefore, guard $2 \times v_1 > v_2 + 2$ evaluates to $15.2 > 11.4$, and therefore the transition to ℓ_2 can be taken. After 3 time units in ℓ_2, not modifying the value of v_2 as $f(\ell_2, v_2) = 0$, the guard to ℓ_3 is satisfied as $9.4 \in [9, 13]$ (recall that $\lambda(p) = 12$). ρ is accepting as it ends in ℓ_3.

Now consider the following alternative sequence ρ': $(\ell_1, (0, 0))$, $(e_1, 5), (\ell_2, (0, 15)), (e_2, 3), (\ell_3, (3, 15))$. This sequence is a *negative* run of $\lambda(\mathcal{A})$, as the transition via e_2 cannot be taken for this valuation ($15 \notin [9, 13]$). However, ρ' is a positive run of $\lambda'(\mathcal{A})$, where $\lambda'(p) = 14.5$.

A graphical representation of (positive and negative) runs focusing on the *evolution of the variables over time* can be obtained directly from the runs. This graphical representation is made of H lines (where H denotes the variables cardinality) obtained as follows: given a (positive or negative) run $(\ell_0, \mu_0), (d_0, e_0), (\ell_1, \mu_1), \cdots$, given a variable v, the initial point is $(0, \mu_0(v))$. That is, each variable v defines graphically a non-necessarily differentiable piecewise linear function.

Example 4. Consider the first run ρ from Example 3. Its associated graphical representation is given in Fig. 8.

Symbolic Semantics. Let us now define the symbolic semantics of PLMAs, as an extension of the semantics of PTAs (see e.g., [8,24,25]) to multi-rates and linear constraints.

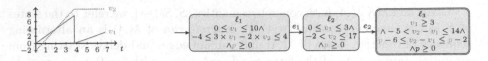

Fig. 8. Graphical run   **Fig. 9.** A parametric
zone graph

Constraints. We first need to define operations on constraints. Given a parameter valuation λ and a variable valuation μ, we denote by $\mu|\lambda$ the valuation over $\mathbb{V} \cup \mathbb{P}$ such that for all variables v, $\mu|\lambda(v) = \mu(v)$ and for all parameters p, $\mu|\lambda(p) = \lambda(p)$. Given a parametric linear constraint $\mathbf{C}$, we use the notation $\mu|\lambda \models \mathbf{C}$ to indicate that $\mu \models \lambda(\mathbf{C})$. We say that $\mathbf{C}$ is *satisfiable* if $\exists \mu, \lambda$ s.t. $\mu|\lambda \models \mathbf{C}$. We will often use geometrical concepts for constraints; in particular, whenever $\mu|\lambda \models \mathbf{C}$, then the valuation $\mu|\lambda$ can be seen as a *point belonging to the polyhedron* $\mathbf{C}$.

We define the *time elapsing* of $\mathbf{C}$ w.r.t. flow $f : \mathbb{V} \to \mathbb{Q}$, denoted by $\mathbf{te}(\mathbf{C}, f)$, as the constraint over $\mathbb{V}$ and $\mathbb{P}$ obtained from $\mathbf{C}$ by delaying all variables by an arbitrary amount of time according to f. That is, $\mu'|\lambda \models \mathbf{te}(\mathbf{C}, f)$ iff $\exists \mu : \mathbb{V} \to \mathbb{R}, \exists d \in \mathbb{R}$ s.t. $\mu|\lambda \models \mathbf{C} \wedge \mu' = te(\mu, f, d)$.

Given $R \subseteq \mathbb{V}$, we define the *reset* of $\mathbf{C}$, denoted by $[\mathbf{C}]_R$, as the constraint obtained from $\mathbf{C}$ by resetting to 0 the variables in R, and keeping the other variables unchanged. We denote by $\mathbf{C}{\downarrow}_\mathbb{P}$ the projection of $\mathbf{C}$ onto $\mathbb{P}$, i.e., obtained by eliminating the variables not in $\mathbb{P}$ (e.g., using Fourier-Motzkin. The application of these operation to a linear constraint yields a linear constraint; this can be computed efficiently using operations on polyhedra [12].

A symbolic state is a pair $(\ell, \mathbf{C})$ where $\ell \in L$ is a location, and $\mathbf{C}$ is a linear constraint called a *parametric zone*.

Definition 4 (Symbolic semantics). *Given a PLMA* $\mathcal{A} = (\Sigma, L, \ell_0, F, \mathbb{V}, V_0, \mathbb{P}, I, f, E)$, *the symbolic semantics of* $\mathcal{A}$ *is the labeled transition system called* parametric zone graph $\mathcal{PZG}(\mathcal{A}) = (E, \mathbf{S}, \mathbf{s}_0, \Rightarrow)$, *with*

- $\mathbf{S} = \{(\ell, \mathbf{C}) \mid \mathbf{C} \subseteq I(\ell)\}$, $\mathbf{s}_0 = (\ell_0, \mathbf{te}((\bigwedge_{1 \leq i \leq H} v_i \in V_0(v_i)), f(\ell_0)) \wedge I(\ell_0))$,
- $((\ell, \mathbf{C}), e, (\ell', \mathbf{C}')) \in \Rightarrow$ *if* $e = (\ell, g, a, R, \ell') \in E$ *and* $\mathbf{C}' = \mathbf{te}(([(\mathbf{C} \wedge g)]_R \wedge I(\ell')), f(\ell')) \wedge I(\ell')$ *with* $\mathbf{C}'$ *satisfiable.*

That is, in the parametric zone graph, nodes are symbolic states, and arcs are labeled by edges of the original PLMA. Observe that, as in PTAs, a symbolic state contains all the valuations after time elapsing (instead of just the valuations after a discrete transition).

If $((\ell, \mathbf{C}), e, (\ell', \mathbf{C}')) \in \Rightarrow$, we write $\mathsf{Succ}(\mathbf{s}, e) = (\ell', \mathbf{C}')$, where $\mathbf{s} = (\ell, \mathbf{C})$. By extension, we write $\mathsf{Succ}(\mathbf{s})$ for $\cup_{e \in E} \mathsf{Succ}(\mathbf{s}, e)$.

A *symbolic run* $\mathbf{r}$ of $\mathcal{A}$ is an alternating sequence of symbolic states of $\mathcal{A}$ and edges starting from the initial state $\mathbf{s}_0$ of the form $\mathbf{s}_0, e_0, \mathbf{s}_1, \cdots$ with $i = 0, 1, \ldots$, $e_i \in E$, and $\mathsf{Succ}(\mathbf{s}_i, e_i) = \mathbf{s}_{i+1}$. (The symbolic runs of $\mathcal{PZG}(\mathcal{A})$ are the runs of $\mathcal{PZG}(\mathcal{A})$.) *edgeAt*$(\mathbf{r}, k)$ denotes e_k, and *stateAt*$(\mathbf{r}, k)$ denotes $\mathbf{s}_k$. When $\mathbf{r}$ is finite, $|\mathbf{r}|$ denotes its *length*, i.e., its number of edges (therefore, a finite symbolic run contains $|\mathbf{r} + 1|$ symbolic states).

Example 5. Consider again the PLMA $\mathcal{A}$ in Fig. 7. Then, $\mathcal{PZG}(\mathcal{A})$ (limited to its reachable states) is given in Fig. 9. The constraints in each location give both the admissible valuations for p for which this location is reachable, and a condition over the continuous variables v_1 and v_2 to remain in this location. Note that (the reachable part of) this PZG is finite, which is not necessarily the case in general.

4.3 Two Other Subclasses of RHAs: PTASs and SBAs

Definition 5. *An RHA* $\mathcal{A} = (\Sigma, L, \ell_0, F, \mathbb{V}, V_0, \mathbb{P}, I, f, E)$ *is a* parametric timed automaton with signals *(PTAS) if:*

1. *the set of variables is partitioned into* $\mathbb{V} = \mathbb{C} \uplus \mathbb{S}$, *where* $\mathbb{C}$ *is a set of standard TA clocks (i.e., variables with rates 1), and* $\mathbb{S}$ *is a set of* signals;
2. *all clock rates are 1, i.e.,* $\forall \ell \in L, \forall c \in \mathbb{C}, f(\ell, c) = 1$;
3. *signals satisfy the following constraints:*
   (a) *all signal rates are unconstrained, i.e.,* $\forall \ell \in L, \forall s \in \mathbb{S}, f(\ell, s) = \mathbb{R}$;
   (b) *a signal cannot be reset, i.e.,* $\forall(\ell, g, a, R, \ell') \in E, \forall v \in R : v \notin \mathbb{S}$; *and*
   (c) *each parametric linear inequality in guards and invariants cannot involve both a standard clock from* $\mathbb{C}$ *and a signal from* $\mathbb{S}$ *(i.e., comparisons of the form* $c \bowtie s$, *with* $c \in \mathbb{C}$ *and* $s \in \mathbb{S}$, *are not allowed).*

Observe that, since the signal rates are $= \mathbb{R}$, the formalism of PTAS is not a subclass of PLMAs (see Fig. 5), as this latter formalism imposes $f(\ell, s) = d$ for some $d \in \mathbb{Q}$. However, in practice, a PTAS will always be composed (using synchronized product) with a set of PLMAs (actually SBAs, see below) constraining the rate of signals (see Lemma 1 below).

Example 6. Consider the PTAS in Fig. 1b. Its clock set is $\mathbb{C} = \{c\}$ while its signal set is $\mathbb{S} = \{s_1, s_2\}$. The set of parameters is $\mathbb{P} = \{p\}$. We have $f(\ell_1, c) = f(\ell_2, c) = f(\ell_T, c) = 1$ (not explicitly depicted in Fig. 1b).

Second, we define a signal bounding automaton as a special LMA used to constrain the admissible behaviors of a signal. Therefore, it contains a single variable (actually a signal), no parameter, and no reset.

Definition 6. *A PLMA* $\mathcal{A} = (\Sigma, L, \ell_0, F, \mathbb{S}, \mathbb{P}, I, f, E)$ *is a* signal bounding automaton *(SBA) if: 1)* $\mathbb{P} = \emptyset$; *2)* $|\mathbb{S}| = 1$; *and 3) no resets are allowed, i.e.,* $\forall(\ell, g, a, R, \ell') \in E, R = \emptyset$.

Example 7. An example of SBA is given in Fig. 2, where $\mathbb{S} = \{s_1\}$. In the SBA figures, we use notation $\dot{s}_1 = d$ in location ℓ to denote $f(\ell, s_1) = d$.

Lemma 1. *Let* $\mathcal{A}$ *be a PTAS with* n *signals. Let* $\mathcal{A}_i, i \in \{1, \ldots, n\}$ *be* n *SBAs such that* $\mathcal{A}_i$ *contains a signal variable* s_i. *Then* $\mathcal{A} \parallel \mathcal{A}_1 \parallel \cdots \parallel \mathcal{A}_n$ *is a PLMA.*

In practice, SBAs can also involve clocks, e.g., to mesure time between signal changes. This is both harmless in theory, and allowed by our implementation.

Algorithm 1: Main algorithm $exemplify(\mathcal{A})$

---

input : A PLMA with symbolic initial state s_0 and accepting locations F

output : A set of negative runs and positive runs

1 Explore $\mathcal{PZG}(\mathcal{A})$ until a state $(\ell_T, \mathbf{C})$ is found, for some $\ell_T \in F$ and some $\mathbf{C}$

/* Pick a run r from s_0 to $(\ell_T, \mathbf{C})$ */

2 $\mathbf{r} \leftarrow PickSymbRun(\mathcal{PZG}, s_0, (\ell_T, \mathbf{C}))$

3 **return** $exemplify3(\mathcal{A}, \mathbf{r})$

---

5   Problem

Expressing Specifications over Signals. In our work, we consider as first input a PTAS featuring a set of n signals, and acting as a *specification automaton*. Given a parameter valuation λ and a specification expressed as a PTAS $\mathcal{A}$ with accepting locations F, the specification is satisfied iff F is reachable in $\lambda(\mathcal{A})$.

Bounding Signal Behaviors. In order to define the admissible behaviors of the signals, we also consider an SBA for each of the signals used in the PTAS.

Since the specification (given by a PTAS) is parametric, we first aim at deriving concrete parameter valuations for which the specification is valid, i.e., for which one accepting state is reachable. Second, for a given concrete valuation, we aim at deriving concrete accepting positive runs, as well as negative runs.

Specification exemplification problem:

INPUT: A PTAS $\mathcal{A}$ featuring n signals, and n SBAs $\mathcal{A}_i, i \in \{1, \ldots, n\}$

PROBLEM: Exhibit a set of parameter valuations λ and a set of concrete accepting positive runs and negative runs of $\lambda((\mathcal{A} \parallel \mathcal{A}_1 \parallel \cdots \parallel \mathcal{A}_n))$

Recall that our general approach is given in Fig. 6. In our approach, we make the following assumption (only required when computing *negative* runs):

Assumption 1. *The PTAS and SBAs must be strongly deterministic.*

6   Exemplifying Bounded Signal Specifications

We propose in this section a heuristics-based method to exemplify runs for an arbitrary PLMA. The entry point is *exemplify* in Algorithm 1. We first explore the PZG until a target state is found (line 1). Then, we exhibit a symbolic run from the initial state s_0 to the target state (line 2). Finally, Algorithm 1 calls *exemplify3*, given in Algorithm 2, that returns (up to) 3 concrete runs: one positive run together with a concrete parameter valuation, one negative run for a different parameter valuation, and one negative run for the same parameter valuation. Let us explain these steps.

Algorithm 2: $exemplify3(\mathcal{A}, \mathbf{r})$: Exemplifying 3 concrete runs

input : A PLMA $\mathcal{A}$, a symbolic run $\mathbf{r}$ from s_0 to $(\ell_T, \mathbf{C})$
output : A set $\mathcal{R}$ of concrete negative runs and positive runs

1 $\mathcal{R} \leftarrow \emptyset$

    /* Part 1: positive run   */

2 $\mu|\lambda \leftarrow exhibitPoint(\mathbf{C})$

3 $\rho \leftarrow reconstructPos(\mathcal{A}, \mathbf{r}, |\mathbf{r}|, (\ell_T, \mu|\lambda))$; $\mathcal{R} \leftarrow \mathcal{R} \cup \{\rho\}$

    /* Part 2a: negative run (different parameter valuation)   */

4 **if** $hasPdeadlock(\mathbf{r})$ **then**

5     $(\lambda_i, (\ell_i, \mathbf{C}_i)) \leftarrow findPdeadlock(\mathbf{r})$; $\mu_i \leftarrow exhibitPoint(\lambda_i(\mathbf{C}_i))$

6     $\rho_{pref} \leftarrow reconstructPos(\mathcal{A}, \mathbf{r}, i, (\ell_i, \mu_i|\lambda_i))$

7     $\rho_{suf} \leftarrow constructNeg(\mathcal{A}, \mathbf{r}, i, |\mathbf{r}|, \mu_i|\lambda_i)$

8     $\rho \leftarrow \rho_{pref} + \rho_{suf}$; $\mathcal{R} \leftarrow \mathcal{R} \cup \{\rho\}$

    /* Part 2b: negative run (same parameter valuation)   */

9 **if** $hasVdeadlock(\mathbf{r})$ **then**

10    $(\mu_i, (\ell_i, \mathbf{C}_i)) \leftarrow findVdeadlock(\mathbf{r}, \lambda)$

11    $\rho_{pref} \leftarrow reconstructPos(\mathcal{A}, \mathbf{r}, i, (\ell_i, \mu_i|\lambda))$

12    $\rho_{suf} \leftarrow constructNeg(\mathcal{A}, \mathbf{r}, i, |\mathbf{r}|, \mu_i|\lambda)$

13    $\rho \leftarrow \rho_{pref} + \rho_{suf}$; $\mathcal{R} \leftarrow \mathcal{R} \cup \{\rho\}$

14 **return** $\mathcal{R}$

6.1 Exploration and Symbolic Run Exhibition

The construction of the PZG is made on-the-fly, using Defintion 4. In our implementation, this is done using a breadth-first search (BFS) manner.

Then, the function $PickSymbRun$ takes as argument the PZG $\mathcal{PZG}$, the initial state s_0, and the target state (here $(\ell_T, \mathbf{C})$), and returns a symbolic run from s_0 to $(\ell_T, \mathbf{C})$ in $\mathcal{PZG}$. The actual function (not given in this paper) is implemented in a straightforward manner in our toolkit using a backward analysis in $\mathcal{PZG}$ from $(\ell_T, \mathbf{C})$ to s_0. The exhibited symbolic run is not necessarily unique and, as heuristics, we use a shortest run (again, not necessarily unique), with "shortest" to be understood as the number of discrete steps. Alternative definitions could be used (e.g., minimal-time run [7]).

After exhibiting a symbolic run, our next step is to derive *concrete* runs from that symbolic run. This is the purpose of $exemplify3(\mathcal{A}, \mathbf{r})$, given in Algorithm 2.

We first explain Algorithm 2 as a whole, and then proceed to subfunctions in the following. The first step in $exemplify3$ is to exhibit a "point", i.e., a concrete variable and parameter valuation in the target state constraint $\mathbf{C}$ (line 2). Since $\mathbf{C}$ is a polyhedron, we use a dedicated function $exhibitPoint(\mathbf{C})$. There is no theoretical difficulty in exhibiting a concrete point in a polyhedron; however, our dedicated function must both be efficient and yield a valuation which is as "human-friendly" as possible, i.e., avoiding random rational numbers and avoiding as much as possible to select "0" if another suitable valuation exists. The body of our function $exhibitPoint$ is given in [10].

6.2 Exhibiting Concrete Example Runs

We then reconstruct a concrete positive run (line 3 in Algorithm 2) from the point $\mu|\lambda$ that was just exhibited in the final constraint. This function *reconstructPos* poses no specific theoretical difficulty, but yields some practical subtleties, discussed in [10]. Note that it is always possible to reconstruct a concrete run from a symbolic run.

The second part of Algorithm 2 (line 4–line 8) consists in exhibiting a negative run (based on **r**) for a different parameter valuation than the one (λ) exhibited in the first part of the algorithm. The heuristics we use is to (try to) exhibit a parameter valuation that *cannot* take one of the transitions of the symbolic run **r**: this is a *parametric deadlock*. If such a valuation exists, then the projection onto the parameters of some constraints along the run **r** is *shrinked*, i.e., this run is possible for some parameter valuations up to some state, and then possible for less parameter valuations.

Parametric deadlock checking was studied in, e.g., [4,9], and *findPdeadlock* is basically based on these former works, except that we used the symbolic semantics of PLMAs instead of PTAs. *findPdeadlock* attempts at exhibiting a parameter valuation that cannot pass one of the edges of a symbolic run **r**. *findPdeadlock* is given in [10].

The third part of Algorithm 2 (line 9–line 13) consists in exhibiting a negative run for the same parameter valuation as the one (λ) exhibited in the first part of the algorithm. Our heuristics is as follows: we try to find a transition within **r** for which some variable valuation (for the parameter valuation λ) cannot take this transition. This can come from an unsatisfied guard or invariant: this is a *non-parametric deadlock*.

findVdeadlock attempts to exhibit a variable valuation μ and a symbolic state **s** of a symbolic run **r** such that there exists a deadlock after **s** for μ, i.e., μ cannot take the edge following **s** along **r**, even after elapsing some time. *findVdeadlock* is given in [10].

6.3 Exhibiting Negative Concrete Example Runs

The reconstruction of a negative run fragment is given in Algorithm 3. It takes as arguments the start (i) and end (j) positions of the symbolic run **r**, as well as the concrete valuation $\mu_i|\lambda_i$ to start from at position i. Algorithm 3 simply starts from the valuation $\mu_i|\lambda_i$, and takes the same discrete actions as in the symbolic run, but with an (arbitrary) duration 1: that is, for each k from i to j, we add a transition $(edgeAt(\mathbf{r}, k), 1)$ (where 1 denotes the duration), and we add the updated valuation $(\mu_i|\lambda_i + (k - i))$, which is equal to $(\mu_i|\lambda_i$ incremented by the number of transitions computed so far $(k - i))$. Note that it would be possible to take any other duration than 1, and apply the resets as in the symbolic run. The fact that this concrete run is an invalid run comes from the fact that the valuation $\mu_i|\lambda_i$ is known to be unable to take the immediately following transition, as it is called at lines 7 and 12 of Algorithm 2 where a parametric (resp. non-parametric) deadlock was exhibited.

Algorithm 3: $constructNeg(\mathcal{A}, \mathbf{r}, i, j, \mu_i | \lambda_i)$: Reconstruct a negative run from a symbolic run fragment

---

input : A PLMA $\mathcal{A}$; A symbolic run $\mathbf{r}$ from s_0 to $(\ell_T, \mathbf{C})$; Start position i
        and end position j ; Starting valuation $\mu_i | \lambda_i$
output : A concrete negative run fragment

1 $\rho \leftarrow \mu_i | \lambda_i$
2 **for** $k = i$ **to** j **do** $\rho \leftarrow \rho, (edgeAt(\mathbf{r}, k), 1), (\mu_i | \lambda_i + (k - i))$;
3 **return** ρ

6.4 Formal Result

Exemplifying runs for parametric timed formalisms is a very hard problem, as the mere existence of a parameter valuation for which a location is reachable in a PTA is undecidable [3]. While our method is mostly heuristics-based, we prove that, *provided at least one parameter valuation allows to reach an accepting location*, then our method is able to infer at least one (positive) concrete run.

Proposition 1. *Let $\mathcal{A}$ be a PLMA with accepting locations F. Assume $\exists \lambda$: $\lambda(\mathcal{A})$ reaches some $\ell_T \in F$. Then, assuming a BFS computation of $\mathcal{PZG}(\mathcal{A})$, exemplify($\mathcal{A}$) terminates, and outputs at least one positive run.*

Our algorithm has no guarantee to exhibit negative runs for several reasons: notably, we use only heuristics, here based on deadlocks: there could be *other* negative runs than those exhibited based on a (parametric) deadlocks. Still, one can guarantee the following:

Proposition 2. *Let $\mathcal{A}$ be a PLMA and $\mathbf{r}$ be a symbolic run of $\lambda(\mathcal{A})$ with a parameter valuation λ. Assume there is a concrete negative run due to parametric (resp. non-parametric) deadlock with the same discrete actions as $\mathbf{r}$. Then, assuming a BFS computation of $\mathcal{PZG}(\mathcal{A})$, exemplify3($\mathcal{A}, \mathbf{r}$) outputs a concrete negative run due to parametric (resp. non-parametric) deadlock.*

7 Proof of Concept

We implemented our exemplification algorithm in IMITATOR [5] (v.3.3-alpha "Cheese Caramel au beurre salé").[1]

All polyhedral operations are implemented using PPL [12]. The approach takes as input a network of PLMAs, and attempts to output a set of runs and parameter valuations. As a heuristics, we try to call up to 6 times Algorithm 1, i.e., we try to exhibit up to 6 symbolic runs, and then for each of them, following Algorithm 2, we derive one parameter valuation and a concrete run, followed by a negative run for a different parameter valuation (if any) and a negative run for the same valuation (if any). All analyses terminate within a few seconds, including graphics generation.

---

[1] Source code, models and results are available at 10.5281/zenodo.6382893.

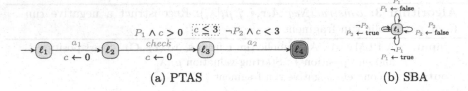

(a) PTAS

(b) SBA

Fig. 10. A non-parametric specification over Boolean predicates

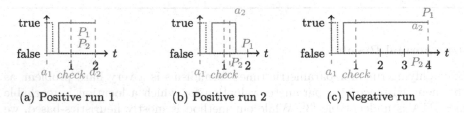

(a) Positive run 1

(b) Positive run 2

(c) Negative run

Fig. 11. Positive and negative runs for Fig. 10

All outputs are textual (in a JSON-like format); however, IMITATOR also automatically outputs basic graphics. The figures in this paper were however (manually) redrawn using LATEX.

Extensions. Thanks to the expressive power of IMITATOR, we can go beyond the formalism presented here. Notably, arbitrary updates (not necessarily to 0, but to parameters, or other variables) are allowed; also, Boolean variables can encode predicates, which can be seen as a simpler setting than signals (see below).

A Non-parametric Specification over Booleans. Assume the following specification: "whenever action a_1 occurs, then following a non-0 time, predicate P_1 must hold; then, strictly less than 3 time units later, a_2 occurs and predicate P_2 must not hold". The PTAS encoding this specification is given in Fig. 10a; the SBA in Fig. 10b simply allows both predicates to switch anytime between true and false.

We give two positive runs in Fig. 11a and 11b and one negative run in Fig. 11c. Observe that the run in Fig. 11c violates the specification because action a_2 occurs exactly in 3 time units (instead of < 3 time units) after *check*.

A Non-parametric Specification over Signals. Recall the motivating specification from Example 1 with the PTAS from Fig. 1a and the SBA in Fig. 2. We assume that initially $s_1, s_2 \in [0, 10]$ (such non-deterministic assignment is allowed by our framework, from V_0 in Definition 2). Three concrete runs are given in Fig. 3, while all six outputs by IMITATOR are given in [10].

A Parametric Specification over Signals. Now recall the parametric specification from Fig. 1b. Our approach derives a parameter valuation $p = 10$, for which this specification can be satisfied, as well as the concrete run in Fig. 4a. Then, our approach derives a parameter valuation $p = 5$ for which the specification may be violated, with a negative run in Fig. 4b: this run is not valid because the two *sense* actions are separated by < 5 time units. Finally, our approach derives a second negative run, this time for $p = 10$, given in Fig. 4c: again, this run is not valid because two *sense* actions occur in a time $\frac{10}{3} < 5$.

8 Conclusion

We presented a first approach to exemplify specifications over signals (as real-valued continuous variables with a piecewise-constant rate), also using regular TA clocks and timing parameters. Our approach's originality is twofold: expressive quantitative specifications (involving notably continuous time, timing parameters and signals), and the use of newly introduced *signal bounding automata* to limit the admissible continuous behavior. Our implementation in IMITATOR makes the process fully automated.

While we do not expect our exemplifying approach to allow for users completely unfamiliar with model checking and timed formalisms to suddenly become experts in these methods, we believe our approach is a first step towards helping users with a low expertise to increase the confidence they have in their specifications.

Future Work. A first future work is to study the theoretical background of our specification formalism, and notably its expressiveness. Also, we so far considered only reachability properties, and our framework shall be extended to liveness/fairness, e.g., using the recent liveness synthesis algorithms for PTAs [6,30]. The strong determinism assumption (Assumption 1) is required by our algorithms, but shall eventually be lifted.

Another direction is to allow more flexible formalisms (e.g., rectangular hybrid automata) to bound the signals.

One of the future directions is to extend our framework to exemplify a more widely used formalism, e.g., LTL, MITL [29], or STL [28]. At least theoretically, this would be straightforward thanks to the high expressiveness of PTASs. In this latter case, we can also benefit from the *positive* run exemplification to exhibit *negative* runs, by taking as input the PTAS corresponding to the *negation* of the original formula.

Further, providing some "coverage" guarantees, with a sufficient number of positive and negative runs, is on our agenda.

One longer-term future work is to use and evaluate our framework to teach students or engineers who are not familiar with formal specifications.

References

1. Alur, R., et al.: The algorithmic analysis of hybrid systems. TCS **138**(1), 3–34 (1995). https://doi.org/10.1016/0304-3975(94)00202-T
2. Alur, R., Dill, D.L.: A theory of timed automata. TCS **126**(2), 183–235 (1994). https://doi.org/10.1016/0304-3975(94)90010-8
3. Alur, R., Henzinger, T.A., Vardi, M.Y.: Parametric real-time reasoning. In: Kosaraju, S.R., Johnson, D.S., Aggarwal, A. (eds.) STOC, pp. 592–601. ACM, New York (1993). https://doi.org/10.1145/167088.167242
4. André, É.: Parametric deadlock-freeness checking timed automata. In: Sampaio, A., Wang, F. (eds.) ICTAC 2016. LNCS, vol. 9965, pp. 469–478. Springer, Cham (2016). https://doi.org/10.1007/978-3-319-46750-4_27
5. André, É.: IMITATOR 3: synthesis of timing parameters beyond decidability. In: Silva, A., Leino, K.R.M. (eds.) CAV 2021. LNCS, vol. 12759, pp. 552–565. Springer, Cham (2021). https://doi.org/10.1007/978-3-030-81685-8_26
6. André, É., Arias, J., Petrucci, L., Pol, J.: Iterative bounded synthesis for efficient cycle detection in parametric timed automata. In: TACAS 2021. LNCS, vol. 12651, pp. 311–329. Springer, Cham (2021). https://doi.org/10.1007/978-3-030-72016-2_17
7. André, É., Bloemen, V., Petrucci, L., van de Pol, J.: Minimal-time synthesis for parametric timed automata. In: Vojnar, T., Zhang, L. (eds.) TACAS 2019. LNCS, vol. 11428, pp. 211–228. Springer, Cham (2019). https://doi.org/10.1007/978-3-030-17465-1_12
8. André, É., Chatain, T., Encrenaz, E., Fribourg, L.: An inverse method for parametric timed automata. Int. J. Found. Comput. Sci. **20**(5), 819–836 (2009). https://doi.org/10.1142/S0129054109006905
9. André, É., Lime, D.: Liveness in L/U-parametric timed automata. In: Legay, A., Schneider, K. (eds.) ACSD, pp. 9–18. IEEE (2017). https://doi.org/10.1109/ACSD.2017.19
10. André, É., Waga, M., Urabe, N., Hasuo, I.: Exemplifying parametric timed specifications over signals with bounded behavior. Technical report abs/2203.13247, arXiv (2022). https://arxiv.org/abs/2203.13247
11. Asarin, E., Caspi, P., Maler, O.: Timed regular expressions. J. ACM **49**(2), 172–206 (2002). https://doi.org/10.1145/506147.506151
12. Bagnara, R., M., H.P., Zaffanella, E.: The parma polyhedra library: toward a complete set of numerical abstractions for the analysis and verification of hardware and software systems. Sci. Comput. Programm. **72**(1–2), 3–21 (2008). https://doi.org/10.1016/j.scico.2007.08.001
13. Barbot, B., Basset, N., Dang, T., Donzé, A., Kapinski, J., Yamaguchi, T.: Falsification of cyber-physical systems with constrained signal spaces. In: Lee, R., Jha, S., Mavridou, A., Giannakopoulou, D. (eds.) NFM 2020. LNCS, vol. 12229, pp. 420–439. Springer, Cham (2020). https://doi.org/10.1007/978-3-030-55754-6_25
14. Basset, N., Dang, T., Gigler, F., Mateis, C., Ničković, D.: Sampling of shape expressions with ShapEx. In: Arun-Kumar, S., Méry, D., Saha, I., Zhang, L. (eds.) MEMOCODE, pp. 118–125. ACM (2021). https://doi.org/10.1145/3487212.3487350
15. Brihaye, T., Geeraerts, G., Ho, H.-M., Monmege, B.: MIGHTyL: a compositional translation from MITL to timed automata. In: Majumdar, R., Kunčak, V. (eds.) CAV 2017. LNCS, vol. 10426, pp. 421–440. Springer, Cham (2017). https://doi.org/10.1007/978-3-319-63387-9_21

16. Cassez, F., Larsen, K.: The impressive power of stopwatches. In: Palamidessi, C. (ed.) CONCUR 2000. LNCS, vol. 1877, pp. 138–152. Springer, Heidelberg (2000). https://doi.org/10.1007/3-540-44618-4_12

17. Cimatti, A., Griggio, A., Magnago, E., Roveri, M., Tonetta, S.: Extending NUXMV with timed transition systems and timed temporal properties. In: Dillig, I., Tasiran, S. (eds.) CAV 2019. LNCS, vol. 11561, pp. 376–386. Springer, Cham (2019). https://doi.org/10.1007/978-3-030-25540-4_21

18. Dawes, J.H., Reger, G.: Explaining violations of properties in control-flow temporal logic. In: Finkbeiner, B., Mariani, L. (eds.) RV 2019. LNCS, vol. 11757, pp. 202–220. Springer, Cham (2019). https://doi.org/10.1007/978-3-030-32079-9_12

19. Daws, C., Yovine, S.: Two examples of verification of multirate timed automata with Kronos. In: RTSS, pp. 66–75. IEEE Computer Society (1995). https://doi.org/10.1109/REAL.1995.495197

20. Halbwachs, N., Proy, Y.-E., Raymond, P.: Verification of linear hybrid systems by means of convex approximations. In: Le Charlier, B. (ed.) SAS 1994. LNCS, vol. 864, pp. 223–237. Springer, Heidelberg (1994). https://doi.org/10.1007/3-540-58485-4_43

21. He, J., Bartocci, E., Ničković, D., Isakovic, H., Grosu, R.: From English to Signal Temporal Logic. Technical report abs/2109.10294, arXiv (2021), https://arxiv.org/abs/2109.10294

22. Henzinger, T.A.: The theory of hybrid automata. In: LICS, pp. 278–292. IEEE Computer Society (1996). https://doi.org/10.1109/LICS.1996.561342

23. Hoxha, B., Mavridis, N., Fainekos, G.: VISPEC: a graphical tool for elicitation of MTL requirements. In: IROS, pp. 3486–3492. IEEE (2015). https://doi.org/10.1109/IROS.2015.7353863

24. Hune, T., Romijn, J., Stoelinga, M., Vaandrager, F.W.: Linear parametric model checking of timed automata. JLAP 52–53, 183–220 (2002). https://doi.org/10.1016/S1567-8326(02)00037-1

25. Jovanović, A., Lime, D., Roux, O.H.: Integer parameter synthesis for real-time systems. TSE 41(5), 445–461 (2015). https://doi.org/10.1109/TSE.2014.2357445

26. Kim, S.K., Carrington, D.A.: Visualization of formal specifications. In: APSEC, pp. 102–109. IEEE Computer Society (1999). https://doi.org/10.1109/APSEC.1999.809590

27. Kurshan, R.P.: Transfer of model checking to industrial practice. In: Handbook of Model Checking, pp. 763–793. Springer, Cham (2018). https://doi.org/10.1007/978-3-319-10575-8_23

28. Maler, O., Nickovic, D.: Monitoring temporal properties of continuous signals. In: Lakhnech, Y., Yovine, S. (eds.) FORMATS/FTRTFT -2004. LNCS, vol. 3253, pp. 152–166. Springer, Heidelberg (2004). https://doi.org/10.1007/978-3-540-30206-3_12

29. Maler, O., Nickovic, D., Pnueli, A.: From MITL to timed automata. In: Asarin, E., Bouyer, P. (eds.) FORMATS 2006. LNCS, vol. 4202, pp. 274–289. Springer, Heidelberg (2006). https://doi.org/10.1007/11867340_20

30. Nguyen, H.G., Petrucci, L., van de Pol, J.: Layered and collecting NDFS with subsumption for parametric timed automata. In: Lin, A.W., Sun, J. (eds.) ICECCS, pp. 1–9. IEEE Computer Society, December 2018. https://doi.org/10.1109/ICECCS2018.2018.00009

31. Ničković, D., Qin, X., Ferrère, T., Mateis, C., Deshmukh, J.: Shape expressions for specifying and extracting signal features. In: Finkbeiner, B., Mariani, L. (eds.) RV 2019. LNCS, vol. 11757, pp. 292–309. Springer, Cham (2019). https://doi.org/10.1007/978-3-030-32079-9_17

32. Pakonen, A., Buzhinsky, I., Vyatkin, V.: Counterexample visualization and explanation for function block diagrams. In: INDIN, pp. 747–753. IEEE (2018). https://doi.org/10.1109/INDIN.2018.8472025
33. Prabhakar, P., Lal, R., Kapinski, J.: Automatic trace generation for signal temporal logic. In: RTSS, pp. 208–217. IEEE Computer Society (2018). https://doi.org/10.1109/RTSS.2018.00038
34. Raskin, J.F.: An introduction to hybrid automata. In: Hristu-Varsakelis, D., Levine, W.S. (eds.) Handbook of Networked and Embedded Control Systems, pp. 491–518. Birkhäuser (2005)
35. Roehm, H., Heinz, T., Mayer, E.C.: STLInspector: STL validation with guarantees. In: Majumdar, R., Kunčak, V. (eds.) CAV 2017. LNCS, vol. 10426, pp. 225–232. Springer, Cham (2017). https://doi.org/10.1007/978-3-319-63387-9_11
36. Tikhonova, U., Manders, M., Boudewijns, R.: Visualization of formal specifications for understanding and debugging an industrial DSL. In: Milazzo, P., Varró, D., Wimmer, M. (eds.) STAF 2016. LNCS, vol. 9946, pp. 179–195. Springer, Cham (2016). https://doi.org/10.1007/978-3-319-50230-4_13
37. Waga, M., André, É., Hasuo, I.: Model-bounded monitoring of hybrid systems. In: Maggio, M., Weimer, J., Farque, M.A., Oishi, M. (eds.) ICCPS, pp. 21–32. ACM (2021). https://doi.org/10.1145/3450267.3450531

Timed Automata Learning via SMT Solving

Martin Tappler[1,2]($\boxtimes$), Bernhard K. Aichernig[1], and Florian Lorber[3]

[1] Institute of Software Technology, Graz University of Technology, Graz, Austria
{martin.tappler,aichernig}@ist.tugraz.at
[2] Silicon Austria Labs, TU Graz – SAL DES Lab, Graz, Austria
[3] Aalborg University, Aalborg, Denmark
florber@cs.aau.dk

Abstract. Automata learning is a technique for automatically inferring models of existing systems, that enables formal verification of black-box systems. In this paper we propose a way of learning timed automata, extended final state machines that can measure the progress of time. We make use of SMT solving to learn timed automata consistent with the observations in a set of timed traces, which can be gathered via active testing or passive monitoring. By imposing a set of restrictions to the learnt models, we ensure that our solutions are not overly general. The presented SMT encoding of the problem allows for two ways of incremental solving and different search orders. We present a prototype implementation with results from case studies and randomly generated timed automata of varying size and complexity. We perform an extensive evaluation over six SMT solvers, using different theories and exploration strategies, as well as incremental and non-incremental solving.

1 Introduction

Automated inference of models is a challenging area researched under the names of process mining [27], specification mining [15], automata learning [13] and model learning [1]. The common goal is to derive a formal model for a black-box system or process, which is used to reason about and verify the system.

Model-based verification techniques such as model-checking are the core of formal verification. However, the used models suffer from three major issues: time and effort needed to create the models, the possible gap between the modelled system and the model, and the error proneness of manually created models. Automated learning of models can significantly aid in these issues. While some supervision and selection of suitable parameters is needed, manual effort is still comparably low. The gap between the system under learning (SUL) and the model is significantly reduced, as the model is built directly from the system observations. Correctness of the model is not guaranteed by passive model learning techniques that rely on recorded data, as these data might not cover all behaviour. However, by providing more data, the model can be further refined.

J. V. Deshmukh et al. (Eds.): NFM 2022, LNCS 13260, pp. 489–507, 2022.
https://doi.org/10.1007/978-3-031-06773-0_26

For real-time systems the verification of properties, such as the adherence to deadlines, is especially crucial. These systems are often modelled as timed automata (TA) [2], which are finite state machines extended by clocks to measure the progress of time. Several tools exist for the verification of TA [14].

In this work, we propose an approach to learn TA via SMT solving, on the basis of timed traces. The approach is passive, i.e., we use existing traces and do not interact with the SUL. We consider TA satisfying three conditions: determinism, isolated outputs, and k-urgency. That is, we expect to learn systems where a trace always leads to the same distinct location, no two outputs are ever enabled at the same time, and outputs are fired within k steps of being enabled. By imposing these restrictions, we avoid overly general solutions, as locations in learnt automata need to split until all restrictions are met.

We present our encoding of the SMT formula created for learning from timed traces, a detailed evaluation of the model learning using three case studies from previous work and several randomly generated automata of differing sizes. We provide extensive results for different SMT solvers, used theories, search orders and incremental solving, thus evaluating the capabilities of different solvers as well as the proposed learning approach. *Our contribution* is the novel application of SMT solving to the learning of TA, the presentation of an encoding of the problem in a highly adaptive and parameterized manner, and a thorough evaluation based on different configurations and SMT solvers.

Structure. After related work, we discuss preliminaries in Sect. 2. Section 3 shows the SMT encoding of the problem. Then, we discuss the implementation and evaluation in Sect. 4 and 5. Finally, we conclude the paper in Sect. 6.

Related Work. Various types of timed models have been studied in model learning. An et al. [4] and Verwer et al. [29] learn real-time automata, automata with only one clock which is reset on every transition. Sen et al. [22] learn continuous-time labeled Markov chains. Vaandrager at al. [28] learn Mealy machines with timers.

In comparison, TA are more expressive and offer good tool support for verification. Approaches for learning TA [3,9,19] have previously mostly been restricted to subclasses of TA, such as event recording automata [10,16] where each event is connected to a clock that is reset when the event is triggered or one-clock timed automata [3]. Tappler et al. [26] learn automata with several clocks, but forbid timing non-determinism via output urgency.

Different technologies are applied for learning, including the L^* algorithm [4], genetic programming [26] and state merging via k-tails [19]. For untimed systems also SAT solving [5,12,20] and SMT solving [23] have been used.

The presented approach builds upon the idea of using SMT solving for model learning [23], but applies it to TA. The restrictions we impose on our models are very close to the ones by Tappler et al. [26], only the urgency of outputs has been slightly relaxed to allow for more expressiveness. Thus, the presented approach newly combines the learning of TA with SMT solving, and eases the restrictions on the learned models compared to previous work.

2 Preliminaries

TA are finite automata enriched with real-valued clock variables [2]. Clocks measure the progress of time while an automaton resides in some location. Transitions can be constrained based on clock values and may reset clocks. We denote the set of clocks by $\mathcal{C}$ and the set of guards over $\mathcal{C}$ by $\mathcal{G}(\mathcal{C})$. Guards are conjunctions of constraints of the form $c \oplus k$, with $c \in \mathcal{C}, \oplus \in \{>, \geq, \leq, <\}, k \in \mathbb{N}$. Transitions are labelled by input and output actions, denoted by Σ_I and Σ_O respectively, with $\Sigma = \Sigma_I \cup \Sigma_O$. Input labels are suffixed by ? and output labels with !. A TA is a tuple $\langle L, l_0, \mathcal{C}, \Sigma, Inv, E \rangle$, where L is a finite non-empty set of locations, $l_0 \in L$ is the initial location, $\mathcal{C}$ are clocks, Σ are discrete actions, Inv is the mapping from locations to location invariants, and E is the set of edges. Location invariants are conjunctions of the form $c \leq d$ and $c < d$. Edges $E \subseteq L \times \Sigma \times \mathcal{G}(\mathcal{C}) \times 2^{\mathcal{C}} \times L$ are five-tuples (l, g, a, r, l'). We write $l \xrightarrow{g,a,r} l'$ for an edge $(l, g, a, r, l') \in E$ with guard g, label a, and clock resets r.

Example 1 (Train model). Figure 1 shows a TA modelling a train at a gate, with $\mathcal{C} = \{c\}$, $L = \{l_0, \ldots, l_5\}$, $\Sigma_I = \{start?, stop?, go?\}$, $\Sigma_O = \{appr!, enter!, leave!\}$, $Inv = \{l_1 \mapsto c \leq 5, \ldots\}$ and $E = \{l_0 \xrightarrow{\top, start?, \{c\}} l_1, \ldots\}$. We underline invariants to distinguish them from guards. From initial location l_0, the train accepts the input $start?$, resetting clock c. After that, it can produce the output $appr!$ if $c \geq 2$, i.e., the train may approach after 2 time units. The invariant forces $appr!$ to be produced within a duration of 3 time units, i.e., while $c \leq 5$.

The semantics of a TA $\mathcal{T}$ is given by a timed transition system (TTS) $[\![\mathcal{T}]\!] = \langle Q, q_0, \Sigma, T \rangle$, with states $Q = L \times \mathbb{R}_{\geq 0}{}^{\mathcal{C}}$, initial state q_0, and transitions $T \subseteq Q \times (\Sigma \cup \mathbb{R}_{\geq 0}) \times Q$, where we write $q \xrightarrow{e} q'$ if $(q, e, q') \in T$. A state $q = (l, \nu)$ consists of a location l and a clock valuation $\nu : \mathcal{C} \to \mathbb{R}_{\geq 0}$ that assigns a real value to every clock $c \in \mathcal{C}$. For $r \subseteq \mathcal{C}$, $\nu[r]$ denotes resets of clocks in r, i.e. $\forall c \in r : \nu[r](c) = 0$ and $\forall c \in \mathcal{C} \setminus r : \nu[r](c) = \nu(c)$. Let $(\nu + d)(c) = \nu(c) + d$ for $d \in \mathbb{R}_{\geq 0}, c \in \mathcal{C}$ denote the progress of time, $\nu \models \phi$ denote that valuation ν satisfies formula ϕ and $\nu \models Inv(l)$ denote that ν satisfies the invariant of l. Finally, $\mathbf{0}$ is the valuation assigning zero to all clocks. The initial state q_0 of the TTS $[\![\mathcal{T}]\!]$ underlying a TA $\mathcal{T} = \langle L, l_0, \mathcal{C}, \Sigma, Inv, E \rangle$ is $(l_0, \mathbf{0})$. Transitions of the TTS are all delay transitions $(l, \nu) \xrightarrow{d} (l, \nu + d)$ for a delay $d \in \mathbb{R}_{\geq 0}$ such that $\nu + d \models Inv(l)$, and all discrete transitions $(l, \nu) \xrightarrow{a} (l', \nu[r])$ for an edge $l \xrightarrow{g,a,r} l'$ such that $\nu \models g$ and $\nu[r] \models Inv(l')$.

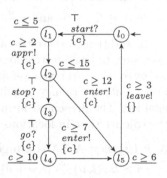

Fig. 1. Train TA.

Timed Traces & Language Inclusion. A timed trace tt is an alternating sequence of delays and actions of length $|tt|$, i.e., $tt = d_1 \cdot a_1 \cdots d_n \cdot a_n \in (\mathbb{R}_{\geq 0} \times \Sigma)^*$. The language $\mathcal{L}(\mathcal{T})$ of a TA $\mathcal{T}$ is the largest set of timed traces tt such that for every tt there is a path in the TTS $[\![\mathcal{T}]\!]$ with the same sequence of actions and delays.

3 Model Learning via SMT Solving

The main idea behind our approach is to encode the properties of the timed automaton we want to learn as an SMT formula. Solving the SMT formula yields a model encoding a timed automaton.

3.1 Setting

We consider the challenging setting of learning from only positive traces, because negative traces showing illegal behaviour are rarely available for black-box SULs. However, learning in this setting is generally impossible even for deterministic finite automata [6]. For this reason, we place common restrictions on TA, which we list below, helping to avoid learning overly general TA.

Assumptions on Timed Systems. Testing based on TA often places assumptions related to determinism on TA [11,24]. We introduce similar assumptions and describe these assumptions on the level of semantics. We use $s \xrightarrow{a}$ to denote $\exists s' : s \xrightarrow{a} s'$ and $s \xrightarrow{a}\!\!\!\!/\ $ for $\nexists s' : s \xrightarrow{a} s'$:

1. *Determinism.* A TA is deterministic iff for every state $s = (l, \nu)$ and every action $a \in \Sigma$, whenever $s \xrightarrow{a} s'$, and $s \xrightarrow{a} s''$ then $s' = s''$.
2. *Isolated Outputs.* A TA has isolated outputs iff whenever an output may be executed, then no other output is enabled, i.e., for every state $s = (l, \nu)$ $\forall o, o' \in \Sigma_O\ s \xrightarrow{o}$ and $s \xrightarrow{o'}$ implies $o = o'$.

In addition to these two assumptions related to deterministic behaviour, it is necessary to place restrictions on the sojourn time in locations. For this purpose, we introduce a relaxed version of output urgency [11] that we coin k-urgency. Strict output urgency requires an output to be fired immediately when it is enabled. The presented form of k-urgency adds timing uncertainty, by limiting the sojourn time in locations where outputs are possible to at most k time units:

3. *k-Urgency.* A TA is k-urgent if $\forall l \in L, \forall \nu \in \mathbb{R}_{\geq 0}{}^{\mathcal{C}}, \forall o \in \Sigma_O, (l, \nu) \xrightarrow{o}$ implies $\nexists d > k : (l, \nu) \xrightarrow{d} (l, \nu + d)$.

The train gate shown in Fig. 1 is k-urgent with $k = 3$.

Based on that, we can define our learning objective. Given a set of timed traces S sampled from a black-box SUL, our goal is to learn a timed automaton $\mathcal{T}$ such that $S \subseteq \mathcal{L}(\mathcal{T})$, i.e., we approximate language inclusion between the SUL and $\mathcal{T}$ on a finite set S. For a large enough set S, this converges to $\mathcal{L}(SUL) \subseteq \mathcal{L}(\mathcal{T})$. The above restrictions ensure that we do not produce overly general automata when we only have access to sampled (positive) traces that should be accepted. Determinism and assuming k-urgency, provide us with negative traces that should not be accepted, e.g., traces with too large delays. Other

---

Algorithm 1. Iterative SMT-Based Learning

Input: $TS, L_{\max}, E_{\max}, M_N, k, el$
Output: learned timed automaton *or* no solution
1: **for** $L_n \leftarrow 2$ **to** $L_{\max}$ **do**
2:     $E_n \leftarrow L_n \cdot el$
3:     **if** $E_n > E_{\max}$ **then return** no solution
4:     $constraints \leftarrow$ CREATECONSTRAINTS(TS, L_n, E_n, M_N, k)
5:     $(result, model) \leftarrow$ SOLVE$(constraints)$
6:     **if** $result$ **then return** CREATETA$(model)$
7: **return** no solution

---

techniques derive knowledge about negative and positive traces differently, e.g., by querying a teacher [4]. Determinism is also an important feature in model-based testing to decide the set of enabled actions after a trace [8]. Hence, our approach enables regression testing based on learned models.

3.2 Main Algorithm

Our SMT formulas consist of three types of constraints: (1) general properties of the considered class of timed automata, like determinism, (2) bounds on the automaton size, (3) language inclusion of timed traces given as training data. In this section, let TS be an ordered sequence of timed traces with one-based indexed access to select $tt_j = TS[j]$.

In common with other approaches to SMT-based learning [23], we try learning TA of bounded size, where the size is determined in terms of the number of locations and edges. We iteratively increase the size until learning is successful or we hit the upper size bound. To simplify searching for an appropriate pair of edge bound E_n and location bound L_n, we define E_n w.r.t. L_n via $E_n = L_n \cdot el$, where el is a constant that can be defined for each experiment. In addition, M_N denotes an upper limit for the constants in clock constraints.

The iterative learning is outlined in Algorithm 1, which takes the timed trace training data, the max. bounds, the upper limits for constants M_N, the bound for k-urgency and el as fixed parameters. In each iteration, the SMT-solver searches for suitable values satisfying all constraints (lines 4 and 5). If they are not satisfiable, we increase the bound constraints unless we hit the upper bounds $L_{\max}$ or $E_{\max}$ (lines 1 to 3). A model of satisfiable constraints encodes a timed automaton consistent with all traces, which is returned in Line 6. The following subsections will focus on these parts and explain the encoding.

3.3 Encoding of the Learnt Timed Automaton

In a single learning iteration with a fixed size bound, we aim to learn a TA $A = \langle C, \Sigma, L, l_0, Inv, E \rangle$, with a given number of locations $|L| = L_n$ and edges $|E| = E_n$. Without loss of generality, we limit ourselves to one clock in the following presentation. Each location l is assigned an invariant, represented by an upper bound $I(l)$. A guard on an edge e is defined by inclusive upper and exclusive lower limits denoted as $g_{up}(e)$ and $g_{lo}(e)$, respectively. Additional clocks could be added by adding additional copies of I, g_{up} and g_{lo} for each new clock. *Restricting Timing Constraints for Efficiency.* Guards encode admissible time intervals for each edge. To enable efficient SMT solving, we restrict guards to encode intervals $[g_{lo}, g_{up})$ that are left-closed and right-open, i.e., guards contain a lower-bound constraint $c \geq g_{lo}$ and an upper-bound constraint $c < g_{up}$, where g_{up} may be set arbitrarily large. If no upper bound is defined we set $g_{up} = M_N$.

This enables a more efficient SMT encoding and allows covering the complete range of clock values. Under a probabilistic interpretation of dense real time that assumes a non-discrete distribution of delays, these types of intervals do not impose a limitation. The probability of observing an event at an exact point in time is generally equal to zero, thus delays do not occur at the interval boundaries. Similarly, we restrict location invariants to use only non-strict inequalities.

Variables and Constants. We represent edges, locations, and action symbols by integers in the intervals $[1 .. L_n]$, $[1 .. E_n]$, and $[1 .. |\Sigma|]$. The determinism constraints are defined solely as constraints over integer constants and uninterpreted functions, whereas we introduce variables to specify constraints related to language inclusion. These variables connect the individual timed steps in a timed trace. For step i and timed trace $tt_j = \mathcal{TS}[j]$, we introduce:

- $e_{j,i}$ ... edge taken by step i of tt_j
- $l_{j,i}$ ... source location of the edge taken by step i of tt_j
- $c_{j,i}$ ... clock valuation before the delay in step i of tt_j
- $c_{j,i}^d$ ... clock valuation after delaying the delay in step i of tt_j

Uninterpreted Functions. We define the following uninterpreted functions to specify constraints, where $G^N = [0 .. M_N]$ are the ranges for guards and invariants. The integer intervals $L_N = [1 .. |L_n|]$ and $E_N = [1 .. |E_n|]$ are the admissible ranges for locations and edges, respectively.

$$
\begin{aligned}
source &: E_N \to L_N & target &: E_N \to L_N \\
label &: E_N \to [1 .. |\Sigma|] & reset &: E_N \to \mathbb{B} \\
g_{lo} &: E_N \to G_N & g_{up} &: E_N \to G_N \cup \{\infty\} \\
I &: L_N \to G_N \cup \{\infty\} & isOutput &: E_N \to \mathbb{B}
\end{aligned}
$$

The first three encode the mapping of an edge to its source location, target location and label, respectively. The next three map from an edge to its clock reset, the lower bound, and the upper bound of its guard. The invariant I maps from a location to its upper time bound. Finally, the last uninterpreted function is a helper function that returns true if the given edge is labelled with an output.

3.4 Constraints

We can now define the constraints on timed automata. They can be grouped into constraints on (1) determinism, (2) size bounds, and (3) language inclusion.

Determinism. We have two types of determinism constraints: (1) standard determinism, which specifies that at most one transition can be enabled for every action at every point in time, (2) isolated outputs, which specifies that no two output transitions can be enabled simultaneously. We express these constraints by specifying that guards of all edges e_i and e_j must be disjoint via:

$$\forall i, j \in E_N, i \neq j :$$
$$(source(i) = source(j) \wedge label(i) = label(j)) \implies$$
$$(g_{up}(i) \leq g_{lo}(j) \vee g_{up}(j) \leq g_{lo}(i)) \qquad\qquad \text{determinism}$$
$$\text{and}$$
$$(source(i) = source(j) \wedge isOutput(i) \wedge isOutput(j)) \implies$$
$$(g_{up}(i) \leq g_{lo}(j) \vee g_{up}(j) \leq g_{lo}(i)) \qquad\qquad \text{isolated outputs}$$

These constraints rely on the guards defining left-closed, right-open intervals.

Bound Constraints. Bound constraints predicate on (1) the number of locations and edges and (2) the ranges of guards and intervals. They are defined as:

$$\forall j: 1 \leq j \leq |\mathcal{TS}| \; \forall i: 1 \leq i \leq |\mathcal{TS}[j]| + 1: 1 \leq l_{j,i} \leq L_n$$
$$\forall j: 1 \leq j \leq |\mathcal{TS}| \; \forall i: 1 \leq i \leq |\mathcal{TS}[j]|: 1 \leq e_{j,i} \leq E_n$$
$$\forall e: 1 \leq e \leq E_n: 0 \leq g_{lo}(e) \leq G_N$$
$$\forall e: 1 \leq e \leq E_n: 0 < g_{up}(e) \leq G_N \vee g_{up}(e) \geq M_\infty$$
$$\forall l: 1 \leq l \leq L_n: 0 \leq I(l) \leq G_N \vee I(l) \geq M_\infty$$

The bound constraints for locations range one step further than the respective constraints on edges to ensure that the location reached by the final action in a trace is valid. The constraints $g_{up}(e) \geq M_\infty$ and $I(l) \geq M_\infty$ specify the absence of upper guard bounds and invariant constraints, respectively. Since SMT solvers do not support encoding ∞ by default, we set M_∞ to a sufficiently large value, such as, the maximal sum of delays in a timed trace. The guard bounds and invariant bounds improve efficiency, but are not strictly necessary, thus a conservative choice of G_N is possible if little domain knowledge is available.

Language Inclusion. Each step in a timed trace is encoded into a set of constraints. These constraints are defined over location and edge variables, which help to connect consecutive steps in a timed trace.

A trace $tt \in \mathcal{TS}$ is a series of delays and actions. When building the formulas, we look at one step of a trace at a time. In step $s_{j,i} = (d_{j,i}, a_{j,i})$, the first index j denotes the trace and the second index i denotes the step. The edge and location taken by a step $s_{j,i}$ are encoded as $e_{j,i}$ and $l_{j,i}$, respectively. All traces start from the initial location, encoded as the integer 1, with the clock value 0.

$$\forall j : l_{j,1} = 1 \qquad\qquad \forall j : c_{j,1} = 0$$

Each step $s_{j,i} = (d_{j,i}, a_{j,i})$ adds the following constraints to our SMT formula:

$$c_{j,i}^d = c_{j,i} + d_{j,i} \qquad\qquad c_{j,i}^d \leq I(l_{j,i}) \qquad (1)$$

$$source(e_{j,i}) = l_{j,i} \qquad\qquad target(e_{j,i}) = l_{j,i+1} \qquad (2)$$

$$label(e_{j,i}) = a_{j,i} \qquad\qquad\qquad\qquad\qquad\qquad (3)$$

$$c_{j,i}^d \geq g_{lo}(e_{j,i}) \qquad\qquad c_{j,i}^d < g_{up}(e_{j,i}) \qquad (4)$$

$$reset_{j,i} \implies c_{j,i+1} = 0 \qquad \neg reset_{j,i} \implies c_{j,i+1} = c_{j,i}^d \qquad (5)$$

$$c_{j,i+1} \leq I(l_{j,i+1}) \qquad a_{j,i} \in \Sigma_O \implies I(l_{j,i}) \leq g_{lo}(e_{j,i}) + k \qquad (6)$$

First, we encode the delay by $d_{j,i}$ time units and enforce that the invariant of the current location holds after delaying (1). Next we encode that the source location and target location of the edge $e_{j,i}$ taken by the current step are $l_{j,i}$ and $l_{j,i+1}$ (2), respectively. These constraints connect the individual steps, since $l_{j,i+1}$ will be the source location of the next step. The next constraint ensures that the label of the current edge is correct. In other words, Constraint 2 and Constraint 3 ensure that for every timed trace tt there is a connected path in the learned automaton with edges labelled by the actions of tt. Hence, these constraints enforce the discrete portion of language inclusion. The following two constraints ensure that the clock valuations satisfy the guard (split into lower and upper bound). The next two constraints update the clock of the next step based on the clock reset. The final two constraints predicate on invariants, where the first ensures the invariant of the next location is satisfied after potentially resetting the clock in Constraint 5. If the current edge is an output, we restrict the invariant of the source location to the lower guard bound of the current edge plus k, enabling a window of at least k time units for an output to be produced. That is, we enforce k-urgency as defined in Sect. 3.1.

3.5 Creating the Learned Timed Automaton

If all constraints specified above are satisfiable, an SMT solver will produce a model that defines all uninterpreted functions and values for all variables. To create a timed automaton from a model (Line 8 in Algorithm 1), we only process the function definitions, since they completely specify all edges, locations, and invariants. Basically, we create a TA with $L = L_N = [1 .. L_n]$, $l_0 = 1$, and $E = E_N = [1 .. E_n]$ and use the uninterpreted function definitions to define the invariants and edges, e.g., using the $source$ function to define source locations.

There may be superfluous locations or edges if L_n or E_n is larger than necessary. If there is valid TA with less than E_n, the SMT solver may choose arbitrary values for some mappings. We account for that by simulating all timed traces from $\mathcal{TS}$ on the learned model while checking which locations and edges are traversed. By removing edges and locations that are not traversed, we simplify the learned timed automaton while ensuring that it still satisfies all constraints.

4   Implementation

The constraints described in Sect. 3 are sufficient to specify a timed automaton that accepts the given training data. However, various implementation aspects, such as the choice of SMT solver, greatly affect the efficiency of SMT solving [7, 17]. As we will show, seemingly innocuous changes can result in significant speed-ups. In this section, we discuss implementation details that affect performance.

Our implementation uses JavaSMT [7] for interfacing with SMT solvers. This library allows us to seamlessly choose among different solvers for a thorough evaluation. Different SMT solvers support different theories to model guard values and clock valuations. We evaluated three different combinations of theories. Finally, incremental solving, i.e., stepwise adding of constraints to a stack interleaved with satisfiability checks, affects performance. The complete implementation and all results from the experiments discussed in Sect. 5 are available in a public git repository at https://github.com/mtappler/smt-ta-learning.

4.1   Theories

The constraints formulated in Sect. 3 predicate on variables and uninterpreted functions of three different data types. These data types comprise (1) discrete structure data, including locations, edges, and action labels, (2) integral timing bounds in guards and intervals, and (3) real-valued clock valuations. We identified three combinations of theories that work well to encode these types.

- *Real & Integer.* We use the theory of real numbers for clock valuations and the theory of integers for discrete data and integer-valued timing bounds.
- *Only Integers.* In this encoding, we use the theory of integers for all types of data. To handle real-valued delays, we multiply every delay with an integer-valued rounding factor r and round it to the nearest integer. We generally set $r = 100$ for our experiments.
- *Only Bitvectors.* The bitvector encoding works just like the integer encoding, but with fixed-size bitvectors instead of integers.

The first encoding is generally preferable since it does not introduce additional imprecision. However, the support of specific theories and efficiency of the implementation varies between solvers, therefore we investigate different encodings.

4.2   Incremental Solving

Our implementation supports incremental learning with two non-orthogonal configuration options, *search order* and *discrete first*, as well as non-incremental learning, where all constraints are pushed and checked at the same time. In any configuration, the guard-bound constraints and determinism constraints are pushed onto the solver stack first.

Search Order. When processing timed traces, we process a single step at a time, thus to process all traces we iterate over all traces and over the length of every trace. The order of iteration leads to two different incremental-solving strategies:

- *Depth-first.* In depth-first processing, we iterate over the traces and create constraints for all steps of a trace at once, pushing the constraints trace by trace. After every trace, we perform a satisfiability check.
- *Breadth-first.* In breadth-first processing, we iterate over the step index from one to the maximum trace length. For a given index i, we create constraints for step i of all traces and push them onto the stack. After processing all steps at index i, we perform a satisfiability check.

Incremental-solving strategies may be faster than non-incremental solving by dividing the learning problem into smaller subproblems. Additionally, they might terminate a learning iteration early if an intermediate satisfiability check fails.

Discrete First. In *discrete first* processing, we perform two passes over the training data. In the first pass, we push constraints involving discrete data onto the stack, such as, the size-bound constraints and $source(e_{j,i}) = l_{j,i}$. In the second pass, we add all constraints related to timing, such as $c_{j,i}^d \geq g_{lo}(e_{j,i})$. The intuition behind this strategy is that we allow the SMT solver to find potential solutions for the discrete part first. Refining these solution by adding timing constraints may be easier than solving everything at once.

5   Evaluation

In this section, we discuss experiments, where we evaluate the different implementation options and configurations discussed in Sect. 4.

5.1   Experiment Subjects

Our experiments were performed on three cases from previous work [26], and randomly generated automata of varying sizes. The three cases are a light switch, a train gate and a car alarm system (CAS). The car alarm system was split into two communicating components. The first component (CAS-Arming) has 9 locations and 18 edges and models arming of the CAS. The second one (CAS-Alarm) has 7 locations and 9 edges and models the switching on and off of the optical and audible alarm. The light switch (Light) and train gate (Train) are models with 5/6 locations and 10/13 edges, respectively. They are the same as in previous work, apart from introducing k-urgent outputs with $k = 3$. Previous work allowed no uncertainty in output timing, i.e., $k = 0$. The 40 random automata range from 3 to 6 locations, with 6 to 10 edges, two input symbols and two output symbols. For each number of locations, we generated 10 automata.

In the evaluation experiments, we treat the original automata as black-box SULs. The training data for learning are timed traces sampled from the SULs using UPPAAL [14]. For the manually created automata, we sample 50 traces and for the randomly generated automata, we sample $l \cdot 10$ traces, where l is the number of locations of the corresponding automaton. We generally set the learning parameter el, which controls the ratio of edges to locations (Algorithm 1), to 2. We set the maximum guard constant G_N to a value higher than the largest guard constant used by the SUL and we set $k = 3$ to enforce k-urgent outputs.

5.2 Performance Criteria

We perform all learning experiments with the SMT solvers BOOLECTOR, CVC 4, MATHSAT 5, SMTINTERPOL, YICES 2, and Z3, in turn evaluating the applicability of these solvers on our kind of problem, with respect to the used theories and support/benefit of incremental solving and different search orders.

We use the learning runtime and the quality of learned models as performance criteria. In order to determine the quality of the learnt models, we simulate randomly generated timed traces on them. As test data serve both, 200 positive and 200 negative traces, i.e., traces that are accepted or rejected by the SUL, to check whether the learned model accepts them. Their simulation provided us with the typical classification results based on true positives (i.e., the trace was a positive trace and could be simulated on the model), false positives (i.e., the trace was a negative trace but could be simulated on the model), true negatives, and false negatives. This allows us to calculate precision, recall, and F1-score, the harmonic mean of precision and recall, for our experiments. For every set of randomly generated automata with a fixed number of locations, we report runtimes and quality metrics averaged over all automata in the set.

Table 1. Model quality metrics for learning random TA of varying sizes with BOOLECTOR and the theory of bitvectors and YICES 2 and the theories of integers and reals.

Model	Metric	BOOLECTOR (BV)	YICES 2 (Integer)	YICES 2 (Real)
3 Locations	Precision	0.93	0.97	0.94
	Recall	0.89	0.89	0.98
	F1	0.91	0.93	0.96
4 Locations	Precision	0.97	0.98	0.97
	Recall	0.90	0.86	0.97
	F1	0.93	0.92	0.97
5 Locations	Precision	0.93	0.96	0.96
	Recall	0.94	0.86	0.99
	F1	0.93	0.91	0.97

5.3 Experiments

In the first analysis, we will mainly look at the model quality metrics, whereas in all other analyses we investigate learning efficiency in terms of runtime.

Model Quality. To investigate the quality of learned models, we examine precision, recall, and F1-score of models learned of random automata with 3 to 5 locations. Since discretization affects these metrics we use BOOLECTOR for constraints over the bitvector theory, YICES 2 and the integer theory, and YICES 2 combined with real-valued delays.

Table 1 contains the results from our experiments on model quality. We can see that the learned models approximate the SULs quite well, as they achieve an $F1$-score larger than 0.9 in general. On the one hand, we see a high precision for learning from discretized delays and real-valued delays. Hence, the learned models are not overly general. The determinism constraints and k-urgency prevent coarse overapproximations. On the other hand, discretization negatively affects recall by increasing the number of false negatives. By employing a rounding factor of $r = 100$, we effectively increase the resolution of guard constraints, which increases the likelihood of erroneously rejecting unseen data. We might counter this issue by increasing the amount of training data. By learning from twice as many timed traces with BOOLECTOR, we were able to increase the recall for 5-location automata from 0.94 to 0.97 (not included in the table). Unfortunately, this increased the runtime by a factor of about 3.5. The differences between bitvectors and integers also result from underspecification that could be mitigated through additional training data.

Table 2. Runtime (in minutes) for learning random timed automata with 3 locations with CVC 4, Z3, and YICES 2 applying incremental and non-incremental solving.

	CVC4 (inc)	CVC4 (non-inc)	YICES (inc)	YICES (non-inc)	Z3 (inc)	Z3 (non-inc)
Mean	0.74	Timeout	0.08	0.62	7.42	0.06
Maximum	1.15	Timeout	0.21	0.78	18.51	0.07
Minimum	0.11	Timeout	0.01	0.29	0.03	0.02

Incremental vs. Non-incremental Solving. In our experiments we observed major differences in how different SMT solvers handle incremental solving. We want to exemplify the potential extent of these differences by discussing runtime measurements for learning 3-location random automata with the three SMT solvers CVC 4, Z3, and YICES 2. Table 2 shows the average, min., and max. runtime for the learning. We use the theory of integers to encode delays in these experiments, but similar observations can be made for other encodings as well.

Both, CVC 4 and YICES 2, show the expected behavior of benefitting from incremental solving. For YICES 2, we can observe a speedup of approximately 7.75 on average, while CVC 4 even requires incremental solving to learn in reasonable time. Our CVC 4 experiments without incremental solving did not terminate within 10 h, which we indicate with *timeout* in the table. In contrast, Z3 suffers from incremental solving, where learning takes more than 100 times as long as in non-incremental mode. A potential explanation is that the incremental solver implementation used by Z3 may be more general and use different solving tactics than the standard integer solver[1]. It may be possible to improve the runtime of solving integer constraints as well by manually specifying certain solver tactics and implementing incremental solving via assumptions. Given the already large configuration space, we opted to use all SMT solvers in their default configuration. Interestingly, incremental solving of bitvector constraints with Z3 is 5 times as fast as non-incremental solving (results are not shown in the table, but are available online). Table 2 also shows that the difference between maximum and average runtime is larger in incremental solving than in non-incremental solving. This results from the fact that incremental solving may stop early if some intermediate subset of all constraints is already unsatisfiable.

Solver Performance. Next, we will examine the difference between individual solvers for learning random timed automata with 3 and 4 locations, respectively. In cases where multiple theories are available and perform differently, we report measurement results for multiple theory-solver configurations. We generally use incremental solving if it is more efficient and non-incremental solving otherwise.

Figure 2 depicts the average runtime of every solver-theory combination. The four missing bars indicate that the respective combination is not available. Although YICES 2 supports bitvectors, we could not run experiments due to an interface-related issue. We truncated the bar for the combination of CVC 4 with bitvectors, because its average runtime of 18 min would have distorted the chart. We can see that the choice of theory and solver can make a substantial difference in runtime. The fastest combination requires only 0.33% of the slowest combination. In general, Z3 with discretization and YICES 2 performed best in the runtime measurements. Considering the lower model quality resulting from discretization, YICES 2 with real-valued delays should be preferred.

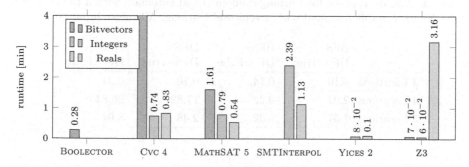

Fig. 2. Average runtimes (minutes) for 3-location random TA for diff. solvers/theories.

---

[1] Issue # 1459 on GitHub (https://github.com/Z3Prover/z3/issues/1459 discusses a similar case involving the floating point theory.

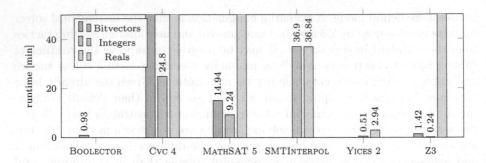

Fig. 3. Average runtimes (minutes) for 4-location random TA for diff. solvers/theories.

Let us examine experiments involving the 4-location random automata to see whether observation from the previous experiments carry over. Figure 3 shows the corresponding average runtime measurements. The four bars that exceed the y-axis limit result from timeouts where the experiments did not terminate within 10 h. We can observe that the runtime increased substantially, at least by factor of three. The relative ordering of solvers combined with discretized delays is mostly the same as in Fig. 2, except that MATHSAT 5 and CVC 4 switched places. Using the theory of reals now requires much more time in comparison with discretized delays. This results from one timed automaton being particularly hard to learn. The eighth automaton took YICES 2–19 min, while the mean and median runtime were 2.94 and 0.57 min. This high runtime results from numerical issues that actually necessitated learning a 5-location automaton. The higher resolution of guards in the discrete encoding of delays enabled more efficient learning of an automaton with four locations.

Table 3. Average runtime for learning random timed automata with 3 to 5 locations using YICES 2 in different modes of incremental learning. All values in minutes.

	BFS DF = True	BFS DF = False	DFS DF = True	DFS DF = False
3 Locations	0.10	0.14	0.10	0.24
4 Locations	2.94	9.22	17.82	26.84
5 Locations	1.57	5.32	2.48	8.64

Table 4. Results from learning timed automata from all case-study subjects using YICES 2 and incremental solving with BFS and discrete-first constraint solving.

		CAS (Arming)	CAS (Alarm)	Light	Train	3 Loc.	4 Loc.	5 Loc.	6 Loc.
Runtime [min]	Mean	362.21	124.19	23.10	382.99	0.10	2.94	1.57	235.56
	Max.					0.16	18.98	6.52	1446.69
	Min					0.02	0.03	0.04	0.29
F1	Mean	0.57	0.92	0.98	1	0.96	0.97	0.97	0.97
	Max.					1	1	1	1
	Min					0.88	0.92	0.98	0.93

Search-Order and Discrete-First Solving. Next, we want to look at the effect of the four different modes of incremental solving, i.e., the combinations of search order (BFS or DFS) and whether discrete-first (DF) constraint processing is enabled. For this purpose, we learn random timed automata with three to five locations using YICES 2 and real-valued delays.

Table 3 contains the average learning runtimes measured in these experiments. We can see that the order of solving indeed makes a difference, except when learning the relatively simple 3-location automata. For learning the 4-location automata, where one is particularly difficult to learn, and the 5-location automata, discrete-first solving with BFS performed best. Comparing the first and second column and the third and fourth column, we can see that especially discrete-first solving improves efficiency leading to a speed up of more than a factor of three. Concerning the other options, BFS appears to be faster than DFS, but the picture is not as clear, especially for the 5-location automata.

Fastest Configuration. Now that we have covered various learning configurations, we conclude the presentation of experimental results by looking at the performance of YICES 2 on all case-study subjects. Due to the favourable quality of learned models, we use real-valued delays, and we apply incremental solving.

Table 4 contains the gathered data comprising the runtime and the F1-score for all models, with minimum, maximum, and mean values for random automata. As in Table 1, which overlaps with Table 4, the F1-score is high in most cases. This means that we can learn models with high precision and recall with the available training data. The CAS-Arming model is an exception with a low F1-value due to a low recall, while its precision is 0.82, as the learned model rejects more traces than it should. A manual analysis reveals that two locations reached, which are after arming the CAS, are merged with the initial location. Additional training data may help to distinguish the merged locations, but learning already takes six hours. Still, the learned automaton models the inputs required to arm the CAS. Unfortunately, we also see a steep increase in runtime when going from three to four locations and from five-location automata to six-location automata, which include the train and the alarm model of the CAS. Learning models with six locations can take up to 24 h. The runtimes required to learn five-location automata appear to be an outlier in this trend.

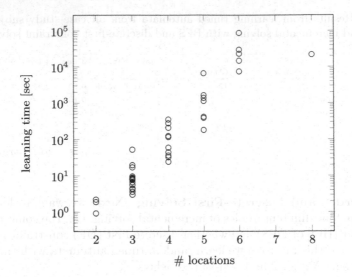

Fig. 4. Scatter plots of learning times from learning all case-study subjects using YICES 2 and incremental solving with BFS and discrete-first constraint solving.

To get a better overview of how learning times are distributed, we show a scatter plots of learning times with YICES 2 in Fig. 4. The x-axis displays the number of locations of the learned timed automata and the y-axis shows the required learning time in seconds in logarithmic scale. We can see that there is an exponential growth trend of the learning time with respect to the number of locations. However, the manually modelled car alarm system component with 8 locations seems to be an exception. We also see that for a fixed number of locations, there is a large variance in learning times. In all cases, expect for learned automata with two locations, there is at least an order of magnitude separating the fastest and the slowest learning time.

Threats to Validity. Using the default parameters for each solver might not achieve a fair comparison between the solvers, as the comparison might differ if every solver was called with optimal parameters. There is great potential in exploring different solver configurations and solving tactics, but we leave this as future work.

We have chosen to compare different SMT solvers rather than to competing learning techniques due to different assumptions on SULs, where some techniques assume knowledge or restrictions concerning resets [4,29] and others require strict output urgency [26,28]. If these assumptions hold, these techniques may perform better than the proposed approach.

6   Conclusion

We have proposed an approach for SMT-based learning of timed automata from a given set of timed traces. We presented the encoding and demonstrated that the approach is feasible and what factors affect performance. For this purpose, we compared six different SMT solvers in several settings. Our experiments showed that learned models achieve a high F1-score, i.e., they accept the language of the SUL with high probability, while rejecting timed traces that are not part of the language. Currently, learning is restricted to models with about 6 locations. It may be possible to learn larger models, like the arming model of the CAS, but we have not seen consistent performance for them. Despite this limitation, model learning for practically relevant systems may be feasible if, for instance, a specific property shall be investigated. Case studies on deterministic learning showed that learned models of communication protocols may have only a few states [21,25]. Alternatively, learning can be enabled by decomposition, which we demonstrate by learning two models of different functionalities of a CAS.

Considering the large runtime differences (up to two orders of magnitude) between different solvers, theories, and ways of processing constraints shown in Fig. 2, Fig. 3, Table 2, and Table 3, we see our results as promising. Future developments in SMT solving may improve runtime in a similar way, thus pushing the limit to 7 or 8 locations. As briefly discussed, it may already be possible to improve efficiency by deriving solving tactics specialized to learning timed automata with a specific solver. Furthermore, restricting the expressiveness of the class of hypothesis models may improve efficiency. For instance, real-time automata [29] may be simpler to learn. In this paper, we aimed to examine a large variety of solver implementation to get a broad picture and to conservatively place restrictions on the hypothesis class. Exploring implementation tactics tailored toward specific configurations, solvers, and classes of timed automata are potential venues for future work. Additionally, the integration of our approach into existing tools, such as the automata learning library AALpy [18], may ease extending and applying our technique.

Acknowledgments. This work has been supported by the "University SAL Labs" initiative of Silicon Austria Labs (SAL) and its Austrian partner universities for applied fundamental research for electronic based systems.

References

1. Aichernig, B.K., Mostowski, W., Mousavi, M.R., Tappler, M., Taromirad, M.: Model learning and model-based testing. In: Bennaceur, A., Hähnle, R., Meinke, K. (eds.) Machine Learning for Dynamic Software Analysis: Potentials and Limits. LNCS, vol. 11026, pp. 74–100. Springer, Cham (2018). https://doi.org/10.1007/978-3-319-96562-8_3
2. Alur, R., Dill, D.L.: A theory of timed automata. Theor. Comput. Sci. **126**(2), 183–235 (1994)
3. An, J., Chen, M., Zhan, B., Zhan, N., Zhang, M.: Learning one-clock timed automata. In: TACAS 2020. LNCS, vol. 12078, pp. 444–462. Springer, Cham (2020). https://doi.org/10.1007/978-3-030-45190-5_25
4. An, J., Wang, L., Zhan, B., Zhan, N., Zhang, M.: Learning real-time automata. Sci. China Inf. Sci. **64**(9), 1–17 (2021). https://doi.org/10.1007/s11432-019-2767-4

5. Avellaneda, F., Petrenko, A.: FSM inference from long traces. In: Havelund, K., Peleska, J., Roscoe, B., de Vink, E. (eds.) FM 2018. LNCS, vol. 10951, pp. 93–109. Springer, Cham (2018). https://doi.org/10.1007/978-3-319-95582-7_6

6. Avellaneda, F., Petrenko, A.: Inferring DFA without negative examples. In: International Conference on Grammatical Inference, pp. 17–29. PMLR (2019)

7. Baier, D., Beyer, D., Friedberger, K.: JavaSMT 3: interacting with SMT solvers in java. In: Silva, A., Leino, K.R.M. (eds.) CAV 2021. LNCS, vol. 12760, pp. 195–208. Springer, Cham (2021). https://doi.org/10.1007/978-3-030-81688-9_9

8. Clemente, L., Lasota, S., Piórkowski, R.: Determinisability of register and timed automata. CoRR abs/2104.03690 (2021). https://arxiv.org/abs/2104.03690

9. Grinchtein, O., Jonsson, B., Leucker, M.: Learning of event-recording automata. Theor. Comput. Sci. **411**(47), 4029–4054 (2010). https://doi.org/10.1016/j.tcs.2010.07.008

10. Grinchtein, O., Jonsson, B., Pettersson, P.: Inference of event-recording automata using timed decision trees. In: Baier, C., Hermanns, H. (eds.) CONCUR 2006. LNCS, vol. 4137, pp. 435–449. Springer, Heidelberg (2006). https://doi.org/10.1007/11817949_29

11. Hessel, A., Larsen, K.G., Nielsen, B., Pettersson, P., Skou, A.: Time-optimal real-time test case generation using UPPAAL. In: Petrenko, A., Ulrich, A. (eds.) FATES 2003. LNCS, vol. 2931, pp. 114–130. Springer, Heidelberg (2004). https://doi.org/10.1007/978-3-540-24617-6_9

12. Heule, M., Verwer, S.: Software model synthesis using satisfiability solvers. Empir. Softw. Eng. **18**(4), 825–856 (2013). https://doi.org/10.1007/s10664-012-9222-z

13. Howar, F., Steffen, B.: Active automata learning in practice. In: Bennaceur, A., Hähnle, R., Meinke, K. (eds.) Machine Learning for Dynamic Software Analysis: Potentials and Limits. LNCS, vol. 11026, pp. 123–148. Springer, Cham (2018). https://doi.org/10.1007/978-3-319-96562-8_5

14. Larsen, K.G., Pettersson, P., Yi, W.: Uppaal in a nutshell. Int. J. Softw. Tools Technol. Transf. **1**(1), 134–152 (1997)

15. Li, W., Forin, A., Seshia, S.A.: Scalable specification mining for verification and diagnosis. In: Sapatnekar, S.S. (ed.) Proceedings of the 47th Design Automation Conference, DAC 2010, Anaheim, California, USA, 13–18 July 2010, pp. 755–760. ACM (2010). https://doi.org/10.1145/1837274.1837466

16. Lin, S.-W., André, É., Dong, J.S., Sun, J., Liu, Y.: An efficient algorithm for learning event-recording automata. In: Bultan, T., Hsiung, P.-A. (eds.) ATVA 2011. LNCS, vol. 6996, pp. 463–472. Springer, Heidelberg (2011). https://doi.org/10.1007/978-3-642-24372-1_35

17. de Moura, L., Passmore, G.O.: The strategy challenge in SMT solving. In: Bonacina, M.P., Stickel, M.E. (eds.) Automated Reasoning and Mathematics. LNCS (LNAI), vol. 7788, pp. 15–44. Springer, Heidelberg (2013). https://doi.org/10.1007/978-3-642-36675-8_2

18. Muškardin, E., Aichernig, B.K., Pill, I., Pferscher, A., Tappler, M.: AALpy: an active automata learning library. In: Hou, Z., Ganesh, V. (eds.) ATVA 2021. LNCS, vol. 12971, pp. 67–73. Springer, Cham (2021). https://doi.org/10.1007/978-3-030-88885-5_5

19. Pastore, F., Micucci, D., Mariani, L.: Timed k-tail: automatic inference of timed automata. In: 2017 IEEE International Conference on Software Testing, Verification and Validation, ICST 2017, Tokyo, Japan, 13–17 March 2017, pp. 401–411. IEEE Computer Society (2017). https://doi.org/10.1109/ICST.2017.43

20. Petrenko, A., Avellaneda, F., Groz, R., Oriat, C.: From passive to active FSM inference via checking sequence construction. In: Yevtushenko, N., Cavalli, A.R., Yenigün, H. (eds.) ICTSS 2017. LNCS, vol. 10533, pp. 126–141. Springer, Cham (2017). https://doi.org/10.1007/978-3-319-67549-7_8

21. De Ruiter, J., Poll, E.: Protocol state fuzzing of TLS implementations. In: Jung, J., Holz, T. (eds.) 24th USENIX Security Symposium, USENIX Security 15, Washington, D.C., USA, 12–14 August 2015. pp. 193–206. USENIX Association (2015). https://www.usenix.org/conference/usenixsecurity15/technical-sessions/presentation/de-ruiter

22. Sen, K., Viswanathan, M., Agha, G.: Learning continuous time Markov chains from sample executions. In: First International Conference on the Quantitative Evaluation of Systems, 2004. QEST 2004. Proceedings, pp. 146–155. IEEE (2004)

23. Smetsers, R., Fiterău-Broştean, P., Vaandrager, F.: Model learning as a satisfiability modulo theories problem. In: Klein, S.T., Martín-Vide, C., Shapira, D. (eds.) LATA 2018. LNCS, vol. 10792, pp. 182–194. Springer, Cham (2018). https://doi.org/10.1007/978-3-319-77313-1_14

24. Springintveld, J., Vaandrager, F.W., D'Argenio, P.R.: Testing timed automata. Theor. Comput. Sci. **254**(1-2), 225–257 (2001). https://doi.org/10.1016/S0304-3975(99)00134-6

25. Tappler, M., Aichernig, B.K., Bloem, R.: Model-based testing IoT communication via active automata learning. In: 2017 IEEE International Conference on Software Testing, Verification and Validation, ICST 2017, Tokyo, Japan, 13–17 March 2017, pp. 276–287. IEEE Computer Society (2017). https://doi.org/10.1109/ICST.2017.32

26. Tappler, M., Aichernig, B.K., Larsen, K.G., Lorber, F.: Time to learn–learning timed automata from tests. In: André, É., Stoelinga, M. (eds.) FORMATS 2019. LNCS, vol. 11750, pp. 216–235. Springer, Cham (2019). https://doi.org/10.1007/978-3-030-29662-9_13

27. Turner, C.J., Tiwari, A., Olaiya, R., Xu, Y.: Process mining: from theory to practice. Bus. Process. Manag. J. **18**(3), 493–512 (2012). https://doi.org/10.1108/14637151211232669

28. Vaandrager, F., Bloem, R., Ebrahimi, M.: Learning Mealy machines with one timer. In: Leporati, A., Martín-Vide, C., Shapira, D., Zandron, C. (eds.) LATA 2021. LNCS, vol. 12638, pp. 157–170. Springer, Cham (2021). https://doi.org/10.1007/978-3-030-68195-1_13

29. Verwer, S., De Weerdt, M., Witteveen, C.: An algorithm for learning real-time automata. In: Benelearn 2007: Proceedings of the Annual Machine Learning Conference of Belgium and the Netherlands, Amsterdam, The Netherlands, 14–15 May 2007

Asynchronous Composition of Local Interface LTL Properties

Alberto Bombardelli[✉][iD] and Stefano Tonetta[✉][iD]

Fondazione Bruno Kessler, Via Sommarive, 18, 38123 Povo TN, Italy
{abombardelli,tonettas}@fbk.eu

Abstract. The verification of asynchronous software components is very challenging due to the non-deterministic interleaving of components and concurrent access to shared variables. Compositional approaches decouple the problem of verifying local properties specified over the component interfaces from the problem of composing them to ensure some global property. In this paper, we focus on symbolic model checking techniques for Linear-time Temporal Logic [24] (LTL) properties on asynchronous software components communicating through data ports. Differently from event-based composition, the local properties can specify constraints on the input provided by other components, making their composition more complex.

We propose a new LTL rewriting that translates a local property into a global one taking into account interleaving with other processes. We demonstrate that for every possible global trace, the local LTL property is satisfied by its projection on the local symbols if and only if the rewritten LTL property is satisfied by the global trace. This rewriting is then optimized, reducing the size of the resulting formula and leaving it unchanged when the temporal property is stutter invariant. We also consider an alternative approach where the local formulas are first translated into fair transition systems and then composed. This work has been implemented inside the contract-based design model checking tool OCRA as part of the contract refinement verification suite. Finally, the different composition approaches were compared through an experimental evaluation that covers various types of specifications.

1 Introduction

Software model checking [1,26] is an algorithmic approach used the verification of programs. It combines different methods based on deductive reasoning, abstraction, and state space exploration. Model checking typically specifies the property to be verified in a temporal logic. One of the most common logic used to express properties of programs is first-order Linear-time Temporal Logic (LTL) [24].

A general problem of model checking is the state space explosion problem. The scalability of the method is exacerbated when considering the asynchronous composition of programs, due to the non-deterministic interleaving of components and concurrent access to shared variables. Compositional approaches usually alleviate the problem by decoupling the problem of verifying local properties

© Springer Nature Switzerland AG 2022
J. V. Deshmukh et al. (Eds.): NFM 2022, LNCS 13260, pp. 508–526, 2022.
https://doi.org/10.1007/978-3-031-06773-0_27

specified over the component interfaces from the problem of composing them to ensure some global property. However, the asynchronous composition of local temporal properties may be tricky when considering software components communicating through data ports.

In this paper, we define the asynchronous composition of local LTL properties based on a rewriting $\mathcal{R}_c$ that maps the local constraints on the input/output data of a component c on the global points in which the component is active. In this case, the formulas can be rewritten to take into account interleaving and conjoined with additional constraints ψ_{constr} to encode for example the persistence of variables that are not written by the active process. In this way, it is possible to verify whether a global property ϕ is satisfied by the composition of local properties, by checking the validity of an following LTL formula in the form: $\bigwedge_{c \in C} \mathcal{R}_c(\phi_c) \wedge \psi_{constr} \to \phi$.

We define the rewriting $\mathcal{R}_c$ for quantifier-free first-order LTL with the "next" operator. In particular, the rewriting of "next", which is important to express input/output properties, needs the use of event-freezing functions, introduced in [28] to relate variables across different time points. We prove that the rewriting is correct, i.e., that for every possible global trace, the local LTL property is satisfied by its projection on the local symbols if and only if the rewritten LTL property is satisfied by the global trace. The main contribution of the paper is an optimized version of the rewriting that takes into account the frame conditions on output data and the stutter invariance of other operators to reduce the size of the resulting formula. We also consider an alternative approach where the local formulas are first translated into fair transition systems and then composed.

The proposed approach has been implemented inside OCRA, which supports a rich extension of LTL and uses a state-of-the-art model checking algorithm implemented in nuXmv [6] as back-ends to check satisfiability. We validated the approach empirically by evaluating the local property and the rewritten one on local traces and their extension with stuttering of local variables. We evaluated the approach on various kind of formulas and components, and compared the different approaches in terms of scalability.

Summarizing, the main contribution of the paper is a rewriting of LTL formulas with the following features:

- it allows to check compositional rules for asynchronous components communicating through input/output data ports;
- it supports compositional reasoning for first-order LTL properties with next and event-freezing functions;
- it is optimized to reduce the size of the resulting formula;
- it has been validated and evaluated on various benchmarks.

The rest of the paper is organized as follows: in Sect. 2, we compare the proposed solution with related works; in Sect. 3, we give some preliminary definitions; in Sect. 4, we formalize the problem; in Sect. 5, we define the rewriting, its optimized version, and the alternative approach based on compilation into transition systems; in Sect. 6, we report on the experimental validation and evaluation; finally, in Sect. 7, we draw the conclusions and some directions for future works.

2   Related Works

When dealing with temporal logics such as LTL for asynchronous systems, one of the main references is the work of Leslie Lamport on Temporal Logic of Action (TLA) [17], later enriched with additional operators [18] and to component-based models in [27]. In fact, we adopt the (quantifier-free) first-order version of LTL [20] with the "next" function which is used to specify the succession of actions of a program. TLA natively supports the notion of stuttering for composing asynchronously programs so that the composition is simply obtained by conjoining the specifications. We focus instead on local properties that are specified independently from how the program is composed so that "next" and input/output data refer only to the local execution. To the best of our knowledge, this paper first addresses the asynchronous composition of local first-order LTL properties. In fact, we rewrite "next" terms using the "at next" operator introduced in [28] to take into account interleaving by referring to the value of variables at the next point in time where the component is not stuttering.

As for propositional LTL, the composition of specifications is studied in various papers on assume-guarantee reasoning (see, e.g., [11,16,21,23]) for both synchronous and asynchronous composition. In the case of asynchronous systems, most works focus on fragments of LTL without the next operator, where formulas are always stutter invariant. Other studies investigated how to tackle down state-space explosion for that scenario usually employing techniques such as partial order reduction [4]. However, our work covers a more general setting, where also the presence of input variables makes formulas non stutter invariant.

Similarly to our work, [4] considers a rewriting for LTL with events to map local properties into global ones with stuttering. In [3], a related rewriting is used within an asynchronous version of HyperLTL. However, contrary to this paper, these works do not consider input variables (nor first-order extension) and assume that every variable does not change during stuttering, resulting in a simpler rewriting. In [15], a temporal clock operator is introduced to express properties related to multiple clocks and, in principle, can be used to interpret formulas over the time points in which a component is not stuttering. Its rewriting is indeed similar to the basic version defined in this paper, but is limited to propositional LTL and has not been conceived for asynchronous composition. The optimization that we introduce to exploit the stutter invariance of subformulas results in simpler formulas easy to be analyzed as shown in our experimental evaluation.

The rewriting of asynchronous LTL is similar to the transformation of asynchronous symbolic transition systems into synchronous ones described in [10]. The work considers connections based on events where data are exchanged only upon synchronization (allowing optimizations as in shallow synchronization [5]). Thus, it does not consider components that read from input variables that may be changed by other components. Moreover, [10] is not able to transform temporal logic local properties in global one as in this paper.

3   Background

3.1   Linear Temporal Logic

In this paper we consider LTL [20] extended with past operators [19] as well as
"if-then-else" (*ite*) and "at next" ($@\tilde{F}$), and "at last" ($@\tilde{P}$) operators from [28].
For simplicity we refer to it simply as LTL.

We work in the setting of Satisfiability Modulo Theory (SMT) [2] and LTL
Modulo Theory (see, e.g., [9]). First-order formulas are built as usual by proposition logic connectives, a given set of variables V and a first-order signature Σ,
and are interpreted according to a given Σ-theory $\mathcal{T}$. We assume to be given
the definition of $M, \mu \models_{\mathcal{T}} \varphi$ where M is a Σ-structure, μ is a value assignment
to the variables in V, and φ is a formula. Whenever $\mathcal{T}$ and M are clear from
contexts we omit them and simply write $\mu \models \varphi$.

LTL Syntax

Definition 1. *Given a signature Σ and a set of variables V, LTL formulas φ
are defined by the following syntax:*

$$\varphi := \top | \bot | pred(u_1, \ldots, u_n) | \neg \varphi_1 | \varphi_1 \vee \varphi_2 | X \varphi_1 | \varphi_1 U \varphi_2 | Y \varphi_1 | \varphi_1 S \varphi_2$$

$$u := c | x | func(u_1, \ldots, u_n) | next(u_1) | ite(\varphi, u_1, u_2) | u_1 @ \tilde{F} \varphi | u_1 @ \tilde{P} \varphi$$

*where c, $func$, and $pred$ are respectively a constant, a function, and a predicate
of the signature Σ and x is a variable in V.*

Apart from $@\tilde{F}$ and $@\tilde{P}$, the operators are standard. $u@\tilde{F}\varphi$ represents the
value of u at the next point in time in which φ holds. Similarly, $u@\tilde{P}\varphi$ represents
the value of u at the last point in time in which φ holds.

LTL Semantic. LTL formulas are interpreted over traces, i.e., infinite sequences
of assignments to the variables in V. We denote by $\Pi(V)$ the set of all possible
traces over the variable set V. Given a trace $\pi = s_0 s_1 \cdots \in \Pi(V)$ and a Σ-
structure M, the semantic of a formula φ is defined as follows:

- $\pi, M, i \models pred(u_1, \ldots, u_n)$ iff $pred^M(\pi^M(i)(u_1), \ldots, \pi^M(i)(u_n))$
- $\pi, M, i \models \varphi_1 \wedge \varphi_2$ iff $\pi, M, i \models \varphi_1$ and $\pi, M, i \models \varphi_2$
- $\pi, M, i \models \neg \varphi$ iff $\pi, M, i \not\models \varphi$
- $\pi, M, i \models \varphi_1 U \varphi_2$ iff there exists $k \geq i, \pi, M, k \models \varphi_2$ and for all $l, i \leq l < k, \pi, M, l \models \varphi_1$
- $\pi, M, i \models \varphi_1 S \varphi_2$ iff there exists $k \leq i, \pi, M, k \models \varphi_2$ and for all $l, k < l \leq i, \pi, M, l \models \varphi_1$
- $\pi, M, i \models X\varphi$ iff $\pi, M, i+1 \models \varphi$
- $\pi, M, i \models Y\varphi$ iff $i > 0$ and $\pi, M, i-1 \models \varphi$

where the interpretation of terms $\pi^M(i)$ is defined as follows:

- $\pi^M(i)(c) = c^M$
- $\pi^M(i)(x) = s_i(x)$ if $x \in V$
- $\pi^M(i)(func(u_1, \ldots, u_n)) = func^M(\pi^M(i)(u_1), \ldots, \pi^M(i)(u_n))$
- $\pi^M(i)(next(u)) = \pi^M(i+1)(u)$
- $\pi^M(i)(u@\tilde{F}(\varphi)) = \pi^M(k)(u)$if there exists $k > i$ such that, for all $l, i < l < k, \pi, M, l \not\models \varphi$ and $\pi, M, k \models \varphi$;
  $\pi^M(i)(u@\tilde{F}(\varphi)) = def_{u@\tilde{F}_\varphi}$ otherwise.
- $\pi^M(i)(u@\tilde{P}(\varphi)) = \pi^M(k)(u)$if there exists $k < i$ such that, for all $l, i > l > k, \pi, M, l \not\models \varphi$ and $\pi, M, k \models \varphi$;
  $\pi^M(i)(u@\tilde{F}(\varphi)) = def_{u@\tilde{P}_\varphi}$ otherwise.

$$- \pi^M(i)(ite(\varphi, u_1, u_2)) = \begin{cases} \pi^M(i)(u_1) & \text{if } \pi, M, i \models \varphi \\ \pi^M(i)(u_2) & \text{otherwise} \end{cases}$$

and the $pred^M, func^M, c^M$ are the interpretation M of the symbols in Σ, and $def_{u@\tilde{F}_\varphi}$ and $def_{u@\tilde{P}_\varphi}$ are some default values in domain of M.

Finally, we have that $\pi, M \models \varphi$ iff $\pi, M, 0 \models \varphi$.

In the following, we assume to have a background theory such that the symbols in Σ are interpreted by an implicit structure M (e.g., theory of reals, integers, etc.). We therefore omit M to simplify the notation, writing $\pi, i \models \varphi$ and $\pi(i)(u)$ instead of respectively $\pi, M, i \models \varphi$ and $\pi^M(i)(u)$.

Moreover, we use the following standard abbreviations: $\varphi_1 \wedge \varphi_2 := \neg(\neg\varphi_1 \vee \neg\varphi_2)$, $\varphi_1 R \varphi_2 := \neg(\neg\varphi_1 U \neg\varphi_2)$ (φ_1 releases φ_2), $F\varphi := \top U \phi$ (sometime in the future φ), $G\varphi := \neg F \neg\varphi$ (always in the future φ), $O\varphi := \top S\varphi$ (once in the past φ), $H\varphi := \neg O \neg\varphi$ (historically in the past φ), $Z\varphi := \neg Y \neg\varphi$ (yesterday φ or at initial state), $X^n\varphi := XX^{n-1}\varphi$ with $X^0\varphi := \varphi$, $Y^n\varphi := YY^{n-1}\varphi$ with $Y^0\varphi := \varphi$, $Z^n\varphi := ZZ^{n-1}\varphi$ with $Z^0\varphi := \varphi$, $F^{\leq n}\varphi := \varphi \vee X\varphi \vee \cdots \vee X^n\varphi$, $G^{\leq n}\varphi := \varphi \wedge X\varphi \wedge \cdots \wedge X^n\varphi$, $O^{\leq n}\varphi := \varphi \vee Y\varphi \vee \cdots \vee Y^n\phi$, $H^{\leq n}\varphi := \varphi \wedge Z\varphi \wedge \cdots \wedge Z^n\varphi$.

Since this paper heavily relies on the release operator, we explicitly define its semantics as follows:

$\pi, M, i \models \varphi_1 R \varphi_2$ iff for all $l \geq i, \pi, M, l \models \varphi_2$ or there exists $k \geq i, \pi, M, k \models \varphi_1$ and for all $i \leq l' \leq k, \pi, M, l' \models \varphi_2$

3.2 Interface Transition Systems

In this paper, we represents I/O components as Interface Transition Systems, a symbolic version of interface automata [13] that considers I/O variables instead of I/O actions.

Definition 2. *An Interface Transition System (ITS) $\mathcal{M}$ is a tuple $\mathcal{M} = \langle V_I, V_O, V_H, \mathcal{I}, \mathcal{T}, \mathcal{F} \rangle$ where:*

- *V_I is the set of input variables, V_O is the set of output variables, V_H is the set of internal variables where $V_I \cap V_O = \emptyset$, $V_I \cap V_H = \emptyset$ and $V_O \cap V_H = \emptyset$.*
- *$V := V_I \cup V_O \cup V_H$ denotes the set of the variables of $\mathcal{M}$*

- $\mathcal{I}$ *is the initial condition, a formula over* $V_O \cup V_H$,
- $\mathcal{T}$ *is the transition condition, a formula over* $V \cup V'_O \cup V'_H$ *where* V'_O *and* V'_H
  are respectively the primed versions of V_O *and* V_H
- $\mathcal{F}$ *is the set of fairness constraints, a set of formulas over* V.

A symbolic transition system $\mathcal{M} = \langle V, S, \mathcal{I}, \mathcal{T}, \mathcal{F} \rangle$ *is an interface transition system without input/output variables (i.e.,* $\langle \emptyset, \emptyset, V, S, \mathcal{I}, \mathcal{T}, \mathcal{F} \rangle$).

Definition 3. *A trace* π *of an ITS* $\mathcal{M}$ *is a trace* $\pi = s_0 s_1 s_2 \cdots \in \Pi(V)$ *such that* $s_0 \models \mathcal{I}$, *for all* i, $s_i \cup s'_{i+1} \models \mathcal{T}$, *and for all* $f \in \mathcal{F}$, *for all* i, *there exists* $j > i$, $s_j \models f$. *The language* $\mathscr{L}(\mathcal{M})$ *of an interface transition system* $\mathcal{M}$ *is the set of all traces of* $\mathcal{M}$. *Given an LTL formula* φ, $\mathcal{M} \models \varphi$ *iff, for all traces* π *of* $\mathcal{M}$, $\pi \models \varphi$.

The asynchronous composition of two ITS is an ITS where the transitions of the two original ITS occurs concurrently. To compose two interface transition systems, their variables must be compatible.

Definition 4. *Two ITS* $\mathcal{M}_1, \mathcal{M}_2$ *are compatible iff they share respectively only input with output (i.e.* $V^1 \cap V^2 = (V_O^1 \cap V_I^2) \cup (V_I^1 \cap V_O^2)$)

The asynchronous composition of ITS should allow certain ITS to run their transitions while the other transition systems freeze. To encode this behaviour symbolically, the composition adds one *stuttering* variable for each interface transition system. A stuttering variable is a Boolean variable that tells whether a specific component is frozen or if it is executing its transition. We denote $st^{\mathcal{M}}$ as the stuttering variable of the ITS $\mathcal{M}$.

Moreover, we introduce new transition conditions $\psi^{\mathcal{M}}_{cond}$ to express the fact that an ITS $\mathcal{M}$ inside a composition do not change their output and internal variables when their stuttering variables are true. Formally, for all ITS $\mathcal{M}$:
$\psi^{\mathcal{M}}_{cond} = st^{\mathcal{M}} \rightarrow \bigwedge_{v \in V_O \cup V_H} (v = v')$

Definition 5. *Let* $\mathcal{M}_1$ *and* $\mathcal{M}_2$ *be two compatible interface transition systems.* $\mathcal{M}_1 \otimes \mathcal{M}_2 = \langle V_I, V_O, V_H, \mathcal{I}, \mathcal{T}, \mathcal{F} \rangle$ *where:*

- $V_I = V_I^1 \cup V_I^2 \setminus ((V_I^1 \cap V_O^2) \cup (V_O^1 \cap V_I^2))$
- $V_O = V_O^1 \cup V_O^2 \setminus ((V_I^1 \cap V_O^2) \cup (V_O^1 \cap V_I^2))$
- $V_H = V_H^1 \cup V_H^2 \cup \{st^{\mathcal{M}_1}, st^{\mathcal{M}_2}\} \cup ((V_I^1 \cap V_O^2) \cup (V_O^1 \cap V_I^2))$
- $\mathcal{I} = \mathcal{I}^1 \wedge \mathcal{I}^2$
- $\mathcal{T} = (\neg st^{\mathcal{M}_1} \rightarrow \mathcal{T}^1) \wedge (\neg st^{\mathcal{M}_2} \rightarrow \mathcal{T}^2) \wedge \psi^{\mathcal{M}_1}_{cond} \wedge \psi^{\mathcal{M}_2}_{cond}$
- $\mathcal{F} = \{\neg st^{\mathcal{M}_1}, \neg st^{\mathcal{M}_2}\} \cup \{\varphi^1 \wedge \neg st^{\mathcal{M}_1} | \varphi^1 \in \mathcal{F}^1\} \cup \{\varphi^2 \wedge \neg st^{\mathcal{M}_2} | \varphi^2 \in \mathcal{F}^2\}$

The definition can be easily generalized to n *ITSs* $\mathcal{M}_1 \otimes ... \otimes \mathcal{M}_n$

Definition 6. *Let* $\mathcal{M} = \mathcal{M}_1 \otimes \mathcal{M}_2$ *be the asynchronous composition of two ITS* $\mathcal{M}_1$ *and* $\mathcal{M}_2$, *let* $\pi = s_0 s_1 ...$ *be a trace of* $\mathcal{M}$. *A pair of consecutive assignments to states* s_i, s_{i+1} *of* π *is called stuttering transition w.r.t.* $\mathcal{M}_1$, $\mathcal{M}_2$ *iff* $s_i \models st^{\mathcal{M}_1}, st^{\mathcal{M}_2}$ *respectively.*

Definition 7. *Let* $\pi = s_0 s_1 \ldots$ *be a trace of an ITS* $\mathcal{M}$ *and* $V' \subseteq V$ *a set of symbols of* $\mathcal{M}$. *We denote* $s_i(V')$ *as the restriction of the assignment* s_i *to the symbols of* V'; *moreover, we denote* $\pi_{|V'} := s_0(V') s_1(V') \ldots$ *as the restriction of all the state assignments of* π *to the symbols of* V'. *Furthermore, we denote* $\mathcal{L}(\mathcal{M})_{|V'} = \{\pi_{|V'} | \pi \in \mathcal{L}(\mathcal{M})\}$ *as the restriction of all the traces of the language of an ITS* $\mathcal{M}$ *to a set of symbols* $V' \subseteq V$.

Definition 8. *Let* $\pi = s_0 s_1 \ldots$ *be a trace of the asynchronous composition of* n *ITS* $\mathcal{M}_1, \ldots, \mathcal{M}_n$. *By fairness constraints on stuttering there are infinitely many points* $i_0, i_1, \ldots$ *such that for all* $j : \pi, i_j \models \neg st^{\mathcal{M}_h}$ *and for all* $k, i_j < k < i_{j+1}.\pi, k \models st^{\mathcal{M}_h}$. *We define the projection of trace* π *over a component* $\mathcal{M}_h$ *as follow:*

$$Pr_{\mathcal{M}_h}(\pi) = s_{i_0}(V_h), s_{i_1}(V_h) \ldots$$

Definition 9. *Let* $\mathcal{M} = \mathcal{M}_1 \otimes \cdots \otimes \mathcal{M}_n$, *let* π *be a trace of* $\mathcal{M}_h$. *We define the inverse operator of* Pr, *denoted by* Pr^{-1}.

$$Pr_{\mathcal{M}_h}^{-1}(\pi) = \{\pi' | Pr_{\mathcal{M}_h}(\pi') = \pi\}$$

4 Formal Problem

4.1 Asynchronous Composition of Properties of ITS

Compositional verification proves the properties of a system by proving the local properties on components and by checking that the composition of the local properties satisfy the global one (see [25] for a generic overview). This reasoning is expressed formally by inference 1, which is parametrized by a function γ_S that combines the components' implementations and a related function γ_P that combines the local properties.

Inference 1. *Let* $\mathcal{M}_1, \mathcal{M}_2, \ldots, \mathcal{M}_n$ *be a set of* n *components,* $\varphi_1, \varphi_2, \ldots, \varphi_n$ *be local properties on each component,* γ_S *is a function that defines the composition of* $\mathcal{M}_1, \mathcal{M}_2, \ldots, \mathcal{M}_n$, γ_P *combines the properties depending on the composition of* γ_S *and* φ *a property. The following inference is true:*

$$\frac{\mathcal{M}_1 \models \varphi_1, \mathcal{M}_2 \models \varphi_2, \ldots, \mathcal{M}_n \models \varphi_n}{\gamma_S(\mathcal{M}_1, \mathcal{M}_2, \ldots, \mathcal{M}_n) \models \gamma_P(\varphi_1, \varphi_2, \ldots, \varphi_n) \quad \gamma_P(\varphi_1, \varphi_2, \ldots, \varphi_n) \models \varphi}{\gamma_S(\mathcal{M}_1, \mathcal{M}_2, \ldots, \mathcal{M}_n) \models \varphi}$$

In our setting, the components $\mathcal{M}_1, \ldots, \mathcal{M}_n$ are represented by ITSs (see Definition 2) and γ_S is defined as the generalization of the asynchronous composition of Definition 5 for n ITS: $\gamma_S(\mathcal{M}_1, \ldots \mathcal{M}_n) = \mathcal{M}_1 \otimes \cdots \otimes \mathcal{M}_n$.

The problem we address in this paper is to define γ_P such that the above inference rule is correct. In order to asynchronously combine the local properties, each property must be rewritten considering stuttering transitions and, evaluating input variables only in active transitions. Formally, we want that for all trace π of $\gamma_S(\mathcal{M}_1, \ldots, \mathcal{M}_n), Pr_{\mathcal{M}_1}(\pi) \models \varphi_1 \wedge \cdots \wedge Pr_{\mathcal{M}_n}(\pi) \models \varphi_n \Leftrightarrow \pi \models \gamma_P(\varphi_1, \ldots, \varphi_n)$. Thus, we require a rewriting function that maps local properties into their global counterparts. This requirement is expressed as follows. For each trace π of an ITS $\mathcal{M}$, for each global trace $\pi^{ST} \in Pr^{-1}(\pi)$: $\pi \models \varphi$ iff $\pi^{ST} \models \mathcal{R}^*(\varphi)$ where φ is a local LTL property in the language of $\mathcal{M}$. As for the event based TS, we need some conditions Ψ_{cond} that we call *frame condition* to guarantee persistency of output variables and to guarantee fairness on components activity. $\Psi_{cond}(\mathcal{M}_1, \ldots, \mathcal{M}_n) := \psi_{cond}^{\mathcal{M}_1} \wedge \cdots \wedge \psi_{cond}^{\mathcal{M}_n} \wedge GF\neg st^{\mathcal{M}_1} \wedge \cdots \wedge GF\neg st^{\mathcal{M}_n}$ where ψ_{cond} is from Definition 5. The final result in this case would be

$$\gamma_P := \mathcal{R}^*(\varphi_1) \wedge \cdots \wedge \mathcal{R}^*(\varphi_n) \wedge \Psi_{cond}(\mathcal{M}_1, \ldots, \mathcal{M}_n)$$

Example 1. Let $\mathcal{M}_1$ be an ITS with c_2 as input variable, c_1 as output variable and $\varphi_1 : c_1 = 0 \wedge G((c_1 < c_2 \wedge c_1' = c_1 + 1) \vee (c_1 \geq c_2 \wedge c_1' = c_1))$ as its local property. Let $\mathcal{M}_2$ be another ITS with c_1 as input variable, c_2 as output variable, p as parameter and $\varphi_2 : c_2 = p \wedge G((c_2' = c_2 - 1)U(c_2 = 0 \wedge c_2' = c_1))$ as its local property. Suppose that we want to prove that the composition of the two properties satisfies the *global* property $\varphi : GF(c_1 = c_1')$. To check if φ holds we check the validity of $\mathcal{R}^*_{\mathcal{M}_1}(\varphi_1) \wedge \mathcal{R}^*_{\mathcal{M}_2}(\varphi_2) \wedge \Psi_{cond}(\mathcal{M}_1, \mathcal{M}_2) \rightarrow \varphi$.

In this example, c_1 is increased only when c_1 is lower than c_2. When considering asynchronous composition, c_2 might change while $\mathcal{M}_1$ is stuttering. In this case, the challenge in finding a correct $\mathcal{R}^*$ is that since c_2 might change while $\mathcal{M}_1$ is stuttering, then the rewriting must evaluate c_2 only when $\mathcal{M}_1$ is active.

4.2 Asynchronous Composition of Properties of Event Based TS

For completeness, we compare the problem defined above with the case of a event-based asynchronous composition, where the transition systems run concurrently with only shared events used for synchronization. If we consider the asynchronous composition of event based TS to represent the function γ_S, we can use the LTL rewriting function T defined in [4] on each $\varphi_1, \ldots, \varphi_n$ inside γ_P to compose the properties. T simply rewrites events and X operators and leaves the other parts of formulas unchanged. We apply T to each φ_i, then, we put these rewritten properties in conjunction with a constraint Ψ that ensures that variables do not change during stuttering transitions and that events do not occur during stuttering transition. $\Psi = \bigwedge_{1 \leq i \leq n}(G(st^{\mathcal{M}_i} \rightarrow \bigwedge_{v \in V^i} v = v' \wedge \bigwedge_{e \in E^i}))$ where V^i and E^i are the sets of respectively variables and events of each $\mathcal{M}^i$. Finally, $\gamma_P(\mathcal{M}_1, \ldots, \mathcal{M}_n) = T(\varphi_1) \wedge \cdots \wedge T(\varphi_n) \wedge \Psi$ In this case, the composition is limited to components with synchronous event communications. Thus, no input variable that is updated by other components can be considered in this model of composition.

5 Rewriting

[1]This section contains the main contributions of this paper. First, a rewriting $\mathcal{R}^*_{\mathcal{M}}$ that transform local LTL properties into their global counterparts. Second,

---

[1] The proofs of the theorems and lemmas of this section can be found in the appendix of the completed version of the paper at: https://es-static.fbk.eu/people/bombardelli/papers/nfm22/nfm-extended.pdf.

an optimised version of $\mathcal{R}^*_\mathcal{M}$, $\mathcal{R}^{\theta*}_\mathcal{M}$, which exploits the concept of *stutter tolerance* (see Definition 14) to reduce the size of the generates formula. Finally, an alternative approach that transforms the local LTL formulas into ITS and then composes the ITS asynchronously.

We introduce the *map* function; a function that maps the position of a state in a local trace to its position in a global trace.

To simplify the notation, we assume to be given an ITS $\mathcal{M}$, a trace π of $\mathcal{M}$, a local property φ and a local term u. For brevity, we refer to $map^{st}_{\pi^{ST}}, \mathcal{R}_\mathcal{M}$, $\mathcal{R}^*_\mathcal{M}$, $\mathcal{R}^\theta_\mathcal{M}$, $\mathcal{R}^{\theta*}_\mathcal{M}$, $Pr^{-1}_\mathcal{M}$ and $st^\mathcal{M}$ as respectively $map_{\pi^{ST}}, \mathcal{R}, \mathcal{R}^*, \mathcal{R}^\theta, \mathcal{R}^{\theta*}, Pr^{-1}$ and st.

Definition 10. *For all* $\pi^{ST} \in Pr^{-1}(\pi)$, *for all* $k \in \mathbb{N}$: $\neg st^{\pi^{ST}}_{occ}(k) := j$ *s. t.* $\pi^{ST}, j \models \neg st$ *and for all* $k \leq l < j : \pi^{ST}, l \models st$. $\neg st^{\pi^{ST}}_{occ}(k)$ *denotes the position of the first occurrence of* $\neg st$ *from point* k. *We also define map as follows: For all* i:

$$map_{\pi^{ST}}(i) := \begin{cases} \neg st^{\pi^{ST}}_{occ}(0) & \text{if } i = 0 \\ \neg st^{\pi^{ST}}_{occ}(map_{\pi^{ST}}(i-1)+1) & \text{if } i > 0 \end{cases}$$

5.1 $\mathcal{R}$ Rewriting

As we mentioned in Sect. 4.1, we want a rewriting that is able to map each local property φ into its global counterpart. In this case, each global property must be satisfied in $Pr^{-1}(\pi)$ iff φ is satisfied in π. We start by proposing a rewriting that maps an LTL formula to another formula such that the augmented traces satisfy the rewritten formula in the active transitions if and only if the original traces satisfy them in the same transitions.

Definition 11. *We define $\mathcal{R}$ as the following rewriting function:*

1. $\mathcal{R}(a) := a$
2. $\mathcal{R}(\varphi \vee \psi) := \mathcal{R}(\varphi) \vee \mathcal{R}(\psi)$
3. $\mathcal{R}(\neg\varphi) := \neg\mathcal{R}(\varphi)$
4. $\mathcal{R}(X\psi) := X(\neg st R(st \vee \mathcal{R}(\psi)))$
5. $\mathcal{R}(\varphi U \psi) := (st \vee \mathcal{R}(\varphi))U(\neg st \wedge \mathcal{R}(\psi))$
6. $\mathcal{R}(Y\varphi) := Y(st S(\neg st \wedge \mathcal{R}(\varphi)))$
7. $\mathcal{R}(\varphi S \psi) := (st \vee \mathcal{R}(\varphi))S(\neg st \wedge \mathcal{R}(\psi))$
8. $\mathcal{R}(func(\psi_1, ..., \psi_n)) := func(\mathcal{R}(\psi_1), ..., \mathcal{R}(\psi_n))$
9. $\mathcal{R}(pred(\psi_1, ..., \psi_n)) := pred(\mathcal{R}(\psi_1), ..., \mathcal{R}(\psi_n))$
10. $\mathcal{R}(ite(\psi, \psi_1, \psi_2)) := ite(\mathcal{R}(\psi), \mathcal{R}(\psi_1)\mathcal{R}(\psi_2))$
11. $\mathcal{R}(next(\psi)) := \psi @\tilde{F}\neg st$
12. $\mathcal{R}(\psi @\tilde{F}\psi_1) := \mathcal{R}(\psi)@\tilde{F}(\mathcal{R}(\psi_1) \wedge \neg st)$
13. $\mathcal{R}(\psi @\tilde{P}\psi_1) := \mathcal{R}(\psi)@\tilde{P}(\mathcal{R}(\psi_1) \wedge \neg st)$

The property of $\mathcal{R}$ is defined in the following lemma:

Lemma 1. *For all π, for all $\pi^{ST} \in Pr^{-1}(\pi)$, for all i:*

$$\pi, i \models \varphi \Leftrightarrow \pi^{ST}, map_{\pi^{ST}}(i) \models \mathcal{R}(\varphi) \qquad \pi(i)(u) = \pi^{ST}(map_{\pi^{ST}}(i))(\mathcal{R}(u))$$

Lemma 1 shows that $\mathcal{R}$ guarantees that satisfiability is preserved in the active transitions of the global traces. However, $map_{\pi^{ST}}(0)$ is not always granted to be equal to 0 (see Definition 9), and thus, we need to find a rewriting that guarantees that satisfiability is preserved also in the first transition.

Definition 12. *We define $\mathcal{R}^*$ as $\mathcal{R}^*(\varphi) := \neg st R(st \vee \mathcal{R}(\varphi))$*

Lemma 2. *For all π, for all $\pi^{ST} \in Pr^{-1}(\pi)$: $\pi^{ST}, map_{\pi^{ST}}(0) \models \mathcal{R}(\varphi) \Leftrightarrow \pi^{ST}, 0 \models \mathcal{R}^*(\varphi))$*

Using Lemma 1 and Lemma 2 together we obtain the following theorem:

Theorem 1. *For all π, for all $\pi^{ST} \in Pr^{-1}(\pi) : \pi \models \varphi \Leftrightarrow \pi^{ST} \models \mathcal{R}^*(\varphi)$*

Theorem 1 shows that $\mathcal{R}^*$ is able to translate a local LTL property into a global property without changing its semantics in term of traces. Using $\mathcal{R}^*$ is possible to transform local properties with I/O variables.

Definition 13. *Let $\mathcal{M}_1, \ldots, \mathcal{M}_n$ be n ITS and $\varphi_1, \ldots, \varphi_n$ be LTL formulas on the language of each $\mathcal{M}_i$. We define $\gamma_P(\varphi_1, \ldots, \varphi_n) = \mathcal{R}^*_{\mathcal{M}_1}(\varphi_1) \wedge \cdots \wedge \mathcal{R}^*_{\mathcal{M}_n}(\varphi_n) \wedge \Psi_{cond}(\mathcal{M}_1, \ldots, \mathcal{M}_n)$*

Corollary 1. *Using γ_P from Definition 13, γ_S from Sect. 4.1, for all compatible ITS $\mathcal{M}_1, \ldots, \mathcal{M}_n$, for all local properties $\varphi_1, \ldots, \varphi_n$ over the language of respectively $\mathcal{M}_1, \ldots, \mathcal{M}_n$, for all global properties φ: Inference 1 holds.*

Example 2. Consider the specifications of Example 1. Through $\mathcal{R}^*$ we can define the asynchronous parallel composition of φ_1 and φ_2:

- $\mathcal{R}^*_{\mathcal{M}_1}(\varphi_1) : \neg st^{\mathcal{M}_1} R(st \vee (c_1 = 0 \wedge G(st^{\mathcal{M}_1} \vee (c_1 < c_2 \wedge c_1@\tilde{F}\neg st^{\mathcal{M}_1} = c1 + 1 \vee c_1 \geq c_2 \wedge c_1@\tilde{F}\neg st^{\mathcal{M}_1} = c_1)))$
- $\mathcal{R}^*_{\mathcal{M}_2}(\varphi_2) : \neg st^{\mathcal{M}_2} R(st^{\mathcal{M}_2} \vee c_2 = p \wedge G(st^{\mathcal{M}_2} \vee ((st^{\mathcal{M}_2} \vee c_2@\tilde{F}\neg st^{\mathcal{M}_2} = c_2 - 1)U(\neg st^{\mathcal{M}_2} \wedge c_2 = 0 \wedge c_2@\tilde{F}\neg st^{\mathcal{M}_2} = c_1))))$
- $\Psi_{cond}(\mathcal{M}_1, \mathcal{M}_2) = G(\neg st^{\mathcal{M}_1} \vee c_1 = c'_1) \wedge GF\neg st^{\mathcal{M}_1} \wedge G(\neg st^{\mathcal{M}_2} \vee c_2 = c'_2) \wedge GF\neg st^{\mathcal{M}_2}$

Each next operator is rewritten as an at next ($@\tilde{F}$). The intuition is that we want to evaluate the variable only in the next transition that does not stutter. c_1 and c_2 are evaluated at the first non stuttering transition, the intuition is that the local initial state is not necessary the global initial state. Finally, using γ_P we can compose φ_1 and φ_2 asynchronously permitting us to check whether or not φ holds. It should be noted that the correctness of the rewriting is guaranteed also removing the constraints on output variables, however this constraint is desirable since it guarantees persistence of data which is a rather realistic property.

5.2 Optimization

The rewriting $\mathcal{R}^*$ is general and works for all the LTL formulas. However, this rewriting increases the size of the formula and consequently, the time required to verify the final specification. There are common cases where it is not necessary to rewrite part of the specification. For example $GF\varphi$ is rewritten as $G(st \vee F(\neg st \wedge \mathcal{R}(\varphi)))$ while it could be rewritten as $GF(\neg st \wedge \mathcal{R}(\varphi))$ (as for fairness constraints). X of a local variable $X\varphi$ is rewritten as $X(\neg stRR(\varphi))$ while by Ψ_{cond} of Sect. 4 it could remain unchanged. This section identifies, formalizes and demonstrates the cases where such optimization can be applied.

We introduce the concept of *stutter-tolerance*. A formula is said *stutter-tolerant* if it keeps the same value when rewritten through $\mathcal{R}$ in all consecutive stuttering transitions.

Definition 14. *An LTL formula φ is said stutter-tolerant w.r.t. $\mathcal{R}$ iff:*
For all π, for all π^{ST} $\in$ *$Pr^{-1}(\pi)$, for all i* : *for all $map_{\pi^{ST}}(i-1) < j <$*
$map_{\pi^{ST}}(i)$:
$$\pi^{ST}, j \models \mathcal{R}(\varphi) \Leftrightarrow \pi^{ST}, map_{\pi^{ST}}(i) \models \mathcal{R}(\varphi)$$

Lemma 3. *Until, yesterday and at last formulas are stutter-tolerant w.r.t. $\mathcal{R}$*

Definition 15. *An LTL formula φ is syntactically stutter-tolerant iff one of the following condition holds:*

- *φ is an until formula or a yesterday formula or an at last formula*
- *$\varphi = \psi_1 \vee \psi_2$ and ψ_1 and ψ_2 are syntactically stutter-tolerant*
- *$\varphi = \neg\psi$ and ψ is syntactically stutter-tolerant*
- *$\varphi = s$ and $s \in V_O \cup V_H$*

Lemma 4. *Syntactically stutter-tolerant formulas are stutter-tolerant w.r.t $\mathcal{R}$*

Using the notion of syntactically stutter-tolerant formula, we define a new optimized rewriting. If the sub-formulas of φ are syntactically stutter-tolerant, then the φ is not rewritten according to $\mathcal{R}$. To demonstrate the correctness of the rewriting, we provide two lemmas that construct the main theorem.

Definition 16. *We define $\mathcal{R}^\theta$ as follows:*

1. $\mathcal{R}^\theta(s) = \mathcal{R}(s)$ *if $s \in V$*
2. $\mathcal{R}^\theta(\varphi \vee \psi) = \mathcal{R}^\theta(\varphi) \vee \mathcal{R}^\theta(\psi)$
3. $\mathcal{R}^\theta(\neg\varphi) = \neg\mathcal{R}^\theta(\varphi)$
4. $\mathcal{R}^\theta(X\psi) = \begin{cases} X(\mathcal{R}^\theta(\psi)) & \text{if } \psi \text{ is synt. st.tol.} \\ X(\neg stR(st \vee \mathcal{R}^\theta(\psi))) & \text{otherwise} \end{cases}$
5. $\mathcal{R}^\theta(\varphi U\psi) = \begin{cases} \mathcal{R}^\theta(\varphi)U\mathcal{R}^\theta(\psi) & \text{if } \psi \text{ is synt. st.tol.} \\ (st \vee \mathcal{R}^\theta(\varphi))U(\neg st \wedge \mathcal{R}^\theta(\psi)) & \text{otherwise} \end{cases}$
6. $\mathcal{R}^\theta(Y\psi) = Y(stS(\neg st \wedge \mathcal{R}^\theta(\psi)))$
7. $\mathcal{R}^\theta(\varphi S\psi) = \begin{cases} \mathcal{R}^\theta(\varphi)S\mathcal{R}^\theta(\psi) & \text{if } \psi \text{ is synt. st.tol} \\ (st \vee \mathcal{R}^\theta(\varphi))S(\neg st \wedge \mathcal{R}^\theta(\psi)) & \text{otherwise} \end{cases}$

8. $\mathcal{R}^\theta(func(\psi_1, ..., \psi_n)) = func(\mathcal{R}^\theta(\psi_1), ..., \mathcal{R}^\theta(\psi_n))$
9. $\mathcal{R}^\theta(pred(\psi_1, ..., \psi_n)) = pred(\mathcal{R}^\theta(\psi_1), ..., \mathcal{R}^\theta(\psi_n))$
10. $\mathcal{R}^\theta(ite(\psi, \psi_1, \psi_2)) = ite(\mathcal{R}^\theta(\psi), \mathcal{R}^\theta(\psi_1), \mathcal{R}^\theta(\psi_2))$

11. $\mathcal{R}^\theta(next(\psi)) = \begin{cases} next(\mathcal{R}^\theta(\psi)) & \text{if } \psi \text{ is synt. st.tol.} \\ \mathcal{R}^\theta(\psi)@F\neg st & \text{otherwise} \end{cases}$

12. $\mathcal{R}^\theta(\psi@F\psi_1) = \begin{cases} \mathcal{R}^\theta(\psi)@F\mathcal{R}^\theta(\psi_1) & \text{if } \psi \text{ is synt. st. tol.} \\ \mathcal{R}^\theta(\psi)@F(\neg st \wedge \mathcal{R}^\theta(\psi_1)) & \text{otherwise} \end{cases}$

13. $\mathcal{R}^\theta(\psi@\tilde{P}\psi_1) = \mathcal{R}^\theta(\psi)@\tilde{P}(\neg st \wedge \mathcal{R}^\theta(\psi_1))$

Lemma 5. *For all π, for all $\pi^{ST} \in Pr^{-1}(\pi)$, for all i:*

$$\pi, i \models \varphi \Leftrightarrow \pi^{ST}, map_{\pi^{ST}}(i) \models \mathcal{R}^\theta(\varphi) \quad \pi(i)(u) = \pi^{ST}(map_{\pi^{ST}}(i))(\mathcal{R}^\theta(u))$$

Definition 17. *We define $\mathcal{R}^{\theta^*}$ as follows:*

$$\mathcal{R}^{\theta^*}(\varphi) := \begin{cases} \mathcal{R}^\theta(\varphi) & \text{if } \varphi \text{ is synt. st.tol.} \\ \neg stR(st \vee \mathcal{R}^\theta(\varphi)) & \text{otherwise} \end{cases}$$

Lemma 6. *For all π, for all $\pi^{ST} \in Pr^{-1}(\pi)$: $\pi^{ST}, map_{\pi^{ST}}(0) \models \mathcal{R}^\theta(\varphi) \Leftrightarrow \pi^{ST}, 0 \models \mathcal{R}^{\theta^*}(\varphi)$*

Theorem 2. *For all π, for all $\pi^{ST} \in Pr^{-1}(\pi) : \pi \models \varphi \Leftrightarrow \pi^{ST} \models \mathcal{R}^{\theta^*}(\varphi)$*

Example 3. Consider the specifications of Example 1. As for Example 2 we can define the asynchronous parallel composition of φ_1 and φ_2 using $\mathcal{R}^{\theta^*}$:

- $\mathcal{R}^{\theta^*}{}_{\mathcal{M}_1}(\varphi_1) : c_1 = 0 \wedge G(st^{\mathcal{M}_1} \vee (c_1 < c_2 \wedge c_1' = c1 + 1 \vee c_1 \geq c_2 \wedge c_1' = c_1)))$
- $\mathcal{R}^{\theta^*}{}_{\mathcal{M}_2}(\varphi_2) : c_2 = p \wedge G((st^{\mathcal{M}_2} \vee c_2' = c_2 - 1)U(\neg st^{\mathcal{M}_2} \wedge c_2 = 0 \wedge c_2' = c_1))$

This example shows how much the optimization can reduce the size of the formula. Since $c_1 = 0$ is an output formula and since G is an until operator, $\mathcal{R}^{\theta^*}$ removes the initial $\neg stR(st \vee \mathcal{R}^\theta(\varphi))$. Furthermore, thanks to Ψ_{cond}, both next expressions can be optimized. Another applied optimization is that the rewriting of φ_2 does not need to add stuttering disjunction on G since until is a syntactically stutter formula. However, since φ_1 and φ_2 are not stutter invariant formulas, both specifications are partially modified by $\mathcal{R}^{\theta^*}$. In particular, inside φ_1 $\mathcal{R}^{\theta^*}$ applies the rewriting of G since next formulas are not stutter tolerant, the same happens with φ_2 where U is rewritten according to $\mathcal{R}$.

5.3   Alternative Approach for Asynchronous Composition

In this section, we consider an alternative approach based on the asynchronous composition of ITS. We exploit the transformation from LTL formula to transition system of [12] to generate ITS to be asynchronously composed. ITS have limited expressibility for initial and transition conditions (see Definition 2). Initial conditions cannot refer to input formula while transition conditions cannot refer to next input formulas. Since LTL does not suffer from this limitation, it is necessary to adapt the ITS construction to fully express all possible LTL properties. Thus, we introduce internal variables that mimic the values of the input variables at each transition; exploiting the asynchronous composition, during stuttering transitions these variables will *guess* the value of the input variables at the next occurrence of not stutter.

Definition 18. *Let $\mathcal{M}$ be an ITS and let φ be an LTL formula over its symbols. We define $LTL2IntTS(\mathcal{M}, \varphi) := \langle V_I, V_O, V_H', \mathcal{I}, \mathcal{T}, \mathcal{F}_\varphi \rangle$ where:*

- *$LTL2TS(\varphi) = \langle V_\varphi, \mathcal{I}_\varphi, \mathcal{T}_\varphi, \mathcal{F}_\varphi \rangle$ is the transition system generated from φ*
- *$V_H' = V_H \cup V^{guess} \cup (V_\varphi \setminus V)$*
- *$\mathcal{I} = \mathcal{I}_\varphi \lceil V_I / V^{guess} \rfloor$*
- *$\mathcal{T} = \mathcal{T}_\varphi \lceil V_I' / V^{guess'} \rfloor \wedge \bigwedge_{\bar{v} \in V^{guess}} (\bar{v} = v)$*
- *$V^{guess} = \{\bar{v} | v \in V_I\}$ where each $\bar{v}$ is a copy of each v*

Lemma 7. *Let $\mathcal{M}$ be an ITS, let φ be an LTL property over the language of $\mathcal{M}$.*

$$\mathcal{M}_\varphi = LTL2IntTS(\mathcal{M}, \varphi) \text{ is a valid ITS and } \mathcal{M}_\varphi \models \varphi$$

Lemma 7 ensures that $LTL2IntTS$ generates an ITS that satisfy the property φ. Thus, using $LTL2IntTS$ with the asynchronous composition of ITS of Definition 5 we generate the composed ITS.

The remainder of this section demonstrates the equivalence between the this approach with the rewriting techniques. The following lemma ensures that a trace π is part of the language of the composition of the ITS defined by $LTL2IntTS$ if and only if the projections of the traces over the local transition systems satisfy the local properties

Lemma 8. *Let $\mathcal{M}_1, \ldots, \mathcal{M}_n$ be n compatible ITS with function γ_S defined according to Sect. 4.1; $\varphi_1, \ldots, \varphi_n$ be local properties of respectively $\mathcal{M}_1, \ldots \mathcal{M}_n$ and $\pi \in \Pi(V)$ be a trace over the symbols of $\mathcal{M} = \gamma_S(\mathcal{M}_1, \ldots, \mathcal{M}_n)$:*

$$Pr_{\mathcal{M}_1}(\pi) \models \varphi_1 \wedge \cdots \wedge Pr_{\mathcal{M}_n}(\pi) \models \varphi_n \wedge \pi \models \Psi_{cond}(\mathcal{M}_1, \ldots, \mathcal{M}_n) \Leftrightarrow \pi \in \mathscr{L}(\gamma_S(\mathcal{M}_{\varphi_1}, \ldots, \mathcal{M}_{\varphi_n}))_{|V}$$

where $\mathcal{M}_{\varphi_1}, \ldots, \mathcal{M}_{\varphi_n}$ are respectively the ITS generated applying $LTL2IntTS$ to the symbols of $\mathcal{M}_1, \ldots, \mathcal{M}_n$ and the properties $\varphi_1, \ldots, \varphi_n$.

From Lemma 8 we derive the following theorem which states that this approach is equivalent with the one based on rewriting.

Theorem 3. *Let $\mathcal{M}_1, \ldots, \mathcal{M}_n$ be n compatible ITS, $\varphi_1, \ldots, \varphi_n$ be local properties of respectively $\mathcal{M}_1, \ldots \mathcal{M}_n$ and $\pi \in \Pi(V)$ be a trace over the symbols of $\mathcal{M} = \gamma_S(\mathcal{M}_1, \ldots, \mathcal{M}_n)$:*

$$\pi \models \gamma_P(\varphi_1, \ldots, \varphi_n) \Leftrightarrow \pi \in \mathscr{L}(\gamma_S(\mathcal{M}_{\varphi_1}, \ldots, \mathcal{M}_{\varphi_n}))_{|V}$$

where $\mathcal{M}_{\varphi_1}, \ldots \mathcal{M}_{\varphi_n}$ are respectively the ITS generated applying $LTL2IntTS$ to the symbols of $\mathcal{M}_1, \ldots, \mathcal{M}_n$ and the properties $\varphi_1, \ldots, \varphi_n$.

6 Experimental Evaluation

[2]The techniques of this paper are implemented inside the contract based design tool OCRA [7] and have been validated through an empirical verification of the rewriting theorems. We implemented a technique that applies Pr and Pr^{-1} to lazo-shaped traces generated from LTL formulas to verify the theorems of the rewritings. Moreover, we also checked that the alternative approach was equivalent to the one proposed for LTL. The validation have been conducted on all LTL specifications of the discrete time example models of OCRA ($\sim$300 formulas) and on 100 randomly generated formulas.[3] We also confronted the approaches with an experimental evaluation.

For completeness, the experimental evaluation considers another technique based on the rewriting of [4] that was already implemented in OCRA and mentioned in Sect. 4.2. We call this rewriting output-only rewriting. Output-only rewriting considers only specifications with local variables and synchronization events. While, to keep the notation readable we did not mention events inside our rewriting, we handle events in our implementation similarly to next operators. To force synchronisation between events, we augment Ψ_{cond} to enable shared events only when its components do not stutter. Due to the limitations of output-only rewriting, the experimental evaluation have been applied only to a sub-set of models. The experiments were run in parallel on a cluster with nodes with Intel Xeon CPU running at 2.27GHz with 8CPU, 48GB. The timeout for each run was four hours and the memory cap was set to 1GB.

The evaluation was applied on different type of models: asynchronous versions of OCRA models, Dwyer LTL patterns [14] parametrized on the number of components and on components with parametrized nested X formulas. The

---

[2] The tar files of the experimental evaluation results can be found at: https://es-static. fbk.eu/people/bombardelli/papers/nfm22/expeval.tar.gz.

[3] The detailed algorithms of the validation can be found in the appendix of the extended version of this paper at:
https://es-static.fbk.eu/people/bombardelli/papers/nfm22/nfm-extended.pdf.

one based on Dwyer LTL patterns [14] considered 3 LTL patterns: *response*, *precedence chain* and *universality* patterns. The models compose the pattern formulas in two ways: as a sequence of n components linked in a bus and as a set of components that tries to write on the output port concurrently. Since the output-only rewriting does not support input port, in the models used in the comparison with the output-only rewriting replace input data readings with synchronizing event exchanging such data.

Each model have been tested with two symbolic model checking algorithms: ic3ia [8] and one based on bdd [22] (only for finite state models) that we will call bdd for brevity; however, due to the limited space we show only plots with the ic3ia algorithm. Figure 1 shows the results of response pattern model with events, universality sequence pattern model with input port and precedence chain model where each component concurrently writes to the global output port.

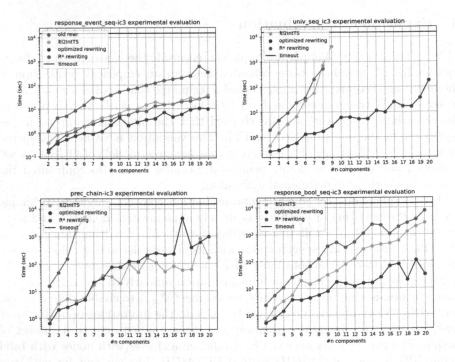

Fig. 1. Pattern experimental evaluations

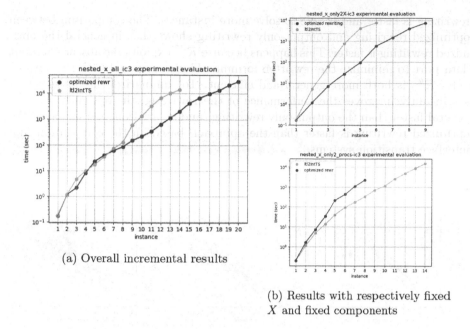

(a) Overall incremental results

(b) Results with respectively fixed
X and fixed components

Fig. 2. Nested X experimental evaluation

The experimental evaluation based on nested X sequence considered 2 parameters: the number of nested X of the global property and the number of components. In this scenario, we confront the approach based on asynchronous composition of ITS with the optimized temporal rewriting. The global property is defined as: $G(G^{\leq n*s}t \to F^{\leq n*s}r)$ where n is the number of nested X, s is the number of components in the system and t and r are two boolean formulas. Local properties are defined as $G(G^{\leq n}t \to F^{\leq n}r)$ where n. Figure 2a shows the overall results of the experimental evaluation, where the y-axis represents the time required to check x global properties while Fig. 2b shows the result restricted to models with $n = 2$ and with $s = 2$.

Figure 3 shows the overall results with scatter plots that confronts the optimized rewriting with the other approaches. In these plots, the y coordinate represents the time to verify the validity of each instance with the *optimized* rewriting while the x coordinate represents the time to verify the validity of each instance with the adversarial approach. If a point is above the dashed line, then the adversarial method performed better; otherwise, the optimized rewriting was faster in verifying the validity of that instance. The optimized rewriting ($\mathcal{R}^{\theta*}$) outperforms the non optimized one ($\mathcal{R}^*$) in almost every model. Intuitively, $\mathcal{R}^{\theta*}$ generates formulas that are smaller than those produced by $\mathcal{R}^*$ (see Example 3 for a comparison between the rewritten formulas). When dealing with nested X, the approach based on asynchronous composition performs better than the optimized rewriting when there are only two components; this is outlined in Fig. 2b. However, even if $ltl2IntTS$ sometimes performs better, in general the optimized rewriting is faster and is able to solve more instances. The comparison between optimized rewriting and output-only rewriting shows that in general the optimized rewriting is faster. This happens because $\mathcal{R}^{\theta*}$ exploits the absence of input data port to minimize the rewritten formula. Thus, compared with the output-only, $\mathcal{R}^{\theta*}$ is both more general and efficient. To summarize: the optimization significantly improves the performance of the rewriting, the optimization is in general faster than the output-only rewriting, and, apart from certain cases, the optimized rewriting is faster than the approach based on the compilation into interface transition systems.

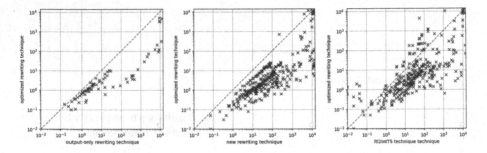

Fig. 3. Scatter plots on all the experiments

7   Conclusions

In this paper, we considered the problem of compositional reasoning for asynchronous systems with LTL properties over input and output variables. We proposed a new rewriting of LTL formulas that allows for checking compositional rules with temporal satisfiability solvers. We provided an optimized version and an alternative solutions based on the compilation of the LTL formulas into transition systems. We finally compare these rewritings con various benchmarks showing the scalability of the approach.

In the future, we will consider various directions for extending the framework including real-time and hybrid specifications, optimizations based on the scheduling of components and other communication mechanisms such as buffered communication, and the application of the proposed rewriting in an extension of Asynchronous HyperLTL [3].

References

1. Baier, C., Katoen, J.-P.: Principles of Model Checking. MIT Press, Cambridge (2008)
2. Barrett, C., Sebastiani, R., Seshia, S.A., Tinelli, C.: Satisfiability modulo theories. In: Handbook of Satisfiability, pp. 825–885. IOS Press, January 2009

3. Baumeister, J., Coenen, N., Bonakdarpour, B., Finkbeiner, B., Sánchez, C.: A temporal logic for asynchronous hyperproperties. In: Silva, A., Leino, K.R.M. (eds.) CAV 2021. LNCS, vol. 12759, pp. 694–717. Springer, Cham (2021). https://doi.org/10.1007/978-3-030-81685-8_33

4. Benes, N., Brim, L., Cerná, I., Sochor, J., Vareková, P., Buhnova, B.: Partial order reduction for state/event LTL. In: IFM (2009)

5. Bu, L., Cimatti, A., Li, X., Mover, S., Tonetta, S.: Model checking of hybrid systems using shallow synchronization. In: Hatcliff, J., Zucca, E. (eds.) FMOODS/FORTE -2010. LNCS, vol. 6117, pp. 155–169. Springer, Heidelberg (2010). https://doi.org/10.1007/978-3-642-13464-7_13

6. Cavada, R., et al.: The NUXMV symbolic model checker. In: Biere, A., Bloem, R. (eds.) CAV 2014. LNCS, vol. 8559, pp. 334–342. Springer, Cham (2014). https://doi.org/10.1007/978-3-319-08867-9_22

7. Cimatti, A., Dorigatti, M., Tonetta, S.: OCRA: a tool for checking the refinement of temporal contracts, pp. 702–705, November 2013

8. Cimatti, A., Griggio, A.: Software model checking via IC3. In: CAV, pp. 277–293 (2012)

9. Cimatti, A., Griggio, A., Magnago, E., Roveri, M., Tonetta, S.: SMT-based satisfiability of first-order LTL with event freezing functions and metric operators. Inf. Comput. **272**, 104502 (2019)

10. Cimatti, A., Mover, S., Tonetta, S.: HyDI: a language for symbolic hybrid systems with discrete interaction, pp. 275–278, August 2011

11. Cimatti, A., Tonetta, S.: Contracts-refinement proof system for component-based embedded systems. Sci. Comput. Programm. **97**, 333–348 (2015). Object-Oriented Programming and Systems (OOPS 2010) Modeling and Analysis of Compositional Software (papers from EUROMICRO SEAA 12)

12. Clarke, E., Grumberg, O., Hamaguchi, K.: Another look at LTL model checking. Technical report, USA (1994)

13. de Alfaro, L., Henzinger, T.A.: Interface automata. In: ESEC/SIGSOFT FSE, pp. 109–120. ACM (2001)

14. Dwyer, M., Avrunin, G., Corbett, J.: Patterns in property specifications for finite-state verification. In: Proceedings - International Conference on Software Engineering, February 1970

15. Eisner, C., Fisman, D., Havlicek, J., McIsaac, A., Van Campenhout, D.: The definition of a temporal clock operator. In: Baeten, J.C.M., Lenstra, J.K., Parrow, J., Woeginger, G.J. (eds.) ICALP 2003. LNCS, vol. 2719, pp. 857–870. Springer, Heidelberg (2003). https://doi.org/10.1007/3-540-45061-0_67

16. Jonsson, B., Tsay, Y.-K.: Assumption/guarantee specifications in linear-time temporal logic. Theor. Comput. Sci. **167**, 47–72 (1996)

17. Lamport, L.: Temporal logic of actions. ACM Trans. Programm. Lang. Syst. (TOPLAS) **16**(872–923), 6 (1994)

18. Lamport, L.: The operators of TLA, June 1997

19. Lichtenstein, O., Pnueli, A., Zuck, L.: The glory of the past. In: Logics of Programs, pp. 196–218 (1985)

20. Manna, Z., Pnueli, A.: The temporal logic of reactive and concurrent systems - specification. Springer (1992). https://doi.org/10.1007/978-1-4612-0931-7

21. McMillan, K.L.: Circular compositional reasoning about liveness. In: Pierre, L., Kropf, T. (eds.) CHARME 1999. LNCS, vol. 1703, pp. 342–346. Springer, Heidelberg (1999). https://doi.org/10.1007/3-540-48153-2_30

22. Meinel, C., Theobald, T.: Algorithms and Data Structures in VLSI Design: OBDD - Foundations and Applications, January 1998

23. Păsăreanu, C.S., Dwyer, M.B., Huth, M.: Assume-guarantee model checking of software: a comparative case study. In: Dams, D., Gerth, R., Leue, S., Massink, M. (eds.) SPIN 1999. LNCS, vol. 1680, pp. 168–183. Springer, Heidelberg (1999). https://doi.org/10.1007/3-540-48234-2_14
24. Pnueli, A.: The temporal logic of programs, pp. 46–57, September 1977
25. Roever, W.-P.: Concurrency Verification: Introduction to Compositional and Non-compositional Methods, January 2001
26. Rozier, K.Y.: Linear temporal logic symbolic model checking. Compu. Sci. Rev. 5(2), 163–203 (2011)
27. Rysavy, O., Rab, J.: A formal model of composing components: the TLA+ approach. Innov. Syst. Softw. Eng. 5, 139–148 (2009)
28. Tonetta, S.: Linear-time temporal logic with event freezing functions. In: Gand, A.L.F. (ed.) vol. 256. EPTCS, pp. 195–209 (2017)

Elucidation and Analysis of Specification Patterns in Aerospace System Telemetry

Zachary Luppen[1](✉)(iD), Michael Jacks[2](iD), Nathan Baughman[2](iD), Muhamed Stilic[2](iD),
Ryan Nasers[2](iD), Benjamin Hertz[3](iD), James Cutler[4](iD), Dae-Young Lee[2](iD),
and Kristin Yvonne Rozier[2](iD)

[1] Space Exploration Technologies Corp., Hawthorne, CA 90250, USA
zachary.luppen@spacex.com, zluppen@gmail.com
[2] Iowa State University, Ames, IA 50010, USA
[3] Collins Aerospace, Cedar Rapids, IA 52498, USA
[4] University of Michigan, Ann Arbor, MI 48109, USA

Abstract. Experimental aerospace projects often require flight vehicle platforms
for testing, such as high-altitude balloons, sounding rockets, unmanned aerial systems (UAS), and CubeSats. The system telemetry transmitted by these vehicles
is crucial to understanding overall performance. A growing desire to implement
greater levels of system autonomy and AI-enhanced control into these systems
merits introducing rigorous safety analysis from formal methods techniques, such
as Runtime Verification (RV). RV depends heavily upon the accuracy and robustness of the specifications it reasons over, and the task of developing a comprehensive set of system specifications often poses a significant challenge. To aid specification development for new systems, we provide an analysis on the process of
implementing RV into four real aerospace systems of increasing complexity. We
design and validate fourteen formal specifications for a real high-altitude balloon
mission and draw on three past formal specification efforts on a sounding rocket,
UAS Traffic Management (UTM) system, and CubeSat to compare specification
patterns and overlapping system needs. We identify four common temporal logic
subformulas for specifications within and between these systems, providing metrics on development resources, frequency, and perceived automation difficulty.
We generalize our results and discuss considerations for automatically generating formal specifications in aerospace projects.

Keywords: Runtime verification · Temporal logic · System health monitoring ·
Formal specification · R2U2 · High-altitude balloon · Sounding rocket · UAS ·
CubeSat · Satellite

This project/material is based upon work supported by the Iowa Space Grant Consortium under
NASA Award No. 80NSSC20M0107. Work partially supported by NSF CAREER Award CNS-
1552934, NASA ECF NNX16AR57G, and NSF PFI: BIC grant CNS-1257011. Thanks to Kaili
Henry and Yang He for their work on specification development and Matthew Nelson for providing resources from HABET. Reproducibility artifacts are available at http://temporallogic.org/
research/AerospaceSystems-NFM22/.
Z. Luppen—The work in this manuscript was performed for the completion of a master's degree
prior to Mr. Luppen's employment at SpaceX. The data referenced herein is not related to nor
gathered from any SpaceX resources.

© Springer Nature Switzerland AG 2022
J. V. Deshmukh et al. (Eds.): NFM 2022, LNCS 13260, pp. 527–537, 2022.
https://doi.org/10.1007/978-3-031-06773-0_28

1   Introduction

Academic, industrial, commercial, and amateur entities profoundly use small aerospace systems to perform small-scale, experimental research [23,29,44,45]. The intended experiments and mission goals for these projects vary greatly, from testing experimental hardware to evaluating cosmic radiation levels at progressive altitudes in Earth's atmosphere [33]. The process of building, designing, and flying these systems is a non-trivial task despite their benefits of low cost and fast turnaround times. In practice, many developers meet unforeseen challenges and setbacks that can occur at practically any stage of a given mission [3,25,46]. Conceivable problems are documented and well-known, but developers generally have the means only to develop a baseline working system due to limited resources, engendering a need for greater system autonomy.

Enabling small aerospace systems to monitor system faults automatically and in real time provides the ability to trigger mitigation actions and optimize performance. Runtime verification (RV) specializes in identifying fault signatures and provides a deeper understanding of a given system's behavior [34,35]. Recent studies have explored the integration of RV into autonomous aerospace systems, like sounding rockets [14], unmanned aerial systems (UAS) [6,13,28], and CubeSats [2,12,32]. However, there have been few efforts to understand the similarities and differences, along with scaled complexity, in applying formal specification and RV to these systems [39]. It is crucial to understand how mission needs compare within and across each system to elicit formal specifications automatically for real-time verification of future designs.

We examine four real aerospace systems designed, developed, and flown/launched independently: a high-altitude balloon, a sounding rocket, a UAS Traffic Management (UTM) system, and a CubeSat. We contribute (1) formal high-altitude balloon specifications and successful RV on the real dataset using the R2U2 RV engine [40], (2) a comparative analysis and identification of patterns in aerospace system specifications, and (3) a map for auto-generating formal specifications. The remainder of this paper is organized as follows. In Sect. 2, we discuss the syntax and formal semantics of Mission-time Linear Temporal Logic (MLTL), the common specification language of these studies. Section 3 briefly outlines each of the four aerospace vehicles and their mission profiles and discusses their respective telemetry data collections. Section 4 describes development and validation of formal specifications for a high-altitude balloon system and scaling to larger systems. We provide metrics and comparisons of formal specifications and patterns identified in all four aerospace systems in Sect. 5. In Sect. 6, we discuss lessons learned and conclude with plans for developing more automated techniques to generate formal specifications.

2   MLTL Syntax and Semantics

We utilize mission-time linear temporal logic (MLTL) for all specifications developed for the aerospace systems [17,37]. MLTL employs closed interval time bounds over a set of bounded natural numbers on all temporal operators, rather than literal time increments.

Definition 1. *(MLTL Syntax) The syntax of a given MLTL formula ϕ comprised of atomic propositions $\mathcal{AP}$ is recursively defined as such:*

$$\phi :: = true \mid false \mid p \mid \neg\phi \mid \phi_1 \wedge \phi_2 \mid \phi_1 \vee \phi_2 \mid \Box_I\phi \mid \Diamond_I\phi \mid \phi_1\mathcal{U}_I\phi_2 \mid \phi_1\mathcal{R}_I\phi_2$$

where $p \in \mathcal{AP}$ is a Boolean and all ϕ are atomic propositions. The symbols utilized in this syntax stand for the following: $\neg$ is not, $\wedge$ is logical and, $\vee$ is logical or, $\Box_I$ is globally, $\Diamond_I$ is eventually, $\mathcal{U}_I$ is until, $\mathcal{R}_I$ is release. I is an interval [lb,ub] from a lower to an upper bound, where lb $\leq$, ub, and lb, ub $\in \mathbb{N}$ [17,37].

As MLTL is derived from linear temporal logic (LTL), a majority of the semantics are identical: $false \equiv true$, $\phi_1 \vee \phi_2 \equiv \neg(\neg\phi_1 \wedge \neg\phi_2)$, $\neg(\phi_1\mathcal{U}_I\phi_2) \equiv (\neg\phi_1\mathcal{R}_I\neg\phi_2)$ and $\neg\Diamond_I\phi \equiv \Box_I\neg\phi$. Note that unlike LTL, MLTL does not possess the next $\mathcal{X}$ operator because it is logically equivalent to $\Box_{1,1}\phi$ [17].

Definition 2. *(MLTL Semantics) A MLTL formula ϕ, over a set of propositions $\mathcal{AP}$, by a computation/trace π starting from position i (denoted as π, i $\models \phi$) has satisfaction recursively defined as follows:*

- π, i $\models true$
- π, i $\models p$ iff $p \in \pi[i]$
- π, i $\models \neg\phi$ iff π, i $\not\models \phi$
- π, i $\models \phi_1 \wedge \phi_2$ iff π, i $\models \phi_2$
- π, i $\models phi_1 \, \mathcal{U}_{lb,ub}\phi_2$ iff $|\pi| \geq i + lb$ and, there exists $j \in [i + lb, i + ub]$ such that π, $j \models \phi_2$ and for every $k < j$, $k \in [i + lb, i + ub]$, π, $k \models \phi_1$.

3 Aerospace Systems

We analyze and compare formal specifications for four separate aerospace systems: a high-altitude balloon, a sounding rocket, a UTM, and a CubeSat. This section briefly describes each system and the exigence for applying formal methodologies. We note that, while each system here is progressively more complex than the last, this is not indicative of aerospace systems as a whole. Additional information and visuals of the telemetry datasets are available at http://temporallogic.org/research/AerospaceSystems-NFM22/.

3.1 High-Altitude Balloon

The Make 2 Innovate (M:2:I) Laboratory, located at Iowa State University (ISU), developed a high altitude balloon as part of its High Altitude Balloon Experiments in Technology (HABET) series [19]. The goal of this program is to design, build, fly, and recover small payloads developed entirely by undergraduate students at ISU [19,20]. This launch tested the functionality and accuracy of a SparkFun NEO-M9N GPS module for use on future HABET projects. While the GPS module proved capable, a handful of extraneous measurements were made that provided ground station operators with inaccurate readings while the balloon remained almost stationary on the ground. While not utilized during this launch, some balloon launch teams include on-board mechanisms to pop, vent, or detach the balloon at a defined altitude (often either for experimentation or to prevent further drift in upper atmospheric winds) measured by the GPS [4,10,22,24,31]. If such a mechanism had been used on this project, extraneous measurements may have led to prematurely popping the balloon and thereby ending the mission. Studies of this system do not exist in current literature.

3.2 Sounding Rocket

The Cyclone Rocketry team at ISU developed a sounding rocket called *Nova Somnium*. Nova Somnium flew at the 2019 Spaceport America Cup near Las Cruces, New Mexico [8,14]. Originally designed to reach an apogee altitude of 10,000 ft AGL, it carried a telemetry system for data transmission back to a dedicated ground station, and an aerobraking control system (ACS). During the launch, the ACS actuated prematurely and resulted in a critical failure of the system. Development of formal specifications and RV analysis of this system is described in greater detail in [14].

3.3 UAS Traffic Management System (UTM)

The UAS considered in the UTM project is an AeroVironment (formerly produced by Pulse Aerospace) VAPOR 55 and is owned and operated by the University of Iowa's Operator Performance Laboratory (OPL) in Iowa City, IA [1,6]. UAS are quickly integrating into the National Air Space (NAS) over the United States, and the Federal Aviation Administration (FAA) expects their use to "expand rapidly" in the coming years. Given that this increased air traffic will likely produce congestion and safety concerns, there is a growing need to integrate UAS with intelligent, automated systems for UAS Traffic Management. Previous studies mapped out RV implementations for three separate aspects of the UTM framework: onboard the VAPOR 55, each ground control system, and within the UTM cloud-based framework [6,13].

3.4 CubeSat

The CubeSat, called the GEO-CAPE ROIC In-Flight Performance Experiment (GRI FEX), was developed by the Michigan eXploration Lab (MXL) [16]. Launched in December 2015 from Vandenberg Air Force Base in California, GRIFEX is a 3U CubeSat carrying a NASA Jet Propulsion Laboratory (JPL)-developed all-digital in-pixel high frame rate read-out integrated circuit (ROIC) being tested for use on future spacecraft [5,16,26,30,36]. Although CubeSats generally have mission lifetimes between 6 months to two years, GRIFEX has been in operation for over five years. Such an abnormally long lifetime provides developers with unique data regarding performance degradation due to solar and cosmic radiation. The majority of GRIFEX operations involve manual processes and was not subject to rigorous formal methodologies during its development phase [16]. Recent efforts characterized the CubeSat's performance degradation to provide further insight on methods for updating formal specifications for a dynamically changing system [18].

4   Methodology

The four aerospace systems described above are reactive to their environments and possess well-defined operational timelines; this merits a specification logic like Linear Temporal Logic (LTL) to provide finite-bounded reasoning for each system [21]. Mission-time Linear Temporal Logic (MLTL) encodes the system requirements generically with integer-bounded time steps that provide ease of mapping to real mission data, providing optional integer bounds on temporal operators [17, 37]. MLTL has been used in many industry-based research projects [2, 6, 7, 11, 13–15, 18, 27, 37, 38, 41–43].

Past studies utilized a similar methodology to develop runtime specifications for aerospace systems [6, 13, 14, 18]. We employ these techniques in developing specifications for the high-altitude balloon, constructing requirements in English from known mission parameters and tracking system coverage to capture as many system constraints as possible. We organize our specifications into the categories defined in [39]: operating ranges (RNG), rates of change (RAT), relationships (REL), control sequences (CTRL), and consistency checks (CHE). Our specification validation and debugging uses previously described methods [14].

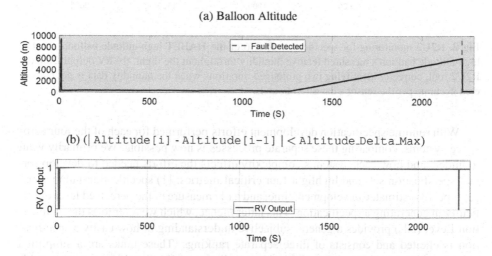

(a) Balloon Altitude

(b) (| Altitude[i] - Altitude[i-1] | < Altitude_Delta_Max)

Fig. 1. R2U2 RV engine [40] monitoring for specification RAT3 of the HABET high-altitude balloon. (a) The high altitude balloon's measured altitude throughout the flight. Half of the duration shown here is when the balloon was secured to the ground for final checkouts. (b) RV output from the R2U2 tool, correctly identifying two faults when the change in altitude between time steps exceeds more than 20 m. The GPS status for the first fault was reported as high-integrity but is clearly an incorrect measurement. The second fault occurred during balloon burst and descent.

To demonstrate the validity of this approach, we examine two specifications and the resulting RV output, produced using R2U2 [40], from the HABET telemetry data obtained during the balloon's mission. Figure 1 shows multiple instances of off-nominal altitude delta measurements. The altitude delta spike seen at the beginning of the time series data occurred while the balloon was affixed to the ground and risked the balloon's systems popping itself, thinking apogee had been reached. The out-of-bounds measurements of the balloon's humidity sensor appear in Fig. 2.

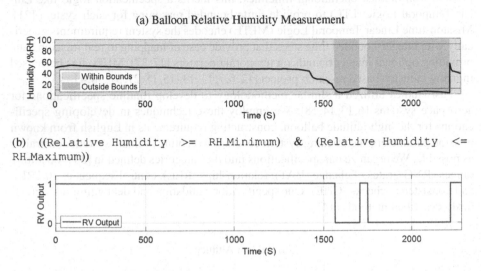

(a) Balloon Relative Humidity Measurement

(b) ((Relative Humidity >= RH_Minimum) & (Relative Humidity <= RH_Maximum))

Fig. 2. R2U2 monitoring for specification RNG6 of the HABET high-altitude balloon. (a) The high altitude balloon's measured relative humidity throughout the flight. (b) RV output from the R2U2 tool, correctly identifying two prolonged durations when the humidity data is not considered accurate per the sensor's datasheet bounds.

With runtime specification development efforts performed for each of the four aerospace systems, comparing these separate processes is now possible. We primarily want to understand how each system's complexity affects the efforts needed to develop formal specification sets and highlight four critical metrics: (1) specification number and (2) type, (3) estimated development time, and a (4) measure of the perceived level of difficulty in generating a specification. This latter metric, which we refer to as the Automation Level (AL) provides a general subjective understanding of how easily a specification is elicited and consists of three separate rankings. These ranks are a simplified version of the automation levels defined in past literature [9]. Specifications ranked **AL 1** require a brief examination of a datasheet to generate and are comparatively easy to extract and formalize. Additionally, most specifications with this ranking are dependent only on component data sheets (rather than mission-specific parameters), and are therefore easily applicable to other systems. One example of this rank would be a specification that dictates a temperature sensor must operate within its operating minimum and maximum; this information is readily available in the component's datasheet. Specifications with rank **AL 2** require a small degree of user/developer input. These specifications require a minor parameter or range adjustment but are still reasonably easy to generate. An example of this rank would be a specification describing the minimum and/or maximum altitudes that an aerospace system should experience; these requirements vary by system. Lastly, specifications with rank **AL 3** require a significant level of user interaction. These specifications are the most difficult to produce. Generally, specifications describing control sequences or mission phase durations fall under this category. Table 1 displays the key metrics of the formal specifications developed for each of the four aerospace systems.

5   Results

We identify four separate generalized temporal logic patterns from the analysis of the aerospace system specifications. The atomic propositions in each pattern can take on varying levels of complexity, ranging from a simple equality check to propositional logic formulas containing multiple sub propositions (e.g., $a0 : !a1 \rightarrow (a2 \parallel a3)$, where $a1, a2, a3$ are defined from system variable comparisons). Table 2 details metrics on each of these patterns and their occurrences within the aerospace system specifications. The first specification pattern, written as $G[0, M](a0)$, appears the most frequently in all four subsystems. The M bound specifies that the specification should hold true for every time step of the entire mission. Specifications with this pattern are well suited to enforcing operating ranges, bounding rates of change, specifying relationships between variables, and checking for logical inconsistencies. Most $G[0, M](a0)$ specifications are AL 1.

Table 1. Specification development summary for the high-altitude balloon, sounding rocket, UTM, and CubeSat examined in this study. Development time estimates account for time spent debugging and validating. The Automation Level (AL) metric provides a measure 1–3 of the difficulty in eliciting specifications for each pattern.

Aerospace system	MLTL spec category	Count	Estimated development time	AL 1	AL 2	AL 3
Balloon	All specifications	14	13 person-hours	6	2	8
	RNG Specifications	7	4 person-hours	6	0	1
	RAT Specifications	6	8 person-hours	0	6	0
	REL Specifications	1	0 person-hours	0	0	0
	CTRL Specifications	0	0 person-hours	0	0	0
	CHE Specifications	0	1 person-hours	0	0	1
Sounding rocket	All specifications	19	50 person-hours	4	7	8
	RNG Specifications	6	14 person-hours	2	3	1
	RAT Specifications	6	15 person-hours	2	4	0
	REL Specifications	0	0 person-hours	0	0	0
	CTRL Specifications	7	21 person-hours	0	0	7
	CHE Specifications	0	0 person-hours	0	0	0
UTM	All specifications	124	69 person-hours	30	87	7
	RNG Specifications	80	12 person-hours	27	53	0
	RAT Specifications	18	18 person-hours	3	15	0
	REL Specifications	18	18 person-hours	2	9	7
	CTRL Specifications	8	21 person-hours	2	6	0
	CHE Specifications	0	0 person-hours	0	0	0
Cube satellite	All specifications	265	77 person-hours	180	25	60
	RNG Specifications	149	39 person-hours	68	25	56
	RAT Specifications	112	32 person-hours	112	0	0
	REL Specifications	4	6 person-hours	0	0	4
	CTRL Specifications	0	0 person-hours	0	0	0
	CHE Specifications	0	0 person-hours	0	0	0

The second pattern, $G[0, M]F[0, N](a0)$, states that $a0$ must be true at least once every N time steps, where $N < M$. This specification pattern is identical to $G[0, M](a0)$ when $N = 0$, but when $N > 0$ allows $a0$ to be periodically violated without violating the specification. This provides the flexibility to handle anticipated stochastic or cyclic behavior. These specifications usually fall into AL 2 or 3 due to the value of N typically needing human definition. ·

The third pattern, $G[0, M](a0 \rightarrow F[0, N]a1)$, represents a temporal relationship between a condition ($a0$) and a behavior ($a1$). Specifications with this pattern primarily encode control sequences. The sounding rocket ACS and UTM system provide air and spacecraft control, so these specification sets benefit most from this pattern. Most of these specifications are AL 3 due to the need for higher knowledge of mission event sequencing and coordination with other systems.

The final pattern we identify, $G[0, M](a0 \rightarrow a0\ U[0, N]a1)$, places a temporal constraint $a1$ on $a0$. Whenever the $a0$ condition is met, $a0$ must continue to hold until $a1$ occurs, and $a1$ must occur within N time steps of $a0$ first being met. Like the previous pattern, this pattern primarily encodes control sequences and typically falls into AL 3.

Table 2. Metrics on the generalized specification forms described in Sect. 5. Under "Aerospace System" we tabulate the number of specifications of each pattern for each aerospace system case study.

Specification pattern	Typical AL	Aerospace system			
		Balloon	Sounding rocket	UTM	**CubeSat**
$G[0, M](a0)$	1	8	8	77	265
$G[0, M]F[0, N](a0)$	2	6	4	35	0
$G[0, M](a0 \rightarrow F[0, N]a1)$	3	0	5	6	0
$G[0, M](a0 \rightarrow a0U[0, N]a1)$	3	0	2	0	0

6 Conclusion

The four common temporal logic subformulas we identify in the aerospace systems are quickly and easily realizable as formal specifications. However, such aerospace systems generally do not see the level of formal reasoning and validation that larger projects do, owing to time and resource constraints. To fully bridge this gap, we suggest a tool that will, given a list of parts/components on a designed mission, reference a database and return a set of temporal logic specifications in the forms of the identified patterns; parts databases already exist for common components and sensors. Development of this tool would be non-trivial but would significantly aid formal specification development for system developers who are not familiar with formal methods.

References

1. AeroVironment, I.: Vapor uas: Helicopter drone with drop delivery (2021). https://www.avinc.com/uas/vapor

2. Aurandt, A., Jones, P., Rozier, K.Y.: Runtime verification triggers real-time, autonomous fault recovery on the CySat-I. In: Proceedings of the 14th NASA Formal Methods Symposium (NFM 2022). Springer, Caltech, California, USA, May 2022

3. Balloonnews, Balloonnews: 10 ways that a high altitude balloon flight can go wrong August 2014. https://balloonnews.wordpress.com/2014/04/10/10-ways-that-a-high-altitude-balloon-flight-can-go-wrong/

4. Basta, T., Miller, S., Clark, R.T.: Weather Balloon Altitude Control System. Montana State University (2014–2015)

5. Bekker, D.L., et al.: Grifex payload data system architecture for on-orbit focal plane array evaluation. In: Proceedings of the American Geophysical Union, Fall Meeting 2012 (2012)

6. Cauwels, M., Hammer, A., Hertz, B., Jones, P.H., Rozier, K.Y.: Integrating runtime verification into an automated UAS traffic management system. In: Muccini, H., Avgeriou, P., Buhnova, B., Camara, J., Caporuscio, M., Franzago, M., Koziolek, A., Scandurra, P., Trubiani, C., Weyns, D., Zdun, U. (eds.) ECSA 2020. CCIS, vol. 1269, pp. 340–357. Springer, Cham (2020). https://doi.org/10.1007/978-3-030-59155-7_26

7. Dabney, J.B., Badger, J.M., Rajagopal, P.: Adding a verification view for an autonomous real-time system architecture. In: AIAA Scitech 2021 Forum, p. 0566, January 2021. https://doi.org/10.2514/6.2021-0566

8. ESRA Board of Directors: 2019 spaceport america cup (2019). http://www.soundingrocket.org/2019-sa-cup.html

9. Fisher, M., Mascardi, V., Rozier, K.Y., Schlingloff, B.-H., Winikoff, M., Yorke-Smith, N.: Towards a framework for certification of reliable autonomous systems. Auton. Agent. Multi-Agent Syst. **35**(1), 1–65 (2020). https://doi.org/10.1007/s10458-020-09487-2

10. Garg, K.: Autonomous Navigation System for High Altitude Balloons. Ph.D. thesis, Luleå Technical University, Graphic Production 2019 (2019)

11. Geist, J., Rozier, K.Y., Schumann, J.: Runtime observer pairs and bayesian network reasoners on-board FPGAs: flight-certifiable system health management for embedded systems. In: Bonakdarpour, B., Smolka, S.A. (eds.) RV 2014. LNCS, vol. 8734, pp. 215–230. Springer, Cham (2014). https://doi.org/10.1007/978-3-319-11164-3_18

12. Gross, K.H., et al.: Formally Verified Run Time Assurance Architecture of a 6U CubeSat Attitude Control System, pp. 1–15. AIAA Infotech (2020). https://doi.org/10.2514/6.2016-0222, https://arc.aiaa.org/doi/abs/10.2514/6.2016-0222

13. Hammer, A., Cauwels, M., Hertz, B., Jones, P., Rozier, K.Y.: Integrating runtime verification into an automated UAS traffic management system. Innovations in Systems and Software Engineering: A NASA Journal, July 2021. https://doi.org/10.1007/s11334-021-00407-5

14. Hertz, B., Luppen, Z., Rozier, K.Y.: Integrating runtime verification into a sounding rocket control system. In: Dutle, A., Moscato, M.M., Titolo, L., Muñoz, C.A., Perez, I. (eds.) NFM 2021. LNCS, vol. 12673, pp. 151–159. Springer, Cham (2021). https://doi.org/10.1007/978-3-030-76384-8_10

15. Kempa, B., Zhang, P., Jones, P.H., Zambreno, J., Rozier, K.Y.: Embedding Online Runtime Verification for Fault Disambiguation on Robonaut2. In: Proceedings of the 18th International Conference on Formal Modeling and Analysis of Timed Systems (FORMATS). Lecture Notes in Computer Science (LNCS), vol. TBD, p. TBD. Springer, Vienna, Austria (September 2020). TBD, http://research.temporallogic.org/papers/KZJZR20.pdf

16. eXploration Lab, T.M.: Grifex (2021). https://exploration.engin.umich.edu/blog/?page_id=2684

17. Li, J., Vardi, M.Y., Rozier, K.Y.: Satisfiability checking for mission-time LTL. In: Dillig, I., Tasiran, S. (eds.) CAV 2019. LNCS, vol. 11562, pp. 3–22. Springer, Cham (2019). https://doi.org/10.1007/978-3-030-25543-5_1

18. Luppen, Z., Jacks, M., Baughman, N., Stilic, M., Nasers, R., Lee, D.Y., Rozier, K.Y., Cutler, J.: Runtime verification of the dynamic performance degradation of the grifex cubesat (under review). In: NASA Formal Methods. Springer International Publishing (2022)

19. M2I: Make to innovate (m:2:i) (2021). https://m2i.aere.iastate.edu/

20. M2I: Project goals (habet) (2021). https://m2i.aere.iastate.edu/habet/project-goals-and-scope-of-work/

21. Manna, Z., Pnueli, A.: Temporal Verification of Reactive Systems: Safety. Springer, New York (2012). https://books.google.com/books?id=lfIGCAAAQBAJ

22. Marshall, R.: Cutdown mechanisms, March 2021. https://sites.google.com/site/ki4mcw/Home/cutdown-mechanisms

23. Merkert, R., Bushell, J.: Managing the drone revolution: a systematic literature review into the current use of airborne drones and future strategic directions for their effective control. J. Air Transp. Manage. **89**, 101929 (2020). https://doi.org/10.1016/j.jairtraman.2020.101929. https://doi.org/10.1016/j.jairtraman.2020.101929

24. Meyer, J.J., Flaten, J.A., Candler, G.V.: Pdf, April 2021

25. Tolmasoff, M., Santos, R.D., Venturini, C.: Improving mission success of cubesats. In: Proceedings of the U.S. Space Program Mission Assurance Improvement Workshop, May 2007

26. Moldwin, M., Sharma, S., Deshmukh, A., Scott, C., Cutler, J.: Machine learning algorithms for spacecraft magnetic field interference cancellation: enabling satellite magnetometry without a boom. Earth and Space Science Open Archive, p. 1 (2019). https://doi.org/10.1002/essoar.10500304.1. https://www.essoar.org/doi/abs/10.1002/essoar.10500304.1

27. Moosbrugger, P., Rozier, K.Y., Schumann, J.: R2U2: monitoring and diagnosis of security threats for unmanned aerial systems. Formal Methods Syst. Design **51**(1), 31–61 (2017). https://doi.org/10.1007/s10703-017-0275-x

28. Muñoz, C., Carreño, V., Dowek, G.: Formal analysis of the operational concept for the small aircraft transportation system. In: Butler, M., Jones, C.B., Romanovsky, A., Troubitsyna, E. (eds.) Rigorous Development of Complex Fault-Tolerant Systems. LNCS, vol. 4157, pp. 306–325. Springer, Heidelberg (2006). https://doi.org/10.1007/11916246_16

29. NASA CubeSat Launch Initiative: CubeSat 101, 1st edn. California Polytechnic State University, San Luis Obispo (Cal Poly) CubeSat Systems Engineer Lab (2017)

30. Norton, C.D., Pasciuto, M.P., Pingree, P., Chien, S., Rider, D.: Spaceborne flight validation of nasa esto technologies. In: 2012 IEEE International Geoscience and Remote Sensing Symposium, pp. 5650–5653 (2012). https://doi.org/10.1109/IGARSS.2012.6352330

31. Papp, D.: Archery release becomes reusable balloon cutdown mechanism, March 2021. https://hackaday.com/2021/03/27/archery-release-becomes-reusable-balloon-cutdown-mechanism/

32. Peng, Z., Lu, Y., Miller, A., Johnson, C., Zhao, T.: A probabilistic model checking approach to analysing reliability, availability, and maintainability of a single satellite system. In: 2013 European Modelling Symposium, pp. 611–616, November 2013. https://doi.org/10.1109/EMS.2013.102

33. Phillips, T., et al.: Space weather ballooning. Space Weather **14**(10), 697–703 (2016). https://doi.org/10.1002/2016SW001410. https://agupubs.onlinelibrary.wiley.com/doi/abs/10.1002/2016SW001410

34. Pike, L., Goodloe, A., Morisset, R., Niller, S.: Copilot: A hard real-time runtime monitor. In: Proceedings of the 1st International Conference on Runtime Verification. LNCS, Springer (November 2010), preprint available at https://leepike.github.io/pub_pages/rv2010.html

35. Pike, L., et al.: Copilot - realtime programming language and runtime verification framework, March 2022. https://copilot-language.github.io/

36. Pingree, P., et al.: Cove, marina, and the future of on-board processing (obp) platforms for cubesat science missions, December 2012

37. Reinbacher, T., Rozier, K.Y., Schumann, J.: Temporal-logic based runtime observer pairs for system health management of real-time systems. In: Ábrahám, E., Havelund, K. (eds.) TACAS 2014. LNCS, vol. 8413, pp. 357–372. Springer, Heidelberg (2014). https://doi.org/10.1007/978-3-642-54862-8_24

38. Rozier, K.Y., Schumann, J., Ippolito, C.: Intelligent Hardware-Enabled Sensor and Software Safety and Health Management for Autonomous UAS. Technical Memorandum NASA/TM-2015-218817, NASA, NASA Ames Research Center, Moffett Field, CA 94035, USA, May 2015

39. Rozier, K.Y.: Specification: the biggest bottleneck in formal methods and autonomy. In: Blazy, S., Chechik, M. (eds.) VSTTE 2016. LNCS, vol. 9971, pp. 8–26. Springer, Cham (2016). https://doi.org/10.1007/978-3-319-48869-1_2

40. Rozier, K.Y., Schumann, J.: R2U2: tool overview. In: Proceedings of International Workshop on Competitions, Usability, Benchmarks, Evaluation, and Standardisation for Runtime Verification Tools (RV-CUBES). vol. 3, pp. 138–156. Kalpa Publications, Seattle, WA, USA, September 2017. TBD. https://easychair.org/publications/paper/Vncw

41. Schumann, J., Moosbrugger, P., Rozier, K.Y.: R2U2: monitoring and diagnosis of security threats for unmanned aerial systems. In: Bartocci, E., Majumdar, R. (eds.) RV 2015. LNCS, vol. 9333, pp. 233–249. Springer, Cham (2015). https://doi.org/10.1007/978-3-319-23820-3_15

42. Schumann, J., Moosbrugger, P., Rozier, K.Y.: Runtime analysis with R2U2: a tool exhibition report. In: Falcone, Y., Sánchez, C. (eds.) RV 2016. LNCS, vol. 10012, pp. 504–509. Springer, Cham (2016). https://doi.org/10.1007/978-3-319-46982-9_35

43. Schumann, J., Rozier, K.Y., Reinbacher, T., Mengshoel, O.J., Mbaya, T., Ippolito, C.: Towards real-time, on-board, hardware-supported sensor and software health management for unmanned aerial systems. Int. J. Prognostics Health Manage. (IJPHM) 6(1), 1–27 (2015)

44. Science, H.A.: Intro to weather balloons (2021). https://www.highaltitudescience.com/pages/intro-to-weather-balloons

45. Seibert, G.: The history of sounding rockets and their contribution to European space research. ESA History Study Reports, November 2006

46. Wong, K.: Nasa's deuce-carrying rocket fails to collect data due to technical glitch, November 2017. https://www.aerospace-technology.com/news/newsnasas-deuce-carrying-rocket-fails-to-collect-data-due-to-technical-glitch-5962942

Robust Computation Tree Logic

Satya Prakash Nayak[1]([✉])[ID], Daniel Neider[1,2][ID], Rajarshi Roy[1][ID],
and Martin Zimmermann[3][ID]

[1] Max Planck Institute for Software Systems, Kaiserslautern, Germany
{sanayak,neider,rajarshi}@mpi-sws.org
[2] Safety and Explainability of Learning Systems Group, Carl von Ossietzky
Universität Oldenburg, Oldenburg, Germany
[3] Aalborg University, Aalborg, Denmark
mzi@cs.aau.dk

Abstract. It is widely accepted that every system should be robust in that "small" violations of environment assumptions should lead to "small" violations of system guarantees, but it is less clear how to make this intuition mathematically precise. While significant efforts have been devoted to providing notions of robustness for Linear Temporal Logic (LTL), branching-time logics, such as Computation Tree Logic (CTL) and CTL*, have received less attention in this regard. To address this shortcoming, we develop "robust" extensions of CTL and CTL*, which we name robust CTL (rCTL) and robust CTL* (rCTL*). Both extensions are syntactically similar to their parent logics but employ multi-valued semantics to distinguish between "large" and "small" violations of the specification. We show that the multi-valued semantics of rCTL make it more expressive than CTL, while rCTL* is as expressive as CTL*. Moreover, we devise efficient model checking algorithms for rCTL and rCTL*, which have the same asymptotic time complexity as the model checking algorithms for CTL and CTL*, respectively.

Keywords: Robustness · Computation tree logic · Linear temporal logic · Model checking

1 Introduction

Specifications for reactive systems are typically written as an implication $\Phi \Rightarrow \Psi$ where Φ is an environment assumption, and Ψ is a system guarantee. However, the specification $\Phi \Rightarrow \Psi$ is satisfied if the environment assumption Φ is violated, no matter how the system behaves. This is clearly inadequate since the environment assumptions will inevitably be violated in the real world: the true environment where the system will be deployed is often not entirely known at design time and, thus, can not be accurately and fully formalized by the formula Φ.

The work was partly funded by Deutsche Forschungsgemeinschaft (DFG, German Research Foundation) grant number 434592664, by Villum Investigator Grant S4OS held by Kim G. Larsen, and by the Danish National Research Center DIREC.

J. V. Deshmukh et al. (Eds.): NFM 2022, LNCS 13260, pp. 538–556, 2022.
https://doi.org/10.1007/978-3-031-06773-0_29

To prevent systems from behaving arbitrarily when the environment assumption is violated, there have been concentrated efforts on improving the specifications for reactive systems by making them robust to the violations of the environment assumption. For instance, the works of Bloem et al. [2], Tarraf et al. [18], Doyen et al. [4], Ehlers et al. [5], and Tabuada et al. [15,16] have provided different ways of introducing robustness for specifications in Linear Temporal Logic (LTL). All these approaches require some additional assumptions or additional quantitative information from the designer. This has motivated Tabuada and Neider [17] to introduce a new logic, called robust LTL (rLTL), which provides robustness without relying on any additional assumptions or input from a designer beyond an LTL formula. Inspired by this logic, the works of Neider et al. [13] introduced robust extensions for Prompt-LTL and Linear Dynamic Logic.

Most work on robustness has been directed at LTL. Branching-time logic, such as Computation Tree Logic (CTL) and CTL*, have received less attention in this regard, with a few exceptions. For instance, the work of French et al. [9] introduces a logic called RoCTL, but they use additional operators that require manual quantification of the violations.

To address this shortcoming, we develop robust extensions of CTL and CTL*, which we call robust CTL (rCTL) and robust CTL* (rCTL*). These logics are inspired by rLTL. Similar to rLTL, our new logics employ multi-valued semantics to track the degree of violations of a specification and are guided by two objectives: first, the syntax of rCTL and rCTL* is similar to the syntax of CTL and CTL*, respectively; second, the notion of robustness in these logics is intrinsic rather than extrinsic, i.e., robustness does not rely on the designers to provide quantitative information about the specification such as the number of violations permitted, ranks, cost, etc.

To demonstrate how our notion of robustness works, consider a specification $\Phi \rightarrow \Psi$ for a robot deployed in an office-like environment. The environment assumption $\Phi = \forall \Box \neg H$ states that humans never visit the initial location of the robot. On the other hand, the robot guarantee $\Psi = \forall \Box \exists \bigcirc R$ states the following: "for all trajectories, regardless of the robot's current position, the robot can return to its initial location in one time step" (Note that such a specification can not be expressed in LTL). Ideally, we would then want the following:

- if humans satisfy the assumption Φ, then the robot should also satisfy the guarantee Ψ;
- however, if humans violate the assumption by visiting the initial location a finite number of times before realizing their mistake and eventually not visiting it anymore, i.e., if they only satisfy $\forall \Diamond \Box \neg H$, then rather than behaving arbitrarily, the robot should also satisfy $\forall \Diamond \Box \exists \bigcirc R$, i.e., the robot eventually should be able to return to its initial location from any point;
- similarly, if humans violate the assumption by not visiting the initial location only infinitely often (or finitely often), i.e., if they satisfy $\forall \Box \Diamond \neg H$ (or $\forall \Diamond \neg H$), then the robot should satisfy $\forall \Box \Diamond \exists \bigcirc R$ (or $\forall \Diamond \exists \bigcirc R$, respectively).

Later in this paper, we show that such a notion of robustness is indeed captured by the semantics of rCTL and rCTL*.

The first two contributions of the paper are robust variants of the logics CTL and CTL*, namely rCTL and rCTL*, respectively. Their semantics rely on a many-valued truth system that captures the various degrees of violation of a specification.

Second, we study the expressive power of rCTL and rCTL* and compare them to existing logics such as LTL, rLTL, CTL, and CTL*. The key results here are that rCTL is more expressive than CTL, while rCTL* has the same expressive power as CTL*.

Third, to demonstrate that rCTL and rCTL* specifications can be effectively used for verification, we provide efficient algorithms for model checking properties specified in these logics. We establish that the time complexity of rCTL and rCTL* model checking is linear and exponential, respectively, in the size of the formula, which is the same as the time complexity of CTL and CTL* model checking, respectively. Thus, robustness can be added to branching-time logics for free.

All proofs omitted due to space restrictions can be found in the full version [12].

2   Notation and Review of Computation Tree Logic

In this section, we review the syntax and semantics of CTL, which expresses properties of Kripke structures.

Throughout this paper, we fix a finite set $\mathcal{P}$ of atomic propositions. A (finite) *Kripke structure* $M = (S, I, R, L)$ over $\mathcal{P}$ consists of a finite set of states S, a set of initial states $I \subseteq S$, a transition relation $R \subseteq S \times S$ such that for all states s there exists a state s' satisfying $(s, s') \in R$, and a labeling function $L: S \to 2^{\mathcal{P}}$. The set $\mathrm{post}(s) = \{s' \in S \mid (s, s') \in R\}$ contains all successors of $s \in S$. A path of the Kripke structure M is an infinite sequence of states $\pi = s_0 s_1 \cdots$ such that $s_{i+1} \in \mathrm{post}(s_i)$ for each $i \geq 0$. For a state s, let $\mathrm{paths}(s)$ denote the set of all paths starting from s. And for a path π and $i \geq 0$, let $\pi[i]$ denote the i-th state of π, and $\pi[i..]$ denotes the suffix of π from index i on.

Syntax. CTL formulas are classified into state and path formulas. Intuitively, state formulas express properties of states, whereas path formulas express temporal properties of paths. For ease of notation, we denote state formulas and path formulas by Greek capital letters and Greek lowercase letters, respectively. CTL state formulas over $\mathcal{P}$ are given by the grammar

$$\Phi ::= p \mid \Phi \vee \Phi \mid \Phi \wedge \Phi \mid \neg \Phi \mid \Phi \Rightarrow \Phi \mid \exists \varphi \mid \forall \Phi,$$

where $p \in \mathcal{P}$ and φ is a path formula. CTL path formulas are given by the grammar

$$\varphi ::= \bigcirc \Phi \mid \Diamond \Phi \mid \square \Phi \mid \Phi \mathbf{U} \Phi \mid \Phi \mathbf{W} \Phi,$$

where $\bigcirc$, $\Diamond$, $\square$, $\mathbf{U}$, and $\mathbf{W}$ denote the operator next, eventually, always, until, and weak until, respectively.

Semantics. Slightly deviating from the usual notation, we define the CTL semantics using a mapping V_{CTL} that maps a state/path and a CTL formula to a truth value in $\mathbb{B} = \{0,1\}$. Given a state s and state formulas Φ, Ψ, CTL semantics is defined as follows:

- $V_{\mathrm{CTL}}(s,p) = \begin{cases} 0 & \text{if } p \notin L(s); \text{ and} \\ 1 & \text{if } p \in L(s). \end{cases}$
- $V_{\mathrm{CTL}}(s, \Phi \vee \Psi) = \max\{V_{\mathrm{CTL}}(s,\Phi), V_{\mathrm{CTL}}(s,\Psi)\}$.
- $V_{\mathrm{CTL}}(s, \Phi \wedge \Psi) = \min\{V_{\mathrm{CTL}}(s,\Phi), V_{\mathrm{CTL}}(s,\Psi)\}$.
- $V_{\mathrm{CTL}}(s, \neg\Phi) = 1 - V_{\mathrm{CTL}}(s,\Phi)$.
- $V_{\mathrm{CTL}}(s, \Phi \Rightarrow \Psi) = \max\{1 - V_{\mathrm{CTL}}(s,\Phi), V_{\mathrm{CTL}}(s,\Psi)\}$.
- $V_{\mathrm{CTL}}(s, \exists\varphi) = \max_{\pi \in \mathrm{paths}(s)} V_{\mathrm{CTL}}(\pi, \varphi)$.
- $V_{\mathrm{CTL}}(s, \forall\varphi) = \min_{\pi \in \mathrm{paths}(s)} V_{\mathrm{CTL}}(\pi, \varphi)$.

Similarly, for a path π, the CTL semantics of path formulas is defined as given below:

- $V_{\mathrm{CTL}}(\pi, \bigcirc \Phi) = V_{\mathrm{CTL}}(\pi[1], \Phi)$.
- $V_{\mathrm{CTL}}(\pi, \Diamond \Phi) = \max_{i \geq 0} V_{\mathrm{CTL}}(\pi[i], \Phi)$.
- $V_{\mathrm{CTL}}(\pi, \Box \Phi) = \min_{i \geq 0} V_{\mathrm{CTL}}(\pi[i], \Phi)$.
- $V_{\mathrm{CTL}}(\pi, \Phi \mathbf{U} \Psi) = \max_{j \geq 0} \min\{V_{\mathrm{CTL}}(\pi[j], \Psi), \min_{0 \leq i < j} V_{\mathrm{CTL}}(\pi[i], \Phi)\}$.
- $V_{\mathrm{CTL}}(\pi, \Phi \mathbf{W} \Psi) = \min_{j \geq 0} \max\{V_{\mathrm{CTL}}(\pi[j], \Phi), \max_{0 \leq i \leq j} V_{\mathrm{CTL}}(\pi[i], \Psi)\}$.

Note that this definition is equivalent to the usual semantics of CTL [1].

3 Robust Computation Tree Logic

In this section, we robustify CTL by generalizing the ideas underlying robust LTL to CTL, obtaining the logic rCTL. We describe the syntax and semantics of rCTL and discuss the relation and differences between rCTL and other temporal logics.

As discussed in the robot example in the introduction, we want to capture the notion of robustness in CTL by ensuring that a small violation in environment assumptions leads to a small violation of system guarantees. To achieve that, we introduce robust semantics for CTL. Following arguments given by Tabuada and Neider [17], we first motivate the semantics of rCTL using an example. Consider the CTL path formula $\Box\, p$, where p is an atomic proposition. The formula can be satisfied in only one way, namely when p holds at every step (i.e., state) of the path. In contrast, the formula can be violated in several ways. Intuitively, $\Box\, p$ is violated in the worst manner when p fails to hold at every step. Then, we would prefer a case where p holds for finitely many steps. Even better would be the case when p holds at infinitely many steps. Finally, among all possible ways $\Box\, p$ can be violated, we would prefer the situation where p fails to hold for at most finitely many steps. Our robust semantics is designed to distinguish between satisfaction and these four different degrees of violation of $\Box\, p$. However, as convincing as this argument might be, a question persists: in which sense can we regard these five alternatives as canonical?

We answer this question by interpreting the satisfaction of $\Box\, p$ as a counting problem. Recall that the semantics of $\Box\, p$ for a path π is given by $V_{\mathrm{CTL}}((\pi, \Box\, p) = \min_{i \geq 0} V_{\mathrm{CTL}}(\pi[i], p)$. Now, observe that the truth value of the CTL formula $\Box\, p$ for a path π only depends on the number of occurrences of 0's and 1's in the infinite word $\alpha = V_{\mathrm{CTL}}(\pi[0], p) V_{\mathrm{CTL}}(\pi[1], p) \cdots \in \mathbb{B}^\omega$ but not on their order. From this perspective, $\Box\, p$ is violated in the worst manner when p fails to hold at every step, which corresponds to the number of occurrences of 1 in α being zero. The next degree of violation of $\Box\, p$ in which p holds at finitely many steps corresponds to having a finite number of 1's. Similarly, the next degree of violation corresponds to having an infinite number of 1's and an infinite number of 0's. Among all the ways in which $\Box\, p$ is violated, the most preferred way corresponds to having finitely many 0's. Finally, the satisfaction of $\Box\, p$ corresponds to having zero 0's. Note that the position where 0's and 1's occur is irrelevant for our argument. Furthermore, note that by successively applying permutations that swap position i with position $i + 1$ and leave all the remaining elements of $\mathbb{N}$ unaltered, one can transform any $\alpha \in \mathbb{B}^\omega$ into words of one of the following five forms: $1^\omega, 0^k 1^\omega, (01)^\omega, 1^k 0^\omega, 0^\omega$. It is not hard to verify that the five cases of violations of $\Box\, p$ that we discussed above amount to the words of the five forms given above. We thus conclude the need for five truth values to describe five different ways of counting 0's and 1's that correspond to five different canonical forms of violations of $\Box\, p$.

According to our motivating example $\Box\, p$, the desired semantics should have one truth value corresponding to true and four truth values corresponding to the different shades of false. It is instructive to think of truth values as elements of $\mathbb{B}^4$. To ease notation, we denote such values by $b = b_1 b_2 b_3 b_4$ or $b = (b_1, b_2, b_3, b_4)$ with $b_i \in \mathbb{B}$. We denote the set of truth values as $\mathbb{B}_4$, which consists of the five truth values $\{0000, 0001, 0011, 0111, 1111\}$. The value 1111 corresponds to true, and the others correspond to different shades of false. The truth values are ordered naturally as $0000 < 0001 < 0011 < 0111 < 1111$.

Syntax. Similar to the syntax of CTL, formulas of rCTL are also classified into state and path formulas. Furthermore, we equip every temporal operator with dots to distinguish the robust operators from the normal ones. rCTL state formulas over $\mathcal{P}$ are formed according to the grammar

$$\Phi ::= p \mid \Phi \vee \Phi \mid \Phi \wedge \Phi \mid \neg \Phi \mid \Phi \Rightarrow \Phi \mid \exists \varphi \mid \forall \varphi,$$

where $p \in \mathcal{P}$ and φ is a path formula. rCTL path formulas are formed according to the grammar

$$\varphi ::= \odot \Phi \mid \diamondsuit \Phi \mid \boxdot \Phi \mid \Phi\ \mathrm{U}\ \Phi \mid \Phi\ \mathbf{W}\ \Phi.$$

Semantics. We now discuss the motivation behind our many-valued semantics for rCTL. The notion of a triangular-norm summarizes all the desirable properties of a many-valued conjunction (see P. Hájek [11] for details), and it is natural to model conjunction and disjunction in $\mathbb{B}_4$ by min and max, respectively. Moreover, as in intuitionistic logic, we define the implication, denoted by $a \rightarrow b$ on the level of truth values, such that $c \leq a \to b$ if and only if $c \wedge a \leq b$ for every $c \in \mathbb{B}_4$. This leads to

$$a \to b = \begin{cases} 1111 & \text{if } a \leq b; \text{ and} \\ b & \text{otherwise.} \end{cases}$$

However, the negation, denoted by $\bar{a}$ on the level of truth values, defined by $a \to 0000$ as in intuitionistic logic, is not compatible with our interpretation that all elements in $\mathbb{B}_4 \setminus \{1111\}$ represent different shades of false and, thus, their negation should be 1111. Therefore, we follow the ideas introduced by rLTL and use *da Costa algebras* to define the negation (see Priest and Graham [14] for details):

$$\bar{a} = \begin{cases} 0000 & \text{if } a = 1111; \text{ and} \\ 1111 & \text{otherwise.} \end{cases}$$

In other words, "true" (1111) gets mapped to "false" (0000), while "shades of false" get mapped to "true".

It should be mentioned that working with a five-valued semantics has its price. As in intuitionistic logic, $\bar{\bar{a}}$ may not be equal to a as evidenced by taking $a = 0111$. Although it is still true that $\bar{\bar{a}} \to a$. Interestingly, we can think of double negation as quantization in the sense that true is mapped to true and all the shades of false are mapped to 0000 (false). Hence, double negation quantizes the five different truth values into two truth values (true and false) in a manner that is compatible with our interpretation of truth values.

Similar to the semantics of CTL, we define the semantics of rCTL by a mapping V, called *valuation*, that maps an rCTL formula and a state/path to an element of $\mathbb{B}_4$. For an atomic proposition $p \in \mathcal{P}$, it is defined classically:

$$V(s, p) = \begin{cases} 0000 & \text{if } p \notin L(s); \text{ and} \\ 1111 & \text{if } p \in L(s). \end{cases}$$

Following the semantics of rLTL, we define the semantics for boolean connectives in rCTL using da Costa algebras, as follows:

$$V(s, \Phi \vee \Psi) = \max \left\{ V(s, \Phi), V(s, \Psi) \right\}.$$
$$V(s, \Phi \wedge \Psi) = \min \left\{ V(s, \Phi), V(s, \Psi) \right\}.$$
$$V(s, \neg \Phi) = \overline{V(s, \Phi)}$$
$$V(s, \Phi \Rightarrow \Psi) = V(s, \Phi) \to V(s, \Psi)$$

For existential path quantification, we want $V(s, \exists \varphi) \geq b$ if there exists a path π from s such that $V(\pi, \varphi) \geq b$. Similarly, we want $V(s, \forall \varphi) \geq b$ if for all paths π from s holds that $V(\pi, \varphi) \geq b$. This leads to:

$$V(s, \exists \varphi) = \max_{\pi \in \text{paths}(s)} V(\pi, \varphi) \quad \text{and} \quad V(s, \forall \varphi) = \min_{\pi \in \text{paths}(s)} V(\pi, \varphi).$$

Now, for path formulas, we formalize the intuition above in the semantics of the temporal operators. Using the counting interpretation as discussed earlier, we define the semantics of $\boxdot$ by

$$V(\pi, \boxdot \, \Phi) = \left(\min_{i \geq 0} V_1(\pi[i], \Phi), \max_{j \geq 0} \min_{i \geq j} V_2(\pi[i], \Phi), \min_{j \geq 0} \max_{i \geq j} V_3(\pi[i], \Phi), \max_{i \geq 0} V_4(\pi[i], \Phi) \right),$$

where $V_\ell(\pi, \varphi)$ denotes the ℓ-th entry of $V(\pi, \varphi)$ for $1 \leq \ell \leq 4$.

The semantics of $\diamondsuit \, \Phi$ mimics the classical semantics in that the truth value of $\diamondsuit \, \Phi$ on π is the maximal truth value of Φ that is assumed at any position of π.

$$V(\pi, \diamondsuit \, \Phi) = \max_{i \geq 0} V(\pi[i], \Phi).$$

Using a similar approach, the semantics for other temporal operators are defined as follows:

$$V(\pi, \odot \Phi) = V(\pi[1], \Phi).$$
$$V(\pi, \Phi \, \mathbf{U} \, \Psi) = \max_{j \geq 0} \min \left\{ V(\pi[j], \Psi), \min_{0 \leq i < j} V(\pi[i], \Phi) \right\}.$$
$$V(\pi, \Phi \, \mathbf{W} \, \Psi) = (\min_{j \geq 0} W_1, \max_{k \geq 0} \min_{j \geq k} W_2, \min_{k \geq 0} \max_{j \geq k} W_3, \max_{j \geq 0} W_4) \text{ where}$$

$$W_l = \max \left\{ V_l(\pi[j], \Phi), \max_{0 \leq i \leq j} V_l(\pi[i], \Psi) \right\}.$$

Example 1. Having defined the rCTL semantics, let us recall the example of the specification for a robot given in Sect. 1: $\Phi \Rightarrow \Psi$, where $\Phi = \forall \Box \neg H$ is the environment assumption that humans never visit the initial location, and $\Psi = \forall \Box \exists \bigcirc R$ is the robot guarantee that from any state in a path there exists a way for the robot to return to its initial location in one time step. The robust version of this formula is $\forall \boxdot \neg H \Rightarrow \forall \boxdot \exists \odot R$. Let us see if this formula captures the robustness property as discussed in Sect. 1.

Now, coming back to our example, suppose $\Phi_1 = \neg H$ and $\Phi_2 = \exists \odot R$. Let us assume $\forall \boxdot \Phi_1 \Rightarrow \forall \boxdot \Phi_2$ evaluates to 1111 for some Kripke structure. Then the following hold.

- If humans never visit the initial location, then in any path, Φ_1 holds at every state. Hence, $\forall \boxdot \Phi_1$ evaluates to 1111. Then by the semantics of $\Rightarrow$, the formula $\forall \boxdot \Phi_2$ also must evaluate to 1111. That means, in any path, Φ_2 also holds at every state. Therefore, from any state of a path, the robot can return to its initial location in one time step. Hence, the desired behavior of the system is retained when the environment assumption holds with no violation.

- If humans violate the assumption by visiting the initial location finitely many times and eventually not visiting it anymore, then for any path, Φ_1 holds eventually at every state. Hence, $\forall \boxdot \Phi_1$ evaluates to 0111. Then, by the rCTL semantics, $\forall \boxdot \Phi_2$ evaluates to 0111 or higher. Hence, in any path, Φ_2 also needs to hold eventually at every state. That means, from any state in a path, the robot can return to its initial location eventually.
- Similarly, if Φ_1 holds at infinitely (finitely) many states in every path, then Φ_2 needs to hold at infinitely (finitely) many states in every path.

Hence, whenever the formula $\forall \boxdot \Phi_1 \Rightarrow \forall \boxdot \Phi_2$ evaluates to 1111, its semantics captures the intended robustness property by which a weakening of the assumption $\forall \boxdot \Phi_1$ leads to a weakening of the guarantee $\forall \boxdot \Phi_2$.

Now, a natural question arises: does the formula still provide useful information when its value is lower than 1111. It follows from the semantics of implication that $\forall \boxdot \Phi_1 \Rightarrow \forall \boxdot \Phi_2$ evaluates to $b < 1111$ only when $\forall \boxdot \Phi_1$ evaluates to a higher value than b, whereas $\forall \boxdot \Phi_2$ evaluates to b. So, the desired system guarantee is not satisfied. However, the value of $\forall \boxdot \Phi_1 \Rightarrow \forall \boxdot \Phi_2$ still describes which weakened guarantee follows from the environment assumption. This can be seen as another measure of robustness: despite $\forall \boxdot \Phi_2$ not following from $\forall \boxdot \Phi_1$, the system's behavior is not arbitrary, a value of b is still guaranteed.

3.1 Expressiveness of rCTL

In this section, we compare the expressiveness of rCTL with other temporal logics such as CTL, LTL, and rLTL. We show that the five truth values of rCTL make it more expressive than CTL. More precisely, there are properties that one can express in rCTL but not in CTL. However, the expressiveness of rCTL and LTL are incomparable; and the same also holds for rCTL and rLTL.

We compare the expressiveness of two classes of logics by comparing the expressiveness of their formulas. For logics A and B, we say A is as expressive as B if for every formula in B there is an equivalent formula in A. Moreover, we say A is more expressive than B if A is as expressive as B but the converse is not true. Furthermore, we say A and B have incomparable expressiveness if neither of A and B is as expressive as the other one. For branching time logics, we only consider the state formulas when comparing the expressiveness.

Now the question is what it means for two formulas to be equivalent. Intuitively speaking, equivalent means "express the same thing". Formally, we define the equivalence of two formulas using their satisfaction sets. For a given Kripke structure, and a state formula Φ, we define the satisfaction set $Sat(\Phi, b)$ of an rCTL formula Φ and with value $b \in \mathbb{B}_4$ to be the set of states s such that $V(s, \Phi) \geq b$. Since the satisfaction sets of an rCTL (state) formula are always associated with a truth value in $\mathbb{B}_4$, we always associate a truth value with an rCTL formula when comparing its expressiveness.

For two rCTL state formulas Φ_1, Φ_2 and two truth values $b_1, b_2 \in \mathbb{B}_4$, we say Φ_1 with truth value b_1 is equivalent to Φ_2 with truth value b_2 if for every Kripke structure it holds that $Sat(\Phi_1, b_1) = Sat(\Phi_2, b_2)$. Similarly, an rCTL formula Φ_1

with truth value b_1 is equivalent to a CTL formula Φ_2 if for every Kripke structure it holds that $\mathrm{Sat}(\Phi_1, b_1) = \mathrm{Sat}_{\mathrm{CTL}}(\Phi_2)$, where $\mathrm{Sat}_{\mathrm{CTL}}(\cdot)$ denotes the satisfaction sets for CTL formulas. The equivalence between an rCTL formula and LTL formula is defined analogously.

Now, comparing the semantics of CTL and rCTL, an induction over the structure of formulas shows that the CTL semantics of a formula containing no implication can be recovered from the first bit of the rCTL semantics. Recall that V_{CTL} and V_1 are the CTL valuation and the first bit of the rCTL valuation, respectively.

Lemma 1. *For any CTL state formula Φ containing no implication, let Φ_r be the rCTL state formula obtained by dotting all temporal operators in Φ. Then for any state s, it holds that $V_{CTL}(s, \Phi) = V_1(s, \Phi_r)$. Consequently, it holds that $\mathrm{Sat}_{CTL}(\Phi) = \mathrm{Sat}(\Phi_r, 1111)$.*

As we know that $\Phi \Rightarrow \Psi$ is equivalent to $\neg \Phi \vee \Psi$ in CTL, hence, one can rewrite any CTL formula into a formula containing no implication. Therefore, by using Lemma 1, rCTL is at least as expressive as CTL.

However, the converse is not true, i.e., there exist rCTL formulas that have no equivalent CTL formula. For example, consider the rCTL formula $\Phi = \forall \boxdot p$ with truth value 0111. For a state s, we have $s \in \mathrm{Sat}(\Phi, 0111)$ if and only if for each $\pi \in \mathrm{paths}(s)$, there exists j such that $p \in L(\pi[i])$ for all $i \geq j$, which is equivalent to each path $\pi \in \mathrm{paths}(s)$ satisfying the LTL formula $\Diamond \Box p$. However, as we know, the formula $\Diamond \Box p$ can not be expressed in CTL (see Baier and Katoen [1] for details). Therefore, there is no CTL formula Ψ such that $\mathrm{Sat}(\Phi, 0111) = \mathrm{Sat}_{\mathrm{CTL}}(\Psi)$. In total, we obtain the following result.

Theorem 1. *rCTL is more expressive than CTL.*

It is known that the expressiveness of LTL and CTL is incomparable, i.e., there exist CTL formulas (i.e., $\forall \Diamond \forall \Box p$) for which there is no equivalent LTL formula, and there exist LTL formulas (i.e., $\Diamond(p \wedge \bigcirc p)$) for which there is no equivalent CTL formula (see Baier and Katoen [1] for details). The same holds for the expressiveness of LTL and rCTL. As we just saw that the first bit of the rCTL semantics captures the CTL semantics (for a formula with no implication), it follows that for the rCTL formula $\forall \Diamond \forall \boxdot p$ (with value 1111), there is no equivalent LTL formula. Furthermore, it is easy to see that the five-valued semantics does not help in expressing $\varphi = \Diamond(p \wedge \bigcirc p)$. Hence, using the proof of inexpressibility of φ in CTL, it can be shown that φ can not be expressed by any rCTL formula either. Intuitively, a Kripke structure satisfies the formula φ if all paths contain a pair of consecutive states where p holds. This property is inexpressible in rCTL as all path formulas are guarded with an existential or universal operator. One can express "all paths contain a state such that p holds at that state and at all (or some) of its successor" in rCTL, which is not the same as the property we want. Therefore, we obtain the following result.

Theorem 2. *rCTL and LTL have incomparable expressiveness.*

In the paper on rLTL [17], Tabuada and Neider showed that LTL and rLTL are equally expressive. Hence, a direct corollary of Theorem 2 is the following:

Corollary 1. *rCTL and rLTL have incomparable expressiveness.*

3.2   rCTL Model Checking

The classical CTL model checking problem asks whether all executions of a system satisfy a given property. However, in the context of rCTL, this question is more involved due to rCTL's many-valued semantics. A natural generalization is whether all executions satisfy a given property with at least a given value $b_0 \in \mathbb{B}_4$. Formally, the rCTL model checking problem is: for a given Kripke structure $M = (S, I, R, L)$, an rCTL formula Φ and a truth value $b_0 \in \mathbb{B}_4$, does $V(s, \Phi) \geq b_0$ hold for all initial states $s \in I$? Our rCTL model checking procedure is shown as pseudocode in Algorithm 1. It is similar to the standard CTL model checking algorithm in that it recursively computes the satisfaction sets $\mathrm{Sat}(\Psi, b)$ for each subformula[1] $\Psi \in \mathrm{Sub}(\Phi)$ and each truth value $b \in \mathbb{B}_4$. To check whether all paths of the Kripke structure starting in an initial state satisfy Φ, it is then enough to check whether all initial states belong to $\mathrm{Sat}(\Phi, b_0)$. Note that $\mathrm{Sat}(\Psi, 0000) = S$ since every state satisfies any rCTL formula Ψ with truth value 0000.

Algorithm 1. rCTL Model Checking

Input: Kripke structure M, rCTL formula Φ and a truth value $b_0 \in \mathbb{B}_4$

    for all $\Psi \in \mathrm{Sub}(\Phi)$ in increasing size **do**

        $\mathrm{Sat}(\Psi, 0000) = S$

        for all $b = 1111$ to 0001 **do**

            Compute $\mathrm{Sat}(\Psi, b)$ as characterized in Table 1

    return $I \subseteq \mathrm{Sat}(\Phi, b_0)$

The key idea of Algorithm 1 is to recursively compute the satisfaction sets using a dynamic programming technique. More precisely, we compute the satisfaction sets by induction over the construction of Φ as shown in Table 1. Since $\mathrm{Sat}(\Psi, 0000) = S$ for any rCTL formula Ψ, Table 1 only shows the case $b > 0000$. To simplify the following presentation of these cases, we split the discussion into three categories: atomic propositions, boolean connectives, and temporal operators.

Atomic Propositions. The valuation for atomic propositions is defined classically, as in the case of CTL. Hence, the satisfaction set $\mathrm{Sat}(p, b)$ of an atomic proposition $p \in \mathcal{P}$ with a value $b > 0000$ is the set of all states whose label contains p.

Boolean Connectives. The computation of the satisfaction sets for the boolean connectives closely follows the semantic definition based on the da Costa algebra. Conjunction and disjunction are implemented using the usual intersection

---

[1] The set of subformulas is defined as for CTL. See Baier and Katoen [1] for details.

Table 1. Characterization of the satisfaction sets

Symbol	$\mathrm{Sat}(\cdot,\cdot)$ for formulas Φ, Ψ and value $b \in \mathbb{B}_4 \setminus \{0000\}$
$p \in \mathcal{P}$	$\mathrm{Sat}(p,b) = \{s \in S \mid p \in L(s)\}$
$\vee$	$\mathrm{Sat}(\Phi \vee \Psi, b) = \mathrm{Sat}(\Phi, b) \cup \mathrm{Sat}(\Psi, b)$
$\wedge$	$\mathrm{Sat}(\Phi \wedge \Psi, b) = \mathrm{Sat}(\Phi, b) \cap \mathrm{Sat}(\Psi, b)$
$\neg$	$\mathrm{Sat}(\neg\Phi, b) = S \setminus \mathrm{Sat}(\Phi, 1111)$
$\Rightarrow$	$\mathrm{Sat}(\Phi \Rightarrow \Psi, 1111) = \bigcap_b \mathrm{Sat}(\Psi, b) \cup (S \setminus \mathrm{Sat}(\Phi, b))$
	$\mathrm{Sat}(\Phi \Rightarrow \psi, b) = \mathrm{Sat}(\Phi \Rightarrow \Psi, 1111) \cup \mathrm{Sat}(\Psi, b)$ for any $b \leq 0111$
$\odot$	$\mathrm{Sat}(\exists \odot \Phi, b) = \{s \in S \mid \mathrm{post}(s) \cap \mathrm{Sat}(\Phi, b) \neq \emptyset\}$
	$\mathrm{Sat}(\forall \odot \Phi, b) = \{s \in S \mid \mathrm{post}(s) \subseteq \mathrm{Sat}(\Phi, b)\}$
$\Diamond$	$\mathrm{Sat}(\exists \Diamond \Phi, b) = \mu T.F_\exists(T, \mathrm{Sat}(\Phi, b), S)$
	$\mathrm{Sat}(\forall \Diamond \Phi, b) = \mu T.F_\forall(T, \mathrm{Sat}(\Phi, b), S)$
$\Box$	$\mathrm{Sat}(\exists \Box \Phi, 1111) = \nu T.F_\exists(T, \emptyset, \mathrm{Sat}(\Phi, 1111))$
	$\mathrm{Sat}(\exists \Box \Phi, 0111) = \mu T_1.\nu T_2.G_\exists(T_1, T_2, \emptyset, \mathrm{Sat}(\Phi, 0111))$
	$\mathrm{Sat}(\exists \Box \Phi, 0011) = \nu T_2.\mu T_1.G_\exists(T_1, T_2, \emptyset, \mathrm{Sat}(\Phi, 0011))$
	$\mathrm{Sat}(\exists \Box \Phi, 0001) = \mu T.F_\exists(T, \mathrm{Sat}(\Phi, 0001), S)$
	$\mathrm{Sat}(\forall \Box \Phi, 1111) = \nu T.F_\forall(T, \emptyset, \mathrm{Sat}(\Phi, 1111))$
	$\mathrm{Sat}(\forall \Box \Phi, 0111) = \mu T_1.\nu T_2.G_\forall(T_1, T_2, \emptyset, \mathrm{Sat}(\Phi, 0111))$
	$\mathrm{Sat}(\forall \Box \Phi, 0011) = \nu T_2.\mu T_1.G_\forall(T_1, T_2, \emptyset, \mathrm{Sat}(\Phi, 0011))$
	$\mathrm{Sat}(\forall \Box \Phi, 0001) = \mu T.F_\forall(T, \mathrm{Sat}(\Phi, 0001), S)$
U	$\mathrm{Sat}(\exists(\Phi \ \mathbf{U} \ \Psi), b) = \mu T.F_\exists(T, \mathrm{Sat}(\Psi, b), \mathrm{Sat}(\Phi, b))$
	$\mathrm{Sat}(\forall(\Phi \ \mathbf{U} \ \Psi), b) = \mu T.F_\forall(T, \mathrm{Sat}(\Psi, b), \mathrm{Sat}(\Phi, b))$
W	$\mathrm{Sat}(\exists(\Phi \ \mathbf{W} \ \Psi), 1111) = \nu T.F_\exists(T, \mathrm{Sat}(\Psi, 1111), \mathrm{Sat}(\Phi, 1111))$
	$\mathrm{Sat}(\exists(\Phi \ \mathbf{W} \ \Psi), 0111) = \mu T_1.\nu T_2.G_\exists(T_1, T_2, \mathrm{Sat}(\Psi, 0111), \mathrm{Sat}(\Phi, 0111))$
	$\mathrm{Sat}(\exists(\Phi \ \mathbf{W} \ \Psi), 0011) = \nu T_2.\mu T_1.G_\exists(T_1, T_2, \mathrm{Sat}(\Psi, 0011), \mathrm{Sat}(\Phi, 0011))$
	$\mathrm{Sat}(\exists(\Phi \ \mathbf{W} \ \Psi), 0001) = \mu T.F_\exists(T, \mathrm{Sat}(\Psi, 0001) \cup \mathrm{Sat}(\Phi, 0001), S)$
	$\mathrm{Sat}(\forall(\Phi \ \mathbf{W} \ \Psi), 1111) = \nu T.F_\forall(T, \mathrm{Sat}(\Psi, 1111), \mathrm{Sat}(\Phi, 1111))$
	$\mathrm{Sat}(\forall(\Phi \ \mathbf{W} \ \Psi), 0111) = \mu T_1.\nu T_2.G_\forall(T_1, T_2, \mathrm{Sat}(\Psi, 0111), \mathrm{Sat}(\Phi, 0111))$
	$\mathrm{Sat}(\forall(\Phi \ \mathbf{W} \ \Psi), 0011) = \nu T_2.\mu T_1.G_\forall(T_1, T_2, \mathrm{Sat}(\Psi, 0011), \mathrm{Sat}(\Phi, 0011))$
	$\mathrm{Sat}(\forall(\Phi \ \mathbf{W} \ \Psi), 0001) = \mu T.F_\forall(T, \mathrm{Sat}(\Psi, 0001) \cup \mathrm{Sat}(\Phi, 0001), S)$

and union of sets, respectively. The set $\mathrm{Sat}(\neg\Phi, b)$ is the complement of all states on which Φ evaluates to 1111 (recall that we assume $b > 0000$). Finally, the implementation of the implication is more involved. By definition, the set $\mathrm{Sat}(\Phi \Rightarrow \Psi, 1111)$ is the set of states s for which $V(s, \Phi)$ is less than $V(s, \Psi)$; in set notation, this is expressed by the intersection of the sets $\mathrm{Sat}(\Psi, b) \cup (S \setminus \mathrm{Sat}(\Phi, b))$ for each $b \in \mathbb{B}_4$. For any other truth value $b \leq 0111$, $\mathrm{Sat}(\Phi \Rightarrow \Psi, b)$ consists of all states where the implication evaluates to 1111 or Ψ evaluates to at least b.

Temporal Operators. For all temporal operators, we compute the satisfaction sets for existential and universal path formulas individually.

A state s satisfies the formula $\exists \odot \Phi$ with a value of at least b if one of its successors satisfies Φ with a value of at least b. Hence, the set $\mathrm{Sat}(\exists \odot \Phi, b)$ is the set of states s such that one of its successors is in $\mathrm{Sat}(\Phi, b)$. Similarly, the set $\mathrm{Sat}(\forall \odot \Phi, b)$ is the set of states s such that all of its successors are in $\mathrm{Sat}(\Phi, b)$.

Next, a state s satisfies the formula $\exists \diamondsuit \Phi$ with a value of at least b if there exists a path from s containing a state that satisfies Φ with a value of at least b. By applying expansion laws similar to those of CTL (see Baier and Katoen [1] for details), this statement is equivalent to s satisfying Φ with a value of at least b or one of its successors satisfying $\exists \diamondsuit \Phi$ with a value of at least b. Hence, as in CTL, $\mathrm{Sat}(\exists \diamondsuit \Phi, b)$ is the smallest subset T of S satisfying $\mathrm{Sat}(\Phi, b) \cup \{s \in S \mid \mathrm{post}(s) \cap T \neq \emptyset\} \subseteq T$. Equivalently, this set equals the least fixed point of the function

$$F_\exists(T, S_1, S_2) = S_1 \cup \{s \in S_2 \mid \mathrm{post}(s) \cap T \neq \emptyset\},$$

where $S_1 = \mathrm{Sat}(\Phi, b)$, $S_2 = S$, and T is the fixed-point variable. To simplify our notation, we use standard notation for fixed points and write $\mu T.F(T, \cdot)$, and $\nu T.F(T, \cdot)$, respectively for the least and greatest fixed point of a function $F(T, \cdot)$ with fixed-point variable T (which is unique for all functions we consider).

Similarly, a state s satisfies the formula $\forall \diamondsuit \Phi$ with a value of at least b if every path starting from s contains a state satisfying Φ with value at least b. Hence, the set $\mathrm{Sat}(\forall \diamondsuit \Phi, b)$ is the least fixed point $\mu T.F_\forall(T, \mathrm{Sat}(\Phi, b), S)$ of the function

$$F_\forall(T, S_1, S_2) = S_1 \cup \{s \in S_2 \mid \mathrm{post}(s) \subseteq T\}.$$

The characterization of the set $\mathrm{Sat}(\exists \boxdot \Phi, b)$ is more complex, and we discuss each truth value separately. Firstly, a state s satisfies $\exists \boxdot \Phi$ with value 1111 if there exists a path from s on which every state satisfies Φ with value 1111. By applying expansion laws similar to those of CTL, this statement is equivalent to s satisfying Φ with value 1111 and one of its successors satisfying $\exists \boxdot \Phi$ with value 1111. Hence, the set $\mathrm{Sat}(\exists \boxdot \Phi, 1111)$ equals $\nu T.F_\exists(T, \emptyset, \mathrm{Sat}(\Phi, 1111))$.

Next, a state s satisfies $\exists \boxdot \Phi$ with a value of at least 0111 if there exists a path from s on which eventually every state satisfies Φ with a value of at least 0111. It is not hard to verify that the set $\mathrm{Sat}(\exists \boxdot \Phi, 0111)$ is equal to the nested fixed point $\mu T_1.\nu T_2.G_\exists(T_1, T_2, \emptyset, \mathrm{Sat}(\Phi, 0111))$ of the function

$$G_\exists(T_1, T_2, S_1, S_2) = \{s \mid \mathrm{post}(s) \cap T_1 \neq \emptyset\} \cup S_1 \cup \{s \in S_2 \mid \mathrm{post}(s) \cap T_2 \neq \emptyset\}.$$

The greatest fixed point of the function containing the last two terms (on the right side) of the above equation represents a property of a path that all states on that path satisfy Φ with a value of at least 0111 and then the least fixed point of the function ensures that there exists a path that has a suffix with that property.

Similarly, a state s satisfies $\exists \boxdot \Phi$ with a value of at least 0011 if there exists a path from s on which there exist infinitely many states satisfying Φ with a value of at least 0011. Note that the property that a path contains infinitely many states satisfying Φ (with a value b) is the dual of the property that a path contains finitely many states satisfying Φ (with a value b). Hence, similar to the last case, it is not hard to see that

$$\mathrm{Sat}(\exists \boxdot \Phi, 0011) = \nu T_2.\mu T_1.G_\exists(T_1, T_2, \emptyset, \mathrm{Sat}(\Phi, 0011)).$$

Finally, a state s satisfies $\exists \boxdot \Phi$ with a value of at least 0001 if there exists a path from s containing a state that satisfies Φ with a value of at least 0001, which is equivalent to satisfying $\exists \Diamond \Phi$ with a value of at least 0001. Hence, $\text{Sat}(\exists \boxdot \Phi, 0001)$ is the set $\mu T.F_{\exists}(T, \text{Sat}(\Phi, 0001), S)$, as above.

Analogously, one can characterize $\forall \boxdot \Phi$ using the fixed points of the functions $F_{\forall}$ and $G_{\forall}$, where

$$G_{\forall}(T_1, T_2, S_1, S_2) = \{s \mid \text{post}(s) \subseteq T_1\} \cup S_1 \cup \{s \in S_2 \mid \text{post}(s) \subseteq T_2\}.$$

Characterizations for $\Phi \cup \Psi$ and $\Phi \mathbf{W} \Psi$ can be obtained similarly. In total, we obtain the result given below.

Theorem 3. *Let $M = (S, I, R, L)$ be a Kripke structure. Then for rCTL formulas Φ and truth values $b \in \mathbb{B}_4 \setminus \{0000\}$, one can compute the sets $\text{Sat}(\Phi, b)$ recursively as specified in Table 1.*

Algorithm 1 computes $5 \cdot |\text{sub}(\Phi)|$ satisfaction sets following the subformula ordering. Using the standard fixed-point iterations, which take linear time in the number of the states, each fixed point can be computed in linear time. Similarly, one can compute the nested fixed points in quadratic time in the number of states. Thus, we obtain the following.

Theorem 4. *The rCTL model checking problem can be solved in time $\mathcal{O}(N^2|\Phi|)$, where N is the number of states of the given Kripke structure, and Φ is the given rCTL specification.*

As we know, the CTL model checking algorithm also takes linear time in the size of the formula [1]. Hence, both model checking problems are in PTIME.

3.3 rCTL Satisfiability

This section considers the satisfiability problem for rCTL, which is: for a given rCTL formula Φ and truth value $b_0 \in \mathbb{B}_4$, does there exist a Kripke structure $M = (S, I, R, L)$ such that $I \subseteq \text{Sat}(\Phi, b_0)$? The rCTL satisfiability can be solved by translating the given rCTL formula and the given truth value into an equivalent μ-calculus formula (see Bradfield and Walukiewicz [3] for definitions) of linear size and then checking the resulting formula for satisfiability. This is always possible relying on the fixed point characterizations described in Sect. 3.2 (see Table 1). Since the satisfiability problem for μ-calculus is EXPTIME-complete [3], rCTL satisfiability is in EXPTIME. A matching lower bound already holds for CTL [6].

Theorem 5. *The satisfiability problem for rCTL is EXPTIME-complete.*

4   Robust CTL*

In this section, we present the robust version of CTL*, named robust CTL*, which combines the features of rCTL and rLTL. We show that rCTL* is more expressive than both and then present an algorithm for rCTL* model checking.

Syntax. Like CTL*, robust CTL* allows path quantifiers $\exists$ and $\forall$ to be arbitrarily nested with temporal operators. The syntax of rCTL* state formulas is the same as in rCTL. Moreover, rCTL* path formulas are similar to rLTL formulas, with the only difference being the use of arbitrary rCTL* state formulas as atoms. rCTL* state formulas over $\mathcal{P}$ are formed according to the grammar

$$\Phi ::= p \mid \Phi \vee \Phi \mid \Phi \wedge \Phi \mid \neg \Phi \mid \Phi \Rightarrow \Phi \mid \exists \varphi \mid \forall \varphi,$$

where $p \in \mathcal{P}$ and φ is a path formula. rCTL* path formulas are formed according to the grammar

$$\varphi ::= \Phi \mid \varphi \vee \psi \mid \varphi \wedge \psi \mid \neg \varphi \mid \varphi \Rightarrow \psi \mid \odot \varphi \mid \Diamond \, \varphi \mid \Box \, \varphi \mid \varphi \; \mathbf{U} \; \psi \mid \varphi \; \mathbf{W} \; \psi.$$

Semantics. As in CTL*, the semantics for rCTL* state and path formulas are analogous to rCTL and rLTL semantics, respectively. Let M be a Kripke structure and Φ, Ψ be rCTL* state formulas and φ, ψ be rCTL* path formulas. Then for a state s, the rCTL* semantics $V(s, \Phi)$ is the same as the rCTL semantics. For a path π, the semantics is analogous to rLTL semantics, as defined below.

- $V(\pi, \Phi) = V(\pi[0], \Phi)$
- $V(\pi, \neg \varphi) = \overline{V}(\pi, \varphi)$
- $V(\pi, \odot \varphi) = V(\pi[1..], \varphi)$
- $V(\pi, \varphi \vee \psi) = \max \left\{ V(\pi, \varphi), V(\pi, \psi) \right\}$
- $V(\pi, \varphi \wedge \psi) = \min \left\{ V(\pi, \varphi), V(\pi, \psi) \right\}$
- $V(\pi, \varphi \Rightarrow \psi) = V(\pi, \varphi) \rightarrow V(\pi, \psi)$

- $V(\pi, \Diamond \, \Phi) = \max_{i \geq 0} V(\pi[i], \Phi)$
- $V(\pi, \Box \, \Phi) = (\min_{i \geq 0} V_1(\pi[i], \Phi), \max_{j \geq 0} \min_{i \geq j} V_2(\pi[i], \Phi),$
  $\min_{j \geq 0} \max_{i \geq j} V_3(\pi[i], \Phi), \max_{i \geq 0} V_4(\pi[i], \Phi))$
- $V(\pi, \varphi \; \mathbf{U} \; \psi) = \max_{j \geq 0} \min \left\{ V(\pi[j..], \psi), \min_{0 \leq i < j} V(\pi[i..], \varphi) \right\}$
- $V(\pi, \varphi \; \mathbf{W} \; \psi) \quad = \quad (\min_{j \geq 0} W_1, \max_{k \geq 0} \min_{j \geq k} W_2, \min_{k \geq 0} \max_{j \geq k} W_3,$
  $\max_{j \geq 0} W_4)$ where

$$W_l = \max \left\{ V_l(\pi[j..], \varphi), \max_{0 \leq i \leq j} V_l(\pi[i..], \psi) \right\}$$

Example 2. Having defined the rCTL* semantics, let us see how the rCTL* formula $\forall(\Box \, \Phi_1 \Rightarrow \Box \, \Phi_2)$ is different from $\forall \Box \, \Phi_1 \Rightarrow \forall \Box \, \Phi_2$, where $\Phi_1 = \neg H$ states that humans are not at the robot's initial location and $\Phi_2 = \exists \odot R$ states that the robot can return to its initial location in one time step, as described in Sect. 1. Assume $\forall(\Box \, \Phi_1 \Rightarrow \Box \, \Phi_2)$ evaluates to 1111. Then the formula $\Box \, \Phi_1 \Rightarrow \Box \, \Phi_2$ must evaluate to 1111 for each path. Hence, the following holds:

- If Φ_1 holds at every state in a path π, then $V(\pi, \Box \, \Phi_1)$ evaluates to 1111. Hence, by the rCTL* semantics, $V(\pi, \Box \, \Phi_2)$ must also evaluate to 1111. That means, Φ_2 also holds at every state in π. Hence, in any path, if humans never visit the initial location, then from every state, the robot can return to its initial location in one time step.

- Similarly, if Φ_1 holds eventually always for some path π, then $V(\pi, \boxdot \Phi_1)$ evaluates to 0111. Then, by the rCTL* semantics, $V(\pi, \boxdot \Phi_2)$ evaluates to 0111 or higher. Hence, Φ_2 also needs to hold eventually always in π. Therefore, if humans visit the initial location a few times and never visit it again in a path, then from any state in that path, the robot can return to its initial location eventually.
- Similarly, if Φ_1 holds at infinitely (finitely) many states in some path π, then Φ_2 needs to hold at infinitely (finitely) many states in π.

As we can see, the semantics of $\forall(\boxdot \Phi_1 \Rightarrow \boxdot \Phi_2)$ captures the robustness property for every path separately, whereas the rCTL formula $\forall \boxdot \Phi_1 \Rightarrow \forall \boxdot \Phi_2$ captures the robustness property jointly for all paths starting from a state.

To understand the difference, let us consider the Kripke structure M with initial state s_0 as shown in Fig. 1 (where transitions are depicted by edges). Suppose the set of states that satisfy (with value 1111) the state formulas Φ_1 and Φ_2 are $\{s_0, s_1\}$ and $\{s_0, s_2\}$, respectively (as shown by the labels in the figure).

There are only two paths starting from s_0, i.e., $\pi_1 = s_0 s_1 s_1 \cdots$ and $\pi_2 = s_0 s_2 s_2 \cdots$. Since Φ_1 holds at every state in the path π_1, we have $V(\pi_1, \boxdot \Phi_1) = 1111$. Moreover, since Φ_1 holds only at the first state in the path π_2, we have $V(\pi_2, \boxdot \Phi_1) = 0001$. Hence, $V(s_0, \forall \boxdot \Phi_1) = \min_{i \in \{1,2\}} V(\pi_i, \boxdot \Phi_1) = 0001$. Similarly, since Φ_2 holds only at the first state of each path, we have $V(\pi_1, \boxdot \Phi_2) = V(\pi_2, \boxdot \Phi_2) = 0001$. Hence, $V(s_0, \forall \boxdot \Phi_2) = 0001$. Therefore, it holds that $V(s, \forall \boxdot \Phi_1 \Rightarrow \forall \boxdot \Phi_2) = 1111$.

However, as we have $V(\pi_1, \boxdot \Phi_2) = 0001 < V(\pi_1, \boxdot \Phi_1)$, it holds that $V(\pi_1, \boxdot \Phi_1 \Rightarrow \boxdot \Phi_2) = 0001$. Similarly, we have $V(\pi_2, \boxdot \Phi_1 \Rightarrow \boxdot \Phi_2) = 1111$. Hence, we have

$$V(s, \forall(\boxdot \Phi_1 \Rightarrow \boxdot \Phi_2)) = 0001 \neq V(s, \forall \boxdot \Phi_1 \Rightarrow \forall \boxdot \Phi_2).$$

This is the case because both of the paths do not satisfy $\boxdot \Phi_1 \Rightarrow \boxdot \Phi_2$ with value 1111 individually, but collectively, the state s_0 satisfies $\forall \boxdot \Phi_1 \Rightarrow \forall \boxdot \Phi_2$.

4.1   Expressiveness of rCTL*

The satisfaction sets and the equivalence between two formulas in rCTL* are defined as for rCTL. Now, as we can see, rCTL* is an extension of both rCTL and rLTL. Therefore, it subsumes both rCTL and rLTL (and hence, it also subsumes LTL). Furthermore, using the discussion in Sect. 3.1, it is easy to see that the rCTL* formula $(\forall \Diamond \forall \boxdot p) \vee (\Diamond p \Rightarrow \Diamond q)$ can not be expressed in rLTL or rCTL. In total, we obtain the following result:

Theorem 6. *rCTL* is more expressive than rLTL, rCTL, and LTL.*

Now, using the same idea as in Lemma 1, one can recover the CTL* semantics of a formula with no implication from the first component of the rCTL*

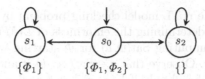

Fig. 1. Example of a Kripke structure

semantics. Conversely, using the same arguments as for the analogous result for rLTL [17, Proposition 5], one can translate each rCTL* formula into four CTL* formulas that captures the four components of the rCTL* semantics. Hence, we obtain the following result.

Theorem 7. *CTL* and rCTL* are equally expressive.*

4.2   rCTL* Model Checking

The model checking problem for rCTL* is analogous to that of rCTL, which is: for a given Kripke structure $M = (S, I, R, L)$, an rCTL* formula Φ and a truth value $b_0 \in \mathbb{B}_4$, does $V(s, \Phi) \geq b_0$ hold for all initial states $s \in I$? As we will see, to solve the rCTL* model checking problem, one can use a combination of rCTL and rLTL model checking. This is similar to CTL* model checking, which combines CTL and LTL model checking.

As in rCTL, for the rCTL* model checking, we use the characterization of the satisfaction sets. Sat(Φ, b) can be computed using Table 1 for every state formula Φ which is either an atomic proposition or can be expressed as a boolean combination (conjunction, negation, etc.) of two subformulas. Otherwise, we use an rLTL model checking algorithm to compute Sat(Φ, b) for a state formula starting with a path quantifier.

Let us first go through the basic concepts of rLTL and its model checking algorithm. As we have described earlier, rCTL* is an extension of rLTL. Both rCTL* path formulas and rLTL formulas are defined using the same grammar, with the only difference being the use of state formulas as atoms in rCTL*. Moreover, the valuation V for rLTL formulas is defined the same way as it is defined for rCTL* path formulas. Furthermore, given a Kripke structure M, an rLTL formula φ, and a set of truth values $B \subseteq \mathbb{B}_4$, the rLTL model checking problem is to determine whether for all paths π starting from an initial state in M, it holds that $V(\pi, \varphi) \in B$. To solve the rLTL model checking, Tabuada and Neider [17] have provided an algorithm to compute a generalized Büchi automaton (see Grädel et al. [10] for definition) recognizing all paths satisfying a given formula with a value $b \in B$ for a given set $B \subseteq \mathbb{B}_4$, as formalized below.

Lemma 2 (Tabuada and Neider [17]). *Given an rLTL formula φ, and a set of truth values $B \subseteq \mathbb{B}_4$, one can construct a generalized Büchi automaton $A_{\varphi,B}$ with $\mathcal{O}(5^{|\varphi|})$ states and $\mathcal{O}(|\varphi|)$ accepting sets that recognizes all paths π such that $V(\pi, \varphi) \in B$.*

Then, one can solve the rLTL model checking problem by translating M into a Büchi automaton and determining the emptiness of $L(M) \cap L(A_{\varphi, \mathbb{B}_4 \setminus B})$.

Coming back to computing $\mathrm{Sat}(\Phi, b)$ for Φ starting with a path quantifier, let us consider $\Phi = \forall \varphi$. Observe that $s \in \mathrm{Sat}(\forall \varphi, b)$ if and only if $V(s, \forall \varphi) \geq b$. Further, $V(s, \forall \varphi) \geq b$ if and only if $V(\pi, \varphi) \geq b$ for all $\pi \in \mathrm{paths}(s)$. The basic idea is now to replace all maximal proper state subformulas Ψ of φ by fresh atomic propositions a_Ψ and use the rLTL model checking algorithm to compute all the states from which all paths satisfy the rLTL formula φ with value at least b. However, we need to make a minor modification in the construction of the Büchi automaton of Lemma 2 such that for each a_Ψ, it holds that $V(s, a_\Psi) \geq b$ whenever $s \in \mathrm{Sat}(\Psi, b)$ and $V(s, a_\Psi) < b$ whenever $s \notin \mathrm{Sat}(\Psi, b)$. This can be done by initializing these atomic propositions with the required truth value.

Similarly, we compute $\mathrm{Sat}(\exists \varphi, b)$ by the rLTL model checking algorithm using the observation that $s \notin \mathrm{Sat}(\exists \varphi, b)$ if and only if $V(\pi, \varphi) < b$ for all $\pi \in \mathrm{paths}(s)$.

Now, one can solve the rCTL* model checking problem using Algorithm 1. However, the time complexity of the algorithm is not the same as in rCTL since the computation of Sat uses the rLTL model checking algorithm, which takes exponential time in the size of the formula (Tabuada and Neider [17]). Hence, the time complexity of the rCTL* model checking algorithm is dominated by the time complexity of the rLTL model checking algorithm.

Altogether, our algorithm runs in polynomial space (as rLTL model checking is in PSPACE [17]). A matching lower bound already holds for CTL* [7].

Theorem 8. *The rCTL* model checking problem is* PSPACE-*complete.*

As we know, CTL* model checking problem is also PSPACE-complete [7]. Hence, both CTL* and rCTL* model checking problems have the same asymptotic complexity.

4.3   rCTL* Satisfiability

This section considers the satisfiability problem for rCTL*, which is: for a given rCTL* formula Φ and truth value $b_0 \in \mathbb{B}_4$, does there exist a Kripke structure $M = (S, I, R, L)$ such that $I \subseteq \mathrm{Sat}(\Phi, b_0)$? One can solve rCTL* satisfiability by translating the given rCTL* formula and the truth value into an equivalent CTL* formula using Theorem 7 and then solving CTL* satisfiability. Since CTL* satisfiability is 2EXPTIME-complete, so is rCTL* satisfiability.

Theorem 9. *The satisfiability problem for rCTL* is* 2EXPTIME-*complete.*

5   Conclusion

Inspired by robust LTL, we first developed robust extensions of the logics CTL and CTL*, named rCTL and rCTL*, respectively. Second, we showed that rCTL is more expressive than CTL, while rCTL* is as expressive as CTL*. Third, we showed that the rCTL and rCTL* model checking problem lie in PTIME and PSPACE, respectively, as do the CTL and CTL* model checking problem.

Tabuada and Neider [17] described *quality* as the dual of robustness. To illustrate this point, consider the CTL formula $\Diamond \Phi \Rightarrow \Diamond \Psi$. According to the motto "more is better" we would prefer the system to guarantee the stronger property $\Box \Diamond \Psi$ whenever the environment satisfies the stronger property $\Box \Diamond \Psi$. And similarly, $\Diamond \Box \Phi$ should lead to $\Diamond \Box \Psi$ and $\Box \Phi$ should lead to $\Box \Psi$. Then, a natural question that arises for further research is whether there is an extension of CTL (and CTL*) that can be used to reason about both robustness and quality.

Another promising direction is to study the synthesis problem for rCTL and rCTL*. One approach would be to extend bounded synthesis (see Schewe and Finkbeiner [8] for details) to rCTL*.

References

1. Baier, C., Katoen, J.: Principles of Model Checking. MIT Press (2008)
2. Bloem, R., Greimel, K., Henzinger, T.A., Jobstmann, B.: Synthesizing robust systems. In: Proceedings of 9th International Conference on Formal Methods in Computer-Aided Design, FMCAD 2009, 15–18 November 2009, Austin, Texas, USA, pp. 85–92. IEEE (2009). https://doi.org/10.1109/FMCAD.2009.5351139
3. Bradfield, J., Walukiewicz, I.: The mu-calculus and model checking. In: Clarke, E., Henzinger, T., Veith, H., Bloem, R. (eds.) Handbook of Model Checking, pp. 871–919. Springer, Cham (2018). https://doi.org/10.1007/978-3-319-10575-8_26
4. Doyen, L., Henzinger, T.A., Legay, A., Nickovic, D.: Robustness of sequential circuits. In: Gomes, L., Khomenko, V., Fernandes, J.M. (eds.) 10th International Conference on Application of Concurrency to System Design, ACSD 2010, Braga, Portugal, 21–25 June 2010, pp. 77–84. IEEE Computer Society (2010). https://doi.org/10.1109/ACSD.2010.26
5. Ehlers, R., Topcu, U.: Resilience to intermittent assumption violations in reactive synthesis. In: Fränzle, M., Lygeros, J. (eds.) 17th International Conference on Hybrid Systems: Computation and Control (Part of CPS Week), HSCC 2014, Berlin, Germany, 15–17 April 2014, pp. 203–212. ACM (2014). https://doi.org/10.1145/2562059.2562128
6. Emerson, E.A., Halpern, J.Y.: Decision procedures and expressiveness in the temporal logic of branching time. J. Comput. Syst. Sci. **30**(1), 1–24 (1985). https://doi.org/10.1016/0022-0000(85)90001-7
7. Emerson, E.A., Lei, C.: Modalities for model checking: branching time logic strikes back. Sci. Comput. Program. **8**(3), 275–306 (1987). https://doi.org/10.1016/0167-6423(87)90036-0
8. Finkbeiner, B., Schewe, S.: Bounded synthesis. Int. J. Softw. Tools Technol. Transf. **15**(5–6), 519–539 (2013). https://doi.org/10.1007/s10009-012-0228-z
9. French, T., McCabe-Dansted, J.C., Reynolds, M.: A temporal logic of robustness. In: Konev, B., Wolter, F. (eds.) Frontiers of Combining Systems, 6th International Symposium, FroCoS 2007, Liverpool, UK, 10–12 September 2007, Proceedings. Lecture Notes in Computer Science, vol. 4720, pp. 193–205. Springer (2007). https://doi.org/10.1007/978-3-540-74621-8_13

10. Grädel, E., Thomas, W., Wilke, T. (eds.): Automata, Logics, and Infinite Games: A Guide to Current Research [outcome of a Dagstuhl seminar, February 2001], Lecture Notes in Computer Science, vol. 2500. Springer (2002). https://doi.org/10.1007/3-540-36387-4

11. Hájek, P.: Metamathematics of Fuzzy Logic, Trends in Logic, vol. 4. Kluwer (1998). https://doi.org/10.1007/978-94-011-5300-3

12. Nayak, S.P., Neider, D., Roy, R., Zimmermann, M.: Robust computation tree logic. arXiv 2201.07116 (2022), https://arxiv.org/abs/2201.07116

13. Neider, D., Weinert, A., Zimmermann, M.: Robust, expressive, and quantitative linear temporal logics: pick any two for free. In: Leroux, J., Raskin, J. (eds.) Proceedings Tenth International Symposium on Games, Automata, Logics, and Formal Verification, GandALF 2019, Bordeaux, France, 2–3rd September 2019. EPTCS, vol. 305, pp. 1–16 (2019). https://doi.org/10.4204/EPTCS.305.1

14. Priest, G.: Dualising intuitionictic negation. Principia: Int. J. Epistemol. **13**(2), 165–184 (2009). https://doi.org/10.5007/1808-1711.2009v13n2p165

15. Tabuada, P., Balkan, A., Caliskan, S.Y., Shoukry, Y., Majumdar, R.: Input-output robustness for discrete systems. In: Jerraya, A., Carloni, L.P., Maraninchi, F., Regehr, J. (eds.) Proceedings of the 12th International Conference on Embedded Software, EMSOFT 2012, part of the Eighth Embedded Systems Week, ESWeek 2012, Tampere, Finland, 7–12 October 2012, pp. 217–226. ACM (2012). https://doi.org/10.1145/2380356.2380396

16. Tabuada, P., Caliskan, S.Y., Rungger, M., Majumdar, R.: Towards robustness for cyber-physical systems. IEEE Trans. Autom. Control **59**(12), 3151–3163 (2014). https://doi.org/10.1109/TAC.2014.2351632

17. Tabuada, P., Neider, D.: Robust linear temporal logic. In: Talbot, J., Regnier, L. (eds.) 25th EACSL Annual Conference on Computer Science Logic, CSL 2016, August 29 - September 1, 2016, Marseille, France. LIPIcs, vol. 62, pp. 10:1–10:21. Schloss Dagstuhl - Leibniz-Zentrum für Informatik (2016). https://doi.org/10.4230/LIPIcs.CSL.2016.10

18. Tarraf, D.C., Megretski, A., Dahleh, M.A.: A framework for robust stability of systems over finite alphabets. IEEE Trans. Autom. Control **53**(5), 1133–1146 (2008). https://doi.org/10.1109/TAC.2008.923658

On-the-Fly Model Checking with Neural MCTS

Ruiyang Xu$^{(\boxtimes)}$ and Karl Lieberherr

Khoury College of Computer Sciences, Northeastern University,
Boston, MA 02115, USA
{xu.r,k.lieberherr}@northeastern.edu

Abstract. Recent progress in AI, which combines deep learning with classical search algorithms, has shown remarkable performance improvements for several challenging board games, such as Go and Chess. In this paper, we propose a method to apply this new technique to model checking problems. In particular, we leverage the game-theoretical semantics of logic expressions (recursive first-order logic in our case) to turn a model checking problem into a two-player perfect information win-lose game. The game can then be played and learned by a deep learning and search algorithm (neural MCTS). The existence of a winning strategy of a player indicates that either the model-checked property can be verified or there is a counterexample. We modified the classical neural MCTS algorithm to ensure it can handle cycles when searching in state space. We also propose a way to incorporate fairness constraints into the learning and search process. We test our idea on two labeled transition systems (one is from a numerical game, and the other is the classical Dining Philosophers problem). Our experimental results show an outperformance of our method compared with reinforcement-learning-based model checking approaches.

Keywords: Neural MCTS · Model checking · On-the-fly

1 Introduction

The world has entered a new era where large distributed concurrent systems have been developed to serve numerous clients worldwide. Those systems cover a large part of our daily life, such as finance and transportation. A tiny mistake in the design could potentially incur a severe security issue and cause economic losses. Therefore, it is crucial to keep the design of those systems correct. That is why model-checking deserves to be paid more attention to nowadays. However, the model-checking community has long been troubled by the *state explosion problem* [7], namely as the number of state variables in the system increases, the size of the system state space grows exponentially.

The past few years have witnessed a combination of search algorithms and machine learning (ML) techniques (i.e., neural MCTS) showing a remarkable

© Springer Nature Switzerland AG 2022
J. V. Deshmukh et al. (Eds.): NFM 2022, LNCS 13260, pp. 557–575, 2022.
https://doi.org/10.1007/978-3-031-06773-0_30

performance improvement when dealing with games that have large state spaces, such as Go and Chess [22–25]. Because states information is learned and stored by neural networks, those algorithms' memory usage can be considered constants. Being motivated by the recent progress of AI in gameplay, we came up with an alternative approach to tackle the state explosion problem. Specifically, it has been known for decades that the game-theoretical semantics [13], which shows a duality between logic and game, can be utilized for model-checking [27]. Although the goal of model-checking is to find errors that can appear in some rare cases, the game-theoretical semantics allows one to reduce the problem of verifying a property into a two-player semantic game defined on the logic used to describe that property. Such a reduction (or gamification) allows one to apply a self-play-based ML algorithm to learn from the game and eventually solve the problem.

A high-level view of the Neural MCTS algorithm for an interpreted sentence ϕ for some logic L with game-semantics is given by the following loop:

Repeat

- Find faulty predictions (TRUE or FALSE) for ϕ and its sub-formulas, called $curriculum(\phi)$, through self-play of $Game(L, \phi)$.
- Learn from the faulty predictions $curriculum(\phi)$, which gives negative reward information based on winning/losing predictions and self-play outcomes.
- Update approximation to value function, which predicates the winning/losing chance, and policy functions, which approximate a serial of Skolem functions used as a strategy to prove or disprove the formula.

Until convergence: there are no faulty predictions for ϕ and its sub-formulas.

Learning based on self-play is basically a process of finding faulty predictions for each player. A faulty prediction is one where the prediction of the game outcome (from the value function) contradicts the actual outcome. Since the game is zero-sum with no draws, the two players will continuously compete by mutually creating curricula for each other to learn until there is no faulty prediction anymore. Consequently, a winning strategy learned by an ML algorithm for that game shows how to verify/falsify that property. It should be noted that even when the two players agree with each other, their prediction might still be wrong because the agreement on a truth value might be based on weak players. This is a common issue for all ML-based model checkers because ML algorithms are probabilistic, and 100% correctness is not guaranteed. Therefore, *"they should favor the discovery of errors rather than focusing on guaranteeing correctness"* [8]. That is also the reason why learning a strategy to falsify a property is especially useful when constructing a counterexample from the model-checking problem.

Leveraging such a duality, in this paper, we show an approach to adapt neural MCTS to on-the-fly model-checking through semantic-game-based gamification. In particular, we use recursive first-order logic as our model specification language, which provides us with a novel approach to generate state representations. In addition to that, we also propose a method to impose fairness constraints by concatenating a normalized counter vector to the state representation. We test our approach on two problems: model-checking an alternating reachability property on a numeric game and a liveness property on the well-known dining philosopher problem. Our preliminary experimental results show that turning model-checking problems into games and solving them with cutting-edge game-play AI technology might be a promising research direction.

2 Preliminary

2.1 Model Checking with L_μ

Modal μ-calculus (L_μ) has been used broadly in model checking, a logic used to describe properties of the target labeled transition system (LTS). An LTS is defined as a tuple (S, I, A, T), where S is a set of states, I is a nonempty subset of S of initial states, A is a set of actions, and relation T formulates transitions among different states, which are labeled with actions. With an LTS, one can abstract and model the possible development of a system. The problem of model-checking a L_μ formula on a transition system is to decide whether the LTS satisfies the formula.

The syntax of L_μ is:

$$\Phi := \textbf{True} \mid \textbf{False} \mid X \mid \Phi \wedge \Phi \mid \Phi \vee \Phi \mid \neg\Phi \mid [A]\Phi \mid \langle A\rangle\Phi \mid \nu X.\Phi \mid \mu X.\Phi,$$

where X ranges over a set of variables, regarded as names of predicates. We also use $\sigma X.\Phi$ to stand for either $\nu X.\Phi$ or $\mu X.\Phi$. The semantics of L_μ can be represented with Monadic Second-order Logic (MSOL) since it has been proved that L_μ is the bisimulation invariant fragment of MSOL [15]. To be specific, let $\Phi[x]$ be the MSOL translation of a L_μ formula Φ, with one free variable x. Then a L_μ formula can be translated into an MSOL formula recursively in the following way:

$$
\begin{aligned}
&X[x] = X(x) \\
&(\Phi_1 \wedge \Phi_2)[x] = \Phi_1[x] \wedge \Phi_2[x] \\
&(\Phi_1 \vee \Phi_2)[x] = \Phi_1[x] \vee \Phi_2[x] \\
&(\neg\Phi)[x] = \neg\Phi[x] \\
&\langle A\rangle\Phi[x] = \exists y \in S.\ (xTy) \wedge \Phi[y] \\
&[A]\Phi[x] = \forall y \in S.\ (xTy) \rightarrow \Phi[y] \\
&\mu X.\Phi[x] = \exists X \subseteq S.\ (\forall y \in S.\ \Phi[y] \rightarrow X(y)) \wedge X(x) \\
&\nu X.\Phi[x] = \exists X \subseteq S.\ (\forall y \in S.\ X(y) \rightarrow \Phi[y]) \rightarrow X(x)
\end{aligned}
\tag{1}
$$

where $X(x)$ means for some set $X \subseteq S$, $x \in X$.

It is to be noted that the definition of fix-point operator **LFP** and **GFP** is intricate, for which we use the explanation from [28]. To put it simply, let $\Phi(x; X)$ be any MSOL predicate parameterized on some set X. And suppose $S_X = \{x|\Phi(x; X)\}$, then a MSOL predicate actually also defines a function which maps X to S_X. The fix-point of the function can be computed by recursively calling the function with its output. To be specific, the **LFP** of a predicate $\Phi(x; X)$ is derived by a sequence of function calls:

$$S_0 = \{x|\Phi(x; \varnothing)\}, S_1 = \{x|\Phi(x; S_0)\}, ..., S_n = \{x|\Phi(x; S_n)\}$$

LFP. $\Phi(x; X) := S_n,$

and similarly, the **GFP** of a predicate $\Phi(x; X)$ can be derived by the sequence: $\Phi(x; X)$ is derived by a sequence of function calls:

$$S_0 = \{x|\Phi(x; S)\}, S_1 = \{x|\Phi(x; S_0)\}, ..., S_n = \{x|\Phi(x; S_n)\}$$

GFP. $\Phi(x; X) := S_n.$

As a result, the fix-point operators and the two modal operators make it possible to express the finite or infinite temporal properties of an LTS.

2.2 Game Theoretical Semantics

Game theoretical semantics is an approach that rebuilds the logical concepts with game-theoretic concepts. A logical formula is interpreted as a game between two players, one in the Proponent role and the other in the Opponent role. The game runs recursively on the computational order of the logical operators. The game ends when a primitive predicate is achieved, and the Proponent wins if the formula evaluates to true; otherwise, the Opponent wins. A winning strategy can be represented by a finite sequence of Skolem functions (which are useful tools to improve the system design) corresponding to the moves made by the player relative to those played by the other one [21].

To better understand the concept, we first introduce the game theoretical semantics of first-order logic (FOL) [13,21]. A semantic game is represented as a tuple (Ψ, P, OP), where the Ψ is a formula interpreted by a structure M. P and OP denote the game role for each of the two players, and, initially, player-1 plays the P role. The game rule can be summarized in Table 1.

Table 1. The game semantics for a FOL formula φ. In this table, OP stands for Opponent, and P stands for Proponent. The game ends at an atomic predicate φ. It is to be noted that the negation switches the role of the two players; namely, strategies for P in a game for $\neg\Psi$ are strategies for OP in the game for Ψ.

Formula	Operation	Subgame
$\forall x \in A : \Psi(x)$	OP picks x_0 from A	$(\Psi[x/x_0]$, P, OP)
$\exists x \in A : \Psi(x)$	P picks x_0 from A	$(\Psi[x/x_0]$, P, OP)
$\Psi \wedge \chi$	OP picks $\Theta \in \{\Psi, \chi\}$	$(\Theta$, P, OP)
$\Psi \vee \chi$	P picks $\Theta \in \{\Psi, \chi\}$	$(\Theta$, P, OP)
$\neg\Psi$	N/A	$(\Psi$, OP, P)
φ	N/A	N/A

The concept of game theoretical semantics can also be extended to L_μ [12,20,27]. However, since L_μ is involved with a transition system, the game rule is more complex (Table 2). Even though the modal operators $[A]$ and $\langle A \rangle$ resemble the quantifiers in FOL, the fix-point operator is utterly distinct, which actually grants L_μ more expressiveness than FOL [18]. As a result, the winning condition is no longer as simple as the one with FOL. Instead of deciding whether a formula can be evaluated as true or false, one may encounter situations where one of the players cannot pick any transition in the system because of a deadlock. Alternatively, one may encounter situations where the game is just running forever because of a cycle in the transition system. In summary, the updated winning condition can be summarized as the following [27]:

- Proponent wins, when either
  - within finitely many moves, the formula can be evaluated to **true** for the underlying transition system.
  - within finitely many moves, the Opponent gets into a deadlock where no transition is available.
  - the game can run forever because of a greatest fix-point operator $\nu X.\Psi$, which indicates that a safety property can always hold.
- Opponent wins, when either
  - within finitely many moves, the formula can be evaluated to **false** for the underlying transition system.
  - within finitely many moves, Proponent gets into a deadlock where no transition is available.
  - the game can run forever because of a least fix-point operator $\mu X.\Psi$, which indicates that a liveness property can never hold.

Table 2. The game semantic for a L_μ formula φ with underlying transition system state S, where $X \triangleleft \sigma X.\Psi$ means X is bound by $\sigma X.\Psi$. Notice that the game might not always end at a primitive predicate. Due to the nature of L_μ, it may end at a deadlock or just run forever.

Configuration	Operation	Subgame
$([A]\Psi)[x]$	OP picks a transition $x \xrightarrow{a \in A} y$	$(\Psi[y],\ \text{P},\ \text{OP})$
$(\langle A \rangle \Psi)[x]$	P picks a transition $x \xrightarrow{a \in A} y$	$(\Psi[y],\ \text{P},\ \text{OP})$
$(\Psi \wedge \chi)[x]$	OP picks $\Theta \in \{\Psi, \chi\}$	$(\Theta[x],\ \text{P},\ \text{OP})$
$(\Psi \vee \chi)[x]$	P picks $\Theta \in \{\Psi, \chi\}$	$(\Theta[x],\ \text{P},\ \text{OP})$
$(\neg \Psi)[x]$	N/A	$(\Psi[x],\ \text{OP},\ \text{P})$
$(\sigma X.\Psi)[x]$	N/A	$(\Psi[x],\ \text{P},\ \text{OP})$
$X[x]$	N/A	$(\Psi[x],\ \text{P},\ \text{OP}),\ X \triangleleft \sigma X.\Psi$
$\varphi[x]$	N/A	N/A

The game semantics of L_μ gives a local view on the model checking problem, while the MSOL semantics of L_μ provides a global view. Typically those fix-point operators, from a global view, define a closure of LTS state in which certain temporal property always holds; yet from a local view, they describe recursive behaviors so that the evolution of LTS forms a cycle. The local view, acquired from game semantics, turns out to be more intuitive to help us understand or design a L_μ property. For instance, $\nu X.\Phi$ defines a "good" cycle which means something good should always happen; otherwise, the system is not well designed; while $\mu X.\Phi$ specify a "bad" cycle which means, eventually something good should happen; otherwise the system is not well designed.

2.3   Learning with Neural MCTS

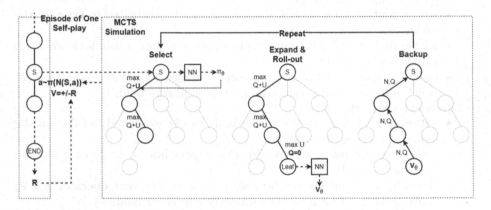

Fig. 1. The workflow of the neural MCTS algorithm.

MCTS has been applied to solving combinatorial games for a long time [6], while recently, combining deep neural networks with MCTS showed success in improving solver competence in many practical combinatorial games. The concept of neural MCTS was proposed independently in Expert Iteration [1], and AlphaZero [25]. In a nutshell, neural MCTS uses the neural network as policy and value approximators. During each learning iteration, it carries out multiple rounds of self-plays. Each self-play runs several MCTS simulations to estimate an empirical policy at each state, then sample from that policy, take a move, and continue. After each round of self-play, the game's outcome is backed up to all states in that game episode. Those game episodes generated during self-play are then stored in a replay buffer, which is used to train the neural network (Fig. 1).

During one self-play episode, for a given state, the neural MCTS runs a given number of simulations on a game tree, rooted at that state to generate an empirical policy. Each simulation, guided by the policy and value networks, passes through 4 phases:

1. **SELECT**: At the beginning of each iteration, the algorithm selects a path from the root (current game state) to a leaf (either a terminal state or an

unvisited state) according to an upper confidence boundary (UCB, [3,4,17]). Specifically, suppose the root is s_0. The UCB determines a sequence of states $\{s_0, s_1, ..., s_l\}$ by the following process:

$$a_i = \arg\max_a \left[Q(s_i, a) + \underbrace{\alpha\pi_\theta(s_i, a)\frac{\sqrt{\sum_{a'} N(s_i, a')}}{N(s_i, a) + 1}}_{U(s_i, a)} \right] \tag{2}$$

$$s_{i+1} = \text{move}(s_i, a_i)$$
$$Q(s_i, a) = N(s_i, a) = 0, \text{if } s_{i+1} \text{ is unvisited}$$

where α is a tunable parameter, $N(s, a)$ counts the times of visiting (s, a) during the MCTS simulations, and $Q(s, a)$ is a state-action value estimator. The UCB is also guided by a policy estimator $\pi_\theta(s, a)$. It has been proved in [9] that selecting actions using Eq. 2 is equivalent to optimize the empirical policy

$$\hat{\pi}(s, a) = \frac{1 + N(s, a)}{|A| + \sum_{a'} N(s, a')}$$

where $|A|$ is the size of the action space, so that it approximates the solution of a regularized policy optimization problem. As a result, MCTS simulation can be regarded as a regularized policy optimization [9]. As long as the value network is accurate, the MCTS simulation will optimize the output policy to maximize the action value output while minimizing the change to the policy network.

2. **EXPAND**: Once the selected phase ends at an unvisited state s_l, the state will be fully expanded and marked as visited. During the next selection iteration, all its child nodes will be considered leaf nodes.

3. **ROLL-OUT**: The roll-out is carried out for any unvisited state s_l. If s_l is a terminal state, the game outcome $R(s_l)$ will be used as the state value backup for the **BACKUP** phase, otherwise, the algorithm will use a value network to estimate the result of the game (from current state s_l) and use that value $V_\theta(s_l)$ for **BACKUP**.

4. **BACKUP**: This is the last phase of an MCTS simulation in which the algorithm backs up the state value and updates the state-action value estimator for each node in the selected states sequence. To illustrate this process, suppose the selected states and corresponding actions and players are

$$\{(s_0, a_0, p_0), (s_1, a_1, p_1), ...(s_{l-1}, a_{l-1}, p_{l-1}), (s_l, -, p_l)\}$$

Let v_l be either the actual game outcome $R(s_l)$ or the estimated outcome $V_\theta(s_i)$. The value is then backed up in the following way

$$\{(s_0, a_0, p_0, v_0), (s_1, a_1, p_1, v_1), ...(s_{l-1}, a_{l-1}, p_{l-1}, v_{l-1}), (s_l, -, p_l, v_l)\},$$

where $v_i = (-1)^{|p_{i+1} - p_i|} v_{i+1}$. In other words, for any two-player game, the leaf state value v_l is backed up in a fashion such that states play by the same player as the leaf state will be assigned the same value v_l, while states play by another player will be assigned the opposite value $-v_l$. The backed up state values are then be used to update the counter N and state-action value estimator Q:

$$N(s_t, a_t) \leftarrow N(s_t, a_t) + 1$$
$$Q(s_t, a_t) \leftarrow Q(s_t, a_t) + \frac{V_\theta(s_r) - Q(s_t, a_t)}{N(s_t, a_t)} \quad (3)$$

Once the given number of simulations has been reached, the algorithm returns the empirical policy $\hat{\pi}(s)$ for the current state s. An action is then sampled from $\hat{\pi}(s)$, and the game moves to the next state by playing that action. In this way, MCTS generates the players' states and actions alternately until the game ends with some outcome R after T steps, which gives an episode for the game. Each episode is defined as a sequence of tuples $(s_i, p_i, \hat{\pi}_i, v_i)$, where s_i is the game state at step i, p_i is the player at step i, $\hat{\pi}_i$ is the empirical policy generated at step i, and $v_i = (-1)^{|p_i - p_T|}R$ is the value signal from the outcome, which will become a contradictory signal once the prediction from the value network is faulty. After a given number of self-plays, all episodes will be stored into a replay buffer so that it can be used to train and update the value network V_θ (with all v_i's) and policy network π_θ (with all $\hat{\pi}_i$'s).

3 Methodology

3.1 Recursive-FOL

In this work, we use recursive first-order logic (recursive-FOL) for model checking a finite LTS. The recursive FOL is essentially an extension of FOL with fix-point operators, which allows a predicate to be defined by referring back to itself. However, unlike L_μ, which defines properties functionally, recursive-FOL provides us more flexibility and allows us to describe model checking properties in a modular way so that a property can be defined with multiple sub-components, which is used later for deriving vector representations (see Sect. 3.2). To be specific, a recursive-FOL property can be defined by the following grammar:

$$
\begin{aligned}
\langle\text{property}\rangle &\models \langle\text{predicates}\rangle \\
\langle\text{predicates}\rangle &\models \langle\text{predicate}\rangle \mid \langle\text{predicate}\rangle ; \langle\text{predicates}\rangle \\
\langle\text{predicate}\rangle &\models \mathbf{LFP}.X(s) := \langle\text{fol-expr}\rangle \\
&\quad \mid \mathbf{GFP}.X(s) := \langle\text{fol-expr}\rangle \\
&\quad \mid X(s) := \langle\text{fol-expr}\rangle \\
\langle\text{fol-expr}\rangle &\models \mathbf{True} \mid \mathbf{False} \mid \varphi(s) \mid X(s) \mid \neg\langle\text{fol-expr}\rangle \\
&\quad \mid \langle\text{fol-expr}\rangle \vee \langle\text{fol-expr}\rangle \\
&\quad \mid \langle\text{fol-expr}\rangle \wedge \langle\text{fol-expr}\rangle \\
&\quad \mid \exists a \in A_s.\ X(s^a) \\
&\quad \mid \forall a \in A_s.\ X(s^a)
\end{aligned}
$$

where φ ranges over all primitive predicates, X ranges over the identifiers of the predicates, s is the LTS state variable for each predicate, A_s is the action space for the current state, and s^a is the successor state that $s \xrightarrow{a} s^a$.

The motivation of applying recursive-FOL to model checking comes directly from the MSOL interpretation of L_μ (see Sect. 2.1). However, different from MSOL, which implies fix-point operator intrinsically, adding a fix-point operator to FOL is tricky and error-prone [11]. Specifically, suppose we have a FOL predicate $\Phi(x; P)$, parameterized by a variable x and another predicate $P(x)$. To make sure an extended FOL formula (say $\mathbf{LFP}.\Phi(x; P)$) is well-formed, the function $F(P) = \{x | \Phi(x; P)\}$ must be monotone, which means either $F(P) \subseteq \{x | P(x)\}$ or $F(P) \supseteq \{x | P(x)\}$. It is to be noted that, in general, whether a FOL predicate $\Phi(x; P)$ is monotone is undecidable. Nevertheless, one can still construct monotone predicates by forcing each occurrence of P in $\Phi(x; P)$ to be positive [10]. In this work, we assume the user always defines a well-formed formula. This assumption comes from a practical consideration that any two-player extensive form game can be abstractly described as:

$$\mathbf{LFP}.\Phi(s, p; P) := Q(s, p) \vee \exists a \in A_s^p. \neg P(s^a, \bar{p}),$$

where s^a is the state following $s \xrightarrow{a} s^a$, $\bar{p}$ is the opposite player of p, $Q(s, p)$ means that the game ends at s and player p wins the game, and $\Phi(s, p; P)$ means that given the current game state s and player p, the current player p will eventually win the game. As a result, the predicate is defined by the formula and the underlying structure of the game states. In other words, if the game can generate infinitely many states, then the formula above is not well-formed.

Next, we show how to transform a L_μ formula to recursive-FOL. Since a modular approach is used to define a predicate, we need to first decompose a L_μ formula into different predicates. For example, suppose the given formula is

$$\nu Z.(p \vee \mu X.(q \vee [A]X)) \wedge \langle A \rangle Z, \tag{4}$$

we can rewrite it into two individual fix-point predicates, with a distinct state variable s as:

$$\mathbf{GFP}.Z(s) := (p[s] \vee X[s]) \wedge ((\langle A \rangle Z)[s]$$
$$\mathbf{LFP}.X(s) := q[s] \vee ([A]X)[s].$$

After decomposing every fix-point operator into individual predicates, we finish by transforming recursively with the following rules:

$$\begin{aligned}
p[x] &= p(x) \\
(\Phi_1 \wedge \Phi_2)[x] &= \Phi_1[x] \wedge \Phi_2[x] \\
(\Phi_1 \vee \Phi_2)[x] &= \Phi_1[x] \vee \Phi_2[x] \\
(\neg\Phi)[x] &= \neg\Phi[x] \\
(\langle A \rangle \Phi)[x] &= \exists a \in A_x. \ Z[x^a] \\
([A]\Phi)[x] &= \forall a \in A_x. \ Z[x^a],
\end{aligned} \tag{5}$$

where p means a primitive predicate that can always be evaluated, given the current state variable x. A_x is the set of all legal actions of an LTS at state x, and x^a represents the state such that $x \xrightarrow{a} x^a$.

The game semantics of recursive-FOL is almost the same as FOL's, except that the winning condition of the L_μ semantic game has been applied. However, it should be pointed out that since the variables of fix-point operators in L_μ have been transformed to unique fix-point predicates, there is no need to track bounded variables anymore. Consequently, the semantic game plays on a group of predicates and jumps from one to another if necessary.

3.2   State Representation

The state representation of any game state for a recursive-FOL semantic game is a vector $[i, p, \xi, \zeta]$, where i is an integer ID number for each predicate (in this case, $i(Z) = 0, i(X) = 1$), and $p \in \{-1, 1\}$ is the player ID. ξ and ζ are two vector components, where ξ is the vectorized representation of the current LTS state s, and ζ is an encoding of the action sequence on the syntax tree, which is initialized to all -1 for each predicate.

The entrance of a semantic game is always a predicate, which can be represented as a syntax tree. Once evaluated step by step, each node is either a logic operator or a predicate. A predicate indicates a leaf node for the current tree, but it also points to an entrance of another tree. We use a preorder traversal to identify each node and vectorize the action sequence on the tree structure, namely ζ.

For illustration, let's use the transformed recursive-FOL formula from Eq. 4, which contains two fix-point predicates:

$$\mathbf{GFP}.Z(s) := (p(s) \lor X(s)) \land (\forall a \in A_s.\ Z(s^a))$$
$$\mathbf{LFP}.X(s) := q(s)s \lor (\exists a \in A_s.\ X(s^a)),$$

where p and q are primitive predicates. The syntax trees of the two predicates can be drawn out as:

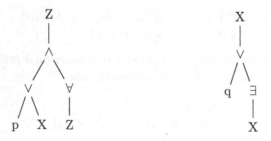

To better understand how to generate ζ properly, let's see the example above. The preorder indexes for each node in the two trees are:

$$[Z : 0, \land : 1, \lor : 2, p : 3, X : 4, \forall : 5, Z : 6]$$
$$[X : 0, \lor : 1, q : 2, \exists : 3, X : 4],$$

which means we can use a length-seven vector to completely encode any action sequences on these two trees during gameplay. All we need is to store the action taken on each node to the corresponding position in the vector. For instance, starting from some $Z(s)$, if a player took the left branch of the $\land$ operator at position 1, and then the other player took the right branch of the $\lor$ operator at position 2, then the vector ζ at leaf node X becomes:

$$[0, 0, 1, -1, -1, -1, -1].$$

Furthermore, if the game continued from predicate X, and one of the players picked the right branch of the $\lor$ operator at position 1, and then chose some move $m \in A_s$ on the $\exists$ operator at position 3, then the vector ζ at leaf node X becomes:

$$[0, 1, m, -1, -1, -1, -1].$$

3.3 MCTS with Fix-point Predicates

Applying neural MCTS to a recursive-FOL semantic game looks straightforward. However, it turns out to be non-trivial. Specifically, a semantic game might have an infinite game sequence composed of a set of states in a cycle. However, one of the players can still win the game as long as we can track the type of the leading fix-point operator (namely, the starting point of a cycle). On the other hand, the neural MCTS algorithm was not designed to handle an infinite game that uses looping states as a winning condition. As a result, we propose some modifications to the previous design to deal with this new situation.

Our method is motivated by the bounded game semantics on L_μ [12]. During the self-play and MCTS simulation, we maintain a stack $\mathfrak{L}$ and a counter $\mathfrak{C}$ to track the number of visits of each fix-point predicate along a game sequence. To be specific, for a given game state s, if s is the root node of some predicate's syntax tree, and also that predicate is a fix-point predicate, then we check if s is in the stack $\mathfrak{L}$. If it is already there, then we continuously pop from the stack the top state t and set $\mathfrak{C}[t] = 0$ until we hit s, then set $\mathfrak{C}[s] = \mathfrak{C}[s] + 1$; otherwise, we just push s to L and set $\mathfrak{C}[s] = 1$. After updating the stack, we check if $\mathfrak{C}[s] > \Gamma$ for some given integer bound Γ. s is considered to be a winning state for the Proponent/Opponent only if $\mathfrak{C}[s] > \Gamma$ and s is the root node of a **GFP/LFP** predicate.

After updating $\mathfrak{L}$ and $\mathfrak{C}$, we concatenate the visiting time of the predicate to the state representation of the corresponding state in the search tree. In other words, each tree node represents a tuple $(s, \mathfrak{C}[s.\mathbf{root}])$, where $s.\mathbf{root}$ is the root state of a predicate's syntax tree that state s is affiliated to. In this manner, neural MCTS no longer needs to deal with a potentially infinite game sequence, but it can still detect a cycle in the state space.

3.4 Fairness as a Challenge

Fairness is an essential concept in model-checking. Informally speaking, the fairness constraint requires that, in a multi-process system, each process should get an equal chance to run when it is able to run. This requirement is crucial, especially when searching for a counterexample of a liveness property. Since a model checking algorithm also decides how to schedule the running of each process, it is trivial for it to fabricate an unrealistic "counterexample" when ignoring the fairness constraint.

Classical model-checking algorithms solve this problem with a global method, which searches for all possible strongly connected components (SCCs) in the state space, then verify each component to see if it satisfies the fairness constraint. However, for a large LTS, the global method becomes intractable because of the state explosion issue.

With that being said, the main motivation to use neural MCTS in model-checking is its ability to handle large state space through a local search. We propose here a local approach to the fairness problem by maintaining a list of process access counter $\mathfrak{F}$. Therefore $\mathfrak{F}[p]$ means process with id number p has been accessed $\mathfrak{F}[p]$ times. The counter list $\mathfrak{F}$ is then be concatenated with state representation. During self-play and MCTS simulation, we check if, at the current state, $|\max(\mathfrak{F}) - \min(\mathfrak{F})| > K$ for some integer constant K. If so, then the current player loses the game immediately. It should be pointed out that $\mathfrak{F}$ needs to be normalized before it is used as an input to the neural network. Consequently, neural MCTS is forced to learn to access every process in a balanced way.

4   Experiments

4.1   Highest Safe Rung Problem

The Highest Safe Rung (HSR) problem is a well-known puzzle [26]. The problem can be described as follows:

Consider throwing jars from a specific rung of a ladder. The jars could either break or not. If a jar is unbroken after a trial, it can be used next time. The highest safe rung is the rung that the jar will break for any trial performed above it. Given three positive numbers k, q, and n, can we always be able to locate the highest safe rung on a n-rung ladder with at most k jars and q trials? (assuming the jars are identical with each other).

The above problem can actually be solved by playing an alternating reachability game [12] between two players, Alice and Bob. In the beginning, Alice claims that within q trials, she would be able to locate the highest safe rung on a n-rung ladder by using at most k jars, or noted as $\mathrm{HSR}(k, q, n)$. Alice first makes a move during the gameplay by selecting a rung m ($1 \leq m < n$) and performing one trial on that rung. And Bob then decides whether the jar will break or not. If the jar is broken, Alice would only have to check rungs below rung m; otherwise, she needs to check rungs above m. As a result, Alice either claims $\mathrm{HSR}(k - 1, q - 1, m)$ if Bob says "break", or $\mathrm{HSR}(k, q - 1, n - m)$ if Bob says "safe". The game will end if either Alice wins by claim something like $\mathrm{HSR}(k, q, 1)$ where ($k \geq 0 \wedge q \geq 0$), or Bob wins by forcing Alice to claim something like HSR(k, q, n) where $((k \leq 0 \vee q \leq 0) \wedge n > 1)$. The original HSR problem can be solved if and only if Alice has a winning strategy.

Finding a winning strategy can be regarded as a model checking problem to verify a reachability property on an LTS. The LTS can be generated by applying the above game rule to a given initial state (k, q, n) (see Fig. 2 for an example). The property can be described as **starting from the initial state, Alice will eventually win the game**. We formulate this property with recursive-FOL predicates:

$$\mathbf{LFP}.X(s) := p(s) \vee \exists a \in A_s. \; Y(s^a)$$
$$Y(s) := q(s) \wedge \forall a \in A_s. \; X(s^a)$$
$$p(s) := s.n = 1$$
$$q(s) := s.n = 1 \vee (s.k > 0 \wedge s.q > 0)$$

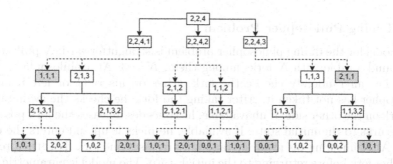

Fig. 2. The LTS for HSR$(2, 2, 4)$ where solid edges are actions taken by Alice, dashed edges are actions taken by Bob. The gray nodes are terminal states where Alice wins.

We carry out our experiment with HSR$(8, 8, 256)$ and HSR$(3, 8, 93)$. For each instance, we run five experiments. In each experiment, we record the number of Proponent's (Alice's) winning games during 100 self-plays. As the hyperparameters, we set the number of MCTS simulations to 25, exploration coefficient α is 4. We use a four-layer multi-layer perceptron (MLP) network with shape $[256, 256, 256, 256]$ for the policy and value neural network. The neural network is trained with the Adam optimizer, with learning being 0.001. The mini-batch size is set to 64, and the training epoch is set to 10. We run the experiment until one of the players consistently wins during the self-play, indicating that a winning strategy has been learned against the other player. We executed these experiments with a Core i7-9750H 4.5 GHz CPU, 16 GB Memory, and a GTX 1650 GPU. It can be seen from the experimental result (Fig. 3) that the neural MCTS can learn a winning strategy for the Proponent in **25** iterations (each iteration takes 10 min on average). Besides, we have also verified the correctness of the learned strategy with the ground truth solution using the Bernoulli Triangle in [29].

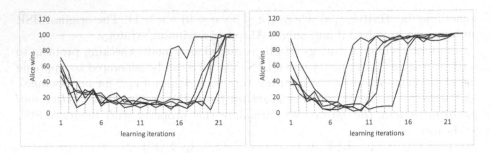

Fig. 3. Experimental results for HSR(8,8,256) (left) and HSR(3,8,93) (right). There are five trials. Each trial has 25 iterations. And each iteration contains 100 self-play. We show the wins of Alice (the Proponent) among 100 games in each iteration. It can be seen from the figure above that Alice has a U-shape learning curve in both cases, which indicates that the two players competed and learned from each other.

4.2 Dining Philosopher Problem

Our model for the dining philosopher problem is straightforward. N philosophers sit around a table with N forks among them, $N \geq 3$. At a philosopher's initial state, he can randomly choose the fork either on his right or left if another philosopher has not taken it. After taking the fork, he checks the availability of the fork on the other side. If unavailable, he concedes, releases the fork possessed, and returns to the initial state. If available, he picks it up and enters the eating state. After finishing his meal, he randomly releases one fork first, then releases the other fork before returning to the initial state. The model is parametric in the number of philosophers, where each philosopher model has ten states (Fig. 4). It is to be noted that we intentionally make our model imperfect so that when all philosophers follow this scheme, some of them may starve. We expect the model checking process to capture this design fallacy by showing us a counterexample.

In this experiment, we are interested in model-checking the property that *if philosopher 0 is hungry, then eventually the philosopher will eat.* This property can also be rewritten as the following recursive-FOL:

$$\textbf{GFP}.Z(s) := (\neg p(s) \vee X(s)) \wedge \forall a \in A_s.\ Z(s^a)$$

$$\textbf{LFP}.X(s) := q(s) \vee \forall a \in A_s.\ X(s^a)$$

$$p(s) := in\ s,\ \text{philosopher 0 is hungry.}$$

$$q(s) := in\ s,\ \text{philosopher 0 is eating.}$$

The recursive-FOL expression is a bit complex. There are two fix-point predicates nested within each other. The first fix-point predicate $Z(s)$ means that *starting from state s, it is always true that if philosopher 0 is hungry, he will eventually eat.* While the second fix-point predicate $X(s)$ means that *starting from state s, no matter how the system evolves, philosopher 0 will eventually eat.*

The experiment is conducted with eight instances, parameterized with N equal to 3 to 10. For each instance, we run five trials. We take down the number of

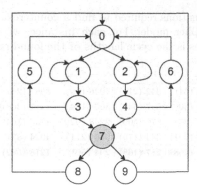

Fig. 4. The LTS for a single philosopher. State 0 is the initial state. State 1 and 2 are first picking attempts, either left or right. A philosopher will stay at one of these two states if he cannot obtain the first fork. After successfully picking his first fork, at state 3 or 4, he will try to pick the second fork. If he cannot obtain the second fork, he will go to either state 5 or 6 to release the fork picked. Otherwise, the philosopher can go to state 7, the eating state. After eating, he releases one of the forks and goes to either state 8 or 9, where he will release the other fork and go back to the initial state.

transitions required in each trial before finding a counterexample. As the hyperparameters, we change the number of MCTS simulations to 5 and the exploration coefficient α to 1. The MLP networks with shape $[128, 128, 128, 64]$ are used for both the policy and value neural network. We run the experiment until the Opponent discovers a counterexample. It should also be noted that fairness is not negligible since we are dealing with a liveness property. We use the approach mentioned in Sect. 3.4 to add fairness constraints to our system, where we set K to be 50. The experimental results are listed in the table below (Table 3). Even though it takes time for neural MCTS to self-play and learn, the running time to find a counterexample is proportional to the number of transitions in the path, while each transition takes **50** ms on average. It can be seen that our results outperform the ones from a reinforcement learning (Q-learning to be precise) based method [5], which takes more running time but only finds a longer path. Moreover, we have also tested this problem with two off-the-shelf model checkers, SPIN [14], and PRISM [19]. Due to the state explosion issue, SPIN can only run up to N=7 on our computer (Table 4), while PRISM only runs up to N = 5 (since PRISM does not support generating of a counterexample for the CTL property in the form of A [G ("hungry" => F "eating")]), we cannot show the path length in this case).

Table 3. Number of transitions required to find a counterexample for model-checking the given dining philosopher model. For each instance, we run 5 experiments. The number in the parentheses is the cycle lengths of the found counterexample.

	N = 3	N = 4	N = 5	N = 6	N = 7	N = 8	N = 9	N = 10
1	27 (14)	27 (17)	102 (54)	342 (271)	1046 (59)	838 (124)	3676 (553)	4742 (4405)
2	55 (48)	77 (63)	344 (309)	597 (547)	300 (154)	1217 (308)	2519(1980)	2727 (1226)
3	113 (39)	186 (175)	204 (37)	679 (509)	2248 (922)	1744 (164)	4664 (728)	2636 (1592)
4	76 (35)	98 (54)	579 (391)	344 (179)	976 (211)	1024 (831)	1956 (1017)	3480 (2350)
5	49 (37)	70 (50)	289 (268)	287 (168)	294 (60)	1218 (582)	1488 (1086)	3651 (1370)

Table 4. Model-checking the dining philosopher model with SPIN [14]. It can be seen that, even though SPIN tends to find shorter cycles, the running time increases exponentially because of the state explosion. As a result, SPIN can only model-check the problem up to N = 7.

	N = 3	N = 4	N = 5	N = 6	N = 7	N = 8
Length	2504 (18)	2165 (8)	2760 (28)	2959 (14)	9660 (12)	N/A
Time(s)	0.03	0.09	0.3	3.84	643	1.93E+03
States	5236	37302	113680	2.09E+06	2.03E+08	5.37E+08

5 Related Work

Model-checking through games was first proposed in [27], where the author applied a game-theoretical semantics to L_μ so that a model-checking problem is transformed into a two-player game. However, unlike our method, the author proposed to solve the game by a pure search algorithm with backtracking techniques. Another limitation to their method is that their system cannot handle fairness. It is to be noted that the work in [12], which is quite similar to the previous one, is more theoretical oriented rather than providing a concrete model checking algorithm. To our knowledge, we are the first work to apply modern gameplay AI to model-checking-problem-derived semantic games.

Applying machine learning to model checking for searching counterexamples has only been found in [2] and [5], both of which are reinforcement learning (Q-learning) based. They both use Büchi Automata to transform the model-checking problem into a graph search problem, which can be solved by reinforcement learning after formulating the graph search problem as a Markov Decision Process (MDP). Our method can treat as a complement to the study in this direction. However, unlike the Q-learning approach, which treats an on-the-fly model-checking task as a single MDP, we use a game-centric system that makes it possible to leverage the power of neural MCTS. We show that our method is superior to the approach from [5], but not the other one. However, [2] is only designed for liveness property, which allows it to encode state space efficiently, therefore mitigating the state explosion problem. Besides, we propose to use recursive-FOL as our model specification language, which is very close to L_μ. As a result, our method supports a more expressive specification than the ones in [5], which only supports LTL.

6   Conclusion

This paper highlights a likely promising approach for model checking systems with large state spaces. Our method is mainly based on two lines of development in computer science: the first one is from the formal methods and logic community, where we use the game-theoretical semantics of a logic to turn a logic expression into a two-player semantic game; the second one is from the AI and machine learning community, where we adapt the neural MCTS, a robust gameplay algorithm based on searching and learning, to play the semantic game derived from the logic specification. In this way, we can solve the classical model-checking problems by leveraging cutting-edge AI techniques. Besides, we propose recursive-FOL as our specification language, which is powerful in expressiveness. We also introduce a way to build fairness constraints in the game process. We compared our result with other model-checker tools and machine learning-based approaches and showed that it outperforms them.

In future work, we also plan to test our method on a more practical set of benchmarks, such as ones from the hardware model checking competition. We also work on improving the efficiency of Neural MCTS by using a meta-learning approach to build the neural network in incremental steps [16].

Finally, it is worth pointing out that, like other ML-based-model-checking methods, since the learned strategy might only win against a potentially suboptimal strategy of the opponent, our method should only be applied to error-detection (i.e., finding counterexamples) instead of certifying the correctness. Although there are some limitations to our approach, the potential of the combination of search and learning is still considerable.

References

1. Anthony, T., Tian, Z., Barber, D.: Thinking fast and slow with deep learning and tree search. In: Proceedings of the 31st International Conference on Neural Information Processing Systems. NIPS 2017, pp. 5366–5376 (2017)
2. Araragi, T., Cho, S.M.: Checking liveness properties of concurrent systems by reinforcement learning. In: Edelkamp, S., Lomuscio, A. (eds.) MoChArt 2006. LNCS (LNAI), vol. 4428, pp. 84–94. Springer, Heidelberg (2007). https://doi.org/10.1007/978-3-540-74128-2_6
3. Auer, P., Cesa-Bianchi, N., Fischer, P.: Finite-time analysis of the multiarmed bandit problem. Mach. Learn. **47**(2), 235–256 (2002)
4. Auger, D., Couëtoux, A., Teytaud, O.: Continuous upper confidence trees with polynomial exploration – consistency. In: Blockeel, H., Kersting, K., Nijssen, S., Železný, F. (eds.) ECML PKDD 2013. LNCS (LNAI), vol. 8188, pp. 194–209. Springer, Heidelberg (2013). https://doi.org/10.1007/978-3-642-40988-2_13

5. Behjati, R., Sirjani, M., Nili Ahmadabadi, M.: Bounded rational search for on-the-fly model checking of LTL properties. In: Arbab, F., Sirjani, M. (eds.) FSEN 2009. LNCS, vol. 5961, pp. 292–307. Springer, Heidelberg (2010). https://doi.org/10.1007/978-3-642-11623-0_17

6. Browne, C., et al.: A survey of monte Carlo tree search methods. IEEE Trans. Comput. Intellig. AI Games **4**(1), 1–43 (2012)

7. Clarke, E.M., Klieber, W., Nováček, M., Zuliani, P.: Model checking and the state explosion problem. In: Meyer, B., Nordio, M. (eds.) LASER 2011. LNCS, vol. 7682, pp. 1–30. Springer, Heidelberg (2012). https://doi.org/10.1007/978-3-642-35746-6_1

8. Clarke, E.M., Wing, J.M.: Formal methods: state of the art and future directions. ACM Comput. Surv. **28**(4), 626–643 (1996)

9. Grill, J.B., et al.: Monte-Carlo Tree Search as Regularized Policy Optimization. arXiv:abs/2007.12509 (2020)

10. Gurevich, Y.: Toward logic tailored for computational complexity. In: Börger, E., Oberschelp, W., Richter, M.M., Schinzel, B., Thomas, W. (eds.) Computation and Proof Theory. LNM, vol. 1104, pp. 175–216. Springer, Heidelberg (1984). https://doi.org/10.1007/BFb0099486

11. Gurevich, Y., Shelah, S.: Fixed-point extensions of first-order logic. In: 26th Annual Symposium on Foundations of Computer Science (SFCS 1985), pp. 346–353 (1985)

12. Hella, L., Kuusisto, A., Rönnholm, R.: Bounded game-theoretic semantics for modal mu-calculus and some variants. In: Proceedings 11th International Symposium on Games, Automata, Logics, and Formal Verification, GandALF 2020, Brussels, Belgium, September 21–22, 2020. EPTCS, vol. 326, pp. 82–96 (2020)

13. Hintikka, J.: Game-theoretical semantics: insights and prospects. Notre Dame J. Formal Logic **23**(2), 219–241 (1982)

14. Holzmann, G.: The model checker SPIN. IEEE Trans. Software Eng. **23**(5), 279–295 (1997)

15. Janin, D., Walukiewicz, I.: On the expressive completeness of the propositional mu-calculus with respect to monadic second order logic. In: Montanari, U., Sassone, V. (eds.) CONCUR 1996. LNCS, vol. 1119, pp. 263–277. Springer, Heidelberg (1996). https://doi.org/10.1007/3-540-61604-7_60

16. Kadam, P., Xu, R., Lieberherr, K.J.: Dual Monte Carlo Tree Search. CoRR abs/2103.11517 (2021)

17. Kocsis, L., Szepesvári, C.: Bandit based monte-Carlo planning. In: Fürnkranz, J., Scheffer, T., Spiliopoulou, M. (eds.) ECML 2006. LNCS (LNAI), vol. 4212, pp. 282–293. Springer, Heidelberg (2006). https://doi.org/10.1007/11871842_29

18. Kolaitis, P.G.: On the expressive power of logics on finite models. In: Finite Model Theory and Its Applications. Texts in Theoretical Computer Science an EATCS Series, pp. 27–123. Springer, Heidelberg (2007). https://doi.org/10.1007/3-540-68804-8_2

19. Kwiatkowska, M., Norman, G., Parker, D.: Probabilistic symbolic model checking with PRISM: a hybrid approach. In: Katoen, J.-P., Stevens, P. (eds.) TACAS 2002. LNCS, vol. 2280, pp. 52–66. Springer, Heidelberg (2002). https://doi.org/10.1007/3-540-46002-0_5

20. Niwinski, D., Walukiewicz, I.: Games for the mu-Calculus. Theor. Comput. Sci. **163**(1&2), 99–116 (1996)

21. Rebuschi, M.: Extended game-theoretical semantics. In: Trobok, M., Miščević, N., Žarnić, B. (eds.) Between Logic and Reality. Logic, Epistemology, and the Unity of Science, vol. 25, pp. 161–182. Springer, Dordrecht (2012). https://doi.org/10.1007/978-94-007-2390-0_9

22. Schmid, M., et al.: Player of Games. CoRR abs/2112.03178 (2021)
23. Schrittwieser, J., et al.: Mastering Atari, go, chess and shogi by planning with a learned model. Nature **588**, 604–609 (2020)
24. Silver, D., Huang, A., Maddison, C.J., Guez, A., Sifre, L., van den Driessche, G., et al.: Mastering the game of go with deep neural networks and tree search. Nature **529**, 484 (2016)
25. Silver, D., Schrittwieser, J., Simonyan, K., Antonoglou, I., Huang, A., Guez, A., et al.: Mastering the game of go without human knowledge. Nature **550**, 354 (2017)
26. Sniedovich, M.: OR/MS games: 4. the joy of egg-dropping in Braunschweig and Hong Kong. Inf. Trans. Edu. **4**(1), 48–64 (2003)
27. Stevens, P., Stirling, C.: Practical model-checking using games. In: Steffen, B. (ed.) TACAS 1998. LNCS, vol. 1384, pp. 85–101. Springer, Heidelberg (1998). https://doi.org/10.1007/BFb0054166
28. Walukiewicz, I.: Monadic second-order logic on tree-like structures. Theoret. Comput. Sci. **275**(1), 311–346 (2002)
29. Xu, R., Lieberherr, K.J.: Learning self-play agents for combinatorial optimization problems. Knowl. Eng. Rev. **35**, e11 (2020)

Requirements-Driven Model Checking and Test Generation for Comprehensive Verification

Devesh Bhatt[1][(✉)], Hao Ren[1], Anitha Murugesan[1], Jason Biatek[1],
Srivatsan Varadarajan[1], and Natarajan Shankar[2][(✉)]

[1] Honeywell Aerospace, Plymouth, USA
Devesh.Bhatt@honeywell.com
[2] SRI International, Palo Alto, USA
shankar@csl.sri.com

Abstract. In this paper, we present a novel approach that seamlessly integrates requirements-based testing and model checking. Given a set of functional *requirements* and *properties*, both generic attributes and application specific constraints, expressed in our CLEAR requirements notation, our approach and the associated tool suite simultaneously generates an extensive set of requirements-based test cases using equivalence classes and synthesizes requirement models. The synthesized models support formal analysis of the properties using state-of-the-art model checkers that serves as a rigorous evidence of the quality and adequacy of the requirements. Further, the result of executing the test cases generated from those high-quality requirements on the implementation, helps ensure that those requirements are indeed met in the implementation. This comprehensive requirements-based approach to verification leverages automation and reduces defects in evidence generation for design assurance as outlined in guidance such as DO-178C and DO-333. We use the ArduCopter, an open-source platform, to illustrate our approach.

1 Introduction

Aerospace design assurance practices *ARP4754A* [20] and associated guidance regarding software aspects of certification *DO-178C* [18] are used by the aviation industry and regulators as a primary means of compliance with airworthiness regulations for airborne software. One of the key principles of such certification is the use of *requirements-based testing* along with coverage metrics to show that the tests sufficiently cover the code structure with bidirectional traceability.

With the publication of DO-333 [19], a formal methods supplement to DO-178C, the use of formal methods has become a recognized means of compliance, streamlining the process for aircraft manufacturers to obtain certification

Supported by DARPA under agreement number FA8750-20-C-0226. The views, opinions and/or findings expressed are those of the authors and should not be interpreted as representing the official views or policies of the Department of Defense or the U.S. Government.

J. V. Deshmukh et al. (Eds.): NFM 2022, LNCS 13260, pp. 576–596, 2022.
https://doi.org/10.1007/978-3-031-06773-0_31

credit. Faster model checkers and theorem-provers and their widespread adoption in industry have meant an opportunity for more scalable and comprehensive formal-methods based software verification pipeline that utilizes them to show *with high confidence, a more exhaustive assessment showing also the absence of errors*, whereas testing can just reveal the *presence of errors* and cannot prove that a software never violates desired property. But testing is still essential to the *test-like-you-fly* certification philosophy which emphasizes verification through testing be performed on the actual software implementation executed on flight platforms and to reduce defect discovery late during operation with dire consequences. Formal verification of a model of the software implementation, however, runs the risk of abstraction divergence between model of the software and software implementation potentially invalidating any verification evidence derived from those models. This abstraction divergence between formal model and the implementation could arise for a plethora of reasons including error in requirements specifications, incorrect implementation of software from those requirements, invalid architectural assumptions and/or platform characteristics.

In this paper, we propose an *integrated, belt-and-suspender approach using formal methods-based requirements-driven model checking and testing*, that leverages the benefits of both verification strategies to meet the certification compliance objectives of DO-178C and DO-333. The cornerstone of this approach is our requirements notation called CLEAR (Constrained Language Enhanced Approach to Requirements) [4,7], that provides natural language flavored constructs to specify a wide range of logical, relational, temporal and arithmetic aspects of system behaviors. CLEAR was exclusively defined with formal syntax and semantics to enable the use of formal-methods based automation tools for early discovery of requirement errors. Text2Test, a novel verification tool developed by Honeywell [3], automatically performs *static analysis* of the CLEAR requirements to ensure their consistency and completeness. Text2Test also simultaneously synthesizes formal models in a logical notation that can be used with a model checker, namely Sally [22], to verify properties, as well as automatically generates test cases for verifying behavior of the implementation. This *simultaneous co-synthesis of the model and tests from the same underlying requirements* ensures no model abstraction gap with respect to implementation arise because properties verified on the model through model checking can be confirmed on the implementation through testing.

Note that, showing absence of misinterpretation of design intent in requirements formalization and construction may often involve human judgment and review, and/or substantial high-fidelity simulations, thereby being a non-trivial validation process itself especially when translating natural language requirement documents into formalized requirement language. This intent validation process is beyond the scope of this paper, which focuses on internal defect analysis of the intrinsic aspect of the requirements. Along with formalized textual requirements, we also formally specify first-class property constructs (e.g. safety, liveness, invariants) for software which are subsequently exploited by a model checker for verification of those properties. While requirements describe specific behaviors for facilitating software design and implementation, properties serves as constraints on the software behavior and preferred evolution of system behavior.

Some properties could also be carefully crafted for the purpose of validating the design intent. These twin specifications allow designers to systematically exploit the *complementarity of model checking and testing* to satisfy some verification objective and achieve higher confidence.

The main contribution of this paper is two-fold: (a) the novel integrated two-pronged specification-verification approach and, (b) the orchestration of appropriate formal notation and tools. The CLEAR notation uniquely allows capturing the detailed behavioral description as well as properties (or invariants) of system; The orchestrated tool-chain Text2Test-Sally allows comprehensive requirement-based static analysis, test generation and model checking without expert human intervention. Further, we use the Advanced Fail Safe module of the ArduCopter rotorcraft to illustrate our approach. Through these contributions, we advance the state-of-the-art practice in certification by proposing a framework that, firstly, eliminates ambiguities and errors in intent specification through requirement formalism, its analysis and strengthened with additional specification of formal properties in a novel manner which has hitherto not been done. Next, the framework reduces adhoc-ness and informality in the verification process by automatically synthesizing both the formal models, on which properties are then verified, and tests that are then systematically shown to be both complete and adequate. Finally, the framework maintains strong bidirectional traceability links between requirements/properties and the evidence from the verification campaign to guarantee strict coverage.

The paper is organized as follows. In Sect. 2, we provide an overview of our integrated verification approach, followed by an outline of the case example in Sect. 3. In Sects. 4 and 5, we explain our requirements notation, and model synthesis, formal analysis and test generation. Finally, we conclude in Sect. 6.

2   Comprehensive and Integrated Verification Approach

Fig. 1 presents our comprehensive verification strategy that combines two verification tracks (i) Formal methods based property checking of a synthesized model directly from requirements thereby ensuring software code that faithfully implements the requirements then also implicitly inherits verified properties of the model which is an abstraction of the implementation, and (ii) Explicit testing of the actual software code implementation that executes on the aircraft with automatically generated tests from the same model to ensure that there is no divergence between model abstraction and implementation as well as delivering a more complete array of tests that are synthesized in a principled manner to ensure comprehensive requirements coverage.

Also observe that in Fig. 1 we start the verification early and directly from the intent specification of the software i.e. software requirements and hence explicitly synthesize both models and tests from those requirements and use that to independently verify software design implementation and code which is typically managed through an independent manual process. The CLEAR notation with formal semantics for requirements is the foundation of this approach—enabling

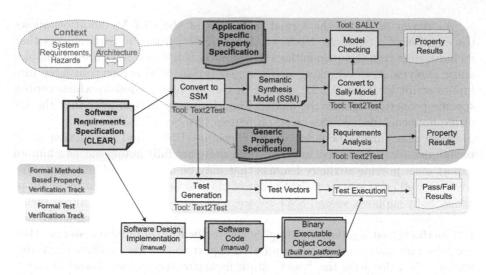

Fig. 1. Verification using requirements emantics, property checking, and testing

model-checking of requirements' properties as well as principled testing of code against the requirements.

The requirements for a software component are developed in the context of system requirements, hazard specifications, and architecture (note: discussion of these is outside the scope of this paper). This context also serves as the basis for deriving either *generic properties*, that the set of software requirements must satisfy in terms of quality (e.g. error free specifications) as it will serve as the foundation to build upon, or *application-specific properties*, that must be satisfied in order to meet some particular aspect of system requirements or to mitigate some hazard. In essence, as shown in Table 1, the *requirements* and *properties* are complementary: requirements are statements describing specific behaviors whereas properties (e.g. safety, liveness, invariants) are behavioral constraints that must not be violated by the software component. Thus, the composite behavior specified by the requirements must also not violate the properties.

Table 1. Verification of both intent specifications: requirements and properties

| | Behavioral Requirements | Properties: *What the system ought to do/not to do* | | |
		Safety	Liveness	Invariants
Purpose	Specific functional behaviors that the system shall do	Something bad will never happen	Something good will eventually (or in bounded time) occur	Desired system constraints
Verification Approach	Testing	Model Checking	Testing and Model Checking	Testing and Model Checking
Exemplars from case study in Sect. 3	If the remaining battery power is critically low, the system shall initiate emergency landing	Once the system is in insufficient battery state, then system shall never transition back to normal battery state	The system shall reach its destination in normal battery state (within x secs)	Emergency landing is always initiated when/after systems reached insufficient battery state

As shown in Fig. 1, the formal semantics of the CLEAR notation allows the creation of a *Semantic Synthesis Model (SSM)* from the requirements that includes state transition semantics and temporal behaviors. SSM directly enables static analysis, model checking, and test generation. SSM is then translated into inputs script for *Sally* [13,22], a state of the art model checker, which verifies specific properties against the model. Then by proxy we can infer that the set of requirements also satisfies these properties (see Sect. 5.2).

Note that current bounded model checking (BMC) and k-induction proof techniques are very effective but they are usually not fully automatic, as a human expert must provide auxiliary lemmas that may be intricate and difficult to discover as well encode their insight order of clauses being checked to prove properties. Sally supports several SMT solvers with improvements for improvements and scalability and extensions to verification algorithms BMC, k-induction and IC3 methods that significantly simplify the verification of infinite systems - they are fully automatic and do not require an expert to provide auxiliary invariants whereby IC3 discovers the "right" state invariants on its own based on novel inference techniques from abstract interpretations [12]. Sally native specification language (MCMT), like it's predecessor SAL on which it is derived from, is naturally expressive to handle state-machine models and it's flexibility also allows for modular composition and selective translations of the overall model. These key Sally capabilities enable automatic translation and thus automatic verification possible in our framework with minimal human interventions.

The CLEAR semantics also enable requirement analysis to verify generic properties such as: all requirements in the set are accurate, verifiable, free of gaps, and consistent (free of conflicts) (see Sect. 5.1). Test generation is also based on these semantics to create comprehensive tests to verify that the code satisfies all behavioral aspects of the requirements including state transitions, boundary conditions, and time-dependent behavior (see Sect. 5.3). The integrated verification argument is summarized as follows:

1. The software behavior and constraints are specified using two complementary means: 1) requirements of specific behaviors in the CLEAR notation, and 2) application-specific properties that are constraints on the behavior.
2. Show that the requirements reflect the proper system intent and are correct:
   - Requirements analysis is performed to verify that the requirements are accurate and free of gaps and conflicts.
   - A state-transition system model is created from the requirements that is used for formal model checking to verify the set of requirements satisfies the application-specific properties.
3. Tests are created and executed on the code to verify that the implementation comprehensively satisfies the behavioral aspects of the requirements.
4. Summary argument: Given 1, 2, and 3 above, one can conclude that software component correctly implements the its behavioral intent in the system.

3 ArduCopter Case Study

We use the open source ArduCopter rotorcraft flight system [1] platform as a case study. The mission goal for the ArduCopter is to perform autonomous surveillance, taking off from a *home/launch* location, following a sequence of *waypoints* and returning to the launch location and finally landing there. It is restricted to fly within a pre-configured operational safety perimeter called *Geofence* - defined with altitude, range, and polygon. There are also a set of pre-defined locations called *rally points* as safe-back up landing or loiter locations. Among the several ArduPilot's functional components, we focus on the *Advance Fail Safe* (AFS) runtime monitor software component that checks if the flight correctly executes the mission plan and initiates contingency recovery actions when any violations are detected.

Table 2. AFS high level functional description

	Contingency	Recovery action
1	Insufficient Battery	If battery level is low and sufficient to return to launch, then return to launch and terminate mission. If battery level is critically low then land immediately and terminate mission
2	GPS Lock Loss	If GPS is lost, then hover at the current location. If GPS recovered within 5 s then resume mission. Otherwise go to last waypoint using IMUs only, land there and terminate mission
3	Max Altitude Geofence breach	If altitude breach is detected, try to drop to the target altitude within 5 s. If desired altitude is achieved, continue with mission. Otherwise, land current location and terminate mission
4	Range Geofence breach	If range breach is detected, try to drop to Target Position within 5 s. If Target Position is achieved, continue with mission. Otherwise, land immediately and terminate mission
5	Polygon Geofence breach	If polygon breach is detected, try to reach target Position within Boundary within 5 s. If Target Position is achieved, continue with mission. Otherwise, land immediately and terminate mission
6	Ground Station Communication Loss	Go to the closest rally point and hover. Attempt to re-establish communication without loss for 5 s. If re-established, complete the remaining mission and record the disruption count. Otherwise, return to launch and terminate mission. If disruption count$> n$, return to launch and terminate mission

For illustrating our approach, we consider a subset of AFS functions, namely six contingency (off-nominal) situations and the desired recovery response actions, as listed in their precedence order in Table 2. Readers can find in [21] details of the formal architectural specifications of the overall system, the properties inherited by the individual software component due to the architectural paradigm when the system and associated software components strictly adhere to the specification and the controlled build process assembles the requisite software component modules with integration guarantees to ensure architectural specification tightly matches with implementation execution on the platform.

4   Requirement Specification and Model Synthesis

4.1   CLEAR: Constrained Language Enhanced Approach to Requirements

Requirements specification, formalization, and analysis have been addressed by several frameworks and tools; most of these provide patterns and templates for specifying conditions and temporal behaviors. VARED [2] uses NLP techniques to translate natural language to linear temporal logic (LTL) for further analysis, however, without attributing formal semantics for the translation. SpeAR [14] allows writing requirements in a natural-language like specifications using a small set of temporal patterns; requirements are translated into a Lustre [16] model for further formal analysis and proofs. The ASSERT platform [11] provides the language SRL for writing requirements using conditions and a small set of temporal patterns, providing some analysis and test generation capabilities but no translation to formal semantics for property proofs. FRETish [10] provides a more general approach to temporal behavior specification, with formal semantics for translation to metric temporal logic (MTL) formulas.

The current methods [10,14] provide quite reasonable approaches for specifying temporal behaviors, but that is not sufficient for specifying complex algorithmic aspects of avionic systems behaviors. CLEAR has been driven to support full-scale development for complex avionics application domains (e.g., flight

```
ID "Type Definitions":
    Define copter_position as instance of type XYZVector.
    Define last_way_point as instance of type XYZVector.
    Define Abormal_Batt_Event as (bat_level <= T_rtl).
ID "GPS_LL Req 2: w_priority":
    While No_Abonormal_Batt_Event is true and Current_GPS_Loss_Count is
    less than Max GPS_Losses_Allowed. when GPS_Fix has been 'Lost' for 3 seconds,
    then the AFS Subsystem shall transition AFS_State to 'GPS Loss Hover'.
ID "GPS_LL Req 4.2: w_priority":
    While AFS_State is 'Flight Terminated due to GPS Loss' and No_Abonormal_Batt_Event
    is true, When distance between copter_position and last_way_point is less than
    location_reached_threshold feet, then the AFS Subsystem shall
    latch copter_command to 'Land Immediately'.
ID "InSuf_Bat Req 1":
    While GPS_Fix is 'Available'. If T_land <= bat_level <= T_rtl,
    then AFS Subsystem shall transition AFS_State to 'Return to Launch Due to Low Battery'
ID "InSuf_Bat Req 2":
    While GPS_Fix is 'Lost', If T_land <= bat_level <= T_rtl,
    then AFS Subsystem shall transition AFS_State
    to 'Land Immediately Due to Low Battery and No GPS'.
ID "InSuf_Bat Req 2.1":
    When AFS_State transitions to 'Land Immediately Due to Low Battery and No GPS',
    then AFS Subsystem shall  latch copter_command to 'Land Immediately'.
ID "InSuf_Bat Req 4":
    When bat_level is less than T_land, then AFS Subsystem shall transition AFS_State
    to 'Land Immediately Due to Battery Critically Low'.
```

Fig. 2. Snippets of AFS requirements in CLEAR notation

control, navigation, flight management, and displays), where complex behaviors include both temporal and algorithmic aspects. CLEAR has a blended notion of temporal and algorithmic behaviors which allows more flexible composition of time-triggered, state based, and event-based behaviors with algorithmic aspects such as set manipulation/selection, interval arithmetic, and mathematical functions. All such aspects are integrated in the underlying semantic synthesis model (SSM) that is used for formal analysis and test generation.

As an example, the CLEAR requirements in Fig. 2 are snippets taken from two sets of requirements: GPS Lock Loss and Insufficient Battery contingencies. Each requirement captures a single specific intent, such as how to respond when a GPS fix is regained after being lost. Multiple requirements together constitute a requirement set corresponding to a system function. Automated checks on these requirements ensure that gaps in the requirement set can be identified and fixed. 'While' clauses specify conditions based on states, and 'When' clauses specify events such as a value crossing a threshold or a particular time interval passing. Events, states, and time intervals can be composed to create conditions that blend different behaviors together, with all elements appearing in the synthesized model. Enumerated values are indicated by single quotes, so 'Lost' and 'Available' are possible values for the variable GPS_Fix, and 'Flight Terminated due to GPS Loss' is a possible value for AFS_State.

CLEAR has a rich expression syntax which also allows user-defined phrases for higher-level concepts, one example of which can be seen in a requirement in the 'distance between' expression. In this example, copter_position and last_way_point are of type XYZVector, a built-in structure consisting of X, Y, and Z coordinates. Custom phrases can also be defined and extended natively in CLEAR. The distance between phrase in CLEAR calculates the Euclidean distance between two such vectors. By providing native support for such concepts, a requirement can more clearly convey the *intent*. While it is possible to generate the same model using the same exponent and addition operators that underly 'distance between', the higher-level phrase better conveys what is meant by this requirement. User-defined phrases can be also created for a variety of computations over time-intervals such as filtered sensor values, moving averages over time. Such temporal phrases can be combined with mathematical phrases—e.g.: "While the 30 s simple moving average of the distance between Coord1 and Coord2 is greater than 400 ft ... ". Additionally, for a proper factoring of intent in complex behaviors, CLEAR also provides constructs to define named expressions and sets that can be parameterized and nested.

Finally, to support a variety of application domains, CLEAR provides over 150 behavior operators including: Boolean, relational, arithmetic, time-dependent (timers, filters, integrators), math functions (basic algebraic, transcendental, and special functions), and multi-dimensional interpolation tables [4].

4.2   Tool Architecture Overview and SSM Creation

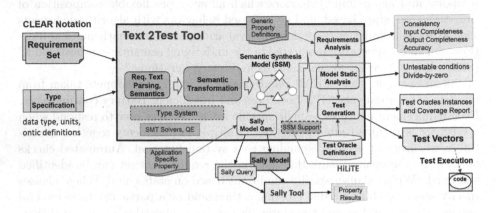

Fig. 3. Verification automation by Text2Test and sally tools

Text2Test is a comprehensive tool that automates several verification activities as shown in Fig. 3. Text2Test takes as inputs the CLEAR requirement set as well as type specifications such as variable data types, units, and definitions of other ontic characteristics of the inputs. It then parses the textual requirements, applies requirement-level semantics, and then creates a semantic-equivalent internal diagram for the requirement set called *Semantic Synthesis Model (SSM)*. Note that, in HiLiTE, SSM is a direct import and translation of a MATLAB/Simulink model. Text2Test borrows from HiLiTE's underlying definition of SSM elements, and constructs SSM from textual requirements and type definitions (the yellow shape in Fig. 3 shows the HiLiTE capabilities used). This SSM forms the basis for model static analysis, test generation (Subsect. 5.3), requirement analysis against generic properties (Subsect. 5.1), and translation to formal model for model checking (Subsect. 5.2). The model static analysis function [5] analyzes SSM to determine range constraints and untestable/anomalous behavior – providing a foundation for requirements analysis and tests generation. While other state-of-the-art formal requirement analysis frameworks (such as FRETish [10]) focus on directly translating structured natural language into temporal logic formulas, Text2Test bridges two ends with a graphical model SSM, allowing a full suite of model-based analysis and test generation. Together with the property-based verification capability using Sally, our tool suite can generate comprehensive and consistent assurance evidence.

Tool Maturity and Scalability: Text2Test capability is constructed upon the model analysis and test generation engine of Honeywell's HiLiTE tool [3,5,6] that has been used extensively in several avionics product certifications including Boeing 787 flight controls and Airbus A350 environment control. HiLiTE has been qualified under DO-178C and DO-330 (Tool Qualification supplement) for performing model static analysis and generating comprehensive tests from requirements expressed in models. Text2Test tool itself has been matured by usage in many industrial avionics product programs using hundreds of requirements.

4.2.1 From Requirement Set to Semantic Synthesis Model (SSM)

Text2Test first parses requirement texts into functional nodes and data-flow edges, forming a raw model of the entire requirement set while preserving the semantics of individual requirements as well as creating traceability. Text2Test then performs a system-level aggregation through multiple structural merging processes. Structural merge is based on graph search and pattern recognition, aiming to fuse low level primitive nodes into those of richer semantics, as well as to eliminate redundancy and preserve traceability. These result in a minimum-scale but semantic-equivalent optimized model for the requirement set called *Semantic Synthesis Model (SSM)* with full traceability.

For instance, a state transition behavior consists of initialization, and a transition function that determines the current state value from the previous state value and/or external transition trigger conditions (triggers for short). The state only updates at active trigger(s), otherwise remain the same as its previous value (user specified state has inertia behavior) through a feedback path. The "while" clause is to specify the previous (source) state value and the "when" clause is to specify the non-state triggering condition, followed by the clause that sets the current (destination) state value. The left side of Fig. 4 shows the partial raw model representing an example of state transition behavior with n triggers, specified across upto n individual requirements in CLEAR. The raw model contains primitive blocks explicitly mapping to CLEAR functional and logical keywords (e.g., *switch* block to "While/When", *not* block to "not"), as well as a *Combiner* block as a routing hub node aggregating all state value set and get for the common state variable. An initialization requirement is simply converted to a *constant* block input to the *Combiner*. Then proper connection is added, forming a feedback loop and other paths.

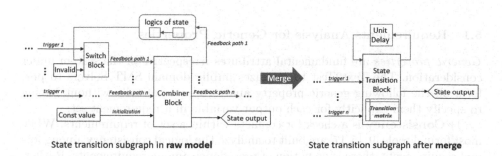

State transition subgraph in **raw model**   State transition subgraph after **merge**

Fig. 4. State transition subgraph before and after merge.

When the state transition block merge starts, the *Combiner* block is firstly replaced by a *StateTransitionBlock* (*STB*) block whose functionality is defined by an (initially empty) inherent transition matrix. Next, each feedback path is analyzed to identify the associated non-state trigger and the source state value(s), which assign the row elements of the state transition matrix (for **semantic richness**), thus the entire feedback path is removed (for **simplicity**), while the non-state trigger is reconnected directly to the *STB* block input. Requirement ID is also recorded as row info (for **traceability**). The *Invalid* block is removed (for **execution**), since the transition matrix is presumptive to be input-complete. The input completeness will be formally verified as a generic property after merge. Lastly, a feedback path of *unit delay* is added outside *STB* (for **temporal correctness**), providing the state value memory for the merged state transition subgraph. The initialization path in the raw model is also removed (for **simplicity**), after initializing *unit delay* accordingly, rendering the *STB* itself as a memoryless non-time dependent block.

Note that, SSM allows *null* node(s) for input-incomplete requirement set. Despite the fact that a *null* node does not execute or propagate value/range through, the model analysis and test generation can still be performed on scenarios that do not require active values from the *null* node, generating verification artifacts of partial coverage to the best extent. This novel "as-is" modeling provides great flexibility in requirement creation and verification of the rapid prototyping and diagnosis scheme. Further, when a requirement set has defect(s), the corresponding SSM truthfully interprets that. The defect(s) as well as their diagnosis traces will be detected by model analysis and systematically reported.

5   Verification Activities and Techniques

In this section, we describe our approach to (a) generic property verification, (b) model checking of application specific properties, and (c) requirements-based test case generation, as outlined in Fig. 1. The artifacts generated by these three verification approaches serve as evidences in assuring the safety of the system in consideration.

5.1   Requirements Analysis for Generic Properties

Generic properties are fundamental attributes irrespective of the system under consideration. The Text2Test tool utilizes public domain SMT Solvers to perform all the following generic property analyses automatically without having to specify them explicitly for each output variable in a requirement set:

1) **Consistency** is a check for conflicts within a set of requirements. While most formal tools [9, 15, 17] are built to analyze the logical consistency among formal requirements, there is no notion of precedence among requirements. Rather, precedence is often baked into each requirement specification (such as a number of negated conditions in the antecedents) masking the intent of precedence in the minds of the specifier. However, the CLEAR notation provides explicit

constructs such as 'order of precedence', that the specifier can use before a set of requirements to obviously indicate the order of its precedence. Consequently, Text2Test's *consistency check* is uniquely designed to account for this precedence construct. For example, among the three breach contingencies to be mitigated by the AFS (Table 2), when more than one occurs at the same time, the response had to be ordered based on the severity and impact of each contingency (per the concept of operations). Though one could have specified this precedence by combinatorially adding the absence of other breaches in each requirement, it not only make the requirements very long, but also masks the intent. However, by using the CLEAR's precedence construct, we concisely specified the mitigation of each breach in order of its severity (as shown in Fig. 5) and Text2Text was able to analyze consistency accordingly.

```
ID "ALT_BRE, RAN_BRE, POLY_BRE Precedence: w_priority":
  AFS Subsystem shall set AFS_State as defined in the following precedence order
    While Condition_For_Breach_Transition is true and Max_Altitude_Breach_Event is detected to be 'Breach',
    the AFS Subsystem shall transition AFS_State to 'Max Altitude Breach'
    While Condition_For_Breach_Transition is true and Polygon_Breach_Event is detected to be 'Breach',
    the AFS Subsystem shall transition AFS_State to 'Polygon Breach'
    While Condition For Breach Transition is true and Range_Breach_Event is detected to be 'Breach',
    the AFS Subsystem shall transition AFS_State to 'Max Range Breach'
  end.
```

Fig. 5. Requirements with precedence construct

In general, if a requirement is considered as a condition-response pair, given a set of condition-response pairs $\{(cond_1^p, resp_1^p), \ldots, (cond_n^p, resp_n^p)\}$ for output variable v with the same priority level p, Text2Text's consistency is formulated as $\left(\oplus(cond_1^p, \ldots, cond_n^p)\right) \vee \left(\neg \bigvee(cond_1^p, \ldots, cond_n^p)\right)$, where the first disjunctive clause is to ensure that only one condition holds at a time and the second clause relaxes that logic to allow the case where no condition holds.

2) **Input and Output Completeness** identifies missing combinations of input conditions and unspecified output values that is crucial to assess the adequacy of requirements. Let $\{(cond_1, resp_1), \ldots, (cond_m, resp_m)\}$ be the set of condition-response pairs for a variable v at all priority levels. In Text2Test, the SMT formulation for the input-completeness check is: $\vee(cond_1, \ldots, cond_m)$. *Output completeness check* is performed by comparing the specified output variable range and the range propagated through the SSM by model static analysis. Text2Test tool meticulously discovers and displays the gaps to the user in a formatted HTML report. When analyzing the AFS communication loss requirements that have a number of conditions in their antecedents, the tool reported a number of missing input combinations and unspecified values of the output. While the resolution to specify more requirements was specific to the case example, the tool was helpful in rigorously quantifying the requirements' adequacy.

3) **Mode-thrashing analysis** aims to prevent the system from a hazardous metastable phenomenon, i.e., unintended switching back-and-forth between two states (general case: cycle through multiple states), often associated with continuous value triggered mode switches at the absence of safe margins. This is

an advanced analysis that comes into play when the requirement set specifies maximum input sensing fluctuation parameter, denoted by $fluc$. The sensed continuous input in_{sensed} subject to sensing fluctuation on top of the ground truth reference in_{ref}, i.e., $in_{sensed} \in [in_{ref} - fluc, in_{ref} + fluc]$, may be used in mutual-exclusive boolean triggering conditions for some downstream state s mode switch. One simple statement of the absence of potential mode-thrashing for an ON/OFF mode switch is that: stable input subject to noise shall not cause unintended contradicting mode switching triggers in consecutive time steps. Its general logic is:

$$((in_{ref} = \text{REF}) \wedge \mathbf{X}(in_{ref} = \text{REF})) \Rightarrow \neg((cond_s^{ON} \wedge \mathbf{X}cond_s^{OFF}) \vee (cond_s^{OFF} \wedge \mathbf{X}cond_s^{ON}))$$

for any possible stable (constant) reference value REF, where $\mathbf{X}$ is the standard temporal operator denoting the "next" time step, and $cond_s^{ON}$ and $cond_s^{OFF}$ are Boolean conditions that set the state s to be ON and OFF respectively. Note that, Text2Test supports above concept and logic are as well as their extension to multiple-mode switches. While no such fluctuation related errors were reported in the subset of requirements we considered for AFS, we have found this generic analysis very useful in many large scale systems where engineers unintentionally missed specifying safety margins among mutual-exclusive triggering conditions through timers, debounces, or hysteresis.

5.2   Sally Integration and Application Specific Property Verification

Sally [13, 22] is a model checker for transition systems with both bounded model checking (BMC) and k-induction engines. Users can alternate the verification engines as needed. Integrating Sally with Text2Test provides advanced capability of specific property verification other than the generic ones, given that the requirement set can be modeled as a transition system. In our tool chain, the integration is achieved by translating Text2Test internal SSM to Sally model. This subsection introduces the model translation process, as well as the enhanced capability enabled by the tools integration and the extension.

5.2.1   From SSM to Sally Model

Model translation: Sally model is a script model with inputs, states, and state transitions. On the other hand, SSM is a functional data-flow graph model which may or may not possess intended state transition behavior. But because of the underlying periodic execution with discrete time steps (each requirement set can have a specified distinct execution period), SSM essentially can be remodeled as a transition system that responds to instantaneous changes. In this translation process, nodes/structures of the SSM are converted to the Sally script segments (declaration, initialization, and state transition), following the rules in Table 3.

Table 3. SSM to Sally Model Translation.

Case I: A system *input* node	
Sally counterparts:	1) **System input declaration:** A system input variable
	2) **State declaration:** An auxiliary input state variable
	3) **State initialization:** None
	4) **State transition:** Next step value of the input state equals to input
Note:	All states update simultaneously lagging by one step of system input(s)

Case II: An *STB* node and the associated *unit delay* and *output* node	
Sally counterparts:	1) **State declaration:** A Sally state variable
	2) **State initialization:** Same value as the *unit delay*'s initial value
	3) **State transitions:** Transition matrix in Sally language
Note:	This structure as a whole corresponds to one single Sally state

Case III: A time-dependent node	
Sally counterparts:	1) **State declaration:** A Sally state variable
	2) **State initialization:** Same value as the node's initial value
	3) **State transitions:** Transfer function in Sally language
Note:	**Case III** excludes the *unit delay* node instances from **Case II** category

Case IV: A non-time-dependent node	
Sally counterparts:	1) **State declaration:** A Sally state variable
	2) **State initialization:** None
	3) **State transitions:** Node's math/logical function in Sally language
Note:	A memoryless state has no initialization

SSM responds to system input(s) instantaneously, while in Sally model states' update responds to system input(s) one time step delay. To eliminate the response delay at the system inputs interface, an auxiliary input state variable is created to be one time step delay of the corresponding system input in Sally model. Thus, the auxiliary input state(s) update simultaneously with the rest of the system, all states as a whole exhibiting equivalent behavior of the SSM.

5.2.2   Checking Application Specific Properties Against Sally Model

Overview: The bottom part of Fig. 3 shows the flow for checking a Specific Property against a Sally model. The Sally integration with Text2Test tool uses the Sally model checker tool taking generic Sally query as input. Meanwhile, the integration supports input and temporal extensions to query formula expressiveness through automatically converting the syntax-richer extended queries to generic Sally queries, as described in the following paragraph and Sect. 5.2.3 respectively.

Specifying Properties With System Inputs: In the generic Sally query .mcmt file, an input condition cannot be directly encoded as part of the query formula, as most other model checkers do. Instead, Sally tool supports an input assumption annex. But it is verbose and more importantly cannot deal with properties containing input-state relationship (such as "State s is always greater than input x."). Our solution in the translated Sally model is to introduce an auxiliary input state for each system input (as shown in Table 3 Case I). Therefore, the integrated tool chain is more flexible with encoding the input state in the query formula.

An Example of Application Specific Property: For the AFS runtime monitor ground station (GS) communication component, a safety property is given as "After the initial step, if the current GS communication disruption count is more than 3, then AFS state shall not be Normal Flight (value 0)". The corresponding Sally query (in SMT2 format) is

(query AFS ($\Rightarrow$ (and *not_initial_step* ($>$ *GS_Comm_Dis_Count* 3))(not (= *AFS_State* 0)))),

where AFS is the system name, and other variables are self-explanatory.

5.2.3   Temporal Extension to Sally Query

Motivation: Generic Sally query does not allow basic temporal operators such as "next." and "pre.", although "next." is used in the Sally model script to denote the next time step. Queries are checked at all time steps without an explicit temporal operator. This is to say, one cannot write a generic query formula about a state s in specific future or past time step(s). This is due to limitation of implementation rather than that of reasoning engines' power. To enrich temporal logic semantics and take most advantage of the reasoning power, temporal extension to Sally query is developed as part of the tools integration.

Approach: Two basic temporal operators $\mathbf{X}$ and $\mathbf{F}$, denoting "next" and "eventually" respectively, and time step syntax sugar are introduced to augment the query language. Let t and $t'_{>t}$ denote the beginning and end time of the temporal domain, and *generic_pred* be an SMT Lib 2.0 format Boolean predicate of the state variables from the generic Sally model, we have the following general form of temporal extended predicates below:

- $\mathbf{X}(t, t')[generic\_pred]$— meaning that "$generic\_pred$ holds for <u>all</u> time steps in between t (not included) to t' (included)."
- $\mathbf{F}(t, t')[generic\_pred]$— meaning that "$generic\_pred$ holds for <u>any</u> time step in between t (not included) to t' (included)."

Note that both t and t' are integer multiple of the system period. They can be negative, 0, or positive numbers, corresponding to past, current, or future time respectively. A temporal extended predicate can be embedded in a larger query formula the same way a generic predicate does. For the AFS emergency landing component, a safety property is given as "If the battery level is below the low threshold, then the system state shall become 0 within 0.2 s." Its temporal formulation is:

$$(\text{query } AFS \ (\Rightarrow (< bat\_lvl \ low\_thresh) \ \mathbf{F}[0, 0.2][(= s \ 0)]))). \tag{1}$$

Property Translation and Sally Model Augmentation: A temporal extended property is translated into an equivalent generic Sally query before Sally tool takes it as input. The translation is a straightforward process of temporal unfolding and (often) shifting. G10 Hz frequency, Formula 1 is unfolded to

$$(\text{query } AFS \ (\Rightarrow (< bat\_lvl \ low\_thresh) \ (\underline{or} \ (= s \ 0)(= next\_s \ 0)(= next2\_s \ 0))))), \tag{2}$$

where $next\_s$ and $next2\_s$ are auxiliary state variables denoting 1 and 2 time steps forward shifts of s respectively. Note the difference between the prefix "$next\_$" in the auxiliary state variable name and the temporal operator "next.". In case that the temporal operator is $\mathbf{X}$ instead of $\mathbf{F}$, Formula 1 is unfolded to

$$(\text{query } AFS \ (\Rightarrow (< bat\_lvl \ low\_thresh) \ (\underline{and} \ (= s \ 0)(= next\_s \ 0)(= next2\_s \ 0))))).$$

Each newly created auxiliary state variable needs to be declared and given a state transition in the Sally model. The state transition is given by the form of assigning the next time step state value. While an auxiliary state variable of the <u>past</u> time step can be easily assigned as "$(= next.prev\_s \ state.s)$", it is not easy to assign a <u>future</u> state variable without introducing more auxiliary variables than what are needed in the property. Naturally, entire Formula 2 can be shifted 2 time steps towards past, resulting in the plain Sally query in the generic form:

$$(\text{query } AFS \ (\Rightarrow (< prev2\_bat\_lvl \ prev2\_low\_thresh)$$
$$(or \ (= prev2\_s \ 0)(= prev\_s \ 0)(= s \ 0))))), \tag{3}$$

where $prev\_s$ and $prev2\_s$ are auxiliary state variables denoting 1 and 2 time steps backward shifts of s respectively.

Now, all state variables in Formula 3 are either on current or past time step. Their declarations and state transitions can be added to the original Sally model without introducing further more auxiliary state variables. The augmented Sally model is thereby a property-specific Sally model, because the choice of auxiliary state variables are property-specific. The entire process is done in an automatic fashion. Lastly, Sally tool verifies the property-specific Sally model against the plain Sally query. The complete data flow is summarized in Fig. 3.

5.3   Test Generation from Requirements

Testing is inherently incomplete and cannot be formalized in logic. The challenge is to make testing more rigorous and bring some notions of sufficiency and "completeness" for covering all relevant aspects of the behaviors expressed in the requirements. To this end, our approach is to base the testing upon the *behavioral operators* embedded in requirements – these are the nodes in the SSM created by the Text2Test tool, as described in Sect. 4.2.1. An *equivalence class* (of tests values) is pre-defined for each specific behavioral aspect of an operator, such that any single set of test operand/result values falling in the equivalence class is sufficient to test that behavior aspect.

To ensure that all behavioral operators present in the requirement set are covered sufficiently by testing, the test generation creates two sets of artifacts:

1. Test Oracles: A set of *test oracles* (test obligations) are created for each instance of a behavior operator in the SSM. A test oracle doesn't encode specific input/output values; rather it symbolically specifies the *equivalence-class* definition of operands and result values for a specific aspect of the operator's behavior. Figure 7 provides an example of equivalence-class specification for the switch operator.
2. Tests: A test created to satisfy a *test oracle* chooses specific value for the operands and results of the operator that satisfy the equivalence-class definition in the test oracle and then propagates these values to component's inputs/outputs as shown in Fig. 8. A test *satisfies* a particular test oracle if: 1) the components input values in the test, as propagated to the particular operator in the SSM graph, match the oracle's equivalence-class definition, and 2) the operator result value in the oracle, as propagated with observability to the component output, matches the test's expected value.

Creation of Test Oracles's Equivalence-Class Definitions. We use the well-established guidance in DO-178C [18] to base the testing criteria of the test oracles as in Fig. 6. These criteria have been matured over industrial product certifications such that the generated tests can detect several classes of design/coding error such as omissions and substitutions of operands, operators, and variable. To support a variety of application domains, Text2Test provides over 150 behavior operators including: Boolean, relational, arithmetic, time-dependent (timers, debounces, filters, integrators), a comprehensive library of basic algebraic, transcendental, and special math functions, and multidimensional interpolation tables. Text2Test tool configuration includes a formal definition of test oracles in the Test Oracle Specification Language for each behavioral operator. A test oracle is essentially an *equivalence class* specification where only one test case is required in each equivalence class. The language allows specification of boundary values, time-based behavior, and range constraints on values.

Each distinct aspect of the behavior of an operator is specified in a test oracle as an equivalence class:

a. Boundary values are used to construct equivalence classes where appropriate (e.g., relational operators)
b. For timers, filters, integrators, and delays, multiple execution steps are specified to verify time-dependent behaviors.
c. For state operators, the reachability of each state and transition is verified.
d. For arithmetic operators and functions:
   Numerically significant values for operands are used
   Separate equivalence classes are constructed around behavior pivot points (e.g., modulo operators)
e. For all operators, unique impact of each operand on the result is verified.
   Note: this ensures that the tests achieve modified condition/decision (MC/DC) structural coverage for Boolean expressions.
a. Behavior of the operator for invalid input values is verified (this satisfies robustness-testing objectives).

Fig. 6. Test oracle criteria for testing behavioral operators of requirements

Figure 7 shows the test oracle definition for the *switch* operator which represents the behavior of the "while ... otherwise ..." clause. Note that the equivalence class formula specifies that the values at the two input operands of the

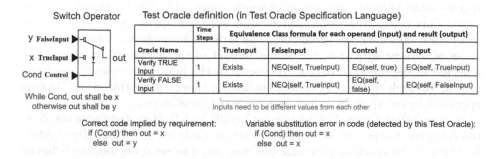

Switch Operator   Test Oracle definition (in Test Oracle Specification Language)

Oracle Name	Time Steps	Equivalence Class formula for each operand (input) and result (output)			
		TrueInput	FalseInput	Control	Output
Verify TRUE Input	1	Exists	NEQ(self, TrueInput)	EQ(self, true)	EQ(self, TrueInput)
Verify FALSE Input	1	Exists	NEQ(self, TrueInput)	EQ(self, false)	EQ(self, FalseInput)

While Cond, out shall be x
otherwise out shall be y   inputs need to be different values from each other

Correct code implied by requirement: Variable substitution error in code (detected by this Test Oracle):
if (Cond) then out = x   if (Cond) then out = x
else out = y   else out = x

Fig. 7. Definition of Test Oracles for the *Switch* Operator

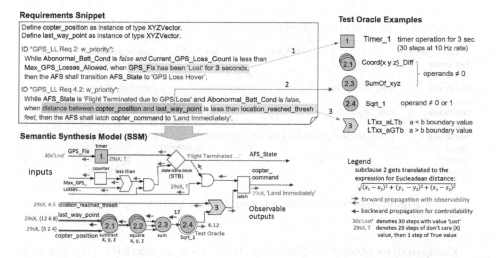

Fig. 8. Example of creation of test oracles and tests from requirements

switch (x and y in the requirement) need to be different so as to verify that the proper branch in the code was chosen. Such test will detect the type of variable substitution error in the code shown in the figure.

Figure 8 shows examples of derivation of test oracles from a requirement set. As aforementioned in Sect. 4.2.1 and Fig. 3, semantic transformations are applied to requirements to create the SSM. The nodes in SSM are the behavioral operators—each having a set of test oracles.

Creation of Tests. The tests are created by iterating over all the operators (nodes) in the SSM, considering one operator under test at a time. The test oracles of the operator under test are enumerated by evaluating each test oracle definition in the embedding context of this operator within the SSM. This yields constraints on the inputs values and expected output values of the operator for the test oracle. The next step is the backward and forward propagation of these constraints and values within the SSM to the component's inputs and outputs, using principles of controllability and observability [8]. Figure 8 shows the backward and forward propagation for the *Sqrt_1* operator's test oracle which require input value 17 and produces result value 4.12. The backward propagation occurs through the sum, square, and subtract operators, yielding {x,y,z} coordinate values for the two inputs. The forward propagation follows the principles of *observability*—i.e., the unique impact of the operator result should be reflected in the observed output. As shown in the figure, this entails also propagating through connected operators including timers, state-transition, Boolean operators to set up input values for several previous steps.

Figure 9 shows some test vectors for Insufficient Battery requirements. Note the reference to the specific test oracle before each set of vectors. Test vectors for the last test oracle require multiple time steps to set up before the behavior result is reached.

FunctionUnderTest	AFS_Insuff_Battery_Req_step				
	No. of Time Steps	Input:1	Input:2	Input:3	Output:1
ColumnName		GPS_Fix	bat_level	copter_position	AFS_State
Test Oracle	AND_59_False[1]		Description	False Output from Input [1]	
Vector	1	0 X		X	6
Test Oracle	AND_59_False[2]		Description	False Output from Input [2]	
Vector	1	1	49.9900017	X	4
Test Oracle	AND_59_All True		Description	True Output	
Vector	1	0	49.9900017	X	6
Test Oracle	STATE_AFS_State_Reach_State_Landed		Description	Reach State: Landed	
Vector	1	0	50.0099983	1000	0
Vector	1 X		51	0.101000004	0
Vector	1	1	51	0.100000001	4

Fig. 9. Test vector snippets for insufficient battery requirements

Compared to other test generation tools such as ASSERT [11], our approach is much more comprehensive, with a rigorous notion of coverage for all behaviors expressed in the requirements. For example, ASSERT mentions "condition, equivalence class, and boundary value analysis", but without imparting any notions of rigor or completeness across all behavior operators. Furthermore, approach for state/time related behaviors and observability is not provided.

6   Future Work and Conclusions

In this paper, we described our approach to formally analyze and generate testcases from requirements in an integrated manner. In our approach, we use the CLEAR notation to unambiguously capture requirements. The Text2Test tool is then used to automatically (a) perform formal analysis of generic properties of the requirements, (b) synthesize requirements models, and (c) generate requirements-based test cases based on equivalence class testing theory. Further, we leverage the Sally tool to model check if the generated model meets the application-specific properties. We used the Advanced Fail Safe (AFS) module of the ArduCopter rotorcraft to illustrate our approach. Our future work is focused on expanding the definition of CLEAR language to specify *ontic* data types with annotations, application-specific behavioral properties, and security and safety requirements and properties. We also plan to specify formal semantics for CLEAR constructs and their translation to SSM, supported by PVS proofs.

References

1. ArduPilot. https://ardupilot.org/ (2020)
2. Badger, J., Throop, D., Claunch, C.: Vared: verification and analysis of requirements and early designs. In: 2014 IEEE 22nd International Requirements Engineering Conference (RE), pp. 325–326 (2014). https://doi.org/10.1109/RE.2014.6912279
3. Bhatt, D., Chattopadhyay, A., Li, W., Oglesby, D., Owre, S., Shankar, N.: Contract-based verification of complex time-dependent behaviors in avionic systems. In: Rayadurgam, S., Tkachuk, O. (eds.) NFM 2016. LNCS, vol. 9690, pp. 34–40. Springer, Cham (2016). https://doi.org/10.1007/978-3-319-40648-0_3
4. Bhatt, D., et al.: Constrained Language Enhanced Approach to Requirements (CLEAR) Requirements-Driven Model Checking and Test Generation 19 User Guide. Technical report, Honeywell International, ARCOS Program Tech Report, August 2021
5. Bhatt, D., Madl, G., Oglesby, D.: System architecture driven software design analysis methodology and toolset. Technical report, SAE Technical Paper (2012)
6. Bhatt, D., Madl, G., Oglesby, D., Schloegel, K.: Towards scalable verification of commercial avionics software. In: Proceedings of the AIAA Infotech@ Aerospace Conference (2010)
7. Bhatt, D., Murugesan, A., Hall, B., Ren, H., Jeppu, Y.: The clear way to transparent formal methods. In: 4th Workshop on Formal Integrated Development Environment - FLoC 2018 (2018)
8. Certification Authorities Software Team (CAST) and others: rationale for accepting masking MC/DC in certification projects. Position Paper 6, Technical report (2001)

9. Cimatti, A., Clarke, E., Giunchiglia, F., Roveri, M.: NuSMV: a new symbolic model verifier. In: Halbwachs, N., Peled, D. (eds.) CAV 1999. LNCS, vol. 1633, pp. 495–499. Springer, Heidelberg (1999). https://doi.org/10.1007/3-540-48683-6_44

10. Conrad, E., Titolo, L., Giannakopoulou, D., Pressburger, T., Dutle, A.: A compositional proof framework for FRETish requirements (2022)

11. Crapo, A., Moitra, A., McMillan, C., Russell, D.: Requirements capture and analysis in assert (tm). In: 2017 IEEE 25th International Requirements Engineering Conference (RE), pp. 283–291. IEEE (2017)

12. Dutertre, B., Jovanovic, D., Navas, J.: Advanced symbolic analysis tools for fault-tolerant integrated distributed systems. NASA/CR-2018-21934, May 2018

13. Dutertre, B., Jovanović, D., Navas, J.A.: Verification of fault-tolerant protocols with sally. In: Dutle, A., Muñoz, C., Narkawicz, A. (eds.) NFM 2018. LNCS, vol. 10811, pp. 113–120. Springer, Cham (2018). https://doi.org/10.1007/978-3-319-77935-5_8

14. Fifarek, A.W., Wagner, L.G., Hoffman, J.A., Rodes, B.D., Aiello, M.A., Davis, J.A.: SpeAR v2.0: formalized past LTL specification and analysis of requirements. In: Barrett, C., Davies, M., Kahsai, T. (eds.) NFM 2017. LNCS, vol. 10227, pp. 420–426. Springer, Cham (2017). https://doi.org/10.1007/978-3-319-57288-8_30

15. Fuxman, A., Liu, L., Mylopoulos, J., Pistore, M., Roveri, M., Traverso, P.: Specifying and analyzing early requirements in tropos. Requirements Eng. 9(2), 132–150 (2004)

16. Halbwachs, N., Caspi, P., Raymond, P., Pilaud, D.: The synchronous data flow programming language lustre. Proc. IEEE 79(9), 1305–1320 (1991)

17. Holzmann, G.J.: The model checker spin. IEEE Trans. Software Eng. 23(5), 279–295 (1997)

18. RTCA Inc.: RTCA DO-178C, Software Considerations in Airborne Systems and Equipment Certification (2011)

19. RTCA Inc.: RTCA DO-333, Formal Methods Supplement to DO-178C and DO-278A (2011)

20. SAE: ARP4754A: Guidelines for Development of Civil Aircraft and Systems. SAE International (2010)

21. Shankar, N., et al.: DesCert: design for certification, DARPA automated rapid certification of software (ARCOS), technical area 1 (TA-1), Phase 1 Report. Technical Report, SRI International (October 21 2021), provided upon request at https://github.com/SRI-CSL/DesCert/tree/master/Reports/Phase1Report

22. SRI International's Computer Science Laboratory: Sally Model Checker. https://github.com/SRI-CSL/sally

Operational Annotations
A New Method for Sequential Program Verification

Paul C. Attie[(⊠)]

School of Computer and Cyber Sciences, Augusta University, Augusta, Georgia
PATTIE@augusta.edu

Abstract. I present a new method for specifying and verifying the partial correctness of sequential programs. The key observation is that, in Hoare logic, assertions are used as selectors of states, that is, an assertion specifies the set of program states that satisfy the assertion. Hence, the usual meaning of the partial correctness Hoare triple $\{f\}\,P\,\{g\}$: if execution is started in *any of the states that satisfy assertion* f, then, upon termination, the resulting state will be *some state that satisfies assertion* g. There are of course other ways to specify a set of states. Given a program α, the *post-states* of α are the states that α may terminate in, given that α starts executing in an arbitrary initial state. I introduce the *operational triple* $[\alpha]\,P\,[\beta]$ to mean: if execution of P is started in *any post-state of* α, then upon termination, the resulting state will be *some post-state of* β. Here, α is the *pre-program*, and plays the role of a pre-condition, and β is the *post-program*, and plays the role of a post-condition.

Keywords: Program verification · Hoare logic

1 Introduction

I present a system for verifying partial correctness of sequential programs. In contrast to Floyd-Hoare logic [6,10], I do not use pre-conditions and post-conditions, but rather *pre-programs* and *post-programs*. An assertion is essentially a means for defining a set of states: those for which the assertion evaluates to true. Hence the usual Hoare triple $\{f\}\,P\,\{g\}$ means that if execution of P is started in *any of the states that satisfy assertion* f, then, upon termination of P, the resulting state will be *some state that satisfies assertion* g. Another method of defining a set of states is with a sequential program α which starts execution in any state, i.e., with precondition *true*. The set of states in which α terminates (taken over all possible starting states) constitues the set of states that α defines. I call these the *post-states* of α.

I introduce the *operational triple* $[\alpha]\,P\,[\beta]$, in which α is the *pre-program*, β is the *post-program*, and P is the program being verified. The meaning of $[\alpha]\,P\,[\beta]$ is as follows. Consider executions of α that start in any state. From the final state of every such execution, P is executed. Let φ be the set of resulting final

© Springer Nature Switzerland AG 2022
J. V. Deshmukh et al. (Eds.): NFM 2022, LNCS 13260, pp. 597–615, 2022.
https://doi.org/10.1007/978-3-031-06773-0_32

states of P. That is, φ results from executing P from any post-state of α. Also, let ψ be the set of post-states of β, i.e., the set of final states that result from executing β starting in any state. Then, $[\alpha]\,P\,[\beta]$ is defined to mean $\varphi \subseteq \psi$. That is, the post-states of $\alpha; P$ are a subset of the post-states of β.

Contributions of the Paper. This paper makes the following contributions:

- *Code derivation/synthesis via trading*: Starting with a pre-program α and post-program β, parts of α can be "traded" into the actual program P, since they are both written in code. This gives a method of deriving program code from specification code, e.g., unwinding an outer loop of the pre-program and then trading it into the program can give initial code for a loop body of the program. This technique is illustrated in Sect. 6. Trading gives flexibility in developing both the program and the pre-program, as code can be freely moved between the program and the pre-program, and in some cases there is benefit to moving code from the program back into the pre-program; see [1] for examples of this. The Trading tactic is not available in logic-based verification methods, e.g., Floyd-Hoare logic [6,10] and separation logic [25].
- *Separation effect*: To deal with pointer-based structures required the extension of Hoare logic to separation logic [25]. For example, in the in-place reversal of a linked list, a key requirement is that the initial list not contain cycles. This requirement is expressible in my framework by a pre-program which a priori constructs an acyclic linked list. Section 6 gives such a pre-program: it declares an array n of Node objects (thereby making them all distinct) and then scans the array setting $n[i]$ to point to $n[i+1]$ (thereby constructing an acyclic linked list).
- *Practical application*: Since the pre-program α and the post-program β are not actually executed, they can be written without concern for efficiency, and they can refer to any well defined expression, e.g., $\delta[t]$ for the shortest path distance from a designated source s to node t. Nevertheless, being expressed as code, they may be easier for developers to write than logic specifications, since code is a formalism that developers are already well familiar with.

2   Related Work

The use of assertions to verify programs was introduced by Floyd [6] and Hoare [10]: a precondition f expresses what can be assumed to hold before execution of a program P, and a postcondition g expresses what must hold afterwards. The "Hoare triple" $\{f\}\,P\,\{g\}$ thus states that if f holds when execution of P starts, then g will hold upon termination of P. If termination is not required, this is known as *partial correctness*, and if termination is required we have *total correctness*. Both precondition and postcondition are expressed as a formula of a suitable logic, e.g., first order logic. Subsequently, Dijkstra introduced the *weakest precondition predicate transformer* [5]: $wp(P, g)$ is the weakest predicate f whose truth before execution of P guarantees termination of P in a state satisfying g. He then used weakest preconditions to define a method for formally deriving a program from a specification, expressed as a precondition-postcondition pair. Later, Hoare observed that the Hoare triple can be expressed operationally, when he wrote "$\{p\}\, q\, \{r\} \triangleq p; q < r$" in [11], but he does not seem to have developed this observation into a proof system.

The formalization of specifications and program correctness has lead to a rich and extensive literature on program verification and refinement. Hoare's original rules [10] were extended to deal with non-determinism, fair selection, and procedures [7]. Separation logic [25] was devised to deal with pointer-based structures.

A large body of work deals with the notion of *program refinement* [2, 20]: start with an initial artifact, which serves as a specification, and gradually refine it into an executable and efficient program. This proceeds incrementally, in a sequence of refinement steps, each of which preserves a "refinement ordering" relation $\sqsubseteq$, so that we have $P_0 \sqsubseteq \ldots \sqsubseteq P_n$, where P_0 is the initial specification and P_n is the final program. Morgan [20] starts with a pre-condition/post-condition specification and refines it into an executable program using rules that are similar in spirit to Dijkstra's weakest preconditions [5]. Back and Wright [2] use *contracts*, which consist of assertions (failure to hold causes a breach of the contract), assumptions (failure to hold causes vacuous satisfaction of the contract), and executable code. As such, contracts subsume both pre-condition/post-condition pairs and executable programs, and so serve as an artifact for the seamless refinement of a pre-condition/post-condition specification into a program.

A related development has been the application of monads to programming [18, 19]. A monad is an endofunctor T over a category C together with a unit natural transformation from 1_C (the identity functor over C) to T and a multiplication natural transformation from T^2 to T. The Hoare state monad contains Hoare triples (precondition, program, postcondition) [12], and a computation maps an initial state to a pair consisting of a final state and a returned value. The unit is the monadic operation return, which lifts returned values into the state monad, and the multiplication is the monadic operation bind, which composes two computations, passing the resulting state and returned value of the first computation to the second [28]. The Dijkstra monad captures functions from postconditions to preconditions [12, 27]. The return operation gives the weakest precondition of a pure computation, and the bind operation gives the weakest precondition for a composition of two computations.

Hoare logic and weakest preconditions are purely assertional proof methods. Monads combine operational and assertional techniques, since they provide operations which return the assertions that are used in the correctness proofs. My approach is purely operational, since it uses no assertions (formula in a suitable logic) but rather pre- and post-programs instead. My approach thus represents the operational endpont of the assertional–operational continuum, with Hoare logic/weakest preconditions at the other (assertional) endpoint, and monads somewhere in between.

3   Syntax and Semantics of the Programming Language

I use a basic programming language consisting of primitive types, arrays, and reference types, assignments, if statements, while loops, for loops, procedure definition and invocation, class definition, object creation and referencing. I assume standard primitive types (integers, boolean etc.) and the usual semantics for reference types: object identifiers are pointers to the object, and the identity of an object is given by its location in memory, so that two objects are identical iff they occupy the same memory. Parameter passing is by value, but as usual a passed array/object reference allows the called procedure to manipulate the original array/object.

My syntax is standard and self-explanatory. I also use [] to denote nondeterministic choice between two commands [9]. For integers i, j with $i \leqslant j$, I use $x := [i : j]$ as syntactic sugar for $x := i [] \cdots [] x := j$, i.e., a random assignment of a value in $i, \ldots, j$ to x. This plays the role of the range assertion $i \leqslant x \leqslant j$ in Hoare logic. I use tt for true, ff for false, and $skip$ for the statement that terminates immediately with no change of state.

My proof method relies on (1) the axioms and inference rules introduced in this paper, and (2) an underlying method for establishing program equivalence. Any semantics in which the above are valid can be used. For concreteness, I assume a standard small-step (SOS) operational semantics [24, 26].

An **execution** of program P is a finite sequence $s_0, s_1, \ldots, s_n$ of states such that (1) s_i results from a single small step of P in state s_{i-1}, for all $i \in 1, \ldots, n$, (2) s_0 is an initial state of P, and (3) s_n is a final (terminating) state of P. A **behavior** of program P is a pair of states (s, t) such that (1) $s_0, s_1, \ldots, s_n$ is an execution of P, $s = s_0$, and $t = s_n$. Write $\{|P|\}$ for the set of behaviors of P.

4   Operational Annotations

I use a sequential program to specify a set of states. There is no constraint on the initial states, and the specified set is the set of all possible final states. If any initialization of variables is required, this must be done explicitly by the program.

Definition 1 (Post-state set). *For a terminating program P,*

$$post(P) \triangleq \{t \mid (\exists s : (s, t) \in \{|P|\})\}.$$

That is, $post(P)$ is the set of all possible final states of P, given any initial state. Infinite (nonterminating) executions of P do not contribute to the post-state set. The complete state set is specified by the program $skip$, and the empty state set by the program $while\ (tt)\ skip$. The central definition of the paper is that of *operational triple* $[\alpha] P [\beta]$:

Definition 2 (Operational triple). *Let α, P, and β be programs. Then*

$$[\alpha] P [\beta] \triangleq post(\alpha; P) \subseteq post(\beta).$$

Recall the meaning of $[\alpha] P [\beta]$: every terminating execution of $\alpha; P$ ends in a state that is also a final state of some terminating execution of β. Thus $[\alpha] P [\beta]$ specifies *partial correctness*, since it deals only with terminating executions, and permits P to have non-terminating executions. Even α and β can have non-terminating executions; these do not change the meaning of the specification, since they do not change the post-state set. If α (β) has only nonterminating executions then $post(\alpha) = \emptyset$, ($post(\beta) = \emptyset$), which is akin to a false precondition (postcondition). So if α or P (or both) has only nonterminating executions, then $[\alpha] P [\beta]$ is vacuously true. If β has only nonterminating executions, then $[\alpha] P [\beta]$ is false, unless α or P (or both) has only nonterminating executions.

4.1   Program Ordering and Equivalence

The next section presents a deductive system for establishing validity of operational triples. The rules of inference use three kinds of hypotheses: (1) operational triples (over "substatements" as usual), and (2) program ordering assertions $P \preceq Q$, and (3) program equivalence assertions $P \equiv Q$.

Definition 3 (Program ordering, $\preceq$). $P \preceq Q \triangleq post(P) \subseteq post(Q)$.

Here P is "stronger" than Q since it has fewer post-states (w.r.t., the precondition tt, i.e., all possible pre-states), and so P produces an output which satisfies, in general, more constraints than the output of Q. This is *not* the same as the usual program refinement relation, since the mapping from pre-states to post-states induced by the execution of P is not considered. Also, the "direction" of the inclusion relation is reversed w.r.t. the usual refinement ordering, where we write $Q \sqsubseteq P$ to denote that "P refines Q", i.e., P satisfies more specifications than Q.

The operational triple is expressible as program ordering, since by Definition 3, $[\alpha] P [\beta] \triangleq \alpha; P \preceq \beta$.

If one increases the set of states in which a program can start execution, then the set of states in which the program terminates is also possibly increased, and is certainly not decreased. That is, the set of post-states is monotonic in the set of pre-states. Since prefixing a program α with another program γ simply restricts the states in which α starts execution, I have the following.

Proposition 1. $\gamma; \alpha \preceq \alpha$.

Definition 4 (Program equivalence, $\equiv$). *Programs P and Q are equivalent iff they have the same behaviors:* $P \equiv Q \triangleq \{\!|P|\!\} = \{\!|Q|\!\}$.

That is, I take as program equivalence the equality of program behaviors. Note that equivalence is *not* ordering in both directions. This discrepancy is because ordering is used for weakening/strengthening laws (and so post-state inclusion is sufficient) while equivalence is used for substitution, and so, for programs at least, equality of behaviors is needed.

Any method for establishing program ordering and equivalence is sufficient for my needs. The ordering and equivalence proofs in this paper are informal, and based on obvious concepts such as the commutativity of assignment statements that modify different variables/objects.

Future work includes investigating proof systems for program equivalence [3,4,13,22,23]. Some of these are mechanized, and some use bisimulation and circular reasoning. I will look into using these works for formally establishing program equivalence hypotheses needed in my examples (which are then akin to Hoare logic verification conditions), and to adapting these systems to establish program ordering, e.g., replace bisimulation by simulation.

5   A Deductive System for Operational Annotations

Table 1 presents a deductive system for operational annotations. Soundness of the system is formally established in the full version of the paper [1]. I do not provide a rule for the **for** loop, since it can be easily turned into a **while**. The following are informal intuition for the axioms and inference rules.

Sequence Axiom. If P executes after pre-program α, the result is identical to post-program $\alpha; P$, i.e., the sequential composition of α and P. This gives an easy way to calculate a post-program for given pre-program and program. The corresponding Hoare logic notion, namely the strongest postcondition, is easy to compute (in closed form) only for straight-line code.

Empty Pre-program. Program P is "doing all the work", and so the resulting post-program is also P. Having *skip* as a pre-program is similar to having *tt* as a precondition in Hoare logic.

Empty Program. This is analogous to the axiom for *skip* in Hoare logic: $\{f\}$ *skip* $\{f\}$, since *skip* has no effect on the program state.

Trading Rule. Sequential composition is associative: $\alpha; (P1; P2) \equiv (\alpha; P1); P2$. By Definitions 1, 4: $post(\alpha; (P1; P2)) = post((\alpha; P1); P2)$. Hence, if the program is a sequential composition $P1; P2$, I can take $P1$ and add it to the end of the pre-program α. I can also go in the reverse direction, so technically there are two rules of inference here. I will refer to both rules as (*Trading*). This *seamless transfer between program and pre-program has no analogue in Hoare logic*, and provides a major tactic for the derivation of programs from operational specifications.

Append Rule. Appending the same program γ to the program and the post-program preserves the validity of an operational triple. This is useful for appending new code into both the program and the post-program.

Substitution Rule. Since the definition of operational annotation refers only to the behavior of a program, it follows that one equivalent program can be replaced by another. This rule is useful for performing equivalence-preserving transformations, such as loop unwinding.

Table 1. Axioms and rules of inference

$[\alpha]\, P\, [\alpha; P]$ $\hspace{6cm}$ *(Sequence Axiom)*

$[skip]\, P\, [P]$ $\hspace{6cm}$ *(Empty Pre-program)*

$[\alpha]\, skip\, [\alpha]$ $\hspace{6cm}$ *(Empty Program)*

$[\alpha]\, P1; P2\, [\beta]$ iff $[\alpha; P1]\, P2\, [\beta]$ $\hspace{3cm}$ *(Trading)*

$$\frac{[\alpha]\, P\, [\beta]}{[\alpha]\, P; \gamma\, [\beta; \gamma]} \hspace{5cm} \textit{(Append)}$$

$$\frac{\alpha \equiv \alpha' \quad P \equiv P' \quad \beta \equiv \beta' \quad [\alpha]\, P\, [\beta]}{[\alpha']\, P'\, [\beta']} \hspace{3cm} \textit{(Substitution)}$$

$$\frac{\alpha \preceq \alpha' \quad [\alpha']\, P\, [\beta]}{[\alpha]\, P\, [\beta]} \hspace{4cm} \textit{(Pre-program Strengthening)}$$

$$\frac{[\alpha]\, P\, [\beta'] \quad \beta' \preceq \beta}{[\alpha]\, P\, [\beta]} \hspace{4cm} \textit{(Post-program Weakening)}$$

$$\frac{[\alpha]\, P1\, [\beta] \quad [\beta]\, P2\, [\gamma]}{[\alpha]\, P1; P2\, [\gamma]} \hspace{3.5cm} \textit{(Sequential Composition)}$$

$$\frac{[\alpha']\, P\, [\alpha]}{[\alpha]\, while(B)\, P\, elihw\, [\beta]} \; \alpha' \cong (\alpha, B), \beta \cong (\alpha, \neg B) \hspace{1.5cm} \textit{(While)}$$

$$\frac{[\alpha']\, P\, [\gamma; \alpha]}{[\alpha]\, while(B)\, P\, elihw\, [\beta]} \; \alpha' \cong (\alpha, B), \beta \simeq (\alpha, \neg B) \hspace{1cm} \textit{(While Consequence)}$$

$$\frac{[\alpha']\, P1\, [\beta] \quad [\alpha'']\, P2\, [\beta]}{[\alpha]\, \textit{if } B \textit{ then } P1 \textit{ else } P2 \textit{ fi}\, [\beta]} \; \alpha' \cong (\alpha, B), \alpha'' \cong (\alpha, \neg B) \hspace{1cm} \textit{(If)}$$

$$\frac{[\alpha']\, P\, [\beta] \quad \alpha'' \preceq \beta}{[\alpha]\, \textit{if } B \textit{ then } P \textit{ fi}\, [\beta]} \; \alpha' \cong (\alpha, B), \alpha'' \cong (\alpha, \neg B) \hspace{1cm} \textit{(One-way If)}$$

Pre-program Strengthening. Reducing the set of post-states of the pre-program cannot invalidate an operational triple.

Post-program Weakening. Enlarging the set of post-states of the post-program cannot invalidate an operational triple.

Sequential Composition. The post-state set of β serves as the intermediate state-set in the execution of $P1; P2$: it characterizes the possible states after $P1$ executes and before $P2$ executes.

While Rule. Given $[\alpha]\, P\, [\alpha]$, I wish to conclude $[\alpha]\, \textbf{\textit{while}}(B)\, P\, \textbf{\textit{elihw}}\, [\beta]$ where β is a "conjunction" of α and $\neg B$, i.e., the post-states of β are those that are post-states of α, and also that satisfy assertion $\neg B$, the negation of the looping condition. Also, I wish to weaken the hypothesis of the rule from $[\alpha]\, P\, [\alpha]$ to $[\alpha']\, P\, [\alpha]$, where α' is a "conjunction" of α and B, i.e., the post-states of α' are those that are post-states of α and that also satisfy assertion B, the looping condition. I therefore define the "conjunction" of a program and an assertion as follows. Let α', α be programs and B a Boolean expression. Then define $\alpha' \cong (\alpha, B) \triangleq post(\alpha') = post(\alpha) \cap \{s \mid s(B) = tt\}$. Note that this definition does not produce a unique result, and so is really a relation rather than a mapping. The construction of α' is not straightforward, in general, for arbitrary assertions B. Fortunately, most looping conditions are simple, typically a loop counter reaching a limit. I therefore define the needed program α' by the semantic condition given above, and leave the problem of deriving α' from α and B to another occasion.

Given a while loop $\textbf{\textit{while}}(B)\, P\, \textbf{\textit{elihw}}$ and pre-program α, let α' be a program such that $\alpha' \cong (\alpha, B)$, and let β be a program such that $\beta \cong (\alpha, \neg B)$. The hypothesis of the rule is: execute α and restrict the set of post-states to those in which B holds. That is, have α' as a pre-program for the loop body P. First assume that B holds initially. Then, after P is executed, the total resulting effect must be the same as executing just α. So, α is a kind of "operational invariant". Given that this holds, and taking α as a pre-program for $\textbf{\textit{while}}(B)\, P\, \textbf{\textit{elihw}}$, then upon termination, we have α as a post-program. On the last iteration of the while loop, B is false, and the operational invariant α still holds. In case B is initially false, the while loop terminates immediately with no change of state. Hence α holds, since it held initially, and B is false. Hence in both cases I can assert β as a post-program for the $\textbf{\textit{while}}$ loop.

While Rule with Consequence. By applying Proposition 1 and (*Post-program Weakening*) to (*While*), I obtain (*While Consequence*), which states that the operational invariant can be a "suffix" of the actual post-program of the loop body. This is often convenient, in practice.

If Rule. Let α be the pre-program. Assume that execution of $P1$ with pre-program $\alpha' \cong (\alpha, B)$ leads to post-program β, and that execution of $P2$ with pre-program $\alpha'' \cong (\alpha, \neg B)$ also leads to post-program β. Then, execution of $\textbf{\textit{if}}\, B\, \textbf{\textit{then}}\, P1\, \textbf{\textit{else}}\, P2\, \textbf{\textit{fi}}$ with pre-program α leads to post-program β.

One-Way If Rule. Assume that execution of $P1$ with pre-program $\alpha' \cong (\alpha, B)$ leads to post-program β. Also assume that any post-state of α is also a post-state of β. Then execution of $\textbf{\textit{if}}\, B\, \textbf{\textit{then}}\, P1\, \textbf{\textit{fi}}$ with pre-program α always leads to post-program β.

A notable omission from the above rules is an assignment axiom. Letting P be $x := e$ in (*Sequence Axiom*), I obtain $[\alpha] \, x := e \, [\alpha; x := e]$. This can be regarded as the operational analogue of the Hoare Logic assignment axiom. The post-program $\alpha; x := e$ can then be further manipulated, e.g., by equivalence transformations, or by being a pre-program for the statement following $x := e$.

6   Example: In-Place List Reversal

I now illustrate the use of operational annotations to derive a correct algorithm for the in-place reversal of a linked list. The full version [1] also contains examples of deriving selection sort, Dijkstra's shortest path algorithm, and binary search tree node insertion, from operational specifications. (*Trading*) is used heavily in all these examples. Throughout, I use informal arguments for program equivalence, based on well-known transformations such as eliminating the empty program *skip*, and unwinding the last iteration of a ***for*** loop. Pre/post-programs are written in bold red italics, and regular programs are written in typewriter.

The input is a size $\ell + 1$ array n of objects of type Node, where $\ell \geqslant 3$, and indexed from 0 to $\ell - 1$. The last element is set to NIL and serves as a sentinel. Node is declared as follows: *class* Node{Node p; other fields...}. Element i is referred to as n_i instead of $n[i]$, and contains a pointer $n_i.p$, and possibly other (omitted) fields. The use of this array is purely for specification purposes, so that I can construct the initial linked list from elements $n_0, \ldots, n_{\ell-1}$. An array also ensures that there is no aliasing: all elements are distinct, by construction. Array n is created by executing Node[] $n := new$ Node[$\ell + 1$]; $n.\ell :=$ NIL. The pre-program and post-program both start with code to declare Node, followed by the above line to create array n. I omit this code as including it would be repetitive and would add clutter.

I start by applying (*Empty Program*), which gives the following:

$$i := [0 : \ell - 3];$$
$$\textbf{\textit{for}} \ (j = 0 \ \textbf{\textit{to}} \ \ell - 1) \ n_j.p := n_{j+1} \, \textbf{\textit{rof}};$$
$$\textbf{\textit{for}} \ (j = 1 \ \textbf{\textit{to}} \ i + 1) \ n_j.p := n_{j-1} \, \textbf{\textit{rof}};$$
$$r := n_{i+1}; s := n_{i+2}; t := n_{i+3}$$

```
skip
```

$$i := [0 : \ell - 3];$$
$$\textbf{\textit{for}} \ (j = 0 \ \textbf{\textit{to}} \ \ell - 1) \ n_j.p := n_{j+1} \, \textbf{\textit{rof}};$$
$$\textbf{\textit{for}} \ (j = 1 \ \textbf{\textit{to}} \ i + 1) \ n_j.p := n_{j-1} \, \textbf{\textit{rof}};$$
$$r := n_{i+1}; s := n_{i+2}; t := n_{i+3}$$

The pre (and post) programs do three things: (1) construct the linked list by setting $n_j.p$ to point to the next node n_{j+1}, including the last "real" node $n_{\ell-1}$, which points to the sentinel n_ℓ, and (2) reverse part of the list, up to position $i+1$, by setting $n_j.p$ to point to the previous node n_{j-1}, for j from $i+1$ down to the second node n_1, and (3) maintain 3 pointers, into positions $i+1$, $i+2$, and $i+3$. The pre (post) programs are simple enough that I take their correctness for granted. The topic of writing correct specifications is of course a major concern of software engineering [29]. One of the possible post-states of the pre (post) programs has $t = n_\ell$; this is the termination state for the overall algorithm, as we will see. Now unwind the last iteration of the second **for** loop of the pre-program. So, by (*Substitution*)

$$i := [0 : \ell - 3];$$
for $(j = 0$ **to** $\ell - 1)$ $n_j.p := n_{j+1}$ **rof**;
for $(j = 1$ **to** $i)$ $n_j.p := n_{j-1}$ **rof**;
$$n_{i+1}.p := n_i;$$
$$r := n_{i+1}; s := n_{i+2}; t := n_{i+3}$$
skip
$$i := [0 : \ell - 3];$$
for $(j = 0$ **to** $\ell - 1)$ $n_j.p := n_{j+1}$ **rof**;
for $(j = 1$ **to** $i + 1)$ $n_j.p := n_{j-1}$ **rof**;
$$r := n_{i+1}; s := n_{i+2}; t := n_{i+3}$$

Now introduce $r := n_i; s := n_{i+1}; t := n_{i+2}$ into the pre-program. Since r, s, t are subsequently overwritten, and not referenced in the interim, this preserves equivalence of the pre-program with its previous version. So, by (*Substitution*)

$$i := [0 : \ell - 3];$$
for $(j = 0$ **to** $\ell - 1)$ $n_j.p := n_{j+1}$ **rof**;
for $(j = 1$ **to** $i)$ $n_j.p := n_{j-1}$ **rof**;
$$r := n_i; s := n_{i+1}; t := n_{i+2};$$
$$n_{i+1}.p := n_i;$$
$$r := n_{i+1}; s := n_{i+2}; t := n_{i+3}$$
skip
$$i := [0 : \ell - 3];$$
for $(j = 0$ **to** $\ell - 1)$ $n_j.p := n_{j+1}$ **rof**;
for $(j = 1$ **to** $i + 1)$ $n_j.p := n_{j-1};$ **rof**;
$$r := n_{i+1}; s := n_{i+2}; t := n_{i+3}$$

Now apply (*Trading*) to move the last two lines of the pre-program into the program, and remove the *skip* since it is no longer needed.

$$i := [0 : \ell - 3];$$
for $(j = 0$ **to** $\ell - 1)$ $n_j.p := n_{j+1}$ **rof**;
for $(j = 1$ **to** $i)$ $n_j.p := n_{j-1}$ **rof**;
$$r := n_i; s := n_{i+1}; t := n_{i+2}$$
$$\mathbf{n_{i+1}.p := n_i};$$
$$\mathbf{r := n_{i+1}; s := n_{i+2}; t := n_{i+3}}$$
$$i := [0 : \ell - 3];$$
for $(j = 0$ **to** $\ell - 1)$ $n_j.p := n_{j+1}$ **rof**;
for $(j = 1$ **to** $i + 1)$ $n_j.p := n_{j-1}$ **rof**;
$$r := n_{i+1}; s := n_{i+2}; t := n_{i+3}$$

To avoid repetitive text, and to anticipate the development of the operational invariant for the while loop that goes through the linked list, I define the abbreviations

$inv \triangleq$

> $for \ (j = 0 \ to \ \ell - 1) \ n_j.p := n_{j+1} \, rof;$
> $for \ (j = 1 \ to \ i) \ n_j.p := n_{j-1} \, rof;$
> $r := n_i; s := n_{i+1}; t := n_{i+2}$

and

$inv' \triangleq$

> $for \ (j = 0 \ to \ \ell - 1) \ n_j.p := n_{j+1} \, rof;$
> $for \ (j = 1 \ to \ i) \ n_j.p := n_{j-1} \, rof;$
> $r := n_{i+1}; s := n_{i+2}; t := n_{i+3}$

Since $r := n_i; s := n_{i+1}$ immediately precedes $\mathbf{n_{i+1}.p} := \mathbf{n_i}$, I can replace $\mathbf{n_{i+1}.p} := \mathbf{n_i}$ by $\mathbf{s.p} := \mathbf{r}$ while retaining equivalence. So, by (*Substitution*)

> $i := [0 : \ell - 3]; inv$
> $\mathbf{s.p} := \mathbf{r};$
> $\mathbf{r} := \mathbf{n_{i+1}}; \mathbf{s} := \mathbf{n_{i+2}}; \mathbf{t} := \mathbf{n_{i+3}}$
> $i := [0 : \ell - 3]; inv'$

Since $s := n_{i+1}$ precedes $\mathbf{r} := \mathbf{n_{i+1}}$ and s is not modified in the interim, I can replace $\mathbf{r} := \mathbf{n_{i+1}}$ by $\mathbf{r} := \mathbf{s}$ while retaining equivalence. Likewise, since $t := n_{i+2}$ precedes $\mathbf{s} := \mathbf{n_{i+2}}$, and t is not modified in the interim, I can replace $\mathbf{s} := \mathbf{n_{i+2}}$ by $\mathbf{s} := \mathbf{t}$. So, by (*Substitution*) applied twice, I obtain

> $i := [0 : \ell - 3]; inv$
> $\mathbf{s.p} := \mathbf{r};$
> $\mathbf{r} := \mathbf{s}; \mathbf{s} := \mathbf{t}; \mathbf{t} := \mathbf{n_{i+3}}$
> $i := [0 : \ell - 3]; inv'$

From $for \ (j = 0 \ to \ \ell - 1) \ n_j.p := n_{i+1} \, rof$, I have $n_{i+2}.p := n_{i+3}$, and I observe that $n_{i+2}.p$ is not subsequently modified. Also I have $t := n_{i+2}$ occurring before the program, and t is not modified until $\mathbf{t} := \mathbf{n_{i+3}}$, so I can replace $\mathbf{t} := \mathbf{n_{i+3}}$ by $\mathbf{t} := \mathbf{t.p}$. Hence by (*Substitution*)

> $i := [0 : \ell - 3]; inv$
> $\mathbf{s.p} := \mathbf{r};$
> $\mathbf{r} := \mathbf{s}; \mathbf{s} := \mathbf{t}; \mathbf{t} := \mathbf{t.p}$
> $i := [0 : \ell - 3]; inv'$

Now apply (*While*) to obtain the complete program, while also incrementing the loop counter i at the end of the loop body.

> $for \ (j = 0 \ to \ \ell - 1) \ n_j.p := n_{j+1} \, rof$
> $\mathbf{r} := \mathbf{n_0}; \mathbf{s} := \mathbf{n_1}; \mathbf{t} := \mathbf{n_2}$

```
i := 0; inv
while (i ≠ ℓ − 2)
        i := [0 : ℓ − 3]; inv
    s.p := r;
    r := s; s := t; t := t.p
        i := [0 : ℓ − 3]; inv′
    i := i + 1;
        i := [1 : ℓ − 2]; inv
elihw
    i := ℓ − 2; inv
```

Upon termination, $i := \ell - 2$ expresses the negation of the looping condition, and so forms part of the post-program of the while loop, together with the operational invariant inv. I add $i := i + 1$ at the end of the loop body to re-establish the invariant. The justification for this is equivalence between $i := [0 : \ell - 3]; inv'$; $i := i + 1$ and $i := [1 : \ell - 2]; inv$, i.e., between (1) the range for i before incrementing, followed by the "modified" invariant inv', followed by the increment of i, and (2) the range for i after incrementing, followed by the invariant inv.

The loop terminates when t reaches the sentinel, i.e., when $t = n_\ell$. Since $t := n_{i+2}$ in the operational invariant, this requires $i = \ell - 2$. The post-program of the loop then gives $for\ (j = 1\ to\ \ell - 2)\ n_j.p := n_{j-1}\ rof$, which means that the last node's pointer is not set to the previous node, since the list ends at index $\ell - 1$. Hence we require a final assignment that is equivalent to $n_{\ell-1}.p := n_{\ell-2}$.

The post-program also gives $i := \ell - 2; r := n_i; s := n_{i+1}; t := n_{i+2}$, which yields $i := \ell - 2; r := n_{\ell-2}; s := n_{\ell-1}; t := n_\ell$. Hence the last assignment can be rendered as $s.p := r$. Also, the loop termination condition can be rewritten as $t \neq \text{NIL}$, since t becomes NIL when it is assigned n_ℓ, which happens exactly when i becomes $\ell - 2$. Hence, using (*Substitution*) and (*Post-program Weakening*), I obtain

```
for (j = 0 to ℓ − 1) n_j.p := n_{j+1} rof
r := n_0; s := n_1; t := n_2
i := 0; inv
while (t ≠ NIL)
        i := [0 : ℓ − 3]; inv
    s.p := r;
    r := s; s := t; t := t.p
        i := [0 : ℓ − 3]; inv′
    i := i + 1;
        i := [1 : ℓ − 2]; inv
elihw;
    i := ℓ − 2; inv
s.p := r
for (j = 0 to ℓ − 1) n_j.p := n_{j+1} rof;
for (j = 1 to ℓ − 1) n_j.p := n_{j-1} rof
```

Now, as desired, the "loop counter" i is no longer needed as a program variable, and can be converted to an auxiliary ("ghost") variable. The result is

$$\textbf{for } (j = 0 \textbf{ to } \ell - 1) \ n_j.p := n_{j+1} \textbf{rof}$$
$$\textbf{r} := \textbf{n}_0; \textbf{s} := \textbf{n}_1; \textbf{t} := \textbf{n}_2$$
$$i := 0; \ inv$$
$$\textbf{while } (\textbf{t} \neq \text{NIL})$$
$$\qquad i := [0 : \ell - 3]; \ inv$$
$$\qquad \textbf{s.p} := \textbf{r};$$
$$\qquad \textbf{r} := \textbf{s}; \textbf{s} := \textbf{t}; \textbf{t} := \textbf{t.p}$$
$$\qquad i := [1 : \ell - 2]; \ inv$$
$$\textbf{elihw};$$
$$i := \ell - 2; \ inv$$
$$\textbf{s.p} := \textbf{r}$$
$$\textbf{for } (j = 0 \textbf{ to } \ell - 1) \ n_j.p := n_{j+1} \textbf{rof};$$
$$\textbf{for } (j = 1 \textbf{ to } \ell - 1) \ n_j.p := n_{j-1} \textbf{rof}$$

Upon termination, $\textbf{s}$ points to the head of the reversed list. The post-program is quite pleasing: it constructs the list, and then immediately reverses it!

7   Operational Annotations for Procedures

Let *pname* be a non-recursive procedure with parameter passing by value, and with body *pbody*. Let $\bar{a}$ denote a list of actual parameters, and let $\bar{f}$ denote a list of formal parameters. An actual parameter is either an object identifier or an expression over primitive types, and a formal parameter is either an object identifier or a primitive-type identifier.

Let r be an identifier matching the return type of *pname*, and not occurring in *pbody*. To avoid complex substitutions I assume that: (1) all local variables/objects in *pbody* do not have the same identifier as any variable/object in the calling context and (2) there is only a single return statement, which is the last statement of *pbody*. These assumptions are not fundamental; they can be removed at the price of somewhat more complex rules.

$$pname(\bar{a}) \ \equiv \ \bar{f} := \bar{a}; \ pbody[skip/\textbf{return}] \qquad (Equiv\ Nonrecursive\ Void)$$

$$r := pname(\bar{a}) \ \equiv \ \bar{f} := \bar{a}; \ pbody[r := e/\textbf{return}(e)] \qquad (Equiv\ Nonrecursive)$$

Equiv Nonrecursive Void handles calls where the returned value does not exist (void return type). *Equiv Nonrecursive* handles assignment of the returned value to r by textually replacing $\textbf{return}(e)$ by $r := e$ in the procedure body. Consider the linked list reversal algorithm above, packaged as a procedure:

```
Node Procedure listRev(Node h) {
      r := h; s := h.p; t := h.p.p;
      while (t ≠ NIL)
            s.p := r;
```

```
        r := s; s := t; t := t.p
        elihw;
        s.p := r;
        return(s)
}
```

Now consider a call $v := listRev(\ell)$ where ℓ is the head of a linked list. By (*Equiv Nonrecursive*), I have:

```
v := listRev(ℓ) ≡ {
        h := ℓ;
        r := h; s := h.p; t := h.p.p;
        while (t ≠ NIL)
                s.p := r;
                r := s; s := t; t := t.p
        elihw;
        s.p := r;
        v := s
}
```

This gives the correct effect for the procedure call $listRev(\ell)$, namely that v points to the head of the reversed list. In particular, both primitive and reference types (as parameters) are handled correctly, and need not be distinguished in the above rules.

For recursive procedures, an inductive proof method is needed, as usual. I use an inductive rule to establish the equivalence between a sequence of two procedure calls and a third procedure call. These correspond, respectively, to the pre-program, the program, and the post-program. The method is as follows:

1. Let α, P, β be recursive procedures which give, respectively, the pre-program, program, and post-program
2. To establish $\alpha; P \equiv \beta$ I proceed as follows:
   (a) Start with $\alpha; P$, replace the calls by their corresponding bodies, and then use a sequence of equivalence-preserving transformations to bring any recursive calls $\alpha'; P'$ next to each other
   (b) Use the inductive hypothesis for equivalence of the recursive calls $\alpha'; P' \equiv \beta'$ to replace $\alpha'; P'$ by β'
   (c) Use more equivalence-preserving transformations to show that the resulting program is equivalent to β

The appropriate rule of inference is as follows:

$$\frac{\alpha'; P' \equiv \beta' \;\vdash\; \alpha; P \equiv \beta}{\alpha; P \equiv \beta} \quad (\textit{Equiv Recursive}) \quad (1)$$

where $\vdash$ means "is deducible from". Thus, if we prove $\alpha; P \equiv \beta$ (pre-program followed by program is equivalent to post-program) by assuming $\alpha'; P' \equiv \beta'$ (a recursive invocation of the pre-program followed by a recursive invocation of the program is equivalent to a recursive invocation of the post-program), then we conclude, by induction on recursive calls, that $\alpha; P \equiv \beta$.

The following example verifies the standard recursive algorithm for node insertion into a binary search tree (BST). Each node n consists of three fields: $n.key$ gives the key value for node n, $n.\ell$ points to the left child of n (if any), and $n.r$ points to the right child of n (if any). The constructor Node(k) returns a new node with key value k and null left and right child pointers. I assume that all key values in the tree are unique. For clarity, I retain red italics for specification code and black typewriter for program code. Procedure insert(T,k) gives the standard recursive algorithm for insertion of key k into a BST with root T.

insert(T, k)::

```
if (T = NIL) T := new Node(k);
else if (k < T.key) insert(T.ℓ, k);
else insert(T.r, k);
```

To verify the correctness of insert(T,k), I define two recursive procedures $ct(T, \psi)$ and $cti(T, \psi, k)$. $ct(T, \psi)$ takes a set ψ of key values, constructs a random binary search tree containing exactly these values, and sets T to point to the root of this tree. $x := select\ in\ \psi$ selects a random value in ψ and assigns it to x. $cti(T, \psi, k)$ takes a set ψ of key values and a key value $k \notin \psi$, constructs a random binary search tree which contains exactly the values in ψ together with the key k, and where k is a leaf node, and sets T to point to the root of this tree.

$ct(T, \psi)$::

> if ($\psi = \emptyset$) $T := $ NIL;
> $else$
>> $x := select\ in\ \psi$;
>> $\psi := \psi - x$;
>> $Node\ T := new\ Node(x)$;
>> $ct(T.\ell, \{y \mid y \in \psi \land y < x\})$;
>> $ct(T.r, \{y \mid y \in \psi \land y > x\})$

$cti(T, \psi, k)$::

> if ($\psi = \emptyset$) $T := new\ Node(k)$;
> $else$
>> $x := select\ in\ \psi$;
>> $\psi := \psi - x$;
>> $Node\ T := new\ Node(x)$;
>> if ($k < x$)
>>> $cti(T.\ell, \{y \mid y \in \psi \land y < x\}, k)$;
>>> $ct(T.r, \{y \mid y \in \psi \land y > x\})$

$$else$$
$$ct(T.\ell, \{y \mid y \in \psi \wedge y < x\})$$
$$cti(T.r, \{y \mid y \in \psi \wedge y > x\}, k)$$

I now verify

$$[ct(T, \varphi)] \, \mathtt{insert(T, k)} \, [ct(T, \varphi \cup k)]. \qquad (*)$$

That is, the pre-program creates a random BST with key values in φ and sets T to the root, and the post-program creates a random BST with key values in $\varphi \cup k$ and sets T to the root. Hence, the above operational triple states that the result of $\mathtt{insert(T, k)}$ is to insert key value $\mathtt{k}$ into the BST rooted at $\mathtt{T}$. I first establish

$$cti(T, \varphi, k) \preceq ct(T, \varphi \cup k). \qquad (a)$$

Intuitively, this follows since $cti(T, \varphi, k)$ constructs a BST with key values in $\varphi \cup k$, and where k must be a leaf node, while $ct(T, \varphi \cup k)$ constructs a BST with key values in $\varphi \cup k$, with no constraint of where k can occur. A formal proof proceeds by induction on the length of an arbitrary execution π of $cti(T, \varphi, k)$, which shows that π is also a possible execution of $ct(T, \varphi \cup k)$. The details are straightforward and are omitted. In the sequel, I show that

$$[ct(T, \varphi)] \, \mathtt{insert(T, k)} \, [cti(T, \varphi, k)] \qquad (b)$$

is valid. From (a,b) and (*Post-program Weakening*), I conclude that (*) is valid, as desired. To establish (b), I show

$$ct(T, \varphi); \mathtt{insert(T, k)} \equiv cti(T, \varphi, k). \qquad (c)$$

from which (b) follows immediately by Definitions 2 and 4.

I establish (c) by using induction on recursive calls. I replace the above calls by the corresponding procedure bodies, and then assume as inductive hypothesis (c) as applied to the recursive calls within the bodies. This is similar to the Hoare logic inference rule for partial correctness of recursive procedures [7].

To apply the inductive hypothesis, I take $ct(T, \varphi); \mathtt{insert(T, k)}$, replace each call by the corresponding procedure body, and then "interleave" the procedure bodies using commutativity of statements, which preserves equivalence. Then I bring the recursive calls to ct and to $\mathtt{insert}$ together, so that the inductive hypothesis applies to their sequential composition, which is then replaced by the equivalent recursive call to cti. This gives a procedure body that corresponds to a call of cti, which completes the equivalence proof. The result is as follows (see [1] for full details):

$$if \ (\varphi = \emptyset) \ \ T := \mathbf{new} \ \mathbf{Node(k)}$$
$$else$$
$$x := select \ in \ \varphi;$$
$$\varphi := \varphi - x;$$
$$\mathbf{Node} \ T := new \ \mathbf{Node}(x);$$

```
if (k < T.val)
    cti(T.ℓ, {y | y ∈ φ ∧ y < x}, k);
    ct(T.r, {y | y ∈ φ ∧ y > x});
else
    ct(T.ℓ, {y | y ∈ φ ∧ y < x});
    cti(T.r, {y | y ∈ φ ∧ y > x}, k)
```

and is the procedure body corresponding to the call $cti(T, \varphi, k)$. By (*Equiv Recursive*), I conclude $ct(T, \varphi); \texttt{insert(T, k)} \equiv cti(T, \varphi, k)$, which is (c) above. This completes the proof.

8   Conclusions

I presented a new method for verifying the correctness of sequential programs. The method does not use assertions, but rather pre-/post-programs, each of which define a set of post-states, and can thus replace an assertion, which also defines a set of states, namely the states that satisfy it. Since pre-/post-programs are not executed, they can be inefficient, and can refer to any mathematically well-defined quantity, e.g., shortest path distances in a directed graph. I illustrated my method using as examples in-place list-reversal and an abbreviated BST node insertion. The full version of the paper [1] also presents derivations of selection sort and Dijkstra's shortest path algorithm, as well as giving full details for BST node insertion.

My approach is, to my knowledge, the first which uses *purely* operational specifications to verify the correctness of sequential programs, as opposed to pre- and post-conditions and invariants in a logic such as Floyd-Hoare logic and separation logic, or axioms and signatures in algebraic specifications [30]. The use of operational specifications is of course well-established for the specification and verification of concurrent programs. The process-algebra approach [8,16,17] starts with a specification written in a process algebra formalism such as CSP, CCS, or the Pi-calculus, and then refines it into an implementation. Equivalence of the implementation and specification is established by showing a bisimulation [16,21] between the two. The I/O Automata approach [14] starts with a specification given as a single "global property automaton" and shows that a distributed/concurrent implementation respects the global property automaton by establishing a simulation relation [15] from the implementation to the specification. Future work includes more examples and case studies, and in particular examples with pointer-based data structures. I am also investigating program refinement in the context of operational annotations, and the extension of the operational annotations approach to the verification of concurrent programs.

References

1. Attie, P.C.: Operational annotations: A new method for sequential program verification. CoRR abs/2102.06727 (2021). https://arxiv.org/abs/2102.06727

2. Back, R., von Wright, J.: Refinement Calculus - A Systematic Introduction. Graduate Texts in Computer Science. Springer (1998). https://doi.org/10.1007/978-1-4612-1674-2
3. Ciobâcă, Ș, Lucanu, D., Rusu, V., Roșu, G.: A language-independent proof system for full program equivalence. Formal Aspects Comput. **28**(3), 469–497 (2016). https://doi.org/10.1007/s00165-016-0361-7
4. Crole, R.L., Gordon, A.D.: Relating operational and denotational semantics for input/output effects. Math. Struct. Comput. Sci. **9**(2), 125–158 (1999). http://journals.cambridge.org/action/displayAbstract?aid=44797
5. Dijkstra, E.W.: Guarded commands, nondeterminacy and formal derivation of programs. Commun. ACM **18**(8), 453–457 (1975)
6. Floyd, R.: Assigning meanings to programs. In: Mathematical Aspects of Computer Science. Proceedings of Symposium on Applied Mathematics, pp. 19–32. American Mathematical Society (1967)
7. Francez, N.: Program verification. Addison-Wesley, International computer science series (1992)
8. Hoare, C.A.R.: Communicating Sequential Processes. Prentice-Hall (1985)
9. Hoare, C.A.R., et al.: Laws of programming. Commun. ACM **30**(8), 672–686 (1987). https://doi.org/10.1145/27651.27653
10. Hoare, C.: An axiomatic basis for computer programming. Commun. ACM **12**(10), 576–580, 583 (1969)
11. Hoare, T.: Laws of programming: the algebraic unification of theories of concurrency. In: Baldan, P., Gorla, D. (eds.) CONCUR 2014. LNCS, vol. 8704, pp. 1–6. Springer, Heidelberg (2014). https://doi.org/10.1007/978-3-662-44584-6_1
12. Jacobs, B.: Dijkstra and Hoare monads in monadic computation. Theor. Comput. Sci. **604**, 30–45 (2015). https://doi.org/10.1016/j.tcs.2015.03.020
13. Lucanu, D., Rusu, V.: Program equivalence by circular reasoning. Formal Aspects Comput. **27**(4), 701–726 (2014). https://doi.org/10.1007/s00165-014-0319-6
14. Lynch, N.A., Tuttle, M.R.: An introduction to input/output automata. CWI-Quarterly **2**(3), 219–246 (1989), centrum voor Wiskunde en Informatica, Amsterdam, The Netherlands. Technical Memo MIT/LCS/TM-373, Laboratory for Computer Science, Massachusetts Institute of Technology, Cambridge, MA 02139, November 1988
15. Lynch, N.A., Vaandrager, F.W.: Forward and backward simulations: I. Untimed systems. Inf. Comput. **121**(2), 214–233 (1995). https://doi.org/10.1006/inco.1995.1134
16. Milner, R. (ed.): A Calculus of Communicating Systems. LNCS, vol. 92. Springer, Heidelberg (1980). https://doi.org/10.1007/3-540-10235-3
17. Milner, R.: Communicating and mobile systems - the Pi-calculus. Cambridge University Press (1999)
18. Moggi, E.: Computational lambda-calculus and monads. In: Proceedings of the Fourth Annual Symposium on Logic in Computer Science (LICS '89), Pacific Grove, California, USA, 5–8 June, 1989, pp. 14–23. IEEE Computer Society (1989). https://doi.org/10.1109/LICS.1989.39155
19. Moggi, E.: Notions of computation and monads. Inf. Comput. **93**(1), 55–92 (1991). https://doi.org/10.1016/0890-5401(91)90052-4
20. Morgan, C.: Programming from specifications, 2nd edn. Prentice Hall International series in computer science, Prentice Hall (1994)
21. Park, D.: Concurrency and automata on infinite sequences. In: Deussen, P. (ed.) GI-TCS 1981. LNCS, vol. 104, pp. 167–183. Springer, Heidelberg (1981). https://doi.org/10.1007/BFb0017309

22. Pitts, A.M.: Operational semantics and program equivalence. In: Barthe, G., Dybjer, P., Pinto, L., Saraiva, J. (eds.) APPSEM 2000. LNCS, vol. 2395, pp. 378–412. Springer, Heidelberg (2002). https://doi.org/10.1007/3-540-45699-6_8

23. Pitts, A.M., Stark, I.D.B.: Observable properties of higher order functions that dynamically create local names, or: What's new? In: Borzyszkowski, A.M., Sokolowski, S. (eds.) MFCS 1993. LNCS, vol. 711, pp. 122–141. Springer, Heidelberg (1993). https://doi.org/10.1007/3-540-57182-5_8

24. Plotkin, G.D.: A structural approach to operational semantics. J. Log. Algebraic Methods Program. **60–61**, 17–139 (2004)

25. Reynolds, J.C.: Separation logic: a logic for shared mutable data structures. In: Proceedings of the 17th Annual IEEE Symposium on Logic in Computer Science, LICS 2002, pp. 55–74. IEEE Computer Society, Washington, DC (2002). http://dl.acm.org/citation.cfm?id=645683.664578

26. Schmidt, D.A.: Programming language semantics. In: Gonzalez, T.F., Diaz-Herrera, J., Tucker, A. (eds.) Computing Handbook, Third Edition: Computer Science and Software Engineering, pp. 69: 1–19. CRC Press (2014)

27. Swamy, N., Hritcu, C., Keller, C., Rastogi, A., Delignat-Lavaud, A., Forest, S., Bhargavan, K., Fournet, C., Strub, P., Kohlweiss, M., Zinzindohoue, J.K., Béguelin, S.Z.: Dependent types and multi-monadic effects in F. In: Bodik, R., Majumdar, R. (eds.) Proceedings of the 43rd Annual ACM SIGPLAN-SIGACT Symposium on Principles of Programming Languages, POPL 2016, St. Petersburg, FL, USA, January 20–22, 2016, pp. 256–270. ACM (2016). https://doi.org/10.1145/2837614.2837655

28. Swierstra, W.: A hoare logic for the state monad. In: Berghofer, S., Nipkow, T., Urban, C., Wenzel, M. (eds.) TPHOLs 2009. LNCS, vol. 5674, pp. 440–451. Springer, Heidelberg (2009). https://doi.org/10.1007/978-3-642-03359-9_30

29. Wing, J.M.: Hints to specifiers. Teaching and learning formal methods, pp. 57–78 (1995)

30. Wirsing, M.: Algebraic specification. In: van Leeuwen, J. (ed.) Handbook of Theoretical Computer Science, Volume B: Formal Models and Semantics, pp. 675–788. Elsevier and MIT Press (1990). https://doi.org/10.1016/b978-0-444-88074-1.50018-4

Towards Formal Verification of HotStuff-Based Byzantine Fault Tolerant Consensus in Agda

Harold Carr[1], Christa Jenkins[2], Mark Moir[3(✉)], Victor Cacciari Miraldo[4],
and Lisandra Silva[5]

[1] Oracle Labs, Burlington, MA, USA
`harold.carr@oracle.com`
[2] University of Iowa, Iowa City, USA
`cwjnkins@uiowa.edu`
[3] Oracle Labs, Wellington, New Zealand
`mark.moir@oracle.com`
[4] Tweag, Utrecht, The Netherlands
`victor.miraldo@tweag.io`
[5] Runtime Verification, Champaign-Urbana, IL, USA
`lisandra.silva@runtimeverification.com`

Abstract. LIBRABFT is a Byzantine Fault Tolerant (BFT) consensus protocol based on HOTSTUFF. We present an abstract model of the protocol underlying HOTSTUFF/LIBRABFT, and formal, machine-checked proofs of their core correctness (safety) property and an extended condition that enables non-participating parties to verify committed results. (Liveness properties would be proved for specific implementations, *not* for the abstract model presented in this paper.)

A key contribution is precisely defining assumptions about the behavior of honest peers, in an abstract way, *independent* of any particular implementation. Therefore, our work is an important step towards proving correctness of an entire class of concrete implementations, without repeating the hard work of proving correctness of the underlying protocol. The abstract proofs are for a single configuration (epoch); extending these proofs across configuration changes is future work. Our models and proofs are expressed in Agda, and are available in open source.

1 Introduction

There has been phenomenal interest in decentralized systems that enable coordination among peers that do not necessarily trust each other. This interest has largely been driven in recent years by the emergence of blockchain technology. When the set of participants is limited by *permissioning* or *proof of stake* [1,2], Byzantine Fault Tolerant (BFT) [3] consensus—which tolerates some *byzantine* peers actively deviating from the protocol—is of interest.

This is an extended version of a conference paper with the same title in the proceedings of the 14th NASA Formal Methods Symposium (NFM 2022). It contains additional details and proof overviews.

© Springer Nature Switzerland AG 2022
J. V. Deshmukh et al. (Eds.): NFM 2022, LNCS 13260, pp. 616–635, 2022.
https://doi.org/10.1007/978-3-031-06773-0_33

Due to attractive properties relative to previous BFT consensus protocols, implementations based on HOTSTUFF [4] are being developed and adopted. For example, the Diem Foundation (formerly Libra Association) was until recently developing LIBRABFT based on HOTSTUFF [5,6]. (LIBRABFT was renamed to DIEMBFT before being discontinued; other variants are emerging.)

Many published consensus algorithms, including some with manual correctness proofs, have been shown to be incorrect [7,8]. Therefore, precise, machine-checked formal verification is essential, particularly for new algorithms being adopted in practice. Some of the papers on HOTSTUFF/LIBRABFT include brief correctness arguments, but they lack many details and are not machine checked. Furthermore, LIBRABFT uses data structures, messages and logic, that differ significantly from versions on which those informal proofs were based.

Our contributions are as follows:

- a precise, abstract model of the protocol underlying HOTSTUFF/LIBRABFT;
- precise formulation of assumptions; and
- formal, machine-checked proofs of core correctness (safety) properties, plus a novel extended condition that enables additional functionality.

Proving correctness for an *abstraction* of the protocol enables verifying any concrete implementation by proving that its handlers ensure the assumptions of our abstract proofs. Our contribution is thus an important step towards proving correctness for an entire class of concrete implementations. However, this class does not include all possible variants. In particular, DIEMBFT recently added an option for committing based on 2-chains, rather than 3-chains, as our work assumes (see Sect. 3.1). Adapting our techniques to accommodate 2-chain-based implementations is future work.

This paper focuses on the metatheory around an *abstraction* of a system of peers participating in the HOTSTUFF/LIBRABFT protocol, and assumptions about which peers can participate, rules that honest peers obey, and the intersection of any two quorums containing at least one honest peer. We state and prove key correctness properties, such as that any two committed blocks do not conflict (i.e., they belong to the same ordered chain of committed blocks).

Our ongoing work [9] aims to use the results presented in this paper to verify a concrete Haskell implementation that we have developed based on the Diem Foundation's open-source Rust implementation [10]. We have built a system model that can be instantiated with data types and handlers, yielding a model of a distributed system in which honest peers execute those handlers and byzantine ones are constrained only by being unable to forge signatures of honest peers. We have ported this implementation to Agda, using a library we have developed [11] to enable the ported code to closely mirror the original, thus reducing the risk of error. We have made substantial progress towards proving that the resulting Agda port satisfies the assumptions established in this paper.

LIBRABFT supports configuration changes (also known as epoch changes), whereby parameters such as the number and identities of participating peers can be changed. The contribution described in this paper is an abstract model for a single epoch and formal, machine-checked proofs of its correctness conditions. Stating and proving cross-epoch properties is future work. Nevertheless, the

Haskell implementation we are verifying supports epoch changes, and our verification infrastructure is prepared for multiple epochs. In particular, our abstract modules are parameterized by an "epoch configuration" structure.

Our models, definitions and proofs are expressed in Agda [12,13], a dependently-typed programming language and proof assistant. We chose Agda for this work because its syntax is similar to Haskell's, making it easier to develop and have confidence in a model of the implementation we aim to verify. This paper is intended to be reasonably self contained and does not require the reader to know Agda. To that end, we will explain Agda-specific features and syntax that are important for following the paper. We encourage interested readers to explore the open source proofs in detail, and we hope that this paper will provide a useful overview and guide that will make them more accessible. For readers who would like to learn about Agda, we recommend starting with the tutorial in [14].

In Sect. 2, we overview salient aspects of HOTSTUFF/LIBRABFT to motivate our approach to abstractly modeling the protocol and formally verifying correctness properties. In Sect. 3, we present the definitions used to develop the formal abstract model of a system of peers participating in the protocol, and to define traditional and extended correctness properties. We also describe their proofs, which are available in open source [9]. Related work is summarized in Sect. 4 and concluding remarks and future work appear in Sect. 5. Additional proof overviews are included in the extended version of this paper [15].

2   An Overview of HOTSTUFF/LIBRABFT

The following overview does *not* fully describe HOTSTUFF and LIBRABFT: it highlights aspects that our abstraction must accommodate to enable our proofs. Details are in the relevant papers and repositories [4–6,9,10].

Peers participating in the HOTSTUFF/LIBRABFT protocol repeatedly agree to extend a chain of *blocks* that is initially empty (represented by a *genesis* record). Each block identifies (directly or indirectly) the block that it extends (or the genesis record if none) via one or more cryptographic hashes. This common *hash chaining* [16] technique ensures that each block uniquely identifies its predecessor, unless an adversary finds a hash collision (e.g., two different blocks that hash to the same value); it is a standard assumption that a computationally bounded adversary cannot do so [17, Chapter 9].

We require that two (*honest*) peers that faithfully follow the protocol cannot be convinced to extend the chain in conflicting ways: if honest peer p_1 (resp., p_2) determines that block b_1 (resp. b_2) is in the chain, then the chain up to one of the blocks *extends* the chain up to the other. This must hold even if some (*byzantine*) peers (up to some threshold, as discussed below) actively misbehave.

A peer can *propose* to add a new block to a chain, and others can *vote* to support the proposal. A proposed block can include a special *reconfiguration* (*epoch change*) transaction, which would change the set of peers participating and/or other parameters. To prevent impersonation, messages are signed.

A valid proposal contains or identifies a *quorum certificate* that represents a *quorum* of votes supporting the previous block. Based on assumptions discussed below, we can be sure that any two quorums each contain a vote from at least one honest peer in common. An honest participant will refuse to vote for a proposal if the requirements for the quorum certificate and previous blocks are not met. This ensures that the quorum certificate associated with each block in a chain satisfies these requirements, even though some peers that contributed votes to the quorum certificates may be dishonest. The conditions for *committing* a block are designed to ensure that honest peers never contribute votes to two quorums that cause conflicting blocks to be committed.

If a byzantine proposer sends different proposals to different peers, a quorum of votes for the same proposal may not be generated. In this case, waiting peers may time out, and initiate a new effort to extend the chain; this can result in competing proposals to extend the same chain with different blocks. To distinguish between proposals, each proposed block has an associated *round*, which must be larger than that of the block that it extends. Because competing proposals are possible, peers collectively build a *tree* of records, and follow specified rules to determine when a given proposal has been committed. The essence of the protocol is in the rules that honest peers must follow, and what information a peer must verify before committing a proposal.

The goal of this work is an *abstract* model of the protocol that is independent of all these details, capturing just enough detail to prove that, if the assumptions are not violated, then honest peers will not commit conflicting proposals.

3   Correctness Properties and Proofs

We prove our high-level abstract correctness properties in module *LibraBFT.Abstract.Properties* (in file `LibraBFT/Abstract/Properties.agda`), which receives several module parameters that can be instantiated in order to relate a particular implementation to the abstract machinery.

> module *LibraBFT.Abstract.Properties*
> $(\mathcal{E} \;:\; EpochConfig)\,(UID \;:\; Set)$
> $(\_\overset{?}{=}UID \;:\; (u_0\; u_1 \;:\; UID) \;\to\; Dec\,(u_0 \;\equiv\; u_1))$
> $(\mathcal{V} \;:\; VoteEvidence\; \mathcal{E}\; UID)$
> where ...

We first describe *EpochConfig*; the other module parameters are explained later. *EpochConfig* represents configuration information for an epoch, including: how many peers participate in the epoch (*authorsN*), their identities (*toNodeId*), and their public keys (*getPubKey*), as well as requirements such as each member having a different public key (*PK-inj*). Members are identified by values of type *Fin authorsN*: the natural numbers less than *authorsN*; for example, we have *getPubKey* : *Member* $\to$ *PK* where *Member* = *Fin authorsN*.

An *EpochConfig* also provides *IsQuorum*, a predicate indicating what the implementation considers to be a quorum. The type of *IsQuorum* is *List Member* $\to$ *Set*; *Set* is Agda's way of representing an arbitrary type. This definition is then used to define another important field of an *EpochConfig*:

$$bft\text{-}assumption : \forall \{xs\ ys\} \rightarrow IsQuorum\ xs \rightarrow IsQuorum\ ys$$
$$\rightarrow \exists[a](a \in xs \times a \in ys \times MetaHonestPK\ (getPubKey\ a))$$

Here, *bft-assumption* requires that the intersection of any two quorums contains at least one honest peer.[1]

Agda supports *implicit* arguments, listed in curly braces, which need not be provided explicitly if their values can be inferred from context, e.g., *IsQuorum xs* implies that *xs* is of type *List Member*. The $\exists[a]\cdot$ notation says that there is an *a* which satisfies the condition—a product of three conditions, in this case. The type of *a* must be implied by context; here, $a \in xs$ implies that *a* is of type *Member*.

To inherit the correctness properties we prove, an implementation must provide an *EpochConfig* as a module parameter. Part of constructing it is proving *bft-assumption* based on whatever assumptions and definition of *IsQuorum* the implementation uses. One common approach is to assume *n* peers with equal "voting power", at most *f* of which are byzantine, and to ensure that $n > 3f$; in this case, a set of peers is a quorum iff it contains at least $2n/3$ distinct peers. *LibraBFT.Abstract.BFT* contains a lemma that can be used to prove that such assumptions imply *bft-assumption*. The lemma is sufficiently general to accommodate LIBRABFT's approach of assigning (potentially non-uniform) *voting power* to peers, and considering a set of peers to be a quorum iff its combined voting power exceeds two thirds of the total voting power.

The remainder of this section is in context of a single *EpochConfig* called $\mathcal{E}$.

3.1   Abstract *Record*s and *RecordChain*s

A *Record* can be a *Block*, a quorum certificate (*QC*) or the epoch's *genesis* (initial) *Record*; precise definitions are below. (These are *abstract* records that may not correlate closely to data structures and message formats used by an implementation; for example, in LIBRABFT, blocks *contain* the previous QC.) HOTSTUFF-based algorithms grow a tree of *Record*s rooted at the epoch's genesis

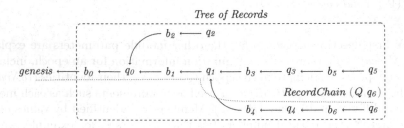

Fig. 1. A tree of *Record*s with a *RecordChain* from *genesis* to abstract *Record* $Q\ q_6$.

---

[1] *MetaHonestPK* is a predicate representing whether a peer owning a key behaves honestly. The *Meta* prefix identifies this as being part of the formal model and not accessible to implementations, which must not depend on knowing who is honest.

record, where nodes contain a *Block* or a *QC*. Paths (called *RecordChains*) from the root begin with the genesis record and then alternate between *Block*s and *QC*s. For example, the existence of a path from the root to a record *r* is captured by the type *RecordChain r* being inhabited. Figure 1 illustrates a tree of *Records*.

While typical implementations carry more information, abstractly, a *Block* comprises its round number, an identifier of type *UID* for itself and for the quorum certificate it extends, if any (a value of type *Maybe UID* is either *nothing* or *just x* for some *x* of type *UID*). *UID* can be any type that has decidable equality, as represented by the second and third module parameters; these are passed to other modules in the *Abstract* namespace as needed. Definitions below are in modules *LibraBFT.Abstract.Records* and *LibraBFT.Abstract.RecordChain*.

Typical implementations obtain a *Block*'s id by applying a cryptographic hash function to some or all of its contents; thus identifiers may not be unique. Our correctness properties are therefore proved modulo "injectivity failures" on (supposedly) unique ids. We do *not* assume that such injectivity failures do not exist, which would make our proofs meaningless because they *can* occur in practice, however unlikely. We elaborate below and in Sects. 4 and 5.

Abstractly, a *Vote* is by a member of the epoch, for a round and *Block* id.

```
record Block : Set where              record Vote : Set where
  constructor mkBlock                   constructor mkVote
  field bRound   : Round                field vRound    : Round
        bId      : UID                        vMember   : Member
        bPrevQC  : Maybe UID                  vBlockUID : UID
```

A quorum certificate (*QC*) represents enough *Votes* to *certify* that a *Block* has been accepted by a quorum of members. It includes the *Block*'s id and round, and a list of *Votes* and evidence that the QC is "valid" (representing properties that honest peers verify before accepting the QC), i.e.:

1. The list of voting *Members* represents a quorum.
2. All *Votes* are for the *Block*'s id.
3. All *Votes* are for the same round.

Honest peers accept a (concrete) *Vote* only if it satisfies implementation-specific conditions captured by the module parameter $\mathcal{V}$ of type *VoteEvidence $\mathcal{E}$ UID*, an implementation-specific predicate on abstract *Votes*. To enable proofs to access the verified conditions, we add a fourth coherence clause to QCs:

4. For each *Vote* in the *QC*, there is evidence that a message was sent containing a concrete representation of the (abstract) *Vote* that satisfies the implementation-specific conditions.

Putting this all together, we have:

```
record QC : Set where
   constructor mkQC
      field qRound       : Round
            qCertBlockId : UID
            qVotes       : List Vote
            qVotes-C1    : IsQuorum (List-map vMember qVotes)
            qVotes-C2    : All (λ v → vBlockUID v ≡ qCertBlockId) qVotes
            qVotes-C3    : All (λ v → vRound v    ≡ qRound)       qVotes
            qVotes-C4    : All V qVotes
```

All (from the Agda standard library) accepts a predicate and a list, and requires that each element of the list satisfies the predicate.

Next, we define a *Record* to be either a *Block*, a *QC*, or the special genesis record *I*. There is a constructor for each case, and the *B* and *Q* constructors take arguments of the appropriate type to form a *Record*.

```
data Record : Set where
   I :            Record
   B : Block →   Record
   Q : QC   →   Record
```

We then say that a record r' *extends* another record r, denoted $r \leftarrow r'$, whenever one of the following conditions is met:

1. r is the genesis *Record* and r' is a *Block* for round greater than 0 and not identifying any previous *Block*.
2. r is a *QC* and r' is a *Block* with a round higher than r's and with a *bPrevQC* field identifying r.
3. r is a *Block* and r' is a *QC* certifying r.

We capture these conditions in the following Agda datatype; $\_\leftarrow\_$ indicates that $\leftarrow$ is an infix operator with two arguments. Values of this type can be constructed using one of three constructors ($I{\leftarrow}B$, $Q{\leftarrow}B$ or $B{\leftarrow}Q$), each of which requires several arguments to establish a value of $\_\leftarrow\_$ for a pair of *Records*.

```
data _←_ : Record → Record → Set where
   I←B  : ∀ {b} → 0 < getRound b → bPrevQC b ≡ nothing
             → I ← (B b)
   Q←B : ∀ {q b} → getRound q < getRound b
             → just (qCertBlockId q) ≡ bPrevQC b
             → Q q ← B b
   B←Q : ∀ {b q} → getRound q ≡ getRound b → bId b ≡ qCertBlockId q
             → B b ← Q q
```

*RecordChain*s are in the reflexive, transitive closure of $\_\leftarrow\_$, starting at the genesis record *I*. Sometimes, we reason about paths starting at records other than

I; we therefore define $RecordChain$ using the more specific $RecordChainFrom$.

data $RecordChainFrom$ $(o$: $Record)$: $Record$ $\rightarrow$ Set where
  $empty$: $RecordChainFrom$ o o
  $step$: $\forall$ $\{r$ $r'\}$ $\rightarrow$ $RecordChainFrom$ o r
            $\rightarrow$ $r \leftarrow r'$
            $\rightarrow$ $RecordChainFrom$ o r'
$RecordChain$: $Record$ $\rightarrow$ Set
$RecordChain$ $=$ $RecordChainFrom$ I

Next, we present definitions needed to specify when a $Block$ can be committed. For $k > 0$, a $\mathbb{K}$-*chain* is a sequence of k $Blocks$, each of which is extended by a QC, such that each $Block$ (except the first) extends the QC that extends the previous $Block$. Furthermore, each adjacent pair of $Blocks$ must satisfy the relation R, which can be instantiated with $Simple$ (which holds for any pair of $Blocks$) or $Contig$ (which holds only if the rounds of the two $Blocks$ are contiguous: the second $Block$'s round is one greater than that of the first; the first parameter to R enables a definition of $Contig$ that does not require a predecessor for the first $Block$; see module $LibraBFT.Abstract.RecordChain$). $\mathbb{K}$-*chains* are defined as follows.

data $\mathbb{K}$-*chain* $(R$: $\mathbb{N}$ $\rightarrow$ $Record$ $\rightarrow$ $Record$ $\rightarrow$ $Set)$
  : $(k$: $\mathbb{N})$ $\{o$ r : $Record\}$ $\rightarrow$ $RecordChainFrom$ o r $\rightarrow$ Set where
  0-*chain* : $\forall$ $\{o$ $r\}$ $\{rc$: $RecordChainFrom$ o $r\}$ $\rightarrow$ $\mathbb{K}$-*chain* R 0 rc
  s-*chain* : $\forall$ $\{k$ o $r\}$ $\{rc$: $RecordChainFrom$ o $r\}$ $\{b$: $Block\}$ $\{q$: $QC\}$
          $\rightarrow$ $(r{\leftarrow}b$: $r \leftarrow B$ $b)$ $\rightarrow$ $(prf$: R k r $(B$ $b))$
          $\rightarrow$ $(b{\leftarrow}q$: B $b \leftarrow Q$ $q)$ $\rightarrow$ $\mathbb{K}$-*chain* R k rc
          $\rightarrow$ $\mathbb{K}$-*chain* R $(suc$ $k)$ $(step$ $(step$ rc $r{\leftarrow}b)$ $b{\leftarrow}q)$

Block b_0 (and those preceding it) are committed if b_0 is the head of a contiguous 3-chain: there is a $RecordChain$ that contains b followed by blocks b_1 and b_2, such that the rounds of blocks b_0, b_1 and b_2 are consecutive. This is called a $CommitRule$ ($kchainBlock$ n c_3 is the nth $Block$ from the end of c_3):

data $CommitRuleFrom$ $\{o$ r : $Record\}$
                    $(rc$: $RecordChainFrom$ o $r)$ $(b$: $Block)$: Set where
  $commit$-*rule* : $(c_3$: $\mathbb{K}$-*chain* $Contig$ 3 $rc)$ $\rightarrow$ $b \equiv kchainBlock$ 2 c_3
            $\rightarrow$ $CommitRuleFrom$ rc b

3.2 First Correctness Property: *thmS5*

We can now explain the first high-level property we prove for our abstract model, *thmS5*. (Because our work has been influenced by versions of the HOTSTUFF [4] and LIBRABFT papers [5,6], some of our properties are named after properties presented informally in those papers. For example, *thmS5* is named after Theorem S5 in [5].) It states that, if two blocks b and b' are committed via $CommitRule$ rc b and $CommitRule$ rc' b', respectively, then one of the blocks is contained in the record chain of the other. This property ensures that all committed *Blocks* are on a single non-branching path in the tree of *Records*.

$$thmS5 : \forall \{q \ q'\} \rightarrow \{rc : RecordChain \ (Q \ q)\} \rightarrow AllInSys \ rc$$
$$\rightarrow \{rc' : RecordChain \ (Q \ q')\} \rightarrow AllInSys \ rc'$$
$$\rightarrow \{b \ b' : Block\} \rightarrow CommitRule \ rc \ b \rightarrow CommitRule \ rc' \ b'$$
$$\rightarrow Either \ NonInjective\text{-}\equiv (Either \ ((B \ b) \in RC \ rc') \ ((B \ b') \in RC \ rc))$$

AllInSys rc means that each record in *rc* is "in" the abstract system according to an implementation-specific predicate over abstract *Records* called *InSys*, which is provided as a module parameter. For purposes of *AllInSys*, a record *r* being "in" a record chain *rc* is captured by a simple recursive definition: if *rc* is formed by extending record chain *rc'* by record *r'*, then *r* is "in" *rc* iff $r = r'$ or *r* is "in" *rc'*. On the other hand, as explained in Sect. 3.4, $\in RC$ represents a more complicated notion of a record being "in" a record chain.

Note that *thmS5* requires that *either NonInjective-$\equiv$* holds *or* one of the committed *Blocks* is in a *RecordChain* ending at the other. The *NonInjective-$\equiv$* disjunct—which is shared by many of the properties discussed below—reflects that we prove *thmS5* modulo injectivity of *Block* ids, as discussed above.

In Sect. 3.6, we explain how we refine the definition of *thmS5* and other properties in order to relate our abstract proofs to the security properties of a concrete implementation that is proved correct using them. For now, however, we can think of the following simplified definition of *NonInjective-$\equiv$*:

NonInjective-$\equiv$: Set
$$NonInjective\text{-}\equiv = \Sigma \ (Block \times Block)$$
$$(\lambda \ \{(b_0 \ , \ b_1) \rightarrow b_0 \not\equiv b_1 \times bId \ b_0 \equiv bId \ b_1 \})$$

The Σ notation is similar to the $\exists[\cdot]\cdot$ notation introduced earlier, except that it specifies the *type* of the existentially quantified value (not just a name, as with $\exists[\cdot]\cdot$) and the condition on the value of that type is expressed as a predicate on that type. Thus, a value of type *NonInjective-$\equiv$* comprises a *pair* of (abstract) *Blocks*—b_0 and b_1—that are *different* but have the *same* id.

3.3 Precisely Defining Protocol Rules

Module *LibraBFT.Abstract.RecordChain.Properties* contains the proof of *thmS5*, which requires module parameters representing assumptions about *Records* that are *InSys*. These assumptions capture the key properties that an implementation must ensure. Part of our contribution is to precisely define these assumptions in an abstract way, independent of any particular implementation.

Implementations described in various papers [4–6] are all based on the same core ideas, but differ substantially in detail. None of these papers gives a precise definition of the core protocol. Early versions of the LIBRABFT papers [5] come closest, providing explicit statements of two "voting constraints".

These voting constraints ("Increasing Round" and "Preferred Round") were a starting point for us, but they are not entirely suitable for our purposes. For example, the "Increasing Round" constraint is originally stated as: *An* *honest node that voted once for B in the past may only vote for B′ if round (B) < round (B′).* However, to interpret this as a protocol rule, we would need to define precisely what it means to have "voted in the past". Our proof efforts revealed that it suffices to require that an honest peer does not sign and send *different* (abstract) votes for the same round (regardless of order):

$$
\begin{aligned}
&VotesOnlyOnceRule \;:\; Set\;\ell \\
&VotesOnlyOnceRule \;=\; (a \;:\; Member) \;\to\; MetaHonestMember\;a \\
&\qquad \to\; \forall\,\{q\;q'\} \;\to\; InSys\,(Q\;q) \;\to\; InSys\,(Q\;q') \\
&\qquad \to\; (v \;:\; a \in QC\;q)\,(v' \;:\; a \in QC\;q') \\
&\qquad \to\; vRound\,(\in QC\text{-}Vote\;q\;v) \;\equiv\; vRound\,(\in QC\text{-}Vote\;q'\;v') \\
&\qquad \to\; \in QC\text{-}Vote\;q\;v \;\equiv\; \in QC\text{-}Vote\;q'\;v'
\end{aligned}
$$

For generality, *InSys* is assumed to return a type from some arbitrary universe [18] with level ℓ. The v parameter is evidence that there is a *Vote* by member a represented in q (a *QC*), and $\in QC\text{-}Vote\;q\;v$ is that (abstract) *Vote*. Thus, *VotesOnlyOnceRule* requires that, if there are two *Votes* for the same round by an honest member a in *QC*s in the system, then the *Votes* are equal.

The second constraint—*PreferredRoundRule*—is more complicated. It is based on the voting constraint called "Locked Round" in early versions of the LibraBFT paper [5]; similar constraints on voting are followed by HOTSTUFF [4] and by later versions of LIBRABFT [6]. The essence of this rule is that, if an honest peer contributes a *Vote* to q (a *QC*) that commits a *Block* (c_3 is essentially a *CommitRule* that commits the *Block* identified by *kchainBlock 2 c_3*), then it does not vote in a higher round for a *Block* unless the round of the *previous Block* is at least that of the committed *Block*. This is a key requirement to avoid voting to commit another *Block* that conflicts with the first.

$$
\begin{aligned}
&PreferredRoundRule \;:\; Set\;\ell \\
&PreferredRoundRule \\
&\quad = \; \forall\,a\,\{q\;q'\} \;\to\; MetaHonestMember\;a \;\to\; InSys\,(Q\;q) \;\to\; InSys\,(Q\;q') \\
&\quad \to\; \{rc \;:\; RecordChain\,(Q\;q)\}\,\{n \;:\; \mathbb{N}\} \;\to\; (c_3 \;:\; \mathbb{K}\text{-}chain\;Contig\,(3+n)\;rc) \\
&\quad \to\; (v \;:\; a \in QC\;q)\,(rc' \;:\; RecordChain\,(Q\;q'))\,(v' \;:\; a \in QC\;q') \\
&\quad \to\; vRound\,(\in QC\text{-}Vote\;q\;v) < vRound\,(\in QC\text{-}Vote\;q'\;v') \\
&\quad \to\; Either\;NonInjective\text{-}\equiv \\
&\qquad\qquad (getRound\,(kchainBlock\,(suc\,(suc\;zero))\;c_3) \;\leqslant\; prevRound\;rc')
\end{aligned}
$$

3.4   The Proof of *thmS5*

Our proof of *thmS5* is similar to the manual proof presented an early version of the LIBRABFT paper [5]. However, a formal, machine-checked proof must address many details that are glossed over in the manual proof. Furthermore, as discussed in Sect. 3.3, making our assumptions about honest peers' *Votes* precise and implementation-independent required somewhat different assumptions.

To help the reader approach the formal, machine-checked proofs in our open-source development [9], we describe below some of its key proofs and properties.

We first introduce two key lemmas. Roughly speaking, *lemmaS2* states that there can be at most one certified *Block* per round. Its proof depends on the *bft-assumption*: for two QCs, there is some honest peer with *Votes* in each. By the assumption that honest peers obey *VotesOnlyOnceRule*, if the blocks certified by the two QCs have the same round, then both *Votes* are for the same *BlockId*. However, this does *not* imply the QCs certify the same *Block*. For this reason, the conclusion of *lemmaS2* is that *either bId is non-injective or $b_0 \equiv b_1$.*

$$
\begin{aligned}
lemmaS2 \ : \ &\forall \{ b_0 \ b_1 \ : \ Block \} \{ q_0 \ q_1 \ : \ QC \} \ \rightarrow \ InSys \, (Q \ q_0) \ \rightarrow \ InSys \, (Q \ q_1) \\
&\rightarrow (p_0 \ : \ B \ b_0 \leftarrow Q \ q_0) \, (p_1 \ : \ B \ b_1 \leftarrow Q \ q_1) \\
&\rightarrow getRound \ b_0 \ \equiv \ getRound \ b_1 \\
&\rightarrow Either \ NonInjective\text{-}\equiv (b_0 \ \equiv \ b_1)
\end{aligned}
$$

Similarly, *lemmaS3* makes the *PreferredRoundRule* apply to QCs.

$$
\begin{aligned}
lemmaS3 \ : \ &\forall \{ r_2 \ q' \} \{ rc \ : \ RecordChain \ r_2 \} \ \rightarrow \ InSys \ r_2 \\
&\rightarrow (rc' \ : \ RecordChain \, (Q \ q')) \ \rightarrow \ InSys \, (Q \ q') \\
&\rightarrow (c_3 \ : \ kchain \ Contig \ 3 \ rc) \ \rightarrow \ round \ r_2 < getRound \ q' \\
&\rightarrow Either \ NonInjective\text{-}\equiv (getRound \, (kchainBlock \, (suc \, (suc \ zero)) \ c_3) \\
&\qquad\qquad\qquad\qquad\qquad\qquad\qquad\qquad \leqslant prevRound \ rc')
\end{aligned}
$$

The proof of *thmS5* depends on a non-symmetric variant of it called *propS4*:

$$
\begin{aligned}
propS4 \ : \ &\forall \{ q \ q' \} \{ rc \ : \ RecordChain \, (Q \ q) \} \ \rightarrow \ AllInSys \ rc \\
&\rightarrow (rc' \ : \ RecordChain \, (Q \ q')) \ \rightarrow \ AllInSys \ rc' \\
&\rightarrow (c_3 \ : \ \mathbb{K}\text{-}chain \ Contig \ 3 \ rc) \\
&\rightarrow getRound \, (kchainBlock \, (suc \, (suc \ zero)) \ c_3) \ \leqslant \ getRound \ q' \\
&\rightarrow Either \ NonInjective\text{-}\equiv (B \, (kchainBlock \, (suc \, (suc \ zero)) \ c_3) \in RC \ rc')
\end{aligned}
$$

Recall that $\in RC$ is a specific representation of what it means for a *Record* to be "in" a *RecordChain* that is precisely defined later, and note that c_3 is a $\mathbb{K}$-*chain Contig 3 rc*, for some *rc*, i.e., a *CommitRule*.

Proof overviews for *thmS5* and *propS4* are in the extended paper [15].

Finally, we explain what it means for a *Block* to be "in" a *RecordChain*, as captured by the $\in RC$ predicate. It is tempting to think that, if *RecordChains* rc and rc' both end at block b, then the requirements of $\_\leftarrow\_$ ensure that rc and rc' are the same *RecordChain*. However, suppose we have $q \leftarrow b$ and $q' \leftarrow b$, where q and q' are QCs. The definition of $\_\leftarrow\_$ requires that *just* ($qCertBlockId \ q$) $\equiv$ *bprevQC b* $\equiv$ *just* ($qCertBlockId \ q'$). This does *not* imply that $q \equiv q'$ because q and q' may include different *Votes*, reflecting the reality that two peers may be convinced to extend the same *Block* by two *different* valid QCs.

Therefore, we need a notion of *equivalent RecordChains* that contain the same *Blocks* and equivalent QCs: two QCs are equivalent iff they certify the same *Block* (i.e., their *qCertBlockId* components are equal). These notions are captured by $\approx RC$ (defined in *LibraBFT.Abstract.RecordChain*), which requires the two *RecordChains* to be "pointwise equivalent" meaning that the corresponding *Records* in the two *RecordChains* are equivalent. A lemma *RC-irrelevant* shows that, if two record chains rc and rc' end at the same *Record*, then they are equivalent (i.e., $rc \approx RC\ rc'$), unless there is an injectivity failure.

The $\mathbb{K}$-*chain*-$\in RC$ property used in the proof of *propS4* states that, if a *RecordChain* rc_1 ends at a block b that is in a $\mathbb{K}$-*chain* based on another record chain rc, then another *Block* that is earlier in the $\mathbb{K}$-*chain* is also "in" rc_1. To enable proving this, $\in RC$ must allow for the possibility that the other *Block* is contained in an equivalent *RecordChain*. The definition of $\in RC$ there-fore has an additional constructor beyond the two obvious ones, which enables the *Record* in question to be "transported" from an equivalent *RecordChain*:

$$
\begin{aligned}
&\mathrm{data}\ \_\in RC\_\{o\ :\ Record\}\ (r_0\ :\ Record)\ : \\
&\qquad\qquad \forall\ \{r_1\}\ \rightarrow\ RecordChainFrom\ o\ r_1\ \rightarrow\ Set\ \mathrm{where} \\
&here\quad :\ \forall\ \{rc\ :\ RecordChainFrom\ o\ r_0\}\ \rightarrow\ r_0\ \in RC\ rc \\
&there\quad :\ \forall\ \{r_1\ r_2\}\ \{rc\ :\ RecordChainFrom\ o\ r_1\}\ \rightarrow\ (p\ :\ r_1\ \leftarrow\ r_2) \\
&\qquad\qquad \rightarrow\ r_0\ \in RC\ rc\ \rightarrow\ r_0\ \in RC\ (step\ rc\ p) \\
&transp\ :\ \forall\ \{r\}\ \{rc0\ :\ RecordChainFrom\ o\ r\}\ \{rc_1\ :\ RecordChainFrom\ o\ r\} \\
&\qquad\qquad \rightarrow\ r_0\ \in RC\ rc0\ \rightarrow\ rc0\ \approx RC\ rc_1\ \rightarrow\ r_0\ \in RC\ rc_1
\end{aligned}
$$

3.5   Traditional and Extended Correctness Properties

Our core correctness property *CommitsDoNotConflict* is *thmS5* without the *NonInjective*-$\equiv$ disjunct. It is proved in *LibraBFT.Abstract.Properties*, which receives an additional module parameter *no-collisions-InSys* providing evidence that there are no injectivity failures between *Blocks* that satisfy *InSys*. Note that, if an implementation reaches a state in which this does not hold, then there is an injectivity failure between *concrete Records* at the implementation level; for a typical implementation, this signifies a collision for a cryptographic hash function among *Records* that are actually in the system, contradicting the standard assumption that a computationally bounded adversary is unable to find such collisions. To prove *CommitsDoNotConflict*, we invoke *thmS5* and then use *no-collisions-InSys* to eliminate the possibility of an injectivity failure.

To invoke *CommitsDoNotConflict* for a particular implementation, we need to provide *AllInSys rc*, where rc is the *RecordChain* for the first *CommitRule* (and similarly for rc'). To enable this, honest voters in typical implementations will vote to extend a *Block* only after verifying that the *Block* extends a *QC* (or the initial *Record*) that the peer already knows is in the system. Thus, a peer that verifies a *CommitRule* based on a record chain rc that ends in a *QC* (q) knows that every *Record* in rc is "in the system": *AllInSys rc*.

Extended Correctness Condition. We are also interested in enabling parties that do not participate in the protocol to verify commits. Suppose a peer p provides to a client c the contents of a *CommitRule* that c can verify. In this case, c cannot invoke *CommitsDoNotConflict* (or *thmS5*), because it does not know the *RecordChain* on which the *CommitRule* is based.

For this purpose, we define and prove a variant of *CommitsDoNotConflict* called *CommitsDoNotConflict'*. This condition ensures that even a party that does not participate in consensus can confirm commits and will not confirm conflicting commits.

$CommitsDoNotConflict'$: $\forall \{o\ o'\ q\ q'\}$
$\rightarrow \{rcf\ :\ RecordChainFrom\ o\ (Q\ q)\}\ \rightarrow\ AllInSys\ rcf$
$\rightarrow \{rc'\ :\ RecordChainFrom\ o'\ (Q\ q')\}\ \rightarrow\ AllInSys\ rc'$
$\rightarrow \{b\ b'\ :\ Block\}\ \rightarrow\ CommitRuleFrom\ rcf\ b\ \rightarrow\ CommitRuleFrom\ rcf\ b'$
$\rightarrow\ Either\ \Sigma\ (RecordChain\ (Q\ q'))\ ((B\ b)\ \in RC\_)$
      $\Sigma\ (RecordChain\ (Q\ q))\ ((B\ b')\ \in RC\_)$

$CommitsDoNotConflict'$ does not require $CommitRules$ based on full $RecordChains$; instead, $CommitRuleFroms$ based on $RecordChainFroms$ suffice. This property shows that a party can validate just the $Records$ required to form a $CommitRuleFrom$, and confirm that the $Block$ it claims to commit has indeed been committed, and that there cannot be another commit that conflicts with it. Here, $(B\ b)\ \in RC\_$ is a predicate over values of type $RecordChain\ (Q\ q')$, so $CommitsDoNotConflict'$ says that, if there are two $CommitRuleFroms$ based on $RecordChainFroms$ that end with a QC and have all of their $Records$ in the system, then (unless there is an injectivity failure), one of committed $Blocks$ is in a $RecordChain$ that contains the other.

To prove this property, we require an additional assumption about the implementation, which is provided as a module parameter $\in QC{\Rightarrow}AllSent$, of type $Complete\ InSys$, where:

$Complete$: $\forall \{\ell\}\ \rightarrow\ (Record\ \rightarrow\ Set\ \ell)\ \rightarrow\ Set\ \ell$
$Complete\ \in sys\ =\ \forall \{a\ q\}\ \rightarrow\ MetaHonestMember\ a$
      $\rightarrow\ a\ \in QC\ q\ \rightarrow\ \in sys\ (Q\ q)$
      $\rightarrow\ \exists[b]\ (\Sigma\ (RecordChain\ (B\ b))\ AllInSys\ \times\ B\ b\ \leftarrow\ Q\ q)$

Here, $Record\ \rightarrow\ Set\ \ell$ is a predicate on (abstract) $Records$ representing what $Records$ an implementation considers to be "in the system".

This assumption (indirectly) requires that an honest peer sends a $Vote$ for a $Block$ id (which may subsequently be represented in a QC) only if it knows that there is a $Block$ with that id and a $RecordChain$ up to that $Block$ whose $Records$ are all "in the system" (for example the peer may have validated all of those $Records$ itself, or it may have validated sufficient information to be confident that all of them have been validated by some honest peer, unless there is a hash collision among $Records$ that are in the system).

The extended version of this paper [15] includes proof overviews for $CommitsDoNotConflict'$, and for a lemma crf$\Rightarrow$cr on which it depends.

3.6 Relating Non-injectivity to Security Properties

Recall from Sect. 3.2 that we prove our abstract properties modulo injectivity of $Block$ ids. However, the simplified $NonInjective$-$\equiv$ disjunct used in the property definitions presented so far is insufficient. The reason is that it is *trivial* to construct two different abstract $Blocks$ with the same id, meaning that we could prove *thmS5* with a single-line proof, independent of the actual protocol. Worse, we could accidentally do the same in context of legitimate-looking proofs.

The issue is that the abstract *Block*s we could trivially construct bear no relation to any real *Block*s and ids produced in the execution of a concrete implementation. To resolve this problem, we strengthen the first disjunct of *thmS5* to *NonInjective-≡-InSys*, defined as follows:

NonInjective-≡-InSys : *Set*
NonInjective-≡-InSys =
    Σ *NonInjective-≡* λ $\{((b_0 , b_1) , \_ , \_) \rightarrow$ *InSys* $(B\ b_0) \times$ *InSys* $(B\ b_1)\}$

This definition requires that the proof not only provides different *Block*s b_0 and b_1 with the same id, but also proof that the implementation considers the *Record*s $B\ b_0$ and $B\ b_1$ to be "in the system". The meaning of "in the system" is specified by the implementation-provided predicate *InSys* and is thus beyond the scope of this paper. However, in ongoing work, we are proving a real implementation correct using the results presented here. In that broader context, we instantiate *InSys* with a predicate that holds only for *Block*s that are contained in network messages that have actually been sent. In this way, from the perspective of that concrete implementation, we ensure that our correctness properties hold unless and until an adversary *actually finds a hash collision* and introduces it into the system. We contrast this approach to some related efforts in Sect. 4.

The *NonInjective-≡* and *NonInjective-≡-InSys* definitions stated above are actually simplified versions of more general definitions we use in our proofs; details are available in our open source development [9]. These more general definitions are required because, at different stages of our proofs, we use different predicates to capture evidence collected so far about the conflicting *Block*s, so that we can build up to the proof for *thmS5* that both *Block*s satisfy *InSys*.

4 Related Work

4.1 HotStuff/LibraBFT

Before open sourcing our work in December 2020 [9], we were not aware of any formal verification work related to the HotStuff/LibraBFT protocols beyond manual proof sketches [4–6]; these are useful and have influenced our work significantly, but are far from detailed, precise proofs. We have since learned of two other pieces of work involving mechanical proofs of correctness of variants of the HotStuff/LibraBFT algorithm, and one involving model checking.

Librachain [19] is a Coq-based model of the data structures used in LibraBFT. It contains a single commit from May 2020, described as "experimental"; we are not aware of any paper describing this work. The Librachain model commits to some structural details that are not central to the core protocol. For example, it assumes that the *QuorumCert* that a new *Block* extends is included in the *Block* record; this is one implementation choice, but certainly not fundamental. Furthermore, the proofs assume various conditions have been validated for the data structures, and are thus intimately tied to the particular implementation types. In contrast, we model an *abstraction* of the core protocol, and establish precise requirements for *any* implementation to enjoy the correctness properties we prove. The Librachain development also uses a hypothesis that the hash function used is injective, which is not true of hash functions that are used in practice. Our properties are proved to hold unless and until a *specific* injectivity failure exists between (abstract) *Records* that are actually "in the system" (see Sect. 3.6); when instantiated with implementations that use cryptographic hash functions to assign ids, this ensures that the result holds unless and until a peer succeeds in finding a specific hash collision, violating the assumption that a computationally bounded adversary cannot do so.

More recently, Leander [20] has described work modeling and proving correctness for one specific, simplified variant of HOTSTUFF. Hashes are not explicitly modeled, but the way the relationship between blocks is modeled amounts to an assumption that hashing is injective. Leander modeled this simplified variant in TLA+ and Ivy, and the paper is focused on comparing the tools for this purpose.

Kukharenko et al. [21] use TLA+ [22] to model check *basic* HOTSTUFF, but not the more practical *chained* variant used by LIBRABFT. Again, our work applies to an abstraction of the protocol that can be instantiated for all versions of HOTSTUFF and LIBRABFT, as well as variants that may not yet exist.

Model checking has the advantage of requiring less work (defining a model and correctness properties and then "pushing the button") than developing precise, machine-checked correctness proofs. It can also provide insight into errors found. Kukharenko et al. ran one of their models with seven participants of which three are byzantine (correctness is not guaranteed in this case), and found a counterexample showing *how* the byzantine peers can violate correctness.

To limit the state space, Kukharenko et al. developed a restricted model, in which a node (analogous to our *Block*) can be extended only by one of two nodes, and a more general model in which any node can extend any other (from some fixed set). The restricted model, with just four peers (one byzantine), took over seven hours to check. The more general model took over 17 d. Our approach imposes no such limitations, and Agda checks our proofs in under one minute. Finally, for the more general model, TLA+ estimates an "optimistic" probability of 0.3 that it has in fact not explored the entire state space due to hash collisions on states, leaving open the possibility of an unfound bug even for this minimal configuration. We consider that Kukharenko et al.'s work complements ours, but does not obviate the need for the machine-checked correctness proofs.

4.2 Other BFT Consensus Protocols

Pîrlea and Sergey present Toychain [23, 24], which models Nakamoto consensus [25] and proves correctness properties about it using Coq [26]. Although Nakamoto consensus differs substantially from HOTSTUFF/LIBRABFT, Toychain is the closest prior work to ours in terms of modeling structures (collections of trees of records) and reasoning about their properties. Their model can be instantiated with different implementation components, and they prove that any implementation that provides components satisfying certain requirements is correct. In contrast, each of the LIBRABFT-related efforts mentioned above [19–21] proves properties about one particular model of HOTSTUFF/LIBRABFT.

While Toychain indeed establishes some generality by enabling instantiation with specific components, we impose no structure whatsoever on an implementation: if the externally visible behaviour of honest peers for a given implementation complies with two precisely stated rules, then that implementation can inherit the correctness properties we have proved of the abstract model.

Toychain initially assumed an injective hash function, which requires trusting that the proofs do not abuse the power granted by a false assumption. Interestingly, subsequent versions of Toychain addressed this issue by removing the assumption that the hash function used is injective. The bulk of Chap. 3 of Pîrlea's thesis [24] is devoted to describing the complexity that this undertaking involved, reporting that *every* proof had to be changed, and citing an example of one proof that grew from 10 lines to 150 to accommodate this enhancement!

In contrast, as described in Sect. 3.6, we have taken a different approach. Our abstract model is aware only of ids assigned to *Block*s that an implementation considers to be "in the system", not hash functions. We too rested our initial development on an unsound foundation by assuming that ids were injective. However, because our abstraction freed us from reasoning about hash functions in our correctness proofs, it was not particualrly disruptive to later augment our proofs to provide evidence of *specific* injectivity failures when necessary, tying those injectivity failures to *Record*s that the implementation considers to be in the system.

The work that is perhaps closest to our broader project is Velisarios [27], which uses the Coq theorem prover [26] and provides a framework for modeling distributed systems with byzantine peers, analogous to our system model. It is based on a Logic of Events [28] approach, in contrast to our state transition system approach. Velisarios is instantiated with definitions modeling PBFT [29] to prove PBFT correct. Coq supports extraction to OCaml, enabling an implementation to be derived from the PBFT model. Agda has support for extracting to Haskell or Javascript. However, we have not experimented with this. The goal of our ongoing work is to model our practical Haskell implementation in Agda and prove correctness for that model using the results presented in this paper.

Alturki et al. [30] use Coq to formally verify correctness of Algorand's [31] consensus protocol. Their correctness condition is slightly different as Algorand's protocol seeks to ensure that exactly one block is certified per round, implying a total order on all certified blocks. Crary [32] reports on work towards verifying correctness for the consensus mechanism of Hashgraph [33] in Coq. Losa and Dodds [34] describe formal verification of safety and liveness properties for the Stellar consensus protocol using Ivy and Isabelle/HOL. Alturki et al. [35] use Coq to formally verify properties for Gasper [2]—Ethereum 2.0's Proof of Stake consensus mechanism. Rather than assuming that any two quorums intersect on at least one honest node, they prove that, if (using our terminology) two conflicting blocks are committed, then there exist two quorums whose common members can have their stake slashed. This property would be satisfied if only the first offense results in slashing; presumably, a stronger property that ties the conflicting blocks to specific quorums related to those blocks could be proved.

There is also work model checking other BFT consensus protocols. For example, Tholoniat and Gramoli [8] have used ByMC [36] to model check RedBelly's consensus algorithm [37]; ByMC is a model checker designed to mitigate the state space blowup for algorithms in which processes wait for a threshold of messages. While basic HOTSTUFF may fit this structure, chained HOTSTUFF does not.

Braithwaite et al. [38] report on work in progress towards model checking Tendermint [39] using TLA+; so far, they have gained useful insight into the algorithm using very small configurations, and have found and fixed some specification bugs as a result. Nonetheless, their experience again highlights the challenges of model checking related to state space and execution time.

5   Concluding Remarks and Future Work

We have presented a formal model of the essence of a Byzantine Fault Tolerant consensus protocol used in several existing implementations, and proved its safety properties—including one that enables non-participants to verify commits—for a single epoch, during which configuration does not change. Extending our proofs to accommodate epoch changes (reconfiguration) is future work.

Our contributions include precisely defining implementation assumptions and correctness conditions, and developing formal, machine-checked proofs of correctness properties for any implementation satisfying the assumptions. Our model, definitions, and proofs are all expressed in Agda, and are available in open source.

Our approach enables verifying implementations by proving only that honest peers obey the rules established by our abstract assumptions, without repeating the hard work of proving the underlying protocol correct each time.

Our *thmS5* property establishes correctness unless it can provide *evidence* of a *specific* injectivity failure between *Blocks* that are *in the system*. Thus our proofs are independent of how specific implementations assign *Block* ids, and ensure that they hold unless and until an injectivity failure actually occurs. In this way, our abstract proofs support proving that implementations that use crypotgraphic hash functions to assign ids behave correctly, based on the standard assumption that a computationally bounded adversary cannot produce a hash collision.

In our broader project [9], we have defined a system model in which messages can be lost, duplicated and arbitrarily delayed, and dishonest peers are constrained only by their inability to forge signatures of honest peers. We have ported our Haskell implementation to Agda using a library we have developed [11], instantiated our system model with its types and handlers, and made substantial progress towards proving that it satisfies the required assumptions.

Beyond that, extending our system model to support proofs of liveness in the partial synchrony model [40] is future work. A pragmatic intermediate point is to prove within our existing system model that, from any reachable state that has *Block*s available to commit, there is some execution in which another *Block* is committed (called *plausible liveness* by Buterin and Griffith [41]). These liveness properties would pertain to a model of a specific *implementation*; liveness properties do not make sense for the abstract model presented in this paper.

References

1. King, S., Nadal, S.: PPCoin: peer-to-peer crypto-currency with proof-of-stake (2012). web.archive.org/web/20171211072318/peercoin.net/assets/paper/peercoin-
-paper.pdf
2. Buterin, V., et al.: Combining GHOST and Casper (2020). https://doi.org/10.48550/ARXIV.2003.03052, arxiv.org/abs/2003.03052
3. Lamport, L.: The part-time parliament. ACM Trans. Comput. Syst. **16**(2), 133–169 (1998). https://doi.org/10.1145/279227.279229
4. Yin, M., Malkhi, D., Reiter, M.K., Gueta, G.G., Abraham, I.: HotStuff: BFT consensus with linearity and responsiveness. In: Proceedings of the 2019 ACM Symposium on Principles of Distributed Computing, PODC 2019, pp. 347–356. Association for Computing Machinery, New York (2019). https://doi.org/10.1145/3293611.3331591
5. Baudet, M., et al.: State machine replication in the Libra blockchain (2019). developers.diem.com/papers/diem-consensus-state-machine-replication-in-the-diem-blockchain/2019-06-28.pdf
6. The LibraBFT Team: State machine replication in the Libra blockchain, May 2020. developers.diem.com/papers/diem-consensus-state-machine-replication-in-the-diem-blockchain/2020-05-26.pdf
7. Cachin, C., Vukolic, M.: Blockchain consensus protocols in the wild. CoRR abs/1707.01873 (2017). arxiv.org/abs/1707.01873
8. Tholoniat, P., Gramoli, V.: Formal verification of blockchain byzantine fault tolerance (2019). https://doi.org/10.48550/ARXIV.1909.07453, arxiv.org/abs/1909.07453
9. BFT consensus in Agda, December 2021. github.com/oracle/bft-consensus-agda/releases/tag/nasafm2022
10. diem.com: Diem github repository (2021). github.com/diem/diem
11. Carr, H., Jenkins, C., Miraldo, V.C., Moir, M., Silva, L.: An approach to translating Haskell programs to Agda and reasoning about them, March 2022. github.com/oracle/bft-consensus-agda/docs/README.md
12. Norell, U.: Dependently typed programming in Agda. In: Koopman, P., Plasmeijer, R., Swierstra, D. (eds.) AFP 2008. LNCS, vol. 5832, pp. 230–266. Springer, Heidelberg (2009). https://doi.org/10.1007/978-3-642-04652-0_5
13. Agda 2.6.1.1 documentation, May 2021. agda.readthedocs.io/en/v2.6.1.1
14. Wadler, P., Kokke, W.: Programming language foundations in Agda (2009). https://doi.org/10.1016/j.scico.2020.102440
15. Carr, H., Jenkins, C., Moir, M., Miraldo, V.C., Silva, L.: Towards formal verification of HotStuff-based byzantine fault tolerant consensus in Agda: Extended version (2022). arxiv.org/abs/2203.14711

16. Spreitzer, M.J., Theimer, M.M., Petersen, K., Demers, A.J., Terry, D.B.: Dealing with server corruption in weakly consistent, replicated data systems. In: Proceedings of the 3rd Annual ACM/IEEE International Conference on Mobile Computing and Networking, MobiCom 1997, pp. 234–240. ACM, New York (1997). https://doi.org/10.1145/262116.262151

17. Menezes, A.J., Vanstone, S.A., Oorschot, P.C.V.: Handbook of Applied Cryptography, 1st edn. CRC Press Inc., USA (1996)

18. Wikipedia: Universe (mathematics), February 2021. en.wikipedia.org/wiki/Universe_(mathematics)

19. Garillot, F., Siles, V.: Librachain, May 2020. github.com/novifinancial/LibraChain

20. Jehl, L.: Formal verification of HotStuff. In: Peters, K., Willemse, T.A.C. (eds.) FORTE 2021. LNCS, vol. 12719, pp. 197–204. Springer, Cham (2021). https://doi.org/10.1007/978-3-030-78089-0_13

21. Kukharenko, V., Ziborov, K., Sadykov, R., Rezin, R.: Verification of HotStuff BFT consensus protocol with TLA+/TLC in an industrial setting. SHS Web Conf. **93**, 01006 (2021). https://doi.org/10.1051/shsconf/20219301006

22. Kuppe, M.A., Lamport, L., Ricketts, D.: The TLA+ toolbox. Electron. Proc. Theor. Comput. Sci. **310**, 50–62 (2019). https://doi.org/10.4204/EPTCS.310.6

23. Pîrlea, G., Sergey, I.: Mechanising blockchain consensus. In: Proceedings of the 7th ACM SIGPLAN International Conference on Certified Programs and Proofs, CPP 2018, pp. 78–90. Association for Computing Machinery, New York (2018). https://doi.org/10.1145/3167086

24. Pîrlea, G.: Toychain formally verified blockchain consensus, April 2020. pirlea.net/papers/toychain-thesis.pdf

25. Nakamoto, S.: Bitcoin: a peer-to-peer electronic cash system (2009). www.bitcoin.org/bitcoin.pdf

26. Bertot, Y., Castran, P.: Interactive Theorem Proving and Program Development: Coq'Art The Calculus of Inductive Constructions, 1st edn. Springer Publishing Company, Incorporated (2010)

27. Rahli, V., Vukotic, I., Völp, M., Esteves-Verissimo, P.: Velisarios: byzantine fault-tolerant protocols powered by Coq. In: Ahmed, A. (ed.) ESOP 2018. LNCS, vol. 10801, pp. 619–650. Springer, Cham (2018). https://doi.org/10.1007/978-3-319-89884-1_22

28. Bickford, M., Constable, R.L., Rahli, V.: Logic of events, a framework to reason about distributed systems. In: 2012 Languages for Distributed Algorithms Workshop, Philadelphia, PA (2012). www.nuprl.org/documents/Bickford/LOE-LADA2012.html

29. Castro, M., Liskov, B.: Practical byzantine fault tolerance. In: Proceedings of the Third Symposium on Operating Systems Design and Implementation, OSDI 1999, pp. 173–186. USENIX Association, USA (1999)

30. Alturki, M.A., et al.: Towards a verified model of the algorand consensus protocol in Coq. In: Sekerinski, E., et al. (eds.) FM 2019 International Workshops. LNCS, vol. 12232 pp. 362–367 (2020). https://doi.org/10.1007/978-3-030-54994-7_27

31. Gilad, Y., Hemo, R., Micali, S., Vlachos, G., Zeldovich, N.: Algorand: scaling byzantine agreements for cryptocurrencies. In: Proceedings of the 26th Symposium on Operating Systems Principles, SOSP 2017, pp. 51–68. Association for Computing Machinery, New York (2017). https://doi.org/10.1145/3132747.3132757

32. Crary, K.: Verifying the hashgraph consensus algorithm (2021). arxiv.org/abs/2102.01167

33. Baird, L.: The Swirlds hashgraph consensus algorithm: fair, fast, byzantine fault tolerance. Technical report SWIRLDS-TR-2016-01 (2016). www.swirlds.com/downloads/SWIRLDS-TR-2016-01.pdf
34. Losa, G., Dodds, M.: On the formal verification of the Stellar consensus protocol. In: 2nd Workshop on Formal Methods for Blockchains (2020). drops.dagstuhl.de/opus/volltexte/2020/13422/pdf/OASIcs-FMBC-2020-9.pdf
35. Alturki, M.A., et al.: Verifying Gasper with dynamic validator sets in Coq (2020). github.com/runtimeverification/beacon-chain-verification/blob/master/casper/report/report.pdf
36. Konnov, I., Widder, J.: ByMC: byzantine model checker. In: Margaria, T., Steffen, B. (eds.) ISoLA 2018, Part III. LNCS, vol. 11246, pp. 327–342. Springer, Cham (2018). https://doi.org/10.1007/978-3-030-03424-5_22
37. Crain, T., Gramoli, V., Larrea, M., Raynal, M.: DBFT: efficient leaderless byzantine consensus and its application to blockchains. In: 2018 IEEE 17th International Symposium on Network Computing and Applications (NCA), pp. 1–8 (2018). https://doi.org/10.1109/NCA.2018.8548057
38. Braithwaite, S., et al.: Formal specification and model checking of the Tendermint blockchain synchronization protocol. In: 2nd Workshop on Formal Methods for Blockchains (2020). drops.dagstuhl.de/opus/volltexte/2020/13423/pdf/OASIcs-FMBC-2020-10.pdf
39. Buchman, E., Kwon, J., Milosevic, Z.: The latest gossip on BFT consensus (2018). https://doi.org/10.48550/ARXIV.1807.04938, arxiv.org/abs/1807.04938
40. Dwork, C., Lynch, N., Stockmeyer, L.: Consensus in the presence of partial synchrony. J. ACM 35(2), 288–323 (1988). https://doi.org/10.1145/42282.42283
41. Buterin, V., Griffith, V.: Casper the friendly finality gadget. CoRR abs/1710.09437 (2017). arxiv.org/abs/1710.09437

DSV: Disassembly Soundness Validation Without Assuming a Ground Truth

Xiaoxin An[✉], Freek Verbeek, and Binoy Ravindran

Virginia Tech, Blacksburg, USA
{xxan15,freek,binoy}@vt.edu

Abstract. Disassembly is a crucial step in binary security, reverse engineering, and binary verification. Various studies in these fields use disassembly tools and hypothesize that the reconstructed disassembly is correct. However, disassembly is a challenging and undecidable problem. Even state-of-the-art industrial disassemblers suffer from issues ranging from incorrectly recovered instructions to incorrectly assessing which addresses belong to instructions and which to data. We thus present DSV: a systematic and automated approach to validate whether the output of a disassembler is sound with respect to the binary. No source code, debugging information, or annotations are required. We apply DSV to 102 binaries of Coreutils with eight different state-of-the-art disassemblers from academia and industry. DSV is able to find soundness issues in the output of all these disassemblers. Using DSV to validate the output of a disassembler increases trust in any research effort built on top of it.

Keywords: Reverse engineering · Disassembly soundness · Concolic execution · Bounded model checking

1 Introduction

Disassembly is a crucial part of many reverse engineering and related sub-disciplines such as decompilation, binary analysis, binary verification, and binary rewriting. Practitioners have a plethora of tools available [1–4] to recover assembly instructions from an executable binary. Still, disassembly is not a solved problem: new techniques are developed based on, among others, machine learning [5], advanced heuristics, and inference [1–3]. These new techniques improve accuracy and soundness.

In most of the reverse engineering work, practitioners implicitly take the premise that the disassembly process is trustworthy. This premise is based on well-developed commercial and open-source disassemblers. For example, Ramblr [6] uses static binary rewriting to implement binary reassembling. The developers take angr [2] as the base platform to disassemble the binary and to rebuild the control flow graph (CFG), which means the correctness of Ramblr highly

© Springer Nature Switzerland AG 2022
J. V. Deshmukh et al. (Eds.): NFM 2022, LNCS 13260, pp. 636–655, 2022.
https://doi.org/10.1007/978-3-031-06773-0_34

relies on the correctness of angr. As an other example, Ghidra [3] is a state-of-the-art tool for decompilation. Its capabilities include control-flow reconstruction, type-inference, and pointer-analysis. However, all the functionalities are based on the assumption that disassembly is done correctly.

Disassembly, however, is by its very nature inherently an *untrustworthy* process. It is an undecidable problem [7,8]. In a context where only the binary is available (e.g., legacy systems or third-party proprietary software), there is *no ground truth* as to what the "correct" assembly instructions are. Even state-of-the-art disassemblers suffer from issues when, e.g., instructions are overlapping, data and instructions are mixed, indirect jump/call targets are unresolved, or a security vulnerability leads to unexpected control flow. Although mainstream disassemblers, such as objdump, Hopper, and IDA Pro, are developed by numerous researchers and are elaborately tested, different kinds of issues of these disassemblers have been discovered and reported [9,10].

In this paper, we propose a formal definition for the soundness of disassembly. Based on this definition, we implement a tool called DSV (short for Disassembly Soundness Validation) to validate whether a binary has been soundly disassembled or not. DSV takes a binary file and the assembly file disassembled from the binary file as inputs, generates "sound" or "unsound" as output, and reports all the "unsound" disassembled instructions. A key characteristic is that DSV does *not* assume a ground truth; in other words, DSV does not presume the availability of source code or debug information.

Essentially, DSV performs a recursive traversal starting at the binary's entry point while validating all reached instructions. DSV over-approximates the semantics of the binary under investigation in two ways. First, the semantics of various instructions are over-approximated by treating their effects on certain state parts as unknown. Second, the jumps and paths that can be traversed at runtime are statically over-approximated. DSV needs to deal with three key problems: unbounded loops, pointer aliasing, and indirect-branch instructions. In order to deal with loops, we employ *bounded model checking* (BMC) [11]. To handle the pointer aliasing problem and indirect branches, we use *concolic execution* [12].

We apply DSV to all the binaries of Coreutils library for eight different disassemblers. Soundness issues are found in each of them. Some examples include:

1. Incorrectly recovering instructions, e.g., Ghidra [3] disassembles 49 0f a3 c8 to bt rax,rcx while the correct result should be bt r8,rcx;
2. Incorrectly recovering immediate values in operands, e.g., Dyninst [13] translates 48 b8 ff ff ff ff ff to mov rax, 0x4611686018427387903, however, the valid instruction is movabs rax,0x3fffffffffffffff;
3. Missing instructions due to underapproximating indirect control flow transfers.

The contribution of this paper consists of:

1. A formal definition for the soundness of disassembly.

2. An automated methodology called DSV (for: Disassembly Soundness Validation) for validating whether the output of a black-box disassembler is sound
   w.r.t. a binary.
3. The application of this methodology to 102 binaries of Coreutils, each for
   eight different disassemblers: angr 8.19.7.25 [2], BAP 1.6.0 [4], Ghidra 9.0.4 [3],
   objdump 2.30, radare2 3.7.1 [1], Dyninst 10.2.1 [13], IDA Pro 7.6, and Hopper
   4.7.3.

Paper Organization. We discuss past and related work in Sect. 2. In Sect. 3,
we introduce a soundness definition for the disassembly process and discuss
the definition's validity. Section 4 illustrates DSV's implementation details. We
discuss soundness issues in existing disassemblers detected by DSV in Sect. 5.
Section 6 reports experimental results obtained by applying DSV to the Coreutils
library. We conclude in Sect. 7.

2   Past and Related Work

We first discuss the main approaches to disassembly. Then, the approaches for
validation of disassembly are discussed.

2.1   Disassembly Techniques

Linear sweep and recursive traversal are the major techniques behind the binary
disassembly process. PSI [14] and objdump are typical linear-sweep disassemblers.
These disassemblers handled the byte sequences in the binaries sequentially.
Linear-sweep disassemblers have superior performance under certain circumstances. For example, some linear sweep disassemblers fulfilled a 100% correctness on SPEC CPU2006 benchmarks generated by gcc and clang [10]. However,
linear sweep disassemblers have poor performance to handle special situations
such as overlapping instructions, inline data, and jump tables.

On the other hand, disassemblers such as IDA pro, Dyninst [13], Ghidra [3], and
Hopper were implemented using recursive traversal. These disassemblers decoded
the instructions following the execution path of the sequential and branching
instructions and tried to resolve the indirect jump addresses. Essentially, they
reconstructed the *control flow* on-the-fly in order to perform disassembly. Recursive traversal handles overlapping instructions and inline data in a more reliable
way than linear sweep disassemblers.

2.2   Soundness Validation

Andriesse et al. [10] checked the false positive and false negative rates for nine
mainstream disassemblers using SPEC CPU2006 and Glibc-2.22 as the benchmarks. The researchers gave a comprehensive comparison between different disassemblers on five critical criteria, including instruction recovery, function starting address relocation, function signature restoration, control flow graph (CFG),

and callgraph reconstruction. They used the ground truth information derived from LLVM analysis, DWARF debugging information, and some manual ancillary work. These ground truths provided critical information for the five criteria.

Paleari et al. [15] developed a methodology called n-version disassembly to apply differential analysis on verifying the correctness of different x86 disassemblers. The writers employed various disassemblers to recover the instruction from the same string of bytes and compared the results to find out the divergences. This paper validates the correctness of single-instruction disassembly, whereas our paper focuses on a complete disassembly process.

Pang et al. [16] manually evaluated the code base of various disassemblers and discussed the algorithm and heuristics used by these disassemblers. They also studied 3,788 binaries from different sources on nine main-stream disassemblers to evaluate the instruction recovery, cross-reference accuracy, function starting point, and CFG construction. They reported incorrectly disassembled cases existing in these disassemblers. The ground truths were automatically collected in the compiling and linking procedures when generating binaries with a method similar to the technique used by Andriesse et al. [10].

3 Definition of Disassembly Soundness

In this section, we provide a definition of the soundness of a disassembly process. Moreover, we discuss a crucial assumption required to ensure that this definition reflects the correctness of a disassembly process without ground truth.

3.1 Soundness Definition

To formulate a formal notion of disassembly soundness, we first introduce the types and notations used in the definition. An element of type Nword is a bit vector with size N. Given a bit vector w, notation $|w|$ provides the size of the bit vector. The type Instruction indicates the type of valid x86-64 instructions. In our soundness definition, an instruction is represented by, among other things, an opcode mnemonic, its operands with size directives, and possibly certain prefixes.

The definition of soundness is based on three components: a function read_bytes that reads bytes from a binary file, a function bytes_of that assembles a single instruction into bytes, and an abstract transition relation $\rightarrow_A$.

The first function read_bytes reads, given an address and a size, a byte sequence from the binary file. In all the following definitions, the type of the address is expressed as 64word, and the type of byte is 8word. Then the type annotation of read_bytes is represented as:

$$\text{read\_bytes} : \text{64word} \mapsto \mathbb{N} \mapsto [\text{8word}]$$

Function bytes_of maps a single instruction to the corresponding byte sequence representation, which is the essential work of any assembler. Although the bytes_of function represents an assembly process, our soundness definition does not consider any specific implementation of an assembler. Function bytes_of is type-annotated as:

$$\text{bytes\_of} : \text{Instruction} \mapsto [8\text{word}]$$

Let $\rightarrow_C$ denote a deterministic concrete transition relation over concrete addresses, and $\rightarrow_C^*$ represents the transitive closure of this transition relation. Modeling this concrete transition relation is impossible: the relation depends on the current state of registers, memory, and flags, but also on the state of peripherals, the OS, etc. Let a_0 be a binary's entry address. An instruction address a is *reachable* at run-time, if and only if:

$$a_0 \rightarrow_C^* a$$

The soundness definition is based on an over-approximative abstraction of this concrete transition relation, which is defined as $\rightarrow_A$. This is a non-deterministic transition relation over addresses: $\rightarrow_A$ is of type $64\text{word} \mapsto \{64\text{word}\}$. This transition relation solely concerns the 64-bit value of the instruction pointer rip of the concrete state and produces a set of next instruction addresses.

Definition 1. *Transition relation $\rightarrow_A$ is a proper abstraction of concrete transition relation $\rightarrow_C$, if and only if, for any reachable concrete states s and s':*

$$s \rightarrow_C s' \implies \text{rip}(s) \rightarrow_A \text{rip}(s')$$

We use $\rightarrow_A^*$ to indicate the transitive closure of $\rightarrow_A$.

Finally, the input of our soundness definition is the output of a disassembler. This output essentially is a partial mapping from byte sequence to instructions. It is denoted as disasm. We also define an auxiliary function disasm_n. Function disasm_n returns, given the current address, the size of bytes that are to be disassembled for the next single instruction. The two functions are of type:

$$\text{disasm} : [8\text{word}] \mapsto \text{Instruction}$$

$$\text{disasm\_n} : 64\text{word} \mapsto \mathbb{N}$$

Definition 2. *Let a_0 be a binary's entry address and let disasm be some disassemblers' output. Output disasm is sound, if and only if:*

$$\forall a \cdot a_0 \rightarrow_A^* a \implies \text{bytes\_of}(\text{disasm}(\beta)) = \beta$$
$$\textbf{where } \beta = \text{read\_bytes}(a, \text{disasm\_n}(a))$$

Definition 2 indicates that for all reachable addresses a inside a binary file, the bytes β of the disassembled instruction $\text{disasm}(\beta)$ located at address a are equal to the actual bytes that are read from the binary. If there exist some reachable instructions whose bytes are not equal to those in the binary, the disassembler is unsound.

This definition is independent of the inner mechanism of a disassembler. Whether a disassembler is implemented using recursive traversal, linear sweep, or machine-learning is irrelevant since we only try to validate the consistency between a binary file and the output of the disassembler.

3.2   Loose Comparison of Instruction Bytes

For each reachable instruction address, Definition 2 compares the bytes produced by reassembling a disassembled instruction with the original bytes from the binary. However, a strict byte-by-byte comparison may incorrectly classify a disassembler as unsound. Consider Fig. 1. The original assembly process is modeled as a asm function, which maps an instruction to the corresponding bytes. This function is part of the trust base, but it is not available.

$$asm : \texttt{Instruction} \mapsto [\texttt{8word}]$$

The ground truth is the original instruction i_0, assembled by the original assembler asm to b_0. Both i_0 and asm are assumed to be unavailable. The black-box disassembler disasm produces an instruction i_1 from b_0. Definition 2 suggests that it suffices to reassemble instruction i_1 into bytes b_1 and then strictly compare b_0 and b_1 to validate the soundness.

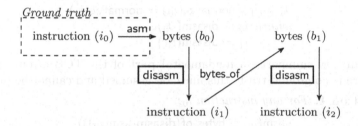

Fig. 1. Comparison per instruction. The dashed box indicates that the ground truth, i.e., the original instruction and original assembler, are unavailable. The disassembler under investigation (disasm) is black-box.

This, however, is not necessarily correct for two reasons. First, the function disasm may produce an instruction different from i_0 but with the same semantics. In such a case, reassembling may not reproduce the same bytes. Second, function bytes_of may be different from the original assembler asm (since that function is unavailable). Thus, even if the disassembler under investigation disasm was able to reproduce the exact instruction i_0, a strict comparison between b_0 and b_1 may still fail in the soundness validation.

Listing 1.1. An example that does not satisfy the soundness definition.

```
objdump(0f1f440000) = nop DWORD PTR [rax+rax*1+0x0]
gcc(nop DWORD PTR [rax+rax*1+0x0]) = 0f 1f 04 00
objdump(0f1f0400) = nop DWORD PTR [rax+rax*1]
```

For example, we employ gcc as the assembler and objdump as the disassembler and get the example in Listing 1.1. In this example, b_0 is 0f 1f 44 00 00, b_1 is

0f 1f 04 00. They are not equivalent. If we solely compare b_0 and b_1, we will make the wrong declaration that the disassembly process carried out by objdump is not sound. However, the disassembled result is sound since nop DWORD PTR [rax+rax*1+0x0] and nop DWORD PTR [rax+rax*1] are semantically equivalent. The reason behind this situation is that gcc would automatically apply optimization when it encounters certain types of instructions.

Thus, instead of a strict comparison, we will use a loose comparison of bytes. The bytes b_1 produced by reassembling are again disassembled. This produces instruction i_2. We will consider b_0 and b_1 loosely equal if these instructions are equal *after normalization*. The *normalization* is executed by a normalize function, which rewrites an instruction to a normalized format following rules such as reformatting assembly code from AT&T format to Intel, removing *1 and +0, and normalizing the representation of memory accesses. The normalized instruction is ensured to be semantically equivalent to the original instruction.

Definition 3. *Let β_0 and β_1 be two byte-sequences. They are loosely equivalent, notation $\beta_0 \simeq \beta_1$, if and only if:*

$$\beta_0 = \beta_1 \lor \mathsf{normalize}(i_0) = \mathsf{normalize}(i_1)$$
$$\textbf{\textit{where}} \ \ i_0 := \mathsf{disasm}(\beta_0),$$
$$i_1 := \mathsf{disasm}(\beta_1)$$

We can now summarise a fundamental part of the TCB of our approach. Since there is no ground truth, this must be assumed and cannot be proven.

Assumption 1. *For any instruction i_0:*

$$\mathsf{asm}(i_0) \simeq \mathsf{bytes\_of}(\mathsf{disasm}(\mathsf{asm}(i_0)))$$

implies that instruction i_0 has been correctly disassembled by function disasm.

4 Validation Algorithm

In Sect. 3, we define the soundness of the output of a disassembler w.r.t. the original binary file. According to that definition, there are three components that must be implemented: read_bytes, bytes_of, and the abstract step function $\rightarrow_A$.

The first two are straightforward. For read_bytes, we employ the readelf utility to get the binary segment information and implement a Python program to read a byte sequence from a binary file directly. To implement function bytes_of, we need to translate *a single instruction* to its byte-sequence representation. The choice of the assembler, whether gcc, clang, or some other, is independent of the disassembler under investigation and of the type of the source binary file.

The third component, an abstract transition relation $\rightarrow_A$, is more involved. A perfect and exact implementation of this component does not exist since it is undecidable which addresses are reachable from the entry point [7]. It is also undecidable to distinguish instructions from raw data [8]. Implementation of $\rightarrow_A$ requires, among other things, dealing with indirect jumps and calls, jump tables, data inlined in code, and overlapping instructions. Specifically, predicting where an indirect branch jumps to is a major challenge for all existing disassemblers.

4.1   Consequences of an Inexact Abstract Transition Relation

We thus, necessarily, implement an *inexact* abstract transition relation. We will use $\leadsto_A$ to denote this inexact implementation of the hypothetical exact abstract transition relation $\to_A$. We introduce the following terminology (here a_0 denotes the binaries' entry point):

White. An instruction address a is white if it is deemed reachable by the implementation $\leadsto_A$, i.e.:

$$a_0 \leadsto_A^* a$$

We can now rephrase the notions of false positive and false negative w.r.t. this terminology. A *false positive* occurs when disassembler-output is deemed sound by DSV, whereas it is incorrect. We define a false positive as the existence of an incorrectly disassembled reachable instruction that is not white. It is thus reachable at runtime and deemed unreachable (and therefore missed) by the implementation $\leadsto_A$. A *false negative*, then, is an incorrectly disassembled unreachable instruction that is white. In other words, it is deemed reachable by the implementation $\leadsto_A$, but unreachable at runtime.

A false positive can happen if the implementation $\leadsto_A$ *under-approximates* the concrete transition relation $\to_C$. In other words, it can happen if it is possible that a reachable instruction is not white. We aim for an implementation that does not suffer from false positives, and therefore require the implementation to be proper (see Definition 1): any reachable instruction is visited. In the case of proper over-approximation, a false negative can happen, i.e., an unreachable instruction may be white.

Finally, we would like to note that there is no decidable way to determine whether an instruction address is reachable or not. There is no ground truth and no reliable way of establishing reachability without source code. In practice, however, it is possible to establish the unreachability of certain parts of the binary. For example, in the current implementation, functions called inside an external __cxa_atexit function are not considered to be reachable (e.g., deconstructors). We thus use the following terminology:

Black. An instruction address is black if it is not white and *it can be established* (e.g., with conservative manual inspection) that it is unreachable.

Grey. An instruction address is grey if it is not white and it is not black, i.e., if it cannot be established whether it is reachable or not.

Given an over-approximative implementation $\leadsto_A$, all instruction addresses reported by some disassembler are either white, black, or grey. The aim is to construct an implementation $\leadsto_A$ that minimizes the number of grey instructions. Only the case where DSV finds an issue in a grey instruction constitutes a false negative.

4.2   DSV Overview

In essence, DSV employs a standard forward BMC exploration loop. At all times, three parameters are maintained:

s: **the current state.** A symbolic state is maintained that contains symbolic expressions for registers, flags, and memory. The initial state solely consists of an assignment of some concrete values to the stack pointer `rsp` and the instruction pointer `rip`.

π: **the current path constraint.** A symbolic predicate is maintained that contains the branching conditions of the current path. Its purpose is to prune inconsistent paths (we check the consistency using the Z3 SMT Solver [17]). Initially, this constraint is true.

Σ: **the stored states.** A key-value mapping with as keys instruction addresses and as values symbolic states. This mapping allows DSV to keep track of which addresses have been visited and to reduce the traversed state space. Initially, this mapping is empty.

DSV first fetches the instruction *i* as disassembled by the disassembler under investigation and validates that instruction (see Sect. 3.2). It then updates Σ by adding the current state σ. It may be the case that the current instruction address was already visited. In that case, a *merge* must happen between the current state *s* and the stored state. If the current state *s* and the merged state *agree* (intuitively: they contain the same information), then no further exploration is necessary. If the instruction address was unvisited, the current state is simply inserted into Σ. DSV then concolically executes instruction *i* to the merged state s_m, given the current path constraint π. This provides a set of pairs of symbolic states and path constraints; one instruction may induce multiple paths. Each of these pairs is explored.

4.3 State and Memory Model

The state consists of assignments of symbolic expressions to flags, registers, and memory. Symbolic expressions consist of expressions with a standard set of operators (e.g., $+, -, \ldots$) and as base operands either immediate values, registers, or flags. Most notably, a symbolic dereference operator is supported that reads data from memory. An operand may also be an unconstrained universally quantified variable. We will use v_f to denote a fresh variable. The symbolic expressions used by DSV are close to that used in existing literature [18].

Since the bit length of all registers is fixed, we model general-purpose registers as a 64-bit Z3 bit-vector and deal with register aliasing accordingly. We set the initial values of all the registers, except for `rip` and `rsp`, to symbolic values and modify the values of registers according to the semantics of instructions. The value of each register can be either symbolic or concrete.

There are different techniques to model memory. To design a space-efficient memory model that simulates the memory changes during the execution of a binary, we model memory as a function mem of type 64word $\mapsto$ ([8word], $\mathbb{N}$). This function maps memory addresses to byte sequences and the size of the region starting at the given address. Function mem is partial, which means that not all addresses at the memory have explicit content. At all times, all regions in the range of mem are separate.

Since we keep the stack pointer concrete, all local variables correspond to memory regions with concrete addresses. The same holds for global variables. Moreover, the Glibc functions malloc and calloc are modeled in such a way that they return a *concrete* address that does not overlap with any existing region in the memory. This concretizes the majority of addresses. Theoretically, this approach may lead to unsoundness issues: for example, if a program successfully allocates memory using malloc, then branches are taken based on whether that (non-null) pointer is greater than some immediate value. To the best of our knowledge, such behavior is undefined according to the C standard.

Assumption 2. *We assume that the control flow of a binary does not depend on the concrete values returned by memory allocation functions or on the concrete value of the stack pointer.*

However, not all memory addresses are concrete: symbolic addresses occur when pointers are returned by external functions that are not linked statically. In these cases, reading from a symbolic memory region returns a fresh symbol. Writing to such a memory region will remove all heap-related regions from the memory but will keep the local stack frame intact.

4.4   Merging and Agreeing

If the address of the current state s was already visited, the current state s and the visited state s_{old} are merged (see Algorithm 1). If the current value v at a key k in s is symbolic, then v is possible to represent any value, and we do not need to change it. However, if the current value v is concrete, we need to compare v with v_{old} at the same key k in s_{old} to decide how to merge v and v_{old} to get the new result.

Algorithm 1. Merging algorithm.

```
 1: function MERGE(s_old, s)
 2:     s_new ← copy(s)
 3:     for all (k, v) ∈ s do
 4:         v_old ← s_old[k]
 5:         if v is a concrete value then
 6:             if v_old is a concrete value then
 7:                 if v ≠ v_old then
 8:                     s_new[k] ← fresh variable
 9:                 end if
10:             else
11:                 s_new[k] ← fresh variable
12:             end if
13:         end if
14:     end for
15:     return s_new
16: end function
```

The current state s is not explored if state s and merged state s_m contain the same information, i.e., if the two state *agree*. Two states agree if they have the same keys and for any key-value pair (k, e) in s and (k, e_m) in s_m the expression e and e_m agree.

Definition 4. *Let* fresh(e) *denote the set of fresh variables in symbolic expression* e. *Two expressions* e_0 *and* e_1 *agree if and only if there exists a bijection* β *between* fresh(e_0) *and* fresh(e_1), *such that* e_0 *and* e_1 *are syntactically equal if all fresh variables* v_f *in* e_0 *are replaced with* $\beta(v_f)$.

Example 1. Consider a loop in which register `rax` is incremented with 4 every iteration. Let the visited state $s_{old} = \{\text{rax} := v_{f_0}, \text{rdi} := v_{f_0} + 100\}$. After one loop iteration, the current state $s = \{\text{rax} := v_{f_0} + 4, \text{rdi} := v_{f_0} + 100\}$. The merged state will be $s_m = \{\text{rax} := v_{f_1}, \text{rdi} := v_{f_0} + 100\}$ and will be stored. States s_m and s do not agree and exploration will continue. However, after one more iteration, we will obtain state $s' = \{\text{rax} := v_{f_1} + 4, \text{rdi} := v_{f_0} + 100\}$. States s' and state s_m will be merged, resulting in $s'_m = \{\text{rax} := v_{f_2}, \text{rdi} := v_{f_0} + 100\}$. States s_m and s'_m do agree, and therefore the loop is not unrolled further.

4.5   Instruction Semantics

There is no need to set up complete semantics for *all* instructions. In our implementation, instruction semantics is constructed to change the value of the `rip` register to guide the symbolic execution. We only need to build up semantics for instructions that – be it directly or indirectly – influence the `rip` register. We will call this the set of *relevant* instructions.

The set of *relevant* instructions include **push**, **pop**, **mov**, **lea**, **call**, **ret**, simple arithmetic instructions, logical instructions, bitwise instructions, jump instructions, etc. According to the statistics taken in some literature [19], these instructions would make up over 96% of instructions in multiple C/C++ applications and web browsers. Advanced instructions such as floating-point instructions and SIMD extensions typically do not impact register `rip`. It is not necessary to construct specific semantics for these instructions.

For all the irrelevant instructions, we use *unknown* semantics by assigning fresh variables any time an irrelevant instruction is executed. In most cases, an instruction has an opcode and different operands, and the content of the destination operand is modified by the instruction. For irrelevant instructions, the semantics assigns some fresh variable v_f to the destination operand, representing that the current status of the corresponding register, flag, or memory is undefined or undetermined. The fresh variables are handled using the symbolic execution rules in our DSV SE engine.

4.6   Concolic Execution

As discussed in Sect. 4.3, we make use of concolic execution that concretizes memory addresses as much as possible while leaving the remainder as symbolic as possible. As such, the branching conditions that are taken are generally symbolic. In the case of a conditional jump based on a symbolic flag value, both paths are taken (sequential execute and jump). This over-approximates reachability.

A key challenge is to resolve indirect-branch addresses. An indirect branch is a control flow transfer (jump or call) where the target is computed instead of an immediate. Indirect branches happen, e.g., in the case of compiled switch-statements, function callbacks, or virtual tables. Three cases may arise:

1. The current state is sufficiently concrete that the computation can be resolved. In this case, exploration continues.
2. The expression that computes the next value of `rip` is symbolic, but the current state and the path constraint contain sufficient information to both bind and over-approximate the set of next addresses. In this case, exploration continues to all next addresses.
3. The current state does not contain sufficient information to bind the set of next addresses; the expression that computes `rip` contains unbounded symbolic values. An error message is produced, and we manually investigate how to resolve the issue. Generally, we need to trace back and see which irrelevant instructions need to be considered relevant. This situation is infrequent since we have modelled the semantics of the most common instructions based on their usage rate.

With the state model for registers, flags, and memory, we carry out the concolic execution to construct a CFG for the machine code. Concolic execution is overapproximative. The vast majority of branches are taken due to the symbolic conditions. Meanwhile, `rsp` is always concrete, and therefore local variables in the stack frame can be read/written. Besides, addresses are concrete in the memory allocation functions. The concrete addresses prevent memory aliasing issues.

In the construction of CFG, indirect jump, indirect call, and return instructions pose a challenge of how to resolve the indirect-branch addresses. The path constraint provides a bound on the set of next addresses. Besides, we introduce a trace-back model to fix the problem of unimplemented instruction semantics. We also implement an algorithm [20] to solve the challenge of jump table without determined upperbound. However, these still exists unresolved indirect-branch addresses in the concolic execution since it is an undecidable problem.

5 Soundness Issues Exposed by DSV

This section summarises some of the soundness issues found by DSV. We mainly focus on instructions that are erroneously recovered by different disassemblers.

In Sect. 6.1, we use DSV to evaluate the disassembly results generated by eight disassemblers on the Coreutils library. Even though most of the reachable instructions for these disassemblers are correctly recovered, there are few exceptions where the disassembled instruction is incorrect w.r.t. the byte sequence. We report on some cases found by DSV, that are inappropriately disassembled by certain disassemblers. Table 1 summarises the found results, which are disagreed for different disassemblers. Some of the disagreements (row 1, 2 of the table) are trivial and can be argued not to impact soundness. Row 3, 4, 5, and 6 of the table consists of actual soundness issues.

Table 1. Examples of instruction recovery results for different disassemblers. All the results are normalized to Intel format.

bytes	objdump	radare2	angr	Hopper	BAP	IDA Pro	Ghidra	Dyninst
f3c3	repz ret	ret			rep ret	rep retn	ret	rep ret
4881a4249000 0000fffbffff	and qword ptr [rsp+0x90], 0xfffffffffffffbff						and qword ptr [rsp+ 0x90],0xfffffbff	
4899	cqo							cdq rax
4d0fa3f7	bt r15,r14						bt rdi,r14	bt r15,r14
48be00000000 00f0ffff	movabs rsi,0xfffff00000000000					mov rsi,0xfffff00000000000		mov rsi,0x-17592186044416
64488b042528 000000	mov rax,qword ptr fs:[0x28]							mov rax,0x28

Row 1 and 2 of Table 1 mainly concerns different representations of the same semantical intent. There are cases where the operands of an instruction are not represented since default behavior is assumed. For instance, both Ghidra and Dyninst (correctly) assume that immediates are sign-extended to fit the destination operand, if necessary. However, minor differences may be relevant. For example, the instructions repz ret and ret have the same semantical intent but their execution time may differ for certain architectures.

Row 3, 4, 5, and 6 concerns semantically different recovered instructions. For instance, Dyninst disassembles 4899 to cdq rax, which is not a valid instruction in x86-64 ISA (note that cdq performs sign-extension to 64 bits, whereas cqo performs sign-extension to 128 bits). An example is shown where Ghidra misrepresents a register (rdi instead of r15). Besides, a 64-bit immediate is wrongly disassembled by Dyninst. Finally, Dyninst sometimes seems to omit representations of segment registers such as ds and fs.

Except for the examples listed in Table 1, there are some ambiguous cases for different disassemblers. The outputs generated by Dyninst do not have any ptr operator to indicate the operand size of a memory operand, which leads to ambiguous semantical behavior. For example, 49837c242800 is translated to cmp [r12 + 0x28],0x0 by Dyninst while the other disassemblers' result is cmp qword ptr [r12 + 0x28],0x0. Without the qword ptr specifying the size of the operand as 64-bit, we cannot determine what the exact value reading from the memory is. Thus the result of the cmp instruction is undetermined.

6   Experimental Results

In Sect. 6.1, we apply DSV on eight different disassemblers: objdump 2.30, radare2 3.7.1, angr 8.19.7.25, BAP 1.6.0, Hopper 4.7.3, IDA Pro 7.6, Ghidra 9.0.4, and

Dyninst 10.2.1, using 102 test cases from Coreutils-8.31. Here, we evaluate the performance of DSV.

All these experiments are carried out on a machine with Intel Core i7-7500U CPU @ 2.70 GHz × 4 and 16 GB RAM. The OS is Ubuntu 20.04.2 LTS, and the Coreutils-8.31 library is compiled using gcc 7.5.0 through the standard build process.

6.1   Coreutils Library

We apply DSV on 102 test cases in the Coreutils library, which are disassembled using eight disassemblers. For each test case, we report the number of instructions: total, white, gray, and black. The definition of *white*, *black*, or *grey* instructions are given in Sect. 4.1. Roughly speaking, white indicates instructions that are proven to be reachable by DSV, and black illustrates unreachable instructions. The grey instructions are those that are reported by the disassembler but are not visited by DSV; the reachability of these instructions is unknown. Table 2 shows the results of basename, expand, mknod, realpath, and dir test cases in the Coreutils library for different disassemblers. These 5 test cases are selected based on the number of total instructions and the diversity of various instruction types.

Instruction Recovery. Most disassemblers are capable to correctly disassemble all the reachable instructions. As shown in Fig. 2, for most of test cases in Coreutils library, objdump, angr, BAP, and IDA Pro achieve an accuracy rate of 100% for single-instruction recovery. Meanwhile, Ghidra and Dyninst make some errors in the disassembly process for some test cases, and the accuracy would decrease to around 97.5%.

Control Flow Recovery. For all test cases, there exists a gap between the number of white instructions, which are reachable instructions detected by DSV, and the number of total instructions; in other words, the number of black instructions can be relatively high. This can be accounted for two reasons.

The first reason is that different disassemblers consider different parts of the binary. For example, BAP generates the instructions from sections .symtab, .debug_line, .debug_ranges, and so on, while some disassemblers may solely generate instructions from .text, .plt, and .plt.got sections.

The second reason lies in the technique that DSV employs to handle external functions. DSV treats external functions as black boxes and does not go inside the external functions to execute them. Internal functions that are called by external functions may be considered black. For example, the internal function close_stdout is called by the external function __cxa_atexit (it calls the close function after program exit). Thus, the close_stdout function is considered black. Some exceptions include __libc_start_main and pthread_create. These two external functions execute the function pointer passed through the rdi register, and the internal functions pointed to are not executed by DSV. Broader coverage, i.e., less black instructions, can be reached by providing semantics to external functions that call internal ones.

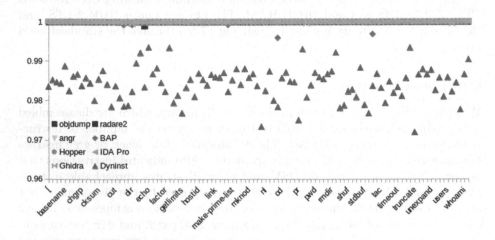

Fig. 2. Ratio of correctly disassembled vs. the white disassembled instructions.

The ratio of grey vs. white instruction is an indication of how accurate control flow has been recovered. If the ratio is low (zero), then the disassembler highly accurately decided which instructions are reachable and which is not. If it becomes higher, this may indicate either that the disassembler coarsely overapproximated which instructions are reachable (many grey instructions), or that the disassembler missed instructions. The ratio is on average about 4%. As shown in Fig. 3, BAP usually has the highest ratio since the instructions whose addresses are stored in indirect jump tables are missed by BAP due to lack of support for indirect branching. Meanwhile, objdump and angr have similar ratio for most of test cases , as we use angr to statically generate a CFG (CFGFast) and to disassemble a binary file, which have similar outputs as objdump.

The amount of white instructions per disassembler is an indication of how many instructions have been reached. objdump, radare2, angr, and Ghidra have similar numbers of white instructions. Meanwhile, BAP has smaller results in all these test cases since it does not employ any heuristics to solve the indirect branch problem caused by jump table. The results for Dyninst are unstable because there are some instruction-recovery errors in the disassembly results.

Soundness Results. Most disassemblers are sound for most of the test cases. We find that Ghidra sometimes incorrectly recovers instructions. There are three other major exceptions.

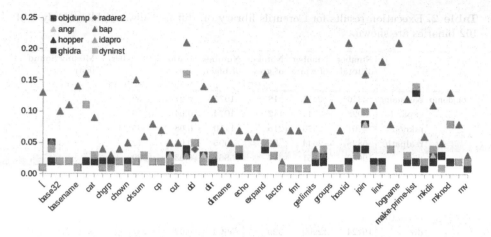

Fig. 3. Ratio of grey instructions to white for different disassemblers.

First, BAP does not resolve indirect branches. Since BAP essentially reports an empty set of next addresses for indirect jump tables – whereas DSV wants to continue exploration – DSV reports a soundness issue. We marked these as missing instructions: the issue is not that BAP incorrectly recovers instructions, but that it misses instructions by "under-approximating" control flow.

Additionally, radare2 sometimes translates instructions to data. For example, in dir test case, radare2 disassembles the bytes ff2552c72100 at address 3888 to data .qword 0x90660021c75225ff, which should be translated to a call instruction to malloc. This kind of mis-translation leads to missing instructions.

In some situations, Hopper is not capable to correctly determining the instruction boundaries. For example, in dir test case, at address 0xf2a8, the disassembler should generate an instruction sub r12d,0x1. However, Hopper classifies it as data and continues the disassembly process from address 0xf2a9.

Another exception is Dyninst. There are various examples showing that Dyninst involves errors on instruction recovery. These errors may cascade since incorrectly recovering instructions may also lead to incorrectly assessing which instruction addresses are to be disassembled. For instance, Dyninst cannot recover control flow for the seq test case from the Coreutils library since incorrectly recovered instructions lead to unrealistic paths.

Table 2. Execution results for Coreutils library on different disassemblers. Only 5 of 102 binaries are shown.

		Number of total	Number of white	Number of grey	Number of black	Ratio of grey vs. white	Number of indirects	Missing instr	Sound
objdump	basename	3310	2217	18	1075	0.01	59		
	expand	3928	2742	112	1074	0.04	79		
	mknod	4101	2775	216	1110	0.08	65		
	realpath	5828	2644	89	3095	0.03	72		
	dir	19029	12751	417	5861	0.03	230		
radare2	basename	3409	2217	18	1174	0.01	59		
	expand	4027	2742	111	1174	0.04	79		
	mknod	4200	2775	214	1211	0.08	65		
	realpath	5927	2644	86	3197	0.03	72		
	dir	19124	12900	320	5904	0.02	231	×	×
angr	basename	3415	2217	18	1180	0.01	59		
	expand	4033	2742	111	1180	0.04	79		
	mknod	4206	2775	214	1217	0.08	65		
	realpath	5933	2644	86	3203	0.03	72		
	dir	19134	12751	413	5970	0.03	230		
BAP	basename	5894	826	114	4954	0.14	37	×	
	expand	7373	1320	205	5848	0.16	56	×	
	mknod	7022	1282	162	5578	0.13	43	×	
	realpath	11368	1251	108	10009	0.09	46	×	
	dir	28906	5718	667	22521	0.12	150	×	×
Hopper	basename	3250	2217	18	1015	0.01	59		
	expand	3845	2742	111	992	0.04	79		
	mknod	4022	2775	68	1179	0.02	65		
	realpath	5636	2644	86	2906	0.03	72		
	dir	18292	12607	350	5335	0.03	230	×	×
IDA Pro	basename	3221	2217	18	986	0.01	59		
	expand	3820	2742	111	967	0.04	79		
	mknod	3995	2775	68	1152	0.02	65		
	realpath	5607	2644	87	2876	0.03	72		
	dir	18220	12751	268	5201	0.02	230		
Ghidra	basename	3256	2217	18	1021	0.01	59		
	expand	3826	2742	99	985	0.04	79		
	mknod	4029	2775	68	1186	0.02	65		
	realpath	5658	2644	86	2928	0.03	72		
	dir	18303	12751	267	5285	0.02	230		×
Dyninst	basename	3269	2222	16	1031	0.01	60		×
	expand	3874	2707	123	1044	0.05	79		×
	mknod	4058	2747	214	1097	0.08	64		×
	realpath	5724	2609	85	3030	0.03	71		×
	dir	18694	12845	329	5520	0.03	230		×

7 Conclusion

Disassembly is a challenging and undecidable problem that lies at the base of various research in reverse engineering, formal verification, binary hardening, and security analysis. Even state-of-the-art disassemblers that have been elaborately designed and tested have soundness issues, such as whether a disassembly accurately reflects the semantical behavior of the binary under investigation. We propose a definition for soundness of the output of a disassembler w.r.t. the original binary. Moreover, we propose DSV, a tool for validating whether a binary has been correctly disassembled. DSV finds incorrectly disassembled instructions and assesses whether the disassembler under investigation could determine at which addresses instructions need to be recovered correctly.

DSV does not assume the existence of ground truth in the form of source code, an LLVM representation, or debugging information. We, therefore, necessarily make assumptions and aim to provide an explicit insight into the trusted codebase. The trusted codebase of DSV contains two key assumptions. First, we assume that the proposed way of loosely comparing byte sequences allows DSV to decide whether a single byte sequence correctly corresponds to a single instruction. Second, DSV employs concolic execution leaving certain parts, such as the stack pointer, concrete. It is assumed that leaving these parts concrete does not influence the reachability of instruction addresses.

DSV has been applied to validate the output of eight state-of-the-art disassembler tools on 102 binaries of Coreutils library. Soundness issues were exposed, ranging from incorrect instruction recovery to incorrectly recovered control flow of the binary (leading to missing instructions).

Future Work: DSV essentially is a binary exploration tool. We argue that DSV demonstrates that the combination of bounded model checking and concolic execution is very applicable in the context of stripped binaries as it mitigates the complexity of some fundamental issues. Even though its current version solely focuses on the validation of disassembly, we aim to use the core algorithm and concepts of DSV for other binary exploration efforts. For example, We aim to use DSV for validating the correctness of generated control flow and call graphs, and generally for exposing "weird" edges [21] and security vulnerabilities in binaries. Currently, DSV is restricted to binaries with the x86-64 format. Since our formal definition is general, we intend to extend our implementation and validation efforts to other ISAs, such as ARM.

Source Code Availability. The complete source code, benchmarks, and experimental results are open-sourced and available at the project website: https://ssrg-vt.github.io/DSV. The source code artifact is archived with a DOI link at: https://doi.org/10.5281/zenodo.6380975.

Acknowledgments. We thank the anonymous reviewers for their insightful comments which greatly improved the paper. This work is supported by the Defense Advanced Research Projects Agency (DARPA) under Agreement No. HR00112090028 and contract N6600121C4028, and the US Office of Naval Research under grants N00014-17-1-2297 and N00014-18-1-2665.

References

1. Radare2: Unix-like reverse engineering framework. https://github.com/radareorg/radare2 (2021)
2. Shoshitaishvili, Y., et al.: Sok:(state of) the art of war: offensive techniques in binary analysis. In: 2016 IEEE Symposium on Security and Privacy (SP), pp. 138–157. IEEE (2016)
3. Rohleder, R.: Hands-on ghidra-a tutorial about the software reverse engineering framework. In: Proceedings of the 3rd ACM Workshop on Software Protection, pp. 77–78 (2019)
4. Brumley, D., Jager, I., Avgerinos, T., Schwartz, E.J.: BAP: a binary analysis platform. In: Gopalakrishnan, G., Qadeer, S. (eds.) CAV 2011. LNCS, vol. 6806, pp. 463–469. Springer, Heidelberg (2011). https://doi.org/10.1007/978-3-642-22110-1_37
5. Park, J., Xu, X., Jin, Y., Forte, D., Tehranipoor, M.: Power-based side-channel instruction-level disassembler. In: 2018 55th ACM/ESDA/IEEE Design Automation Conference (DAC), pp. 1–6. IEEE (2018)
6. Wang, R., et al.: Ramblr: making reassembly great again. In: NDSS (2017)
7. Rice, H.G.: Classes of recursively enumerable sets and their decision problems. Trans. Am. Math. Soc. **74**(2), 358–366 (1953)
8. Wartell, R., Zhou, Y., Hamlen, K.W., Kantarcioglu, M.: Shingled graph disassembly: finding the undecideable path. In: Tseng, V.S., Ho, T.B., Zhou, Z.-H., Chen, A.L.P., Kao, H.-Y. (eds.) PAKDD 2014. LNCS (LNAI), vol. 8443, pp. 273–285. Springer, Cham (2014). https://doi.org/10.1007/978-3-319-06608-0_23
9. Meng, X., Miller, B.P.: Binary code is not easy. In: Proceedings of the 25th International Symposium on Software Testing and Analysis, pp. 24–35 (2016)
10. Andriesse, D., Chen, X., Van Der Veen, V., Slowinska, A., Bos, H.: An in-depth analysis of disassembly on full-scale x86/x64 binaries. In: 25th USENIX Security Symposium (USENIX Security 16), pp. 583–600 (2016)
11. Biere, A., Cimatti, A., Clarke, E.M., Strichman, O., Zhu, Y.: Bounded model checking (2003)
12. Sen, K., Marinov, D., Agha, G.: Cute: a concolic unit testing engine for c. ACM SIGSOFT Softw. Eng. Notes **30**(5), 263–272 (2005)
13. Bernat, A.R., Miller, B.P.: Anywhere, any-time binary instrumentation. In: Proceedings of the 10th ACM SIGPLAN-SIGSOFT Workshop on Program Analysis for Software Tools, pp. 9–16 (2011)
14. Zhang, M., Qiao, R., Hasabnis, N., Sekar, R.: A platform for secure static binary instrumentation. In: Proceedings of the 10th ACM SIGPLAN/SIGOPS International Conference on Virtual Execution Environments, pp. 129–140 (2014)
15. Paleari, R., Martignoni, L., Fresi Roglia, G., Bruschi, D.: N-version disassembly: differential testing of x86 disassemblers. In: Proceedings of the 19th International Symposium on Software Testing and Analysis, pp. 265–274 (2010)
16. Pang, C., et al.: Sok: all you ever wanted to know about x86/x64 binary disassembly but were afraid to ask. arXiv preprint arXiv:2007.14266 (2020)
17. de Moura, L., Bjørner, N.: Z3: an efficient SMT solver. In: Ramakrishnan, C.R., Rehof, J. (eds.) TACAS 2008. LNCS, vol. 4963, pp. 337–340. Springer, Heidelberg (2008). https://doi.org/10.1007/978-3-540-78800-3_24
18. Cadar, C., Dunbar, D., Engler, D.R., et al.: Klee: unassisted and automatic generation of high-coverage tests for complex systems programs. In: OSDI, vol. 8, pp. 209–224 (2008)

19. Akshintala, A., Jain, B., Tsai, C.C., Ferdman, M., Porter, D.E.: X86–64 instruction usage among c/c++ applications. In: Proceedings of the 12th ACM International Conference on Systems and Storage, pp. 68–79 (2019)
20. Cifuentes, C., Van Emmerik, M.: Recovery of jump table case statements from binary code. Sci. Comput. Program. **40**(2–3), 171–188 (2001)
21. Shapiro, R., Bratus, S., Smith, S.W.: Weird machines in ELF: a spotlight on the underappreciated metadata. In: 7th USENIX Workshop on Offensive Technologies (WOOT 13) (2013)

Probabilistic Hyperproperties
with Rewards

Oyendrila Dobe[1], Lukas Wilke[2], Erika Ábrahám[2], Ezio Bartocci[3],
and Borzoo Bonakdarpour[1(✉)]

[1] Michigan State University, East Lansing, MI, USA
borzoo@msu.edu
[2] RWTH Aachen University, Aachen, Germany
[3] Technische Universität Wien, Vienna, Austria

Abstract. *Probabilistic hyperproperties* describe system properties that
are concerned with the probability relation between different system
executions. Likewise, it is desirable to relate performance metrics (e.g.,
energy, execution time, etc.) between multiple runs. This paper introduces the notion of *rewards* to the temporal logic HyperPCTL by extending the syntax and semantics of the logic to express the accumulated
reward relation among different computations. We demonstrate the
application of the extended logic in expressing side-channel timing countermeasures, efficiency in probabilistic conformance, path planning in
robotics applications, and recovery time in distributed self-stabilizing
systems. We also propose a model checking algorithm for verifying
Markov Decision Processes against HyperPCTL with rewards and report
experimental results.

Keywords: Markov models · Hyperproperties · Rewards · Model
checking · Policy

1 Introduction

Stochastic phenomena appear in many systems such as those that interact with
the physical environment (e.g., due to environmental uncertainties, thermal fluctuations, random message loss, and processor failure). Traditionally, the specification of systems that deal with uncertainties are expressed in some form of probabilistic temporal logic such as PCTL and PCTL* [5]. These logics can express the
properties of *single* probabilistic computation trees. The temporal logic HyperPCTL [2]
generalizes PCTL to express *probabilistic hyperproperties* by allowing quantification over
multiple computation trees and expressing the probability relation among them. For

This research was partially supported by the United States NSF SaTC Award 2100989,
WWTF ICT19-018 grant ProbInG and the DFG Research and Training Group
UnRAVeL.
O. Dobe and L. Wilke—First co-authors.

J. V. Deshmukh et al. (Eds.): NFM 2022, LNCS 13260, pp. 656–673, 2022.
https://doi.org/10.1007/978-3-031-06773-0_35

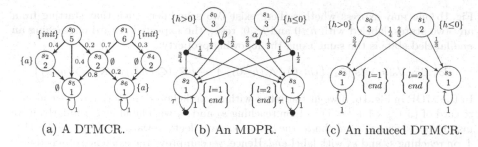

(a) A DTMCR.   (b) An MDPR.   (c) An induced DTMCR.

Fig. 1. Example Markov models.

instance, consider the Markov Decision Process (MDP) in Fig. 1b. The HyperPCTL formula

$$\forall\hat{\sigma}.\forall\hat{s}(\hat{\sigma}).\forall\hat{s}'(\hat{\sigma}).\ \left((h > 0)_{\hat{s}} \wedge (h \leq 0)_{\hat{s}'}\right) \Rightarrow \left(\mathbb{P}\lozenge(l = 1)_{\hat{s}} = \mathbb{P}\lozenge(l = 1)_{\hat{s}'}\right)$$

requires that the probability of reaching a state with proposition $l = 1$ from any pair of states $\hat{s}$ and $\hat{s}'$ labeled by $h > 0$ and $h \leq 0$ respectively, should be equal for the Discrete Time Markov Chain (DTMC) induced by any scheduler $\hat{\sigma}$.

In addition to the probability relation between certain events and computations, it is natural to analyze the average behavior of Markov models as well as the interrelation of average behaviors in different executions. For example:

– *Service-level agreements* (e.g., average system response time and uptime) are generally concerned with average performance metrics of a system among a set of executions. This is, of course, a system-wide performance requirement rather than the property of individual executions.
– *Side-channel timing* leaks can potentially reveal sensitive information through execution time of a function call. The execution time can be captured as a reward model where each instruction is associated with a cost and the probabilistic hyperproperty expresses that every pair of executions should exhibit the same expected execution cost.
– *Distributed algorithms* often use randomization to break symmetry in order to tackle impossibility results. Although one can reason about the expected performance of a randomized distributed algorithm by the traditional reward models, from a design perspective, it is desirable to determine and mitigate states from where convergence to the objective of the algorithm takes much longer than others.

These examples clearly motivate the need to somehow augment probabilistic hyperproperties with reward constraints.

With this motivation, our first contribution in this paper is to make the connection between reward models and probabilistic hyperproperties. In the context of a hyperproperty, analogous to the probability relation between multiple executions in a HyperPCTL formula, a reward mechanism should be able to express the expected reward relation along different quantified computation trees. To this end, we extend the syntax and semantics of HyperPCTL by allowing arithmetic functions over expected rewards and comparing them over multiple executions. For instance, for the MDP in

Fig. 1b one may express whether there exist two schedulers such that starting from any two states, labeled with $h>0$ and $h\leq0$, resp., the expected reward of reaching an *end*-labeled state is the same using the following property:

$$\exists\hat{\sigma}_1.\exists\hat{\sigma}_2.\forall\hat{s}(\hat{\sigma}_1).\forall\hat{s}'(\hat{\sigma}_2).\left((h>0)_{\hat{s}} \wedge (h\leq0)_{\hat{s}'}\right) \to \left(\mathcal{R}_{\hat{s}}(\lozenge\, end_{\hat{s}}) = \mathcal{R}_{\hat{s}'}(\lozenge\, end_{\hat{s}'})\right)$$

In the MDP in Fig. 1b, if we instantiate $\hat{s}$ with s_0, and choose the action α, we collect a reward of $(3 + \frac{3}{4} \times 1 + \frac{1}{4} \times 1) = 4$, on reaching s_2 and s_3 with label *end*. Similarly, if we instantiate $\hat{s}'$ with s_1, and choose the action α, we collect a reward of $(3+\frac{2}{3}\times1+\frac{1}{3}\times1) = 4$, on reaching s_2 and s_3 with label *end*. Hence, we can prove the existence of schedulers that satisfy the above property in the MDP in Fig. 1b. On a closer look, no matter which action we choose at s_0 and s_1, the property is always satisfied. Also, if we instantiate $\hat{s}$ and $\hat{s}'$ with any other states different from s_0 resp. s_1, the property is vacuously true. On the contrary, if we replace the equality of rewards with inequality then the property is false as there are no such schedulers. Besides comparing reward values, our HyperPCTL extension offers further expressive power to e.g. measure accumulated rewards in an execution until an observable property, say termination, gets satisfied in another one.

Our second contribution in this paper is an algorithm for model checking Hyper-PCTL formulas with rewards for MDPs. Since the general verification problem is known to be undecidable [2], we focus on memoryless non-probabilistic schedulers which yields a decidable problem, for which we propose a model checking algorithm based on logical problem encoding and SMT solving. We have implemented a prototype of our method and analyzed it experimentally on three case studies: (1) side-channel timing attacks, (2) probabilistic performance conformance, and (3) randomized path planning for multi-agent robotics applications.

Organization. In Sect. 2, we present preliminary concepts. We introduce our proposed extension of HyperPCTL with rewards in Sect. 3 and discuss its applications in Sect. 4. We present our model checking algorithm and associated experimental results in Sects. 5 and 6, respectively. Related work is discussed in Sect. 7. Finally, we conclude in Sect. 8.

2 Preliminaries

By $\mathbb{R}$ ($\mathbb{R}_{\geq0}$) we denote the real (non-negative real) numbers, and by $\mathbb{N}$ the natural numbers including 0. For any domain D and any $v = (v_0,\ldots,v_{n-1}) \in D^n$, we define $v[i] = v_i$ for $i \in \{0,\ldots,n-1\}$. The concepts below have been adapted from [5] and extended to work for hyperlogics.

2.1 Discrete-time Markov Models with Rewards

When defining costs or rewards for Markov models, we can assign rewards to states or transitions. In this work we limit to the assignment of *non-negative* rewards to *states* and support multi-dimensional reward *vectors*.

Definition 1. *A Discrete Time Markov Chain with (k-ary) rewards (DTMCR) is a tuple $\mathcal{D} = (S, P, \mathsf{AP}, L, rew)$ with (1) a non-empty set of states S, (2) a transition function $P : S \times S \to [0,1] \subseteq \mathbb{R}$ with $\sum_{s'\in S} P(s,s') = 1$ for all $s \in S$, (3) a finite set of atomic propositions AP, (4) a labeling function $L : S \to 2^{\mathsf{AP}}$ and (5) a reward function $rew: S \to \mathbb{R}_{\geq0}^k$.*

Figure 1a shows an example DTMCR with unary rewards. Assume a DTMCR $\mathcal{D} = (S, P, \mathsf{AP}, L, rew)$. An *infinite path* is a sequence of states $\pi = s_0 s_1 \ldots \in S^\omega$ with $P(s_i, s_{i+1}) > 0$ for all $i \in \mathbb{N}$. A non-empty prefix of an infinite path is a *finite path* $\pi = s_0 \ldots s_{n-1} \in S^+$ of length $|\pi| = n \in \mathbb{N} \setminus \{0\}$. Let $Paths_s^{\mathcal{D}}$ ($fPaths_s^{\mathcal{D}}$) be the set of all infinite (finite) paths starting in $s \in S$. A state $t \in S$ is *reachable* from $s \in S$ if there exists a path in $fPaths_s^{\mathcal{D}}$ ending in t. A state $s \in S$ is *absorbing* iff $P(s, s) = 1$.

For a finite path $\pi \in fPaths_s^{\mathcal{D}}$, we define its *cylinder set* $Cyl^{\mathcal{D}}(\pi)$ as the set of all infinite paths with π as a prefix. The probability of the cylinder set of $\pi \in fPaths_s^{\mathcal{D}}$ is defined as $\mathrm{Pr}_s^{\mathcal{D}}(Cyl^{\mathcal{D}}(\pi)) = \Pi_{i=0}^{|\pi|-1} P(s_i, s_{i+1})$. For sets $R \subseteq fPaths_s^{\mathcal{D}}$ we have $\mathrm{Pr}_s^{\mathcal{D}}(R) = \sum_{\pi \in R'} \mathrm{Pr}_s^{\mathcal{D}}(\pi)$, where R' contains all finite paths from R that have no extensions in R. These notions induce for each $s \in S$ the *probability space*,

$$\left(Paths_s^{\mathcal{D}}, \left\{ \bigcup_{\pi \in R} Cyl^{\mathcal{D}}(\pi) \mid R \subseteq fPaths_s^{\mathcal{D}} \right\}, \mathrm{Pr}_s^{\mathcal{D}} \right).$$

Note that the cylinder sets of two finite paths starting in the same state are either disjoint or one is contained in the other.

For a reward function $rew \colon S \to \mathbb{R}_{\geq 0}^k$ and $i \in \{0, \ldots, k-1\}$ we define $rew_i \colon S \to \mathbb{R}_{\geq 0}$ to assign the *ith state reward* $rew_i(s) = rew(s)[i]$ to all $s \in S$. The *ith cumulative reward* for a finite path, $\pi = s_0 s_1 \ldots s_{n-1}$ is defined as $rew_i(\pi) = \sum_{j=0}^{n-1} rew_i(s_j)$. Note that non-negative rewards assure monotonic increase of cumulative rewards with path extensions.

To argue about simultaneous runs across two DTMCRs, we define their parallel composition.

Definition 2. *Assume two DTMCRs $\mathcal{D}_i = (S_i, P_i, \mathsf{AP}_i, L_i, rew_i)$ with k_i-ary rewards, $i \in \{1, 2\}$. We define the* parallel composition *$\mathcal{D}_1 \times \mathcal{D}_2 = (S_1 \times S_2, P, \mathsf{AP}_1 \cup \mathsf{AP}_2, L, rew)$ with $(k_1 + k_2)$-ary rewards, such that for all $(s_1, s_2), (s_1', s_2') \in S \times S$:*
(1) $P((s_1, s_2), (s_1', s_2')) = P_1(s_1, s_1') \cdot P_2(s_2, s_2')$, (2) $L((s_1, s_2)) = L_1(s_1) \cup L_2(s_2)$ and (3) $rew((s_1, s_2)) = (rew_1(s_1), rew_2(s_2))$.

Next, we extend the probabilistic nature of DTMCRs with non-determinism.

Definition 3. *A Markov Decision Process with k-ary rewards (MDPR) is a tuple $\mathcal{M} = (S, Act, P, \mathsf{AP}, L, rew)$ with (1) a non-empty set of states S, (2) a non-empty finite set of actions Act, (3) a transition function $P : S \times Act \times S \to [0, 1] \subseteq \mathbb{R}$ such that for each $s \in S$ we have $\sum_{s' \in S} P(s, \alpha, s') \in \{0, 1\}$. For all $\alpha \in Act$, there is at least one action that can be chosen in each state, such that $\alpha \in Act(s) = \{\alpha \in Act \mid \sum_{s' \in S} P(s, \alpha, s') = 1\}$ and for $\alpha \in Act \setminus Act(s), \sum_{s' \in S} P(s, \alpha, s') = 0$, (4) a finite set of atomic propositions AP, (5) a labeling function $L : S \to 2^{\mathsf{AP}}$, and (6) a reward function $rew : S \to \mathbb{R}_{\geq 0}^k$.*

Figure 1b shows an example MDPR. In each state, for the next execution step, any of the enabled actions can be chosen non-deterministically. *Schedulers* are used to eliminate this non-determinism.

Definition 4. *A scheduler for an MDPR $\mathcal{M} = (S, Act, P, \mathsf{AP}, L, rew)$ is a tuple $\sigma = (Q, act, mode, init)$ with (1) a countable set of modes Q, (2) a function $act : Q \times S \times Act \to [0, 1] \subseteq \mathbb{R}$ such that for every $s \in S$ and $q \in Q$,*

$$\sum_{\alpha \in Act(s)} act(q, s, \alpha) = 1 \quad and \sum_{\alpha \in Act \setminus Act(s)} act(q, s, \alpha) = 0 ,$$

(3) a mode transition function $mode : Q \times S \to Q$ and (4) $init : S \to Q$ assigning each state of $\mathcal{M}$ a starting mode.

Let $\Sigma^{\mathcal{M}}$ be the set of all schedulers for $\mathcal{M}$. A scheduler is *finite-memory* if Q is finite, *memoryless* if $|Q| = 1$, and *non-probabilistic* if $act(q, s, \alpha) \in \{0, 1\}$ for all $q \in Q$, $s \in S$ and $\alpha \in Act$.

Definition 5. *Assume an MDPR $\mathcal{M} = (S, Act, P, \mathsf{AP}, L, rew)$ with k-ary rewards and a scheduler $\sigma = (Q, act, mode, init)$ for $\mathcal{M}$. Then $\mathcal{M}$ and σ induce the DTMCR with k-ary rewards $\mathcal{M}^{\sigma} = (S^{\sigma}, P^{\sigma}, \mathsf{AP}, L^{\sigma}, rew^{\sigma})$, where $S^{\sigma} = Q \times S$,*

$$P^{\sigma}((q,s),(q',s')) = \begin{cases} \sum_{\alpha \in Act(s)} act(q,s,\alpha) \cdot P(s,\alpha,s') & \text{if } q' = mode(q,s) \\ 0 & \text{if } q' \neq mode(q,s) \end{cases}$$

with $L^{\sigma}(q, s) = L(s)$ and $rew^{\sigma}(q, s) = rew(s)$, for all $q \in Q$ and $s \in S$.

If σ is memoryless, we sometimes omit its mode and write (s) instead of (q, s). For the MDPR in Fig. 1b and a scheduler that chooses action α in states s_0, s_1 and action τ in states s_2, s_3, the induced DTMCR is shown in Fig. 1c.

Different executions in several models can be seen as executions in the composition of the models. To simplify notation, in this paper we restrict ourselves to comparing executions in the same model, leading to the notion of *self-composition*.

Definition 6. *Assume an MDPR $\mathcal{M} = (S, Act, P, \mathsf{AP}, L, rew)$ and a sequence $\sigma = (\sigma_0, \ldots, \sigma_{n-1}) \in (\Sigma^{\mathcal{M}})^n$ of schedulers for $\mathcal{M}$. For $i \in \{0, \ldots, n-1\}$, let $\mathcal{M}_i = (S, Act, P, \mathsf{AP}_i, L_i, rew)$ with $\mathsf{AP}_i = \{a_i \mid a \in \mathsf{AP}\}$, and $L_i : S \to 2^{\mathsf{AP}_i}$ with $L_i(s) = \{a_i \mid a \in L(s)\}$. We define the n-ary self composition of $\mathcal{M}$ under σ as the DTMCR $\mathcal{M}^{\sigma} = (S^{\sigma}, P^{\sigma}, \mathsf{AP}^{\sigma}, L^{\sigma}, rew^{\sigma}) = \mathcal{M}_0^{\sigma_0} \times \ldots \times \mathcal{M}_{n-1}^{\sigma_{n-1}}$.*

In the above definition, $\mathcal{M}_i^{\sigma_i}$ is the DTMCR induced by $\mathcal{M}_i$ and σ_i. Note that the reward of a state $\boldsymbol{s} = ((q_0, s_0), \ldots, (q_{n-1}, s_{n-1})) \in S^{\sigma}$ in the n-ary self-composition $\mathcal{M}^{\sigma}$ is the sequence $rew^{\sigma}(\boldsymbol{s}) = (rew(s_0), \ldots, rew(s_{n-1}))$, i.e. the ith state reward in the jth execution is $rew_{j,i}^{\sigma}(\boldsymbol{s}) = rew_i(s_j)$. For a finite path π in $\mathcal{M}^{\sigma}$, we denote its cumulative ith reward in the jth execution as $rew_{j,i}(\pi) = \sum_{k=0}^{|\pi|-1} rew_{j,i}(\pi[k])$.

3   HyperPCTL with Rewards

3.1   HyperPCTL Syntax

Hyperproperties of executions in an MDPR can be specified using the logic HyperPCTL. As shown in Fig. 2, a *quantified formula* φ^q starts with a sequence of quantifiers over scheduler variables $\hat{\sigma} \in \hat{\Sigma}$, fixing

$$
\begin{aligned}
\varphi^q &::= \forall \hat{\sigma}.\varphi^q \mid \exists \hat{\sigma}.\varphi^q \mid \varphi^{sq} \\
\varphi^{sq} &::= \forall \hat{s}(\hat{\sigma}).\varphi^{sq} \mid \exists \hat{s}(\hat{\sigma}).\varphi^{sq} \mid \varphi^{nq} \\
\varphi^{nq} &::= \mathbf{true} \mid a_{\hat{s}} \mid \varphi^{nq} \wedge \varphi^{nq} \mid \neg\varphi^{nq} \mid \varphi^{ar} \sim \varphi^{ar} \\
\varphi^{ar} &::= \mathbb{P}(\varphi^{path}) \mid \mathcal{R}_{\hat{s},i}(\varphi^{path}) \mid f(\varphi^{ar}, \ldots, \varphi^{ar}) \\
\varphi^{path} &::= \bigcirc \varphi^{nq} \mid \varphi^{nq} \, \mathcal{U} \, \varphi^{nq} \mid \varphi^{nq} \, \mathcal{U}^{[k_1,k_2]} \, \varphi^{nq}
\end{aligned}
$$

Fig. 2. HyperPCTL syntax

the schedulers under which executions are considered. Inside, a *state-quantified formula* φ^{sq} defines a sequence of quantifiers over state variables $\hat{s} \in \hat{S}$, where each quantifier specifies a new execution from a given state under a given scheduler. Note that different executions might use the same scheduler.

In the scope of these quantifiers is a *non-quantified state formula* φ^{nq}, which can be the constant `true`, an atomic proposition indexed with a state variable, a conjunction, a negation, or a relational constraint comparing two arithmetic expressions via $\sim\in\{>$ $,\geq,=,\neq,<,\leq\}$. *Arithmetic expressions* are constructed from probability expressions, reward expressions or applying arithmetic function symbols (e.g., addition, subtraction, multiplication, etc., where constants are 0-ary functions) to arithmetic expressions. Note that the reward operator $\mathcal{R}$ is indexed with a state variable $\hat{s}$ specifying the execution for which we consider the reward, and an integer i specifying the reward component; for models with unary rewards, like in our examples, we skip the second index (as it is always 0). Finally, the parameters of probabilistic and reward expressions are *path formulas*, which apply one of the temporal operators, next ($\bigcirc$), unbounded until ($\mathcal{U}$), or bounded until ($\mathcal{U}^{[k_1,k_2]}$, $k_1 \leq k_2 \in \mathbb{N}_{\geq 0}$) to non-quantified state formulas.

A HyperPCTL *formula* is a quantified formula in that every occurrence of an indexed atomic proposition $a_{\hat{s}}$ is in the scope of a state quantifier for $\hat{s}(\hat{\sigma})$, which in turn is in the scope of a scheduler quantifier for $\hat{\sigma}$. W.l.o.g., in the following we assume that each scheduler or state variable is quantified at most once.

In addition to standard syntactic sugar $\vee, \rightarrow, \Diamond, \square, \ldots$, we can express expected cumulative reward over the next $t \in \mathbb{N}$ steps and expected reward in the state reached after t steps as follows:

$$\mathcal{R}_{\hat{s},i}(C_t) = \mathcal{R}_{\hat{s},i}(\mathbf{true}\,\mathcal{U}^{[t,t]}\mathbf{true}) \text{ and } \mathcal{R}_{\hat{s},i}(I_t) = \begin{cases} \mathcal{R}_{\hat{s},i}(C_t) - \mathcal{R}_{\hat{s},i}(C_{t-1}) & \text{if } t>0 \\ \mathcal{R}_{\hat{s},i}(C_t) & \text{else} \end{cases}.$$

3.2   HyperPCTL Semantics

HyperPCTL formulas are evaluated recursively in the context of an MDPR $\mathcal{M}$, a sequence σ of actions and a sequence s of states, both of the same length. Intuitively, the length of these sequences says how many executions we run in parallel, and the ith elements in these sequences specify the ith execution of the scheduler and the initial state in the induced DTMCR, respectively. An MDPR $\mathcal{M}$ satisfies a HyperPCTL formula φ (written $\mathcal{M} \models \varphi$) iff $\mathcal{M},(),() \models \varphi$.

In the semantic rules below, the substitution $\varphi[\hat{\sigma}\rightsquigarrow\sigma]$ remembers the instantiation of a scheduler variable $\hat{\sigma}$ by a scheduler $\sigma = (Q, act, mode, init)$ through syntactically transforming in φ each $\forall\hat{s}(\hat{\sigma})$ and $\exists\hat{s}(\hat{\sigma})$ into $\forall\hat{s}(\sigma)$ and $\exists\hat{s}(\sigma)$, resp. When instantiating the nth state quantifier $\forall\hat{s}(\sigma)$ or $\exists\hat{s}(\sigma)$ by a state s, we "start" an nth execution in state $(init(s),s)$ of $\mathcal{M}^\sigma$, which corresponds to extending the previously $(n-1)$-ary self-composition of $\mathcal{M}$ to *arity* n. We remember this by adding σ and s at the end of the corresponding sequences in the context (using concatenation $\circ$), and applying the substitution $\varphi[\hat{s}\rightsquigarrow n]$ to replace each indexed atomic proposition $a_{\hat{s}}$ and each reward operator $\mathcal{R}_{\hat{s},i}$ in φ by a_n and $\mathcal{R}_{n,i}$, respectively.[1] We recall from [2] the semantics of constructs that are not related to rewards:

---

[1] Instead of syntactical substitutions, we could also use binding functions to map scheduler variables to schedulers and state variables to indices in the state sequence in the context.

$$\mathcal{M}, \sigma, s \models \forall \hat{\sigma}.\varphi \qquad \textit{iff } \mathcal{M}, \sigma, s \models \varphi[\hat{\sigma} \rightsquigarrow \sigma] \textit{ for all } \sigma \in \Sigma^{\mathcal{M}}$$

$$\mathcal{M}, \sigma, s \models \exists \hat{\sigma}.\varphi \qquad \textit{iff } \mathcal{M}, \sigma, s \models \varphi[\hat{\sigma} \rightsquigarrow \sigma] \textit{ for some } \sigma \in \Sigma^{\mathcal{M}}$$

$$\mathcal{M}, \sigma, s \models \forall \hat{s}(\sigma).\varphi \qquad \textit{iff } \mathcal{M}, \sigma \circ \sigma, s \circ (\textit{init}(s), s) \models \varphi[\hat{s} \rightsquigarrow |\boldsymbol{\sigma}|] \textit{ for all } s \in S$$

$$\mathcal{M}, \sigma, s \models \exists \hat{s}(\sigma).\varphi \qquad \textit{iff } \mathcal{M}, \sigma \circ \sigma, s \circ (\textit{init}(s), s) \models \varphi[\hat{s} \rightsquigarrow |\boldsymbol{\sigma}|] \textit{ for some } s \in S$$

$$\mathcal{M}, \sigma, s \models \mathbf{true}$$

$$\mathcal{M}, \sigma, s \models a_i \qquad \textit{iff } a_i \in L^{\sigma}(s)$$

$$\mathcal{M}, \sigma, s \models \varphi_1 \wedge \varphi_2 \qquad \textit{iff } \mathcal{M}, \sigma, s \models \varphi_1 \textit{ and } \mathcal{M}, \sigma, s \models \varphi_2$$

$$\mathcal{M}, \sigma, s \models \neg\varphi \qquad \textit{iff } \mathcal{M}, \sigma, s \not\models \varphi$$

$$\mathcal{M}, \sigma, s \models \varphi_1^{ar} \sim \varphi_2^{ar} \qquad \textit{iff } [\![\varphi_1^{ar}]\!]_{\mathcal{M},\sigma,s} \sim [\![\varphi_2^{ar}]\!]_{\mathcal{M},\sigma,s}$$

$$[\![\mathbb{P}(\varphi_{path})]\!]_{\mathcal{M},\sigma,s} \quad = \quad \mathrm{Pr}^{\mathcal{M}^{\sigma}}(\{\pi \in \textit{Paths}_s^{\mathcal{M}^{\sigma}} \mid \mathcal{M}, \sigma, \pi \models \varphi_{path}\})$$

$$[\![f(\varphi_1^{ar}, \ldots, \varphi_k^{ar})]\!]_{\mathcal{M},\sigma,s} \quad = \quad f([\![\varphi_1^{ar}]\!]_{\mathcal{M},\sigma,s}, \ldots, [\![\varphi_k^{ar}]\!]_{\mathcal{M},\sigma,s})$$

We are left with the semantics for $\mathcal{R}_{j,i}(\varphi^{path})$ (note that instantiating a state quantifier for $\hat{s}(\sigma)$ replaces each $\mathcal{R}_{\hat{s},i}$ occurrence by $\mathcal{R}_{j,i}$, where j is the position of the quantifier). The value of $\mathcal{R}_{j,i}(\bigcirc \varphi^{nq})$ is the current ith reward plus the expected ith reward of the successor state in the jth execution, if the probability that the successor state satisfies φ^{nq} is 1; otherwise, the value is undefined. The value of $\mathcal{R}_{j,i}(\varphi_1^{nq} \mathcal{U} \varphi_2^{nq})$ is the expected cumulative ith reward in the jth execution, accumulated until the first time a (global self-composition) state is reached that satisfies φ_2^{nq}, in case the probability of satisfying $\varphi_1^{nq} \mathcal{U} \varphi_2^{nq}$ is 1; otherwise, the value is undefined. The semantics of $\mathcal{R}_{j,i}(\varphi_1^{nq} \mathcal{U}^{[k_1,k_2]} \varphi_2^{nq})$ is similar, but the rewards are accumulated until the first satisfaction of φ_2^{nq} within time $[k_1, k_2]$. Formally, the semantics for $[\![\mathcal{R}_{j,i}(\varphi^{path})]\!]_{\mathcal{M},\sigma,s}$ is as follows, given that $[\![\mathbb{P}(\varphi^{path})]\!]_{\mathcal{M},\sigma,s} = 1$. If that is not the case, $[\![\mathcal{R}_{j,i}(\varphi^{path})]\!]_{\mathcal{M},\sigma,s}$ is undefined.

$$fPaths_s^{\mathcal{M}^{\sigma}}(\varphi_1^{nq} \mathcal{U} \varphi_2^{nq}) \quad = \quad \{s_0 \ldots s_n \in fPaths_s^{\mathcal{M}^{\sigma}} \mid \mathcal{M}, \sigma, s_n \models \varphi_2^{nq} \textit{ and }$$
$$\mathcal{M}, \sigma, s_i \models \varphi_1^{nq} \wedge \neg\varphi_2^{nq} \textit{ for } i = 0, \ldots, n-1\}$$

$$fPaths_s^{\mathcal{M}^{\sigma}}(\varphi_1^{nq} \mathcal{U}^{[k_1,k_2]} \varphi_2^{nq}) \quad = \quad \{s_0 \ldots s_n \in fPaths_s^{\mathcal{M}^{\sigma}} \mid k_1 \leq n \leq k_2 \textit{ and }$$
$$\mathcal{M}, \sigma, s_n \models \varphi_2^{nq} \textit{ and }$$
$$\mathcal{M}, \sigma, s_i \models \varphi_1^{nq} \textit{ for } i = 0, \ldots, k_1 - 1 \textit{ and }$$
$$\mathcal{M}, \sigma, s_i \models \varphi_1^{nq} \wedge \neg\varphi_2^{nq} \textit{ for } i = k_1, \ldots, n-1\}$$

$$[\![\mathcal{R}_{j,i}(\bigcirc \varphi^{nq})]\!]_{\mathcal{M},\sigma,s} \quad = \quad rew_{j,i}^{\sigma}(s) + \sum_{s' \in S^{\sigma}} P^{\sigma}(s, s') \cdot rew_{j,i}^{\sigma}(s')$$

$$[\![\mathcal{R}_{j,i}(\varphi_1^{nq} \mathcal{U} \varphi_2^{nq})]\!]_{\mathcal{M},\sigma,s} \quad = \quad \sum_{\pi \in fPaths_s^{\mathcal{M}^{\sigma}}(\varphi_1^{nq} \mathcal{U} \varphi_2^{nq})}(\mathrm{Pr}^{\sigma}(\pi) \cdot rew_{j,i}^{\sigma}(\pi))$$

$$[\![\mathcal{R}_{j,i}(\varphi_1^{nq} \mathcal{U}^{[k_1,k_2]} \varphi_2^{nq})]\!]_{\mathcal{M},\sigma,s} \quad = \quad \sum_{\pi \in fPaths_s^{\mathcal{M}^{\sigma}}(\varphi_1^{nq} \mathcal{U}^{[k_1,k_2]} \varphi_2^{nq})}(\mathrm{Pr}^{\sigma}(\pi) \cdot rew_{j,i}^{\sigma}(\pi))$$

Since adding rewards to HyperPCTL causes arithmetic values to be potentially undefined, we need to extend the above semantics to handle the propagation of undefined values. For each syntactic case, the above semantics remains unchanged if all involved statements used in the definition are defined. It would be an easy job to set the values in all other cases to undefined. However, even if some of the arguments are undefined, we still might be able to conclude a defined value. For example, if one of the operands in a conjunction is false then the conjunction is inevitably false, even if the other operand is undefined. In extension to the above semantics for the cases when all terms used in the definition are defined, below we fix the semantics for the remaining cases with the objective to reduce the occurrence of undefined values.

We extend the Boolean domain of true (1) and false (0) with undefined ($\bot$). We use the $\models$ relation as before when all sub-expressions (and thus the formula) are known to be defined, and use $[\![\cdot]\!]$ otherwise. Logical constants as well as atomic propositions are always defined. The value of a conjunction is undefined iff none of the operands is false and not both operands are true, whereas a negation is undefined iff the negated formula is undefined.

The value of a universally state-quantified formula $\forall \hat{s}(\sigma).\varphi$ is undefined if the value of φ is undefined for at least one instantiation of the formula with a state and is not false for any other instantiation. Likewise, the value of an existentially state-quantified formula $\exists \hat{s}(\sigma).\varphi$ is undefined if the value of φ is undefined for at least one instantiation of the formula with a state and is not true for any other instantiation. The undefinedness of scheduler quantifiers is analogous.

Also the domain of arithmetic values gets extended with the undefined value $\bot$. Arithmetic function applications $f(\varphi_1, \ldots, \varphi_k)$ and arithmetic constraints $\varphi_1 \sim \varphi_2$ are undefined iff any of their parameters are undefined. However, for probabilistic until $\varphi = \mathbb{P}(\varphi_1 \mathcal{U} \varphi_2)$ we can exploit available information to increase the number of defined cases, even if the satisfaction of one of the operands is undefined in the current state, as shown in Table 1. The information we exploit for the semantics in a state s are the probabilistic until values in the successor states, or more precisely, the value of $p = \sum_{s' \in S^\sigma} P(s, s') \cdot [\![\varphi]\!]_{M,\sigma,s'} \in [0,1] \cup \{\bot\}$, which we consider undefined iff one of the successor probabilities is undefined.

Row	$[\![\varphi_1]\!]$	$[\![\varphi_2]\!]$	p	$[\![\varphi]\!]$
1	*	1	*	1
2	0	0	*	0
3	$\bot$	0	0	0
4	$\bot$	0	$\neq 0$	$\bot$
5	1	0	*	p
6	0	$\bot$	*	$\bot$
7	$\bot$	$\bot$	*	$\bot$
8	1	$\bot$	1	1
9	1	$\bot$	$\neq 1$	$\bot$

Table 1. Semantics of $\varphi = \mathbb{P}(\varphi_1 \mathcal{U} \varphi_2)$, partly depending on $p = \sum_{s' \in S^\sigma} P(s, s') \cdot [\![\varphi]\!]_{M,\sigma,s'} \in [0,1] \cup \{\bot\}$. Here, $[\![.]\!]$ is short for $[\![.]\!]_{M,\sigma,s}$.

Table 1 extends the original probabilistic until semantics from above with the undefined cases, using $*$ to denote an arbitrary (defined or undefined) arithmetic value. This table is split into three parts. The first part states that if φ_2 is true then the formula value is 1. The second part covers the case where φ_2 is false, where the violation of φ_1 leads to the violation of the formula, and if φ_1 is true then the formula probability equals the value of p. An interesting case in the second block is when φ_1 is undefined: though in most cases the formula is also undefined, if we know that the probability to satisfy the until formula in the future is 0 then we can safely state that the probability to satisfy the same in the current state is also 0. Similarly in the third block, if φ_1 is true in the current state and the probability to satisfy the until formula in the future is 1 then, irrelevant of the value of φ_2, the probability to satisfy the until formula from the current state is always 1.

Reward expressions are undefined if the respective path property is not satisfied with probability 1. For the reward expression $\mathcal{R}_{j,i}(\bigcirc \varphi)$, this is the only case in which it is undefined. To evaluate $\varphi = \mathcal{R}_{j,i}(\varphi_1 \mathcal{U} \varphi_2)$, if φ_2 is true in the current state then we need to know only the current state's reward; in this case the reward is defined independent of the successor states. If φ_2 is false currently then the reward is computed from the current state reward plus the expected successor φ-values, thus undefinedness of the reward expression in a successor state causes undefinedness in the current state. However, if φ_2 is undefined in the current state then we do not know which of these two cases apply; the only case where this does not matter is if the reward expression evaluates in all successor states to 0, namely then the value of φ is the current state reward. Thus if φ_2 is undefined in the current state then the reward expression is undefined in all but this special case, even if the probability of the until formula is 1.

The definedness of bounded until formulas is similar to the unbounded case for both probability and reward expressions, except that we now also need to account for the bounds.

However, with these definitions, we only exploit some but not all information, to determine the definedness of a property. Assume, for example, the property that from a state s, the probability to eventually satisfy φ is less than p. It might be the case that in some states reachable from s the value of φ is undefined, triggering the above probability to be undefined by our algorithm. However, φ might be reachable along another path with a probability larger than p, in which case we could have safely stated that it is at least p. Hence, it can be a direction of future research to find a tighter bound on the definedness of a property.

4   Applications of HyperPCTL with Rewards

4.1   Timing Attacks

Side-channel timing leaks can potentially reveal sensitive information. For example, RSA uses the modular exponentiation algorithm on the right to compute $a^b \bmod n$, where a is the message and b is the encryption key. This implementation is flawed because of the *if* in line 6. Due to the lack of an *else* branch, its execution will take longer if b contains more 1-bits. An attacker could therefore run a thread in parallel to measure the execution time of the algorithm to derive the number of 1-bits in the encryption key.

```
1  void mexp(){
2    c = 0; d = 1; i = k;
3    while (i >= 0){
4      i = i-1; c = c*2;
5      d = (d*d) % n;
6      if (b(i) == 1){
7        c = c+1;
8        d = (d*a) % n;
9      }
10   }
11 }
```

To prevent such vulnerabilities, we would like the execution time to be independent of the bit values in the encryption key, which is captured by assigning a reward of 1 to each state in the MDPR. Here, each state represents the current position in the code and loop iteration. This results in the following HyperPCTL formula:

$$\forall \hat{\sigma}_1.\forall \hat{\sigma}_2.\forall \hat{s}(\hat{\sigma}_1).\forall \hat{s}'(\hat{\sigma}_2). (init_{\hat{s}} \wedge init_{\hat{s}'}) \rightarrow (\mathcal{R}_{\hat{s}}(\lozenge \, end_{\hat{s}}) = \mathcal{R}_{\hat{s}'}(\lozenge \, end_{\hat{s}'})).$$

4.2   Probabilistic Conformance

The aim here is to ensure that an implementation conforms with the system it is simulating [2]. We consider the implementation of a 6-sided die with repeated tossing of a fair coin using the Knuth-Yao algorithm [22]. For conformance, the probabilistic distribution of reaching the 6 sides of a die should be equal in both cases. We model this problem with an MDP consisting of two components: the first component describes the die and its states represent the faces of the die after being rolled. The second component describes the multiple coin tosses and its states represent the unique combined results of the tosses. Extending this model with rewards allows us to synthesize *efficient* implementations: if we assign to every state, except the absorbing states, a reward of 1, the expected reward on reaching one of the absorbing states in the coin implementation will be equal to the expected number of coin tosses in it. If we limit the rewards collected in such a path, we can filter the implementations with minimum intermediate states. The following formula specifies that the expected number of coin tosses in such an implementation must be less than 4:

$$\exists \hat{\sigma}.\forall \hat{s}(\hat{\sigma}).\exists \hat{s}'(\hat{\sigma}).dieInit_{\hat{s}} \rightarrow \left(\varphi \wedge \mathcal{R}_{\hat{s}'}(\lozenge(\bigvee_{l=1}^{6}(die = l)_{\hat{s}'})) < 4 \right)$$

with $\varphi = coinInit_{\hat{s}'} \wedge \bigwedge_{l=1}^{6} (\mathbb{P}(\lozenge(die = l)_{\hat{s}}) = \mathbb{P}(\lozenge(die = l)_{\hat{s}'}))$.

4.3 Cost Analysis in Multi-Agent Path Planning

We consider the examples in Fig. 3 where two robots R_1, R_2 aim to reach the target cell *end* starting their journey from two different initial cells $(start_1, start_2)$. The robots' behavior is modeled as an MDPR where each cell occupied represents a state. Nondeterministic actions represent all possible moves of the robot from each cell, while the successful maneuvering after having executed an action is captured by a probability distribution.

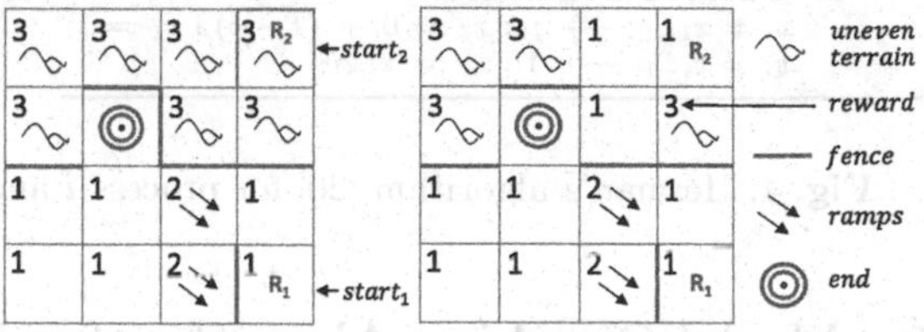

Fig. 3. The maze on the left satisfies φ_{target}, while on the right it violates φ_{target}.

Fences prevent a robot to move in a certain direction disabling possible actions in a particular cell, while the presence of ramps or uneven terrain can increase/decrease the probability of correct robot maneuvers. The occupancy of each state has a cost in terms of energy consumption modeled as a positive reward. We want to check that for all possible (memoryless) schedulers, when robots R_1, R_2 start their mission from their respective initial conditions and they can both reach the target state with probability 1, then the expected energy consumption for robot R_1 is less than the expected energy consumption for robot R_2. This can be expressed as the following probabilistic hyperproperty:

$$\varphi_{target} = \forall \hat{\sigma}.\forall \hat{s}(\hat{\sigma}).\forall \hat{s}'(\hat{\sigma}).\psi \rightarrow \Big(\mathcal{R}_{\hat{s}}(\Diamond \, end_{\hat{s}}) < \mathcal{R}_{\hat{s}'}(\Diamond \, end_{\hat{s}'}) \Big), \text{ where}$$

$$\psi = \Big(start_{1\,\hat{s}} \wedge start_{2\,\hat{s}'} \wedge \mathbb{P}(\Diamond \, end_{\hat{s}}) = 1 \wedge \mathbb{P}(\Diamond \, end_{\hat{s}'}) = 1 \Big).$$

4.4 Probabilistic Self-stabilizing Systems

In distributed systems, randomization is often used to break symmetry between processes to tackle impossibility results. For instance, self-stabilizing token circulation in a ring is impossible in a non-probabilistic setting but Herman's algorithm [20] (see Fig. 4) uses randomization to ensure recovery to a *stable state* (i.e., there is only one token circulating) with probability one. In such an algorithm, from certain initial states, convergence to a stable state may be faster than others and if faults hit those states with a higher probability, it reduces the average convergence time significantly. Thus, designers of self-stabilizing algorithms often use state encodings to tackle slow recovery [11]. The following formula intends to check whether there exists a state from which the convergence time is twice slower than from some other state:

$$\forall \hat{\sigma}.\exists \hat{s}(\hat{\sigma}).\exists \hat{s}'(\hat{\sigma}).\Big(\mathcal{R}_{\hat{s}}(\Diamond \, stable_{\hat{s}}) > 2 \cdot \mathcal{R}_{\hat{s}'}(\Diamond \, stable_{\hat{s}'}) \Big)$$

Note that Herman's algorithm yields a DTMCR and, thus, the choice of scheduler quantification is irrelevant.

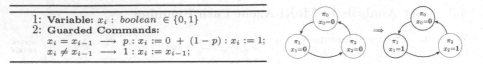

1: **Variable:** x_i : *boolean* $\in \{0,1\}$
2: **Guarded Commands:**
$x_i = x_{i-1} \longrightarrow p : x_i := 0 + (1-p) : x_i := 1;$
$x_i \neq x_{i-1} \longrightarrow 1 : x_i := x_{i-1};$

Fig. 4. Herman's algorithm [20] for process i and example for three processes.

5   Model Checking Algorithm for Reward Operators

HyperPCTL provides an increased level of expressiveness over PCTL and PCTL*, causing the model checking problem for MDPRs to be undecidable even without rewards, as shown in [2]. To achieve decidability for HyperPCTL without rewards, in [2] we restricted the domain of scheduler quantification to *memoryless non-probabilistic schedulers*. For this restricted domain, the model checking problem is NP-complete (or coNP-complete) when the scheduler quantification is existential (or universal). We provided a model checking algorithm by logically encoding HyperPCTL satisfaction problems as linear real-arithmetic formulas and use an SMT solver to check the encodings for satisfiability. Elaborate explanations of encoding non-reward operators can be found in [2].

After adding rewards, the model checking problem restricted to finite memoryless schedulers is still decidable. Similar to the standard model checking problem for Markov Reward Models, computing the expected reward earned until a certain set of states is reached, has a polynomial time complexity in the size of the MDP: the problem can be solved by determining a linear real-arithmetic equation system via graph reachability analysis and solving it. This means adding rewards does not change the class of complexity of the model checking problem as identified in [2].

However, adding rewards to the problem requires a major adaption of the logical encoding. The reason is that expected reward values might be undefined, and undefinedness might propagate from the inner sub-formulas to the formula value. The main contributions of this section are (1) to extend the model checking algorithm from [2] to encode the semantics of reward-related HyperPCTL expressions and (2) to modify the previous encodings to model undefinedness propagation for the remaining language components. To ease understanding, in the following we consider unary-reward models and a single existential scheduler quantifier in our properties; extension to multi-dimensional rewards and several scheduler quantifiers without quantifier alternation is doable by little modifications to the algorithms. Given their finite domain, support for scheduler quantifier alternation is possible, too, but it would require more involved extensions.

Assume as input an MDPR model $\mathcal{M}$ and a HyperPCTL formula φ. In [2] we used Boolean variables $holds_{s,\varphi}$ to encode the truth value of a Boolean-valued formula φ in state s. In this work, we replace the two-valued domain for these variables by a three-valued domain over the values *true* (1), *false* (0) and *undefined* ($\bot$). Furthermore, we use variables $val_{s,\varphi}$ to store the

---

Algorithm 1: Main SMT encoding algorithm

Input: $\mathcal{M} = (S, Act, P, AP, L, rew)$: MDPR;
φ: HyperPCTL formula.

Output: Whether $\mathcal{M}$ satisfies φ.

1 **Function**
    Main$(\mathcal{M}, \varphi = \exists \hat{\sigma}.Q_1 \hat{s}_1(\hat{\sigma})\ldots.Q_n \hat{s}_n(\hat{\sigma}).\varphi^{nq})$:
2 | $E := \bigwedge_{s \in S}(\bigvee_{\alpha \in Act(s)} \sigma_s = \alpha)$
3 | $E := E \wedge \text{Semantics}(\mathcal{M}, \varphi^{nq}, n)$
4 | $T := E \wedge \text{Eval}(\mathcal{M}, \varphi, \{1\})$
5 | $U := E \wedge \text{Eval}(\mathcal{M}, \varphi, \{\bot, 1\})$
6 | **if** $check(T) = SAT$ **then return** *TRUE*
7 | **else if** $check(U) = SAT$ **then return** *UNDEF*
8 | **else return** *FALSE*

Algorithm 2: SMT encoding for the meaning of an input formula

---

Input: $\mathcal{M} = (S, Act, P, AP, L, rew)$: MDPR; φ: quantifier-free HyperPCTL
formula or expression; n: number of state variables in φ.
Output: SMT encoding of the meaning of φ in n-ary self-composition of $\mathcal{M}$.

1 **Function** Semantics$(\mathcal{M}, \varphi, n)$:
2   **if** φ *is true* **then** $E := \bigwedge_{s \in S^n} holds_{s,\varphi}{=}1$
3   **else if** φ *is* $a_{\hat{s}_i}$ **then**
4          $E := (\bigwedge_{s \in S^n, \, a \in L(s_i)}(holds_{s,\varphi}{=}1)) \wedge (\bigwedge_{s \in S^n, \, a \notin L(s_i)}(holds_{s,\varphi}{=}0))$
5   **else if** φ *is* $\neg\varphi'$ **then**
6          $E := \text{Semantics}(\mathcal{M}, \varphi', n) \wedge \bigwedge_{s \in S^n}(holds_{s,\varphi'}{=}0 \rightarrow holds_{s,\varphi}{=}1) \wedge$
7          $\bigwedge_{s \in S^n}(holds_{s,\varphi'}{=}1 \rightarrow holds_{s,\varphi}{=}0) \wedge \bigwedge_{s \in S^n}(holds_{s,\varphi'}{=}\bot \rightarrow holds_{s,\varphi}{=}\bot)$
8   **else if** φ *is* $\varphi_1 \wedge \varphi_2$ **then** $E := \text{SemanticsConjunction}(\mathcal{M}, \varphi, n)$
9   **else if** φ *is* $\varphi_1^{ar} \sim \varphi_2^{ar}$ **then** $E := \text{SemanticsComp}(\mathcal{M}, \varphi, n)$
10   **else if** φ *is* $f(\varphi_1^{ar}, \ldots, \varphi_k^{ar})$ **then** $E := \text{SemanticsArithmetic}(\mathcal{M}, \varphi, n)$
11   **else if** φ *is* $\mathbb{P}(\bigcirc\varphi')$ **then** $E := \text{SemanticsNext}(\mathcal{M}, \varphi, n)$
12   **else if** φ *is* $\mathbb{P}(\varphi_1 \mathcal{U} \varphi_2)$ **then** $E := \text{SemanticsUnboundedUntil}(\mathcal{M}, \varphi, n)$
13   **else if** φ *is* $\mathbb{P}(\varphi_1 \mathcal{U}^{[k_1,k_2]}\varphi_2)$ **then** $E := \text{SemanticsBoundedUntil}(\mathcal{M}, \varphi, n)$
14   **else** $E := \text{RewSemantics}(\mathcal{M}, \varphi, n)$
15   **return** E

---

numerical value of an arithmetic expression φ in state s. To also encode the definedness
of arithmetic values, we introduce additional Boolean variables $def_{s,\varphi}$ which should be
true iff the corresponding value is defined. Finally, to encode a scheduler, we use for
each state of $\mathcal{M}$ a variable σ_s to store the chosen action.

The starting point of the encoding is Algorithm 1, which begins by encoding the
scheduler choice[2] in line 2. The semantics of the non-quantified inner formula φ^{nq}
under a given scheduler choice in each of the states is encoded in line 3. This basic
encoding E is extended in two directions: formula T encodes that φ can be made
true by some suitable quantifier instantiation, whereas U encodes that φ can be made
true or undefined. Only if none of these two cases apply (i.e. if both formulas are
unsatisfiable), we conclude that $\mathcal{M}$ does not satisfy φ. Not listed in the algorithm is
the case of a universal scheduler quantifier, where we use negation to get an existential
formula, apply the listed algorithm, and negate the answer.

The semantics of formulas is encoded by Algorithm 2. We omit the pseudocode
of sub-algorithms that were needed also without rewards; these are similar to those
in [2] but get extended with the encoding of definedness as explained in Sect. 3.2.
Relevant for rewards is line 14, calling the method RewSemantics in Algorithm 3 to
encode the semantics of the reward operators. In the case of rewards over the next
operator $\varphi = \mathcal{R}_{\hat{s}_i}(\bigcirc\varphi')$, we first encode the probability $\mathbb{P}(\bigcirc\varphi')$; φ is undefined if this
probability is not 1 (line 5). If the probability is defined, then the reward is the expected
reward of the successors in the ith execution (line 7).

---

[2] For n scheduler quantifiers, we would simply need to include such a scheduler encoding for each of the schedulers $\sigma_1, \ldots, \sigma_n$, and in the rest of the encoding, refer to the respective schedulers σ_i instead of σ.

Algorithm 3: SMT encoding for the meaning of reward operators

Input: $\mathcal{M} = (S, Act, P, \mathsf{AP}, L, rew)$: MDPR; φ: quantifier-free HyperPCTL
formula or expression; n: number of state variables in φ.
Output: SMT encoding of the meaning of φ in n-ary self-composition of $\mathcal{M}$.

1 **Function** RewSemantics($\mathcal{M}, \varphi, n$):
2   **if** φ *is* $\mathcal{R}_{\hat{s}_i}(\bigcirc\varphi')$ **then**
3      $E := $ Semantics($\mathcal{M}, \mathbb{P}(\bigcirc\varphi'), n$)
4   **foreach** $s = (s_1, \dots, s_n) \in S^n$ **do**
5        $E := E \wedge ((val_{s, \mathbb{P}(\bigcirc\varphi')} \neq 1 \vee \neg def_{s, \mathbb{P}(\bigcirc\varphi')}) \leftrightarrow \neg def_{s, \varphi})$
6   **foreach** $\alpha = (\alpha_1, \dots, \alpha_n) \in Act(s_1) \times \dots \times Act(s_n)$ **do**
7          $E := E \wedge ([def_{s, \varphi} \wedge \bigwedge_{j=1}^{n} \sigma_{s_j} = \alpha_j] \rightarrow [val_{s, \varphi} = rew(s_i) +$
            $\sum_{s' \in supp(\alpha_1) \times \dots \times supp(\alpha_n)}((\prod_{j=1}^{n} P(s_j, \alpha_j, s'_j)) \cdot rew(s'_i))])$

8   **else if** φ *is* $\mathcal{R}_{\hat{s}_i}(\varphi_1 \mathcal{U}^{[k_1, k_2]}\varphi_2)$ **then**
9      $E := $ SemanticsBoundedUntil($\mathcal{M}, \mathbb{P}(\varphi_1 \mathcal{U}^{[k_1, k_2]}\varphi_2), n$)
10     $E := E \wedge $ RewardBoundedUntil($\mathcal{M}, \varphi, n$)

11   **else if** φ *is* $\mathcal{R}_{\hat{s}_i}(\varphi_1 \mathcal{U} \varphi_2)$ **then**
12     $E := $ SemanticsUnboundedUntil($\mathcal{M}, \mathbb{P}(\varphi_1 \mathcal{U} \varphi_2), n$)
13     $E := E \wedge $ RewardUnboundedUntil($\mathcal{M}, \varphi, n$)

14 **return** E

Algorithm 4: SMT encoding for reward of unbounded until

Input: $\mathcal{M} = (S, Act, P, \mathsf{AP}, L, rew)$: MDPR; φ: HyperPCTL unbounded until
formula of the form $\mathcal{R}_{\hat{s}_i}(\varphi_1\mathcal{U}\varphi_2)$; n: number of state variables in φ.
Output: SMT encoding of φ's meaning in the n-ary self-composition of $\mathcal{M}$.

1 **Function** RewardUnboundedUntil($\mathcal{M}, \varphi = \mathcal{R}_{\hat{s}_i}(\varphi_1\mathcal{U}\varphi_2), n$):
2    $\varphi' := \mathbb{P}(\varphi_1 \mathcal{U} \varphi_2); \quad E := \mathbf{true}$
3   **foreach** $s = (s_1, \dots, s_n) \in S^n$ **do**
4      $E := E \wedge (holds_{s, \varphi_2} = 1 \rightarrow (val_{s, \varphi} = rew(s_i) \wedge def_{s, \varphi}))$
5      $E := E \wedge ((val_{s, \varphi'} \neq 1 \vee \neg def_{s, \varphi'}) \rightarrow \neg def_{s, \varphi})$
6   **foreach** $\alpha = (\alpha_1, \dots, \alpha_n) \in Act(s_1) \times \dots \times Act(s_n)$ **do**
7        $E := E \wedge ((val_{s, \varphi'} = 1 \wedge def_{s, \varphi'} \wedge holds_{s, \varphi_2} \neq 1 \wedge \bigwedge_{j=1}^{n} \sigma_{s_j} = \alpha_j) \rightarrow$
8        $[val_{s, \varphi} =$
         $rew(s_i) + \sum_{s' \in supp(\alpha_1) \times \dots \times supp(\alpha_n)}((\prod_{i=1}^{n} P(s_j, \alpha_j, s'_j)) \cdot val_{s', \varphi}) \wedge$
9        $(\neg def_{s, \varphi} \leftrightarrow [(\bigvee_{s' \in supp(\alpha_1) \times \dots \times supp(\alpha_n)} \neg def_{s', \varphi}) \vee$
10       $(holds_{s, \varphi_2} = \bot \wedge val_{s, \varphi} \neq rew(s_i))])])$

11 **return** E

To encode the reward of unbounded until formulas, we first need to encode the probability of the until formula, since this probability needs to be 1 for a defined reward value. Then we call the RewardUnboundedUntil method from Algorithm 4, which implements the semantics of the reward of unbounded until from Sect. 3.2. Undefinedness is covered in line 5, when the probability of the unbounded until is either not defined or

Table 2. Experimental results. **VR:** Verification result. **TA:** Timing attack. **PC:** Probabilistic conformance. **RO:** Robotics example. **HS:** Herman's algorithm. **IJ:** Israeli-Jaflon's algorithm. $\checkmark$: the result is true. $\times$: the result is false.

Case study		VR	Running time (s)			#SMT formulas	#sub formulas	#states	#transitions
		Encoding	Solving	Total	Variables				
TA	1-bit key	$\times$	0.11	0.01	0.12	344	1008	8	10
	16-bit key	$\times$	16.41	3.69	20.10	19244	49728	68	100
	30-bit key	$\times$	143.49	44.64	188.13	62868	160160	124	184
	45-bit key	$\times$	774.53	1304.98	2079.51	137448	348080	184	274
PC	$s = (0)$	$\checkmark$	5.03	2.03	7.06	7281	34681	20	186
	$s = (0,1,2)$	$\checkmark$	6.66	8.91	15.57	7281	61631	20	494
	$s = (0,\dots,4)$	$\checkmark$	8.82	35	43.82	7281	88581	20	802
	$s = (0,\dots,6)$	$\checkmark$	11.64	53.05	64.69	7281	115531	20	1110
RO	3×3	$\checkmark$	0.87	0.05	0.92	2179	7622	18	66
	3×3	$\times$	0.93	0.05	0.98	2179	7622	18	66
	4×4	$\checkmark$	3.55	0.28	3.83	6561	21572	32	160
	4×4	$\times$	3.43	0.25	3.68	6561	21476	32	148
	5×5	$\checkmark$	13.07	0.5	13.57	15651	48302	50	250
	5×5	$\times$	13.19	0.98	14.17	15651	48302	50	250
	6×6	$\checkmark$	44.52	1.04	45.56	32041	96096	72	398
	6×6	$\times$	44.65	7.48	52.13	32041	96096	72	398
HS	$n = 3$	$\checkmark$	0.1	0.01	0.11	489	4655	8	28
	$n = 5$	$\checkmark$	0.95	0.13	1.08	2369	7047	32	244
IJ	$n = 3$	$\checkmark$	0.08	0.01	0.09	169	698	7	21
	$n = 4$	$\checkmark$	0.24	0.04	0.28	601	2194	15	56
	$n = 5$	$\checkmark$	0.89	0.33	1.22	2233	7010	31	140
	$n = 6$	$\checkmark$	3.93	19.39	23.32	8569	23362	63	336

not 1, and in the lines 9–10, when the probability of the unbounded until is 1, φ_2 is not true and either a successor reward is undefined, or φ_2 is undefined and the successor rewards are not zero. The method `RewardBoundedUntil` for reward expressions with bounded until, not shown here, is similar to the unbounded case, but needs additional bookkeeping about the time interval within which φ_2 needs to be satisfied.

6 Evaluation

We have implemented a prototype of the presented algorithm by extending our tool Hyper-Prob [10] to support rewards. The implementation has been coded in Python using the libraries Lark [24] for parsing the input formula, and Stormpy [26] for parsing the input MDPR. The generated constraints are then solved by the SMT solver Z3 [25]. Our implementation cannot handle all possible cases

---

Algorithm 5: Encoding certain formula values

Input: $\mathcal{M} = (S, Act, P, \mathsf{AP}, L, rew)$: MDPR;
    φ: HyperPCTL formula; $v \subseteq \{0, 1, \}$.
Output: Encoding that
    $\mathcal{M}, (), () \models \exists \hat{\sigma}.Q_1 \hat{s}_1 \dots . Q_n \hat{s}_n.(\varphi^{nq} \in v)$.
1 **Function** Eval($\mathcal{M}, \varphi = \exists \hat{\sigma}.Q_1 \hat{s}_1 \dots . Q_n \hat{s}_n.\varphi^{nq}$,
    v)**:**
2   **foreach** $i = 1, \dots, n$ **do**
3   **if** $Q_i = \forall$ **then** $B_i := " \bigwedge_{s_i \in S} "$ **else**
        $B_i := " \bigvee_{s_i \in S} "$
4   **return** $B_1 \dots B_n \ (holds_{(s_1,\dots,s_n),\varphi^{nq}} \in v)$

of undefinedness. We currently do not calculate the extent of partial definedness of a property in a model. We check whether the states queried in the property are reachable with a probability of one and proceed in calculation of rewards in such cases. Hence, we have evaluated case studies, where the reachability probabilities are always one.

The concept of rewards have eased the modeling of case studies with respect to counting of expected steps needed to reach a state. Hence, for timing attack and probabilistic conformance case studies, the number of transitions and states are less when compared to the models used in [2]. The implementation also returns a witness/counterexample whenever possible, allowing us to synthesize schedulers. Note that, though the ensemble of schedulers in the executions (i.e. σ in the semantical context) define a scheduler in the self-composition, not all schedulers of the self-composition can be defined this way, posing a major difference between scheduler synthesis for PCTL and for HyperPCTL.

For the **TA** case study, we have modeled the problem with $\{1, 16, 30, 45\}$-bit encryption keys. We have verified the HyperPCTL formula described in Sect. 4.1. The property does not hold on the given model and our implementation finds this bug. Since our implementation can handle only one scheduler quantifier, we have added a second copy of the model to the input MDPR such that the single scheduler can assign different actions to the states in the two copies of the model.

For the **PC** case study, we have verified the property described in Sect. 4.2. We have started with a model with all possible transitions, represented non-deterministically, from the initial state s_0. For all other states, we allowed only the transitions that will give us a correct solution. We challenged our implementation to synthesize a scheduler that will satisfy the required probabilities within the given reward bound. We scaled the model by incrementally allowing all possible combination of transitions using non-deterministic actions in each state and limited the expected coin tosses to be 4 for each experiment. For all the cases, our implementation was successful in finding a solution, which we verified manually as correct.

For the **RO** case study, we have verified the property described in Sect. 4.3. We have scaled the model in terms of maze size and verified both positive and negative cases of path finding. On self-stabilizing systems, we have verified several properties and described one of them in Sect. 4.4. This property is satisfied and we have successfully found a witness. We have reported the timing data for this property in Table 2. We have verified the property in models representing both Herman's (**HS**) and Israeli-Jaflon's (**IJ**) [21] algorithms. Since, Herman's algorithm is only valid for odd processes, we tried verification over $\{3, 5\}$ processes. For Israeli-Jaflon's, we tried it over $\{3, 4, 5, 6\}$ process.

The experiments have been performed in a Docker container running on a system with 2.3 GHz i7 processor and 32 GB of RAM. Because of the incomplete implementation of handling of undefined values, which would add a significant number of additional constraints, the reported execution times are lower than they would normally be. From Table 2, it is clear that the execution times for even relatively small MPDRs are large. This is because of the inherent complexity of the problem, to which reward operators add a new dimension of complexity.

7   Related Work

The classical temporal logics for probabilistic systems [19], for example PCTL and its extension with reward operators [17,23], cannot express probabilistic hyperproperties, because they can only refer to a single path at a time. There has been considerable work to overcome this shortcoming for non-probabilistic hyperlogics in terms of automated verification [8,14–16] and monitoring [4,6,7,12,13,18,27] of HyperLTL specifications. However, none of these are relevant to probabilistic systems. The work in [3] overcomes this limitation by introducing HyperPCTL, a temporal logic that can express probabilistic hyperproperties over discrete-time Markov chains. In [1] we addressed the problem of computing the regions of parameter configurations of discrete-time Markov chains satisfying/violating a formula φ in a fragment of HyperPCTL. In [2], we enriched the syntax and semantics of HyperPCTL with the possibility to quantify simultaneously over schedulers and probabilistic computation trees. However, reasoning about rewards was not supported in [2], while it is considered in this paper for the first time.

An orthogonal attempt to solve the model checking problem has been addressed in [9], where the authors present the temporal logic PHL that allows quantification over schedulers, but path quantification of the induced DTMC is achieved by using HyperCTL*. To overcome the undecidability problem of model checking with their logics, the authors provide two approximate methods for proving and refuting only universally quantified formulas in PHL for memoryful schedulers. However, this work does not handle reward models as well.

Other works related to probabilistic hyperproperties comprises of approaches based on *statistical model checking* (SMC) [28,29] using an extension of HyperPCTL that allows explicit path quantification over the probability operator. However, these approaches do not consider the use of rewards either.

8   Conclusion

In this paper, we studied probabilistic hyperproperties with rewards. To this end, we extended the temporal hyperlogic HyperPCTL with reward operators that associates quantified computation trees with interrelated accumulated rewards. We also proposed an SMT-based algorithm for model checking these formulas for MDPRs. We have created a prototypical implementation and used it to analyze a few case studies. Due to the high complexity of the problem, more efficient model checking algorithms are greatly needed. An orthogonal solution is to design less accurate and/or approximate algorithms such as statistical model checking that scale better and provide certain probabilistic guarantees about the correctness of verification. Another interesting direction is using counterexample-guided techniques to manage the size of the state space.

References

1. Ábrahám, E., Bartocci, E., Bonakdarpour, B., Dobe, O.: Parameter synthesis for probabilistic hyperproperties. In: Proceedings of LPAR 2020: The 23rd International Conference on Logic for Programming, Artificial Intelligence and Reasoning. EPiC Series in Computing, vol. 73, pp. 12–31. EasyChair (2020). https://doi.org/10.29007/37lf

2. Ábrahám, E., Bartocci, E., Bonakdarpour, B., Dobe, O.: Probabilistic hyperproperties with nondeterminism. In: Hung, D.V., Sokolsky, O. (eds.) ATVA 2020. LNCS, vol. 12302, pp. 518–534. Springer, Cham (2020). https://doi.org/10.1007/978-3-030-59152-6_29

3. Ábrahám, E., Bonakdarpour, B.: HyperPCTL: a temporal logic for probabilistic hyperproperties. In: McIver, A., Horvath, A. (eds.) QEST 2018. LNCS, vol. 11024, pp. 20–35. Springer, Cham (2018). https://doi.org/10.1007/978-3-319-99154-2_2

4. Agrawal, S., Bonakdarpour, B.: Runtime verification of k-safety hyperproperties in HyperLTL. In: Proceedings of CSF 2016: The IEEE 29th Computer Security Foundations, pp. 239–252. IEEE Computer Society (2016). https://doi.org/10.1109/CSF.2016.24

5. Baier, C., Katoen, J.P.: Principles of Model Checking. The MIT Press, Cambridge (2008)

6. Bonakdarpour, B., Sanchez, C., Schneider, G.: Monitoring hyperproperties by combining static analysis and runtime verification. In: Margaria, T., Steffen, B. (eds.) ISoLA 2018. LNCS, vol. 11245, pp. 8–27. Springer, Cham (2018). https://doi.org/10.1007/978-3-030-03421-4_2

7. Brett, N., Siddique, U., Bonakdarpour, B.: Rewriting-based runtime verification for alternation-free HyperLTL. In: Legay, A., Margaria, T. (eds.) TACAS 2017. LNCS, vol. 10206, pp. 77–93. Springer, Heidelberg (2017). https://doi.org/10.1007/978-3-662-54580-5_5

8. Coenen, N., Finkbeiner, B., Sánchez, C., Tentrup, L.: Verifying hyperliveness. In: Dillig, I., Tasiran, S. (eds.) CAV 2019. LNCS, vol. 11561, pp. 121–139. Springer, Cham (2019). https://doi.org/10.1007/978-3-030-25540-4_7

9. Dimitrova, R., Finkbeiner, B., Torfah, H.: Probabilistic hyperproperties of Markov decision processes. In: Hung, D.V., Sokolsky, O. (eds.) ATVA 2020. LNCS, vol. 12302, pp. 484–500. Springer, Cham (2020). https://doi.org/10.1007/978-3-030-59152-6_27

10. Dobe, O., Ábrahám, E., Bartocci, E., Bonakdarpour, B.: HYPERPROB: a model checker for probabilistic hyperproperties. In: Huisman, M., Păsăreanu, C., Zhan, N. (eds.) FM 2021. LNCS, vol. 13047, pp. 657–666. Springer, Cham (2021). https://doi.org/10.1007/978-3-030-90870-6_35

11. Fallahi, N., Bonakdarpour, B., Tixeuil, S.: Rigorous performance evaluation of self-stabilization using probabilistic model checking. In: Proceedings of SRDS 2013: The 32nd IEEE International Conference on Reliable Distributed Systems, pp. 153–162. IEEE Computer Society (2013). https://doi.org/10.1109/SRDS.2013.24

12. Finkbeiner, B., Hahn, C., Stenger, M., Tentrup, L.: RVHyper: a runtime verification tool for temporal hyperproperties. In: Beyer, D., Huisman, M. (eds.) TACAS 2018. LNCS, vol. 10806, pp. 194–200. Springer, Cham (2018). https://doi.org/10.1007/978-3-319-89963-3_11

13. Finkbeiner, B., Hahn, C., Stenger, M., Tentrup, L.: Monitoring hyperproperties. Formal Meth. Syst. Des. 54(3), 336–363 (2019). https://doi.org/10.1007/s10703-019-00334-z

14. Finkbeiner, B., Hahn, C., Torfah, H.: Model checking quantitative hyperproperties. In: Chockler, H., Weissenbacher, G. (eds.) CAV 2018. LNCS, vol. 10981, pp. 144–163. Springer, Cham (2018). https://doi.org/10.1007/978-3-319-96145-3_8

15. Finkbeiner, B., Müller, C., Seidl, H., Zalinescu, E.: Verifying security policies in multi-agent workflows with loops. In: Proceedings of CCS 2017: The 15th ACM Conference on Computer and Communications Security (CCS). ACM (2017). https://doi.org/10.1145/3133956.3134080

16. Finkbeiner, B., Rabe, M.N., Sánchez, C.: Algorithms for model checking HyperLTL and HyperCTL*. In: Kroening, D., Păsăreanu, C.S. (eds.) CAV 2015. LNCS, vol. 9206, pp. 30–48. Springer, Cham (2015). https://doi.org/10.1007/978-3-319-21690-4_3

17. Forejt, V., Kwiatkowska, M., Norman, G., Parker, D.: Automated verification techniques for probabilistic systems. In: Bernardo, M., Issarny, V. (eds.) SFM 2011. LNCS, vol. 6659, pp. 53–113. Springer, Heidelberg (2011). https://doi.org/10.1007/978-3-642-21455-4_3

18. Hahn, C., Stenger, M., Tentrup, L.: Constraint-based monitoring of hyperproperties. In: Vojnar, T., Zhang, L. (eds.) TACAS 2019. LNCS, vol. 11428, pp. 115–131. Springer, Cham (2019). https://doi.org/10.1007/978-3-030-17465-1_7

19. Hansson, H., Jonsson, B.: A logic for reasoning about time and reliability. Formal Aspects Comput. **6**, 102–111 (1994). https://doi.org/10.1007/BF01211866

20. Herman, T.: Probabilistic self-stabilization. Inf. Process. Lett. **35**(2), 63–67 (1990). https://doi.org/10.1016/0020-0190(90)90107-9

21. Israeli, A., Jalfon, M.: Token management schemes and random walks yield self-stabilizing mutual exclusion. In: Proceedings of PODC 1990: The Ninth Annual ACM Symposium on Principles of Distributed Computing, pp. 119–131 (1990). https://doi.org/10.1145/93385.93409

22. Knuth, D., Yao, A.: The complexity of nonuniform random number generation. In: Algorithms and Complexity: New Directions and Recent Results. Academic Press (1976)

23. Kwiatkowska, M., Norman, G., Parker, D.: Stochastic model checking. In: Bernardo, M., Hillston, J. (eds.) SFM 2007. LNCS, vol. 4486, pp. 220–270. Springer, Heidelberg (2007). https://doi.org/10.1007/978-3-540-72522-0_6

24. LARK. https://lark-parser.readthedocs.io/

25. de Moura, L.M., Bjørner, N.: Z3: an efficient SMT solver. In: Proceedings of TACAS 2008, pp. 337–340 (2008)

26. STORMpy. https://moves-rwth.github.io/stormpy/

27. Stucki, S., Sánchez, C., Schneider, G., Bonakdarpour, B.: Gray-box monitoring of hyperproperties. In: ter Beek, M.H., McIver, A., Oliveira, J.N. (eds.) FM 2019. LNCS, vol. 11800, pp. 406–424. Springer, Cham (2019). https://doi.org/10.1007/978-3-030-30942-8_25

28. Wang, Y., Nalluri, S., Bonakdarpour, B., Pajic, M.: Statistical model checking for hyperproperties. In: Proceedings of CSF 2021: The IEEE 34th Computer Security Foundations, pp. 1–16. IEEE (2021). https://doi.org/10.1109/CSF51468.2021.00009

29. Wang, Y., Zarei, M., Bonakdarpour, B., Pajic, M.: Statistical verification of hyperproperties for cyber-physical systems. ACM Trans. Embed. Comput. Syst. **18**(5s), 92:1–92:23 (2019). https://doi.org/10.1145/3358232

Hypercontracts

Inigo Incer[1]([✉]), Albert Benveniste[2], Alberto Sangiovanni-Vincentelli[1],
and Sanjit A. Seshia[1]

[1] University of California, Berkeley, USA
inigo@berkeley.edu
[2] INRIA/IRISA, Rennes, France

Abstract. Contract theories have been proposed to formally support distributed and decentralized system design while ensuring safe system integration. We propose *hypercontracts*, a general model with a richer structure for its underlying model of components, subsuming simulation preorders. While general, the new model provides a richer algebra for its notions of refinement, parallel composition, and quotient. Further, it allows the introduction of new operations. Building on top of these foundations, we propose *conic hypercontracts*, which are still generic but come with a finite description.

1 Introduction

The need for compositional algebraic frameworks to design and analyze reactive systems is widely recognized. In these frameworks, distributed and decentralized system design and verification are based on a proper definition of *interfaces* that support the specification of subsystems having a partially specified context of operation, and subsequently guaranteeing safe system integration. Over the last few decades, we have seen the introduction of several algebraic frameworks: interface automata [7,10–12,22], process spaces [24], modal interfaces [4,19–21,29], assume-guarantee (AG) contracts [5], rely-guarantee reasoning [9,15,17,18], and their variants. The interface specifications state (*i*) what the component guarantees and (*ii*) what it assumes from its environment in order for those guarantees to hold, i.e., all these frameworks implement a form of assume-guarantee reasoning.

These algebraic frameworks share a notion of a component, of an environment, and of a specification called a *contract* to stress the give-and-take dynamics between the component and its environment. They all have notions of satisfaction of a specification by a component, and of contract composition. To unify many contract frameworks, high-level theories have been proposed of which existing contract theories are instantiations. Bauer et al. [3] describe how to build a contract theory if one has a specification theory available. Benveniste et al. [6] provide a meta-theory that builds contracts starting from an algebra of components. Here, several operations on contracts are proposed. Further, it has been shown how this meta-theory can describe, among others, interface automata, assume-guarantee contracts, modal interfaces, and rely-guarantee reasoning. This meta-theory is, however, low-level, specifying contracts as unstructured sets of environments and implementations. As a consequence, important concepts such as parallel composition and quotient of contracts are expressed in terms that are considered too abstract—see [6], Chap. 4. For example, no closed form formula is given for the quotient besides its abstract definition as adjoint of parallel composition. This paper introduces a theory, called *hypercontracts*, that will address these drawbacks.

Assume-guarantee (AG) contracts [5] require users to state the assumptions and guarantees of the specification explicitly, while interface theories express a specification as a game played between the specification environments and implementations. Experience tells that designers find the explicit expression of a contract's assumptions and guarantees natural (see [6] Chap. 12), while interface theories are perceived as a less intuitive mechanism for writing specifications; however, interface theories in general come with the most efficient algorithms, making them excellent candidates for internal representations of specifications. Some authors ([6] Chap. 10) have therefore proposed to translate contracts expressed as pairs (assumptions, guarantees) into some interface model, where algorithms are applied. This approach has the drawback that results cannot be traced back to the original (assumptions, guarantees) formulation.

Further, AG contracts only support environments and implementations that can be expressed using trace properties; while many attributes of interest can be expressed using trace properties, there are important system attributes, such as non-interference [14], that are *hyperproperties* [8], falling outside the class of trace properties. Hypercontracts allow environments and implementations to be expressed using arbitrary hyperproperties.

To elaborate on this point, the most basic definition of a property in the formal methods community is "a set of traces." This notion is based on the *behavioral* approach to system modelling, in which we assume an underlying set of behaviors $\mathcal{B}$, and properties are defined as subsets of $\mathcal{B}$. In this approach, design elements or components are also defined as subsets of $\mathcal{B}$. The difference between components and properties is semantics: a component collects the behaviors that can be observed from that component, while a property collects the behaviors meeting some criterion of interest. Then, a component M satisfies a property P, written $M \models P$, when $M \subseteq P$, that is, when each behavior of M is in the set of behaviors satisfying P. Properties of this sort are called *trace properties*. Several important design requirements can be expressed with properties, for example, *safety*. But there are system characteristics such as mean response times, security attributes, and reliability that can only be determined by analyzing multiple traces. The theory of hyperproperties [8] was introduced to express these more general design attributes.

Formally, *hyperproperties* are subsets of $2^{\mathcal{B}}$. Recall that each element of $2^{\mathcal{B}}$ defines a semantically-unique component. Thus, a component M satisfies a hyperproperty H if $M \in H$. An assume-guarantee theory that supports the expression of arbitrary hyperproperties is a major contribution of this paper.

As we present our theory, we will use the following running example.

Example 1 (Running example). Consider the digital system shown in Fig. 1a[1]. Here, we have an s-bit secret data input S and an n-bit public input P. The system has an output O. There is also an input H that is equal to "zero" when the system is being accessed by a user with low-privileges, i.e., a user not allowed to use the secret data, and equal to "one" otherwise. We wish the overall system to satisfy the following requirement: for all environments with $H = 0$, the implementations can only make the output O depend on P, the public data, not on the secret input S.

A prerequisite for writing this requirement is to express: "the output O depends on P, the public data, but not on the secret input S". We claim that this requirement cannot be captured by a trace property. Suppose for the sake of simplicity that all variables are 1-bit-long. A trace property that may express the independence from the secret for $O = P$ is

$$
P = \left\{
\begin{array}{l}
(P = 1, S = 1, O = 1), \\
(P = 0, S = 1, O = 0), \\
(P = 1, S = 0, O = 1), \\
(P = 0, S = 0, O = 0)
\end{array}
\right\}.
$$

A valid implementation $M \subseteq P$ is the following set of traces:

$$
M = \left\{
\begin{array}{l}
(P = 1, S = 1, O = 1), \\
(P = 0, S = 0, O = 0)
\end{array}
\right\}.
$$

However, the component M leaks the value of S in its output. We conclude that independence does not behave as a trace property, and therefore, neither does non-interference. To overcome this, simply list all the subsets of P that satisfy the independence requirement:

$$
\left\{
\begin{array}{l}
(P{=}1, S{=}1, O{=}1), \\
(P{=}0, S{=}1, O{=}0), \\
(P{=}1, S{=}0, O{=}1), \\
(P{=}0, S{=}0, O{=}0)
\end{array}
\right\},
\left\{
\begin{array}{l}
(P{=}1, S{=}1, O{=}1), \\
(P{=}1, S{=}0, O{=}1)
\end{array}
\right\},
\left\{
\begin{array}{l}
(P{=}0, S{=}1, O{=}0), \\
(P{=}0, S{=}0, O{=}0)
\end{array}
\right\}
$$

This precisely defines a subset of 2^B, i.e., a hyperproperty.

In our development, we will use hypercontracts first to express this top-level, assume-guarantee requirement, and then to find a component that added to a partial implementation of the system results in a design that meets the top-level specification.   □

---

[1] This system is similar to those presented in [23, 28] to illustrate the non-interference property in security.

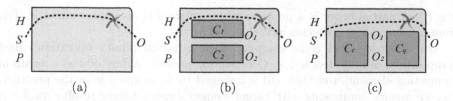

Fig. 1. (a) A digital system with a secret input S and a public input P. The overall system must meet the requirement that the secret input does not affect the value of the output O when the signal H is de-asserted (this signal is asserted when a privileged user uses the system). Our agenda for this running example is the following: (b) we will start with two components C_1 and C_2 satisfying respective hypercontracts $\mathcal{C}_1$ and $\mathcal{C}_2$ characterizing information-flow properties of their own; (c) the composition of these two hypercontracts, $\mathcal{C}_c$, will be derived. Through the quotient hypercontract $\mathcal{C}_q$, we will discover the functionality that needs to be added in order for the design to meet the top-level information-flow specification $\mathcal{C}$.

Contributions. We provide a theory called *hypercontracts* which generalizes existing theories of AG contracts while treating assumptions and guarantees as first-class citizens. This new AG theory supports arbitrary structured hyperproperties, including non-interference and robustness.

Our theory of hypercontracts is built in three stages. We begin with a theory of components. Then we state what are the sets of components that our theory can express; we call such objects compsets—compsets boil down to hyperproperties in behavioral formalisms [23]. From these compsets, we build hypercontracts. We provide closed-form expressions for hypercontract manipulations. Then we show how our hypercontract theory applies to two specific cases: downward-closed hypercontracts and interface hypercontracts (equivalent to interface automata). The main difference between hypercontracts and the meta-theory of contracts [6] is that hypercontracts are more structured: the meta-theory of contracts defines a theory of components, and uses these components to define contracts. Hypercontracts use the theory of components to define compsets, which are the types of properties that we are interested in representing in a specific theory. Hypercontracts are built out of compsets, not out of components.

To summarize, our key contributions are the following: (i) a new model of *hypercontracts* possessing a richer algebra than the metatheory of [6] and capable of expressing any lattice of hyperproperties and (ii) a calculus of *conic hypercontracts* offering finite representations of downward-closed hypercontracts.

2 Preliminaries

Many concepts in this paper will be inherited from **preorders**. We recall that a preorder $(P, \leq)$ consists of a set P and a relation $\leq$ which is transitive (i.e., $a \leq b$ and $b \leq c$ implies that $a \leq c$ for all $a, b, c \in P$) and reflexive ($a \leq a$ for all

$a \in P$). A partial order is a preorder whose relation is also antisymmetric (i.e., from $a \leq b$ and $b \leq a$ we conclude that $a = b$).

Our preorders will come equipped with a partial binary operation called composition, usually denoted $\times$. Composition is often understood as a means of connecting elements together and is assumed to be monotonic in the preorder, i.e., we assume composing with bigger elements yields bigger results: $\forall a, b, c \in P.\ a \leq b \Rightarrow a \times c \leq b \times c$. We will also be interested in taking elements apart. For a notion of composition, we can always ask the question, for $a, b \in P$, what is the largest element $b \in P$ such that $a \times b \leq c$? Such an element is called *quotient* or *residual*, usually denoted c/a. Formally, the definition of the quotient c/a is

$$\forall b \in P.\ a \times b \leq c \text{ if and only if } b \leq c/a, \tag{1}$$

which means that the quotient is the right adjoint of composition (in the sense of category theory). A synonym of this notion is to say that composing by a fixed element a (i.e., $b \mapsto a \times b$) and taking quotient by the same element (i.e., $c \mapsto c/a$) form a Galois connection. A description of the use of the quotient in many fields of engineering and computer science is given in [16].

A partial order for which every two elements have a well-defined LUB (aka join), denoted $\vee$, and GLB (aka meet), denoted $\wedge$, is a lattice. A lattice in which the meet has a right adjoint is called Heyting algebra. This right adjoint usually goes by the name exponential, denoted $\rightarrow$. In other words, the exponential is the notion of quotient if we take composition to be given by the meet, that is, for a Heyting algebra H with elements a, c, the exponential is defined as

$$\forall b \in H.\ a \wedge b \leq c \text{ if and only if } b \leq a \rightarrow c, \tag{2}$$

which is the familiar notion of implication in Boolean algebras.

3   The Theory of Hypercontracts

Our objective is to develop a theory of assume-guarantee reasoning for any kind of attribute of reactive systems. We do this in three steps:

1. we consider components coming with notions of preorder (e.g., simulation) and parallel composition;
2. we discuss the notion of a compset and give it substantial algebraic structure—unlike the unstructured sets of components considered in the metatheory of [6];
3. we build hypercontracts as pairs of compsets with additional structure—capturing environments and implementations.

In this section we describe how this construction is performed, and in the next we show specialized hypercontract theories.

3.1   Components

In the theory of hypercontracts, the most primitive concept is the component. Let $(\mathbb{M}, \leq)$ be a preorder. The elements $M \in \mathbb{M}$ are called *components*. We say that M is a subcomponent of M' when $M \leq M'$. If we represented components as automata, the statement "is a subcomponent of" is equivalent to "is simulated by."

There exists a partial binary operation, $\|: \mathbb{M}, \mathbb{M} \rightarrow \mathbb{M}$, monotonic in both arguments, called *composition*. If $M \parallel M'$ is not defined, we say that M and M' are *non-composable* (and *composable* otherwise). A component E is an environment for component M if E and M are composable. We assume that composition is associative and commutative.

Example 2 (running example, cont'd). In order to reason about possible decompositions of the system shown in Fig. 1a, we introduce the internal variables O_1 and O_2, as shown in Fig. 1b. They have lengths o_1 and o_2, respectively. The output O has length o. For simplicity, we will assume that the behaviors of the entire system are stateless. In that case, the set of components $\mathbb{M}$ is the union of the following sets:

- For $i \in \{1, 2\}$, components with inputs H, S, P, and output O_i, i.e., the sets
$\{(H, S, P, O_1, O_2, O) \mid \exists f \in (2^1 \times 2^s \times 2^n \rightarrow 2^{o_i}). O_i = f(H, S, P)\}$.
- Components with inputs H, S, P, O_1, O_2, and output O, i.e., the set
$\{(H, S, P, O_1, O_2, O) \mid \exists f \in (2^1 \times 2^s \times 2^n \times 2^{o_1} \times 2^{o_2} \rightarrow 2^o). O = f(H, S, P, O_1, O_2)\}$. We also consider components any subset of these components, as these correspond to restricting inputs to subsets of their domains.

In this theory of components, composition is carried out via set intersection. So for example, if for $i \in \{1, 2\}$ we have functions $f_i \in (2^1 \times 2^s \times 2^n \rightarrow 2^{o_i})$ and components $M_i = \{(H, S, P, O_1, O_2, O) \mid O_i = f_i(H, S, P)\}$, the composition of these objects is

$$M_1 \parallel M_2 = \left\{(H, S, P, O_1, O_2, O) \left| \begin{array}{l} O_1 = f_1(H, S, P) \\ O_2 = f_2(H, S, P) \end{array} \right. \right\},$$

which is the set intersection of the components's behaviors.   □

3.2   Compsets

CmpSet is a lattice whose objects are sets of components, called *compsets*. Thus, compsets are equivalent to hyperproperties when the underlying component theory represents components as sets of behaviors. In general, not every set of components is necessarily an object of **CmpSet**.

CmpSet comes with a notion of satisfaction. Suppose $M \in \mathbb{M}$ and H is a compset. We say that M *satisfies* H or conforms to H, written $M \models H$, when $M \in H$. For compsets H, H', we say that H *refines* H', written $H \leq H'$, when $M \models H \Rightarrow M \models H'$, i.e., when $H \subseteq H'$.

Since we assume **CmpSet** is a lattice, the greatest lower bounds and least upper bounds of finite sets are defined. Observe, however, that although the partial order of **CmpSet** is given by subsetting, the meet and join of **CmpSet** are not necessarily intersection and union, respectively, as the union or intersection of any two elements are not necessarily elements of **CmpSet**.

Example 3 (Running example: non-interference). Non-interference, introduced by Goguen and Meseguer [14], is a common information-flow attribute, a prototypical example of a design quality which trace properties are unable to capture [8]. It can be expressed with hyperproperties, and is in fact one reason behind their introduction.

Suppose σ is one of the behaviors that our system can display, understood as the state of memory locations through time. Some of those memory locations we call *privileged*, some *unprivileged*. Let $L_0(\sigma)$ and $L_f(\sigma)$ be the projections of the behavior σ to the unprivileged memory locations of the system, at time zero, and at the final time (when execution is done). We say that a component M meets the non-interference hyperproperty when

$$\forall \sigma, \sigma' \in M.\ L_0(\sigma) = L_0(\sigma') \Rightarrow L_f(\sigma) = L_f(\sigma'),$$

i.e., if two traces begin with the unprivileged locations in the same state, the final state of the unprivileged locations matches.

Non-interference is a downward-closed hyperproperty [23,28], and a 2-safety hyperproperty—hyperproperties called *k-safety* are those for the refutation of which one must provide at least k traces. In our example, to refute the hyperproperty, it suffices to show two traces that share the same unprivileged initial state, but which differ in the unprivileged final state.

Regarding the system shown in Fig. 1a, we require the top level component to generate the output O independently from the secret input S. We build our theory of compsets by letting the set 2^M be the set of elements of **CmpSet**. This means that any set of components is a valid compset. The components meeting the top-level non-interference property are those belonging to the compset $\{(H, S, P, O_1, O_2, O) \mid \exists f \in (2^1 \times 2^n \to 2^o).\ O = f(H, P)\}$, i.e., those components for which H and P are sufficient to evaluate O. This corresponds exactly to those components that are insensitive to the secret input S. The join and meet of these compsets is given by set union and intersection, respectively.   □

Composition and Quotient. We extend the notion of composition to **CmpSet**:

$$H \parallel H' = \left\{ M \parallel M' \ \middle| \ \begin{array}{l} M \models H,\ M' \models H',\ \text{and} \\ M \text{ and } M' \text{ are composable} \end{array} \right\}. \tag{3}$$

Composition is total and monotonic, i.e., if $H' \leq H''$, then $H \parallel H' \leq H \parallel H''$. It is also commutative and associative, by the commutativity and associativity, respectively, of component composition.

We assume the existence of a second (but partial) binary operation on the objects of **CmpSet**. This operation is the right adjoint of composition: for compsets H and H', the residual H/H' (also called *quotient*), is defined by the universal property (1). From the definition of composition, we must have

$$H/H' = \{M \in \mathbb{M} \mid \{M\} \parallel H' \subseteq H\}. \tag{4}$$

Downward-closed Compsets. The set of components was introduced with a partial order. We say that a compset H is *downward-closed* when $M' \leq M$ and $M \models H$ imply $M' \models H$, i.e., if a component satisfies a downward-closed compset, so does its subcomponent. Section 4.2 treats downward-closed compsets in detail.

3.3 Hypercontracts

Hypercontracts as pairs (environments, closed-system specification). A hypercontract is a specification for a design element that tells what is required from the design element when it operates in an environment that meets the expectations of the hypercontract. A hypercontract is thus a pair of compsets:

$$\mathcal{C} = (\mathcal{E}, \mathcal{S}) = (\text{environments, closed-system specification}).$$

$\mathcal{E}$ states the environments in which the object being specified must adhere to the specification. $\mathcal{S}$ states the requirements that the design element must fulfill when operating in an environment which meets the expectations of the hypercontract. We say that a component E *is an environment of hypercontract* $\mathcal{C}$, written $E \models^E \mathcal{C}$, if $E \models \mathcal{E}$. We say that a component M *is an implementation of* $\mathcal{C}$, written $M \models^I \mathcal{C}$, when $M \parallel E \models \mathcal{S}$ for all $E \models \mathcal{E}$. We thus define the set of implementations $\mathcal{I}$ of $\mathcal{C}$ as the compset containing all implementations, i.e., as the quotient:

$$\text{implementations} = \mathcal{I} = \mathcal{S}/\mathcal{E}.$$

A hypercontract with a nonempty set of environments is called *compatible*; if it has a nonempty set of implementations, it is called *consistent*. For $\mathcal{S}$ and $\mathcal{I}$ as above, the compset $\mathcal{E}'$ defined as $\mathcal{E}' = \mathcal{S}/\mathcal{I}$ contains all environments in which the implementations of $\mathcal{C}$ satisfy the specifications of the hypercontract. Thus, we say that a hypercontract is saturated if its environments compset is as large as possible in the sense that adding more environments to the hypercontract would reduce its implementations. This means that $\mathcal{C}$ satisfies the following fixpoint equation: $\mathcal{E} = \mathcal{S}/\mathcal{I} = \mathcal{S}/(\mathcal{S}/\mathcal{E})$.

At a first sight, this notion of saturation may seem to go against what for assume-guarantee contracts are called contracts in canonical or saturated form, as we make the definition based on the environments instead of on the implementations. However, the two definitions for AG contracts and hypercontracts agree. Indeed, for AG contracts, this notion means that the contract $\mathcal{C} = (A, G)$ satisfies $G = G \cup \neg A$. For this AG contract, we can form a hypercontract as follows: if we take the set of environments to be $\mathcal{E} = 2^A$ (i.e., all subsets of A)

and the closed system specs to be $\mathcal{S} = 2^G$, we get a hypercontract whose set of implementations is $2^{G \cup \neg A}$, which means that the hypercontract $(2^A, 2^G)$ is saturated.

Hypercontracts as pairs (environments, implementations). Another way to interpret a hypercontract is by telling explicitly which environments and implementations it supports. Thus, we would write the hypercontract as $\mathcal{C} = (\mathcal{E}, \mathcal{I})$. Assume-guarantee theories can differ as to the most convenient representation for their hypercontracts. Moreover, some operations on hypercontracts find their most convenient expression in terms of implementations (e.g., parallel composition), and some in terms of the closed system specifications (e.g., strong merging).

The lattice **Contr** *of hypercontracts.* Just as with **CmpSet**, we define **Contr** as a lattice formed by putting together two compsets in one of the above two ways. Not every pair of compsets is necessarily a valid hypercontract. We will define soon the operations that give rise to this lattice.

Preorder. We define a preorder on hypercontracts as follows: we say that $\mathcal{C}$ *refines* $\mathcal{C}'$, written $\mathcal{C} \leq \mathcal{C}'$, when every environment of $\mathcal{C}'$ is an environment of $\mathcal{C}$, and every implementation of $\mathcal{C}$ is an implementation of $\mathcal{C}'$, i.e., $E \models^E \mathcal{C}' \Rightarrow E \models^E \mathcal{C}$ and $M \models^I \mathcal{C} \Rightarrow M \models^I \mathcal{C}'$. We can express this as

$$\mathcal{E}' \leq \mathcal{E} \text{ and } \mathcal{S}/\mathcal{E} = \mathcal{I} \leq \mathcal{I}' = \mathcal{S}'/\mathcal{E}'.$$

Any two $\mathcal{C}, \mathcal{C}'$ with $\mathcal{C} \leq \mathcal{C}'$ and $\mathcal{C}' \leq \mathcal{C}$ are said to be *equivalent* since they have the same environments and the same implementations. We now obtain some operations using preorders which are defined as the LUB or GLB of **Contr**. We point out that the expressions we obtain are unique up to the preorder, i.e., up to hypercontract equivalence.

GLB and LUB. From the preorder just defined, the GLB of $\mathcal{C}$ and $\mathcal{C}'$ satisfies: $M \models^I \mathcal{C} \wedge \mathcal{C}'$ if and only if $M \models^I \mathcal{C}$ and $M \models^I \mathcal{C}'$; and $E \models^E \mathcal{C} \wedge \mathcal{C}'$ if and only if $E \models^E \mathcal{C}$ or $E \models^E \mathcal{C}'$.

Conversely, the least upper bound satisfies $M \models^I \mathcal{C} \vee \mathcal{C}'$ if and only if $M \models^I \mathcal{C}$ or $M \models^I \mathcal{C}'$, and $E \models^E \mathcal{C} \vee \mathcal{C}'$ if and only if $E \models^E \mathcal{C}$ and $E \models^E \mathcal{C}'$.

The lattice **Contr** has hypercontracts for objects (up to contract equivalence), and meet and join as just described.

Parallel Composition. The composition of hypercontracts $\mathcal{C}_i = (\mathcal{E}_i, \mathcal{I}_i)$ for $1 \leq i \leq n$, denoted $\|_i \mathcal{C}_i$, is the smallest hypercontract $\mathcal{C}' = (\mathcal{E}', \mathcal{I}')$ (up to equivalence) meeting the following requirements:

- any composition of implementations of all $\mathcal{C}_i$ is an implementation of $\mathcal{C}'$; and
- for any $1 \leq j \leq n$, any composition of an environment of $\mathcal{C}'$ with implementations of all $\mathcal{C}_i$ (for $i \neq j$) yields an environment for $\mathcal{C}_j$.

These requirements were stated for the first time by Abadi and Lamport [1]. Using our notation, this composition principle becomes

$$
\mathcal{C} \parallel \mathcal{C}' = \bigwedge \left\{ \begin{array}{c} (\mathcal{E}', \mathcal{I}') \\ \in \mathbf{Contr} \end{array} \middle| \left[\begin{array}{l} \mathcal{I}_1 \parallel \dots \parallel \mathcal{I}_n \leq \mathcal{I}', \text{ and} \\ \mathcal{E}' \parallel \mathcal{I}_1 \parallel \dots \parallel \hat{\mathcal{I}}_j \parallel \dots \parallel \mathcal{I}_n \leq \mathcal{E}_j \\ \text{for all } 1 \leq j \leq n \end{array} \right] \right\}
$$

$$
= \bigwedge \left\{ \begin{array}{c} (\mathcal{E}', \mathcal{I}') \\ \in \mathbf{Contr} \end{array} \middle| \left[\begin{array}{l} \mathcal{I}_1 \parallel \dots \parallel \mathcal{I}_n \leq \mathcal{I}', \text{ and} \\ \mathcal{E}' \leq \bigwedge_{1 \leq j \leq n} \frac{\mathcal{E}_j}{\mathcal{I}_1 \parallel \dots \parallel \hat{\mathcal{I}}_j \parallel \dots \parallel \mathcal{I}_n} \end{array} \right] \right\}, \tag{5}
$$

where the notation $\hat{\mathcal{I}}_j$ indicates that the composition $\mathcal{I}_1 \parallel \dots \parallel \hat{\mathcal{I}}_j \parallel \dots \parallel \mathcal{I}_n$ includes all terms $\mathcal{I}_i$, except for $\mathcal{I}_j$.

Example 4 (Running example, parallel composition). Coming back to the example shown in Fig. 1, we want to state a requirement for the top-level component that for all environments with $H = 0$, the implementations can only make the output O depend on P, the public data. We will write a hypercontract for the top-level. We let $\mathcal{C} = (\mathcal{E}, \mathcal{I})$, where

$$
\mathcal{E} = \{M \in \mathbb{M} \mid \forall (H, S, P, O_1, O_2, O) \in M . H = 0\}
$$
$$
\mathcal{I} = \{M \in \mathbb{M} \mid \exists f \in (2^n \to 2^o) . \forall (H, S, P, O_1, O_2, O) \in M . H = 0 \to O = f(P)\}.
$$

The environments are all those components only defined for $H = 0$. The implementations are those such that the output is a function of P when $H = 0$.

Let $f^* : 2^n \to 2^o$. Suppose we have two hypercontracts that require their implementations to satisfy the function $O_i = f^*(P)$, one implements it when $S = 0$, and the other when $S \neq 0$. For simplicity of syntax, let s_1 and s_2 be the propositions $S = 0$ and $S \neq 0$, respectively. Let the two hypercontracts be $\mathcal{C}_i = (\mathcal{E}_i, \mathcal{I}_i)$ for $i \in \{1, 2\}$. We won't place restrictions on the environments for these hypercontracts, so we obtain $\mathcal{E}_i = \mathbb{M}$ and

$$
\mathcal{I}_i = \{M \in \mathbb{M} \mid \forall (H, S, P, O_1, O_2, O) \in M . s_i \to O_i = f^*(P)\}.
$$

We now evaluate the composition of these two hypercontracts: $\mathcal{C}_c = \mathcal{C}_1 \parallel \mathcal{C}_2 = (\mathcal{E}_c, \mathcal{I}_c)$, yielding $\mathcal{E}_c = \mathbb{M}$ and

$$
\begin{aligned}
\mathcal{I}_c = \{M \in \mathbb{M} \mid &\forall (H, S, P, O_1, O_2, O) \in M . \\
&(s_1 \to O_1 = f^*(P)) \wedge (s_2 \to O_2 = f^*(P))\}.
\end{aligned}
$$

Mirror or Reciprocal. We assume we have an additional operation on hypercontracts, called both mirror and reciprocal, which flips the environments and implementations of a hypercontract: $\mathcal{C}^{-1} = (\mathcal{E}, \mathcal{I})^{-1} = (\mathcal{I}, \mathcal{E})$ and $\mathcal{C}^{-1} = (\mathcal{E}, \mathcal{S})^{-1} = (\mathcal{S}/\mathcal{E}, \mathcal{S})$. This notion gives us, so to say, the hypercontract obeyed by the environment. The introduction of this operation assumes that for every hypercontract $\mathcal{C}$, its reciprocal is also an element of **Contr**. Moreover, we assume that, when the infimum of a collection of hypercontracts exists, the following identity holds:

$$
\left(\bigwedge_i \mathcal{C}_i \right)^{-1} = \bigvee_i \mathcal{C}_i^{-1}. \tag{6}
$$

Hypercontract Quotient. The *quotient* or residual for hypercontracts $\mathcal{C} = (\mathcal{E}, \mathcal{I})$ and $\mathcal{C}'' = (\mathcal{E}'', \mathcal{I}'')$, written $\mathcal{C}''/\mathcal{C}$, has the universal property (1), namely $\forall \mathcal{C}'.\ \mathcal{C} \parallel \mathcal{C}' \leq \mathcal{C}''$ if and only if $\mathcal{C}' \leq \mathcal{C}''/\mathcal{C}$. We can obtain a closed-form expression using the reciprocal:

Proposition 1. *The hypercontract quotient obeys* $\mathcal{C}''/\mathcal{C} = \left((\mathcal{C}'')^{-1} \parallel \mathcal{C}\right)^{-1}$.

Proof.

$$
\mathcal{C}''/\mathcal{C} = \bigvee \{\mathcal{C}' \mid \mathcal{C} \parallel \mathcal{C}' \leq \mathcal{C}''\} = \bigvee \left\{ (\mathcal{E}', \mathcal{I}') \;\middle|\; \begin{bmatrix} \mathcal{I} \parallel \mathcal{I}' \leq \mathcal{I}'', \\ \mathcal{E}'' \parallel \mathcal{I} \leq \mathcal{E}', \text{ and} \\ \mathcal{E}'' \parallel \mathcal{I}' \leq \mathcal{E} \end{bmatrix} \right\}
$$

$$
= \left(\left(\bigvee \left\{ (\mathcal{E}', \mathcal{I}') \;\middle|\; \begin{bmatrix} \mathcal{I} \parallel \mathcal{I}' \leq \mathcal{I}'', \\ \mathcal{E}'' \parallel \mathcal{I} \leq \mathcal{E}', \text{ and} \\ \mathcal{E}'' \parallel \mathcal{I}' \leq \mathcal{E} \end{bmatrix} \right\} \right)^{-1} \right)^{-1}
$$

$$
\overset{(6)}{=} \left(\bigwedge \left\{ (\mathcal{I}', \mathcal{E}') \;\middle|\; \begin{bmatrix} \mathcal{I} \parallel \mathcal{I}' \leq \mathcal{I}'', \\ \mathcal{E}'' \parallel \mathcal{I} \leq \mathcal{E}', \text{ and} \\ \mathcal{E}'' \parallel \mathcal{I}' \leq \mathcal{E} \end{bmatrix} \right\} \right)^{-1}
$$

$$
= \left(\bigwedge \left\{ (\mathcal{I}', \mathcal{E}') \;\middle|\; \begin{bmatrix} \mathcal{E}'' \parallel \mathcal{I} \leq \mathcal{E}', \\ \mathcal{I}' \parallel \mathcal{I} \leq \mathcal{I}'', \text{ and} \\ \mathcal{I}' \parallel \mathcal{E}'' \leq \mathcal{E} \end{bmatrix} \right\} \right)^{-1}
$$

$$
= \left((\mathcal{C}'')^{-1} \parallel \mathcal{C}\right)^{-1}. \qquad \square
$$

Example 5 (Running example, quotient). We use the quotient to find the specification of the component that we need to add to the system shown in Fig. 1c in order to meet the top level contract $\mathcal{C}$. To compute the quotient, we use (10), as the hypercontracts we state consist of subset-closed compsets. We let $\mathcal{C}/\mathcal{C}_c = (\mathcal{E}_q, \mathcal{I}_q)$ and obtain $\mathcal{E}_q = \mathcal{E} \wedge \mathcal{I}_c$ and

$$
\mathcal{I}_q = \{ M \in \mathbb{M} \mid \exists f \in (2^n \to 2^o) \forall (H, S, P, O_1, O_2, O)
$$
$$
\in M.\, ((s_1 \to O_1 = f^*(P)) \wedge (s_2 \to O_2 = f^*(P))) \to (H = 0 \to O = f(P)) \}.
$$

We can refine the quotient by lifting any restrictions on the environments, and picking from the implementations the term with $f = f^*$. Observe that f^* is a valid choice for f. This yields the hypercontract $\mathcal{C}_3 = (\mathcal{E}_3, \mathcal{I}_3)$, defined as $\mathcal{E}_3 = \mathbb{M}$ and

$$
\mathcal{I}_3 = \{ M \in \mathbb{M} \mid \forall (H, S, P, O_1, O_2, O) \in M.
$$
$$
((s_1 \to O_1 = f^*(P)) \wedge (s_2 \to O_2 = f^*(P))) \to O = f^*(P) \}.
$$

A further refinement of this hypercontract is $\mathcal{C}_r = (\mathcal{E}_r, \mathcal{I}_r)$, where $\mathcal{E}_r = \mathbb{M}$ and

$$
\mathcal{I}_r = \{ M \in \mathbb{M} \mid \forall (H, S, P, O_1, O_2, O) \in M.\, ((s_1 \to O = O_1) \wedge (s_2 \to O = O_2)) \}.
$$

By the properties of the quotient, composing this hypercontract, which knows nothing about f^*, with $\mathcal{C}_c$ will yield a hypercontract which meets the non-interference hypercontract $\mathcal{C}$. Note that this hypercontract is consistent, i.e., it has implementations. As hypercontract refinements have smaller compsets of implementations, it is possible for a refined hypercontract to lack implementations.   □

Merging. The composition of two hypercontracts yields the specification of a system comprised of two design objects, each adhering to one of the hypercontracts being composed. Another important operation on hypercontracts is viewpoint merging, or *merging* for short. It can be the case that the same design element is assigned multiple specifications corresponding to multiple viewpoints, or design concerns [5, 25] (e.g., functionality and a performance criterion). Suppose $C_1 = (\mathcal{E}_1, \mathcal{S}_1)$ and $C_2 = (\mathcal{E}_2, \mathcal{S}_2)$ are the hypercontracts we wish to merge. Two slightly different operations can be considered as candidates for formalizing viewpoint merging:

- A *weak merge* which is the GLB; and
- A *strong merge* which states that environments of the merger should be environments of both C_1 and C_2 and that the closed systems of the merger are closed systems of both C_1 and C_2. If we let $C_1 \bullet C_2 = (\mathcal{E}, \mathcal{I})$, we have

$$\mathcal{E} = \vee\{\mathcal{E}' \in \mathbf{CmpSet} \mid \mathcal{E}' \leq \mathcal{E}_1 \wedge \mathcal{E}_2 \text{ and } \exists C'' = (\mathcal{E}'', \mathcal{I}'') \in \mathbf{Contr}. \ \mathcal{E}' = \mathcal{E}''\}$$

$$\mathcal{I} = \vee \left\{ \mathcal{I}' \in \mathbf{CmpSet} \ \middle| \ \begin{array}{l} \mathcal{I}' \leq (\mathcal{S}_1 \wedge \mathcal{S}_2)/\mathcal{E} \text{ and} \\ (\mathcal{E}, \mathcal{I}) \in \mathbf{Contr} \end{array} \right\}.$$

The difference is that, whereas the commitment to satisfy $\mathcal{S}_2$ survives under the weak merge when the environment fails to satisfy $\mathcal{E}_1$, no obligation survives under the strong merge. This distinction was proposed in [30] under the name of weak/strong assumptions.

3.4   An Example on Robustness

Now we explore assume-guarantee specifications of autonomous vehicles. We will deal with their safety and the robustness of their perception components. In order to consider the perception components, we will build our model using a pair (X, O), where $X \in S$ is the input image, belonging to a set S of images, and $O \in CS$ is the classification of the image X, an element of the classification space CS. To deal with safety, we will consider pairs $(v, \Delta s)$, where v represents the state of the vehicle with domain SP, and Δs is the maximum amount of time that it takes the vehicle to come to a full stop. Thus, every component $M \in \mathbb{M}$ is of the form

$$M = \left\{ (X, O, v, \Delta_s) \in S \times CS \times SP \times \mathbb{R}^+ \mid \exists f \in S \to CS. \ O = f(X) \right\}.$$

As discussed in Seshia et al. [33], certain robustness properties of data-driven components are hyperproperties. Robustness properties usually take the form

$d(x, y) < \delta \Rightarrow D(f(x), f(y)) < \varepsilon$, where d and D are distance functions. The property says that points that are close should have similar classifications. As two points are needed to provide evidence that a function is not robust, these are 2-safety hyperproperties. We will state a specification for our vehicles that requires their perception components to be robust. Suppose the input space S is partitioned in sets S_i. We want our vehicle to meet the following top-level specification:

$$\mathcal{C} = \left(\mathbb{M}, \left\{ M \in \mathbb{M} \;\middle|\; \begin{array}{l} \forall (x_k, o_k, v_k, \Delta s_k), (x_l, o_l, v_l, \Delta s_l) \in M. \\ \bigwedge_i x_k, x_l \in S_i \to |o_k - o_l| \leq \varepsilon \end{array} \right\} \right).$$

Suppose our vehicle obeys the specification $\mathcal{C}_a$ given by

$$\mathcal{C}_a = \left(\mathbb{M}, \left\{ M \in \mathbb{M} \;\middle|\; \begin{array}{l} \forall (x_k, o_k, v_k, \Delta s_k), (x_l, o_l, v_l, \Delta s_l) \in M. \\ \bigwedge_i x_k, x_l \in S_i \to |o_k - o_l| \leq \varepsilon_i \end{array} \right\} \right).$$

This specification says that the perception component in each region S_i should have a robustness ε_i. Suppose that there is a $j \in \mathbb{N}$ such that $\varepsilon_i \leq \varepsilon$ for all $i \leq j$ and $\varepsilon_i > \varepsilon$ otherwise. The contract quotient is $\mathcal{C}_q = (\mathcal{E}_q, \mathcal{I}_q)$, where $\mathcal{E}_q = \mathcal{I}_a$ and

$$\mathcal{I}_q = \frac{\left\{ M \in \mathbb{M} \;\middle|\; \begin{array}{l} \forall (x_k, o_k, v_k, \Delta s_k), (x_l, o_l, v_l, \Delta s_l) \in M. \\ \bigwedge_i x_k, x_l \in S_i \to |o_k - o_l| \leq \varepsilon \end{array} \right\}}{\left\{ M \in \mathbb{M} \;\middle|\; \begin{array}{l} \forall (x_k, o_k, v_k, \Delta s_k), (x_l, o_l, v_l, \Delta s_l) \in M. \\ \bigwedge_i x_k, x_l \in S_i \to |o_k - o_l| \leq \varepsilon_i \end{array} \right\}},$$

where we used the horizontal bar to denote the compset quotient. By the definition of the contract quotient, any refinement of $\mathcal{C}_q$ is a solution to our problem, namely, what is the specification that we have to compose with a specification $\mathcal{C}_a$ in order for the result to meet a goal specification $\mathcal{C}$. We thus compute a refinement of the quotient that we just obtained:

$$\mathcal{C}_b = \left(\mathbb{M}, \left\{ M \in \mathbb{M} \;\middle|\; \begin{array}{l} \forall (x_k, o_k, v_k, \Delta s_k), (x_l, o_l, v_l, \Delta s_l) \in M. \\ \bigwedge_{i>j} x_k, x_l \in S_i \to |o_k - o_l| \leq \varepsilon \end{array} \right\} \right).$$

Observe how using the quotient we were able to obtain a specification $\mathcal{C}_b$ that contains exactly what needs to be fixed in the component adhering to hypercontract $\mathcal{C}_a$ in order for it to meet the top-level specification $\mathcal{C}$. Moreover, the specification $\mathcal{C}_b$ does not contain any information about $\mathcal{C}_a$.

One of the uses of hypercontracts is in handling multiple viewpoints. Suppose that the robust perception specification is given to a vehicle on top of other specifications, such as safety. For example, suppose there is a specification that says that if the state of the vehicle v is inside a safety set T, then the amount of time Δs that it takes the vehicle to come to a full stop is a most P. We can write the spec

$$\mathcal{C}_s = (v \in T, \Delta s < P).$$

By using strong merging, we can get into a single top-level hypercontract the specification of the perception and the safety viewpoints, as follows:

$$\left(v \in T, \left\{ M \in \mathbb{M} \; \middle| \; \begin{array}{l} \forall (x_k, o_k, v_k, \Delta s_k), (x_l, o_l, v_l, \Delta s_l) \in M. \\ \Delta s_k, \Delta s_l < P \wedge \bigwedge_i x_k, x_l \in S_i \rightarrow |o_k - o_l| \leq \varepsilon \end{array} \right\} \right).$$

This specification summarizes the perception and safety viewpoints of the vehicle. As robustness is a hyperproperty, we cannot use AG contracts to reason about the specifications in this example, but hypercontracts enable us to do so.

4   Behavioral Modeling

In the behavioral approach to system modeling, we start with a set $\mathcal{B}$ whose elements we call behaviors. Components are defined as subsets of $\mathcal{B}$. They contain the behaviors they can display. A component M is a subcomponent of M' if M' contains all the behaviors of M, i.e., if $M \subseteq M'$. Component composition is given by set intersection: $M \times M' \stackrel{\text{def}}{=} M \cap M'$. If we represent the components as $M = \{ b \in \mathcal{B} \mid \phi(b) \}$ and $M' = \{ b \in \mathcal{B} \mid \phi'(b) \}$ for some constraints ϕ and ϕ', then composition is $M \times M' = \{ b \in \mathcal{B} \mid \phi(b) \wedge \phi'(b) \}$, i.e., the behaviors that simultaneously meet the constraints of M and M'. This notion of composition is independent of the connection topology: the topology is inferred from the behaviors of the components.

We will consider two contract theories we can build with these components. The first is based on unconstrained hyperproperties; the second is based on downward-closed hyperproperties.

4.1   General Hypercontracts

The most expressive behavioral theory of hypercontracts is obtained when we place no restrictions on the structure of compsets and hypercontracts. In this case, the elements of **CmpSet** are all objects $H \in 2^{2^{\mathcal{B}}}$, i.e., all hyperproperties. The meet and join of compsets are set intersection and union, respectively, and their composition and quotient are given by (3) and (4), respectively. Hypercontracts are of the form $\mathcal{C} = (\mathcal{E}, \mathcal{I})$ with all extrema achieved in the binary operations, i.e., for a second hypercontract $\mathcal{C}' = (\mathcal{E}', \mathcal{I}')$, the meet, join, and composition (5) are, respectively, $\mathcal{C} \wedge \mathcal{C}' = (\mathcal{E} \cup \mathcal{E}', \mathcal{I} \cap \mathcal{I}')$, $\mathcal{C} \vee \mathcal{C}' = (\mathcal{E} \cap \mathcal{E}', \mathcal{I} \cup \mathcal{I}')$, and $\mathcal{C} \parallel \mathcal{C}' = \left(\frac{\mathcal{E}'}{\mathcal{I}} \cap \frac{\mathcal{E}}{\mathcal{I}'}, \mathcal{I} \parallel \mathcal{I}' \right)$. From these follow the operations of quotient, and merging.

4.2   Conic (or Downward-Closed) Hypercontracts

We assume that **CmpSet** contains exclusively downward-closed hyperproperties. Let $H \in$ **CmpSet**. We say that $M \models H$ is a maximal component of H when H contains no set bigger than M, i.e., if $\forall M' \models H.\ M \leq M' \Rightarrow M' = M$.

We let $\overline{H}$ be the set of maximal components of H:

$$\overline{H} = \{M \models H \mid \forall M' \models H.\ M \leq M' \Rightarrow M' = M\}.$$

Due to the fact H is downward-closed, the set of maximal components is a unique representation of H. We can express H as

$$H = \bigcup_{M \in \overline{H}} 2^M.$$

We say that H is k-*conic* if the cardinality of $\overline{H}$ is finite and equal to k, and we write this

$$H = \langle M_1, \ldots, M_k \rangle, \text{ where } \overline{H} = \{M_1, \ldots, M_k\}.$$

Order. The notion of order on **CmpSet** can be expressed using this notation as follows: suppose $H' = \langle M' \rangle_{M' \in \overline{H}'}$. Then

$$H' \leq H \text{ if and only if } \forall M' \in \overline{H}'\ \exists M \in \overline{H}.\ M' \leq M.$$

Composition. Composition in **CmpSet** becomes

$$H \times H' = \bigcup_{\substack{M \in \overline{H} \\ M' \in \overline{H}'}} 2^{M \cap M'} = \langle M \cap M' \rangle_{\substack{M \in \overline{H} \\ M' \in \overline{H}'}}. \tag{7}$$

Therefore, if H and H' are, respectively, k- and k'-conic, $H \times H'$ is at most kk'-conic.

Quotient. Suppose H_q satisfies

$$H' \times H_q \leq H.$$

Let $M_q \in \overline{H}_q$. We must have

$$M_q \times M' \models H \text{ for every } M' \in \overline{H}',$$

which means that for each $M' \in \overline{H}'$ there must exist an $M \in \overline{H}$ such that $M_q \times M' \leq M$; let us denote by $M(M')$ a choice $M' \mapsto M$ satisfying this condition. Therefore, we have

$$M_q \leq \bigwedge_{M' \in \overline{H}'} \frac{M(M')}{M'}, \tag{8}$$

Clearly, the largest such M_q is obtained by making (8) an equality. Thus, the cardinality of the quotient is bounded from above by $k^{k'}$ since we have

$$H_q = \left\langle \bigwedge_{M' \in \overline{H}'} \frac{M(M')}{M'} \right\rangle_{\substack{M(M') \in \overline{H}. \\ \forall M' \in \overline{H}'}}. \tag{9}$$

Contracts. Now we assume that the objects of **CmpSet** are pairs of *downward-closed compsets*. If we have two hypercontracts $\mathcal{C} = (\mathcal{E}, \mathcal{I})$ and $\mathcal{C}' = (\mathcal{E}', \mathcal{I}')$, their composition and quotient are, respectively,

$$\mathcal{C} \parallel \mathcal{C}' = \left(\frac{\mathcal{E}}{\mathcal{I}'} \wedge \frac{\mathcal{E}'}{\mathcal{I}}, \mathcal{I} \times \mathcal{I}' \right) \text{ and } \mathcal{C}/\mathcal{C}' = \left(\mathcal{E} \times \mathcal{I}', \frac{\mathcal{I}}{\mathcal{I}'} \wedge \frac{\mathcal{E}'}{\mathcal{E}} \right). \tag{10}$$

5   Conclusions

We proposed hypercontracts, a general model of contracts providing a richer algebra than the metatheory of [6]. We started from a generic model of components equipped with a simulation preorder and parallel composition. On top of them, we considered compsets (or hyperproperties, for behavioral formalisms), which are lattices of sets of components equipped with parallel composition and quotient; compsets are our generic model formalizing "properties." Hypercontracts are then defined as pairs of compsets specifying the allowed environments and either the obligations of the closed system or the set of allowed implementations—both forms are useful.

We specialized hypercontracts by restricting them to conic hypercontracts, whose environments and closed systems are described by a finite number of components. Conic hypercontracts include assume-guarantee contracts as a specialization. We illustrated the versatility of our model on the definition of contracts for information flow in security and robustness of data-driven components.

The flexibility and power of our model suggests that a number of directions that were opened in [6], but not explored to their end, can now be reinvestigated with more powerful tools: contracts and testing, subcontract synthesis (for requirement engineering), contracts and abstract interpretation, contracts in physical system modeling.[2] In particular, as monitoring hyperproperties [13] is more tractable than model checking them, hypercontracts are a promising tool to enable compositional testing of hyperproperties in reactive systems.

Furthermore, results on contracts were recently obtained in the domain of control systems. In particular, Phan-Minh and Murray [26,27] introduced the notion of reactive contracts. Saoud et al. [31,32] proposed a framework of assume-guarantee contracts for input/output discrete or continuous time systems. Assumptions vs. guarantees are properties stated on inputs vs. outputs. With this restriction, reactive contracts are considered and an elegant formula is proposed for the parallel composition of contracts. Bartocci et al. [2] recently introduced information-flow interfaces, a theory that enables assume-guarantee reasoning over information-flow properties. Hypercontracts are complementary to this theory, as they support arbitrary classes of hyperproperties. These recent

---

[2]   Simulink and Modelica toolsuites propose requirements toolboxes, in which requirements are physical system properties that can be tested on a given system model, thus providing a limited form of contract. This motivates the development of a richer contract framework to help requirement engineering in Cyber-Physical Systems design.

developments offer the opportunity of exploring further avenues of research to link these new concepts.

Acknowledgments. We are very grateful to our reviewers for their comments. This work was supported by NSF Contract CPS Medium 1739816, by the DARPA LOGiCS project under contract FA8750-20-C-0156, and by the Chateaubriand Fellowship of the Office for Science & Technology of the Embassy of France in the United States.

References

1. Abadi, M., Lamport, L.: Composing specifications. ACM Trans. Program. Lang. Syst. **15**(1), 73–132 (1993)
2. Bartocci, E., Ferrère, T., Henzinger, T.A., Nickovic, D., da Costa, A.O.: Information-flow interfaces. In: International Conference on Fundamental Approaches to Software Engineering, pp. 3–22 (2020)
3. Bauer, S.S., et al.: Moving from specifications to contracts in component-based design. In: de Lara, J., Zisman, A. (eds.) FASE 2012. LNCS, vol. 7212, pp. 43–58. Springer, Heidelberg (2012). https://doi.org/10.1007/978-3-642-28872-2_3
4. Bauer, S.S., Larsen, K.G., Legay, A., Nyman, U., Wasowski, A.: A modal specification theory for components with data. Sci. Comput. Program. **83**, 106–128 (2014)
5. Benveniste, A., Caillaud, B., Ferrari, A., Mangeruca, L., Passerone, R., Sofronis, C.: Multiple viewpoint contract-based specification and design. In: de Boer, F.S., Bonsangue, M.M., Graf, S., de Roever, W.-P. (eds.) FMCO 2007. LNCS, vol. 5382, pp. 200–225. Springer, Heidelberg (2008). https://doi.org/10.1007/978-3-540-92188-2_9
6. Benveniste, A., et al.: Contracts for system design. Found. Trends Electron. Des. Autom. **12**(2–3), 124–400 (2018)
7. Bujtor, J., Vogler, W.: Error-pruning in interface automata. In: 40th International Conference on Current Trends in Theory and Practice of Computer Science SOFSEM 2014, pp. 162–173, Novy Smokovec, Slovakia, 26-29 January 2014
8. Clarkson, M.R., Schneider, F.B.: Hyperproperties. J. Comput. Secur. **18**(6), 1157–1210 (2010)
9. Coleman, J.W., Jones, C.B.: A structural proof of the soundness of rely/guarantee rules. J. Log. Comput. **17**(4), 807–841 (2007)
10. de Alfaro, L., Henzinger, T.A.: Interface automata. In: Proceedings of the 8th European Software Engineering Conference Held Jointly with 9th ACM SIGSOFT International Symposium on Foundations of Software Engineering, ESEC/FSE-9, pp. 109–120. ACM New York, NY, USA (2001)
11. de Alfaro, L., Henzinger, T.A.: Interface theories for component-based design. In: Henzinger, T.A., Kirsch, C.M. (eds.) EMSOFT 2001. LNCS, vol. 2211, pp. 148–165. Springer, Heidelberg (2001). https://doi.org/10.1007/3-540-45449-7_11
12. Doyen, L., Henzinger, T.A., Jobstmann, B., Petrov, T.: Interface theories with component reuse. In: Proceedings of the 8th ACM & IEEE International conference on Embedded software, EMSOFT 2008, pp. 79–88, Atlanta, GA(2008)
13. Finkbeiner, B., Hahn, C., Stenger, M., Tentrup, L.: Monitoring hyperproperties. Formal Meth. Syst. Des. **54**(3), 336–363 (2019). https://doi.org/10.1007/s10703-019-00334-z

14. Goguen, J.A., Meseguer, J.: Security policies and security models. In: 1982 IEEE Symposium on Security and Privacy, Oakland, CA, USA, 26–28 April 1982, pp. 11–20, Oakland, CA, USA, 1982. IEEE Computer Society (1982)
15. Hayes, I.J., Jones, C.B.: A guide to rely/guarantee thinking. In: Bowen, J.P., Liu, Z., Zhang, Z. (eds.) SETSS 2017. LNCS, vol. 11174, pp. 1–38. Springer, Cham (2018). https://doi.org/10.1007/978-3-030-02928-9_1
16. Incer, I., Mangeruca, L., Villa, T., Sangiovanni-Vincentelli, A.L.: The quotient in preorder theories. In: Raskin, J.-F., Bresolin, D. (eds.) Proceedings 11th International Symposium on Games. Automata, Logics, and Formal Verification, Brussels, Belgium, September 21–22, 2020, volume 326 of Electronic Proceedings in Theoretical Computer Science, pp. 216–233. Open Publishing Association, Brussels, Belgium (2020)
17. Jones, C.B.: Specification and design of (parallel) programs. In: IFIP Congress, pp. 321–332, Paris, France (1983)
18. Jones, C.B.: Wanted: a compositional approach to concurrency. In: McIver, A., Morgan, C. (eds), Programming Methodology, pp. 5–15, New York, NY, 2003. Springer, New York. https://doi.org/10.1007/978-0-387-21798-7_1
19. Larsen, K.G., Nyman, U., Wąsowski, A.: Interface input/output automata. In: Misra, J., Nipkow, T., Sekerinski, E. (eds.) FM 2006. LNCS, vol. 4085, pp. 82–97. Springer, Heidelberg (2006). https://doi.org/10.1007/11813040_7
20. Larsen, K.G., Nyman, U., Wąsowski, A.: Modal I/O automata for interface and product line theories. In: De Nicola, R. (ed.) ESOP 2007. LNCS, vol. 4421, pp. 64–79. Springer, Heidelberg (2007). https://doi.org/10.1007/978-3-540-71316-6_6
21. Larsen, K.G., Nyman, U., Wąsowski, A.: On modal refinement and consistency. In: Caires, L., Vasconcelos, V.T. (eds.) CONCUR 2007. LNCS, vol. 4703, pp. 105–119. Springer, Heidelberg (2007). https://doi.org/10.1007/978-3-540-74407-8_8
22. Lüttgen, G., Vogler, W.: Modal interface automata. Logic. Meth. Comput. Sci. 9(3) (2013)
23. Mastroeni, I., Pasqua, M.: Verifying bounded subset-closed hyperproperties. In: Podelski, A. (ed.) Static Analysis. pp, pp. 263–283. Springer International Publishing, Cham (2018)
24. Negulescu, R.: Process spaces. In: Palamidessi, C. (ed.) CONCUR 2000. LNCS, vol. 1877, pp. 199–213. Springer, Heidelberg (2000). https://doi.org/10.1007/3-540-44618-4_16
25. Passerone, R., Incer, I., Sangiovanni-Vincentelli, A.L.: Coherent extension, composition, and merging operators in contract models for system design. ACM Trans. Embed. Comput. Syst. 18(5s) (2019)
26. Phan-Minh, T.: Contract-Based Design: Theories and Applications. PhD thesis, California Institute of Technology (2021)
27. Phan-Minh, T., Murray, R.M.: Contracts of Reactivity. Technical report, California Institute of Technology (2019)
28. Rabe, M.N.: A temporal logic approach to information-flow control. PhD thesis, Universität des Saarlandes (2016)
29. Raclet, J.-B., Badouel, E., Benveniste, A., Caillaud, B., Legay, A., Passerone, R.: Modal interfaces: Unifying interface automata and modal specifications. In: Proceedings of the Seventh ACM International Conference on Embedded Software, EMSOFT 2009, pp. 87–96. ACM New York, NY, USA (2009)
30. Sangiovanni-Vincentelli, A.L., Damm, W., Passerone, R., Frankenstein, T.: Contract-based design for cyber-physical systems. Eur. J. Control 18(3), 217–238 (2012)

31. Saoud, A., Girard, A., Fribourg, L.: On the composition of discrete and continuous-time assume-guarantee contracts for invariance. In: 16th European Control Conference, ECC, 12–15 June 2018, pp. 435–440, Limassol, Cyprus. IEEE (2018)
32. Saoud, A., Girard, A., Fribourg, L.: Assume-guarantee contracts for continuous-time systems. working paper or preprint. Automatica **134**, 109910 (2021)
33. Seshia, S.A., et al.: Formal specification for deep neural networks. In: Lahiri, S.K., Wang, C. (eds.) Automated Technology for Verification and Analysis. pp, pp. 20–34. Springer International Publishing, Cham (2018)

Monitorability of Expressive Verdicts

Felipe Gorostiaga[1,2,3] and César Sánchez[1(✉)]

[1] IMDEA Software Institute, Madrid, Spain
{felipe.gorostiaga,cesar.sanchez}@imdea.org
[2] Universidad Politécnica de Madrid (UPM), Madrid, Spain
[3] CIFASIS, Rosario, Argentina

Abstract. Online runtime verification is a formal dynamic technique that studies how to monitor formal specifications incrementally against an input trace. Often, an observed prefix of a behavior is not enough to emit a definite verdict and the monitor must wait to receive more information. Monitorability classifies the set of properties depending on the feasibility to obtain a verdict after a finite observation. Havelund and Peled [20] classified LTL properties according to whether an observation can be extended to a definite answer.

In this paper we present a framework that extends the classification of Havelund and Peled to verdict domains that are richer than Booleans, obtaining a monitorability setting under which some of the verdicts (but not others) can be discarded after a sequence of observations. We study two instances of this setting, quantitative temporal logics and partially ordered domains for stream runtime verification, and we illustrate using examples the different elements of the taxonomy. Finally, we also consider how assumptions on the set of behaviors can improve monitorability, and how imprecise observations can impair monitorability.

1 Introduction

Runtime verification (RV) is a dynamic formal technique for system reliability that studies how events, emitted from a system under study, adhere to a given formal specification. Runtime verification focuses on two main problems: (1) how to generate a monitor from a given specification, and (2) algorithms that take a monitor and process a sequence of input events produced by the system, typically in a incremental manner, attempting to produce a definite verdict. In this paper we use *behavior* to refer to the trace of the system—that is, one infinite sequence of events that a system can produce—and *observation* as the finite sequence of events that monitor receives.

Static formal verification techniques like model checking [14,28] attempt to prove that every behavior of the system satisfies a given specification. In contrast, in runtime verification monitors must decide based on observations. Runtime verification sacrifices completeness to provide an applicable formal extension of testing and debugging. See [19,26] for surveys on runtime verification and the recent book [4].

© Springer Nature Switzerland AG 2022
J. V. Deshmukh et al. (Eds.): NFM 2022, LNCS 13260, pp. 693–712, 2022.
https://doi.org/10.1007/978-3-031-06773-0_37

Early specification languages studied for runtime verification were based on temporal logics, typically LTL [6,13,21], regular expressions [32], timed regular expressions [2], rules [3], or rewriting [30]. Since monitors only see an observation and not a complete behavior, the semantics of temporal logic must be adapted for finite traces. One solution is to adapt the semantics for finite traces [13] that provide a definite answer upon the "termination" of the trace. Another solution is to give a definite answer only if all the behaviors that extend the observation satisfy the specification (declaring satisfaction), or if all such extensions violate the specification (declaring violation). Otherwise, the monitor can produce a temporary "*I don't know*" verdict [6], with the hope to later refine it into a conclusive verdict. The idea of producing an inconclusive verdict was already introduced in the context of stream runtime verification [11] and later used in variants of LTL for finite traces, like LTLf [12] and MLTL [29].

A basic *soundness* criteria states that monitors should never give a verdict that can be later reverted by an extended observation [7]. However, sound monitors can still switch from an indecisive verdict into a definite verdict. The soundness requirement is semantic, in the sense that it is based on the semantics of the logic itself by considering all possible traces that are compatible with the given observation. Monitors can be formally understood as an implementation of a computational function that maps observations into verdicts [20,33,34] that respects the soundness requirement. Therefore, monitoring algorithms correspond to an incremental execution of the monitor as a function. From this perspective monitorability corresponds to the question of the existence of such a computable function.

One of the first definitions of monitorability, given by Pnueli and Zaks [27], establishes that an LTL property is monitorable after an observation u if there is an observation u' that extends u for which the verdict is definitely a violation or there is an observation u' that is an extension of u for which the verdict is a satisfaction. There are properties that are always monitorable for violation, in the sense that every violating behavior has a finite prefix (observation) that is sufficient to determine the violation. For a second class of properties this witness only exists for some behaviors, and for the rest of the properties there is never such a witness observation (these definitions are analogous replacing violation by satisfaction). Havelund and Peled present in [20] a complete taxonomy for LTL, introducing the terms AFR (always finitely refutable), SFR (sometimes finitely refutable) and NFR (never finitely refutable). Their counterparts for a satisfaction verdict are AFS, SFS and NFS. In this paper we study extensions of this taxonomy for more expressive (non-Boolean) verdicts.

It is useful for specification engineers to have very expressive logics to define their properties, but additional expressiveness usually comes at the price of higher complexity in the decision problems and more inefficient algorithms. Since the early languages used in RV were borrowed from static verification where decidability is crucial, these languages only allowed Boolean verdicts. However, runtime verification solves a simpler problem than model-checking so some researchers have been extending the expressivity of RV specification languages.

Examples include logics that can quantify over the data in the events [5,20], extensions of automata with the ability to store and compare data [9], and quantitative semantics for temporal logics [15]. Another direction to extend the expressivity of monitors is Stream Runtime Verification [10,11,16,18,31] that abstract the data used in the monitoring algorithms in temporal logics to arbitrary data. In this paper we extend the Havelund and Peled notions of monitorability to the setting of richer verdicts by studying whether a subset of the possible verdicts can be discarded after witnessing a finite trace. In [12] the monitorability necessarily refers to the ability to give a conclusive verdict after a finite observation, but the logics we consider are defined over infinite traces. In contrast, LTLf [12] and similar logics are interpreted over finite traces. Also, logics that guarantee that verdicts are obtained after a finite number of steps (by the semantics of the logic or some assumption on the input trace), like MLTL [29], are immediately in AFS and AFR.

The standard monitoring studies monitors that are correct for any system under observation, which is considered unknown during the generation of the monitor. However, one can often monitor more effectively for particular systems or under *assumptions* about what the system can do. For example, [36] improves LTL monitoring using a model of the system to prune the set of possible future observations, and [33] considers how to improve the monitoring of hyperproperties using approximations of the system. Similarly, [22] illustrates properties that are not monitorable but become monitorable if one assumes that the input observation satisfies a given LTL formula. In practice, the events obtained from the system may not be perfect, which can affect the monitoring. For example, in [25] the authors study the possibility that events or event values are unknown, so the monitor must deal with the set of possible observations, therefore emitting sets of verdicts. In [23], the authors define the concept of *trace mutations* to capture divergences between observations and behaviors, and study how different mutations affect the monitorability of a property. We present in Sect. 5 an example of a system and monitoring with richer verdicts that can be monitored under assumptions and event uncertainties, and instantiate the monitorability landscape for the properties monitored. This paves the way for a systematic analysis of monitoring of rich verdicts under assumptions and uncertainties.

In summary, the contributions of the paper are: (1) an extension of the Havelund and Peled taxonomy of monitorability to richer verdicts and in particular to totally and partially ordered domains; and (2) an instantiation of the taxonomy to quantitative temporal logics and to partially ordered domains based on stream runtime verification.

Finally, note that our taxonomy of properties, like the one introduced by Havelund and Peled, is based on the ability of monitors to produce verdicts. Other taxonomies of properties exist. For example, [8] classifies properties based on the use of the temporal operators involved.

The rest of the paper is structured as follows. Section 2 includes the preliminaries. Section 3 introduces the generalization of the monitorability framework to expressive verdicts. This is instantiated to quantitative temporal logics in Sect. 4, where the set of verdicts is totally ordered, and to partially ordered domains in Sect. 5. Finally, Sect. 6 contains some final remarks.

2   Preliminaries

We use streams (infinite sequences) to represent the *behavior* exhibited by a system. A stream of type D is an infinite sequence of values of D, and we denote the type of the streams of type D as D^ω. We will usually use *record types* to represent the information of different aspects of the system under study. The type $\langle p_0 :: D_0, \ldots, p_n :: D_n \rangle$ represents a record that contains a finite number of entries and assigns a value of type D_i to every variable p_i for $0 \le i \le n$. For example, $s \stackrel{\text{def}}{=} (\langle p : true \rangle \langle p : true \rangle \langle p : false \rangle^\omega) \in \langle p :: Bool \rangle^\omega$ is the stream of $\langle p :: Bool \rangle$ values where p starts with two *true* values and remains *false* thereafter. Given a record value $r \stackrel{\text{def}}{=} \langle p_0 : v_0, \ldots, p_n : v_n \rangle$ we use $r(p_i)$ to refer to v_i for $0 \le i \le n$. Given a stream $\sigma \in D^\omega$ and a natural number $i \in \mathbb{N}_0$ we use $\sigma(i)$ to refer to the element of type D at position i in σ. Similarly, we use σ^i to refer to the stream $(\sigma(i) \, \sigma(i+1) \, \ldots)$. For example, $s(0)(p) = true$, $s(50)(p) = false$, and $s^1 = (\langle p : true \rangle \langle p : false \rangle^\omega)$.

We use finite sequences to represent *observations* of the behavior of a program. A sequence of type D is a finite sequence of values of D, and we denote the type of the sequences of type D as D^*. The length of a sequence ls is the number of elements in ls, written as $|ls|$. For example, $l \stackrel{\text{def}}{=} [\langle p : true \rangle \langle p : true \rangle \langle p : false \rangle \langle p : false \rangle \langle p : false \rangle] \in [\langle p :: Bool \rangle]$ is the stream of assignments of Boolean values to p, which starts with two *true* values and is succeeded by three *false* values. We say that a sequence $ls \in D^*$ of length $|ls| = n$ is a prefix of a stream $s \in D^\omega$ and write $ls \prec s$ if the first n elements of s coincide with the n elements of ls. We also say that s is a continuation of ls. We say that $ls \in D^*$ is a subsequence of a stream $s \in D^\omega$ and write $ls \sqsubset s$ if there is an index i such that $ls \prec s^i$. We also say that s is an expansion of ls. For example, $|l| = 5$, $l \prec s$ (this is, s is a continuation of ls), and obviously $l \sqsubset s$ (this is, s is an expansion of ls). The sequence $[\langle p : false \rangle \langle p : false \rangle \langle p : false \rangle]$ is also a subsequence of s, because it is a prefix of s^2.

Let $\mathsf{AP} = \{p_0, \ldots, p_n\}$ be a finite set of atomic propositions and $R \stackrel{\text{def}}{=} \langle p_0 :: Bool, \ldots, p_n :: Bool \rangle$ the record type that assigns a Boolean value to each atomic proposition in AP. The syntax of LTL is:

$$\varphi ::= T \mid a \mid \varphi \vee \varphi \mid \neg\varphi \mid \bigcirc \varphi \mid \varphi \, \mathcal{U} \, \varphi$$

where a is an atomic proposition, $\vee$ and $\neg$ are the usual Boolean disjunction and negation, and $\bigcirc$ and $\mathcal{U}$ are the next and until temporal operators. The semantics of LTL associate behaviors $\sigma \in R^\omega$ with formulas as follows:

$$\sigma \models T \quad \text{always} \qquad\qquad \sigma \models \varphi_1 \vee \varphi_2 \text{ iff } \sigma \models \varphi_1 \text{ or } \sigma \models \varphi_2$$
$$\sigma \models a \quad \text{iff} \quad \sigma(0)(a) = true \qquad \sigma \models \neg\varphi \quad \text{iff } \sigma \not\models \varphi$$
$$\sigma \models \bigcirc\varphi \quad \text{iff} \quad \sigma^1 \models \varphi$$
$$\sigma \models \varphi_1 \, \mathcal{U} \, \varphi_2 \text{ iff} \quad \text{for some } j \ge 0 \; \sigma^j \models \varphi_2, \text{ and for all } 0 \le i < j, \sigma^i \models \varphi_1$$

Common derived operators are $\varphi_1 \wedge \varphi_2 \stackrel{\text{def}}{=} \neg(\varphi_1 \vee \varphi_2)$, $\varphi_1 \mathcal{R} \varphi_2 \stackrel{\text{def}}{=} \neg(\neg\varphi_1 \mathcal{U} \neg\varphi_2)$, $\Diamond\varphi \stackrel{\text{def}}{=} T \mathcal{U} \varphi$ and $\Box\varphi \stackrel{\text{def}}{=} \neg\Diamond\neg\varphi$.

2.1   LTL Property Classification

In [20], the authors give a property classification according to the capability of a monitor to reach a verdict witnessing a finite trace. The original definitions are the following. For a given property φ:

Safety/Always Finitely Refutable (AFR). When φ does not hold on a behavior, a failed verdict can be identified after a finite prefix.

Guarantee/Always Finitely Satisfiable (AFS). When φ is satisfied on a behavior, a satisfied verdict can be identified after a finite prefix.

Liveness/Never Finitely Refutable (NFR). When φ does not hold on a behavior, a refutation can not be identified after a finite prefix.

Morbidity/Never Finitely Satisfiable (NFS). When φ is satisfied on a behavior, satisfaction can not be identified after a finite prefix.

The authors define two extra property classes that are not given a name:

Sometimes Finitely Refutable (SFR). For some behaviors that violate φ, a refutation can be identified after a finite prefix; while for other behaviors violating φ, a refutation cannot be identified with a finite prefix.

Sometimes Finitely Satisfiable (SFS). For some behaviors that satisfy φ, satisfaction can be identified after a finite prefix; while for other behaviors satisfying the property, satisfaction cannot be identified with a finite prefix.

Figure 1 shows the landscape of property classes along with an example LTL property for every class.

We can see, for example, that $\Diamond p$ belongs to **Guarantee** and Liveness. This property is NFR because given any finite prefix of a trace where the property does not hold, we can construct an alternative continuation where it does hold, simply making the next value of p be *true*. The property is also AFS because we can find the first index when p becomes *true* and any continuation of that prefix makes the property *true*.

3   A Richer View of Monitorability

In this section we generalize the framework of Havelund and Peled in [20] to consider richer verdicts (beyond Boolean values). Similar to the approach in [20], we base our work on the ability of a monitor to reach a verdict witnessing a finite observation. Note that the finite satisfiability of a property means that with a finite observation we can *dismiss* the value *false* as the result, and the finite refutability of a property means that with a finite observation we can *dismiss* the value *true* as the result. The main intuition is to focus on the dismissibility of verdict values.

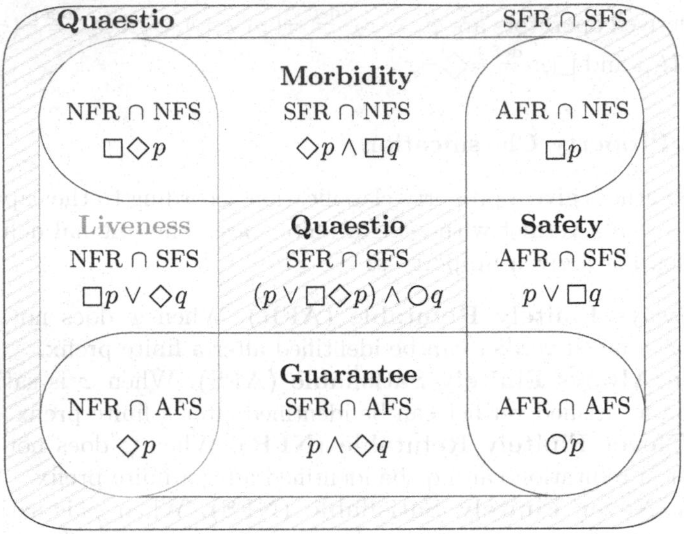

Fig. 1. Landscape of property classes according to [20].

Consider a formalism whose semantics $[\![\cdot]\!]$ is defined over behaviors of type I^ω and that assigns verdicts of type D. For example, classical LTL is defined over records of Boolean values and its semantics assigns Boolean verdicts.

We say a value $v \in D$ is *Finitely Dismissible* for a formula φ and a behavior $s \in I^\omega$ if there is an observation $ls \in I^*$, $ls \prec s$ such that for all s' continuation of ls, $[\![\varphi]\!](s') \neq v$. We say a value $v \in D$ is *Finitely Admissible* for a formula φ and a behavior $s \in I^\omega$ if there is an observation $ls \in I^*$, $ls \prec s$ such that for all possible continuations $s' \in I^\omega$ (this is, all the streams $s' \in I^\omega$ such that $ls \prec s'$), $[\![\varphi]\!](s') = v$. Notice that the only value that can be Finitely Admissible for φ over s is $[\![\varphi]\!](s)$.

We say that a set of values $D' \subseteq D$ is *None Finitely Dismissible* (NFD) for a formula φ and a behavior s if every $v \in D'$ is not Finitely Dismissible for φ and s. Analogously, we say that a set of values $D' \subset D$ is *All Finitely Dismissible* (AFD) for a formula φ and a behavior s if every $v \in D'$ is Finitely Dismissible for φ and s. Notice that the empty set is both NFD and AFD. We say that a set of values $D' \subset D$ is *Some Finitely Dismissible* (SFD) if it is not AFD nor NFD.

We can extend the definition of Finite Admissibility to sets of values but they are of little use in our work.

Lemma 1. *If v is Finitely Admissible for a formula φ and a behavior s then $D \backslash \{v\}$ is AFD for φ and s.*

Proof. Since v is Finitely Admissible for φ and s, there is a finite sequence $ls \prec s$ such that for every continuation s' of ls, $[\![\varphi]\!](s) = v$. We can therefore dismiss any value in $D \backslash \{v\}$ with the finite prefix ls. $\square$

The converse holds for finite domains.

Lemma 2. *If $D\backslash\{v\}$ is AFD for a formula φ and a behavior s and D is finite, then v is Finitely Admissible for φ and s.*

Proof. There is an index for every element v' in $D\backslash\{v\}$ that indicates the shortest length of the finite prefix after which v' can be dismissed for φ over s. After a prefix of the maximum length of those indexes (which are finite), we will have dismissed every $v' \neq v$ in D, and as a consequence the semantics of any continuation over φ is v. $\qquad\square$

However, if D is infinite, Lemma 2 does not hold.

Lemma 3. *If $D\backslash\{v\}$ is AFD for a formula φ and a behavior s and D is infinite, then it is not necessarily the case that v is Finitely Admissible for φ and s.*

Proof. Let there be a property φ that assigns the maximum value of the field p (of type $\mathbb{N}$) in the behavior if it exists, and ∞ otherwise. The verdict is of type $\mathbb{N} \cup \{\infty\}$ and for the behavior $s \overset{\text{def}}{=} (\langle p : 1 \rangle \ \langle p : 2 \rangle \ \langle p : 3 \rangle \ \ldots)$, the semantics of φ is $[\![\varphi]\!](s) = \infty$, any natural number is finitely dismissible and yet ∞ is not finitely admissible: we can simply repeat the last value of a prefix forever, creating a continuation whose semantics over φ is a natural number. $\qquad\square$

We will show two more (counter) examples for bounded, dense verdict domains in Sects. 4.2 and 4.3.

4 Boolean and Quantitative Totally Ordered Domains

In this section we generalize the classification of Havelund and Peled to totally ordered sets, according to the dismissibility of values with respect to the result. Note that this is the same criterion as in the original definitions.

4.1 Property Classes

If the type D of the verdicts of a formalism is a totally ordered set equipped with an order relation $(D, \leq)$, we can classify the properties according to their value-dismissibility as follows. Let $v = [\![\varphi]\!](\sigma)$ be the semantics of the property φ for behavior σ. We use $v_<$ for the set of values lower than v and $v_>$ the set of values greater than v, that is $v_< \overset{\text{def}}{=} \{v'|v' < v\}$ and $v_> \overset{\text{def}}{=} \{v'|v' > v\}$. We say a property is AFD$_>$ if the set of values greater than its verdict for any behavior is AFD. We define AFD$_<$, NFD$_>$ and NFD$_<$ analogously. A property is SFD$_>$ if for some executions, some values greater than its verdict are finitely dismissible while other are not. The definition of SFD$_<$ is analogous. With these definitions we can redefine the property classes for rich, totally ordered domains as follows:

Safety/AFD$_>$. We say that a property is a *Safety* property if the set $v_>$ is All Finitely Dismissible for any behavior σ (this is, the monitor can dismiss every value greater than the result with a prefix). In other words, if you set a maximum tolerable threshold t and the result is below the threshold, you will know it after a finite prefix.

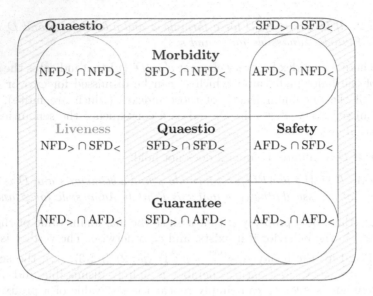

Fig. 2. Landscape of property classes for totally ordered domains

Guarantee/AFD$_<$. We say that a property is a *Guarantee* property if the set $v_<$ is All Finitely Dismissible for any behavior σ (this is, the monitor can dismiss every value lower than the result with a prefix). In other words, if you set a minimum score t and the result is higher than it, you will know it with a finite prefix.

Liveness/NFD$_>$. We say a property is a *Liveness* property if the set $v_>$ is None Finitely Dismissible for any behavior σ (this is, the monitor can never dismiss any value greater than the result processing any prefix). In other words, if you set a maximum tolerable threshold t and the result is below it, you will not know it with a finite prefix.

Morbidity/NFD$_<$. We say a property is a *Morbidity* property if the set $v_<$ is None Finitely Dismissible for any behavior σ (this is, the monitor can never dismiss any value lower than the result with a prefix). In other words, if you set a minimum score t and the result is higher than it, you will not know it with a finite prefix.

We define two additional sets of properties:

SFD$_>$. In some traces the monitor can dismiss some values higher than the result with a prefix, but not others.

SFD$_<$. In some traces, the monitor can dismiss some values lower than the result, but not others.

Figure 2 shows the landscape of property classes for rich, totally ordered domains. Note that the definitions of **Safety** and Liveness are incompatible for verdict domains with more than one element, and so are the definitions of **Guarantee** and **Morbidity**, which means that a property cannot be both a **Safety** and a

Liveness property, nor can it be both a **Guarantee** and a **Morbidity** property. However, it is possible that a property belongs to two classes, and also that a property does not belong to any of the classes described above.

We see that our definitions maintain the classification of the original properties presented in [20] if we consider the Boolean domain with the usual order relation *false* < *true*. Recall that according to our definitions, a **Safety** property is one such that a monitor can always dismiss the values greater than the result with a finite prefix. This is equivalent to say, in the Boolean ordered set, that if the result is *false* then a monitor can always dismiss the set {*true*} with a prefix. Since the domain is finite, Lemma 2 implies that the value *false* is always Finitely Admissible, and thus, a failed verdict can be identified after a finite prefix. A similar analysis can be made for the rest of the classes.

In the following sections we will give a witness for every class and sensible multiclass for different formalisms and domains.

4.2   Quantitative LTL

In [15] the authors define quantitative semantics for LTL, which generalize the semantics from Boolean to a richer type. Input streams are streams of real numbers in the range $[0, 1]$. The syntax is the same as for classic LTL. The semantics is given recursively over the terms and assigns a value in the range $[0, 1]$ for every term with respect to a behavior that assigns a real number in the range $[0, 1]$ to every proposition, this is, in QLTL, $R \overset{\text{def}}{=} \langle p_0 :: \mathbb{R}_{[0,1]}, \dots, p_n :: \mathbb{R}_{[0,1]} \rangle$.

$$[\![T]\!](\sigma) \overset{\text{def}}{=} 1 \qquad\qquad [\![\varphi \vee \psi]\!](\sigma) \overset{\text{def}}{=} [\![\varphi]\!](\sigma) \sqcup [\![\psi]\!](\sigma)$$

$$[\![a]\!](\sigma) \overset{\text{def}}{=} \sigma(0)(a) \qquad\qquad [\![\neg\varphi]\!](\sigma) \overset{\text{def}}{=} 1 - [\![\varphi]\!](\sigma)$$

$$[\![\bigcirc\varphi]\!](\sigma) \overset{\text{def}}{=} [\![\varphi]\!](\sigma^1)$$

$$[\![\varphi \,\mathcal{U}\, \psi]\!](\sigma) \overset{\text{def}}{=} sup_{i \geq 0}([\![\varphi]\!](\sigma^0) \sqcap \cdots \sqcap [\![\varphi]\!](\sigma^{i-1}) \sqcap [\![\psi]\!](\sigma^i))$$

where $x \sqcap y \overset{\text{def}}{=} \min(x, y)$ and $x \sqcup y \overset{\text{def}}{=} \max(x, y)$.

Following the syntax of the derived operators, their semantics in QLTL are $[\![\varphi \wedge \psi]\!](\sigma) \overset{\text{def}}{=} [\![\varphi]\!](\sigma) \sqcap [\![\psi]\!](\sigma)$, $[\![\Diamond\varphi]\!](\sigma) \overset{\text{def}}{=} sup_{i \geq 0}[\![\varphi]\!](\sigma^i)$, and $[\![\Box\varphi]\!](\sigma) \overset{\text{def}}{=} inf_{i \geq 0}[\![\varphi]\!](\sigma^i)$.

Since the generalization of the property classes to quantitative values presented in Sect. 4.1 is consistent with the generalization of the semantics of LTL to quantitative values in QLTL, the formulae presented in Sect. 2.1 belong to the same classes.

Lemma 4. *The following hold:*

- *The property $\Diamond p$ belongs to* **Guarantee** *and* Liveness,
- *the property $\Box p$ belongs to* **Safety** *and* **Morbidity**,
- *the property $\bigcirc p$ belongs to* **Safety** *and* **Guarantee**,
- *the property $\Box \Diamond p$ belongs to* **Morbidity** *and* Liveness,
- *the property $p \wedge \Diamond q$ only belongs to* **Guarantee**,

- *the property $\Box p \lor \Diamond q$ only belongs to* Liveness,
- *the property $p \lor \Box q$ only belongs to* **Safety**, *and*
- *the property $\Diamond p \land \Box q$ only belongs to* **Morbidity**.

Proof. We show the proof that $\Diamond p$ belongs to **Guarantee** and Liveness. $\Diamond p$ is NFD$_>$ because given any finite prefix of a trace where the supremum is $v \neq 1$, we can construct an alternative continuation where it is greater than v simply making the next value 1. If the verdict is $v = 1$, the complement set would be trivially NFD. It is AFD$_<$ because the verdict v is the minimum element greater or equal than the infinite values of p throughout the trace. Let $v' < v$. If no element in $(v', v]$ occur in the trace, then the result would be v'. Otherwise, the occurrence of such value would dismiss v' as a possible result.   □

The verdict of a QLTL property is a real number in the range $[0, 1]$, i.e. an infinite set, and thus it is subject to the case where the set of values different from the result is AFD but the result itself is not Finitely Admissible.

Lemma 5. *There is a QLTL property φ and a behavior s such that $v = [\![\varphi]\!](s)$ is not Finitely Admissible, but $[0, 1]\backslash\{v\}$ is AFD.*

Proof. Consider the property $(\Diamond p \land q)$ and a behavior s such that, at every instant i, the value of q is $\frac{1}{2}$ and the value of p is $\sum_{n=0}^{i} \frac{1}{4 \times 2^n}$, this is, p produces values closer to $\frac{1}{2}$, but never $\frac{1}{2}$ exactly. Then, in QLTL, $[\![\Diamond p]\!](s) = \frac{1}{2}$, the set $[0, \frac{1}{2}) \cup (\frac{1}{2}, 1]$ is All Finitely Dismissible, but the result $\frac{1}{2}$ is not Finitely Admissible.   □

4.3   Discounting in LTL

The temporal logic Disc$^{\mathrm{LTL}}[\mathcal{D}]$ generalizes LTL by adding discounting temporal operators [1]. According to the authors, the logic is in fact a family of logics, each parameterized by a set $\mathcal{D}$ of discounting functions. A function $\eta : \mathbb{N} \rightarrow [0, 1]$ is a *discounting function* if $\lim_{i \to \infty} \eta(i) = 0$, and η is strictly decreasing. Input streams are Boolean, as in classic LTL, but verdicts are real numbers in the range $[0, 1]$.

For a given a set of discounting functions $\mathcal{D}$, the logic Disc$^{\mathrm{LTL}}[\mathcal{D}]$ adds to LTL the operator $\varphi \, \mathcal{U}_\eta \, \varphi$. The semantics of this logic is given recursively over the terms and assigns a value in the range $[0, 1]$ for every term with respect to a behavior, assigning 0 to an input value of *false* and 1 to an input value of *true*.

$$[\![T]\!](\sigma) \overset{\text{def}}{=} 1 \qquad\qquad [\![\varphi \lor \psi]\!](\sigma) \overset{\text{def}}{=} \max\{[\![\varphi]\!](\sigma), [\![\psi]\!](\sigma)\}$$

$$[\![a]\!](\sigma) \overset{\text{def}}{=} \begin{cases} 1 & \text{if } \sigma(0)(a) = true \\ 0 & \text{otherwise} \end{cases} \qquad [\![\neg\varphi]\!](\sigma) \overset{\text{def}}{=} 1 - [\![\varphi]\!](\sigma)$$

$$[\![\bigcirc\varphi]\!](\sigma) \overset{\text{def}}{=} [\![\varphi]\!](\sigma^1)$$

$$[\![\varphi \, \mathcal{U} \, \psi]\!](\sigma) \overset{\text{def}}{=} \sup_{i \geq 0}\{\min\{[\![\psi]\!](\sigma^i), \min_{0 \leq j < i}\{[\![\varphi]\!](\sigma^j)\}\}\}$$

$$[\![\varphi \, \mathcal{U}_\eta \, \psi]\!](\sigma) \overset{\text{def}}{=} \sup_{i \geq 0}\{\min\{\eta(i)[\![\psi]\!](\sigma^i), \min_{0 \leq j < i}\{\eta(j)[\![\varphi]\!](\sigma^j)\}\}\}$$

Property Classification. The properties in Sect. 4.2 belong to the same categories, which is reasonable because they do not use discounting functions. For the same reason, and since the observations are Boolean values, the possible values are $\{0,1\}$ and thus the semantics and the property classes coincide with those of classic LTL.

Lemma 6. *Properties of the form* $\varphi\,\mathcal{U}_\eta\,\psi$ *belong to* **Safety** *and* **Guarantee**.

Proof. Let $v = \sup_{i \geq 0}\{\min\{\eta(i)[\![\psi]\!](\sigma(i)), \min_{0 \leq j < i}\{\eta(j)[\![\varphi]\!](\sigma(j))\}\}\}$ for a trace σ.

Let $v' \in (v, 1]$ (if the set $(v, 1]$ is empty, it can be trivially dimissed). Since both $[\![\psi]\!]$ and $[\![\varphi]\!]$ are in the range $[0, 1]$ at any index, then there is an index k such that $\eta(k) < v'$. After index k and since no value greater than v' ever happened (it would be greater than the verdict and thus the supremum), v' can be dismissed as a verdict.

Let $v' \in [0, v)$ (if the set $[0, v)$ is empty, it can be trivially dimissed). Following the same reasoning, there is an index k after which $\eta(k) < v$. At index k, v is guaranteed to be the result. $\qquad\qquad\Box$

$Disc^{LTL}[\mathcal{D}]$ provides us with another example where the set of non-verdicts is All Finitely Dismissible but the correct result is not Finitely Admissible.

Lemma 7. *There is a* $Disc^{LTL}[\mathcal{D}]$ *property* φ *and a behavior* s *such that* $v = [\![\varphi]\!](s)$ *is not Finitely Admissible, but* $[0, 1]\backslash\{v\}$ *is AFD.*

Proof. Consider a behavior s such that p is always *false*, and the $Disc^{LTL}[\mathcal{D}]$ property $\varphi = \Diamond_\eta p(s)$. The temporal operator $\Diamond_\eta$ is defined as $\Diamond_\eta\varphi \stackrel{\text{def}}{=} T\mathcal{U}_\eta\varphi$. From the semantics of $\mathcal{U}$ and T, we see that

$$[\![\varphi]\!](s) = \sup_{i \geq 0}\{\min\{\eta(i).\sigma(i)(p), \min_{0 \leq j < i}\{\eta(j).1)\}\}\}$$

$$= \sup_{i \geq 0}\{\min\{\eta(i).0, \min_{0 \leq j < i}\{\eta(j))\}\}\} = \sup_{i \geq 0}\{\min_{0 \leq j < i}\{\eta(j))\}\}\}$$

Then, $[\![\varphi]\!](s) = 0$, the set $(0, 1]$ is All Finitely Dismissible, but the result 0 is not Finitely Admissible. $\qquad\qquad\Box$

5   Towards Partially Ordered Domains

In this section we generalize the property classes definitions presented so far to partially ordered domains. We also introduce the notions of *assumptions* (via gray box monitoring) and *imprecise observability* to capture different relations between behaviors and observations, and we see how these notions impact in property classification in a concrete example.

5.1   Property Classes for Partially Ordered Domains

We first generalize the definitions of the property classes presented in Sect. 4.1. If the type of the verdicts of a formalism is a partially ordered set, we still classify the properties according to their value-dismissibility. Let $v = [\![\varphi]\!](\sigma)$, $v_{\not\geq}$ the set of values in D not greater or equal than v and $v_{\not\leq}$ the set of values in D not lower or equal than v, that is $v_{\not\leq} \overset{\text{def}}{=} \{v'|v' \not\leq v\}$ and $v_{\not\geq} \overset{\text{def}}{=} \{v'|v' \not\geq v\}$. We now redefine the property classes for rich, partially ordered domains:

Safety/AFD$_{\not\leq}$. We say a property is a *Safety* property if the set $v_{\not\leq}$ is All Finitely Dismissible for any behavior σ (this is, the monitor can dismiss every value not lower or equal than the result with a prefix).

Guarantee/AFD$_{\not\geq}$. We say a property is a *Guarantee* property if the set $v_{\not\geq}$ is All Finitely Dismissible for any behavior σ (this is, the monitor can dismiss every value not greater than the result with a prefix).

Liveness/**NFD$_{\not\leq}$.** We say a property is a *Liveness* property if the set $v_{\not\leq}$ is None Finitely Dismissible for any behavior σ (this is, the monitor can never dismiss any value not lower or equal than the result with a prefix).

Morbidity/NFD$_{\not\geq}$. We say a property is a *Morbidity* property if the set $v_{\not\geq}$ is None Finitely Dismissible for any behavior σ (this is, the monitor can never dismiss any value not greater or equal than the result with a prefix).

Again, we also define two additional sets of properties:

SFD$_{\not\leq}$. In some traces the monitor can dismiss some values not lower or equal than the result with a prefix, but not others.

SFD$_{\not\geq}$. In some traces, the monitor can dismiss some values not greater or equal than the result, but not others.

It is easy to see that for totally ordered domains the set of values not greater or equal than a value is equal to the set of values lower than it, hence these new definitions simply extend the classifications presented in Sect. 4.1 to partially ordered sets. The landscape of the new property classification is the same as the one in Fig. 2, but with the subscripts $>$ replaced by $\not\leq$ and the subscripts $<$ replaced by $\not\geq$.

5.2   Gray Box Monitoring (Assumptions)

So far we have considered that any stream of states is a possible behavior of the system, following a black box approach in which the monitor has no information about the conduct of the system. However, trace analysis for value dismissibility must only take into account *plausible* behaviors of the system under scrutiny and thus we can use *assumptions* to limit the set of behaviors contemplated. We call this a *gray box* approach. An assumption, as defined in [22], is a set of behaviors that contains the traces that comply with the assumption. Assumptions can make properties fit into the categories presented in the previous section that would otherwise be uncategorizable.

For example, we saw in Sect. 2.1 that the LTL property $\Box p \vee \Diamond q$ only belongs to the Liveness property class. However, under the assumption that $\Box(p \vee q)$, the property becomes a tautology and thus, it is trivially both a **Safety** and **Guarantee** property. The same LTL property $\Box p \vee \Diamond q$ becomes a **Safety** property under the assumption that once q becomes *false*, it will remain *false* forever, i.e., $\Box(\neg q \rightarrow \Box \neg q)$.

Recall that a value v is finitely dismissible (resp. admissible) if the semantics of a property for every continuation of an observation is different from (resp. equal to) v. When we use assumptions, we only need to consider the continuations of the observation ls that intersect the assumption A: $\{s' \in I^\omega \cap A | ls \prec s'\}$.

5.3 Imprecise Observations

Sometimes observations are imperfect, in the sense that some parts of the observation are missing. In practice, this could be due to technical impossibility, bad instrumentation, privacy concerns, faulty communication, or because the monitor is incorporated to an already running system. Up to this point we have considered observations to be a prefix of the behavior, but in this section we generalize the relationship between observations and behaviors via an abstraction function *obs*, which indicates the different ways a behavior can be observed.

The observation function is a representation about how a behavior can be perceived by the monitor. The choice of the observation function has an impact on property classification. For example, we saw in Sect. 2.1 that the LTL property $\bigcirc p$ is a **Safety** and **Guarantee** property, but it becomes a Liveness and **Morbidity** property under loss or corruption of events, stuttering, or incorrect event order arrival.

In the example shown in Sect. 5.4 below, our *obs* function captures the error (mutation in the terminology of [23]) of losing a prefix of the behavior, as a way to represent the scenario in which we start to monitor a system that is already running and thus the initial state is unknown. We also show a set of *obs* functions that implement a *controlled corruption* mutation in which events of a certain kind are replaced by a *no-value* event, representing the situation in which the system under analysis is not properly instrumented or privacy concerns prevent the monitor from detecting specific events, and thus some events are unobservable.

5.4 Example: Resource Sharing

This example illustrates that if assumptions are present, sometimes it is possible to effectively monitor liveness and safety properties. The monitors considered in this example try to compute a verdict value at every time instant, instead of a single verdict corresponding to the valuation of a formula at the initial position for the input trace observed. We model these streams of valuations in stream runtime verification [31] where the output of the verdict stream provides the sequence of verdict values for each time instant.

In the scenarios presented so far, the monitor gains information about the behavior by incrementally observing a prefix of the behavior. That is, the monitor observes the set of finite prefixes of a trace, which acts as the abstraction function of a behavior. In other words, the observations of the monitor is computed from a behavior s as $obs_{\prec}(s) \overset{\text{def}}{=} \{ls \mid ls \prec s\}$. However, property classification can also be applied to scenarios where the beginning of a trace is unknown, that is, where observations miss a prefix. We can represent this case, considering that observations $ls \in D^*$ are not prefixes of behaviors $s \in D^\omega$ but subsequences of them. The behavior abstraction we consider in this situation is the function that returns each of the (finite) subsequences of a stream, this is, $obs_{\sqsubset}(s) \overset{\text{def}}{=} \{ls \mid ls \sqsubset s\}$.

Consider for example a monitor that observes the lock/free operations of semaphores of a concurrent program. Our task is to study a monitor that produces a verdict indicating, at every point in time and for every resource, which process is the holder of the lock (if any). We start by introducing some intermediate definitions and properties before we describe the monitor.

The input stream $e \in EventT^\omega$ indicates the successive events that take place during the execution of the concurrent program. In [17] the authors show how to represent event-based systems using a synchronous language. As proposed in that work, we use a special constant nop to represent the absence of an event in an instant. We assume that at most one event can happen at every instant. Let $ProcessT$ be the set of processes in the system, and let $ResourceT$ be the set of resources. A process can *lock* or *free* a resource.

The output (verdict) stream $acquired \in AcquiredT^\omega$ is calculated from e and computes which process is holding which resource at every instant keeping a map that assigns a process to a resource. Formally, the types $EventT$ and $AcquiredT$ are defined as:

$$EventT \overset{\text{def}}{=} \{nop\} \cup (ProcessT \times ResourceT \times \{lock, free\})$$

$$AcquiredT \overset{\text{def}}{=} ResourceT \mapsto ProcessT$$

A nop event represents that no event happened in an instant. A (p, r, o) event indicates that process p has performed operation o over resource r. The resources that are not a key of the map in $AcquiredT$ are unlocked, and we define maps as sets of key-value pairs with at most one value associated with a key.

We define a partial order relation between maps: for two maps m and m', we say that $m \leq m'$ iff every key-value pair in m is in m'. Formally, $m \leq m' \overset{\text{def}}{=} \forall (k, v) \in m, (k, v) \in m'$. For example, the empty map $\emptyset$ is lower or equal than any map. The maps $m_0 = \{(0, 10)\}$ and $m_1 = \{(1, 20)\}$ are not comparable (i.e., $m_0 \not\leq m_1$ and $m_0 \not\geq m_1$) but they have a supremum which is the map $m_2 \overset{\text{def}}{=} \{(0, 10), (1, 20)\}$ (this is, $m_0 \leq m_2$, $m_1 \leq m_2$ and also for every other m_2' such that $m_0 \leq m_2'$ and $m_1 \leq m_2'$, then $m_2 \leq m_2'$). On the other hand, the maps $\{(0, 10)\}$ and $\{(0, 20)\}$ are not comparable and they do not have a supremum.

By observing *lock* events the monitor can dismiss some values that are not lower than the verdict, and by observing *free* events the monitor can dismiss some values that are not greater than the verdict. We will see why in Lemma 8.

We classify the property of resource ownership using gray box monitoring and with respect to system assumptions. We first define two possible assumptions about the system:

$$willFree \overset{\text{def}}{=} \Box((p, r, lock) \rightarrow \Diamond(p, r, free))$$
$$willLock \overset{\text{def}}{=} \Box(r \notin keys(acquired) \rightarrow \Diamond(\_, r, lock))$$

The assumption *willFree* limits the traces to those in which whenever a process locks a resource, then at some point in the future the process will free the resource. Similarly, *willLock* restricts to traces in which whenever a resource is available, some process will eventually lock it.

Let us also consider two functions that override events.

$$noLock(e) \overset{\text{def}}{=} \begin{cases} nop & \text{if } e = (\_, \_, lock) \\ e & \text{otherwise.} \end{cases} \qquad noFree(e) \overset{\text{def}}{=} \begin{cases} nop & \text{if } e = (\_, \_, free) \\ e & \text{otherwise.} \end{cases}$$

The function *noLock* overrides *lock* events with *nop* events, while the function *noFree* overrides *free* events with *nop* events.

We can use the functions *noLock* and *noFree* in the observability abstraction *obs* to represent the inability of the monitor to perceive *lock* or *free* events. We define three functions that abstract behavior to observations using *mapS* to map a function over a set of observations and *mapL* to map a function over a finite sequence of events:

$$obs_{noLock}(s) \overset{\text{def}}{=} mapS \ (mapL \ noLock) \ (obs_\sqsubseteq(s))$$

$$obs_{noFree}(s) \overset{\text{def}}{=} mapS \ (mapL \ noFree) \ (obs_\sqsubseteq(s))$$

$$obs_{blind}(s) \overset{\text{def}}{=} mapS \ (mapL \ (noLock \circ noFree)) \ (obs_\sqsubseteq(s))$$

An observation of a behavior using obs_{noLock} is a finite subsequence of the behavior where all the *lock* events have been replaced by *nop*. Analogously, obs_{noFree} represents the inability of the monitor to perceive *free* events, and obs_{blind} represents the inability of the monitor to perceive both *lock* and *free* events.

Lemma 8. *The property* acquired *can belong to any class depending on the assumptions of the system and on the events the monitor can actually perceive.*

Proof. We sketch here the proof that *acquired* is a **Guarantee** property under the assumption *willFree* with observation function $obs_\sqsubseteq$. Let m be the map at the beginning of the monitoring, and let $m' \not\geq m$. This means that there is a $(r, p) \in m$ which is not in m'. In other words, there is a resource r which has been acquired by a process p and has not yet been freed. Due to the assumption, the process p will eventually free r, conveying the information that (r, p) was part of the initial map and at that point the monitor can dismiss m' as a candidate.

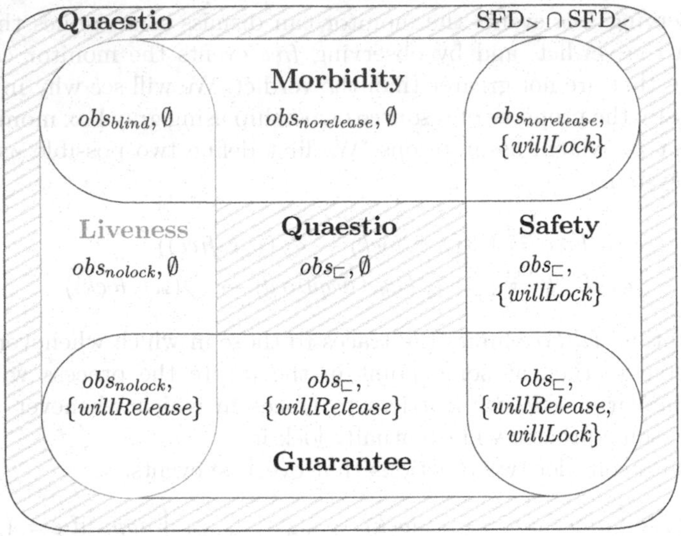

Fig. 3. Classifications of *acquired* with respect to observability and assumptions

We will see that the property is SFD$_{\not\subseteq}$ under the assumption *willFree*. Let m be the map at the beginning of the monitoring, and let $m' \not\subseteq m$. This means that there is a $(r, p) \in m'$ which is not in m. If the monitor witnesses the lock of r, it can dismiss m', but it cannot dismiss maps $m' \not\subseteq m$ that contain as keys resources that are not locked after the monitoring starts.   □

We explain now the classification of the property *acquired* based on value-dismissibilty with respect to *obs* and system assumptions (see Fig. 3).

- *acquired* is a **Guarantee** property under the assumption *willFree*. Let m be the map at the beginning of the monitoring, and let $m' \not\supseteq m$. This means that there is a $(r, p) \in m$ which is not in m'. In other words, there is a resource r which has been acquired by a process p and not yet released. Due to the assumption, the process p will eventually release r, conveying the information that (r, p) was part of the initial map and at that point the monitor can dismiss m' as a candidate. The property is SFD$_{\not\subseteq}$ under the assumption *willFree*: let m be the map at the beginning of the monitoring, and let $m' \not\subseteq m$. This means that there is a $(r, p) \in m'$ which is not in m. If the monitor witnesses the lock of r, it can dismiss m', but it cannot dismiss maps $m' \not\subseteq m$ that contain as keys resources that are not locked after the monitoring starts.
- *acquired* is a **Safety** property under the assumption *willLock*. The proof is analogous to the previous one. Let m be the map at the beginning of the monitoring, and let $m' \not\subseteq m$. This means that there is a $(r, p) \in m'$ which is not in m. Due to the assumption, some process will eventually lock r, conveying the information that (r, p) was not part of the initial map and

at that point the monitor can dismiss m' as a candidate. We will see that the property is SFD$_{\not\geq}$ under the assumption $willLock$. Let m be the map at the beginning of the monitoring, and let $m' \not\geq m$. This means that there is a resource r locked in m which is not so in m'. If the monitor witnesses the release of r it can dismiss m', but it cannot dismiss maps $m' \not\leq m$ that contain as keys resources that were locked before monitoring started and are not released after that.

– $acquired$ is in both a **Safety** and **Guarantee** property if both assumptions hold, but it does not belong to any of the classes if there are no assumptions regarding lock behavior. The reasoning follows from previous classifications.

– If the observability function is obs_{noFree} and thus the monitor cannot detect $free$ events, it cannot dismiss values not greater or equal than the result and belongs to the class **Morbidity**. Let m be the map at the beginning of the monitoring, and let $m' \not\geq m$. This means that there is a resource r locked in m which is not so in m'. Since the monitor cannot witness the release of r, it cannot dismiss m'. The property is SFD$_{\not\leq}$: let m be the map at the beginning of the monitoring, and let $m' \not\leq m$. There exists an $(r, p) \in m'$ which is not in m. If the monitor witnesses the lock of r it can dismiss m', but it cannot dismiss maps $m' \not\leq m$ with resources that are not locked after the monitoring starts.

– If the observability function is obs_{noLock} the property belongs to the class Liveness. Let m be the map at the beginning of the monitoring, and let $m' \not\leq m$. This means that there is a $(r, p) \in m'$ which is not in m. Since the monitor cannot witness the lock of r, it cannot dismiss m'. The property is SFD$_{\not\geq}$: let m be the map at the beginning of the monitoring, and let $m' \not\geq m$. This means that there is a resource r locked in m which is not so in m'. If the monitor witnesses the release of r it can dismiss m', but it cannot dismiss maps $m' \not\leq m$ with resources that were locked before monitoring started and are not released after that.

– If the observability function is obs_{blind} and thus the monitor can detect neither $lock$ nor $free$ events, it cannot dismiss any map and belongs to both **Morbidity** and Liveness. This follows from the reasoning of the previous items.

– $acquired$ is a Liveness and **Guarantee** property under assumption $willFree$ with the observability function obs_{noLock} because obs_{noLock} makes the property a Liveness property, and the assumption makes it a **Guarantee** property.

– $acquired$ is **Safety** and **Morbidity** under the assumption $willLock$ if the observability function is obs_{noFree} because obs_{noFree} makes the property a **Morbidity** property, and the assumption makes it a **Safety** property.

6   Conclusion

In this paper we have presented a generalization of the classification of Havelund and Peled [20] to expressive verdicts. We have introduced general definitions for admissibility and dismissibility of verdicts and instantianted these to totally ordered and partially ordered domains. Then we have illustrated the taxonomy to quantitative logics like quantitative LTL and discounting LTL. Future work includes studying other quantitative logics like *Counting LTL* [24], where the semantics distinguish the steps necessary until satisfactions, and *Robust LTL* [35]. We also plan to extend our framework to general verdicts in the setting of stream runtime verification.

References

1. Almagor, S., Boker, U., Kupferman, O.: Discounting in LTL. In: Ábrahám, E., Havelund, K. (eds.) TACAS 2014. LNCS, vol. 8413, pp. 424–439. Springer, Heidelberg (2014). https://doi.org/10.1007/978-3-642-54862-8_37
2. Asarin, E., Caspi, P., Maler, O.: Timed regular expressions. J. ACM **49**(2), 172–206 (2002)
3. Barringer, H., Goldberg, A., Havelund, K., Sen, K.: Rule-based runtime verification. In: Steffen, B., Levi, G. (eds.) VMCAI 2004. LNCS, vol. 2937, pp. 44–57. Springer, Heidelberg (2004). https://doi.org/10.1007/978-3-540-24622-0_5
4. Bartocci, E., Falcone, Y. (eds.): Lectures on Runtime Verification. LNCS, vol. 10457. Springer, Cham (2018). https://doi.org/10.1007/978-3-319-75632-5
5. Basin, D.A., Klaedtke, F., Müller, S., Zalinescu, E.: Monitoring metric first-order temporal properties. J. ACM **62**(2), 1–45 (2015)
6. Bauer, A., Leucker, M., Schallhart, C.: Runtime verification for LTL and TLTL. ACM Trans. Softw. Eng. Methodol. **20**(4), 14 (2011)
7. Bauer, A., Leucker, M., Schallhart, C.: The good, the bad, and the ugly, but how ugly is ugly? In: Sokolsky, O., Taşıran, S. (eds.) RV 2007. LNCS, vol. 4839, pp. 126–138. Springer, Heidelberg (2007). https://doi.org/10.1007/978-3-540-77395-5_11
8. Chang, E., Manna, Z., Pnueli, A.: Characterization of temporal property classes. In: Kuich, W. (ed.) ICALP 1992. LNCS, vol. 623, pp. 474–486. Springer, Heidelberg (1992). https://doi.org/10.1007/3-540-55719-9_97
9. Colombo, C., Pace, G.J., Schneider, G.: Dynamic event-based runtime monitoring of real-time and contextual properties. In: Cofer, D., Fantechi, A. (eds.) FMICS 2008. LNCS, vol. 5596, pp. 135–149. Springer, Heidelberg (2009). https://doi.org/10.1007/978-3-642-03240-0_13
10. Convent, L., Hungerecker, S., Leucker, M., Scheffel, T., Schmitz, M., Thoma, D.: TeSSLa: temporal stream-based specification language. In: Massoni, T., Mousavi, M.R. (eds.) SBMF 2018. LNCS, vol. 11254, pp. 144–162. Springer, Cham (2018). https://doi.org/10.1007/978-3-030-03044-5_10
11. D'Angelo, B., et al.: LOLA: runtime monitoring of synchronous systems. In: Proceedings of the 12th International Symposium of Temporal Representation and Reasoning (TIME 2005), pp. 166–174. IEEE CS Press (2005)
12. De Giacomo, G., Vardi, M.Y.: Linear temporal logic and linear dynamic logic on finite traces. In: Proceedings of the 23rd International Joint Conference on Artificial Intelligence (IJCAI 2014), pp. 854–860. AAAI Press (2013)
13. Eisner, C., Fisman, D., Havlicek, J., Lustig, Y., McIsaac, A., Van Campenhout, D.: Reasoning with temporal logic on truncated paths. In: Hunt, W.A., Somenzi, F. (eds.) CAV 2003. LNCS, vol. 2725, pp. 27–39. Springer, Heidelberg (2003). https://doi.org/10.1007/978-3-540-45069-6_3

14. Emerson, E.A., Clarke, E.M.: Characterizing correctness properties of parallel programs using fixpoints. In: de Bakker, J., van Leeuwen, J. (eds.) ICALP 1980. LNCS, vol. 85, pp. 169–181. Springer, Heidelberg (1980). https://doi.org/10.1007/3-540-10003-2_69

15. Faella, M., Legay, A., Stoelinga, M.: Model checking quantitative linear time logic. Electron. Notes Theoret. Comput. Sci. **220**(3), 61–77 (2008). Proceedings of the Sixth Workshop on Quantitative Aspects of Programming Languages (QAPL 2008)

16. Faymonville, P., Finkbeiner, B., Schirmer, S., Torfah, H.: A stream-based specification language for network monitoring. In: Falcone, Y., Sánchez, C. (eds.) RV 2016. LNCS, vol. 10012, pp. 152–168. Springer, Cham (2016). https://doi.org/10.1007/978-3-319-46982-9_10

17. Gorostiaga, F., Danielsson, L.M., Sánchez, C.: Unifying the time-event spectrum for stream runtime verification. In: Deshmukh, J., Ničković, D. (eds.) RV 2020. LNCS, vol. 12399, pp. 462–481. Springer, Cham (2020). https://doi.org/10.1007/978-3-030-60508-7_26

18. Gorostiaga, F., Sánchez, C.: Striver: stream runtime verification for real-time event-streams. In: Colombo, C., Leucker, M. (eds.) RV 2018. LNCS, vol. 11237, pp. 282–298. Springer, Cham (2018). https://doi.org/10.1007/978-3-030-03769-7_16

19. Havelund, K., Goldberg, A.: Verify your runs. In: Meyer, B., Woodcock, J. (eds.) VSTTE 2005. LNCS, vol. 4171, pp. 374–383. Springer, Heidelberg (2008). https://doi.org/10.1007/978-3-540-69149-5_40

20. Havelund, K., Peled, D.: Runtime verification: from propositional to first-order temporal logic. In: Colombo, C., Leucker, M. (eds.) RV 2018. LNCS, vol. 11237, pp. 90–112. Springer, Cham (2018). https://doi.org/10.1007/978-3-030-03769-7_7

21. Havelund, K., Roşu, G.: Synthesizing monitors for safety properties. In: Katoen, J.-P., Stevens, P. (eds.) TACAS 2002. LNCS, vol. 2280, pp. 342–356. Springer, Heidelberg (2002). https://doi.org/10.1007/3-540-46002-0_24

22. Henzinger, T.A., Saraç, N.E.: Monitorability under assumptions. In: Deshmukh, J., Ničković, D. (eds.) RV 2020. LNCS, vol. 12399, pp. 3–18. Springer, Cham (2020). https://doi.org/10.1007/978-3-030-60508-7_1

23. Kauffman, S., Havelund, K., Fischmeister, S.: What can we monitor over unreliable channels? Int. J. Softw. Tools Technol. Transf. **23**(4), 579–600 (2021). https://doi.org/10.1007/s10009-021-00625-z

24. Laroussinie, F., Meyer, A., Petonnet, E.: Counting LTL. In: Proceedings of the 2010 17th International Symposium on Temporal Representation and Reasoning (TIME 2010), pp. 51–58. IEEE (2010)

25. Leucker, M., Sánchez, C., Scheffel, T., Schmitz, M., Thoma, D.: Runtime verification for timed event streams with partial information. In: Finkbeiner, B., Mariani, L. (eds.) RV 2019. LNCS, vol. 11757, pp. 273–291. Springer, Cham (2019). https://doi.org/10.1007/978-3-030-32079-9_16

26. Leucker, M., Schallhart, C.: A brief account of runtime verification. J. Logic Algebr. Program. **78**(5), 293–303 (2009)

27. Pnueli, A., Zaks, A.: PSL model checking and run-time verification via testers. In: Misra, J., Nipkow, T., Sekerinski, E. (eds.) FM 2006. LNCS, vol. 4085, pp. 573–586. Springer, Heidelberg (2006). https://doi.org/10.1007/11813040_38

28. Queille, J.P., Sifakis, J.: Specification and verification of concurrent systems in CESAR. In: Dezani-Ciancaglini, M., Montanari, U. (eds.) Programming 1982. LNCS, vol. 137, pp. 337–351. Springer, Heidelberg (1982). https://doi.org/10.1007/3-540-11494-7_22

29. Reinbacher, T., Rozier, K.Y., Schumann, J.: Temporal-logic based runtime observer pairs for system health management of real-time systems. In: Ábrahám, E., Havelund, K. (eds.) TACAS 2014. LNCS, vol. 8413, pp. 357–372. Springer, Heidelberg (2014). https://doi.org/10.1007/978-3-642-54862-8_24

30. Roşu, G., Havelund, K.: Rewriting-based techniques for runtime verification. Autom. Softw. Eng. **12**(2), 151–197 (2005)

31. Sánchez, C.: Online and offline stream runtime verification of synchronous systems. In: Colombo, C., Leucker, M. (eds.) RV 2018. LNCS, vol. 11237, pp. 138–163. Springer, Cham (2018). https://doi.org/10.1007/978-3-030-03769-7_9

32. Sen, K., Roşu, G.: Generating optimal monitors for extended regular expressions. ENTCS **89**(2), 226–245 (2003)

33. Stucki, S., Sánchez, C., Schneider, G., Bonakdarpour, B.: Gray-box monitoring of hyperproperties. In: ter Beek, M.H., McIver, A., Oliveira, J.N. (eds.) FM 2019. LNCS, vol. 11800, pp. 406–424. Springer, Cham (2019). https://doi.org/10.1007/978-3-030-30942-8_25

34. Stucki, S., Sánchez, C., Schneider, G., Bonakdarpour, B.: Gray-box monitoring of hyperproperties with an application to privacy. Form. Methods Syst. Des. **58**, 1–34 (2021). https://doi.org/10.1007/s10703-020-00358-w

35. Tabuada, P., Neider, D.: Robust linear temporal logic. In: Proceedings of the 25th EACSL Annual Conference on Computer Science Logic (CSL 2016), vol. 62 of LIPIcs, pp. 10:1–10:21. Schloss Dagstuhl - Leibniz-Zentrum für Informatik (2016)

36. Zhang, X., Leucker, M., Dong, W.: Runtime verification with predictive semantics. In: Goodloe, A.E., Person, S. (eds.) NFM 2012. LNCS, vol. 7226, pp. 418–432. Springer, Heidelberg (2012). https://doi.org/10.1007/978-3-642-28891-3_37

BDDs Strike Back
Efficient Analysis of Static and Dynamic Fault Trees

Daniel Basgöze[1], Matthias Volk[2(✉)] (iD), Joost-Pieter Katoen[1,2] (iD),
Shahid Khan[1] (iD), and Marielle Stoelinga[2,3] (iD)

[1] Software Modeling and Verification, RWTH Aachen University,
Aachen, Germany
[2] Formal Methods and Tools, University of Twente, Enschede, The Netherlands
m.volk@utwente.nl
[3] Department of Software Science, Radboud University, Nijmegen, The Netherlands

Abstract. Fault trees are a key model in reliability analysis. Classical static fault trees (SFT) can best be analysed using binary decision diagrams (BDD). State-based techniques are favorable for the more expressive dynamic fault trees (DFT). This paper combines the best of both worlds by following Dugan's approach: dynamic sub-trees are analysed via model checking Markov models and replaced by basic events capturing the obtained failure probabilities. The resulting SFT is then analysed via BDDs. We implemented this approach in the STORM model checker. Extensive experiments (a) compare our pure BDD-based analysis of SFTs to various existing SFT analysis tools, (b) indicate the benefits of our efficient calculations for multiple time points and the assessment of the mean-time-to-failure, and (c) show that our implementation of Dugan's approach significantly outperforms pure Markovian analysis of DFTs. Our implementation STORM-DFT is currently the only tool supporting efficient analysis for both SFTs and DFTs.

1 Introduction

Fault trees [47,51,54] are a common formalism in reliability engineering and required by standards in a broad range of industries [27,33,51]. A fault tree represents a Boolean function and models how overall system failures depend on the failure of basic system components. Fault tree analysis (FTA) is commonly performed by translating a fault tree into a binary decision diagram (BDD) and calculating the relevant metrics on this BDD [43,50]. BDDs yield compact representations of fault trees enabling the analysis of large systems [17]. Ongoing improvements in BDD tools such as parallelisation [20] allow for modern implementations of FTA via BDDs.

This work has been partially funded by NWO under the grant PrimaVera number NWA.1160.18.238, European Union's Horizon 2020 research and innovation programme under the Marie Skłodowska-Curie grant agreement No. 101008233 (*Mission*), and the ERC Consolidator Grant 864075 (*CAESAR*). Khan is funded by a HEC-DAAD stipend.

© Springer Nature Switzerland AG 2022
J. V. Deshmukh et al. (Eds.): NFM 2022, LNCS 13260, pp. 713–732, 2022.
https://doi.org/10.1007/978-3-031-06773-0_38

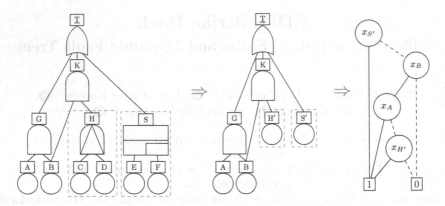

Fig. 1. DFT modularisation

Fault trees are static in nature and their expressiveness is limited. *Dynamic fault trees (DFT)* [21] support ordered failures, spare management and functional dependencies. The flexibility and increased expressiveness of DFTs however requires more involved analysis methods. BDDs cannot represent DFTs directly as DFTs consider failure sequences instead of Boolean combinations. A common approach is to translate DFTs into Markov models [10,22,56]. Gulati and Dugan [31] proposed a modular DFT analysis approach combining several analysis techniques. It divides the DFT into independent sub-parts which are analysed individually. *Modularisation thus allows to use the best of both worlds: Markov models for dynamic parts and BDDs for static parts.*

The idea of modularisation is depicted in Fig. 1. First, dynamic modules, i.e., sub-trees containing dynamic elements, are identified (the blue boxes in the left-most tree). Each dynamic module is analysed independently with state-of-the-art analysis techniques for Markov models [56]. Afterwards, each dynamic module is replaced by a single basic event which represents the corresponding failure probabilities (tree in the middle). The remaining (static) fault tree is then translated into a BDD (right most part) and is analysed by BDD techniques. Modularisation works especially well when the dynamic parts are contained at the bottom of the fault tree and the static parts are on top. As dynamic parts commonly model single components, this structure is present in most DFTs.

Related Work. FTA via BDDs was first presented in [43] and [17], and successively improved in [25,50]. BDD-based analysis of static fault trees (SFTs) is supported by academic tools such as SCRAM [40], XFTA [45] and SHARPE [55], as well as commercial tools, e.g., RISKSPECTRUM [3]. We refer to [47] for a detailed overview on BDD-based FTA.

For DFTs, various analysis techniques exist. Common approaches translate DFTs into models such as Markov models [10,22,56], Bayesian networks [38] and Petri nets [39], or are based on Monte-Carlo simulation [15,41]. There also exist analysis techniques based on extensions of BDDs such as sequence decision diagrams [44], sequential BDDs [58], multiple-valued decision diagrams [36] or conditional BDDs [60]. These approaches use BDDs to enumerate all failure sequences leading to a system failure so as to compute the overall system unreliability. To the best of our knowledge, no tool support exists for any of the BDD approaches for DFTs and their scalability for large DFTs remains unclear.

For SD fault trees [35]—another extension of static fault trees with limited dynamic behaviour—efficient analysis techniques exist via minimal cut sets [35] and abstraction [4]. However, expressiveness of SD fault trees is limited compared to DFTs as they only allow dynamic behaviour in basic system components.

Our DFT approach is based on modularisation [31] which was first implemented in the DIFTREE tool [23] and its successor GALILEO [53]. However, both tools are not available anymore for more than a decade. Recent work [56] has implemented modularisation for DFTs but is limited to independent sub-trees that must be direct children of the top event. In addition, [56] analyses static FTs by translation to Markov models.

Implementation. We implemented the BDD translation for static fault trees (SFTs) in the STORM model checker [32] and use the multi-core BDD library SYLVAN [20]. Our implementation STORM-DFT supports computing minimal cut sets (MCS), the unreliability and several importance measures such as the Birnbaum index [8]. STORM-DFT exploits vectorisation and thus enables to compute a metric for multiple time bounds at once. In addition, we support the calculation of the mean-time-to-failure (MTTF) via approximation. For DFTs, we implemented the modularisation approach exploiting both the BDD translation and our efficient DFT analysis via Markov models [56].

Evaluation. Experiments on a benchmark set of 215 SFTs and 124 DFTs yield:

- On SFTs, STORM-DFT is competitive compared to existing tools such as SCRAM [40] and XFTA [45] and is significantly faster when analysing multiple time points due to vectorisation.
- The variable ordering in STORM-DFT is not yet optimal and can lead to larger BDDs and subsequently longer run times.
- On DFTs, our BDD-based modularisation is significantly faster than both plain Markov-model analysis [56] and an existing realisation of (top-down) modularisation [56] based on pure Markov-model analysis.

Our implementation is publicly available in the open-source tool STORM-DFT[1]. We also provide an artifact of the experimental evaluation containing the scripts, tool configurations and fault tree models[2].

Contributions. In summary, the main contributions of this paper are:

- A competitive implementation of SFT analysis via BDDs in STORM [32].
- Vectorisation for multiple time bounds and an approximation for MTTF.
- A fast implementation of a modern version of modularisation using BDDs.

Our implementation STORM-DFT is the only state-of-the-art analysis tool for both static and dynamic fault trees.

---

[1] https://www.stormchecker.org/.
[2] https://doi.org/10.5281/zenodo.6390998.

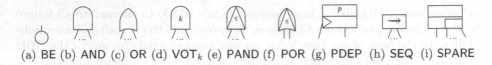

(a) BE (b) AND (c) OR (d) VOT$_k$ (e) PAND (f) POR (g) PDEP (h) SEQ (i) SPARE

Fig. 2. Node types in ((a)–(d)) static and (all) dynamic fault trees.

Structure of the Paper. We introduce fault trees and binary decision diagrams in Sect. 2. Section 3 presents the analysis of (static) fault trees using BDDs. We evaluate the approach in Sect. 4. Section 5 presents the analysis of dynamic fault trees via modularisation and using BDDs for static parts. We evaluate the approach in Sect. 6. We conclude in Sect. 7 and present future work.

2 Preliminaries

2.1 Fault Trees

Fault trees (FTs) model how failures can occur and propagate in systems [47,51, 54]. FTs are *directed acyclic graphs* in which the leaves are called *basic events* (BEs) and intermediate nodes are called *gates*. A BE represents an (atomic) system component which fails according to a given failure distribution. Failures of BEs are propagated through the system according to the gates and eventually lead to a failure of the unique root of the graph, the *top event*. *Dynamic fault trees (DFTs)* [21] are the most prominent extension of fault trees and their additional gates allow for more realistic modelling. Note that we do not consider repairs.

Definition 1 (Dynamic fault tree). *A* dynamic fault tree (DFT) *is a tuple* $\mathcal{F} = (V, \sigma, \mathit{Type}, \mathit{top}, \Theta)$ *where*

- *V is a finite set of nodes.*
- $\sigma : V \to V^*$ *defines the ordered children of a node (also called the inputs).*
- *Type* $: V \to \{BE, AND, OR, VOT_k\} \cup \{PAND, POR, PDEP, SEQ, SPARE\}$ *defines the type of a node.*
- *top* $\in V$ *is the top event.*
- $\Theta : \{v \in V \mid \mathit{Type}(v) = BE\} \to \Omega$ *maps each BE to a failure distribution from* Ω *the set of probability distributions.*

A VOT$_k$-gate satisfies $1 \le k \le |\sigma|$. A *static fault tree (SFT)* is a DFT where the node types *Type* are restricted to $\{BE, AND, OR, VOT_k\}$. In DFTs, we restrict the failure distributions of BEs to exponential distributions to allow for analysis based on Markov models. We say a "DFT $\mathcal{F}$ is failed" if *top* is failed.

We shortly introduce the different node types; the precise semantics is given in [34]. The graphical representation of each node type is given in Fig. 2.

Basic events (BEs) fail according to their associated failure distributions. Commonly, an exponential failure distribution with a failure rate λ is used.

Static gates represent Boolean logic functions. The AND-gate fails if all its inputs fail. The OR-gate fails if at least one input fails. The VOT$_k$-gate is a generalisation and fails if at least k inputs fail.

Priority gates extend the static gates with the additional constraint that the inputs have to fail in order from left to right. Failures out of this order render the gate *fail-safe* and it can never fail. The PAND-gate fails if all inputs fail from left to right. The POR-gate fails if the leftmost child fails before all other gates.

Dependencies encode functional dependencies of the system. If the first child of the PDEP$_p$ fails, all other children fail with probability p.

Sequence enforcers ensure that children only fail in order from left to right.

Spare gates model spare management. Initially, the first child is used. If it fails, the next child is claimed and used, and so forth. The SPARE fails if all its children failed. Children can be shared by multiple SPAREs, but can only be used exclusively by one SPARE. Using a child activates the corresponding components and can increase the associated failure rate.

Example 1 (Fault tree). Consider the DFT on the left of Fig. 1. The top event T fails for example if both BEs A and B fail. The DFT also fails if B and PAND H fail. The PAND only fails if the first child C fails before D.

Fault Tree Analysis. Fault trees are analysed w.r.t. the failure of the top event. Common metrics are the *unreliability* within a given time bound and the *mean-time-to-failure (MTTF)*. For SFTs, the *minimal cut sets* play an important role. Cut sets with only a few elements for example indicate system vulnerabilities.

Definition 2 (Minimal cut sets). *Let $\mathcal{F}$ be a* static *fault tree. A* minimal cut set (MCS) *for $\mathcal{F}$ is a set $M \subseteq BE$ such that:*

1. *the failure of all BEs in M leads to the failure of $\mathcal{F}$, and*
2. *M is minimal, i.e., no subset $M' \subsetneq M$ leads to the failure of $\mathcal{F}$.*

2.2   Binary Decision Diagrams

Binary decision diagrams (BDDs) [1,13] are graphs based on the Shannon expansion [48]. We introduce BDDs by example and refer to [14] for more details.

A BDD $\mathcal{B}$ encodes a Boolean function f over variables $x_1, \ldots, x_n$. Nodes in $\mathcal{B}$ represent variables of f and follow a given variable ordering. Outgoing edges of a node x represent the two possible assignments of variable x: the solid line represents $x = 1$, the dashed line $x = 0$. Leaves represent functions 1 and 0.

Example 2 (BDD). Consider the BDD on the right of Fig. 1. The BDD represents the function $f = x_{S'} \vee (x_B \wedge (x_A \vee x_{H'}))$. The satisfying assignments of f are obtained by following all paths from the root to the 1-leaf.

3   SFT Analysis via BDD

Translation from SFT into BDD. An SFT $\mathcal{F}$ is translated into a BDD by simply calculating the BDD-representation of the propositional formula representing the

718   D. Basgöze et al.

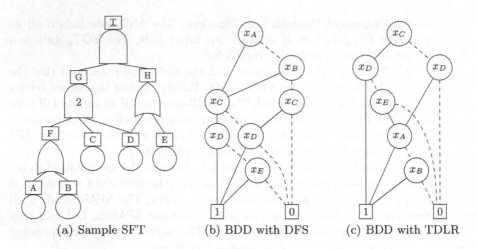

(a) Sample SFT   (b) BDD with DFS   (c) BDD with TDLR

Fig. 3. SFT and corresponding BDDs for different variable orders

failure behaviour of $\mathcal{F}$ [43]. The algorithm follows a simple recursive bottom-up approach which combines the BDDs of sub-trees according to the logic gates. The VOT_k-gate is translated by exploiting the Shannon decomposition [48].

Variable Ordering. The variable ordering employed for the BDD is important as different orderings can result in significantly different BDD sizes [2,49]. Common variable orderings are *depth-first search (DFS)* [43] and *top-down left-right (TDLR)* [2]. Finding optimal variable orderings is still ongoing research [11,42].

Example 3 (BDDs for SFT). Consider the SFT depicted in Fig. 3(a). The corresponding BDD for the DFS ordering $x_A <_{\text{Var}} x_B <_{\text{Var}} x_C <_{\text{Var}} x_D <_{\text{Var}} x_E$ has 7 nodes and is given in Fig. 3(b). The BDD for variable ordering TDLR $x_C <_{\text{Var}} x_D <_{\text{Var}} x_E <_{\text{Var}} x_A <_{\text{Var}} x_B$ has 6 nodes and is depicted in Fig. 3(c).

3.1   Computing Minimal Cut Sets

Minimal cut sets are a common metric for SFTs. Several approaches exist to compute MCS [47], and we focus on the BDD-based approach [43]. We are interested in all paths of the BDD that reach the 1-leaf, i.e., lead to a failure of the SFT. All variables reached by the 1-edge on such a path form a *solution* of the BDD. Each solution is a cut set. The aim is to compute all minimal solutions, i.e., solutions whose proper subsets are not a solution.

A naïve approach computes the solutions for each (sub-)BDD in a bottom-up way. The solutions of a node v are then the union of the solutions of the 1-successor of v extended with v, and the solutions of the 0-successor. However, the resulting solutions are not necessarily minimal [6,43].

The algorithm of [43] exploits the fact that SFTs can only encode monotonic switching functions (a.k.a. *coherent* FTs). From the original BDD $\mathcal{B}$, a new BDD $\mathcal{B}'$ is constructed whose solutions are exactly the minimal solutions of $\mathcal{B}$.

This construction uses the 'without'-operator on BDDs to exclude parts of the 1-successor which are already included in the 0-successor; see [6,43] for details.

3.2 Computing Unreliability

Let X by the random variable representing the failure of BE x. We use $P_t(f_x) := P(X \leq t)$ to denote the probability that x fails within time bound t. A common metric is the *unreliability* $P_t(\mathcal{F}) := P_t(f_{top})$, i.e., the probability that the SFT $\mathcal{F}$ with TLE *top* fails within time bound t. This metric can easily be computed on the BDD by employing Shannon decomposition: $P_t(f) = P_t(f_x) \cdot P_t(f|_{x=1}) + (1 - P_t(f_x)) \cdot P_t(f|_{x=0})$. The algorithm works independently of the calculation for $P_t(f_x)$ and can therefore be applied to any failure distribution of the BEs.

Computing Sensitivity Measures. Importance measures [47,54] are used to assess how sensitive the overall system is w.r.t. sub-systems. The *Birnbaum importance index* [8] is a prominent metric. For BE e in SFT $\mathcal{F}$ at time t, the Birnbaum index is given by the conditional probabilities $\mathrm{BI}_t(\mathcal{F}, e) := P_t(\mathcal{F} \mid e) - P_t(\mathcal{F} \mid \neg e)$, where $\neg e$ represents that e has not failed. The calculation is done on the BDD corresponding to $\mathcal{F}$, cf. [25]. Additional metrics are computed based on the Birnbaum index [25], e.g., the *critical importance factor*, the *Vesely-Fussell importance factor* [28], the *risk achievement worth* and the *risk reduction worth* [16].

Vectorisation for Multiple Time Bounds. Investigating the unreliability over time requires computing the unreliability for a large number of different time bounds. The calculation for multiple time bounds can easily be parallelised, because the computations are independent: the failure probability of the top event within time bound t only depends on the failure probabilities of the BEs within t. We employ *vectorisation* [26] where multiple probabilities— corresponding to different time bounds—are stored within a single vector and computed concurrently. Vectorisation exploits both temporal and spatial locality in modern CPU caches as well as *SIMD instructions* (single instruction multiple data) which operate on arrays of values at once.

3.3 Computing the MTTF

Vectorisation naturally leads to approximation methods as we can efficiently evaluate many time bounds at once. We exploit this for the *mean-time-to-failure (MTTF)*, i.e., the expected time point the SFT $\mathcal{F}$ fails at. It is calculated by $\int_0^\infty P_t(\mathcal{F}) \, dt$. We numerically approximate the improper integral by sampling a large number of time bounds on the BDD obtained for the SFT. We use two different methods from [18]. The first method, *proceeding to the limit*, computes a sequence of integrals $\int_{r_i}^{r_{i+1}} P_t(\mathcal{F}) \, dt$ until the result of an integral is less than a given error ε. Our implementation uses varying steps sizes which start at 10^{-10} and a default error of $\varepsilon := 10^{-12}$. The second method, *change of variable*, aims to "squeeze" the unbounded interval $[0, \infty)$ into the bounded interval $[0, 1)$ using integration by substitution. The latter method always uses the same number of samples (default 10^6) and works good for functions slowly approaching zero.

The former method uses a variable number of samples and performs better for functions which approach zero relatively fast or change rapidly; see [6] for details.

3.4 Implementation

We implemented the SFT analysis in the STORM-DFT[3] tool based on the STORM model checker [32] and use the multi-core library SYLVAN [20] for creating and handling BDDs. We list the main implementation details in the following.

Multi-core BDD. SYLVAN natively enables multi-core computations on BDD [19]. STORM-DFT exploits this when performing the translation from SFT to BDD.

Complement Edges. The implementation uses *complement edges* [12] which negate the corresponding function and it allows to use a single terminal node.

Variable Ordering. The implementation uses the order of BEs given in the input file (in Galileo format[4]) as the variable ordering for the BDD. That way, we support arbitrary variables orderings which can be explicitly given by either the user or a pre-processing step. Currently, STORM-DFT supports the DFS and TDLR variable orderings via pre-processing steps.

Caching. During the translation, intermediate BDDs are not cached in order to reduce the memory consumption. Caching can be explicitly enabled for specific events if needed.

Vectorisation. STORM-DFT uses the EIGEN library [30] for vectorisation. The *chunk-size*, i.e., the number of time points computed in parallel, can be configured from the command-line. We refer to [6] for details on the optimal chunk-size.

Properties. Apart from standard metrics presented before, our implementation supports properties defined in a fragment of *continuous stochastic logic (CSL)* [5]. More precise, STORM-DFT supports (time-bounded) reachability formulas of the form $\mathbb{P}_{=?}(\lozenge^{\leq t}\phi)$ for state formula ϕ and time bound t.

4   Evaluation of SFT Approach

We evaluate the fault tree analysis via BDDs as implemented in STORM-DFT on a range of benchmarks and compare with existing tools. For reproducibility, we provide an artifact online[5] which contains the analysis scripts, tool configurations and fault tree models used in our experimental evaluation.

4.1 Configurations

We use STORM-DFT version 1.6.3. In the default configuration, STORM-DFT is single-threaded, uses a chunk-size of 1024 for vectorisation and uses the DFS variable ordering. We also evaluate STORM-DFT in a configuration using the TDLR variable ordering and in configurations using multiple cores.

---

[3] https://www.stormchecker.org/.
[4] https://dftbenchmarks.utwente.nl/galileo.html.
[5] https://doi.org/10.5281/zenodo.6390998.

Table 1. SFT benchmark sizes

	Aralia	Sprinkler	Railway	Industry	Random	Random (large)
#BEs	25–1567	31	22–54	36–184	150	500
#Gates	20–1622	35	69–259	21–67	70–122	261–316

We compare the SFT analysis in STORM-DFT with two existing tools: SCRAM[6] (version 0.16.2) and XFTA[7] (version 2.0.1).

SCRAM [40] is an open-source probabilistic risk analysis tool which supports the *Open-PSA Model Exchange* format [52]. It performs SFT analysis using BDDs and supports metrics such as MCS, unreliability and importance measures. Before analysis, SCRAM simplifies the SFT's graph structure. The BDD variable ordering then follows the topological ordering on the simplified SFT.

XFTA [45] is a free-to-use tool for the analysis of fault trees and similar models. It is hosted by the AltaRica Association. XFTA uses its own object-oriented design language *S2ML+SBE* as input, but also supports the Open-PSA format. The analysis is performed by either generating the MCS and calculating the metrics on them or by creating a BDD and computing the metrics via the BDD. For the variable ordering, the children of gates are sorted beforehand and then the DFS ordering is used.

4.2 Benchmarks

We use the following collection of SFT benchmarks for our evaluation:

- 40 examples from the Aralia benchmark set[8]. We excluded 3 non-coherent SFTs containing a negation-gate as STORM-DFT does not support them.
- 3 models of wet-pipe fire sprinkler systems in Australian shopping centres [37]
- 8 examples modelling train routing options w.r.t. infrastructure failures in railway station areas [57].
- 3 industrial models for components of a lock used in water navigation.
- 161 randomly generated SFTs using a script provided by the SCRAM tool. 128 of the random SFTs have 150 BEs and 33 are large SFTs with 500 BEs.

We provide statistics on the benchmarks in Table 1. We give the minimal and maximal number of BEs and gates for each benchmark set.

We analyse each fault tree w.r.t. four queries: all minimal cut sets (*MCS*), the *unreliability* at time point $t = 1$, the *unreliability for 10 000 time points* that are uniformly distributed within the interval $[0, 10]$, and the *Birnbaum importance index* at time point $t = 1$.

---

[6] https://github.com/rakhimov/scram.

[7] https://altarica-association.org/members/arauzy/Software/XFTA/XFTA2.html.

[8] https://github.com/rakhimov/scram/tree/develop/input/Aralia.

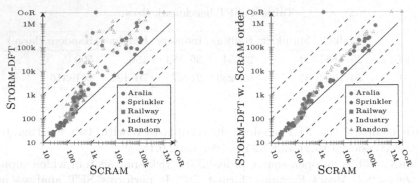

(a) BDD sizes STORM-DFT DFS vs SCRAM (b) BDD sizes STORM-DFT using variable
ordering from SCRAM vs SCRAM

Fig. 4. Comparison of BDD sizes for different variable orderings for MCS

4.3 Results

We ran STORM-DFT, SCRAM and XFTA on all 215 examples w.r.t. the four different queries. We ran the experiments on a desktop machine with an AMD
Ryzen™ 9 5950X and 32 GB of RAM running Arch Linux. In the multi-core configuration, we used 16 cores. The timeout was set to 5 min and the memory was
limited to 30 GB. We asserted that the obtained results are the same for all three
tools. In the following, we provide detailed comparisons of the tools. Additional
results and details can be found in the extended version of this paper [7].

We present the comparisons as scatter plots such as in Fig. 5. All scatter plots
are in log-log scale and indicate—in most cases—the time (in seconds) it took
each tool to compute a query. Line *OoR* indicates *out of resources* and represents
either a timeout or memory out. All points below the diagonal indicate examples
which STORM-DFT could solve faster than the other tool. All points below the
first (second) dashed line correspond to SFTs for which STORM-DFT was one
(two) order(s) of magnitude faster than the other tool. Similarly, for every point
above the diagonal, the other tool was faster.

BDD Sizes. First, Fig. 4 compares the number of nodes in the BDDs which
provides an idea of the respective memory consumption. Figure 4(a) compares
the sizes of the BDDs obtained by STORM-DFT and SCRAM. The largest BDDs
which could be analysed contain more than a million nodes. In general, SCRAM
yields smaller BDDs, for larger BDDs even by more than one order of magnitude.
The main reason is that SCRAM uses a slightly different variable ordering which
seems to yield smaller BDDs.

The influence of the variable ordering is further investigated in Fig. 4(b).
Here, we extract the variable ordering from SCRAM and employ it in STORM-
DFT. We see that using the SCRAM variable ordering in STORM-DFT improves
upon the default DFS ordering and yields smaller BDD sizes—in particular
for larger SFTs. However, SCRAM still yields smaller BDDs than STORM-DFT.

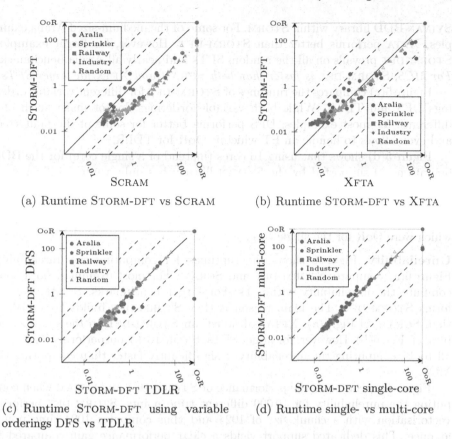

(a) Runtime STORM-DFT vs SCRAM

(b) Runtime STORM-DFT vs XFTA

(c) Runtime STORM-DFT using variable orderings DFS vs TDLR

(d) Runtime single- vs multi-core

Fig. 5. Comparisons for the computation of MCS

Reasons for the discrepancy could be that the BDD implementation in SCRAM is specifically tailored to SFTs or that the self-reported number of BDD nodes in both tools are computed in different ways.

Using good heuristics for the variable ordering is crucial for a small memory footprint; the heuristics in STORM-DFT can be further improved.

MCS. We compare the runtimes for computing the MCS in Fig. 5. Figure 5(a) compares STORM-DFT and SCRAM. We first see that the SFTs corresponding to the sprinkler, railway and industry case studies can be solved within 1 s by both tools. This also holds for other tools/configurations and metrics. As these SFTs are not a challenge, we focus on the Aralia benchmark and random SFTs in the remainder. STORM-DFT is faster than SCRAM in nearly all cases. One possible reason is that SCRAM outputs the MCS in an XML format which requires more I/O-operations than the simple list output of STORM-DFT.

When comparing STORM-DFT with XFTA (cf. Fig. 5(b)), the picture is more diverse. XFTA is faster than STORM-DFT on most examples which can be solved within 1 s. This is mostly due to the overhead resulting from initializing the

SYLVAN BDD library within STORM. For some of the medium-sized Aralia examples, XFTA performs better than STORM-DFT. However, for larger examples, STORM-DFT prevails on all the random SFTs and nearly all Aralia benchmarks. *For MCS, STORM-DFT is faster than both SCRAM and XFTA for larger SFTs.*

Figure 5(c) compares the runtimes of STORM-DFT for different variable orderings DFS and TDLR. While both variable orderings do not make much of a difference for most examples, DFS performs better for some of the fault trees and even allows to handle an FT which is OoR for TDLR.

Figure 5(d) shows that using 16 cores (instead of a single core) for the BDD operations as supported by the SYLVAN library has only a minor influence on the runtime. One reason is that most operations performed on the BDDs are fairly basic and therefore do not profit much from parallelization. However, for some large examples, the configuration with multiple cores allows to handle SFTs which were OoR for the single core.

Unreliability. Figure 6 shows the runtimes for computing the unreliability. Figure 6(a) compares STORM-DFT and SCRAM. For most examples, both tools compute the unreliability within 1 s. For larger benchmarks, SCRAM outperforms STORM-DFT. The main reason is that STORM-DFT builds larger BDDs than SCRAM, cf Fig. 4(a). XFTA is faster than STORM-DFT on the small examples, cf. Fig. 6(b). However, for larger SFTs, STORM-DFT outperforms XFTA. For all tools, computing the unreliability is significantly faster than computing the MCS.

Figure 6(c) compares the performance of STORM-DFT and SCRAM when computing the unreliability for 10 000 different time points. STORM-DFT performs vectorisation with a chunk-size of 1024 and thus computes 1024 time points at once. This dedicated support yields a clear performance gain compared to SCRAM which computes each time point sequentially. For larger SFTs, STORM-DFT is more than one order of magnitude faster. The same holds true when comparing to XFTA, cf. Fig. 6(d).

STORM-DFT is slower when computing the unreliability for one time bound, but is significantly faster than SCRAM and XFTA for multiple time bounds.

Importance Measures. Last, we consider the computation of the Birnbaum importance index for all BEs in a SFT. We omit the results for SCRAM as SCRAM needs to compute the MCS for computing the Birnbaum importance index for all BEs. As STORM-DFT does not need this computation, the comparison would be unfair. We provide the results in the extended version of this paper [7].

Figure 7(a) compares the runtime for STORM-DFT and XFTA when computing the Birnbaum importance index for all BEs at a single time point. We see that most examples are solved within 1 s. XFTA performs better on the larger examples. Figure 7(b) compares both tools when computing the Birnbaum importance index for 1000 time points. Here, STORM-DFT is orders of magnitude faster than XFTA and provides results where XFTA runs out of resources.

When computing the Birnbaum importance index for all BEs, XFTA is faster for single time points whereas STORM-DFT is orders of magnitude faster for multiple time points.

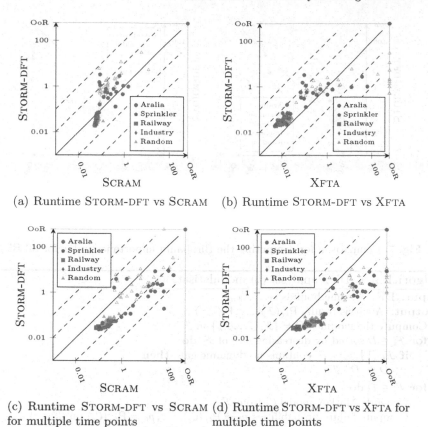

(a) Runtime STORM-DFT vs SCRAM   (b) Runtime STORM-DFT vs XFTA

(c) Runtime STORM-DFT vs SCRAM   (d) Runtime STORM-DFT vs XFTA for
for multiple time points   multiple time points

Fig. 6. Comparisons for the computation of the unreliability

5   DFT Analysis via BDD and Modularisation

Dynamic fault trees extend SFTs by capturing dynamic failure behaviour such
as ordered failures, spare management or functional dependencies. Analysis of
DFTs therefore needs to keep track of the history of failures and BDDs cannot be
easily used. In this approach, we combine SFT and DFT analysis using *modularisation* [31]. Modularisation is a "divide-and-conquer"-approach which splits the
DFT into *modules*, i.e., independent sub-trees. Each module is analysed independently and the corresponding results are combined in the end. Modularisation
thus allows to exploit the "best" analysis technique for each module individually.

Modules containing dynamic elements are analysed by translating the corresponding sub-DFT into a Markov model [56]. The state space of the Markov
model is created by exhaustively exploring all possible BE failures of the DFT.
Each transition corresponds to the failure of a BE and the successor state represents the status of the DFT after the BE failure. The transition rate is given
by the failure rate of the BE. Our translation employs several optimisation tech-

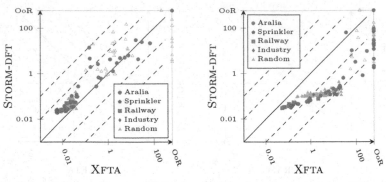

(a) Runtime STORM-DFT vs XFTA for single time point

(b) Runtime STORM-DFT vs XFTA for multiple time points

Fig. 7. Comparison for computing the Birnbaum importance index for all BEs

---

Algorithm 1. DFT analysis via modularisation

Input: DFT $\mathcal{F}$, time bounds $t_1, \ldots, t_n$
Output: Analysis results $\mathsf{P}_{t_1}(\mathcal{F}), \ldots, \mathsf{P}_{t_n}(\mathcal{F})$
  Compute the modules $D = \{\mathcal{F}_1, \ldots, \mathcal{F}_k\}$ in $\mathcal{F}$
  for $\mathcal{F}_i \in D$ sorted by decreasing size of $\mathcal{F}_i$ **do**
    if $\mathcal{F}_i \setminus \bigcup_{\mathcal{F}' \neq \mathcal{F}_i} \mathcal{F}'$ contains no dynamic gate **then**
      $D := D \setminus \mathcal{F}_i$
  for $\mathcal{F}_i \in D$ **do**
    Generate Markov model $\mathcal{C}_i$ from $\mathcal{F}_i$
    Compute failure probabilities $p_1 = \mathsf{P}_{t_1}(\mathcal{C}_i), \ldots, p_n = \mathsf{P}_{t_n}(\mathcal{C}_i)$ on $\mathcal{C}_i$
    Create BE B_i such that $\mathsf{P}_{t_j}(B_i) = p_j$ for all $1 \leq j \leq n$
    Replace $\mathcal{F}_i$ by B_i in $\mathcal{F}$
  Build BDD $\mathcal{B}$ from $\mathcal{F}$
  Compute results $r_1 = \mathsf{P}_{t_1}(\mathcal{B}), \ldots, r_n = \mathsf{P}_{t_n}(\mathcal{B})$ on $\mathcal{B}$
  return $r_1, \ldots, r_n$

---

niques to mitigate a state space explosion. The optimisations encompass discarding irrelevant failures and exploiting symmetries, see [56] for the details.

Note that modularisation can only be used for computing probabilities, e.g., the unreliability. The MTTF cannot be computed compositionally as combining expectations is difficult [9]. Thus, other approaches are necessary such as the approximation from Sect. 3.3 or composing independent Markov models [56].

Algorithm. We shortly describe our implementation of the DFT analysis via modularisation based on [31]. Algorithm 1 presents the pseudo-code. We use the DFT in Fig. 1 as an example and compute the unreliability within time bound t. We start the analysis by identifying the modules in the DFT using the algorithm of [24]. The algorithm traverses the fault tree in a depth-first left-most order and stores the order in which nodes are visited. A node v is a root of a module if all its descendants are visited in-between the first and last visit of v.

The algorithm runs in linear time and yields a unique list of modules. Minor adaptions of the algorithm are required to adequately handle SEQ and FDEP, cf. [6]. Next, we only keep the dynamic modules, i.e., modules containing at least one dynamic element. We iteratively remove a module if its corresponding elements not contained in other modules only contain static gates. That way, we remove modules containing only static elements and modules which are a subset of dynamic modules. This step results in a unique set of dynamic modules. The example DFT contains two dynamic modules (indicated by dashed blue boxes on the left DFT in Fig. 1). Next, each dynamic module is translated to a Markov model and analysed according to the given metric [56]. The complete dynamic module is then replaced by a single BE which matches the calculated failure probabilities. In our example, BE H' is chosen such that it has the same probability to fail within time bound t than the whole module of H. In the end, the resulting fault tree (on the right in Fig. 1) contains only static elements. Thus, this SFT can be analysed using the BDD approach presented in Sect. 3.

Static modules could of course also be replaced by corresponding BEs. As building the BDD is efficient, we opt to directly analyse the resulting SFT instead. Specific dynamic structures such as the first child of a PAND or SEQ could also be further modularised following [59]. However, the application of these modularisation rules is very limited and results in semi-Markov chains. This approach is therefore not considered here.

Implementation. We implemented the modularisation in STORM-DFT using the BDD implementation described in Sect. 3.4. A DFT is analysed by translating it into a Markov model as in [56]. While STORM-DFT already supports a modularisation, this top-down approach is only applicable to children of the top-level event. In contrast, the new implementation is applicable to dynamic modules located anywhere in the DFT. Moreover, the Markov models for dynamic modules are cached such that multiple queries can be performed on the same model. This is not possible in the previous implementation which regenerates each model for a new metric. The caching is in particular useful when computing multiple time points and exploiting vectorisation on the resulting SFT.

6   Evaluation of DFT Approach

We evaluate the DFT modularisation and compare with existing approaches.

Configurations. We compare the modularisation using BDDs with two existing approaches within STORM-DFT [56]: the translation to a continuous-time Markov chain (CTMC) and the top-down modularisation.

Benchmarks. We use the following DFT benchmarks:

- 68 DFTs from the FFORT benchmark collection [46].
- 40 DFT obtained by using the SFTs from the Aralia benchmark set and replacing one BE by the DFT ftpp.1-1 from the FFORT benchmark set.

Table 2. DFT benchmark sizes

Benchmark set	#BEs	#Static gates	#Dyn. gates	#BEs mod.	#Static gates mod.
Adapt. SFT	32–1574	26–1628	3	25–1623	21–1623
Adapt. Railway	194–545	153–487	19–54	22–54	40–168
Adapt. VGS	54–99	31–59	6–20	1–79	0–39
FFORT	6–87	1–50	0–44	1–50	0–21

- 8 DFTs modelling infrastructure in railway station areas [57] and slightly adapted to contain modules.
- 8 DFTs modelling configurations for a vehicle guidance system (VGS) [29] and adapted by removing irrelevant FDEPs.

Table 2 gives statistics on these benchmarks: the minimal and maximal number of BEs, static and dynamic gates in the original DFT as well as the numbers for the SFT after modularisation.

We run the three configurations of STORM-DFT on the 124 DFTs. We compute the *unreliability* at a time bound t either given by the largest bound specified in FFORT or we use $t = 100$ otherwise. For *multiple time bounds*, we use 1000 time bounds uniformly distributed over the interval $[0, t]$. We used the same machine and settings (timeout 5 min, 30 GB memory) as in Sect. 4.1.

6.1 Results

Unreliability. Figure 8 compares the computation of the unreliability. Figure 8(a) compares the modularisation using BDDs with the CTMC approach. The new BDD approach solves nearly all DFTs within 1 s and outperforms the CTMC approach by several orders of magnitude. Modularisation is therefore offering clear performance benefits compared to plain CTMC analysis.

Figure 8(b) compares the new BDD-based modularisation with the existing top-down modularisation. The new approach prevails for all larger DFTs. The BDD modularisation solved the adapted SFTs within 0.1 s while the top-down approach required up to 100 s. On these DFTs, top-down modularisation is not applicable and thus, the entire DFT must be translated into a CTMC.

The advantage of the BDD modularisation becomes even clearer for multiple time bounds, cf. Fig. 8(c). The BDD modularisation is significantly faster than the top-down modularisation for most of the considered DFTs. On most DFTs, the BDD modularisation is able to compute 1000 time points within 1 s. The main reasons for the performance improvement on multiple time points are the caching of the intermediate Markov models and the use of vectorisation on the resulting BDD, cf. Sect. 3.2.

The BDD-based modularisation is significantly faster than both the plain CTMC approach and the existing top-down modularisation.

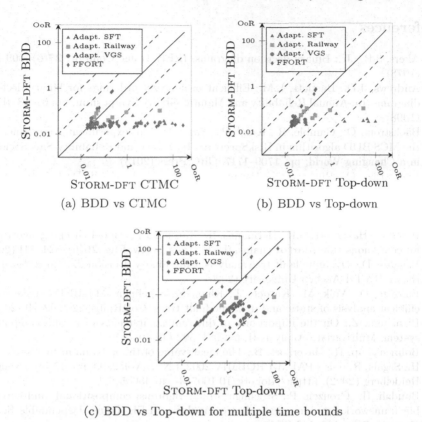

(a) BDD vs CTMC

(b) BDD vs Top-down

(c) BDD vs Top-down for multiple time bounds

Fig. 8. Comparisons of runtimes for the computation of the unreliability

7 Conclusion

We presented an implementation for fault tree analysis based on BDDs in the
STORM-DFT tool. Our implementation is competitive compared to existing tools
and performs significantly better when computing multiple time points. We also
presented an implementation for DFT analysis based on modularisation. The
modular analysis allows to use the best techniques for each sub-tree and outperforms existing approaches. STORM-DFT is currently the only available tool
supporting modularisation for efficient DFT analysis.

Future Work. Further improvements are needed to obtain smaller BDDs during the translation, for example by improving the heuristics for variable orderings such as using heuristics from SCRAM. The modularisation cannot be fully
exploited if large dynamic modules are present. A possible research direction is
to approximate the results for sub-modules, either by smaller fault trees or by
the approximation approach of [56].

730   D. Basgöze et al.

References

1. Akers, S.B., Jr.: Binary decision diagrams. IEEE Trans. Comput. **27**(6), 509–516 (1978)
2. Andrews, J.D., Bartlett, L.M.: Efficient basic event orderings for binary decision diagrams. In: Annual Reliability and Maintainability Symposium, pp. 61–68. IEEE (1998)
3. Bäckström, O., Gamble, R., Krcal, P., Wang, W.: An experimental assessment of the MCS BDD algorithm in RiskSpectrum. In: Safety and Reliability-Safe Societies in a Changing World, pp. 1709–1717. CRC Press (2018)
4. Bäckström, O., Butkova, Y., Hermanns, H., Krčál, J., Krčál, P.: Effective static and dynamic fault tree analysis. In: Skavhaug, A., Guiochet, J., Bitsch, F. (eds.) SAFECOMP 2016. LNCS, vol. 9922, pp. 266–280. Springer, Cham (2016). https://doi.org/10.1007/978-3-319-45477-1_21
5. Baier, C., Haverkort, B.R., Hermanns, H., Katoen, J.P.: Model-checking algorithms for continuous-time Markov chains. IEEE Trans. Softw. Eng. **29**(6), 524–541 (2003)
6. Basgöze, D.: Dynamic fault tree analysis using binary decision diagrams. Bachelor thesis, RWTH Aachen University (2020)
7. Basgöze, D., Volk, M., Katoen, J., Khan, S., Stoelinga, M.: BDDs strike back: efficient analysis of static and dynamic fault trees. CoRR abs/2202.02829 (2022)
8. Birnbaum, Z.: On the importance of different components in a multicomponent system. Multivariate Analysis-II, pp. 581–592 (1969)
9. Bohnenkamp, H., Haverkort, B.: The mean value of the maximum. In: Hermanns, H., Segala, R. (eds.) PAPM-PROBMIV 2002. LNCS, vol. 2399, pp. 37–56. Springer, Heidelberg (2002). https://doi.org/10.1007/3-540-45605-8_4
10. Boudali, H., Crouzen, P., Stoelinga, M.: A rigorous, compositional, and extensible framework for dynamic fault tree analysis. IEEE Trans. Dependable Secur. Comput. **7**(2), 128–143 (2010)
11. Bouissou, M., Bruyere, F., Rauzy, A.: BDD based fault-tree processing: a comparison of variable ordering heuristics. In: European Safety and Reliability Association Conference, ESREL (1997)
12. Brace, K.S., Rudell, R.L., Bryant, R.E.: Efficient implementation of a BDD package. In: DAC, pp. 40–45. IEEE Computer Society Press (1990)
13. Bryant, R.E.: Graph-based algorithms for Boolean function manipulation. IEEE Trans. Comput. **35**(8), 677–691 (1986)
14. Bryant, R.E.: Binary decision diagrams. In: Handbook of Model Checking, pp. 191–217. Springer, Cham (2018). https://doi.org/10.1007/978-3-319-10575-8_7
15. Budde, C.E., Ruijters, E., Stoelinga, M.: The dynamic fault tree rare event simulator. In: Gribaudo, M., Jansen, D.N., Remke, A. (eds.) QEST 2020. LNCS, vol. 12289, pp. 233–238. Springer, Cham (2020). https://doi.org/10.1007/978-3-030-59854-9_17
16. Cheok, M.C., Parry, G.W., Sherry, R.R.: Use of importance measures in risk-informed regulatory applications. Reliab. Eng. Syst. Saf. **60**(3), 213–226 (1998)
17. Coudert, O., Madre, J.C.: Fault tree analysis: 10/sup 20/prime implicants and beyond. In: Annual Reliability and Maintainability Symposium, pp. 240–245. IEEE (1993)
18. Davis, P.J., Rabinowitz, P.: Methods of Numerical Integration. Academic Press, Cambridge (1984)
19. van Dijk, T.: Sylvan: multi-core decision diagrams. Ph.D. thesis, University of Twente, The Netherlands (2016)

20. van Dijk, T., van de Pol, J.: Sylvan: multi-core framework for decision diagrams. Int. J. Softw. Tools Technol. Transf. **19**(6), 675–696 (2017)
21. Dugan, J.B., Bavuso, S.J., Boyd, M.A.: Fault trees and sequence dependencies. In: Annual Reliability and Maintainability Symposium, pp. 286–293 (1990)
22. Dugan, J.B., Bavuso, S.J., Boyd, M.A.: Dynamic fault-tree models for fault-tolerant computer systems. IEEE Trans. Reliab. **41**(3), 363–377 (1992)
23. Dugan, J.B., Venkataraman, B., Gulati, R.: DIFtree: a software package for the analysis of dynamic fault tree models. In: Annual Reliability and Maintainability Symposium, pp. 64–70. IEEE (1997)
24. Dutuit, Y., Rauzy, A.: A linear-time algorithm to find modules of fault trees. IEEE Trans. Reliab. **45**(3), 422–425 (1996)
25. Dutuit, Y., Rauzy, A.: Efficient algorithms to assess component and gate importance in fault tree analysis. Reliab. Eng. Syst. Saf. **72**(2), 213–222 (2001)
26. Eijkhout, V.: Introduction to High Performance Scientific Computing. lulu.com (2011)
27. Federal Aviation Administration: System safety handbook (2000)
28. Fussell, J.: How to hand-calculate system reliability and safety characteristics. IEEE Trans. Reliab. **24**(3), 169–174 (1975)
29. Ghadhab, M., Junges, S., Katoen, J.P., Kuntz, M., Volk, M.: Safety analysis for vehicle guidance systems with dynamic fault trees. Reliab. Eng. Syst. Saf. **186**, 37–50 (2019)
30. Guennebaud, G., Jacob, B., et al.: Eigen v3 (2010). http://eigen.tuxfamily.org
31. Gulati, R., Dugan, J.B.: A modular approach for analyzing static and dynamic fault trees. In: Annual Reliability and Maintainability Symposium, pp. 57–63. IEEE (1997)
32. Hensel, C., Junges, S., Katoen, J.P., Quatmann, T., Volk, M.: The probabilistic model checker storm. Int. J. Softw. Tools Technol. Transf. 1–22 (2021). https://doi.org/10.1007/s10009-021-00633-z
33. ISO: ISO 26262: Road vehicles - Functional safety. Standard, International Organization for Standardization, Geneva, Switzerland (2011)
34. Junges, S., Katoen, J.-P., Stoelinga, M., Volk, M.: One net fits all. In: Khomenko, V., Roux, O.H. (eds.) PETRI NETS 2018. LNCS, vol. 10877, pp. 272–293. Springer, Cham (2018). https://doi.org/10.1007/978-3-319-91268-4_14
35. Krcál, J., Krcál, P.: Scalable analysis of fault trees with dynamic features. In: DSN, pp. 89–100. IEEE Computer Society (2015)
36. Mo, Y.: A multiple-valued decision-diagram-based approach to solve dynamic fault trees. IEEE Trans. Reliab. **63**(1), 81–93 (2014)
37. Moinuddin, K., Innocent, J., Keshavarz, K.: Reliability of sprinkler system in Australian shopping centres-a fault tree analysis. Fire Saf. J. **105**, 204–215 (2019)
38. Montani, S., Portinale, L., Bobbio, A., Raiteri, D.C.: Radyban: a tool for reliability analysis of dynamic fault trees through conversion into dynamic Bayesian networks. Reliab. Eng. Syst. Saf. **93**(7), 922–932 (2008)
39. Raiteri, D.C.: The conversion of dynamic fault trees to stochastic Petri nets, as a case of graph transformation. Electron. Notes Theor. Comput. Sci. **127**(2), 45–60 (2005)
40. Rakhimov, O.: Scram probabilistic risk analysis tool (2018). https://doi.org/10.5281/zenodo.1146337
41. Rao, K.D., Gopika, V., Rao, V.V.S.S., Kushwaha, H.S., Verma, A.K., Srividya, A.: Dynamic fault tree analysis using Monte Carlo simulation in probabilistic safety assessment. Reliab. Eng. Syst. Saf. **94**(4), 872–883 (2009)

42. Rauzy, A.: Some disturbing facts about depth-first left-most variable ordering heuristics for binary decision diagrams. Proc. Inst. Mech. Eng. Part O: J. Risk Reliab. **222**(4), 573–582 (2008)
43. Rauzy, A.: New algorithms for fault trees analysis. Reliab. Eng. Syst. Saf. **40**(3), 203–211 (1993)
44. Rauzy, A.: Sequence algebra, sequence decision diagrams and dynamic fault trees. Reliab. Eng. Syst. Saf. **96**(7), 785–792 (2011)
45. Rauzy, A.: Probabilistic safety analysis with XFTA. AltaRica Association (2020)
46. Ruijters, E., et al.: FFORT: a benchmark suite for fault tree analysis. In: ESREL. Singapore: Research Publishing (2019)
47. Ruijters, E., Stoelinga, M.: Fault tree analysis: a survey of the state-of-the-art in modeling, analysis and tools. Comput. Sci. Rev. **15**, 29–62 (2015)
48. Shannon, C.E.: A symbolic analysis of relay and switching circuits. Electr. Eng. **57**(12), 713–723 (1938)
49. Sinnamon, R.M., Andrews, J.: Improved efficiency in qualitative fault tree analysis. Qual. Reliab. Eng. Int. **13**(5), 293–298 (1997)
50. Sinnamon, R.M., Andrews, J.D.: Fault tree analysis and binary decision diagrams. In: Annual Reliability and Maintainability Symposium, pp. 215–222. IEEE (1996)
51. Stamatelatos, M., Vesely, W., Dugan, J., Fragola, J., Minarick, J., Railsback, J.: Fault Tree Handbook with Aerospace Applications. NASA, Washington, DC (2002)
52. Steven, E., Antoine, R.: Open-PSA Model Exchange Format. The Open-PSA Initiative (2007)
53. Sullivan, K.J., Dugan, J.B., Coppit, D.: The Galileo fault tree analysis tool. In: FTCS, pp. 232–235. IEEE Computer Society (1999)
54. Trivedi, K.S., Bobbio, A.: Reliability and Availability Engineering - Modeling, Analysis, and Applications. Cambridge University Press, Cambridge (2017)
55. Trivedi, K.S., Sahner, R.A.: SHARPE at the age of twenty two. SIGMETRICS Perform. Eval. Rev. **36**(4), 52–57 (2009)
56. Volk, M., Junges, S., Katoen, J.P.: Fast dynamic fault tree analysis by model checking techniques. IEEE Trans. Ind. Inform. **14**(1), 370–379 (2018)
57. Volk, M., Weik, N., Katoen, J.-P., Nießen, N.: A DFT modeling approach for infrastructure reliability analysis of railway station areas. In: Larsen, K.G., Willemse, T. (eds.) FMICS 2019. LNCS, vol. 11687, pp. 40–58. Springer, Cham (2019). https://doi.org/10.1007/978-3-030-27008-7_3
58. Xing, L., Tannous, O., Dugan, J.B.: Reliability analysis of nonrepairable coldstandby systems using sequential binary decision diagrams. IEEE Trans. Syst. Man Cybern. Part A **42**(3), 715–726 (2012)
59. Yevkin, O.: An improved modular approach for dynamic fault tree analysis. In: Annual Reliability and Maintainability Symposium, pp. 1–5. IEEE (2011)
60. Zhou, S., Xiang, J., Wong, W.E.: Reliability analysis of dynamic fault trees with spare gates using conditional binary decision diagrams. J. Syst. Softw. **170**, 110766 (2020)

Approximate Translation from Floating-Point to Real-Interval Arithmetic

Daisuke Ishii$^{(\boxtimes)}$, Takashi Tomita, and Toshiaki Aoki

Japan Advanced Institute of Science and Technology, Nomi, Japan
{dsksh,tomita,toshiaki}@jaist.ac.jp

Abstract. Floating-point arithmetic (FPA) is a mechanical representation of real arithmetic (RA), where each operation is replaced with a rounded counterpart. Various numerical properties can be verified by using SMT solvers that support the logic of FPA. However, the scalability of the solving process remains limited when compared to RA. In this paper, we present a decision procedure for FPA that takes advantage of the efficiency of RA solving. The proposed method abstracts FP numbers as rational intervals and FPA expressions as interval arithmetic (IA) expressions; then, we solve IA formulas to check the satisfiability of an FPA formula using an off-the-shelf RA solver (we use CVC4 and Z3). In exchange for the efficiency gained by abstraction, the solving process becomes quasi-complete; we allow to output unknown when the satisfiability is affected by possible numerical errors. Furthermore, our IA is meticulously formalized to handle the special value NaN. We implemented the proposed method and compared it to four existing SMT solvers in the experiments. As a result, we confirmed that our solver was efficient for instances where rounding modes were parameterized.

Keywords: Floating-point arithmetic · Interval arithmetic · SMT solvers

1 Introduction

A key technique to perform calculations on reals efficiently is *floating-point arithmetic* (FPA; Sect. 3) [15,21], although there will be numerical errors caused by rounding reals into FP numbers. The decision procedure on the logical theory of FPA is important for verifying numerical programs, hardware models, etc., while accounting numerical errors. Indeed, such a theory and dedicated decision procedures have been developed and implemented in recent SMT solvers (e.g. [3]). Many solvers are based on a technique called *bit blasting* [5,6] that encodes a satisfiability problem on FPA into that on bit vectors (BVs). Despite the high performance of SAT solvers and several improvements (Sect. 2), the FPA solvers

This work was partially supported by JSPS (KAKENHI 18K11240).

J. V. Deshmukh et al. (Eds.): NFM 2022, LNCS 13260, pp. 733–751, 2022.
https://doi.org/10.1007/978-3-031-06773-0_39

are less scalable than the real arithmetic (RA) solvers; especially when solving instances described by the same arithmetic formulas, the former is slower (sometimes in orders of magnitude) than the latter.

This paper aims to realize an efficient method by using RA solvers instead of bit blasting. The proposed method represents an FPA expression with a rational interval that encloses every valuation in FP numbers for the expression. This abstraction, which assumes arbitrary rounding modes and mild estimation of rounding errors, slightly limits the method's target problem and completeness. However, we expect to solve practical FPA problems with this approach by leveraging the efficiency of an off-the-shelf RA solver. In addition, it is interesting to compare bit blasting with our method, as it explores the optimal decision procedure at the boundary between Boolean and continuous domains.

The contributions described in this paper are as follows:

- *A method to solve FPA formulas by encoding them into formulas on real intervals.* We formalize interval arithmetic (IA) for this purpose that handles the special FP number NaN (not a number) correctly (Sect. 4). A linear function for error estimation, an *interval extension* scheme for FPA formulas, and an encoding method from the FPA logic to the real-interval logic are presented. *Weak* and *strong* modes are used for encoding, and their correspondence with δ-variants [12] is discussed. The method has been implemented as a tool that translates between SMT-LIB descriptions for FPA formulas and for RA formulas that embed the interval extension (Sect. 5). We have also implemented a Z3PY script that solves FPA formulas.
- *Experiments to confirm the efficiency of the proposed method by comparison with four other SMT solvers* (Sect. 6). We prepared FPA problem instances in three sets, in which a set is a typical FPA benchmark and two sets consist of instances with no rounding mode setting. In the experiments, we obtained promising results when comparing our method to existing FPA solvers. We confirmed that our method (the Z3PY script or manual solving with CVC4) solved the most number of problems for each set except for the FPA benchmark. We also confirmed that the number of inconclusive (unknown) results by our solver were small ($<10\%$) in all but one of the six categories.

Examples. Let f be a real function. Suppose we want to check the satisfiability of an FPA formula $\varphi_{\mathbb{F}} := f_{\mathbb{F}} >_{\mathbb{F}} +0_{\mathbb{F}}$, which is a direct translation of an RA formula $\varphi := f > 0$, obtained by replacing every syntactic element in φ with an FPA counterpart (with a rounding mode configuration). We can feed them to an SMT solver supporting FPA and RA; then, the solving process for $\varphi_{\mathbb{F}}$ is often less efficient than solving φ. When we can estimate an error bound $\delta := |f - f_{\mathbb{F}}|$, checking variant formulas $\varphi^- := f > -\delta$ and $\varphi^+ := f > \delta$ by the RA solver might be more efficient. If φ^- is unsat or φ^+ is sat, then so is $\varphi_{\mathbb{F}}$; otherwise, this method could answer "unknown" (f can be in the δ-neighborhood of zero). The proposed method in this paper translates f into an expression $\boldsymbol{f}$ based on an IA, which evaluates to an interval that overapproximates $f_{\mathbb{F}}$ assuming any rounding modes; then, δ is obtained as the width of $\boldsymbol{f}$.

The case $f_{\mathbb{F}}$ evaluates to the special value NaN makes this method complicated. The satisfiability of a negative predicate $\varphi'_{\mathbb{F}} := \neg(f_{\mathbb{F}} \leq_{\mathbb{F}} +0_{\mathbb{F}})$ might be checked using the same formulas φ^- and φ^+. However, if we assume that $f_{\mathbb{F}}$ evaluates to either NaN or other FP numbers, it is not correct; $\varphi'_{\mathbb{F}}$ is sat regardless of other assignments, because NaN $\leq_{\mathbb{F}} +0_{\mathbb{F}}$ does not hold. Therefore, we use variant formulas φ'^- and φ'^+, prepared specifically for negative predicates. We define φ'^- to be true regardless of other assignments if it is not certain that $f_{\mathbb{F}}$ is not NaN; in contrast, satisfiability of φ'^+ depends on the regular assignments.

2   Related Work

The FPA theory solvers contained in SMT solvers have been actively developed over the last ten years or so, as summarized in [3,31].

Bit blasting [5,6] is a major approach applied in many SMT solvers including Z3, CVC4 and MATHSAT. It converts an FPA formula to a Boolean formula by encoding an FP number into a set of Boolean variables and FP operator circuits into Boolean formulas. Because the size of an encoded formula easily becomes large, many approximation methods have been studied (e.g. [2,5,14,23, 25]). Brain et al. [3] have implemented a reference bit-blasting engine included in CVC4. This paper proposes a non-bit-blasting solver based on an RA solver, with competing results in the experiments. The number of encoded real variables is proportional to the number of original FP variables, and we confirmed that memory usage is lower on average than in other solvers.

There are several works that encode FPA in RA. Leeser et al. [17] have proposed precise FPA embedding in an extended RA. The performance of their solver REALIZER was not competitive in our preliminary trial. Mixed-real-FPA [23,24] has been proposed to encode FPA, where some formulas are approximated by real formulas with rounding operations removed and other formulas are left unchanged. Their procedure tries to encode a formula into a mixed formula that has the same solution as the original. Zeljić et al. [30] have proposed an approximation refinement framework based on a similar idea. In contrast to that the methods in [23,24,30] approximate FPA by mixed-real-FPA, ours encodes an overapproximation of FPA formulas in RA; the result of solving the encoded formula is sound, whereas the above methods require verification after solving.

In decision procedures, IA-based techniques [20,28] play a crucial role in various ways. For RA logic formulas, there are solvers based on intervals bounded by FP numbers [10,11,19,22,29]; in contrast, we approximate FPA formulas using real intervals. IA-based decision procedures tend to be incomplete but can be δ-*complete* [12]; the same idea is applied in our encoding method.

IA is used frequently in FPA solvers to accelerate their process by approximating FP numbers. Typically, it is coupled with bit blasting and algorithms such as CEGAR [5] and non-chronological backtracking [2,14,25]. MATHSAT implements the method in [2]. OBJCP [31,32] and COLIBRI [18] are CP-based solvers implementing constraint propagation algorithms and other techniques e.g. diversification [31] and distance constraints [18]. Bit-blasting solvers and

CP solvers use intervals bounded by FP numbers, whereas ours uses intervals bounded by rational numbers. COLIBRI also uses integer and real intervals, but the details have not been made public.

IA is also used in the static analysis of numerical programs [1,8,9,13,26,27]. It is typically used for abstraction of numerical computation and to compute bounds for rounding errors. Methods to compute tight bounds [8,26] have been proposed; our method can adopt these methods to improve the accuracy. In terms of abstraction of FP expressions, Sect. 4 can be regarded as a variant of the formalization in e.g. [27]. However, our method differs in that 1) we aim at efficient solving of FPA logic formulas and 2) we formalize NaN cases that is essential in the FPA logic. [1] formalizes IA involving special values but it assumes a limited form of constraints.

Another branch of solvers applies an approach that encodes an axiomatization of FP numbers in the theory of reals and integers [4,7,9]. Our method can be considered to be in line with this approach, except that ours axiomatizes an interval extension of FPA in which rounding operations are overapproximated.

3   Floating-Point Arithmetic

FP numbers [15,21] are machine-representable approximations of real numbers. They are represented as BVs, and we consider various sets of FP numbers parameterized with the size of BVs (we limit the radix to 2).

Definition 1. *Let eb and sb be the sizes of* exponent *and* significand *bits, respectively. An* FP number *is represented by a pair* (M, e) *of two integers such that* $|M| \leq 2^{sb} - 1$ *and* $e \in [e_{\min}, e_{\max}]$, *where* $e_{\max} = 2^{eb-1} - 1$ *and* $e_{\min} = 1 - e_{\max}$; *it is interpreted as a real number* $M \times 2^{e-sb+1}$. *In addition, we use special data. There are two* signed zeros -0 *and* $+0$ *(we denote either of them by* 0 *if the difference does not matter). Infinities* $-\infty$ *and* $+\infty$ *represent numbers outside the representable bounds. Another special value* NaN *represents the result of exceptional evaluations.* $\mathbb{F}_{eb,sb}$ *and* $\mathbb{F}^*_{eb,sb}$ *denote the sets of FP numbers with fixed bit sizes, where* $\mathbb{F}_{eb,sb} = \mathbb{F}^*_{eb,sb} \setminus \{-\infty, +\infty, \text{NaN}\}$. *We simply denote* $\mathbb{F}$ *and* $\mathbb{F}^*$ *when bit sizes are not important.*

For 64-bit double-precision FP numbers, $eb = 11$ and $sb = 53$. In a multi-sort context, we also denote an FP number n by $n_{\mathbb{F}}$.

Definition 2. *We consider the sets of extended reals* $\mathbb{R}^+ := \mathbb{R} \cup \{-\infty, +\infty\}$ *and* $\mathbb{R}^* := \mathbb{R}^+ \cup \{\text{NaN}\}$. *We interpret an FP number by mapping to the corresponding element in* $\mathbb{R}^*$ *using the function* $v : \mathbb{F}^* \to \mathbb{R}^*$. $v(\mp 0)$ *evaluates to* 0.

Distribution of FP numbers is not uniform, and errors increase as the value increases. Figure 1 illustrates the errors when x is *rounded to farthest* in $\mathbb{F}_{4,4}$. Errors can be estimated using parameters

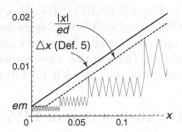

$$ed := 2^{sb-1} \quad \text{and} \quad em := 2^{e_{\min}-sb+1},$$

which represent the inverse of the slope that approximates the error function, and the error bound for subnormal FP numbers such that $|M| < 2^{sb-1}$, respectively.

Fig. 1. Rounding error.

In FPA (arithmetic with FP numbers), we apply four operators $\circ \in \{+, -, \times, \div\}$, other operators e.g. absolute value $|\cdot|$, and comparison operators. Although their semantics follows from the real interpretation, FP numbers are not closed under those operations, so the results are *rounded* to neighboring FP numbers, causing numerical errors. Each rounded operation should be associated with one of the six *rounding modes*, e.g., the mode "*round to nearest ties to even (RNE)*" rounds to a closest FP number; when two FP numbers are of the same distance, one with an even M is chosen. The set of modes are denoted by $\mathbb{M}$. In the SMT-LIB format, there are two equation operators: `fp.eq` and `=`; in the sequel, we denote them by $=$ and $\equiv$, respectively. `fp.eq` ($=$) is usually used in numerical programming and `=` ($\equiv$) is the bit equality. The main difference between the two is that NaN $=$ NaN does not hold but NaN $\equiv$ NaN does, and the former does not distinguish between the zeros but the latter does.

The semantics of FPA is specified in the IEEE-754 standard [15], formalized in several works e.g. [4,7], and mechanically specified by the SMT-LIB `FloatingPoint` theory.[1] Notably, for the special data, dedicated arithmetic rules are applied, e.g., $+\infty - +\infty$ and $+\infty \times 0$ evaluate to NaN, and $x =$ NaN does not hold, where x is an arbitrary FP number.

We consider logic formulas involving FPA predicates.

Definition 3. *The grammar of FPA formulas is as follows:*

$$F ::= T \gg T \mid \neg F \mid F \vee F$$
$$T ::= c \mid id \mid uop(T) \mid bop(rm, T, T)$$

where $\gg \in \{\equiv, =, \geq, >\}$, c *is a literal of a sort* $\mathbb{F}_{eb,sb}$, *and* id *is a variable name. uop are unary operations* $-(\cdot)$ *and* $|\cdot|$, *which do not require rounding, and bop are binary operations* $+$, $-$, $\times$ *and* $\div$, *associated with a rounding mode.*

We assume that formulas are well-sorted, insisting that every subformula is sorted in $\mathbb{F}_{eb,sb}$ with the same eb and sb. In the other sections, we also denote FPA constructs such as $\gg$ and c by $\gg_{\mathbb{F}}$ and $c_{\mathbb{F}}$ to indicate the sort.

---

[1] https://smtlib.cs.uiowa.edu/theories-FloatingPoint.shtml.

The SMT-LIB's FPA theory supports multi-precision FPA and multi-sort FPA mixed with BV, integers and reals, wherein additional sort-conversion operators are needed. The theory also provides additional predicates, e.g. `fp.isNaN` and `fp.isNegative`. Our implementation (Sect. 5) supports many of these features, but some are left for future work.

4   Abstraction of FPA with Interval Arithmetic

Section 4.1 introduces basics about IA and defines an interval extension of FP operators. In Sect. 4.2, we consider logic formulas involving interval predicates and how to convert an FPA formula into that system. Then, the soundness basis of the proposed method is described.

4.1   Interval Arithmetic

IA [20] is a traditional method for the abstraction of continuous domains e.g. reals. In this paper, we introduce intervals with rational bounds in $\mathbb{R}^*$ (the codomain of v in Definition 2) to approximate FPA.

Definition 4. *Intervals are* $\boldsymbol{x} = [\underline{x}, \bar{x}] := \{\tilde{x} \in \mathbb{R}^+ \mid \underline{x} \leq \tilde{x} \leq \bar{x}\}$, *where* $\underline{x}, \bar{x} \in \mathbb{Q} \cup \{-\infty, +\infty\}$, *and* $\underline{x} \leq \bar{x}$. *Point intervals such that* $\underline{x} = \bar{x} = x$ *are also denoted by* $[x]$. *Furthermore, we consider intervals that additionally contain* NaN; *they are denoted either as* $[\underline{x}, \bar{x}] \cup \{\text{NaN}\}$ *or as* $\boldsymbol{x}$ *when considering generic intervals. We denote the set of intervals by* $\mathbb{I}^*$.

Interval $[-\infty, +\infty]$ represents the entire domain $\mathbb{R}^+$ bounded by $-\infty$ and $+\infty$. Point interval $[+\infty]$ represents the set $\{+\infty\}$. We do not consider the empty set and $\{\text{NaN}\}$ as intervals to make the analysis simple in return for a slight increase of abstraction.

To abstract the rounding of a real number $\tilde{x} \in \mathbb{R}^+$ to an FP number $x \in \mathbb{F}^+_{eb,sb}$ (with an arbitrary mode), we consider an interval $\boldsymbol{x}$ such that $v(x) \in \boldsymbol{x}$. It is preferable to have a tight $\boldsymbol{x}$, but accurate encoding of its bounds will be costly when later handling with SMT solvers; thus, we use a linear approximation of rounding operators, at the expense of inaccuracy. They are based on the numerical error analysis in Sect. 3.

Definition 5. *We assume a set of FP numbers* $x \in \mathbb{F}^+_{eb,sb}$. *The rounding operators* ∇x *and* $\triangle x$ *are defined respectively by:*

$$\nabla x := \begin{cases} -\infty & \text{if } x - \frac{|x|}{ed} - em < \min \mathbb{F}, \\ x - \frac{|x|}{ed} - em & \text{otherwise}, \end{cases}$$

$$\triangle x := \begin{cases} +\infty & \text{if } x + \frac{|x|}{ed} + em > \max \mathbb{F}, \\ x + \frac{|x|}{ed} + em & \text{otherwise}. \end{cases}$$

For example, $\nabla 0.1 = 0.0855469$ and $\triangle 0.1 = 0.114453$, assuming $\mathbb{F}^+_{4,4}$.

Lemma 1. *For $\tilde{x} \in \mathbb{R}$, its rounded value $x \in \mathbb{F}^+_{eb,sb}$ with any mode, and $\boldsymbol{x} :=$ $[\nabla\tilde{x}, \triangle\tilde{x}]$, $\tilde{x} \in \boldsymbol{x}$ and $v(x) \in \boldsymbol{x}$ hold.*

Given an FPA operator $op_\mathbb{F}$ with n arguments (assumed to be total functions), its *interval extension* $\mathbb{I}^{*n} \to \mathbb{I}^*$ evaluates to intervals enclosing the possible rounded results. In ordinary IA, interval extensions of real functions are considered (e.g. in [20,28]). In the same way, we consider interval extension for FPA expressions, but in our case, handling of "NaN cases," e.g. $+\infty \times_\mathbb{F} 0$, needs attention. In this regard, we will enclose any FPA expressions that may evaluate to NaN in an interval containing NaN. Based on the widening operators and the handling of NaN, we define the interval extensions of FPA operators.

Definition 6. *Let $op_\mathbb{F}$ be an n-ary FPA operator $\mathbb{M} \times \mathbb{F}^{*n}_{eb,sb} \to \mathbb{F}^*_{eb,sb}$, $op_\mathbb{R}$ be an operator $\mathbb{R}^{*n} \to \mathbb{R}^*$ (ideal counterpart of $op_\mathbb{F}$ in RA), $\vec{x}$ be an interval vector in $\mathbb{I}^{*n}$, S be the set $\{op_\mathbb{R}(\vec{x}) \mid \vec{x} \in \vec{\boldsymbol{x}}\}$, $S_{\backslash\mathrm{NaN}} := S \setminus \{\mathrm{NaN}\}$. The interval extension of $op_\mathbb{F}$ is defined by*

$$op_\mathbb{I}(\vec{\boldsymbol{x}}) := [\nabla \inf S_{\backslash\mathrm{NaN}}, \triangle \sup S_{\backslash\mathrm{NaN}}] \cup \begin{cases} \{\mathrm{NaN}\} & \textit{if } \mathrm{NaN} \in S, \\ \emptyset & \textit{otherwise.} \end{cases}$$

Given an expression f that conforms to the syntax T in Definition 3, its interval extension is obtained by inductively applying the interval extension to every operator in f.

For example (assuming $\mathbb{F}^+_{4,4}$), $[1] \times_\mathbb{I} [0.5] +_\mathbb{I} [0, +\infty] = [0.435547, +\infty]$; $[0] \times_\mathbb{I} [-\infty, +\infty] = [0] \cup \{\mathrm{NaN}\}$; $[1] \div_\mathbb{I} [0] = [-\infty, +\infty]$. Efficient methods to compute $[\nabla \inf S, \triangle \sup S]$ for basic operators, handling only the bounds of the arguments, have been developed for numerical IA libraries; see [20,28]. In practice, we can have more accurate interval extensions in various ways as long as the resulting intervals are sound, e.g., we can evaluate $[1] \times_\mathbb{I} [0.5]$ as $[0.5]$. The following lemma summarizes the soundness of interval extensions.

Lemma 2. *Consider an FPA operator $op_\mathbb{F}$ and its interval extension $op_\mathbb{I}$. Let $\vec{\boldsymbol{x}}$ be an interval vector and $\boldsymbol{f}$ be $op_\mathbb{I}(\vec{\boldsymbol{x}})$. We have:*

$$\forall m \in \mathbb{M}, \ \forall \vec{x} \in \vec{\boldsymbol{x}}, \ v(op_\mathbb{F}(m, \vec{x})) \in \boldsymbol{f}.$$

The lemma is proved using the WHY3 tool for our implementation of the four operators (Sect. 5.4).

4.2 Approximation of FPA Formulas by IA Formulas

This section considers *weak* and *strong* abstractions of FPA formulas, based on the interval extensions. The basic idea here is borrowed from the δ-decision procedure [12] that formalizes a numerical process, given a bound δ for allowed numerical errors. We apply the idea to the domain of $\mathbb{F}^*$ and do not specify δ but let the interval-extended operations determine it.

We introduce IA logic formulas in mode weak ($? = -$) or strong ($? = +$).

Definition 7. *Let* ? *be* − *or* + *and it be fixed in a formula. The grammar of IA formulas, denoted by φ^- or φ^+, is as follows:*

$$F ::= T \gg_?^{[\neg]} T \mid F \wedge F \mid F \vee F$$
$$T ::= c \mid id \mid uop(T) \mid bop(T,T)$$

where $\gg_?^{[\neg]}$ *is parameterized in three ways: 1)* $\gg^{[\neg]}$ *represents* $\gg$ *or* $\gg^\neg$; *2)* $\gg \in \{\equiv, =, \geq, >\}$ *and* $\gg^\neg \in \{\not\equiv, \neq, <, \leq\}$; *3)* $\gg_?$ *is instantiated as* $\gg_-$ *or* $\gg_+$. *c and id represent constants (interval literals) and variables in* $\mathbb{I}^*$, *and uop and bop represent interval operators.*

Modes − and + are prepared for the soundness of decisions of unsat and sat, respectively (Lemma 3 and Theorem 1). For the soundness, there is no logical negation operator as in [12] but we have negated comparison operators in $\gg_?^\neg$. Two kinds of operators $\gg_?$ and $\gg_?^\neg$ handle "positive" and "negative" literals separately in the encoding process (Definition 8).

The semantics of IA formulas are straightforward, with assignments of free variables in $\mathbb{I}^*$ and evaluating interval extensions. However, in the following, we will modify $\mathbb{I}^*$ slightly to make a sound satisfiability checking. The interpretation of inequalities $f \gg_?^{[\neg]} g$ in two modes ? $\in \{-, +\}$ differs in whether or not to allow uncertain cases such that interval evaluations f and g result in non-point intervals and intersect. The two groups of operators $\gg_?$ and $\gg_?^\neg$ are not only negated but also different in the way they handle NaN. The semantics of the comparison operators should be appropriately defined so that the following lemma holds.

Lemma 3. *Consider the following subset of $\mathbb{I}^*$:*

$$\mathbb{I}_\#^* := \{x \in \mathbb{I}^* \mid \exists \hat{x} \in \mathbb{F}_{eb,sb}^*, \ \hat{x} \in x\}.$$

Let f and g be interval extensions of m-ary and n-ary FPA expressions f and g, respectively. We have:

$$f \gg_- g \text{ is unsat} \Rightarrow f \gg_\mathbb{F} g \text{ is unsat},$$
$$f \gg_-^\neg g \text{ is unsat} \Rightarrow \neg(f \gg_\mathbb{F} g) \text{ is unsat},$$
$$\exists (\vec{x}, \vec{y}) \in \mathbb{I}_\#^{*m+n}, \ f(\vec{x}) \gg_+ g(\vec{y}) \Rightarrow f \gg_\mathbb{F} g \text{ is sat},$$
$$\exists (\vec{x}, \vec{y}) \in \mathbb{I}_\#^{*m+n}, \ f(\vec{x}) \gg_+^\neg g(\vec{y}) \Rightarrow \neg(f \gg_\mathbb{F} g) \text{ is sat}.$$

The lemma is proved using WHY3 to confirm that every comparison operators are correctly defined, but for limited forms of f and g (Sect. 5.4).

Because assignments with intervals that do not contain any FP numbers (e.g. [0.1]) are possible, we must prohibit them in $\mathbb{I}_\#^*$ to make a sound decision for strong interval extension. In an actual encoding, the condition "$\exists \hat{x} \in \mathbb{F}_{eb,sb}^*, \hat{x} \in x$" can be made simpler and weaker, e.g., as $\underline{x} \leq \triangledown \bar{x}$ or $\triangle \underline{x} \leq \bar{x}$. In the decision with weak interval extension, it is sufficient to assume only point intervals (and point intervals appended with {NaN}) because any FP number can be represented by a point interval; in addition, an evaluation with point intervals will give the best approximation.

As an example of the operators, instances of $>_?^{[-]}$, which are $>_-$, $\leq_-$ (i.e. $>_?^-$), $>_+$ and $\leq_+$ (i.e. $>_+^-$), when rhs is $[0]$ are defined in a logic on $\mathbb{R}^*$ as follows:

$$\boldsymbol{f} >_- [0] :\Leftrightarrow \bar{f}_{\backslash\mathrm{NaN}} > 0, \qquad\qquad \boldsymbol{f} >_+ [0] :\Leftrightarrow \mathrm{NaN} \notin \boldsymbol{f} \wedge \underline{f} > 0,$$

$$\boldsymbol{f} \leq_- [0] :\Leftrightarrow \mathrm{NaN} \in \boldsymbol{f} \vee \underline{f}_{\backslash\mathrm{NaN}} \leq 0, \qquad \boldsymbol{f} \leq_+ [0] :\Leftrightarrow \bar{f}_{\backslash\mathrm{NaN}} \leq 0,$$

where $\boldsymbol{f}_{\backslash\mathrm{NaN}}$ denotes $\boldsymbol{f} \setminus \{\mathrm{NaN}\}$. Since $\mathrm{NaN} >_{\mathbb{F}} 0$ does not hold, NaN cases are disallowed by $>_+$ for the soundness, whereas they are ignored by $>_-$ for the completeness of the case where f is not NaN. On the other hand, since the negative literal $\neg(\mathrm{NaN} >_{\mathbb{F}} 0)$ holds, NaN cases are handled differently by $\leq_?$.

Let $\boldsymbol{f}$ be an interval extension of f, δ be the width of $\boldsymbol{f}$ (i.e. $\bar{f} - \underline{f}$), and $\delta_{\mathbb{F}}$ be the upward rounded value of δ in $\mathbb{F}_{eb,sb}$. When contrasted with the $\bar{\delta}$-decision procedure [12], checking the satisfiability of $\boldsymbol{f} \gg_- [0]$ is equivalent to checking whether $f \gg -\delta_{\mathbb{F}}$ is satisfiable or $f \gg 0_{\mathbb{F}}$ is not satisfiable; likewise, checking $\boldsymbol{f} \gg_+ [0]$ (with the above conditioning) is equivalent to checking whether $f \gg 0_{\mathbb{F}}$ is sat or $f \gg \delta_{\mathbb{F}}$ is unsat.

Next, we consider translation from FPA into IA. To encode FPA, some expressions in RA are also used to describe boundary conditions of intervals.

Definition 8. *The* weak extension φ^- *or* strong extension φ^+ *is translated from an FPA formula φ by the following steps:*

1. *Transform φ into a negation normal form.*
2. *Transform each literal into an interval inequality of the form $\boldsymbol{f} \gg_?^{[-]} \boldsymbol{g}$; positive (resp. negative) literals are encoded using operators $\gg_?$ (resp. $\gg_?^-$), e.g., $f < g$ into $\boldsymbol{g} >_? \boldsymbol{f}$ and $\neg(f < g)$ into $\boldsymbol{g} \leq_? \boldsymbol{f}$. Other than that, translation is straightforward (constants to point intervals, operators to their interval extensions, etc.).*
3. *When $? = +$, each variable x in φ is translated into an interval variable $\boldsymbol{x}$, appended with a constraint $\underline{x} \leq \nabla\bar{x}$ (or $\triangle\underline{x} \leq \bar{x}$). When $? = -$, variables are forced to be a point interval with constraint $\underline{x} = \bar{x}$.*

From the above definitions and lemmas, the following theorem holds.

Theorem 1. *Let φ be an FPA formula and φ^- and φ^+ be weak and strong interval extensions of φ, respectively.*

- *If φ^- is not satisfiable, then so is φ.*
- *If φ^+ is satisfiable, then so is φ.*

For example, consider an unsat FPA formula $\varphi :\Leftrightarrow x >_{\mathbb{F}} 0 \wedge -x >_{\mathbb{F}} 0$; φ^- is not satisfiable because no point intervals satisfy the two predicates; φ^+ is also not satisfiable due to the definition of $\boldsymbol{f} >_+ [0]$ (because no interval $\boldsymbol{x}$ satisfies both $\underline{x} > 0$ and $-\bar{x} > 0$). An FPA formula $\varphi' :\Leftrightarrow \neg(x >_{\mathbb{F}} 0) \wedge \neg(-x >_{\mathbb{F}} 0)$ is satisfiable with the assignment $x := 0_{\mathbb{F}}$ or $x := \mathrm{NaN}$. Its interval extensions

$\varphi'^?$ are of the form $\boldsymbol{x} \leq_? [0] \wedge -\boldsymbol{x} \leq_? [0]$ (constraint is also appended to φ'^+ in Step 3); then, φ'^- is satisfiable with $\boldsymbol{x} := [0]$ or any $\boldsymbol{x}$ containing NaN; φ'^+ is not satisfiable because the auxiliary constraint forbids $\boldsymbol{x} := [0]$ (although it can be exceptionally allowed).

5   Implementation

We have implemented a solver for FPA formulas via translation into weak and strong interval extensions; our implementation expresses IA formulas in real arithmetic (RA) and solves them using an SMT solver (we use CVC4 and Z3). In addition, we have prepared several benchmark problems for the experiments (Sect. 6). The process is illustrated in Fig. 2. In the following, we denote "IA embedded in RA" by RIA. The main process of the proposed solver is twofold: 1) Translation from FPA to RIA; 2) An incremental solving process in which the FPA precision is gradually improved to accelerate the overall process. For benchmarking, we prepared two sets of problems in FPA; also, we prepared a set by translating problems in RA into FPA or RIA.

The artifacts developed in this work are available at https://doi.org/10.5281/zenodo.6387089.

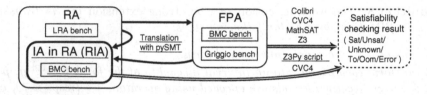

Fig. 2. Process of experiments. Underlined items are newly developed.

5.1   Encoding IA in RA

Given an FPA formula φ, our translator generates RIA descriptions that encode φ^- and φ^+. As long as φ consists of linear expressions, the translation is done in linear RA. Example translation from an FPA formula $\times(\text{RNE}, 0.1_{\text{RNE}}, x) >_{\mathbb{F}} 1$ is shown in Fig. 3, where 0.1_{RNE} is a rounded value with mode RNE. In the beginning, **Lines 1–38** define the vocabularies of RIA. At **Line 2**, we prepare the RInt datatype to represent intervals, defined as tuples of the bounds and a flag indicating whether NaN is contained. At **Lines 12–16**, the downward rounding operator is defined following Definition 5. Placeholders *ed* and *em* should be filled with concrete values. The symbol `ri.max_value` represents the maximum representable number prepared for the considered FP sort, and `ri.large_value` is constrained as `ri.large_value > 2 ri.max_value` and is used to represent $+\infty$. At **Lines 20–30**, the interval multiplication operator is defined following

```
1   ;; Definition of datatype RInt representing I*.
2   (declare-datatype RInt ((tpl (ri.l Real) (ri.u Real) (p_nan Bool) )))
3
4   ;; ...
5   ;; Definition of ▽(v).
6   (define-fun ri.r_dn ((v Real)) Real
7     (let ((w (- v (/ (ite (>= v 0) v (- v)) ed) em)))
8       (ite (>= w (- ri.max_value)) w (- ri.large_value)) ) )
9
10  ;; ...
11  ;; Definition of x + y.
12  (define-fun ri.add ((x RInt) (y RInt)) RInt
13    (let ( (l (ri.r_dn (+ (ri.l x) (ri.l y))))
14           (u (ri.r_up (+ (ri.u x) (ri.u y)))) )
15      (tpl l u (or (p_nan x) (p_nan y) (and (is_ninf x) (is_pinf y))
16                   (and (is_pinf x) (is_ninf y)) )) ) )
17
18  ;; ...
19  ;; Definition of x × y.
20  (define-fun ri.mul ((x RInt) (y RInt)) RInt
21    (ite (>= (ri.l x) 0)
22      (ite (= (ri.u x) 0)
23        (ite (and (not (is_ninf y)) (not (is_pinf y))
24                  (not (p_nan x)) (not (p_nan y)) )
25          ri.zero ;; [x] = [0]
26          ri.zero_nan ) ;; [x] = [0] and [y] = -+inf
27        (ite (>= (ri.l y) 0)
28          (ite (= (ri.u y) 0)
29            ;; Other 18 cases are omitted.
30            ) ) ) ) )
31
32  ;; ...
33  ;; Definitions of f >_ [0] and f >_ g.
34  (define-fun ri.gt0 ((f RInt)) Bool
35    (or (is_pinf f) (> (ri.u f) 0)) )
36
37  (define-fun ri.gt ((f RInt) (g RInt)) Bool
38    (or (is_pinf f) (is_ninf g) (ri.gt0 (ri.sub_exact f g))) )
39
40  ;; ...
41
42  (declare-const x RInt)
43  (assert (= (ri.l x) (ri.u x)))
44  (assert (=> (p_nan x) (= x ri.nan)))
45
46  (assert (ri.gt (ri.mul (ri.of_real (/ 1 10)) x) (ri.exact 1.0)))
```

Fig. 3. Example of IA encoding in RA (? = −).

Algorithm 1: Incremental solving process.

Input : Precision bound (eb, sb), $? \in \{-, +\}$, FPA formula φ
Output: unsat, sat or unknown

1 $\varphi^? := \text{ENCODE}(?, \varphi)$;
2 **for** $(eb', sb') :\in [(4, 4); (5, 11); (8, 24); (11, 53); (15, 113)]$ **do**
3     $eb'' := \min\{eb, eb'\}$; $sb'' := \min\{sb, sb'\}$;
4     $r := \text{CHECKSATASSUMING}(\varphi^?, \text{DEFCONSTANTS}(eb'', sb''))$;
5   **if** $(? = - \wedge r = \text{unsat}) \vee (? = + \wedge r = \text{sat})$ **then return** r **end**
6 **end**
7 **return** unknown;

---

a typical algorithm, e.g. [16]. If a NaN case may be involved, the functions compute the bounds of a normal interval obtained for the other cases and set the flag p_nan; for example, the branch at **Line 26** might involve NaN cases, i.e., x or y contains NaN, or $0 \times \mp\infty$, so it results in the interval $[0] \cup \{\text{NaN}\}$. At **Lines 34–38**, definitions of comparison operators follow the discussion in Sect. 4.2. In the definition of function ri.gt, operator ri.sub_exact is used for subtraction without widening the resulting interval. Finally, at **Lines 42–46**, the example formula is specified. The variable x is constrained to be $\underline{x} = \bar{x}$ (cf. Step 3 of Definition 8) and to be $[-\infty] \cup \{\text{NaN}\}$ when emulating the NaN assignment.[2]

Multi-precision Encoding Scheme. To encode formulas involving multi-precision FP numbers, we use a modified encoding scheme. It assumes a list of precisions (eb_i, sb_i) that appear in a formula (each precision is represented by an integer i). Then, the scheme uses a set of rounding operators prepared for each precision and modified operator functions with an additional precision parameter.

5.2 Translators

We have implemented a translator from FPA descriptions to RIA descriptions. It is realized by extending the implementation of PYSMT,[3] a PYTHON library for the SMT format containing a parser, printers, etc. We implemented support for FPA, intermediate representation of vocabularies of IA, and translation and printing scripts. Embedding in RA was implemented in the printers. The translator runs in several ways e.g. for weak or strong mode; it can also generate formulas in which precisions are abstracted for incremental solving. To facilitate the experiments in Sect. 6, we have also implemented translators from RA to FPA and RIA. The development repository is at https://github.com/dsksh/pysmt.

---

[2] For simplicity of encoded formulas, we have chosen not to handle the interval $\{\text{NaN}\}$; instead, we assign the value $[-\infty] \cup \{\text{NaN}\}$ (for φ^-) or $[-\infty, +\infty] \cup \{\text{NaN}\}$ (for φ^+).
[3] https://github.com/pysmt/pysmt.

5.3 Solver Script

We have implemented a PYTHON script to solve RIA formulas. The script runs two processes for mode $-$ or $+$ in parallel; it results in unsat or sat if either of the processes obtains a sound result; otherwise, it results in unknown. The script is based on Z3PY 4.8.12.[4] It assumes FPA with a *precision bound* (eb, sb) that represents the finest precision assumed in φ. ENCODE$(?, \varphi)$ generates an interval extension $\varphi^?$ with the abstract precision mode, which encodes while leaving the precision parameters (e.g. ed and em) undefined. The main loop of Algorithm 1 tries to solve under several precisions configured from coarser to exact ones. The CHECKSATASSUMING process invokes the RA solver of Z3 while assuming a precision bound temporarily.

5.4 Formal Verification Using Why3

We have (partially) verified the correctness of the proposed method using WHY3,[5] a verification platform with plugged-in theorem provers. Lemmas 2 and 3 have been verified as follows. We first defined a real interval type and a predicate "$x \in \boldsymbol{x}$" (where $x \in \mathbb{R}^*$ and $\boldsymbol{x} \in \mathbb{I}^*$) in WHY3's input language. Then, Lemma 2 was verified for the four operators $+, -, \times$, and $\div$. For every operator $\circ$, we implemented the interval extension as procedure $\boldsymbol{f} : \mathbb{I}^* \times \mathbb{I}^* \to \mathbb{I}^*$ and verified the Hoare triple $\{\boldsymbol{x}, \boldsymbol{y} \in \mathbb{I}^*\} \; r := \boldsymbol{f}(\boldsymbol{x}, \boldsymbol{y}) \; \{\forall m \in \mathbb{M}, x \in \boldsymbol{x} \wedge y \in \boldsymbol{y} \Rightarrow \circ(m, x, y) \in r\}$. It resulted in a number of verification conditions and they were discharged using the back-end provers i.e. ALT-ERGO[6] and COQ.[7] Next, Lemma 3 was verified for the predicates $\boldsymbol{x} \gg_?^{[\neg]} [0]$ and $\boldsymbol{x} \gg_?^{[\neg]} \boldsymbol{y}$ where $\boldsymbol{x}$ and $\boldsymbol{y}$ are limited to identifiers. We defined the comparison operators as WHY3 predicates and their properties (cf. Lemma 3) as WHY3 lemmas. The lemmas were then proved using ALT-ERGO and COQ. Ishii et al. [16] have verified interval operators, which are an overapproximation of four arithmetic operators in reals. This work used a similar basic verification process and auxiliary lemmas. The WHY3 description is available at https://github.com/dsksh/fp_rint_why3.

6 Experiments

We have conducted experiments to answer the following questions: (**RQ1**) How efficient is the proposed method when compared to the state-of-the-art FPA solvers? (**RQ2**) To what extent does the incompleteness of the method affect the results in practice? We have experimented using three sets of problem instances.

In the experiments, we solved FPA formulas via encoding into RIA. Formulas were then solved in three ways: 1) Using the solver script (Sect. 5.3) with non-incremental setting; 2) With incremental setting; 3) Using CVC4 1.8[8] with

---

[4] https://github.com/Z3Prover/z3.
[5] http://why3.lri.fr.
[6] https://alt-ergo.ocamlpro.com/.
[7] https://coq.inria.fr/.
[8] https://cvc4.github.io.

manual selection of conclusive results. We refer to our method with either of the settings 1–3 as "RIA." For comparison, we also solved with the exiting FPA solvers Z3, CVC4 (linked with SYMFPU [3]), COLIBRI v2176 [18], and MATHSAT 5.6.6[9] (with an ACDCL-based FPA solver enabled). Experiments were run on a 2.2 GHz Intel Xeon E5-2650v4 with a memory limit of 3 GB. The timeout was set to 1200 s. We did not measure the time taken for translation, but only the time taken for the solving process for FPA or RIA formulas.

6.1 Bounded Model Checking

In the first experiment, we performed the bounded model checking (BMC) of discrete-time dynamical systems as a practical use case. We aimed to prepare problem instances that require precision and investigate the extent to which the results become unknown. In BMC with a bound $k \in \mathbb{N}$, paths of a target system of length k were encoded into an FPA formula φ in $\mathbb{F}_{11,53}$ (rounding modes were left unspecified), and we verified whether an output o of a path reaches a threshold th by checking the satisfiability of $\varphi \wedge o \geq th$. As target systems, we considered a 1D feedback integrator, a 2D second-order filter, and a rotation on a 2D plane; a transition of the systems involves 2, 5 or 6 arithmetic operations, respectively.

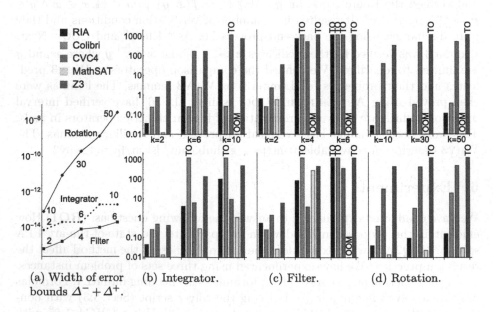

(a) Width of error bounds $\Delta^- + \Delta^+$.   (b) Integrator.   (c) Filter.   (d) Rotation.

Fig. 4. Results of BMC. Chart (a) shows required perturbations to make each BMC conclusive. (b)–(d) show the execution time for unsat (upper) and sat (lower) instances. "TO" and "OOM" represent executions resulted in timeout and out of memory.

---

[9] https://mathsat.fbk.eu.

For each system, we performed BMC with three ks; results are shown in Fig. 4. We checked for each system and k a boundary threshold $\tilde{th}$ whose perturbation switches the satisfiability. We then obtained the *error bounds* $\Delta^- < 0$ and $\Delta^+ > 0$ such that the proposed method outputs unsat or sat when $th := \tilde{th} - \Delta^?$. Finally, we solved the RIA or FPA formulas encoding the unsat and sat instances perturbated for Δ^- and Δ^+. We compared the execution time of the prepared solvers; wherein, the non-incremental RIA solver (setting 1) was used to have best results since every instance requires fine precision.

6.2 Benchmark Problems

The second experiment is based on the following two sets of benchmark problems.

– *Linear arithmetic (LA) benchmark.* For evaluation in a continuous domain, which is essentially the subject of FPA, we translated instances in the QF_LRA section of the SMT-LIB benchmarks[10] into FPA instances by simply converting data sorts (from $\mathbb{R}$ to $\mathbb{F}_{11,53}$), operators, etc. Each real constant is converted to an exact FP constant if possible, otherwise they are converted to a rounded value. Since the set is large, we picked the instances whose originals

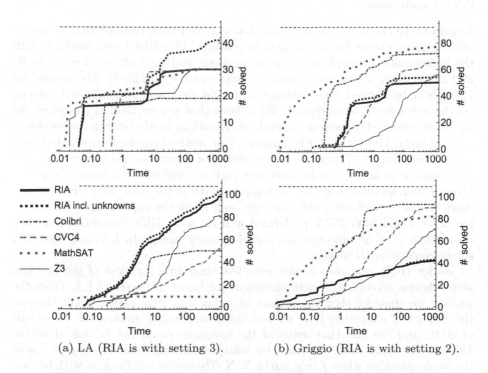

Fig. 5. Results on benchmark problems (unsat (upper) and sat (lower) instances).

10 http://smtlib.cs.uiowa.edu/benchmarks.shtml.

were solvable by Z3 within the 30s.[11] Because the proposed method abstracts the rounding modes of FPA operators, we parameterized the rounding modes in formulas and represented them by unconstrained variables. Also, every free and unassigned variable was asserted that it is not NaN.

– *Griggio benchmark.* The Griggio suite, taken from the SMT-LIB benchmarks, offers challenging problems for bit-blasting solvers and has been used in several experiments [3,18,31]. Here, we use the suite as a standard FPA problem set to evaluate our solver. Some instances involve multiple precisions and concrete rounding modes are given in most cases.

Figure 5 shows the cactus plots of the number of solved instances versus time (with semi-logarithmic scale), assuming each instance is solved in parallel. For our solver, results counting unknowns are also shown with dotted lines. The setting 3 (using CVC4) or 2 (incremental) solved more instances than the others for LA or Griggio, respectively. For instances for which the solution was previously unknown, the solution obtained by any solvers was assumed to be correct; two instances of LA were excluded because the outputs did not match among the solvers.

6.3   Discussions

Regarding **RQ1**, we obtained results that were better or comparable to those of other solvers, except for the Griggio benchmark. Our RIA-based method (with the appropriate settings) solved the most unsat and sat instances for the BMC and LA sets (in which the rounding modes are not specified). The results for Griggio, a benchmark that includes instances designed for dedicated solvers, on the other hand, were dismal. We believe that our method is inefficient for instances where the decision depends on rounding mode settings or combinations of normal and special FP numbers. Our method can be incorporated with precise encoding of FP numbers e.g. handling of exact rounded values as in [17]. Development of an efficient method with such a translation is a future challenge. Overall, our method was able to compete with other dedicated FPA solvers. Also, no solver performed outstandingly well in all the experiments. For example, CVC4 and MATHSAT performed well for some BMC instances, but they resulted in a lot of timeouts and out-of-memory errors. In LA, only the RIA solver could solve 21 instances.

As for **RQ2**, unknown results were less than 10% for most of the problem sets, whereas around 30% were unknowns for unsat instances of LA. From the results, we consider that the impact of unknowns were rather small because the impact of execution time on scalability was much greater (cf. the result of BMC and the fact that many of the instances could not be solved within 1200 s). The main cause was that we inhibit falsifying inequalities $f \gg_\sqsupseteq^\sim g$ of the weak extension when f or g can be NaN. This cause can be dealt with by case

---

[11] Instances using the `ite` function were omitted; many of `LassoRanker` and `meti-tarski` instances were removed to balance the number.

analyses, e.g., detection of assignments to a free variable, and we have actually implemented some analyses in our translators. Otherwise, unknowns occur more often as the number of operations increases and by the *wrapping effect* (cf. the rotation system in BMC). Reduction of errors using e.g. Affine form instead of interval vectors will be a future work. In addition, we use rounding operators in Definition 5 based on a mild estimation of errors. We consider that the use of linear formulas improved the efficiency of the solving process while providing sufficient accuracy.

The RIA incremental solver performed better than the non-incremental solver using Z3 for Griggio; for LA, non-incremental solving using CVC4 was better than incremental probably due to the performance of CVC4 in solving linear formulas. In BMC, non-incremental performed better than incremental because all the instances required double precision. When it is decidable with a coarser precision and/or the lemmas learned along the way accelerate the solving process, the incremental solver outperforms.

7 Conclusion

We have proposed an IA logic to approximate FPA formulas and a dedicated solver using RA solvers of CVC4 and Z3. Despite using an off-the-shelf RA solver, we obtained experimental results that were competitive with those of other FPA solvers; we confirmed that our solver is effective for a subset of FPA (BMC and LA) where rounding modes are parameterized. Although the solver was shown inefficient for the FPA benchmark Griggio, it solved the most numbers of instances for two such problem sets.

Future research issues include dealing with unknown cases, improving performance with e.g. ACDCL [2] and distance constraints [18], and to expand the supported FPA predicates.

References

1. Bagnara, R., Bagnara, A., Biselli, F., Chiari, M., Gori, R.: Correct approximation of IEEE 754 floating-point arithmetic for program verification. Constraints **308**, 1–41 (2022). https://doi.org/10.1007/s10601-021-09322-9
2. Brain, M., D'Silva, V., Griggio, A., Haller, L., Kroening, D.: Deciding floating-point logic with abstract conflict driven clause learning. Formal Methods Syst. Des. **45**(2), 213–245 (2013). https://doi.org/10.1007/s10703-013-0203-7
3. Brain, M., Schanda, F., Sun, Y.: Building better bit-blasting for floating-point problems. In: Vojnar, T., Zhang, L. (eds.) TACAS 2019. LNCS, vol. 11427, pp. 79–98. Springer, Cham (2019). https://doi.org/10.1007/978-3-030-17462-0_5
4. Brain, M., Tinelli, C., Rüemmer, P., Wahl, T.: An automatable formal semantics for IEEE-754 floating-point arithmetic. In: Symposium on Computer Arithmetic, pp. 160–167. IEEE (2015). https://doi.org/10.1109/ARITH.2015.26
5. Brillout, A., Kroening, D., Wahl, T.: Mixed abstractions for floating-point arithmetic. In: FMCAD, pp. 69–76. IEEE (2009)

6. Clarke, E., Kroening, D., Lerda, F.: A tool for checking ANSI-C programs. In: Jensen, K., Podelski, A. (eds.) TACAS 2004. LNCS, vol. 2988, pp. 168–176. Springer, Heidelberg (2004). https://doi.org/10.1007/978-3-540-24730-2_15

7. Conchon, S., Iguernlala, M., Ji, K., Melquiond, G., Fumex, C.: A three-tier strategy for reasoning about floating-point numbers in SMT. In: Majumdar, R., Kunčak, V. (eds.) CAV 2017. LNCS, vol. 10427, pp. 419–435. Springer, Cham (2017). https://doi.org/10.1007/978-3-319-63390-9_22

8. Darulova, E., Izycheva, A., Nasir, F., Ritter, F., Becker, H., Bastian, R.: Daisy - framework for analysis and optimization of numerical programs (tool paper). In: Beyer, D., Huisman, M. (eds.) TACAS 2018. LNCS, vol. 10805, pp. 270–287. Springer, Cham (2018). https://doi.org/10.1007/978-3-319-89960-2_15

9. Daumas, M., Melquiond, G.: Generating formally certified bounds on values and round-off errors. In: 6th Conference on Real Numbers and Computers, pp. 55–70 (2004)

10. Franzle, M., Herde, C., Ratschan, S., Schubert, T.: Efficient solving of large non-linear arithmetic constraint systems with complex Boolean structure. JSAT **1**, 209–236 (2007)

11. Gao, S., Avigad, J., Clarke, E.M.: δ-Complete decision procedures for satisfiability over the reals. In: Gramlich, B., Miller, D., Sattler, U. (eds.) IJCAR 2012. LNCS (LNAI), vol. 7364, pp. 286–300. Springer, Heidelberg (2012). https://doi.org/10.1007/978-3-642-31365-3_23

12. Gao, S., Avigad, J., Clarke, E.M.: Delta-decidability over the reals. In: Proceedings of Symposium on Logic in Computer Science (LICS), pp. 305–314 (2012)

13. Goubault, E., Putot, S.: Static analysis of numerical algorithms. In: Yi, K. (ed.) SAS 2006. LNCS, vol. 4134, pp. 18–34. Springer, Heidelberg (2006). https://doi.org/10.1007/11823230_3

14. Haller, L., Griggio, A., Brain, M., Kroening, D.: Deciding floating-point logic with systematic abstraction. In: FMCAD, pp. 131–140. IEEE (2012)

15. IEEE: 754–2008 - IEEE Standard for Floating-Point Arithmetic (2008)

16. Ishii, D., Yabu, T.: Computer-assisted verification of four interval arithmetic operators. J. Comput. Appl. Math. **377** (2020). https://doi.org/10.1016/j.cam.2020.112893

17. Leeser, M., Mukherjee, S., Ramachandran, J., Wahl, T.: Make it real: effective floating-point reasoning via exact arithmetic. In: DATE, pp. 7–10. EDAA (2014). https://doi.org/10.7873/DATE2014.130

18. Marre, B., Bobot, F., Chihani, Z.: Real behavior of floating point numbers. In: SMT Workshop, pp. 1–12 (2017)

19. Michel, C., Rueher, M., Lebbah, Y.: Solving constraints over floating-point numbers. In: Walsh, T. (ed.) CP 2001. LNCS, vol. 2239, pp. 524–538. Springer, Heidelberg (2001). https://doi.org/10.1007/3-540-45578-7_36

20. Moore, R.E.: Interval Analysis. Prentice-Hall, Upper Saddle River (1966)

21. Muller, J.M., et al.: Handbook of Floating-Point Arithmetic, 2nd edn. Birkhäuser, Basel (2018)

22. Older, W., Benhamou, F.: Programming in CLP (BNR). In: Position Papers for the First Workshop on Principles and Practice of Constraint Programming, pp. 239–249 (1993)

23. Ramachandran, J., Wahl, T.: Integrating proxy theories and numeric model lifting for floating-point arithmetic. In: FMCAD, pp. 153–160 (2016). https://doi.org/10.1109/FMCAD.2016.7886674

24. Salvia, R., Titolo, L., Feliú, M.A., Moscato, M.M., Muñoz, C.A., Rakamarić, Z.: A mixed real and floating-point solver. In: Badger, J.M., Rozier, K.Y. (eds.) NFM 2019. LNCS, vol. 11460, pp. 363–370. Springer, Cham (2019). https://doi.org/10.1007/978-3-030-20652-9_25
25. Scheibler, K., Neubauer, F., Mahdi, A., Franzle, M., Teige, T., Bienm, T.: Accurate ICP-based floating-point reasoning. In: FMCAD, pp. 177–184 (2016). https://doi.org/10.1109/FMCAD.2016.7886677
26. Solovyev, A., Baranowski, M.S., Briggs, I., Jacobsen, C., Rakamarić, Z., Gopalakrishnan, G.: Rigorous estimation of floating-point round-off errors with symbolic Taylor expansions. ACM Trans. Program. Lang. Syst. **41**(1) (2018). https://doi.org/10.1145/3230733
27. Titolo, L., Feliú, M.A., Moscato, M., Muñoz, C.A.: An abstract interpretation framework for the round-off error analysis of floating-point programs. In: Dillig, I., Palsberg, J. (eds.) VMCAI 2018. LNCS, vol. 10747, pp. 516–537. Springer, Cham (2018). https://doi.org/10.1007/978-3-319-73721-8_24
28. Tucker, W.: Validated Numerics. Princeton University Press, Princeton (2011)
29. Tung, V.X., Van Khanh, T., Ogawa, M.: raSAT: an SMT solver for polynomial constraints. Formal Methods Syst. Des. **51**(3), 462–499 (2017). https://doi.org/10.1007/s10703-017-0284-9
30. Zeljić, A., Backeman, P., Wintersteiger, C.M., Rümmer, P.: Exploring approximations for floating-point arithmetic using UppSAT. In: Galmiche, D., Schulz, S., Sebastiani, R. (eds.) IJCAR 2018. LNCS (LNAI), vol. 10900, pp. 246–262. Springer, Cham (2018). https://doi.org/10.1007/978-3-319-94205-6_17
31. Zitoun, H., Michel, C., Michel, L., Rueher, M.: An efficient constraint based framework for handling floating point SMT problems (2020). https://doi.org/10.48550/arXiv.2002.12441
32. Zitoun, H., Michel, C., Rueher, M., Michel, L.: Search strategies for floating point constraint systems. In: Beck, J.C. (ed.) CP 2017. LNCS, vol. 10416, pp. 707–722. Springer, Cham (2017). https://doi.org/10.1007/978-3-319-66158-2_45

Synthesis of Optimal Defenses for System Architecture Design Model in MaxSMT

Baoluo Meng[✉] ⓘ, Arjun Viswanathan, William Smith, Abha Moitra, Kit Siu, and Michael Durling

GE Research, Niskayuna, NY 12309, USA
{baoluo.meng,arjun.viswanathan,william.d.smith,moitraa,siu,
durling}@ge.com

Abstract. Attack-Defense Trees (ADTrees) are widely used in the security analysis of software systems. In this paper, we introduce a novel approach to analyze system architecture models via ADTrees and to synthesize an optimal cost defense solution using MaxSMT. We generate an ADTree from the Architecture Analysis and Design Language (AADL) model with its possible attacks, and implemented defenses. We analyze these ADTrees to see if they satisfy their cyber-requirements. We then translate the ADTree into a set of logical formulas, that encapsulate both the logical structure of the tree, and the constraints on the cost of implementing the corresponding defenses, such that a minimization query to the MaxSMT solver returns a set of defenses that mitigate all possible attacks with minimal cost. We provide an initial evaluation of our tool on a delivery drone system model which shows promising results.

Keywords: AADL system architecture model · Attack-defense tree analysis · Synthesis of optimal defenses · MaxSMT

1 Introduction

System security has attracted worldwide attention as society has grown increasingly dependent on computer-based systems. To address the security concerns of systems, many risk analysis techniques have been introduced over the years in order to identify potential system failure and mitigate risks before the system is fielded. *Attack trees* [15] are a prominent methodology to visually depict the security vulnerabilities of a system. They have been used in the analysis of threats against systems in the fields of defense and aerospace. Attack trees capture attacks in a tree structure, where the root node represents the attacker's goal and child nodes refine the goal with details involved in achieving the goal. *Attack-defense trees (ADTrees)* [13] extend attack trees with the notion of defenses against attacks, with the objective of reducing the consequences of attacks. In an ADTree, defense and attack nodes are distinguished node types, and in addition to refinements of nodes via children of the same type of node, child nodes can be *counter-measures* of the opposite kind of parent node. Such trees are

© Springer Nature Switzerland AG 2022
J. V. Deshmukh et al. (Eds.): NFM 2022, LNCS 13260, pp. 752–770, 2022.
https://doi.org/10.1007/978-3-031-06773-0_40

able to capture both the attacks and the defenses of a system in an adversarial model, and as such, can be used to analyze the sufficiency of attack mitigation techniques of the system.

Implementing defenses requires various amount of effort, time, and money. A challenging problem is to select a set of defenses that is able to mitigate all threats while incurring minimal cost of implementation. In this work, we use MaxSMT solvers to synthesize a set of optimal-cost defenses that mitigate all possible attacks on a system. A prototype was implemented in a tool called VERDICT— in conjunction with the model-based architectural analysis (MBAA) component, model-based architectural synthesis (MBAS) calculates a set of defenses for all known attacks at minimal cost. We make the following contributions in this paper.

- We describe an approach that converts an AADL system architecture model to an attack-defense tree and an evaluation of these ADTrees in terms of a set of cyber-requirements.
- We encode the ADTree along with the costs of implementing defenses as a MaxSMT problem so that the solver can find a least-cost defense solution that satisfies all requirements.
- We present the analysis and synthesis features in the VERDICT toolchain which provides an implementation of the above functionalities.
- We show an evaluation of the synthesis capability on a high-fidelity AADL model of a delivery drone system.

Section 2 presents our specifications of attacks, defenses, and attack-defense trees. Section 3 presents a translation of AADL models to ADTrees and our method of analyzing whether an ADTree satisfies its requirements. Section 4 describes the interaction with the SMT solver in determining a minimum-cost set of defenses for the system. Section 5 is an evaluation of the VERDICT toolchain on an AADL model of a delivery drone system. Section 6 discusses some related work and Sect. 7 discusses directions our work can move in the future, along with a summary.

2   Preliminaries

In this section, we formalize our problem and solution space. We consider attacks from the MITRE Common Attack Pattern Enumeration and Classification (CAPEC) library [1] that targets embedded systems and defenses (controls) from the National Institute of Standards and Technology's (NIST's) 800-53 security standard [2]. A toy drone example is used through the paper to illustrate various features.

2.1   Attack and Defense Specification

This work is based on two standards drafted by the Radio Technical Commission for Aeronautics (RTCA)—DO-326, the Airworthiness Security Process Specification [3] and DO-356, the Airworthiness Security Methods and Considerations [4]

– both providing guidance against threats to aircraft systems. The standards specify the acceptable level of risk corresponding to the level of severity of successful attacks. The severity of successful attacks is categorized into 5 levels based on their effects on the aircraft, crew, and passengers: Catastrophic, Hazardous, Major, Minor, and No Effect. These levels, along with the corresponding levels of risk acceptable in the system, are presented in the first two columns of Table 1.

Table 1. Mapping between the severity of consequence, acceptable level of risk, design assurance level (DAL), DAL score (Score) and development objectives (with independence).

Severity level	Acceptable level of risk	DAL	Score	Objective (W/Independence)
Catastrophic	1×10^{-9}	A	9	66 (25)
Hazardous	1×10^{-7}	B	7	65 (14)
Major	1×10^{-5}	C	5	57 (2)
Minor	1×10^{-3}	D	3	28 (2)
No effect	1	E	0	0 (0)

We represent by L the set of severity levels, and by ρ the set of acceptable risk levels. The top-level event of an ADTree represents the attacker's goal, which is measured in terms of confidentiality (C), integrity (I) and availability (A) of the outports of the system. The attacker's goal is to sabotage the system by compromising its components. Attacks on components are ultimately propagated to the outports of the system through internal connections. The system fails if the CIAs of its outports are compromised. To mitigate attacks, the system designer has to implement defenses in components with various degrees of rigor, which can prevent failure of the system. The previously mentioned standards map the rigor of defense implementation, called *Design Assurance Levels (DALs)*, to a security consideration score or DAL score—columns 3 and 4 of Table 1. DAL A is the highest rigor defense and E is the lowest. DALs originated in DO-178 and were reused in DO-254. These standards were developed to ensure that software and complex hardware were developed with enough rigor and could be proved to be absent of bugs with potentially severe consequences. To bring the system within an acceptable risk level of attacks, and to prevent the system from failing with the associated severity level, its developers need to implement the component to the respective DAL score and meet appropriate development objectives from the fifth column. For example, if the failure of software can have a Catastrophic consequence, one must show compliance to 66 objectives as part of the software development process, 25 of which need to be performed by independent developers. The implementation of defenses incurs efforts and cost, which increase with the DAL score, and the goal of this work is to synthesize a set of defenses that mitigate all attacks at an optimal (minimal) cost.

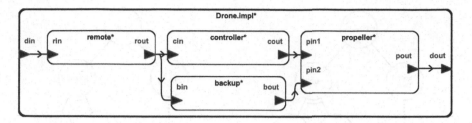

Fig. 1. The AADL structure diagram for the toy drone model

We will use CIA to denote the set consisting of the properties confidentiality (C), integrity (I) and availability (A) ($CIA = \{C, I, A\}$), and DAL, the set of possible DAL scores ($DAL = \{0, 3, 5, 7, 9\}$). We also consider the sets: A of possible attacks, D of possible defenses, and S of components of a system.

2.2 Attack-Defense Trees

ADTrees are rooted, labeled, finite trees that represent scenarios of security attacks against a system, and the countermeasures taken against these attacks. The nodes of an ADTree are either *attack nodes*—represented as red circles—or *defense nodes*—represented as green rectangles, and the nodes are labeled either with attack or defense goals, or with logical gates that connect these goals. A node's children represent either *refinements* (represented by straight line edges) of the same node type or *countermeasures* (dotted line edges) of the opposite node type. Refinements can either be conjunctive, (denoted in diagrams with an arc below the parent node) in which case, all the refinements' goals must be achieved for the parent's goal to be achieved; or disjunctive, where at least one of the refined goals must be achieved for the parent's goal to be achieved. Non-refined nodes (leaves) are called *basic actions*. The root of an ADTree represents the attacker's goal, which can be refined down to a logical formula over the basic actions (leaves) by expanding on the refinements performed by nodes (conjunctions and disjunctions).

Example 1. Consider the following model that abstracts a simple drone. The model is represented using an architecture diagram in Fig. 1. A remote control allows the user to direct the drone. The drone consists of a controller that implements its logic, and a propeller that helps the drone move. As a security measure, the drone consists of a backup controller which implements a much simpler logic than the main controller. The user of the remote may invoke the single functionality of the backup which brings the drone back to its base.

A wireless connection connects the remote to the controller and to the backup, both of which have a wired connection to the propeller. Figure 2a shows the ADTree that models the attacks and defenses of the drone system, supposing that we care about the integrity of the drone's propeller, that is, we want the propeller to move as instructed by the remote, and return back safely to the owner if that isn't feasible. Consider the following attacks:

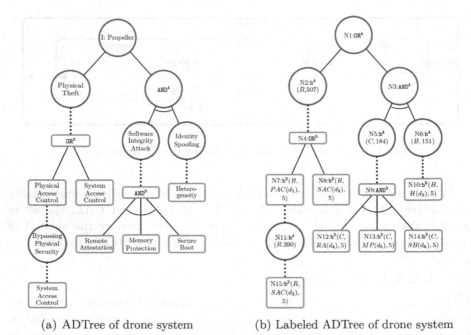

(a) ADTree of drone system   (b) Labeled ADTree of drone system

Fig. 2. Example toy drone system

1. Physical Theft Attack (CAPEC–507) on the remote.
2. A combination of a Software Integrity Attack (CAPEC–184) on the controller, and an Identity Spoofing Attack (CAPEC–151) on the backup controller.

Either Physical Access Control or System Access Control of the remote can defend against Physical Theft, but CAPEC–390 (Bypassing Physical Security) is a *dependent attack* that becomes applicable once Physical Access Control is implemented, and can only be defended against by implementing System Access Control. Three defenses—Remote Attestation, Memory Protection, and Secure Boot—are necessary for the controller to mitigate CAPEC-184 and Heterogeneity alone implemented on the backup controller can protect it against the identity spoofing attack. In Fig. 2b, we label the nodes, attacks, and defenses, and also use the notation from our ADTree definition (Definition 1). We also give label R for the remote sub-system, C for the controller, and B for the backup controller. All defenses are implemented to DAL-score 5.

Definition 1. *An* ADTree T *is generated by the following grammar.*

$$T \rightarrow T^A \mid T^D$$
$$T^A \rightarrow b^A(s, a) \mid OR^A(T^A, \ldots T^A) \mid AND^A(T^A, \ldots, T^A) \mid C^A(T^A, T^D)$$
$$T^D \rightarrow b^D(s, d, \delta) \mid OR^D(T^D, \ldots T^D) \mid AND^D(T^D, \ldots T^D) \mid C^D(T^D, T^A)$$

Superscripts A and D represent attack and defense entities, respectively. T represents terms or trees, OR encapsulates disjunctive refinements of a node, AND *represents conjunctive refinements of a node, and C encapsulates the action of a node and its countermeasure. b represents basic actions—for attack nodes, they are parameterized by a component and an attack; and for defense nodes, they are parameterized by a component, a defense, and implemented DAL-score. An attack tree, denoted T^A, is an ADTree with root of type A and a defense tree, denoted T^D, is a tree with root of type D. We define a function root that returns the root node of an ADTree.*

We use an inductive definition of ADTree in Definition 1 from Kordy et al. [14]. Defenses are implemented to a particular DAL-score, and the defense nodes (that are basic actions) are parameterized by this DAL-score, along with the component that they defend and the defense itself. DAL-scores can only take values from column 4 of Table 1. Although our definition allows for any kind of ADTree, in practice, we only consider ADTrees with attack root nodes. This suits our goal of using ADTrees to analyze the attacker's actions. An interesting feature of our ADTrees is that we allow repetition of defense and attack nodes. That is, multiple b^A and b^D nodes in our trees can have the same label $((s, a)$ or $(s, d, \delta))$. The only restriction we place is that when two b^A or b^D nodes have the same label, their child-node structure must be identical.

3 ADTree Analysis

In this section, we describe how our tool uses ADTrees to analyze a system architecture modeled using AADL (Architecture Analysis and Design Language) [10], which provides a framework and language for early analyses of a system's architecture with respect to performance-critical properties. Our tool builds an ADTree from an AADL model, a specification of possible attacks, possible defenses, implemented defenses, and cyber-requirements to satisfy. This tree is evaluated in terms of the likelihood of success of an arbitrary attacker, given a set of defenses.

3.1 Defense Models

Within VERDICT, the analysis of the AADL model receives information primarily from the Security Threat Evaluation and Mitigation (STEM) component [17]. STEM identifies possible CAPEC attacks, possible NIST-800-53 defenses and defenses implemented in the components of the system. STEM provides this data in the form of a defense model $\mathbb{M}$ with two types of relations: an implemented defense model $\mathbb{M}_I$ and an applicable defense model $\mathbb{M}_A$.

A *defense model* $\mathbb{M}$ is a relation containing tuples that relate components of a system to defense–DAL-score pairs, and attack–CIA pairs. Each tuple signifies the applicability of an attack (if any) to a component, and either the applicability or implementation of a set of defenses to the same component to respective DAL-scores. We distinguish 3 types of defense models, and define two of them as follows. The third, the synthesized defense model, is defined later.

1. An *implemented defense model* $\mathbb{M}_{\mathbb{I}}$ represents defenses currently implemented in the system. We say $(s, a, \gamma, \Delta) \in \mathbb{M}_{\mathbb{I}}$ iff in component s, γ attack a is applicable, and for each $(d, \delta) \in \Delta$, defense d is implemented to DAL-score δ, where $s \in S, a \in A, \gamma \in CIA, d \in D, \delta \in DAL$.

2. An *applicable defense model* $\mathbb{M}_{\mathbb{A}}$ represents defenses applicable in the system. We say $(s, a, \gamma, \Delta) \in \mathbb{M}_{\mathbb{A}}$ iff in component s, γ attack a is applicable, and for each $(d, \delta) \in \Delta$, defense d is applicable to DAL-score δ.

In the defense models that it provides, STEM guarantees that basic action nodes with the same labels have the same sub-trees, as required by our mechanism in Sect. 2.2.

Example 2. Consider the ADTree from Example 1 in terms of the following cyber requirement: $q : (d_{out} : \mathtt{I})$ with Major (1×10^{-5}) severity level. In other words, q requires the integrity of outport d_{out} to be resilient to attacks of Major severity level. While the tree from Fig. 2 models the applicable defense model, we show two different implementations of defenses. The applicable defense model $\mathbb{M}_{\mathbb{A}}$ (Fig. 2) consists of the following set of tuples:
$\{(R, CAPEC\text{--}507, \mathtt{I}, \{(d_1, 5)\}), (R, CAPEC\text{--}507, \mathtt{I}, \{(d_2, 5)\}),$
$(B, CAPEC\text{--}151, \mathtt{I}, \{(d_3, 5)\}), (C, CAPEC\text{--}184, \mathtt{I}, \{(d_4, 5), (d_5, 5), (d_6, 5)\}\}.$
The implemented defense model $\mathbb{M}_{\mathbb{I}}$ consists of the following set of tuples.
$\{(R, CAPEC\text{--}507, \mathtt{I}, \{(d_2, 7)\}), (C, CAPEC\text{--}184, \mathtt{I}, \{(d_4, 9), (d_5, 7), (d_6, 5)\})\}$
A second implementation is specified using $\mathbb{M}_{\mathbb{I}}'$ as follows.
$\{(R, CAPEC\text{--}507, \mathtt{I}, \{(d_1, 5)\}), \{(C, CAPEC\text{--}184, \mathtt{I}, \{(d_4, 3)\}),$

3.2 ADTree Construction

In this subsection, we briefly explain the ADTree construction algorithm `ADTree`, without fully specifying it (doing this in an extended version of the paper[1]). `ADTree` operates on the following parameters:

1. *mod*, the AADL model of a system, that specifies ports P, connections C, components S, and cyber-relations R between ports of the system, where cyber relations are internal to a component, and specify how the conjunctions or disjunctions CIA vulnerabilities of inports propagate to the CIA vulnerabilities of outports. An example cyber relation is `in1:I or in2:I => out1:I`, which states that compromise of the integrity of `in1` or `in2` would lead to the compromise of the integrity of `out1`.

2. Q, the set of cyber requirements, where each cyber-requirement q is a logical formula over (p, γ) atoms, $p \in P, \gamma \in CIA$, with a corresponding level of severity $l \in L$.

3. $\mathbb{M}$, a defense model.

---

[1] Extended version of the paper: https://github.com/baoluomeng/2022_NFM/tree/main/synthesis_extended.pdf.

and returns an ADTree T corresponding to the requirements in Q on the AADL model *mod* considering attacks and defenses in M. The details about the language (VERDICT annex) specifying cyber relations and cyber requirements can be found in Meng et al. [16].

The algorithm constructs an ADTree for each requirement, and combines them using an OR^A node. The tree for each requirement is constructed by backtracing through the connections in the model, starting at the relevant outport, and checking for the CIA property specified by the requirement. During backtracing the logical structure of the requirements and cyber-relations are reflected in the logical structures of the corresponding ADTrees. Finally, the algorithm also runs through the constructed tree to remove any redundant nodes.

Example 3. Using the cyber requirements Q consisting of the single requirement q: (d_{out} : I) with Major severity level and the applicable defense model from Example 1, ADTree can construct the ADTree in Fig. 2b.

3.3   ADTree Evaluation

An ADTree represents the goal of the attacker, and an evaluation of the tree specifies the likelihood of success of the attacker in achieving this goal. The evaluation of the ADTree was introduced by Siu et al. [18]. We formalize it as a recursive function M as follows, and call it *measure*.

$$
\begin{aligned}
M(T) := \text{match } T \text{ with} \\
\mid\ &b^A(s,a) \rightarrow 1 \\
\mid\ &b^D(s,d,\delta) \rightarrow 1e^{-\delta} \\
\mid\ &OR^A(T_1,\ldots,T_n) \rightarrow \max(M(T_1),\ldots,M(T_n)) \\
\mid\ &OR^D(T_1,\ldots,T_n) \rightarrow \min(M(T_1),\ldots,M(T_n)) \\
\mid\ &AND^A(T_1,\ldots,T_n) \rightarrow \min(M(T_1),\ldots,M(T_n)) \\
\mid\ &AND^D(T_1,\ldots,T_n) \rightarrow \max(M(T_1),\ldots,M(T_n)) \\
\mid\ &C^A(b^A(s,a),T^D) \rightarrow \min(M(b^A(s,a)),M(T^D)) \\
\mid\ &C^D(b^D(s,d,\delta),T^A) \rightarrow \max(M(b^D(s,d,\delta)),M(T^A))
\end{aligned}
$$

Basic attack nodes are always assigned a value of 1 for likelihood of a successful attack. Assigning a number to the level of attack is quite difficult and would hold true for only a short period of time, and not for the lifetime of a system. According to Javaid et al. [12], the issue with deciding the likelihood of various attacks is that "the risk values may be different for different researchers according to the information available and level of analysis. Hence, more emphasis should be put on countermeasures for threats which receive high priority." Thus, we chose to assume a worst-case likelihood for attacks (from the point of view of defending the system) and give more fine-grained scores for defenses.

Satisfaction. A cyber-requirement q specifies the severity level l of a CIA of an outport of the system. A defense model $\mathbb{M}$ corresponding to AADL model *mod satisfies* q, $\mathbb{M} \vdash q$, if $M(T_q) \leq \rho$ where $T_q = \text{ADTree}(mod, q, \mathbb{M})$ and ρ is the acceptable level of risk corresponding to l from Table 1. In this case, we also say that T_q satisfies q, or $T_q \vdash q$. Intuitively, implementing the defenses from $\mathbb{M}$ in *mod* results in an ADTree whose attacks are mitigated. Satisfaction of a requirement by a model (resp. ADTree) is naturally extended to a set of requirements.

$$\mathbb{M} \vdash Q \quad \text{if } \forall q \in Q, \ \mathbb{M} \vdash q$$

A tree constructed from $\mathbb{M}_A$ satisfies its requirements, by definition, while one constructed from $\mathbb{M}_I$ may or may not.

Example 4. The following are the evaluations of the ADTrees from our applicable and implemented defense models. $M(\text{ADTree}(mod, q, \mathbb{M}_A)) = 1 \times 10^{-5}$; $M(\text{ADTree}(mod, q, \mathbb{M}_I)) = 1 \times 10^{-7}$; $M(\text{ADTree}(mod, q, \mathbb{M}_I')) = 1$.

Thus, $\mathbb{M}_A$ and $\mathbb{M}_I$ satisfy q while $\mathbb{M}_I'$ does not. An evaluation using the applicable defense model is always within the level of severity corresponding to the requirement. The evaluation of $\mathbb{M}_I'$ shows that the implementation does not succeed in stopping the attacker because the bypassing physical security attack is not defended at all, and neither of CAPEC–184 and CAPEC–151 are defended sufficiently. $\mathbb{M}_I$, on the other hand, is able to satisfy the requirement.

4   ADTree Synthesis

While the goal of analysis is to construct an ADTree from an AADL model and determine whether the cyber-requirements are satisfied (alternatively, whether the attacks corresponding to the ADTree are mitigated), synthesis constructs an optimal set of defenses based on a cost model for these defenses and (possibly) on the currently implemented defenses.

We define the concepts of synthesized defense models, and cost models.

Definition 2. *Synthesized Defense Model. A synthesized defense model* $\mathbb{M}_S$ *is the set of optimal defenses to implement, output by synthesis. If* $(s, a, \gamma, \Delta) \in \mathbb{M}_S$, *then for each* $(d, \delta) \in \Delta$, *the implementation of defense d to DAL-score δ in s is part of the optimal solution to mitigate γ attack a.*

Definition 3. *Cost Model. The cost model* $\mathbb{C}$ *associates a cost with each component–defense–DAL-score triple from the tuples in a defense model. Given defense d, sub-component s, and DAL-score δ, the cost of implementing d in s to δ is the non-negative real number represented by* $\mathbb{C}(s, d, \delta)$.

$$\mathbb{C} : S \times D \times DAL \rightarrow \mathbb{R}_{\geq 0}$$

We define the cost model of a defense model $\mathbb{M}$ as follows.

$$\mathbb{C}(\mathbb{M}) = \forall (s, a, \gamma, \Delta) \in \mathbb{M}, \sum_{(d, \delta) \in \Delta} \mathbb{C}(s, d, \delta)$$

The only restriction we place on cost models is that costs must be monotonically increasing with respect to the DAL-scores, that is, $\delta_i > \delta_j \rightarrow \mathbb{C}(s, d, \delta_i) \geq \mathbb{C}(s, d, \delta_j)$, for any $s \in S$, $d \in D$, and $\delta_i, \delta_j \in DAL$. This reflects the expectation that higher DALs are more expensive to implement (or at least, not cheaper). The synthesis problem seeks an optimal solution with respect to $\mathbb{C}$. The cost may represent financial cost, time required for implementation, or perhaps some compound or abstract definition of cost. For simplicity, one might consider a cost model that assigns the DAL-score as the cost of a component–defense–DAL-score triple, $\mathbb{C}(s, d, \delta) = \delta$ (for arbitrary s, d, and δ).

Example 5. Recollect the requirement q for our example drone system:

$$q : (d_{out} : \text{I}) \text{ with Major } (1 \times 10^{-5}) \text{ severity level}$$

As we informally stated in Example 4, one implementation of the defenses doesn't satisfy q, another does, and the applicable defenses also satisfy q, by definition.

$$\mathbb{M}_A \vdash q$$
$$\mathbb{M}_I \vdash q$$
$$\mathbb{M}'_I \nvdash q$$

Now, we define a cost model $\mathbb{C}$ for the drone system.

$$\mathbb{C}(s, d, \delta) = \begin{cases} 2\delta, & \text{for } (Remote, d_1, \delta) \\ 2\delta, & \text{for } (Remote, d_2, \delta) \\ 4\delta, & \text{for } (Backup, d_3, \delta) \\ 2\delta, & \text{for } (Controller, d_4, \delta) \\ 2\delta, & \text{for } (Controller, d_5, \delta) \\ 3\delta, & \text{for } (Controller, d_6, \delta) \\ \delta, & \text{otherwise} \end{cases}$$

$\square$

4.1   Synthesis Problem Statement

The goal of synthesis is to construct a set of defenses to mitigate all attacks with the least cost. We distinguish 3 cases to synthesize solutions for.

1. Ignore implemented defenses. In this case, the job of synthesis is to synthesize a defense model $\mathbb{M}_S$ from scratch such that $\mathbb{M}_S \vdash Q$ and $\mathbb{C}(\mathbb{M}_S)$ is minimal. This case finds a globally minimal solution, in the sense that every other solution which mitigates the attack-defense tree must have a cost greater than or equal to the cost of $\mathbb{C}(\mathbb{M}_S)$. It resembles the early design phase of a system, when defenses have not yet been implemented.
2. Use implemented defenses. There are two possible cases to consider here.

(a) $\mathbb{M}_I \vdash Q$. In other words, all possible attacks are mitigated and the requirements in Q are satisfied by the implemented defenses in $\mathbb{M}_I$. In this case, synthesis tries to optimize the implemented defenses. $\mathbb{M}_S$ is an optimization of $\mathbb{M}_I$ using any combination of:

    i. eliminating unnecessary defenses—removing tuples from $\mathbb{M}_I$

    ii. downgrading current defenses—replacing $(s, a, \gamma, \{(d, \delta_i), \Delta_R\})$ in $\mathbb{M}_I$ with $(s, a, \gamma, \{(d, \delta_j), \Delta_R\})$ such that $\delta_j < \delta_i$

    This case resembles a situation where successful defenses have already been implemented, but can be downgraded or removed to save costs. Here, we restrict addition of new defenses to save costs.

(b) $\mathbb{M}_I \nvdash Q$. In other words, the requirements in Q are not satisfied by the implemented defenses in $\mathbb{M}_I$. In this case, synthesis corrects the implemented defenses with the least amount of change possible. $\mathbb{M}_S$ is a modification of $\mathbb{M}_I$ using some combination of:

    i. implementing new defenses—adding triples to $\mathbb{M}_I$

    ii. upgrading current defenses—replacing $(s, a, \gamma, \{(d, \delta_i), \Delta_R\})$ in $\mathbb{M}_I$ with $(s, a, \gamma, \{(d, \delta_j), \Delta_R\})$ such that $\delta_j > \delta_i$

    A real-life application of this situation is one where defenses have been implemented, unsuccessfully, and need to be improved to mitigate attacks, at minimal additional cost. The already implemented defenses are considered sunk costs that cannot be recovered and thus are not downgraded or removed.

4.2   MaxSMT Encoding for Synthesis

The problem of optimizing the defense costs is stated as a MaxSMT problem and sent to Z3's MaxSMT solver [8]. The input to the MaxSMT solver is an SMT-LIB [6] script (with some extensions for the optimization commands) that includes (i) declarations of variables, (ii) assertions of formulas, and, (iii) an expression over the variables to optimize, given the constraints asserted. Our MaxSMT encoding depends on the case we are encoding from Subsect. 4.1.

In all 3 cases, we do the following. For each component–defense pair (s, d) $((s, \_, \_, \{(d, \_), \_\}) \in \mathbb{M}_A)$, we declare a variable $v_{s,d}$ which stands for the real number representing the synthesized cost of implementing defense d in component s to a particular DAL δ (for each $(s, \_, \_, \{(d, \delta), \_\})$ that we care about, we add a constraint on $v_{s,d}$, as we will show). Since we allow repeated labels, notice that during the creation of these $v_{s,d}$ variables, multiple nodes in the tree might necessitate the creation of the same variable. Some mechanism, such as a hash table, would have to check that variable declarations aren't repeated in the SMT script. Constraints, however, can be repeated.

For each variable $v_{s,d}$, we assert that the cost is non-negative. Then, we encode the ADTree($mod, Q, \mathbb{M}_A$) as an assertion, where mod is the AADL model of the system, Q is the set of requirements, and $\mathbb{M}_A$ is the applicable defense model. Since $\mathbb{M}_A$ satisfies Q, this assertion sets a baseline on the synthesized model. The following function F converts an ADTree to a quantifier-free first-order formula, which is asserted.

$$F(T) := \text{match } T \text{ with}$$
$$\mid \texttt{OR}^{\texttt{A}}(T_1, \ldots, T_n) \rightarrow F(T_1) \wedge \ldots \wedge F(T_n)$$
$$\mid \texttt{OR}^{\texttt{D}}(T_1, \ldots, T_n) \rightarrow F(T_1) \vee \ldots \vee F(T_n)$$
$$\mid \texttt{AND}^{\texttt{A}}(T_1, \ldots, T_n) \rightarrow F(T_1) \vee \ldots \vee F(T_n)$$
$$\mid \texttt{AND}^{\texttt{D}}(T_1, \ldots, T_n) \rightarrow F(T_1) \wedge \ldots \wedge F(T_n)$$
$$\mid \texttt{C}^{\texttt{A}}(\texttt{b}^{\texttt{A}}(s, a), T^{\texttt{D}}) \rightarrow F(\texttt{b}^{\texttt{A}}(s, a)) \vee F(T^{\texttt{D}})$$
$$\mid \texttt{C}^{\texttt{D}}(\texttt{b}^{\texttt{D}}(s, d, \delta), T^{\texttt{A}}) \rightarrow F(\texttt{b}^{\texttt{D}}(s, d, \delta)) \wedge F(T^{\texttt{A}})$$
$$\mid \texttt{b}^{\texttt{A}}(s, a) \rightarrow \bot$$
$$\mid \texttt{b}^{\texttt{D}}(s, d, \delta) \rightarrow v_{s,d} \geq \mathbb{C}(s, d, \delta)$$

$\texttt{OR}^{\texttt{A}}$ nodes are translated to conjunctions and $\texttt{AND}^{\texttt{A}}$ nodes to disjunctions because the ADTree is concerned with the success of the attacker while the MaxSMT encoding is concerned with the success of defending any possible attack. If an attacker needs a conjunction ($\texttt{AND}^{\texttt{A}}$) of attacks to succeed, it suffices from the defender's point of view to stop at least one of the attacks successfully, and hence the disjunction in the MaxSMT encoding. The reasoning for using conjunctions for $\texttt{OR}^{\texttt{A}}$ nodes is similar. Finally, we need to minimize the cost, which is done by using the **minimize** command in the SMT-LIB script over the sum of all variables representing the costs of defenses.

The variables declarations, assertions and the optimization command are common in all cases. Additions to the assertions are unique to each case of the problem statement and we consider each of the 3 cases (all assertions must be added before the optimization command in the script).

Case 1. Since we ignore implemented defenses, the constraint from $\mathbb{M}_{\texttt{A}}$ – ($F(\texttt{ADTree}(mod, Q, A, \mathbb{M}_{\texttt{A}}))$) suffices to restrict the synthesized solution to one that mitigates all attacks. Additionally, the optimization command assures a global optimum.

Case 2(a). Since the implemented defenses satisfy the requirements, we assert constraints from $\mathbb{M}_{\texttt{I}}$—for each $(s, \_, \_, \{(d, \delta), \_\}) \in \mathbb{M}_{\texttt{I}}$, assert $v_{s,d} \leq \mathbb{C}(s, d, \delta)$. We also restrict implementation of new defenses—for each $(s, a, \gamma\{(d, \delta), \Delta_R\}) \in \mathbb{M}_{\texttt{A}}$ such that there exists no $(s, \_, \_, \{(d, \_), \_\}) \in \mathbb{M}_{\texttt{I}}$, assert $v_{s,d} = 0$. Given the lower bounds from $\mathbb{M}_{\texttt{A}}$, and the upper bounds from $\mathbb{M}_{\texttt{I}}$, the MaxSMT solver finds the minimal cost solution, without adding any new defenses.

Case 2(b). Since the implemented defenses do not satisfy the requirements and the cost of implementing them is considered sunk, we assert them as lower bounds—for each $(s, \_, \_, \{(d, \delta), \_\}) \in \mathbb{M}_{\texttt{I}}$, assert $v_{s,d} \geq \mathbb{C}(s, d, \delta)$. For defenses that don't work, the constraints from $\mathbb{M}_{\texttt{A}}$ supersede the lower bound specified by the constraints from $\mathbb{M}_{\texttt{I}}$.

The MaxSMT encoding for each case is summarized as follows.

Case 1:

> For each $s \in S, d \in D$, declare-var $v_{s,d}$
> For each $v_{s,d}$, assert $v_{s,d} \geq 0$
> assert $F(\text{ADTree}(mod, Q, A, \mathbb{M_A}))$
> minimize $\displaystyle\sum^{s \in S, d \in D} v_{s,d}$

Case 2(a):

> For each $s \in S, d \in D$, declare-var $v_{s,d}$
> For each $v_{s,d}$, assert $v_{s,d} \geq 0$
> assert $F(\text{ADTree}(mod, Q, A, \mathbb{M_A}))$
> For each $(s, d, \delta) \in \mathbb{M_I}$, assert $v_{s,d} \leq \mathbb{C}(s, d, \delta)$
> For each $(s, d, \delta) \notin \mathbb{M_I}$, assert $v_{s,d} = 0$
> minimize $\displaystyle\sum^{s \in S, d \in D} v_{s,d}$

Case 2(b):

> For each $s \in S, d \in D$, declare-var $v_{s,d}$
> For each $v_{s,d}$, assert $v_{s,d} \geq 0$
> assert $F(\text{ADTree}(mod, Q, A, \mathbb{M_A}))$
> For each $(s, d, \delta) \in \mathbb{M_I}$, assert $v_{s,d} \geq \mathbb{C}(s, d, \delta)$
> minimize $\displaystyle\sum^{s \in S, d \in D} v_{s,d}$

4.3 SMT Model Evaluation

All our calls to the MaxSMT solver are expected to be satisfiable. A solution where all possible defenses are implemented to the highest possible DAL would trivially satisfy the problem (while likely being unnecessarily expensive):

$$\forall (s, a, \gamma, d, \delta) \in \mathbb{M_A}, (s, a, \gamma, d, 9) \in \mathbb{M_S}$$

The response from the solver varies in its optimization of defense cost. The variables $v_{s,d}$ in our SMT encoding model the cost of implementing defense d in component s to some DAL-score. Thus, when the SMT solver returns an optimal solution as a model, it returns an optimal cost for each component-defense pair. We need to build $\mathbb{M_S}$ from this for which we need the DAL-score for each component-defense pair. We define the inverse cost function $\mathbb{C}^{-1}$ that given a component-defense-cost triple, returns the DAL-score to implement the defense to in the component. Since a component–defense pair could have the same cost for multiple DAL-scores (the monotonicity requirement does not prevent this), the inverse isn't over an injective function. We break ties by preferring higher DAL-scores, given equal costs.

$$\mathbb{C}^{-1}(c, s, d) = \mathtt{max}\{\delta_i \mid \mathbb{C}(s, d, \delta_i) = c\}$$

Thus, as a minimal cost solution, for each component s and defense d, the SMT solver returns a cost as the real value of $v_{s,d}$. $\mathbb{M}_\mathbb{S}$ is then constructed as follows.

$$\forall v_{s,d}, \forall a \in A, \text{ such that } (s, a, \gamma, \{(d, \delta), \Delta_R\}) \in \mathbb{M}_A,$$
$$(s, a, \gamma, \{(d, \mathbb{C}^{-1}(v_{s,d}, s, d))\}) \in \mathbb{M}_\mathbb{S}$$

This is the minimal cost defense model synthesized by the MaxSMT solver.

Example 6. We construct synthesized defense models from the satisfiable solution returned by the SMT solver for the toy drone system using the cost model in Example 5 as follows.

- **Case 1.** Without any additional restrictions, the SMT solver returns values 0, 10, 20, 0, 0 and 0 respectively, for $rd1$, $rd2$, $bd3$, $cd4$, $cd5$ and $cd6$, which are its recommended costs for the defenses. Applying the cost inverse function, we have the following DALs to implement the components to. $\mathbb{C}^{-1}(0, R, d_1) = 0$; $\mathbb{C}^{-1}(10, R, d_2) = 5$; $\mathbb{C}^{-1}(20, B, d_3) = 5$; $\mathbb{C}^{-1}(0, C, d_4) = 0$; $\mathbb{C}^{-1}(0, C, d_5) = 0$; $\mathbb{C}^{-1}(0, C, d_6) = 0$. This is an optimal cost solution unrestricted by any implementation constraints. The total cost is 30.
- **Case 2(a).** The SMT solver returns cost 0 for $rd1$ and $bd3$, cost 10 for $rd2$, $cd4$, and $cd5$, and 15 for $cd6$. Applying the cost inverse function, we have that d_1 and d_2 are to be implemented to DAL 0 and 5 in the remote, d_3 to DAL 0 in the backup controller, and d_4, d_5, and d_6 all to DAL 5 in the main controller. Here, since the implemented defenses already satisfy the requirement, new ones aren't added, and instead, synthesis suggests reductions. The global optimal solution would choose d_3 over d_4, d_5 and d_6, but since the latter are already implemented, synthesis only suggests DAL reductions where applicable (to d_4 and d_5). The total cost of the synthesized solution is 45, which is cheaper than the implementation which costs 61.
- **Case 2(b).** The SMT solver returns costs 10, 10, 20, 6, 0 and 0 for $rd1$, $rd2$, $bd3$, $cd4$, $cd5$, and $cd6$ which translate to DALs 5, 5, 5, 3, 0 and 0, respectively. Since the unsatisfactory defenses have already been implemented, their cost is considered a sunk cost (16 here). The SMT solver specifies what defenses need to be added to satisfy the requirements—d_2 and d_3 in this case. The total cost of the synthesized solution is 46.

Notice that the same defense can be applicable to a component to defend 2 different attacks. For example, system access control defends against both CAPEC–507 and CAPEC–390. Because our encoding doesn't take into account attacks (and it doesn't need to), once synthesis suggests to implement such a defense, we add all possible occurrences of it to $\mathbb{M}_\mathbb{S}$. While this redundance is necessary for soundness of the formalism, it can be ignored during implementation. In fact, it isn't necessary to map synthesized defenses to attacks they mitigate at all, we do it in the formalism just to be able to make synthesized solutions comparable with applicable and implemented solutions.   □

5   Evaluation

A prototype of ADTree-based security analysis and synthesis was implemented in the VERDICT toolchain [16,19], which is a plugin for the OSATE tool [5].

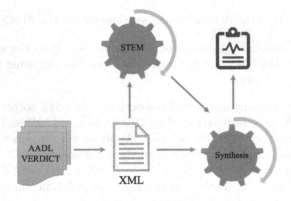

Fig. 3. The architecture of synthesis module in VERDICT.

The architecture of synthesis module in VERDICT is shown in Fig. 3. The input to synthesis is a system architecture model in AADL annotated with cyber-relations and cyber requirements in VERDICT annex. The model will be translated into an intermediate representation in XML that will be further consumed by several modules in VERDICT. For synthesis, it will first be converted to the input to STEM tool, which will identify applicable attacks and also applicable or implemented defenses depending on the running mode of synthesis. The output from STEM and the XML model will then be leveraged by the synthesis module for attack-defense tree analysis and synthesis as described in Sects. 3 and 4.

We perform an evaluation on a high-fidelity architecture model of a delivery drone to demonstrate the capabilities of the tool. In addition, the tool was leveraged by Raytheon Technologies to evaluate on DoD applications development showing promising results [7]. The VERDICT tool is publicly available[2].

A notional architecture for the delivery drone is shown in Fig. 4. The AADL model[3] consists of 12 inter-connected components and is annotated with meta-level properties, defense properties, cyber relations and cyber requirements.

---

[2] VERDICT Tool GitHub: https://github.com/ge-high-assurance/VERDICT.

[3] The Delivery Drone AADL Model: https://github.com/baoluomeng/2022_NFM/tree/main/DeliveryDrone.

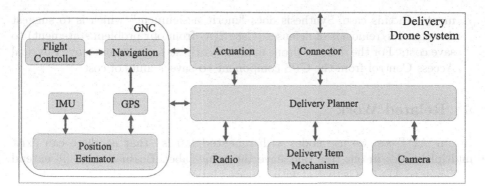

Fig. 4. A notional architecture diagram for the delivery drone model.

Meta-level properties such as component type and pedigree, come built-in with the AADL model. Given this system, the STEM component of the VERDICT toolchain identifies possible CAPEC attacks and NIST 800-53 defenses. These attacks and defenses are fed to the synthesis tool for further processing. The defense property is a numerical DAL-score from δ, and represents the rigor of implemented defense in each component of the system, and is used to construct $\mathbb{M}_{\mathbb{I}}$. Cyber relations and requirements are declared in an annex language to AADL – VERDICT. For example, one cyber requirement defines a successful mission of delivering a package to its destination, while requiring the drone to be resilient to malicious commands that attempt to obtain an improper delivery of a package. The requirement depends on the integrity of the output *delivery_status*, which is used as a starting point from which the system architecture is traced, to build the ADTree for analysis. Furthermore, the consequence of successful attack is Hazardous, requiring corresponding defenses to be implemented to at least DAL-score 7.

To demonstrate its optimizing capabilities, we invoke the Synthesis tool on the model for 3 cases (corresponding to the ones specified in Sect. 4.1) using the default cost model - one where the cost for each defense-DAL pair is the DAL score itself.

– **Case 1.** The implemented defenses are ignored, and a *global* optimal solution is returned. Synthesis suggest a list of defenses with minimal costs to be implemented to DAL 7 so that all cyber requirements can be satisfied. The total cost for the implementation is 273.
– **Case 2.** Implemented defenses are taken into consideration by Synthesis, and these don't satisfy the requirements. Synthesis suggests implementing two defenses for the *deliveryItemMechanism* component: Supply Chain Security and Tamper Protection, both to DAL 7, which would allow for the requirements to be satisfied. These would mitigate CAPEC-439 (Manipulation During Distribution) with an additional cost 14.
– **Case 3.** Once the suggested defenses in case 2 are implemented in the model, they would be considered by Synthesis sufficient to satisfy all cyber require-

ments. In this case, Synthesis does "merit assignment" which is to suggest downgrades/removals of defenses (Case 2(a) from our problem statement) to save costs. For the delivery drone model, Synthesis suggest to remove Physical Access Control from the GPS component to save 7 units of cost.

6   Related Work

In our ADTrees, we use nodes with repeated labels—that is, there can exist multiple nodes in our tree that have the same label. Bossuat et al. [9] extend ADTrees to AD-DAGs to deal with repeated labels. In our work, by guaranteeing that these nodes will have the same child-structure, we are able to maintain the ADTree formalism, and also maintain soundness by handling repetitions during our SMT-encoding.

Fila et al. [11] and Kordy et al. [14] find an optimized set of defenses to mitigate an ADTree using integer linear programming. We use an SMT-based optimization approach, and also build our trees from AADL models of the system. Additionally, we are able to incorporate implementations of defenses that may or may not satisfy the requirements specified by the ADTree and suggest solutions based on these variations (cases 2(a) and 2(b) from Sect. 4.1). We use the formalism of attack-defense trees introduced by Kordy et al. [13] to specify our ADTrees.

7   Conclusion and Future Work

We propose a security analysis technique for system architecture designs via attack-defense trees, and a novel technique to synthesize optimal cost defenses for the components of a model. We translate the AADL model of a system into an ADTree, and encode this ADTree along with the cost of implementing its defenses into a MaxSMT query, such that a satisfying model of the SMT query is a minimum-cost defense for the system, that mitigates all applicable attacks. We utilize advancements in the ADTree literature and SMT technology, in building our formalism of the process of converting an AADL model to an ADTree and then to an optimization query to a MaxSMT solver. We provide an implementation of our technique as the Synthesis functionality in the VERDICT tool chain. One potential extension to our formalism and our tool is to allow a single defense to defend attacks over multiple components and connections – *extensibility* of defenses.

Acknowledgement & Disclaimer. Distribution Statement "A" (Approved for Public Release, Distribution Unlimited). This research was developed with funding from the Defense Advanced Research Projects Agency (DARPA). The views, opinions and/or findings expressed are those of the author and should not be interpreted as representing the official views or policies of the Department of Defense or the U.S. Government.

References

1. MITRE Common Attack Pattern Enumeration and Classification (CAPEC). https://capec.mitre.org/. Accessed 21 Mar 2022
2. National Institute of Standards and Technology 800-53. https://csrc.nist.gov/publications/detail/sp/800-53/rev-5/final. Accessed 21 Mar 2022
3. Radio Technical Commission for Aeronautics(RTCA) DO326 - Airworthiness Security Process Specification. https://www.rtca.org/. Accessed 21 Mar 2022
4. Radio Technical Commission for Aeronautics(RTCA) DO356 - Airworthiness Security Methods and Considerations. https://www.rtca.org/. Accessed 21 Mar 2022
5. The OSATE Tool (2021). https://osate.org/about-osate.html
6. Barrett, C., Fontaine, P., Tinelli, C.: The Satisfiability Modulo Theories Library (SMT-LIB) (2016). www.SMT-LIB.org
7. Barzeele, J., et al.: Experience in designing for cyber resiliency in embedded DOD systems. In: INCOSE International Symposium, vol. 31, pp. 80–94. Wiley Online Library (2021)
8. Bjørner, N., Phan, A.-D., Fleckenstein, L.: νz- an optimizing SMT solver. In: Baier, C., Tinelli, C. (eds.) TACAS 2015. LNCS, vol. 9035, pp. 194–199. Springer, Heidelberg (2015). https://doi.org/10.1007/978-3-662-46681-0_14
9. Bossuat, A., Kordy, B.: Evil Twins: Handling Repetitions in Attack–Defense Trees. In: Liu, P., Mauw, S., Stølen, K. (eds.) GraMSec 2017. LNCS, vol. 10744, pp. 17–37. Springer, Cham (2018). https://doi.org/10.1007/978-3-319-74860-3_2
10. Feiler, P.H., Lewis, B., Vestal, S., Colbert, E.: An overview of the SAE architecture analysis & design language (AADL) standard: a basis for model-based architecture-driven embedded systems engineering. In: Dissaux, P., Filali-Amine, M., Michel, P., Vernadat, F. (eds.) Architecture Description Languages, pp. 3–15. Springer, US, Boston, MA (2005)
11. Fila, B., Wideł, W.: Exploiting attack-defense trees to find an optimal set of countermeasures. In: 2020 IEEE 33rd Computer Security Foundations Symposium (CSF), pp. 395–410 (2020). https://doi.org/10.1109/CSF49147.2020.00035
12. Javaid, A.Y., Sun, W., Devabhaktuni, V.K., Alam, M.: Cyber security threat analysis and modeling of an unmanned aerial vehicle system. In: 2012 IEEE Conference on Technologies for Homeland Security (HST), pp. 585–590. IEEE (2012)
13. Kordy, B., Mauw, S., Radomirović, S., Schweitzer, P.: Foundations of attack–defense trees. In: Degano, P., Etalle, S., Guttman, J. (eds.) FAST 2010. LNCS, vol. 6561, pp. 80–95. Springer, Heidelberg (2011). https://doi.org/10.1007/978-3-642-19751-2_6
14. Kordy, B., Wideł, W.: How well can I secure my system? In: Polikarpova, N., Schneider, S. (eds.) IFM 2017. LNCS, vol. 10510, pp. 332–347. Springer, Cham (2017). https://doi.org/10.1007/978-3-319-66845-1_22
15. Mauw, S., Oostdijk, M.: Foundations of attack trees. In: Won, D.H., Kim, S. (eds.) ICISC 2005. LNCS, vol. 3935, pp. 186–198. Springer, Heidelberg (2006). https://doi.org/10.1007/11734727_17
16. Meng, B., et al.: Verdict: a language and framework for engineering cyber resilient and safe system. Systems 9(1), 18 (2021)
17. Moitra, A., Prince, D., Siu, K., Durling, M., Herencia-Zapana, H.: Threat identification and defense control selection for embedded systems. SAE Int. J. Transp. Cybersecur. Privacy 3(11-03-02-0005), 81–96 (2020)

18. Siu, K., Herencia-Zapana, H., Prince, D., Moitra, A.: A model-based framework for analyzing the security of system architectures. In: 2020 Annual Reliability and Maintainability Symposium (RAMS), pp. 1–6. IEEE (2020)
19. Siu, K., et al.: Architectural and behavioral analysis for cyber security. In: 2019 IEEE/AIAA 38th Digital Avionics Systems Conference (DASC), pp. 1–10. IEEE (2019)

Certified Computation
of Nondeterministic Limits

Michal Konečný[1] , Sewon Park[2] , and Holger Thies[2]([⊠])

[1] Aston University, Birmingham, UK
m.konecny@aston.ac.uk
[2] Kyoto University, Kyoto, Japan
sewon@kurims.kyoto-u.ac.jp, thies.holger.5c@kyoto-u.ac.jp

Abstract. The computational content of constructive metric completeness is the operator that computes limits of Cauchy sequences. It can
be used to construct certified programs that compute interesting transcendental real numbers from sequences of approximations. The desired
nondeterministic version of it would be to nondeterministically compute
real numbers from nondeterministic approximations. However, it is not
obvious how nondeterministic metric completeness should be formalized.

We extend previous work on the formalization of exact real computation by primitive properties of nondeterminism. We show that by these
properties, various forms of nondeterministic metric completeness can be
derived without extending the axiomatic structure of constructive real
numbers. We further implement our theory in the Coq proof assistant
and use Coq's code extraction features to extract efficient exact real computation programs using several forms of nondeterministic computation.

Keywords: Constructive real numbers · Formal proofs · Exact real
number computation · Program extraction · Nondeterminism

1   Introduction

Exact real computation is an elegant approach in which real numbers and other
continuous mathematical structures are treated as basic entities in programming
languages that can be manipulated exactly without introducing rounding errors.
This is often realized by having an abstract data type for real numbers which
keeps track of errors in the background and increases the working precision when
necessary. Algorithm designers therefore can focus solely on the mathematical
problem itself, without thinking about representation issues of real numbers. Of
course this elegance comes at a price and exact real arithmetic is usually less

Holger Thies is supported by JSPS KAKENHI Grant Number JP20K19744. Sewon
Park is supported by JSPS KAKENHI Grant number JP18H03203. This project has
received funding from the EU's Horizon 2020 research and innovation programme under
the Marie Skłodowska-Curie grant agreement No 731143. The authors thank Franz
Brauße and Norbert Müller for helpful discussions.

© Springer Nature Switzerland AG 2022
J. V. Deshmukh et al. (Eds.): NFM 2022, LNCS 13260, pp. 771–789, 2022.
https://doi.org/10.1007/978-3-031-06773-0_41

efficient than the more common approach of using fixed-length floating point approximations. Nonetheless, there are many applications where robustness and reliability are more important than mere efficiency and exact real computation is a feasible alternative in these cases. Furthermore, optimized implementations of exact real computation achieve to minimize the overhead in many cases [1, 16, 21].

In general, the above mentioned properties of exact real computation also facilitate the process of formal verification as it is not necessary to deal with the difficulties of formalizing floating point arithmetic [4]. Indeed, there are already several works dealing with the verification of exact real number computations e.g. [2, 10, 22, 24, 28], and many more and verifying operations like basic arithmetic is usually straightforward.

On the other hand, the continuous semantics of exact real computation come with their own difficulties. In particular, the seemingly simple process of making a decision, that is, choosing one branch of a program if a condition holds and another if it does not, is often non-trivial as it involves discontinuities.

Consider for example the simple comparison operator $<$ on the reals, usually chosen to be a function from reals to the Booleans. As the function is not continuous, there is no way to make this operator computable. More generally, any total, continuous function from the reals to the Booleans is necessarily constant, and thus no interesting operation can be computed.

There are essentially two ways to deal with this problem:

(i) Partiality: Consider the partial function $<$ of type $\mathbb{R} \times \mathbb{R} \rightharpoonup \mathsf{bool}$ such that $x < y$ is undefined if $x = y$. In this case, the semantics are identical to the usual mathematical interpretation, but programs fail to terminate if two equal numbers are compared [30, Theorem 4.1.16].

(ii) Nondeterminism: Extend the notion of computation to multivalued functions $f : A \rightrightarrows B$. The comparison may be replaced by a multivalued soft comparison $x <_k y = \{tt \mid x < y + 2^k\} \cup \{ff \mid y < x + 2^k\}$ [6, 19]. That is, if the two numbers are far enough apart, the correct Boolean value will be returned, but if the numbers are close, any of the two values can be returned nondeterministically.

While (i) is a simple solution, non-termination of programs is usually extremely undesirable. Exact real computation software therefore often implements primitive operations to construct nondeterministic functions. Examples include AERN's `select` [16], or `choose` in iRRAM [21] and Ariadne [1,8]. These frameworks are used to compute highly accurate approximations of numerical problems and nondeterministic operations have been applied in practical situations. However, the formal semantics of this kind of nondeterminism has been less studied.

In recent work [14], we presented a formalization of constructive real numbers in a simple dependent type theory. Our formalization was designed as a framework to extract certified exact real computation programs from constructive proofs, and closely model some of the features of exact real computation such as nondeterminism. For example, when proving a theorem of the form $\Pi(x : \mathsf{R}).\ P\,x \rightarrow \mathsf{M}\Sigma(y : \mathsf{R}).\ Q\,x\,y$, a user automatically gets an exact real computation program that for any input $x \in \mathbb{R}$ such that $P(x)$ holds, nondeterministically computes $y \in \mathbb{R}$ such that $Q(x, y)$ holds. This is realized by mapping the axiomatized real number type R in the type theory to the abstract data type of real numbers in an exact real computation software. In the cited paper, the practicality of the approach is demonstrated by implementing the axiomatization in Coq and mapping to data types and operators in AERN using Coq's program extraction mechanism [17,18]. A main goal of our implementation is to not only provide provably correct but also efficient computation, comparable to native implementations in exact real computation frameworks.

A unique feature of exact real computation, making it more powerful than e.g. symbolic or algebraic computation, is the ability to construct real numbers by limits of certain user-defined sequences [5,23]. While it is clear how the limit computation should be axiomatized in the logical language [3,7,27], it has been under debate how to deal with the case when nondeterminism is involved in the limit computation [11,15]. Note that this situation occurs quite naturally even for simple operations such as computing square roots of complex numbers.

Early versions of iRRAM therefore already provided a simple nondeterministic limit operation as primitive [21, § 10.3] which the authors of the software recently suggested to replace by a more generic operation for nondeterministic limits [11]. However, an important open question that remained is, besides the practicality, if the nondeterministic limit operation is sound, natural, and primitive, i.e. needs to be introduced as an axiom in the axiomatization of constructive real numbers or if it can be derived from a more general principle.

Inspired by [11] and personal communication with the authors, we were able to answer this question: In the current work we specify *nondeterministic dependent choice*, a simple and natural principle of the nondeterminism itself that makes the limit operation suggested in [11] and some other forms of nondeterministic limits derivable. It automatically ensures that the nondeterministic limit operations are sound and that they naturally arise due to the characteristics of nondeterminism applied to the ordinary metric completeness. It moreover suggests that, assuming the computational language is rich enough, there is no need to introduce a nondeterministic limit primitive in exact real computation.

To demonstrate the practicality, we extended our Coq implentation proposed in [14] in the suggested way. Our implementation offers a framework where users can obtain certified programs using nondeterministic limits simulated in the AERN framework. We present some basic examples, extract AERN programs from them and show that they behave well in terms of efficiency.

2   Background and Overview

Let us first briefly summarize the theory from [14] and describe some minor modifications to the original work. Although we mostly have a concrete implementation in the Coq proof assistant in mind, we formulate our results in a more general type-theoretic setting and hope that this also makes it accessible to readers less familiar with Coq. Formal descriptions of dependent type theories can be found in various literature including [29, Chapter 1].

We assume to work in a dependent type theory with basic types $0, 1, 2, N, Z$, an à la Russel universe of classical propositions Prop, and an à la Russel universe of types Type (with an implicit type level). We assume that the identity types $=$ are in Prop and that Prop is a type universe closed under $\rightarrow, \times, \vee, \exists, \Pi$, containing two types True, False : Prop which are the unit and the empty type respectively. It is a universe of classical propositions in that for example $P \vee Q$: Prop denotes the classical fact that P or Q holds which differs from $P + Q$: Type the sum type denoting there to be a computational procedure deciding if P or Q holds. Similarly, when we have a family of classical propositions $P : X \rightarrow$ Prop, the type $\exists(x : X). \, Px$: Prop belonging to Prop denotes the classical existence of $x : X$ satisfying Px while the ordinary dependent pair type (also called Σ-type), $\Sigma(x : X). \, Px$: Type belonging to Type denotes the constructive existence. Note that Prop shares the same constructs for function types (implications) $\rightarrow$, product types (conjunctions) $\times$, and dependent function types, also called Π-types, (universal quantifiers) Π with Type.

In order to make Prop classical, we assume the (classical) law of excluded middle $\Pi(P : \text{Prop}). \, P \vee \neg P$ (where $\neg P :\equiv P \rightarrow \text{False}$), the (classical) propositional extensionality $\Pi(P, Q : \text{Prop}). \, (P \leftrightarrow Q) \rightarrow P = Q$ (where $P \leftrightarrow Q :\equiv (P \rightarrow Q) \times (Q \rightarrow P)$), and the (classical) countable choice of the form $\Pi(A : \text{Type}). \, \Pi(P : N \rightarrow A \rightarrow \text{Prop}). \, (\Pi(n : N). \, \exists(x : X). \, Pnx) \rightarrow \exists(f : N \rightarrow A). \, \Pi(n : N). \, Pn(fn)$. Note the use of the classical $\exists$, as opposed to the constructive Σ and that we did not assume countable choice in [14].

We also assume the general functional extensionality $\Pi(A : \text{Type}). \, \Pi(P : A \rightarrow \text{Type}). \, \Pi(f, g : \Pi(x : A). \, Px). \, (\Pi(x : A). \, fx = gx) \rightarrow f = g$ and the Markov principle $\Pi(f : N \rightarrow \text{Prop}). \, (\Pi(n : N). \, (fn) + \neg(fn)) \rightarrow (\exists(n : N). \, fn) \rightarrow \Sigma(n : N). \, fn$.

From [14], we keep the axiomatization of *Kleenean*, saying that there is a type constant K admitting two distinct constants true, false : K. We write $\lceil k \rceil$ for $k = \text{true}$. K denotes semi-decidable decision procedures. For example, we assume $\Pi(x, y : R). \, \Sigma(k : K). \, \lceil k \rceil = (x < y)$ to say that comparison over the reals is semi-decidable. Here $<$ of type $R \rightarrow R \rightarrow \text{Prop}$ is an axiomatized term constant.

We keep all the axioms of real numbers from op. cit. except for classical completeness. In [14] we had two different formulations of completeness. The first is constructive completeness saying that for any $f : N \rightarrow R$ which is a (fast) Cauchy sequence, there constructively is a real number $x : R$ which is the limit point of the sequence. The other is classical completeness which says for any classical predicate $P : R \rightarrow \text{Prop}$ that is classically nonempty and bounded above, there classically exists the least upper bound. In our modified theory we can prove that constructive completeness implies classical completeness using classical countable choice and hence removed the classical completeness axiom.

The soundness of the axioms in [14] is argued by extending a realizability interpretation in the category of assemblies over Kleene's second algebra [13, 26] by mapping types into assemblies and terms into morphpisms in the category [[25], Sect. 4 and Sect. 5]. An assembly over Kleene's second algebra is a pair of a set A and a binary relation $\Vdash_A \subseteq \mathbb{N}^{\mathbb{N}} \times A$ that is surjective in the sense that for any $x \in A$, there is $\varphi \in \mathbb{N}^{\mathbb{N}}$ such that $(\varphi, x) \in \Vdash_A$. The binary relation is often written in infix notation and φ is said to realize x when $\varphi \Vdash_A x$ holds. Given two assemblies $(A, \Vdash_A)$ and $(B, \Vdash_B)$, a function $f : A \to B$ is defined continuous (computable) if there is a continuous (computable[1]) partial Baire space function $\tau : \mathbb{N}^{\mathbb{N}} \rightharpoonup \mathbb{N}^{\mathbb{N}}$ that tracks f in the sense that for any $(\varphi, x) \in \Vdash_A$, it holds that $\tau(\varphi) \Vdash_B f(x)$. The category of assemblies over Kleene's second algebra is the category of such assemblies and computable functions.

In [14], we propose a nondeterminism monad M such that for any type X : Type, we automatically get a type MX : Type modeling the result of a nondeterministic computation in X. Formally speaking, we consider a type transformer F : Type $\to$ Type a monad in our type theory when it is accompanied with

(i) a function lift $\mathsf{lift}^F : \Pi(X, Y : \mathsf{Type}). (X \to Y) \to (F X) \to F Y$
   (write $\mathsf{lift}^F_{X,Y}$ for $\mathsf{lift}^F X Y$),
(ii) a proof that F and lift^F form a functor

$$\mathsf{lift}^F_{X,X}(\mathsf{id}_X) = \mathsf{id}_{F X} \text{ where } \mathsf{id}_{X:\mathsf{Type}} :\equiv \lambda(x : X).\ x, \text{ and}$$

$$\mathsf{lift}^F_{X,Z}(f \circ g) = (\mathsf{lift}^F_{Y,Z} f) \circ (\mathsf{lift}^F_{X,Y} g) \text{ where } f \circ g :\equiv \lambda(x : X).\ f(g\,x)$$

   for all X, Y, Z : Type, $g : X \to Y$, and $f : Y \to Z$,
(iii) a unit $\mathsf{unit}^F : \Pi(X : \mathsf{Type}). X \to F X$ (we write unit^F_X for $\mathsf{unit}^F X$),
(iv) a proof that the unit is a natural transformation

$$(\mathsf{lift}^F_{X,Y} f) \circ \mathsf{unit}^F_X = \mathsf{unit}^F_Y \circ f$$

   for all X, Y : Type and $f : X \to Y$,
(v) a multiplication $\mathsf{mult}^F : \Pi(X : \mathsf{Type}). (F (F X)) \to F X$
   write mult^F_X for $\mathsf{mult}^F X$),
(vi) a proof that the multiplication is a natural transformation

$$\mathsf{mult}^F_Y \circ (\mathsf{lift}^F_{F X, F Y}(\mathsf{lift}^F_{X,Y} f)) = (\mathsf{lift}^F_{X,Y} f) \circ \mathsf{mult}^F_X$$

   for all X, Y : Type and $f : X \to Y$, and
(vii) proofs of the three monad coherence conditions

$-$ $\mathsf{mult}^F_X \circ \mathsf{unit}^F_{F X} = \mathsf{id}_{F X}$
$-$ $\mathsf{mult}^F_X \circ (\mathsf{lift}^F_{X, F X} \mathsf{unit}^F_X) = \mathsf{id}_{F X}$
$-$ $\mathsf{mult}^F_X \circ \mathsf{mult}^F_{F X} = \mathsf{mult}^F_X \circ (\mathsf{lift}^F_{F (F X), F X} \mathsf{mult}^F_X)$

for all X : Type. Note the analogy in the definition with monads in category theory.

The monad M in the type theory is interpreted as a monad $\mathbf{M}$ in the category of assemblies over Kleene's second algebra whose action on an assembly $(A, \Vdash_A)$ is $(\mathbf{P}_+(A), \Vdash_{\mathbf{M}A})$ where $\mathbf{P}_+(A)$ is the set of nonempty subsets of A and the realization relation is defined by

$$\varphi \Vdash_{\mathbf{M}A} S \quad :\Leftrightarrow \quad \exists x \in A.\, \varphi \Vdash_A x.$$

---

[1] in the sense of computable analysis [30].

The monad on a function is defined by $\mathbf{M}(f) := S \mapsto \bigcup_{x \in S}\{f(x)\}$. Note that the lifted function is tracked by the same Baire space function that tracks f. The monad is interesting as it classifies computable nondeterministic functions in computable analysis.[2]

The main novel contributions in this work deal with extending the formalization of nondeteterminism from our previous work. We suggest a different set of axioms for the nondeterminism monad. Our new formalization is expressive enough to define various notions of nondeterministic completeness useful in practical applications. The new set of axioms is more expressive in the sense that all the properties of nondeterminism used in [14] are still derivable.

3   The Nondeterminism Monad

Nondeterminism is expressed by a monad in our type theory such that when we have a type X : Type, we automatically have a nondeterministic version $\mathsf{M}X$: Type of it. A term of the nondeterministic type is regarded as the result of a nondeterministic computation in X. As the underlying set of $\mathsf{M}X$ in the model is the set of non-empty subsets of the underlying set of X, we suggest a characterization of the monad by relating it with the classical non-empty power-set monad that we can construct within the type theory:

$$\mathsf{P}_+X :\equiv \Sigma(S : X \to \mathsf{Prop}). \ \exists(x : X). \ S\,x$$

We can confirm that it forms a monad with function lift, unit, and multiplication:

$$\mathsf{lift}^{\mathsf{P}_+}_{X,Y} f \quad :\equiv \quad \lambda((S, -)). \ \big(\lambda(y : Y). \ \exists(z : X). \ (y = f\,z) \times (S\,z), -\big)$$

$$\mathsf{unit}^{\mathsf{P}_+}_X x \quad :\equiv \quad \big(\lambda(y : X). \ x = y, -\big)$$

$$\mathsf{mult}^{\mathsf{P}_+}_X x \quad :\equiv \quad \big(\lambda(y : X). \ \Sigma(z : \mathsf{P}_+X). \ (\pi_1\,z\,y) \times (\pi_1\,x\,z), -\big)$$

Here, the occurrences of $-$ represent some classical proof terms. A (dependent) pair (a, b) such that $a : X$ and $b : P\,a$ is of type $\Sigma(x : X). \ P\,x$ or $\exists(x : X). \ P\,x$ where the ambiguity is only for the simplicity in our presentation. And, π_1 is the first projection of pairs (Σ-types).

We assume that there is a type constructor M : Type $\to$ Type, a function lift $\mathsf{lift}^{\mathsf{M}}$, a unit $\mathsf{unit}^{\mathsf{M}}$, and a multiplication $\mathsf{mult}^{\mathsf{M}}$ which form a monad in our type theory. In order to relate it with the classical non-empty power-set monad, we assume that there is a submonoidal natural transformation

$$\mathsf{picture} : \Pi(X : \mathsf{Type}). \ \mathsf{M}X \to \mathsf{P}_+X.$$

which we write $\mathsf{picture}_X$ for picture X. It is a submonoidal natural transformation in that (i) it is a natural transformation, (ii) for any X : Type, $\mathsf{picture}_X$ is monic $\Pi(x, y : \mathsf{M}X). \ \mathsf{picture}_X\,x = \mathsf{picture}_X\,y \to x = y$, and (iii) the coherence conditions which on the unit is $\mathsf{picture}_X \circ \mathsf{unit}^{\mathsf{M}}_X = \mathsf{unit}^{\mathsf{P}_+}_X$ and on the multiplication is $\mathsf{picture}_X \circ \mathsf{mult}^{\mathsf{M}}_X = \mathsf{mult}^{\mathsf{P}_+}_X \circ \mathsf{picture}_{\mathsf{P}_+X} \circ (\mathsf{lift}^{\mathsf{M}}_{\mathsf{M}X\,\mathsf{P}_+X}\mathsf{picture}_X)$ hold.

---

[2] Nondeterministic functions are also known as *multivalued* functions.

We call the natural transformation "picture" because we regard $\mathsf{picture}_X\, x$, when $x : \mathsf{M}X$ is a nondeterministic element, as a classical picture showing the elements x represents. Let us make the definition

$$\mathsf{pic}_X : \mathsf{M}X \to (X \to \mathsf{Prop}) :\equiv \lambda(x : \mathsf{M}X).\ \pi_1(\mathsf{picture}_X x)$$

which discards the second entry of $\mathsf{picture}_X\, x$ such that we can conveniently use $\mathsf{pic}_X\, x\, y : \mathsf{Prop}$ to express that $y : X$ is a possible outcome of $x : \mathsf{M}X$.

We further characterize the nondeterminism by that the classically lifted picture $\mathsf{lift}^{\mathsf{P}_+}_{\mathsf{M}X,\mathsf{P}_+X}\, \mathsf{picture}_X : \mathsf{P}_+(\mathsf{M}X) \to \mathsf{P}_+(\mathsf{P}_+X)$ constructively admits an inverse; i.e., $\Pi(X : \mathsf{Type}).\ \Sigma(i : \mathsf{P}_+(\mathsf{P}_+X) \to \mathsf{P}_+(\mathsf{M}X)).\ \big(i \circ (\mathsf{lift}^{\mathsf{P}_+}_{\mathsf{M}X,\mathsf{P}_+X}\, \mathsf{picture}_X) = \mathsf{id}_{\mathsf{P}_+(\mathsf{M}X)}\big) \times \big((\mathsf{lift}^{\mathsf{P}_+}_{\mathsf{M}X,\mathsf{P}_+X}\, \mathsf{picture}_X) \circ i = \mathsf{id}_{\mathsf{P}_+(\mathsf{P}_+X)}\big)$ holds. The following diagram shows the relation between the two monads.

The last building block in relating the two monads is a destruction method. When we have a nondeterministic object $x : \mathsf{M}X$, we assume that we can obtain a term of type $\mathsf{M}\Sigma(y : X).\ \mathsf{pic}_X\, x\, y$. Namely, when we have a nondeterministic object x, we can nondeterministically get a pair (y, t) where $y : X$ and t is a reason why y can be nondeterministically obtained from x.

We carry some of the original characterizations of the nondeterministic monad from [14]. For any two semi-decidable decisions $x, y : \mathsf{K}$, if promised that either of x or y holds classically, we can nondeterministically decide whether x holds or y holds:

$$\mathsf{select} : \Pi(x, y : \mathsf{K}).\ (\lceil x \rceil \vee \lceil y \rceil) \to \mathsf{M}(\lceil x \rceil + \lceil y \rceil).$$

We further carry over the assumption that if a type X is subsingleton, we can eliminate the nondeterminism on $\mathsf{M}X$:

$$\mathsf{elimM} : \Pi(X : \mathsf{Type}).\ (\Pi(x, y : X).\ x = y) \to (\mathsf{M}\, X) \to X.$$

Remark 1. When we have a nondeterministic object $x : \mathsf{M}X$, regarding it as the result of some nondeterministic computation, it is desirable to analyze properties of the possible outcomes of the nondeterministic computation x. For a classical predicate $P : X \to \mathsf{Prop}$, we can express *all possible outcomes* $y : X$ *of* x *satisfy* $P\, y$ by $\Pi^{\mathsf{M}}(y : x).\ P\, y :\equiv \Pi(y : X).\ \mathsf{pic}_X\, x\, y \to P\, y$ and *some possible outcomes* $y : X$ *of* x *satisfy* $P\, y$ by $\exists^{\mathsf{M}}(y : x).\ P\, y :\equiv \exists(y : X).\ (\mathsf{pic}_X\, x\, y) \times (P\, y)$.

3.1   Nondeterministic Dependent Choice

Suppose any sequence of types $P : \mathsf{N} \to \mathsf{Type}$ and a nondeterministic procedure that runs through the types $f : \Pi(n : \mathsf{N}).\ (Pn) \to \mathsf{M}(P(n+1))$. We can think of a procedure of repeatedly and indefinitely applying the nondeterministic procedure: e.g., $f_n(\cdots f_2(f_1(f_0\, x_0))) \cdots)$ where $x_0 : P0$. Though the expression is not well-typed, intuitively, in the computational point of view, when we apply it repeatedly, we get, nondeterministically, a sequence that selects through Pn. Starting from x_0, we get nondeterministically $x_1 : P0$ from $f\, 0\, x_0 : \mathsf{M}(P0)$. Then, according to the nondeterministic choice $x_1 : P0$ amongst $f\, 0\, x_0 : \mathsf{M}(P0)$, we again get nondeterministically $x_2 : P1$ from $f\, 1\, x_1 : \mathsf{M}(P1)$. Repeating this forever, we get a specific (nondeterministic) sequence where each entry depends on the nondeterministic choices that have been made in the previous entries.

In our type theory, we already have a tool to express repeated applications, the primitive recursion $\mathsf{N\text{-}rec}_{\lambda(n:\mathsf{N}).\ \mathsf{M}(Pn)}$ which is of type

$$\mathsf{M}(P0) \to (\Pi(n : \mathsf{N}).\ \mathsf{M}(Pn) \to \mathsf{M}(P(n+1))) \to \Pi(n : \mathsf{N}).\ \mathsf{M}(Pn).$$

Given $f : \Pi(n : \mathsf{N}).\ (Pn) \to \mathsf{M}(P(n+1))$ and $x_0 : P0$, applying the recursion on $\mathsf{unit}^{\mathsf{M}}_{P0}x_0$ and $\lambda(n : \mathsf{N}).\ \lambda(x : \mathsf{M}(Pn)).\ \mathsf{mult}^{\mathsf{M}}(\mathsf{lift}^{\mathsf{M}}(f\,n)\,x)$ denotes exactly applying f repeatedly on x_0. However, the result of the application does not preserve any information on the dependency between the sequential nondeterministic choices as we can see that the result is of type $\Pi(n : \mathsf{N}).\ \mathsf{M}(Pn)$.

For example, let us consider $Pn :\equiv \mathsf{R}$ and

$$f\,n\,x :\equiv \begin{cases} 0 \text{ or } 1 & \text{if } n = 0, \\ x & \text{otherwise.} \end{cases}$$

When we repeatedly apply the procedure on $1/2$, we expect to have one of the two sequences $1/2, 0, 0, 0, 0, \cdots$ or $1/2, 1, 1, 1, 1, \cdots$ nondeterministically. However, when we apply the primitive recursion, all we can get is the sequence of the nondeterministic real numbers $1/2, (0 \text{ or } 1), (0 \text{ or } 1), \cdots$ which is less informative, forgetting all the information about the dependencies that f creates. Hence, we need a separate and more expressive principle but with computational behavior identical to primitive recursion.

Suppose any sequence of types $P : \mathsf{N} \to \mathsf{Type}$ and a sequence of classical binary relations $Q : \Pi(n : \mathsf{N}).\ Pn \to P(n+1) \to \mathsf{Prop}$. The binary relation is where the dependencies between sequential choices are encoded. For the above example, $Q\,n\,x\,y$ can be set to $n > 0 \to x = y$. We call a function of type

$$\Pi(n : \mathsf{N}).\ \Pi(x : Pn).\ \mathsf{M}\Sigma(y : P(n+1)).\ Q\,n\,x\,y$$

an M-*trace* of Q. Note that admitting a trace automatically ensures that Q is a (classically) entire relation: $\Pi(n : \mathsf{N}).\ \Pi(x : Pn).\ \exists(y : P(n+1)).\ Q\,n\,x\,y$.

The nondeterministic dependent choice (M-dependent choice for short) says that for any M-trace of Q, there is a term of type

$$\mathsf{M}\Sigma(g : \Pi(n : \mathsf{N}).\ Pn).\ \Pi(m : \mathsf{N}).\ Q\,m\,(g\,m)\,(g\,(m+1))$$

satisfying a coherence condition that will be described below. In words: From a trace of Q, we can nondeterministically get a sequence g that runs through Q.

Given any M-trace f of Q, now there are two different ways of constructing a term of type $\Pi(n : \mathsf{N}). \, \mathsf{M}(P\,n)$, forgetting the information on the dependencies. The first is to naively apply the primitive recursion on f which is shown in the beginning of this subsection. The second is to apply the following operation

$$\mathsf{to\_fiber}^{\mathsf{M}}(g : \mathsf{M}\Pi(n : \mathsf{N}). \, P\,n) :\equiv \lambda(n : \mathsf{N}). \, \big(\mathsf{lift}^{\mathsf{M}}(\lambda(h : \Pi(n : \mathsf{N}). \, P\,n). \, h\,n)\,g\big)$$

on the M-lifted first projection of the M-dependent choice. The coherence condition states that the two operations of forgetting the information on the paths are identical (c.f. Fig. 1).

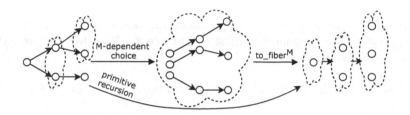

Fig. 1. Intuitive picture on the coherence condition for the M-dependent choice

We assume that our type theory admits M-dependent choice.

Remark 2. The name nondeterministic dependent choice comes from the observation that when repeating the above with the double negation monad or the propositional truncation monad (assuming they are provided by the type theory), the principle becomes the classical dependent choice and intuitionistic dependent choice, respectively.

Remark 3. In [14], it was axiomatized that there is a term constant ωlift such that for any $P : \mathsf{N} \to \mathsf{Type}$, it holds that $\omega\mathsf{lift}\,P : (\Pi(n : \mathsf{N}). \, \mathsf{M}(P\,n)) \to \mathsf{M}\Pi(n : \mathsf{N}). \, P\,n$ is a section of $\mathsf{to\_fiber}^{\mathsf{M}}$. In other words, for any $f : \Pi(n : \mathsf{N}). \, \mathsf{M}(P\,n)$, it holds that $\mathsf{to\_fiber}\,(\omega\mathsf{lift}\,f) = f$. From a computational point of view, it says, when we have a sequence of nondeterministic computations, we can nondeterministically choose one sequence of (deterministic) computations.

The property is used to derive an operator computing deterministic limits from nondeterministic sequences. Observe that the ωlift can be derived from the M-dependent choice when we simply let $Q\,n\,x\,y :\equiv \mathsf{True}$. Hence, we conclude that the new set of axioms for the nondeterminism presented in this paper is more expressive than the previous one.

4 Nondeterministic Limits

A defining feature of exact real computation is the ability to compute certain limits of user-defined sequences. Its counterpart in the axiomatization of real numbers is the principle of metric completeness.

There are three distinct cases where we need to compute limits: (1) when a deterministic sequence of real numbers converge to a deterministic point, (2) when a sequence of nondeterministic real numbers converge to a deterministic point, and (3) when a sequence of nondeterministic real numbers converge to a nondeterministic point. The first case is exactly the ordinary metric completeness which is realized by the primitive limit operations in exact real number computation software.

In this section, we derive the other forms of limits from the ordinary constructive completeness and our new more expressive nondeterminism monad.

4.1   Deterministic Limits of Nondeterministic Sequences

Consider the case where there is a single real number we want to obtain and we have a nondeterministic procedure approximating said number.

Suppose we have a nondeterministic sequence $f : \mathsf{N} \to \mathsf{MR}$ that is a (fast) Cauchy sequence meaning that

$$\mathsf{is\_Cauchy}^M\, f := \Pi(n, m : \mathsf{N}).\ \Pi^M(x : f\,n).\ \Pi^M(y : f\,m).\ -2^{-n-m} \leq x - y \leq 2^{-n-m}$$

(see Remark 1 for the definition of Π^M). That is, any choices of $f\,n$ and $f\,m$ will be at most $2^{-(n+m)}$ far apart from each other and thus any possible sequence will be a fast Cauchy sequence, converging to a unique limit point that we define by the relation

$$\mathsf{is\_limit}^M\, x\, f := \Pi(n : \mathsf{N}).\ \Pi^M(y : f\,n).\ -2^{-n} \leq x - y \leq 2^{-n}.$$

We can prove that for any nondeterministic Cauchy sequence, there deterministically and constructively exists the limit.

Lemma 1. *Within our type theory, we can construct a term of the type*

$$\Pi(f : \mathsf{N} \to \mathsf{MR}).\ \mathsf{is\_Cauchy}^M\, f \to \Sigma(x : \mathsf{R}).\ \mathsf{is\_limit}^M\, x\, f.$$

In words, a nondeterministic sequence converges to a point if all possible candidates of the nondeterministic sequence converge to the point.

In practice, we often already have a classical description of real numbers that we want to construct. For example, when we compute a square root of a real number $x : \mathsf{R}$, we first define it classically by $S : \mathsf{R} \to \mathsf{Prop} := \lambda(y : \mathsf{R}).\ x = y \times y$ then prove $\Sigma(y : \mathsf{R}).\ S\,y$.

For any real number $x : \mathsf{R}$ and a classical description of real numbers $S : \mathsf{R} \to \mathsf{Prop}$, define the notation: $x \sim_n S := \exists(y : \mathsf{R}).\ (S\,y) \times |x - y| \leq 2^{-n}$ saying that x approximates a real number represented by S by 2^{-n}. Then, we can derive the following version of metric completeness:

$$(\exists!(x : \mathsf{R}).\ S\,x) \to (\Pi(n : \mathsf{N}).\ \mathsf{M}\Sigma(y : \mathsf{R}).\ y \sim_n S) \to \Sigma(y : \mathsf{R}).\ S\,y.$$

Here, $\exists!(x : X).\ P\,x$ is for the classical unique existence abbreviating $\exists(x : X).\ (P\,x) \times \Pi(y : X).\ P\,x \to x = y$.

Example 1 (Real square root). Any non-negative real number classically admits a unique non-negative square root. Consider any real number x : R with a term of type $x \geq 0$. Let $S :\equiv \lambda(y : R). (y \geq 0) \times (x = y \times y)$. Of course, the classical property can be proven in our system which will yield a term of type $\exists!(y : R). S\,y$. In [14], we use Heron's method with nondeterministic scaling to nondeterministically approximate the non-negative square root. Heron's method is a simple and well known method to approximate the square root of a real number x by the inductively defined sequence $x_0 := 1$ and $x_{i+1} := \frac{1}{2}\left(x_i + \frac{x}{x_i}\right)$. The sequence converges quadratically to $\sqrt{x}$ in the interval $\frac{1}{4} \leq x \leq 2$, meaning $|\sqrt{x} - x_i| \leq 2^{-2^i}$ and thus can be used to construct a fast Cauchy sequence converging to the square root for any x in said interval. Outside of this interval, we can nondeterministically find a scaling factor z : Z such that $\frac{1}{4} \leq 4^z x \leq 2$, approximate the square root of the scaled number and rescale it appropriately.

Applying the second version of the metric completeness to the defined sequence, we can obtain

$$\sqrt{} : \Pi(x : R). x \geq 0 \to \Sigma(y : R). (y \geq 0) \times (x = y \times y).$$

Note that we need to consider the case $x = 0$ separately, see [14] for details.

4.2 Nondeterministic Limits

Suppose we are given a classical description of real numbers $S : R \to$ Prop that is classically sequentially closed. Define is_seq_closed S to for the following type:

$$\Pi(f : N \to R). (\Pi(n : N). (f\,n) \sim_n S) \to \exists(x : R). (S\,x) \times \text{is\_limit}\,x\,f.$$

A *nondeterministic refinement procedure* is a procedure that for each natural number n and real number x_n with a promise $x_n \sim_n S$, nondeterministically computes a 2^{-n-1} approximation to some (possibly different) real number in S which is at most 2^{-n-1} apart from x_n. That is, a nondeterministic refinement procedure is a function f of type

$$f : \Pi(n : N). \Pi(x : R). x \sim_n S \to M\Sigma(y : R). \left(|x - y| \leq 2^{-n-1}\right) \times \left(y \sim_{n+1} S\right).$$

We will show that given such a nondeterministic refinement procedure, we can apply the M-dependent choice to nondeterministically get a point in S which we call the limit point of the procedure. To this end, we define

$$P\,n :\equiv \Sigma(x : R). x \sim_n S \quad \text{and} \quad Q\,n\,x\,y :\equiv |\pi_1 x - \pi_1 y| \leq 2^{-n-1}.$$

See that the refinement procedure f can be easily adjusted to become a M-trace of Q. The M-dependent choice on it with an initial approximation x_0 : $M\Sigma(y : R). y \sim_n S$, yields a sequence $g : N \to R$ that is consecutively close, i.e. $\Pi(n : N). |(g\,n) - (g\,(n+1))| \leq 2^{-n-1}$, and converges to S's elements, i.e. $\Pi(n : N). g\,n \sim_n S$. As S is sequentially closed and we can prove that g is Cauchy, applying the ordinary limit on S constructively yields a point in S. Hence, applying the lift^M on the procedure and postcomposing it to the result of the M-dependent choice yields the nondeterministic limit.

Theorem 1. *Within our type theory, we can construct a term of type*

$\Pi(S : \mathsf{R} \to \mathsf{Prop}).\ \mathsf{is\_seq\_closed}\ S \to$

$\quad \mathsf{M}\Sigma(y : \mathsf{R}).\ y \sim_0 S \to$

$\quad \left(\Pi(n : \mathsf{N}).\ \Pi(x : \mathsf{R}).\ x \sim_n S \to \mathsf{M}\Sigma(y : \mathsf{R}).\ \left(|x - y| \leq 2^{-n-1}\right) \times (y \sim_{n+1} S)\right) \to$

$\quad \mathsf{M}\Sigma(y : \mathsf{R}).\ S\,y$

4.3   Nondeterministic Limits with Additional Information

The nondeterministic refinement in the previous subsection requires to consecutively refine any possible previous approximation to a better approximation of
a limit. However, in practice it is often more reasonable to think of the case
where all possible approximations throughout the indefinite refinement procedure share some invariant properties. That is, we only have to consider a subset
of all possible 2^{-n} approximations to be given as inputs of the n'th refinement.

Let us, for example, again consider the nondeterministic function

$$f\,n\,x :\equiv \begin{cases} 0 \text{ or } 1 & \text{if } n = 0, \\ x & \text{otherwise,} \end{cases}$$

from Sect. 3.1. Starting with $1/2$, the function nondeterministically generates
the two sequences $1/2, 0, 0, \cdots$ and $1/2, 1, 1 \cdots$. Both are Cauchy sequences that
converge to 0 and 1 respectively, thus we would consider 0 and 1 possible limit
points. However, note that f is not an admissible refinement procedure in the
previous sense: When 2^{-n} is given as a 2^{-n} approximation to 0, f returns 2^{-n}
which is not a 2^{-n-1} approximation to any of 0 or 1. In other words, we lose the
information that when applying f, we only encounter either 0 or 1 when $n > 0$.

We would like to use the invariant property of f to build a more effective
nondeterministic limit operation. Let $S : \mathsf{R} \to \mathsf{Prop}$ be a classical description
of real numbers that is sequentially closed. We declare an invariant property of
approximations $I : \mathsf{N} \to \mathsf{R} \to \mathsf{Type}$ that is preserved throughout the refinements.
We can encode I in P at the step of applying the M-dependent choice:

$$P\,n :\equiv \Sigma(x : \mathsf{R}).\ (x \sim_n S) \times I\,n\,x.$$

A similar derivation as in the previous section yields the following more informative limit operation:

Theorem 2. *Within our type theory, we can construct a term of type*

$\Pi(S : \mathsf{R} \to \mathsf{Prop}).\ \Pi(I : \mathsf{N} \to \mathsf{R} \to \mathsf{Type}).\ \mathsf{is\_seq\_closed}\ S \to$

$\quad \mathsf{M}\Sigma(y : \mathsf{R}).\ (y \sim_0 S) \times I\,0\,y \to$

$\quad \left(\Pi(n : \mathsf{N}).\ \Pi(x : \mathsf{R}).\ (x \sim_n S) \times I\,n\,x \to\right.$

$\quad\quad \left.\mathsf{M}\Sigma(y : \mathsf{R}).\ \left(|x - y| \leq 2^{-n-1}\right) \times (y \sim_{n+1} S) \times (I\,(n+1)\,y)\right) \to$

$\quad \mathsf{M}\Sigma(y : \mathsf{R}).\ S\,y$

Note that the required nondeterministic refinement procedure accepts additional information on its input $I\,n\,x$: Type, on which we can do effective reasoning as it is indexed through Type. For example, in the above case of 0 and 1, we can let $I\,n\,x :\equiv n > 0 \to (x = 0) + (x = 1)$ such that in the beginning of each refinement step $n > 0$, we can effectively test if x is 0 or 1. The price to pay is that in each step we have to construct a Boolean term which indicates whether the refinement is 0 or 1 which then is used in the next refinement step. Figure 2 illustrates this example.

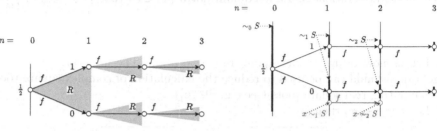

(a) An M-*trace* of $Q\,n\,x\,y \equiv |x - y| \leq 2^{-n}$ converging to $S = \{0, 1\}$

(b) Without the invariant I, the refinement procedure f is not admissible.

Fig. 2. Using an invariant property of f to define a limit

Remark 4. The iRRAM C++ framework provides a similar operation `limit_mv`. The operator computes the limit of a nondeterministic sequence using an additional discrete hint `choice` that restricts the possible values of the limit [20].

5   Examples

Let us illustrate the use of the limit operations introduced in the previous section with some examples. Multivalued functions play an important role in complex analysis and the area therefore provides a multitude of examples including n-th roots, logarithms and inverse trigonometric functions. In Sect. 5.1, we present what is perhaps the simplest of these examples, the complex square root.

A second, more theoretical, example where nondeterministic approximation turns out to be useful, is to show that any two real number types that satisfy our axioms are isomorphic. We present this example in Sect. 5.2.

5.1   Computing Complex Square Roots

We prove the constructive and nondeterministic existence of square roots of complex numbers using a simple method described e.g. in [20]. The square root of a number $z \in \mathbb{C}$ is a number $x \in \mathbb{C}$ such that $x^2 = z$. If x is a square root of z then so is $-x$ and there are no other square roots. Thus, for every $z \neq 0$

there are exactly two square roots. In the case of the square root on nonnegative reals (Example 1) we could simply choose one of the two square roots to get a singlevalued branch. However, it is well known that no such continuous choice exists for the whole complex plane: The square root has a branch point at $z = 0$ and thus there is no singlevalued, continuous square root function in any region containing $z = 0$ as an interior point. We show that we can, however, prove the nondeterministic existence of a square root constructively in our theory.

In order to express the statement, we first extend our theory to a type of complex numbers. We define the type as a pair of real numbers, i.e. $C :\equiv R \times R$ with its field operations and a maximum norm $|\cdot| : C \to R$.

For any sequence $f : N \to C$ that is Cauchy, we can untangle the real and imaginary parts and obtain the limit point by applying the ordinary limit operator. Similarly, we can extend the nondeterministic limit operator to C.

Let us now return to the square root operation. The following well-known algebraic formula can be used to reduce the calculation of complex square roots to calculating real square roots (see e.g. [9, §6]).

Let $z = a + ib$, then

$$\sqrt{\frac{\sqrt{a^2 + b^2} + a}{2}} + i\mathrm{sgn}(b)\sqrt{\frac{\sqrt{a^2 + b^2} - a}{2}}$$

is one of the square roots of z. Of course, this function is not computable as sgn is not continuous in 0. However, if $z \neq 0$, we can nondeterministically choose one of the cases $a < 0$, $a > 0$, $b < 0$, $b > 0$ and apply the formula (in case $a > 0$ or $a < 0$, a slight adaption of the formula using $\mathrm{sgn}(a)$ instead of $\mathrm{sgn}(b)$ is used).

Thus, using Example 1, we can show the following restricted version of the existence of a complex square root

$$\sqrt{}_0 : \Pi(z : C).\ z \neq 0 \to M(\Sigma(x : C).\ x \cdot x = z). \tag{1}$$

Finally, we apply Theorem 2 to also include the case $z = 0$. Recall that given a 2^{-n} approximation x_n of a square root of z that satisfies a certain predicate I that we will define later, we need to choose a $2^{-(n+1)}$ approximation x_{n+1} of a square root of z with $|x_{n+1} - x_n| \leq 2^{-(n+1)}$ and such that x_{n+1} satisfies I. We proceed as follows. In the beginning, at each step n we nondeterministically choose one of the two cases $|z| < 2^{-2(n+2)}$ or $|z| > 0$. In the first case, 0 is a good enough approximation for any square root of z. In the second case, we know $z \neq 0$ and thus can apply (1) to get the exact value of a square root. However, once we have selected the second case, for any later elements of the sequence we just return the previous value x_n. Thus, all possible sequences the refinement procedure returns have the form $0, 0, 0, \ldots, 0, x, x, x, \ldots$, where x is a square root of z. Further, if we returned 0 at the n-th step, we know that $|z| < 2^{-2(n+2)}$ and therefore for any square root x, $|x| < 2^{-(n+2)}$ and returning x at step $n + 1$ is a valid refinement of the previous approximation.

Thus, the invariant property of the sequence defined in this way is given by the relation $I\,n\,x : \mathsf{Type}$ defined by

$$I\ n\ x :\equiv \left((|z| \leq 2^{-2(n+2)}) \times (x = 0)\right) + (x \cdot x = z).$$

Applying Theorem 2 with this I, we get

$$\sqrt{} : \Pi(z : \mathsf{C}).\ \mathsf{M}(\Sigma(x : \mathsf{C}).\ x \cdot x = z).$$

5.2 Equivalence of Axiomatic Real Numbers

To prove that the set of axioms we devised to express exact real number computation is expressive enough, we prove that any two types R_1 and R_2 satisfying the set of axioms are type-theoretically equivalent. As our type theory is extensional, they are equivalent if we can construct the mutually inverse functions $\iota_1 : \mathsf{R}_1 \to \mathsf{R}_2$ and $\iota_2 : \mathsf{R}_2 \to \mathsf{R}_1$. The basic idea of the construction is similar to [12] where an effective model-theoretic structure of real numbers is suggested.

From the classical Archimedean principle of real numbers, for any $x : \mathsf{R}_1$, there classically is $z : \mathsf{Z}$ which bounds the magnitude of x in the sense that $|x| < z$ holds. Applying nondeterministically the Markov principle, we can construct the nondeterministic rounding operator:

$$\mathsf{round} : \Pi(x : \mathsf{R}_1).\ \mathsf{M}\Sigma(z : \mathsf{Z}).\ z - 1 < x < z + 1.$$

Recall that the usual rounding is not computable due to discontinuity of the classical rounding function [30, Theorem 4.3.1]. Then, by scaling, we can construct a term of type

$$\mathsf{dyadic} : \Pi(x : \mathsf{R}_1).\ \Pi(n : \mathsf{N}).\ \mathsf{M}\Sigma(z : \mathsf{Z}).\ |x - z \cdot 2^{-n}| \le 2^{-n}$$

which nondeterministically approximates the binary magnitude of real numbers.

By using the destruction principle of the nondeterminism and doing some clerical work, we get the fact that for any real number $x : \mathsf{R}_1$, there exists a sequence of nondeterministic integers $f : \mathsf{N} \to \mathsf{MZ}$ such that every section $g : \mathsf{N} \to \mathsf{Z}$ of f is an approximation sequence of x in the sense that $\mathsf{is\_limit}\,x\,(\lambda(n : \mathsf{N}).\ (g\,n) \cdot 2^{-n})$ holds.

Note that the description thus far implicitly used the integer embedding in R_1. Taking out the embedding explicitly, we can prove that for any sequence of integers $g : \mathsf{N} \to \mathsf{Z}$, if its induced dyadic sequence is Cauchy in one type of real numbers, it also is Cauchy in the other one. Hence, from f, using the other integer embedding $\mathsf{Z} \to \mathsf{R}_2$, we can get a sequence of nondeterministic real numbers in R_2 where every section is a Cauchy sequence in R_2. Thus, after proving that the limit points of such sequences is unique, we can apply the deterministic limit of nondeterministic sequences (Lemma 1) to construct a real number in R_2.

Intuitively, we use the space of sequences of nondeterministic integers as an independent stepping stone connecting the two axiomatic types R_1 and R_2. In our axiomatization of nondeterminism we can analyze each section of a sequence of nondeterministic integers so that we can apply a limit operation in R_2.

The other direction $\mathsf{R}_2 \to \mathsf{R}_1$ can be constructed analogously, and the two mappings being inverse to each other can be proved easily, concluding that the two axiomatic types R_1 and R_2 are equivalent.

6 Implementation and Experimental Results

All mathematical concepts and results presented in this paper have been fully formalized in Coq. The formalization is released under the MIT open-source licence and is included in https://github.com/holgerthies/coq-aern.

Moreover, we extracted Haskell/AERN code from our formalisation of the complex square root that uses our nondeterministic limit operator. The extraction mechanism realizes our axioms as appropriate Haskell/AERN terms, including axioms for real number operations and the nondeterministic choice operator as described in [14, Appendix B] adapted for the changes described here. In particular, M-dependent choice translates to ordinary primitive recursion in the Haskell translation. This is due to the fact that M itself vanishes, i.e., it becomes the Haskell's identity monad, as real number computations in Haskell/AERN are intrinsically nondeterministic already.

Figure 3 shows the execution times of this extracted code on a sample of inputs and with various target precisions. We use logarithmic scales to make the differences easier to see. Slower performance at zero reflects the fact that the limit computation uses the whole sequence, unlike away from zero where only a finite portion of the sequence is evaluated and the faster converging Heron iteration takes over for higher precisions. The closer the input is to zero, the later this switch from limit to Heron takes place when increasing precision. For very large inputs, there is a notable constant overhead associated with scaling the input to the range where Heron method converges. In [14] we evaluated the performance of our implementation of the real square root and showed that it is comparable to a hand-written Haskell/AERN implementation. Comparing with the execution times from Fig. 3, it can be seen that the performance of our complex square root appears to be comparable to the performance of the real square root and thus is in turn again comparable to a hand-written implementation.

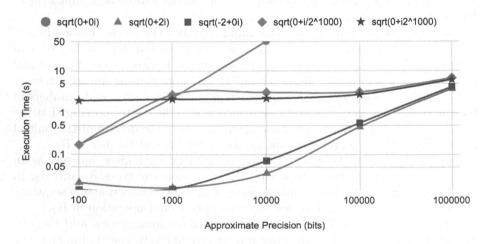

Fig. 3. Execution time of the extracted complex square root function

7   Conclusion

Nondeterminism and the computation of limits are two central features of exact real computation. Extending our previous work, in the current work we devised a sound and powerful framework for formal verification of exact real computation which allows the use of nondeterministic computation in multiple ways. Following recent discussions on the implementation of multivalued limits in exact real computation frameworks, we concluded that we do not need to include a multivalued limit as a primitive operation, but can derive several useful forms of multivalued limit operations from a more natural principle in our theory.

As a simple but important example for a function where nondeterministic limits turn out to be useful, we proved the existence of a complex square root in our constructive theory. Of course, there are several other examples of functions that are necessarily multivalued and we plan to add some of these in future work. We further plan to extend our framework by polynomial root finding and matrix diagnonalization which essentially require nondeterministic limits.

References

1. Balluchi, A., Casagrande, A., Collins, P., Ferrari, A., Villa, T., Sangiovanni-Vincentelli, A.: Ariadne: a framework for reachability analysis of hybrid automata. In: Proceedings 17th International Symposium on Mathematical Theory of Networks and Systems. Kyoto (2006)
2. Berger, U., Tsuiki, H.: Intuitionistic fixed point logic. Ann. Pure Appl. Log. **172**(3), 102903 (2021). https://doi.org/10.1016/j.apal.2020.102903
3. Bishop, E.A.: Foundations of Constructive Analysis (1967)
4. Boldo, S., Melquiond, G.: Computer Arithmetic and Formal Proofs - Verifying Floating-point Algorithms with the Coq System. ISTE Press (2017). https://www.elsevier.com/books/computer-arithmetic-and-formal-proofs/boldo/978-1-78548-112-3
5. Brattka, V.: The emperor's new recursiveness: the epigraph of the exponential function in two models of computability. In: Ito, M., Imaoka, T. (eds.) Words, Languages & Combinatorics III, pp. 63–72. World Scientific Publishing, Singapore (2003), iCWLC 2000, Kyoto, Japan, 14–18 March 2000
6. Brattka, V., Hertling, P.: Feasible real random access machines. J. Complex. **14**(4), 490–526 (1998). https://doi.org/10.1006/jcom.1998.0488, https://www.sciencedirect.com/science/article/pii/S0885064X98904885
7. Bridges, D.S.: Constructive mathematics: a foundation for computable analysis. Theor. Comput. Sci. **219**(1), 95–109 (1999). https://doi.org/10.1016/S0304-3975(98)00285-0, https://www.sciencedirect.com/science/article/pii/S0304397598002850
8. Collins, P., Geretti, L., Casagrande, A., Zapreev, I., Zivanovic, S.: Ariadne (2005–20). http://www.ariadne-cps.org/
9. Cooke, R.L.: Classical Algebra: its Nature, Origins, and Uses. John Wiley & Sons (2008)

10. Cruz-Filipe, L., Geuvers, H., Wiedijk, F.: C-CoRN, the constructive coq repository at Nijmegen. In: Asperti, A., Bancerek, G., Trybulec, A. (eds.) MKM 2004. LNCS, vol. 3119, pp. 88–103. Springer, Heidelberg (2004). https://doi.org/10.1007/978-3-540-27818-4_7

11. Brausse, F., Norbert Müller, R.R.: Intensionality and multi-valued limits. In: Proceedings 15th International Conference on Computability and Complexity in Analysis (CCA), p. 11 (2018)

12. Hertling, P.: A real number structure that is effectively categorical. Math. Log. Q. **45**, 147–182 (1999). https://doi.org/10.1002/malq.19990450202

13. Hofmann, M.: On the interpretation of type theory in locally cartesian closed categories. In: Pacholski, L., Tiuryn, J. (eds.) CSL 1994. LNCS, vol. 933, pp. 427–441. Springer, Heidelberg (1995). https://doi.org/10.1007/BFb0022273

14. Konečný, M., Park, S., Thies, H.: Axiomatic reals and certified efficient exact real computation. In: Silva, A., Wassermann, R., de Queiroz, R. (eds.) WoLLIC 2021. LNCS, vol. 13038, pp. 252–268. Springer, Cham (2021). https://doi.org/10.1007/978-3-030-88853-4_16

15. Konečný, M.: Verified exact real limit computation. In: Proceedings 15th International Conference on Computability and Complexity in Analysis (CCA), pp. 9–10 (2018)

16. Konečný, M.: aern2-real: A Haskell library for exact real number computation. https://hackage.haskell.org/package/aern2-real (2021)

17. Letouzey, P.: A new extraction for Coq. In: Geuvers, H., Wiedijk, F. (eds.) TYPES 2002. LNCS, vol. 2646, pp. 200–219. Springer, Heidelberg (2003). https://doi.org/10.1007/3-540-39185-1_12

18. Letouzey, P.: Extraction in Coq: an overview. In: Beckmann, A., Dimitracopoulos, C., Löwe, B. (eds.) CiE 2008. LNCS, vol. 5028, pp. 359–369. Springer, Heidelberg (2008). https://doi.org/10.1007/978-3-540-69407-6_39

19. Luckhardt, H.: A fundamental effect in computations on real numbers. Theor. Comput. Sci. **5**(3), 321 – 324 (1977). https://doi.org/10.1016/0304-3975(77)90048-2, http://www.sciencedirect.com/science/article/pii/0304397577900482

20. Müller, N.T.: Implementing limits in an interactive realram. In: 3rd Conference on Real Numbers and Computers, 1998, Paris. vol. 13, p. 26 (1998)

21. Müller, N.T.: The iRRAM: exact arithmetic in C++. In: Blanck, J., Brattka, V., Hertling, P. (eds.) CCA 2000. LNCS, vol. 2064, pp. 222–252. Springer, Heidelberg (2001). https://doi.org/10.1007/3-540-45335-0_14

22. Müller, N.T., Uhrhan, C.: Some steps into verification of exact real arithmetic. In: Goodloe, A.E., Person, S. (eds.) NFM 2012. LNCS, vol. 7226, pp. 168–173. Springer, Heidelberg (2012). https://doi.org/10.1007/978-3-642-28891-3_17

23. Neumann, E., Pauly, A.: A topological view on algebraic computation models. J. Complex. **44**, 1–22 (2018)

24. Park, S., et al.: Foundation of computer (algebra) analysis systems: Semantics, logic, programming, verification. arXiv e-prints pp. arXiv-1608 (2016)

25. Reus, B.: Realizability models for type theories. Electron. Notes Theor. Comput. Sci. **23**(1), 128–158 (1999)

26. Seely, R.A.G.: Locally cartesian closed categories and type theory. Math. Proc. Camb. Philoso. Soc. **95**(1), 33–48 (1984). https://doi.org/10.1017/S0305004100061284

27. Specker, E.: Nicht konstruktiv beweisbare Sätze der analysis. J. Symb. Logic **14**(3), 145–158 (1949)

28. Steinberg, F., Thery, L., Thies, H.: Computable analysis and notions of continuity in Coq. Logical Meth. Comput. Sci. **17**(2) (2021). https://lmcs.episciences.org/7478

29. Univalent Foundations Program, T.: Homotopy Type Theory: Univalent Foundations of Mathematics. https://homotopytypetheory.org/book, Institute for Advanced Study (2013)

30. Weihrauch, K.: Computable Analysis. Springer, Berlin (2000). https://doi.org/10.1007/978-3-642-56999-9

The Power of Disjoint Support Decompositions in Decision Diagrams

Lieuwe Vinkhuijzen(✉) ⓘ and Alfons Laarman ⓘ

Leiden University, Leiden, The Netherlands
{l.t.vinkhuijzen,a.w.laarman}@liacs.leidenuniv.nl

Abstract. The relative succinctness and ease of manipulation of different languages to express Boolean constraints is studied in knowledge compilation, and impacts areas including formal verification and circuit design. We give the first analysis of Disjoint Support Decomposition Binary Decision Diagrams (DSDBDD), introduced by Bertacco, which achieves a more succinct representation than Binary DDs by exploiting Ashenhurst Decompositions. Our main result is that DSDBDDs can be exponentially smaller than BDDs.

1 Introduction

Decision Diagrams are data structures for the representation and manipulation of Boolean functions. They are used for probabilistic reasoning [4,13], verification [18,22,36], circuit design [30,31,37,38] and simulation of quantum computing [25,34,35]. Since Bryant [11] popularized the Binary Decision Diagram (BDD), there has been a proliferation of different decision diagrams which use different architectures, e.g., ZDD [23], TBDD [12,33], SDD [15], uSDD [32], FBDD [17]. Darwiche and Marquis [16] analytically compare the succinctness and tractability of manipulation operations (e.g., computing the logical OR of two functions) of these different diagrams and other representations such as CNF, resulting in a *knowledge compilation map*. In particular, they elucidate the inherent tradeoff between succinctness and tractability: Some diagrams can be exponentially more succinct, but do not admit efficient manipulation and/or query operations, or vice versa (e.g., d-DNNF [16] strictly contains DDs and allows model counting in polynomial time, but no efficient algorithm for computing the logical OR is known; and SDDs can be exponentially more succinct than BDDs [10]).

The Disjoint Support Decomposition BDD [6,26] (DSDBDD[1]) augments a BDD with disjunctive decompositions (sometimes called Ashenhurst-Curtis decompositions [1,3]). They are canonical like BDDs and support the same queries and operations as BDDs (model counting, conjunction, negation, etc.). DSDBDDs have so far been deployed in only few applications, mostly in circuit

---

[1] No name has been given to this diagram, so we use DSDBDD in accordance with conventions in the literature.

© Springer Nature Switzerland AG 2022
J. V. Deshmukh et al. (Eds.): NFM 2022, LNCS 13260, pp. 790–799, 2022.
https://doi.org/10.1007/978-3-031-06773-0_42

verification [27]. In order to know whether efforts to deploy them elsewhere are likely to be fruitful, we make an initial step towards placing DSDBDDs on the knowledge compilation map. Our main result is that DSDBDDs can be exponentially smaller than BDDs. To this end, we give a function that yields the separation, drawing on the theory of expander graphs to show that its BDD cannot be small. As corollaries, we also clarify the relation between other languages. Finally, we also point out some open questions.

2   Background and Related Work

A Binary Decision Diagram is a data structure used to represent and manipulate Boolean functions; formally it can be defined as follows.

Definition 1 (Binary Decision Diagram (BDD)). *A BDD is a rooted, directed acyclic graph. It has two leaves, labeled* TRUE *and* FALSE, *which represent the constant* TRUE *and* FALSE *functions. A non-leaf node is called a* Shannon node; *it is labeled with (the index of) a variable and has two outgoing edges, called the* low *edge and the* high *edge. Each node v represents a Boolean*

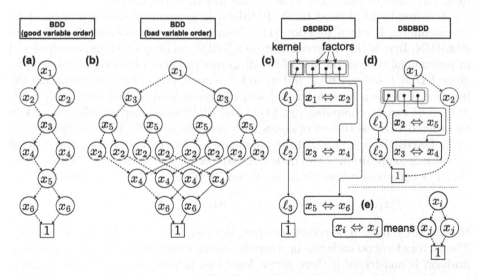

Fig. 1. (a) and (b): BDDs for the function $f \triangleq (x_1 \Leftrightarrow x_2) \wedge (x_3 \Leftrightarrow x_4) \wedge (x_5 \Leftrightarrow x_6)$. Low (high) edges are drawn as dotted (solid) arcs. The FALSE Leaf and arcs which go to the FALSE Leaf are not drawn. These two BDDs use different variable orders: (a) uses $x_1 < x_2 < x_3 < x_4 < x_5 < x_6$, whereas (b) uses $x_1 < x_3 < x_5 < x_2 < x_4 < x_6$, which is why (b) is much bigger than (a). (c): a DSDBDD for the same function. The root node is a decomposition node, whose kernel and factors are indicated. For sake of clarity and compactness, in several parts of the figure we have "collapsed" the small BDD representing $x_i \Leftrightarrow x_j$ by drawing it as a single rectangle (e). (d): a DSDBDD which represents the function $f = \neg x_1 \wedge \neg x_2 \vee x_1 \wedge ((x_2 \Leftrightarrow x_5) \wedge (x_3 \oplus x_4))$ and whose root node is not a Decomposition node.

function $[\![v]\!]$, *as follows. If a node* v *is labeled with variable* x *and has low edge to* v_0 *and high edge to* v_1, *then it represents the function* $[\![v]\!] \triangleq \neg x \wedge [\![v_0]\!] \vee x \wedge [\![v_1]\!]$. *A BDD is ordered if, on each path from the root to a leaf, each variable appears at most once and always in the same order. It is* reduced *if there are no equivalent nodes, representing the same function, and there is no node whose low and high edges point to the same node.*   ◇

Figures 1(a) and (b) show examples of BDDs. The two BDDs represent the same function, $f \triangleq (x_1 \Leftrightarrow x_2) \wedge (x_3 \Leftrightarrow x_4) \wedge (x_5 \Leftrightarrow x_6)$. They have a different shape, because they employ different variables orders, $x_1 < x_2 < x_3 < x_4 < x_5 < x_6$ and $x_1 < x_3 < x_5 < x_2 < x_4 < x_6$, respectively. In fact, if we generalized the functions and variable orders from $n = 6$ to $n > 6$, the corresponding BDD would stay linearly sized in the first case, but in the latter would become exponentially sized, in the number of variables. The effect of variable orders in BDDs is well known [9].

In the figure, the value $f(x)$ of an assignment x can be found by traversing the diagram as follows. One starts at the root node. A node is labeled with a variable x_i; if $x_i = 0$, we traverse the low (dotted) edge; otherwise, if $x_i = 1$, we traverse the high (solid) edge, until we arrive at a Leaf. To avoid cluttering the diagram, edges to the FALSE Leaf are not drawn in the figure.

A reduced and ordered BDD (ROBDD) is a canonical representation of its corresponding Boolean function [11]. From now on, we assume all BDDs are ROBDDs. Bryant [11] observed that such BDDs can be queried and manipulated in polynomial time in the size of the diagrams (number of nodes). For example, given BDDs f and g, with k and m nodes, respectively, a BDD representing the function $f \wedge g$ can be constructed and the number of models of f (i.e., $\vec{x}$ s.t. $f(x) = 1$) can be computed in $\mathcal{O}(km)$ and $\mathcal{O}(k)$ time, respectively. *Layer* i in an ordered BDD, is the set of nodes with variable label x_i (possibly empty).

A DSDBDD [5,6,14,21,26–29] augments a BDD by considering the disjoint support decompositions of its nodes. A *disjoint support decomposition* of a function f decomposes it into its *kernel* k and its *factors* $j_1, \ldots, j_m$, as follows:

$$f(x_1, \ldots, x_n) = k(\ell_1, \ldots, \ell_m) \text{ with } \ell_i \triangleq j_i(x_{i,1}, \ldots, x_{i,n_i}) \tag{1}$$

Here factor j_i takes n_i variables as input; the variables ℓ_i are "dummy variables". The factors have no variables in common, so the numbers n_i sum to n. A decomposition is non-trivial if there are at least two factors, and one factor reads at least two variables. Ashenhurst [3] was the first to develop a theory of disjoint support decompositions of Boolean functions and to give an algorithm which finds the decomposition given f's truth table, requiring time exponential in the number of variables. He showed that by repeatedly decomposing the functions k and j_i, the fixpoint reached is uniquely determined by f, up to complementation of the factors, and up to permutation of the order in which they appear as inputs to the kernel. This tree of functions is sometimes called the *Ashenhurst-Curtis decomposition* of f.

In [5], Bertacco and Damiani describe and implement an efficient algorithm to build a DSDBDD as follows. If a Shannon node in a BDD represents a function which allows a non-trivial decomposition, this node and its children are replaced by a dedicated *decomposition node* pointing to BDDs representing its kernel and its factors. These factors may themselves be decompositions, allowing 'nesting' of decompositions. This process is repeated until no Shannon node is eligible. Thus, a hybrid diagram is obtained, in which some nodes indicate decompositions (see Definition 2). Because of Ashenhurst's unique decomposition theorem [3], DSDBDDs are canonical like BDDs. The goal is that the new diagram is smaller than BDD, since this method may remove more nodes than it adds, but analytically little was known about this up to now.

Definition 2 (Disjoint Support Decomposition Diagram (DSDBDD)).
A DSDBDD is a BDD whose internal nodes are either Shannon nodes or decomposition nodes. A decomposition node v has an outgoing edge to an internal node v_{ker} called its kernel and outgoing edge to its factors $v_1, \ldots, v_m$. It represents the function $[\![v]\!] = [\![v_{ker}]\!]([\![v_1]\!], \ldots, [\![v_m]\!])$, like in Eq. 1. The diagram satisfies the following three rules:

1. *If v is a factor of a decomposition node, then v satisfies $[\![v]\!](0, \ldots, 0) = 1$*
2. *Two factors $[\![v_i]\!]$ and $[\![v_j]\!]$ of a decomposition node have disjoint support, i.e., $vars([\![v_i]\!]) \cap vars([\![v_j]\!]) = \emptyset$, for $i \neq j$, where $vars(f)$ denotes the set of variables on which f depends.*
3. *The factors $v_1, \ldots, v_m$ of a decomposition node satisfy $\min vars([\![v_i]\!]) < \min vars([\![v_j]\!])$ for $i < j$, where $\min$ is relative to the diagram's variable order.*

◇

Figure 1(c) shows a DSDBDD for the same function f as Fig. 1(a) and 1(b). Since this function can be expressed as a formula referencing each variable once, the DSDBDD can easily decompose it, obtaining the kernel $k = \text{AND}$ on three variables. The factors are $x_i \Leftrightarrow x_{i+1}$ for $i = 1, 3, 5$. We remark that this succinct decomposition is available to a DSDBDD regardless of the variable order, whereas the BDD may have exponential size unless the right variable order is found. Figure 1(d) shows that the root of a DSDBDD is not necessarily a decomposition node.

Let us briefly motivate the three rules in Definition 2, which are similar to those formulated by Bertacco and Damiani [5]. The purpose of the rules is to keep the query and manipulation operations tractable, i.e., to prevent the diagram from becoming more expressive than intended. Notably, without rule 2, we no longer have efficient algorithms for querying and manipulating such a diagram; for example, model counting would be NP-hard, because, a 3-CNF formula may now be represented as a decomposition with kernel AND, and whose factors are disjunctions on three variables. Rule 1 compensates the fact that, according to Ashenhurst's Theorem, a decomposition is unique up to complementation of the factors. For example, if a function f has a decomposition $f = k(\ell_1, \ldots, \ell_m)$ with $\ell_i = j_i(x_{i,1}, \ldots, x_{i,n_i})$ as in Eq. 1, then another decomposition is $f = k'(\neg\ell_1, \ldots, \neg\ell_m)$, where k' takes the values $k'(\ell_1, \ldots, \ell_m) \triangleq k(\neg\ell_1, \ldots, \neg\ell_m)$. More generally, for each factor, the complementation may be chosen independently, leading to exponentially many possible decompositions. Rule 1 uniquely determines the choice of complementation by enforcing that, for each factor, $j_i(0, \ldots, 0) = 1$. Similarly, rule 3 compensates for the fact that a decomposition is unique up to permutation of the kernel's input variables. For example, we may write the function f above as $f = k''(j_m, \ldots, j_1)$ where $k''(\ell_1, \ldots, \ell_m) \triangleq k(\ell_m, \ldots, \ell_1)$.

Technically, the kernel of a decomposition node takes as input variables that are not inputs to f. The question which variables of the kernel to identify with which variables of the DD can be an important design decision for DSDBDD package implementations, and for obtaining canonicity. The diagram can be made canonical by imposing additional rules. Since such a canonical diagram is included in the above definition, a separation between BDDs and Definition 2 implies a separation with the canonical version. Therefore, we omit the strengthening of Definition 2 to obtain canonicity for the purposes of this work.

DSDBDDs supports the same queries and manipulation operations as BDDs (i.e., conjunction, disjunction, negation, model counting, etc.). These algorithms greedily minimize the DD by checking, whenever a new node is constructed, whether the node allows a decomposition, and then building this decomposition before proceeding. The worst-case running times of the algorithms are polynomial in the size of the BDDs (but not necessarily in the size of the DSDBDDs). In the best case, the running time is much better; in that case, the operands of, e.g., CONJOIN, are two decompositions whose kernels read exactly the same factors. In this case the operation can take advantage of the fact that, if $j_1, \ldots, j_m$ are functions such that f_1, f_2 decompose as $f = k_1(j_1, \ldots, j_m)$ and $f_2 = k_2(j_1, \ldots, j_m)$, then

$$f_1 \wedge f_2 = (k_1 \wedge k_2)(j_1, \ldots, j_m) \tag{2}$$

This allows the CONJOIN algorithm to work only on k_1 and k_2, whose diagrams may be exponentially smaller than the BDDs of f and g. In the worst case,

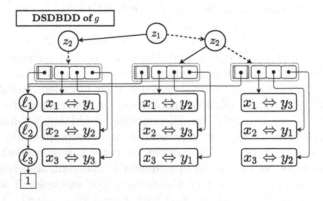

Fig. 2. The DSDBDD of the function g, in Eq. 4 when $n = 3$. The permutations used are $\pi_0 = (1)(2)(3), \pi_1 = (1, 2, 3), \pi_2 = (1, 3, 2)$. The rectangle containing $x_i \Leftrightarrow x_j$ represents the BDD of the function $x_i \Leftrightarrow x_j$, as shown in Fig. 1(e).

however, the decompositions share no factors, so that CONJOIN must "unfold" these decomposition nodes into BDDs and the operation is done on the BDDs; hence, the running time is polynomial in the size of the BDDs. Bertacco and Plaza implemented these operations in the publicly available software package STACCATO [26,27]. They find that their package is competitive with CUDD both in terms of time and memory, on the task of compiling a Boolean circuit into a DD.

Similar ideas appear in AND/OR multi-valued DDs (AOMDDs) [20], which are canonial, and in BDS-Maj diagrams [2]. In BDS-Maj, the kernel is always chosen to be the Majority function on three inputs, and the factors may share variables, unlike in a DSDBDD.

3   Succinctness Separation Between DSDBDD and BDD

Theorem 1 shows an example of a *separating function* g (Eq. 4) which has a small DSDBDD but exponential-sized BDD, *for every variable order*. It is based on three multiplexed copies of the order-parameterized function f, with variable orders π_0, π_1, π_2. By abuse of notation, we use z both as a bit-string, and as the integer $z \in \{0, 1, 2\}$ which the bit-string represents in base 2. The function f is well known to yield exponential BDDs for non-interleaved variable orders, as our generalized Lemma 1 shows. We state it without proof.

$$f[\pi](x_1, \ldots, x_n, y_1, \ldots, y_n) \triangleq (x_1 \Leftrightarrow y_{\pi(1)}) \wedge \cdots \wedge (x_n \Leftrightarrow y_{\pi(n)}) \tag{3}$$

$$g(z, x_1, \ldots, x_n, y_1, \ldots, y_n) \triangleq f[\pi_z](x_1, \ldots, x_n, y_1, \ldots, y_n) \text{ for } z \in \{0, 1, 2\}. \tag{4}$$

Lemma 1. *Let $\pi \in S_n$ and σ be an order over $\{x_1, \ldots, x_n, y_1, \ldots, y_n\}$ (the variables $f[\pi]$). For $1 \le i \le n$, say that x_i and $y_{\pi(i)}$ are partners. Let L be the first n variables according to σ. If k elements in L have their partner outside of L, then a BDD of $f[\pi]$ with variable order σ has at least 2^k nodes on layer n.*

By choosing distinct permutations π, π', the functions $f[\pi], f[\pi']$ will disagree on which variables are partners. Theorem 1 shows that there exist many irreconcilable choices for permutations $\pi_0 - \pi_2$ in g, because the corresponding "partner graph", connecting two partner variables according to either permutation, is an *expander*, i.e., has high connectivity.

Theorem 1. *Let π_0, π_1, π_2 be permutations chosen uniformly and independently at random from S_n. Then it holds that, with high probability, for every variable order σ over $\{x_1, \ldots, x_n, y_1, \ldots, y_n\}$, at least one of the BDDs for $f[\pi_0], f[\pi_1], f[\pi_2]$ has size $2^{\Omega(n)}$ and hence the BDD for g is also large.*

Proof. Let G be the undirected bipartite graph with nodes $V = \{x_1, \ldots, x_n, y_1, \ldots, y_n\}$ and edges $E = E_0 \cup E_1 \cup E_2$ with $E_j = \{(x_i, y_{\pi_j(i)}) \mid 1 \le i \le n\}$. Then G is an expander with high probability by Theorem 4.16 in

[19]. That is, there is a constant $\varepsilon > 0$ (independent of n) such that, with high probability, for all sets of vertices $L \subset V$, if $|L| \leq n$, then

$$\frac{|N(L) \setminus L|}{|L|} \geq \varepsilon \qquad \text{where } N(L) = \{w \mid \exists v \in L : (v, w) \in E\} \qquad (5)$$

Let σ be a variable order of V (the variables of the functions $f[\pi_j]$), and let L be the first n variables according σ. Then there are at least $\varepsilon \cdot n$ vertices in $\overline{L}$ connected to L. Since each vertex is connected to at most 3 edges, it holds that one of the edge sets E_j is responsible for at least $\varepsilon \cdot n/3$ edges crossing over from L to $\overline{L}$. Let $K = E_j \cap (L \times \overline{L})$ be a set of pairs $(x_i, y_{\pi_j(i)})$ such that x_i is in L, but its partner $y_{\pi_j(i)}$ is $\overline{L}$. It follows from Lemma 1 that the corresponding function $f[\pi_j]$ has a BDD of size at least $2^{|K|} = 2^{\Omega(n)}$. Since $g_{|z:=j} = f[\pi_j]$, and since a BDD is at least as large as the BDDs of its subfunctions, g also has at least $2^{\Omega(n)}$ nodes. This holds w.h.p. over the choice of permutations.   □

The DSDBDD of g is shown in Fig. 2, for $n = 3$. For larger n, the DSDBDD simply has more "rows", i.e., there are still three decomposition nodes, and they have n factors. The DSDBDD of g therefore has only $\mathcal{O}(n)$ nodes for larger n.

An immediate corollary is that the same relation holds between DSDBDDs versus ZDDs [23], Tagged BDDs [33] and CBDDs [12], since these decision diagrams are all at most a factor n smaller than BDDs on any function.

4   Conclusion and Future Work

We have analyzed the Disjoint Support Decomposition Binary Decision Diagram and found that it strictly dominates BDD and ZDD in terms of memory, up to polynomial overhead. That is, DSDBDDs can be exponentially smaller than BDDs. It remains an open question how DSDBDDs relates to other very expressive DDs; notably, it would be good to know its relation to SDDs, FBDDs, non-deterministic BDDs (∨-BDD [7,8]) and d-DNNF. In addition, it would be interesting to map the complexity of DSDBDDs of the different operations considered by Darwiche & Marquis [16].

To the best of our knowledge, DSDBDDs have not been deployed on large, real-world problems as encountered, e.g., in model checking and synthesis. Given that we showed that DSDBDDs can be exponentially more succinct, and they retain canonicity of BDDs, it could be worthwhile to test the scalability of DSDBDD in practice. In a similar vein, the integration of disjoint support decompositions into other decision diagrams could be considered. Minato [24] shows how to find the DSDs of the nodes in a ZDD; a next step would be to integrate this into the Boolean operations of ZDDs, as was done in [26,27], so that the diagram remains small during compilation. Other promising candidates for integration with DSDs are FDDs and SDDs; we are not aware of any work in this direction.

Acknowledgements. The authors wish to thank Holger Hoos for insightful discussions and for many useful comments on drafts of this paper, and the anonymous NFM reviewers for helpful feedback.

References

1. Al-Rabadi, A.N., Perkowski, M., Zwick, M.: A comparison of modified reconstructability analysis and Ashenhurst-Curtis decomposition of Boolean functions, Kybernetes (2004)
2. Amarú, L., Gaillardon, P.-E., De Micheli, G.: BDS-MAJ: A BDD-based logic synthesis tool exploiting majority logic decomposition. In: Proceedings of the 50th Annual Design Automation Conference, pp. 1–6 (2013)
3. Ashenhurst, R.L.: The decomposition of switching functions. In: Proceedings of an International Symposium on the Theory of Switching, April 1957 (1957)
4. Baier, C., Katoen, J.-P.: Principles of Model Checking. The MIT Press, Cambridge (2008)
5. Bertacco, V.: The disjunctive decomposition of logic functions. In: Proceedings of the International Conference on Computer-Aided Design (ICCAD 1997), November 1997, pp. 78–82 (1997)
6. Bertacco, V., Damiani, M.: Boolean function representation based on disjoint-support decompositions. In: Proceedings International Conference on Computer Design. VLSI in Computers and Processors, pp. 27–32. IEEE (1996)
7. Bollig, B., Buttkus, M.: On the relative succinctness of sentential decision diagrams. Theory Comput. Syst. **63**(6), 1250–1277 (2019)
8. Bollig, B., Farenholtz, M.: On the relation between structured d-DNNFs and SDDs. Theory Comput. Syst. **65**(2), 274–295 (2021)
9. Bollig, B., Wegener, I.: Improving the variable ordering of OBDDs is NP-complete. IEEE Trans. Comput. **45**(9), 993–1002 (1996)
10. Bova, S.: SDDs are exponentially more succinct than OBDDs. In: Thirtieth AAAI Conference on Artificial Intelligence (2016)
11. Randal, E.: Bryant, Graph-based algorithms for Boolean function manipulation. IEEE Trans. Computers **35**(8), 677–691 (1986)
12. Bryant, R.E.: Chain reduction for binary and zero-suppressed decision diagrams. In: Beyer, D., Huisman, M. (eds.) TACAS 2018. LNCS, vol. 10805, pp. 81–98. Springer, Cham (2018). https://doi.org/10.1007/978-3-319-89960-2_5
13. Dal, G.H., Laarman, A.W., Hommersom, A., Lucas, P.J.F.: A compositional approach to probabilistic knowledge compilation. Int. J. Approximate Reasoning **138**, 38–66 (2021)
14. Damiani, M., Bertacco, V.: Finding complex disjunctive decompositions of logic functions. In: Proceedings of the International Workshop on Logic & Synthesis, pp. 478–483 (1998)
15. Darwiche, A.: SDD: a new canonical representation of propositional knowledge bases. In: Proceedings of the Twenty-Second International Joint Conference on Artificial Intelligence-Volume Two, pp. 819–826. AAAI Press (2011)
16. Darwiche, A., Marquis, P.: A knowledge compilation map. J. Artif. Intell. Res. **17**, 229–264 (2002)
17. Gergov, J., Meinel, C.: Efficient Boolean manipulation with OBDDs can be extended to FBDDs. Universität Trier, Mathematik/Informatik, Forschungsbericht, pp. 93–12 (1993)

18. Hong, X., Ying, M., Feng, Y., Zhou, X., Li, S.: Approximate equivalence checking of noisy quantum circuits. arXiv preprint arXiv:2103.11595 (2021)
19. Hoory, S., Linial, N., Wigderson, A.: Expander graphs and their applications. Bull. Am. Math. Soc. **43**(4), 439–561 (2006)
20. Mateescu, R., Dechter, R., Marinescu, R.: And/or multi-valued decision diagrams (AOMDDs) for graphical models. J. Artif. Intelli. Res. **33**, 465–519 (2008)
21. Matsunaga, Y.: An exact and efficient algorithm for disjunctive decomposition. In: Proceedings of Synthesis and System Integration of Mixed Technologies (SASIMI 1998, Japan), October 1998
22. McMillan, K.L.: Symbolic model checking: an approach to the state explosion problem, Ph.D. thesis, 1992, UMI No. GAX92-24209
23. Minato, S.: Zero-suppressed BDDs for set manipulation in combinatorial problems. In: Proceedings of the 30th ACM/IEEE Design Automation Conference, pp. 272–277. IEEE (1993)
24. Minato, S.: Finding simple disjoint decompositions in frequent itemset data using zero-suppressed BDD. In: Proceedings of IEEE ICDM 2005 Workshop on Computational Intelligence in Data Mining, pp. 3–11 (2005)
25. Niemann, P., Wille, R., Miller, D.M., Thornton, M.A., Drechsler, R.: QMDDs: efficient quantum function representation and manipulation. IEEE Trans. Comput. Aided Des. Integr. Circuits Syst. **35**(1), 86–99 (2015)
26. Plaza, S., Bertacco, V.: Boolean operations on decomposed functions. In: Proceedings of the 24th International Workshop on Logic & Synthesis, pp. 310–317 (2005)
27. Plaza, S., Bertacco, V.: STACCATO: disjoint support decompositions from BDDs through symbolic kernels. In: Proceedings of the 2005 Asia and South Pacific Design Automation Conference, pp. 276–279 (2005)
28. Sasao, T.: FPGA design by generalized functional decomposition. In: Sasao, T. (ed.) Logic Synthesis and Optimization, The Kluwer International Series in Engineering and Computer Science, vol. 212, pp. 233–258. Springer, Boston (1993). https://doi.org/10.1007/978-1-4615-3154-8_11
29. Sasao, T., Matsuura, M.: DECOMPOS: an integrated system for functional decomposition. In: International Workshop on Logic Synthesis, vol. 1998, pp. 471–477 (1998)
30. Soeken, M., Frehse, S., Wille, R., Drechsler, R.: RevKit: a toolkit for reversible circuit design. J. Multiple Valued Log. Soft Comput. **18**(1), 55–65 (2012)
31. Soeken, M., Tague, L., Dueck, G.W., Drechsler, R.: Ancilla-free synthesis of large reversible functions using binary decision diagrams. J. Symb. Comput. **73**, 1–26 (2016)
32. Van den Broeck, G., Darwiche, A.: On the role of canonicity in knowledge compilation. In: Twenty-Ninth AAAI Conference on Artificial Intelligence (2015)
33. van Dijk, T., Wille, R., Meolic, R.: Tagged BDDs: combining reduction rules from different decision diagram types. In: Proceedings of the 17th Conference on Formal Methods in Computer-Aided Design, FMCAD Inc, pp. 108–115 (2017)
34. Viamontes, G.F., Rajagopalan, M., Markov, I.L., Hayes, J.P.: Gate-level simulation of quantum circuits. In: Proceedings of the 2003 Asia and South Pacific Design Automation Conference, pp. 295–301 (2003)
35. Vinkhuijzen, L., Coopmans, T., Elkouss, D., Dunjko, V., Laarman, A.: LIMDD a decision diagram for simulation of quantum computing including stabilizer states, arXiv preprint arXiv:2108.00931 (2021)
36. Vinkhuijzen, L., Laarman, A.: Symbolic model checking with sentential decision diagrams. In: Pang, J., Zhang, L. (eds.) SETTA 2020. LNCS, vol. 12153, pp. 124–142. Springer, Cham (2020). https://doi.org/10.1007/978-3-030-62822-2_8

37. Wille, R., Drechsler, R.: BDD-based synthesis of reversible logic for large functions. In: Proceedings of the 46th Annual Design Automation Conference, pp. 270–275 (2009)
38. Zulehner, A., Wille, R.: Improving synthesis of reversible circuits: exploiting redundancies in paths and nodes of QMDDs. In: Phillips, I., Rahaman, H. (eds.) RC 2017. LNCS, vol. 10301, pp. 232–247. Springer, Cham (2017). https://doi.org/10.1007/978-3-319-59936-6_18

Incremental Transitive Closure for Zonal Abstract Domain

Kenny Ballou[✉][iD] and Elena Sherman[iD]

Boise State University, Boise, USA
{kennyballou,elenasherman}@boisestate.edu

Abstract. The Zonal numerical domain is an efficient, weakly-relational abstract domain in static analysis by abstract interpretation. Compared to the Interval domain, the Zonal domain is capable of discovering weak relations between two program variables. To reason about Zonal states, it is imperative that they are transformed into a canonical closed form. This task is accomplished through the transitive closure operation commonly implemented as the all-pairs shortest path algorithm, with $O(n^3)$ complexity, where n is the number of program variables.

In this work, we explore the closed form of Zonal states in the context of a data-flow analysis framework. Also, we present an incremental transitive closure algorithm that preserves a closed form of an updated Zonal state. The algorithm reduces the overall analysis complexity to $O(n^2)$. We evaluate our approach by performing intra-procedural Zonal analysis on 63 real-world programs. The results show an improvement in runtime, especially on large programs. For example, an hour-long analyzer run with the traditional Zonal implementation has been reduced to a minute with the proposed incremental Zonal variant.

1 Introduction

Abstract interpretation (AI) [4] is an essential technique for supporting various software engineering and programming languages tasks. Used in the context of data-flow analysis framework [7], AI assists a static analyzer with computing invariants over program variables. Then areas such as program verification [2,16] or compiler optimization [1,6] exploit these invariants to accomplish their tasks.

To capture the abstract semantics of a program, AI employs abstract numerical domains, which vary in their expressive power. The Interval domain abstracts program variables into a single continuous interval. Relational numerical domains, such as the Zone and Octagon domain [9,10], are more expressive because they represent relations between program variables. However, the expressiveness of relational numerical domains comes with a higher runtime cost [9]. The Zonal domain is the most efficient among relational domains, but it still timeouts on large programs because of its cubic complexity in terms of program variables [10]. This complexity comes from the transitive closure algorithm for computing canonical representations for Zonal states, which is imperative when comparing Zonal states or identifying infeasible states.

© Springer Nature Switzerland AG 2022
J. V. Deshmukh et al. (Eds.): NFM 2022, LNCS 13260, pp. 800–808, 2022.
https://doi.org/10.1007/978-3-031-06773-0_43

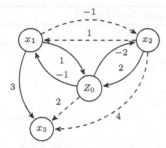

(a) Graph representation of a Zonal state. Dashed edges are implicit relations.

$$\begin{array}{c} \\ Z_0 \\ x_1 \\ x_2 \\ x_3 \end{array} \begin{array}{cccc} Z_0 & x_1 & x_2 & x_3 \\ \begin{pmatrix} 0 & -1 & -2 & \boxed{2} \\ 1 & 0 & \boxed{-1} & 3 \\ 2 & \boxed{1} & 0 & \boxed{4} \\ \top & \top & \top & 0 \end{pmatrix} \end{array}$$

(b) Difference Bounded Matrix encoding of the graph on the left. Dashed boxes denote implicit relations.

Fig. 1. A directed graph for $x_1 = 1$, $x_2 = 2$ and $x_1 - x_3 \leq 3$ and the corresponding difference bounded matrix encoding.

In this work, we investigate the full closure property of Zonal abstract states in the context of a data-flow static analysis framework. While previous work [10] defines transfer functions on the Zonal domain regardless of its full closure property, we observed that the fixpoint algorithm frequently compares the Zonal states from the current and previous iterations, which requires invocation of the closure algorithm. This observation prompted us to explore whether the efficiency of transfer functions for fully closed Zonal states can be improved.

We evaluated three implementations of Zonal states in an intra-procedural branch-sensitive data-flow analysis framework on 63 real-world programs. We constructed our experiment to answer the following two research questions:
RQ1: In the context of data-flow analysis, does the propagation of fully closed Zonal states improve runtime efficiency of the analysis?
RQ2: In the context of data-flow analysis, is the proposed incremental transitive closure algorithm more efficient than a conventional closure implementation?

Before we answer these questions in Sect. 4, we first present necessary background on Zonal abstract domain and then proposed algorithm in Sect. 3. We conclude with the paper's summary and directions for future work.

2 Zonal Abstract Domain

The Zonal [10] abstract domain is a weakly-relational domain that includes only constraints of the form $x - y \leq c$, where x and y are program variables and c is a numerical constant, in our case an integer. To represent constraints of the form $x \leq c$ in the above canonical form, a special "zero" variable, Z_0, is introduced. Since its value is always 0, the constraint becomes $x - Z_0 \leq c$. The set of linear inequalities represents a bounding region of program variables' possible values.

Representation. The advantages of Zonal domain are that its state can be efficiently represented as a directed graph, and operations on states reduce to graph operations. Figure 1a gives a graph example and Fig. 1b the corresponding

Algorithm 1. Forget operation for a traditional Zonal state

```
 1: function CLOSEANDFORGET(k)
 2:     for i = 0 to N do                                    ▷ Close connected paths
 3:         for j = 0 to N do
 4:             if (i ≠ j ∧ j ≠ k) then
 5:                 M_ij ← min (M_ij, M_ik + M_jk)
 6:             end if
 7:         end for
 8:     end for
 9:     for i = 0 to N do                              ▷ Forget constraints connected to k
10:         if i ≠ k then
11:             M_ik ← ⊤
12:             M_ki ← ⊤
13:         end if
14:     end for
15: end function
```

encoding as a difference-bounded matrix (DBM) [5]. Here, a constraint $x - y \le c$, is an edge with weight c from the source node x and the target node y. The constraints encoded in Fig. 1a (in solid lines) are $x_1 = 1$, i.e., $x_1 - Z_0 \le 1$ and $Z_0 - x_1 \le -1$, $x_2 = 2$ and $x_1 - x_3 \le 3$. Dashed lines represent implicit relations, while the absence of edges indicate unbounded relations between variables. Thus, no edge from x_3 to x_1 indicates the unbounded relation $x_3 - x_1 \le +\infty$.

The DBM representation places source nodes in rows and target nodes in columns in the same order, and weights between them are elements of the matrix, e.g., the x_1 row and the x_3 column represents the relationship $x_1 - x_3 \le 3$, and ⊤ values indicate unbounded relations. The values in dashed boxes are implicit relations that are computed by a transitive closure algorithm.

Canonical Form. To efficiently compare two Zonal states using their DBM encoding, and perform other essential operations used in a data-flow framework (e.g., `intersection`, `least-upper bound`), it is essential that Zonal states are in the same canonical representation. In the previous example, the set of constraints with solid lines and the same set augmented with implicit constraints (dashed lines) describe the identical bounded region, yet their DBMs are different. Miné [10] proposed a canonical form by transitively closing the set of constraints in a Zonal state. That is, the canonical form where all constraints are explicit, no additional constraints can be inferred. This form is often called *fully closed*.

Essentially, the transitive closure adds implicit constraints, but also tightens the constraints represented by the DBM. Thus, given a DBM M, the transitive closure of M with $n = |M|$ yields the following property: $\forall i, j, k \in \{0, 1, \ldots n\}$, $m_{ij} \le m_{ik} + m_{kj}$ on elements of M. To transform M into this canonical form, researchers commonly use an all-pairs shortest path algorithm, such as the Floyd-Warshall algorithm [3]. Unfortunately, it has $\Theta(n^3)$ complexity. In fact, this algorithm is primarily the reason for Zonal domain analysis has $O(n^3)$ complexity [10].

Operations. A transfer function of a Zonal state interprets semantics of a statement in terms of removal of existing constraints, i.e., `forget` operation,

---

Algorithm 2. Incremental Closure Algorithm

```
 1: function INCREMENTALCLOSURE(s, t, c, M)
 2:     N ← length(M), W ← {t}
 3:     if ADDCONSTRAINT(s, t, c) then
 4:         for i = 0 to N do
 5:             if ADDCONSTRAINT(s, i, M_st + M_ti) then
 6:                 W ← W ∪ {i}
 7:             end if
 8:         end for
 9:         for i = 0 to N do
10:             for w ∈ W do
11:                 ADDCONSTRAINT(i, w, M_is + M_sw)
12:             end for
13:         end for
14:     end if
15: end function
```

---

and addition of a new constraint, i.e., add operation. The add operation only requires updating a single element of the state's DBM.

However, the forget operation for traditional Zonal states requires additional care, since removing an edge causes all implicit constraints to also disappear, which results in precision loss. Thus, if in Fig. 1a the implicit constraints $x_3 \geq -2$ inferred by $x_1 - x_3 \leq 3$ and $x_1 = 1$ is not made explicit before reassigning x_1 (which leads to removing all incoming and outgoing edges from the x_1 node), then the value of x_3 becomes less restricted. As such, the forget operation has an intermediate path closure step (lines 2–8 of Algorithm 1) that discovers all implicit paths through the node marked for removal. Afterwards, the algorithm removes all constraints connected to the removed node (lines 9–14). Note, this operation does not remove the variable, instead it removes the constraints associated with the variable, thus making it unbounded. Algorithm 1 presents pseudocode for forget as in previous work [10] and has $O(n^2)$ complexity.

If a data-flow framework propagates fully closed Zonal states, however, then the first part of the algorithm on lines 2–9 becomes unnecessary. Thus, for *closed* Zonal states, the complexity of forget operation becomes $O(n)$. This complexity reduction comes with a cost – the framework should transform states to their fully closed form ($O(n^3)$). Although, a data-flow framework already requires *closed* Zonal states to perform state comparisons, feasibility checks, and other operations. Hence, the fully closed property of a Zonal state could eliminate invocation of closure algorithm in the context of the framework.

3   Incremental Closure

Since the data-flow framework favors the fully closed form, we investigate whether we can modify the transfer function's operations add and forget such that for a given fully closed Zonal state they produce a new, fully closed state.

In this case, a constraint removal through forget operation is the same as for closed Zonal states. If a state is fully closed, then a removal of an edge maintains such a property since no new inferred constraints could be discovered. But add operation requires additional considerations. For Zonal states, we propose a novel incremental closure algorithm, which after adding a constraint, also discovers all minimal constraints that can be inferred through that edge. The algorithm computes edges between the source node's parents and the target node's children.

Algorithm 2 presents the pseudocode for the DBM encoding. The parameters s and t are indices of the closed DBM M for the source and the target nodes, and $c \in \mathbb{Z}$ is the constant. If the added constraint is tighter than the existing one, i.e., `AddConstratint` returns true, then it proceeds to discover new implicit constraints. Then the algorithm constructs a worklist of all children which are affected by the addition of the new constraint (lines 4–8). Using this worklist and the parents of s, the algorithm computes the minimum constraint between all the parents of s and the children of t (lines 9–12). The complexity of the incremental transitive closure algorithm is $O(n^2)$ from the two nested loops on the same lines.

Following is a proof of correctness for Algorithm 2.

Theorem 1. *Given a fully closed Zonal state in DBM encoding and a new constraint with s, t and c parameters, the* `IncrementalClosure` *algorithm computes a correct, fully-closed DBM.*

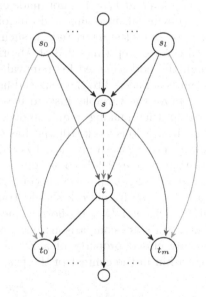

Fig. 2. Example graph representation of M during induction step. The dashed cyan edge represents the additional edge $(s \rightarrow t)$; blue edges represent parents of s connecting to t; magenta edges represent s connecting to children of t; and green edges represent parents of s connecting to children of t. (Color figure online)

Proof. Let V be a finite set of program variables such that $s, t \in V$.

We prove by induction on the number of edges of M, with the full closure property as our induction hypothesis.

Case 1. *Base Case.* Our DBM M has $k = 0$ edges and it is closed. Since $m_{ij} = \top$ $\forall i, j \in \{0, 1, \dots |V|\}$. Therefore, our full closure property, $\forall i, j, h \in \{0, 1, \dots, |V|\}, m_{ij} \leq m_{ih} + m_{hj}$, holds.

Case 2. *Induction.* We assume DBM M with k edges, M is fully closed, and no edge exists between node s and t, i.e., $s - t \leq \top$.

Adding edge $s \rightarrow t$, we have $k + 1$ edges.

Let $S = \mathrm{parent}(s) \cup \{s\}$ and $T = \mathrm{children}(t) \cup \{t\}$. The edges to be recomputed consists of edges from $s_l \rightarrow t_m, \forall s_l \in S$ and $\forall t_m \in T$. We need to show the full closure property holds.

Case (a) *Parents of s connect to t.* This case connects to blue edges in Fig. 2.

$\forall s_l \in S$, we connect

$$m^{*}_{s_l t} \leftarrow \min\left(m_{s_l t}, m_{s_l s} + m_{st}\right)$$

where $m^{*}_{s_l t}$ is the new edge weight for edge $s_l \rightarrow t$.

Case (b) *s connects to members of T.* This case connects to magenta edges in Fig. 2.

$\forall t_m \in T$, we connect

$$m^{*}_{s t_m} \leftarrow \min\left(m_{s t_m}, m_{st} + m_{t t_m}\right)$$

where $m^{*}_{s t_m}$ is the new edge weight for edge $s \rightarrow t_m$.

Case (c) *S connects to T.* This case connects to green edges in Fig. 2.

$\forall s_l \in S$ and $\forall t_m \in T$, we connect

$$m^{*}_{s_l t_m} \leftarrow \min\left(m_{s_l t_m}, m_{s_l s} + m_{st} + m_{t t_m}\right)$$
$$\leftarrow \min\left(m_{s_l t_m}, m_{s_l s} + m^{*}_{s t_m}\right)$$

where $m^{*}_{s_l t_m}$ is the new edge weight for edge $s_l \rightarrow t_m$.

Since either $m_{s_l t_m}$ was already constrained by some h or the addition of edge $s \rightarrow t$ induced a new minimum which was computed above, therefore, $m_{s_l t_m} \leq m_{s_l h} + m_{h t_m}, \forall h \in \{0, 1, \dots |V|\}$ holds. $\square$

4   Evaluations and Results

To evaluate the proposed approaches, we implemented three Zonal branch sensitive intra-procedural analyses: *traditional, closed* and *incremental*. We used the Soot (v. 4.2.1.) data-flow framework [14] that has been extended to support numerical abstract domains [11]. We evaluated these implementations on real-world programs and compared their runtimes. We used the obtained data to answer our two research questions.

Benchmarks. Our benchmark set consists of 63 real-world Java methods with non-trivial number of integer operations [12]. To better evaluate the scalability

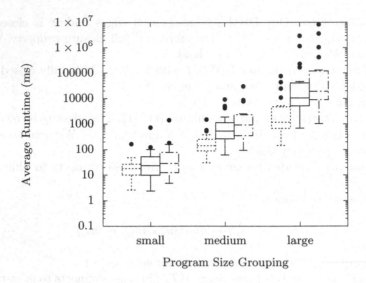

Fig. 3. Average runtime grouped by program sizes. Dotted boxes – *incremental*, solid boxes – *closed*, and dashed – *traditional* Zonal abstract domains.

of Zonal implementations, we partitioned the methods into three (3) groups: "small", "medium", and "large". The median instruction count for "small", "medium", and "large" is 23, 156, 468, respectively.

Environment. To avoid inconsistencies within JVM startup times and other experiment supporting operations, we record only the time each analyzer spends performing fixed-point computations. We run each Zonal implementation five times on each program and use the average time as data points.

Results. Figure 3 shows runtime results of our experiments as box plots (milliseconds, log scale y-axis) for each benchmark group (x-axis). The data shows that *closed* (solid boxes) performs slightly better than *traditional* (dashed boxes) Zonal states. Although both Zonal variants invoke the full closure operation at each statement, *closed* uses the full closure property to avoid invocation of this operation at merge and widening points, and when computing branch feasibility. Moreover, the forget operation for *closed* has a linear complexity, while the same operation for *traditional* has a quadratic complexity.

Thus, these improvements contribute to *closed* outperforming *traditional* implementation. However, after performing a t-test, we found no statistically significant differences for all program sizes for $p \leq 0.05$ (for the large group, runtimes become significantly different at $p \leq 0.07$). This small difference in *closed* over *traditional* is due to the dominating cubic complexity of the transitive closure algorithm. Thus, we see a slight improvement of *closed* Zonal state implementation over *traditional*, which indicates that propagating fully closed Zonal states is more efficient in the context of data-flow analysis.

We observe that *incremental* is more efficient compared to *closed*, especially for the large program group. Also, the growth of *incremental* is less steep than the other two variants, because the former is dominated by the quadratic and the latter by the cubic growth complexity in terms of program variables. The data for large program supports this difference in complexity, where the median runtime for *incremental* is about 10^3 ms, while for *closed* is about 10^4 ms.

T-test analyses show no statistical differences for the small group, but found them for the other two groups. The p value for *incremental* vs. *closed* for the medium group is 0.004 and for the large group is 0.002. Thus, we can conclude that our proposed incremental transitive closure algorithm is more efficient than a conventional closure algorithm in the context of a data-flow framework.

5   Conclusion

In this paper, we analyzed propagation of fully closed Zonal abstract states in the context of a data-flow static analysis framework. In addition, we proposed a novel incremental transitive closure algorithm for the Zonal abstract domain and showed analytically and experimentally that it reduces analysis time by an order of magnitude, especially on larger programs.

The representation of DBMs are borrowed from previous work in the model checking community [5,8,15]. This work may be relevant to applications within model checking techniques that require canonical representation of DBMs. In future work, we intend to extend the incremental closure algorithm to allow for more efficient implementations of other canonical forms besides the fully closed canonical form. For example, a canonical form that eliminates relations between constant values, or a minimal canonical form [8].

Acknowledgments. The work reported here was supported by the U.S. National Science Foundation under award CCF-19-42044.

References

1. Abate, C., et al.: An extended account of trace-relating compiler correctness and secure compilation. ACM Trans. Program. Lang. Syst. **43**(4), 1–48 (2021). https://doi.org/10.1145/3460860
2. Blanchet, B., et al.: A static analyzer for large safety-critical software. In: Proceedings of the ACM SIGPLAN 2003 Conference on Programming Language Design and Implementation, pp. 196–207. PLDI 2003, Association for Computing Machinery, New York, NY, USA (2003). https://doi.org/10.1145/781131.781153
3. Cormen, T., Leiserson, C., Rivest, R., Stein, C.: Introduction to Algorithms, chap. 26.2. Computer science, McGraw-Hill (2009). https://doi.org/10.11708/9446, https://books.google.com/books?id=aefUBQAAQBAJ
4. Cousot, P., Cousot, R.: Abstract interpretation: a unified lattice model for static analysis of programs by construction or approximation of fixpoints. In: Proceedings of the 4th ACM SIGACT-SIGPLAN symposium on Principles of programming languages, pp. 238–252. POPL 1977, ACM, New York, NY, USA (1977). https://doi.org/10.1145/512950.512973

5. Dill, D.L.: Timing assumptions and verification of finite-state concurrent systems. Lecture Notes in Computer Science, pp. 197–212 (1990). https://doi.org/10.1007/3-540-52148-8_17
6. Katz, S.: Program optimization using invariants. IEEE Trans. Softw. Eng. **4**(05), 378–389 (1978). https://doi.org/10.1109/TSE.1978.233858
7. Kildall, G.A.: A unified approach to global program optimization. In: Proceedings of the 1st Annual ACM SIGACT-SIGPLAN Symposium on Principles of Programming Languages, pp. 194–206. POPL 1973, ACM, New York, NY, USA (1973). https://doi.org/10.1145/512927.512945
8. Larsen, K., Larsson, F., Pettersson, P., Yi, W.: Efficient verification of real-time systems: compact data structure and state-space reduction. In: Proceedings Real-Time Systems Symposium, pp. 14–24. IEEE Computer Society (1997). https://doi.org/10.1109/real.1997.641265,https://doi.org/10.1109/REAL.1997.641265
9. Miné, A.: The octagon abstract domain. Higher Order Symbol. Comput. **19**(1), 31–100 (2006). https://doi.org/10.1007/s10990-006-8609-1
10. Miné, A.: A new numerical abstract domain based on difference-bound matrices. In: Danvy, O., Filinski, A. (eds.) PADO 2001. LNCS, vol. 2053, pp. 155–172. Springer, Heidelberg (2001). https://doi.org/10.1007/3-540-44978-7_10
11. Sherman, E.: Redesigning soot's data-flow analysis framework for abstract interpretation. In: Companion Proceedings for the ISSTA/ECOOP 2018 Workshops, pp. 78–84. ISSTA 2018, Association for Computing Machinery, New York, NY, USA (2018). https://doi.org/10.1145/3236454.3236506,https://doi.org/10.1145/3236454.3236506
12. Sherman, E., Dwyer, M.B.: Exploiting domain and program structure to synthesize efficient and precise data flow analyses (t). In: 2015 30th IEEE/ACM International Conference on Automated Software Engineering (ASE), November 2015. https://doi.org/10.1109/ase.2015.41
13. Tange, O.: Gnu parallel 20210722 ('blue unity'), July 2021. https://doi.org/10.5281/zenodo.5123056,https://doi.org/10.5281/zenodo.5123056, GNU Parallel is a general parallelizer to run multiple serial command line programs in parallel without changing them
14. Vallée-Rai, R. Co, P., Gagnon, E., Hendren, L., Lam, P., Sundaresan, V.: Soot - a java bytecode optimization framework. In: Proceedings of the 1999 Conference of the Centre for Advanced Studies on Collaborative Research, p. 13. CASCON 1999, IBM Press (1999)
15. Yovine, S.: Model checking timed automata. In: Rozenberg, G., Vaandrager, F.W. (eds.) EEF School 1996. LNCS, vol. 1494, pp. 114–152. Springer, Heidelberg (1998). https://doi.org/10.1007/3-540-65193-4_20
16. Zhu, H., Magill, S., Jagannathan, S.: A data-driven CHC solver. In: Proceedings of the 39th ACM SIGPLAN Conference on Programming Language Design and Implementation, pp. 707–721. PLDI 2018, Association for Computing Machinery, New York, NY, USA (2018). https://doi.org/10.1145/3192366.3192416

Proof Mate: An Interactive Proof Helper for PVS (Tool Paper)

Paolo Masci[1]([⊠]) and Aaron Dutle[2]

[1] National Institute of Aerospace, Hampton, VA, USA
paolo.masci@nianet.org
[2] NASA Langley Research Center, Hampton, VA, USA
aaron.m.dutle@nasa.gov

Abstract. This paper presents Proof Mate, an interactive proof helper for the PVS verification system. The helper is integrated in VSCode-PVS, the Visual Studio Code extension for PVS. It extends the capabilities of VSCode-PVS by introducing new functionalities for suggesting proof commands, sketching proof attempts, and repairing broken proofs during interactive proof sessions. This work further aligns VSCode-PVS to the functionalities provided by modern development tools, with the ultimate aim to facilitate the adoption of formal methods in engineering practices and education.

Tool available at: https://github.com/nasa/vscode-pvs

1 Introduction

The capabilities of formal methods tools have classically been measured by aspects such as the expressiveness of the specification language, the level of automation, and the scalability of the analysis when dealing with complex systems. In recent years, an additional metric started to play an important role, linked to the usability of the tool front-end. The current generation of proof engineers, and likely future generations, favor graphical front-ends over command line versions. Functionalities like auto-completion, integrated help, and point-and-click interactions are now considered baseline features that any modern tool front-end is expected to provide.

Developers of formal methods tools are upgrading the front-end of their tools to meet this new baseline. An example is VSCode-PVS [4], which upgrades the Emacs front-end of PVS [7] to Visual Studio Code, a mainstream open-source code editor widely popular in the developer community. VSCode-PVS provides editor functionalities such as autocompletion, hover information, live diagnostics, interactive proof tree visualizer and editor, among several others.

This work introduces Proof Mate, a new interactive tool for VSCode-PVS that further extends the capabilities of the PVS front-end with new functionalities for proof development, proof editing and proof repair.

P. Masci—Research by the first author is supported by the National Aeronautics and Space Administration under NASA/NIA Cooperative Agreement NNL09AA00A.

J. V. Deshmukh et al. (Eds.): NFM 2022, LNCS 13260, pp. 809–815, 2022.
https://doi.org/10.1007/978-3-031-06773-0_44

2   Theorem Proving in PVS and VSCode-PVS

The Prototype Verification System (PVS [7]) is an interactive theorem prover (ITP) based on a sequent calculus for classical higher-order logic, used extensively by NASA Langley Research Center's formal methods team (see, e. g., [2, 6]). Specifications and properties are written in a human-readable ".pvs" file, but contrary to many other ITPs, proofs are stored in a separate proof file using an internal representation [5], and not generally intended for direct reading or editing. Proofs are constructed interactively in PVS using proof commands, which are applied to a *sequent*. A sequent has the structure $A_1..A_n \vdash C_1..C_n$, where A_i are called antecedent formulas, and C_i are consequent formulas. A proof command manipulates the sequent (with some commands branching to several sequents). A branch is closed (i.e., proven) when an antecedent is false, a consequent is true, or the same formula appears in the antecedent and consequent. An example proof command is `assert`, which expands and simplifies definitions. Proofs can consist of many branches and hundreds of proof commands, stored as a list.

While the original PVS Emacs interface allows for *viewing* a proof in either text or tree form, *editing* a proof in this form is difficult even for expert users, and cannot be performed during an interactive proof session. VSCode-PVS [4] is a new front-end that integrates PVS in the Visual Studio Code editor. In VSCode-PVS, proof commands are entered in the Prover Console and displayed as a proof tree in a side panel called Proof Explorer (see Fig. 1). Proof Explorer improves the viewing and navigation of proofs by incorporating a collapsible, filesystem-like view. Edit operations in Proof Explorer, however, are intentionally constrained, because the proof tree shown is intended to always reflect the proof structure computed by PVS. This way, the user knows exactly what will be saved in the proof file at the end of a proof session.

3   Proof Mate

Proof Mate extends the capabilities of VSCode-PVS by introducing new functionalities for suggesting proof commands, sketching proof attempts, and repairing broken proofs during interactive proof sessions. The tool is integrated in the front-end as a side panel characterized by interactive tree views, inline actions, and a toolbar (see Fig. 1). Proof Mate has a similar look and feel to Proof Explorer, but because it is not tied directly to the proof being attempted, it offers much more flexibility to experiment with and write proof segments.

Suggesting Proof Commands. Proof Mate provides hints for proof commands during a proof session, while the proof engineer is proving a theorem. Hints are selected using heuristics based on common proof patterns in PVS. The heuristics are encoded into templates which ensure that the selected commands are applicable. One example is: "if a consequent formula starts with FORALL or an antecedent starts with EXISTS, then recommend skolemization commands (i.e., `skosimp*` or `skeep`)." Another example is: "if a formula has the form expr

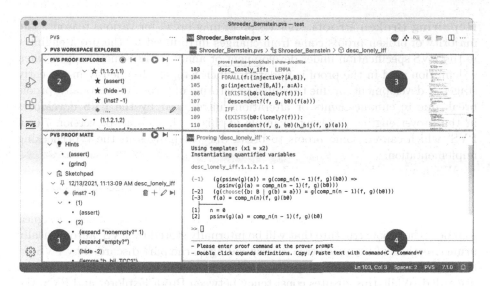

Fig. 1. Proof Mate (1), Proof Explorer (2), Editor (3) and Prover Console (4)

= IF expr THEN expr ENDIF, recommend commands for lifting the innermost contiguous branching structure out to the top level (i.e., `lift-if`)." When none of the other heuristics are matched, general simplification procedures are recommended (i.e., `assert` or `grind`). The hints are automatically computed by Proof Mate during interactive proof sessions, every time a new sequent is returned by PVS. A tooltip providing a brief description of the proof command is shown when hovering the mouse over a recommendation. Point-and-click interactions can be used to select a recommendation and send it to the prover console for execution.

Sketching Proof Attempts. Proof Mate provides a sketchpad that can be used by proof engineers to create and edit *proof clips*. While the look and feel of the sketchpad resembles that of Proof Explorer, proof clips shown in the sketchpad are designed to reflect proof ideas in the mind of the proof engineer developing the proof, as opposed to mirroring the proof tree that is internally created by PVS. Because of this, proof clips can be edited freely. Multiple proof clips can be created and stored in the sketchpad. Each clip is automatically labeled with a timestamp or a custom name provided by the proof engineer. Edit operations allowed on sketchpad clips include renaming, addition, deletion, and copy/paste of proof commands and proof branches. Copy/paste operations are also allowed between the sketchpad and Proof Explorer. All operations can be performed with point-and-click interactions. Inline action buttons are provided for frequent operations. Proof clips are maintained across different proof sessions, allowing re-use of proof sketches created for other proofs. Interactive controls are available for executing proof commands and playback of proof clips.

Repairing Broken Proofs. A PVS proof may break for various reasons. The majority of broken proofs come from changes introduced by the proof engineer in the PVS specification under development or analysis. This may happen when a definition used in the proof is updated, which happens frequently in the early stages of development, or due to simple refactoring of terms. Occasionally, proofs break due to enhancements or alterations introduced by the PVS developers in the prover engine. A recent example of this is the release of version 7.0 of PVS, which caused some proofs to break due to changes in the typechecking implementation.

When a proof breaks, and PVS attempts to rerun the proof, some fragments of the proof structure are often discarded[1]. This may happen when, for example, a `split` command previously created 3 branches, but due to some change in the specification, only 2 branches are now created. Proof Explorer, which is designed to reflect the proof structure that will be internally stored by PVS, automatically prunes sections of the proof tree corresponding to the part discarded by PVS. In the hypothetical example, the proof commands for the missing branch would be discarded. While this ensures consistency between Proof Explorer and PVS, the net result is that a fragment of the proof is effectively lost. Proof Mate seamlessly detects these situations and saves to the sketchpad the proof fragments that would otherwise be lost. Proof engineers can inspect the fragments saved in the sketchpad to understand what caused the break and edit/execute the fragments to repair the proof.

Figure 1 shows a situation where a proof, that was previously complete, broke during a proof re-run. In the original proof, PVS was generating two sub-goals (i.e., two branches) after (`inst? -1`). In the proof re-run, PVS is not generating sub-goals. In this situation, PVS discards the two branches and, consequently, Proof Explorer automatically prunes all nodes after (`inst? -1`). Proof Mate saves the pruned fragments in the sketchpad, as a clip rooted in (`inst? -1`)— this provides a visual cue that can help proof engineers map the content of the sketchpad with that of Proof Explorer. In this example, the proof was broken because of a definition change introduced in the PVS specification. The repair action involved executing the first command in the first branch of the proof clip (i.e., `assert`). While the repair in this case was indeed simple, it can occur that the most difficult branch of a proof is the one that is pruned after being broken, and Proof Mate makes the repair simple.

4 Architecture and Implementation

The high-level architectural diagram shown in Fig. 2 illustrates how Proof Mate is integrated in VSCode-PVS and the Language Server Protocol[2] (LSP) architecture. Being a front-end module, Proof Mate is part of the client side of the LSP

---

[1] It should be noted that the entire broken proof is retained until a user intentionally saves a new version. Even while repairing a broken proof, the repair may be abandoned without saving and the original (broken) proof will persist.

[2] https://microsoft.github.io/language-server-protocol.

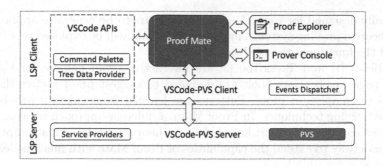

Fig. 2. Proof Mate Architecture integrated in VSCode-PVS (blocks represent functional components, arrows indicate exchange of data or events between components).

architecture. It communicates with three VSCode-PVS components. *VSCode-PVS Client* is used for sending a request to execute a proof command to the VSCode-PVS server through the LSP connection. The client is also used for receiving notifications about changes in the proof structure, in particular deletion of nodes and proof branches. These events are used by Proof Mate for seamless detection and handling of broken proofs. *Proof Explorer* provides a shared clipboard that is used by Proof Mate when performing copy/paste operations from/to Proof Explorer. *Prover Console* provides APIs for writing text in the console. These APIs are used by Proof Mate to provide feedback to the user when, e.g., point-and-click interactions with Proof Mate trigger the execution of a command. The *VSCode APIs* are used by Proof Mate for creating the visual elements of the view, as well as to link the view to the global command palette and clipboard of the Visual Studio Code editor.

Implementation. Proof Mate is entirely implemented in TypeScript, a version of the JavaScript language annotated with type information that can be statically checked for type correctness. A class `ProofMate` implements the functionalities of the module. The class inheritance mechanism is used to define the class as an extended version of Proof Explorer and build on existing code. Overall, the implementation of the Proof Mate module includes approximately 2K lines of TypeScript code. Only minor additions were necessary in the other modules to correctly integrate Proof Mate in the VSCode-PVS front-end.

5 Related Work

Pumpkin [8,9] is a proof repair tool for the Coq proof assistant. The tool provides a semi-automatic *repair-by-example* approach to proof repair. The basic intuition is that a same breaking change may cause similar problems in different proofs. When a proof breaks, the proof engineer can therefore develop an example patched proof, and then use automatic differencing techniques and proof term transformations to synthesize a template patch candidate that can potentially fix other proofs that were broken in a similar way. While this approach is specifically designed for Coq, the concept appears to be generally applicable to other theorem proving systems, including PVS, and will be explored to automate some of the functionalities of Proof Mate.

Tactician [1] and TacticToe [3] are interactive proof helpers for Coq and HOL4, respectively. Both tools are designed to suggest proof tactics than can be used to complete a proof. Patterns are learned from existing proofs using machine learning techniques. In Proof Mate, a different approach is taken, based on a direct encoding of expert knowledge into heuristics rules. An attempt is currently underway to extend the capabilities of Proof Mate with machine learning, targeted at suggesting lemmas.

PeaCoq [10] is an experimental front-end designed to help novice users develop a proof. The tool uses a *visual diff view* to highlight the effects of the refactoring changes on the proof tree. Color-coded text is used to highlight differences between the old and the new version of the proof script. A similar kind of visualization was considered for VSCode-PVS, where changes in the proof tree were directly visualized in Proof Explorer using strikethrough text for the highlighting of deleted fragments. This possible solution was discarded because of usability issues—the window quickly became cluttered and hard to navigate.

6   Conclusion and Future Work

Proof Mate brings a collection of new capabilities to the users of VSCode-PVS, by suggesting relevant proof commands, providing a sketchpad for proofs or proof sections to be assembled outside the interactive prover, and assisting in repairing broken proofs in a number of ways. In contrast to most other interactive theorem provers, PVS does not support editing of proofs outside of the sequential interactive console in a simple way. Proof Mate fills this role and others, providing a playground for copying, editing, writing, and even suggestion of proof sections without restriction, and during a live proof session.

Each of the functionalities that Proof Mate provides (suggestion, sketching, repairing) are ripe for modification and improvement. The current command suggester is based on pattern matching of particular statements in the sequent. While this is certain to find *a* command that will apply, there are more sophisticated methods for finding relevant commands. Future efforts will incorporate more sophisticated techniques such as machine learning to find commands that may be more relevant to the user. One example under current development is a suggester for appropriate lemmas to be used.

The proof sketching functionality in Proof Mate can also be extended in several ways. Currently, Proof Mate allows for a block of commands to be selected and used in the interactive prover console. A small extension would be to facilitate a user creating a custom *local strategy* from these commands, including variables that could be replaced on use. This is a step toward the larger goal of making the PVS strategy language more user-friendly and applicable. A much more ambitious goal is the translation of a natural language proof of a theorem or statement into a proof inside of PVS. While a full proof is unreasonable to expect, a system that could identify and sketch the main skeleton of a proof from a natural language description could aid in the formal verification.

The proof repair function of Proof Mate takes the pruned branches of a previous proof attempt and copies it to the sketchpad. While this catches a large number of broken proofs, there are situations where the sequent diverges prior to where Proof Mate catches the change, and so repair is more difficult. For example, if a change in a specification adds a statement to the antecedent, there can be a long sequence of successful commands (hiding formulas, calling lemmas, etc.) before the first true "break" in the proof. Adding functionality to find this divergence point is more difficult, since the proof is stored as a sequence of commands and does not carry information about the sequent(s) resulting from a command. Another possible enhancement would be for Proof Mate to save not just the pruned sequent, but store the actual repair that was used, since a repair in one proof is often needed in other similar repairs.

References

1. Blaauwbroek, L., Urban, J., Geuvers, H.: The tactician. In: Benzmüller, C., Miller, B. (eds.) CICM 2020. LNCS (LNAI), vol. 12236, pp. 271–277. Springer, Cham (2020). https://doi.org/10.1007/978-3-030-53518-6_17

2. Dutle, A., Moscato, M., Titolo, L., Muñoz, C., Anderson, G., Bobot, F.: Formal analysis of the compact positionreporting algorithm. Formal Aspects Comput. **33**(1), 65–86 (2020). https://doi.org/10.1007/s00165-019-00504-0

3. Gauthier, T., Kaliszyk, C., Urban, J.: Learning to reason with HOL4 tactics. CoRR abs/1804.00595 (2018), http://arxiv.org/abs/1804.00595

4. Masci, P., Muñoz, C.A.: An integrated development environment for the prototype verification system. In: Monahan, R., Prevosto, V., Proença, J. (eds.) Proceedings Fifth Workshop on Formal Integrated Development Environment, F-IDE@FM 2019, Porto, Portugal, 7th October 2019. EPTCS, vol. 310, pp. 35–49 (2019). https://doi.org/10.4204/EPTCS.310.5

5. Muñoz, C.: Batch proving and proof scripting in PVS. NIA/NASA Langley, NASA/CR-2007-214546, NIA Report No. 2007–03 (2007)

6. Muñoz, C., Narkawicz, A.: Formal analysis of extended well-clear boundaries for unmanned aircraft. In: Rayadurgam, S., Tkachuk, O. (eds.) NFM 2016. LNCS, vol. 9690, pp. 221–226. Springer, Cham (2016). https://doi.org/10.1007/978-3-319-40648-0_17

7. Owre, S., Rushby, J.M., Shankar, N.: PVS: a prototype verification system. In: Kapur, D. (ed.) CADE 1992. LNCS, vol. 607, pp. 748–752. Springer, Heidelberg (1992). https://doi.org/10.1007/3-540-55602-8_217

8. Ringer, T.: Proof Repair. Ph.D. thesis, University of Washington (2021)

9. Ringer, T., Porter, R., Yazdani, N., Leo, J., Grossman, D.: Proof repair across type equivalences. In: Proceedings of the 42nd ACM SIGPLAN International Conference on Programming Language Design and Implementation, pp. 112–127 (2021). https://doi.org/10.1145/3453483.3454033

10. Robert, V.: Front-end tooling for building and maintaining dependently-typed functional programs. Ph.D. thesis (2018)

Runtime Verification Triggers Real-Time, Autonomous Fault Recovery on the CySat-I

Alexis Aurandt(✉), Phillip H. Jones(✉), and Kristin Yvonne Rozier(✉)

Iowa State University, Ames, IA 50010, USA
{aurandt,phjones,kyrozier}@iastate.edu

Abstract. CubeSats are low-cost platforms that are popular for conducting spaceborne experiments, however they are known to have high failure rates (∼25% failure rate). In order to improve the likelihood of success of Iowa State University's first CubeSat (CySat-I), we integrate Runtime Verification (RV) on the CySat-I to allow for fault detection at runtime. Although CubeSats have been previously identified as a possible target for RV, this is the first time that a RV engine has been deployed on a CubeSat. We utilize the R2U2 runtime verification engine due to its low overhead; we embed R2U2 directly on the On-Board Computer (OBC) to monitor the current state of the CySat-I. R2U2 continuously monitors the different subsystems on the CySat-I, and R2U2's fault detection triggers predefined fault recovery strategies. Since the Electrical Power System (EPS) is a common source of failure, we specifically focus on this subsystem. We design a list of twenty-two specifications from English requirements corresponding to the EPS and translate them into Mission-time Linear Temporal Logic (MLTL). We perform mock launches on Earth with external fault injection to illustrate that R2U2 successfully reasons about faults and the CySat-I effectively performs fault recovery. We demonstrate that the CySat-I can successfully recover from eight unique EPS faults at runtime in a timely manner with no errors. During our mock launches, R2U2 discovered a potential error in the manufacturer's firmware related to the EPS's under-voltage event monitoring, and this led to a more in-depth investigation of the error by the manufacturers.

Keywords: Online runtime verification · R2U2 · Temporal logic · Formal specification · Fault recovery · CubeSat

1 Introduction

Since the first CubeSat was launched in 2003, the number of CubeSats launched each year has increased exponentially, and as of December 2021, a total of 1,663 CubeSats have been launched [12,24,27]. This exponential growth in CubeSats is due to their low-cost and capability for fast development. CubeSats allow for both academic institutions and commercial sectors to gain easy space access with limited resources and time requirements. With the increase in popularity of CubeSats, the technology and

Supported by NSF:CPS Award 2038903. Reproducibility artifacts available at http://temporallogic.org/research/CySat-NFM22.

© Springer Nature Switzerland AG 2022
J. V. Deshmukh et al. (Eds.): NFM 2022, LNCS 13260, pp. 816–825, 2022.
https://doi.org/10.1007/978-3-031-06773-0_45

research behind CubeSats has also advanced. This has lead to a decrease in failure rate over the years, but the failure rate is still troubling at approximately 25% [27].

Failure within CubeSats is common due to a lack of proper integration and system testing before launching [14,24,25]. Furthermore, universities tend to have higher failure rates than their commercial counterparts due to more constrained resources and development schedules [13,14,24,26]. If more time is dedicated to integration and system testing, most causes of failure could be discovered before the satellite is ever launched. Since fast development time is one of the attributes that make CubeSats attractive, most CubeSats will never have fully exhaustive integration and system testing before becoming spaceborne. Runtime Verification (RV) provides a unique mitigation. RV adds an independent check for real-time triggering of appropriate fault recovery strategies. Additionally, RV is a useful tool for finding errors in the system during testing on Earth; it provides different coverage than traditional system testing to allow for finding difficult errors with less effort.

Most CubeSat failures originate in the Electrical Power System (EPS), Attitude Determination and Control System (ADCS), and the communications system [2,13,24]. These subsystems are mission-critical; if any of these subsystems fail, the entire satellite experiences failure. A recent study formally verified a CubeSat's ADCS at design time to provide runtime assurance [8]. Also, [15] provides a case study of deploying runtime verification on a simulated CubeSat communications system. We focus on the EPS as it has never been evaluated for formal verification and it contributes to approximately one-third of CubeSat failures [13].

The CySat-I's Onboard Computer (OBC) has strict real-time constraints as it is responsible for commanding and monitoring all the other subsystems. The OBC is also restricted to 2MB of program memory [6]. The Realizable, Responsive, Unobtrusive Unit (R2U2) is a unique RV engine in that it requires little overhead and has a fast response time [18,21]. In addition, R2U2 has been previously deployed on several resource-constrained hard real-time systems [3,9,10]. The CySat-I team selected R2U2 as the RV engine due to its configurability for resource-constraints, real-time verdict streaming, and proven unobtrusive monitoring of other real-time systems, e.g., [4,10,19]. Our implementation of fault recovery with the aid of R2U2 is currently planned to launch onboard the CySat-I in October 2022.

We contribute (1) elicitation of twenty-two realistic EPS specifications from English requirements translated into Mission-time Linear Temporal Logic (MLTL), (2) external fault injection to demonstrate that the CySat-I autonomously recovers from eight unique EPS faults in real-time, and (3) firmware error discovery during testing with the help of R2U2. Our categorization technique for the elicitation of EPS specifications is generalizable for application to other mission-critical systems. The remainder of the paper is organized as follows. Section 2 outlines the CySat-I architecture. Section 3 details the implementation of R2U2 on the CySat-I. Section 4 describes the development of the twenty-two specifications. Our mock launch setup with external fault injections appears in Sect. 5. We analyze the mock launch results and plot data revealing a firmware error in Sect. 6. In Sect. 7, we draw conclusions and explore future plans.

2 System Description

The CySat-I is a 3U CubeSat (10 cm × 10 cm × 30 cm) that was designed by students at Iowa State University through the Aerospace Department's Make to Innovate program [17]. The CySat-I is composed of a mix of commercial off-the-shelf (COTS) and custom components interconnected in a stack by PC/104 connectors as shown in Fig. 1. The OBC, EPS, and UHF are COTS components from Endurosat. The OBC hosts a STM32F427 ARM Cortex processor [6] serving as the brain of the satellite; it is responsible for coordinating the other subsystems. The EPS manages how the solar panels charge the batteries and

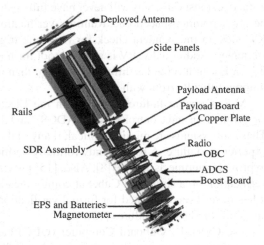

Fig. 1. Exploded view of the CySat-I and all of its components

manages when different power buses and subsystems are powered on/off. The Ultra-High Frequency Radio (UHF) is responsible for deploying the antenna and communicating with the ground station. The ADCS, a COTS component from CubeSpace, is responsible for orientating the satellite towards Earth. The boost board is a custom component that amplifies the 5 V produced by the EPS to the 7.4 V required by the ADCS. The payload is another custom component, and it consists of a FPGA that hosts a Linux-based software defined radio (SDR). The payload's SDR reads measurements from an array of low-noise amplifiers (LNAs) to measure soil moisture on Earth [16].

3   Implementation

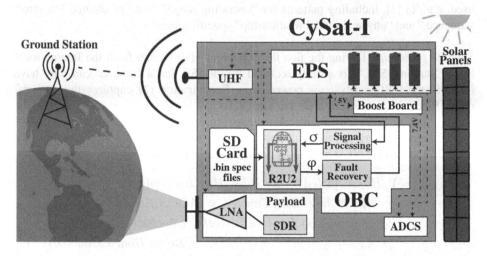

Fig. 2. R2U2 Integration. Specification binary files are loaded into R2U2 from a SD card. EPS data is gathered and processed during "Signal Processing", and this outputs the signals (σ) that are inputted into R2U2. Based on the loaded specifications, R2U2 supplies the output verdict (φ) for each of the inputs (σ). The output verdicts (φ) are used by the OBC's "Fault Recovery" to autonomously trigger the applicable EPS mitigation action. The power supply lines are indicated by dashed lines.

We deploy R2U2 directly onto the OBC of the CySat-I using the STM32CubeIDE [22]. The C version of R2U2 requires 16 KB of the OBC's 2 MB program memory (0.8%), which leaves plenty of room for the CySat-I mission software (180 KB). We translated the CySat-I mission requirements from the Endurosat EPS user manual [5,7] and the CySat-I concept of operations manual [11] into MLTL specifications. MLTL concisely captures the strict temporal mission requirements and is a native language of R2U2 [18,21]. We compiled the specifications and loaded the specification binaries onto the OBC's SD card. The OBC loads the specifications once into R2U2 upon initial boot-up. FreeRTOS, a real-time operating system, manages the OBC's tasks [1]. FreeRTOS launches a five second periodic task that will gather and process status information from the EPS, input the signals into R2U2, and store the `false` output verdicts produced by R2U2 into an array. The OBC evaluates this array, and whenever a `false` output verdict occurs (i.e., a specification is violated), a predefined mitigation strategy is triggered. Figure 2 illustrates this integration of R2U2 into the CySat-I.

4 Runtime Specification Development

We elicit specifications according to the categorization scheme presented in [20] and used, e.g., in [3], including patterns for "operating range," "rate of change," "control sequence," and "physical model relationship" specifications.[1]

Satellite power up. During the first thirty minutes after launch from the International Space Station (ISS), it is strictly required by the ISS that a CubeSat can only have its EPS and OBC subsystems powered on. Specification (1) captures this requirement. Since the FreeRTOS task that runs R2U2 is launched every five seconds, the $G_{[0,360]}$ part of this specification covers the first thirty minutes of the mission (i.e., 5 s * 360 = 30 min). During this time, all power buses (except for the 3.3 V bus required for the OBC) and all enable signals must be in the off/disabled state.

$$G_{[0,360]}\{\neg 5V\_Bus\_Enabled \wedge \neg LUP\_5V\_Bus\_Enabled \wedge$$
$$\neg LUP\_3.3V\_Bus\_Enabled \wedge \neg ADCS\_Active$$
$$\wedge \neg Payload\_Enabled \wedge \neg UHF\_Enabled \wedge$$
$$\neg Boost\_Board\_Enabled\} \quad (1)$$

Power bus requirement. Specification (2) captures that any time the UHF is enabled at least thirty minutes after launch, then the latch-up protected (LUP) 3.3 V bus must also be enabled. The LUP 3.3 V bus is a UHF input required for proper operation. The $G_{[360,M]}$ part of the specification established that this specification must hold from thirty minutes after launch till the end of the mission indicated by M. Corresponding requirements for the boost board and payload form specifications (3) and (4).

$$G_{[360,M]}\{UHF\_Enabled \rightarrow LUP\_3.3V\_Bus\_Enabled\} \quad (2)$$

$$G_{[360,M]}\{Boost\_Booard\_Enabled \rightarrow 5V\_Bus\_Enabled\} \quad (3)$$

$$G_{[360,M]}\{Payload\_Enabled \rightarrow 5V\_Bus\_Enabled\} \quad (4)$$

Under-voltage Event. Whenever the EPS's output power buses fall below a given voltage threshold, the EPS's lifetime *under-voltage event* counter increments [5]. Specification (5) uses this information to compare the current value (value at mission time i) of this status value to its previous value (value at mission time $i - 1$). If these are not equal, then an *under-voltage event* has occurred. In this specification, $G_{[0,M]}$ checks that the requirement holds from the beginning to the end of the mission.

$$G_{[0,M]}\{Num\_Under\_Voltage_i == Num\_Under\_Voltage_{i-1}\} \quad (5)$$

---

[1] All twenty-two specifications with categorization appear here: http://temporallogic.org/research/CySat-NFM22.

I2C Communication. The OBC communicates with the EPS over an I2C bus interface. It was documented in [2] that I2C communication errors can cause EPS failure. To mitigate this mode of failure, we instrumented the OBC's I2C driver to report and accumulate communication errors (e.g., NACKs, transaction timeouts). Specification (6) detects whenever a new I2C error occurs. If the total number of I2C errors at the current mission-time does not equal the total number of errors at the previous mission time, then this specification does not hold. In the event that R2U2 detects the failure of this specification, it triggers the fault mitigation action of resetting the I2C bus.

$$G_{[0,M]}\{Num\_I2C\_Errors_i == Num\_I2C\_Errors_{i-1}\} \tag{6}$$

5   Evaluation Methodology

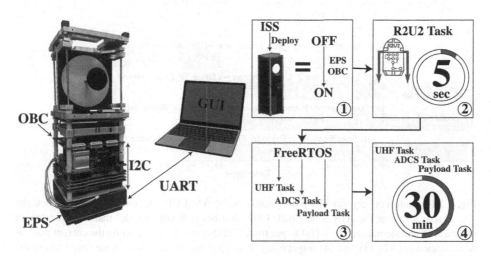

Fig. 3. Mock Launch. Left: The physical CySat-I PC/104 stack without the external structures (e.g., solar panels) and its setup during the mock launches. Right: Mock launch sequence.

We conduct mock launches to evaluate the correct implementation of our specifications, deployment of R2U2 within the CySat-I, and implementation of our fault recovery mechanisms. Within the CySat-I PC/104 stack, the EPS communicates with the OBC via an I2C bus. The EPS also has a UART connection available over a USB port. Endurosat provides a GUI that can interact with the EPS's UART interface while the EPS is plugged into the PC/104 stack. This setup is depicted in Fig. 3. We leverage this GUI during mock launches to inject power bus faults by turning buses on/off and subsystem enable faults by enabling/disabling different subsystems. As shown in Fig. 3, a mock launch consists of: 1) powering on the EPS and OBC (i.e., emulating the CySat-I being launched from the ISS), 2) FreeRTOS on the OBC starting the R2U2 task that runs every five seconds, 3) FreeRTOS starting simplified tasks for the other subsystems, and 4) all subsystem tasks waiting thirty minutes before starting modified operation. We record and analyze the input status signals of R2U2 and the output verdicts generated by R2U2 during the mock launch fault-injection campaigns. These logs allow us to determine if faults are being detected as expected and if fault mitigation strategies are being appropriately triggered.

6   Results and Analysis

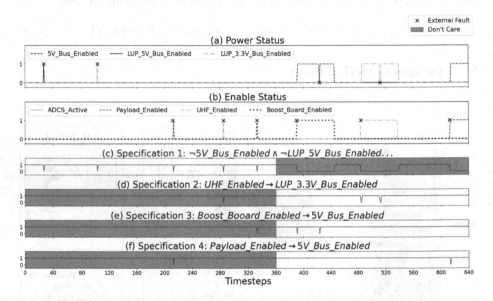

Fig. 4. EPS fault recovery. (a) The power status of the 5 V, LUP 5 V, and LUP 3.3 V buses. (b) The enable status of the ADCS, payload, UHF, and boost board. An 'X' marker indicates an injection of an external fault. (c)–(f) Output from R2U2 correctly determining the current state of specification (1), (2), (3), and (4) respectively. A shaded region indicates a time range where the OBC does not care about the output of R2U2 within its fault recovery.

R2U2 is a stream-based RV engine that reevaluates specifications at each time step creating an implicit global operator. Therefore, we reduce our specifications that we instruct R2U2 to reason over as depicted in Figs. 4 and 5. Recall that specification (1) is only applicable for the first thirty minutes after launch, specifications (2), (3), and (4) are only applicable after the first thirty minutes, and specifications (5) and (6) are always applicable. In order to apply a specification for a certain time interval, the OBC monitors the current time step of R2U2. If not within the applicable time interval for a specification, the OBC does not care what R2U2 is outputting and does not apply a mitigation action, which is indicated by the shaded region in Fig. 4.

Figure 4 illustrates an approximately hour-long mock launch with fault recovery for four unique specification faults (i.e., specification (1), (2), (3), and (4)).[2] Within the

---

[2] All eight specification faults appear here: http://temporallogic.org/research/CySat-NFM22.

first thirty minutes, none of the plotted power buses or subsystem enables are allowed to be enabled. During this period, we inject power bus and subsystem enable faults. Each time a fault is injected, two actions are observed: 1) R2U2 indicates a fault by providing a `false` verdict for specification (1), and 2) our fault recovery mechanism is triggered shown by the violating enable being disabled autonomously by the next time step. After the initial thirty minutes, we inject faults that either enable a subsystem before its required power bus is powered on or we disable a power bus while its corresponding subsystem is still enabled. In both cases, a mitigation strategy enabled the appropriate power bus by the next time step. While the time steps observed by R2U2 are five seconds, the response time of our fault recovery (i.e., time from fault detection to correction) is approximately 7 ms.

Figure 5 depicts the discovery of an error within the EPS firmware, which provides a real-world example of the benefit of using RV during testing. During a mock launch, R2U2 detected the number of *under-voltage events* changing. Upon closer examination, the value spikes from a value of ten (the expected value during this mock launch) to a value of 2308 briefly before returning back to a value of ten. After discovering this erroneous behavior with the EPS's firmware, we contacted the manufacturer who is currently investigating the issue.

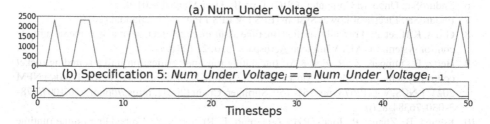

Fig. 5. Potential EPS Firmware Error. (a) The value of the *under-voltage event* counter. (b) Output from R2U2 correctly determining the current state of specification (5) to indicate a change in the *under-voltage event* counter.

7 Conclusion

In order to increase the CySat-I's chance for having a successful mission, we deployed R2U2 on the CySat-I to trigger fault recovery and monitor for errors during testing. R2U2 was able to successfully reason over twenty-two MLTL specifications and detect faults in real-time. R2U2 and our fault recovery mechanisms will ensure that several faults that could occur during the CySat-I's mission can be successfully recovered from. Additionally, if R2U2 had not been deployed on the CySat-I, we would have never uncovered the EPS firmware bug concerning the *under-voltage event* counter. The ability to perform fault recovery in real-time during the mission of the CySat-I is advantageous for the other mission-critical subsystems onboard (e.g., the ADCS and UHF); appropriate fault recovery for these subsystems can reduce the failure rate of future CubeSats. In future work, the R2U2 engine can trigger appropriate fault mitigation strategies for all mission-critical subsystems of a CubeSat, and RV can continue to be explored for CubeSat testing on Earth to assist in discovering elusive errors. We are also pursuing to publish our twenty-two EPS specifications as a benchmark to a public database (e.g., StarExec [23]).

References

1. Amazon Web Services: The FreeRTOS^{TM} Reference Manual (2017)
2. Bouwmeester, J., Langer, M., Gill, E.: Survey on the implementation and reliability of Cube-Sat electrical bus interfaces. CEAS Space J. **9**(2), 163–173 (2016). https://doi.org/10.1007/s12567-016-0138-0
3. Cauwels, M., Hammer, A., Hertz, B., Jones, P., Rozier, K.Y.: Integrating runtime verification into an automated UAS traffic management system, pp. 340–357 (09 2020). https://doi.org/10.1007/978-3-030-59155-7_26
4. Dabney, J.B., Badger, J.M., Rajagopal, P.: Adding a verification view for an autonomous real-time system architecture. In: Proceedings of SciTech Forum, 2021–0566, AIAA, January 2021. https://doi.org/10.2514/6.2021-0566
5. EnduroSat: Electrical Power System (EPS I & EPS I Plus) - I2C Protocol User Manual (2019)
6. EnduroSat: Onboard Computer (OBC) Type II - User Manual (2019)
7. EnduroSat: Electrical Power System (EPS I & EPS I Plus) User Manual (2020)
8. Gross, K.H., et al.: Formally verified run time assurance architecture of a 6u CubeSat attitude control system. In: AIAA Infotech Aerospace, p. 0222 (2016)
9. Hertz, B., Luppen, Z., Rozier, K.Y.: Integrating runtime verification into a sounding rocket control system. In: Dutle, A., Moscato, M.M., Titolo, L., Muñoz, C.A., Perez, I. (eds.) NFM 2021. LNCS, vol. 12673, pp. 151–159. Springer, Cham (2021). https://doi.org/10.1007/978-3-030-76384-8_10
10. Kempa, B., Zhang, P., Jones, P.H., Zambreno, J., Rozier, K.Y.: Embedding online runtime verification for fault disambiguation on Robonaut2. In: Bertrand, N., Jansen, N. (eds.) FOR-MATS 2020. LNCS, vol. 12288, pp. 196–214. Springer, Cham (2020). https://doi.org/10.1007/978-3-030-57628-8_12
11. Kilcoin, M., Kempa, B., Goldenberg, J., Nelson, M., Gonzalez-Torres, T.: Cysat-1 concept of operations (2020). https://iastate.box.com/s/zf6xbwwc3jb9hwshc6hc52evx2e60s13
12. Kulu, E.: Nanosatellite & CubeSat database. https://www.nanosats.eu/database
13. Langer, M., Bouwmeester, J.: Reliability of CubeSats - statistical data, developers' belief, and the way forward. In: Proceedings of the 30th Annual AIAA/USU Conference on Small Satellites (2016)
14. Langer, M., Weisgerber, M., Bouwmeester, J., Hoehn, A.: A reliability estimation tool for reducing infant mortality in CubeSat missions. In: 2017 IEEE Aerospace Conference (2017). https://doi.org/10.1109/AERO.2017.7943598
15. Luppen, Z.A., Lee, D.Y., Rozier, K.Y.: A case study in formal specifications and runtime verification of a CubeSat communications system. In: AIAA SciTech Forum (2021). https://doi.org/10.2514/6.2021-0997
16. Nelson, M.E.: Implementation and evaluation of a software defined radio based radiometer. Master's thesis (2016)
17. Nelson, M.E., Lee, D.Y., Kilcoin, M., Gordon, L., Brown, W.: Preparing CySat-1: a look at Iowa state university's first CubeSat. In: Proceedings of the 34th Annual Small Satellite Conference (2020)

18. Reinbacher, T., Rozier, K.Y., Schumann, J.: Temporal-logic based runtime observer pairs for system health management of real-time systems. In: Ábrahám, E., Havelund, K. (eds.) TACAS 2014. LNCS, vol. 8413, pp. 357–372. Springer, Heidelberg (2014). https://doi.org/10.1007/978-3-642-54862-8_24

19. Rozier, K.Y.: R2U2 in space: system and software health management for small satellites. In: Spacecraft Flight Software Workshop (FSW), December 2016. https://www.youtube.com/watch?v=OAgQFuEGSi8

20. Rozier, K.Y.: Specification: the biggest bottleneck in formal methods and autonomy. In: Blazy, S., Chechik, M. (eds.) VSTTE 2016. LNCS, vol. 9971, pp. 8–26. Springer, Cham (2016). https://doi.org/10.1007/978-3-319-48869-1_2

21. Rozier, K.Y., Schumann, J.: R2U2: tool overview. In: RV-CuBES 2017. An International Workshop on Competitions, Usability, Benchmarks, Evaluation, and Standardisation for Runtime Verification Tools. Kalpa Publications in Computing, vol. 3, pp. 138–156. EasyChair (2017). https://doi.org/10.29007/5pch

22. STMicroelectronics: STM32CubeIDE User Manual (2020)

23. Stump, A., Sutcliffe, G., Tinelli, C.: StarExec: a cross-community infrastructure for logic solving. In: Demri, S., Kapur, D., Weidenbach, C. (eds.) IJCAR 2014. LNCS (LNAI), vol. 8562, pp. 367–373. Springer, Cham (2014). https://doi.org/10.1007/978-3-319-08587-6_28

24. Swartwout, M.A.: The first one hundred CubeSats: a statistical look (2013)

25. Venturini, C., Braun, B., Hinkley, D., Berg, G.: Improving mission success of CubeSats. In: Proceedings of the 32nd Annual AIAA/USU Conference on Small Satellites (2018)

26. Venturini, C.C.: 8 steps improving small set mission success. https://aerospace.org/article/8-steps-improving-small-sat-mission-success

27. Villela, T., Costa, C.A., Brandão, Alessandra, M., Bueno, F.T., Leonardi, R.: Towards the thousandth CubeSat: a statistical overview. Int. J. Aerosp. Eng. **2019** (2019). https://doi.org/10.1155/2019/5063145

Correction to: From Verified Scala to STIX File System Embedded Code Using Stainless

Jad Hamza, Simon Felix, Viktor Kunčak, Ivo Nussbaumer, and Filip Schramka

Correction to:
Chapter "From Verified Scala to STIX File System Embedded Code Using Stainless" in: J. V. Deshmukh et al. (Eds.):
NASA Formal Methods, **LNCS 13260,**
https://doi.org/10.1007/978-3-031-06773-0_21

In the original version of this paper, Fig. 3 was not displayed as it should have been. It is now included in this erratum.

The original version of this chapter can be found at
https://doi.org/10.1007/978-3-031-06773-0_21

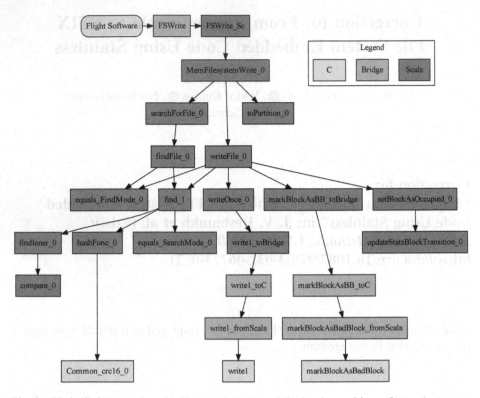

Fig. 3. Flight Software using the file system (top), and the hardware drivers (bottom) were not modified. Only the file system was ported to Scala. Bridge functions, written in C, connect the two implementations when function signatures differ.

Author Index

Printed in the United States
by Baker & Taylor Publisher Services